IVÁN BALASSA—
GYULA ORTUTAY

*Hungarian Ethnography
and Folklore*

HUNGARIAN ETHNOGRAPHY AND FOLKLORE

IVÁN BALASSA— GYULA ORTUTAY

WITH A PREFACE BY ALEXANDER FENTON

CORVINA KIADÓ

Title of the Hungarian original:
MAGYAR NÉPRAJZ
CORVINA KIADÓ, BUDAPEST, 1979

Text translated by
MARIA AND KENNETH BALES
Poems translated by
LÁSZLÓ T. ANDRÁS
Consultants:
ALEXANDER FENTON AND MÁRIA KRESZ

Drawings by
ATTILA BÁNÓ
Maps and diagrams by
MARIANNE KISS
Cover by
FERENC BARABÁS

Photos by:
DEZSŐ ANTAL, RUDOLF BALOGH, TAMÁS BROCKÓ, VILMOS DIÓSZEGI, KÁROLY
ESCHER, EDIT FÉL, BÉLA GUNDA, SÁNDOR GÖNYEI, TIBOR GYERKÓ, ISTVÁN
GYÖRFFY, IVÁN HEVESY, TAMÁS HOFER, MÁRTON KANKOVSZKY, ZOLTÁN KAL-
LÓS, KATA KÁLMÁN, ATTILA KÁROLY, KÁROLY KOFFÁN, KÁLMÁN KÓNYA,
KÁLMÁN KÓRIS, PÉTER KORNISS, ISTVÁN KOVÁCS, TAMÁS KOVÁCS, ALBERT
KRESZ, MIKLÓS LANTOS, OLGA LESZIK, MARGIT LUBY, GÉZA MEGAY, GÁBOR
MINARIK, ZOLTÁN MÓSER, JÁNOS MANGA, BALÁZS MOLNÁR, LÁSZLÓ NAGY,
GERTRUD PALOTAY, JÁNOS REISMANN, ZSUZSA SÁNDOR, BÁLINT SÁROSI, KATA
SUGÁR, JENŐ SZABÓ, KÁROLY SZELÉNYI, LEVENTE SZEPSI SZŰCS, JÁNOS SZEREN-
CSÉS, MARGIT TÓTH, ERNŐ VADAS, AURÉL VAJKAI

ISBN 963 13 0922 3

Printed in Hungary, 1984
Kner Printing House Dürer Workshop

Preface

by Alexander Fenton

In 1949 Gyula Ortutay wrote in his preface to the first issue of *Folia Ethnographica,* published by the Ethnographic Institute of the Pázmány Péter University of Budapest, that it fulfilled a long-felt need, and that for a long time the results of researches in Hungarian ethnology had been inaccessible to foreign colleagues who did not understand Hungarian. The intention of *Folia Ethnographica,* using Russian, English and French, was to give an account of Hungarian work on the one hand, and to provide comparative data for international purposes on the other.[1]

The first issue of 30 years ago is worth looking at more closely, for the trends that it was setting. Károly Marót wrote in it about history and ethnology. He did not use the word ethnology in the way in which it is used now (in the present publication "ethnology" or "regional ethnology" is equated, as now agreed between European scholars, with "Volkskunde", "folk life", etc.), but rather contrasted it with the discipline of history, by which the past should be examined "wie es eigentlich war", as it really was, to use Ranke's expression. Ethnology for Marót had to do with poetical and religious values, which were not factual, and could therefore be misleading in any attempt to make a historical reconstruction. For most present-day European scholars, ethnology is a historical discipline, and it might appear that there has been a complete *volte-face* since Marót's time. Yet this is not so. Marót was, of course, writing in the spirit of the intellectual fashion of his period, but in his specific examination of the myth of the separation of Sky and Earth, he was concerned to observe that a historical attitude forbade statements about myths originating at definite points in time. Thus his approach was historical, and his view of ethnology was critical in a sound historical way. His refusal to force the strait-jacket of preconception on historical evidence is an attitude not different from the one we should now have.[2]

Material aspects of history were looked at by Professor István Tálasi in his article on peasant farming, poaching and fishing,[3] that is, the basic sources of food-production and food-getting, which provided not only the means for subsistence at a local level, but also—in terms of cattle and later grain—a primary source of international trade. Tálasi was not so much giving information here about techniques, practices, equipment and tools, however, as examining the types and methods of study carried out up to the 1940s by his compatriots. From the 18th century, some attention was being given to the life of the peasantry and to their occupations, coinciding broadly with the period when feudal conditions and feudal service bonds were moving towards an overdue end. This was mainly from the angle of geography and economics, however, and interest of this kind continued till the later 19th century. A more scientific interest in the collection and analysis of the concrete details of material culture did not really develop till the 1890s.

Even so, it had a body of earlier sources of a related kind from which it could quarry, such as the plentiful practical farming literature, which, as in Britain, compared current with older situations. Historical perspective over 150 to 200 years can be got as a result, and this is a kind of source of which ethnologists can still make much use.

Iván Balassa has himself taken up this line of activity to good effect. His doctoral thesis on maize, and his study of the history of the plough and of ploughing, are major works that draw heavily on such sources, as do a host of articles published by him.[4] He was also responsible for setting up, within the Agricultural Museum, a Historical Archive of Agricultural Implements, which contains, amongst other things, the results of surveys of such implements in other Hungarian museums.

Since about 1950, too, a series of subject monographs has appeared on aspects of cultivation under Professor Tálasi, generally following the "Wörter und Sachen" approach, and with a historical orientation that often lays emphasis on the medieval period. Much attention is paid to the cultivation of grain, to changes in work techniques and productivity, and to analysis of the social motives that underlie production. The subjects include tobacco, maize, potatoes and paprika, and take into consideration questions of diffusion, acceptance, etc., as well as comparative material from neighbouring countries. The technical circumstances of cultivation remain most prominent, however. These studies take the subject through to the industrial period, in Hungary beginning essentially in the latter half of the 19th century, and have continued unbroken.[5] Attention was also paid to crop-raising, at home and in neighbouring countries, as indicated by a substantial volume on grain cultivation in East and Central Europe, edited by Balassa in 1972.[6]

The life and equipment of herdsmen has been a favourite topic of study, partly influenced by the earlier nomadism of the Hungarians, though in this respect they are also an organic part of South-East Europe. Volumes on animal husbandry and the culture of shepherds, published in 1961 and 1969, exemplify the methods of approach through working techniques, language and ergology, applied here over an area stretching from South-East Europe to Western Asia.[7] In recent years some detailed regional and general studies of pastoral life have appeared from Debrecen, under the general editorship of Professor Béla Gunda.[8]

Since the 1930s there has been active research into settlement patterns and buildings. I. Szabó has used ethnological concepts for historical purposes in his study of the development of villages, and a number of local studies of buildings have also appeared from Debrecen. Usually questions of chronology are given priority in buildings studies, and the influence of joiners and masons on the art of building in the last century and a half has been examined.

A development of recent years has been the holistic ethnological study of particular regions. A number of attractive regional handbooks has come from the Gondolat Press,[9] and another recent example deals with the marshy Kis-Balaton and its surroundings.[10] Studies of themes, such as the history of the way in which country folk have made use of the resources of the forests,[11] also continue to flow from the pens of Hungarian ethnologists.

19th-century researchers concentrated on ethnic character and origins, seeing Hungarian peasant agriculture as having a double origin, either Asiatic, or German and Slav derived. The distribution of material data such as the treading out of grain in the open-air by the feet of animals, the underground storage of grain in pits, etc., was cited to illustrate the theory. J. Csaplovics, writing in 1822, was the one who brought such ethnic problems into ethnological perspective. Cropraising, and the life and equipment of herdsmen and fishermen were subjected to scrutiny, and related to linguistic[12] and archaeological evidence.

The ideas and conclusions of the earlier researchers have been modified now in the light of increased knowledge, but this is normal and natural in any growing subject. The important thing is that there should be a system, even if only used as a provisional framework, if a subject is to get past the stage of simple collection. And this stage was well and truly passed by Hungarian scholars. There was at first the emphasis on origins, perhaps a natural result of a search for identity. Part of this was a search for traces of the traditions of the past surviving into the present, as happened also in Britain;[13] but with the work of István Györffy and his contemporaries in the 1920s, ethnology began to be given an integrated shape which led in the 1930s to a desire for a comprehensive synthesis. This was attempted in the volumes of *A Magyarság Néprajza* (The Ethnography of the Hungarians. 1933–37), a remarkable work by the standards of any country, which not only presented factual data, but also helped to stimulate and guide the work of post-1930 ethnologists, making them aware of the importance of a social outlook besides the usual historical problems. The first edition was sold out before it even got on to the market. At the same time relevant museum collections were being built up, and in 1949 Tálasi, in looking at agriculture as a whole and some of its constituent factors, and the ramifications of its links with the entire civilization of the country and the mental world, made a plea for a synthesis of the whole. He has had to wait for 30 years for the present book by Balassa and Ortutay.

The same long-term trend-setting volume of *Folia Ethnographica* included an article by Linda Dégh.[14] She outlined the ancestry of the discipline of folklore, and showed, partly by assessing the work of individual collectors and scholars, how attitudes to the subject and the methodology of approach have changed since the age of 19th-century romanticism, when folk literature and what it had to say about the national self was the primary object. In pursuing the public collection of folk literature, customs, language, dances, the Hungarian Academy of Sciences, founded through the inspiration of István Széchenyi (whose father, Ferenc, was involved in the founding of the Hungarian National Museum), played a strong directional part.

Subsequently the character of the country itself changed. It was then an underdeveloped country in both the economists' and geographers' senses. The people in general were not town dwellers. The market towns were agricultural centres, and industrial centres with a brisk trade and full supporting services were lacking. Handicrafts were very much in the hands of incoming craftsmen, especially Germans. The aristocracy kept out of the way in Austria or Transylvania, and the nobility lived on their estates in a certain degree of isolation from each other. The serfs had no opportunities for education or improvement—and indeed their full liberation in Hungary is so recent that a living writer, Gyula Illyés, could describe their feudal conditions of existence from personal knowledge, in his book *People of the Puszta*.[15] Out of such a background came an almost feverish search for origins, for identity. After the end of the century, when the Hungarian Ethnological Society was founded, its journal *Ethnographia* at first reflected this concern with ancient history, philology and literature, the motifs of folk-poetry being seen as one of the chief sources of ancient history.

There was much discussion about whether or not folklore and material culture should be separate. Investigators of mental culture with a literary bias in their training, and of material culture with an archaeological, geographical and technical bias, tended to go their own separate ways in the 1920s. On both sides, attitudes to collection and research were conditioned by the times. In folk-tale collecting, for example, the reconstructing of a "type", and observation of variants, played a dominant role. The question of evolution was scarcely considered, and in this respect, a great deal is owed to the work of the musicians, people like Bartók and Kodály, through whom folklorists learned the virtues of total as opposed to selective collection, and began to look at the complete repertoires of folk-singers and tellers of tales, or even of the inhabitants of an entire village.

A further step towards what might be called applied folklore (or indeed applied ethnology) was taken by folklorists like Gyula Ortutay, who realized that help in agrarian reform could be given through an understanding of the complex mentality of the people (including all ethnic groups). They sought to examine the entire peasant society, and to see the elements of their subject (including the individual) in the perspective of the communal framework of peasant life. This was all the more easily possible because folk tales are still alive, so that the links between the individual and the community, the ways of presentation, the dynamics of new creation, and so on, can be readily examined. The degrees of contact and divergence between folk-poetry and literary poetry were studied. Application or functionalism became part of the approach, as did an increasing ability to interpret the past due to the full recording of data as a sound base for subsequent analysis. It came to be considered that no traditions were meaningless, and that elements of culture were not necessarily survivals from one generation to another, but were always being re-created, or at least adapted as the people's circumstances changed from generation to generation. Transmission was seen as a matter of revival rather than survival, and this has sometimes led to the view that the scope of ethnology was the present. This more sociological orientation, however, which now marks the subject in many countries, need not deny the historical background, for this is essential in order to estimate the present correctly. In this respect, in the field of ballad research, one may point to two recent studies of the French origins of the ballad in medieval Hungary, and of Hungary as a centre of diffusion in East Central Europe.[16]

In my own view ethnology is a discipline concerned with the past as much as with the present, the one leading up to the other. But it is a complex discipline, as life is complex, and it has many facets attracting workers whose individual backgrounds and skills will dictate each individual approach. Each contributes to the whole, and the present book is a courageous attempt to view the total subject, updating and amending in the light of modern research the material presented 30 years ago in *A Magyarság Néprajza*. This double achievement is a clear indication of the established nature and strength of ethnological studies in Hungary, as also is the fact that the time has already come when books of over 400 pages about the history of Hungarian ethnology[17] can be written. The American Hungarian Foundation has listed 314 items in a bibliography of English language resources on the subject.[18] This, in conjunction with the present book and its bibliography, gives the English-speaking world a change to come to grips with Hungarian ethnology, and to profit from it accordingly.

What, to an observer like myself, are the characteristics of present-day Hungarian ethnology? I have been both impressed and inspired by the wealth of literature produced on the subject. The three dimensions of material, mental and social culture are generally held to be the corner-stones of ethnology, but perhaps no other country has been so much aware of ethnic criteria as a further essential element. It has been said that social culture has never developed in Hungary as an independent branch of ethnology, since so many aspects are covered by related disciplines,[19] but still there exist monumental studies, such as the three volumes on the village of Átány by Fél and Hofer,[20] and the present compendium of wide experience and knowledge pays much attention too to social culture. This is an area on which future writers will undoubtedly build. At the same time I find it good that the material culture of the past and present remains prominent in the work that goes on. There has been a swing in some countries to a preference for a more sociological type of approach, and this has had its effect in Hungary too, but the everyday, concrete facts of the material by which people live must remain the firm base on which alone ethnological theory can confidently be built. Since 1958, the co-ordinated collection of data for the *Hungarian Ethnological Atlas* by almost every active ethnologist in the country (which Gyula Ortutay helped to make possible) has given ethnological work in Hungary a degree of cohesion that is rare. And in 1977 there appeared from the press the first volume of another vast project, the *Hungarian Ethnological Lexicon, A—E.*[21] (Since then, the other four volumes have also been published.) The record is enviable, and I welcome the present achievement of Gyula Ortutay, for whom it is now, sadly, a memorial, and of Iván Balassa. The ideals of the first volume of *Folia Ethnographica* have been substantially achieved.

Notes

[1] *Folia Ethnographica* 1949. I/1. 4.

[2] MARÓT, K.: "History and Ethnology", *ibid*, 1949. I/1. 24–33.

[3] TÁLASI, I.: "Research into Hungarian Peasant Farming, Poaching and Fishing", *ibid*, 44–71.

[4] BALASSA, I.: *A magyar kukorica. Néprajzi tanulmány* (Hungarian Maize. Ethnographical Study), Budapest, 1960; BALASSA, I.: *Az eke és a szántás története Magyarországon* (The History of the Plough and Ploughing in Hungary), Budapest, 1973. For a bibliography of Balassa's writings, see *Ethnographia*, 1977. LXXXVIII/2–3. 210–223.

[5] SZABÓ, M.: "Undersökningar av ungersk folkkultur ett alternativ inom europeisk etnologi", In *Nord Nytt* 1972/4. 244–246. For a recent example of a study of the agriculture of a clearance village, see Takács, L.: *Egy irtásfalu földművelése*, Budapest, 1976.

[6] BALASSA, I. ed.: *Getreidebau in Ost- und Mitteleuropa*, Budapest, 1972.

[7] FÖLDES, L. ed.: *Viehzucht und Hirtenleben in Ostmittel- Europa*, Budapest, 1961; FÖLDES, L. ed.: *Viehwirtschaft und Hirtenkultur. Ethnographische Studien*, Budapest, 1969.

[8] For example, BENCSIK, J.: *Pásztorkodás a Hortobágy területén a XVIII. század végétől* (Animal-herding on the Northern Hortobágy from the late 18th Century), Debrecen, 1969; SZABADFALVI, J.: *Az extenzív állattenyésztés Magyarországon* (Extensive Animal Husbandry in Hungary) (Műveltség és Hagyomány XII), Debrecen, 1972; DAM, L.: *A Nagy-Sárrét népi építészete* (Folk Architecture of Nagy-Sárrét), Debrecen, 1975; SELMECZI KOVÁCS, A.: *Csűrös építkezés és gazdálkodás Észak-Magyarországon* (The Construction of the *csűr* and Farming in Northern Hungary), Debrecen, 1976.

[9] A series of 10 volumes up to 1977, including I. TÁLASI's *Kiskunság*, Budapest, 1977.

[10] TAKÁCS, L.: *A Kis-Balaton és környéke* (The Little-Balaton and Environs), (Somogyi Almanach 27–29), Kaposvár, 1978 (English summary).

[11] HEGYI, I.: *A népi erdőkiélés történeti formái* (Historical Forms of Peasant Forest Foraging), Budapest, 1978.

[12] Cf. BENKŐ, L. and IMRE, S.: *The Hungarian Language*, The Hague, Paris, 1972. 171. ff. (the lexical stock of Hungarian).

[13] E.g. MADARASSY, L.: *A nomád pásztorkodás a kecskeméti pusztákon* (Nomadic Herding on the Kecskemét *puszta*), 1912; SZABÓ, K.: *A Hortobágy puszta és élete* (The Hortobágy *puszta* and its life), 1914; MITCHELL, A.: *The Past in the Present: What is Civilisation?*, 1880.

[14] DÉGH, L.: "History of Hungarian Folklore", in *Folia Ethnographica*, 1949. I/1. 72–98.

[15] ILLYÉS, GY.: *People of the Puszta*, Budapest, 1967.

[16] VARGYAS, L.: *Researches into the Medieval History of Folk Ballad*, Budapest, 1967; and VARGYAS, L.: *A magyar népballada és Európa (Hungarian Folk Ballads and Europe)*, Budapest, 1976.

[17] SOZAN, M.: *The History of Hungarian Ethnography*, Syracuse University, 1972.

[18] HOWELL, D. R.: *Hungarian Ethnography: A Bibliography of English Language Sources* (Hungarian Research Center, American Hungarian Foundation), Virginia, 1975.

[19] Szabó 1972. 248.

[20] FÉL, E. and HOFER, T.: *Proper Peasants. Traditional Life in a Hungarian Village*, Chicago, 1969; *Bäuerliche Denkweise in Wirtschaft und Haushalt*, Göttingen, 1972; *Geräte der Átányer Bauern*, Copenhagen, 1974.

[21] ORTUTAY, GY. ed.: *Magyar Néprajzi Lexikon A—E*, Budapest, 1977; *F—Ka*, Budapest, 1979; *K—Né*, Budapest, 1980; *N—Szé*, Budapest, 1981; *Sz—Zs*, Budapest, 1982.

Foreword

The Hungarians, who were Finno-Ugric in origin but who incorporated Turkic elements into their culture, occupied their country in the Carpathian Basin at the very end of the 9th century. Their culture, which was characteristic of the steppe, was influenced by the economic and social conditions of Central Europe, the conversion to Christianity, and the numerous neighbouring nations. For this reason it has been said that "Hungary is Europe in a nutshell". Here, folk cultures combine the traditions of East and West into a unit unique to and characteristic only of Hungary. In our work we attempt to illuminate her multiple yet unified character from as many aspects as possible.

Every book is meant for a smaller or larger community of readers. The author's job is the harder, his responsibility the greater, the wider the circle to which he wishes to offer something new. We feel this burden increasingly now that we have undertaken to inform experts and interested laymen alike about what our discipline has concluded regarding the traditional culture of the Hungarian people. The task is difficult not only because we must explore the most important territories of life, but also because we must do so in such a way as to disperse those romantic conceptions which even today often cling to the Hungarian people.

Though experts and lay public make different demands in regard to a book, the two can be reconciled. This is why we attempt a general synthesis without becoming immersed in smaller, or what we judge to be less significant, details. For the experts we include at the end of the volume a selected bibliography, with the help of which they can further research areas of interest to them. We serve both groups by including sufficient sketches, maps and photographs to make the message more understandable and more interesting. There are many debated questions in our field, since the raw material now being uncovered in ever growing quantities continues to raise new problems. We therefore first summarize the results of the debates already settled, or thought by us to have been settled, so that the reader can see the most recent but already established conclusions.

We wish to offer an outline summary of the entire field of Hungarian folk knowledge, a summary which extends into areas of social, material, and intellectual culture, social, material anthropology and folklore. This culture was for centuries primarily a tradition carried and reshaped by the peasantry, who from the time of its development in the Middle Ages was forced for the most part to be self-sufficient both in the material and intellectual areas. This type of culture is much older and more comprehensive than the culture of the ruling classes, and can with justice be called communal, since the widest strata of people passed it on to succeeding generations through tradition.

However, this culture itself developed, was reshaped, changed. It preserved relics, historical and ethnic characteristics from the Hungarian past, to some extent in the field of material culture, to a greater extent in the field of folklore. Economic and social changes shaped the living conditions of the peasantry, sometimes through slow progress, sometimes with such a rapid tempo that it was difficult to keep up, but to which they needed to adjust and become accustomed, whether they liked it or not. So the peasants' culture developed, changed seemingly by itself, but in fact through the compelling effect of outside forces.

Although Hungarian folk culture changed and developed as a result of economic and social factors, many other elements also played a part in this process, of which it suffices to mention only a few.

Landlords and peasants lived alongside each other within the area of one settlement. The manor-house where the peasants performed their services stood as an example to the humble peasant huts. Often the same carpenter who worked for the landlord made the furnishings for the cottages, at least from the 18th century on. And upper-class culture at every period tried to link itself with the aristocratic, and through them with European trends. Thus the great cultural, artistic currents of Europe, although often a century late and much diluted, still got through to the Hungarian peasants.

The church at different periods also left a significant mark on the culture of the peasants. The buildings of churches, standing at the centre of the villages, gave provincial reflections to European architectural directions, that is, they were the provincial versions of these directions. Church holidays and the name days of the saints left an imprint on the world of custom. Analogies and stories with European currency found their way through the sermons into Hungarian folk poetry. For example, the influence of Gregorian chants is still alive today. The influence of Calvinist psalms, whose French melodies originated in the 16th century, can also be shown.

As a result of different nations living together within the Carpathian Basin, their folk culture mutually influenced one another. This can be demonstrated especially in areas of contact, where the composition of a significant number of the villages is mixed. However, certain cultural elements can also be often found far from border regions, and furthermore not infrequently in a significant part of a linguistic region.

We can untangle and explore all this if present-day ethnology follows with attention the historical direction of the phenomena. Going backwards in time, such surviving documents as written memoirs, illustrations and existent objects can be made to tell their story. In this way we can determine the course of development, and once in a while the origin as well, of a device, a work method, or a certain type of folk poetry. We know of numerous instances where ethnographical investigations can be linked up ultimately with the results of archeological research.

By the Middle Ages the peasantry was no longer homogeneous. Those who were more or less prosperous were distinguishable from indigent servants and were also well separated from the village artisans. During the last two hundred years the social differentiation gradually became more marked, especially within the sphere of economics. An even greater disparity developed between the culture of the prosperous and that of poor peasants, agricultural labourers and seasonal labourers of the latifundia. Hungarian ethnology considers that the description and analysis of the differentiation of folk culture is one of its most important tasks, and where ways and opportunities are offered, we relate our work to this.

Folk culture, therefore, is not in itself homogeneous and its bearers do not have the same ability to develop it further. Gifted story-tellers and singers not only create variations of their art, but in the spirit of tradition, they also create something new. In the past women of outstanding skill in weaving or sewing gained reputations similar to those of certain shepherds. People came from afar to order an ornamental whip or buy ornate woodcarvings. Agricultural tools were improved and working methods changed mostly by innovators hidden under the veil of anonymity. Outstanding story-tellers and singers were remembered in the same way as masters of ceremonies at weddings, who had to fulfil the function of organizer, versifier and dancer in one person. The peasantry appeared to be a homogeneous mass only when viewed from a distance, since outstanding individuals in the different strata were creators in certain areas of peasant culture and under limited conditions, and their innovations could be built into the whole.

The description of such a complicated process is possible only if we break up peasant culture into chapters, as we do in this book, according to outside points of a view. Furthermore, we do this according to the method developed in our discipline, which separates material culture from folklore only in order to facilitate research. These will be preceded by another chapter, in which we pin-point certain phenomena present in social or community culture, i. e., we shall analyse the relationships between people, and between people and society. This division and systematization serve to make the survey easier. Phenomena co-exist or are connected to each other in everyday life, in the past as in the present. The man who ploughed might be the same as the one who was a redoubtable teller of tales and singer of songs, or who at another time organized a burial and maybe, in the appropriate season, a harvesting group. But the reader must do this synthesizing for himself; the authors can only try to offer help in this effort.

This aim is also served by our introduction, which acquaints the reader with the outline history of Hungarian ethnology, its past and present directions, and some basic characteristics of its current organization and function. Hungarian folk culture is most intimately linked to the history of the entire people and nation. This synopsis provides an ethnological framework within which the reader can place his own knowledge. Similarly, a short excursion into the territory of Hungarian linguistics will introduce the most important ethnic groups and ethnographic regions of the Hungarian people, which differ from each other in more or less significant characteristics. Their names will recur frequently, so the reader can already greet them as familiars. Besides, as we have introduced the main features of Hungarian ethnography, so shall we also outline how and what elements or units of folk culture fit into the socialist culture.

Introduction

Material of an ethnological character can already be found in the medieval Hungarian chronicles and charters. A 12th-century writer who signs himself ANONYMUS, educated at French universities, refers to the peasants' "false tales and the bards' prattling songs", which, as a historian, he was scornful of, yet willingly or unwillingly he still used them. Chronicles and religious literature later on also preserved many ethnographical features for us. From the 11th century, geographical names in charters often refer to the devil, witches, and pagan sacrificial places, but these are incidental. We can make good use of certain of these data, but they can in no way provide the basis of Hungarian ethnology. This we can connect with the name of MÁTYÁS BÉL (1685–1749), who published his five and a half volume work, *Notitia Hungariae novae Historico geographica,* between 1735–42. He deliberately attempted the precise and faithful description of the eleven counties he introduced. He compared the observed ethnographic phenomena with the corresponding ones of the nationalities who lived together with the Hungarians, and often referred to regional divergences and ethnic groups. Therefore we can rightly call him the forerunner of descriptive ethnography and comparative ethnology in Hungary, though the fact that he wrote in Latin, and that a considerable part of his works remained unpublished, significantly reduced their usefulness and consequently their influence.

Among the ever-increasing literature relating to folk knowledge in the 18th century the life's work of Lutheran clergyman SÁMUEL TESSEDIK (1742–1820) rises above the rest, especially his book entitled *A paraszt ember Magyarországban, mitsoda és mi lehetne* (The Peasant in Hungary, What He Is and What He Might Become), Pécs, 1786. He was the first to point out the importance of the intellectual culture of the peasantry, their social stratification, and peculiarities of life style. He carefully described their economic backwardness and superstitions, and sought to eliminate the latter by teaching practical knowledge to young peasants in his agricultural school. Similarly, GERGELY BERZEVICZY (1763–1822) was much occupied with the question of peasant culture, in connection with which he called attention to its intellectual and economic ramifications. For him the basic issue was the earliest possible ending of the serfs' poverty, allied with the raising of their educational standards.

During the first third of the 19th century, historians and linguists consciously paid increasing attention to learning about national traditions, which in turn led to the accumulation of more and more ethnographical information. *Tudományos Gyűjtemény* (Scientific Collection), 1817–1841, a periodical of wide scope that was as good as any in its time, contained ethnographic essays in almost every issue. The essay by JÁNOS CSAPLOVICS (1780–1847) entitled "Ethnographiai értekezés Magyarországról" (An Ethnographical Essay on Hungary) appeared here in 1827. Here he took as a goal a complete survey of all the peoples in

Hungary, who, though living alongside each other, still maintained certain diversities. He was the first to formulate the statement "Hungary is Europe in a nutshell", implying that almost every European ethnographical question can be examined in this territory. He realized most of his aims in a larger work, written in German (*Gemälde aus Ungarn,* Pest, 1822).

The systematic collecting and working up of folk literature started after a number of spasmodic attempts in 1841, when the Kisfaludy Society advertised a competition for the collection of folksongs. The noted follower of HERDER and the GRIMM brothers, JÁNOS ERDÉLYI (1814–1868), published his three- volume work *Népdalok és Mondák* (Folksongs and Sagas) between 1846 and 1848, in which he presented selections from the vast amount of material gathered by him and his co-workers. By then the book by JÁNOS KRIZA (1811–1875), the Unitarian bishop from Transylvania, entitled *Vadrózsák* (Wild Roses) had reached completion in manuscript form, although due to difficulties over publication it saw the light only in 1863. In 1872 publication began of the volumes of the *Magyar Népköltési Gyűjtemény* (Hungarian Folk Poetry Collection), of which the last, the eleventh volume, was published in 1924. The most effective folklore researcher of the last quarter of the century was LAJOS KÁLMÁNY (1852–1919), whose seven volumes and numerous essays are still an indispensable source, especially for researchers of the South Lowlands.

Already, the research and recording of beliefs and superstitions was taking place sporadically in the first half of the 19th century, but it was ARNOLD IPOLYI (1823–1886) who systematically collected these and attempted to reconstruct from them the elements of Hungarian ancient religion (*Magyar mythologia,* Pest, 1854). Although his methods and conclusions are largely outdated, he was undoubtedly the initiator of one direction of ethnological research, the effects of which can be felt to the present day.

Research into material culture began later and proceeded more slowly than for folklore. Although the National Museum's Department of Ethnography was founded in 1872, it merely vegetated for two decades. It began to develop in earnest in 1896, when, for the millennium of the Magyar Conquest of Hungary, an open-air museum was opened representing the entire country and consisting of 24 farmyards and a church. Twelve farmyards represented the Hungarian population, 12 the other nationalities. After their dismantling, the objects exhibited there were acquired by the Ethnographical Museum.

OTTÓ HERMAN (1835–1914) published in 1887 his mammoth two-volume work *A magyar halászat könyve* (The Book of Hungarian Fishing), which has served as a prototype study ever since. This theme was further developed by JÁNOS JANKÓ (1868–1902) in his comparative study that looked toward ancient history, *A magyar halászat eredete* (The Origin of Hungarian Fishing), 1900.

In 1889 the *Magyar Néprajzi Társaság* (Hungarian Ethnographical Society) was formed to unite the ever-growing camp of Hungarian ethnographers, and from then it has remained the most universal social organ of Hungarian ethnography. Its main journal, *Ethnographia,* has been published continuously since 1890. Associated with it from 1900 on has been the *Néprajzi Múzeum Értesítője* (The Bulletin of the Ethnographical Museum), which, though temporarily discontinued during the years of the two world wars, reappeared in 1954 in the form of a yearbook. These are the two basic publications in which both theoretical studies and the results of field research appear. In the first year of *Ethnographia* LAJOS KATONA (1862–1910) published his study entitled "Ethnographia, ethnologia, folklore" which was abreast of the times and standards of Europe and is virtually the starting point for the principle and theory of Hungarian ethnological research.

The First World War, and the difficulties following it, impeded and retarded the development of Hungarian ethnography. Development was especially hindered by the fact that for long there was no department of ethnography at the university. Finally, in 1929 SÁNDOR SOLYMOSSY (1864–1945) became chairman at the University of Szeged; then in 1934 ISTVÁN GYÖRFFY (1884–1939) was appointed Professor of Ethnography at the University of Budapest. At Szeged, teaching relates primarily to folklore, and at Budapest to material culture.

The most outstanding event of the period between the two world wars was that an eminent editorial group assembled a digest of the ethnography of the Hungarians in a four-volume work entitled *A Magyarság Néprajza* (The Ethnography of the Hungarians), 1933–1937, which still gives the only and most complete overview of the subject, despite the fact that it is partly outdated. Two volumes deal with material culture, the other two with folklore.

Closely connected with ethnology is a good tradition of collecting and discussing of folk music. Collection goes back to the first half of the 19th century, but it really began to thrive in 1895, when BÉLA VIKÁR (1859–1945) began to record songs with a phonograph. BÉLA BARTÓK (1881–1945) and ZOLTÁN KODÁLY (1882–1967) followed this tradition. Their names became world famous, not only because of their work of collecting and their scientific recordings, but also because of their compositions based on folk music, and last but not least, because they incorporated folk music into the national culture.

Before the Second World War, GYULA ORTUTAY (1910–1978) initiated a new direction on research into folk tales, which, besides considering the achieved results, put a special emphasis on demonstrating the creative method of outstanding individual story-tellers. He initiated the *Új Magyar Népköltési Gyűjtemény* (The New Hungarian Folk Poetry Collection) in 1940, and 18 volumes have appeared since.

After 1945, the reorganization of Hungarian ethnology accelerated. The work began with calculating and evaluating the results of the past and with setting tasks for the future. The *Magyar Népkutatás Kézikönyve* (Manual of Hungarian Folk Research), 1947–48, which assessed the work completed in certain topics of ethnography, served this purpose. It is unfortunate that this excellent initiative has not been so far completed.

The greatest achievement of the new era was the establishing of two chairs of ethnology at the University of Budapest and one each at Debrecen and Szeged, since this satisfactorily solved the problem of educating a new generation. Under the direction of the Hungarian

Academy of Sciences, systematic collecting and recording in all fields of ethnology began in 1950. Since that year, the results have been made known abroad by the journal *Acta Ethnographica,* published in Russian, German, English and French.

Before 1945, there were only twenty or twenty-two full-time ethnological researchers. Today there are one hundred and seventy. Because researchers are working in different places, synchronization of their work is important. This task is fulfilled by the *Magyar Tudományos Akadémia Néprajzi Főbizottsága* (the High Committee of Ethnology of the Hungarian Academy of Sciences) whose members include the most outstanding researchers, also representing some ethnological institutions.

Among the institutes, the *Néprajzi Kutató Csoport* (Ethnographical Research Group) belongs directly to the Hungarian Academy of Sciences. The number of its scientific research workers approaches thirty. Work is carried on in three departments. The Department of Folklore

1. The Village Museum of Göcsej
Zalaegerszeg

2. The Village Museum of Göcsej
Zalaegerszeg

has the most important projects and the greatest number of researchers. The primary goal of the Institute for the future is to develop research in this direction. The Department of Material Culture is smaller in staff, but it is the instigator of several important research projects (among them the *Ethnographical Atlas*). The Department of Social Culture was formed last, but it is developing fast, since its area of research has been much less explored in Hungary in comparison to the others.

The oldest and largest institute is the *Néprajzi Múzeum* (Ethnographical Museum). The number of artifacts exhibited there approaches 200 thousand. The following departments implement the work: the *Hungarian Department* collects, stores, and organizes artifacts relating to Hungarian ethnology, as well as artifacts of nationalities living together with or neighbouring the Hungarians. The *International Department* collects from every region which is not under the auspices of the Hungarian Department. Especially significant are its Finno-Ugric, Oceanian, and African collections. Notes referring to artifacts, manuscripts, the results of field research, posthumous papers of outstanding ethnologists, are housed in the *Ethnological Documentation Department*. The number of sketches and photographs there must be in the hundreds of thousands. The collection of documents referring to the history of ethnological research is the most important collection of its kind in Hungary. The *Folk Music Collection* preserves phonograph-cylinders, and, from a later date, tapes, records and notes dating from the end of the past century. The monumental material comprising the musical notations of BÉLA VIKÁR, BÉLA BARTÓK, ZOLTÁN KODÁLY and LÁSZLÓ LAJTHA (1892–

1963) is of inestimable value, and is augmented by the collection of folk instruments. The *Library* is a public reference library, where the number of books approaches 80,000.

Among the provincial museums, 27 ethnographic collections contain over 5,000 artifacts each; five of them contain more than 10,000, and three of them approach or exceed 20,000 objects. Manuscripts, photographs and drawings are also included in these collections. The collecting and organizing activities of the provincial museums are directed overall by the Ethnographical Museum of Budapest. Nearly fifty researchers are working in provincial museums at this date.

Among the ethnological types of museums, we must make a special note of the *village museums,* often called *skanzen* in Hungary, after the

3. The Village Museum of Vas County
Szombathely

Swedish example. Between the two world wars there was only enough
money to move and re-erect a few relics of peasant architecture here and
there. The situation became appropriate for the building of such
museums in the 1960s. A fisherman's hut and a cottier's cottage have
been exhibited since 1966, on their original site in Tihany, on the shore
of Lake Balaton. The *Göcseji Szabadtéri Múzeum* (Village Museum of
Göcsej), opened in 1967, has 33 buildings altogether, representing the
rural architecture of South-Western Hungary. The *Vasi Falumúzeum*
(Village Museum of Vas County), opened at Szombathely in 1973, has
25 buildings encompassing 7 complete farmyards arranged as though
along a street, as was usual on the Western Border. In the eastern part of
the country, at Nyíregyháza, several dwellings and farm buildings of the
Sóstói Falumúzeum (Village Museum of Sóstó) mark the beginning of
this enterprise. Besides these, certain typical peasant dwellings are
preserved locally and function as local museums in different parts of the
country.

The central *Magyar Szabadtéri Múzeum* (Hungarian Ethnographical
Village Museum) is still being expanded north of Budapest on the
outskirts of Szentendre, a town which lies along the bank of the Danube.

21

Its first section was opened in autumn 1973. The scale of this great enterprise is such that according to the plans there will be 53 dwellings, 58 farm buildings, and 74 other buildings brought in and constructed during one decade. The buildings have already been chosen from the entire country. Besides traditional peasant furnishings, 24 different trades and handicrafts will also be preserved along with 33 complete workshops.

It is possible to survey a specific area of ethnology only if all the material data possible have been accumulated. It is worth mentioning such undertakings, because they illustrate well the main directions of Hungarian ethnology.

The *Néprajzi Történeti Archívum* (Ethnological Historic Archives) contains the data from unpublished and published certificates, codices and indexes of ethnological relevance prior to 1526. The major part of these data refers to material culture, and with their aid a vivid picture can

5. The Hungarian Ethnographical Village Museum, Szentendre Farmsteads from Kispalád and Botpalád

be made of the medieval Hungarian settlement, home, furniture, eating habits, attire, transportation methods and trade.

A *Mezőgazdasági Munkaeszköztörténeti Archívum* (Historical Archives of Agricultural Tools) includes descriptions and photographs of archaeological, historical and ethnological objects, and indicates the work processes that were carried out with these tools. The number of identified work tools approaches one hundred thousand.

The work on the *Magyar Néprajzi Atlasz* (Hungarian Ethnographical Atlas) began in 1959, based on 240 research locations in Hungary. In addition, research was carried on in 24 villages in Czechoslovakia, and 22 villages in Yugoslavia. The drawing of the final draft of the maps is in progress and the first proofs will shortly go to press. Material for the ethnological atlases of certain regions, the counties of Szolnok and Baranya, is being collected and prepared for publication by the provincial museums of these areas.

The largest joint undertaking of Hungarian folklore research is the *Magyar Népmese Katalógus* (Catalogue of Hungarian Folk Tales). Its

6. The Hungarian Ethnographical Village Museum, Szentendre
House from Kispalád

research workers have already documented all the tales that have appeared in print, analysed the most important manuscript collections, and will continue to do further exploration in this area. Work commenced recently on the *Magyar Monda Katalógus* (Catalogue of Hungarian Legends), but the collection of already printed myths has been largely completed and the analysis of manuscript sources begun.

The *Népdalszövegek Katalógusa* (Catalogue of Folksong Texts) is almost complete, and extends both to printed and to manuscript sources. Because the sorted material is so bulky that its publication at present is completely out of the question, it is available for research only in manuscript form. The collection of the *Magyar Népzene Tára* (Treasury of Hungarian Folk Music) extends to songs and texts written down both in the past and more recently. Its extensive volumes appear in Hungarian and in foreign languages, and the publication of several is now in progress.

We have mentioned only a few of the important and central undertakings of Hungarian ethnology, but there are also some others that only partially or indirectly touch upon Hungarian ethnological science. The *Sámánhit Archívum* (Shaman Archives) is the most important of these. It contains the photographs, descriptions, and sketches of museum objects referring to Eurasian shamanism, and includes published and handwritten collections, notes and tapes that are preserved in the museums and centres of research in Eurasia. The recently deceased VILMOS DIÓSZEGI

7. The *Palots* house
Balassagyarmat, Palóc Museum

(1923–1972), founder of the Archive, completed it with his wide-range collecting in the Soviet Union.

Two large undertakings of Hungarian ethnology affect every researcher. One is the *Néprajzi Lexikon* (Encyclopedia of Ethnography), which gives the definitions of fundamental ethnological concepts, and provides alphabetical description of objects and phenomena in five large and richly illustrated volumes. It was published by the Hungarian Academy of Sciences.

Secondly, the Ethnological High Committee of the Hungarian Academy of Sciences decided to prepare and publish the new summary of *Magyar Néprajz*. The first volume gives a historical survey, expounds the ethnogenesis of Hungary, and examines the stratification of Hungarian folk culture in different areas. Two volumes will deal with material culture, two with folklore, and one with social anthropology. Preparations for the six-volume work have already begun.

Hungarian ethnologists can publish their articles not only in the periodicals already mentioned *(Ethnographia, Néprajzi Értesítő, Acta Ethnographica)*, but also in different yearbooks. The Ethnological Research Institute publishes annually (since 1966) articles mainly written by its co-workers under the title *Népi Kultúra—Népi Társadalom* (Folk Culture—Folk Society). The Ethnological Institute of the University of Debrecen has published the annual volumes of *Műveltség és Hagyomány* (Learning and Tradition) since 1960. These contain several shorter contributions, and from time to time a single study filling the entire book. The primary objective of the *Néprajzi Közlemény* (Ethnographical Communiqué) is to give information about collected raw material from the notes, but it also contains full reviews. The Hungarian Ethnographic Society has been publishing in six yearly issues the *Néprajzi Hírek* (News on Ethnography), containing the latest results of Hungarian ethnology. Every year the last issue contains as complete a bibliography as possible of Hungarian ethnology published in the previous year.

There are also several ethnological studies in the yearbooks of the national and provincial museums. Their annual numbers total about twenty.

Studies in the form of books are brought out by publishing companies. Most ethnographical books are published by Akadémiai Kiadó (the Publishing House of the Hungarian Academy of Sciences), in Hungarian, and sometimes in a foreign language. The most important role in introducing and popularizing the results of Hungarian ethnology in foreign languages has been assumed by Corvina Kiadó.

The Ethnogenesis of the Hungarian People and their Place in European Culture

The Hungarians constitute the largest group of the Finno-Ugric language family, followed in numbers by the Finns, then the Estonians and some other smaller and larger groups in the Soviet Union. Based on the testimony of linguistics, archeology, the study of plant and animal species and other sciences, the original home of the Finno-Ugric peoples has been located west of the Volga–Kama region, where they lived in the near vicinity of each other until about the third millennium B.C. These fishing-hunting peoples, according to the evidence of archeology and linguistics, already practised husbandry and even primitive agriculture before they began to disperse. The Hungarians were located in the original homeland near the Voguls (Mansi) and Ostyaks (Khanti), together with whom they created the Ugric branch, but the vocabulary of Hungarian shows that they also maintained contact with the Permian branch. Very little remains for posterity from the material culture of the Finno-Ugric and Ugric period. Here and there in the area of fishing and hunting we can suspect some inheritance in certain tools or methods of procedure. There is more of this early cultural stratum hidden in the intellectual culture. In lamentations and in certain carols, in children's games, in the beliefs about the soul, and in shamanism, there occur certain elements of Hungarian ethnic history which are traceable to its early phase (cf. also pp. 670–72).   The Ugrians (the Voguls, Ostyaks, Magyars) separated slowly in the middle of the third millennium B.C. from the Finn–Permian branch (the Finns, Estonians, Zyryans [Komi], Votyaks [Udmurt], Cheremissians [Mari], Mordvinians, Lapps, etc.).

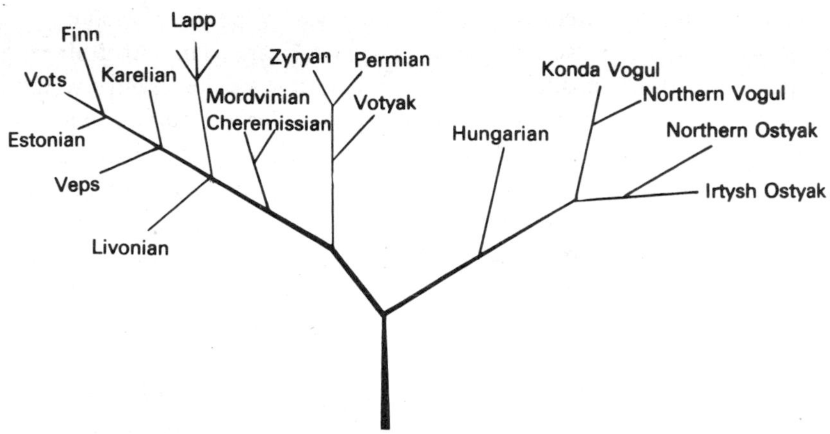

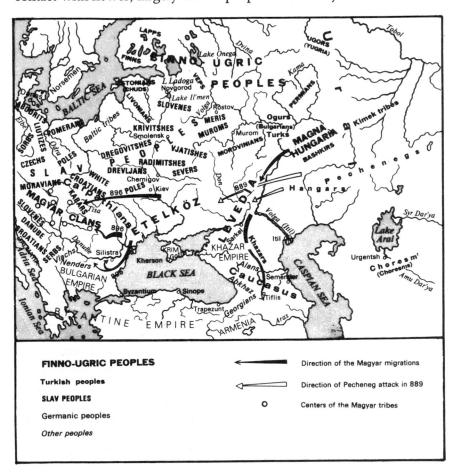

Fig. 1. The relationship of the Finno–Ugric peoples

The separation of the Magyars and the later Ob-Ugrians (Voguls, Ostyaks) must have taken place between 1000 and 500 B.C. The so-called Ananyino culture, to which presumably the pre-Magyars also belonged, existed during this period. By then they were building earthworks, and their tools made of bone have remained in large number. The ancient Magyars, pushed from the Volga–Kama region towards south–south–east, emerged from the forest belt into the world of the wooded steppes.

Not only did the land change around them, but they also came into contact with newer, largely Turkic peoples. Thus they learned the most

Fig. 2. Eastern Europe in the 9th century, and the early Hungarian settlements

FINNO-UGRIC PEOPLES

Turkish peoples

SLAV PEOPLES

Germanic peoples

Other peoples

⟵ Direction of the Magyar migrations

⟵ Direction of Pecheneg attack in 889

o Centers of the Magyar tribes

27

important branches of animal husbandry: the domestication of sheep, cattle, and horses. They were nomadic during the period of pasturing. At this time they also became acquainted with the basic elements of plough agriculture, which presupposes a partially settled existence. Their contact with the Turkic peoples must have been strong, because Byzantine sources in the beginning called them Turks, and other sources mention them also by a Turkish name, calling them *Onugrians,* ten tribes. The naming of our people in most European languages derives from this word: (H)Ungarus, Ungar, Vengri, etc., while the Hungarians call themselves *Magyars* after the tribal name *Magyer* of Ugrian origin.

During the move southward the Magyars reached the foothills of the Caucasus, where, at least from the 8th century, they became members of the Khazar Khaganate. This empire, possessing a well-developed animal husbandry, field, garden and grape culture, already wore the features of a nearly feudal state and in this the Magyars also participated. In the 9th century seven Magyar tribes, also joined by one Khazar and a rebel *Kabar* tribe, moved on towards the west and occupied the large territory that stretched to the Lower Danube. By then even the Byzantine sources called them *Magyars.* They were engaged not only in nomadic husbandry, but in agriculture as well, and settled mostly along the river in semi-permanent dwellings.

The traces of contact with the various Turkic peoples can be shown primarily in the characteristics of husbandry, especially nomadic animal husbandry, in the plough cultivation of fields, and in vine growing. Some characteristics can be found in building construction and in clothing as much as in the processing of hemp with certain implements that remind us of these peoples. In the area of folklore, many elements survived almost until the present day, though they might show up in different structures. Examples are the learning of a kind of *runic script* and the expansion of shamanism, the major characteristics of which are preserved in the person of the *táltos* (shaman). The trail of pentatonic melodies, characterized by the exact repetition of the melody a fifth lower, can be followed through the Turks to Inner Asia, and this type of melody constitutes about ten per cent of Hungarian folksongs. We can also find traditions referring to this period in the range of customs relating to weddings and burials.

It was in South Russian territory that the Magyars first met different Eastern Slavic tribes, such as the *Poljan* and *Severjan,* from whom, instead of the Khazars, they collected the taxes. They warred with them and sold the prisoners to Byzantine merchants at the Black Sea port. Their contacts left imprints not only of wars but of peace as well. They gained additional knowledge of fishing, and became acquainted with the tools and methods of group work. Their agricultural knowledge also expanded; they probably learned the use of the wheeled plough from the Slavs. Some elements of their body of beliefs, e.g. relating to witches, also originated from this period.

The warring, nomadic groups of the Magyars broke into the Carpathian Basin from 862 on and interfered in the conflicts of the peoples who lived there. At this time the head of the Magyar tribal confederacy went to war with about 20,000 horsemen, beyond which we must suppose a body of people adequate to support them, so that the number of families must have numbered at least 100,000, and the total numbers reached and possibly exceeded half a million.

The Magyars, while helping the Byzantines, defeated the Bulgarians, who in turn took revenge by releasing the Pechenegs who pushed from the east against the Magyars just at the time when their military force was roaming far afield. On seeing the devastated settlements and fearing renewed attacks, the entire confederacy of tribes realized that there was nothing else to do but to push into the Carpathian Basin. This they did and in the course of a few years they had occupied it.

The Carpathian Basin, throughout its history, has given a home to many peoples, some of whom passed on their culture to their successors. Such were the Celts (4th century B.C.), who were known as the disseminators of iron tools. Then came the Romans, who left behind in Transylvania (Dacia) and Transdanubia (Pannonia) such a culture that even the centuries of the period of migration could not sweep away certain of its elements.

The Magyars found many different kinds of peoples in the relatively sparsely populated Carpathian Basin. The Bulgarians had settled on the central great steppes and a part of Transylvania. At other places different Slavic peoples had settled in pockets: Moravians, Danubian Slovenians, White Croatians, Slovakians, and others. A remnant of the Frankish rule of Charlemagne, Bavarians lived at the western boundaries. Only one substantial state stood in the way of the Magyars, the Moravian principality, stretching from the west to the Garam, but this too they defeated. The conquered peoples adjusted to the Magyars, but the Magyars also adapted themselves to them and so began the interaction of Magyar and Slav that continues even today.

For more than half a century the contact of the Magyars with Europe meant war, with roaming and marauding to the west. They exploited the dismemberment and eternal warfare of the feudal West. They attached themselves to one or another ruler and fought in Italy, Germany, and got as far as Switzerland, France, and on one occasion even Spain. The head of the tribal confederacy looked favourably upon such military excursions, not only because they helped to keep the military force fit, but also because the practice held off western attacks while he was organizing his own country. The speed of the Magyar light cavalry, their terrible arrows, and their new fighting method not only brought victory, but also gave rise to general fear in Europe, until the united German armies inflicted a decisive defeat upon them at Augsburg in 955. In the course of their roaming the Magyars looked at a completely different and for them new world; they met the new and for them strange European culture.

However, this did not basically change their half-settled, half-nomadic way of life. The change took place at the time when, following efforts made by Byzantine missionaries, King Stephen I (997–1038) took up Roman Christianity. He urged, and occasionally forced, the entire Magyar nation to do the same. By this step the Magyars avoided attrition, which had led to the disappearance of many peoples during the period of migration in the Carpathian Basin. They retained their language and their independence, but a large part of the culture, the world of beliefs and the customs they brought with them vanished, changed, or were amalgamated with other cultural elements.

Ultimately, Christianity came to the Magyars through Slavic mediation. Accordingly, they were acquainted with a great many new words, concepts, objects, and phenomena. Some examples are: *keresztény* (Christian), *pap* (priest), *barát* (friar), *apát* (abbot), *apáca* (nun), *szent* (saint), *pokol* (hell), *csoda* (miracle), *malaszt* (divine grace), *vecsernye* (vespers); some of the names of weekdays: *szerda* (Wednesday), *csütörtök* (Thursday), *péntek* (Friday), *szombat* (Saturday); and among major holidays, *karácsony* (Christmas). The Magyars also became acquainted with the new social order primarily with the aid of the Slavs: *császár* (emperor), *király* (king), *ispán* (bailiff), *tiszt* (officer), *kenéz* (magistrate), *udvarnok* (Lord High-Steward), *bajnok* (champion), and a string of other concepts. However, from the point of view of ethnology, the influence that affected the Magyars in the area of agriculture is even more important. Significant changes took place in the system of working the soil: *parlag* (waste land), *ugar* (fallow), and in the method of cultivation and harvesting. In particular the domestication of garden vegetable production: *bab* (beans), *cékla* (beets), *mák* (poppy seed), *retek* (radish), *uborka* (cucumber) can be attributed to the Slavic peoples with whom they lived together. The influence of close ties may be found in many fields: crafts, trades, family relationships, houses, dwellings, nutrition, clothing, and many others. Not all influences were, of course, one-way, as is shown by the fact that in the Slovakian language the words of Hungarian origin approach one thousand. New concepts and new attainments were linked to these expressions.

Contact with the Germans at the western border region had already begun at the time of the conquest of Hungary. This was especially strengthened in the time of Stephen I, who brought in and settled Bavarian–Austrian knights, priests and burghers. However, already during the 12th and 13th centuries peasants and artisans whose descendants are still living in the region of Szepes (Czechoslovakia) and Transylvania came in much greater numbers. This influence affected primarily city life, the guilds and trades, but also certain new objects and concepts reached the peasantry (*tönköly* [German wheat], *bükköny* [vetch], *csűr* [hayloft], *istálló* [stable], *kaptár* [beehive], *major* [farmstead of an estate], *puttony* [butt], etc.), which seem to indicate development toward more intensive farming.

The Hungarians soon came into contact with Italians also, but Italian influence was much less compared to Slav and German influence. Some of the technical terms of navigation (*sajka* [small boat], *bárka* [bark], *gálya* [galley]), and of commercial life (*piac* [market]) left marks mainly on city culture. Buildings of Italian masters who worked here (churches, forts, castles) transposed European forms of architecture into peasant styles. The turn of the 12th and 13th centuries saw significant French and Walloon settlements. Besides priests and monastics, peasants came too, who left clearly visible marks in areas such as viniculture.

Slavic, German, French, and other Western influences can be traced not only in the material culture but in the folklore as well. Amongst the ruling classes the great cultural change came earlier, but it gradually became observable among the peasantry also. One of the transmitters of the new culture was the Church, which introduced a completely new intellectual culture to the Hungarians through its liturgy, its saints and the associated legends, and through customs connected with church holidays. In the courts of the king and the high nobility, western heroic songs were propagated by bards, while the one-time pagan bards were driven back among the people, and the priests cruelly persecuted them along with the memories of the old world of beliefs. The separation of the epic literary forms slowly began at this period. Side by side with heroic songs now legends, myths and ballads began to play an increasing role. An early stratum of the ballads very likely came to the Carpathian Basin with the Walloon-French settlers. The folklore of the Hungarian peasantry, while retaining many elements from the previous period, slowly set out on the European road. That this change did not take place without a jolt is shown by the recurrent pagan rebellions, but the ever-strengthening economic and intellectual process proved irreversible.

All this was supported by the fact that Eastern political ties, although not broken completely, became significantly weaker. The kings of the House of Árpád (until 1301) still maintained their ties, primarily based on kinship, with Kiev and Byzantium, which represented Eastern Christianity, but it was no longer an economic and cultural influence touching upon the entire nation.

In 1241–42 the Tartars destroyed a significant part of the country. The nomadic Cumanians and after them the Jazygians appeared at this time on the country's central, flat areas, well suited for extensive animal husbandry. This meant the strengthening of the pagan tradition in the second half of the 13th century, since even some kings (Ladislas IV, or Ladislas the Cumanian) revered ancient customs. However, during the next centuries the Cumanians and Jazygians assimilated into the Hungarians, whose social development represented a higher stage, and so only a few words and objects were accepted into the Hungarian language and culture (*buzogány* [mace], *csődör* [stallion], *komondor* [sheep dog], *balta* [hatchet], *csákány* [pick ax]).

The bulk of the Hungarians were working people divided already in the Middle Ages into several social groups, more or less differentiated from one another. The situation and living conditions of servants, of permanent or free serfs, freemen *(szabadok)* and the artisans changed in every era. A ninth of the produce was paid to the landlord for their land, and a tenth of the produce to the Church, besides which the people had to do labour service and occasionally give money and gifts. The amount of gifts changed according to what the landlord needed at certain times. In general it may be observed that towards the end of the Middle Ages, the situation of peasants increasingly declined. The result was that the number of local peasant risings, smaller and larger ones, multiplied.

The peasant rebellion in 1514 led by Dózsa was the largest and most notable. After a cruel defeat, the legal rights of peasants were drastically cut back, permanent serfdom was declared, the right to move was prohibited, and the amount of work due to the landlord was increased to a whole day or two days a week or often even more. Furthermore, all this happened just at the time when the Turkish Empire posed an immediate threat to Hungary. In 1526 the Turks defeated the Hungarian army at Mohács, a town along the Danube; the king, Louis II, fell on the battlefield and the historical period began when the country was divided into three parts. The Turks ruled the central and southern areas, the House of Habsburg acquired the northern and western regions, and in Transylvania a more or less independent principality was set up.

Although this period, which lasted to the end of the 17th century, was one of the most difficult periods of Hungarian history, cultural development did not come to a halt. The great artistic and intellectual currents of Europe arrived and had their full effect here: the Renaissance, Humanism, the Reformation. The printing of books expanded, more and more schools were established. The most difficult situation for Hungarian peasants was within the territories occupied by the Turks, where taxes, ransoms, robberies, and the burning of villages were everyday occurrences. In spite of all this, peasant culture continued to develop even in this period. The three-unit house (room + kitchen + room) spread over a larger and larger territory, and at the same time some pieces of furniture appeared, new in form and function. In those market towns which were spared by the Turks, trade flourished. Even articles of clothing taken over from the Turks (*kalpag* [hat], *csizma* [boots], *papucs* [slippers], *dolmány* [dolman]) were made, and new foods (*tarhonya* [granulated dry pastry made of flour and eggs]) were adopted. A large proportion of the cultural goods of Ottoman Turkish origin came to the Hungarians through a South Slavic filter.

In Transylvania peasant culture was shaped by the mutual interaction of the Hungarians, Rumanians and Saxons who lived next to or near each other. The Hungarians supplied agricultural goods, the Rumanians supplied animals, while the Saxons supplied the products of the artisans. The multiplicity of Renaissance style and the influx of Turkish industrial products and their effects on folk culture can easily be traced here.

The population of the country's northern region became more dense in this period, since primarily nobles, but in part even serfs fled in large numbers to this area from the southern region. However, even in this territory they could not escape the robberies of the Imperial mercenary troops, who often surpassed even the Turks in cruelty. German influence can be more strongly felt here, but it affected the peasantry to a lesser degree.

Turkish occupation had barely ended at the end of the 17th century when the Hungarians again took up arms to free themselves from Habsburg oppression. After the loss of the fight for independence (1703–1711), led by Ferenc Rákóczi II, the Habsburgs gave the most fertile areas of the pillaged and depopulated country to those Austrian–German landlords who earned merit during the war. At this time the migration from north to south began, the result of which was that the Hungarian groups who had previously fled from the Turks to the north, now swarmed down to the Great Plain. Slovaks also settled in the same area. The German influx exceeded even these in numbers,

32

mainly in Transdanubia, but also in certain areas of the Great Plain and Upper Hungary. Thus, by the end of the 18th century the Hungarians totalled barely fifty per cent of the population. All this again affected Hungarian peasant culture, although only to a smaller degree, because settlement pockets of the various nationalities either assimilated to the Hungarians or took on significant elements of Hungarian culture.

The relative peace of this century, in comparison with those preceding, meant the strengthening of the peasantry, even though their burdens had grown. Beside services in kind, they had to provide the landlords with 52 days of work with a horse each year or 102 days of work on foot, and had also to undertake several days' long hauling. The inner structure of agriculture also changed: extensive animal husbandry decreased, the significance of farming grew, new crops (potato, maize, green pepper, tobacco) became widely spread. The house and its furnishings developed further, and certain elements of folk customs, which live on to this day, appeared largely then, for the first time. Hungarian folksongs of a new style were formed and the most characteristic dances developed. By the end of this period, which came to an end with the freeing of the serfs in 1848, the characteristic traits of Hungarian folk culture became clearly evident, and may be studied in collections of museums and also in lingering tradition.

The social differentiation of peasantry owning land became increasingly obvious by the second half of the last century. A growing chasm can be observed between the rich peasant who owned 20–50 hectares and the poor peasant who struggled on 1–5 hectares. A greater number of the poor peasants became destitute, and to their numbers may be added those indigent agricultural labourers, the masses of labourers on the great estates, who numbered millions. Special groups emerged amongst such rural workers: seasonal labourers, pick and shovel men, melon pickers, tobacco pickers. Each group has specific traits of culture typical only of that profession. Yet this period, in spite of everything, is the era when Hungarian folk arts flourished. Costumes, homespun and embroidery became more colourful; the supply of new materials from industry was playing an important part in this proliferation. The most artistic products of the potter's craft and the best painted furniture originate from this period, which by and large closes with World War I. Generally, the richest and the poorest among the strata of the peasantry were first to give up their traditions. The richest did so to make easier their approach to the ruling class, and the poorest out of economic necessity as a result of the basic change in their form of life.

Beginning in 1920, with the breaking up of the Austro-Hungarian Monarchy, the nationalities living in Hungary formed their own states in accordance with the peace treaty, and the present borders of Hungary were drawn up. Within these live 10.5 million citizens, and Hungarian is the mother tongue of 95 per cent of them. Among the nationalities, Germans, Slovakians, South Slavs and Rumanians live in Hungary in larger numbers.

After 1945 the Hungarian nation tried to obliterate the serious wounds caused by the war, and from 1948–49 it has worked on erecting socialist economic life, society, and culture. Of outstanding importance for the

Hungarian peasantry is the year 1961, when following the pattern of a great many earlier examples, they entered the path of collective farming. The past two decades show that for them this was as significant a change of fortune as the change from fisher-hunter to nomadic husbandman, or the basic change in life style and culture after the settlement in the Carpathian Basin, or changes brought about by being freed from the burden of serfdom. The character, organization, and assignment of labour changed decisively, resulting in basic adaptations in, for example, the organization of the family. The individual farm outbuildings are gradually disappearing from beside the new houses, since they are needed less and less. With the change of life style produced by the effect of schools and of the media of mass communication, a new culture is evolving, into which everything worth preserving from the old culture is being built. It follows from what has been said above that our synopsis of Hungarian folk culture relates largely to the past, which is revealed, evaluated, and introduced by both ethnology and historical science.

Besides the 10 million Hungarians living within the borders of the country, there are outside the country a large number of Hungarians, whose mother tongue is Hungarian. Thus there are 406,116 in Czechoslovakia, 520,938 in Yugoslavia, 1,811,983 in Rumania, 164,960 in the Soviet Union (1967–68 data), and about 50,000 in Austria. Beside this there are almost one million in the USA, and approximately half million who live in smaller or larger groups in various parts of the world. From the point of view of ethnological research, the Hungarians living outside Hungary are important not only because of their numbers, but also because as a result of their isolated situation they have often well preserved many old traits.

This brief summary simply is intended to acquaint the reader with the major changes of fortune of the Hungarian people in the thousand-year process of development of its culture. Only in this way is it possible to understand the culture of the Hungarian people, which is built on foundations brought from the East, developed in Central Europe, and connected with general European progress.

Hungarian Ethnic Groups, Ethnographic Regions and Pockets of Survival

The folk culture of the Hungarians is uniform in its basic structure and major characteristics, just as the dialects are not divided by differences that hinder comprehension. Yet we have recorded smaller and larger groups, regions, and pockets surrounded by other ethnic groups, which differ more or less from their immediate or distant neighbours. This difference, however, is never manifested in the entirety of the culture, but perhaps only in certain phenomena, or at most in groups of phenomena. Certain ethnic groups that remain as pockets within the Hungarian whole are separated from their neighbours by characteristic elements. The differentiating elements take new shapes and change just as the entirety of folk culture is not a static unit, because it is constantly renewing itself and abandoning features that for some reason have become superfluous.

We are able to trace the roots of the formation of ethnic groups back to the Magyar Conquest. Among the eight tribes that settled here there could well have been differences in origin, culture, and occupation, even though these differences may have been washed away by later eras. The diversified geographical conditions in the mountains, steppes, and swampy regions of the Carpathian Basin affected the development of local cultures as factors determining life style. Differences were emphasized by historical factors such as the fact that in the age of feudalism certain groups and areas enjoyed greater or lesser privileges that differentiated them from the other groups. Similarly, in various sections of the country economic and social differences also contributed to the development of ethnic groups, in which in certain cases we can discover the feeling of identity. Some groups of Hungarians living near the Rumanians, South Slavs and Slovakians took over particular characteristics into their own culture that emphasized their separation. All this makes it beyond doubt that ethnic groups, ethnological regions and pockets are formations that look back upon a longer or shorter historical past.

Broadly speaking, we can separate or distinguish them only by taking the following considerations into account. The people who live in isolated pockets in the main incorporate the typical characteristics of their own ethnic group, which differentiate them from their neighbours, and by means of which they can also draw their own boundaries. This is comparable to what the representatives of the surrounding villages or ethnic groups tell about their neighbours. The picture is completed by the characteristics which for some reason are not mentioned by the members of the group in question. We must especially be aware of the feeling of identity and its manifest forms, which may be expressed in endogamy or in some other form.

We can determine the characteristic traits of the culture of certain ethnic groups primarily with the aid of already assembled and evaluated ethnological material, and by relating them to their environment, and perhaps comparing them with those of other ethnic groups in which some of these traits might have originated. Ethnological maps and in general the cartographic delineation of phenomena can provide excellent service in determining the diffusion of elements.

In the case of ethnic groups, the mutual historical sense of cohesion dominates, and often spreads across geographical and administrative boundaries. Geographical factors determine the border in the case of ethnological regions, when the peoples of a mountain district, a swamp area, a river valley, or a vine-growing region belong together. In the determination of a linguistic or ethnic pocket it is the language surrounding the group in question on every side that dominates. Although the delimitation is from a variety of points of view, still the differentiation of the groups is determined by the special colouring of their culture. Thus, if in one case we encounter the naming of a group of people, and in another we make use of the regional or area designation, we are referring in both cases to a certain relatedness with an ethnic tinge of the people who live there. This can appear in very diverse forms, through occupation and costume, or custom to folk poetry.

The most important intellectual cohesive force of a nation is language, the significance of which is ever more increasing in our times. The most recent research shows that we cannot use the dialect in every respect to determine ethnic groups. As a rule, phonetic and linguistic boundaries only exceptionally coincide with the territories of ethnic groups. Research in word geography offers much better opportunities, but unfortunately we can make use of this in full confidence only in the rare instances when a page of the *Atlas of Hungarian Dialects* projects on the map the concept suited exactly to our purpose.

After all we can attempt only in broad outlines the introduction of the most important ethnic groups, ethnological regions, and pockets of survival of the Hungarian people. Reaching over present-day borders, partly from geographical, partly from historical consideration, we can divide that part of the Carpathian Basin into four large sections where the mother tongue of the people who live there is Hungarian. Transdanubia (the *Dunántúl*) is the western territory bordered by the Danube and the Dráva rivers, and there are also smaller Hungarian areas in Austria. Upper Hungary (the *Felföld*) contains the northern hill and mountain area and reaches into Slovakia. The Great Plain *(Alföld)* is the central plain of the Carpathian Basin, which continues into Yugoslavia on the south. The Hungarian ethnic groups of Transylvania *(Erdély)* in places even sweep through the crest of the Eastern Carpathians. We will follow this geographical division in the following chapters.

Transdanubia   In the centre of the rather more hilly than mountainous terrain of Transdanubia (the *Dunántúl*) lies the largest lake in Hungary, the 70-km-long Balaton. This is the area, once known as Pannonia, where certain Celtic–Roman traditions exist in folk culture, absorbed by the Hungarians into their culture in the same way as they absorbed certain Croatian–Slovakian and, in the western areas, German elements. The latter was also made possible by the fact that environmentally some of this area belonged to the Alps, the effects of which can be similarly shown in agriculture and building style.

Göcsej occupies a significant territory in the south-western corner of the country. This is a rolling, hilly region, which is difficult to cultivate. The main occupation of the population is animal husbandry and agriculture, including the growing of buckwheat and vines. Parts of the villages are settled on cleared woodlands, and these groups of houses are called *szeg,* which appears in village names such as *Kustánszeg.* In the past the families did not disperse, but lived on one lot or near each other in the typical form of a joint family. It can happen that the house and the farm buildings surround a small sized, U-shaped yard, which is closed off in front by a fence and a gate. These fenced houses disappeared only in the recent past. The custom of minstrelsy, which preserves pagan elements connected with the Christmas holiday cycle, survives until the present. In the 18 villages of the neighbouring *Hetés,* lying south-west of Göcsej, in a comparable environment, a similar culture developed.

The lower section of the *Őrség* comprises the 18 villages in the valley of the Zala and Kerka rivers. Its inhabitants, as the name shows (*őrség*—guards), are the descendants of the medieval border guards. They settled in the forest and formed a *szer* (kinship group) by families, which grew into smaller villages, but in many places they have preserved their characteristics until today. Some of these small settlements are called after the name of the family, e. g. Kovács-szer, Szabó-szer. In the past animal husbandry characteristic of the Alpine region was the basis of their existence, as in the poor soil grain seeds gave very meagre returns for their labour. The scattered settlements amidst ploughed fields, orchards, and grazing land lend a special charm to this region. In the Austrian Burgenland, in the valley of the Pinka, hide the few Hungarian villages of the *Felsőőrség* (Felsőőr, Alsóőr, Őrisziget, Jobbágyi), which were the westernmost settlements of the Hungarians who defended the borders against attacks coming from the west during the Middle Ages. This group has preserved much tradition in its language and customs, but in its culture German influences prevail.

The people of the *Hanság* lived in a swampy, boggy area. Their main occupations, beside animal husbandry, were fishing, hunting, the processing of reeds and bulrushes as a cottage industry, and peat cutting. During the second half of the last century large parts of the swamps were drained and in their place a flourishing agriculture developed. The last remnants of the swamps have recently been drained.

The people of the *Rábaköz* live in the villages of the flat land between the Rába and Rábca rivers. The typical central market town of the area is Kapuvár, which may mark, as indicated by its name, the site of gate (*kapu*—gate, *vár*—castle) of the defence system that stretched through here. Many animals and much produce changed hands at its famous markets. It differs from neighbouring regions in its building style, its special white embroidery, and the rich folk costume of some of its villages.

On the right bank of the Rába run two mountain ranges: one is the *Kemeneshát,* and to the north of it rises the *Sokoró.* The former customs and costumes of the people of *Kemenesalja* and *Sokoróalja* are different from those of their neighbours, and they proudly display these features even today.

The people of *Szigetköz* live on the closed island between the Great Danube and the Mosoni Danube. They keep many animals on their irrigated pastures and meadows, which provide the means of existence of the population. The water played a determining role in their life, for while it devastated much, it also fertilized the meadows.

Here we cross the Danube and find one of the largest Hungarian ethnic groups in Slovakia, the people of *Csallóköz*. In the past they called this region *Aranykert* (the Garden of Gold), because they used to wash gold out of the sands of the Danube. The innumerable stagnant and flowing waters of the Danube outline the borders of the villages, offering a means of existence to fishermen and husbandmen, whilst often ruining the work of the peasants. In the past, part of the population, especially in Komárom and its vicinity, engaged in shipping. The galleys loaded with grain travelled all the way to the Black Sea. During the Turkish rule they got even as far as Istanbul, and they also shipped fish to Vienna.

North and north-east of the Csallóköz we find *Mátyusföld,* named after an all-powerful landlord of the 14th century, Máté Csák. The folklore traditions of this region are flourishing even today, and its children's games are especially well known. Even farther north live the Hungarians of the *Zobor region,* who constitute the most northerly contiguous settlements of Hungarians. They have therefore preserved many archaic characteristics, the most familiar of which occur in the customs, folksongs and ballads.

Now we return to the right bank of the Danube, where, proceeding to the south, the *Bakony Mountains* rise, with small settlements hiding in the valleys. A good proportion of the villages have been inhabited since the time of Árpád. The people's life, especially in the past, was determined by the forest. The pigherds of the Bakony are already mentioned in documents dating from the 13th century. They were, like all peoples living in the forest, masters of woodcarving. They made tools for agricultural and home use in such quantities that they travelled to distant markets with them. With the shrinking of the forest, agriculture more and more eclipsed both husbandry and woodworking.

The densely populated villages of the *Balaton Highlands* stretch all the

9. Rural buildings
Szigliget, Veszprém County

38

way down to the lake shore. On the volcanic soil of the hillsides of the region, with its Mediterranean-like climate, excellent vines grow, and fishing assures the livelihood of a significant portion of the population. The stone buildings of the villages, with their historic-style porticos, spread over a large area.

We arrive, after crossing the Balaton, to *Somogy* (Somogy "country"), the part toward the Balaton called *Outer Somogy;* the part toward the Dráva, *Inner Somogy.* In general, the earlier life style of the population was determined by animal husbandry. The feeding of swine on mast, the use of the forest, and the processing of wood gave way to agriculture with the shrinking of the forest area. In *Zselicség* which lies south of Kaposvár, the most beautiful objects were carved by swineherds. The rich and varied folk costumes of the region, its white and colourful embroidery, are known far and wide. The peasant towns, occupied with agriculture, rose to middle-class standards relatively early.

In the south-western corner of Baranya County, between the Dráva and Okor rivers, we find the settlements of the *Ormánság.* This was a wet, swampy area at one time, with ridges of land rising out of it only here and there. This is where its name comes from (*ormán*—a protrusion).

39

Because of the danger from floods, the people built their houses on huge beams, wove the walls from wicker, and plastered these with mud. They engaged in fishing, animal husbandry and increasingly in agriculture. They fed their swine on mast in the forest, and pastured their famous herds of horses in the meadows. It is worth mentioning that one of their occupation in the 18th and 19th centuries, the making of potash, led to the destruction of the forest. Their characteristic costumes suggest South Slavic influence, and the use of white for mourning was long preserved here. The prosperous peasantry, which rapidly rose into the middle-class, tried to prevent its property from being broken up by having only one-child families.

The Hungarian villages of the *Drávaszög* are located in the corner of Transdanubia, which is now part of Yugoslavia, whilst the four Hungarian villages of Slavonia, Kórógy, Szentlászló, Haraszti and Eszék, are south of the Dráva river. They occupy island-like positions in the South Slav environment and their inhabitants intermarry with each other; earlier they also kept marital contacts with Baranya County. They

11. A dwelling in the vineyard
Nagykutas, Zala County

fished, hunted, and lived from husbandry in the past. Agriculture gained ground during the last century. They are differentiated from the villages that settled north of them by their archaic costume, language, and folk poetry.

The extent of the *Sárköz,* near the Danube in Tolna County, is difficult to determine. Five villages form its core (Őcsény, Decs, Sárpilis, Alsónyék, Báta), but certain elements of its culture can be found in Baranya or even in Slavonia. Some villages join it on the left bank of the Danube (Érsekcsanád, Szeremle). After the regulation of the waterways in the 19th century, agriculture came to replace exploitation of the resources of the river. The effects of the great local tradition of home-spun, of embroidery of white sewn on a black background, and colourful, rich folk costumes which flourished in the prosperity of the second half of the last century, and also of its folklore traditions, can be found on neighbouring groups.

Among the numerous smaller or larger ethnic groups of Trans-danubia, *Mezőföld* also deserves mention. It lies mostly on flat lands south of Lake Velence, between the Sárvíz, then the Sió and the Danube. The inhabitants of its large villages were early to follow urban culture, whilst the labourers of the former large estates developed a particular, individualistic culture, rich in folklore traditions.

Upper Hungary

The largest ethnic group of Upper Hungary (the *Felföld*) is the *Palots.* Their name means Cumanian in various Slavic languages, which might refer to their origin, but it is more likely that only their neighbours thought them to be Cumanian. Today, the traces of their relationship to the Cumans, which lives in tradition, cannot be easily discovered. Their settlements extend from the course of the Garam all the way to the centre of Borsod County, and in some places, even further. All the people in the north up to the Hungarian linguistic border are Palotses. Their boundaries are even more difficult to define on the south, because after the expulsion of the Turks, the prolific population emigrated even into the Southern Great Plain.

Precisely because the Palotses are dispersed over such an extremely large territory, we can differentiate several sub-groups among them. In general we speak of Western and Eastern Palotses. Among the former, the Palotses of Hont and Nógrád counties differ from each other. Several villages of the *Medvesalja* are just as isolated from the other villages as the settlements of *Galgamente,* whose rich embroidery, folk costumes, songs and dances are known far and wide. The smaller and larger groups of the Eastern Palotses are tied to certain geographic units. There is *Erdőhát,* south of the Sajó and Rima rivers. Its people, the *Barkó,* are so much like the Palotses that according to some they are part of this group. The *Hegyhát* is the hilly area enclosed by the streams Sajó, Bán and Hangony, while the *Homok* indicates a part of the valley of the stream called Tarna.

In spite of the differences among the various groups of the Palotses, the common features that unite them are still very numerous. The peculiarity of their dialect, which extends to several large areas, is taken

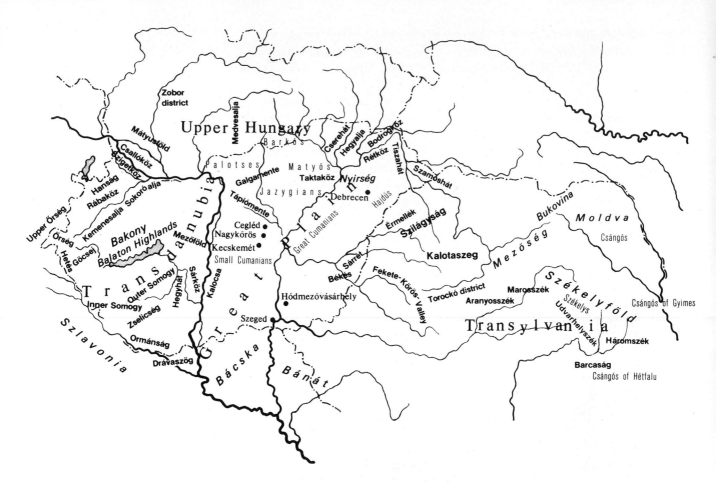

Fig. 3. Hungarian ethnic groups and ethnographical regions in the Carpathian Basin

as a basic determinative mark by many. The organization of the joint family prevailed with them for a long time. Shepherding played an especially important part in their animal husbandry, which is quite uniform, and its connections point toward Transylvania and Slovakia. They are also bound by many characteristics in house construction, homespuns, costumes, and folk poetry. We can point to Slovakian influence on the northern stretch of this group, especially in customs and beliefs, such as, e.g. *kiszehajtás* (throwing a straw dummy into the brook on Palm Sunday to avert the plague).

The *Cserehát* contains the villages between the Bódva and Hernád rivers. On the southern and eastern slopes of the Zemplén Mountains are the villages and market towns of *Tokaj-Hegyalja*. Life here in the past as well as in the present is determined by its far-famed vine growing. Because of the wine trade Greek, Serbian, Russian, Polish, Slovakian and German merchants lived here, a fact which can be felt in the culture, especially in connection with grapes, wine, and certain small crafts. To the north lie the 15 villages of *Hegyköz*. The difficult living circumstances of the people here are characterized by forestry work, animal husbandry and fruit growing.

On the border between Upper Hungary and the Great Plain, but already on the plains, live the *Matyós* in one larger and one smaller village (Mezőkövesd, Szentistván). Their Roman Catholic religion played a major role in their culture. Their name, as they proudly proclaim, is

12. Catholic church
Hollókő, Nógrád County

a diminutive form of the name of the great Hungarian king of the 15th
century, Matthias. They were peasants and husbandmen, but most of
their land was occupied by great estates, so that from the second half of
the last century they were compelled to sign up as seasonal labourers (for
4–6 months) and thus earn a living in various parts of the country. The
common, so-called *hadas* settlements of joint families and their organization (*had*—troop) can be well demonstrated until the most recent times.
They have developed an extraordinarily colourful, rich embroidery and
folk costume since the second half of the last century. Their material
culture points toward the Great Plain, whilst their folklore seem closer
to that of the Palotses.

Great Plain

The numerous ethnic groups of the Great Plain (the *Alföld*) are even more difficult to take stock of. We shall start with those who were held together by privileges reaching back into the past which decisively influenced the development of their folk culture.

The *Cumanians,* of Turkish origin, arrived in Hungary while fleeing from the Tartars in the middle of the 13th century. The kings designated quarters for their needs in the central part of the Great Plain. At first they were engaged mostly in herding, then they settled down and in a few centuries assimilated into the Hungarians. They lived largely in market towns, where they jealously guarded their privileges against the influx of peasants and nobles. In 1702 the Habsburgs stripped them of their privileges, which they had to buy back after four decades from an Order of Teutonic Knights to whom their land was donated.

The *Great Cumanians,* with Karcag as their headquarters and largest town, occupied the central part of the region east of the Tisza *(Tiszántúl),* while the *Little Cumanians* lived between the Danube and the Tisza with the town of Kiskunfélegyháza as their headquarters. This is where their "captain" resided. Cumanian family and community organizations survived almost unaltered until the final termination of their privileges (1876). The religion of the great majority of Cumanians is Calvinist. They have preserved several items of the costumes of the Great Plain almost to the present day. More traits of Oriental origin may be discovered in their folk poetry, music, and world of beliefs than in those of other ethnic groups.

The *Jazygians* live around the Zagyva, a tributary on the right of the

13. Cumanian men
Kunszentmiklós, Bács-Kiskun County

14. Village scene
Jászjákóhalma, Szolnok County

Tisza river, and are in contact with the Palotses to the north. They are Indo-Europeans, Alans in origin, and having arrived at the same time as the Cumanians, they too enjoyed similar privileges. Together they formed one high organization with a "captain" who resided in Jászberény. After the expulsion of the Turks, the prolific Jazygians swarmed south and populated the regions of *Little Cumania,* of the Trans-Tisza region (east of the Tisza), and even the southern Great Plain, the Bácska and Bánát. For the most part they are Roman Catholics. Agriculture gained ground faster with them than with the Cumanians. Their characteristic costumes and rich world of beliefs differentiate them from their neighbours. Their sense of identity is strong even today.

The *Hajdú* towns and villages can be found in the central part of the Tiszántúl, mostly in the present-day Hajdú-Bihar County. They gained their name from their occupation: *hajdú* meaning herdsmen, drivers, and *hajt* meaning to drive. Later many of them became mercenary foot soldiers. István Bocskai (1557–1606), Prince of Transylvania, settled about ten thousand Hajdús on his estates in the Great Plain in 1605 and assured them so-called "Hajdú privileges": they had to provide military service, but they were exempt from all taxes to state and landlord. Extensive animal husbandry survived the longest in· the Kunság and Hajdúság, where agriculture for a long time served only to fulfil local needs. In both places, from the 17th century on, the system of scattered farms developed which became centres at first of animal husbandry, and later of agriculture. Most of the Hajdús are Calvinists, though some are Roman Catholic.

The larger and smaller market towns of the Great Plain and the bigger privileged royal towns can also be regarded as ethnic pockets, because the inhabitants have a strong feeling of identity and developed their own character in the effort to preserve their privileges. We can speak of this especially at places where the peasantry held in its hand the governing of the town. Such closely knit three towns between the Danube and the Tisza are *Cegléd, Nagykőrös,* and *Kecskemét.* Their character was determined by the coexistence of the prosperous peasantry, the labourers who lived in their shadow, and the artisans. Extensive agriculture first developed at these places, and concentrated primarily on vegetable and fruit production and vine growing. Similarly important in the southern Great Plain is *Szeged* on the bank of the Tisza, with its huge area of scattered farms, its swarming groups that extended far to the south. Szeged's river people and fishermen formed a separate group, as did its characteristic artisans: knife makers, slipper makers, braid makers, etc., who carried their wares to faraway lands. Szeged is the oldest centre of Hungarian paprika growing, which become an independent line of occupation. *Hódmezővásárhely,* north of Szeged along the Tisza, stands out from its environment by its rich decorative folk art. The Calvinist school with its long history in *Debrecen,* a city in the Tiszántúl, has exerted significant cultural influence on the surroundings from the 16th century. The so-called *civis* (civilian) concept was extended equally to prosperous peasants, artisans with property, and merchants. Debrecen is an important trade centre, centrally sited between Transylvania, Pest and Upper Hungary. Its typical products, the *szűr* (an overcoat made of thick woollen cloth or frieze), the *guba* (an overcoat made of woollen cloth with tafts of wool woven into it), sheepskin garments, earthenware vessels, and the products of harness makers became famous far and wide.

Among the large number of peoples of the Great Plain we must also mention the people around *Kalocsa,* most of whom moved to this area from all parts of the country after the expulsion of the Turks. They are just as much masters of paprika growing as are the people of Szeged, yet even in this, they preserve many individual characteristics. Their multicoloured embroidery, wall paintings and the most colourful folk costumes not only differentiate them in Hungary, but also make them known all over the country.

Bácska, the lower section of the area between the Danube and the Tisza, is in Yugoslavia, while *Bánát,* the plain bordered by the Maros–Tisza–Danube, belongs partly to Rumania, partly to Yugoslavia. The original Hungarian population was largely extinguished during the Turkish rule, and new Hungarian inhabitants moved back again to this area only in the 18th century. For this reason, almost every village is a separate ethnographic unit, and in their culture traces of elements they brought along have amalgamated with elements taken from that of other people. From the point of view of its historical and ethnological part, *Békés* is a similar area; here the Hungarian majority lived together with Rumanians, Slovakians, and Germans. Although certain characteristics of the folk culture and of folk art that developed indicate distant origins, still it is characteristically of the Great Plain.

The largest swampy, boggy area of the Tiszántúl, east of the Tisza, is called *Sárrét*. Two of its areas are differentiated: *Nagysárrét* is in Bihar County along the river Berettyó, *Kissárrét* is along the river Körös, extending into Békés County. The original population largely died off during the Turkish wars. Their place was taken by the Cumanians and Hajdús in large numbers. It was characteristically a water-dominated world until the middle, and in some places until the end, of the last century. The major occupations of the population are fishing, hunting, meadow husbandry and the processing of reeds and bulrushes. After drainage, here too, agriculture became prevalent. Many characteristics referring to an Oriental past have survived in its world of beliefs.

The life of the people of *Nyír* and *Rétköz* was shaped by the floods of the Tisza and the swamps that remained all the year around. Agriculture was possible only on the smaller or larger islands. Alongside cabbage, which had been grown for a long time, potatoes and sunflowers soon gained ground. The twenty-eight connected settlements of Rétköz did not end at the Tisza, but continued in the *Bodrogköz,* where the almost fifty settlements in the island of the Bodrog–Latorca–Tisza are held together by a more or less similar culture. Special mention should be made of the joint family organization, its rich art of homespun, its varied world of beliefs, its tales and myths. On the right bank of the Tisza, between Tokaj and Tiszadob, lie the settlements of *Taktaköz,* the former culture of which resembles in several ways those we have been discussing.

Tiszahát includes the plain north of the Tisza, *Szamoshát* the plain on the south bank of the Szamos. Here too, water regulated life in the past. In the wide expanses of the floody plain and oak and beech forest enormous herds of swine fattened. Carts and tools were made from the timber. The homespun, embroidery, simple folk costume and rich folklore traditions of the people survived until today.

Transylvania

The name Transylvania *(Erdély)* indicates an area beyond the forest, so called since the 12th century because huge forests separated it from the Great Plain. This is also why its territory is detached, but in addition, from the 14th century, its history also developed differently as it became one of the independent parts of Hungary until 1848. Its western parts, called *Partium,* were not parts of Transylvania although they belonged under the authority of the prince of Transylvania. Here we shall speak of several smaller Hungarian groups, which in regard to their characteristics belong to the Great Plain, yet are all found in Rumania.

Strictly speaking the *Érmellék* is still part of the plains of Bihar, and its culture is also typical of the Great Plain, but its first-rate vine culture differentiates it from the latter. *Szilágyság* is a hilly area in the western half of Transylvania and so in many connections it is tied to the Great Plain, although traits typical of Transylvania already dominate. Only a few villages belong together. The others are surrounded like islands by the Rumanians (Désháza, Diósad, Tövishát, Várvölgy, Szer, etc.). Their rich decorative art, their traditions of folk music and folk poetry vary almost from village to village.

A partly Hungarian linguistic pocket, consisting of 13 villages in the *Valley of the Fekete-Körös,* west of Belényes, deserves close attention if only because of its isolation. Their culture points in many respects toward Kalotaszeg and the inner part of Transylvania. The character of their costume is rather like that of the Great Plain, where they used to go in groups to harvest. By the time they returned home, the grain had ripened even in their colder climate. Among their former occupations forest-animal husbandry is worth mentioning.

Kalotaszeg lies west of Kolozsvár, almost by the Bihari Alps, along the rivers Kalota, Sebes-Körös, and Nádaspatak. The villages are situated in three groups. The people of *Felszeg* live along the Körös and Kalota and consider themselves as the most distinctive group of Kalotaszeg. The region of *Alszeg* is in the valley of the Almáspatak that falls toward the Szilágyság, while in the gradually narrowing valley of the Nádaspatak, toward Kolozsvár, nestle the villages along the river Nádas. Kalotaszeg consists of about 30 to 40 villages. The centre, and the settlement with the largest number of inhabitants, is Bánffyhunyad. From here also many people went to the Great Plain to harvest, and by the time they returned their own grain was ready to cut. Huge hay-growing meadows and mountain pastures served as the basis for their animal husbandry. Their home industry was remarkably highly developed, especially hemp processing. The rich folk costume of Kalotaszeg influenced the surrounding areas also (see Ill. 199). The chain-stitch or closed square chain-stitch embroidery with its ornamental foliage pattern designed on linen *(írásos)* has become known in faraway lands. Many beautiful relics of woodcarving may be found in this formerly forested region, for instance, finely wrought gates, distaffs, ornamental yokes, grave posts.

The central, mildly hilly area of Transylvania is known as *Mezőség*. Many Hungarian linguistic pockets exist here, almost every one of which developed a folk culture specifically its own. Such are the few Hungarian villages of the *Borsa Valley* and *Szék,* whose rich culture of song and dance, still alive today, has become universally known. And even in Kolozsvár itself, the Hungarian inhabitants of parts of the town called *Hóstát, Hidelve,* and the adjoining villages of *Kolozsmonostor* and *Szamosfalva* have preserved many ethnological traits. Among the iso-

16. Men going off on a Sunday Jobbágytelke, former Maros-Torda County

lated Hungarian villages *Szakadát* is worth mentioning, distinctive from its neighbours by characteristic costumes, building style, and customs.

Torockó and *Torockószentgyörgy* in the former Torda County have been most important centres of iron mining and processing in Transylvania from the beginning of the Middle Ages. Their products travelled far. A specific type of costume and embroidery differentiated them even from neighbouring villages.

The largest Hungarian ethnic group of Transylvania is formed by the *Székelys*, most of whom live in the Eastern Carpathians. Their name and origin are equally subject to debate. Recent research shows that they occupied their present country as border guards when they moved there in the 11th and 12th centuries from the western borders of Hungary to defend the eastern borders from the attacks of Cumanian and Pecheneg tribes. This military organization also showed up during later centuries and determined the life circumstances of the Székelys. Socially they stratified into highest nobles *(primor),* followed the *lófő* or lesser nobles *(equites).* The latter went to war on their own horses with their own weapons. The foot Székelys *(pixidarii),* who did not possess a horse, went to camp on foot. Although there were differences of wealth among the Székelys, large estates developed to a lesser degree here than in other parts of the country.

The one-time military administration established its so-called *szék* (seat) within the Székelys. *Udvarhelyszék* was called *anyaszék* (the mother seat) by historical sources; its population is mostly Calvinist and Unitarian. *Csíkszék* is entirely Catholic, while the population of *Háromszék*—consisting of *Kézdiszék, Orbaiszék,* and *Sepsiszék*—is Calvinist and Catholic. The villages of *Marosszék* belong to several religions. *Aranyosszék* lies somewhat isolated west of *Székelyland.* Later on some smaller areas joined these units. Thus *Miklósvárfiszék,* consisting of ten villages, joined Háromszék, and *Bardócfiszék* and *Kereszturfiszék* joined Udvarhely. Furthermore, there are smaller ethnic groups and ethnological regions amongst the units, which often cross their borders. Thus *Erdővidék* designates the relatedness of *Bardócszék* and *Miklósvárfiszék,* each in a valley of a stream, to *Udvarhelyszék.*

In its foundation and main characteristics the folk culture of the Székelys is as much identical to that of other ethnic groups of the Hungarians as is their language, and it is only as a consequence of their history and isolation that they have preserved many archaic features. Their life style is characterized by foresting, alpine shepherding, and agriculture. Forest gleaning is highly developed; most Székelys know how to process wood. Voluntary co-operative work *(kaláka)* is general, so that they built their houses and barns from wood with the help of neighbours, relatives and friends. Among their monumental woodcarvings, the Székely gate (see Fig. 21, Ill. 57 and Plate I) and grave posts stand out. Formerly horses and cattle played the leading role in the alpine husbandry, but have lately given way to sheep. The basins of *Csík, Gyergyó* and *Háromszék* are suited to agriculture, but in some places mountainsides are ploughed so steep that even to climb up is a difficult task. Besides woodcarving, homespun and stitched embroidery have

17. Rural scene
Antalok-pataka, former Csík County

gained important roles in decorative art. Their costumes differentiate them according to each seat.

Székely folklore is extraordinarily rich. Folksongs, especially folk ballads, preserve very fine versions. The folk tales and the different varieties of legends are still appreciated at peasant gatherings. Singing and instrumental folk music indicate a great past just as much as their dances do.

The Székelys in the course of their history were often forced to gather into smaller or larger groups to seek refuge out of the country. Thus in 1764, after a terrible massacre by the imperial military forces of the Habsburgs, several thousand Székelys fled outside the Carpathians into Bukovina and settled there amid great hardships. One segment moved from here in 1880 to the southern Danube banks. Almost all of those who were left behind set forth in 1941 and these Székelys of Bukovina (see also p. 67) found a new country first in the southern Great Plain, in Bácska, later on in Transdanubia, and the present Tolna and Baranya counties. The scientific examination of the integration of their culture in a new environment is an exceptionally exciting task.

The Hungarians who live outside the Carpathians in Moldavia are called *Csángó*. Most of them migrated here from northern Transylvania in the Middle Ages. They have preserved a great many archaisms in the completely Rumanian environment, but the influence of the surrounding Rumanians is felt both in their culture and in their language. Not

51

infrequently, their folk music and their dances have survived in medieval form.

The Székelys also sent out swarming groups toward the Carpathians. Thus we can find near Brassó in the region of *Barcaság* the Lutheran *Csángós* of *Hétfalu* ("Seven villages"), who are not only excellent farmers, but formerly as carters carried the products of the Brassó artisans as well as their own products on the roads of Rumania and Transylvania. The *Csángós of Gyimes* moved into the mountain pass of Gyimes in the 16th to the 18th centuries, to the vicinity of the road that led towards Moldavia. Administratively, in the past they did not belong to Csíkszék (see Plates XV and XVI).

★

To complete the survey we should speak of the Hungarian groups living in America and in Western Europe as well. This, however, is almost impossible on the basis of our present knowledge. The immigrants originated from different ethnic groups and ethnological regions, and represented different social classes and strata. Thus it is difficult to speak of them in the same vein as above. Also, folkloristic and ethnological research aimed at elucidating this problem has only just begun. However, we can already observe that tradition lives vigorously in the customs of alimentation. Furthermore the immigrants consciously strive to keep alive traditions of folksong and dance. They have also preserved customs concerning baptism, wedding and burial.

I. Social Anthropology

The study of the effects of social anthropology is a rather neglected area in the literature of Hungarian ethnology. Even if we happen to find the subject reviewed in digests, it is assigned a place somewhere between material culture and folklore. However, we have decided to begin the discussion with social anthropology, keeping in mind that the subject is closely bound to both the material and intellectual culture of the Hungarians. Consequently, and by way of introduction, the reader should now familiarize himself with concepts he is likely to find everywhere in the pages of this book. As the demarcation is extremely difficult, we have listed here questions that could have been mentioned in either of the other two areas. We do this partly because life is a complete whole in which everything is interrelated, and partly because we would like to emphasize the importance of social culture.

Starting with the smallest social unit, the nuclear family, and by examining blood and artificial relationships, we shall introduce the institution of neighbourhood, the stratification of the population of Hungarian villages and also of market towns, the organization of villages, and the possibilities for linking smaller and larger regions and areas. Furthermore, we shall speak of those labour migrations that have affected the entire country and beyond, and which, becoming especially brisk from the second half of the last century, have played a significant role in the exchange of cultural attainments between distant regions.

We shall also introduce, in large outlines, the historical role of the Churches in the Hungarian village, as well as the pilgrimages, and the fairs, which were large gatherings often involving whole national territories. They were not only important factors in the dispersal of cultural goods, but also contributed new aspects to both the material and intellectual culture of the Hungarian folk.

The Nuclear and the Extended Family

The family is the smallest unit of society which rests on material and intellectual foundations, and the form and content of it changes periodically. The small or nuclear family *(kiscsalád)* consists of the parents and the children up to the time they leave the economic unit of this community and establish their own family. In the case of the large or extended family *(nagycsalád)*, three or maybe four generations (grandparents, parents, children, grandchildren) live on one lot, often in one house, working together in a patriarchal system. Many transitional steps have developed between these two family forms, and according to the most recent research which has also taken distant historical times into account, both can be found among the Hungarians, often within the same settlement.

On the History of Family Organization

Linguistics and archeology have brought to light many new details, especially during the last decades, about the Magyar family at the earliest periods. It can be determined on the basis of archeological finds that in the course of the second millennium B. C. the patriarchal form gradually became stronger and that by the end of the period it had even become predominant. This is the reason why matriarchal elements appear only fragmentarily in Hungarian traditions and even then only in the rarest instances.

The Hungarian terminology of family organization goes back largely to the Finno-Ugric period. The original meaning of *ős* (ancestor) in the 12th century is still *apa* (father), with the following terms, still in use: *atya* (father), *anya* (mother), *fiú* (son), *öccs* (younger brother), *atyval* (stepfather), *fial* (stepson)—the last two originally compound words, now known only through historical sources—*árva* (orphan), *férfi* (man), *férj* (husband), *feleség* (wife), *meny* (daughter-in-law), *vő* (son-in-law), *ipa* (father-in-law), *napa* (mother-in-law), *ángy* (elder brother's wife). The following were added in the Ugric period: *apa* (father), *leány* (daughter) (originally a compound), *iafia* (also an original compound at present meaning distant relative). Larger units with collective names also belong to these: *rokon* (relative; its original meaning is "near"), *had* (troop), *szer* (kin), *vér* (blood). It seems apparent from this survey, which cannot be called complete, that the Magyars, along with the Finno-Ugrians, lived in families that at this time already were patrilineal. This terminology also shows that we are reckoning with a special version of the extended family. We can also be sure they belonged in clans. It is quite certain that as they became a people of the steppes, and as they came into closer contact with various Turkic peoples, the extended family organization and patriarchal characteristics became more and more marked.

The cemeteries that are being excavated in growing numbers tell

54

a great deal about family organization in the 10th century, immediately following the Conquest. Large family burials can be observed among some of the wealthy in the cemeteries, consisting of 15 to 20 graves, usually forming a single line. These contain parents, children, and grandchildren who belong together through blood lineage. The oldest man led the community descended from him and his wife and, because of his role, was buried in the centre; around him were laid the members of the patriarchal extended family in the order of their rank, age, and sex. However, at the same period the nuclear family, in the modern meaning of the term, can also be found among the wealthy, where the sons, after founding their own family, received their share of the inheritance and moved to the land gained in this way. There were many advantages to this system. First of all, they spread over a larger territory the stock which could easily be damaged by epidemics, robbery and natural disasters, and so reduced these dangers. Secondly, one member of the family always represented the interest of the family in different places. Such a division plays an important role even in the origin myth of the Magyars. The first-born sons of Ménmarót, Magyar and Hunor, in the story of the mythical stag "departed from their father and moved to a separate tent"; later they moved on looking for suitable quarters for themselves on land farther away. The youngest son always stayed with the aging parents, and, after his father's death, could step into his inheritance. We can also find remnants of this custom in folk tales, and basically this remained of the characteristic features of Hungarian family organization until the most modern times.

18. *Matyó* family
Mezőkövesd

During the last decades more and more cemeteries of the common people and servants from the period of the Conquest have been and are being excavated. In these the graves appear in small groups, in interrupted rows, and separated from each other. In spite of the relatively small number of relics it is possible to ascertain significant differences in wealth. Modern research proves that the extended family form involved only one part of the wealthiest layer of the Magyars of the Conquest, while the majority of the common people must have lived in small family units.

Written sources tell us a great deal, although not in great detail, about questions of medieval family organization. Thus, for example, the laws of Ladislas I, at the end of the 11th century, differentiated in respect to taxes between grown sons who lived in their father's house in a common household with him and those who had their own dwellings. This, however, can be found not only amongst the common people, but amongst the landed nobility as well, who, in order to keep the land together, had not partitioned their holdings, although in some cases certain large families among them also fell apart into small families.

Researchers examining the composition of 17th-century peasant families in the north-western corner of the linguistic territory came to the conclusion that the form of the family is correlated most closely with the size of its wealth. If the wealth is so great that it requires many working hands, equipment, and animal stock, then the extended family can care for it more effectively. However, in cases where the land was of small extent, so that the extended family could in no way have existed on it together, we come upon small families. Accordingly, we can state that the extended family is an organization which adapted to the economic conditions in every period, and although it contains many ethnic elements in its form, its existence, disappearance, and reoccurrence was primarily regulated by the necessity resulting from the extent of the land and size of the animal stock.

In many places in the 19th century the extended family survived on lands held in villeinage, a survival facilitated by the landlords' attempt to prevent the fragmentation of peasant property. The number of such peasant families grew increasingly less from the second half of the 19th century, but in some places this form of family survived right to the middle of this century, thus providing an opportunity to study its form and character in different parts of the linguistic territory.

Family Organization

We can best get acquainted with the family, and the extended family, by enumerating the rights, obligations and tasks of its members.

The head of the extended family is the *gazda,* who is the absolute and incontrovertible master of all members of the family. He was able to shut out members of the family from the unit. Usually the *gazda* was the oldest, most experienced member of the family, and if they lived in an extended large family, not his son, but usually his brother followed him after his death, based on seniority. This method of inheritance goes back to the distant past, occurring, for example, in the succession of the House of Árpád during the 11th to the 13th centuries.

The *gazda* disposed of all the material goods of the family freely and without any obligation of accountability. Thus he could submit to sell both his inherited and acquired land, he could spend, drink up, or even give away its sale price, and he could do so without being called to account for it by members of the family. Although this happened only on rare occasions, we mention it simply to indicate the extent of the *gazda*'s unrestricted authority. The majority of the *gazda*s always strove to acquire more, either to buy fresh land or to gain parts of hitherto undivided fallow land. Thus in the age of serfdom the entire family cleared the forest, dried out swampy areas, and broke in pasture land, after which they did not have to pay ninth dues and tithes. From the middle of the 19th century the *gazda* tried to increase his property by acquiring the land of people financially ruined or dead. Although he asked the opinion of his grown and married sons at the time of purchase, their opinion did not change his decision.

He alone disposed of all produce that grew on the land and even in the

57

20. Cumanian peasant *(gazda)*
Great Plain

garden around the house. He separated what seemed to be sufficient for the year's food from what he wanted to sell at the weekly market or at the fair. He kept the key of the granary always on himself, so that no one could enter without him. Similarly, he alone issued the wine and brandy, and he kept a strict note of the change in quantity. He kept all the money coming from various sources in a box that would lock well, or perhaps in an earthenware vessel, but we know of some who carried the money around their neck.

The basic expenditures of the large family were paid by the *gazda*. He also paid the different taxes, acquired and repaired the agricultural tools, and bought new stock. He was responsible only for the purchase of the major articles of clothing for the members of the family. Thus, boots, frieze mantles, coats, and later on shoes were bought at big fairs. But all *gazda*s tried to urge members of their household to make the greater part of their own clothes from flax, hemp, and, where possible, wool. Whatever went beyond that, the wife tried to juggle out of the price of milk, eggs, and chickens, although in many places the *gazda* tried to keep track even of this sum.

The *gazda* maintained the right to the income of the family not derived directly from his own property. Thus certain male members of even prosperous Palots families went down to the Great Plain to harvest. They brought back their share of crops and the family could bake milk loaves out of that for themselves all year. The *gazda* utilized the surplus working power of the extended joint family in other ways as well. He sent his sons to the forest for daywork where an opportunity was offered, or perhaps they undertook a haulage. The income from all this was at the command of the *gazda,* and at the most he gave some of it back to those who earned it. He provided smaller sums to his unmarried sons on Sunday, so they could go to the inn.

The *gazda* directed all the work on the property, although in this—especially during his later years—he did not physically participate in most cases. He decided who among his sons, sons-in-law, daughters and daughters-in-law would do what work on a certain day, and determined the quantity of the work. He himself usually worked around the house, repairing tools and buildings leisurely, so as not to tire himself out. He visited the fields only periodically to supervise the work. He took part in actual work mostly during harvesting and did hauling only if others in the family were doing some more urgent chores.

He also kept in his hand the formation of his family, thus determining, mostly on economic considerations, the marriage partners of his sons and daughters. He had the right to scold or even beat anyone within the family, although he did this to adults only in the most extreme cases. Primarily it was the children who suffered physical punishment. Although the village community debated abuses of patriarchal authority, no opinion of any kind whatsoever could effectively influence the father's decision.

The *gazda* looked upon the sons' introduction to work and other knowledge as his task, while his wife, the *gazdasszony,* saw to rearing the daughters, something the father did not concern himself with. A small boy usually rode on the cart so that he could get used to the road and horses; at the age of six he was already guarding the geese and the chickens against predators, at first in the yard and later in the pastures outside the village. A ten-year-old child was already hoeing, although it is true that he did only half a row and the adults did the rest of it for him. The father got his son used to the scythe by the age of fifteen. At first he cut fodder, then grass. They started him on grain harvesting (unless necessity brought it about otherwise) only after the age of eighteen, and until then he learned how to lay in swaths, and at some places how to bind and stack sheaves. The *gazda* always enjoyed working with his sons and even more with his grandsons; he told them tales and stories, and gave accounts of his experiences in soldiering. This is why songs, ballads, and tales descended from grandparents to grandchildren rather than from parents to children.

The *gazda* represented the family in negotiations with relatives and neighbours as well as before various village, state, and church bodies. A special place was due to him in church together with the other *gazda*s which was passed down to them through heredity. At the market he always disposed by himself of the produce, animals, and products that were to be sold, and in buying he at best asked advice only from the member of the family older than himself.

The few features listed above show that the authority of the head of the large family was made evident in every respect. This was also the case in the narrower nuclear family, with the difference that here a great deal more work fell to the share of the head of the family. The *gazda* was almost without exception that member of the family who possessed the widest range of knowledge. Generally, he tried to pass his knowledge on to his family. The best among them became the peasant leaders of the village, organizers of weddings and burials, and also represented the interests of the larger community.

The other prominent individual, who on the whole was totally subordinate to the *gazda,* is the *gazdasszony*. Generally she is the wife of the *gazda,* and only rarely did it happen that, after the death of the *gazda,* and if her son agreed to it, she continued to be *gazdasszony*. Her task was—with the help of her daughters and daughters-in-law—first of all to do the housework and the work around the house. She did not take much part in work in the field, at most she carried food out to the workers at the time of the big harvests.

Her most important task was cooking, as well as baking bread and processing the milk. All of this she would not let out of her hands as long as she was able, and usually she employed the help of the oldest *menyecske* (young wife). Raising and feeding the small stock was among her tasks along with accounting for eggs. She used the profit gained from milk and poultry for the clothing of the family. Out of it she also helped her daughter when she parted from the family and covered the trifling expenses of her grandchildren. She kept secret the amount of her income, for the *gazda* held it to belong to the common income.

The burden of clothing the family also lay on the *gazdasszony*'s shoulders. Thus the processing of hemp and flax, from pulling it out of the ground to the weaving of the homespun, counted as one of her most important tasks. From the prepared linen, the women sewed the undergarments, and in many cases the outer garments, of both men and women, but the *gazdasszony* also had to get together year by year the dowry of the girls growing to marriageable age. In areas where these tasks are still practised the number of her chores was increased by the processing of wool and even by the sewing of cloth garments. Naturally, keeping the house and washing was her burden too, as well as taking care of the vegetable garden and gathering, storing and preserving her produce—all of which meant a good deal of care.

At the same time the *gazdasszony* was also a mother, who held the rearing of her children to be one of her most important tasks. While they were young, all the cares of the children of both sexes rested on her shoulders. Later she was occupied much more with the girls, although the making and keeping clean of the boys' clothing continued to be her responsibility. Daughters and daughters-in-law were used only as helpers in housekeeping by the mother, who always gave them specific tasks, while reserving for herself the general organizing of the work.

Housework was always subordinate to farm work. The job designated by the *gazda* had to be done first, and only if time allowed could other things follow. The *gazdasszony* was the go-between for the *gazda* and the members of the family. They told her all their wishes, and she, at the right time and in the right way, passed them on to the *gazda*.

The unmarried lads *(legények)* and married men formed the most important part of the large family's work force. The oldest son, or in the case of an extended large family, the brother of the *gazda* as the next in line, had a certain sphere of authority in directing the work. But this was limited only to the organization of tasks designated by the *gazda*.

One of the most important duties of the young men or lads and the married men was to take care of the livestock. They were always the ones who worked with the oxen and horses and who supplied them with fodder, and they also milked the cows, which on the Great Plain especially was the men's job. Harnessing and driving the animals, and the agricultural work performed with animals was always carried out by the young men and the married men, as was all the work done with the scythe. Threshing, the treading out of grain, and in general all the work that required greater physical power fell to their lot.

A special place was due among the men to the *vő* (son-in-law), that is, to the man who married the *gazda's* daughter and moved in with her family. According to the conditions of property, the connection here could be of various kinds. If the young man lived in good material circumstances, similar to those of the bride, the marriage came about mostly to join properties. In this case the situation of the new husband equalled that of the *gazda's* son, and he came to the girl's house with a trousseau of clothes, just as brides did in other cases. The son-in-law who brought little or no property, and especially livestock, into the marriage had a more difficult status. He lived more or less at the level of a hired hand and could not let his voice be heard in any matter. His wife gave orders even in the smaller family, since he shared in the property through her. Sometimes the *gazda's* daughter was married to the hired hand, either because she got pregnant and no other solution could be found, or because they judged him diligent, or perhaps because for some reason no one had asked to marry the girl (e.g. because of physical disability). Such a son-in-law was held in even lower esteem than a hired hand, although it often happened that after the death of the *gazda* and of his successor, the son-in-law himself became the *gazda*.

It could also happen that the son-in-law could no longer stand the humiliating situation and moved out. He could ask in such cases to be paid for the time he spent there at least as much as they would have paid a servant. It could also happen that the wife died, and if the *gazda* was satisfied with the son-in-law's work, and could not do without it, then he tried everything to keep him there for the future. In such a case, the widowed son-in-law might marry a younger sister, or else, he could choose a wife from among the relatives. In rare instances he was even permitted to bring an outsider or widow to the house. However, if there was no possible solution, he was able to leave. At such times he also took his children away and for his work he generally got one and a half times as much as he could have earned as a hired hand. This was the main reason why the *gazda* tried to keep him on the family together with his children, who were the working force of the future.

The women of the family and the extended family are partly descendants of the *gazda,* partly the wives of his grown sons, the *menyecskék* (young wives). The daughters had more rights and the mother overlooked more of their doings than those of the daughters-in-law. This, however, did not mean that they did not have to participate in agricultural work in the fields. Among the chores of the daughters at home was to care for the garden, especially the flower garden in front of the house, and to take part in processing the hemp, but they rarely participated in housekeeping. A daughter's most important task was to get married as soon as possible, in spite of the fact that folk wisdom held that "one girl is better off than a hundred young wives". The daughters who were under direct supervision of the *gazdasszony* worked much less than the young wives and could take part in much more entertainment.

Basically the young wife who came from another family became a member of her husband's family in every respect and assimilated into it entirely. In certain parts of the linguistic territory she called her husband's elder brother *nagyobbik uram* (my older husband), and his younger brother *kisebbik uram* (my younger husband). If her husband died, some male member of the family often married her, because they did not readily let a good worker out of the family. The young wives also participated in all agricultural work. The extent of this changed through time. Thus only the women harvested with the sickle, while the men used only the scythe. In the latter case the women laid what had been cut in swaths. They could work around the house only if the *gazda* permitted it. At such times the *gazdasszony* indicated the necessary chores in the house and in the garden, or perhaps she sent them with milk, eggs, and chicken to the market. Generally the *gazdasszony* or the oldest of the wives cared for the children, for, compared to the others, she had greater authority and could order the young ones about. The wife had to help in the field work even when she was nursing, and at best she could go home at noon to feed her young one and on her return bring lunch back with her.

Divorce was a rare occurrence during the last century even in Protestant areas. In the case of divorce the wife moved back to her parents and took along her smaller children. Among the poorer folk, the older boy went with his mother, while the older daughter stayed with her father. Since the men were the breadwinners, and the girls and women took care of the house, the divided family was thus capable of living on.

The extended family, and often even the nuclear family, kept certain orphaned, or unmarried relatives. These took part in all the work according to their strength, but they did not have any rights and they were made to feel at all times that they were being kept out of charity. Although they could sit at the table, such men in most cases were assigned their sleeping quarters in the barn.

Peasant families that possessed property too large to cultivate themselves, kept some farm hands *(cseléd),* servants, and maidservants. To a certain degree these were looked upon as members of the family during

the time of their service. The words *család* and *cseléd* (family—farm
hand), of Slavic origin, indicates this phenomenon. The word has been
split into these two senses from the 16th century on. The first part of it
came to mean permanently "family" *(család),* the second "farm hand"
(cseléd). Farm hands were hired for one year. The youngest often had not
yet reached the age of ten and got nothing but food and perhaps some
pieces of second-hand clothing. Their task was most often to guard
animals and to do small jobs around the house. The grown farm hands
did all the work around the animals and in the fields. They earned less
working for the peasants of the village than on the large estates. Thus
farm hands derived from the poorest layer of peasant society, so that to
them even the meagerly dished-out food meant a great deal. Usually 6 to
8 quintals of grain, a pair of boots, and some little spending money made
up the bulk of their salary. They could not get married, for the *gazda*
insisted upon this condition during hiring. A maid servant *(szolgáló)*
could only be found among more prosperous peasants when the

gazdasszony needed help because of the size of the house or because of the state of her health.

Family life was regulated in every respect by strict patriarchal customs. This was also expressed in the order of the meals. The *gazda,* as the head of the family, sat at the head of the table. Alongside him sat his sons according to age, followed by the sons-in-law, and finally by the servants. The *gazda* reached into the dishes first, and consequently he took the best pieces. The rest of them followed in a pre-arranged order. In certain parts of the linguistic territory the women could not even start eating until the men had finished. Then they gave food to the children and also helped themselves to the left-overs. Usually they did not even sit at the table but ate their food off their knees, sitting on little stools or on the threshold. Breaking a loaf was mostly the job of the head of the family, who in Catholic areas first drew a cross with the point of the knife on the bottom of the bread. Thus the bread is a real symbol of the extended family, and while they lived on "the same bread" *(egy kenyéren),* that is to say, farmed together, this served as a common tie among them.

With regard to sleeping quarters the prevailing order changed from area to area but was the same in the same region. Thus in the Great Plain the *gazda* and his wife slept in one bed, in the front part of the room close to the window. The other one or two beds were used by the grown son and his wife, while the children slept together in box-like cots that could be pulled out from under the beds, or perhaps together with the old folk in the corner between the wall and the oven. The young men and the farm hands spent the night in the barn, because in this way they could take care of the animals better, and also it was harder to keep track of their staying out at night. In many places, the *gazda* slept from spring to autumn on the porch, where not only was the air more fresh but he could also keep an eye on the yard. In Palots areas the men slept in the front room called the *első ház* (first house), while the womenfolk found shelter in an unheated chamber or *kamara* with a tiny window. Here most of the space was taken up by beds, interspersed with chests containing the personal belongings of each girl or woman. Across the door stood the bed and chest of the *gazdasszony,* and around it, those of the rest according to rank. The children grew up in this chamber. They could be taken into a heated area only for bathing. Above each woman's bed on a rod hung her dresses and her Sunday boots.

The patriarchal nature of family organization is demonstrated in the order of inheritance. During the last century, changing forms of inheritance developed according to region, depending in the first instance on the extent of state pressure to assure that female members of the family could inherit land when the property was divided as a consequence of the breaking up of the extended family. That is to say, we cannot speak of inheriting in the case of the extended family, since after the death of the old *gazda* his oldest son or perhaps his brother generally took over the entire property and the direction of the work along with it. After the death of a heavy-handed *gazda,* tensions and disruptive forces usually broke up the family, and then the questions that arose about inheritance were similar to those in the case of the nuclear family.

Generally, daughters did not inherit landed property among the Hungarian peasantry. When they were married off they got their under- and outer-garments, differing in quantity and quality according to regions. Formerly they got a dower-chest and later a bed, a chest, or some other kind of furniture. The prosperous sometimes also gave a cow or calf, so that the young wife could cover her expenses out of its profit. Sometimes they gave the young wife a piece of the hemp fields outside the village. Since the second half of the last century, daughters have also received their share from the property, but usually they got compensation only in the form of money. The inheriting of land by daughters on an equal basis with sons began to spread only in this century, but it never became customary.

The sons did not in every instance receive an equal share. The oldest son, if he left the family because of his marriage, usually got from the land and perhaps from the stock the share due to him. This was generally smaller than what he would have received from an equal distribution, because they clearly did not want to impair the productivity of the remaining land. The youngest son stayed with the parents longest by the law of nature, and accordingly he inherited the house and its furnishing, and the land that was left after satisfying his brothers and sisters, along with the agricultural equipment. For this he nursed the old folk in their afflictions, and took care of their burial. In such cases the older siblings received only some souvenirs from the furnishing of the house. The right of the youngest son to the house of his parents was not only recognized by Hungarian lawbooks from the 16th century, but was also made mandatory, and certain records from the beginning of the 12th to 13th centuries already mention this. The peculiar situation of the youngest son is widely reflected in the folk tales and other creations of folk poetry. The father could disinherit his son from the property, but this happened very rarely. Beginning with the 19th century it happened more often that a talented child was further educated by his parents to be a teacher or priest or, more rarely, to pursue some other profession. In this case he either did not receive a share from the inheritance or got a reduced share on the assumption that his rights were already satisfied by the sum spent on his education.

The tangible property belonging to the family was identified by an ownership mark, so that it was easily recognizable and ownership proven with its help (cf. p. 259). The most commonly known is the animal mark or brand, used primarily on horses and cattle. This was inherited within the family through several generations and usually contained the initials of the *gazda*. If there was more than one similar brand within a village, they were differentiated by an *X* or star or some other sign. It could also happen, in the interest of more specific

Fig. 4. Branding iron. Hungarian Plain. End of the 19th century

Fig. 5. Brand marks for cattle. Kecskemét.
19th century

distinction, that they used the mark of the settlement along with the family mark if they wanted to drive the stock a distance. Everybody knew the mark of a certain family in the village, and so they burned it on agricultural implements as well. We even know instances when they marked the gravepost with it, indicating the family to which the deceased had belonged. In vine-growing regions they used the branding iron to mark the barrels (cf. p. 408).

Sheep and pigs were marked by trimming and notching their ears in a certain way which passed through generations within one family, but in some places the notching of the sheep's ear indicated its age. Compared to the above, the marking of the small stock was less regular. Marks were cut into the web on the feet of geese and ducks, while a chick's toenail was removed. If they wandered off, they could be easily identified with these aids. The women sewed marks into their clothes and underwear, so that they should not get mixed up during washing. However, these marks designated not the family, but rather the individual members within it.

The Troop, Clan, Kindred

The nuclear and extended family is an economic unit bearing the same name, which in the majority of cases lives on the same plot of land, in the same house. On the other hand, the clan *(nemzetség)* or the troop *(had)* do not belong together economically. Tighter and looser ties are indicated by a common family name, by a careful recording of descent from the same paternal ancestor, and by the defence of their mutual interest. It is very difficult to differentiate between the clan and the troop, because in some cases they are only synonyms for the same thing appearing in different regions, while in other places where they live next to each other certain differences are observable between them. Generally speaking the clan consists of a larger, the troop of a smaller unit.

The *nem, nemzet, nemzetség* (clan) is the name for an institution of kinship comprising several nuclear or extended families regionally, but not infrequently within the same territory as well. We can trace its existence, in the case of the nobles, right from the Conquest, and for serfs from the 16th century, when family names became increasingly fixed. This, however, does not mean that it was not generally known much earlier.

The clan was maintained through seven generations in the old days, but this number steadily decreased in the last century, until in more recent times it has extended only through three generations. The living and the dead alike are included in the clan, generally extending from great-grandparents all the way to third and fourth cousins. The old members of the clan kept track of all this, and we know one Székely from Bukovina who listed by name 273 people who belong to and have belonged to his clan. The Magyar clans were strictly exogamous, that is to say, they did not permit marriage within their ranks. This prohibition became more and more limited as the boundaries of the clan narrowed, and later extended only to second cousins. The wife usually did not belong to the clan of the husband but kept her own. Her connection with it was shown in the first place by the retention of her maiden name in village usage. Her clan provided a defence for her if she suffered some grave injustice from her husband. The theory of patriarchal seniority asserted itself vigorously within the clan, so that the oldest, most respectable and wealthiest members held it together. Because the role of the clan in peasant societies differs according to region or group, instead of generalizing, we shall give as specific instances two archaic forms from the eastern half of the linguistic region.

The Székelys from Bukovina migrated from the Székelyföld in the 18th century to Bukovina and settled where they are now in the south-eastern corner of Transdanubia in 1945 (cf. p. 51). From the middle of the 18th century they have kept track of the clans, a practice that has begun to fade only during the last decades. There was an order of prestige among the clans, primarily based on the conditions of property.

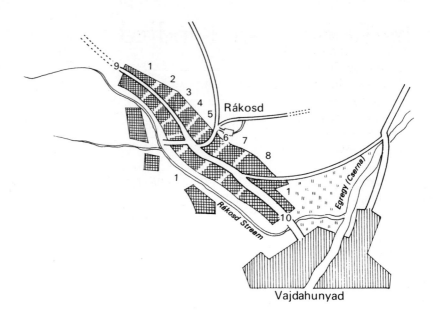

Fig. 6. The division according to clans in a village. Rákosd, former Hunyad County. Early 20th century
1. Recent settlers, 2. Bertalan, 3. Jakab, 4. Balázsi, 5. Dávid, 6. Farkas, 7. Gergely, 8. Pető families, 9. Upper village 10. Lower village

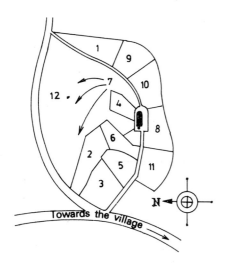

Fig. 7. The cemetery is the mirror image of the village. Rákosd, former Hunyad County. Early 20th century
1. Strangers, 2. Bertalan, 3. Jakab, 4. Balázsi, 5. Dávid, 6. Farkas, 7. Gergely, 8. Váradi-Pető families, 9. Guests, 10. Priests, 11. Bikfalvi-Farkas, 12. Second-rank families

Governing each clan there was a head, who represented the entire community. He played a leading role during the times of weddings and burials. Newborn babies were introduced to him, as were the new wives. When they slaughtered a pig, they sent him a sample. He represented the young before the law, he bought for them and in their stead horses and cows at the fair. At times he called together the leading members of the clan to discuss more important questions, to set right the conflicts and quarrels within the clan. The head of the clan also participated in the governing of the village, because he represented a larger unit. The most respected men, the judges, also came from among them.

Clan consciousness was first and foremost expressed in helping each other within the clan. Communal work was undertaken at time of house construction and large-scale harvesting. If one of the members was struck by a natural disaster, everyone tried to help to get him on his feet. They visited the sick, they followed the dead to the burial together, and they participated in weddings together. The clan also possessed special marks. Thus in the Csibi family the men wore a peacock feather in their hats, which they passed on to the younger generation only after they grew old. Blood feuds, alive even in this century, claimed many victims. The clan tried to retaliate for any offence against its members, in many cases attacking a member from the other clan who actually had nothing to do with the hurt suffered.

A differentiation according to clans on the basis of conditions of property was noted in the village Rákosd in Transylvania, distinguishing between new or old settlers. Here the separation of certain clans can be demonstrated by the way they settled. The more prominent, leading clans lived on the lower, more spacious, more fertile territory of the village, while the poorer ones who settled later chose a place for themselves on the upper part, where the soil was poorer and where, because of the proximity of the forest, they also suffered more damage from the wild beasts and from robbers. The clans also parcelled out among themselves the cemetery that lay around the church, and here too the order of settlement prevailed. Similarly, they kept the same strict order in the seating at church, since every clan could use only its own bench both on the side of the men and that of the women. They entered the church in this order, whilst strangers and guests occupied the seats designated for them. The young wife left the bench of her own clan and sat with her mother-in-law and her sisters-in-law.

While the concept of the clan is known throughout the entire linguistic territory, the *had* can be found in a relatively small area amongst the Palotses, in the Jászság, Kunság, Hajdúság, Bodrogköz and Nyírség. It binds the families too on the basis of paternal lineage, but it seems as if it was a smaller unit than the clan. In many cases it was mixed up with the concept of the extended family, or was even identified with it. More modern observation proves that it also embraces a shorter period of time, because it includes only the living and not the dead. Its size even among the living extends only to three or perhaps four generations. Thus in a village in the Bodrogköz, a man called Hegedűs, who moved in from the other side of the Tisza as a son-in-law together with his grown sons and grandsons, in about six decades became the founder of the Hegedűs troop. The *had* in this area, therefore, is a concept of such a kind that, according to circumstances, can always be updated with newer content.

However, the *had* can also be connected with certain military organizations of the Cumanians and Hajdús, which prevailed in their basic forms until the middle of the last century. The so-called *hadas* settlements (according to *had*) located in these areas point to this phenomenon. Here families related to each other settled in a certain part of the village or market town, and in many cases families bearing identical names and belonging to one band lived there in 4 to 20 separate houses. They farmed independently but helped each other in work and in any kind of difficulty. In the Jászság they use the *had* designation when the old folk live in the settlement and the young people farm out on the farmstead, although in this case we are talking about a large family which farms together but lives separately.

The kindred *(rokonság)* has a wider scope than the troop. It includes not only paternal but also maternal descent, and in some places artificial relations as well, but never the dead. The significance of kindred has grown especially during the last decades, as the clan has been pushed vigorously into the background. Generally, kindred is counted up to the third or second generation, but in most cases it ends with first cousins. This is the limit of which kindred invite each other to weddings, at which it is proper to go to burials, and at which families try to help each other if need arises.

Artificial Kindred, Neighbourhood

We will mention only a few from among the numerous versions of artificial kindred. Because research has been insufficient, we know these ties only sparsely, nor do we have the necessary overall view into the extent of their permeation. Such, for instance, is the "milk brotherhood" *(tejtestvérség),* formed when a mother for some reason could not nurse her child and one of the neighbours, relatives, or godmothers took care of the infant. They kept track of this relationship and spoke of it all through life, and in some areas it was even held to be a barrier to marriage. Milk brothers in most cases held together and helped each other as much as if they were blood brothers.

Earlier, the tasting of each other's blood played a big role in adopting the other as a brother or kin, through which the participants became related to each other. Anonymus (12th century) mentions in his chronicle that the Magyar chieftains made a blood compact before the Conquest (end of the 9th century). According to the old custom, the seven chieftains let their blood trickle into a vessel and with this act ratified the oath they took to Álmos, head of the tribes. This blood oath was not to be broken, and they all kept it until their death. It has been noted many times in later Hungarian history that two men, or perhaps small or large groups, became relatives through such a blood compact and inherited each other's property like real brothers.

We can find traces of becoming brothers through blood in some places among the peasantry, for example, among the Székelys of Bukovina. The children play together, but there are always some among the friends who would like to maintain life-long contact with each other. They decide by mutual wish to adopt each other as brothers. This can happen only between members of the same sex who have descended from different clans. The day for adopting blood brothers is the second day of Our Lady, August 16, when they go off to a place where no one else is present. They prick the tip of their middle finger with a needle and taste the trickling blood. With this they become brothers, which is also reflected in the way they address each other. They can count on each other in time of hardship, but this relation has no consequence in property inheritance.

Basically, adoption *(örökbefogadás)* is also a form of artificial kindred, which usually came about when the marriage of the *gazda* was barren and the family wanted to ensure the inheritance of property. They selected a boy, usually from among the relatives, and adopted him to their name. This also happened when the child's father or both parents died off. In such cases some relatives adopted a child or children even if they already had offspring. The adopted children shared the property equally with the natural children.

The most widely spread form of artificial kindred is choosing future godparents, the general name of which is *koma* (cf. p. 604). The Magyars borrowed this word and most certainly the concept itself from one of the Slavic languages, and it spread along with Christianity. According to the instruction of the Church, there can only be one pair of *koma*s, but in peasant practice there are often as many as four, or even thirty. The parents choose the godparents from among their old boyhood companions and girlfriends, but they must be already married. Generally, in the past they were not chosen from among the relatives. The latter practice spread only during the last half of the 19th century. Among the *koma*s there is a main *koma* pair *(főkomapár),* whose name is also noted in the register of birth. The main godmother *(főkomaasszony)* holds the child over the baptismal font.

The parents try to plan for *koma*s even before the child is born. After their choice they make inquiries to find out if for some reason their request might be refused. If the response is favourable, then after the birth of the child the father goes and asks them ceremoniously. A *koma* pair should in turn invite the other party to act as *koma*s for them if they should have a child, and failure to do so counts as a crass insult even today.

The system makes an extremely strong tie not only between child and godparents, but among the parents as well, who not infrequently help each other more than if they were blood relations. But a strong tie is

Fig. 8. The number of godparents at the turn of the century in the Carpathian Basin.
1. One pair of godparents, the same for each child
2. One pair of godparents, a different pair for each child
3. Several pairs of godparents, the same for all children (siblings)
4. Several pairs of godparents, a different one for each child
5. All four variations present

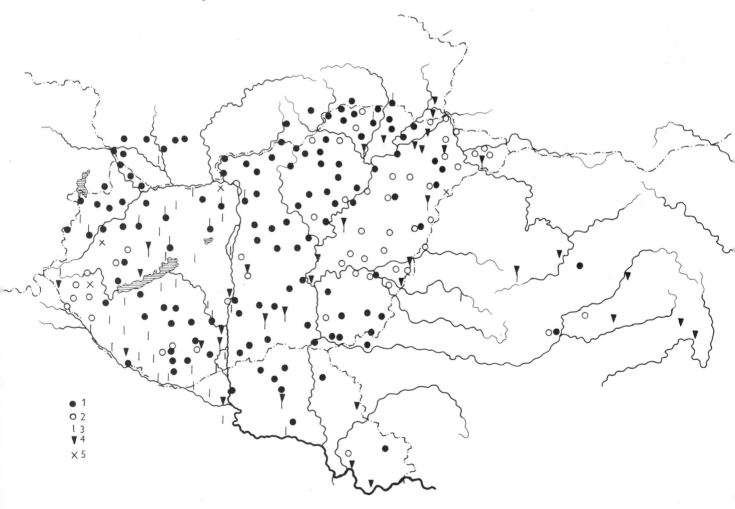

● 1
○ 2
| 3
▼ 4
× 5

formed among various *koma*s also, which is reflected in the way the *koma*s address each other. Acting as godparent was forbidden or opposed only in two cases. If the woman was menstruating or was pregnant, she could not hold the child under the baptismal water, and the responsibility then went to one of the *koma* women, to whom, in this case, the name *édeskoma* (sweet koma) was due. Engaged couples could not be *koma*s, because to do so, according to belief, would have led to the breaking up of their relationship.

An extremely strong connection, equal in value to artificial kindred, is the neighbourhood *(szomszédság)*, which is based on living immediately next to each other. The word *szomszéd* (neighbour) belongs to the oldest Slavic loans in the Hungarian language, and probably became part of it at the time of the development and general diffusion of the village settlements. Relations and neighbours were one and the same in certain parts of the settlement, since relations in many places lived near each other. The importance of the neighbourhood institution is made clear from proverbs such as "One good neighbour is worth more than a hundred bad relatives".

Neighbours are distinguished according to their location. The neighbour at the side of the settlement is the *first neighbour,* the one whose house is on the opposite side is the *back neighbour,* and the one at the foot of the lot is the *next-door neighbour.* The building and maintaining of fences is organized in such a way that everybody is obliged to build and maintain the eastern side. Everybody digs the post-holes of his own lot. Along the high fence only a half-roofed shed can be built. Furthermore, the manure heap had to be placed at least five metres away from the property line.

The fence, or hedge, is an exceedingly important boundary. If trees are planted on it, the fruit belongs to both owners. If the tree is rooting further in but a branch overhangs the other side, the neighbour can pick its fruit and even has the prerogative of cutting it off. In many places the well is placed on the property line, because in this way the cost of digging it is only half for each neighbour and both can use it equally. According to unwritten law, the owner of the property can kill the poultry, dogs, and cats that wander on his lot, but as this can lead to long-term animosity, it is rarely done. The owner has to maintain the wall of the house overlooking the neighbour's property, but this extends mostly to plastering, for it is whitewashed only very rarely.

Contact between neighbours was partly social, partly economic in character. Neighbouring families got together by age groups. The children played together and perhaps guarded the stock together. The women visited each other several times a day for a little chat, maybe for a longer chat in the evening, and above all they got together for spinning. Gatherings of the men, called *tanyázás* in the Great Plain, were most regular. In the evening, after feeding and watering the stock, neighbours got together in the barn. An especially developed form of this is the so-called *ólaskert,* where the men gathered and shortened the long winter evenings with talking and story telling.

Generally, the economic ties are even stronger, since hardly a day passed when they did not borrow some domestic tool from each other.

If they were short of salt, paprika, or bread before baking time, the wife or child ran and asked some from the neighbour. They had to return such a loan exactly, or even in heaped measure, as it is told also in the proverb: "Borrowed bread must be returned". They always returned borrowed tools, plates and platters carefully cleaned. Another form of contact was to send samples of fresh baking and bread to the neighbour, just as they had to send a sample when the pig was killed.

Neighbours were called upon to help in any kind of work even before the immediate relatives. They were counted on to help build the house and dig the well and to hold down the pig when it was slaughtered. Neighbours were present at family holidays, and they usually went to market together. It also frequently happened that they helped each other to carry out agricultural work on a basis of total equality.

The economic aspect of the neighbourhood relationship lasted for a long time and in some respects it can even be found today. Social contact, however, is being pushed more and more into the background. As the result of the speedy and almost complete permeation of radio and even more of television, evening visits have mostly stopped and the gatherings in the barn—even where they keep stock privately around the house—can no longer be found. The peasant population is progressively turning inward on the example of the cities, and consequently the place of meeting is primarily the place of work and not the home.

Classes and Social Strata in the Hungarian Village

The population of the Hungarian villages was not homogeneous even in the Middle Ages, since property differences and occupational variations led to the development of groups of different character and interest, as also did religious differences and variations by age groups. All this can be measured in the area of economic and social life just as much as it shows up in the cultural sphere. The freeing of the serfs in 1848 ended part of the feudal obligations, and from then on there appeared within the peasantry even more marked property and attitudinal differences. The interests of the rich peasant strata tied them to the ruling class, while the indigent peasantry was growing closer to the industrial proletariat. In the following we will point in broad outline to the most important of the property-occupation groups, primarily at the turn of the century, and will follow some places and cases all the way to 1945.

Nobles and Lords We must mention at least a few of the characteristics of the nobles *(nemes)* and the lords because they basically determined the economic life of the peasantry, as some remnants of the feudal ties remained even after the serfs had been freed. Beginning with the Middle Ages, the nobility had also stratified considerably. The lowest layers, the so-called common nobles *(köznemes)*, who, because they lacked property, were referred to as "nobles of seven plum trees", in many cases possessed only a house and a little land, which, like the serfs, they cultivated themselves. They clung fiercely to their privileges, according to which they paid no taxes and could participate in the political life of the country. Their education and habits lay extremely close to, and in many cases were identical with, those of the peasantry. In outward appearance their broadcloth clothes and sword differentiated them from the serfs, whom they looked down upon and would not mix with. The middle strata of the nobility, the landowners, possessed independent estates, which were largely cultivated by the serfs who, in addition, also had to pay them shares of produce.

Their mansions, inside and out, imitated those of the high nobility, as did their traditions. The high nobles and high lords, often not even Hungarian in origin, usually did not live on their estates but spent the greater part of the year in their palaces in Vienna, Buda, Pozsony, or perhaps further west, and only infrequently came home to the estate run by stewards and overseers. Their culture or often even their language had not much in common with the Hungarians.

After the freeing of the serfs a good part of the lesser nobility blended into the peasantry, while a proportion tried to find a position as officials, as did those middle nobles who could no longer exist on the income of their estates. The estates of the high nobility, extending to many thousands and not infrequently to many tens of thousands of hectares, remained almost untouched until 1945 and were cultivated by the army of millions of farm labourers and rural agricultural labourers.

The relationship between the landlord and the peasantry was of an economic nature, based primarily on exploitation. We must also mention one of the cultural aspects of this relationship. The style of mansions and castles undoubtedly affected folk architecture, and often the same master erected both types of buildings (cf. p. 188). The wealthier peasants attempted to copy, albeit with a time lapse, the better agricultural equipment of the large estates. Certain elements of clothing, of weaving and embroidery arrived to the villages through acquaintance with their upper-class equivalents, and these contacts can be demonstrated even in the dissemination of poetic material, since servants and maids could transmit them easily. Similarly measurable is the influence of what we can attribute to upper-class culinary arts. Undoubtedly this was one channel through which certain European cultural elements reached the Hungarian peasantry.

The Village Intelligentsia

A significant number of village intellectuals originated from the peasantry, or perhaps can be traced back to it through several generations. Their situation was peculiar, since in most cases despite their origin they had to serve the often contradictory interests of the state and of the landlords. Because of their situation, in their mode of existence they imitated partly the landlord, partly the urban middle class. Their significance in the spreading of general culture is of very great importance, varying according to period, place, and often the individual.

The priest, the minister and the teacher usually rose from the peasantry, and this signified the first step in the escape from peasant life. These occupations were closely tied to each other, since during the last century exclusively, and even up to 1948, the great majority of schools were maintained by one of the churches. The role played by priests, ministers, teachers and cantors as intermediaries between literature and folk art was very important. This stratum played a great role in bringing about this mutual exchange. The priests, and especially the Protestant ministers, sought out foreign lands after they had finished studying theology at home and brought back with them not only religious but also a great deal of worldly knowledge as well. Thus they became acquainted with windmills in Holland in the 17th century, and the first domestic copies built were based on their findings. In the 18th and 19th centuries it again was the priests who acquainted their parishioners with several new forms of the plough. We must mention especially the Lutheran minister of Szarvas, Sámuel Tessedik, who not only brought to light the miserable conditions of the peasants of the Great Plain, but also established an agricultural school where the children of the peasants could learn the basic elements of farming. Those schools in Hungary where teachers, priests, and ministers were trained kept a lively contact with European culture, and became yet another channel through which European culture reached, though greatly delayed, the Hungarian peasantry.

Naturally, not every stratum acquired general culture. In this respect it is enough to mention that in 1881 more than 50 per cent of the population of Hungary over the age of six was illiterate. The distribution of illiteracy varied: in the central area the percentage was much smaller, while in the fringe areas it was much greater, and in some places almost reached 90 per cent.

The notary and the parish clerk were representatives of state authority, who, although officially elected in the village, still carried out the decisions and instructions of the county. Formerly a doctor could not be found even in ten villages because they preferred to settle in market towns, and the villagers had to try to cure themselves.

The village intellectuals came into contact with the peasantry only in an official capacity; social contact with them was rare. Perhaps they put in an appearance at some festive occasion such as peasant weddings.

The Rich Peasants

A characteristic figure of the Hungarian village was the rich peasant or, as they called him in some parts of the Great Plain, *basaparaszt* (pasha peasant). The development of this stratum had already begun in the age of serfdom, since certain families were able to increase their movable and landed property considerably despite feudal restrictions. Especially in the Great Plain, it was possible to increase the number of animals in the stock, while in other areas they increased their stock through selling and buying. After the liberation of the serfs opportunities increased for the rich peasants who possessed some capital. They began to use not only day labourers but also permanent farmhands to cultivate their growing amounts of land. In most cases they exploited their employees even more than the large estates did, if for no other reason, than because they were always present themselves, and did not tolerate anyone's resting or standing around but constantly urged their labourers to work.

A significant proportion of the rich peasants kept the form of the extended family, since work opportunity was plentiful on the property, and it was also necessary for one member of the family, while working alongside the farmhands, to be constantly inspecting their work. Their houses differed from the traditional cottages of the village more in size than in form. Their farm buildings were much larger and more spacious as required, so that they could lodge all the produce and stock. They were the first among the peasants to introduce new, improved, and at the same time more expensive work implements, with which they tried to increase the yield of the land.

In broad outlines their culture and traditions conformed to those of the other peasant strata. Their clothes were also similar, only they bought their holiday clothes of better quality and more expensive material. This peasant stratum stood closest to the village intellectuals, and so they liked to marry their daughters to teachers and ministers and attempted to adapt their life style to them. For this reason the new kinds of furniture appeared in their houses first, their women parted first with folk costumes, and even in their kitchen they liked to use upper-class novelties. To generalize broadly, this stratum parted earliest with some of their former traditions.

The leaders of the village rose from among the rich peasants, members of the magistracy, the judges, and other office holders. This was partly because they could afford the time to handle communal affairs, and partly because they liked to attach themselves to the professional leaders of the village. They could also represent the interests of their families in this way.

The Middle Peasants

The landholdings of the middle peasants *(középparaszt)* varied between 5 and 15 hectares, an area that can be cultivated by a family workforce, and so at most they hired shared labourers only for harvesting, which needed to be done in a hurry. They could handle the work only if the entire family laboured from dawn to dusk. But even in this way if two years of poor harvest followed one another, it was very difficult for them to extricate themselves from debt.

Their property, cultivated with the traditional tools and methods, generally yielded less than that of the rich peasants. Because they rarely

22. Middle peasant man
Jászalsószentgyörgy, Szolnok County

77

had money to buy tools we can find in their circle commonly owned implements and machines, which they bought and used together. A few of the fortunate ones struggled up into the rich peasantry, but very frequently they slid down into the stratum beneath them.

The middle peasants hired day labourers rarely and would not themselves accept such jobs. They were therefore the most inward-turning stratum of the peasantry. They clung to tradition in furnishing their houses and in both eating and clothing themselves. Just like the rich peasants, they too strove to educate their children, and their sons' success as teacher or priest meant for them the first step upward.

The Poor Peasants

The poor peasants rarely possessed more than 1 to 5 hectares of land. This was not even enough to provide bread or to produce enough corn to fatten a pig. So the poor peasant was compelled to work as a wage labourer and to take on share harvesting and other work for share, so that he could support his family, even if with great difficulty. His little land was more a hindrance to him than anything else, since he also needed to do the necessary work on it.

The houses of this group were more humble than those of the former, mostly having only two rooms. Their furnishings were traditional, but at the same time they were the first to buy cheap factory-made furniture and utensils, as necessity forced them to do so. They stoutly guarded their traditions, especially concerning folk poetry, because they were comparatively often together at social gatherings and common work projects, and always welcomed and appreciated a good singer and story-teller. This explains why most folk poetry has been collected from this stratum and that of rural agrarian labourers.

The Rural Agricultural Labourers

The poor peasants and the rural agricultural labourers stood exceedingly close to each other. In most cases only a cottage and a bit of land formed the difference, which could disappear into nothing in the case of a long-term illness or a bad harvest. Their numbers were extremely high and even between the two world wars amounted to one third of the total population.

One part of them strove to move into the higher stratum of the peasantry, but a decisive majority judged this to be futile, since too many such experiments failed. Thus they grew closer and closer to the industrial workers in their life style and organization. Their miserable situation forced them to abandon the traditional culture in clothing, in furniture, and in many other respects, yet at the same time they not only maintained, but also enriched their intellectual culture.

Their inhuman fate urged them to organize, which, however, did not always succeed in meeting with similar movements on the part of the industrial workers. During the last decades of the past century they often came into conflict with the authorities. Not infrequently the police and soldiers beat down their campaigns aimed at dividing the land of the landowners. Their situation became so bad in so many areas that it caused a mass migration to America. Between 1890 and 1914 more than one million indigent farm labourers sought better living conditions in the USA, and most of these never returned home.

In what follows we will introduce several characteristic groups of rural agricultural labourers. Some of these exist over the entire language territory while others are limited to certain areas. Their characteristic is that, contrary to the occupational layers (tobacco, melon, onion, paprika, etc. growers), they did not sell any products, but only their own manpower. Furthermore, in most cases they had to accept work in faraway places.

Share Labourers

For centuries the landless farm labourers performed agricultural work primarily for a certain portion of the yield. This labour method really expanded after the freeing of the serfs, when the large estates that did not possess capital suddenly lost the free labour of the serfs. There was no other choice but to hire share labourers to harvest, to cultivate and harvest corn, and to cultivate various industrial crops. There came from all this such a jumble of connections that it hindered the labourer's free movement and tended to tie him more closely to one place.

Share harvesters in the 18th century still received a sixth or seventh portion of the crop for their work (cf. pp. 504-7). By the turn of the 19th to 20th centuries this share decreased to a tenth or eleventh portion and both the cutter and binder of the sheaves received this amount together. From the beginning of the last century these conditions were fixed in writing on the large estates. The harvesting *gazda* had usually concluded these harvesting contracts in February with the steward of the estate in the name of the harvesters. They agreed upon the ratio of the share and, furthermore, upon how the work was to be done and how much time they would need to do it. If somebody fell sick, they let him go and at most paid him for the work already finished. The *gazda* supplied drinking water, but the labourers had to pour it into jugs and carry it around. If a storm scattered the sheaves they had to gather them together as often as was necessary.

Several methods of having meals developed. The large estates generally doled out weekly a so-called payment in kind consisting of bread, bacon, flour, vegetables, perhaps lard, vinegar, and always brandy, or in some areas wine, of varying quantity, out of which the woman who cooked for the harvesters prepared the midday dinner and sometimes the supper. At other places the estate customarily took charge of the cooking, but because this gave ample opportunity to cheat, the labourers preferred payment in kind. The providing of cooked meals survived for a long time in the case of the rich and middle peasants, where the food of the one or two harvesting couples was the same as that of the *gazda*.

Harvesting usually lasted from two to four weeks, and since the harvesters started early, normally before dawn, they went home only if they worked in the vicinity of the village. In most cases they slept outside, or perhaps sought shelter at the nearest farmstead. On the large estates they emptied one of the barns at such times and the share harvesters slept there on straw.

They made contracts in various ways. There were those who hired

23. A cotter woman
Öszöd, Somogy County

themselves out only for the harvest itself, which was over with the stocking of the sheaves. Others also assumed responsibility for carting in the crop, loading the cart and lifting the shocks. There were some who also saw to the treading out and threshing, and later the work of machine-threshing, which gave them a certain extra income.

They had to complete harvesting in a definite time or else the seed dropped from the ear, which meant a great loss to the *gazda*. The harvesting labourers, in order to increase their share, went on strike immediately before harvest or during it to assert their rights. At such times the gendarmes beat down their efforts. They carried off the organizers and put them in jail, while the intimidated remainder started to work again. The landowners feared harvesting strikes from the end of the last century on, and as a consequence they tried to tie down the workers in various ways. One method of this was the cultivation of share maize.

Generally, this work was given only to those who took on harvesting.

Depending on circumstances, it amounted to one or two hectares. This was ploughed, seeded, and handed over by the estate to the share labourer, who hoed it three times, harvested it, and cut and stacked it. For this work earlier he got half the crop, later on one third, then one fourth of it. But if he participated in the harvester strike his cornfield was taken away from him, which meant that the following winter he was unable to fatten a pig.

From the turn of the century, various industrial crops, especially sugar beet, gained significance on the large estates. They tried to devise the cheapest possible means of paying for labour on them. Therefore they made a contract with the share harvesters and share labourers of corn that required them to do any kind of work for the customary daily wage all through the year, whenever the estate was in need of them. This meant that the share labourer could not go anywhere, for example to take on a more profitable job, because the estate, if the labourer did not show up immediately, broke the contract and he lost the foundation of his livelihood.

This contract stipulated not only the above conditions, but also that the share labourer was obliged to do without pay for a few days any kind of work designated by the employer. During this time he got neither a daily payment or wage, nor food. In the previous ways of organization, but especially in this so-called "working-off" system, the direct continuation of feudal serf services can easily be recognized. The share

24. Harvesting
Great Plain

harvesters usually were obliged to provide services during one or two days, mostly carting in the unthreshed grain without being paid for it. The labour on the fields of maize meant an even higher rate of unpaid work. In the Great Plain it varied between one and three days per cadastral acre (1.42 acres), but in certain counties of Transdanubia it even reached as much as seven days.

After threshing, the harvesters carried their share home on a cart hired communally and paid for the cost proportionately. In some places they succeeded in charging it to the estate. In the evening or even during the noon break, the harvesters often sang, and songs about harvesting occur often. They liked to listen to tales, myths, true stories, soldiering experiences, and the one who knew a lot of these gained great respect.

The share harvesters, under the leadership of certain *gazda*s, worked together sometimes for decades, and hung together not only in work, but in everyday life, in the village and in entertainments as well.

Seasonal Workers

The seasonal workers *(summás)* contracted with the estate for five to seven months to do all kinds of agricultural work for a specified sum (cf. pp. 506–7). (The expression *summás* derives from the Latin word "summa".) The work lasted from early spring to late autumn and thus the employer saved himself the amount of winter wages, when he could give no regular work to the labourers. This stratum developed in the last quarter of the 19th century to a smaller or greater degree in many parts of the Hungarian linguistic territory. However, in certain areas this system

25. Harvest festival Boldog, Pest County

assured the livelihood of a significant portion of the population, e.g. of the Matyós of Mezőkövesd, who went regularly to do seasonal work. More than half of the population of the village earned its bread far away.

Among the people of Mezőkövesd it was first of all the poor peasants and the rural labourers, both men and women, who volunteered for this work. The children of the *gazda* went along only if there appeared to be much surplus labour in the large family. The estate entrusted the *summásgazda* and *bandagazda* with the getting together of the band, and the volunteers gathered at his dwelling at the sound of a drumbeat. They had to get a work certificate and if they joined, they signified their willingness by handing this to the *gazda*. The *bandagazda* dealt with all the problems of the workers, and smoothed over any conflicts among them. Only he could keep contact with the representative of the estate. He was told about the division of labour, and was given the payments in money and in kind for division. For this organizational work he got twice the determined wage.

26. Harvesters eating their midday meal
Great Plain

83

Wages in kind were measured out weekly to seasonal workers. They included flour, bacon, vegetables (beans, peas, lentils), sometimes meat and always brandy in varying quantities. Some cash was also added, which they tried to save up for the winter months. A portion of the goods in kind went to the *gazdasszony,* usually the wife of the *gazda,* who provided warm food at least once a day and baked the bread. She got the necessary help from the band to do this work.

In the early days seasonal workers went to the place of work in carts, later they went by train, the expense being covered by the estate. Their lodging was in sheds, barracks or even in barns, where they spent the night on the ground on straw mattresses, or mostly on straw. Their working hours lasted from sunrise to sunset, and they were expected to be at the place of work by the time the sun rose, no matter how far it was from their lodging. They had a half-hour break in the morning and again in the afternoon, and one hour at noon. They had to work six full days, which in the summer months exceeded 16 hours a day in length.

The seasonal workers had to do all kinds of work, the hoeing of corn, the thinning of beets, and harvesting, at which they worked in pairs, the partner usually being a wife or daughter. The hauling in and threshing was just as much a part of their work as the gathering of corn and beets. When rain prevented work in the fields, tasks were found for them in the barn, in or around the farm buildings, and in the granary.

The only day of rest was Sunday, when they did their cleaning up, since during the week they usually fell upon their beds in their clothes. The women and girls washed for themselves and for the men. In most places the landlord put in the contract that they were obliged to go to church. Also on Sunday they got a chance to repair broken hand implements and if after all this they still had some time, then they talked, told stories, and sang, especially in the afternoon and evening hours.

The younger ones at such times grouped together and visited some neighbouring workband, where they were usually offered refreshments. Frequently a zither or accordion was brought out and there was dancing. This dance gathering on Sunday afternoons, the so- called *cuháré,* spread so widely that later on it was adopted in Mezőkövesd also. Others went to the neighbouring villages to make new acquaintances and to drink in the tavern.

Pick and Shovel Men

The large-scale regulating of rivers and the construction of railroads, which required a great deal of earth moving, started in the second half of the last century. This was accomplished by the pick and shovel men *(kubikos)* from the southern half of the Great Plain, who were landless or possessed land only in rare cases (cf. p. 507). They were paid according to the vat (containing 25 gallons) of earth they lifted out, and the payment, unlike that of the farm labourers described above, generally was made in money.

The pick and shovel men also worked in bands, led by the *gazda,* and it was among his duties to organize the group. Therefore, when he heard from the newspaper or by word of mouth of some larger undertaking, he travelled there on his own or at shared expense to look over the situation and the opportunities to make money. If he found everything satisfactory, then he began to gather the band in such a way that he first assured a place for his good men and his relatives, among whom he picked out the foremen and their substitutes.

The *bandagazda* of the pick and shovel men worked along with the others, but at the same time he checked the engineers' accounting so that he would not be cheated. In most cases he did not get paid more and would not accept more for this work. He always stood up for the rights of himself and his fellows and always represented their interest against the employer. All this indicates that their well-organized work groups, loyal to each other, already stood closer to the industrial than to the agricultural workers.

The most important tools of the pick and shovel man were the spade, the shovel, and the hand barrow. He always carried these with him and, as they were his own property, repaired them and adjusted them to the work. The hand barrow is a one-wheeled implement, made of planks, with the aid of which the dug-out earth could be moved to greater or smaller distances. On a flat surface the work was easier and they could do more of it, but help was needed to push the hand barrow up a steep hill. In such cases the man hitched his 10 to 14-year-old son in front of the hand barrow. They often took these children along to working places at great distances. They got no special pay for this, but their input showed up in their father's income. This was one method of teaching the children the job of the pick and shovel man. In some places there were cart *gazda*s also, who hauled the dug-out earth on a two-wheeled, square

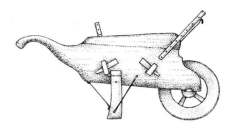

Fig. 9. Side view of the wheelbarrow of a pick and shovel man. Region of Szentes, Csongrád County. First half of 20th century

27. Pick and shovel men awaiting employment
Budapest, Teleki Square

cart, pulled by one horse to the designated area. Cart drivers and children who could drive horses worked alongside them.

For more extensive construction work, barracks or other temporary lodgings were raised for the pick and shovel men, but in most cases they built their huts themselves before they commenced work. They picked sheltered areas at the bottom of the bank where the work was being done or at the edge of the forest, and used all the raw material they found locally (leafy branches, reeds, rushes, sod, etc.). If they stayed for a longer period, they made a dug-out hut in the ground, resembling structures made by the shepherds and field guards. The labourers usually carried a rush matting with them, which, when spread out on the spade handle, offered protection from both rain and sun. They lit the fire outside the hut in the summertime, but in winter they had to find a place for that too inside.

Everyone saw to his own feeding, the main basis for which they brought from home, chiefly bread, bacon, and various dry noodles, as well as onions. Bacon served for the daytime meals because, since the pick and shovel men worked at time-rates, they kept the rest period as short as possible. Generally they had time for warm food only in the evening, when everybody cooked the *tarhonya* or *lebbencs* (pastry cut into big squares) soup in their kettle, with plenty of onion, and, if supplies permitted, with bacon.

28. Pick and shovel men at work
Great Plain

Sunday meant a day off in their work. Then, if they lived close, they went home to replenish their food stock and change clothing, to see their

86

family, and to do some chores around the house. If not, they spent the day cleaning themselves, washing and sewing, because the professional pick and shovel men always tried to take care of themselves even in their difficult situation. If they worked near a settlement they went in there. They looked around and took good note of things useful to them, which is why they played an important role in spreading the elements of material and intellectual culture.

As there were fewer occasions for story-telling, they preferred to tell jokes, narrations and personal adventures. Besides the contemporary folksongs, they were already quite familiar with the rallying songs and marches of a political nature. They even added to these and produced rhymed sayings (cf. pp. 507–8). Although not many have been recorded, in the *kubikos* villages of the South Great Plain people still remember many such rhymes. Most of these lamented the hardship of work, the fight with the elements, the lack of money, the distance from the family, and the hardship of life, as for example:

> *The land wrings us dry as dust,*
> *The ploughs our palms with sores encrust,*
> *Our pants and shirts are bare and mired.*
> *The Lord must be god-awful tired.*

Agricultural Hands on Large Estates

We have already mentioned the hired hands or *cseléd* of the *gazda* (cf. pp. 63–4), but in the manors of the large estates there lived in much larger numbers the various strata of agricultural hands, also called *cseléd*, totally defenceless and in very difficult material circumstances. Their system developed in a basically similar fashion throughout the linguistic territory, since the large estate organization also developed in a uniform way (cf. pp. 505–6).

The steward ran a large estate, while the details were directed by the bailiffs *(ispán)*. The *gazda*s and the overseer carrying a cane *(botos ispán)* directly controlled the agricultural servants, day labourers, and seasonal workers under the supervision of the bailiff. The bulk of agricultural labourers were the *béres,* who worked with the oxen, and *kocsis,* who drove the horses. Their leader was the first *béres* and the first *kocsis* respectively, who guided the work directly and got two or three quintals (100 kg) more produce annually for this.

Agricultural hands were always hired by the year, and if they did what was asked, their engagement was extended for the following year. However, if any objection was raised against them, among which talking back was regarded as the most offensive, then they could not stay. In such a case they got a few days to try to find a job on the neighbouring estates. But if word got around that they were disobedient, that is, that they stood up for their rights, then they would not be hired anywhere, and at the end of the year the estate removed them by force, if need be, from their dwellings, so they and their family had to seek refuge with some relative who lived in the village, until they got a job somewhere.

The form of the agricultural hands' dwelling was very similar over the

Fig. 10. Ground-plan of homes for
agricultural hands on large estates.
General. Beginning of 20th century

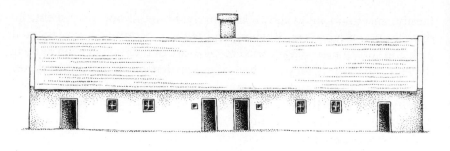

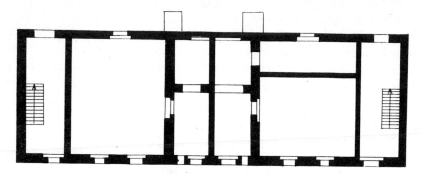

entire country from the beginning of the 19th century. In the earliest
form, four rooms opened onto one great kitchen and in each room two
families were quartered. This meant that often more than fifty adults and
children lived together. Later only one family lived in a room, and
occasionally only two rooms opened onto the kitchen, but basically the
institution of the common kitchen survived right up to 1945. Across
from the dwelling the pigsty and hen house were placed, and where they
permitted the keeping of cows, the stable. In many places the labourers
also got a small field of arable land, a little over half a hectare in size, on
which they usually planted potatoes and maize, since this made it
possible to keep poultry and pigs.

   The quantity and content of the agricultural hands' annual payment in
kind differed significantly according to time and place, so we shall
simply indicate its constituent elements. Its most important part was the
12 to 16 quintals of grain (wheat or rye), usually measured out quarterly.
Added to this was a definite amount of money, which in value was
always significantly less than the price of the grain. Usually they received
a pair of boots, later on a pair of brogues, some salt, and according to the
natural resources of the area, fuel for heating. To this was added in the
older times the keeping of a cow at the estate's expense, a custom that
ended in many places between the two world wars, a certain amount of
land, and perhaps hemp and vegetable gardens. The women cultivated
these with the help of the children.

   There was a strict order for the work both in summer and winter.
Reveille in spring was at three to four o'clock in the morning. The *béres*
saw to the stock first of all, then he could go back for a brief time to eat
breakfast, after which the carts were driven together to the field. Here
the tasks to be done were determined exactly. Work was interrupted by
the lunch break, after which it continued until late afternoon. After
returning home the animals needed to be cleaned, fed and watered. This

meant that they got home around 8 o'clock, too late to be of any help in the work at home.

In winter the reveille bell was rung later, but even then they were given some kind of work. This is when they hauled the crop to market, to the railroad station, and over long distances. They had to repair carts and farm tools, turn the wheat over in the granary, shell the maize, and cut down and haul the trees from the forest. Still there was more time left for conversation, when in the barn the men welcomed a chance to tell both "true" stories and fairy tales.

Sunday did not excuse the agricultural hands from work, since they had to take care of the stock from morning to evening even then. They tried to help during the day in cultivating and harvesting their land allowance, but in most places the landlord insisted that the labourers go to church and kept a vigorous eye on them. However, Sunday still meant some easing of things. This was the time when the young people got together for conversation, singing, and sometimes even for a little dancing. The farmstead and the manor of the estate were usually located far from the village, so that they could not have had much contact with it. Besides, the villagers looked down on the agricultural labourers and did not welcome them, so that most of them spent their lives isolated from the village. Consequently the number of illiterates among them was considerably higher than in the villages, although in some places, and especially in the 20th century, the estates established schools.

The traditional culture of the agricultural hands was largely in harmony with their surroundings as a less colourful version of it. The furnishing of the dwellings consisted of the same pieces of furniture, but they could not afford painted furniture. The traditional way of arrangement was pared down by merciless necessity. They gave up folk costume soonest, and their diet was a poorer version of the villagers'. Usually they married among each other, and they tried to celebrate the wedding as festively as possible. They clung very much to their traditions and kept many old beliefs for a very long time. Perhaps this explains the fact that in the 20th century various religious sects made great progress among them, while at the same time, because of their defencelessness and dispersion, we can hardly find a trace of organizing activity in the defence of their own interests.

Among the agricultural hands of the large estate, a special place was due to the liveried coachman (parádéskocsis) who drove a carriage of the landlord or the steward. The herdsmen (pásztor) of the estate also belonged among the servants, but because of their higher wages and wider authority, they did not mix much with them. The highest rank among them was given in most cases to the cattle herd (gulyás), who frequently inspected and directed the work of the rest of the herdsmen. The hunter and the forester were also paid in kind, but their tasks separated them completely from the rest.

Beginning with the last quarter of the 19th century, the large estates began to use various power machines. Thus, alongside artisans—the blacksmith, cartwright, etc.—now mechanics and locksmiths also appeared. The artisans received a higher salary in money and in kind than all the other labourers, and were called by the title úr, "mister".

Artisans did not share with anyone their independent house. They could work for other people for cash, and all this assured them a higher standard of material comfort in comparison to the agricultural labourers. Most of them already had little in common with the traditional culture.

Smaller Groups and Occupations

The above mentioned strata and groups made up the overwhelming majority of the population of the Hungarian villages and market towns, but a few other groups are also worth mentioning. From among the poor, indigent peasants came the park or field guard *(csősz)* and the keeper *(kerülő),* who officially were called field guards. These were hired by the village community and were usually paid in kind (grain, corn). From autumn to winter, but especially during the time of harvest, they lived outside the village, near the fields, and made their temporary huts from leafy branches, corn stalk, and reeds. In the Great Plain they climbed on a tall tree *(látófa)* so they could see far over the tall growing corn. They had to pay for damage caused by thieves or wandering animals, if they were unable to name the culprit. The field guards of the large estates usually came from among its superannuated labourers, who, for a reduced payment in kind, welcomed a chance at this difficult and responsible job.

While beekeeping and hunting occurred only as supplementary occupations during the last century (cf. pp. 232-38), the fishermen *(halász)* carried on their job as an independent, year-around occupation in the Hungarian villages. Generally, two-thirds of the better quality fish from the waters of the landlord had to be handed in, while the fishermen could dispose of the rest. They took time off only during harvesting, when, as share harvesters, they tried to earn grain for the winter. Fishing was through the centuries an occupation handed on from father to son, and if possible fishermen married among each other, or looked for a match among the poor peasants, because the *gazda*s looked down on them, expressing their attitude with a saying from the Great Plain:

> *Birdcatcher, fisher, hunter*
> *They're never free from hunger!*

Their simple, usually two-roomed houses huddled at the edge of the settlement. They built if they could by the water, to be as close as possible to their work. The many drying nets or nets waiting to be repaired, and in the Great Plain the bottle-gourd climbing up on trees, betrayed from afar the occupation of the people living in the house.

The families of the *herdsmen* (cf. pp. 246-51) lived in the village or at the manor, while the head of the family and the grown sons spent a large part of the year out in the pasture with the stock. The herdsmen rarely mixed with the peasants and labourers, and even among themselves they maintained separation according to the kind of animal they guarded. Among the herdsmen, when they reached the status of head herdsmen, could be found many prosperous men, who acquired considerable wealth through clever exchanges, marketing, and in earlier times by accepting stolen animals into the flock. However, the shepherds were reckoned the wealthiest of the herdsmen. They grazed their own sheep along with the flock of the community or of the large estate and gained both from its progeny and milk profit, so that they often became completely independent. However, no matter how wealthy some of them became, in most cases they could not participate in the communal life of the village, so they kept their separateness, willy-nilly. Only a few of the herdsmen who drove the animals of the village out to pasture every day accepted this occupation for life, or passed it on to their family. These herdsmen came mostly from among the poor peasants, rural workers. At other times the job served as a temporary expedient for bankrupt men, or sometimes older, retired men volunteered to do it.

A significant role was played by the carriers (*fuvaros*) (cf. p. 270) before the building of the railroads, and often even after that, in hauling products. They came from among *gazda*s who owned little land, or from among the poor peasants. In the latter case, this counted as a basic occupation. Generally the poor man bought two horses and a wagon, though with great difficulties, and undertook hauling for smaller and greater distances. But since he had no land and he could get feed for his animals only through share work, he was compelled to turn to the large estate. Here he got a meadow to mow for the third or fourth part of the yield, and could cut the aftermath for half of its yield. In return, he agreed to transport the cut grain and to convey the threshed-out grain to the railroad station, some of it free, some of it for a predetermined daily wage, but he always had to be on call at the time fixed by the estate. Socially these carriers did not rise from among the poor peasantry, since the death of a horse or some other misfortune threw them right back among the hired hands. However, there were also some hauliers who carried goods back and forth on roads linking parts of the country or countries together. These were mostly hired by merchants travelling to remote markets. They knew the roads, the local circumstances, the taverns that provided lodging, and the dangers on the road extremely well, so that their work was well paid. There are parts of the country where the bulk of the population lived from hauling.

Artisans

In the following, we will mention a few rural trades (carpenter, miller, tanner, weaver, furrier, boot-maker, *szűr*- and *guba*-maker, potter, etc.), giving separate consideration to their organization by examining the role they fulfilled in the life of villages and market towns, and in Hungarian peasant society in general.

In some cases the activities of rural industry remained within the framework of the home as cottage industry (e.g. spinning and weaving, woodworking) (cf. pp. 302-9-371), in other cases they are independent professions (e.g. weaving, skin processing, etc.). There were also some occupations ever since the Middle Ages which may be considered as specialized work, such as that of potters, smiths, millers, etc. The attempts of professional artisans to defend their occupation against those who only worked occasionally as bunglers, and who tried to be free from all supervision and avoided paying taxes, was only natural. This is

29. The sign–board of a potter
Nagyatád, Somogy County

30. Front of a guild chest, 1800
Miskolc

one of the reasons for the existence of professional guilds, the organization of which, along with its Austrian-Bavarian name *(céh),* came from the west, primarily from the German linguistic territory (cf. p. 661).

The guilds are first mentioned in the 14th and 15th centuries, but at other periods they linked together only the artisans working in the same or related areas of the larger towns. The numbers of guilds increased after the Turks left, especially from the 18th century on, when the craftsmen in cottage industries also joined some of the corresponding guilds in neighbouring cities. Although a decree in 1872 terminated them officially and replaced them with another organizational form, guilds continued to exist in the old, familiar form until the turn of the century.

The rights and responsibilities of certain guilds were regulated by the guild charter *(privilegium* or *céhlevél),* which was updated and renewed from time to time according to need. They kept this important document and its versions in the guild chest along with the records, the seal on which the tools of the guild figured symbolically, the tablet that communicated the invitation to meetings, and the money that came in from donations and fines.

The process of becoming a guild member was strictly regulated. It was uniform throughout the country and did not change much during the centuries. It was, to start with, difficult to become an apprentice, because besides his parents two guild members also had to vouch for the young boy. Apprenticeship usually lasted for three years, but this was lengthened at some times and in some places. The apprentice got no salary; indeed his parents usually paid for him, either to the guild or directly to the master. At the most his employer gave him some articles of clothing. He had no rights at all, but his duties were numerous. Besides learning the trade, he had to clean the shop, help in the kitchen and garden, carry water, deliver the finished goods, bring home raw materials. He got a very meagre board for all this work, and physical punishment was very much part of training. When he had learned the trade he became a journeyman, and on this occasion he entertained all

93

the other journeymen of the guild, who accepted him into their midst with drink.

From here on he could no longer be friends with the apprentices, for he belonged to the company of journeymen, whose "paternal master" *(atyamester)* strove to defend their rights against the employer. The journeyman received, besides board, a regular weekly salary, but for this he had to work from dawn to dusk. He had to pay for any damage he caused and he had to give an account of all his doings to his master. The journeyman was obliged to travel partly within the country, partly outside it. The surviving books of itinerant journeymen show unquestionably that Hungarian journeymen often reached the towns and cities of Western Europe. This made it possible for them to get acquainted with new techniques and materials, and keep an eye on European fashions. Thus, journeying was a very important factor in Hungarian folk industry, and within it, in the development of the clothing industry and the formation of folk costumes.

The journeyman, after learning all the tricks of his trade from his master and on his travels, could register to make his masterpiece *(remek)*. For this occasion he made some especially beautiful and valuable work of art, which was judged by the masters of the guild, and if they found it acceptable, they admitted its maker, after he had paid a predetermined "tax", among the masters. From then on he could take on work himself and could hire apprentices and journeymen; that is to say, he became a fully-fledged member of the guild.

The members of the guild chose a head master *(céhmester)*. He defended the rights of all members, guarded the money and documents, presided over meetings and feasts, supervised the work of the masters, and dealt with those who had offended the guild's rules. He represented the entire guild to the outside world, to the authorities as well as to customers. He was aided in his duties by the guild clerk *(céhjegyző)*.

Meetings were held regularly. A meeting began with the opening of the guild chest, and went on until the chest was locked again (Ill. 165–7). Here they decided about using money and admitting masters, assessed rights and wrongs and imposed punishment. The guild's customs and regulations prescribed the many-sided support for the members. For example, sick journeymen received nursing both day and night, they supported the impoverished and the old with money, participated collectively in the burial of dead members and of their relations. Also, during Carnival, most of the guilds held a guild ball, which gave an opportunity for young people to get acquainted.

The artisans who gathered in the guilds played an important part in the life of the city or village. The master craftsmen were members of local government and participated as a group in paying special taxes and doing community work. In the case of walled cities, they were responsible for the defence of certain bastions and wall sections. Similarly they played a significant role in the life of the church. Their flags were kept mostly within the church and they paraded together in processions. Furthermore, the guild obliged its members to attend Mass on Sundays.

The dealers of various articles did not for the most part belong to the peasant community of the village in terms of origin and culture; they mostly settled into the local community from somewhere else. Socially, they ranked just below the intelligentsia. However, they generally did not take part in the leadership of the village and in its collective activities. They tried to establish good relationships with everybody, because in selling and buying they depended on the rural population, as did the people of the villages on them.

The livestock dealer *(kupec)* gathered animals and dispatched them to market, or perhaps sold them to a butcher or sausage maker. He usually extended his operation beyond a single village, and kept an eye on price fluctuations between certain areas. Because the grain merchant *(gabonakereskedő)* possessed storage room for larger quantities of grain, he was more tied to one locality. From early spring he would lend grain and money at a considerable interest, and in this way tied down the following year's yield for a set price. Generally he bought up all kinds of grain and tried to hold them back until spring, when he could sell it for a large profit either locally, or to the wholesale merchants. He often owned the mill too, or the miller expanded his operation to buying up grain, so that the grain merchant could increase his income considerably in either case.

There was a shopkeeper *(boltos)* even in the smallest village. The local shop would be in the centre of the settlement, so that it could be easily approached from all directions. Most village groceries were general stores, where it was possible to buy salt, spices, vinegar, petroleum, and any other goods that were needed daily in peasant housekeeping. Articles of clothing, farm tools, etc., were rarely stocked, because the peasants purchased these at fairs. At the store they could pay not only with money but also with produce, mostly eggs, flour, and the like. The grocer always credited them less than the current rate, so that he could profit doubly from them. In areas where part of the population got its pay in one sum (e.g. share labourers, seasonal workers, agricultural labourers, etc.), he advanced money on a promissory note, but charged interest.

The tavern keeper *(korcsmáros)* was an important personage in every Hungarian village. Even in the smaller villages there was often more than one tavern. The tavern keeper's house was built along the main road to catch the traffic. The tavern usually consisted of a larger taproom, with a railed-off counter made of planks, where the bottles remained safe if fighting broke out. It was rarely possible to eat a meal at the village taverns, because they were primarily set up for drinking. Wine and brandy were sold, beer only much later. The tavern keeper, like the grocer, would also sell on credit, which he collected with interest. The sons of the farmers brought bags full of wheat, often stolen from their own father, if they did not have enough cash to pay for a drink. The tavern was the meeting place of men; a woman would step in only to try to call her husband home. Bowling alleys were attached to taverns from the second half of the last century, and in these men gathered together on Sunday afternoons for conversation and play.

Collective Work and Social Gatherings

We have seen above some forms of work performed for money and for shares on the large estates or on peasant property (cf. pp. 79-90). We became familiar with the working organization within the family and with its direction. However, beside this, work in the interest of the community or joint work to help each other also played a big role in the life of the village. In many cases participation was made attractive by the combination of work and entertainment.

Since community work benefits all participants, villagers did it using their own food and perhaps at the conclusion offered a little drink to the leaders of the village. Generally, more men than women participated in such work. Thus in the Székelyland, and in other places also, if damage caused by wolves increased highly to the loss of the stock, a hunt was organized, and the men of the village, armed with sticks, axes, and fire-arms, pursued the game until they had killed it or chased it to neighbouring areas.

Caring for pastures also counted as communal work. The men went out in early spring to smooth down the molehills, to clear away bushes and dry thorns, to repair the wells and troughs, and, in mountainous areas, to clean out the springs. Everybody took food for himself, as only drink was given by the magistracy or by the organization owning the pasture. The maintenance of the roads between the fields and of the march stones was done likewise during spring.

In many places the village and the church also possessed land which was cultivated and harvested communally. The profit was used to cover common expenses. It was a similar situation when the lands of the

33. Reaping hay
Szék, former Szolnok-Doboka County

priests or magistrates were cultivated by the village community, but the owners had to take care of the harvesting themselves. It was proper for such office holders to offer food and drink to those who did the work for them.

Work done on the basis of mutual help was even more important both in its scope, its social and economic reverberations. This kind of gathering is called *segítség* (help) and in some places of the eastern linguistic region *kaláka, móvá* or *kocetá*. We shall mention only a few of the numerous forms which extended to almost all areas of economic life.

The *housebuilding kaláka* was universal, and in many places people still practise it today. They start out by collecting and bringing together the basic building materials. Then, when the *gazda* signals that the work should begin, a start is made by those who volunteered to dig the foundation. When this job is completed, they drink a toast to it. Next the walls are erected and the roof timbers put on, and on completion of these tasks they hold a *bokréta ünnepség* (garland celebration), still held today even in the cities. Meanwhile the *gazda* diligently takes note of the participants' names, because he knows that he has to work the same number of days in return. The biggest celebration on completion is the house warming, to which all helpers are invited. On the menu there is usually pork stew made with paprika and washed down with wine. Songs and toasts asking for a blessing are also inevitable parts of the celebration.

In the Székelyland, they held the *csűrdöngölő kaláka* (barn stamping

97

kaláka) to pack down the clay floor of the house or barn. Mostly young people participated, who, singing as they went, trod with slow rhythmic steps on every part of the floor and tried to make the smoothed floor as hard as possible. One of the known dances of the Székelyland must have developed from this movement. Its name, *csűrdöngölő,* has preserved its origin.

Among the agricultural tasks, the *hay gathering* and the carrying in of hay was done with mutual help in many places, for example at Kalotaszeg. At this time, the entire village went out and dealt with the hayfields of the participants one by one. The men cut the grass, while the women gathered and then tossed the hay. Stacking and carrying in the hay were again the tasks of the men.

In cultivating the soil many things were done together, beginning with the *hauling of the manure.* The men carried the manure in carts, taking it from one yard after the other, and at each place the participants were given refreshment. In hilly regions they carried the manure on their backs to the steep hillsides, but this work, unlike the carting, belonged among the women's tasks.

During harvest they helped each other only on smaller properties. The so-called *aratókaláka* (harvesting *kaláka*) was customary until very recently. The *gazda* spoke a day before to those he had chosen, to go out to the fields together. Harvesting was done all day long, but not with great exertion, and the *gazda* provided food and drink. In the evening

35. Men playing cards
Méra, former Kolozs County

98

a warm supper awaited them at his house, and the harvesters stayed together for a few hours and had a dance.

Almost all the stages of treading out and threshing grain, the gathering in of potatoes and maize (cf. pp. 90, 91, 210, 213), and the processing of hemp and flax (cf. p. 302) were done with communal work, refreshments and entertainment always playing an important role. In many cases the latter was its *raison d'être* and its more important part.

Thus in the western part of Transdanubia, hardly any work was actually done when the young girls had the task of guarding the grapes. When the grapes began to ripen the girls would go out to the vineyards on the outskirts of the village and frighten birds picking grapes by shouting and singing aloud. Songs including the name of a maiden and a lad were often included, to the pleasure of the young men listening nearby, since these revealed which girl's heart was attached to whom. In the Sárköz, the girls paraded out to the vineyard arm in arm after Sunday church service, and young men could escort them to the gate of the vineyard. From this time on nobody was allowed to cross the boundary of the vineyard for a week. The chosen young man saw to supplying his girlfriend with food. Around dusk, he filled his basket with eatables for the next day. At the gate he handed it over to the waiting girl, and after a brief conversation, he had to part from her.

Another branch of collective work was based not on equality but on need, and provided draught power and better machinery for the needy. Most of the poor peasants did not possess horses or cattle, so that they could not plough their land themselves. One of the *gazda*s or perhaps a haulier did this job for them, and in return they had to provide four to six days of hand labour per cadastral acre. The produce of the fields was transported into the village in the same way, and this put an especially heavy burden on the poor peasants. In such cases there were no refreshments or entertainment offered. When the use of the first manually handled grain-separator began to spread, they were bought by dealers. They would lend out machines in exchange for one or more days of hand labour for the use of the grain-separator.

Self-governing Bodies
of the Village

Having discussed the smaller parts of the inner structure of the Hungarian village, we move on to the larger structure which extended to everything and everyone in the community. Needless to say, this larger organization bore the marks of elements borrowed from the outside, but there are also those the inhabitants created for themselves or else adapted to their needs.

The leader of the village, the *bíró,* possessed different jurisdictions and tasks at various periods. As the original meaning of the title *hatalommal bíró* (possessor of power) indicates, the administering of justice was the most important role he played. We find that the precursor of the office appeared simultaneously with the development of the Hungarian villages, beginning in the 11th century. His task was to uphold order in the village, to collect taxes, or rather to promote taxes, and, furthermore, to judge petty cases. According to local need the legal customs of certain settlements were set in village laws from the end of the Middle Ages, and the village mayor guaranteed the upholding of these.

Election of the village *bíró* counted as one of the biggest events of the village, since much depended on not only who the new mayor was, but also on what family or clan he belonged to. In the early morning the village drummer or *kisbíró* announced the place of the election and the names of the nominees. The retiring mayor asked the pardon of those whom he had in some way offended since he came to office and at the same time made a suggestion in regard to his successor. Only the members of the magistracy elected the mayor, either by popular acclaim or by voting by name. The outgoing village mayor handed over to the new one the village staff *(bíróbot),* the key to the village chest, and the village seal. This was followed by the election of the officers for smaller posts. Finally they all accompanied the new village mayor to his home, where he invited the members of the council and the more prosperous and influential *gazdas* in for a toast. At some places they planted a tree in front of his house to commemorate the election. At this time they carried the pillory there from the house of the old mayor, symbolizing with this that the meting out of justice has changed hands.

During the second half of the last century the course and jurisdiction of village mayoral elections were standardized nationally. Mayors were elected every three years, and for this the high magistrate of the district nominated three men. The citizens could vote for the one most suitable to them. Naturally the nominees came from among the most prosperous *gazdas* and from among those whom the leaders of the district and of the country knew would represent the interest of state authority. The mayor's task extended to three areas. He directed the autonomous management of the village and carried out the decisions of the council and the magistrate. Secondly, he enforced the decrees and laws of the country and the state in the village. Finally, he acted as judge within

Fig. 11. Marks of stamps used by village communities.
1. Tápé, Csongrád County. 1641
2. Kislőd, Veszprém County. 1841
3. Magyaralmás, Fejér County. 1788

a relatively limited circle, which extended mostly to stealing from the fields, disturbances of the peace, settling smaller property suits, and regulating the disorderly.

Other deputies also carried out specific tasks in the handling of smaller transgressions. Thus we can frequently find references to *törvénybíró* (law judge), *mezőbíró* (field judge) and other assignments in memoirs and notes. Besides these, from the Middle Ages on, two to ten *esküdt*s (jurymen), were selected according to the size of the settlement, for the direct assistance of the village mayor. As they were familiar with all the problems of the village, later village mayors emerged from among them. Generally, one of them always had to stay at the village hall, to record the complaints and to notify the mayor if the question at issue came under his jurisdiction. He participated at the execution of distraints, and made suggestions in the affairs of the poor and in helping them.

The *kisbíró* (village drummer) was the permanent employee of the village who was on duty all day, and for this he got a certain amount of payment in kind and clothing. From the end of the 19th century, this was changed to cash in more and more places. He had to call clients to the village hall and deliver notices. Drumming was his most important task, followed by his reading news of common interest and calls for marketing, repeated at various points of the village.

In every village, there were also night watchmen *(éjjeliőr* or *bakter)*, who received a pre-determined payment in kind, clothes and boots. There were at least two, but in larger settlements, sometimes more. Their service started in the evening with the lighting of lamps, and ended in dawn. One always stayed at the village hall, while the other made a tour of the village, and as a sign that he was fulfilling his task

37. Drumming out the news
Szentistván, Borsod-Abaúj-Zemplén
County

satisfactorily, he blew a horn each hour and sang, or recited verses. It was among his tasks to address strangers and those coming around late, to inspect taverns, and to prevent thieving. He took the captives to the town hall and locked them up in the jail. He was responsible for his work directly to the village mayor. The fire watchers *(tűzőr)* watched the village night and day, from the tower of the church, and in summertime they kept an eye on the outlying fields as well. If they detected a fire somewhere, they set the bells ringing irregularly, a sign of fire, and signalled the direction of the flames with a flag or a lantern.

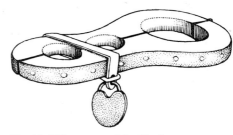

Fig. 12. Pillory to punish offenders. Nagyszalonta, former Bihar County. Second half of 19th century

The village *bíró,* the jurymen, and the members of the magistracy represented the village to the state. A distinguished place was due to them at church, weddings, and all sorts of other gatherings. They represented the interest of the village in questions which affected several villages or perhaps the entire district at once.

The common lands that were not divided among the *gazda*s of the village and were intended for various purposes were handled communally, often by the pasture association *(legelőtársulat),* found in almost every Hungarian village. This association was especially important, because after the liberation of the serfs, the landlord gave the serfs (if he gave at all) a part of his pasture in one piece. This land was not divided; instead, it was shared by each land-owning former serf, according to the size of his arable field and the number of animals he kept. Thus the cottiers, the predecessors of poor peasants, and the rural workers were deprived of pasture, or else, in some places, they had to pay a high price for the right to let their animals graze. The members of the association collected a certain amount of money annually for the upkeep of the pasture, the cleaning of wells, and especially for the wages of the shepherds. Out of this they paid the old *gazda,* who was later called "president", and the pasture of farmstead *gazda*s as well, who directly supervised the order of pasturing. They elected a treasurer and, according to the size of the pasture, other members of the association every three years. The pasture association at the end of the year picked out the herdsmen from among the volunteers who promised to be the most satisfactory. Such herdsmen got, besides their wages, a pre-determined payment in kind for each animal.

The last form of the forest communalty *(erdőbirtokosság)* also developed after the liberation of the serfs, when the forest lands of the landlord and of the peasants were separated from each other. They kept the latter together also at the insistence of the state, since their division would soon have led to the complete destruction of the forest. The proportion of the shares was divided according to the size of the property in land, and it was possible to buy and sell this share independently. Such forest rights assured a share in the profit of tree felling, or its adequate equivalent in kind, to the owner. At the head of the forest communalty stood the president, formerly the forest *bíró,* who with the help of the *gazda*s, but always on the basis of a majority decision, decided about cutting, new planting, and the amount of contributions. The work of the forest *bíró*s was inspected and directed by the organs of the national forest administration, but in spite of it, these forests did not reach the level of the national forests and those that belonged to the landlords.

The Churches and Religious Life

The Churches of the various denominations played a very important role in the life of the Hungarian villages because they influenced to a considerable degree the moral norms, customs, and the shaping of family life. The abandonment of paganism took place in the 10th and 11th centuries, and the Hungarians uniformly followed the Catholic religion till the first half of the 16th century, when the decisive majority became Protestant. The vigorous Counter-Reformation of the 17th century, in which the majority of the landed nobility participated alongside the priests, changed the situation considerably. The theory of *Cuius regio, eius religio* succeeded to a great extent, and Catholicism meant an advantage for the native population as well as to the new inhabitants who came to settle in Hungary. Accordingly, from the 18th century on, the majority of Hungary's population has been Catholic.

Sixty-two per cent of the entire population was Catholic in the first half of the century, above all in Transdanubia and in the northern part of the country. The 22 per cent that were Reformed Presbyterians lived primarily in areas east of the Tisza, while the 6 per cent that were Lutherans lived in various parts of the country. The majority of the

38. Maidens of Mary, ready for procession
Mezőkövesd

104

Hungarians of Transylvania belonged to the various Protestant sects although in large and unbroken Hungarian areas (Csíkszék) we can find only Catholics. In the villages of mixed religion, the members of different denominations were separate from each other in customs and often in costumes and eating habits. The Church usually prohibited, or at least disapproved of, marriages between them.

The organization of the Church influenced intellectual life, and in fact almost completely defined it through the centuries. This can be explained by the fact that the Church maintained the schools from the lowest to the highest grades, and that the world view of the Church asserted itself through these. However, the Church—in Hungary primarily the Catholic Church—was also a secular power that possessed landed property. Thus, the Catholic Church of Hungary, together with the various monastic orders, held, even half a century ago, 10 per cent of all the arable land, in addition to the land grants of the parish parsons. Thus the Church, as landlord, exploited its agricultural workers in the way we have seen above, just as did the secular owners of landed estates.

Generally the Churches collected a tax, a tithe, from their members. The amount of this changed from time to time by area or even by village. It consisted partly of money, partly of contributions in kind, which generally had to be paid in the autumn, after harvesting. Besides this, they collected alms-boy contributions every Sunday, part of which, in the case of Catholics, was due to the Pope as "Peter's pence". The priest was paid a fixed amount of surplice fee to carry out priestly functions such as baptism, marrying and burial.

The village organization of the Catholic church was directed centrally. The parson was appointed by the bishop, while the president of the Church Council was elected locally by the most prosperous and most devout members of the Church. The sexton and sacristan helped the parson to prepare the mass, kept the church clean, and usually also saw to bellringing and delivering messages. They enjoyed a predetermined payment, earlier primarily in kind, and got a special remuneration for tolling the bell for the dead.

The village organization of the Protestant Churches is more democratic, and the minister is elected by the congregation. In the past, if for some reason he proved unsatisfactory, the congregation could even send him away. The church warden stood at the head of the presbytery and counted as the secular head of the local congregation. He handled the money of the church and when necessary, gave an account to the presbytery. The sexton was partly the minister's substitute, and partly his helper during the sacrament of Holy Communion, at which the

40. Interior of a Calvinist church
Szenna, Somogy County

Az 1938 ban konfirmált növendékek ajándéka.

41. In church
Vista, former Kolozs County

more prosperous church members successively offered the wine and bread. The bell ringer, as a permanent and paid employee, did all the chores.

Attending Sunday service was made obligatory by the consensus of Church and village opinion. The women stayed at home in the morning so that they could prepare dinner on time, and in the afternoon the men stayed so that they could feed the animals. Only the old, particularly elderly old women who had free time, participated in weekday worship. After the Sunday service the men stayed together for a while in front of the church to discuss the latest news and events. At such time the village drummer announced decrees of common interest.

The function of the Church was to stand by the three major functions of life and in due fashion fulfil their ceremonies. Essentially, it admitted the infant into the Church with baptism, it blessed the relationship of two people in marriage, and accompanied the dead on the last trip to the cemetery. It noted all this in the register, which the Hungarian churches kept from the 17th century, but more generally only from the 18th century. The state took over the function of registering from the end of the last century and, although the churches continued to record, the state authorities did not accept these records.

42. Sunday, after church
Szék, former Szolnok-Doboka County

The Church also played an important role in the matter of morals. Thus, it punished severely those who wore clothes unsuited for public morals as interpreted by the Church, who created a disturbance, drank, swore, or fornicated. They were put on the pillory, or condemned to begging the Church's pardon, at which time they had to confess their sins in front of the entire congregation and promise to change for the better.

Church music affected folk music from the Middle Ages on. Examples of the literature of sermons appear in the tales and myths of the peasants. The Churches were also the originators and disseminators of certain dramatic plays of religious content.

Parish Feasts, Markets and Fairs

A significant proportion of Hungarian peasants wandered to faraway places for seasonal work, and in this way they got to know other regions and brought home new utensils, methods of work and new customs, many of which were adopted and became general. Pilgrimages, markets and fairs where the people of many villages, or of a larger area—often of entire parts of the country—gathered together, for centuries provided special opportunities for the exchange of produce, knowledge, and customs. These meetings—opportunities for conversation and for making acquaintances—were important occasions for the exchange of material and spiritual goods, and their effect is present even today.

The *búcsú* (pilgrimage), is a Hungarian word of ancient Turkish origin, which included in the language of origin the meaning "absolution, forgiving of sin". In the Hungarian language, from the Middle Ages, the word got the supplementary sense of "dispensation, pilgrimage, church festival". The Catholic Church developed the *búcsú* in this form, announcing forgiveness of sins to the participants, and yet in many cases we can discover pre-Christian features in the practice, the remnants of the pagan Magyars practising their ancient customs during the 11th and 12th centuries in the depths of the forest, among rocks and springs. The respect for springs continued, and the Church, as it did all over Europe, tried to increase the belief in the miraculous powers of watering places. Series of legends developed around such springs, usually connected with Jesus and Mary. Thus, in the Székelyland, the pilgrimage around Lake St. Anna acquired a great fame, but pilgrims who hoped for cure from the water also congregated by several springs every year (Székelyudvarhely, Olasztelek, Esztelnek, etc.). In the Palots area pilgrims came from far away to the springs at Mátraverebély and Hasznos until very recent times, just as they came to a spring in the Bakony, the miraculous powers of which had been circulated in a legend. The Church usually raised a chapel on these places and tried to shape the beliefs about them to serve its own purposes.

At other places, pilgrimages were connected with certain holy pictures of statues placed in various churches and believed to effect miracles. The Greek Catholics held Máriapócs to be such a place, while the people from Szeged made pilgrimages to Radna. In Southern Transdanubia the pilgrimage to Andocs gained the biggest fame. A popular place for pilgrimage at Szeged was the church in the lower town. Every August the settlers who had moved out of here returned on foot from 30 to 40 km away to its picture of the Black Mary. Almost the entire Catholic population of Székelyland participated in the pilgrimage to Csíksomlyó. Carrying banners and singing, they marched, often for days, to the holy place, where the people of the village gave them room and board for nothing or for very little. In some places the custom of sleeping in church was preserved, as it was believed that in sleep the cure, the miracle, is more likely to happen. At some places it was reckoned to be a girl market, where the girls appeared with their full dowry. The merchants set up tents, where not only souvenirs and relics, but often articles of clothing could be bought as well. The showmen, the merry-go-round men were just as much part of the pilgrimage as the taverns, the selling of drinks, and dances. While the older folks and the sick endeavoured to touch and kiss the miraculous statue or picture, the younger ones thought primarily of entertainment.

The pilgrimage of certain villages was connected with the name day of a church's saint. This gathering included even more secular elements. Outsiders usually came only from the neighbouring villages, because these are primarily the holidays of the village, and even the people who have migrated to other villages or even to other countries try to return home for them. The obscuring of the religious character can also be seen in the fact that even the Protestant inhabitants of the village participate in the festivities. Visiting the church is limited primarily to the older generation.

The Protestants also held pilgrimage-like gatherings that were usually connected with some outstanding historical events or other anniversaries. Thus, the citizens of Debrecen annually marched out to the Great Forest on the anniversary of the freeing of their women and daughters from the hands of the Turkish janissaries. The folk celebration of the Székely Unitarians falls at the time of the breaking of the new bread, while at other places they celebrate the day when they announced the freeing of the serfs.

43. Market
Jászberény

While the basic prompting for the pilgrimages of various character originated with the Church, elements of a more or less secular nature being added, the market *(piac)* and fair *(vásár)* are first of all commercial in character, but at the same time their importance for social and cultural exchange was at least as valuable. The circle of attraction of one or another fair also coincided with the occurrence of certain ethnological phenomena.

Hungarian word usage differentiates between market and fair because the two words cover different concepts. The *piac,* from the Italian *piazza,* retains its original meaning of a relatively frequent, perhaps weekly, small-scale market in the main square of the town. Such markets may have existed already in the Middle Ages, as is suggested by the names of towns that include the name of a weekday: Tardos*kedd* (Tardos-Tuesday), Csík*szereda* (Csík-Wednesday), *Csütörtök*hely (Thursday-Place), *Péntek*falu (Friday-Village), *Szombat*hely (Saturday-Place), etc.

Vásár (fair), is a pre-Conquest Iranian loanword, which also turns up often in Hungarian place names: Kézdi*vásár*hely, Maros*vásár*hely, Hód-mező*vásár*hely, Asszony*vásár*a, Marton*vásár,* etc. The Hungarian word for Sunday *(vasárnap),* originates from the word *vásár,* which in essence designates the day of the fair. Throughout the entire Middle Ages and even later, the Church fought against fairs held on Sundays and holy days. In many places they were satisfied with prohibiting sales before Church service. In certain parts of Transylvania they held Sunday fairs until very recently. The other two names of national fairs: *sokadalom* (multitude) and *szabadság* (freedom), emphasize their characteristics. The first indicates that a multitude of many people gathered from wide areas, the second implies that here selling and buying could take a less restricted form.

The *market* and *fair* have left their mark on the settlement in which they played a big role. Originally the market place was situated in the centre of town, usually around the church. Accordingly a square developed. It will suffice to mention only a few among the many examples. We can find squares in place of former haymarkets at Kézdivásárhely, Kolozsvár, Hódmezővásárhely, Kecskemét, and even in Budapest whose former Haymarket Square *(Szénatér)* is today's Kálvin tér. At other places the market was located not at a square but on a wide centrally located street, occupied by vendors on both sides, so that traffic could flow freely along the middle. The main street of Debrecen is like this, and was called *Piac utca* for a long time. No matter where the market was located, on the street or on a square, it was surrounded by a string of stores, taverns, inns, and most of the time it was the trade and administrative centre of the town or village.

Market-days were held in the market towns on almost every working day of the week, while in larger places there may have been even more than one at the same time in different parts of the town. Here, as well as in those villages that possessed the right to markets, the main market day was held on a specific day, and furthermore, in most places down to the most recent times, at some central location of the settlement. Their removal has begun only during the last decades. People from the settlement or from its immediate vicinity brought to these markets small livestock, vegetables, fruit, grain, flour, bacon, and other food products. The permanent vendors, the *kofa*s, sold these on trestle tables, while the occasional vendors offered their wares from the ground. The local potter, wheelwright and other artisans also put out their goods. More permanent stands were set up at markets that held sales several times a week, and in these merchants sold articles of clothing and various cheap goods. The seller brought only a sample from his large quantity of grain, and if price and quality both suited the buyer, they concluded the sale at the merchant's house.

The markets also served as an opportunity to sell unemployed work power. The day labourers looking for work stood on a smaller area, which they called "men-market" or "spitting place". Here the *gazda*s hired day labourers for one or more days. If the labourers failed to find a place by 7 or 8 a.m., they dispersed, since they were not able to start work that day. The market *bíró* supervised the order of the market. During earlier centuries, he rented the right to collect market dues from the settlement. During the last decades this has been done by an official collector.

The best and largest fairs and *national fairs* usually took place where large regions and territories of different character meet. Thus we find fairs going back to the Middle Ages where the Great Plain and the mountain regions meet. We find them primarily in those market towns which possessed considerable industry. This is how the fairs of Debrecen, Gyula, Szatmár, Nagyvárad became famous. They mobilized not only the entire countryside, but caused artisans and merchants to come on carts even from great distances and frequently from other countries.

Beginning with the Middle Ages, generally four fairs were held annually. If possible, these fell on the same day of each year. Local circumstances influenced this, but in the past the name day of the town's patron saint was never omitted from among them. Basically, however, the fairs were adjusted to the order of economic life. Research in Transylvania during the past years has shown that in the course of the year outstanding seasons for fairs developed; for example, there was a spring season, the months of April and May, when mainly the stock changed hands before being driven to pasture. The end of June and the beginning of July was essentially the time of getting ready for harvest, and items necessary for this were acquired at summer fairs. September and October were the months for autumn fairs to buy and sell produce and animals before winter came. The first part of December was the time for fairs to acquire winter clothes. The most important among those listed, in volume and otherwise, were the spring fairs.

The fairs had divided into two parts in early times. The fair where wares were displayed was usually inside the city until the most recent times. If these could not fit into the square, they expanded into the neighbouring streets. Here, primarily the artisans and merchants from far and near sold all the things needed for the inhabitants of the villages and market towns. (See Plate III.) A fair was considered a holiday, and not only local government offices but even the schools closed, since the necessary clothing for the children was acquired at this time. The fairs

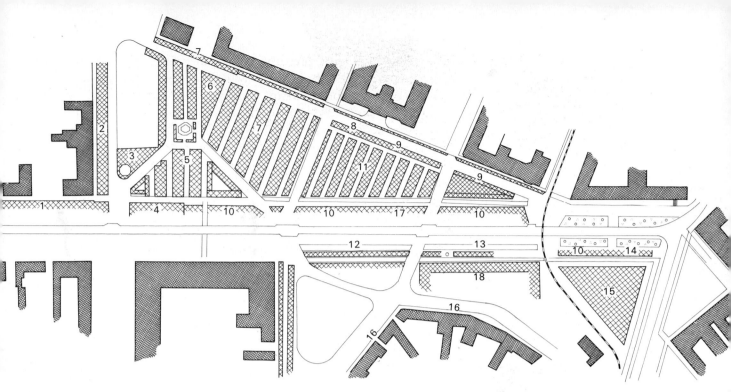

Fig. 13. The ground-plan of the fair for commodities. Gyula, Békés County. 1935
1. Second-hand ware
2. Cabinet-makers and upholsterers
3. Furriers 4. Harness-makers and ropemakers 5. Drapers from Gyula and Békéscsaba
6. Drapers 7. Tailors for men
8. Coppersmiths 9. Hardware merchants
10. Vendors of sweets 11. Hatmakers, bazaar-keepers, basket-weavers, glaziers, etc. 12. Slipper-makers
13. Butchers 14. Photographers.
15. Spectacle-show 16. Rag-dealers.
17. Gingerbread dealers 18. Bootmakers

for crops and stock *(terményvásár, állatvásár)* were usually located outside the city, since the large number of animals would not have fitted into the inner areas. The people of the settlements and of the vicinity brought the products and animals they wanted to dispose of, and with the money they could immediately purchase all the items they needed in the booths at the goods fair. A lot of time was of course necessary to arrange all the buying and selling, so that the big fairs lasted for two or three days.

The location of the goods fairs with stalls *(kirakodó vásár)* was assigned by the leaders of the settlement, who also collected money from the vendors. At first the better places were generally occupied in order of arrival, but for the last few centuries, artisans of similar trades have taken booths in certain rows, making it much easier to shop and to compare prices. In this case the artisans decided on the sequence by drawing lots or by the old method of the order of arrival. The bigger merchants often sent a man ahead so that he assured them the best selling spots.

The artisans, travelling usually in carts, tried to arrive on the afternoon or evening of the day before the fair and started immediately to set up wood-framed canvas tents. In front of these a table was placed, and on it were put the smaller wares, while the larger ones were set up in the back of the tent. As they had to guard the tent from thieves day and night, the *gazda* or one of his helpers slept there, while they parked the cart in the yard of an inn or at the lodging of a local acquaintance.

The important character of fairs as gathering places is well shown by the fact that most of those who came had no intention of buying or selling. They came only to meet acquaintances, friends, and relatives who lived far away, and to get information about prices. But no one was likely to return home without a present, the so-called *vásárfia* ("son of the fair") was due both to the women and children. The children mostly got jackknives, whistles, candy, honey cakes and toys, while the women and girls received kerchiefs, jewelry, rosaries, pretzels and round cakes.

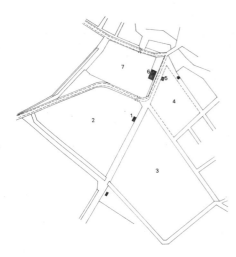

Fig. 14. Ground-plan of the livestock fair. Gyula, Békés County. 1894. 1. Entrance. 2. Horse market. 3. Cattle market. 4. Swine market. 5. Customs building. 6. Slaughterhouse. 7. Bathing place

The vendors who sold these usually took their place in the central part of the fair and offered their wares with loud calls and frequently with verses. The peripatetic vendors usually walked around here, and they were called *bosnyák* (Bosnian) even if they belonged to some other nationality. They tempted the buyers with jewelry, jackknives, mirrors, chains and sometimes watches from a tray bound to the neck.

Clothes merchants were accorded the highest ranking at fairs, especially furriers *(szűcs)* belonging to a guild and the peasant furriers who sold both short and long sheepskin coats *(ködmön)* and mantles *(suba)*. The *guba*-makers (makers of rough woollen coats and blankets) made their products for men, women, and children. The tailors *(szabó)* offered, first of all, articles of clothing, complete suits made from broadcloth. Boots were offered both by boot-makers *(csizmadia)* selling from booths and by vendors who carried their ware on a stick, so it was possible to buy somewhat more cheaply from them. Slipper-makers *(papucsos)* mostly put their wares on the ground, as did potters *(fazekas)*. Many visited the booths of hat- and cap-makers *(süveges, kalapos)* to

44. Selling cow-bells Hortobágy, near Debrecen

114

bargain for headgear. The junk dealers *(ócskás)* took shelter along the outskirts of the commodities fair, where used clothing exchanged hands.

The carpenters or cabinet-makers *(asztalos)* also occupied an important place in the display or goods fair. They exhibited all the pieces of furniture necessary to furnish a room in the style of that particular region. They sold more chests than anything else, since chests were needed in every house and the bottom was apt to rot fairly quickly since they stood on the ground. Beds, tables and benches were less frequently purchased, since these furnishings were more likely to last through two generations. The rope-makers *(köteles)* and harness-makers *(szíjgyártó)* offered halters, harness and bridles necessary to hitch up animals. The coppersmiths *(rézárus)* and hardware merchants *(edényes)* were usually located in the same row.

The fair also provided, to some extent, for intellectual needs. Booksellers sold books, usually their own publications. Prayer books, adventure stories, and above all almanacs were most in demand. Almanacs not only contained interesting articles and stories but also predicted the coming weather and gave the time and place of country fairs. Those vendors who sold, not in booths, but on the ground, on a piece of canvas, stories about highwaymen, outlaws and heroes, competed with the booksellers. Consequently, the broadside pamphlets they sold became known as "canvas" literature *(ponyvairodalom)* or *ponyva* ("canvas"). A special place is due to the chroniclers *(históriás)*, who put in verse certain imagined or actual, perhaps even current, event, such as a robbery or murder. The authors had these verses printed at a provincial press and read parts of them at fairs and sold the prints.

The predecessors of the chroniclers were those who presented pictures of certain events and introduced them to the audience with verses of varying length, for which afterwards they were given a few pennies. It is possible to connect the origin of some more recent ballads with the activity of these "picture pointers" *(képmutogató)*. In Transylvania and Western Transdanubia, the painters of religious icons on glass also sold their wares. The inartistic portrayals of kitchen wall hangings, another popular product sold at the fairs, contributed a great deal to making certain spheres of decorative folk art shallow.

The showmen and clowns usually stayed on one part of the fair-grounds. A merry-go-round was rarely absent. As payment, the children who pushed it to go round and round could get a free ride after four or five turns. A circus tent was put up the day before the fair and the members of the circus would go around the village or town accompanied by loud music calling attention to their arrival. The bear-dancer led his bear on a chain attached to the nose of the animal, who made a few unhappy dance-like movements to the sound of a trumpet. Fortune-tellers had guinea pigs or parakeets that could pull slips of paper out of a box, and from these the people who were willing to sacrifice some money could find out their past and future.

Among the markets for produce the most important was the grain market *(gabonavásár)*, held in the autumn. Grain was also sold in the spring, because those who were able to store it till then got a higher price. Usually special market places were designated for this, which have survived in many areas in square names such as *Búza piac* (wheat market) (in Brassó, Miskolc, Nyíregyháza, etc.). The buyer dug deep into the grain sacks that were hauled on carts, because often the cleanest and best grain was poured into the top of the sack. If the sale was concluded, the buyer put the sacks on his own cart. If the buyer was a local person, the seller carried his grain home and a little refreshment was always provided for him. There was a separate place for the selling of hay, wool, reeds, and other produce.

Usually, a ditch was dug around the stock market *(állatvásár)* below the settlement, so that if the animals should go wild, they could not disperse. The livestock market was divided into further parts, with a separate place for the cattle, horse, sheep, and pigs, so that the animals should not mingle. Some animals were driven on foot, while piglets and fattened pigs were carried in carts with a covered top. A hut for issuing passes was built on the edge of the market place, and here the written procedures necessary for selling the animals were seen to. A smithy was usually present, and the cooks' stall. Carts were sold, and sleds in the winter, and the makers of agricultural implements could easily market their wares (ploughs, harrows, pitchforks, rakes, etc.).

Herdsmen were the chief visitors to the animal fairs held in the mountain regions and on the plains. They came with their families, so that their daughters could get to know and marry herdsmen if possible.

45. The fair at the Hortobágy bridge
near Debrecen
Hortobágy

Fairs held on the name days of Elek, Illés, and Vendel were all counted as herdsmen celebrations, where the feasting and dancing lasted late into the night. Herdsmen were hired at the animal fairs held on Mihály and Dömötör day. They purchased at this time herdsmen supplies and replaced articles of clothing, and bought or traded crooks and whips.

The droving of stock over great distances demanded knowledge and great natural skill. The drovers *(hajcsár)* were, until the end of the last century, important people in the animal trade, but subsequently, the railroad has displaced them increasingly. Their knowledge was handed down from father to son, and among them various strata also developed. The poorer ones served others all their lives and drove the stock purchased by the merchants to distances of often several hundred kilometres. Others, after acquiring a little capital, bought animals themselves and sold the stock at a profit, because they always knew at which market they could dispose of their stock at a higher price. They covered a thirty-kilometre-long journey a day, during which they had to be careful that the animals did not cause any damage to the crops or the fences, and at the same time they had to defend the stock from predators, thieves, and outlaws. The taverns were usually located on the cattle-droving roads a day's journey apart. Here they could often find a cattle fold to keep the animals together, although the drovers still guarded them vigilantly all the time because they could never tell where trouble might come from.

A typical character at the fairs was the gypsy horse dealer *(cigány kupec)*, who mainly dealt in horses. He bought and sold, often taking commissions—that is, he bought for someone else. He generally moved as part of a group of horse dealers. They knew the good points of horses perfectly and knew their exact value, and they always considered to whom and for what purpose they could pass on the purchased animal. The gypsy horse dealers worked together and tried to push the price down, and when they sold, they attempted by various practices and methods to mislead the buyer.

At the fair, everything was bargained for. Only a foolish person would pay the named price. First, the owner of the merchandise put a value on the item he wanted to sell. The buyer usually left this unanswered, indicating by his silence that he thought the price too high. He walked on, but if he was attracted by the merchandise, he turned back to it. If the seller recognized him, he asked the buyer to make an offer. When that happened, bargaining started, and was followed attentively by several people. This went on until the gap began to close. At this time they halved the difference and the deal was settled with a handshake.

When selling stock or larger quantities of grain, it was often the custom to drink a toast to "wet the bargain" *(áldomás)* (cf. pp. 659-60), paid for by the seller. The deep historical roots of this practice may be demonstrated by quoting Anonymus, the 12th-century Hungarian chronicler, who alludes to big celebrations held by the Hungarians after certain victories.

To wet a bargain at the fair, a place was necessary where it was possible to sit down and rest. Such were the cooks' stalls *(lacikonyha),* located in tents along the fringes of the fair. Roast meat and sausages were served, and wines of different quality to go with them. Usually the owner and his wife cooked and baked, and served the food. The owner of the cook's stall came from the poorer folk, who could only afford equipment he was able to carry to fairs at a day's distance, in his own, or more often in a rented cart. He generally looked on this as a temporary expedient and hoped after scraping together a little money to rent a tavern or pub and later on to buy it outright.

A very important role was played at the fairs by the inns, pubs, and places where carts could be parked. These were huge sheds, which stood on pillars in the yard. If there was room, the horses were tied up in the barn, where they ate the fodder the owners brought along, or else the innkeeper's men took care of everything. Gypsies played music from morning to night in the tavern, and hot food was served at all times, while some people ate out of their haversack and ordered only wine. In many places a whole system of friendship among the guests developed. The fairgoers always stopped at the same place and became good friends. In the market towns, where the village children attended higher grades, the parents who came to the fair were welcomed by the family who gave lodging to the child. The parents tried to repay hospitality by the generous quantity of foodstuffs they brought with them.

The primary function of the fairs undoubtedly was the mutual exchange of produce that came into being as the result of the division of labour. But the effects of the fairs in the area of culture are at least as important. With the exchange of products from different areas, a levelling took place between large territories in costume and frequently in work implements as well. The fairgoers learned the news, and heard of certain important events as versified orally or in print. They got access to books, and could buy the almanacs that were, for a long time, one of the most important forms of intellectual nourishments for the peasantry. The fairs, like the pilgrimages, played an extremely important role until recent decades as the meeting places of the more or less separate groups of people and in the exchange of material and intellectual culture.

II. Material Anthropology

The material culture of the Hungarian people is intimately connected with their social civilization and, through the transmission of tradition, this is valid too of their intellectual culture, or folklore. A basic knowledge of social culture is needed to understand material and intellectual culture better, hence its introduction at the beginning of our discussion. We shall refer to it throughout the following chapters and shall try to make it easier for the reader to see everything as a whole, as already mentioned in the Introduction.

In the chapters on material anthropology we shall also deal with the most important customs and beliefs in order to demonstrate the close relationship of these to the former. The alterations in material culture are followed by changes in folklore, but such changes take root slower. In fact, it often happens that the insistence on custom or belief hinders the proliferation of new tools (e.g.: the steel plough) and new working methods. At other times the social and economic organizations impeded the rapid spread of tools that facilitate work (e.g.: the scythe), because they would have reduced the number of agricultural workers needed.

We shall also deal here with the various branches of folk art, though lately they are often discussed together with folklore. We follow the older ethnological procedure only because in this section of our book we deal almost exclusively with historical material, and in the past, ornamentation did not play such a definite role, it was eclipsed by practical considerations. We therefore think it excusable to deal with it as part of the material culture of the past, though we realize that we are dealing with a borderline case which connects other categories formed in the interest of scholarly organization.

Settlement, Building, House Furnishing

Let us approach the Hungarian village in our imagination in such a way that we first pass through the fields, then take a look at the village settlement, stopping at the lots, and finally turning to the houses and agricultural buildings and to the life and work that goes on inside them.

The Outskirts of the Settlement

Today, the *határ,* an outskirt of fields, surrounds every closed settlement, village or town. The Hungarian term *határ* means both boundary and the whole territory within the boundary—fields, forests, pasture, etc.—surrounding the houses and their lots. Hungarian settlements came into existence in the early Hungarian Middle Ages, and in many cases written sources from the 11th century already make reference to these. Archeological excavations prove that settlements, consisting of a few houses and dug-out dwellings sunk into the ground, often changed location and that their firm siting came about only from the 13th and 14th centuries. We know more about the history of towns and villages beginning with this period. Many settlements of the Great Plain became uninhabited during the Turkish rule. After the retreat of the Turks at the end of the 17th century, boundaries around the numerous, now completely resettled towns developed anew and solidified only gradually. Beginning from the Middle Ages we can already often read about *határjárás,* the inspection of landmarks, when the connecting

46. Farmstead Kecskemét

boundaries of the villages involved were determined by the landlord or by a committee formed by the county. A small mound was raised on the connecting points, especially if three boundaries ran together, and a stone placed on top of it. Often written documents fixed the boundary mark, an event made even more memorable by flogging some of the young men who were present with switches, so that they should remember this event and the exact place of the border even in old age. These hills and stones were held to be the meeting places of witches and troubled spirits, and it was hoped that boils could be cured by rubbing them with a handful of soil taken from here.

The outskirts of the villages slowly changed into cultivated areas, first of all, in the immediate vicinity of the settlements. The virgin sod was broken, forests were cut down, the swamps were drained, and the dried-out areas put under the plough. The process of clearing can be traced from the Middle Ages almost to the present day. Under feudalism the spirit of enterprise was further encouraged by the fact that for a certain length of time after reclamation the serfs did not have to pay duty and do labour for the reclaimed fields. On the other hand, the landlord could always redeem the reclaimed land for a small sum and could attach it to the estate under his own control. In many places permission from the landlord was required to clear the fields, and if this was not given, the land could be taken away without compensation.

Two ways of clearing fields were known. In the case of slash and burn (*égetéses irtás),* the bark was cut from the trees all the way around and when the trees had become desiccated, fire was set to the entire forest. At other times the forest was cut down completely, leaving perhaps only the branches which, after they dried out, were burned along with the bushes. The big stumps were generally left to rot in the ground for several years, because it was easier to remove them this way. Clearing was extremely hard work. Clearing one hectare occupied forty to eighty days of a man, depending on what kind of trees the forest consisted of. The cleared areas were first used as pasture and hayfield, and only after a few years were put under the plough.

The tools used for clearing were the *axe, pick-axe, two-pronged hoe* and

121

flat hoe. Characteristic were the *billhooks* or *slashing hooks,* with which they cleared the shrubby areas, and cut the branches of the larger, felled trees. First hoed plants were put into the cleared area and only afterwards did they plough and sow it with grain. In Western Transdanubia, they cultivated clearings for six to eight years, then used them as forests again for thirty to fifty years, so that the poor soil would regain its fertility. The cleared fields that had good soil slowly amalgamated with the cultivated fields of the settlement, and were used as grazing land or left fallow for a few years only if the soil needed rest.

Clearing of swampy and boggy areas was different. These had to be freed first of all from the standing water and protected against the returning floods. On their own, the peasants could carry out this big job only on small areas. For larger areas they had to rely on co-operation or, from the first half of the 19th century, on state-directed flood control. They burned the dried-out marshes and bogs and burned off the remnants of the water plants that had been deposited in thick layers during the centuries. These covered the ground profusely in some places, thinly in others, and had to be levelled out for ploughing and sowing to follow. Such marsh soil proved to be extremely fertile at first. It did not need to be fertilized for decades. However, the roots of reeds were very hard to destroy, so that on such fields, if there was much moisture, reeds appeared even a century later.

On the outskirts of the town and village, country taverns, forester's houses, water mills, and temporary huts of herdsmen were erected, their locations determined by natural economic circumstances.

48. Farmsteads
Kecskemét

122

The scattered settlement *(szórványtelepülés)* is not frequent in the Hungarian linguistic region, with the exception of the peasant farmsteads common in the Great Plain; such do exist in some places among the Székelys, and among the Csángós of Gyimes (cf. Ill. 17). It seems that this form can be found only in areas 500 metres above sea level. We must look for its origin in the attempt to escape feudal duties, and in herding.

We find the so-called *szeres* (kinship) settlement in the south-western part of Transdanubia, Göcsej and Alsóőrség. Here four, five, or even fewer houses line up on the ridge of the hills and ten to fifteen of these form a village. Originally the arable fields lay in the immediate vicinity of the houses. For the most part descendants of one family live in one *szer,* as the names of such settlements imply: *Győrffy-szer, Szabó-szer.* In the meantime when fields became exhausted and new areas were cleared, the agricultural area and the place of settlement moved further apart. To balance this, new buildings were constructed, so that the *szer* moved on from time to time, drew asunder, and then regrouped. In recent times their development into closed villages has become more definite. Although this form of settlement is known throughout Europe, it can be brought into direct relationship with neighbouring Styrian (Austrian) forms corresponding to it.

Hill villages *(hegyközség)* came into being primarily in the grape-growing regions of Transdanubia, where the poor population, living mostly on wine making, moved out from some closed settlement. The houses and yards are located at greater distances from each other. Just as at the *szeres* settlements, these were connected by footpaths, and in some places by cart roads, which formed a vast, confused network.

The early lodgings *(szállás)* of the Great Plain were temporary erections built on the outskirts of settlements to which they belonged. From the end of the 18th century the earlier name *szállás* was displaced, except in the southern part of the linguistic territory, by the word *tanya* (farmstead), originally a word fishermen used for their abode. The Hungarian farmstead areas form the largest region of connected scat-

tered settlement in Europe. This type of settlement is characteristic of the area between the Danube and Tisza, and the southern and central Tiszántúl. Only in the north, although still on the plain, do villages of closed settlement type occur again.

The historical roots of the farmsteads go back to the era prior to the Turkish occupation, although the first remains of their predecessors can be shown in towns where the surrounding boundary areas were large enough to include the fields of the destroyed villages into the area. In the beginning sufficient fodder for winter maintenance was gathered around the buildings where the animals were outwintered. Only the men stayed here with the animals through the winter. The farmstead was created and further developed by economic necessity. Through the years, as the pastures were broken up and with the development of individual

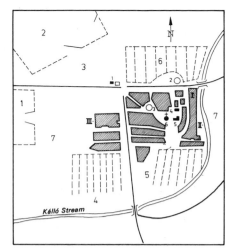

Fig. 15. Fenced gardens of various functions around a village. Konyár, former Bihar County. Late 19th century. 1. The new vineyard. 2. The old vineyard. 3. Playground. 4. Cabbage patches 5. Stable-yards. 6. Threshing yards. 7. Pasture.

51. A grave-post in the cemetery Magyarvalkó, former Kolozs County

50. A well with a steep on a farmstead Karcag

52. Cemetery
Szentegyházasfalu, former Udvarhely
County

ownership, the outlying farmstead became a general agricultural centre. The entire family lived on it from early spring until autumn, so that they could do the necessary work without losing time by travelling. Later on the young people lived out there all the year round, while the old people stayed in their city or village homes. In some cases there were families whose permanent dwellings were the farmsteads and whose connections with the parent settlement decreased.

The farmsteads, therefore, were attached to some closed settlement. Many things show this very tight economic and social tie, such as road access. Farmsteads are easily accessible on the roads that branched out of the villages like spokes on a wheel, though the farmsteads themselves were not interconnected by a road network. The farmstead is the scene of agricultural activity, and the household at the parent settlement serves primarily to process and store produce. The farmstead perfectly accomplished the separation of production, of processing and of use. From the point of view of taxation, marketing, and local government, the farmstead is connected to the village. Baptism, wedding and burial also tie them there by and large; they have no independent cemetery, but they lay their dead to rest in the cemetery of the town.

The farmsteads determine the entire character of certain cities and regions. An example is one of the largest Hungarian cities, Szeged. The first farmsteads appeared at the end of the 17th century, but their numbers could not have been large even at the beginning of the 18th century. They multiplied greatly and by the second half of the century their numbers approached a thousand. In 1880, out of the city's population of 73,676, there were 27,789 living permanently on farmsteads, while in 1930 the figure was 45,450 out of 135,071. This means that the larger part of the population occupied in agriculture lived and worked on farmsteads.

After 1945, as a result of land reform, some 75,000 new farmsteads were built over the entire country. The number of farmsteads began to decrease from the beginning of the 1950s, especially after the collectivization, since they have largely lost their original advantage, proximity to the place of production. Many people moved into the parent settlement, creating new homes. Others continued to stay out. Farmsteads lying near the settlement merged into it, or will soon be reached by the village. More recently some people have kept the farmstead and the garden around it as well as their dwelling in the closed settlement and spend their weekends and part of the summer out there. Such places no longer have anything to do with production but serve as a place of rest after work of a different kind in the city. In many places farmstead centres came into existence with schools, local government offices, a store, tavern, culture house, and their magnetic attraction soon created the seed of a closed village.

A significant proportion of the farmsteads still exists, and in 1970 about eight per cent of the total population of the country lived on such scattered settlements. It is a difficult task to supply the farmsteads with

53. Cemetery
Szatmárcseke, Szabolcs-Szatmár County

electricity, schools, culture houses, stores and road networks. According to the official position, "The forced liquidation of the historically developed farmstead system is contrary to both individual and communal interests. We can reduce the present boundaries of the farmstead region only through far-sighted planning and through central support which takes into consideration the local situation". However, the task is enormous, since half of the population of the region between the Danube and Tisza, not including the population of the cities, lives on farmsteads even today. Families are assisted by allotment of lots, building loans, and jobs in the closed settlement, and are encouraged to move in on a completely voluntary basis. Young people especially use these opportunities, while the majority of the old folk prefer to stay in the familiar surroundings. The yearly decrease of the farmsteads amounts to about one per cent, so that we can reckon on their slow disappearance, as also of scattered settlements that have lost their function.

We find orchards and vineyards in the Great Plain and elsewhere. In the Nagykunság, these are generally divided in width and length into several strips of land, at the end of which stand a *hut* and a *shed*. These are generally one-roomed structures, and their fireplace, heating equipment preserved many antiquities, especially in the Great Plain. They are not fit for permanent dwellings, and people spend the night in them only during work or when guarding the crop.

On the outskirts of larger settlements lie the animal markets, which are otherwise used as occasional pastures. We shall discuss the different forms of temporary herdsman's buildings located on distant pastures later, as well as of the mills located on the edge of the settlement.

However, we may mention here the location of *cemeteries* in respect to the settlements (cf. pp. 635–6). The Magyars of the Conquest presumably chose their place of burial at some distance from their dwellings. However, by the 11th century royal decrees had ordered the building of churches, and inhabitants of villages could not move away from these. They had to lay their dead for eternal rest around the church, as it happened through the entire course of the Middle Ages, even if for lack of space the dead had to be buried on top of each other in the church-yard *(cinterem)*.

The authorities began to urge, sporadically in the 18th century, and more and more strongly in the 19th century, that cemeteries be located outside the village, mainly for reasons of health. At the end of the 19th century, a law prohibited burials around the church, except where the church was located on the outskirts of the village. Thus there are still some graveyards which surround the church. Most of them are no longer used for burial, but we can name some still in use today in various parts of the linguistic region. Thus we can find some in the Székelyland, not infrequently even in cities (Sepsiszentgyörgy), but especially in villages (Telkibánya, Abaúj County; Gyenesdiás, Zala County) and the second largest city of the country, Miskolc, has a cemetery that is surrounded by the settlement itself.

The cemetery outside the village is usually bordered by a ditch with a lilac, box-thorn or other type of hedge on its bank. A permanent fence

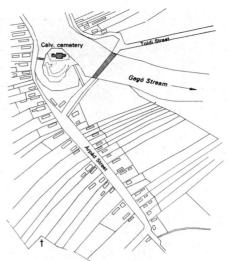

Fig. 16. A village with houses arranged along the street. Nagyszekeres, former Szatmár County. Late 19th century. The graveyard of the Calvinists is around the church, the cemetery of the Roman Catholics is on the rim of the settlement

54. Grave-post
Szenna, Somogy County

55. Heart-shaped grave-post
Karancsság, Nógrád County

56. Tombstone, 1791
Tök, Pest County

and ornamental gate are found only in regions rich in wood and woodcarving tradition. Such can be seen mostly in the Székelyland and Kalotaszeg. Many significances are assigned to the cemetery ditch. This is where the executed, the outlaws who fell in fight, the unbaptized infants, and the suicides were buried, and this is where they burned the straw which had been in the bed of the deceased.

Hungarian cemeteries have an older and a newer form. There are no paths in the former, the graves lying in apparent chaos but parallel to each other. The dead in these graves lie in the east-west direction, so that they turn their faces towards the rising sun, a custom traceable to the Conquest. In the places where the practice of recording family origin along the male line is especially alive, they buried those belonging together by blood in a designated part of the cemetery. When opening new cemeteries the authorities divided the area into parcels in which neither the practice of facing east nor the communal burial of the large family has any significance.

In the past, cemeteries were often planted with fruit trees, and more recently with locust trees, which augmented the income of the church that owned the cemetery or of the field keeper. The flower cult appeared in peasant cemeteries only at the beginning of this century. Earlier they formed a mound, then flattened it out, so that the grass grew over it.

130

They mowed the cemeteries regularly, especially in the older, completely grassy areas.

The Catholics erected a wood or stone cross by the head of the deceased. Among later ones we find some carved in heart shapes after Baroque examples, while others imitated the human shape. The grave posts of the Calvinists were much more varied than those mentioned above. We can find some of a definitely anthropomorphic character in the central part of the country and along the Danube. They are column shaped in wide areas of Upper Hungary, and the notching in front gives information about the age of the dead. In a considerable part of the region east of the Tisza the upper part of the column ends in a peak which tilts forward slightly, and so its shape resembles that of a boat cut in half and stood in the ground. In Transylvania and in a large part of the area between the Danube and Tisza, richly carved, ornamental columns perpetuate the memory of the dead. The age and origin of these practices are subject to debate. There are some who believe them to be pre-Conquest, while others think they spread after the Reformation as a counterpart of the cross.

In certain areas the signs on the grave posts indicate whether it is a woman or man, young man or girl, or perhaps child who rests in the grave. In other areas age is marked by colour. A light colour, blue or white, indicates the young, brown the middle aged, black the more elderly. The latter colour is gaining ground more and more strongly and in certain cemeteries there are only black grave posts. In old Hungarian cemeteries the colour red indicates violent death (someone who died in a war, in a fight, was a victim of murder, etc.).

The cemetery is the village of the dead, where the ancestors rest, they and their belongings protected by superstition. This is why fruit can be picked from the trees only by the field keepers, why flowers cannot be picked here, why bushes and trees cannot be injured, and why grave posts and crosses cannot be stolen. The belief is held that the wronged dead will come for the stolen object at midnight and demand its return.

Beside the structures already listed we find the outskirts of towns and village farmyards containing corn-barns *(csűr)*, sheds *(pajta)* and sheep- and pigpens *(akol, ól)*, living quarters *(szállás)* and loading platforms *(rakodóhely)*. These are closely connected to the inner core of the settlement. Many of these farmyards form a type of settlement typical of part of the Hungarian linguistic territory: the settlement ethnographical literature calls the "double inner-plot" *(két beltelkes* or *kertes)* system. (The Hungarian word *kert* originally meant *fenced* and therefore may mean a fenced farmyard; recently the word mostly means garden.) The basis of this system was as follows: in the core of the settlement, the houses without a larger yard, not separated from each other by streets or fences, were surrounded by a ring of farmyards. In the latter animals were kept, either in the open air or in stables, fodder was stored there, and certain farm chores such as treading out grain or threshing it, etc., were carried out. Men lived and worked on the farmyards all or most of the time. They would build open fireplaces in the stables and gathered together to talk, sing and tell stories. The stables with a fireplace were called heatable stables *(tüzelős ól)*. Therefore, in a certain phase of their

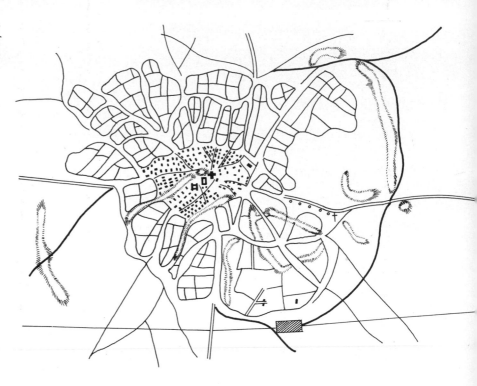

Fig. 17. A settlement with double inner plots. Nagyabony, Pest County. First half of 19th century

development, these farmyards fulfilled in many respects a function similar to the *tanya* farmsteads by separating the agricultural activities from those performed in the dwelling house.

István Györffy discovered this system of settlement form half a century ago in relation to the Hajdú towns, and since then a growing amount of research has found variations of it in an ever-increasing area. It is frequent in the strip between Upper Hungary and the Great Plain, it is rarer in the region east of the Tisza, and it occurs sporadically between the Danube and Tisza. There are several examples of this form of settlement among the Palotses of Upper Hungary, and recent research has also demonstrated its existence in Transdanubia. The latter in-

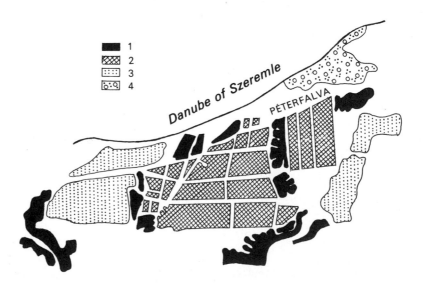

Fig. 18. A village with stable-yards called *szálláskert*. Szeremle, former Bács County. First half of the 20th century. 1. Stable-yards. 2. Settlement of dwelling houses. 3. Plough lands and vegetable gardens. 4. Wood

stances, however, differ in some significant characteristics from their eastern equivalents. The stables stood in the pasture ground and were much more scattered, while the granary and the threshing barn were connected to the stable, though earlier they had stood completely separate from it. Recently its existence has been reported even north of the Csallóköz.

All these data prove not only its wide diffusion but also its antiquity. Beginning with the first half of the 19th century the population of the village or town increased so much that dwelling houses began to be built in the ring of farmyards. In this way the *kert* merged with the settlement. The smaller inner lots and the larger outer lots betray, even today, the former method of dividing the settlement into an interior core of houses surrounded by a ring of farmyards.

In many cases, whole villages were surrounded by a hedge or a ditch, to be entered at the end of the street. This was closed off at night by a gate leading to the fields called the crop-gate *(vetéskapu),* so that the stock could not get to the fields and do damage to the crops.

In the case of the double-inner holdings system, each farmyard with a stable in it *(akloskert)* was separated from the other by ditches, walls built out of manure, and banks packed of earth. Hedges of box-thorn were planted in this so-called *garágya,* "earthwork". This prevented animals from straying even if their guards were absent. The roads from the ring of stable-yards widened outwards like a funnel towards the outskirts of the settlement broadening as the number of stock increased driven out to pasture in the morning. These roads were not closed off with gates, for the system of fields was such that the nearby pastures lay immediately outside the settlement, and these did not need to be protected from the animals.

The Hungarian word *falu,* village, is Finno-Ugric in origin, which testifies to the fact that the ancient Hungarians were already familiar with some form of group settlement. These settlements assume a more definite shape in the laws of King Stephen I, which compelled every ten villages to build a church. This suggests not only the development of organized settlements, but also the existence of village organizations. At the same time, the inner holding *(belső telek)* began to evolve. This was a holding on which stood the house and the farm buildings including the *yard* that served as the place of work, and the smaller or larger *garden*. In the Middle Ages the lots were surrounded by fences over the majority of the country, and contemporary descriptions also mention, in almost every instance, a *gate*. At one time taxes were determined on the basis of the number of gates to a lot.

Over the period that can be covered by ethnographical research, lots were separated by fences of various materials and shapes in most parts of the Hungairan linguistic territory, their form depending on the natural resources and on the customs of the regions. Thus in the Székelyland posts were dug into the ground and connected with three parallel laths, filling the space between with horizontal spars of pine two to three metres high. In the Great Plain, a wattle of willow was woven between

Patterns of Village Settlement and the Organization of Lots

Fig. 19. A small wooden gate with carvings. Tiszakóród, former Szatmár County. Late 19th century

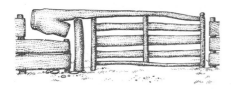

Fig. 20. A gate moving on the stock of a log. Penyige, former Szatmár County. Early 20th century

57. Székely double-gate Máréfalva, former Udvarhely County

the posts stuck in the ground. Poorer folk made their short-lived fences from reeds bound with rushes or from sunflower or corn stalks. Fences made of planks, lath, or even of rod iron have spread in recent times.

We find the most beautiful constructions of gates with bindings *(kötött kapu)* and with dove-cots *(galambos kapu)* in the Székelyland (cf. Plate I). These combine a double entrance, a small one for pedestrians and a large one for carts, into a single, mature structure, rich in tradition. Formerly, gates were only carved, and the first painted ones are known from the end of the 18th century. In Kalotaszeg the freestanding, roofed small gates were carved ornamentally, and similar occur in the region of Tiszahát and in the Little Plain as well. The single-leaved wicker gates that slide on sleigh runners and the crossbar gates of the Upper Tisza region *(tőkés kapu),* which survived until the most recent times, have a long past. In the latter case, a single log holds up a wide gate-board and

134

Fig. 21. A *Székely* gate. Kisborosnyó, former Háromszék County

a post serves as its axle. The crossbar reaches past the gate post and provides a counterbalance for lifting and turning the gate-board.

The shape of the lots and the location of the buildings essentially determine the order of the entire settlement. We can regard the irregular or square- and rectangular-shaped lots as the oldest, going back to the Middle Ages. At that time settlements with street lots *(utcás-szalagtelkes falu)* were prevalent over most of the Hungarian linguistic region. Later on, when the lots were further divided as the growing families raised houses or farm buildings next to or behind each other, houses became more crowded. The core of such agglomerated villages *(halmazfalu)* developed near the church, a settlement type of medieval origin that even later official organizing could not abolish completely.

The other form of settlement connected with the feudal organization of holdings is called the "ribbon lot" system *(szalagtelkes)*. This type remained mostly in hilly regions. Houses stand with their gables towards the street, with one or two windows also facing the street. In front of each, and matching the width of the house, is the small garden,

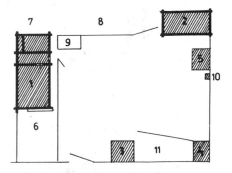

Fig. 22. The ground-plans of a farmyard with a group of buildings. Kalotaszeg, former Kolozs County. Late 19th century. 1. Dwelling house. 2. Barn. 3. Granary. 4. Pigpen. 5. Manure heap. 6. Flower garden. 7. Vegetable garden. 8. Orchard. 9. Cellar. 10. Back house. 11. Fold for milking sheep

40 footsteps

16 footsteps

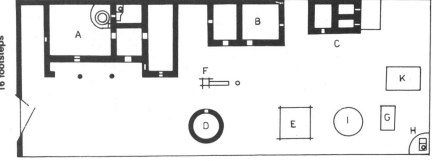

Fig. 23. The ground-plan of a farmyard with buildings arranged on a row. Karcag, Szolnok County. A. Dwelling house. B. Stable and pantry C—D. Chicken- and pigpen. E. Manure heap. F. Well. G. I. K. Stacks of fodder. H. Back house

135

58. A single gate
Szombathely, Village Museum of Vas
County

58. A single gate
Szombathely, Village Museum of Vas
County

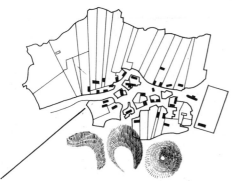

Fig. 24. The ground-plan of an
agglomerated village. Zselickislak,
Somogy County. 19th century

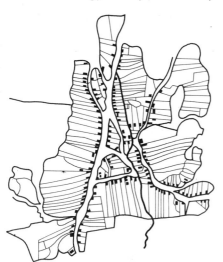

Fig. 25. A village with the plots and houses
arranged in rows along the streets. Szada,
Pest County. 1860

where only flowers are planted, the care of which is the job of the housewife or oldest daughter. Behind the dwelling house follow the buildings of the pantry, stable, and maybe the barn, which often closes off the yard crosswise, so that the stock cannot get into the vegetable garden that lies behind it.

This form is especially typical of Eastern Europe, where the feudal order of settlement was achieved much more consistently and clearly than in Central or Western Europe. Within these main types numerous variations can be distinguished. Such, among others, are the holdings with a double courtyard *(kettős udvarú telek)*. In these, a yard is kept up for the stock on the street side, so that they need not be driven through the entire lot. The house and living yard come next, followed by the barn, hay shed, and maybe a garden. We can find this form of settlement at some places in Transylvania, but versions of it also occur in the Great Plain and the Ormánság. Rows of ribbon lots form the so-called linear or street villages *(soros falu, utcás falu)*, which form the bulk of the present settlements, especially as, from the 18th century on, the increasingly frequent reorganizations of the villages proceeded in this direction.

The houses of village leaders and the more prosperous villagers were located in the centre of the village, near the church, while the poor

59. Settlement around a medieval fortress
Nagyvázsony, Veszprém County

60. Village with streets
Tab, Somogy County

61. Village with streets
Erdőbénye, Borsod-Abaúj-Zemplén
County

peasants and the rural workers had their living quarters at the edges of the settlement. Usually the gypsy colony came after these at a short distance, beyond the fringe of the village.

The Houses
and Farm Buildings

Let us step inside the yard and examine the buildings we find there one by one. Let us examine the material they are made of, their division, and their relation to each other.

The Walling
of the Houses

In forest regions wood was, and in part still is, the most important basic material for all building projects. The much greater expanse of medieval forests made possible a more general use of wood in architecture. The word *ró* (join), describing the work process, and *ács* (carpenter), the name of the artisan who does the work, are both pre-Conquest words (the first Finno-Ugric, the second Old Turkic), showing that the Magyars learned this technique early. Recent work in archeology and ethnography has enumerated an increasing number of arguments to prove that the ancestors of the Hungarians had already become acquainted with wood-architecture on the South Russian plains. As written records increase from the beginning of the 11th century,

138

sporadic data also occur in relation to wooden buildings. That wooden architecture became more general is all the more plausible because the Carpathian Basin falls into the forest region of Central Europe, where this mode of building was frequent even before the Magyar Conquest.

A wooden house was built directly on the ground, or perhaps on larger beams, and in some places they put a stone foundation around the entire base of the house. Primarily pinewood was used for building, because it was the easiest to process and because it gives the lightest and largest beams, but oak structures also occurred. The log was cut in half and rounded or roughed out cornerwise and thus built into the house. The logs were joined at the corners, fitting them into each other with a dovetail joint. Naturally, gaps occurred between the round logs which were filled in with moss. They either left the logs in the natural state or plastered them. In that case notches were cut on the outside of the wood, so that the mud plaster should adhere better. As a next step in development, the beams were split in half (for example in the region of Göcsej), then sawed and thus smooth surfaces were gained in the interior of the building. The technique of fitting slabs into styles *(zsilipelés)* appears to be a newer building technique, in which a groove was carved into the styles that were fastened into the foundation log and then dovetailed beams—well processed and cut the same size—were fitted into these.

A great advantage of a wooden house is that it retains heat in the winter and is cool in the summer. On the other hand it easily is destroyed by fire, and often entire villages burned to the ground. Wooden houses are relatively quick to take apart and move. As early as the 13th century, landlords prohibited their serfs to carry their houses away with them, but they were allowed to sell them locally. From 1495 on a national law prohibited serfs from removing any kind of building fastened to the ground.

The most monumental survivals amongst the wooden structures are *belfries* and *church towers,* which preserved Gothic and Renaissance elements in their construction (cf. Ill. 4,15,51). The most beautiful ones have survived in Transylvania, especially in the region of Kalotaszeg. The ground-plan is usually rectangular, the lower section terminating in an arcade, out of which soars the usually octagonal spire. Four small turrets on each corner make the structure even more attractive. The influence of this style towards the north of Transylvania can also be demonstrated, and the villages of the Tiszahát have preserved some beautifully shaped belfries up to the present day. The lower section of these spread out like a skirt, and thus provide a larger area around the bole, where the old folk can gather before or after the church even in rainy weather. The belfries of Western Transdanubia are more simple (cf. Ill. 3). The four small spires are missing, and there is a smaller arcade or none at all. The lower section is elongated and better emphasizes the unity of the building.

Forests decreased more and more in the central part of the Carpathian Basin from the 18th century on, and as a consequence, wood as building material became less important. Larger sized beams (main girder beams, purlins, bressummers) were shipped on rafts along the rivers that flow from the Carpathians toward the Great Plain. In present-day Hungary

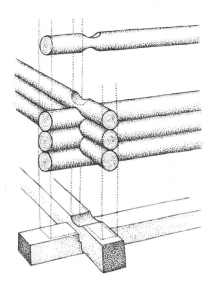

Fig. 26. Setting the logs into an ordinary cross beam. Székelyland, early 20th century

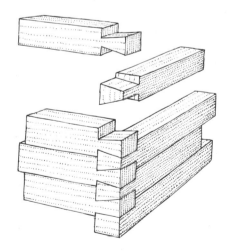

Fig. 27. Setting the wood with grooves called "tooth-of-a-wolf" or "tail-of-a-swallow". Székelyland, early 20th century

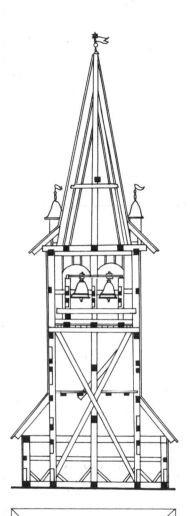

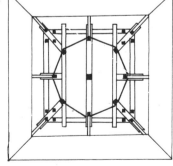

Fig. 28. The cross-section and the ground-plan of a belfry hewn out of wooden beams. Szabolcsbáka, former Szabolcs County. 1770s

we find wooden buildings only occasionally in the Palots areas, and in somewhat greater numbers in Western Transdanubia. In the Hungarian linguistic regions of Transylvania, on the other hand, especially in Székelyland, 90 to 100 per cent of the houses were built from wood according to a 1910 survey, and even today a good proportion of the houses are still built from logs.

The other natural building material is *stone*. Its importance for peasant buildings grew at the time when the thinning of the forest in the mountain regions led to a search for some easily accessible building material. The regions where an earlier period of building with stone can be demonstrated are Upper Hungary, the Palots region, Tokaj-Hegy-alja, and Transdanubia, especially the area north of the Balaton. At other places, if stone was available at all, it was used only for the foundation of the building. In the Bakony the quarried or field gathered stones are shaped only at a corner. Cementing was done in three ways: by putting clay soil between the rocks; much stronger and more generally used is the process of mixing a thick mortar from lime and sand and filling the gaps between the stones with this; and earlier by mixing a thin mortar from lime and sand, or perhaps from broken rocks, and pouring this between the fitted rock in such a way that it completely filled the gaps.

Lime is not only an important material for architecture, but also, especially since the 18th century, for limewashing houses. At places where larger quantities of suitable limestone could be found, lime burning was also done. The largest number of lime burners worked in the Bükk Hills, in the hills of Eastern Transdanubia, and in Transylvania. Quarried limestones were piled into huge kilns, where they turned into raw lime after being burned with wood for 72 hours. When a large quantity was collected, either the lime burners themselves or the hauliers put it on a cart that was covered with rush matting or canvas and took it to the Great Plain or other areas poor in limestone. Here they sold it, or, earlier on, exchanged it for goods in kind.

Stone served not only as raw material for building; artificially excavated caves, houses, barns, and chambers were also made from it. We find examples of such primarily in the Bükk Hills, and in the hills around Buda. Such caves can be traced back to the 16th century. At every period they served as dwellings for the poor. However, in the Bükk Hills cave-architecture (dwellings, cellars, hives, etc.) is more complicated and might have Oriental origins. (Research in this field has only begun.)

In the central part of the Carpathian Basin *soil* served as the basic building material at every period. According to data from a 1910 statistical survey, the walls of more than 50 per cent of the houses in the country were made of soil, and their numbers were rising steadily. There are several ways of using soil for walls, and here we must restrict ourselves to only a few.

Two basic forms of *timber framework* construction can be distinguished from each other. In one case the upright beams are cut into the groundsill, and these are held together on top by a cornice beam. In this way the frame was especially solid in construction and stood solidly on the ground. In the other case, the upright beams were dug one metre deep into the ground, but these too were held together on top with

62. Wooden belfry
Nemesborzova, Szabolcs–Szatmár
County

141

a beam. Although this frame was sunk in the ground it was not as solid as the previous one. The frame made by such methods has walls made of various materials.

Reed played an important part in the making of walls in the regions Sárrét and Kiskunság, and other places as well, where this formerly so important plant grew in large quantities. In the 12th century, Otto, the bishop of Freisingen, speaks of reed houses. Besides houses and farm buildings, larger structures were also made of reed, such as the Presbyterian church of Komádi at the end of the 17th century. Commencing the work, the stronger beams were dug into the ground at the corner of the building, weaker ones at the centre, and were tied together on top by lathing. The longest and thickest reeds were sorted out and the ends dug into the ground, gathered together in two places by wicker, rolled in at the edges, the reed cut at the desired height of the wall. The space for the door was left out, the window space was cut from the wall with a scythe-like tool. After this, the builders applied several coatings of mud mixed with chaff on both sides, until the gaps between the reeds were completely filled. When they achieved the desired thickness, they smoothed the wall inside and out. However, no matter how hard they tried, reed walls could be recognized by their unevenness from afar, though if well-built they could last for a hundred years.

The half-timbering was in most cases filled in with wickerwork. This method of walling is extremely old. Archeologists digging in the Carpathian Basin have found wattle in many places dating from the New Stone Age and the Bronze Age. Stakes were frequently placed between the beams of a *wattle wall* in order to strengthen the wickerwork. This form was well known amongst the Slavic peoples who lived in the region at the time the conquering Magyars settled. That the Hungarians also used it can be demonstrated from the Middle Ages on. It spread as a fortress building technique. Wattle walls were erected two to three metres apart and the space between was filled with earth. The outsides were plastered, thus protecting them from being set on fire.

An extraordinarily large number of versions of the wattle wall are known, from split wicker cut in half, to thin willow and furze wicker. Methods changed from region to region and by periods. In one characteristic form holes are bored at inch intervals into the foundation log, stakes are put into them, and strips of sapwood or wicker are woven into the spaces between. It also happened in some places that prefabricated wattle wall insets of predetermined size were made, and these were built into the corresponding frame structure all at once.

The various kinds of wattle matting were plastered with mud, with yellow earth or clay got from a pit near the village. This was broken up finely with a hoe, watered, and mixed with chaff, bits of straw or broken rushes. In some places horses were used to trample the mixture, and at other places men stamped it barefoot until it cohered, was free from lumps, and tensile. At first it was plastered roughly on the wicker matting, then, after reaching the height of 30 to 40 cm, the plaster was smoothed inside and out. The great advantage of such building in flood regions is that the waves wash away the mud rapidly and can flow through the wattle matting without knocking down the walls. After the flood waters withdraw, the walls can be plastered again.

Larger buildings, country mansions and churches were also made with this technique. Thus in Békés, during the first half of the 18th century, the population newly settling in Mezőberény, a village destroyed under the Turks, built their first church from wicker. They raised a church with the same technique at Sára in Zemplén County, which was replastered after a flood withdrew.

As forests diminished, the number of houses with wattle walls increased for a while. The number of houses that were made entirely of earth rose even more markedly. Mud to make these was prepared by methods described above. Among these techniques the so-called "swallow walling" *(fecskerakás)* was especially widespread. First, a ditch was dug in the ground half a metre deep, and filled with mud. Mud was piled on the standing wall with a fork, but only a metre high at one time. They let each course settle for a length of time depending on the weather, and then continued the work. When the desired height was reached and adequate time for settling was allowed, the wall was carved straight with a spade, the window and the door opening were cut out, and the door casing put in right away. This method is frequently used in the Great Plain and the eastern section of Transdanubia, but it occurs at other places as well.

The pounded wall *(vertfal)* is, to a certain degree, a variation, and basically made in a similar fashion. At ground level, the mud is put between a framework of two planks, and pounded hard with a club made especially for this purpose. This process is repeated until the desired height is reached. Formerly the openings were cut after the walls were already finished, but lately suitable moulds were fitted into the desired spot and filled in well all round. Houses have been built this way up till the present day, primarily in the region east of the Tisza.

Since the 16th and 17th centuries, houses have been built from elements made from earth. The most primitive form of this kind of element is the mudball *(csömpölyeg)*, about the size of a child's head and slightly elongated, and used while still wet. In the southern Great Plain, lathing is nailed at irregular intervals onto logs or stakes and the mudballs pounded onto and between these. At other places the mudballs were put next to and on top of each other without such aids, just as in the case of swallow walling. In such instances the wall is allowed to settle. When it is finished, it is plastered, two or three times outside and once inside, then smoothed and, when completely dry, whitewashed.

The *hant* is really a piece of sod, which, on firm pastures could always be cut up into the desired shapes. We often find it in the Hungarian earthworks of the 16th century. Thus in the eastern part of the Great Plain, the four battlements of Nagyvárad were thereafter regularly laid with sod against the Turks. Those who mastered this skill merited a very important place, gaining mention in 1669: "masons, sodlayers, bricklayers". The carefully laid sodwalls were plastered and occasionally even whitewashed. Hearths were also built with sod. In recent times sod has almost ceased to be used, occurring rarely even in the walls of farm buildings.

The material most widely used at present for building is *adobe*. These are bricks, made out of mud mixed with bits of straw, chaff, husks and sedge, and sundried but not fired. It first appeared sporadically in the first half of the 18th century, but the authorities and landlords strongly urged its use in order to decrease the destruction of the forests. People refused to take to this way of building for a long time, and it became widespread only in the 19th century, and in certain regions only at the end of this period. Adobe was the basic walling material during the first half of this century in the regions of the Great Plain, Transdanubia, and in the Mezőség of Transylvania, and has begun to decrease in use somewhat only during the last two decades.

Adobe is mixed usually outside the village beside the so-called adobe-making pits, where suitable material has been dug out. More rarely the clay is carried into the yard and the adobe made there. The mud is kneaded in the fashion described above, which is generally a job for the men. Formerly it was spread into the desired thickness and the required sizes cut out of it with a spade. Recently the mud has been pressed into a mould made out of planks. It is smoothed, the frame lifted up, and the finished adobe bricks piled up next to each other in rows. The women also participate in the mixing itself. The dried adobe bricks are piled into a triangular, open-work pyramid, with its top plastered against the snow and rain. Thus the bricks can last for several years until they are used up. The poor peasants and hired labourers make their own adobe bricks. However, adobe making is a characteristic gypsy occupation. They get chaff and husks from the customer, who otherwise makes payment, usually per 100 bricks, in money or in kind.

From the adobe bricks many kinds of walls can be made. It is cemented together with mud or mortar, and in some places black earth is put between two rows, which not only makes the wall stronger but also prevents the seeping up of moisture. Recently bricks have been used for foundations and a few rows of them are mixed with the adobe bricks, serving both as insulation and as strengthening. Otherwise *bricks* rarely occurred in the past as a building material among the peasants, although archeological excavations can show traces of it in village buildings. It became more widely used only in recent times. Its origin is probably western, as its name, *tégla* of German origin, also implies.

The walling of the house depended very greatly on the prevailing natural and economic circumstances, and changes in these can be well measured. The same can also be said of the roof structure and roofing, which is so closely related to the wall that its determining character can always be interpreted from it.

Roof Structure and Roofing

There are no houses without an attic in the Hungarian linguistic region, but we know of farm buildings where horizontal beams are placed on the walls to form a loft, and hay or straw is piled on them to a depth of two or three metres (chickens' houses, ice huts, etc.). There must have been roofs and roof structures on Hungarian housing very early. The words *héj,* roof, and *hiu,* attic, imply this: both are of Ugric or perhaps Finno–Ugric origin.

144

The roof structure of Hungarian houses can be divided into three well distinguishable groups: the *szelemenes* (purlin type), the *szarufás* (rafter type), and the *széklábas* (chair leg) type roof structure.

The essence of the purlin type roof structure is the cross beam or purlin *(szelemen)* which runs under the gable, holds up the weight of the roof, and keeps the weight of the roof from pressing sideways on the walls. This is why this solution is primarily used for buildings of wicker and earth. The oldest and at the same time the most general form of this structure is the one where the long cross beam, usually carved out of pine or linden wood, is held up at both ends of the building by a forked upright post *(ágas)*, dug into the ground. If the building is long, another one is dug in the middle of the building. Wooden hooks *(horgasfa)* are hung onto the cross beam, which occasionally rest on the wall itself, but mostly rest on the cornice, otherwise called the *sárgerenda,* that runs along the top of the wall. The *master beam* of relatively recent origin runs through the entire length of the house, dividing it into two equal parts. It rests on the gable- and cross-walls and runs in the same plane as the cornice beams.

There are several known ways of supporting the cross beam, which are probably more recent than the one above. Such is the *félágas* ("half-a-post") structure, which rests either on the shorter cornice beam or on the end of the main centre beam. In the latter case the main centre beam needs to be supported on the wall of the building, so that it can withstand the strain. Another way of supporting it is known in the Palots area, which is called *boldoganya,* "happy mother" (with reference to the Virgin), and may have connections with the cult of the house. In some areas, in the case of stone buildings, the cross beam is put on the top of the gable, when there is no need for further support. Finally, the cross beam can be upheld by beams placed diagonally *(ollóláb)*, primarily in western Transdanubia, although this construction has spread east all the way to the Great Plain. The two long beams of the pincers rest perpendicularly on the cornice beam, while the shorter upper stems enclose the cross beam, and above this come together the double trussing which is attached to the cornice beam. This reinforcement makes the roof structure extremely solid. It seems that the solution originates from the Slovenian areas and its adoption was hastened by the difficulties of getting large-sized trees fit for uprights.

The purlin type of roof structure is known from the New Stone Age. Hungarians adopted very early the word *szelemen,* which is of Slavic origin, as is shown by its phonology. The Magyars may have become acquainted with this form of roof structure on the South Russian steppes. It can still be found among the South Slavs, in the Ukraine, and among the Poles, Slovakians, and Czechs as well. This architectural tradition very likely links up Hungary to the East. Today the cross beam roof structure can be found now and then in old houses and farm buildings.

The rafter *(szarufa)* type roof structure must have been an element of wood architecture originally, and is of considerable age in places where the abundance of wood created a high level of carpentry skills. The inverted V-shaped rafter beam rests on the cornice beam, reinforced in

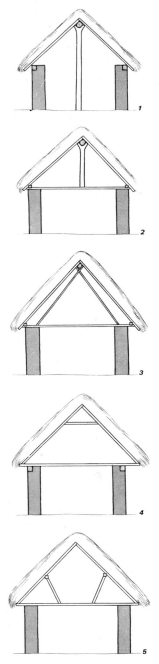

Fig. 29. The most frequent constructions of roofs in the territory of the Hungarian language in the 19th–20th century
1. A ridgebeam *(purlin)* supported by forked posts. 2. As above, the half-posts standing on the attic. 3. The ridgebeam supported by scissor beams. 4. Rafter construction. 5. Construction with side beams

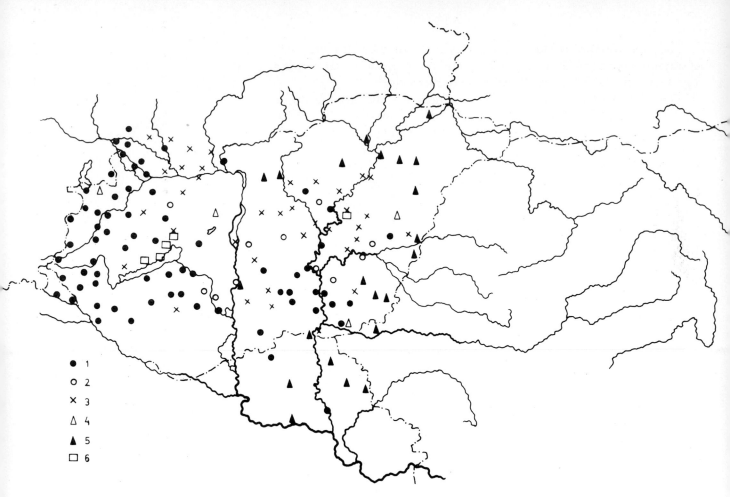

Fig. 30. The ways of supporting the ridgebeam *(purlin)* at the end of the 19th century 1. Solely by scissor beams 2. Mostly as above, in some cases by posts 3. Both constructions occur 4. In most cases forked upright posts, in few cases scissor beams 5. Solely forked upright posts. 6. Gable

its upper third by a tie, the *kakasülő* (roost). If the house has a porch, then the rafter beam is longer on the front side and extends over the cornice beam, thus providing eaves over the porch. If the roof extends at the gable-ends of the house with corner rafters *(szeglet-szarufa),* a hipped roof results on both ends of the house. This served primarily as a protection for the front of the house against rain. In the Palots areas a front porch or eaves *(esővető)* are built for this purpose. These used to be wider in the past but have recently become narrower. It is very likely that the rafter type of roof structure spread from the West towards the East, and it first became general in areas where wood was used for building, in Transylvania and Upper Hungary. However, we can find it in recent times in almost all parts of the Hungarian linguistic region.

The chair-leg *(széklábas)* type of roof construction is relatively new and infrequent in peasant architecture. The rafters are supported on both sides by beams posted together on top by shorter double beams. There is a so-called centre cross-beam that runs along the length of the building at the meeting of the posts and the double beams. This roof structure and its more complicated versions require highly developed carpentry skills.

Once the carpenter has finished the roof structure, it has to be covered. In the Hungarian linguistic territories the covering varies according to the available natural resources, and may be a thatched roof of straw or reed, or it may be wooden shingles, and recently brick-tile, slate or tin.

The most widely used covering was *straw,* threshed by treading, and thatch *(zsúp)*, which comes from threshing with a flail. Thus we can suppose that the use permeated into areas of treading and threshing. Recently both forms have virtually disappeared, only a few examples remaining in the eastern part of the linguistic region, and here and there in the west. Their inflammability and the strong prohibition by the authorities have contributed to the eclipse of such thatched roofs.

Before thatching was begun, lathing was fastened perpendicularly onto the rafters and wooden pegs were fastened to their ends and in some places into their sides. On these pea straw (east of the Tisza) or buckwheat straw (Transdanubia) was piled first, because this held the foundations strongly together. Straw then followed, 15 to 20 cartloads being sufficient for a steeper roof. The straw was stamped down layer after layer so that it would pack down well, then it was raked smooth so the rain could run off it more easily. Because a significant portion of the straw-thatched houses were built without a chimney, the smoke permeated the straw and almost soldered it into one piece, so much so that when it was necessary, it had to be beaten apart with axes. With small repairs, a well-packed straw roof could last for a century.

Sheaves of rye-straw fit for thatching are not loosened during threshing, but are only beaten, tied and put away for winter and then threshed and shaken out all over again. Two sheaves are tied into one thatching sheaf. There are two methods known for making a roof from thatch. One is spreading out *(teregetés)*, in which the loosened sheaves, ears up, are spread on the lathing and fastened to it at every 5 to 6 cm with wicker or, later on, with wire. Following it, and somewhat lower, comes a new layer. When the spreading is completely done, the rows are pounded smooth with a piece of wood made especially for this purpose.

The other method is more complicated. The threshed-out thatch is tied into knots. Some have a knob, others are gathered into two branches, but no knob is twisted at the end. Differently shaped knots are used for fringing, finishing, and for forming the central part of the roof. Because of the combustible nature of straw, there were experiments with plastering straw roofs in the 18th century, but this practice did not catch on. On the other hand, it is customary at some places to coat the thatching sheaves with mud in order to prevent their catching fire. On the top of the roof a human head, an animal, a star, and cross may be formed out of straw. The origin of this custom probably lies in warding off demons.

Reed, being the plant of wet, flooded, swampy areas, is the primary roofing material of such regions. Because plenty of reed grew in the Great Plain and in a significant part of Transdanubia, especially before the rivers were regulated, roofs thatched with reeds are frequent even today. In the Bodrogköz an older and newer form of this is known. The older way was to start off by spreading the sheaves on the bottom and tying them to the lathing by wicker twists. The bottom part of the next bunch was laid above the shoulder of the previous bunch, so that the roof could be covered in four rows, yet in such a way that the roofs should remain stepped even after thatching was completed. The ridge was fringed with reeds or two boards nailed together were placed on it. The newer type of reed-thatched roof is made in a similar fashion, the only difference being that, starting from the bottom, they pound the edges smooth, so that the roof is not only more beautiful and uniform, but rain runs off it better.

The various forms of *shingle* are primarily connected with wood buildings. The smaller ones are split and a groove cut into one side so that the narrowed-down edge of another shingle can slip into it. Every single piece is fastened to the lathing with nails. In some regions of Székelyland, shingles are made out of metre-long thick beech planks and fastened by laying them on top of each other.

In some villages of the Palots region roofs are covered with slate that is mined nearby. Brick roof-tiles are comparatively recent, and have been replaced in some places by factory-made slate or tin, the use of which has eclipsed the traditional roof covering methods.

Layout, Fireplace and Lighting

The earliest form of the Hungarian house probably had one room. This conclusion is supported by the fact that the word *ház* (house) designates both the structure itself and the room, later called *szoba*. That is why the present-day peasant usage speaks about *elsőház,* front room, and *hátsóház,* backroom. Excavations from the 11th to the 13th centuries discovered one-roomed pits, although even then there undoubtedly were larger structures with raised walls. These pit-houses were sunk 100 to 120 cm deep into the ground, so that only part of the building along with the roof was projecting. There are records from the 14th and 15th centuries of houses with two and three divisions or rooms, and this is also authenticated by excavations.

This is why the formerly one-room house, from which the baking

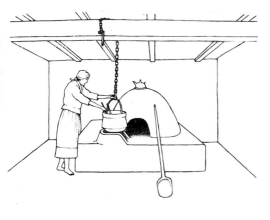

Fig. 31. A smoky kitchen with a bank. Kadarkút, Somogy County. Early 20th century. The oven is in the background, in the front, a Balkan type of cauldron is hanging from a chain

63. Chimneyless kitchen of a cottage built on a log foundation Szenna, Somogy County

ovens and, during the major part of the year, even the open fireplace
were placed out of doors, became a structure suitable for containing
a permanent fireplace. Such a joint house, where the division of room,
kitchen, and pantry can be found, could be 15 to 21 metres long and 4 to
6 metres wide. The floor space of the living room itself might be 6x8
metres in size. In such a building, the kitchen is in the centre, as it is later.
With this the Hungarian house had arrived at a degree of development
which, although refined in its minor details, did not develop further in
basic character.

The *fireplace* played the greatest role in earlier and later development.
The various versions of the fireplace within the house can be easily
ascertained. Nothing proves its importance better than the fact that the
fireplace is the centre of Hungarian family life and its figurative meanings
are still alive in the Hungarian language: *háztűznézni,* "to have a look at
the fireplace", that is, to look over the bride's and bridegroom's house
before the wedding; *családi tűzhelyet alapítani,* "to found a family fireplace", that is, to get married and to move to a separate house. When the
new bride is led into the house of the new bridegroom, she is taken
around the fireplace and with this becomes a member of the family,
possessing definite rights.

In the single-room houses dating from the 10th to the 13th centuries
and sunk half into the ground, ovens have been excavated which were
on the same level as the house, were dug into the ground, and extended

149

65. Székely open fireplace
Székelyland, Rumania

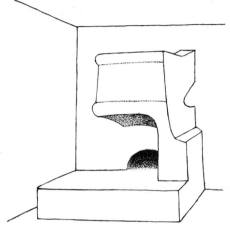

Fig. 34. A variation of the open fireplace
called *kabola* in the corner of the house.
Karcsa, former Zemplén County. Early
20th century

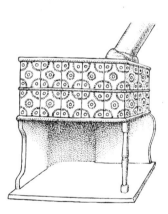

Fig. 35. An open fireplace of the house
called *cserepes*. Siklód, former Udvarhely
County. Early 20th century

66. Open fireplace with chimney
Gyimesközéplok, former Csík County

beyond the wall of the building. Beside these, some clues that have been discovered suggest the existence of a protective roof over the open fireplaces in the immediate vicinity of the buildings. Broken pieces of clay pots excavated around the area testify that cooking took place outside the house during a significant part of the year. Ovens were also found near the buildings, sunk into the ground, repeatedly rebuilt and used for decades. Because the phonetic and semantic explanation of the Hungarian word *kemence* (oven) can come only from Russian, the word and the building itself must belong to the Magyar culture that had evolved on the South Russian steppes.

As is apparent from the above, the hearth arrangements of the Hungarian house were divided from the beginning into *open* and *closed* fireplaces. It is unnecessary to divide them in time and space, because generally they existed alongside each other and supplemented each other functionally. The open fireplace served to heat and to light the room, and was used for cooking and baking. The closed fireplace was used for cooking and baking only.

Among the changing variety of open fireplaces, the clay corner bank, a round or square bench about 30 cm high, is frequent in the southern part of Transdanubia. On this the open fire was lit in the *szenes ház* (house with embers). Because the bank was directly attached to the wall, a wattle wall the height of a man plastered with mud was raised in order to protect the log wall from getting too hot. Cooking was done in a cauldron that hung over the open fire from a chain attached to a beam. In this area of Transdanubia the pear-shaped copper kettle was used, which originated in the Balkans. The smoke of the open fire went out through the door, which is why such buildings were called *füstös ház* (smoky house), or *konyha* (kitchen), since the smoke covered its walls with soot.

Such open fireplaces were used not only for cooking, but also for roasting. The so-called firedog (*tűzikutya*) was used for the latter. Firedogs were placed on each side of the fire to support the pieces of skewered meat. Flat stones were also put on these open fireplaces which became so hot that meat or some sorts of griddle cakes could be baked quickly. The baking bell (*sütőharang*) was also used on the open fireplace. A stone was heated, then covered with the baking bell which, in Transdanubia, was made of baked clay and in Transylvania, was carved of stone. Griddle cakes and meat baked very well under it.

In the Tiszántúl cooking was done on a clay stand built in the centre of the kitchen, which was located between two rooms. This platform was 50 to 60 cm high and at most one metre square. The open chimney that encircled the entire kitchen functioned not only to extract smoke but also to smoke meat, bacon, and sausage that was hung up there.

The hearth (*kandalló*) is one of the characteristic forms of open fireplaces. In it the fire burns on a low bank. Above it is a chimney of plastered wicker or, in a more developed version, of tiles which leads the smoke to the attic or to the porch. Earlier, such a hearth stood in the living room and often was built together with the oven. Generally we can find versions of it in the eastern part of the Hungarian linguistic region. It is known in Transylvania from the 16th and 17th centuries. Its

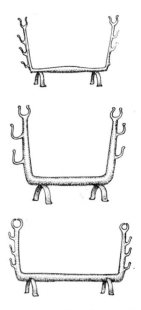

Fig. 32. Symmetrical andirons with four feet called "firedogs". 1. Darufalva, Sopron County, 19th century. 2. Meszlen, Vas County, 19th century. 3. Debrecen, 19th century

Fig. 33. Baking bells. Transylvania. Second half of 19th century

67. Oven in a Palots house
Balassagyarmat, Palóc Museum

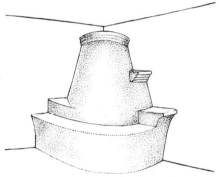

Fig. 36. A round oven named *búbos kemence*. Kiskunhalas, Bács-Kiskun County. 1930s

location and form testify to its Mediterranean, more precisely to its Italian, origin. Perhaps it came into the castles of Transylvania at the time of the Renaissance and found its way into the peasant houses from there.

We can find the most varied and most beautiful examples of such hearths in Székelyland under the names *góc, pest,* and they are described as *cserepes,* tiled, after the material and method of their making. Their smoke-catcher, rectangular in shape, is covered with tile on all sides, and so retains the heat better. Smoke is led up to the attic through a chimney stack. Not only was a 15 to 20 cm high bench built for the hearth, but it was also closed off on one side by means of a wall and supported on the opposite side with a richly carved leg. As this construction makes it impossible to hang the kettle from a beam, they constructed a pivoting wooden leg *(üsttartó kollát)* that turns the kettle over the fire. Pots were put on a three-legged, low iron stand (*vasláb* or ironleg), and baked pancakes on a flat stone. Various types of such hearths and similar

152

68. Open fireplace with a cooking stove
Ziliz, Borsod-Abaúj-Zemplén County

Fig. 37. An oven with a chimney and
banks around it. Former Borsod County.
Early 20th century

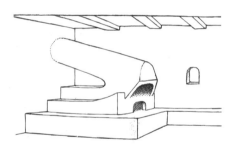

Fig. 38. An oven with a long chimney like
a pipe. Former Borsod County. Early 20th
century

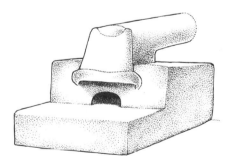

Fig. 39. An oven with a chimney.
Martonyi, former Borsod County. Early
20th century

ones existed in the eastern half of the Hungarian linguistic region. To a certain extent, they formed a transition to ovens with an enclosed fire.

The shape of the ovens *(búbos* or *boglyakemence)* in the Great Plain was square or, like hayricks, barrel-shaped or round on top. First its frame is made out of stakes and woven with wicker, then plastered with mud mixed with pieces of sherds. The mouth of such a hearth opens into the kitchen. Its size depends on how many loaves of bread are to be baked in it. Seven to eight large loaves of bread fit into the largest ones, which can occupy a quarter of the room; in the smaller ones there is room for only three loaves. The oven is heated with straw, corn stalks, and, formerly, with reeds. Frequently, in the Great Plain cow dung was kneaded with straw, formed into squares, and dried. This peat *(tőzeg)* provided a good steady heat. Besides cooking, such a fireplace was used primarily for heating, and a bank suitable for sitting on, ran around its edge, while there was a small nook *(sut, kuckó)* in its inner corner that served as a resting or often as a sleeping place for children or old folk.

The Palots hearth is low, long, and rectangular in shape, with benches running along its free-standing side. Earlier the smoke went out through the opening cut on the narrower front side and usually left the building through the door of the house. In the next phase of development a 50 to 60 cm diameter chimney stack *(kürtő)* was set over the mouth of the hearth like an umbrella, which channelled the smoke to the attic. Later a chimney was raised in the middle of the building, and this created the cylinder-shaped pipe *(síp)*, through which the smoke was drawn to the porch and then outside. Although cooking and baking was done on this hearth, its primary purpose was to keep the room warm. The children slept on top of it, and the men lay down on its bench for a brief rest. They spread corn and various types of grain on it to dry during the day. Usually twigs and wood were burned in it, and the light coming out of its opening let the women see while spinning.

We can assume that the baking oven moved out of the house in Székelyland centuries ago. The more prosperous built a separate baking house *(sütőház)*, while others placed the oven behind the building under

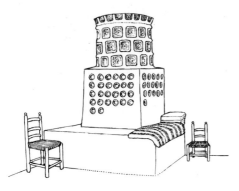

Fig. 40. A stove built out of "cupped" tiles. Decs, Tolna County. Early 20th century

the eaves. They built it on benches, at the front of which they could cook in a kettle hanging over an open fire. So here, as well as frequently in other places, the open and closed fireplace occurred simultaneously.

Ovens built outdoors are frequently encountered throughout the greater part of the linguistic region, but especially in its western half. These ovens are partly low, partly rick-shaped, and were placed in a distant corner of the yard or garden, in order to decrease the fire risk. In some places, the ovens were built outside the village because of this consideration. In such cases more than one family could use them just as they used the common, open-air baking ovens that were raised on the manors of the large estates between the dwellings of agricultural labourers. In these forms we can perhaps presume Mediterranean influence creeping in from the south, where outdoor hearths were favoured on account of the climate.

The stove (kályha) represented the further development of the completely enclosed fireplaces in Hungary, which came from the West, first

69. Round oven
Tápé, Csongrád County

154

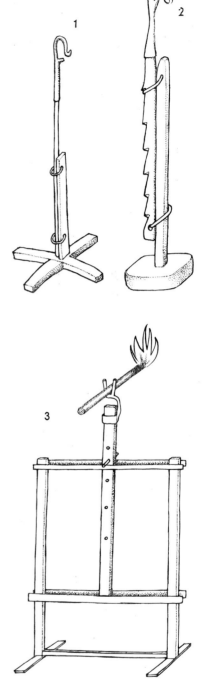

into the castles and country homes of the nobility, and thence to the peasant houses. Early models imitated the baking ovens, except that earthenware vessels were put into the clay, which increased both heat retention and heat emanation. The earthenware tiles, called *kályhaszem,* "stove eye", are rectangular, shaped like a bowl, concave and are made mostly by potters of Transdanubia. We know of such stoves from the region between the Danube and Tisza from excavations, but their later use here is rare. In Transdanubia, on the other hand, stoves expelled the baking ovens completely from the houses and were used only for heating.

Open fireplaces also lit the room. In this respect the light that seeped out of the opening of the hearth was very important, just as was the light that came from the door of the oven. When people were looking for something in a further corner of the room or when they went out to the porch, they took a small piece of burning wood out of the fire and gave light with it. This, or a piece of ember, picked up quickly by hand or with tongs, served to light a pipe.

Fig. 41. A crane to hold taper-wood. 1. Szalafő, Vas County. Early 20th century. 2. Kondorfa, Vas County. Early 20th century. 3. Hejce, Abaúj County. Early 20th century

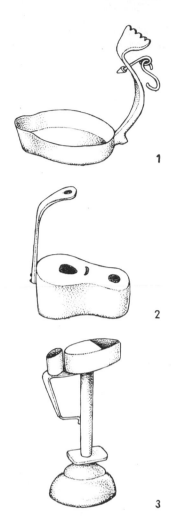

The specially made and split splinters, taper-wood *(fokla)*, made in most places out of pinewood, must have developed out of this occasional usage. On the other hand the Palots dried the thinner branches of the hazelnut, hornbeam, or willow trees, then beat them with an axe head until their fibres separated. These were parched for a short time in the hearth, then stored on its top. They lit one end and placed it on the edge of the bench of the hearth. The Hungarians of Slavonia, in the western part of Transdanubia, stuck them into potatoes, but in other places people made holders *(foklatartó)* for this purpose. Such a crane holder is a tall stand, resting on a base the same height as the furniture, especially the table, so that its light can shine on the table. Splinters were fastened to an iron pin at the top end of the holder, which thus gave some light all round the room. The Csángós of Gyimes pour pine pitch between four or five thin splinters and thus increase the light given by the lit bundle. Others pour the pine pitch into a small dish, mix dry spruce splinters with it, and light it.

More than anything, oils of various kinds were used for lighting. Rape, pumpkin, acorn, and later on sunflower oil gave the clearest light. The oil was put into small dishes such as night-lights *(mécs)*, made by potters, and the wick was held up by a small, wooden, light float *(úszó)*. Now and then lard was used, perhaps even butter, but only if there was no suitable oil.

One of the most widely spread means of lighting is the candle, first made from beeswax, then from tallow, and later from stearin. Primarily sheep and cow tallow was used for this purpose. They poured one-third boiling water and two-thirds tallow together in a big vessel and

Fig. 42. Oil-lamps. 1. Jákótelke, Kolozs County. 2. Bozok, former Hont County. 3. Oil-lamp with a candlestick. Veszprém County. Early 20th century

71. Vessel for dipping candles Kecskemét, Katona József Museum

156

continued to keep it warm. They dipped a wick into it, upon which the liquid gradually settled. The name of this process is candle dipping (*gyertyamártás*). Later they poured the tallow into a tin or glass shape, around a previously fixed wick. This already had become the occupation of small craftsmen, the *candle makers*. Candles were fastened into quite varied holders made of clay, metal, glass, wood, or other materials, which made it a great deal easier to use them. Candles were used out-of-doors or in the barn only when placed in a holder surrounded on four sides by a cow bladder, plates of horn, or later on, glass. Some such lanterns were made of tin with ornamental openings for the light to shine through.

The kerosene lamp and the various kinds of factory-made lamps that accompanied it appeared at the end of the last century. It has been replaced—in many places only in the last decades—by electricity.

Among the Hungarian peasantry, the lighting of the evening light took place with a certain amount of ceremony. It was carried out by the mistress of the house or the oldest daughter, and the members of the family, or the strangers who might happen to be there, wished each other good evening.

Furniture Arrangement in the Dwelling Houses

The form of furniture, especially its decoration, changed relatively rapidly in response to the prevailing fashion of the time and the historical development of ornamental folk art. However, permanent rules prevailed in the manner of furnishing the buildings, rules determined by such factors as the character of the work done there, life style, and, last but not least, tradition. Therefore, change in this respect was much more slow, and the new elements were fitted into the former system.

Several historical periods may be differentiated in furnishing the room of a peasant house. In the earlier period banks of clay were built against the walls all around, and were used for sitting, sleeping, and keeping certain articles of clothing. The clay banks were replaced by wooden benches, standing on posts hammered into the ground and having no backs. Among the Palotses a general use of clay and wooden banks still existed in the last century, but in our century they can be found only among the Csángós. The place of the hearth, even in this period, was in the interior wall of the room, and close to those still in use a few decades ago among herdsmen and farmstead dwellers of the Great Plain. A round opening could be cut in the centre of the table so that the cauldron could be placed into it and the family would eat out of the cauldron communally. Nails were hammered into the wall to hang up footwear and articles of clothing, and maybe sometimes little shelves were fixed up for containing smaller objects. Clothes were also hung on rods fastened from beams.

At the end of the Middle Ages and the beginning of modern times began the gradual separation of work and living space within the peasant room, as a result of which, besides the banks, new pieces of furniture began to appear: the table, the chest, the bed, and the chair. The table gained a special significance among these and was placed in the corner opposite the fireplace. Its original form probably was a board standing

157

on four legs hammered into the ground, later replaced by drawered *(fiókos)* tables and tables with a "pantry" below them *(kamarás asztal).* These carried the signs of various stylistic trends. The table was surrounded by two benches standing against the corner, on which the place of honour belonged to the head of the house and, next to him, to the eldest son. The housewife could get a place only at the fireplace side, but in a significant part of the Hungarian linguistic territory women and girls were not allowed to sit down to the table, but ate their food sitting on small chairs or on the threshold after the men had finished.

As the table gained acceptance, the room was divided into two sections. The place of work developed around the fireplace, where they cooked and, according to need, did work on a bigger or smaller scale such as woodcarving, repairing of smaller tools, washing, etc. We can rightly call the table and its vicinity the sacred corner *(szent sarok);* they inserted the "foundation sacrifice" *(építőáldozat)* into this part of the house. From bones found under this corner of the building we know that roosters were used as foundation sacrifices from around the 11th up to the 13th centuries. The burying of horse and dog skulls also occurred, and in one of the great Hungarian ballads of medieval origin the forever crumbling walls of the fortress Déva were fortified by walling in the ashes of the wife of Stonemason Kelemen (cf. pp. 524–527). In Catholic areas pictures of holy images, the bridal wreath, and perhaps a cross and a household altar, as well as statues brought back from pilgrimages, are placed in the inner corner of the house. In

73. Room interior
Hollókő, Nógrád County

74. Highly stacked bed in the "Sárköz House"
Decs, Tolna County

159

Protestant areas, prints depicting national heroes, the picture of the master of the house as a soldier, the Bible on a small wall shelf, a book of psalms, penny novels, calendars, notes and official documents are put here. The prettiest plates are also hung on these walls in pairs.

The *beds* are placed parallel to each other on two sides of the wall. Among these the one standing in the corner opposite the table is the highest ranking. This is used by the man of the house and his wife. The other bed in the opposite corner, behind the door, is the sleeping place of the newlyweds. Between the bed of the newlyweds and the hearth is a small and simple bed-like plank structure standing on four legs, on which the children sleep.

At each end of the two benches surrounding the table, place is provided for a *chest* for keeping clothes. The chests were replaced in the second half of the last century by a three- or four-drawered chest of drawers *(komót, sublót)*. Above the chest is a slightly forward tilted mirror, and behind that there is a place well suited for putting away

75. Interior of a peasant house
Mezőkövesd

160

books, newspapers and documents. They put memorabilia on top of the commode, such as presents from the fair: ginger bread, coloured pots, small statues, glasses, a cross, a piggy bank, etc.

In this form of furnishing, benches were not used much, so that they lost their multiple function. At first they were put around the table, but it could happen that one was placed in front of the bed. In many places they preferred to put chairs there, usually two, in rare cases three, because these could be pulled up to the empty sides of the table at mealtimes. This furnishing was at most completed by a flat cupboard *(falitéka)* or corner cupboard *(saroktéka),* in which they kept books, medicine, brandy, and in general such things as it was desirable to keep under lock and key.

If there were two rooms in the house, to the left and right of the kitchen, then these were furnished similarly with more or less identical furniture. The difference was only that they put the better, newer, more ornamental furniture in the "clean" or "best" room *(tiszta szoba),* used rarely, and only for guests.

The corner arrangement that could be called typical throughout the entire Hungarian linguistic territory began to break up during the second half of the last century. Until then there were two windows in

the room, close to the table that stood in the corner, one window on the street side, and one on the yard side. As a consequence it was possible to ascertain even from the outside where the sacred corner stood. The next phase was two windows looking out symmetrically onto the street side, and in this case the table was placed between these windows across from the door. Behind it, instead of the two benches, only one chest-seat was placed, in which clothes were stored, but if necessary it could also serve for sleeping. A mirror, plates and pictures were hung above it. Some were hung over the beds, which stood parallel to each other against the walls, so that in such an arrangement the sacred corner essentially ceased to exist, or at any rate some of its elements moved to the two sides.

In this parallel form of arrangement they placed two chests at the foot of the beds left and right of the table, or placed a piece of furniture there which followed the chest in time sequence and served to store clothes such as a *wardrobe,* or a *sideboard.* In most parts of the linguistic region this method of arranging furniture eclipsed the corner arrangement in less than half a century.

We can scarcely speak of the traditional arrangement of the kitchen, since until the most recent times there was very little furniture in the Hungarian kitchen. The kitchen, consequently, preserved its archaic character better than the living room. Here structures shaped from clay and used for baking and cooking remained longer. Most kitchen utensils were hung on the wall in a prescribed order. The reason why the kitchen interior developed more slowly rests in the fact that usually smoke was channelled from the room through the kitchen, above which a chimney was raised. Thus the kitchen generally did not keep up with the development of the rest of the building, as vaulting, which meant the complete removal of smoke, developed only much later.

Only in the front part of the kitchen, in the so-called *pitvar,* porch, the door of which opened onto the yard, was it possible to put furniture. An example is the low bench on which water containers stood. Another more furniture-like piece is the sideboard *(tálas)* for storing kitchen dishes; the top part was for putting plates behind a rail; larger cooking pots were kept in the broader lower section of the sideboard. (On furniture, cf. also pp. 381-89.)

After having thoroughly examined the architecture and interior of the house, let us step out into the yard and get acquainted with the buildings there. Some of these were for the various animals, crops were stored in others, while these or other buildings were used for doing certain jobs.

The largest building of agricultural type is the barn, called *pajta* in the western part of the linguistic territory, and in the east *csűr*. This type of building may be found in regions where, chiefly for climatic reasons, crops could not be kept outdoors for a lengthy time, and where formerly the grain was threshed with a flail, not trodden out. For this reason, barns were not built in the Great Plain, and were much less frequent in the eastern part of Transdanubia than in Western Transdanubia, and have been built in the Little Plain only during the last centuries. The real home for barns is the Palots area and the adjacent regions stretching south, Western Transdanubia, and Transylvania.

As the division and use of the barns differ by regions, we can only attempt to introduce a few types.

In the region of Göcsej, the barn called *pajta* is divided into three parts. Open, pillared and closed versions occur equally. Threshing with a flail was done in the central part, large enough for a loaded cart to drive in. The grain was stored in the loft *(pajtafia)*. After the introduction of machine threshing, fodder was kept in the loft. The closed barn was built on the inner lot, usually of logs. The roof structure has a central arch which provides for better use of the loft. The hipped roof was covered with thatch, just as were houses earlier.

The barns *(gabonapajta)* of nearby Somogy were placed around the

Outbuildings of the Farmyard

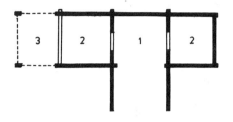

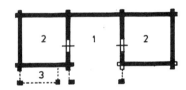

Fig. 43. The ground-plan of a closed barn. Göcsej, Zala County. Early 20th century. 1. Threshing ground. 2. Lean-to of barn. 3. Shed

78. Cellar built of logs. Vineyard in Csurgó–Nagymárton, Somogy County

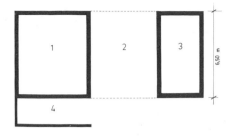

Fig. 44. The ground-plan of a wooden barn with two compartments. Nyíri, former Abaúj County. Late 19th century

79. Barn built on a structure of logs Szenna, Somogy County

settlement at 600 to 800 metres distance, in the threshing yard. They were built of huge foundation logs, approximately 12 to 16 metres long and 6 to 7 metres wide. Wicker was woven into the frame and this was sometimes plastered with a thin layer of clay. The mostly open inside area was shut off by means of two wicker gates turning on posts, located across from each other on the long side (see Ill. 10). The roof was covered with thatch. Formerly the sheaves were carried here after harvest and placed in such a way that space for the cart stayed open in the centre of the barn. Young men guarded the grain at night. In Somogy the grain was trodden out on the open area in front of the barn. This was usually finished by September, and from then on only chaff, straw, and thatch was left inside the barn. Threshing machines replaced the treading out of grain from the turn of the century, and from this time on hay and other fodder were stored in the granary, from which the quantities necessary during the winter were carried by cart and sled to the village stables.

The barns general in the Bakony hills varied in length between 12 and 17 metres and the width between 7 and 8 metres. Smaller, more primitive forms are located in one line with the house, as if a continuation of it, but the larger ones closed off the back of the yard by lying at right angles to the house. The former were generally built on a wooden foundation, the latter on stone. The walls are wattle in the first case, while the larger barns often had walls and plank doors on both sides, so that the barn can be shut up completely. The gable of the roof often

overhangs on the yard side, and the chaff is kept in the shed thus created. Sometimes the entrance is lengthened towards the yard, and carts are kept here, and farm implements of various sizes hanging on the walls. The area of the barn is used primarily for threshing and for storing grain, and only lately is fodder also put into it. The size and building style of the barn indicated the economic standing of the smallholder.

Most versions of the Palots barn *(csűr)* were built of wood. Large stones were piled up for its foundation and the corner structure of logs was laid on them. Perpendicular beams were fitted on the corners which held up the cornice beams running around on top. The sides were made either from legs cut for insertion in a mortise or from thick planks. The thatched roof rests on rafters. The building consists of three divisions. The larger area is the threshing ground *(szérű),* where the treading out or the threshing with flails is done. Both sides of the barn are open. Enclosure with a plank gate is a recent development. Beams reach across the threshing ground, called the *szérűtorok* ("throat"), where the most valued fodder is stored. The other division is the *csűrág* ("branch"), where the harvested grain is put. At some places further partitions are made and in such a *fiók* ("drawer") the farmer fits up for himself a small workshop with a workbench and woodcarving tools. Wooden

81. Barn with triple sections Inaktelke, former Kolozs County

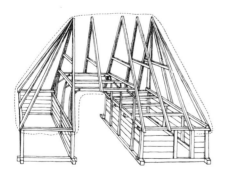

Fig. 45. The construction of a barn comparable to a yoke. Kalotaszeg, former Kolozs county. 1940s

forks, rakes, and other farm implements are made here, and broken worktools of the house repaired.

East of the Palots area, in the Hegyköz of Abaúj, the majority of the *barns* have three divisions. The threshing ground is at the centre, divided on two sides from the *fiók* by the *kármentő* ("rescuer of loss"), an approximately 150–180 cm high wall. Above the threshing barn stretches the *csűrtorok* ("throat"), which serves primarily for storing fodder. The threshing yard of the barn is closed front and back by gates, which may be left off, if carts are parked there regularly. The barns stand at right angles to the house at the end of the yard; vegetable gardens and fruit orchards lie behind them. Ventilation was controlled by opening and closing the granary doors, and after threshing, they also winnowed the grain here. The barns were made of wood, with the corner-post construction, but there are barns with wattle walls, at times even plastered. Barns built on stone foundations gained ground later with walls made of wattle or perhaps of planks. The roofs are generally thatched, or only in some places covered with shingle, tile, or lately with tin. Here too, the three-divisioned barn is a sign of prosperity and larger holdings; the smaller farmers had a one side-partition *fiók* only.

The so-called *jármos-csűr* (yoke-like barn) can be found in Transylvania, especially in Kalotaszeg. These barns got their name from the slightly bent beams that run parallel through the centre. Such barns consist of three parts. In the centre is the *granary*, built high enough for a stacked cart to drive into and yet so that hay can easily be placed into the lofts of the attics, *hij*, of all three parts. The barn is usually located in the

166

section to the right of the entrance from the direction of the yard. They keep the stock here, while the other side, the "tent" *(sátor)*, is suited for storing all kinds of produce or implements. The most important work in the barn is threshing and winnowing the grain. The barn's function is manifold: among others, Sunday afternoon dances are held here. The barn is usually built at the end of the square holding, at right angles to the house, so that its gate will be located across from the entrance of the holding.

However, if the holding slopes toward the back and is threatened with flooding after rain, they then assign it a place parallel to the house or perhaps even across from it. They put the entire structure on foundation logs and they fit the beams or thick planks into the notches of the pillar *(sasfa)*, perpendicular to the foundation ties. The roof structure is of the rafter type. Sticks 60 cm long are beaten into the ends of the rafters, and these support the thatch which is held down on top by V-shaped timbers. Single-covered roofs also occur, though rarely. The roof may be lengthened on the yard side to form a chaff-pen, pigpen, chicken-coop, etc.

The barn of the Székely people is such a large-scale structure that it is an equal partner of the house. Here, amongst the many variations, we will mention a barn type from the district of Kászon. The length varied between 11 and 20 metres, while the width reached as much as 7 to 10 metres. The central area *(csűrköze)*, usually closed off, is at least four metres wide, because only then was it possible to work in it with a flail. Here too, the stable for the horses and cows was located on one side, while on the other side, the *odor,* they put the grain. Smaller buildings were attached to it on the outside, such as the *pig-pen* and *goose-pen,* etc. They built the barn, like the house, out of unhewn pine logs. The logs for the foundation were even larger and big stones were placed at the quarter ties. The central part of the barn had an attic made of planks 8 to 10 cm thick, chosen especially for this purpose, thus no seeds could get lost at threshing time. The height of the stable rarely reached two metres. The hay placed in its attic provided good warmth even during the winter. They tied the animals along the shorter, outer wall. The rafter construction of the roof was mostly covered by shingles. The granary door, made of wooden planks, turned on a wooden hinge and was locked with a large-sized wood lock, partly to protect the valuables kept there, partly to keep out children, who often caused damage or even fire.

The barns introduced from different areas relate to each other according to a basic floor plan, even if their material, shape and roof structure differed from each other according to local conditions, economic demands, and customs. Their basic function is the storing of grain, its threshing and cleaning. Beside this, the more valuable, better quality fodder, especially hay, was also stored here, and this function, after the mechanization of threshing, gained more and more ground. In the eastern part of the linguistic region, but sporadically at other places as well, some were turned into stables, while the pens outside under the eaves provided for the smaller animals.

The next buildings of the farmyard are the buildings providing

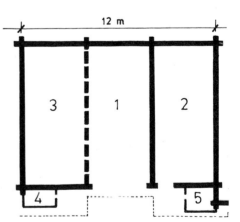

Fig. 46. A barn. Kászonimpér, Csík County. 1911. 1. The "in-between" of the barn. 2. Stable. 3. Place for fodder, called *odor.* 4. Chicken-pen. 5. Pigpen

82. Barn built of logs with a thatched roof
Székelyvarság, former Udvarhely County

protection for the animals. Originally most of these structures were designated in the Hungarian language by the pre-Conquest, old Turkish word *ól* (stable, pen). This was later replaced by the word *akol* (fold), of Slavic origin, and the newer Italian–German derivative, *istálló* (stable). In general usage the latter is applied in regard to livestock, while *ól* is heard in regard to pens for pigs and small animals.

A most simple form is the so-called *állás* (stall), a roof standing on poles, which primarily gives protection against rain. The stock stood around and ate out of the manger placed in the middle, and often circular in shape. For the winter fodder, perhaps manure and reeds were packed around such a structure, especially if they feared that the young animals might freeze. The *ól,* a structure with sides, might have developed in this way.

One characteristic form, widely spread in the Great Plain, is the *tüzelős ól,* a pen with a fireplace. This structure, without an attic, survived longest in the farmyards *(ólas kert)* and farmsteads *(tanya).* Its side was usually built on some version of the earth wall, while the roof was covered by reeds, plastered underneath as protection against fire. Usually the animals were not tied up, only separated by rails. An open fire was lit inside, where the men who would work out-of-doors in the yards could warm themselves and gather in the evening to talk. (See Ill. 36.) Among the Matyó people the fireplace was dug in a corner of the pen, to the left or right of the door, and was lined with stone or brick. This was the best place for making a fire since the smoke could leave

168

quickly through the door. They made clay benches or a bed resting on poles hammered into the ground *(dikó)* in these stables, where the *gazda,* his unmarried son, or maybe a farm hand spent the night.

Today stables are much more developed structures with an attic and gables, and in the majority of cases, are located as a continuation of the house. The stables for horses and cows are almost identical in appearance, the only noticeable difference being simply that a wider door is left in the latter, so that the big-horned Hungarian cattle can get through comfortably. If the unit is large enough, a manger is built at both ends, thus separating, at least in this way, the horses and cows. But, if it is at all possible, they are kept in separate buildings, because horses prefer warmth and are fed more often. They set up a *dikó* in the stable, where the unmarried son gladly slept, since in this way his night wanderings could be less controlled. Amongst the more prosperous farmers this was the place of the farm hand, so that he could be near the animals.

The *pigpens* were not as uniform. In some places they were attached to the barn, in the Great Plain we find them under the maize loft, and at other places they are independent structures with runs of various sizes. In the timber-rich areas of Transdanubia and Upper Hungary, one of the most beautifully raised carpentry buildings is the *hidas* (pigsty), which implies with its names ("bridge-like") that its bottom was lined with thick planks. It was built on a foundation into which as many poles were placed as needed for the partitions they wanted to have in the building. The lath-frame or corner-post construction was used. They chiselled mortises into these and cut tenons into the planks for insertion into the mortises, then lowered the planks onto them. Consequently it was possible to take the pen apart and transport the structure very quickly. A feeding trough was built into it with a fastened swinging board *(leppentyű);* this they could raise from the outside and so pour the swill and maize into the trough.

Only in recent times were *pens for the small livestock* built attached to the barn, sometimes in a form similar to the pigpen. Earlier in the Great Plain round, reed-walled chicken-coops could be seen, resembling in shape the herdsmen's hut, although smaller in size. Otherwise the poultry spent the night on trees, in the cartshed, and in sheds. *Dovecotes* occur all over the linguistic region. A tin collar is fastened to the perpendicular supporting pole, to prevent the cat from climbing up it.

Here we must also mention the various *hay-holding structures,* the significance of which must have been much greater formerly, when no hay was put into the barn, or only rarely. The majority of these consist only of a roof on wooden or brick pillars. The hay holders, called *sop,* are made of wood in Upper Hungary, and the sides of some among these are built from logs or planks. Among the hay-holding structures, we must also mention the *abora* or barracks, frequently found along the upper region of the Tisza. A sliding square-based roof is mounted on four thick poles, and as the fodder decreases, they lower it so the rain cannot splash under it.

The storing of crops for possible bad years was thought to be one of the most difficult tasks of peasant farming. The smaller farmers and poor farm labourers solved the problem easily, because the pantry and the

Fig. 47. A pigpen built on logs, bridge-like, called *hidas*. Bény, former Esztergom County. Late 19th century

Fig. 48. Barracks for sheltering hay with a liftable roof. Upper Tisza region. Early 20th century

Fig. 49. Underground pits for storing
cereal. 1–2. Pereszteg, former Sopron
County. 3–4. Bottle-shaped pits (general).
5. A well–like pit dug in sandy ground, its
opening narrowed with wooden beams

attic provided sufficient room for them. In the pantry the grain was kept in corn bins *(szuszék* or *hombár)* until the new harvest. *Barrels* made of soft wood, and plastered wicker corn bins of a square shape were also used for storage. All this, however, was not sufficient for the farmers who worked the wide fields in the villages and towns of the Great Plain, and also produced for the market, because they preferred to keep their grain until spring in the hope of a higher price.

The pit *(verem)* is one of the most general forms of grain storage, which was used in basic form with varied intensity in the entire Carpathian Basin, although its real home is the Great Plain. There were two versions: the square *grave pit,* which can be dug only into perfectly dry soil, and the *pear-shaped pit,* which offered a great deal more safety. The former was used for short periods, and only in the case of a large harvest, because it could not be shut off from the air.

The *pit cutters,* who usually came from Upper Hungary in the spring, dug out the pear-shaped pits. For a stipulated price they scooped out the earth with buckets, then burned the inside with straw until it became similar to earthenware. They thoroughly aired it and lined it with straw, after which grain could be poured into it. The seed kept in it for years, sometimes for decades, unless the ground water came up. On the large estates they even made pits lined with bricks, plastered and smoothed. They closed off the mouth of the pit with straw, sand and ashes to keep out vermin. In some places a thick layer of grain was spread over the pit and water. The germinating roots formed such a thick layer that no air could get through.

Grain pits were dug in the yard, across from the entrance of the house, perhaps on the street right under the window, so that they could be guarded more easily against thieves. In some places they were grouped together outside the village on one spot and a field guard looked after the pits night and day. In parts of the Great Plain, where the ground water comes up high, they built, from the end of the 18th century and on the analogy of underground pits, above-ground structures of adobe and mud, which resembled large stacks up to 4 or 5 metres high.

In many parts of the linguistic region pantries *(kamra),* separate or attached to the house, were general and were equally used to store grain and other food staples. The different versions must have developed when the second room, opening from the kitchen, which formerly had been a pantry, was used as a second living room. In such cases an extra pantry was added to the building, with a door opening into the yard, and from there on it fulfilled the function of a storage room. In many places, such as Southern Transdanubia, Palócföld, and in certain parts of Transylvania, the pantries are separate buildings, located on different parts of the yard, but always clearly visible from the house.

The pantries of the Ormánság, called *kamra,* in accordance with its southern links, is placed opposite the house and served first of all as the sleeping place of the young couple and also as a storage room. Later on the latter function generally gained ground, mostly articles of clothing being kept here. At one time the Palots *pantry* was probably a separate building, as examples show in the neighbouring Slovak areas. Its function developed as above, but it was attached to the house.

Fig. 50. An elevated pantry called *kástu.*
Szalafő, Vas County. 19th century

The characteristic granary structure of South-Western Transdanubia is the *kástu*. This is a detached one-level, or rarely two-storied structure, which is the granary for the farmer. Here he keeps food staples to be used later on. The word itself is Slovenian in origin, and the building has Slovenian and Austrian links. The *kástu* was always built in a part of the yard that could be observed from the window. Its basic material is wood, and its method of building is similar to the log houses of which it is a smaller version. It is equal in area to a room in the house, or a second-floor version of it. They stored the grain and food in the upper storey, approachable by a wooden ladder, while tools were stored on the ground floor, which also doubled as a workroom where in bad weather the farmer could repair the tools. The building has no window, only a door. Earlier the roof was exclusively of thatch, later of shingles. The *kástu* generally did not survive into the period of tile roofing.

In the Danube–Dráva region a type of grain bin occurs which has

83. A storehouse *(kástu)*
Szalafő, Pityerszer, Vas County

171

sledge runners *(szántalpas hombár).* We can follow its links south, and very likely it was the descendant of the similarly designed herdsman's huts on sledge runners. These were earlier made of wicker, plastered on the inside, and covered with reeds. At the beginning of large-scale grain production, it was made in similar form but out of planks, and roofed with tiles. It needed to be mobile, and thus could be moved away from a dangerous area in case of fire. This type could be found, first of all, in mixed ethnic areas where Hungarians, Croatians, and Catholic Serbians lived together, and can be found even today in Sokác settlements.

On the larger peasant farmsteads, separately standing buildings were erected as a granary *(magtár),* for storing large quantities of grain. Such buildings of mud and brick occur all over the linguistic area but chiefly in the Great Plain, where these buildings succeeded the pits as storage place. In the areas of peasant farmsteads the granary is erected in the yard of the village or town house of the farmer, because it was more secure there. Here, too, it was generally built across from the house, on the opposite side of the holding, with its end towards the street, so that people could keep an eye on it. The interior was partitioned with planks. The sides of these reached to the roof, while in front the planks were slipped into grooves. The grain was let out into bushels at the bottom through an opening that could be closed up, and from the bushels the grain was poured into sacks.

There is no point in listing further the numerous varieties of granaries because most types repeat each other and are not always typical of a certain region. Let us turn instead to the *maize storing structure,* most significant in the Carpathian Basin. We can trace it only to the 18th century, when the production of this new plant increased significantly. The oldest form seems to be the one woven from wicker around four poles, which were dug into the ground and placed 100 to 150 cm apart from each other in width and 3 to 4 m apart in length. It was put in an area sheltered from the wind, because this narrow structure toppled over easily. However, it was not made wider, because then the cobs inside would not have dried out. On the maize bin *(kukoricakas* or *góré)* usually a lower and upper gate were cut. This was filled through the top and emptied through the bottom opening. At some places the top was fastened on in such a way that it would be easy to take off and pour in the corn cobs or take them out through the opening. Such maize bins were in general use until very recent times in the southern part of Transdanubia, in the Upper Tisza region, and in Transylvania. Earlier they could be found in certain parts of the Great Plain.

More recently maize is stored in wooden framed bins, also called *góré,* with lath sides. The first reference to these comes from the last decades of the 18th century. Such bins stood on 120 to 200 cm high wooden or stone legs, on which the quarter ties were laid. Perpendicular pillars were wedged into these and held together on top by a cornice beam. They put sufficiently tight lathing on the sides to keep the cobs from falling out and to prevent the birds getting at the maize. Its width varies between 120 to 200 cm. On big farmsteads they built two of them under one cover, and these were divided inside by a gangway. A chickencoop, or a pig-, duck- and goose-pen, was put under the raised

structure, which made use of the grain that fell out through the cracks. The place of the maize bin in the yard is not determined exactly, but it is usually placed across from the entrance of the house, often in such a way that its longer side is built toward the street. This is one of the most widely used farm storage buildings in the yards of Hungarian peasants.

Pits designed for various purposes are also numerous in the yard. In the Great Plain (at Derecske in Bihar County), a so-called stack-pit *(boglyásverem)* is known. It is usually 150 to 200 cm deep, somewhat more in its width and 3 to 4 m in length. A low plastered wicker wall is raised in front of it and acacia beams are placed on it. Then on top a 3 to 4 m high haystack is put which keeps the pit quite warm. Parsnips, potatoes, and cabbage are stored in these pits.

Cellars are dug under many houses, especially in mountain regions, with doors located at the narrower end of the building, facing the street. Temporary pits in the yard and garden are also frequent where from autumn until spring beets and potatoes are stored. In Transylvania, in Székelyland, they dig a pit or cellar under the pantry inside the house, so it is directly approachable from the house. In other regions they can get down into the smaller-size cellars from the porch.

Besides the above, other different sized buildings can be found in the yard and garden, such as the various sheds *(szín),* among which the largest and most important is the cartshed *(szekérszín).* The name of the wood cutting shed *(favágószín)* shows its function. Chaff is kept in a separate building. Usually around the manure heap is the place for the wicker and walled or plank privy *(budi).* The wood carving shed *(faragó-*

173

szín) is an ever present structure, especially in forest regions. In many places, they built a *summer kitchen* opposite the house to protect the home from heat and flies. The shed for *beehives,* and a *plum drying oven,* are mostly placed in the garden.

A well is present in every yard. Its most characteristic form is the sweep-pole well *(gémeskút).* (cf. Ill. 14,50.) This form occurs everywhere where the ground water is not far from the surface, from Transdanubia to Székelyland. Its real home is the Great Plain, because here water wells up at a depth of 4 to 5 metres. This form of well, the origin of which must be sought in the south, cannot lift water out from much deeper. The other form is the draw well *(kerekeskút),* popular throughout Europe, in which a rope or chain wrapped around a cylinder pulls up the bucket. In regions rich in springs, most wells are lined with large tree trunks, *bodonkút,* with their inside hollowed out. There is a trough along the well, longer or shorter according to the number of animals. Such troughs used to be hewn out of a single tree.

Regional Differences in Hungarian Architecture

We have familiarized ourselves with the most important exterior and interior characteristics of the house and farm buildings. In some places we have also referred to the popularity of certain forms. We shall now summarize what kind of building style is typical of certain regions and how it harmonizes with the ethnic groups and the area. We cannot at this point venture more than the introduction of five more or less separate areas from the point of view of architecture, with the certain knowledge that among these, innumerable forms of transition are possible.

Southern Transdanubia

This is the hilly, at one time largely forested area that lies largely south of the Balaton and stretches to the Dráva. It is thickly settled with villages, mostly small in population, in some of which the double inner-lot type of settlement can be demonstrated until the most recent times. Most of the villages, excepting the settlement type villages of the 18th century, are agglomerations. A significant part of these were changed into settlements along streets and partly into settlements with ribbon holdings when the fields and villages were officially regulated in the first half of the 19th century. A significant part of the agricultural work used to be done in the threshing yard, but already in the last century this practice was sporadical, though it could be still observed between the two world wars. Only the most valuable and most important part of the produce, especially that for human consumption, was kept in the yard and in the house.

In earlier times building material was primarily wood, but undoubtedly wattle on a foundation of beams always had great importance. The building rested on a foundation of huge logs and its roof was covered almost exclusively with straw thatch. Reed thatch took the place of this along the Balaton and around rivers and swamps. Here the use of clay is newer in origin and the use of adobe has been spreading generally only for a century. The so-called *karóköz* building is known in Somogy and Baranya, where they build a frame of stakes for the wall. It appears that

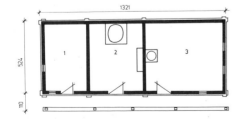

Fig. 51. The ground-plan of a house with a porch. Zádor, Baranya County. 19th century. 1. Pantry. 2. Kitchen. 3. Dwelling room

formerly they used *sods* in this area and even made ovens out of it. They fitted the cut-out pieces of sod into an oven shape, plastered them with clay on the outside, and pressed the surface with planks. When the clay dried they removed the planks and cut a hole in front for making fire and putting in bread.

We can explain the partitioning and ground-plan of the Southern Transdanubia house by the fireplace. Originally the house consisted of a single room, on one side of which stood the bank of the hearth *(padika)*, round-, or in some places square-shaped, made of clay, on which they cooked in a copper cauldron hanging from a beam. Primarily the old people used this room, while the young folk spent the night in the separate bedchamber, located outside the house. This *szenes ház,* a house with an ember hearth, later on became, along with its open fireplace, a separate room attached to the house, but it kept its name. Its ancient origin is proved by the custom that asking for the girl's hand took place in here for three consecutive days, and only afterward was the young man's father and godfather led into the house. The fact that the two rooms have separate outdoor exits also shows that the two rooms originate from different times. At this degree of development, the room already had a closed oven, which was heated from the kitchen. As the development of the house continued they built one more room on the

other side of the kitchen. This in many cases made unnecessary the separate bedchambers in the yard.

The one-roomed house with an ember fire is related to a Balkan type of house, which retained certain characteristics from the age of the Romans. The demonstrable connection with the Balkan house is manifested not only in the form of the fireplace, but in the implements belonging to it: *baking bell, copper kettle,* etc. At the same time the Hungarians influenced their southern neighbours by introducing the various forms of the tile stoves, and the house with a divided ground-plan. In Hungarian ethnographic literature they also call this kind of house, which preserves great antiquities, the Pannonian–Balkan form.

The largest farm buildings of this area are the barns or *sheds,* (see Ill. 10) placed both outside or inside the settlement. These are made of wattle and built on thick foundation logs. In the Ormánság, they built a stable onto one of the barns, a development probably of recent times. The huge wicker maize bins or lofts *(kukoricakas)* can be found in the entire area, but the most beautiful examples are in Somogy County (Ill. 84.).

Western and Central Transdanubia

We can include the entirety of Western Transdanubia, the Balaton region, and the Bakony in this area, a varied, hilly, slightly mountainous, forest-covered region, producing grain at some places and, more importantly, grapes on its gentle slopes. It is among the most beautiful regions of the country. The climate and vegetation of its western section reflects the proximity of the Alps, while its huge walnut and chestnut groves bring to mind the Mediterranean.

This region is characterized by tiny villages huddling near each other and by small towns, most of which preserved their continuity even under the Turks and some of which, furthermore, never came under permanent rule. Current research has failed to find a trace of the double inner-lot settlement. On the other hand, this region is characterized by

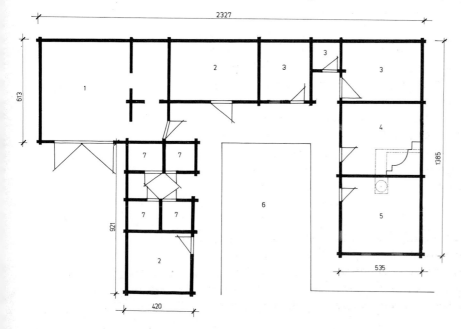

Fig. 52. The ground-plan of a fenced house. Szalafő, Vas County. 19th century. 1. Barn. 2. Stable. 3. Pantry. 4. Kitchen. 5. Room. 6. Manure heap. 7. Pigpen

86. House
Szalafő, Pityerszer, Vas County

177

87. Façade decoration on a house
Szentbékkálla, Veszprém County

the line of scattered houses, threading mostly along the ridges of hills. Originally the plough fields lay adjacent to the houses. The majority of the settlements are agglomerations, a large number of which became street-type settlement later. These settlements have the longest historical past in the north-western areas.

The building material of the houses was primarily wood in the south-west, although this was for a long time eclipsed by stone north of the Balaton (cf. Ill. 9). People mostly used thatch for the roofing of the houses, except that around the Balaton reed was used everywhere. Reed-thatched houses can still be found in the region today. The purlin roof supported by scissor beams was always a basic way of constructing the roof in this region even in the historical past.

One-unit houses still occurred at the end of the 18th century, the enormous size of the room sufficient large for the entire family to live together. Here an open fireplace was used and an oven, which was of a man's height. They called this the smoky house *(füstös ház)*, because it

178

did not have any kind of device to divert or catch smoke. It was related in shape to those of the alpine regions. A pantry was attached to this in many places, so that the fire remained in the smoke house. The pantry was a smokeless, cold room, while the "smoke house" continued to be a smoky, warm room. The problem of heating the room was solved first with an oven, later with a tile stove. This change occurred only after the problem of diverting smoke was solved by means of a chimney, and the tile stove could be stoked from the inside. This great change took place during barely one and a half century and altered the one-unit smoke house into a two-roomed smoke-kitchen house. This path was essentially followed not only by the wattle houses of Göcsej, Veszprém, and the Rábca region, but also by the porticoed, pillared, proud stone houses of the Balaton region.

The typical fenced house *(kerített ház)* of Göcsej developed from this one-unit house. The first step was taken when a third room was built onto the two-unit house. The rooms of young couples did not stand separately any more, but were attached to the existing building, although in such a way that the door of every room opened to the outside so they did not need to pass back and forth from one to the other (cf. Ill. 11). The one or more stables, the pigpen and the chicken-coop adjoined the dwelling rooms, leaning against them. A few sheds, less frequently a barn and granary room, surrounded the yard, which generally speaking was never larger than 100 to 200 square metres. It was shut off in front from the street side by a high fence and a gate, which was always carefully locked for the night. Usually the larger form of buildings, such as the barn, granary room, and separate pantry *(kástu),* were not built into the fenced house. Similarly, they always dug the well at another part of the holding (cf. Ill. 1, 2).

The most ornamental part of the houses of Göcsej is the gable made of ornamentally sawn, carved, and painted boards which was protected by the front of the roof. Usually a large cross was cut in the centre of the design and, to the left and to the right of this, by the attic window, open-work flowers were sawn with curving stems growing out of clay pots. The pillars holding the façade were also carved very richly. All this was painted in white, blue, and red, and the free area between the flowers was enlivened with colourful dots. The blinding whiteness of the wall

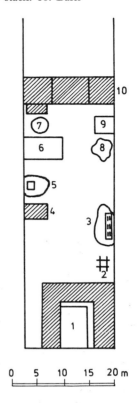

Fig. 53. The ground-plan of the courtyard of a fenced house. Göcsej. Early 20th century. 1. Fenced house. 2. Well. 3. Place to chuck wood. 4. Elevated pantry. 5. Manureheap, back-house. 6. Straw stack. 7. Oats. 8. Heap of gravel. 9. Hay-stack. 10. Barn

Fig. 54. The ground-plan of a stone house with a porch. Balatonhenye, Veszprém County. 19th century.
1. Room. 2. Kitchen. 3. Pantry. 4. Stable

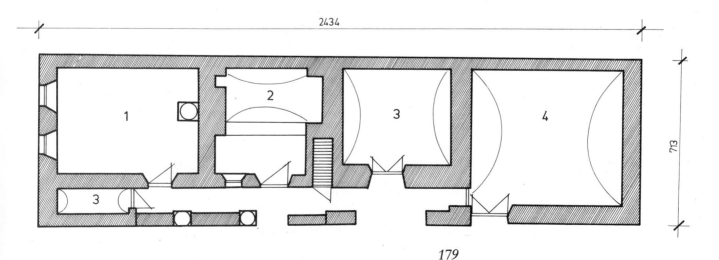

179

88. House
Kővágóőrs, Veszprém County

89. House
Balatonzamárdi, Somogy County

underneath further emphasized the painted carvings and sawn ornaments.

The largest region of stone architecture is north of the Balaton. The houses accord with the forms discussed above regarding ground-plan of the room, kitchen and pantry and their separate entrances. A specially decorative feature is the colonnaded portico, extremely varied in form and reflecting different European stylistic trends. Although these existed also in other parts of the linguistic territory, principally to protect the main wall and entrance of the house, because of the many possibilities stone architecture offers, it was in this region that the most beautiful and well-proportioned porticoes developed. The good artistic effect is increased by the plaster ornamentation of the façade, richly inspired by the Renaissance, Baroque and in some cases, by the Neo-Classic styles.

The most common farm building in the entire area is the kind of barn called *torkos pajta*. This, too, varies by region in building material. It may be made of log, of wattle, or, as the house, of stone. A typical building of the Göcsej and Őrség is the usually one-level, rarely two-level *kástu*, a pantry building that was used also to store grain and as the workshop of the farmer (cf. Fig. 50, Ill. 83).

Upper Hungary includes the mountain area from the river Garam to the Hernád, and in some traits as far as the Bodrog river, extending to the Slovak linguistic boundary to the north, and entering into the steppes of the Great Plain to the south. This dwelling area is uniform, although the north-south running river valleys and the watersheds divide its regions. The soil and the natural endowments are mostly poor, and therefore necessity has preserved many ancient features.

Dwelling Sites of Upper Hungary and the Palots Region

90. Log cottage
Ájfalucska, former Abaúj-Torna County

91. A cave dwelling
Alsóborsod, Borsod County

92. House
Borsod County

182

The type of divided settlement can be found not only in flat areas but also at the foot of the mountains, or in some places, even in mountainous regions. As the Turkish rule reached only until the lower border of this area, the form of village settlement preserved a number of medieval characteristics. Many agglomerate villages exist, some of which loosened up and developed street systems only in recent times. We can also find good examples of the "spindle" *(orsós)* type of settlement.

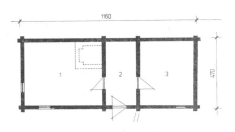

Fig. 55. The ground-plan of a dwelling house. Márianosztra, Nógrád County. 20th century. 1. Room. 2. Kitchen, called *pitvar*. 3. Pantry

The Palotses built out of wood until the time that the forests thinned out. They either built their walls from plain logs or used corner-post construction, or else they lowered thicker planks into the grooves of perpendicular beams. Only in the last hundred years have clay buildings become accepted and eventually widely used, out of necessity. In rare cases, the roof structure is of the purlin type, but more frequently of the rafter type, and is covered almost exclusively with straw thatch. The Palotses were always outstanding craftsmen in thatch work.

As far as it can be traced historically, the hearth was built into the room and was stoked from the inside. A small bench in front of it was used for cooking and baking over an open fire (cf. Ill. 68, 69). Such large, flat-shaped hearths with the open fireplace may be found towards the north, among the Slovak population. On the other hand, the spread of the stack-shaped oven came to the north in the 19th century from the Great Plain. The "cold porch" *(hideg pitvar),* without a fireplace, was attached to the house and was used more or less as a storage room. When the fireplace was moved to the porch, a *pantry* was attached to the first.

The Palots house, with its size and partitioning, was suited to the extended family, often consisting of 25 to 30 members. The family stayed together along the male lines, under the leadership of the farmer; that is to say, the grown sons brought home their wives and lived together forming a single economic unit. The family stayed together in the extraordinarily large-sized room all day in winter, they cooked and ate there. But the room served as the sleeping place only for the men, because the women along with the small children slept in the unheated chamber that opened from the porch. Usually mosquito netting separated the beds from each other, which gave protection against mosquitoes and flies in the summer and also against the cold in the winter. The young men preferred to sleep in the stable and in the barn, in the attic of the house, or in the hay during the summer.

Among larger farm buildings, the most important is the barn, which had three sections in rich households, two in poor ones. Among the smaller buildings let us mention the pigpen *(hidas),* present in every yard. Such were also made for sale and shipped in a dismountable form to more southerly regions.

Dwelling Sites of the Great Plain

This area comprises the largest territory. As far as architecture is concerned, the Great Plain extends far toward the south, and also seems to reach the Little Plain through the north-eastern corner of Transdanubia. This landscape is completely flat, margined by gentle slopes. In the past, flooded plains and permanent marshes occupied its major part, while in the Nyírség, and between the Danube and Tisza, sand pre-

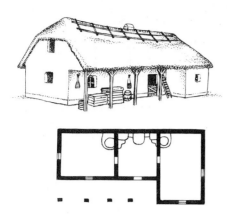

Fig. 56. The ground-plan of a house with a porch. Bihartorda, former Bihar County. Early 20th century

93. House
Komádi, Hajdú-Bihar County

vailed. All these natural factors, along with the cold winters, extremely hot summers, and the lowest rainfall in the Carpathian Basin, influenced architecture significantly.

The Hajdú towns of the Tiszántúl represent the classic form of the double inner-lot type of settlement. Few villages remained on the area once occupied by the Turks, but some of them were resettled. Therefore villages with regulated streets are numerous, since new settlers had to build in such an order.

The history of this dwelling region is known primarily from archaeological excavations. Houses from the 10th to the 13th centuries that were sunk half into the ground have been discovered, consisting of a single large room of 10 to 12 square metres. In one case an oven was found in the corner of the house, dug into the ground on the same level as the floor, though in this period the majority of ovens were built outdoors, outside the houses. But archaeologists can show village houses from the 13th century that had two rooms and were rectangular in shape. One of these may have had wicker walls standing mainly above the ground. More and more data testify that from this time on the partitioning of the peasant houses into two and later three rooms began.

The walling material of the Great Plain house is primarily clay. The wicker wall appears to be earliest, followed by the stamped mud-wall,

184

and most recently the adobe wall which has eclipsed everything else. The roof structure is of the purlin type, supported by two, perhaps three forked uprights. Reed was used first of all for covering, but in some places they substituted rush and sedge (cf. Ill. 14). Straw roofs also occurred, but only in a pressed version, since treading was the basic method of threshing grain and they possessed only pressed straw.

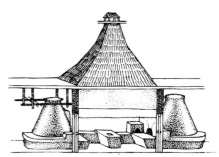

Fig. 57. Section of a house. Bihartorda, former Bihar County. Early 20th century. In the kitchen, note the fireplace on a bank, in both rooms a round oven to be heated from the kitchen, one surrounded by rods for drying clothes

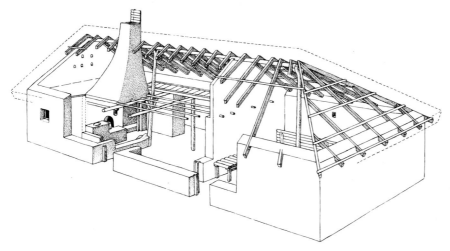

Fig. 58. Stable with a fireplace. Karcag-Berek, Szolnok County. 1851

In regard to the fireplace installations, it is noteworthy that the oven built outside but stoked from the inside of the house survived in many places, among others, on the Little Plain. Otherwise, the problem of channelling the smoke was solved here at the earliest time. The central partition unit of the house was divided into two parts. A skirted chimney, usually made of wicker and plastered, reached above the roof through the attic and channelled out all the smoke from the house. Open fires were used on clay banks in the kitchen, or cooking was done in openings along the edges of the banks. A large oven, round or rectangular or of some other shape, was built in both rooms, and stoked from the kitchen (cf. Ill. 67). The replacement of the oven by a stove did not happen, because the available heating fuel (reed, straw, maize, and sunflower stalks) preserved the oven until the most recent times.

We are going to mention separately two smaller areas within this large region. One is the Little Plain, which lies along the western branch of the Danube, and to the south and north of it (Czechoslovakia) and can largely be followed to the Hungarian linguistic border (Zobor region). In the three-unit house, the doors of the two rooms opened onto the porch. The oven was located outside the building and its mouth opened from the back wall of the kitchen. The stoke-hole of the rooms opened into the kitchen, and they built a bank in front of it. So far, the type of fire bank placed in the centre of the kitchen has not been found in this area. The rooms were heated with tile stoves until the most recent times, but large-sized low ovens also occurred in some places.

The other small area under discussion lies in the north-eastern corner of the Hungarian linguistic region, in the valley of the Tisza and its tributaries. Wood has a greater role in building, manifest in fences, gates, granaries and belfries. One characteristic of architecture here is the colonnaded portico that surrounds the house in some cases on two, and

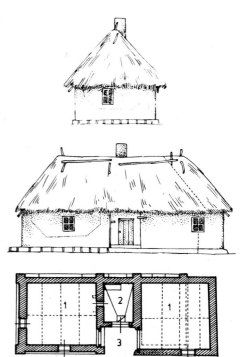

Fig. 59. Side and front view of a house and its ground-plan. Milota, former Szatmár County. 19th century. 1. Room. 2. Kitchen *(pitvar)*. 3. Open porch

in others on three sides. Numerous versions of the hearth with a perpendicular chimney are noteworthy among fireplace installations. Many characteristics show that the architecture of this area is a transition in the direction of the Great Plain, the Palócföld, and, most of all, toward Transylvania (cf. Ill. 4–6), with which the ethnography of this area has much in common.

Most of the farm work was done outdoors in the Great Plain, so no barn is present in this region. Barns occur only in the flat areas bordering on the mountains, as well as in the two small regions mentioned above, as a result of an attempt at intensive farming. In the Great Plain yard, we usually find the stable, smaller pens, cart and chaff sheds, as the extension of the house, only with lower roofs, and perhaps granaries and pits.

Dwelling Sites of Transylvania and the Székely Region

This area includes historical Transylvania and the Székely-Csángó areas that spread from there toward the east. The territory is extraordinarily varied from the architectural point of view, for the long association with Saxons and Rumanians can also be measured in architectural effects. The region is hilly and mountainous, interspersed with high mountains, plateaus, and the plains of river valleys.

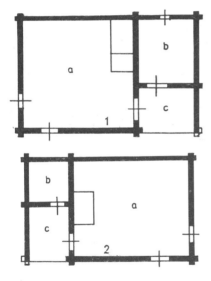

Fig. 60. Ground-plans of the former type of Székely house consisting of two units. 1. Gyimes, former Csík County. 2. Uzon, former Háromszék County. 18th–19th centuries. a) Room *(ház),* b) pantry *(kamra),* c) porch *(eresz)*

94. House Torockó, former Torda-Aranyos County

95. House
Mikóújfalu, former Háromszék County

The settlements are extremely numerous in type. We find examples with streets and ribbon holdings as well as agglomerate villages, usually built close around the church. There are numerous examples of clan settlements, reflecting even today the fact that the families once divided the land of the village among themselves. As the family grew, newer buildings were constructed on the common land, or perhaps parts of it fenced off, but the exit continued to be the same. The existence of such settlements can be demonstrated in many cases not only in the villages, but in the cities as well (Kézdivásárhely). The double inner-lot type of settlement characteristic of the Great Plain cannot be found in Transylvania. This, however, does not mean that in the mountains we cannot find structures for hay and also lodgings for woodcutters and herdsmen, inhabited for only certain parts of the year. Isolated settlements are present among the Székelys, but occur primarily among the Csángós of Gyimes (cf. Ill. 17).

The basic element of building construction on a large part of Székelyland is the pine log. We find stone buildings first of all at Udvarhelyszék, Torockó, while Saxon-influenced brick buildings have spread to many areas. Houses are built of clay primarily in the villages of the Mezőség. Shingles, or much larger wooden plates *(dránica)* were used, especially in

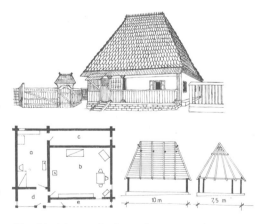

Fig. 61. A house, its front view, ground-plan and construction. Csíkménaság, Csík County. 1830.
a) Small room *(kicsi ház)*, b) big room *(nagy ház)*, c) pantry *(kamra)*, d) porch *(eresz)*, e) veranda *(tornác)*

187

the timber building zone, on the rafter type of roof structure, while at other places many versions of thatch roof occur. Tile roofs have gained ground only during the last fifty years.

One of the most characteristic features of the Székely house is the *eresz*, porch, having mostly three sides, and really used as an entrance to the house. The biggest difference between the Székely and the other Hungarian houses is that the Székely house does not really have a kitchen, that is to say, the sleeping, living, and cooking quarters are not divided into separate rooms. The various types of open hearths were equally used for heating, cooking, baking, and lighting. Because these could fulfil all necessary functions, the kitchen developed only in recent times.

The hearth was located either in the eaves or in a building especially built for it, called the *bake house*. It had a fireplace, a hearth, and a few simple pieces of furnishing. It was lived in from early spring to late autumn. Besides the bake house, the shed *(szín)* is also an important building in the yard. Here they kept the cart, the tools, and sometimes even stored grain. The barn *(csűr)* was used for storing the harvested crops, and one or maybe both of its sides served as a barn. The holding was closed by a gate from the street side, the masterpiece of Hungarian wood construction.

The Influence of Historical Styles on Folk Architecture

The development of Hungarian houses and farm buildings was influenced, first of all, by social-economic circumstances, by natural endowments, and by tradition; certain regional differences thus came into existence. Added to these was the influence of the architectural traditions of the neighbouring peoples and nationalities. However, the influence of the great historical stylistic periods is also present in folk architecture. These reached the peasantry after considerable delay as imitations of churches, fortresses, castles and manor houses, often coming through the hands of the masters who built them.

Certain elements that were organically incorporated into the body of peasant architecture remained primarily in the peripheral regions of the linguistic territory. The reason for this is that regions, because of their isolation, were more apt to conserve various influences, and also because Turkish rule in the 16th and 17th centuries did not eradicate the majority of earlier buildings. The most beautiful wooden buildings are located in such regions: houses, towers, belfries, the Székely gate, magnificent both in structure and ornamentation, and the most beautiful house frontispieces. It is extremely difficult—and in their entirety it is impossible—to tie these to a specific period, because they always occur transformed and adjusted to the entire composition. Still, let us examine some of them.

The belfry of Transylvania and the Tiszahát preserves Gothic tradition in its form, especially the four turrets (cf. Ills. 4, 15, 51, 62). Its balcony, however, resembles Renaissance examples. The carpentry technique of the Székely gate can be traced all the way back to the Gothic.

The Renaissance, especially in Transylvania, prolifically affected, often even centuries later, folk ornamental art. The painted wooden panelling of church ceilings, the frontal plates of its choirs are the direct descendants of the flowering of the Renaissance, and even if they were created by village or town masters known by name, they are still a living, influential part of ornamental peasant art (cf. Ills. 40, 220, Plate XXII). The same is true of the tiles decorating peasant stoves and hearths, on which the stylistic marks of the Gothic and Renaissance periods can be recognized even if they happened to have been made in the 18th or 19th centuries. This is also true of the carvings of the Székely gate, and of the increased use of colouring on it from the end of the 18th century. The roots of all this reach back to the richest period of the Renaissance in Transylvania. Behind the light colonnaded porticos of Transdanubia, we can feel intimation of the Italian-style loggias of the castles and manor houses.

A whole line of castles and country houses was influenced, primarily in the Great Plain, by Neo-Classic architecture. We can find its influence here most strongly in the peasant Neo-Classic pillars of the porticos. At other places, the protruding porticos, standing out from the front of the house, changed to a certain degree the ground plan of the house. Neo-Classic characteristics are also traceable in the great variety of stucco ornamentation of the front of the house.

All these more or less important elements became part of Hungarian folk architecture in a united form, in such a way that they closely amalgamated with its older and newer elements. Often a way of constructing a wall or the shape of a fireplace may be traceable to the New Stone Age, and occurs together with elements dating from the Renaissance and Baroque periods, yet together these elements create a harmonious unit. All this is proof of the creative ability of the Hungarian folk, which also makes itself known, although in different forms, of every peasant culture.

Life in the House and the Farmyard

While describing the interior of the house and the yard, we have often referred to the life and work that went on there. It is impossible to give a survey of this for the entire linguistic territory, since the differences are great not only in regard to the division of the house, but also as regards life style and the work carried out there. However, we can determine one thing: that the house itself, especially during summertime, is only a temporary place of rest for both men and women, during the intermissions of work in the fields or the yard. Work moves into the house during the winter, primarily around the fireplace, which meant woodcarving and repairing of tools for the men, but only when cold weather prevented them from doing it outside. Besides the cooking and baking, the women also did the washing there, processed the hemp and flax, and did numerous daily or occasional chores.

Daily work started at early dawn. The farmer and his sons rose at four o'clock, but before they went out to the stables they lit the fire so that the women could get up as soon as they left. Only the children and the old people rested a little longer. Breakfast followed after feeding the stock, cleaning out the manure, and a brief clean-up for themselves. Then the men and, if the work demanded it, the girls and women as well, went out to the fields to work, or did the daily chores around the house. They fed and watered the stock again at around three in the afternoon, after which they themselves ate. In wintertime, there was a little peaceful period left before bedtime, during which they talked, visited neighbours, and told stories and adventures to each other.

In the house, not only the daily life but the process of infrequent or unusual events were regulated as well. Thus they whitewashed the entire house inside and out, usually at Easter, or in September. They carried out the furniture and scrubbed it, replastered the clay floor of the house, and where it was made of planks, they thoroughly scrubbed it, chores which added mostly to the burden of the women.

Women also had to cope with the various vermin, first of all with mice and cockroaches. At the same time the protecting of the house snake was also one of their tasks. The belief that in the walls of every house lives a snake who protects the inhabitants of the house from trouble and sickness prevailed almost throughout the entire linguistic region. Its destruction, whether intentional or unintentional, was believed to bring misfortune on the whole family or on one of its members.

Among the big events of life, weddings turn the familiar order of the house and the yard upside down the most. At such times all furniture is carried out of the larger room and benches are set up along the walls, and in front of them tables made of planks are laid on sawing stools and chairs. Room is reserved for the musicians in the corner, around the fireplace. Even from the back room the furniture is put into the shed or granary, and that room is where food and wine are served. When the dancing starts, the older folk withdraw here for drinking and talking. The cooking is usually done outdoors or under the sheds. During the summer, they usually put up a large tent in the yard for the guests.

There is no such great rearranging of the house at the time of death. They lay the body out in the clean room with the face toward the door. The mirror is covered, the table is taken out, and the bier is surrounded with benches and chairs, providing a resting place for those who keep vigil with the body. Leave-taking and lamentation take place in front of the house, in the yard. Food and drink are offered to those coming back from the cemetery to the burial feast out of doors, or the table is set in the other room. If there is no second room, then they ask the neighbours to provide room for the funeral feast.

The godparents are generally the only ones invited to the baptismal feast, and this barely causes a change in the order of the house. When a spinning room is set up, usually just the table is taken out and benches and chairs are brought in so that more people can sit down. However, if as a conclusion to the spinning, or for some other occasion, a ball is arranged, then everything has to be hauled out just as at the time of a wedding. However, the next day the house is whitewashed, and the kicked up floor is plastered anew. During the summer, balls are held in the yard or, in the eastern part of the linguistic territory, even in the barn. There is no need to rearrange the furniture when people are invited to strip feathers, but more sitting room is provided.

The porch, the yard, and perhaps the granary are the scenes of some

190

jobs carried out by mutual assistance. The most frequent among these is corn-husking and beating out the sunflower seeds, called *bugázás*. At such times people not only work, but tell stories and sing, and finally have a dance.

The dog defends the yard from unauthorized entries, but dogs are never let into the house. At best a dog can seek shelter in the barn, under a shed, or in the granary, or dig himself a warm resting place in the haystack.

Fire was the greatest calamity of the overcrammed villages and adjacent barns, and often created rubble out of entire sections of villages. If fire was caused by lightning, milk was first poured on it, in the belief that water would not extinguish it. The whole village runs together at a fire and tries to put it out and keep it from spreading, women by using bucket chains, men by quickly beating off the roof.

Acquiring Raw Material from Flora and Fauna

Having to provide the necessary raw material for food, clothing and house building, peasant economy was forced to be self sufficient through the centuries. Consequently it produced scarcely more than what it was able to use up. The feudal system also encouraged this tendency, for as feudal duties increased along with increases in production, it was not in the interest of the peasantry to increase the yield of the land with new methods, or to incorporate larger territories. This is why feudalism became the obstacle to increased production.

Although this held true for the entire peasant economy, still, specialization began early, partly within settlements, partly—because of natural resources, special knowledge and traditions—varying by villages and by regions. Within the settlements, specialists worked in certain occupations, such as, from the Middle Ages on, blacksmiths, wheelwrights, coopers, etc. Similarly, the processing of skin and of wool largely became the task of artisans. Village artisans were not separated socially sharply from the peasantry, but usually participated in cultivating the land, carrying out their trade primarily during the break between agricultural tasks (cf. pp. 91-95).

Certain natural resources also advanced specialization. For example, salt was transported from faraway areas, just as merchants hauled the half-finished or finished products of well-known iron producing and processing centres that had developed during the early Middle Ages, to faraway lands, where they sold or bartered these. The population of areas where wood was plentiful carved agricultural tools, carts, and furniture. They hauled lime and charcoal from the mountain regions to the Great Plain. Dishes, plates and pitchers from the pottery centres were carried to great distances by cart. All this meant not only exchanging and proliferating certain merchandise, but it also assured a permanent contact between parts of the country and, in some cases, between different ethnic groups living far away from each other.

The many-phased acquisition of raw material was strongly connected with the form of the settlement, shaping the exterior and interior order of the yard and agricultural buildings. Among the natural, economic, and social determinants, traditions and ethnic characteristics rated a significant place. The picture created by all these factors changes so much that it is very difficult to survey in its entirety. Consequently, it is possible only to point out certain of its characteristics.

Food Gathering

By the time of the Hungarian Middle Ages, food gathering did not play a significant role in relation to productive activity, but it doubtless did at an earlier time in supplementing food. Man simply took from nature all he could use but did not pay attention to replenishing or preserving it. Gleaning, therefore, can be carried out successfully only over very large

areas. Consequently, it follows that as the population increased in numbers and as the country became more and more a cultivated region, the amount of food gathering decreased continually. However, it has not completely disappeared even today, since the collecting of mushrooms, herbs, and certain fruits (raspberry, wild strawberry) still survives.

The nature of the soil and climate determines the nature of wild-growing plants, and the natural plant cover determines the method and tools of food gathering. For this reason, food gathering is different in the world of the swamps, or on the steppes of the Great Plain, from food gathering in the mountain forests.

Up until the middle—but in many places until the end—of the last century the central part of the country was covered by a permanent swamp region, which was renewed every year by the flooding of the rivers. This offered many kinds of food and numerous raw materials. The *water chestnut (Trapa natans),* flourished in the quieter still waters. It was harvested in the early autumn days from a boat. Its prickly fruit got caught on a piece of ragged felt or a sheep's tail they pulled through the water. In other places water chestnuts were found in such quantities that they raked them out of the water, or fished them out with a piece of fur through a hole cut in the ice. People boiled them and ate the white,

Fig. 62. Gathering water chestnuts with a piece of woolly sheepskin through a hole in the ice. Tisza region, 1920s

193

Fig. 63. Selling water chestnuts at the market. Debrecen. Early 20th century.
a) A cup for measuring water chestnuts.
b) A hook used when cutting off the thorns from the cooked water chestnuts

crumbling, chestnut-like interior, or they kneaded it into dough or, by mixing it with flour, even made bread of it. A favourite food of the people of the Great Plain was the millet-like glyceria *(harmatkása).* They held a sieve under it early in the morning and shook the seeds out. They ate it mixed with eggs as griddle cakes. Herdsmen baked the floury stem of the *bulrush (Typha L.)* in a fire. Biscuits were also made out of it. The sources refer to it mostly as famine food.

A great treasure of swampy regions is *reed (Phragmites),* which was harvested in the winter after the water had frozen. It was cut with a long-handled scythe, the so-called *toló,* made with a stout blade, to each end of which a long pole was fastened and it was pushed through the reeds. When enough reeds gathered in the centre, they lifted them out and tied them in sheaves, then piled these in conical heaps at the edge of the swamp or on one of its islands. Reeds were used not only for roofing the house, but were also made into fences and windbreaks for the stock. Reeds were put under the child in the crib and also into the grave, against groundwater. Thus reeds accompanied men living in the swamps from the cradle to the grave.

The gathering of the *bulrush (Typha L.)* took place in August either from a boat or by wading in the water, in which case a serious battle had to be fought with the leeches that proliferated. The bulrushes were taken home (cf. Ill. 151) after having been dried on the shore, to make baskets, bags, beehives (cf. Ill. 116), and covers out of. Some villages outstanding for bulrush mat-making survived for a long time, and shipped their products to faraway markets.

A characteristic food-gathering figure of the Great Plain swamps was the *pákász.* He spent his entire life in the marshes, among the reeds, his hut standing on a salient part of one of the islands. He rarely had a family and went into the village only if he wanted to exchange some fish, game, or feathers for food. He collected water chestnuts, gathered the glyceria and the bulrush, fished and caught birds with his hands or with tools. He sought out the nests of the waterfowl and took their eggs and their already edible young by the thousand. He acquired the most beautiful feathers for the hats of the village lads, who always gave him food or good money for them. This man of a peculiar life style disappeared at the end of the last century, when the swamps were dried.

Medicinal herbs constitute an important product of food gathering. As a Hungarian proverb has it, "There is medicine in weeds and trees". Actually, folk medicine used plants in many very versatile ways, some of which are still employed today. Such are, among others, the *camomile (Matricaria R.)* which was picked with a comb-like tool, and the fruit of the *cranberry (Vaccinium L.).* In the winter, medicinal tea is brewed from the flowers of the *linden tree (Tilia L.).* They dried the various roots and stored them thus for the winter, for the time of sickness. The folk use of medicinal herbs is often in agreement with the advice of medieval books on medicine, which slowly filtered down and became part of folk knowledge.

The true home of food gathering is the mountain region, the forest. At one time even the trees were felled in such a way that no one thought of their replacement. They cut the huge timbers in the winter. Some

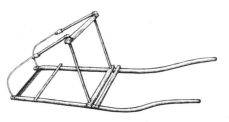

Fig. 64. Reed-pusher for reaping reeds on the ice. Gárdony, Fejér County. Around 1950

they chopped up on the spot and took home that way, others were marked with a proprietary sign in order to avoid losing them and slid them down to the valley whole. From here they were carried to the river, where everybody looked for his own as indicated by the mark that had been put on after felling. Huge rafts were made from the timber and floated in this way down to the Great Plain.

Many things were made out of the wood. *Charcoal* was burned, some on the spot, or potash, indispensable for glass making, was prepared. *Axle grease* was also made from wood. Some cut notches into pine trees and allowed the resin that came out of the wounds to drip into vessels made from bark. When the sap begins to circulate in the trees during spring, they tap them. The birch is especially suited for this. The *nyírvíz* or, as the Székely call it, *virics,* is a sweetish liquid, which was used fermented in the past. It was sold far and wide at the Great Plain fairs of the 18th and 19th centuries.

The forest region is extremely rich in *mushrooms*. In many places

97. Splitting wicker
Kiskunfélegyháza

people are familiar with it and regularly gather 30 to 40 edible varieties. The forest not only provides heating fuel, but the fallen leaves when gathered are an excellent bedding for the stock and, in times of great need, are mixed with other fodder to serve as famine food until grass sprouts in the spring. In many places they even cut the bark off the trees and collect the fruits of the forest in vessels made out of it. In times of famine, people used the cut off, dried, and ground-up bark of the beech tree and acorns, from which, mixed with flour, they made bread.

There are many ways to make use of the fruits of the trees. Thus, wild fruit (apple, pear) is dried and in some places vinegar or refreshing drinks are made out of them. Jam was made from the fruit of the dog-rose bush, from raspberry and wild strawberry.

The economic significance of food gathering is not great, but its unusually large variety implies in most cases a long historical past. During the past two centuries, its significance grew especially at times when the plough lands were ruined by the ravages of war or when a long-lasting drought devastated the crop.

Farming

This is one of the most important activities and the foundation of acquiring food. Through agriculture man was able to free himself to a large degree from the caprices of nature and significantly more people were able to live on a much smaller area. This is why civilization rose to higher levels in those parts of the world where great agricultural civilizations appeared.

The Magyars were thought to be entirely nomadic husbandmen during the centuries preceding and following the Conquest (9th to 11th centuries).

The latest research, however, no longer defines this question so unequivocally. A great many words testify that in the time of contact with the Bulgaro-Turks, the Magyars already had acquired certain agricultural knowledge, as is indicated by many Hungarian words (*eke*, plough; *tarló*, stubble field; *sarló*, sickle; *búza*, wheat; *árpa*, barley; *szérű*, threshing yard, etc.). This knowledge increased when they became acquainted with the famous garden culture of the Khazar Khaganate and learned the basic elements of vine growing (*szőlő*, grape; *bor*, wine; *seprő*, lees, etc.). They could also have learned from the Eastern Slav peoples of the South Russian steppes, who possessed a highly developed agriculture. When the Magyars appeared in the Carpathian Basin, a significant proportion were already occupied in agriculture. This is proven by archaeological sources and also by written notes.

The System of Hungarian Farming

The earliest form of land-use most certainly was the *parlagolás* (leaving land uncultivated), by which they left off cultivating the exhausted land and broke up new land to replace it. The used land was left to rest for 8 to 10 years or even longer and only then was it cultivated again. Naturally this method could survive only as long as there was enough land. It was renewed after the Turks withdrew (18th century), even in areas where it had not been used earlier. In the Great Plain the exhausted plough land was left to pasture. The stock fertilized it, grass grew over it, and thus it regained its productivity.

The opposite of *parlag* is *ugar* (fallow). Both words are Slavic in origin and testify that we took over this system from one of the Slavic peoples. They divide the fields into two or three sections and through the year keep half or one-third resting. On this basis we can speak of *two-* or *three-course rotation* farming. The stock grazes the fallow land for a year and fertilizes it to a certain degree. The turned-over weeds and roots also help to rejuvenate the land. In areas of husbandry the two-, and in other places the three-course system of rotation prevailed, though finally the latter became generally used.

This system spread increasingly from the 13th century on and basically prevailed up to the 19th century. By then at most places the fallow lands were sown, usually with spring wheat, and even more with fodder or root crops. On those parts of the country where the fallow system prevailed, we find permanent plough fields outside the villages beginning from the Middle Ages. These were cultivated without rest. Their name, *tanor, tanorok,* originally meant a plough field fenced with spiky branches. The name, of Slavic origin, also indicates this. The cleared area *(irtás)* was not divided into the rotating land system but was sowed every year.

In the Carpathian Basin we differentiate farming methods of the *mountain* and *hill regions* and that of the *Great Plain*. Leaving fields fallow *(ugar)* is primarily connected to the previous method. It was also characterized by the longer use of the sickle here, by the tying of the grain crop into sheaves stacked in the shape of a cross, and by beating the seeds out with a threshing flail. This work was carried out in the barn where harvested grain was often stored until winter. In the Great Plain the major part of the farm work was done out of doors, which is why we do not find barns in this area. The grain crop was cut with a scythe in earlier times and gathered with rakes into bunches. These were hauled into the threshing yards set up at the end of the plough fields, and threshed by treading out, usually with horses. In the plains grain was kept mostly in underground pits that had been hardened and cleaned by burning.

The separation of the two systems can be shown primarily in the 18th and 19th centuries. For a long time, the Great Plain style of farming was thought to be a nomadic tradition going back to the time of the Conquest, but more recent research has proved that it began to develop only in the 16th century, its characteristics having been strengthened during the Turkish occupation, and especially afterwards. However, the differences began to fade in the second half of the 19th century as the result of similar tendencies in general development.

Soil Cultivation

Among the hand tools for cultivating the soil, one of the most important is the *spade*. The wooden spade was fitted with an iron shoe, which not only made the work easier but also prevented wear. It seems that the symmetrical forms with the two-sided blade with a double step are known in the central and western half of the linguistic region, while the

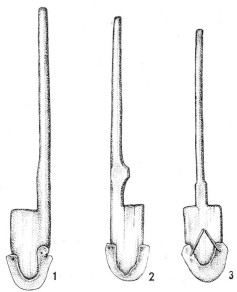

Fig. 65. Wooden spades with iron "slippers". 1–2. Magyarvalkó, former Kolozs County. 3. Székelyland

Fig. 66. Shapes of spades and their distribution in Hungary. Early 20th century

Fig. 67. Plough to be used alternatively, Magyarvalkó, former Kolozs County. Late 19th century

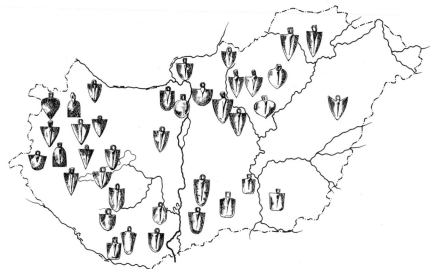

Fig. 68. Plough with the stilt leading to its sole. Szimó, former Komárom County. Late 19th century

asymmetrical, one-sided blade is known in the eastern region. Historical sources mention spades with blades completely of iron from the 16th century. These were shipped from small foundries to distant lands. They have similar forms all over the country, and only perhaps in the placing and size of the blade top are there smaller differences.

The *hoe* is much more varied. Some of half-moon shape are linked to the Balkans. The square ones seem to come from the west. Great variety is shown among the pointed hoes, the characteristic forms of which are designated by the name of the place or region where they are primarily used. We can estimate the number of the types of the various hoes to be at least one hundred, all of which were well known by the small foundries and hoe factories that sent the appropriate form to merchants everywhere. In the mountain region a shorter handle, and in flat areas a longer handle was fitted to the differently shaped hoes in order to accommodate them to working conditions.

In recent times, there is more and more evidence that the pre-Conquest Magyars knew and practised plough farming in the 7th to 9th centuries. First of all, the Hungarian vocabulary testifies to this. The word *eke* (plough) itself is Bulgaro-Turkic in origin; the word *köldök*, the term for the piece of wood which connects the plough beam with the mouldboard of the plough, is from the same source. If we add to this that the terminology of the plough has many words of Finno-Ugric origin (*talp*, mouldboard; *ekefő*, share beam; *szántóvas*, plough share; *laposvas*, flat iron; *hosszúvas*, long iron; *vezér*, head; *szarv*, handle), then we have before us a furrow-turning plough capable of cultivating the cropland. Archeological evidence also proves that the true Magyars could have become acquainted with such a plough either in the Bulgarian Khaganate or in the Khazar Khaganate. Such a large quantity of plough irons has turned up from the excavations there as to prove the wide use of the plough.

On the great South Russian steppes the Magyars also met various Eastern Slavic peoples who possessed a highly developed plough cul-

98. Ploughing
Kökényespuszta, Nógrád County

ture. Some further terms prove that the ploughs of these peoples could have been more developed than the ones earlier known to the Magyars (*gerendely,* plough beam; *taliga,* forecarriage; *ösztöke,* goad; etc.). In recent years Soviet archeologists have excavated in the Ukraine numerous asymmetrical plough shares dating from the 9th and 10th centuries, which proves that these Slavic tribes had already known and used the plough with a forecarriage that could be turned to one side and that improved considerably the quality of the cultivation of the soil. The plough thus arrived at a degree of development which cannot be surpassed even today, as only the pulling power has increased since then.

We must mention that among the finds in Hungary, asymmetrical plough shares and coulters appeared only in the 12th–13th centuries. This may be because the value of iron was so great at this time that iron objects survived only when the settlement was destroyed so suddenly that it was not possible to save them. In other cases, people used even completely worn iron objects for the most varied purposes. Perhaps this may be the reason why no asymmetrical plough irons and coulters have turned up so far from the 10th and 11th centuries.

In the 19th century, the peasants themselves made the frame of the plough in areas rich in wood. However, there were many villages in the mountain regions of the Carpathian Basin, where the population was occupied with plough making. They hauled their merchandise, adjusted to local demands, to the fairs of the Great Plain in the spring and exchanged them for grain or sold them for money. In certain villages and towns *plough makers* operated, but in most places the frames of the ploughs were shaped by the cartwrights and wheelwrights.

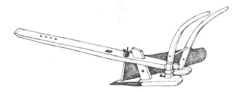

Fig. 69. Plough with its stilt socketed into the sole. (Debrecen type plough). Kunmadaras, Szolnok County. Second half of 19th century

Fig. 70. Asymmetrical plough-carriage. Berzence, Somogy County. Early 20th century

199

The wooden plough had only two iron parts: the plough share and the coulter. Earlier these were made by the village blacksmith. Beginning with the 17th century, town and country assessments set their prices exactly. Later on the foundries produced a significant part of them, and the task of the blacksmith was limited to their furnishing and shaping. In most settlements the first obligation of the *village blacksmith* was to see to sharpening the plough share and the coulter in return for the wages paid him by the farmers.

It is not a difficult task to describe the Magyar wooden ploughs. They form two large groups, symmetrical or asymmetrical. All of the mouldboard ploughs and the majority of their frames are rectangular. Their plough beam is mostly straight so that only in such smaller, isolated areas as the southern part of the linguistic region do we find ploughs with a curved beam. Within the larger units, the ploughs of Hungary can be divided into smaller groups on the basis of the relation between and the location of the handle and the mouldboard.

Symmetrical ploughs are symmetrical in every respect, including the plough share. Such were the *furrow-turning ploughs,* on either side of which was fastened a mouldboard. Thus the ground was turned equally to the left and to the right. This form proliferated generally in the Middle Ages, but it was used only in peripheral areas by the 19th century. The *reversible plough,* which was completely symmetrical and had a single handle, most likely developed from this. The symmetry is broken only by the mouldboard, which can be switched from one side to the other, and along with it the coulter as well. This plough, by following the same path on the return, is especially well suited to ploughing hillsides. This form of the plough was widely used in Transylvania and was known as well in Slovakia and in certain regions of Gömör. Most recent studies have concluded that it most likely developed in the Carpathian Basin in several places independently from each other during the 16th and 17th centuries.

One of the most characteristic forms of the asymmetrical plough is the one on which the handle and mouldboard are carved out of a single piece of wood. This made the structure extremely sturdy. It was consequently especially well suited for breaking up hard, grassy soils. They ploughed with this during the past century in the northern and southern part of the Tiszántúl, in the Palots region and the areas south of them, between the Danube and the Tisza, and in the larger, eastern half of Transdanubia as well. We can therefore say that they used this form over the greater part of the Magyar linguistic territory.

If we search in the west for traces of this *stilt-sole* type of plough, it cannot be found, or only very rarely, and even then it can be proved to be borrowed in some way from the Hungarians. However, if we look for its proliferation toward the east, we find that is was used in Moldavia and in the Ukraine as well as in the great Russian steppes all the way to the Volga, and in some places was introduced by Russian settlers even to Siberia. Written and pictorial descriptions note the occurrence of these ploughs in the Ukraine and in Russia by at least the 15th century; furthermore, we know of data regarding the use of this type at the same time in Hungary as well. Thus, on the basis of linguistic, archaeological, historical, and ethnographical data, it is very likely that the Magyars became acquainted with this kind of plough in the 9th century. Because it was suited to the soil conditions in the Carpathian Basin, the type continued to be used here right up to the 19th century, when the half iron and iron ploughs completely replaced it.

In the central part of the Tiszántúl, that is, in the region east of the Tisza, in Transylvania, and in the western part of Transdanubia as well, wooden ploughs were used, the two handles of which were joined onto a separate, flat mouldboard. This heavy tool was dragged by six to eight oxen, in order to turn the soil 10 to 15 cm deep. This plough supposedly developed from the most simple type of rooting plough.

In the Carpathian Basin, almost every plough has a forecarriage. This assures the balanced movement of the plough, and with its help the depth and width of the ploughing can be controlled. The fairly uniform kinds can be divided into two broad groups.

The two wheels of the symmetrical *forecarriage of a plough* are identical, the beam being located in the centre. There is no way to control the forecarriages on the furrow-turning plough. The width of the furrow can be determined on the forecarriages of the reversible plough by a wood or iron arch shaped in a half circle, the *cságató*. The depth is determined in both cases by the degree to which they push the forecarriage under the plough beam.

The wheels of the *forecarriage of the asymmetrical plough* are different in size. The larger moves along in the furrow, the smaller one on the unploughed ground. The beam of the forecarriage is pushed to the right and above it the plough beam is connected to the bolster. The *cságató* determines the width of the ploughing; it starts out from the left side of the axle and is attached to the beam of the forecarriage by means of holes set at the desired distance. Such a forecarriage of the mouldboard is generally known in the entire Carpathian Basin, where it can be found more frequently to the east and less so towards the west.

The half iron ploughs, at first made in western countries and later imitated at home, appeared in Hungary during the first half of the last century. The first factory, the Vidacs Plough Factory, opened in the 1840s. The number of such ploughs in use in the country in 1848 can be estimated at 2 to 3 per cent, and even ten years later the number did not reach 10 per cent. In 1871, in the large grain producing areas (Great Plain, Little Plain), their numbers already surpassed 90 per cent, yet remained mostly at under 10 per cent in the peripheral regions. However, by 1920, except in some areas of the Carpathian Basin where ancient modes continued to prevail, wooden ploughs largely had disappeared and had been replaced by the all-iron plough.

One important adjunct of the mouldboard plough is the goad pattle (*ösztöke*). This consists of a small iron blade and a short wooden handle. They cleaned the mud from the plough share with it and picked out the weeds that got stuck in its crevices. It was held in the hand, because it could be used to urge on a lazy beast, or else was fixed by the handle and only taken out when there appeared to be a need for it.

The plough was hauled to the field in a cart or by a plough slip (*ekecsúsztató*), of which the most simple form is a V-shaped piece of wood. The plough is rolled onto it in such way that its handle slides on the ground while the plough beam is fastened to the forecarriage of the plough, and in this fashion it is dragged to the desired spot. Its advantage is that by carrying the plough on the slipe they spared the animals. Its disadvantage is that it wrecked the road, so that the authorities strongly forbade its use. As a result, wheeled versions developed later on, some of which grew practically into small carts.

In the Carpathian Basin, during the Middle Ages and even in later times, cattle, primarily oxen, pulled the plough. They harnessed six to eight oxen to larger ploughs on more difficult soil, and two to four oxen to smaller ploughs. In such cases one man drove, that is, directed the oxen, while the other held the plough handle. Oxen were more and more replaced by horses from the 18th century on, especially in the Tiszántúl, where they preferred the faster moving horses for getting around between the farmsteads. We find in many places, especially in the 19th and 20th centuries, that cows were put to the yoke in ploughing, but always at the hands of the poorest peasants. The bison as a plough animal occurs first of all in Transylvania and in smaller numbers in the southern part of Transdanubia.

The first spring ploughing is the great event of peasant life. Usually they would not start on Friday, which was thought to be a day of ill omen, but on the lucky days of Tuesday and Thursday. When they first went out into the fields they sprinkled the cart, and even the man sitting on it, with water, so that he would be lucky all year round. They pulled the plough, which was laid onto the slipe, through some bread and an egg placed at the gate (Krasznokvajda, Abaúj County). If the egg remained whole they took it along and ploughed it into the first furrow, to assure a plentiful harvest.

The reversible plough always returned alongside the same track, ploughing in the opposite direction and as a consequence the mouldboard and coulter were reversed at the end of the field. The mouldboard plough could turn the soil only to one side, so that they had to take a wide turn with it, which is why they also called it *detour plough*. At the time of *joint ploughing,* they marked the centre of the field precisely and drew a furrow on it. They turned the next furrow immediately next to and toward the first one so that it created a ridge in the middle. They started the *ploughing apart* at the right corner of the field, so that the plough turned the soil toward the edge of the field. It was not necessary to mark the centre at this time, because the two last furrows marked it anyway at the end.

They ended up, after finishing the first furrow, on the opposite side of the field from where they began, turning the soil outward, and always turning to the left. Thus, at completion, a wide, deep furrow was formed in the middle of the field. They interchanged the two ploughing methods annually or often at each ploughing.

They used ridge and furrow ploughing *(bakhátas szántás)* on soil that was wet and hard to dry out. They divided the field into small strips 2 to 3 metres wide, and ploughed each of them by the joint ploughing system. Thus a ridge formed in the centre, from which the water drained easily into the furrows between. They used this ploughing method

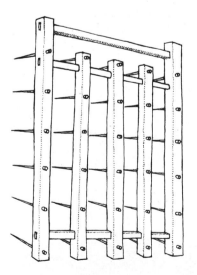

Fig. 71. Harrow, a wooden frame with iron teeth. Nyíri, Abaúj County. 1950s

chiefly in western Hungary, but it also occurred in some of the swampy regions of the Great Plain.

Historical data show that, in connection with rotation farming, the practice of annually ploughing three times for the autumn grain had already developed generally by the end of the Middle Ages. The plough was entered most deeply at the last ploughing, which was then followed by sowing. For a long time they turned the soil only once in the spring for the spring grain. In the Great Plain, but especially in the Tiszántúl after the Turkish occupation, they ploughed for the autumn grain only once, rarely twice, and this practice survived even into the 20th century.

As the ploughed soil is usually lumpy, the *toothed harrow* is used to break it up. Its rectangular forms appear to be the older, its triangular forms the newer. They used the *spike harrow* generally in the central part of the Carpathian Basin, while at other places they used it sporadically, primarily to cover over the seeds.

The most generally grown grain from the Middle Ages on is *wheat (Triticum aestivum),* which at one time was differentiated according to spring and autumn types. *Rye (Secale cereale)* is grown primarily on sandy and hilly areas. But it also happens that these two most important bread cereals are mixed to produce "double" or, by another name, *abajdoc,* which is very popular in certain regions. In addition to these, there are several cereal grains which have partially or entirely died out today. Such are *spelt (Triticum spelta)* and *einkorn (Triticum monococcum),* the production of which can be traced in the Carpathian Basin as far back as the New Stone Age. The fact that it has a brief growing season, makes excellent porridge, and prospers in newly broken turfy ground, preserved *millet (Panicum miliaceum)* among the cereal grains for a long time. *Buckwheat (Polygonum fagopyrum)* was grown especially in the high mountains because it tolerates the cold well. It survived the longest as a porridge cereal in Székelyland and around the western border.

Some kinds of grains are primarily used as fodder for animals. Among these the most important is *barley (Hordeum vulgare),* one of the oldest cultivated plants in the Carpathian Basin. Much newer in origin are *oats (Avena sativa),* the real home of which can be found in the area north of Hungary. Both cereals are primarily used as fodder, and only out of necessity is food made out of them.

Seed grain was always selected with the greatest care. For this purpose the seeds that flew the farthest against the wind at the time of winnowing were put aside. Since this is the seed most ripe and heaviest, it is consequently the most suitable for sowing. At other times a canvas was spread on the bottom of the cart when they hauled the sheaves in, and kept the seeds that fell on it for sowing, because they were the best. The seeds to be sown were soaked in water, and what settled gave the richest harvest.

The day of sowing was related to natural phenomena and to observations. The autumn wheat had to be sown into the soil after the fall of the oak and ash leaves, while the spring wheat was to go into the furrow after the first appearance of the badger and the crow. It was a general rule

Sowing

that "sowing has to be done in the dust in the fall, in the mud in the spring". Barley is to go into the ground when the wild plum is in bloom or when the cuckoo begins to sing.

Other traditions either prohibit sowing on certain days or relate it to some saint's name day. Accordingly they have to leave out the day of *Blighted Peter,* because grain sown on that day will be blighted. Sowing is prohibited in the entire week of *Matthew,* because only the chaff would sprout from the seed, which is why they call this whole week "chaff week".

In more recent times the *tablecloth* has been substituted in most places by a sack for holding the seed. The sower went out to the field early in the morning and took very good care not to meet a woman on his way, because no luck would follow his work then. He put his hat down at the end of the field and asked God's blessing on his sowing. Then he began the sow. It is a tranquil, rhythmic work, which cannot be hurried. There were some who sowed stepping on one leg, that is, threw the seed at every second step, and there were some who threw it on each step. The sower was careful not to sow too wide, because then the blades grew up sparsely. This work is amongst the most delicate, demanding much practice and, above all, a sense of judgement.

Ploughing and sowing were always done by men, women rarely taking part in it even as helpers. After the blades grew out, weeds growing in the grain were weeded with a small, shovel-like iron *(acatoló)*. This, however, was always the job of children and women, with men supervising on the large estates.

Apart from weeding, the growing grain requires little care. At most the birds need to be frightened away with *scarecrows* when the grain begins to turn yellow. The growing phases of the wheat are determined as follows: the grain begins to grow into the stalk on Saint George's day (April 24); the ears appear in May; it stops growing on the day of Guy (June 15); and its root breaks on the day of Peter and Paul (June 29). From here on it just ripens and the harvest can begin.

Harvest day was carefully chosen. Harvesting was not begun during new moon, and the day of Elias was also thought to be unlucky, because lighting might strike. If the first day of harvest was to fall on a Friday, enough had to be cut down on Thursday for a sheaf, so that the main work of harvesting should not begin on a day thought to be unlucky.

One of the tools of the harvest is the sickle *(sarló)*, which is a pre-

Harvesting and Harvesting Customs

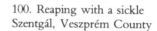

100. Reaping with a sickle
Szentgál, Veszprém County

Fig. 72. Scythe-sickle. Nagyborzova, former Abaúj County. 1950s

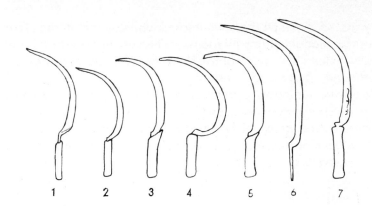

Fig. 73. Sickles. 1–3. "Magyar" sickles.
Cigánd, former Zemplén County.
4. "Tót" (Slovakian) sickle, from the same
place. 5. Upper Tisza region.
6. Jászberény, Szolnok County. 7. Former
Gömör County. Late 19th century

Conquest word in the Hungarian language, adopted from the Turkic. We differentiate two basic types: the *toothed sickle* and the smooth bladed *kaszasarló.* Two types of the latter were known in the Carpathian Basin, distinguished by the curvature and the way of attachment to the handle. One is the *curved form,* the blade of which, starting out from the handle, continues straight for a good while and bends only toward the end. It seems to be a general European type, its equivalents were already found in Hungary by the Magyars. The other widens out just above the handle, becomes arched and only then continues upward. This generally is stronger and in many cases also thicker than the other one. Up-to-date research considers these to be more likely Eastern in origin, because similar ones have been found in Hun and Avar graves as well as in graves dating from the Conquest. This form eclipsed the previous form. These tools were used only for cutting down grain. The smooth-bladed sickle, on the other hand, was earlier used for cutting grass, and later, especially beginning with the last century, it was used in many places for harvesting. After the scythe gained ground, the sickle was used for gathering together the sheaves.

Harvesting with the sickle is mostly woman's work, and men seldom participated in it, apart from the youngest and the oldest. The harvester grasped as many stalks as would fit in his hand, cut it with an upward movement, and put it on strawbands already laid out. The sheaves were always tied by the men, whose task it also was to pile them into stacks of various sizes. Harvesting with the sickle has become less important, especially since the 19th century, until today it occurs only sporadically, in peripheral and in mountain regions.

The other grain-cutting tool is the *scythe.* But while the toothed sickle is a tool used exclusively for cutting cereal crops, the scythe originally was used mowing grass. The Hungarian scythe is a slightly curving steel blade, 70–110 cm long, with a ridged back along its outer edge. Its shaft is 170–220 cm long, depending on the height of the person using it. It has one handle in the mountainous regions, two in the steppes. With the twin handles the scythe can be lowered closer to the ground and a shorter stubble cut. The blade is fastened to the shaft with a ring and set at an angle suitable for the work to be done. At harvest times, especially in the Great Plain, they fasten on it a cradle called a *csapó,* slasher, made out of 2 or 3 twigs, in order to spread the cut stalks better (cf. Fig. 74). The Palotses cover it with linen to further reduce the dropping of seeds. For

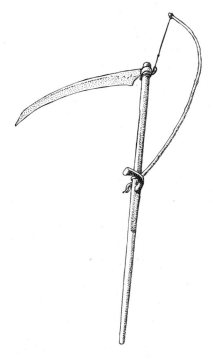

Fig. 74. A scythe with a slasher. Great
Plain.
First half of 20th century. General

206

the same reason they tie a rake or fork on the scythe in certain parts of Transdanubia and Upper Hungary. The blade of the scythe is hammered on an iron anvil, and, if it becomes blunt, sharpened with a whetstone.

We possess data regarding the use of the scythe for harvesting cereal crops only from the 16th and 17th centuries. The agricultural literature of the late 18th century and of the 19th century recommends it as a better and more progressive working tool. From this time on it completely eclipsed the sickle. Only men worked with the scythe, whereas women gathered the sheaves. Binding and gathering the sheaves was again considered masculine work.

Earlier, scythes were used to cut sheaves in a row. In the Great Plain the rows were then pulled together and small stacks, called *vontató,* were made out of them. Two or three forkfuls of crops were made to stand with ears upright in the centre and the rest stacked around them, with

101. Reaping with scythes
Diósjenő, Nógrád County

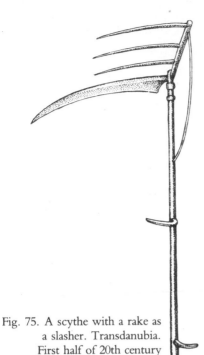

Fig. 75. A scythe with a rake as a slasher. Transdanubia. First half of 20th century

102. a. Wooden holder for whetstone Hungary b. Corn dolley Gégény, Szabolcs-Szatmár County c. Corn dolley Sárospatak

the ears outwards. At man's height, the stack was shaped to a point and covered. A thick rope was fixed around the bottom, about half a metre from the ground, hitched to a horse or an ox and thus hauled to the *threshing barn*. During the first half of the 19th century, four-wheeled, low wagons appeared in the Great Plain, with which it was possible to carry the grain in the ear without much loss. This way of handling cereal grains like mowed hay was continued longest with spring cereals.

Shearing the autumn cereals was usually done by *cutting into* the crop: that is, the cut stalks leaned toward the still-standing wall of grain. In this case a woman or a girl followed the cutter with her back to him and gathered the cut grain with a wooden hook or sickle. When enough of these were gathered, she laid them on strawbands already spread out for this purpose. The tied sheaves were stacked in the shape of a *cross,* just as in harvesting with a sickle. They placed the sheaves into the four sides of the *cross* in such a way that the ears lay inside on top of each other, while the cut ends pointed outward. They laid a sheaf on top of it, the name of which is *pap* (priest) in most of the linguistic area. The number of sheaves in the cross varies by regions. However, in the Middle Ages they counted with a system of sixty in most places, and so the *félkalangya* (half shock of corn) consisted of 15, the *kalangya* (shock of corn) of 30, and the *kepe* (double shock) of 60 sheaves. The counting system of sixty is probably ancient European in origin and came to the Hungarians most likely through Slavic mediation.

The conclusion of the harvest was a day of celebration, richly marked

208

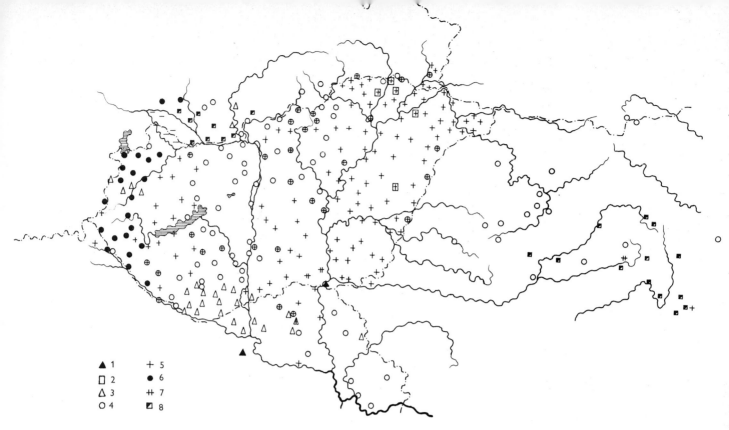

▲ 1	+ 5
▢ 2	● 6
△ 3	╫ 7
○ 4	◪ 8

by customs and superstitions. The family that harvested for itself did not put on much of a celebration at the end of the work, and among the poorer folk this came about only if they had done the work with mutual help. At such times the duty of being host fell to the *gazda* of the house, during the work as well as at the time of its completion.

The more prosperous farmers would engage share harvesters. When he first went out to oversee the work, the women and girls tied his legs with strawropes, and only let him go free if he gave them money, or promised wine and food. There was a belief that, if this was not done, the wheat would yield poorly. A few stalks were left after they finished harvesting, so that storm and shower would not cause damage to the crop in the following year.

The share harvesters also purposely left some grain standing on the stalk on the day of *completion,* which they cut down the following morning. The girls made a bell-like arrangement of wild flowers and corn with its ears. In some places corn-dollies were woven in the shape of a spiral or a tablet, according to local custom (cf. Ills. 102 b-c). Hanging the garland on a stick, the lads or maidens carried it to the yard of the farmer, singing as they went, or accompanied by gypsy music (cf. Ill. 26). There the farmer's wife sprinkled a few drops of water on the garland, to prevent blight on the next year's crop, while the leader of the harvesters greeted the farmer with a poem. They hung the garland on the main beam over the table, and underneath it served lunch or dinner, always accompanied by wine. The *harvest ball* followed, lasting until midnight, or often even until dawn. In many places the harvest garland was preserved until Christmas and then given to the birds, while at other places, they hung up the most beautiful ones in the church or a chapel, or on a roadside cross.

Fig. 76. The number of sheaves in each stock of harvested crops. 20th century.
1. 7 sheaves. 2. 9 sheaves. 3. 10 sheaves.
4. 13–15 sheaves. 5. 17–18 sheaves.
6. 20–21 sheaves. 7. 22 sheaves.
8. 26–30 sheaves

Treading and Threshing

Grain on the stalks that had been tied into sheaves was stored in the barn, if such existed. In the Great Plain and the eastern part of Transdanubia, they stored some of it in the open air in stacks *(asztag),* and some they trod out immediately. They carried it to the storage place on carts, stacked in one of the two ways known in the Carpathian Basin. In the Great Plain and generally in flat regions, two long *poles* are fastened onto the sides of the cart and the sheaves put on the cart so lengthened, with the ears facing inward. The sheaves are roped to the two ends of the poles. In mountain areas the carts are longer and their sides higher. In these areas cart ladders are not used, but a hay pole, *nyomórúd,* is laid on top of the sheaves and fastened to the four corners of the cart, so that the harvested grain cannot slide apart even if the cart should turn over. We find equivalents of the former towards the east, and of the latter rather towards the west.

From the Middle Ages on there were two processes for separating the grain: treading out *(nyomtatás),* which was done by animals, and threshing *(cséplés),* carried out with a flail. The former process mostly relates to South-Eastern Europe, while for the latter we must look to Central Europe. Treading out is the method used in the extensive agriculture of the Great Plain, a method further reinforced during the economic decline caused by the Turkish rule. Flail threshing prospered in the mountain and hill regions. They preferred to tread the grain in the eastern half of Transdanubia during the middle of the last century, while threshing with a flail was more general in the western half.

103. Treading out the corn
Átány, Heves County

104. Winnowing the corn
Mezőkövesd

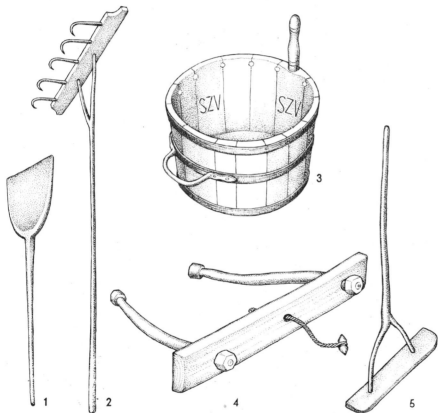

Fig. 77. Implements used when treading out crops. Kardoskút, Békés County. Early 20th century. 1. Shade for winnowing. 2. Rake for gathering chaff. 3. Noggin or bushel. 4. Wooden implement to draw together the threshed cereal. 5. Implement to shove the cereal together

The threshing floor used for treading out was mostly beside the ploughed field, or at some other place in the farmyard, the *threshing yard*, or at the loading place outside of the village (cf. Plate VII). Weeds were cleared from an area, which was in the shape of a circle or ellipse, then it was dug up and clay soil carried onto it. They spread chaff and straw on it and watered it whilst trampling it by horses or perhaps by carts. When the ground became smooth they scattered chaff and straw on it so that it would not crack in the strong sunshine.

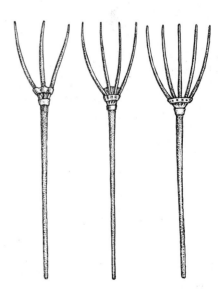

Fig. 78. Wooden forks with split spikes prongs or tines. 1. Szegvár, Csongrád County, 1896. 2. Kémér, former Szilágy County, 1942. 3. Doboz, Békés county, 1934

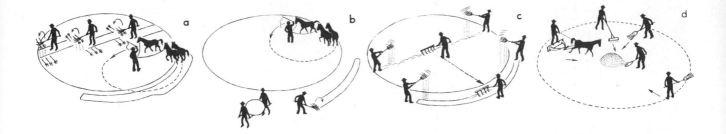

Fig. 79. Phases of treading out crops with horses. Kardoskút, Békés County. First half of 20th century. a) Turning around the heap of crops. b) Horses treading out the crops and men carrying away the empty straw. c) Winnowing, dividing the cereal from the chaff. d) Collecting the cereal in a heap called *garmada*

105. Threshing with a flail Óbánya, Baranya County

They "made the bed" *(beágyazás)* for treading on the completed threshing floor, that is to say, they covered the entire area, thickly and evenly, with loosened sheaves. They then led the horses on it, 2 to 8, according to need and availability. Because the work was hard both for horse and man, they relieved them if it was possible. In most cases the whip-man *(ostoros)* stood in the centre and drove the horses (less frequently oxen) in a circle, adjusting the length of the tether, so that the horses walked on all parts of the bed of grain equally. Another method was to set a post into the centre of the threshing floor, and the rope of the circling horses wound around it. Thus they moved in decreasing circles towards the centre. In some places, carts were also used for treading out. They yoked the horses and drove the carts around on the grain. When the grain on the stalk had broken down sufficiently on the bed of grain *(ágyás)*, it was turned over with a wooden fork and shaken so that the

seeds would fall out of it. They repeated this process three times, and only then did they fling the straw off. They pushed the chaff and seeds to the edge of the threshing ground in a heap *(garmada),* and waited for a suitable wind for winnowing.

Threshing with the flail was always done inside the settlement, in the yard or in the barn. In both places they would prepare a square threshing floor, stamp it down, and plaster it over, so that not a single grain should be lost. The flail *(csép)* consists of two parts, the handle *(nyél)* and the souple *(hadaró),* which was half as long. The two are linked by a thong in such a way that the souple can rotate. In most cases everyone makes this tool for himself, and there are always a few pieces around, hanging on the beams of the barn. They lay down two rows of tied sheaves with the ears facing each other. They thresh these, then turn them over with the handle of the flail and thresh the other side as well. At this stage the ripest seeds fall out, and are stored for sowing. Next they untie the sheaves and carry out a fresh, more thorough threshing, and after they have beaten out every seed they brush the straw off with the help of the flail. They first clean the chaffy seed with a rake, then collect the seeds in a corner of the barn. If several people are doing the threshing then they beat rhythmically, the rhythm changing according to how many people are working together. The number of the threshers can be told from a distance by the noise of beating.

The seeds left after treading out or threshing have to be cleaned of

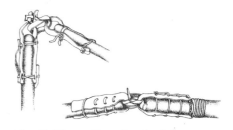

Fig. 80. Ways of fastening the flail to its handle. a) Magyarszerdahely, Zala County. b) Szalonna, Borsod County, 1930s

106. Threshing with a flail
Szentgál, Veszprém County

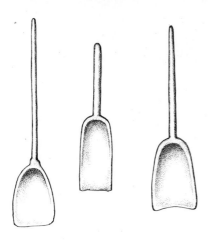

Fig. 81. Winnowing spades. a) Szegvár, Csongrád County. b) Oltszem, former Háromszék County, c) Füzér, former Abaúj County. Late 19th century

chaff and bits of straw. The most general method is winnowing *(szórás),* which was done in a different way in the Great Plain and in the hill and mountain regions. They waited for the wind on the plain, and when it came they threw the grain up against it with a long-handled wooden shovel. The heaviest, ripest seeds could easily fly against the wind and thus reached the ground the fastest, while the refuse grain and the chaff fell at the winnower's feet. Another man stood at the side and tried to drive off the remaining waster from the clean seeds with a wide wicker broom.

It is relatively easier to create a draught in the barn by opening the two doors, located opposite each other. Here, between the doors, they threw up the chaffy grain in a half circle, in the direction of the wind, but with a much shorter-handled shovel. In some places they did this whole process sitting down and with a very short-handled wooden shovel, both granary doors remaining shut. In this case only the resistance of the air does the job of winnowing.

Even after winnowing, the grain was still not completely clean. Therefore, they poured it into a trough and picked out the visible dirt, the bits of soil, by hand, before taking it to the mill. In some places they washed it thoroughly and spread it out to dry.

The cleansing processes described above were closely connected with treading out and with flail-threshing of grain, and disappeared with the mechanical threshing and winnowing of the grain.

Hoed Plants

Hoed plants, the majority of which were imported from America, moved into plough-land cultivation from the 17th century. These gained an ever-growing significance both as fodder for the animals and as food for the people. Together with the new plant culture, new knowledge, tools and procedures also became naturalized. At first the new plants were grown in the garden, but soon they were moved out to the ploughed fields, where they first of all took over the place of the fallow field and, in this way, advanced the break-up of the rotation system and in some places even caused its termination.

The *potato (Sloanum)* is one of the most important food staples of our century, which today occupies about five per cent of the country's cultivated land. It appeared on the plough lands in the 18th century, but did not spread easily among the peasants, because its method of cultivation was contrary to methods with which they were familiar. The lean years of the 19th century, in conjunction with vigorous urging by the authorities and landlords, helped its domestication. Its propagation was also advanced by the fact that in most places they did not have to pay a tithe on it. Its regional locations developed at this time (Nyírség, Somogy, Vas counties), where the plough lands planted with potatoes exceed more than ten per cent of the total cultivated land. Producing for the market began in these areas already at the beginning of the 19th century. Planting is done in the spring with hoes, planting sticks *(cuca),* or by following the plough and planking it into every third furrow. It is hoed two or three times, then in the autumn dug out from the ground with a flat or, in some places, a two-forked spade. During the 19th century, especially in regions where potatoes were grown in large quantities, they were taken up with the plough, which was used to split the drill. They were stored in prism-shaped pits, covered with straw and soil as protection from frost, and to keep them until spring. Smaller quantities were stored in cellars, or in pits in the yard or garden.

Today the *sunflower (Helianthus annuus L.)* is the most important oil-supplying plant in Hungary. Its proliferation is even more recent than that of the potato. Although we can find drawings of it in 16th-century books on botany, it was treated at that time as an ornamental plant in the gardens of the upper nobility. Familiarization with its excellent oil at the end of the 18th century suddenly boosted its popularity. At first it was planted in the garden around the house, and only during the first half of the 19th century was the cultivation moved out to the plough land. Its larger-scale production began only in the second half of the century, primarily at places where, for religious reasons, people did not cook with pig lard during a large portion of the year but used oil instead. On the plough fields it is still planted on the borders of potato and cornfields, especially on peasant farmsteads, and its planting in whole fields has come about only during our century, even on the large estates. They

107. Potato picking
Bercel, Nógrád County

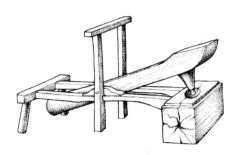

Fig. 82. A large wooden mortar with the pestle moved by feet for pounding paprika, called *külü*. Szeged. 1930s

planted it in larger quantities in the Nyírség, in the southern and south-eastern part of Transdanubia, and in between the Danube and the Tisza. The cut-down heads were carted home, dried in the granary, on the porch, or on an out-of-the-way part of the yard, then the seeds were beaten out with sticks and beaters. This is usually an evening's work done with help, but it is also a time of entertainment that gives a chance for story telling and singing.

The *paprika (Capsicum annuum L.)* is a spice originating in America, without which it is impossible to imagine the Hungarian kitchen. It occurred already in the gardens of the nobility in the 16th century, but it was then grown only as a flower or medicine. It became popular among the peasants in the 18th century. In all likelihood this wave may have come from the south, perhaps through the Bulgarian gardeners or through the Catholic Serbians who also wandered in from the south. Two significant cultivation regions developed in early times, which exist until today. One is at Szeged and its surrounding region, and the other is north of these around Kalocsa. There is one significant difference in the method of production at the two places. At the former they grow the seedlings in hothouses and then plant them outside, while at the latter they throw the paprika seeds directly into the ground and thin them out after they have come up. The paprika is a very delicate plant which needs to be hoed two or three times. It also needs a lot of water, especially until the seedlings have taken root. In the past they began to pick it after the birthday of the Virgin Mary (8 September), but recently they have started somewhat earlier, at the end of August. The gathered paprika is first dried for a short time, then strung up. This is communal work reaching late into the night, and gives a chance for entertainment. The core of the completely dried paprika is removed, broken up, cleaned, then ground in a wooden mortar *(külü)* operated on foot, or in the case of larger quantities, in a paprika mill with a grindstone.

Tobacco (Nicotiana L.) had already become known in Hungary by the 16th century, but at first it was used only as medicine. The Turks also had a role in its dispersion. Decrees prohibiting smoking became increasingly frequent from the 17th century on, but these led to no results. At the beginning of the 18th century, tobacco was grown not only in gardens but on the fields as well, and tobacco regions involving certain villages and regions came into existence. The smoothing of tobacco is also work done in company, like the jobs mentioned above. The growers of paprika and tobacco, because the plants require special skills, developed into an occupational group, but while the former were assured a relatively good livelihood, the tobacco growers, who cultivated land rented from the large estates, for the most part barely surpassed the living standards of the farmhands of the large estates.

Maize (Zea mays) had already appeared in production by the first half of the 17th century in Hungary. This undemanding plant spread rapidly and quickly found its way from the garden to the fields, especially because for a long time farmers had to pay no tithe or ninth for it. The area planted increased more and more, until today it has approached, and at times even surpasses, that used to grow wheat. Today one quarter

of the entire Hungarian sowing area bears crops of maize, but in certain regions it exceeds 30 or even 40 per cent.

The cultivation of maize differs greatly from that of other, earlier known cereal types, although at first they tried to adjust it to others. They simply threw the carefully selected seeds in the ground and ploughed over them, or sowed them on the ploughed field and harrowed them in. They generally put the date of sowing on St. George's Day (April 24). There are several superstitions attached to the sowing. Thus, in the southern part of Transdanubia,the first seeds were sown with closed eyes, through the slit of the skirt, so that the rodents should not find it. In the Nyírség, smoking was prohibited during sowing, to keep the blight away from the crop. In Szatmár County, the belief was that if you looked into the sun during sowing, then your wish for lots of red ears among the crop would be fulfilled. Egg yolks were eaten at the completion of the sowing in Kemenesalja, so that the ears should be all the more yellow.

Sowing in rows or drills replaced scattered sowing in the 19th century. They used a four-toothed *marker,* with which they marked the maize rows on the ploughed field. Along this they threw the seeds into holes pierced with a stick or made with a boot-heel, and covered them with the feet. Two people worked together when sowing with a hoe. One lifted the soil with the hoe, the other threw 3 or 4 seeds under it. Many people eliminated the drawing of lines by dropping the seeds into every third furrow at ploughing, which was covered by the plough during the next turn. To make sowing in rows easier, various sowing devices, fastened onto the plough beam, appeared during the last century, made from wood by handy peasants or from iron by the local blacksmith.

During the 19th century they hoed the maize once for weeds and once to earth up the stalks. The first hoeing took place shortly after the maize came up, when only the most strongly developed plants were left growing in one cluster. Earth was hoed up around the maize stalks immediately before harvesting. Many people opposed this procedure from the second half of the century, and it indeed ceased on the large estates. However, in the peasant farmsteads this hoeing up survived in most parts of the country till the period of collectivization, because they believed that the stalks supported in this way were less likely to be bent or knocked over by the wind. The horse hoe *(lókapa)* appeared at the beginning of the last century. Its earliest form was actually similar to a symmetrical plough of smaller size. It only showed up at larger peasant farmsteads in the second half of the 19th century, while it never really reached the poor peasants. The superstition that palms rubbed with soil from the first stroke of the hoe will not blister is linked with hoeing in Göcsej. In southern Transdanubia they hoed during the last quarter of the moon, because it was thought that the weeds could be better destroyed then.

The fact that it is hard to see far into the tall, growing maize, was favourable to thieves. Therefore, from the beginning of the ripening the field keeper stayed in the fields all the time. He raised by his hut a 4 to 5 m high pillar similar to those of the herdsmen, on which, to make climbing easy, he fastened some rungs crosswise. Thus he could survey

109. Corn husking
Mezőkövesd

218

at any time the maize he had been entrusted to guard. Field keepers were paid in maize, getting 30 to 100 ears for each cadastral acre as well as a part of any thief's fine. Otherwise they had to pay for all damage that befell the crop. Keepers came out of the ranks of older farmhands and herdsmen.

Maize generally ripens in September, which is when the picking takes place (cf. Ill. 34). Two forms have been known from the earliest times, depending on how the ears are broken off the stalk, whether with or without the husk attached. In the latter case, they use a small wooden opener (bontófa) that can be fastened to the wrist, with which they rip open the husk and twist out the clean ear. The shape of such wooden openers corresponds with the ones used at one time by the American Indians. Numerous data indicate that it may have become part of the Hungarian peasant's stock of tools during the turn of the century through migrants who had been to America. Originating from the large estates, clean picking spread increasingly.

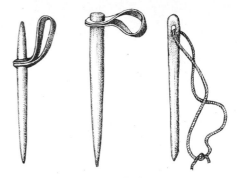

Fig. 83. Wooden pegs for husking corn from the cob. Békés County. 1930s

The other method is to pick the ears with the husk on and carry them home in carts. The cobs were piled into big heaps in the yard or barn and the relatives and neighbours were called over for the evening to help husk them. This counted as the most pleasant work and entertainment during the mild, early autumn evenings. Husking cobs is important work and has to be done urgently, because the ears cannot be kept long in their husks without danger of spoiling. Much tradition and many customs are connected with husking. Thus, a special significance is given to those who find a red ear: it means that the lucky young man or girl is going to get married next year. Red ears hung at the front of the house signal that there is a marriageable girl inside.

Rarely is *masquerading* left out of husking, when the young men try to scare the girls. They put on white sheets, paste on beards and mous-taches made from maize silk, and perhaps carve a death's head or mask from a pumpkin. They go thus from one place to another. Songs are likely to come forth during husking, especially songs connected in some way with maize. This gathering is an excellent opportunity for story telling, although not so much for the long fairy tales as for the scarey, superstitious legends which are listened to in great silence. Story telling is the job of the older folks, who are often invited only for that purpose. Usually fruit, boiled potatoes, and corked maize sprayed with poppy seeds and sweetened with honey is served to the helpers. Sometimes they also have some sweet pastries and a few glasses of wine. When they have finished the work, they dance to the sound of a zither or, earlier, of a bagpipe. At large huskings they even hired a gypsy musician. The dance rarely lasted past midnight, since next day at dawn picking had to continue.

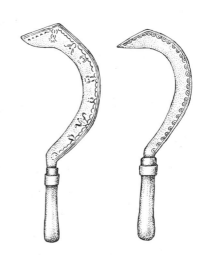

Fig. 84. Old types of billhooks for cutting maize. Csongrád County. Late 19th century

Not only the ear of maize was made use of but the stalk of the corn as well, which counted as a medium-grade fodder. During the first half of the 19th century, in many places the stalk was left outside, and in winter time the cattle grazed it on the spot. During the second half of the last century the shortage of fodder became so great that it was regularly gathered in. This was done with a sickle, reed cutter, stalk cutter made out of a scythe blade, axe, or hoe, the implement differing regionally or by the size of the land holding. The stalks were tied into sheaves, which were stood on their ends, stacked in cones, and hauled home during the winter frost. They were placed in the yard or threshing yard, and fed to the cattle by spring. The remaining segments, just like the *stump* which was carefully taken out of the ground, were the most important heating fuel on the plain from the beginning of the last century.

Shelling maize is a winter occupation, with a great many variations. The most simple way to shell maize is by hand if it is dry enough. At other times they rub two ears together, but even more frequently they rub the seeds off with a cob. To make this easier, first a few rows are pushed off with a pointed iron tool. At some places a blade is driven into the edge of a small chair and the ears repeatedly pulled over it, the seeds falling into the basket placed underneath. The sheller, a utensil that fits onto the hand appears to be more recent. Its teeth pick off the seeds from corncob. Shelling chairs, the fronts of which are studded with nails, are based on essentially the same idea. It used to be customary to thresh maize in the south-western part of Transdanubia and in Transylvania. In Transylvania, the threshing basket is also used. When cobs are put into it and beaten with bent sticks or wooden mallets, the seeds fall out of its plank bottom through small holes. Various sizes of shelling machines proliferated from the middle of the last century.

From a comparison of historical, linguistic, and ethnographic data, it appears that two centres of maize growing developed in the Carpathian Basin: one is Transylvania, the other Transdanubia, especially its southern part. The new plant appeared early in both places. Its method of cultivation and use clearly shows that in one place the Rumanians, and in the other the South Slavs may have been the mediators.

Maize replaced in the diet the porridge plants (millet, buckwheat, einkorn, barley) and took over their nutritional role. The role of these plants in feeding animals, principally in the fattening of pigs, was likewise eclipsed. When the practice of fattening for the market increased, from the beginning of the last century, the area of maize sown increased simultaneously. Its role in human diet has since gradually decreased and its use pushed increasingly in the direction of fodder. Today food is prepared from maize regularly only in certain parts of Transylvania and in a few parts of Transdanubia.

Processing Cereals

Cereal grains first have to be crushed to prepare them for human consumption. The simplest and most ancient tool for this purpose is the *wooden mortar,* which is carved out of a single piece of wood. In it the grain was crushed, formerly with a wooden, more recently with an iron pestle. It is still used in the peripheral areas, but at most to crack millet and corn for the chickens, or less frequently to crush poppy seeds or perhaps paprika.

A technically more developed version of the mortar is the large sized *külü,* which they set in motion by foot or by shifting the body weight. Some had several grinding holes, and a corresponding number of men could work simultaneously. They dehusked millet and buckwheat with these, and used them until very recently for crushing paprika.

A faster and more profitable process is the grinding of cereal seeds between two stones. The bottom stone is always fixed, while the top stone can be turned. The grain to be ground is allowed to trickle in through the eye in the centre of the top stone. This simple hand tool, traceable to ancient times, has survived sporadically in peasant households until today. Earlier it was used to grind flour for meal, later on to grind salt and fodder for the animals. Two versions of it are known. In one the handle is fastened directly on the top stone so that it can be brought into motion only with a strong effort. We can find versions of this form from Roman times, and its connections are primarily towards the west. The handle of the other type is fastened to an overlying beam, so that it is easier to use. This method appears frequently among the Eastern Slavs also.

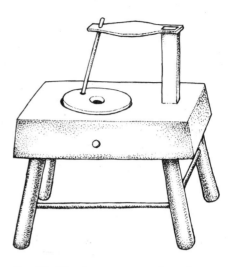

Fig. 85. Wooden mortars and pestles. a) Göcsej, Zala County. b) Former Bereg County. Late 19th century

Hungarian grain production, which was large in quantity and looked back over a considerable past, also gave rise to the creation of a long line of mills driven by water, animals, or wind. The word *malom* (mill) itself and the attached *molnár* (miller), as well as a whole series of names for parts, are Slavic in origin, and are words which the Magyars may have learned already before the end of the 10th century. The name most likely referred to a water mill, since in the following century (1083–95) a whole string of mills is mentioned in the Bakony. It is probable that mills driven by animals gained ground at a later period, while windmills, which originated in the west and appeared only in the 17th century, really gained ground only during the next century.

Two broad groups of *watermills* can be differentiated in the Carpathian Basin. One is the horizontal type with a scoop wheel, the other the vertical water-wheel type. The former occurs relatively rarely. The wheel turns horizontally in the water, and a spindle rises perpendicularly from its centre, with its top end fastened directly to the upper millstone. Thus the wheel turns the millstone by direct drive, with no intermediate gearing. This type is known in southern Transylvania as well as in the Dráva region, so that its ties can probably be sought in the direction of the Balkan Peninsula.

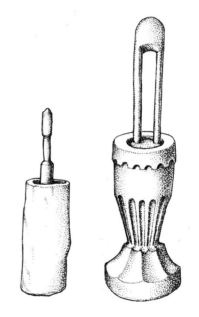

Fig. 86. Hand-mill. Szalonna, Borsod County. 1930s

The vertical watermill can also be divided into two broad groups, one undershot *(alulcsapós),* and the other overshot *(felülcsapós).* The former were built on wide, quietly flowing rivers, so that they were also called *hajómalom* (boat mill). The entire mill and the adjoining mill house were shaped like an ark so that they could be towed to a safe place when the ice flood began. The somewhat smaller store-boat *(tárhajó),* attached to the boat mill, not only housed the grain to be ground, but at the same time also supported the outer end of the axle of the huge wheel. It was made entirely of wood, primarily of oak, except that the cog-wheels were carved out of hornbeam. The daily output of the boat mill can be assessed at approximately 10–12 ql, which was greater than the performance of windmills but less than that of animal-powered mills.

The number of *overshot watermills* always greatly exceeded the number of undershot mills, since it was easy to channel the dammed-up water of any little stream from above onto the paddles of the wheels. The watermills were made and repaired by the millers themselves, who were also excellent carpenters. Usually the miller's family lived in a house

110. A "dry" mill drawn by a horse
Szarvas

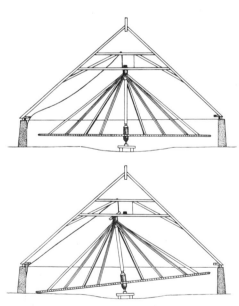

Fig. 87. The construction of the round-
about of a "dry" mill when not
functioning, and when ready to be drawn
by a horse. Szarvas, Békés County. 19th
century

attached to the mill. The miller hired help, an assistant or apprentice, only in larger mills which had several pairs of stones. He collected a duty on the milled grain, and either rendered an account of it to the landlord or redeemed the rental dues for the whole year in one sum.

Dry mills *(szárazmalom)* were driven by animal power and their occurrence in Hungary can be traced all the way to the Middle Ages. Nothing shows their significance better than the fact that 7,966 of them were still operating in the country in 1863, but their numbers were reduced to 651 forty years later. The dry mill consisted of two parts. One was the *kerengősátor* (turning tent) or horse-walk, in which the horses turned the huge wheel that brought the millstone into motion. The other was the *millhouse,* where the grinding mechanism was housed and where there was also space for the grain waiting to be milled or for the ground flour. The person wanting to have his grain milled had to provide the turning power, for the miller merely ran the turning mechanism. Usually he had a long time to wait, because the work progressed slowly. The men who gathered from the village or from neighbouring settlements liked to talk and tell stories to shorten the slowly passing hours. Thus the mills fulfilled an important function not only in spreading news, but in spreading certain intellectual traditions as well.

One version of the dry mill was the treadmill *(tiprómalom)*. Its large wheel was clad with sloping planks, on which the animal moved, seemingly climbing upwards but actually remaining in one place. In this way the big wheel came into motion, and by means of cog-wheel gearing it turned the millstone.

222

Windmills *(szélmalom)* are relative latecomers to Hungary. They spread primarily in the Great Plain in parts of certain regions of Transdanubia. The more primitive form is the post windmill *(bakos szélmalom),* built on a huge central beam rising perpendicularly from the ground. With its help the mill could be turned in the proper direction to catch the wind. This type of mill is generally used in the Mediterranean region, coming to the western part of Europe perhaps at the time of the Crusades and moving to Hungary from there, but it never came into general use and only a few pictures and notes preserve its memory. In the southern part of the Great Plain (Hódmezővásárhely), there were still in the recent past a few small sized *wind grinders* that worked on the same principle.

111. Working in a mill
Gyimesközéplok, former Csík County

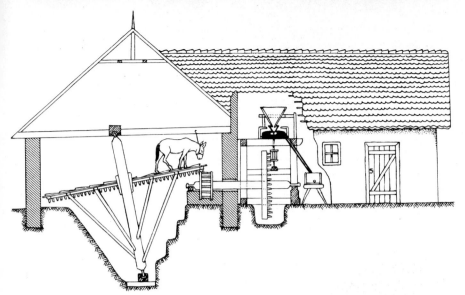

Fig. 88. The construction of a treadmill. Bakonypeterd, Veszprém County. 1930s

The windmills that are best known, and of which a few have come down to us, belong to the so-called *tower*-mill type, the equivalents of which are found primarily in Holland. It is thought that its plans were first brought back by those Protestant students who frequently visited the universities of Holland from the 17th century on. The tower was built of adobe, or more frequently of baked bricks. The millers not only built the wall, but also did the carpentry work, which required extraordinary precision. They joined together the beams, carved the cog-

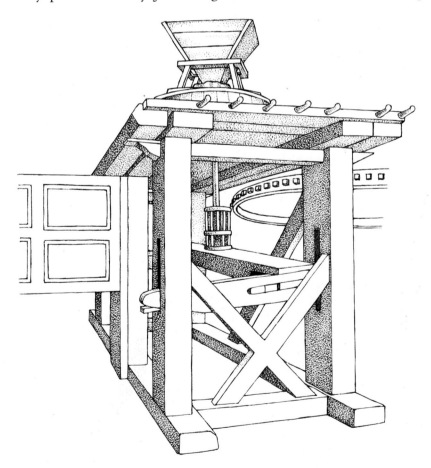

Fig. 89. The construction of a grinder for oily seeds. Mekényes, Békés County. Early 20th century

112. Windmill
Kiskundorozsma, Csongrád County

wheels, made the frame of the sail, and ornamented the cover plates of the interior machinery with rich carvings. They divided the structure into several floors. The stones, the driving mills, and storage room were located in separate areas. The four-vaned sail, attached to the roof section on the outside, could be moved, along with the entire roof, to face the direction desired with the help of a long beam from below. The use of windmills lasted longer than that of dry mills. 475 were registered in the entire country in 1863, ten years later their number had increased to 854, and in 1906 the number was still 691. The majority were operating between the Danube and Tisza.

We can also list among the mills the oil presses *(olajütő)*, the various versions of which can be found over the entire linguistic region. They pressed out the oil primarily from pumpkin, hemp, flax, sunflower seeds, and acorns.

Grapes and Wine

Viniculture has always had great importance in Hungarian life. Words originating from before the Conquest prove that the Magyars had already become acquainted with the cultivation of this plant in the Khazar Khaganate. Examples are *szőlő,* grape; *bor,* wine; *szűr,* strain; *seprő, dregs; ászok,* gauntry for barrels; *homlit,* provine; *bujt,* plant; *lyuk,* hole; *pince,* cellar, etc. The most recent research demonstrates that traces of tools and procedures brought from the east can best be found in the north-eastern part of the linguistic territory. Transdanubia also displays characteristics resembling one-time Roman traditions. The rich body of knowledge was influenced in many respects by the Walloons who settled in Hungary in the 12th–13th centuries and were well acquainted with viniculture, and again by the Serbs and other South Slav peoples who were fleeing from Turkish rule, and later by the Germans arriving from the west.

During the last century, 3 to 5 per cent of the cultivated land of the country was covered by grapes. However, this percentage was drastically changed by the phylloxera plight that brought destruction in the last quarter of the 19th century. Whereas in the 19th century grapes growing on sandy soil made up about 14 per cent of the entire grape-growing area, the percentage has been considerably increased in our century, because phylloxera cannot breed in sandy soil. So today 41 per cent of the entire grape region flourishes on clay soil, and 59 per cent on sand; that is to say, grapes were only partially re-established in the traditional wine regions following the phylloxera plight.

Accounts have been kept of outstanding wine-producing regions since the Middle Ages. Among those that look back in particular on a great and long tradition are Sopron, Eger, Villány and Szekszárd, where red wine is produced primarily. Among the white wine regions the most outstanding ones are Tokaj-Hegyalja, Balaton-felvidék, Gyöngyös, Mór, etc. It is worth mentioning the *furmint* among the numerous old species; it supposedly preserves the memory of the one-time Walloon settlement at Tokaj-Hegyalja.

Cultivation of the grapes usually starts in March with opening and pruning. They believe that this procedure has to be done when the first

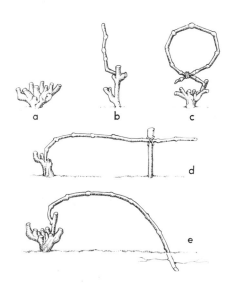

Fig. 90. Vine-stocks and methods of growing vine-shoots. Region of Gyöngyös. 20th century.
a) Dressing the shoot to clear eyes.
b) Dressing the shoot upwards like a rod
c) Dressing the shoot to form a hoop
d) Binding the shoot to a support
e) Digging the end of the shoot underground

226

fruit trees begin to bloom. Pruning is an extremely important operation, because the quantity and quality of the yield can be regulated by it. Formerly, in a considerable part of the country they pruned to a *kopaszfej* (bald top), that is, they left eyes only on the round-shaped vine stock. At the end of the last century a characteristic form of pruning to two or three eyes began to eclipse this even in Tokaj-Hegyalja. In Transylvania and at the foot of the Mátra Mountains, the ring-type cultivation *(karikás művelés)* was the fashion. The vine stalks, left long, were tied back on two sides all the way to the root, so that facing each other they formed a figure eight.

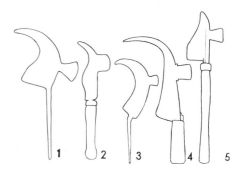

Fig. 91. Pruning knives. 1. Tokaj, the region of Hegyalja. 2. Tihany. 3. Former Bács County. 4. Former Torontál County. 5. Székesfehérvár. Second half of 19th century

The tool for pruning is the characteristically shaped pruning knife *(metszőkés),* which can be traced back to ancient times. Numerous versions are known in the country, all preserving significant regional peculiarities. From this point of view special attention should be paid to those forms on which we find a narrower or broader head on the side opposite the blade, with which they can clean off the dried-up parts of the stalk and bark, at the time of pruning. Some of its versions occur in the southern part of Transdanubia and at Tokaj-Hegyalja. While it is very difficult to determine their origins, we can at any rate speculate on the possible mediation of the Celts, and perhaps in this case we can also suppose that Walloon settlers brought versions with them and that they spread to certain regions of the Great Plain. Using this tool with a quick, pushing motion, the pruner makes a round, horizontal cut on the stalk instead of a longish one. The advantage is that the sap can drain off on all sides at the place of the cut. Pruning scissors appeared during the middle of the last century and, by the beginning of the present century, had replaced the pruning knives completely.

In the past grape vines were hoed only twice, and the weeds were cut with a sickle if the vineyard became too weedy before harvesting. Wine became an article of merchandise early, especially in certain regions, and consequently they tried to improve its quality by better methods of cultivation. Thus they were already urging a third hoeing at Tokaj-Hegyalja during the 16th to 17th centuries, a practice which spread into other grape-growing regions only in the 19th century. Part of the grapes in Hungary were not grown in rows until the end of the last century. Hoeing these, consequently, consisted primarily of clearing out the weeds and loosening the soil. However, in the greater part of the country rows of grapes were hoed to a so-called saddle back *(bakhát),* that is, a ditch was formed around the stalk which assured it a larger quantity of water.

When the wine is in bloom, it is thought best not to go into the vineyard at all, because this would only cause damage. The keeper takes care of the entire vineyard. When the grapes began to ripen the saddle backs are raked so that every footprint will show on them. And the keeper continually walks the hill, trying to scare away the birds that cause damage with a clapper and with loud cracks of his whip.

In the past the beginning of the vintage was determined precisely by the authorities, and, before the freeing of the serfs, by the landlord. Vintage began in the southern regions in September, in many cases in connection with the day of St. Michael (September 29), while at Tokaj-

227

113. Preparations for vintage
Sióagárd, Tolna County

Hegyalja, the farthest northern location, they waited to start the harvest until the day of Simon–Jude (October 28). Thus vintage could last into November, and it has happened that clusters of grapes have been picked in snow or from under the snow.

Vintage is a time both of work and celebration. From early morning, mostly women and girls pick the clusters of grapes into pails *(cseber),* and buckets, and the men carry them in a *puttony* (butt) on their backs to the gathering place (See Plate V). At noon a dinner, cooked outside, and wine await the workers, while towards evening a gipsy usually turns up and, in many places, they finish the day's work with dancing. The

228

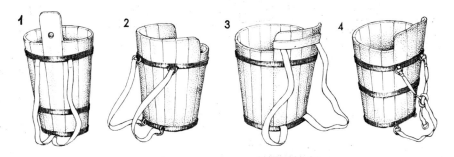

Fig. 92. Various forms of butts. 1. Buda. 2. Zala County. 3. Gyöngyös. 4. Tokaj, the region of Hegyalja. First half of 20th century

114. Winepress from 1750 Hills north of Balaton

helpers can take home as many grapes as fit into their picking vessels, and naturally they can count on help in return during their own vintage.

The celebratory nature of the vintage is also demonstrated by the fact that in the 17th to 19th centuries courts of law ceased in the villages and towns at such times, and the students were given a vacation. When the grape harvest was completed on all the fields, a big parade was organized on the streets, people riding in carts and on horseback. Among the permanent characters was a joke master, a gipsy, and some of the horsemen dressed as Turks, supposedly as a relic of the Turkish occupation. A bell-shaped garland was made out of grapes, and handed to the first citizen of the town. A ball was usually held at the completion of the vintage.

Processing grapes into wine required a great deal of work. First they compressed the grapes in tubs, then crushed them with their bare feet. Pressing followed after that. The oldest presses in the Carpathian Basin are the so-called *bálványos sajtók* (presses with a large beam). Their huge

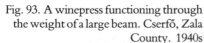

Fig. 93. A winepress functioning through the weight of a large beam. Cserfő, Zala County. 1940s

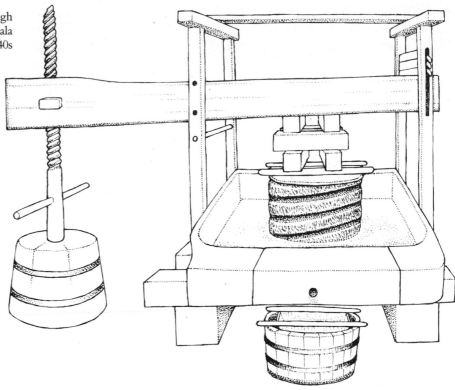

beam pressed the grapes surrounded by a willow basket or by a box of plank with holes in it. In its simplest form a stone pulled down the beam, while on the more complicated ones the desired pressure could be set by a huge wooden screw. The largest versions, in many cases 8 to 10 m long and 3 m high, were used mostly on bigger estates. Large quantities of grapes could be pressed with such winepresses and they did a very thorough job.

The middle spindle press (*középorsós sajtó*) was used mostly on smaller holdings. The upper beam was placed on a wooden spindle, or later on an iron one, and by turning it the grapes placed in a wooden box were pressed out. Most recent research, also supported by the statistics of the last century, has shown that presses were used much more extensively in the regions of Transdanubia than in the north-eastern half of the linguistic territory. The reason for this can be found in the fact that quality mattered more in the latter area, and wine made with a press is always poorer. Differentiation was made between *pure wine* and *pressed wine,* and naturally the price of the former was much higher than that of the latter.

In certain areas, primarily at Tokaj-Hegyalja, different kinds of wines were made from the same grapes in the 16th and 17th centuries. That is to say, in this region, if the autumn was favourable, the dessication of grapes began. The world famous *Tokaj aszú* is made of such grapes. They either pick off the dried grapes separately from the stalk and put them into small vessels, or they pour all the grapes from the butts onto a huge selecting table and the women pick out the *aszú* (dried) grapes.

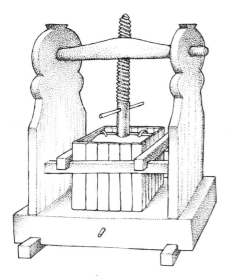

Fig. 94. A winepress functioning through a wooden screw in its centre. Second half of 19th century

They let these stand first in a perforated tub and then the essence drips out by itself. Its sugar content is so high that it has difficulty in fermenting. Afterwards they pour as many butts of *aszú* grapes into the basic unit—which from the 18th century on has been the 140 l *gönci hordó* (barrel of Gönc)—as are needed to make *aszú* wine of a certain degree of strength and sweetness. Generally 3 to 6 butts of *aszú* are used. This mixture also ferments slowly. It is kept in barrels for 3 to 4 years until it settles completely, and only then does it go into bottles that have been the same in shape for almost two centuries.

The most important condition for ripening and preserving wine is keeping it in the *cellar*. There is again a great difference between Transdanubia and the eastern areas in regard to the cellar. In the former region we find large-size wine houses in the vineyards, built of logs and stones, where there is room for the press and all kinds of tools necessary for processing the grapes. From here an entrance leads to the cave-like cellar, cut into stone or a loess wall (cf. Plate IV). In the east, on the other

115. Bottom of barrel with the relief of St. Urban
Hungary

231

hand, for example at Tokaj-Hegyalja, the cellars can always be found within the settlement, or perhaps on the edge of it, in a cluster. They are generally very deep, so that the wine is kept summer and winter at 10 to 12° C. Only in the rarest instances, and only recently, a wine house has been built over the cellar, because generally the work of processing is done outside. At the most an entrance shed is built in front of the cellar, where they put the press, which has come into use during the last hundred years and can be found today at every holding.

Thus, in the cultivation of the grape, we find the same duality that has been pointed out several times already: the western part of the Carpathian Basin has connections in the western, south-western directions, while the eastern part maintains connections in many characteristics, toward the east, south-east.

Animal Husbandry

The raw material originating from animals is used partly as food, partly as clothing. Just as in the case of vegetable products, the method of acquisition can take on the character of food gathering, in the sense that man only takes away from nature, but does not take care of reproduction. Alternatively, it may have the character of breeding, when man cares for the animal, provides it with fodder, and selects the best specimens for further breeding. In the areas of apiculture, hunting, and fishing, all of which we shall discuss below, we can find both stages of development, but we can talk only about the second method in regard to animal husbandry.

Apiculture

Beekeeping is among the most ancient occupations of the old Hungarians, as indicated by the words of Finno-Ugric origin such as *méh,* bee; *méz,* honey; *odú,* bee dwelling, hole; *ereszt,* bee colony. 11th-century sources already mention villages and families which provided honey to their lord. In the north-eastern corner of the linguistic territory so-called stone hives have survived, dating from the same period, holes cut into the rock for keeping bees. A number of names of villages— *Méhes, Fedémes* (bee-house)—testify to significant apicultural activity over most parts of the linguistic territory from the 11th to 13th centuries.

The most primitive form of apiculture has the character of food gathering. The apiarist goes out to the edge of the forest and captures, in a vessel made out of horn or wood, bees sucking flowers. When enough of them are buzzing inside the vessel, he lets one out and watches the direction of its flight. He follows it as long as he can see it. Then he lets out another and follows it also. He repeats this procedure until he arrives at the hollow tree where the bees live. Then he closes up the tree, kills the entire family with smoke and takes away the honey.

It also happened that they did not kill the bees but left them in the tree and took the honey from them only from time to time. In such cases, a property sign was carved on the trunk of the tree, and a wooden board was fastened in front of the hive and a hole bored in it for the bees to get in and out. When they thought that enough honey was collected, they removed the wooden board, smoked out the bees, and took away the

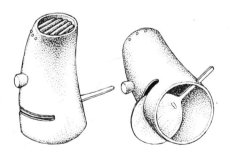

Fig. 95. A horn for catching bees. Domaháza, former Borsod County. 1940s

honey. They always left enough in the hive for the colony to survive until spring. While *live tree* apiculture was not known to have existed in the Carpathian Basin according to former literature, more recent research has found it in several places.

Bees could be actually cared for only if they were kept in one place and in the *apiary*. Apiaries were erected in peaceful, quiet spots, so that no one should disturb the diligently working families. Thus apiaries were often set up in a forest, on certain islands in swampy areas, but most frequently an area was separated off within the settlement in a fenced part of the garden. The simplest are the bee gardens, surrounded by a fence, where the hives stand on the ground or on low legs. Walls, usually made of wattle, surround the *fenced apiaries* on all sides. They run a half-sided roof all around inside it, under which the hives *(köpü, kas)* sit on shelves, facing into the yard. The advantage of this arrangement is that it is easy to close the hives off from the outside world. Drinking water is placed in the centre of the yard, while the beekeeper generally lives in the hut attached to the outside of the structure. This form, called *kelenc,* can so far be shown to have existed only in the north-eastern part of the linguistic territory. Most widespread are the *partly roofed* apiaries, on the wooden boards of which the openings of the bee dwellings face towards the south-east. One section of these consists of a shed that provides only a little protection against the rain, but most such sheds are surrounded on three sides by planks and wicker walls, and in this enclosed area the smaller tools of apiculture are kept.

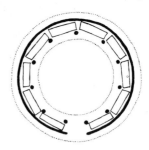

Fig. 96. The ground-plan of a round closed-in courtyard of beehives. Györgyfalva, former Kolozs County. Early 20th century

116. Beehive
Vajdácska, Borsod-Abaúj-Zemplén County

233

117. Drumming the bees into a new hive
Komádi, Hajdú-Bihar County

In forested regions, the bee dwellings are called *köpü,* carved or burned out of logs usually hollow inside. These wooden hives are often richly ornamented with carvings. In forest-poor areas, hives called *kas* are woven out of bulrushes or straw, and their size and shape vary by regions. In other places they cut down a willow tree at the same height as the beehives and split it into several forks. They force these apart and weave them around with supple branches. Afterwards the branches are plastered with clay mixed with cow dung which provides good protection for the bees in the winter. During the winter a bulrush or straw cope is put over the hives in the western part of the linguistic territory, so that they do not have to store them in covered areas. The bee dwelling called *kaptár,* made mostly out of planks after western examples, gradually eclipsed the traditional hives from the second half of the last century, which still have survived sporadically until today.

234

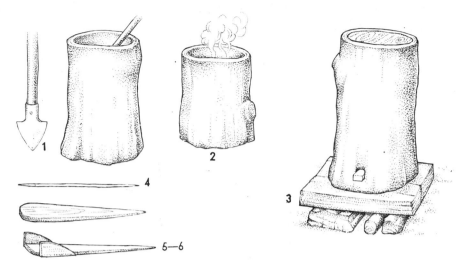

Fig. 97. The preparation and the construction of a wooden beehive. Former Szatmár County. Early 20th century. 1. Fluting out the interior.
2. Preparing the hive through burning out the interior. 3. The prepared hive and its construction. 4. Honeycomb. 5. Planks for the hive

One of the great events of beekeeping is the *flying out in spring*. According to folk belief, the time must be selected carefully, because bees are weak on Monday and Saturday, and become envious and quarrelsome on Tuesday, Friday and Sunday. Therefore most people recommend Wednesday or Thursday, because then the bees will be strong and diligent all through the year. But to make them really tame it is thought necessary to pass them through the wool of a white sheep, well washed with sand, when they first leave the hive in the spring. The beekeeper who preferred his bees to be quarrelsome and thieving would pass them through a wolf's windpipe, or smear the opening of the hive with rooster blood. Thus the bees defended it against every intruder.

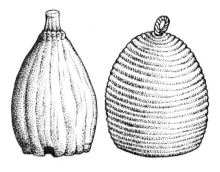

Fig. 98. Forms of beehives. a) Made out of wicker and plastered. Transylvania. b) Woven out of bulrush. Former Borsod County. First half of 20th century

In the summer, the swarming of the bees begins when the new family gathers and tries to find a new home at a distance. At such times beekeepers try to bring the swarm to a stop by cracking a whip, clattering, spraying water, and throwing pieces of clothing in the air. If the bees settle on a tree, they then fasten a hive on a long pole and shake them into it, carry them back into the apiary, and settle the family in a permanent hive.

For a long time in Hungarian peasant apiculture they kept the swarm for the next year but smothered the mother family with smoke and then took the honey away from them. Later on they covered the full hive with another hive and the beekeeper kept beating the bottom one until the bees, annoyed by the noise, moved into the top hive. Thus they could take away the necessary amount of honey without destroying the family. In the autumn honey merchants *(barkács)* appeared, who took out the honeycomb along with the honey, stuffed it into barrels, and carried it to the market.

Honey as a sweetener played an extraordinarily large role in the Hungarian peasant kitchen, and earlier it was also used in the diet of the nobility. It is the indispensable basic material of honey cakes, but nectar is also made from it. The wax was primarily used for candle making. As these functions were curtailed beekeeping decreased significantly, yet even today, along with modern apiculture, the traditional peasant procedures of beekeeping can be found in every village.

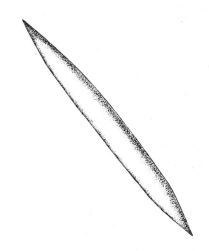

Fig. 99. Sharpened flinging stick. Little Cumania (Kiskunság). Early 20th century

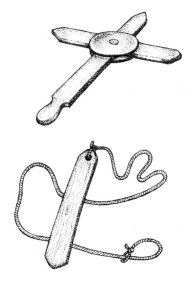

Fig. 100. Hitting sticks. Region of Debrecen. Early 20th century.

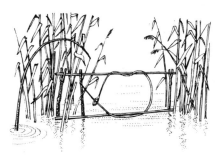

Fig. 101. A snare for catching waterfowl. Sárköz region. Early 20th century

Hunting

Hunting has been a man's job at all periods; the task of the women was the skinning and the preparing of the game. Some elements of Magyar hunting can be traced back even before the Conquest. Thus arrows with a V-shaped head were shot at water birds, because it got stuck in the reeds on account of its shape, and was then reusable. Hungarian archeologists have found a number of examples of these in graves dating from the Conquest, and the Ugric relatives of the Magyars also used such arrows until recently. Similarly, we can trace the equivalents of certain types of snares and traps back to pre-Conquest times. Anonymus, the first Hungarian chronicler (12th century), also proclaimed the importance of hunting: "Whereon in the year 884 the Magyars started out, the young men were at hunting nearly every day, and from that day until the present, the Magyars above other nations are better at hunting."

The new homeland offered largely the same opportunities for hunting as did the South Russian steppes. The peasantry, however, was gradually left out of it, especially in 1504 when King Wladislas gave the right of hunting to the nobility. From then on both serf and commoner were rigorously punished if caught hunting. Thus the methods of hunting amongst the peasants and the nobility developed in different directions. The latter soon turned to firearms, while the former retained the old methods which they could practise in secret, at most improving the forms and in some places augmenting their numbers.

We wish to mention only a few of the numerous methods, procedures, and implements of hunting. The simplest and, in earlier times, the most common one was *beating* the game. Even in the last century wolves were hunted in this way. They chased the wolf on horseback and beat it with a whip with a wire on its end, which twined about the wolf's neck and choked him. The largest bird of the Carpathian Basin, the huge-bodied bustard *(túzok, Otis torda)* could not fly up with its frozen wings when there was a freezing drizzle. At such times the entire flock could be driven into the yard of one of the peasant farmsteads with a whip and killed there for their excellent meat.

Variously shaped *sticks* were also used for hunting, with which they struck down rabbits or wild ducks that were too slow on the take-off from the water. *Flinging sticks* were made of hardwood, sharpened on both ends, and they threw it rotating towards the animal to be killed in such a way as to make the largest possible wound. The *hitting stick,* for a kind of *lapwing (Tringidae),* was made of two pieces of wood laid crosswise on top of one another, and thrown spinning among water birds that gathered at the sound of a decoy whistle.

The *sling shot* deserves an important place among hunting implements, for it is equally suited for bringing down birds and smaller game. Made of soft leather, it has another piece of leather in the middle, 6 to 8 cm wide, to hold the missile, which is made of stone or dried mud. The hunter ties one end of the leather strap to his wrist, while holding the other end in his palm. He spins the sling several times over his head, lets one strap go, and the projectile flies out with great force. In the 18th and 19th centuries even the field keepers used this weapon, with which they tried to keep away not only the destructive birds but thieves as well.

Hungarian peasants used many different kinds of *snares,* knotted from horsehair, string, twine, or wire and placed in the path of the game. A horsehair snare was sufficient for the smaller birds. They tied 20 to 30 loops on a wooden board, on seeds which were spread and, as the bird was picking up the seeds, its neck sooner or later got caught in one of them. Similar snares, rigged up on a husked corncob, quickly trap the neck of a hungry bird. One version is the *pulling snare,* equally used in water and on land. They put a strong supple twig into the ground, bend it down and fasten it with a suitable small peg. They tie the end of the snare to this and place it in the path of the game. It if pushes the peg the twig is freed and the snare pulls the catch up in the air by the neck.

At one time bird-catching was practised with a *net* in the shape of a wide circle. Charters from the Middle Ages allude to the royal net carriers, and even note the names of a few characteristic fouling nets. Quails were chiefly caught with nets. They covered an area of grass or growing grain with it and enticed the quails by imitating their call. Once the birds had arrived under the net they suddenly startled them, and the birds, trying to fly up, could not escape. They also spread a net over the holes of foxes and badgers, so the hunted animals could not get away. They still hunt game with nets today, when trying to catch the game alive to settle them on other territories.

Smaller birds, primarily singing birds, are usually captured with *liming.* The necessary gluey material is usually boiled out of mistletoe. It is spread on the prominent branches of bushes, near which is hung a call bird in a cage. The bird that comes to its call and settles on the bush is caught by the sticky *bird lime.*

One of the oldest hunting tools traceable to the Finno-Ugric period is the *bow trap,* which is primarily used for catching gophers. Its most important part is the bow, led through a longish, narrow box. A flat wooden board, studded with nails on the end, goes in and out of it. With this they tighten the bow and fasten it with a small peg. The trap is placed on the gopher hole. When the animal touches it, the peg loosens easily and, driven by the elastic power of the bow, the forward sliding wooden board captures or kills the gopher. We find various versions of this trap among the hunting tribes of northern Europe and northern Asia, and certain data establish its proliferation into western Europe as well.

The *crushing trap,* which killed the game by dropping a piece of wood or stone on it, was also known in many places. Today's versions are reduced in size and are mostly used for mouse or rat traps. Formerly, using logs of wood, they caught larger predators, bears, or deer with this method.

Catching game in a pit was once practised over a wide area, generally for large game. They dug pits for wild boar in the southern part of Transdanubia, using a surrounding fence to lead the animal into the pit it was thus unable to avoid. *Wolf pits* were longest in use in swampy, boggy regions. When the water froze, the starving wolves ventured right to the edge of the village, and often even into the yards. At such times a pit 2 to 3 m deep was dug along their regular path, and a stake or several stakes were beaten into the bottom of it. They covered the top

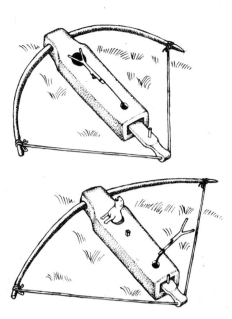

Fig. 102. A bow trap ready to catch its prey and with a caught gopher. Great Plain. 1930s

Fig. 103. Cross-section of a wolf pit. Great Plain. Late 19th century

with reeds, bulrush, or weeds, and for bait, they put a piece of meat or even a live goose in the middle of it on a long pole. The wolf, slipping by, noticed the desirable meal and jumped for it, but the weak roof broke under him and he fell into the pit where he was either impaled on the stakes or killed by the men with pitchforks.

Various methods of hunting with the help of animals was widespread. Rabbit, deer, and often wild boar were chased with a dog until the game collapsed. In the Middle Ages hunting and catching birds with a falcon or eagle was primarily the amusement of the nobility, but the peasantry practised certain forms until almost the most recent times. They would keep an eye on the nest of the *osprey* and *fish hawk*, built on trees in the swamp, and when the mother brought smaller game and fish for her young, they could take it away from them. Thus they forced the mother to bring more and more prey.

Peasant hunting, because of its prohibitions, played at most only a supplementary role during every period in providing food. Nevertheless, it was practised by everybody. There are still some specialists around today who know and practise various methods of trapping.

Fishing The Magyars had lived around waters in their ancient homeland and fishing has been among their most important occupations. A number of fish names *(hal, fish; meny, burbot; keszeg, bream; őn, baleen)* and names of utensils and erections *(háló, net; para, cork; halúsztató fa, wooden fish trough; vejsze, fish weir; horog, hook; hajó, boat),* all of Finno-Ugric origin, testify to its role in the past. In the course of their wanderings the ancestors of the Hungarians learned much from the Slavic peoples of the South Russian steppes, especially in regard to fishing. This is proved by words such as *varsa* (fish weir), and the technical word characteristic of large-scale fishing, *tanya* (the area of water and shore where the fisherman casts his net). And since big rivers, lakes, smaller streams, and endless swamps favoured this occupation in the new homeland, it has persisted until today. Charters of the 11th and 13th centuries already mention fishermen, who supply the required amount of fish to their lord, and even speak of entire villages that lived primarily from fishing. The profession of fishing was sustained during the following centuries, fishermen having to hand over two-thirds of their catch to the landlord, although they could keep all the smaller fishes. Fishing played an important role in providing supplementary food in the past, since every peasant who lived near water fished, mostly with implements he could handle alone.

The simplest kind of fishing is done with the bare hands. This is the oldest method of catching fish and requires a very thorough knowledge of the habits and bodily structure of fishes. In this method, the fisherman stands against the flow of the water in fast mountain streams and, when he spots the fish, tries to catch it by its gills and throw it on the bank. In standing water the fisherman submerges with open eyes and tries to approach his victim with slow movements. He runs his hand along it to locate its gills exactly. He quietens the thrashing of the caught fish with his other hand, until he can reach the shore.

The *fish spear* is one of the oldest and most generally used fishing implements, the one-pronged or multi-pronged varieties being known over a wide area. The tip of the prong is bent back, so that it will not tear out of the body of the fish. (If the fish should free itself, it bleeds to death because of the big wound.) The spear-fisher wades into the water, or waits on the shore, but mostly watches from the bow of the boat for the fish to appear. The spear could be used with greater success during spawning, but it caused great damage in the fish stock. Therefore, its use has been prohibited by law since the end of the last century, although its use still occurs even today. It is worked for preference at night. A torch is lit on the bow of the boat, and the fish that are attracted by the unusual light are an easy prey. The accessory to this method of fishing is the short-handled, curved *gaff*, with which the larger and strongly thrashing fish are lifted into the boat.

A characteristic tool of the small fisherman who works alone is the *groper,* a basket woven up out of twigs for catching fish, used in swamps, flooded areas, and along river banks, in water no deeper than one metre. Its oldest forms were woven from wicker, and more recently they have covered its frame with netting, and even rigged up a long handle on it, so that the man wading in the water can reach forward with it and in this

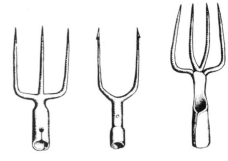

Fig. 104. Harpoons. 1. Nagyvarsány, former Szabolcs County. 2. Nagykálló, former Szabolcs County. 3. Petneháza, former Szabolcs County. Early 20th century

118. Placing fish-traps in front of a large fish-net
Kopács. former Baranya County

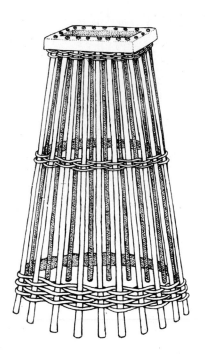

Fig. 105. Wicker groper. Békés County. 1930s

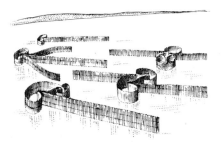

Fig. 106. Types of fish weirs. Lake Balaton. Late 19th century

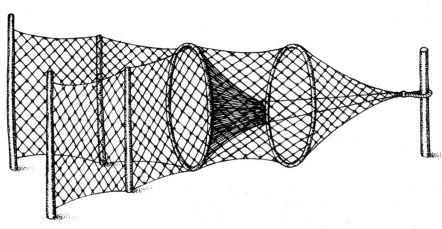

Fig. 107. Net fish-trap with two wings. River Kraszna. Early 20th century

way does not scare off the fish. A bottomless wicker basket, for example a beehive with its end cut off, is suitable for this method of fishing. It depends largely on chance, the fisherman pushes the groper here and there, and if he feels the impact of a fish, he reaches inside and lifts it out by hand. This simple form of fishing is known in many places but we must look primarily towards the east for its exact equivalents.

Trap fishing relies on the habit of fish to keep their direction. That is, once it has started off in one direction, a fish changes it only if it runs into some obstacle. It feels the obstacle with its nose, because it is seeking a passage, a way out of it. The fisherman counts on this behaviour when he sets up a *fish weir*. This is usually made of reeds and is raised at least half a metre above the water. The mouth of the fish weir drives the fish towards the winding *funnel,* which is built so that the fish can not again escape from it. Periodically, the fisherman lifts the fish out of the funnel and into the boat with the aid of the *scoop*. In Székelyland they block up the fast running mountain rivers and larger streams with dams made of stones *(cége),* from which the fish can escape only through the opening left in the centre. This is where they place the fish trap, the *fish weir,* usually made from wicker. Although the fish forces itself through its small opening, it cannot get out again. At other places they make the enclosure out of thick gates, the space between which is closed by wattle work, and with this they direct the fish toward the winged, *netted fish weir* that is set up at the opening (e.g. Bodrogköz).

Fishing by lifting relies on the fish's attempt to escape danger downward or sideways when it senses it, and, as it is swimming above the net that has been lowered into the water, the fish gets caught. The *dipping net* is the characteristic tool of the small fisherman who fishes alone, and would not be used much by a professional fisherman. They tie two hoops across and to the end of each they fasten the corner of a square net. They fish with it mostly from the shore, rarely from a boat. The fisherman watches when the fish appears above the net, so that by lifting the net he can capture it. This method of fishing is related to enclosing. In this case they fish from the seat raised above the weir opening, because it is easy to catch the fish as it passes through.

A kind of *cast fishing* is also used by small fishermen, who fish alone. They weave or cut out the *pöndör* or *rokolya net* in the shape of a circle. The fisherman knows that as the fish cannot descend perpendicularly, it

119. Fisherman with his net
Komádi, Hajdú-Bihar County

therefore tries to go downward sideways. The net, because of the lead weights placed along its edge, sinks faster than the fish descends. The fisherman first of all knots the rope on his left wrist. This rope, formerly made of horsehair and more recently of hemp, is attached to the centre of the circle. The fisherman then flings the net onto his left shoulder like a cloak. He puts into his mouth one part of the lead cord that surrounds the net, and holds on to it with his teeth. Then, on the shore or in the bow of a boat, he turns on his heel with a sudden motion, spreading the net evenly over the water. Because of the lead weight the edge of the net sinks faster and closes up rapidly below, so the fish cannot escape from it. This type of net is known in the region of the Mediterranean and has also reached the Black Sea, and it can be presumed that the Magyars had already become acquainted with it there.

When fishing with a *hook,* there are usually several hooks on a single line. This is often 60 to 80 m long and kept afloat by buoys made of a hollowed-out gourd. One end is fastened on the shore, and a hook dangles at every metre length. Huge hooks were used to catch *sturgeon (Acipenser Huso),* which swam upstream from the Black Sea, the weight often reaching one or two quintals. At such times a rope would be set across the Danube, to which the large-sized, many-forked hooks were attached. Wooden buoys kept the rope on the surface. Sometimes the rope of the hook was fastened to a post and placed on the shore or on a raft, with a cowbell tied on it. When the fish took, the cowbell rang and brought the fisherman quickly to the scene.

Among the innumerable kinds of nets used in Hungarian fishing, we

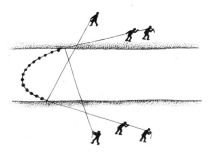

Fig. 108. The organization of a fisher company fishing with a large net. Tiszaörvény, Szolnok County. Early 20th century

shall mention only the kind used for fishing sweeps. The smallest example is the *bicentral net,* which rarely reached 6 to 8 m in length and one and one-half m in width. Two men worked with it, each holding a stick fastened to an end of the net. When they felt the splashing of the fish, they lifted it out of the net with a smaller net. Much larger than the former is the so-called *old net,* or by another name, *large net,* which is basically an enlarged version. It often extends in length to 80–120 m. Even larger than this is the *drag net,* which differs from the big net in that it has a *sack (káta)* at its end, which gathers the fish which can then be taken out together. The big net and drag net are the largest pieces of equipment used on Hungarian fishing sweeps, which they keep dry, and is repaired on the water's edge on *poles* resting on huge beams. As one men cannot handle the huge nets alone, several unite their strength and labour, and sometimes jointly put in the money necessary for the equipment. The fishers share the takings in a pre-arranged way. Such fishing groups are called *bokor* (cluster), *kötés* (bond), and *felekezet* (sect), and are typical of Hungarian fishing. The large size and structure of the

120. Gourd for keeping mudfish
Haraszti, former Verőce County

121. Fishing under the ice
Sára, Borsod-Abaúj-Zemplén County

net require that every member of the group have a definite task, and everybody must obey the *master* or *gazda*. He is the one who leads the fishing, decides when it should begin and end, and defines the scope of everybody's activity. He himself participates in fishing as a steerman. His substitute is the *first apprentice, vicemester* (vice-master), or *kis-gazda,* who pulls the bow of the boat and carries out the most difficult tasks. The number of young men is between 4 and 12, depending on the size of of the net and the extent of the water surface. If the net is owned communally, the catch is shared equally; if it belongs to the *gazda,* then he gets 3 to 5 shares and the men get one share each.

The Hungarian fisherman calls every section of the water and shore where he drags his net *tanya* and divides this territory on the basis of how many times they can cast out the net. The division of fish waters into *tanya*s indicated both the territory and its economic yield. Presumably the Magyars learned the organization and terminology of communal fishing before the Conquest, in the vicinity of the Eastern Slavs.

Fishermen did not rest even in wintertime when the waters freeze. They cut the thin ice with a spear, or struck at it so hard with a hatchet or wooden club that they could easily lift the dazed fish out through the hole. They even used the big net or the drag net under the ice. At such times the fisherman tied an iron *crampoon* on his boots, so that he could move around with complete safety. A huge entrance hole was cut into the ice, and the net was put in it. Then smaller holes were made in a wide circle, through which the cord of the net was passed with a stick. This rope went all the way to the take-out hole. This is the way of fishing wide areas under the ice, and it usually brings good results.

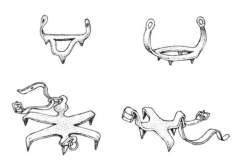

Fig. 109. Crampoons for winter fishing on ice. General. Early 20th century

243

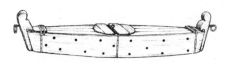

Fig. 110. Ark made out of boards for holding fish. Vencsellő, former Szabolcs County, 1930s

Fig. 111. Monoxylon, a canoe hollowed out of a log *(bödönhajó)*. Lake Balaton. Second half of 19th century

The nets were knotted from hemp yarn by means of old-fashioned *net-knitting needles* by the fisherman himself or by his wife. The size of the mesh varied, according to the purpose of the net. There are, for example, nets with double walls, which further entangle sharp-nosed fish. The nets made by the women of certain areas were known and used far and wide.

The caught fish had to be kept for a varying length of time. That purpose was served by the boat-shaped *bárka* (fishing ark) that had holes on the side and could be sealed on top. Formerly, it was made of reeds or wicker. Back- or hand-baskets to carry the fish home or to market were also made of wicker.

Fishermen moved on the water using various forms of *boats*. The oldest type was made from a single log scooped inside or burned out with embers. These were replaced by the more safely moving *flat boats,* constructed of planks. The large-sized nets could be placed more easily on these. Boats were directed and moved with a stake in shallower water and with paddles of different shapes in deeper water.

The characteristic vehicle of water locomotion was the *raft,* fabricated from wood or sheaves of reed. The former was for hauling logs in rivers and the latter to move between swamps and marshes. The *ferry* has served, and is still serving today, to move men and freight across rivers. These are large-sized, flat-bottomed crafts for transport, which can even take four loaded carts over to the other side at one time. They were pulled over by hand power, along a rope stretched between the two banks, taking advantage of the water current; in shallower water they were poled towards a ramp cut into the shore line.

Animal Husbandry

Husbandry had a greater economic importance than agriculture in certain areas during the Middle Ages, and even in later centuries. This was also apparent in the second half of the last century, since in 1870 in Hungary there was one head of cattle to every three men, one horse to every seven men, and one sheep to every man. On the other hand, by 1931 they reckoned only one head of cattle to every fifth Hungarian citizen, one horse to every tenth, and one sheep to every sixth. These ratios also show that through the centuries the economy of the country shifted increasingly towards agriculture.

Husbandry played an outstanding role not only in nutrition (meat, milk), but also in providing many kinds of basic materials for clothing (wool, leather). But as we go back in time it is also increasingly one of the most important factors of agriculture itself, because the animal stock provided manure and gave the draught power indispensable to cultivating the soil and gathering the harvest.

The Magyars already knew the words *ló* (horse), and *eb* (dog), in the Finno-Ugric period, but they really became livestock raisers only after meeting the Bulgaro-Turks. Even if we do not count all the Magyar words connected with keeping the numerous kinds of livestock, an indication of the differentiation of cattle alone by sex and age has been preserved in the Hungarian language by many pre-Conquest Turkish words: *üsző* (heifer); *tinó* (young bullock); *borjú* (calf); *tulok* (steer); *bika*

244

(bull); *ökör* (ox). We also borrowed from this source the words *kecske* (goat), and *disznó* (pig). It is quite sure that, although they knew and practised farming, for the conquering Magyars animal husbandry was still the more important part of the economy.

The Magyars' knowledge of animal husbandry was further increased in the Carpathian Basin. They learned important elements of hay cultivation from various Slavic peoples, which clearly proves that the ancestors of the Hungarians already provided, on a regular basis, for the wintering of stock. The devastation of the Tartars and the settling of the Cumanians in the 13th century reinforced the nomadic characteristics of animal keeping on the central steppes of the Great Plain.

Two more important influences affected Hungarian animal husbandry. One was the influence of the Walachian herdsmen, who, originating in various parts of present-day Transylvania and Havasalföld, got to the northern part of the Carpathian Basin, as far as the Moravian territories, and especially influenced the Palots shepherds. Such connections could also be demonstrated in the animal keeping of the eastern half of the Great Plain, coming from the Rumanian shepherds called *bács* also by Transylvanian Hungarians who frequented the Great Plain region of the Tiszántúl. Western breeds of cattle came especially from the 18th century on, mostly to Transdanubia, whose traces can be found even to this day.

During the centuries, various forms of Hungarian animal husbandry developed. These categories actually shade into each other; they never appeared in pure form, and transitional forms may be found in many variations.

It is characteristic of *extensive husbandry* that the stock spends the entire year out of doors. In winter the herd is driven into the protection of various covered or half-covered structures, erected in sheltered places of marshes, and forests. Here a certain amount of fodder is laid in stock for the time when a heavy snowfall makes grazing impossible. In the Great Plain the peasant farmsteads were the centres of such winter animal keeping during the initial period of their development. Equivalents can be found now and then in the mountain region, though they are different in their historical development. Stock kept under this system also brought their young into the world outdoors. The large quantity of stock was marketed for slaughter or was brought up and trained to be draught animals.

In *semi-extensive husbandry* the stock stay on the pasture from spring until late autumn, usually until the snow falls. Afterwards they are kept in stables, in covered pens, or in other structures, but still grazed in the winter if the weather permitted. This form of husbandry was general not only in the Great Plain but also appeared in Székelyland, where the *horses* grazed outdoors from early spring until the first snowfall, when they were driven into highland sheds for lodging. Here they were not tied but received fodder regularly and were let outside when the weather was suitable.

Nomadic husbandry combines many characteristics of the two previous forms and keeps the stock primarily on pasture over the largest part of the year. One of its features is that the herdsmen and the flock return to a given settlement but spend a significant part of the year either wandering or at a single, well-defined place. Thus movement is possible between winter and summer lodgings. In the winter, the flock is driven to a place where suitable pasture or cheap fodder is available. Thus they masted pigs in oak forests in the winter, often driving the herd several hundred kilometres for this purpose. Wandering in pursuit of pasture occurred in the Carpathian Basin until the most recent times.

Although traces of *stable keeping* can be shown from the Middle Ages on, yet it became general and predominant only after a considerable part of the pastures had been broken in, and after the pastures of the peasants had been separated from those of the nobility, subsequent to the freeing of the serfs. This meant a major decrease in the pasture available to peasants, who were thus forced to stable their animals and keep them on fodder. From spring until late autumn the stock were driven out each day to the pasture on the edge of the village, but fodder was also given in the evening at the stable. At night, the adolescent children took the horses and oxen that had participated in farmwork out to the fallow fields and pasture, so that they would not eat the very scarce fodder.

Regional Varieties of Breeds

The conquering Magyars brought with them domestic animal species that were able to stand up to wandering, constant grazing, and, in general, extensive husbandry. However, through the years, especially from the 18th and 19th centuries on, and in accordance with changing economic circumstances, these mixed to a considerable degree with and eventually were completely replaced by breeds that came partly from the west, partly from the south, and were better fitted to new demands. Historical perspective can be got today by evaluating the bones of domestic animals resulting from renewed excavations, especially in recent times.

The most valued domestic animal of the Magyars was the *horse,* the value of which is shown by the practice of burying the horse's head and four legs by the side of the Magyar warrior. In many cases the saddle was also put into the grave. These horses were low in the withers, had relatively small heads, and powerful tendons. They withstood hunger and fatigue very well. However, through time, the horse stock changed significantly as the result of Italian, Arabian, and later on, various western influences. The *Székely* and the *parlagi* (scrub) horse, which survived on certain parts of the Great Plain until the recent past, best preserved the build of body and the endurance of the early Magyar type.

The *grey Hungarian horned cattle* show many ancient features even at the present day (cf. Ill. 98). The greyish white animal, high at the withers and with enormous horns, was first of all an important source of draught power, but valued also because of its fine quality meat, and was readily bought at western markets during the Middle Ages. This breed gave relatively little milk, but the milk was high in fat content. It was undemanding, in the winter living on the most scanty fodder. In Transylvania there is a breed of it somewhat smaller but otherwise possessing similar characteristics. Equivalents can be looked for in the direction of the great Russian steppes. The *riska* is smaller bodied but

246

gives much more milk than the previously mentioned cattle and was primarily kept in the southern part of Transdanubia. It supposedly came to Hungary from the Balkans. From the 18th century, when the value of milk increased, various western breeds, primarily Swiss, were brought to the large estates. These eclipsed the older breeds and, through cross-breeding, created new species.

The Hungarian sheep *(juh)* actually belongs to the *racka* variety (cf. Ill. 126). Two types existed, one in the Great Plain, the other in Transylvania. A characteristic of the former is the twisting, upward growing horn, equal in length on both ram and ewe. Its long wool is especially suited for the weaving of strong, durable cloth, and its prepared skin for sheepskin coats. The Transylvanian variety is related to ones in Moldavia. The twisted horn of the ram stretches in two directions almost horizontally. Among the various regional species the *scrub sheep,* which already may have been indigenous to this area before the Conquest, still survived in the 17th century. From the 18th century, the *merino,* ultimately Spanish in origin, and giving much finer wool, pushed out the older species, at first on the estates of the landlords and later from the pastures of the peasants as well.

The ancient species of the *pig* disappeared almost without a trace and even faster than other kinds of livestock. These were mostly long-legged, reddish-coloured animals, noteworthy for their undemanding nature. We know two varieties: the *szalontai,* or by another name *red pigs,* which lived primarily in the swamps of the Great Plain and was driven into the oak forest only in the winter; and the *bakonyi,* which is its variant in the mountain region of Bakony. During the second half of the 18th century a breed called *milos* spread from the Balkans. A special type developed in the Carpathian Basin, the *mangalica,* in which the presence of the breeds that had lived in Hungary earlier can also be discovered. This is primarily a lard producing pig. Its light coloured hair is curly, and it can be raised outdoors and easily driven long distances. We can observe its disappearance during the last decades, its place having been taken by the English meat producing pig.

The most faithful helper of the herdsmen is the dog, among the breeds of which the *komondor* is most important. This sheepdog not only kept the stock together, but with its mate also beat back the attacks of wolves. The word itself is Cumanian in origin, which perhaps can throw light on the origin of the dog; that it is primarily kept in the Great Plain also supports this theory. The *kuvasz* is similar in build but somewhat smaller. It occurs primarily in Transylvania and in the more southern regions, and its homeland might be looked for in the Balkans. Today the *puli* is the best known Hungarian sheepdog. Its predominantly black, shaggy coat and small size differentiate it basically from the others above.

The *donkey* is the helper of the shepherd, used first of all for travelling and for hauling goods (cf. Plate VIII). The *bison* is typically a powerful animal that gives little but thick milk. It is mentioned in records from the Middle Ages on and occurred in large numbers only in Southern Transdanubia and in Transylvania (cf. Ill. 134 and Plate X).

The keeping of domestic fowl (chicken, goose, duck, turkey, guinea fowl, etc.) was always general among the Hungarian peasants, but while caring for the former animals was the duty of men, taking care of the latter was always a job for the women.

The Organization of the Herdsmen

Herdsmen looked after the various animals that grazed in flocks and they themselves were differentiated according to the kind of animal of which they were in charge. In most areas the cattleherd *(gulyás)* was regarded as the most important since at one time he kept a certain number of his own cattle among those of the owner. On the Great Plain, cattle herds rode on horses, and the ornamental long whip and the stick which they carried were at the same time their tools, weapons, and ornaments. The horseherd *(csikós),* the guard of the horses, was next in order of importance, standing in fact on a similar level to that of the cattle herds but differentiated from them by his clothing, which varied from region to region (cf. Plate IX). He never used a club, his most important tool being the long whip. *Shepherds* came next in rank, even though they were generally amongst the wealthiest herdsmen (cf. Plate VIII). The shepherd not only was able to keep sheep himself, but increased his income with certain emoluments paid for double births, milk, and wool. The swineherds *(kondás)* were the least esteemed and at the same time came from the poorest social layer, a fact reflected in their wages. The men who looked after extensive or half-extensive flocks passed on

122. Cattleherd
Borsod-Abaúj-Zemplén County

123. The chief cattleherd
Dévaványa, Békés County

248

their herdsman's knowledge, both rational and irrational, mostly within the family. Thus the history of certain herdsman families can be followed through several generations.

The situation is different with those herdsmen who drove the stock out daily; they were differentiated even in name from the above. Thus cattle were driven by the *csordás,* the pigs by the *csürhés,* both of whom are lower in social rank than their equivalents who tended the extensive or half-extensive flocks. This was usually the occupation of the poor, indigent peasants, and they gladly left it as soon as something better turned up. In the last decades, gypsy herdsmen have been hired in more and more places to tend the village flock because no one else will take on this job.

The leader or *gazda* of the herdsmen who tend one flock is called the *számadó.* The owner entrusts the stock to him, and he is financially responsible for the animals. This is why he is usually a man owning livestock himself, who grazes his stock along with that of the owner. This is the guarantee that possible losses can be replaced from his own. In the organization, the *elsőbojtár* or *számadó bojtár* is substitute of the

124. Cattleherds having their noon meal
Hortobágy

125. Driving the cattle out in the morning
Szék, former Szolnok-Doboka County

126. Shepherd leaning on his crook
Hortobágy

számadó and his right hand man. The *elsőbojtár* is also allowed to own
a definite number of animals. In many places he keeps track of all the
animals and inspects their numbers from time to time. The other *bojtár*s
come after him according to age and the amount of time served, there
being as many of them as are absolutely necessary to tend the flock.
There were even *kisbojtár*s *(tanyás, lakos)* on the farmsteads of the Great
Plain herdsmen, who did not tend the stock during the daytime but were
busy preparing cooked food for the return of the *számadó* and the *bojtár*s.
At night they were not allowed to sleep because they had to keep an eye
on the stock. They went to town for the week's food, on foot or in a cart,
which is why they were also called *carters*.

Herdsmen were engaged and employed at different times according
to the period or region. In the Kiskunság the contract was from the day
of Demetrius until the day of Demetrius—that is, for a year. When it
came to an end, the *számadó* handed over the stock he was entrusted with
to its owner. Employment of the herdsmen in half-extensive husbandry
lasted from the driving-out until closing—that is to say, during the
grazing season. The herdsman driving out daily is actually like a yearly

127. Driving out the swine
Hollókő, Nógrád County

farm hand. He was usually hired during Christmas week. At this time they took time to wet the bargain and the new herdsmen drank a glass with the local farmers, who selected them.

In certain stock-keeping areas, they called the spring animal fair the *herdsmen's market,* because that is where herdsmen were hired. Cattle-herds as well as horseherds, shepherds, and swineherds came to the fair if they wanted to exchange their old place for a new one, and settled the matter of payment with their master.

In recent times the accounting of the village stock took place on the Sunday before the day of St. George (April 24). The herdsman at such time went from house to house and wrote down who wanted to have him drive out how many animals. At the same time he collected from the farmers part of his year's wages, a process which was followed in the evening by the wetting of the bargain in the tavern.

Flocks

The number of animals in the flock was never determined exactly. The pasture and the availability of water decided that. Generally a herd of cattle and a herd of horses consisted of about 500 animals, but in the Kiskunság they often talked of herds containing 800 to 1,000 cattle. The number of pigs in the herd of swine often surpassed a thousand. However, the number of sheep was always less, because processing the milk is possible only in smaller units. Generally one man and one dog came to be thought of as sufficient to herd a hundred head of livestock, and fewer to tend pigs.

The long past of Hungarian animal husbandry is also proved by the fact that the Hungarian language has several names for each flock made up of different animals. Flocks can be designated exactly by the age, sex, and size of the animals kept in them. Formerly the term *nyáj* (flock, herd) was used for all kinds of stock, but later they spoke of the *ménes,* a special name for herds of horses (cf. Plate IX). The *ciframénes* (fancy herd) of Debrecen meant a breeding herd formed of selected mares, while the *renyheménes* (lazy herd) consisted of draught and castrated horses at times when they were not working. However, the *szilajménes* (wild herd) was made up of horses who were not yet broken to the saddle nor to harness, who had not yet been in the stable and had spent summer and winter out of doors.

The *gulya* consisted of a large number of calves, young bullocks or cows, entrusted to the *számadó*. The flock could belong to a city, a village, or perhaps to a large estate. The *számadó* got his emoluments in one sum, and he was obliged to keep a definite number of *bojtár*s on this. The *cifragulya* consisted of a selected breeding stock. The *szűzgulya* (virgin flock of cattle) contained the three- to four-year-old animals, not yet used for breeding. The *törzs* (basic), *rideg* and *szilajgulya* (wildflock) were kept outdoors all the year round. The smaller animal stock of one owner was grazed in a *kurtagulya* (short flock).

Today the name *nyáj* (flock) refers primarily to sheep (cf. Plate VIII). *Falka* is the name for a smaller group, in which they usually guard the sheep of a single owner.

Formerly, the *konda* (herd of swine) spent the entire year outdoors.

The swine rooted in the swamp and pasture from the spring, while they fattened on acorns from the early autumn. In some places, the *konda* is still called *disznónyáj,* that is, a herd of swine.

Grazing and Watering

Besides the wide steppes of the Great Plain and the permanent pastures of the mountain region, the fallow fields of rotation farming assured the possibility of grazing for the animal stock. In the Great Plain, directly on the edges of the settlement, lay those fields to which the stock that spent the night at home was driven every day. Beyond that came the belt of ploughed fields, and then the vast pastures grazed by the stock stayed out from spring until autumn, or throughout the entire year. However, this was the case only in the towns and villages of the Great Plain possessing widely-spread boundaries, while elsewhere during the last two centuries it has been primarily the fallow fields that have constituted the ever-decreasing pasture area.

The grazing of extensively kept stock took place in a definite order. First horses and cattle were let on because they grazed only the higher meadows; then came the sheep, which ate the grass down to the root. Pigs could never go to the common pasture, because the other animals would not graze after them. Their area lay near the rivers and swamps. Here they could root the rush, get fish to eat, and lie about in the water.

The cold was very hard on the stock that spent the winter outdoors. At this period they drove the horses to the pasture first, because they could most easily cut up the snow cover with their hoofs. The Hungarian sheep are said to have quarried out the meagre fodder hiding even under the deepest snow. Cattle are the most helpless, because they can obtain little food with their cloven hoofs, which are easily damaged. Therefore fodder was laid in first of all for cattle. If the stock was really starving they even gobbled up the walls of the wind screen or the roofs of the huts, piled up with weeds of all kinds, just to survive somehow until the grass sprouted in the spring.

128. Milking sheep
Szék, former Szolnok-Doboka County

129. Sheep shearing
Great Plain

During the first half of the 19th century, the pastures were not sharply divided from each other. The herdsmen of the Kiskunság talk even today of the happy times of their grandfathers, when the stock drank out of the Tisza one week, and out of the Danube the next. The herdsmen of Transylvania started their descent at the beginning of winter toward the lower-lying Great Plain regions. The records prove that in the early 19th century many such flocks were outwintered in the vicinity of Nagykunság and Debrecen. There were also some herdsmen from Transylvania who drove their flock over the Carpathians into the plains of Wallachia and returned to the mountain pastures only in the spring.

The swineherds of the Great Plain set off for the oak forests of Upper Hungary usually in September, so that they would be there by St. Michael's Day (September 29), when the grazing prohibition is lifted from the acorning areas. Feeding on acorns lasted mostly until St. Nicholas' Day (December 6), so that by Christmas they could drive home the fattened, or at least improved, herd and perhaps feed them well for a few weeks more at home. The stock spent the 8 to 10 weeks outdoors, the herdsmen raising a hut only for themselves, making it out of wood and covering it with soil.

The occasion when the half-extensive stock, and the stock that

254

returned home regularly, were first driven out was a real holiday. In Catholic areas they said a Mass in honour of St. Wendelin; then, after they had drunk briefly, they turned the stock loose. The herdsman carried out those superstitious acts by which he hoped to assure the health of the stock and to hold them together. He would put smoke around the pasture, and draw a circle around it with a stick, so that no animal could wander out of it. On the night of St. George's Day (April 24) the witches tried to collect the profit of the cows by gathering it in the form of morning dew and carrying it home.

The herdsman had a great deal of trouble other than grazing the animals. In particular he had problems with watering. This was relatively simple in forest and mountain pastures, because the flock could be driven to a nearby stream or spring. Watering is much more difficult on the pastures of the steppes. Formerly the Great Plain herdsmen watered the stock from the so-called *kopolya* or *sírkút*. They dug a huge pit into the ground down to water level, then cut a path into the bank on both sides leading to it. They drove the animals down on one path, and, after drinking, they climbed up on the other.

The characteristic watering place of the Great Plain is the *gémeskút* (cf. Ills. 14, 50), a well with a steep. It was dug wide, so that water could be lifted out of it with several buckets at the same time. Formerly they put reeds on the inside of the well fastened on with spars. But if there was not enough wood in the great plains to line the well, they shored up the sides with *clods of earth,* and *tussocks.* The roots of the grass entwined in the wet

130. Sheep shearing
Szék, former Szolnok-Doboka County

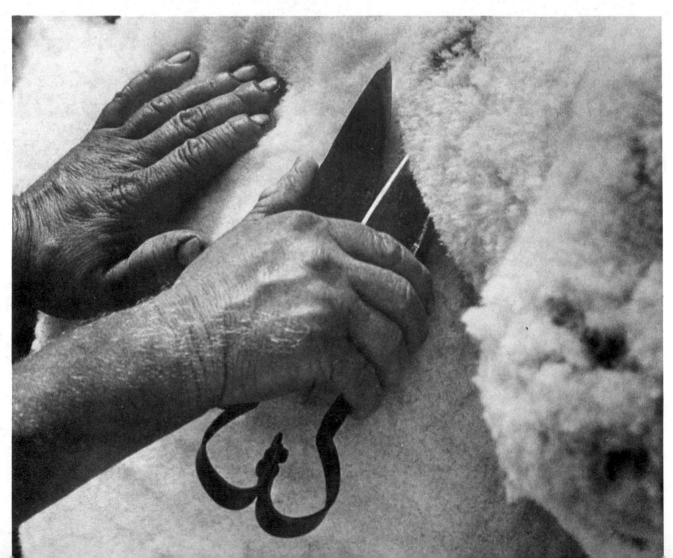

131. Watering the flock
Hortobágy

well and held with such force that it was difficult to cut through them even with a hatchet.

Drawing water is the hardest work of the Great Plain herdsmen. The stock, especially on hot summer days, drink four to five times. Each time the *bojtár* has to pull up several hundred buckets of water. There are two or three buckets to a well. A board is placed inside the well, and standing on it, the water is poured into the long trough.

Foraging

Given the natural endowments of the Carpathian Basin, it was impossible to supply the stock in winter by grazing only. Thus, a certain amount of fodder may have been gathered even around the time of the Conquest, as suggested by one or two words originating from pre-Conquest times. However, the Magyars basically learned to make hay in the Carpathian Basin, supposedly from several Slavic sources. Numerous Hungarian words derive from this source: *kasza* (scythe); *villa* (pitchfork); *pázsit* (turf); *perje* (meadow grass); *széna* (hay); *kazal* (stack), etc. At the same time, certain words prove that the Magyars themselves further advanced some of their earlier knowledge.

The hayfields long remained in the communal possession of the *gazda*s

256

of a village, and each year they decided by lot how to divide portions of the common field among themselves. Such drawing of lots must have taken place originally by means of an arrow, and therefore the divided hayfield was called *nyilas* (arrow), a name preserved in many geographic names. The first hay *(agg-, anyaszéna)* is mown in the first half of June, before harvest (cf. Ill. 33). They always do this with a scythe, and if the grass is thick enough, they then fasten a cradle made of withes, or a rake made of wood on the scythe, with which to lay the swath neatly.

The mown swath was handled in different ways in different regions according to the demands of the climate. In the Great Plain and in the dry areas of Transdanubia, the swaths are turned after the first cutting, but there is no need to do so in the case of the second or perhaps third cutting *(sarjú)*. In the mountainous areas and in areas generally more abundant in moisture, the swaths are scattered with pitchforks right away, to dry better (See Plate VI). The gathered hay is piled into a stack on a one- or

132. Mowing with scythes
Szék, former Szolnok-Doboka County

257

three-legged rack in such a way that the bottom will not reach the ground and the stack can thus dry more easily.

Gathering is done with a *pitchfork* or *rake.* Pitchforks are made of wood and are generally three-pronged. The dried hay is pushed into small round heaps with them, or maybe into *sausages,* heaps longitudinal in form. Three to four swaths are gathered with the rake, with which at first they make smaller, and later larger units. During this time the half-dry hay is being further aired and dried out. Finally they heap it in stacks *(boglya)* in the meadow and keep it there until it can be transported to a permanent place. They store it in the barn, in the hayloft, or perhaps outdoors in ricks *(boglya, kazal).* Even 20 to 30 cartloads of hay may be put into these, and the stock feed on it through the entire winter.

A whole line of cultivated fodder crops appeared from the end of the 18th century: clover *(Trifolium L.),* alfalfa *(Medicago satica),* then, in the 19th century maize, closely sown for fodder *(csalamádé, misling),* and many other plants. All this is closely connected with the appropriation of pastures by the large estates from the peasants, who were then increasingly compelled to keep the stock in the stable on fodder.

The crops of plough lands also offered various kinds of fodder for the stock. Barley straw is best, but animals were also given chaff out of necessity, as well as dried maize stalks.

Even during the last century certain old forms of foraging turned up again, though only at times when, because of a great drought, the stock could get through the winter only with great difficulty. First of all,

133. Gathering hay
Maconka, Heves County

258

134. Collecting hay
Vista, former Kolozs County

foliage must be mentioned, carefully collected in the fall and trampled into a pit that was dug in the ground, where the leafage often lasted until spring. In many cases people cut leafy branches, and, in the spring, budding branches for the stock to eat until they could be driven out to pasture.

Branding and Guarding

Animals were marked primarily by *branding*. The branding iron *(billyog-zó)* is an iron implement with the head shaped in the form of the initials of the owner or, in the case of a larger community, its identifiable sign (cf. pp. 65–6 and Figs. 4, 5). It is made red hot, and used to brand the rump of the animal, or, in the case of sheep, they smeared paint on it making a mark in that way. The mark was not for the benefit of the herdsman, who could tell every single member of the stock entrusted to him anyway, but for the owner. Animals change so much from spring to autumn that the owner does not always recognize it and can identify his own only with the help of the branding mark. Branding, therefore, provided a check on the herdsman and also helped to find and identify stolen stock.

At a primitive level, any piece of hot iron is sufficient for branding an identifying mark. Thus they burned =, *V,* or + signs into the back shoulder blade of the animal with a plough iron, a coulter. The branding irons of more prosperous farmers, passed on from father to son, were known and kept track of far and wide. Special marks differentiated the common stock of the village or town.

Smaller animals were not branded but marked by nicking. Thus bits were cut off the ears of sheep or marks cut into them. Around Kecskemét, the special mark of every larger sheep-keeping family was generally known. For example, sheep belonging to the Deák family were marked on the left ear with the shape of an arrow, and a piece in the shape of a swallow's tail was taken out from the right ear of the stock of the Szappanos family. For geese and ducks, the various marks were cut into the webs of the feet.

The stock carries such differentiating marks through its entire life. However, there are also temporary marks. Thus the shepherd carves small marks out of wood, one larger, the other smaller: two small-sized sickles, locks, chairs, violins, etc. and fastens one on the neck of the mother, the other on the neck of the lamb, so that at nursing time kinship can easily be recognized. When mother and young get used to each other, the shepherd removes the marks and puts them away for next year.

Fig. 112. Rods with notched marks. Great Plain. Second half of 19th century

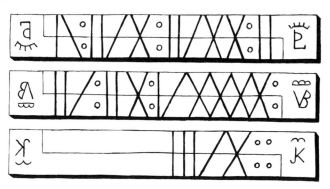

The head shepherd took account of the stock that was handed over to him by *notching.* This is the counting method, the way of keeping a check, used by herdsmen who do not read and write. With it they could always check the number of the animals entrusted to their hands. They mostly used the *half* or *paired notching,* by notching the number of the animals on a stock, then splitting the stick in half. One half stayed with the herdsman, the other with the farmer. They did the splitting in such a way that the marks could be read separately, but if the two halves were placed together it was immediately possible to see any change. New births were recorded by the herdsman on the stock notching (*tőkerovás*), deaths on the carrion notching (*dögrovás*). The expression *"dögrovásra kerül",* be destroyed, perish, and *"dögrováson van",* to be on one's last legs, was taken over from the vocabulary of the herdsmen.

The dog is always the herdsman's faithful helper in shepherding,

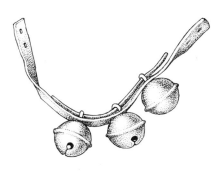

Fig. 113. Rattles to ring fixed on the neck of a lamb or a *puli* dog. Debrecen, 1920s

260

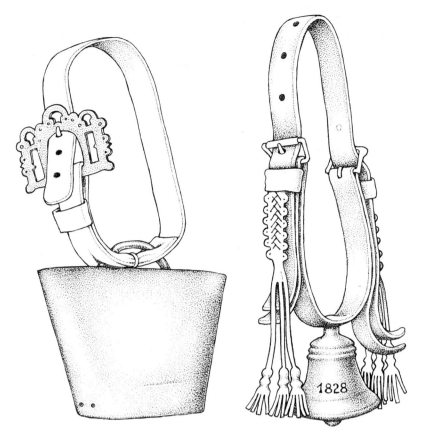

Fig. 115. Cowbell, called *kolomp*, with its strap. Hortobágy, former Hajdú County. 1920s

Fig. 116. Cowbell, called *csengő*, with its strap ending with ornamentally plaited thongs. Debrecen. 1828

keeping together the stock, but there are other means of making the often very difficult job of guarding easier. Among these the *cowbell, bell,* and *rattle* deserve principal place. These are hung on the animal's neck and can signal its whereabouts, or can help the lead animal to direct the entire flock. The cowbell is made of plate iron, bent into shape and soldered together with copper (cf. Ill. 44). The more copper used, the more pleasant its sound becomes. We find many versions ranging from almost half a metre in size to a few centimetres, the latter worn on the neck of the sheep. These are the well-known products of certain regions, but some gypsy clans also make them with a great deal of expertise. The *bell* is actually a reduced copy of church bells. It is cast from copper to which a little tin or perhaps silver is added. A good price had to be paid for large bells that had a beautiful sound, and on some occasions certain exceptional specimens were exchanged for a young head of cattle. Cowbells were mostly tied on the necks of cattle, occasionally a bell was put on an ox, and only bells were put on horses. The *rattle* is a metal ball of small size with an opening cut on its lower end. Iron pellets shaken inside it give the clattering, rattling sound. It is generally tied on a sheep, a pig, or maybe a dog. Rattles are tied on a horse only when it is hitched onto a sled during the winter, at which time the rattles are used alongside and carefully synchronized with the bell, so that people coming from the opposite direction could take notice of and avoid the quietly gliding sled.

The *stick* is the most important among the hand tools of herdsman. All use it with the exception of the horseherd. Most herdsmen made the stick themselves, but specialists particularly skilled in the craft can also be

Fig. 114. Herdsmen with their staffs wearing a high Cumanian cap called *süveg*. Karcag, Szolnok County. 1787

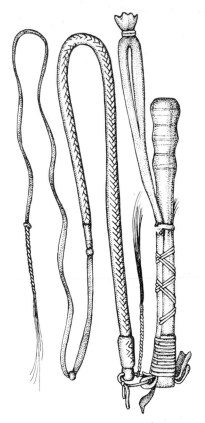

Fig. 117. Short-stocked long whip of herdsmen. Hortobágy, former Hajdú County. Early 20th century

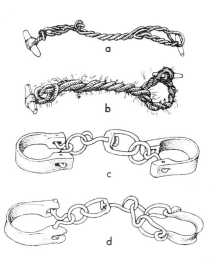

Fig. 118. Various forms of fetters.
a) A fetter made out of hemp-rope. b) Out of rope, hemp mixed with horsehair.
c) Out of wood. d) One end is wooden, the other iron. Szentes, Csongrád County.
Second half of 19th century

found. Oak, dogwood, plum, or wood from the pear tree is preferred for the basic material. They often notch it with a jackknife while it is still live on the tree so that it grows scabrous. It is cured for a long time, often even put under the manure heap to develop the suitable colour. Its sheen comes from rubbing it with lard. Herdsmen not only shepherded with the stick, but formerly it also served as a good throwing weapon against wolves. Holding it between his legs, the herdsmen could even sit on it. When he pushed it into the ground and threw his cloak on it, the makeshift tent would offer a little shade in the scorching Great Plain sun. Shepherds of Transdanubia carve a hook at the end of the staff, while shepherds of the Tiszántúl cast the crook from copper. They not only shepherd the animals with it, but by hooking the hind leg of the sheep, can easily select the one wanted. The swineherd used a *hatchet* with a handle that was approximately one metre long. This was not only an excellent defensive weapon, but was also used to kill the piglet that was destined to be eaten and to cut mistletoe off the tree for the stock.

The *whip* is always short handled and is the inevitable tool of every herdsman except the shepherd. Straps are split into narrow ribbons, then braided around a hemp rope into 6, 8, or 12 strands, and smoothed into a handsome rounded form by wetting. A wider strap goes on the end, to which they tie a *lash* made out of horsehair. The whips of horse and cattle herds are lighter, and those of the swineherds heavier, because they even braid wire into the lash, which in turn is fastened to the handle not by a strap but by a copper ring. Driving the stock is done not only by flicking the animals with the whip, but also by cracking it to make loud sounds like gunshots, which tell the flock the direction of the drive.

A hobble *(nyűg* or *béklyó)* is put on an animal that grazes alone or in smaller groups and on the horse the herdsman constantly uses, so that it cannot wander far. The *nyűg* is made of horsehair or hemp, and with it two of the horse's legs are tied together, or perhaps the opposite fore and hind legs of two horses are linked, so that they can graze slowly but have no chance of running away. The simpler form of the *béklyó* was carved out of wood. The blacksmith makes it of iron and puts a lock on it to try to prevent theft. The hobble is closely attached to the horse's pastern, its short chain allowing only small steps. According to a herdsmen's superstition, even a well-designed hobble can be opened with a plant called *vasfű* (iron grass), which is why they searched for it everywhere from spring on.

A wooden board is hung before the eyes of a wild bull or cow, so that its range of vision is restricted. A ring is put into the pig's nose so it cannot root up the yard and wreck the pen. Cattle and bison are led by a ring hooked into their nostril. The clog hung about a dog's neck curtails it in its movement to such a degree that it cannot wander far off.

The herdsmen were most afraid of stampedes of the herd. The most generally-known method of producing one was to burn hat-grease or cow hooves, the smell of which makes the stock wild, so that they cannot be prevented from bolting, and gallop away. Stampedes also happen when the stock can no longer bear the stinging of flies and try to escape the pain by bolting *(bogárzás)*. There were stories about some herdsmen who possessed knowledge by which they could make the

Fig. 119. Catching a colt out of the horseherd with a tether and a cart-rope. Hortobágy—Tiszacsege, former Hajdú County. 1930s

herds of others stampede, whilst still protecting their own from every danger. Related superstitions are known primarily in the Great Plain and belong among the oldest Hungarian folk beliefs.

To catch an unbroken animal out of the herd was a very difficult task. Horseherds used a lasso or, by a word of Cumanian origin, an *árkány* (lariat) (cf. Plate IX). They herded the horses to the well, then the herdsman approached the selected horse, scared it, and, when its head was stuck up, threw the loop over it. He held the lariat until one of his mates put the halter over the horse's head. Hungarian grey cattle were caught in a different way. They fastened a loop at the end of a long pole and tried to cast it over the horn and down to the base. They wound the

Fig. 121. Catching wild Hungarian cattle from a herd with a tether. Vukmaroca, Slavonia. Around 1910

rope that subdued the wild animal on the well-sweep, but the frantic animal often had to be pressed to the ground by a cart ladder until it wore itself out.

Animal Healing

The healing of animals was also among the herdsman's task. He carried it out by methods and procedures that were partly rational, partly irrational. They did not bother much about curing the wild (szilaj) stock, since their numbers were so great: there were always many left. Part of the loss was recovered from the skin of the dead stock. The most noted animal doctors came from among the shepherds, especially after the merino sheep came to be bred in the entire Carpathian Basin. They used an ointment made of quicksilver, turpentine, and suet on mangy sheep. A sheep suffering from the staggers was helped by an operation. Its head was cut open and the little sack of pus that had caused the illness was lifted out.

Rabies is the most dangerous sickness among dogs. They tried to forestall it by naming dogs after rivers, because it was believed that water protects animals from destructive illnesses. That is why Tisza, Bodrog, Duna, Sajó, etc., are the most widespread names for dogs. The dog spread its rabies through biting the peacefully grazing stock. They usually became aware of the stock's illness only when the signs of rabies were already showing. At this point only the famous and widely known rabies doctor could help, and he generally cured the stock of its sickness. He accepted only food and drink for his work, and as a consequence these peasant doctors generally remained poor.

If the ruminant animal eats too much green fodder at one time, it blows up. In the case of sheep, they are chased around, and as a result of this method the outflow of air begins. An iron tube is inserted by the shoulder blade of bloated cattle and the air that was caught inside is led to escape.

In most villages there was a man who knew about the sicknesses of animals. He bled the stock according to need and let out as much blood as he judged to be unnecessary. Afterwards he sewed up the wound and the animal could go on grazing.

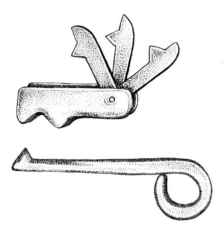

Fig. 120. Implements for cutting veins. a) Zala County. b) Szentes, Csongrád County. Second half of 19th century

Buildings for the Stock and Herdsmen

We have already dealt with buildings raised within the settlement for the stock and for the fodder. We will now give an account of the temporary structures that were renewed annually, and by which they tried to protect, at least to some degree, the men and animals on the pasture from the rigours of the weather, and to keep the stock together.

The herd that wintered outdoors needed protection not so much against the cold as against the wind. Therefore they drove them for the night close to the forest, into the curve of a bank, or to a river bed, where they could find some shelter. In completely flat areas, they set up a wind screen made of reeds (szárnyék). This branched off in several direction, so that the stock could always find a sheltered side. For sheep, they just barely dug the ends of the reeds into the ground, and folded the reed wall at two or maybe three places. However, they set the windscreen for

horses and cattle on top of a high earthen mound, because in this way the
animals were unable to knock it over.

Most structures were used to keep the stock together and to protect
them from predators, which is why there was no roof above their walls.
The simplest form was circular, made of branches, for the pigs masting

135. Sheep fold
Gyimes, former Csík County

on acorns. They closed off the entrance with round timbers or by a makeshift gate. Thus the herdsman could sleep peacefully, for his herd was not threatened by the dangers of wandering away or being attacked.

In the Great Plain they fenced off the place to lodge sheep at night, using wicker hurdles fastened to stakes. These were moved from pasture to pasture and then set up again. This was done regularly on fallow land, moving each or every other day, so that the stock would fertilize all parts of the land with their night manure *(kosarazás)*. They made such enclosures for horses, cattle and sheep out of round timbers of various sizes. In the former two instances these were permanent fixtures, the stock always being driven back from the surrounding pastures. In the latter instance they were continually moved, according to the pastures. They call the latter *esztena* in the eastern part of the linguistic region, while the narrow section where they let the sheep pass through for milking is designated by the word *esztrenga*. Since both names came from the Rumanians, we can look upon this as one element of the Wallachian influences manifested in shepherding.

There were also covered structures on the pasture, usually open on one or another of their sides, or sometimes open all round. In front of them they usually frame up a corral *(karám)*, made of beams, spars, or reeds. This kind of corral, called *akol* or *állás* (pen), is the main provision for the protection of the livestock. Because the merino sheep cannot bear the cold nor spend the night under the open sky, they raised a sheep-fold *(hodály)* for them, a roofed building closed even at the sides. These, made out of the traditional building materials (soil, reeds, etc.), appeared only during the first half of the 19th century.

The pig herds required the least protection. The undomesticated sow farrowed in a pit which she dug herself, or which might be artificially deepened for her. At the bottom of this the piglet grew in safety until it gained strength and could be let free.

The shepherd who lived outdoors required protection, like his stock, and the structures for this purpose were formerly just as simple as those for the stock. Many shepherds did not build any kind of shelter or place

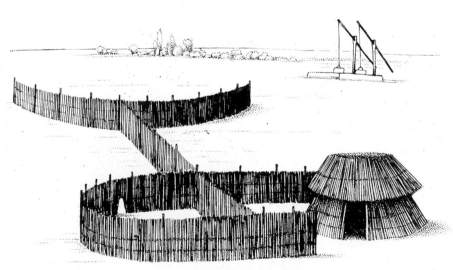

Fig. 123. Fold and windbreak with a hut built of reeds. Karcag, Szolnok County. Early 19th century

266

of relief for themselves. For them only the sheepskin coat *(suba)* provided some protection from early spring till late autumn. That is why they were called *gúnyás pásztor,* herdsmen with garbs. They mostly carried their simple equipment from one place to the other on the back of a donkey.

The simplest structure is the windbreak *(szélfogó),* a reed hurdle that can be propped up at one side and under which the herdsman can put his more precious belongings and seek shelter in pouring rain. It was made

136. A flock of sheep
Szék, former Szolnok-Doboka County

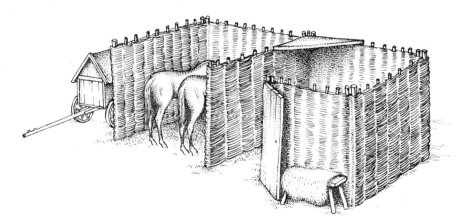

Fig. 124. Fold called *cserény.* Bene, Little Cumania (Kiskunság), Bács-Kiskun County. Early 19th century

267

of wicker, later of wooden planks, and was turned in the direction from where the rain or sun hit the strongest.

It was possible to transport a considerable part of the herdsman's buildings. Such, for example, is the wattle fold *(cserény)* used between the Danube and the Tisza. At first it was woven of wicker panels. Its ground plan is square, to which was often added a wing, fenced on three sides. Here they tied the horses that were used all the time. One corner of the wattle fence was covered and there the shepherd kept his garbs, his chest, and various smaller belongings. The height of the wattle fence permits the herdsman, when standing up, to look out and keep his eye on the stock. At first only half of it was covered, later on it was covered completely so that it would give the greatest protection against the weather. Thus it slowly became a hut, a permanent structure, which remained mostly on the same spot through the entire year. Originally, the wattle fence was the most characteristic shelter of the herdsman on the move; when the stock had grazed up the pasture and moved on, the herdsman could set it up again on the new pasture.

In certain areas of Transylvania and in the central part of the Tiszántúl, they used huts on wheels as shepherd's dwellings. They were rectangular in shape and rolled at first on solid, then later on spoked wheels. The sides and saddle-shaped roof structure were covered with planks. With animals hitched to them, they could be moved even on trackless land. The origin of this type of building can probably be looked for on the migration routes of Wallachian herdsmen, and we can trace its contacts in the Balkans as well.

Among the buildings that were harder to move and were usually renewed only annually, the *vasaló* of the Hortobágy merits mention. This is the shelter and kitchen of the herdsman, and a store for his clothes. It is circular, and made of reed walls which lean inward, but do not meet at the top. The head herdsman's larger chest is placed across the entrance, and the young herdsmen's smaller chests are lined up to the right of the entrance. Several footstools are also found inside, while many spoons, forks, knives, awls, and other tools useful to have at hand are stuck behind the hem of the reeds. An open fire burns in the centre,

Fig. 125. Herdsman's hut called *vasaló*.
Hortobágy, former Hajdú County.
Around 1920

137. The cabin of the shepherd who
guards the flock at night
Csíkszentdomokos, former Csík County

and on this the herdsmen's boy *(tanyás)* prepares the cooked food. The
herdsmen of the Hortobágy are so attached to the *vasaló* that they build it
even beside their permanent hut, but in this case they only use it for
cooking.

One of the most characteristic herdsman buildings is the circular
kontyos kunyhó (rick-shaped hut), up to four or five metres in diameter.
A door is generally left on its southern side, with a panel of reeds or, later
on, of planks. Inside, there are sleeping places and chests, and smaller
tools are placed on its inward leaning wall. They never light a fire in this
type of hut, but rather cook in front of it. The swineherds who were
masting the pigs in the winter also built round huts, but out of split logs.
They laid straw, then soil or perhaps sods, on the notched structure.
They lowered its base and in some places made benches suitable to lie on.
A fire burned in the centre, the smoke passing through the door or
through the small opening left in the roof. By means of material and
linguistic evidence, current research can trace the past of this form of hut
back to the Finno-Ugric period.

After the time when the territories of the pastures had been consolidated, the buildings also became permanently located. Herdsmen's huts
were already by this time generally built of mud or adobe, their roofs
being of saddle shape and covered with reeds or straw. Usually such huts
are located near the pens and corrals.

The Great Plain herdsmen often used the guard's tree *(őrfa, állófa)*.
This is a topped tree with branches, 5 to 7 metres high, which they dig
into the ground near, or in front of, the hut or wattle fence. The
functions of such a tree are many. The herdsman climbs up on it to signal
to his mate in charge of the flock grazing at a distance, or perhaps to
watch the movement of the stock. Cattle rubbed against the tree and
polished it completely, but at the same time left alone the easily
damageable structures made of reeds or wicker. The herdsmen hung
knapsacks on the tree or the raw meat that was to serve as a meal. In
earlier times it was also looked upon as a sign. Only the head shepherd
could use the land for grazing where he had it dug into the ground. At

269

times, in the region between the Danube and Tisza, it was placed on different sides of the wattle fence so that the stock that lay around it would fertilize every area.

Breaking in the Stock and the Means of Transportation

One of the greatest values of livestock (cattle, horses) is that, hitched to the yoke, they plough the land, haul in produce, drive the dry mill, carry finished or half-finished products to the market, and do many other such tasks of basic importance in peasant farming (cf. Ill. 138–40). This is why draught animals were broken to the yoke with a great deal of care and by a well-defined method.

In the case of unbroken animals driven to pasture, the calf usually stayed with the mother. A young herdsman selected one of these calves, to become a draught animal and tied it to a stake near the farmstead. Its mother nursed it when the herd returned from the pasture. They gave it more rope after weaning, so that he could graze around. It thus became used to the herdsman. Such pre-training is unnecessary in the case of domestically kept animals. Young bullocks were broken in at three years of age, generally in the autumn, less frequently in early spring. It was hard, despite the previous training, to extract the selected young animal from the wild herd. When it had quietened down, they led it, tied

138. Women carrying sacks Vista, former Kolozs County

behind the cart, into the yard of the farmstead or village dwelling, and
there they tied it to a tree. They put neither food nor drink in front of it,
but kept offering it to the animal. If the animal accepted it, it was
becoming tame, and they could start breaking him to the yoke.

The yoke (járom or iga) is a frame of wood, into which two oxen can
be hitched next to each other. They put this around the ox's neck and
close it off on the side by the yoke pin, usually made of iron, so that it
cannot pull his head out. In the yoke the ox pulls along the centrally
placed shaft by the strength of its neck and withers. The end of the pole is
fastened to the cart or the forecarriage of the plough by a thick pin.
Several pairs of oxen are connected consecutively by means of poles.
This kind of carriage is always driven with a long-handled whip, usually
made of rope and capable of reaching to the first pair of oxen
(cf. Fig. 121).

The young bullocks selected for breaking in are first matched according to size and by the shape of their horns. After that comes the attempt
to put their necks into the yoke, which is usually such a difficult task that
it requires the strength of several men. Once this has been done, they are
hitched before and behind already trained, older pairs of oxen. The
training is mostly done with a cart, whose wheels are tied in place, or
perhaps making them used to work by ploughing or harrowing. If one
of the young bullocks continually tries to break out of the yoke, they try
to break him with the spiked tinószoktató (bullock breaker), that is pulled
onto the yoke pin. Months pass before the animal learns to do every kind
of work and understand the words that signal starting, stopping, and
turning, and it finally becomes an ox.

Breaking in a horse also starts with catching it. To do so a rope
(pányva) is thrown on the neck of the selected horse, but as it tries to get
loose by every means, it takes three to four men to control the animal.
When it tires, they put a tether made of hemp over the horse's head, and
the saddle on its back, then the bridle and the bridle bit. After this the most
able, venturesome young herdsman can start to break in the horse.

The Hungarian saddle is extremely simple, composed of four pieces

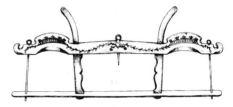

Fig. 126. Ornamented yoke. Tiszabercel,
Szabolcs County. 1930s

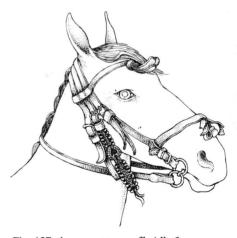

Fig. 127. A peasant type of bridle for
a saddled horse. Debrecen. First half of
19th century

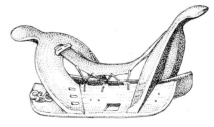

Fig. 128. A peasant type of wooden saddle.
Great Plain. Late 19th century

Fig. 129. Horse of a horseherd with horse gear. Bugac-puszta, former Bács County. 1930s

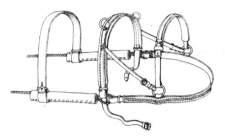

Fig. 130. Driving harness. Debrecen. First half of 20th century

of wood. Two longish wooden plates fit closely and directly onto the horse's back, with the *pommel* carved in the shape of a half circle, fitting into the place and holding them together. Leather is stretched over the projecting parts. This form of saddle is completely different from the one built on a ∧ -shaped wooden base in the western part of Europe.

We can find related kinds in the East, and the Finno-Ugric origin of the word for saddle, *nyereg,* itself implies a long past. The Hungarian saddle assures much easier movements for the rider, and especially for the horse, a fact which confirms the military successes of the Magyars at the time of the Conquest. Beginning in the 18th century, this saddle form was also naturalized in the west with the troops that were set up on the pattern of the Hungarian hussars.

When the horse is sufficiently obedient under the saddle, it can be put in *harness.* They use the *breast harness* throughout the Hungarian linguistic region. Only with the introduction of the western, cold-blooded horses did the *collar harness* spread on the larger estates and in the western section of the linguistic territory. Two horses are generally harnessed to the pole, but occasionally a third horse pulls the cart from the right. Four horses are hitched in pairs in line ahead, while in the case of five, the two behind and the three in front really make the cart fly. In these cases the driver often drives from the back of the left rear horse and directs and urges on those harnessed in front with his long whip.

At first they made a young colt pull a tree stump, and when he was used to doing that, they hitched him in front of the cart as the third horse, the *lógós* (trace horse). When he no longer misbehaved, the colt was made, along with the mare his mother or another older horse, to serve as the *nyerges* or *rudas,* the left or right hand horse, depending on the position that best suited its size.

140. On the way home from reaping Galgagyörk, Pest County

141. Sleighing
Drágszél, Bács-Kiskun County

The simplest means of conveyance are the *sleds,* which slide on the ground or on snow. Hay is hauled on a sled, and certain types of husbandman's buildings are erected on them (Transylvania), as well as wicker granaries, which can thus be dragged farther away from where they stood (the Southern Great Plain). Recently sleds are used only to draw on snow. The short Székely *bakszán* was used to transport timber logs, fastened on one end to the sled. In Upper Hungary, two such sleds accommodated the length of wooden logs. There is also a form of sled in general use over a large part of the linguistic region which slides on two runners having upright fronts to which are fastened cart-like sides or maybe a wicker frame which suits for carrying a load or people.

Fig. 131. Slay to be drawn by a horse. Debrecen. Around 1940

The simplest forms of vehicles on wheels are two-wheeled, and drawn by a horse, more rarely a donkey. Herdsmen used such carts to carry their equipment and food from the settlement to the pasture. The *talyigás* (barrowman) of Debrecen and Miskolc was the haulier for the poor, while *navvies* carried soil to the designated area at the time when the great works of regulating the rivers and building the railways were going on, beginning in the second part of the previous century. A wooden box-body sits over the spoked wheels. Between the double shafts, which are continuations of the side-beams for the bottom of the cart, they hitch one horse and so can haul a considerable load. One version of this, mounted on springs and serving to transport people, is the tumbril *(kordé),* which even spread into towns (Nyíregyháza).

The most common form of wheeled transport is the *wagon,* which is fairly uniform over much of the Carpathian Basin. It may even have originated by connecting the two-wheeled carts, for even today most

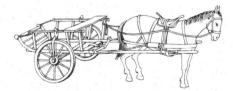

Fig. 132. Tumbril cart with a single horse. Miskolc. It sometimes occurs even today

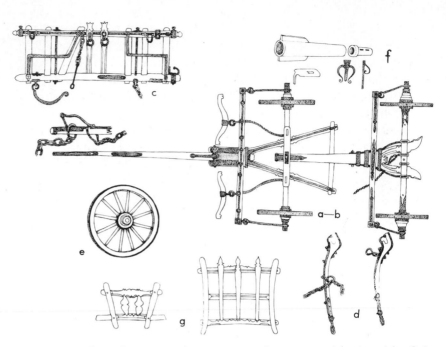

Fig. 133. The construction and details of heavy wagon made of wood with its ironings. Debrecen. First half of 20th century. a–b) The lower framework of the wagon. c) Its sides. d) The woods for holding the sides in place, called "lőcs". e) A wheel. f) The axle. g) The front and back rack

wagons can be taken apart into two sections, or, with the aid of the *stretcher* that runs centrally along their bottom, can be adjusted to the required length. The difference between horse- and ox-traction comes from the fact that the horse pulls by traces, the shaft only serving to give direction, whereas the ox transfers its draught power directly through

142. Horses drinking
Jászjákóhalma, Szolnok County

the pole. The front two wheels can be turned as required around the centre *pin* until one hits against the lower plank of the wagon body. The rear wheels cannot be turned. Nowadays the wheels are equal in size, but formerly the *wheelwright* made the rear wheels larger. The wheels consist of four, five or six felloes, with two spokes mortised into each, so that the wheels have eight, ten or twelve spokes.

The difference between the wagons of the Great Plain and those of the mountain region lies not so much in construction as in size and fittings. The former are much shorter and are equipped with a *vendégoldal* (frame), so that more can be loaded on them both in width and in length. Otherwise wagons are lined with a wicker frame, suitable for carrying corncobs or other produce. The vehicle of the mountain region is significantly longer, and its high and latticed sides make loading easier. Because the roads vary in quality they cannot load it high.

Originally the coach *(kocsi)* must have been a version of the wagon. It got its name from Kocs, a town in Komárom County, which during the Middle Ages was one of the most important stations on the highway that connected Buda and Vienna. They called the light vehicle made here *kocsi-szekér,* which later served almost entirely to transport people. The entire mechanism, and along with it its name, spread into Western Europe (English: *coach,* German: *Kutsche,* Swedish: *kusk,* Italian: *cocchio,* French: *coche,* Spanish: *coche*). In the course of later development a spring- or suspension-framed, carriage-like vehicle evolved from it.

The wagon is not only indispensable to the peasant, but from the Middle Ages on, it was the most important means of transportation and commuting that served to exchange the products of various regions. In the towns and villages, the *carters,* possessing the equipage and vehicles, formed a special social group. Certain villages occupied themselves almost exclusively with hauling. Thus, for example, the hauliers of Tokaj-Hegyalja carried wine to Poland and Russia, and brought back furs, clothing material, and special food-stuffs. The carters who carried farm implements, lime, and charcoal to the Great Plain returned loaded with grain. The hauliers carried the products of potters, weavers, and furriers to markets. Therefore they played a significant role not only in spreading news, but also in disseminating products and cultural goods. The *mail coach* by and large just carried people, so that its importance lay in spreading news and in carrying the post.

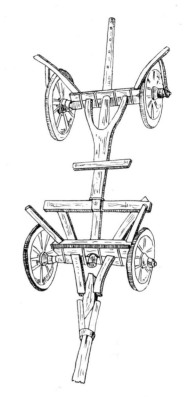

Fig. 134. Lower framework of a wagon used in hilly land. Nyíri, former Abaúj County. 1950s

Alimentation

The material discussed above in broad outline gave us an acquaintance with the acquisition, growing, and preparation of various plant and animal raw materials, and with their transport to the places where they are processed and consumed. The greater part was used up on the spot by the producers themselves, and only in certain areas did production for market begin earlier in quantities larger than needed for home consumption. This applied to wine already in the 16th to 17th centuries, and certain special produce (paprika, tobacco, fruit, etc.) from the 19th century, and finally to cereals.

In the peasant diet, ancient procedures and dishes lived and are living side by side with the newest ones. The old ones came back into existence especially during times of famine, such as in certain years of the last century, when people not only ate the buds of trees, but ground and baked the bark of trees into bread. Differences among the social layers of the peasantry showed most clearly in the diet. Dishes primarily of vegetable origin dominated the meals of the poor, while fat meat was consumed in much larger quantities by the rich peasants. The dietary requirements of various religions also greatly influenced food, so that historical and social stratification are clearly perceptible within a single settlement.

It is certain that traces of a Finno-Ugric inheritance can also be shown in Hungarian alimentation in names, if in no other way (*fazék,* pot; *köles,* millet; *vaj,* butter; *kenyér,* bread; *főz,* cook; *forr,* boil; *süt,* bake; *eszik,* eat; *iszik,* drink, etc.). *Lé (leves,* soup) principally means fish soup among the related peoples, whereas among the Hungarians it became generally used as a concept for thin food, which counted until the most recent times as the most important food of the Hungarian peasantry. The Magyar people must have learned a lot about milk processing during the migrations from various Turkic peoples (*köpü,* churn; *író,* buttermilk; *sajt,* cheese; *túró,* cottage cheese, etc.). The influence of the alimentary culture of the Slavic peoples also shows up in the vocabulary (*ecet,* vinegar; *kása,* mush; *kalács,* milk loaf; *kolbász,* sausage; *kovász,* leaven; *laska,* noodles; *pecsenye,* roast; *pogácsa,* bun; *szalonna,* bacon; *tészta,* pastry; *zsír,* lard, etc.), and also in dishes that are still made today (e.g. cabbage and beet dishes). The Germans also influenced the peasant kitchen in many cases, but generally through transfers from the meals of the upper class (*cukor,* sugar; *piskóta,* sponge cake; *früstük,* breakfast; *szaft,* gravy; *szósz,* sauce, etc.). Certain Italian influences also came to us the same way (*palacsinta,* thin pancake; *mazsola,* raisin; *torta,* cake, etc.). If we add to all this the possibilities provided by the range of regional basic materials and inner development, then we have before us the extraordinarily manifold and complicated nature of the Hungarian peasantry's alimentation.

So far ethnographic research has not cleared up satisfactorily the changes in the historical periods of Hungarian and, within it, of peasant alimentation. Today, basic research makes it possible to carry out this extremely important work, but until it has been carried out, we must be satisfied with introducing primarily the peasant order of meals, the procedures for preparing meals and the most important groups of dishes of the previous century.

Furnishing the Kitchen

We have spoken above (cf. Ills. 63–69) of the most important forms of the open and closed fireplaces, on which raw food was cooked or baked.

Most cooking vessels were made of pottery. The ornamentation of milk jugs *(köcsög)* was simple. Of these, poorer households possessed four or five, the richer ones often more than twenty. Earthenware pots, varying in size, were generally left in their original colour: red, gray-black, or white. The largest among them have a volume of 25 to 30 litres, and are used at weddings to cook soup and stuffed cabbage. They were used partly on the open fire, partly on the hearth. Because such large cooking pots were used only rarely and on special occasions, they were generally kept in the attic and filled with vegetables and dry fruit. The earthenware pan is actually a larger, elongated platter, with or without legs, with turned up sides. Meat is roasted in it, in plenty of lard, on an iron tripod placed over the open fire, or placed on the bottom of the hearth. Sometimes its shape imitates the shape of the fowl that is baked in it.

The man who eats in the field or regularly goes there often fries bacon

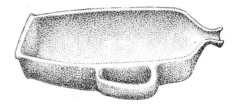

Fig. 135. Earthenware baking pan. Great Plain. Late 19th century

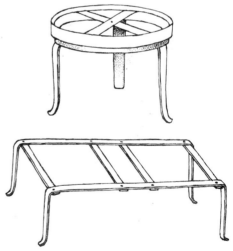

Fig. 136. Tripod for a pot when cooking on an open fire and a similar four-legged stand. Monor, Pest County. 1930s

143. Kitchen with stove Bábonymegyer, Somogy County

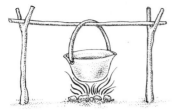

144. Cauldron in the sheep fold Gyimes, former Kolozs County

Fig. 137. Ways of hanging up a cauldron when cooking out of doors. Monor, Pest County. 1930s

Fig. 138. Wooden buckets for dipping into water and for storing water. Őriszentpéter, Vas County. Around 1940

for himself even today. The grate *(rostély)* is a square iron lattice on legs, under which embers are heaped to roast the meat. Cast-iron pots and pans were also used in the peasant kitchen.

The most widely used iron vessel was the cauldron *(bogrács),* which they call *üst* in Transylvania. One form is round, and its edge turns outward.

Its equivalent variations can be traced through the Eastern Slavs all the way to the Caucasus. The other form is pear-shaped, its edge upstanding and straight. This type is found in the southern part of the linguistic region and is equivalent to Balkan forms. Soup and meat is cooked in a cauldron, over an open fire. Kettles made of copper are larger than the former, and were used for boiling bacon, blood sausage, to melt down fat, or boil fodder for the stock. Such cauldrons were used in built-in fireplaces primarily in Transdanubia and the Great Plain. The latter type of cauldron is western in origin and came to Hungary only in the nineteenth century.

Among the vessels used for storing water, the *bucket* was earlier made of wood, and its sheet metal versions spread only from the second half of the 19th century. The different types of jugs *(korsó)* served both to carry and store water. The unglazed, red and black versions are preferred

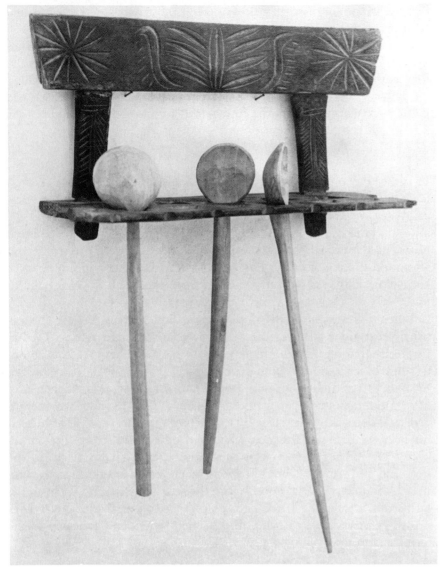

Fig. 139. Unglazed earthenware jugs for holding and carrying water. Great Plain. Early 19th century

145. Spoon-rack
Semjén, Borsod-Abaúj-Zemplén County

146. Wooden bowl with two handles
Szuhahuta, Heves County

because in the summer the fieldworkers can bury its base in the ground so that the evaporating water remains cool inside.

Differently shaped and formed cooking vessels made of various materials, along with the many supplementary utensils, are generally kept in the kitchen (cf. pp. 149–53). If their shape permits, they are hung on the wall, along with the plates used for eating. The larger vessels and platters are usually kept in the cupboard placed in the foreground of the kitchen. It is a relative newcomer to the peasant house.

The Order of Meals

In earlier days the Hungarian peasant, according to traditions that go back to medieval times, ate only twice a day: in the morning a meal called *reggeli, früstök,* or *ebéd,* a word later used for lunch, and in the afternoon the *ebéd* or *vacsora.* During the wintertime, this practice lasted nearly till the present, and is closely connected to the early morning and afternoon stoking of the heating contrivance. However, during times of hard work this system is modified to three meals, and occasionally to five.

When the spring work of ploughing and sowing begins, people usually eat three meals a day. The two main meals remain, but in between, at noon (*délebéd,* midday meal), they eat bread, bacon, onion, or some other cold meal from their knapsack, or maybe fry some bacon. In some towns of the Tiszántúl, people stay on the fields for several days at a time if the outskirts cover large distances (e.g. Hajdúböszörmény). On such occasions it was usually the farmer's task to cook a hot meal at noon in the kettle. Herdsmen who lived outdoors also ate three times a day (in the region between the Danube and Tisza). Early in the morning the youngest herdsboy *(lakos)* cooked a breakfast consisting mostly of meat, while at noon, when the stock was grazing far from the farmstead, the young herdsmen ate only bacon and dried meat with bread. A meat dinner awaited them again when they returned to the farmstead in the evening.

147. Two pottery dishes

The number of meals also increased during the main summer work, especially during harvest and threshing time, when the greatest exertion is necessary. People ate something early in the morning and drank brandy with it, so that they would not start work on an empty stomach, then around 8 o'clock came a breakfast of cold food. They had a one-hour break at noon, and if they harvested for themselves, the women carried the meal out. A brief rest followed again in the afternoon around 5 o'clock, which was accompanied by a cold meal, and when they quit working after dark, they again had warm food at home, or in the case of the share harvesters, at the overnight lodging.

It will be apparent that meals were adjusted to the work on hand. A significant difference existed between everyday and festive food. It is interesting to note that the latter has best preserved an archaic character, while at the same time being the most receptive to accepting new elements. On Sunday, people always tried to have chicken soup and boiled fowl and, more recently, some sort of pastry. The meat of cattle counted as a feast and a rare food, but on the other hand pork was eaten in some form even on weekdays.

A standard menu was associated with the major holidays, although it varied according to region and religion. Thus the Catholics ate fasting kinds of foods on Christmas Eve: cabbage soup, bean soup, fish, and pastry without lard. The Calvinists eat pork-, beef-, or chicken soup and milk loaf, as fasting regulations do not restrict them even on this day, so that in some areas even stuffed cabbage occurs. The situation is different on Good Friday, because then all religious denominations fast. Some kind of sour soup (*cibere,* cabbage soup), lardless milk loaf and popcorn is the food for the day. On Easter Sunday chicken soup, milk loaf and turnovers occur most frequently; Catholics at this time eat pork. Ham is blessed and eaten still while the holiday lasts. Eating spring lamb is a novel practice that has spread only recently.

Special powers are attributed to certain foods, so that their consumption is tied to certain days. Thus mush is eaten at the New Year, in the belief that it will bring luck all the year round. Lentils eaten on Friday make the girls beautiful by Sunday. Small seeds (millet, poppy seeds, etc.) are eaten before sowing to make the harvest more plentiful. Eggs are eaten for the same reason, having in general always represented fertility in peasant superstitions.

Special meals are also associated with the outstanding events of life. The godmothers bring the midday meal to the women in confinement. This generally parallels the Sunday meal, although they always try to make some new dish or pastry, especially something that has just come into vogue. The chicken soup plays a great role in the order of the wedding feast, and in the Great Plain they cook a pastry made into snail-shapes in it. Boiled meat is eaten with horseradish or beets. Rarely are stuffed cabbage rolls absent from traditional food, especially in the central part of the linguistic region. We can find different versions of the wedding mush practically everywhere. It appears to be the oldest element of the diet. At wakes only brandy and bread is served, perhaps bacon, milk loaf, and recently leavened pastry. Only in rare cases do the mourners eat a meal of cooked food.

Storing and Preserving Raw Materials

Fig. 140. An open construction for drying prunes. Former Szatmár County. Early 20th century

We have already spoken about storing raw material (cf. pp. 169–174), but most of it must still undergo some processing until it can be used. From the second half of the 19th century, many types of flour were ground in the mills, and this flour was helped to differentiate its uses. In peasant households flour was stored in the pantry for a month or two. Flour bins served this purpose, in some places barrels and jars. Maize flour cannot be kept in this way for an extended period because it sours easily, which is why they usually ground it not at the mill but rather on a home grinder, and grinding only as much as could be used up right away.

Some raw materials were preserved in various ways. One of the most important processes is *pickling*. This is the method for storing cabbages, cucumbers, beets, turnips, and many other plants for a longer time, and sometimes this is a way of making them more enjoyable. The most important among these is sauerkraut, which has always enjoyed great popularity. The cabbage is shredded with a cabbage shredder made especially for this purpose (formerly it was simply chopped up with a knife), then stuffed or stamped into large barrows. It is salted, then pressed down with a board by means of a large stone, more recently with a screw. Complete cabbage-heads are placed in between the layers, because the whole leaves of cabbage are necessary for making cabbage rolls *(töltött káposzta)*. In the northern and western regions of the linguistic territory, beets and turnips are also pickled, and soup is made of them. Cucumbers, soured by different processes, are served with meat as a treat.

Various kinds of fruit are *desiccated,* especially plums, apples, pears, and less frequently apricots. The simplest method is to lay them out in the sun on a wickerwork tray, but as this requires a great deal of time, drying hearths are often used instead. These are low ovens located in small, separate buildings. Fruit, previously desiccated in the sun, is placed on top of these hearths, on large-sized wicker trays with 2 to 3 cm high edges. The heat penetrates from below and the fruit dries fast. Dried fruit is not only the favourite treat of children, but is also particularly good for cooking fasting soups *(böjtös leves)*. The drying of mushrooms is general in mountain areas where great quantities of different kinds grow.

Storing meat for a longer time caused a great deal of difficulty, since the meat of slaughtered animals could not be eaten all at once either in the herdsmen's or in the peasant households. The herdsmen of the Great Plain cut up the meat of the sheep or calf into small pieces, salted it, put paprika on it, then cooked it in the kettle without water and, by shaking it from time to time, turned it. When it was thoroughly cooked, they spread it on a mat in a shady place. It desiccated completely in 2 to 3 days and could be poured into a sack. Each morning, the young herdsmen took a handful out of this and as they followed the herd, ate it with bread. If the possibility arose, they threw it into boiling water and prepared it just like raw meat. We can assume that this may have been the food of the wandering Magyars, who could easily carry it with them in their saddle bags. A famous Italian chronicler took note of the Hungarian practice in the 14th century, for according to him, in the course of the Italian military campaign of King Louis I, the Hungarian warriors fed on dried meat which they kept in the satchels. Sources from the 19th century and earlier alike mention the drying and smoking of fish.

Pork was not desiccated in peasant households, but preserved with *salting* and *smoking*. After the feast that followed pig-killing, the meat was kept in brine for several weeks, then dried, and hung in the smoky attic or the upper part of the open chimney, more recently in a separate building built especially for this purpose. Here the smoke slowly penetrated the meat so it could be kept safely in the attic or in a cool pantry till the main work periods of the summer and sometimes until new fresh meat became available. The technique of smoking came to Hungary from the west and spread through the entire Hungarian linguistic region.

Another, newer method of preserving meat, called *browning,* is known over a relatively large area. The cooked meat is placed into a large-sized earthenware or tin dish and melted lard is poured over it. As it solidifies, the meat is sealed from the air, and so can be kept even until summer.

Drying was also used to preserve the various pastas kneaded for soups, such as the generally known pasta of the Great Plain, *lebbencs.* Pasta is kneaded out of flour and eggs, stretched thin, and dried until it loses all its moisture. It is then broken up into palm-sized bits and put in white sacks, where it keeps for several months. *Tarhonya,* which is made of similarly kneaded pasta, is also generally known over the same area. It is first pressed through a leather sieve, then a wire sieve, and finally the few-millimetre-sized crumbs are dried in the shade. This too can be kept for months, even for a year. Soups made with these pastas spread initially as the food of herdsmen, of people working in the fields, of railway workers, and of pick and shovel men. Today, even in city diet, commonly known soups are made with both, but especially with the latter.

Among milk products, cottage cheese *(túró)* is stored in a sheepskin bag (Székelyland) or perhaps kneaded in dishes made of tree bark, so that it takes on its odour. Butter is preserved by browning and storing for an extended period in clay pots.

Soups

Various soups *(lé)* occupy a prominent place in the menu of the Hungarian peasantry, for a major meal is unthinkable without them. That is why they say in a story from the Palots area that "of soup alone there were seven kinds".

The most appreciated among soups is bouillon or meat soup *(húsleves)* made of poultry, of pork—especially spare ribs—and sometimes of beef. The meat cooked in it is eaten either with or separately from the soup. Different kinds of pastas are cooked in the soup. In the Great Plain, foremost among these is the *csiga* (snail shaped noodles), which is cooked in the soup for wedding dinners or on other festive occasions. These are made of small pieces of pasta cut into squares and curled with a small rod of wood or iron on the reed of the weaver's loom. Making them is an occasion for popular winter evening gatherings. They also put ribbon, diamond, strawberry leaf, and other differently shaped pasta into the meat soup.

Amongst the long line of sour soups, we should mention the *cibere* or *kiszi,* some variety of which is known over the entire linguistic region. Hot water is poured on bran, and just as it begins to ferment, they strain it and mix it with egg and milk. Such soup is also made out of dry fruit. Both have a significant role among fasting dishes. *Cabbage soup* is found in a soured form, although not as often as among Eastern Slavs.

An outstanding place belongs to the soups made out of leguminous plants (beans, peas, less frequently lentils). These were grown either in the garden or along with maize, planted between the rows, so every household had plenty of them. Such soups were usually thickened with flour and enriched with smoked meat.

Soups made with pasta are mostly the food of herdsmen and field workers. In the Great Plain they cooked it out of *lebbencs* and *tarhonya* and made it so thick that the spoon stood upright in it. Both pastas are browned with lard or bacon, with onion, paprika, and more recently potatoes added to it, and cooked together.

Preparation of Plant Foods

The acquisition of basic materials of plants had always played a minor, subsidiary role in historical times, and their significance decreased through the years.

The plants for mushes (millet, spelt, buckwheat, etc.) were sown in many places in earlier centuries, and were an integral part of alimentation. The short growing-time for millet makes late sowing possible, even after harvesting or after flooding. It also grows in the mountains. By the 18th century, corn became widespread and replaced the mushes, except on the peripheries of the linguistic territory. The consumption of corn in various ways developed primarily among the Hungarians of Transylvania and in Somogy and Szabolcs. From the second half of the 19th century, wheat-rye also became a staple of the peasant diet.

Due to the class structure of the peasantry, the use of cereals showed differences even within one village. The poorest peasants were forced to make do with mush, and continued to grow plants for mush. In other places these remained due to weather conditions, as for example, in the mountains, where corn won't survive. In the Great Plain, the poor peasants mixed the flour of corn with wheat flour to make bread. But by the 20th century, the use of mushes, especially the ones made of corn, was restricted to the poorest folk, so they were rarely consumed by well-to-do peasants. Only in some cases has it survived almost to this day: as a traditional food at weddings (mush with milk), or at men's gatherings (mush with mutton).

Porridges, Mushes

Mush was an important food in the past, but less so in this century. The original basic materials (millet, buckwheat, spelt) are now grown only sporadically, their place has been taken primarily by maize. The grain is first ground into coarse meal *(dara)* or in the case of rice, which has recently become widespread, left whole. We shall mention only a few of the extremely varied and numerous ways of preparing mush.

In the Great Plain, mush made of millet is first cooked in salt water. When the water had boiled down completely, the mush is turned out or left in the pot and eaten with lard and milk. The *puliszka* (maize porridge) of Transylvania differs from this only a little. Finely ground maize meal is thrown all at once into rapidly boiling water and, as it cooks, it sticks together in one big lump. When it is ready, it is turned out on a wooden board, sliced up, and eaten, mostly with milk. The *bálmos* is similarly a dish of Transylvania. Among the many ways of preparing it, the most frequent is to pour the whey back on the cheese and let it drip down again. Then the juice that was improved in this way is boiled, and sifted maize meal dribbled into it.

The *meaty mushes* are the dishes for feasts or community work. In the Őrség they cook millet or buckwheat mush in meat stock and season it with pepper and salt. They put the pieces of meat into it after the stock has boiled down completely and pour onion, browned in lard, on top. Sometimes they also mix a roux with it, to make it more filling. *Ludaskása* (goose mush) is made in the same way, and it figures among the more prestigious dishes. *Kitolókása* ("farewell" mush) is served at a wedding, and in many places a pretzel is put on top of it. This marks the conclusion of the wedding.

The dishes listed and introduced above are all, with the exception of the *puliszka,* poured porridges, which means that the grits or flour is cooked slowly and with constant stirring in boiling water. Beside these, the Hungarian peasantry also eats *mashed porridge.* They make these from grits, beans, pealed and chopped up potatoes. The latter dish has spread, primarily from the middle of the last century, in the form of mushy dishes, even among the peasantry, but its preparation in the form of a cooked and thickened vegetable has occurred only rarely.

One important group of the mushy foods is called *sterc.* Flour is browned in a raw or half cooked state, then boiling water poured on it and it is eaten mostly with lard. The name of these dishes and of their method of preparation points to an origin through the mediation of the Austrian kitchen, and we can emphasize their western connections. There are two basic forms of *sterc.* Flour is browned in a pan for the dry *sterc* and hot water is poured on it when it begins to change its colour. When this boils down lard is put under the meal and they keep stirring it until it turns to crumbs. Recently mashed potatoes are mixed into it, which shows very well the adaptation of the new raw material to an old technique. Mush *sterc* is made by throwing the meal into boiling water all at once, and this sticks together in one big lump. They pour off the water from under it after half an hour of cooking, then break it apart with a wooden spoon and brown it on lard until it turns into crumbs. This method of preparation has disappeared almost completely and can be found only sporadically in various parts of Transdanubia.

Tarts Tarts *(lepény)* are kneaded of flour, with the addition of salt and water, then cut into shapes of different size and baked so that the tart stays in one piece. The importance of tarts during the past centuries must have been significantly greater, yet certain kinds are still in existence today. In Hungary, a kind referred to in ethnographical literature as *soft tart bread* is widely spread. These were still made and consumed over the entire Hungarian linguistic region around the turn of the century.

Its material can be extremely varied, according to the locally predominant cereal type. This is why it is made from wheat and rye or barley. It is made of buckwheat in Western Transdanubia, but there are also certain kinds made of maize meal and potatoes. Salt is the most important ingredient on flavouring the tart-loaf, but in some regions pepper is also put into it, and in the more southerly areas it is sprinkled with paprika. Less frequently poppy seeds are also used, either kneaded into it or sprinkled on top. The tart, 20 to 30 cm in diameter, is shaped out of the finished dough and its thickness rarely exceeds 2 to 3 cm. *Pretzels* of varying size are also shaped out of the same dough. They are up to 15 to 20 cm in size in Western Transdanubia, while they are only 4 to 5 cm in the eastern part of the country. In certain villages there are specialists whose occupation is pretzel making. The pretzels are sold in neighbouring villages or at big fairs. Especially famous are the *pretzels from Debrecen,* purchased eagerly even today as presents from the fair. In the eastern half of the linguistic territory a small loaf was shaped out of dough, its height reaching to 6–7 cm, but its diameter not exceeding 15 cm. Similar loaves were baked in the Bodrogköz as a treat for the Christmas carollers.

The baking of flat tarts took place in different ways. One of the oldest procedures is to spread the dough on hot stones. Very often the flat stone in front of the fireplace served this purpose. Baking in embers, in ashes, survived for a long time in regions of open fireplaces and hearths. The great antiquity of this method of baking is proved by the tales in which the hero's mother packs biscuits *(pogácsa) baked in ashes* for his big trip. In a large part of Transdanubia and in the Great Plain they baked the tart-loaf in the hearth.

Hard tart-loaf *(kemény lepénykenyér)* is made exclusively from wheat flour, and its diffusion is more limited and has been steadily decreasing for centuries. Its dough is prepared as for the soft tart-loaf, but is stretched knife-blade thin (3 to 4 mm) and baked in the hearth or on top of the cooking stove. It is rarely eaten directly but rather is broken up into small pieces and dunked for a moment into hot water. It belongs, in certain areas, among fasting foods.

One form of *palacsinta* (thin pancake) can also be listed in the above category—the kind that is mixed from flour, salt and water until quite thin and then poured on a red hot stone. Its more recent version is done in a frying pan and has milk and egg mixed into its mass.

Many different kinds of tarts were made of maize. Noteworthy among these is the *málé* (polenta), many varieties of which are known in the Carpathian Basin. In Debrecen maize meal was mixed in a large earthenware cooking pot and allowed to stand, to sweeten. They greased the bottom of a cake pan and poured the mush into it, smoothed it neatly, and then dribbled lard on top. It is generally baked in the oven, but in some regions it was put on a red hot slab of stone. If it did not get sweet enough during resting, then sugar, or earlier honey was mixed into the dough. Originally it may have been a bread supplement, but today it is eaten from time to time as a treat.

The round-shaped *görhe* (Tiszántúl) or, by its Transdanubian name *prósza, kukoricapogácsa* (maize biscuit), is made of similar mush. In some places in the Tiszántúl they also knead lard or oil into the dough, and perhaps made it tastier with some milk and sugar. It was mostly baked in the oven and was eaten instead of bread.

All the various kinds of tarts share one characteristic, namely that their dough is not leavened. This differentiates them from the outwardly similar-looking loaves made of leavened dough, mostly of bread dough.

Bread and Milk Loaf

The Hungarian word for bread, *kenyér,* comes from an ancient Permian language, and we can find its equivalent in the Zyrian, Votyak, and Mordvinian languages as well, only there it means: grits, coarse meal. That is, the word has survived, but the concept originally designated by it has moved through a thousand year long road of historical development, until it has come to mean the leavened common bread of today. Although such leavened bread, made of cereal, looks back on a long past, it was not baked generally in all sections of the linguistic territory. Thus among the eastern Székelys, in the Bodrogköz, and also at other places, it has eclipsed only in more recent times mushy foods and unleavened kinds of tart loaf.

The most important basic material of bread in the central part of the Carpathian Basin is wheat, while rye is often primarily in three regions: the West and Central Transdanubia, between the Tisza and the Danube, and on the rolling hills of the Nyírség in the Tiszántúl. Besides wheat the *kétszeres* (*abajdóc,* mixture of wheat and rye) was grown in many places, especially in regions connected with the areas named above. Barley was made into bread primarily in Székelyland, and another version baked out of maize occurs in the entire area of Transylvania, as well as in the southern part of Transdanubia.

Preparation of the flour begins the evening before bread baking day. As much flour is brought from the pantry as is needed for as many loaves as they want to bake. First the housewife sifts the flour and pours it in a *tub,* formerly made of beech wood, later of aspen or willow wood. Then comes the leavening process, two forms of which are known over the linguistic territory. According to one method, they separate a small portion of flour and mix the leaven with it, then cover it with the *kovászfa* (leaven wood) on the trough, and let the dough mature for several hours. When it has risen, it is kneaded into the rest of the flour, together with the necessary salt and water, and the whole dough is left to rest, so that it may rise. In this way, therefore, the sequence is: *leavening, maturing of the leaven, kneading,* and *rising of the dough.* By the other method, they mix and knead together the necessary raw material (flour, water, salt, leaven) all at once, that is to say, they omit leavening. The latter method occurs only rarely.

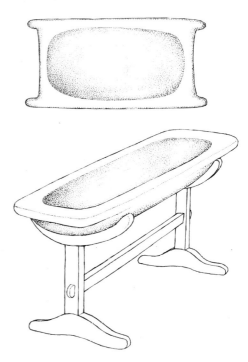

Fig. 141. Wooden tub for kneading dough to make bread. Szalafő, Vas County. 1930s

Fig. 142. A wooden "leaven-stick" *(kovászfa),* placed on the tub in which the dough is rising underneath the cloth which covers it. Great Plain. Late 19th century

The leavening agent may be acquired in many different ways. The simplest method is to put away as much of the leaven after breadmaking as was considered enough for the next baking. Generally, however, *leaven* is made out of bran for a longer period, for half a year or for the whole year, and mix hops, acacia flowers, the skins of pressed grapes, or the foam of fermenting grape juice are also mixed with it, which all gives the desired taste to the bread. Shop-bought *yeast* has spread from the end of the last century, for this, along with the leavening agent, ensures that the bread will rise perfectly. A good housewife always has leaven at home, which she does not like to lend to others, because she thinks that this might have a bad effect on the bread.

Kneading is the hardest of a woman's chores, made even harder by her having to do it generally at night, because it takes until midnight for the leaven to rise. Then she strains as much warm water on the flour as is needed for the quantity, and breaks the leaven apart. She then kneads in this fashion: she puts her four fingers into the dough, squeezes them together, and pushes the dough forward with her clenched fist. This work goes on for about two hours, until holes form in the dough and it parts easily from the side of the tub. Then she folds the dough up,

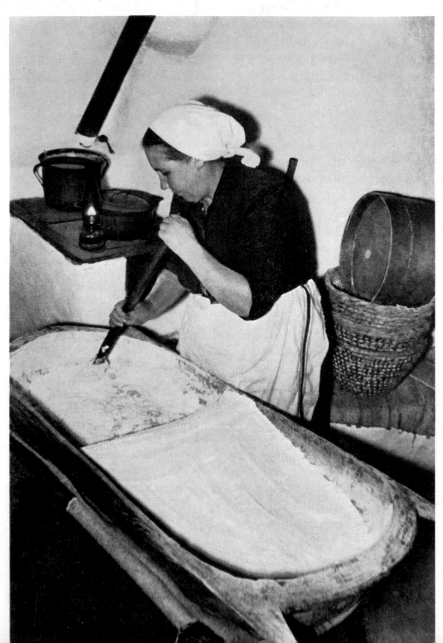

148. Baking bread: mixing leaven
Komádi, Hajdú-Bihar County

149. Baking bread: forming the dough into loaves
Komádi, Hajdú-Bihar County

150. Basket for the dough of a loaf
Cigánd, Borsod-Abaúj-Zemplén County

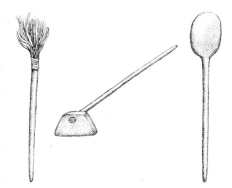

places it in one end of the tub, covers it, and lets the whole thing rise.

She takes a little rest afterwards, but soon starts to heat the oven. This is always done in such a way as to leave one of its interior sides clean. When it is sufficiently hot, she pulls the embers out with a *szénvonó* (ember-peel), after which she can start to shape the risen bread dough. For this baskets are used made out of bulrush or straw, or in forest

Fig. 143. Utensils used when placing the bread into the oven. a) Brush *(pemet)*. b) Wooden implement to draw away the hot ashes. c) Peel for placing the bread into the oven. Region of Őrség. 1930s

289

151. Bread basket
Cigánd, Borsod-Abaúj-Zemplén County

Fig. 145. Straw basket to hold bread.
Jászapáti, Szolnok County. Late 19th
century

152. Bread inside an oven
Átány, Heves County

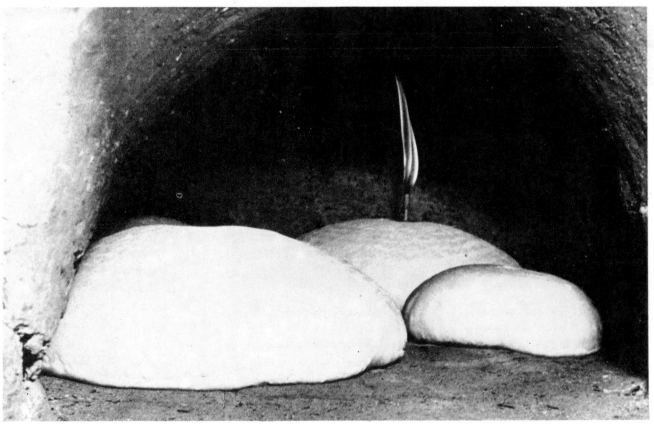

290

regions vessels carved out of wood. Each is lined with a cloth and the basket is filled with dough. They let the shaped dough rest a while, and finally begin putting it into the oven with the help of the *baker's shovel.*

This can be done when the bottom of the oven is hot enough to send out sparks when it is touched by the *poker.* They light to a small piece of wood and set it into the centre of the first loaf, so that it lights up the entire hearth. The large-sized and always round-based loaves generally take three hours to bake in the ovens of the Great Plain. For the small loaf *(cipó),* which is about half the size of the others, a shorter time is sufficient. When they take the loaves out, the bottom of the loaf is brushed clean with whisks made out of a goose wing in the Great Plain, and the top part is washed with lukewarm water to attain a nice, shiny reddish-brown colour.

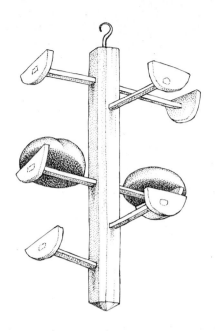

Fig. 144. Bread-rack. Velem, Vas County. Late 19th century

Baking bread was generally done once a week for the whole week, and according to the saying: "a good housewife bakes on Saturday and washes on Monday" (Hódmezővásárhely). This meant fresh bread on the Sunday table. To cut the first slice of bread is the task of the head of the family, who in Catholic areas drew a cross on the bottom of it. The bread he had begun to slice was generally kept in the front room, covered, at the end of the bench, or in the table drawer. They kept whole loaves in the pantry on variously shaped bread racks, or perhaps in baskets woven from bulrush, so that the mice could not get at them.

A piece of the dough may be broken off, or the dough scraped off the side of the bread tub, and this is kneaded together into a bun-like fist-sized bun, *vakaró,* a favourite early morning treat of children. The *lángos* (flat bread), stretched into tart shape, was also baked of bread dough and was made tastier with sour cream. They put it into the oven near the opening, because half an hour's baking was sufficient and it could be taken out more easily from there. *Lángos* bread is a favourite morning meal on a bread-baking day.

The milk loaf *(kalács)* is also made of raised dough, primarily for holidays or other outstanding occasions. The best kind is kneaded out of flour, milk, sugar, and perhaps eggs, then allowed to rise. Its original form is round, as its name, taken from Slavic, also implies. Milk loaf may be formed deftly by hand; human and dove shapes were popular. A long cylinder form braided from dough was also popular. Milk loaves shaped similarly to pretzels, with open-work like a window *(ablakos)* or like a key *(kulcsos)* are usually made for weddings and are used to treat the wedding party. A flask or bottle, filled with wine, was decorated with a round-shaped milk loaf with a hole in the centre pulled on its neck and presented to the priest who officiated at the wedding. Recently various moulds have become popular, depicting fishes, doves, roses. These are made of earthenware or tin. One baked loaf version is the *kuglóf,* known primarily in Transdanubia. It came from the Austrian kitchen during the first half of the 19th century.

Most of the raised pastries are also baked in the oven, although some were baked over an open fire. Among these we can mention the *kürtőskalács* (pastry horn), well known in Transylvania. Finger-wide dough is rolled on a wooden stick and turned over the open fire until it is baked through. The flat bread called *lángos* is fried in lard. It is made of

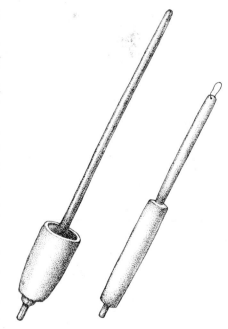

Fig. 146. Stick for baking a pastry rolled like a funnel *(kürtőskalács).* a) Székelyland b) Kalotaszeg. Late 19th century

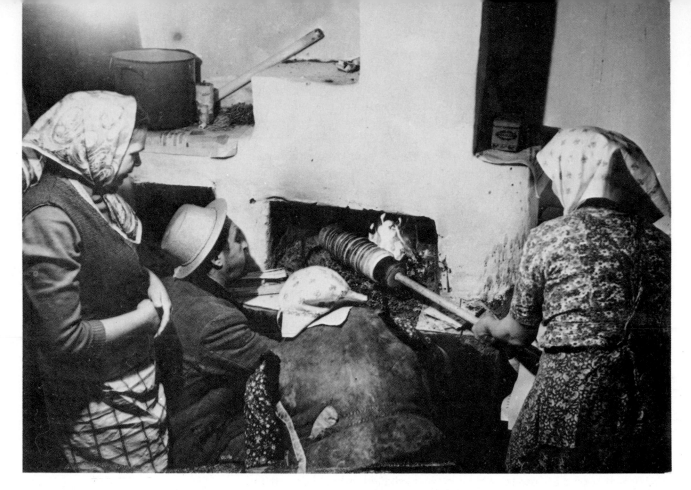

153. Baking pastry horn wound around a stick
Jobbágytelke, former Maros-Torda County

dough similar to bread or milk loaf dough, and is widely spread not only in the villages but in the cities as well. The *csöröge* (fritter-like pastry) is cut out with different moulds, formed into different shapes, and fried in lard or oil.

Pastries made of raised dough are still generally used in peasant households, although they are slowly being eclipsed.

Noodles

The simplest of the noodles are the *galuska* (dumplings), the material of which is largely identical with that of mush. It is cut with a spoon into boiling water, strained and flavoured with lard, butter, cottage cheese, and during lent, with oil. In some places they spread cottage cheese and cracklings on top of dumplings.

Gombóc (round dumpling) is eaten in soups but also occurs as a separate dish. Flour and potato are mixed into its dough. The dumpling is filled in most cases with plums, or cottage cheese, or jam.

The basic mass of *noodles* is kneaded together on a wooden board out of flour, salt, eggs, and water. It is stretched into huge sheets and cut into different shapes. When dry, noodles are cooked in water and therefore are called "cooked pasta" *(főtt tészta)*. Noodles are flavoured with lard, cottage cheese, jam, walnuts, poppy seeds, or some other seasoning. *Derelye* (jam pockets) is made in the following way: jam is put between two layers of stretched out dough, cut into square pieces, and cooked in water.

Noodles have a very important place in peasant diet. Hardly a day passes without it being served in some shape or form. Kneading noodles, especially where the family was large, was a serious task for the housewife.

Pastries constitute the most recent layer in the meals of the Hungarian peasantry and are generally associated with some occasion or holiday. Baking small cakes with baking powder and baker's ammonia started only in this century. At first, these were baked for weddings, later for other holidays, especially for Easter.

Wedding cakes with icing have spread during the last half century to such an extent that today 50 to 100 pieces are brought for large weddings. Specialists in cake making are generally known in each village.

Not only are cakes made in different shapes (cock, house, church, horse, etc.) but are also richly decorated with different kinds of motifs. Cakes can have a ritual role in wedding proceedings in most places. Thus, for instance, in Boldog (Pest County) the groom used to redeem his bride from the dance with a red apple, but today he has to give a cake, shaped like a pair of doves. This also indicates that in certain areas the development of edibles is influenced by fashion as well as by tradition and economic endowments.

Baked Pastries

154. Making strudel
Buzsák, Somogy County

Meat Dishes   Meat dishes play an important role in the life of the Hungarian people, but not to the same extent in each social layer. The proportion of meat dishes was much greater in the diet of herdsmen than in that of share harvesters, seasonal workers, and day labourers. The prosperous peasants consumed much more meat through the year than the poor ones, who usually reserved meat for the times of great work or for holidays. In the Great Plain, they ate meat without any garnishing, the use of pickled vegetables being much less frequent here than, for example, in Transylvania.

Although the produce of hunting counted for relatively little among various kinds of meats, the way of preparing game preserved many ancient features. Thus, to bake a bird, it is covered, the feathers still on, with a thick layer of mud, and thrust into the embers. The feathers are peeled off along with the hardened mud, under which the meat has browned.

The ways of preparing fish are extremely varied. Fish is baked on a spit, roasted over an open fire, or fried in a frying pan. However, the most general method in the southern part of the linguistic territory is still the *fish soup*. Its popularity practically marks the road by which paprika spread. Fish is cooked with *paprika* in the southern regions, while it is seasoned with onion further north. Fish soup and other peasant methods of preparing fish permeated generally into the kitchens of the city and of restaurants.

Poultry provides the permanent and most easily available meat supply of peasant households. Amongst poultry, chicken takes the first place (hen, cock). In preparing chicken, boiling methods dominated: hen-meat soup and boiled meat are both general and festive meals. Poultry, cooked in paprika and water, is a popular but not an old element of the peasant kitchen, while even more recent is baked and stuffed hen. Although duck and geese are common throughout the entire linguistic territory, their role in traditional festive eating is smaller than that of the chicken. The poor kept geese and duck mainly for their feathers, with which they stuffed pillows. Poor people ate duck and geese less frequently than the rich, and sold most of them at a market. Fattening geese and ducks with maize became general from the beginning of the last century, since which time fattened duck and goose have gained ground strongly in city and upper class diet.

During the times that followed the Conquest and through the entire Middle Ages, horse meat was eaten everywhere, but its significance decreased later on, so much so that in the last century its consumption was limited mostly to herdsmen. We know about some parts of the Great Plain (e.g. Jászság) where the poorer folk fattened donkeys for lard.

On certain parts of the linguistic territory, mutton played a very important role both in everyday and in festive eating. *Mush with mutton* used to occur in the menu of the Great Plain herdsmen and also among the food of villagers. Later it diminished as everyday food, while at the same time it became something of a ceremonial dish, especially at meals concluding major work projects (harvest, vintage). The meat of Hungarian sheep is much tastier than that of the merino sheep, so that as long as it was possible the former was used to make meat dishes, cooked with paprika and onions in its own juice.

Beef, no matter how numerous the cattle stock, never played a definitive role in the diet of the Hungarian peasant. Special ways of preparing it did not develop, and it occurred relatively rarely in festive dishes. Boiled meat cooked for soup was eaten as a separate entrée. In the central part of the linguistic region they made *goulash meat* and soup out of beef. In the former case they put the meat, cut into small pieces, on onion browned in lard and let it cook in its own juice, then seasoned it with paprika. In the case of gulyás soup *(gulyásleves)*, they added water, more recently potatoes, to the meat, and sometimes cooked some dumplings with it. Both types of food became universal, not only in the Hungarian kitchen, but on the menus of restaurants all over the world under the name of *gulyás*. Nevertheless, pork stood very much in the centre of the peasant diet. It provided the most important basic material, *lard,* which is still a major element of Hungarian cooking. *Bacon,* which was eaten and still is eaten both *raw, steamed,* and *smoked,* used to be counted as the most important food of the people. Only recently has its use slowly begun to decline. Pork, preserved by smoking or by other methods, provided the backbone of the meals served during the major agricultural work projects. That is why even the poorer social layers of the peasantry tried to kill at least one pig and why the more prosperous ones processed several fattened pigs.

The *disznótor* (pig-killing feast) is one of the biggest events of peasant households and comes before Christmas or in January. The completion of the fattening is timed so as to preserve part of the meat for a longer period by freezing.

Most *gazda*s kill the pig and do its primary processing themselves, but there are several skilled men (*hentes,* butcher; *böllér,* slaughterer) in every village, whom they gladly invite and generally pay in kind. The pig is killed early in the morning. This is followed by the *perzselés* (scorching), that is, burning of the hair with straw. Recently, but mostly only in the west, the practice of scalding with hot water has begun to spread, although in most places they are convinced that the bacon is much tastier after scorching. The scorched pig is thickly covered with mud, which is shaved off with a knife in order to remove the remaining hair.

After this begins the carving of the animal, which is turned on its back. Carving begins with the four hams. Then the innards are removed, and the women join the work. They clean out and thoroughly wash the intestines and the stomach. After that the men carve out the spine with the meat attached to it *(spareribs),* which is made into the most popular kind of soup. The various pieces of meat are gathered, chopped up, seasoned with onion, pepper, and paprika, and stuffed into the small intestines thus making *sausage,* which can be kept right through the summer after it is smoked. Various, and regionally different *blood and liver sausages* are made from liver, blood, and lungs, with the addition of mush, more recently of rice, and with suitable seasoning. These keep in the cold for several weeks. They also mix bits of meat, skin, and tongue and fill the stomach with this mass. It is eaten smoked.

Pig-killing is also an occasion for a social gathering, because relatives and neighbours come over on the first day and generally get sparerib soup, cabbage with meat *(toros káposzta),* or less frequently fresh sausage and blood sausage, and spend the time drinking wine and talking. The next day the bacon is rendered for lard and the meat and bacon are salted in preparation for smoking. The housewife prepares *samples* to be given to relatives and neighbours, who reciprocate with similar food gifts.

Milk and Milk Processing

The milk of cows and sheep have the greatest importance in the diet of the Hungarian peasantry. A few sources also mention the drinking of horse milk, but in the historical period under discussion we know of only rare occurrences of this earlier practice.

Although the Hungarian grey cow gave little milk, the fat content of the milk was quite high. Cows in extensively kept herds were not milked, and the calf could suck as much as it wanted. Only a few milk cows were tied at the farmstead for the needs of the herdsmen, who mostly drank the milk fresh but also processed it in the fashion of yoghurt. In the Great Plain the *tarhó* is the best known among these, and the Magyars very possibly acquired the method of making it from one of the Turkic peoples before the Conquest. They boil the milk in a large-sized vessel, then let it cool until they can just bear putting their finger in it. Then they mix *rennet* into it, which is usually nothing else but *tarhó* put aside from the previous making. After the vessel is closed, the milk sets in a few hours. If they leave it open, the setting time increases to 8 to 12 hours. When it is thick enough for a straw to stand upright in it, it is ready to eat.

Fig. 147. Jugs for milk. Őrség, Vas County. 1930s

In peasant households, milk is usually drunk fresh. If they pour it into milkpots *(köcsög)* it sets and becomes sour, and this is much liked, especially in summer. The fat, of lighter weight, rises to the top of the milk and forms cream *(tejszín),* or to the top of coagulated milk, forming sour cream *(tejfel).* It still contains much water. When cream is freed from water, it turns into *butter.*

The simplest method of making butter is to shake cream in a vessel until the butter condenses out of it. We find this method both in the western (Göcsej) and eastern (Székelyland) linguistic territories. The equivalent of the old method can be demonstrated primarily among the Eastern Slavs. Various churning vessels made of wood and earthenware, later of tin, spread widely, in which plungers on a shaft are moved up and down until the butter condenses. The left over *buttermilk* is a favourite drink of children, and what they leave is given to piglets. Making butter is amongst the oldest methods of milk processing, since it is partly Finno-Ugric and Ugric in its terminology *(vaj,* butter; *ráz,* shake), partly Bulgarian–Turkish *(köpü,* churn; *író,* buttermilk; *túró,* cottage cheese). If the buttermilk is skimmed and warmed, it becomes knotted and turns into *cottage cheese.* The liquid is pressed out of it and is then hung up to dry in sacks. Baked or cooked pastries and noodles are filled and flavoured with it.

Fig. 148. Wooden milk-churn. Szalafő, Vas County. 1930s

Processing sheep's milk is usually the task of the shepherds (cf. Ill. 128), who are sometimes assisted by their wives or daughters.

The sheep stock of the peasants was guarded by a common shepherd, and the sharing of the milk developed differently in various parts of the linguistic territory. In the Tiszántúl (Hajdúszoboszló), generally six *gazda*s put 20 to 30 sheep together into the hands of one shepherd. Everyone got the produce of one complete milking (morning and evening) for a six day period, while the yield of the seventh day belonged to the shepherd. If they put the stock together by tens, that is, if the number of the owners doubled, then the share fell to each person only every second week. In Transylvania the sheep were driven out to the pasture with some celebration on St. George's Day (April 24). At this time everybody milked his own sheep and measured and marked down the yield exactly. Sharing through the entire course of the summer was based on the first milking. The practice of giving the yield of the milk in rental *(árenda)* had already spread among the Palotses during the last century. The shepherd gave 2 kg of fresh cheese to the owner for each ewe that could be milked, regardless of her yield, for the entire duration of the milking season.

Sheep were always milked by the men. Milking, broadly speaking, lasted for four months, from May until early September, and yielded 1 to 4 dl a day per ewe. They force the ewes into a tight enclosure, and drive them toward the shepherd. He catches them one at a time, milks each dry, then lets it go. The pail *(sajtár)* used to be made of wood but now is made of sheet iron. Between its two handles they stretch a string that supports a small mug, into which the milk always goes because it

Fig. 149. Earthenware milk–churn with its lid and dasher. Szomoróc, Vas County. 1930s

155. Churning butter
Kazár, Nógrád County

would otherwise raise too much froth in the big vessel (cf. Ill. 128). The sweet sheep's milk is not used directly; cheese and cottage cheese is made out of it.

To do this, rennet *(oltó)* is needed. The Palots shepherds used the stomach of a young lamb or sucking calf. They cleaned it well, salted it, and next day washed the salt out of it and blew it up. They put it away to dry and, when they wanted to use it, cut a piece off, soaked it in warm milk, or maybe poured whey on it, and so could use it by the next day. They did the same in the Great Plain, but there they also dry and store the milk that was left in the stomach of a three-week-old calf.

They let the fresh milk stand for a while, then put as much rennet into it as was needed for the quantity. When it has coagulated, they break it up thoroughly by hand or with a spoon, and again let it rest for a short time in this condition. Afterwards they put it all into a homespun cloth and wring the whey out. In some places it is freed from most of the moisture by means of a press. They make the cheese round *(gomolya)* in the Great Plain, and in other places they pour it into moulds that give it the most diverse shapes. Finally they further dry it in an airy, but not a sunny place.

Cheese is usually eaten with bread, but in July and August, when the ewe's milk gets very strong, they make cottage cheese with it. It is crumbled, salted, and kneaded into a wooden or clay vessel and in this way kept for a longer time. In Transylvania and among the Csángós of Moldavia they store it in sheepskin bags, and often even smoke it. *Zsendice* is made out of the whey that drips from the cheese by adding one tenth of sweet ewe milk to it and stirring it over the fire until it becomes a cheesy, mushy mass. They eat it together with its whey. It was used regularly until very recent times, and was warmly recommended by the peasants as a remedy for tuberculosis.

Drinks and Spices

The most important drink is water taken from the wells in the yards, and from good-tasting springs. There are many springs in the mountain regions, especially in Székelyland and Upper Hungary where the water is slightly tart in taste and more or less aerated *(borvíz, csevice),* which the population of the surrounding area became used to. They even shipped it to distant settlements in pitchers on carts fixed up for this purpose. In the Great Plain they pushed a pierced straw deep into the marshy soil and sucked up the fresh, clean water.

Among the alcoholic beverages, wine *(bor)* has had the greatest importance in all ages (cf. p. 226). It was regularly consumed in wine-growing regions by both men and women. In other areas it was drunk only on festive occasions, at major work periods, and pig-killing feasts. Among hard spirits the various fruit *pálinka* (brandies), mostly plum and apricot proliferated from the 18th century and were distilled in most peasant houses, in spite of strong prohibition by the authorities.

Home-made beer was made in many places during the 19th century. In Székelyland it was made equally out of wheat, corn, and barley. They sprouted the washed cereal in the attic, then dried it on a gently fired hearth *(szalad).* It was crushed, maybe ground, in a hand mill, placed in

156. Wine-flasks covered with leather
Hungary

a tub with a hole in the bottom, then hot water was poured on it. They put bread crust, onion peel and hops into it, partly for colour, partly for taste. It was stirred when the yeast caused the beer to ferment, and after it settled down, it was strained and drunk for the time that it kept (that is, for a few weeks).

Hydromel, widely known from the Middle Ages on, lost its significance only during the last century. It was made of honey and water mixed in a 1:2 proportion and then boiled. It was cooled and strained through a heavy cloth, then the thick liquid was stored in barrels. In many places its production was associated with honeycake makers. The fermented *boza* of the Great Plain, especially of the Kunság, also belongs among the various beers. Baked corn cakes were mashed, water was poured on the mash, and the whole was fermented. The *boza* became light in colour while it was fermenting. When it settled, they strained it.

Various vinegars, made in every house, were used as flavouring. *Wine-* and *apple-vinegar* are known over a large area. People chop up apples for the latter, grate them, pour on water, and when it is fermented, in a few weeks or perhaps a month, it is strained and used to provide the pleasant tart taste of many dishes.

Salt, indispensable for the preparation of dishes, was shipped to the Great Plain from the mines of the Eastern Carpathians in wheeled vehicles, or by boats on the Tisza. Salt wells were used in certain regions of Székelyland (Marosszék), and the women knew initially in what proportion they had to mix salt and sweet water for the preparation of certain dishes.

Pepper used to be in most general use among the spices, but from the end of the 18th century this was completely pushed into the background everywhere except in Transylvania by the newcomer from the south, *paprika*. In Transylvania, they liked to use *tarragon* and flavoured both soup and meat with it. They put *saffron* into soups, which not only gave a pleasant taste but lent food a rich golden colour. Peasants also endeavoured to make their dishes tastier with *onion, garlic, marjoram, dill, anis, horseradish,* and other spices.

Folk Costumes

An extraordinary number of factors influence national costumes, where alterations occur perhaps at a somewhat faster rate than in other areas of peasant culture. Change accelerated over the last two centuries, partly because increasingly more manufactured and factory products were added to the basic materials produced mostly at home.

During the Middle Ages and the following centuries, most of the basic materials were produced by the peasants themselves. They spun and wove linen out of hemp and flax and even did most of the wool processing themselves. They practised the most simple way of preparing skins, although the main elements of process and supply moved into the hands of village and town specialists since early times. However, these differed depending on whether they prepared the skins *(tawer, currier)* or processed them *(furrier, bootmaker, shoemaker)*. The processing of wool remained within the domestic framework for a long time, but a number of small trades making wool into clothing became independent relatively quickly *(tailor, szűr maker, frieze maker, button maker, hatter)*. The making of linen by peasant women survived longest, although the importance of the products of small artisans (e.g. *weavers*) increased after the end of the 18th century. Factory-made products gained importance after the middle of the 19th century. Materials of broader width and richer colours caused great changes in the appearance of clothing. The high period of Hungarian folk costumes may be reckoned from this time and lasted for half a century—from the middle of the 19th century until the beginning of World War I—and in the border regions it lasted even longer.

Tradition is an especially noteworthy factor in the development of folk costumes. It also has social implications, in that certain strata of the peasantry define their costumes by an unwritten law that is nevertheless a bindingly valid order of the community. In the same way, tradition prescribes the norms of clothing for certain age groups, which are also strongly influenced by the role of each member within the family. Thus costume changes when a girl gets married, after the first child is born, and at the time when she must finally put on the clothes befitting an old woman after the birth of the first grandchild. Tradition also defines the costumes worn for special occasions (e.g. baptism, wedding, burial, etc.).

Various authorities interfered with the development of folk costumes, just as the Church did, by setting certain rules. County authorities prohibited especially expensive and ornamental hats, *szűr* mantles, and richly embroidered sheepskin jackets, primarily those that imitated the clothing of the nobility or were even equal to it. Such interference was always justified as the protection of the poor from the excessive expense of certain pieces of clothing, which could cause bankruptcy, or for which they might attempt robbery in order to acquire the necessary amount of money. In fact, the authorities tried to prevent the people's costumes from approximating those of the nobility. The Church, which directed its measures against overt gaudiness, fought against worldly vanity. The last great demonstration of this prohibition took place in 1924 in Mezőkövesd, where all the sequins and gold lace were ordered to be removed and were burned ceremoniously, and their use, along with the use of pure silk yarn in embroidery, was prohibited by a Catholic priest.

Despite all prohibitions, the clothing of the nobility changed more rapidly than folk costume, and had an effect on peasant dress. And because the nobility maintained familiarity with foreign garments, primarily those of the Western nobility, many new elements of clothing reached the Hungarian peasantry, though with a time lapse. The influence, however, was reciprocal, because in certain periods of anti-Habsburg protest, the nobility put on the garb of the peasantry, or at least took over some of its features in their dress.

Many factors have influenced folk costumes, and the effects of these influences are known in detail only from the evidence of the last hundred years. Therefore, what follows refers primarily to this latter period.

Raw Materials

The raw materials of clothing are extremely varied. In Hungary chiefly linen, mostly hemp and less frequently flax linen, broadcloth, and felt made from wool, and of many different kinds of sheepskin and leather were used for pieces of garments. From earliest times these provided the basis for the clothing of the Magyar people. We shall now take a closer look at their processing.

Processing Hemp and Flax

The ancient Magyars must already have possessed some kind of home-spun cloth before the Conquest, since the names *kender* (hemp), *csepű* (tow), *orsó* (spindle), and *tiló* (swingle) are Bulgaro-Turkish in origin. If we add to these the words *fon* (spin) and *sző* (weave), traceable to the Finno-Ugric period, there can be little doubt that this domestic occupation, at least in part, belongs to the most ancient Hungarian crafts. The Hungarian word *len* (flax) originates from the Slavic, but its earlier significance in the Carpathian Basin cannot compare with that of hemp. It is certain that Slavic peoples introduced a more differentiated processing of fibrous plants to the Hungarians. The terminology also shows Slavic influence: *gereben* (flax-comb), *guzsaly* (distaff), *motolla* (hand reel), *cséve* (spool), *esztováta* (weaver's loom), and its parts: *borda* (reed), *nyüst* (heddle), etc. Furthermore, the general designation of the artisan who did the weaving *(takács)* also derives from one of the Slavic languages.

Until recently, and sometimes even today, each peasant family planted as much flax and hemp as they could process during the year. The 50 to 150 square fathom fields of hemp lay close to the village, outside of the fields of crop rotation. This area of land could be inherited by the daughters as well as the sons, since the produce of the land was turned into linen as the result of their work. Furthermore, because the

Fig. 150. Swingle made out of a single log for beating and for swingling fibres. Region of Takta, former Zemplén County. Around 1940

302

158. Breaking hemp: a swingle
Gyimes-Bükkhavas, former Csík County

Fig. 151. A swingle with a double blade for
fine processing. Region of Takta, former
Zemplén County. Around 1940

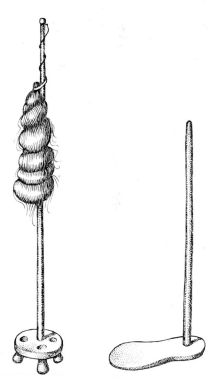

Fig. 152. Two kinds of distaffs, one with
a stool to support with the feet, the other
with a board to sit on. Magyarvalkó,
former Kolozs County. 1930s

159. Combing out hemp
Karcsa, Borsod-Abaúj-Zemplén County

same crop went into the small plots each year, they fertilized it and cultivated it thoroughly. Flax especially demanded much attention. The cultivation of the soil and the early sowing of the hemp were jobs for men. The woman prepared the clean seed for sowing and cooked scrambled eggs for her husband for breakfast, so that the planted seeds would yield plenty of beautiful yellow-white linen. Sowing was quickly done and the empty sack or the cloth used for sowing was thrown up high in the air, so that the plants would grow just as high.

There was not much work with hemp until it was harvested, because it was sown so thickly that all the weeds were smothered. Pulling the flax out of the ground by its roots *(nyűvés)* takes place in July, and of hemp in August. It is dried for a few days, then the sheaves are soaked and stacked on top of each other in a ditch, backwater, or a creek. It is pressed with stones and mud, perhaps tied down, and left until it has softened sufficiently. The time it takes to soften depends equally on the thickness of the stalk, on the weather, and on the temperature of the water. Then the sheaves are taken out, and washed and dried. In fine, sunny weather, a few days are enough for this process.

The dried hemp is *scutched* roughly, then *stripped* more finely. They do this with a tongued implement that stands on legs, its function being to separate the woody fibres of the hemp by beating, and to soften up the usable fibres. Further cleaning takes place with the help of an implement made of nails *(gereben)* pounded into a board, different versions of which exist in various regions of the Hungarian speaking territory. Breaking hemp through trampling by foot or by means of a large rubbing implement *(dörzsölő)* or two scutchers *(szösztörő)* was known only in some regions. The tow is put away, tied together and completely prepared for spinning, and taken out again only when outdoor chores have been finished, late in the autumn.

The oldest implement of *spinning* is the distaff *(guzsaly)*, which in a few cases is held in the armpit, but usually women sit on its base, although in some places the distaff is stuck into a low stool and the woman holds it with her feet on the floor. She ties the tow to the upper part of the distaff, leads the thread out of it with her left hand, wetting it continually while spinning it, and winding the thread with her right hand evenly onto the *spindle*. A great many carved, richly ornamented distaffs may be found, often given by young men to their sweethearts as gifts. The foot-operated spinning wheel *(kerekes-guzsaly* or *rokka)* appeared at the end of the 18th century in the Carpathian Basin. Its name is Italian in origin, but it is presumed to have come to Hungary through Austrian–German mediation. Although more can be spun with this foot-operated instrument than with the distaff in a given period of time, it did not spread everywhere and replaced the *distaff* only very slowly. In certain areas it never gained ground (Bodrogköz), because by the time it had appeared, the domestic processing of hemp was on the decline.

Spinning is not only work, it is also an opportunity for entertainment, because during spinning conversation comes naturally. The *adolescent girls* and *girls of marriageable age* met in the spinning houses of their own community, separately from the younger and older women. For this purpose they either rented a whole room, or were able to use a room at

Fig. 154. An implement for spooling yarn. Désháza, former Szilágy County. 1948

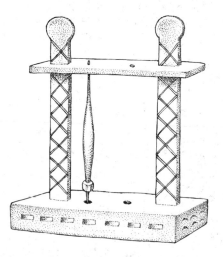

Fig. 153. A stand for bobbins. Magyarvalkó, former Kolozs County. 1930s

160. Working on a spinning-wheel
Sukoró, Fejér County

a house where there were few girls and women in the family and, in return for the room, they spun the roughest hemp of their hosts also. To go to the spinning house, girls did not dress in a festive way, but they wore nicer clothes than for every day. Each girl brought along her distaff and spindle, together with the material to be spun. A permanent and customary sitting arrangement developed. The older girls sat near the door, and the younger girls in the rear part of the room. They started spinning rapidly, because the work slowed down later on, when the young men arrived after having fed and watered the animals and cleaned the stable. Time passed with cheerful conversation. Those who were good story-tellers, knew superstitions and scary tales were especially welcome. Later on in the evening came time for singing and for various games. If a young man picked up a girl's dropped spindle, it was returned only in exchange for a kiss. In the Great Plain the young people often danced to zither music. They did not stay late and, at a signal from the housewife, everyone left together. Spinning was not only an opportunity to get together for work and entertainment, but also functioned as the match-making institution of the village where young people became acquainted with each other.

The spun yarn is wound on a one-forked hand reel *(motolla)* or on a four-forked turnable reel, which measures the length while reeling it. The amount going around the reel once is called yarn length *(szál),* and equals four times the width of the reel. As the length of this varies from

161. The loom of a professional weaver
Nagyvázsony, Veszprém County

162. Beating out the wash at the river Miske, Bács–Kiskun County

region to region, the word *szál* does not indicate some absolute measurement. The first composite unit, varying by regions, three times the *szál,* is the *ige,* or the *kispászma,* which is 50 to 100 times larger. The other composite unit is the *nagypászma,* which is 40 to 100 times longer than the previous unit. The *darab (matring,* skein), consists of 2 to 15 other composite units. With the help of this extremely complicated system of counting, they could always keep exact track of the quantity of completed thread and estimate the length of the linen that can be woven from it.

Another communal job at the end of winter is yarn washing *(fonalmosás).* The yarn is first boiled in lye and ashes, then washed thoroughly either at home or in the icy waters of rivers and lakes (e.g. Bodrogköz). Men help in wringing it out and also in hauling it home from the river or creek. The yarn, dried on the porch or on the fence, is wound into *balls* according to the previously mentioned system of counting, and stored in this form until weaving begins in early spring.

The warping of the loom *(fonalfelvetés),* which precedes weaving, determines both the width and length of the cloth. The warping wheel *(vető)* is made out of four rods which turn on a central spindle, the lower end resting on a board on the ground, the top being fastened to a beam in the ceiling. As a consequence, its size, which is determined by domestic circumstances, can vary widely within the same settlement. The yarn is taken off the warping wheel very carefully, several people helping in this work. They usually thread it onto the loom or maybe put it aside until the next day. In general, by reviewing the methods of counting in reeling and warping, we can still reconstruct the almost forgotten numerical system based on the number 60 that has barely survived in some parts of the Carpathian Basin.

The most ancient form of the loom *(osztováta)* is the vertical loom, but its use in connection with linen weaving is only remembered sporadically. Among the peasant looms currently in use the oldest type appears to be the one that had its poles fastened into a foundation log lying on the ground. This was succeeded by a form, in general use today, standing on

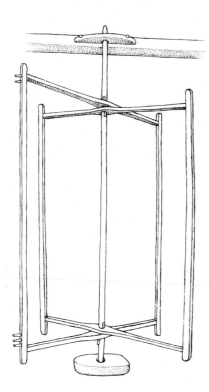

Fig. 155. A warping wheel *(vetőkaró)* for setting the yarn, fixed to the beam of the room. Region of Takta, former Zemplén County. Around 1940

163. Beating out the wash Kalotaszentkirály, former Kolozs County

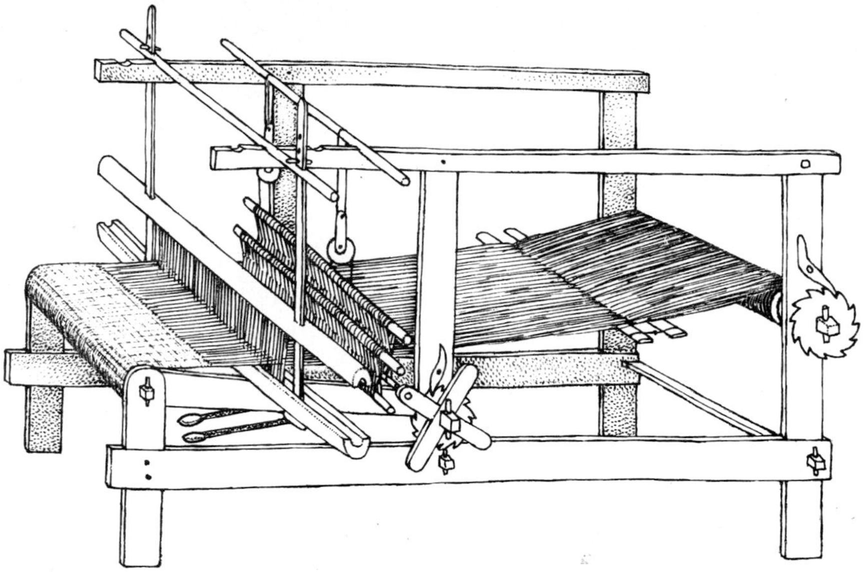

Fig. 156. Loom. Region of Takta, former
Zemplén County. Around 1940

four posts. A cylindrical beam, which fits onto two posts, holds the
yarn; the yarn is guided through the heddles *(nyüst),* which hang from
a beam. In front of the heddles are the reeds *(borda),* with which the yarn
is beaten, after the shuttle *(vetélő)* has been through the shed to weave the
cloth. Two posts hold a beam, also cylindrical, onto which the cloth is
rolled as it is woven. It is possible to weave cloth 50 to 65 cm wide on
a peasant loom, and this dimension significantly influenced the articles of
clothing made from it. The finished cloth is taken off the loom, is dipped
in water, then hung on a fence or spread on the grass, and bleached in the
spring and early summer sun to get it as white as possible.

Simple underwear was sewn out of *plain linen.* Both the warp and the
weft were made of hemp or flax yarn until the middle of the last century.
Since the second half of the 19th century, cotton yarn was used for the
warp in many places, while the weft was hemp or flax. This type of linen
was called half-cotton linen *(félpamutvászon),* and is not nearly as coarse
as its pure hemp predecessor.

The processing of hemp and flax up to the weaving of the cloth is
typically women's work; only the sowing, harvesting, and pulling of
the plant was done by the men. On the other hand, the artisan
weavers—always men—, who have been frequently mentioned since
the beginning of the Middle Ages, first worked at the cities but later on in
the villages as well. They, however, wove ready-made yarn either
which they bought or was brought to them by village women as
payment or for share weaving. Sometimes they were also asked to
weave smooth linen, because wider material could be made on the
weaver's loom, but peasant women came to them more for special types
of cloth, for more ornate and more novel materials (cf. p. 396).

Processing Wool

Although the hair of most animals is suitable for some kind of processing, the wool of sheep has the greatest importance among Hungarians.
Formerly, they processed the wool of the long-haired Hungarian sheep,
but since the last century the finer merino sheep are bred even by the
peasants, and this created a great change in articles of clothing made out

of wool. The Hungarian sheep were sheared generally twice a year, the merino only once, in the spring.

The peasant method of processing wool was discouraged after the great wool boom in the first half of the last century, and it survived for the most part only among the Székelys and other Hungarian groups living in Transylvania. There shearing is done around St. Urban's Day (May 25th). The sheep are driven into the sheepfold of the *gazda* responsible for the flock to be sheared, then the sheep are driven back to the pasture the very same day. Shearing was often done on the highland pastures and the unwashed wool was carried home in sacks.

Larger bits of dirt and manure are picked out of the *oily wool* and the wool is soaked in lukewarm water for half an hour, then beaten thoroughly with a mallet in a creek or other water and carefully dried. After this comes the process of *teasing,* or tearing of the wool into small pieces, and the separation of white fibres from black. It is carded thoroughly with a square-shaped wool comb, and the wool is then ready for spinning. Although hemp is spun in the winter, women try to spin wool during the summer, using a spindle as they do in the case of hemp. They do this quickly, because the women want to start weaving the wool in the autumn, before the time comes to process the hemp. Wool-weaving reeds are set on the loom used otherwise for weaving hemp; there are also slight differences in the way of warping.

As the finished broadcloth is still too loosely woven for making clothing, they take it to a fulling mill *(kalló malom),* where, beaten by heavy mallets, the material becomes more compact. The fulling *(ványolás)* may take as long as 24 hours, during which time the broadcloth is taken out three times and folded up. During the fulling process the cloth generally shrinks to half its original size, but it also becomes much more resistant and is warmer in use. Fulling is done in the spring, when water is not so cold any more. People used to come from great distances to a famous fulling mill.

The *gubacsapás,* the making of a type of frieze mantle with a horizontal cut, was traditionally the work of professional artisans. They clean, tease, and spin the wool as described before. Artisans weave it on a *guba loom,* which serves especially this purpose, producing a cloth with woollen tufts twisted in as the weaving progresses, while the other side remains smooth. Because this *guba* cloth is also loosely woven, it also goes to the fulling mill, where it is pounded until it becomes a stiff material that is easy to make into garments.

Frieze for the *szűr* mantle is made in a manner similar to that in which the Székelys make broadcloth. This cloth is a dense material with a rather fleecy surface. Fulling compresses the threads so closely together that the inexperienced eye can easily mistake it for *felt.* However, felt, unlike the others mentioned before, is not made by weaving but by a pressing technique. It is based on the nature of wool which sticks together tightly when pounded together so that the individual threads cannot ever be separated. The makers of a high cap *(süveggyártó)* and the foot-cloth makers *(kapcakészítő),* who are mentioned in early charters, worked with similar felt-like material.

164. Woman spinning from a distaff
Lészped, Moldavia

Processing Skin

The processing of skin is an extremely old craft, though it became partly specialized early in the case of certain articles of clothing. Herdsmen have preserved most primitive methods and processes of skin preparation almost until the present day. Herdsmen primarily tried to make use of the skins of animals that had perished. Among various herdsmen, shepherds best understood the preparation of skin—sheepskin naturally —out of which they made many simple articles of clothing. Around the Hortobágy the method is to carefully scrape from the flayed sheepskin, which was then stretched out and dried in a shady place. If very dirty, it was washed and dried again. Afterwards it is smeared thoroughly with a mixture of salt and alum, bran is sprinkled on it, it is folded, and put away. After a few days, the skins are crushed, simply by hand, or softened by pulling it to and fro over a blunt scythe-blade. In the course of this work chalk dust or flour is sprinkled on the skin from time to time, from which it becomes completely white. A dye may be brewed out of Brazil wood, oak-apple, gall and vitriol. This is smeared lukewarm onto the skin, which then takes on a beautiful black colour as a result.

A similar method of processing used for leather was also practised earlier by Hungarian tanners, whose products were mentioned

165. Shoemakers at work: detail of a painted guild-chest, 1800 Borsod-Abaúj-Zemplén County

166. A hide-dresser at work: detail from a painted guild chest, 1800 Borsod-Abaúj-Zemplén County

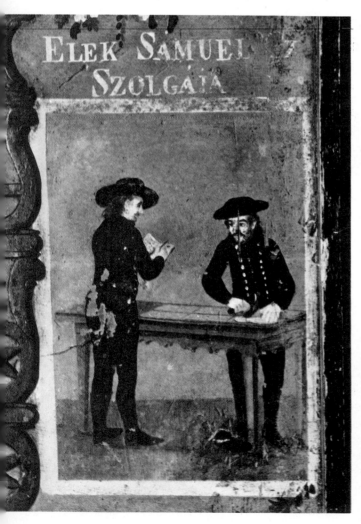

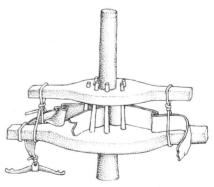

Fig. 157. Implement for softening leather
dressed with alum. Kézdivásárhely,
former Háromszék County. 1930s

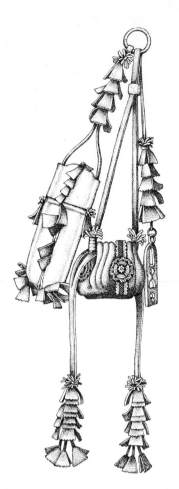

Fig. 158. Leather kit used by herdsmen with a case for a knife, a bag for the flint and the tinder and a steel. Great Plain. Second half of 19th century

appreciatively even by French sources in the second half of the 18th century (Diderot, *Encyclopedia,* Paris, 1772). Their method was as follows: they removed the hair from the flayed skin with a knife, without any kind of chemical interference. Thus the roots of the hair remained in the skin and made it more compact and resistant. It was worked over thoroughly and trampled on with a salt and alum solution. When this had soaked completely into the skin, it was dried, at first in the shade, then by holding the skins over warm embers. By this means the pores expanded and easily soaked up the hot tallow smeared all over the skin. This method was used primarily on ox-skin, which as a result, turned white. Tanning took only 2 to 4 weeks, as opposed to the tannic method used generally in Europe, which in many cases required up to 3 or 4 years. This fact, and the more compact leather made by this method of processing, made it the preferred method in Western Europe also. This process was practised primarily in Central Asia, in the Near East, as well as in the southern part of the Mediterranean Basin during the Middle Ages. On the basis of this it may be supposed that the Magyars were already familiar with this method of leather processing before the Conquest.

Beginning with the Middle Ages *tanners* used another method. They thoroughly smeared the soaked skin with lime and kept it in that manner for 2 to 3 weeks. After this the hair or wool could easily be removed. They collected the wool, washed it and sold it to the *guba* makers. The meat and epithelium were carefully removed from the hide which was steeped for a while in a liquid made from chicken manure. After this preparation the tanning *(cserzés)* followed, the basic material of which was the stripped and crushed bark of oak trees and gallnuts. The hide was kept in this liquid steeping solution for the necessary length of time, to which was added more tanning material every day, so that the acid would stay at the same level. When the cut hide turned yellow inside, the tanning process could be completed. Tanning was followed by a brief

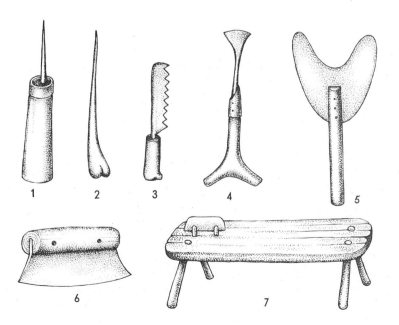

Fig. 159. Utensils for dressing leather. Sárrétudvari, former Bihar county. Around 1940. 1. Awl. 2. A bone for picking holes. 3. Knife to scratch with. 4. Utensil for stretching out leather. 5. Iron implement for softening leather. 6. Knife for cutting off the flesh. 7. Long bench with a knife for softening leather

314

drying, then by treating the hide with fat and then by dyeing it. This method of processing is characteristic of Europe, South Asia, and Asia Minor, but it became increasingly generally used in Hungary also, and replaced the other method.

One of the plants used for tanning especially in Transdanubia around the Balaton was *fustic* (Rhus cotinus, *szömörce*), supposedly propagated by the Turks. This is demonstrated by the fact that the person who works with it is called *tobak,* which is the equivalent of the Ottoman Turkish word meaning "tanner". This plant assured a good quality of tanning. The finest boots were made out of *cordovan leather.*

Elements of Folk Costume

The basic elements of folk costume can be found equally distributed in similar form throughout small and large geographic areas. Attire characteristic of certain regions developed from the combination of these elements. Costume has been constantly changing throughout history. Although some of the details of this process are not known today, we can still attempt to review this progression, at least in an overview.

Historical Strata

Very little is known about the earliest period of Hungarian folk costume. The few words of Finno-Ugric and Ugric origin (*öv,* belt; *szíj,* strap; *szalag,* ribbon, etc.) do not reveal much about the essentials of clothing. The number of words for clothing increased during contact with the Bulgaro-Turks (*saru,* sandal; *csat,* buckle; *ködmön,* sheepskin jacket; *köpönyeg,* mantle; *szirony,* a thong used for sewing and embroidering leatherware; *bársony,* velvet; *gyöngy,* pearl and also beads; *gyűrű,* ring, etc.). Among these words is the word *bagaria* (Russian leather), which brings to mind the name of the Bulgaro-Turks, even though it may have come to the Magyars later by another route.

Archeological finds and later descriptions give some information about the folk costume of the conquering Magyars. Women, like the men, wore trousers. The fact that only one kind of saddle is known from this period, one which could be ridden only when wearing trousers, also bears this out. The shirt was high collared and cut straight, and a belted mantle was worn over it. The sleeves were so long that they even covered the hands. Women wore a headdress or a peaked cap on their heads and covered their feet and lower legs with soft leather or felt sandals. The clothing of the men was, in its main features, exactly like that of the women. The belt was very important, because they hung the sword, the quiver for arrows, and other small objects on it. The head must have been mostly shaved, leaving 2 or 3 locks only, according to the Oriental custom.

After the Conquest, primarily through constant contact with Slavic peoples, numerous new elements were added to Hungarian costume, as the vocabulary testifies: *ruha* (clothes), *gúnya* (garb), *kabát* (coat), *csuha* (cowl), *nadrág* (trousers or breeches), *palást* (cloak), *szoknya* (skirt), *harisnya* (stocking), *kapca* (foot rag), *posztó* (broadcloth), etc. Technical vocabulary shows that during the Middle Ages Hungarians also adopted western influences (*suba,* sheepskin coat; *köntös,* garment; *atlasz,* atlas;

tafota, taffeta, etc.). It is also certain that the costumes of the Pechenegs, Jazygians, and Cumanians, who arrived with the last wave of the migration period in the 13th century, again brought new fashions from the east to Hungary.

All this proves that new and old elements were mixed in Hungarian costume during the Middle Ages. This is the period when certain articles of clothing developed which were held to be Eastern in origin by foreign contemporaries. Among these both nobles and peasants wore *suba* and *turca,* and differences appeared only in the tanning, quality, and ornamentation of the garment. The first description mentioning a *suba* occurs in 1290, but it is possible that sheepskin cloaks were known before the Conquest. Even kings wore cloaks called by this name in the Middle Ages, and we know that King Matthias (1458–1490) had one hundred of them distributed as presents among the retinue of the Czech King Ladislaus. Similarly, the history of other sheepskin garments and the *ködmön*-jacket can be traced back to the Middle Ages. Peaked caps *(süveg)* made of felt are also known from archaeological evidence.

The conquering Turks exercised great influence over the clothing of both peasants and nobility in the 16th and 17th centuries, even in those areas not under their direct influence (e.g. Transylvania, Upper Hungary). Simpler, straight cuts, the increased use of colour, and even the spread of some new materials were elements of this significant Oriental influence. This effect is marked by certain words: *aba* (broadcloth), *dolmány* (dolman), *kalpag* (hat), *kaftán* (caftan), *papucs* (slipper), *csizma* (boot), etc., although some of these words came to the Hungarians through the South Slav peoples.

As the result of the political situation, German influence increased during the following centuries (*kalap,* hat; *kacagány,* leopard's skin thrown loosely over one shoulder; *kanavász,* canvas; *karton,* calico; *galand,* tape; *pántlika,* ribbon; *lajbi,* waistcoat; *pruszlik,* bodice; *zeke,* jerkin, etc.), which also indicates the increased use of manufactured products. Contact with Slavic peoples was pronounced primarily among the peasantry and resulted in many mutual influences. The following words became known to the Hungarian language at this time: *gatya* (long drawers), *kabát* (coat), *sapka* (cap), *karima* (rim), *pelenka* (diaper), etc. The *guba,* found generally in the north-eastern part of the Great Plain, became increasingly popular during the 17th century. As a result, *guba*s were worn from the region of Ungvár and Munkács all the way to Debrecen, where, according to records, Ruthenian women were called upon to introduce the new weaving technique.

Naturally, Hungarian folk costume not only incorporated outside influences, but various regions also developed their own styles as an essential part of their own history. Hungarian costumes significantly influenced surrounding peoples, such as the Rumanians, Slovakians, Serbs, and Croats, and we can even trace the route of certain articles of apparel towards the Germans, Poles, and Ukrainians, although that is not our task at the present.

A large number of traditional beliefs among the Hungarian people are connected with hair. Damage to the hair signifies injury to the individual himself. That is why cutting hair off was still one of the strictest ancient punishments, even during the last century. Keeping a lover by eating a bit of his or her hair, and many other superstitions, prove its importance in peasant life.

In the past, the hair style of men was extremely varied. Records from the 18th century mention the Palots and Cumanian areas, where many men still shaved their heads and left only a forelock on top. This old custom certainly gained strength during the Turkish rule. Even young men wore shoulder-length hair until the middle of the last century. This style went out of fashion when the young men were recruited into the army and had their hair cut, and thus short hair slowly became fashionable among the young. Older men braided their hair on two sides and then pinned it up. This style was replaced by the *rounded* hair style which was cut at the nape and held together in the back by one or two combs. This style could still be found occasionally among the herdsmen of the Great Plain during the first decade of the 20th century.

Moustaches with waxed, pointed whiskers were considered a man's chief ornament. The moustache became fashionable during the second half of the 18th century, in spite of its being strongly prohibited by the authorities. Straight and curly styles of whiskers became usual by the beginning of this century. Such moustaches, however, have almost completely disappeared during the last decades, just as the wearing of

Hair and Headdress

Fig. 160. An old man with two plaits in his hair. Apáti-puszta, Tolna County. Late 19th century

168. Woman braiding her hair
Boldog, Pest County

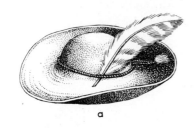

Fig. 161. Hats with large brims. a) Hat for a cowman. Hortobágy, former Hajdú County. b) Hat with a large brim. Udvarhely County. Early 19th century

beards, which was customary only in certain areas (e.g. Southern Transdanubia). A certain type of beard known as the "Kossuth beard" was worn in some places as a political protest, after the defeat of the 1848–49 War of Independence.

Throughout the entire Hungarian speaking area, women wore their hair long and never cut it. The name for unmarried girls was *hajadon* (bare-headed), which refers to their not wearing anything on their heads. Formerly girls braided their hair into two or three, and later one braid, and tied coloured ribbons into each braid. In a few places in the country girls pinned up their hair into a bun made of many small braids (Kalocsa, Sióagárd). Married women wore their braided hair pinned in a knot on the top of the head. In fact, the last act of the wedding is the pinning up of the hair of the young wife *(felkontyolás)*.

At one time the majority of men's head coverings were made from animal hide or wool felt. The material used for the *fur cap* is sheepskin, generally black in colour and peaked in shape. It is generally worn in the winter, even today. The famous *Cumanian cap* or *cap of Tur* was made of felt. Recent research proves that even during the first half of the last century this hat was worn by Hungarians all over the country, and not only by the Cumanians. It is a tall, cylindrical form of headgear, and may have come to the peasants from the old traditional soldier's outfit. The wearing of wide-rimmed felt hats spread during the first half of the last century. We often read in the official ordinances of this time that the wearing of the wide-rimmed, so-called "peasant outlaio hats" was prohibited. Gradually the rim of the hats decreased in size. Their smaller-rimmed successors still may be seen worn on the heads of the husbandmen of the Hortobágy. The wide-rimmed hat style lasted for a long time among the Székelys and Csángós, and also among the neighbouring peoples (e.g. Slovaks). Inexpensive straw hats appeared from the middle of the last century, and became popular in certain parts of the Hungarian speaking territory especially during the time of major summer work.

The Hungarian peasant always wears a hat and does not take it off unless he is eating or is in church or some especially honoured, unfamiliar place. He is not much used to lifting it; at most he tilts it a little with his finger if he wants to greet somebody. It is such an inevitable fixture of his attire that in many places they even place it over the face of the dead. Boys and especially young men would stick the feathers of various birds in their hats. Eagle and crane feathers were primarily the prerogative of the nobility, while commoners had to be satisfied with cock or bustard feathers, up until the time the serfs were liberated. Herdsmen of the Great Plain kept the custom of wearing feathers in their hats longest. Since the beginning of the last century, the bridesmen who invite people to the wedding have worn flower bouquets or feather grass in their hats, and newly conscripted young men bind coloured ribbons onto their hats.

The girls wear a *párta,* an ornately decorated headpiece on their heads, which covers the forehead but leaves the top of the head uncovered. Some predecessors of this headdress have been found in graves dating from the period of the Conquest, but many of the later type of

318

169. Two young wives *(menyecske)* in festive headdress
Kazár, Nógrád County

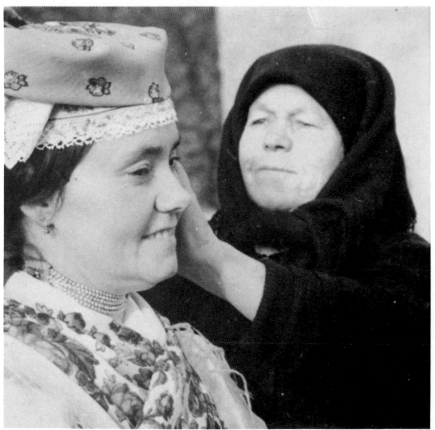

170. Arranging the headdress of a young wife *(menyecske)*
Kazár, Nógrád County

171. Headdress of a middle-aged woman
Kazár, Nógrád County

172. Headdress of an aged woman
Kazár, Nógrád County

II. Indigo-dyers at work. A signboard for the hostel of journeymen, 1862

◁ I. Székely gate. Máréfalva, former Udvarhely County

III. A stall for indigo-dyed cottonware at a fair. Véménd, Baranya County

IV. Wine cellar. Upper Balaton region

V. Vintage. Upper Balaton region

VI. Hay-making women
Vista, former Kolozs County

VII. Treading out grain on an estate, 1855. Great Plain

VIII. Shepherds, 1855. Great Plain

IX. Catching a horse with a lasso, 1855. Great Plain

X. Buffalo herdsman, 1855. Upper Balaton region

XI. A young wife *(menyecske)*. Kapuvár, Győr-Sopron County

XII. Women and girls in festive costumes. Sióagárd, Tolna County

XIII. Girls wearing their costumes ▷
Kazár, Nógrád County
XIV. A girl dressed in her Sunday best ▷
Vista, former Kolozs County

XV. A couple wearing everyday clothes
Gyimes-Bükkhavas, former Csík County

XVI. Men wearing their costumes
Gyimes-Bükkhavas, former Csík County

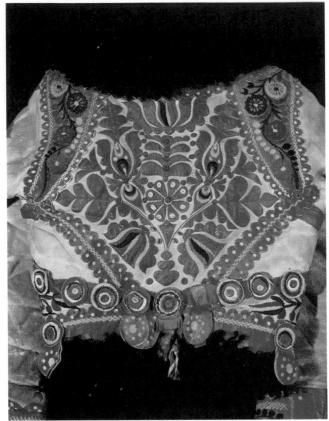

XVII. A woman's sheepskin jacket
Tordaszentlászló, former Torda-Aranyos County

XVIII. Back of a woman's sheepskin jacket
Transdanubia

XIX. Woman's sheepskin jacket. Maconka, Heves
County

XX. Sleeves of women's sheepskin jackets. Transdanubia

XXI. Detail of a *suba* (sheepskin cloak). Kisújszállás, Szolnok County

headdresses came to the peasantry through the mediation of the nobility. The *párta* was worn on holidays and special occasions, and was valued as the symbol of maidenhood. This meaning is expressed in the saying that a girl "stayed in her *párta*", that is to say, she remained an old maid. The most beautiful kinds of maiden's headdresses were worn in the district of Sárköz, in Debrecen, in the villages of Kalotaszeg, and in Torockó.

Folk belief assigns greater magical power to a married woman's hair than to a girl's, and that is the reason why a married woman must always keep her head covered. The coif or headcovering (*főkötő*) serves this purpose, the shape, colour and form of which vary greatly according to region, the age of the wearer, the weather, and the occasion. Usually an under-headdress holds the bun of hair in place, and a more ornate one is fitted on top of that for festive occasions. This headdress is made stiff with some cardboard-paper. Various versions developed in the Hungarian-speaking regions. The most usual coifs are shaped like a cylinder or a column. The Matyós wear a conical coif, while in certain parts of Transdanubia the coif is formed into flat, square shape. Ruffles, bows, and ribbons are sewn on the front. In certain regions, after the birth of the first child, the young wife wears a red headdress, the colours becoming darker as the number of her children increases, and finally she

173. Married young woman's headdress Kalocsa

174. Bride in her bridal wreath Boldog, Pest County

321

wears the black colour befitting a grandmother. During the past decades such headgear has disappeared almost completely, having been replaced by a kerchief tied over the head, whose colours darken as the wearer grows older.

Underwear

Underwear is usually made out of linen, more recently replaced with cambric *(gyolcs)* for Sunday wear, the Hungarian name evoking the name of the German town, Cologne. Most of the articles of clothing were of linen, as was much of women's outer clothing until recently. This is the reason why women are called *white servants, linen servants,* and *white folk* all over the country. Clothing made of flax or hemp linen used to be worn as outer garments during the summer, and as underwear in winter, with another garment worn over it.

The most important piece of underwear is the *blouse* or chemise, which is found in both a long and short version. The cut may be either with the sleeves gathered into the neck or with the sleeves sewn on to the shoulders. The short blouse or shift, which evokes Renaissance tradition, reaches past the waist just far enough to be held to the body by tying the skirt over it. The chemise covers the body to mid-calf. In the case of the first type of blouse, the sleeves were inserted directly into the collar, thus making it possible to gather the shirt's front. This style was still popular during the last century but gradually was replaced by the second type of blouse having sleeves sewn to the shoulders. Blouses function equally as under or outer garments. The front, cuffs, and shoulder sections may be richly ornamented, especially for young people and in certain regions (Kalotaszeg and Sárköz).

Women wear a petticoat called *pendely* with the short-waisted blouse, which surrounds the lower part of the body like a skirt. The blouse and petticoat were often sewn together, and this is how the chemise came into being. If the petticoat is worn as underwear, it is unseemly to let it be seen under the outer garment, but if it is used as an outer garment, it is treated as such. In such cases they pleated it carefully and even ornamented it in various ways.

Men's shirts can also be long or short, the latter, found especially in the Great Plain, are even shorter than the waist. The shirt of the bridegroom played an important role at weddings. It was made at the bride's house and carried in procession to the bridegroom, who wore it at the wedding. Although he might put it on again occasionally, he would preserve his festive shirt for his funeral. There was no collar on the oldest type of shirts, only a band or binding was sewn around the neck. The shirt with a folded collar is a newcomer, appearing at the end of the last century, and in many places is called "soldier's shirt" *(katonaing),* indicating its origin. As cambric was becoming more popular than linen, this type of shirt became extremely loose-fitting. The gathered sleeves were sewn into the shoulders of shirts called *borjúszájú ing* or *lobogós ujjú ing* (shirts with very wide sleeves). In the case of shirts with sleeves gathered into a cuff, which appear to be newer in origin, the lower part of the sleeve is gathered. The front and the cuffs of men's shirts were embroidered in some places with white-work (Somogy,

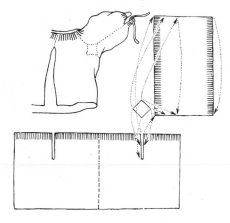

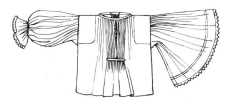

Fig. 162. A blouse for a woman with the sleeves gathered into the neck. Lóc, Nógrád County. Early 20th century

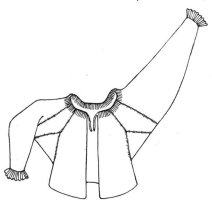

Fig. 163. T-shaped blouse for a woman with the cuff gathered on one of the sleeves, the other left open. Palotsland. Early 20th century

Fig. 164. The type of shirt called *borjúszájú ing.* Martos, former Komárom County. 1930s

322

Nógrád, and Tolna Counties) or colourful needlework (e.g. Matyóföld, Kalotaszeg). The material used for shirts is always white; only the horse-herdsmen of the Hortobágy wear dark blue shirts. Although a man's shirt is considered an undergarment, it is used as an outer garment in many places, especially in regions where its ornamentation especially justifies it as such.

The men's undergarment, the *gatya,* a long pantaloon, was made of white linen. In some places the edges were trimmed with fringes and occasionally they were ornamented with embroidery (Transdanubia). This piece of clothing, like the petticoat, could also function as both an under and outer garment. During the 19th century a double pair of *gatya* were worn during the winter, one over the other. The linen *gatya* was changed regularly, but if two were worn, they dipped the upper one in ashy water, smeared it with lard and bacon ring, and wore it until it fell apart. A wider variation of the *gatya,* the *bőgatya,* appeared as an outer garment with the adaptation of cambric. The more widths of cambric that went into its cutting, the more handsome it was considered to be. These *gatya*s were worn only on festive occasions along with the wide-sleeved shirt.

Outer Wear

Today the difference between women's and men's clothing is primarily defined by the skirt or the trousers. The skirt, called *kabát* in the north-eastern linguistic territory, covers the lower part of the body. Its length varies from above the knee versions (e.g. Buják), through those reach-ing the mid-calf (Őrhalom), to the ones covering the ankles (Matyós). Several starched petticoats are worn underneath, often as many as ten, in order to appeal to the peasant concept of beauty, a preference for rounded shapes. These are worn with *hip cushions* for extra roundness. In some regions the skirt is sewn to the *bodice* or fastened with suspenders which assures not only more comfort, but also makes dressing easier. Skirts are not always sewn together in front. The *muszuj* or *bagazia* of Kalotaszeg, for instance, is no more than a back apron, pleated and tied in front (cf. Ill. 199). The apron worn over it covers the front opening. This traditional form of garment indicates how the styles of skirts developed. In many regions skirts were ornamented by smocking, and some women were especially proficient in making these.

The material of skirts may be extremely varied. In Székelyland they make the *rokolya* out of colourful homespun and the outer skirt out of a solid-coloured fabric. The place of origin of the wearer can be ascertained immediately from the colouring of her skirt. The fabrics produced by small industry have played an important and ever-growing role in the evolution of Hungarian folk costumes from the end of the 18th century on. Artisans known as *bluedyers* appeared in Europe in the 18th century and used a technique of cloth production brought from East Asia known as batik; it came to Hungary via the Uplands and Transdanubia from the Czech–Moravian, Austrian, and German areas. Within a very short time, bluedyeing workshops of various sizes were in operation throughout the entire Carpathian Basin. There they printed patterns, mostly of western origin, on material which was either their own or brought to them by the peasants. Various blue-dyed materials began to play an increasingly important role in everyday wear, and even in holiday wear (cf. Plates II, III). For women's wear on festive occasions, however, especially in wealthy areas or among the more prosperous members of the peasantry, this material became less important as use of manufactured products spread, such as velvet, silk brocade, woven stuffs and other materials, from the middle of the 19th century on.

The apron *(kötény)* is an indispensable element of women's wear. It is used on weekdays to protect the skirt, and for holiday wear as well. For this reason, it is one of the most richly ornamented pieces of the Hungarian woman's costume. The apron also played an important role in the world of beliefs, especially the bridal apron, which the young wife would put away carefully, and keep to cover her sick children with, thus ensuring their quick recovery. The *loose apron* covers the skirt almost completely, while the *narrow apron* made of only one width of cloth, covers it only in front. Ornamentation of holiday aprons is extremely varied. There are homespun aprons, but usually aprons are covered with embroidery, and lace and ribbons sewn on their edges. Significant differences are apparent between the aprons of married women and the aprons of girls, mostly in colour, material, and ornamentation.

Women wore a bodice *(pruszlik)* over their blouses, of which there are two basic types. The older one is shorter than the waist and its neck is more widely cut out. This style has survived longest in the southern part of the Hungarian-speaking territory. The neck is closed on the other form, which extends past the waist. This style was worn in the northern areas. Usually the bodices are richly ornamented, primarily with embroidery and by embellishing the edges in various ways. The diffusion of wearing the bodice can be connected to the expansion of city fashion from the second half of the last century.

In men's wear breeches *(nadrág)* replaced the *gatya*, or rather turned it into underwear. This transformation of the male peasant costume began in many areas scarcely a century ago and was basically completed by the end of the last century. In many places oral tradition tells us about the first appearance of breeches in the village (e.g. Bodrogköz). They were made of black or blue broadcloth, with a flap in front that folds down. Earlier they were even lined inside. There are also data showing that breeches were worn turned inside out on weekdays and with the right side out on holidays. The breeches of the Székely men, called *harisnya* (e.g. hose), are one of the most archaic forms (cf. Ill. 16 and p. 361). Their present cut developed from the uniform of the Székely border-guards in the second half of the 18th century. The colour and shape of their black and red braiding mark the social rank of the wearer. The material was generally white, but today braiding trim appears on gray material also.

Men wore a sleeveless waistcoat *(mellény, lajbi),* made of black and dark blue broadcloth and, less often, of silk. Its characteristic feature is that both its back and front are made of the same material, as opposed to the later version which was worn under the coat. As this later waistcoat can be seen only from the front, it is acceptable to make the back from

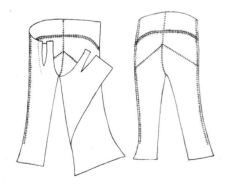

Fig. 165. The cut of the Székely hoses called *harisnya,* and a finished pair. Csíkszentandrás, former Csík County. 1930s

cheaper cloth. There are many forms of waistcoats, some with high collars, other with a cut-out neck, some embellished with ornate buttons and braidings. Often ornamental rows of buttons made of silver, tin, pewter and nickel are sewn on. Generally these articles of clothing are among the most ornamental examples of men's wear.

The belt *(öv)* is an important piece of men's wear worn both over and under top clothes. The *tüsző* or, by its Transylvanian name, *sziju,* is made of thick leather and tied directly onto the waist. It not only serves as a pocket but also protects the body and keeps it warm. A belt about 3 to 4 inches wide made of thick leather was worn as outer wear in many parts of the Hungarian-speaking territory during the last century. We know they were worn among the Palots people and the Matyó. The widest are the belts worn in Transylvania, such as ones from Torockó, which are embroidered with coloured thongs. Besides securing the garment, such belts also served the function of carrying various objects (tobacco pouch, lighter, etc.) that were hung on them, with the money hidden inside.

We often find ornamental frog closings, braid, and bound buttons, which were made in the shops of the *gombkötő* (button making) artisans. These embellished the outer wear of women and especially men. In the 17th and 18th centuries these artisans worked primarily for the nobility, but in the 19th century, when the use in broadcloth in folk wear increased, peasants gradually became major customers of braid and button makers. A great quantity of frog closings, braid and buttons appeared on pants and waistcoats, but by the beginning of the 20th century, this old craft which had been indispensable to Hungarian fashion was eclipsed and it finally disappeared altogether.

Mantles and Coat-like Outer Wear

It is easier to understand coat-like outer wear if we consider the most important types and those known over the widest territory according to their material. A significant proportion of garments were cut from material woven of wool, or perhaps felt, while others were made of fur or leather, among peasants mostly of sheepskin.

The most widespread form of coat-like outer wear is the *szűr* mantle. Although it has sleeves, in most places the sleeves are not used as such but are sewn up one end so that small utensils may be kept in them (cf. Ill. 37). In some places (Transdanubia), the sleeves became shorter until they atrophied completely. The word *szűr* itself probably originated from the first syllable of the word *szürke* (gray), which refers to its earliest colour. The mantle was sewn out of rectangular pieces, further proof of the great antiquity of this article of clothing.

Although the *szűr* was worn by men from Transdanubia as far east as the region of Kalotaszeg in Transylvania, certain regional variations can still be differentiated.

Thus in Transdanubia the *szűr* is generally very short, its large, square collar reaching all the way down to the waist. This collar was also used to cover the head in rainy weather. The *szűr* of the Palotses is of the most simple type, with little ornamentation.

In the region east of the Tisza, and Kalotaszeg, the *szűr* had a short

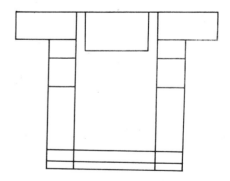

Fig. 167. Cut of the mantle called *szűr.* Kisújszállás, Szolnok County. Early 20th century

stand-up collar and was called *nyakas szűr* (collared *szűr*). Since the beginning of the last century the *szűr* has been richly ornamented with appliqués or embroidered embellishments, while formerly only its edges were decorated with colourful materials.

The most highly ornamented and embellished versions of the *szűr* were worn by young men, while married men, especially in their old age, wore *szűr*s decorated primarily with black. The *szűr* is a most expensive piece of peasant wear, yet every young man tried to buy one by the time he was ready to get married. When going to propose, he left his *szűr* at the girl's house as if by accident, and watched with great trepidation the next day to see if they hung it out in front of the house. If they did, it meant he was not considered a desirable suitor. If it was not outside, however, his best men could go to the house to ask for the girl's hand. This is why the expression *"kitenni a szűrét"* (to put one's *szűr* out) is a vernacular phrase meaning "to throw somebody out".

The *szűr* was not worn in Székelyland; instead garments called *cedele* (Kászon), *zeke* (Udvarhely), or *bámbán* (Csíkszék and Háromszék) were worn. These were also made from broadcloth and belong to an ancient type of clothing from south-eastern Europe. Formerly these were cut out of a single length of cloth, more recently an added bottom part was sewn into it. These garments reached to mid-calf during the last century, then gradually became shorter. They were embellished with black braid and, at certain places, edged with green or dark blue broadcloth. In earlier times there was never a collar; collars came into fashion only later.

176. Horseherd wearing a *szűr* mantle
Hortobágy

327

Fig. 168. The cut of the mantle called *guba*.
Matolcs, former Szatmár County. Early
20th century

Fig. 166. Man's jacket. Erked, former
Szilágy County. 1916

The festive *cedele* was ornamented more richly, with two rows of braid trim. It was worn thrown on the shoulder in warmer weather, while in the cold it was tied around the waist, usually with a belt made of horsehair.

The *guba* is known over a relatively smaller area but maintains a close connection with the various articles of clothing of Europe's eastern and western regions (cf. Ill. 44). It was made out of rectangular lengths of *guba* broadcloth (cf. p. 310), with a round hole cut for the head. The sleeves were much longer than the arm, which eliminated the need for gloves. The *guba* was worn in very cold weather; otherwise it was carried thrown over the shoulder. In the course of its continuous diffusion, the *guba* reached the line of the Danube during the 19th century, but it was never worn on the western side of the Danube. A *guba* may be black or gray, the former being in many places the attire of the prosperous farmers, while the latter was worn by the poorer peasants. Speaking very broadly, however, the *guba* was associated with less prosperous people, as indicated by the proverb "*Guba* with *guba*, *suba* with *suba*" which means that the poor should associate with and marry only the poor, and the rich only the rich. The *guba* was worn by both men and women, although those of the women were much shorter, reaching only to mid-thigh.

The garments mentioned above are all long. However, broadcloth was also used to make clothing which reached only to the waist or just a little past it. These broadcloth *jackets* could be found in different forms

328

and colours over a large part of the Hungarian-speaking regions. In many places this jacket was called *dolmány,* and had a stand-up collar. In other places the collar was folded down and richly braided. Certain versions, such as the dolman-like *mente,* was worn thrown over the shoulders, a practice that came into use in connection with hussar costume.

Fig. 169. A shepherd holding his staff wearing a *suba* and a cap called *süveg.* Debrecen—Balmazújváros. 1740

Among sheepskin garments, the *suba* was worn over the greatest part of the Great Plain (cf. Ill. 37). It belongs to the category of cloak-like garments, and simple, unornamented versions of it were worn, not only by herdsmen, but also by carters and the people of the distant farmsteads. The most embellished examples were worn by the prosperous peasants of the towns. The *suba* protects its wearer against rain and cold,

Fig. 170. The cut of a round cloak called *suba,* made out of 12 sheepskins. Former Bács County. Early 20th century. 1. Front piece. 2. Side piece. 3. Back piece. 4. Shoulder piece. 5. Addition to each skin where the front legs are missing

178. The embroidery of a *suba* sheepskin cloak
Kisújszállás, Szolnok County

179. Women wearing *ködmön* jackets Nagycigánd, Borsod-Abaúj-Zemplén County

and also serves as bed and cover and, if necessary, as a table, because by spreading it on the ground one can eat from it. In the cold it is a suitable cover to spread on the back of a sweating horse. When the *suba* starts to get ragged, it is put in the corner of the oven, on a mean bed or on a bed in the stable, where it still provides good service.

The *suba* is circular in shape when spread out, as it consists of individual triangular pieces of sheepskin (cf. Ill. 37). The simplest *suba* consists of only 3 to 4 pieces, which were cut and sewn by the herdsmen themselves. But a very beautiful festive *suba* was made of 12 to 15 sheepskins and assembled by so-called *Hungarian furriers,* who travelled to distant fairs with their finished goods. The *suba* was richly embroidered, which is why an extremely high price had to be paid for it. It was meant to last for a lifetime, and poorer folk, especially day labourers and farm hands could not afford to buy one. Men's *suba*s are generally white or yellow, the women's are usually brown. The people of the peasant towns of Transylvania and of Transdanubia preferred the same colours.

Herdsmen made the most simple leather garments themselves. The *hátibőr* (back hide) of the Great Plain is made of a single sheepskin, the two hind legs tied at the waist, the two front ones at the neck, so that it covers only the back. The *mejjes* (chest warmer) consists of two parts,

330

180. Short sheepskin *bunda* of the Hajdú
district
Debrecen

331

one worn on the back, the other on the chest. It is held together on both sides by binding. Such a garment had no sleeves, and was only rarely ornamented. On a more elaborated version the skin was sewn up on one side and fastened on the other with buttons (Székely, Csángó). The front was embellished with rich embroidery. Men and women both wore several versions (cf. Plate XVI).

Sleeved sheepskin jackets *(ujjas ködmön)* are known over the entire linguistic territory (cf. Plates XVII–XIX). Some reach to above the waist, others down to mid-thigh. We find both straight cut and flounced bottom *ködmön* styles. The former is often so short that it does not even cover the waist (South Transdanubia, see Plate XX), although in earlier times in some places it was long enough to cover the knees (Great Plain). Women often tie a shawl under the *ködmön,* in which case the neck is cut out, while those worn by men often have a high neck. The type with a flounced bottom is worn mostly in the Great Plain. This type of *ködmön* flares out from the waist, and is thus especially suitable for riding a horse. It was often used as wear in the army; supposedly, King Matthias had 8,000 of these jackets made by Great Plain furriers in the second half of the 15th century when he was preparing to besiege the famous fortress of Southern Hungary, Szabács. The bottom and front of the *ködmön* jackets were trimmed with fur and those of the women embroidered richly, those of the men less so (cf. pp. 389–9).

The different kinds of sheepskin coats were made by artisans called *Hungarian furriers,* who were experts not only at sewing but at embroidering as well. They never worked with broadcloth. On the other hand the so-called *German furriers* made garments that were made of broadcloth outside and lined with sheepskin. This garment first appeared among the nobility, then it spread increasingly among the peasantry as well, especially from the middle of the 19th century.

Footwear

The extremely varied Hungarian footwear of earlier times became more similar from the last century on, even in colour. One of the oldest forms of footwear is the *bocskor* (laced-up sandal). Although the origin of the word is not known, we know that the word was borrowed from the Hungarians by the neighbouring Slavic peoples, which indirectly proves its antiquity. This type of footwear is without a doubt one of the most ancient, and its antiquity is proved not only by records but also by lyrics of minstrel songs, which mention the birchbark sandals of the minstrels of the first Hungarian king, Stephen I (997–1038). The related Finno-Ugric peoples wore similar footwear until recent times. It appears that different versions of the *bocskor* were worn even by the nobility in the 17th century, as it was noted that the poet Miklós Zrínyi wore a "full laced-up sandal" on the hunt that ended so tragically with the loss of his life.

The *bocskor* was the most generally-worn footwear of Eastern Europe. A round- and wrinkle-toed version was worn in the Great Plain. There were loops *(telek)* or openings on the edge of the *telkes bocskor,* which was fastened to the shin with thongs that were pulled through them. The majority of the different *bocskor*s of Transylvania are

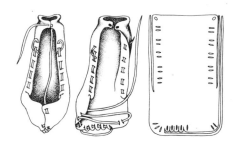

Fig. 171. The preparation of "Magyar" sandals *(bocskor)*. Nagyecsed, former Szatmár County. 1920s

pointed and sewn all the way down along the toe. The covered sandals *(fedeles bocskor)* used in the southern part of the Great Plain and in Transdanubia were made up of two parts and the front was completely closed. Herdsmen wore the *bocskor* longest. The harvesters made them for themselves out of boot-tops because this light wear provides good protection against rough stubble. The surrounding peoples (Rumanians and Serbs) preserved this old-fashioned footwear longer than the Hungarians.

The *bocskor* was rarely worn with bare feet, except sometimes in the summer. In the winter and in rainy weather people wrapped their feet with a foot cloth *(kapca)* made of leather, wool or linen, smeared thoroughly with lard to make it more resistant against cold and water. In some areas (Tiszántúl, Palócföld) leggings were wrapped above the *bocskor* to protect the shins. These were made of leather and laced up with thongs through the holes on the sides. This became the transition to boots.

Among the boots the *saru* (a kind of sandal) appears to be the most ancient and is a scarcely remembered form. The word is a pre-Conquest word adopted from Turkic. During the *saru*'s long historical development, many different kinds of footwear were included in the meaning of this word. From the surviving examples and notations one element seems especially permanent, an element which, among others, differentiates it from the boot: that is, its upper part is sewn to the sole by turning it outward, which made it possible to use not just one but, according to need, two or three soles. This solution is related to various western types of footwear.

The word *csizma* (boot) appears first in the last years of the 15th century, but it is undoubtedly Ottoman Turkish in origin and perhaps came to Hungary through south Slavic intermediation. The boot is a high-topped type of footwear sewn together at first on the two sides. Its toe was pointed and, in many cases, turned upward. The sole is sewn, then turned. Its heel is carved out of wood, the leather turned down over it, and a heel iron fastened to it. At first only the upper class wore it, and while the peasantry began to take on its use only in the 18th century, it became really widely used only in the 19th century and often (e.g. Székelyland) only at the end of the century.

The boot is generally a festive form of footwear. The men's are black almost without exception, and ornamentation was put on them only now and then. The young men liked to put spurs on them, so they could beat out the rhythm during dancing. Since the beginning of this century the technique of making boots has changed, and now the upper part is sewn together on the back. Women wore many different kinds of coloured boots, mainly red and yellow. They embellished the top with embroidery, studded the heel with nails, and put a copper heel iron on it (Kalotaszeg). Variously shaped shoes have begun to replace boots only during the last decades.

Carters and other men doing work standing in the cold wore the *botos*. This word, supposedly medieval in origin and known throughout Europe, was perhaps introduced by the French settlers. The *botos* is made by the hatmakers out of felt and broadcloth. Later the word *botos*

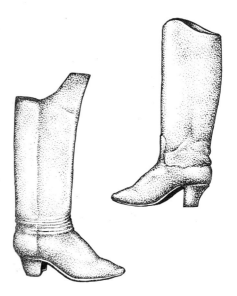

Fig. 172. Boots. a) A red boot for a woman, the type sewn at the back. Mezőkövesd. First half of 20th century. b) The type sewn on the side with a nailed-on sole. Rimóc, Nógrád County. First half of 20th century

was used to designate a leather-soled boot, only the top part of which was made of broadcloth or felt. The *bakancs* (ankle boot), the name of which is very likely the derivative of the word *boka* (ankle), appeared at the beginning of the 16th century. It is a type of footwear reaching the ankle, and in every period was used for work.

Women's light footwear, worn less frequently by men, is called the *papucs* (slipper). Ottoman Turkish in origin, it appeared first in the second half of the 16th century. It consists of two parts, an upper part which covers the foot, and the sole. The slippers of younger women and girls have higher heels and the upper part is richly embroidered, especially in areas where they wear colourful, knitted stockings with them on holidays. Older women and men wear lower heeled or heelless slippers. Men fasten them to their feet with thongs. Wearing slippers was originally confined to the southern Great Plain, where the most outstanding slipper-makers worked (Szeged).

Regional Forms of Hungarian Folk Costumes

We have reviewed the basic materials of Hungarian folk costumes as well as the articles of clothing made from them, and the most important changes they went through. These factors, appearing in different combinations, create the characteristic folk costume of a certain region. We have tried in the foreword to introduce the different ethnic groups, ethnological regions, and isolated settlements of the Hungarian people. Besides architecture, folk costumes are the most visible part of folk culture. It is therefore reasonable to examine the broad regions of the Hungarian speaking territory from the point of view of folk costume.

Naturally we cannot attempt to introduce in detail folk costumes of every region and ethnic group. We speak only in generalities, paying special attention to those areas where folk costumes flourished in the recent past or can be found even today. We thus will attempt to make the reader acquainted with some of the important features of Hungarian peasant culture not only by grouping them by subject matter but also by showing, as much as possible, their geographic proliferation.

Transdanubia

Because of its location, western influence came to Transdanubia first, both in material and in the cutting and sewing of certain articles of fashion. Mutual influences can be demonstrated most easily in the southern region of Transdanubia with Croats and Slovenians, because of contacts and proximity. The traditions of Serbs and other South Slav groups spread to the north along the Danube, influencing Hungarian folk costumes, especially through use of greater colour and richness. At the same time, Hungarian influences also penetrated to the west and south, but it is not up to our present study to examine that subject.

Only remnants of folk costumes are known from the *Göcsej* and *Hetés* regions. Girls wore long braids with long ribbons in back that reached down to their heels. Married women rolled their hair on a piece of wood, later made from cardboard. A type of headdress called *pacsa* for festive wear was shaped out of white linen, starched, and decorated; we can find its equivalent among the Croats. Linen skirts were worn with aprons, which were also made out of linen. The short sheepskin coat was prominent among the winter wear, and was variegated by red cordovan and ornamented with white and yellow leather appliqué. Formerly men's shirts were so short that they did not cover the waist, longer shirts coming into use only during the second half of the last century, when the front was embroidered with white cotton yarn. The *gatya* (drawers), made out of one to one and a half widths of linen, was supplanted in the middle of the last century by a festive version, sewn out of five or six widths of material, fringed at the bottom. An apron decorated by stripes was also worn by men. Breeches made out of broadcloth only appeared around the middle of the last century. The *bocskor* was generally worn in winter and summer, supplemented in the cold weather by leggings wrapped around shins. A thong was wound around the leggings so precisely that the legging could not be seen under it. A braid-trimmed bodice was worn over the shirt, and the older people wore sheepskin vests. A short *szűr* was worn over that or, in the case of someone more prosperous, the large *szűr*.

181. Young married woman
Kapuvár, Győr–Sopron County

335

182. Bride and groom
Kapuvár, Győr–Sopron County

The costumes of the *Rábaköz* were worn longest by the people of
Kapuvár. On holidays, married women tied an embroidered white
batiste or tulle kerchief over their coifs. A favoured material for the rich
garments of women was red velvet sprinkled with gilded stars. Even
blue satin was used for dresses, which is unique among Hungarian folk
costumes. A long silk apron was tied in front of the skirt (cf. Plate XI).
The costume is extremely rich and, from the middle of the last century,
was made mostly of various manufactured materials. Men also wore
richly ornamented clothes. They pinned a large bouquet to their small
fur caps. We find detailed embroidery on the cambric shirt, and flowers
embroidered even on the legs of the under-drawers. The shirt is cut out
of brocade with roses in it, and is further embellished with ribbons. Men
wore an apron made of lusterine embroidered with flowers. Their hard-
topped boots matched both the pale blue winter broadcloth suit and the
summer wear.

It is worthwhile taking a closer look at the women's attire in Martos

(Martovec) of the *Csallóköz*. The girls wore a gathered, black ribbon in their hair, tied over the forehead. Young wives could also wear such a band, but usually their headdress was trimmed with gold lace and silk ribbons. The hair of the married women was knotted on a comb. Several silver chains or garnet necklaces were worn. One basic element of the women's costume is the petticoat, which was made of five widths of hemp linen and which was worn with straps. They usually wore a wide-sleeved shirt, tinted blue. The bodice was cut out in the front and back and it reached the waist; festive versions were made of cotton, silk, and other factory-made materials. Wearing skirts became fashionable only during the last century. A shawl was worn over the shoulders. Young people even put rattles into the heels of their red boots, the top part of which was wrinkled all the way around, while the older people wore black boots. Certain characteristics of this costume can be traced to the Palotses.

Törökkoppány of Somogy County, in the southern part of Transdanubia, is noteworthy among the numerous villages where folk costumes were worn. What makes the headgear of the girls interesting is that, contrary to the general custom, they wore their hair in a knot, like married women. A small, hard headdress, called *pille,* richly decorated

184. Middle-aged couple and their young son wearing second-best clothes in summertime
Martos, former Komárom County

338

with beads, goes on top of it. Holiday skirts were made of velvet, and
underneath a thick rear cushion was worn to make the figure seem
bulkier. One characteristic of the men's wear is the long shirt, which was
not tucked into the pants but worn hanging loose, with lace often
embellishing the bottom.

The folk costume of the *Ormánság* has many ancient characteristics.
For example, the white colour of mourning survived here, seen mostly
in the garments of the older women. The girls wore their hair in two
braids decorated with red ribbons, their heads left uncovered. The
married women covered their heads with headdresses of a certain shape
and colour, according to their ages. The young wives up to the age of 35
wore red, wide-ribboned headdresses; between the ages of 35 to 40 they
mixed in ribbons of blue. The blue ribbons, along with white and green
ones, were worn more and more up to age 50, when the ribbons were
completely taken off and the headdress became white. The skirt called
bikla was made of linen, on top of which younger women wore a shirt

339

186. Young women in their best clothes
Érsekcsanád, Bács-Kiskun County

made of tulle. They also wore a festive tulle shirt over their linen shirts. From the beginning of the 20th century, black completely replaced wearing white among the old. This was the result of the growing influence of city culture.

We find the most ornamented costumes of Transdanubia along the Danube, in the region of *Sárköz*, which developed from the middle of the last century as the result of sudden prosperity following the draining of marshes. The girls wore a *párta* over their foreheads, the newer version of which, consisting of three parts, was called "velvet" *(bársony)*. The women pinned their hair on the top of their head in a half crown and covered it with an oblong headdress. They embroidered this with white yarn on a black background, because here black was considered to befit

340

a young person. Until the birth of the first child, young wives wrapped their heads with a *bíbor,* made of voile, the end embroidered with silk and gold, which they wore in such a way that the embroidery could be displayed to advantage. They wore necklaces made out of coins or other ornaments. Men's costumes varied only slightly from that of the surrounding areas. A high fur cap was worn over long hair, and in the summer they also used to wear wide-brimmed hats. The dolman coat *(szűrdolmány)* was made of white broadcloth, its cut and length in accordance with the waist-length shirt. The sides of the dolman were decorated with red and green appliqués of broadcloth or leather. Men in this area also wore the embroidered *szűr* and *suba.*

Among the numerous folk costumes of eastern Transdanubia, which varied from village to village, that of the village of *Fadd* in Tolna County is the most interesting. One of its most archaic features is the women's blouse, which is so short that it does not even reach the waist. The petticoat *(pendely)* was worn even on holidays, and served as the bottom

187. Young wives in their costumes
Decs, Tolna County

skirt. The bodice was sewn together with the skirt. Shoulder shawls and jewellery were found here, just as in the Sárköz. Sheepskin jackets *(ködmön)* and red boots completed this attractive costume.

The folk costume of *Sióagárd* (Tolna County) is characterized by a short coat, made of silk, worn over the blouse-like, narrow-waisted shirt. The apron is embroidered richly with colourful yarn, as is the bodice in recent times. Cloth slippers are worn with colourfully patterned, thick stockings (cf. Plate XII).

Upper Hungary

The largest ethnic unit of the Highlands is the Palots *(palóc)*, within which certain groups can be differentiated on the basis of their folk costumes. A few smaller groups towards the south are known primarily because of their rich folk costumes and are also included in our description.

Many people have admired the varied and beautiful headdresses of the

188. Girl
Sióagárd, Tolna County

189. Dressing the newly wed wife
Kazár, Nógrád County

343

Palots women. Sándor Petőfi, among others, wrote as follows when he travelled through the land of the Palots on foot: "I went from Losonc to Balassagyarmat... the village of Ludány was on the way, where I saw the most beautiful bonnets in my life. When I get married, I will have one brought from there for my wife." The coifs in *Őrhalom-Hugyag* are similar, although there are differences even within the region. Here even the homespun linen was fulled and used for underwear. Shoulder shawls were not worn from the beginning of the century, and as a consequence, the bodice neck became closed and was richly ornamented. The skirt is the most characteristic part of the local costume. It reached to mid-calf or even to the ankle, and is made of heavy brocade and velvet with ornate fringes for holiday use, or of lighter blue-dyed material for everyday use. A homespun apron, patterned with red, was tied in the front. A half century ago this was replaced by an apron made from the same material as the skirt. Men's clothing is much more simple. The basis of it is a suit made of black broadcloth. They also wore the *suba* and the *szűr* and different versions of the sheepskin *ködmön*. Boots are generally worn as holiday footwear.

The folk costumes of several villages around Szécsény *(Hollókő, Rimóc, Lóc)* show numerous similar characteristics. Colourful ribbons embellish the girls' braids, while the composite headdress and headkerchief of married women covers part of their foreheads. The young girls wear light-coloured beads, the middle-aged women wear blue and green necklaces, but it is considered improper for older women to wear any beads at all. The shirt is usually made of linen, although they also used tulle. On top of that goes the narrowly folded shawl, so that most of the shirt remains visible. The embroidered leather bodice was worn mostly by the more prosperous people. Women liked to use blue-dyed material for skirts, as its dark colour set off the apron, which reached almost all the way around the short skirt, so short that its wearer's calf was visible above the top of the boot. The men of Lóc and Hollókő wore modestly embroidered linen shirts and black vests ornamented with red, green, or black buttons, according to the wearer's age. The black satin apron, which was colourfully embroidered on the bottom, was generally worn.

The folk costume of *Buják* is considered extreme in many respects. The girls' hair, braided into a single braid, is decorated with a ribbon tied only on the end. The married women wear a very peculiar headdress, on top of which they fasten a bouquet made of silver and gold yarn and beads. They wear multiple necklaces. The wide sleeves of the bodice, together with the upright flounce of the shoulder shawl, emphasize the upper body. The most striking elements, however, are the skirts, many of which are worn at the same time, and which are the shortest of all the Hungarian costumes. A ribbon of a contrasting colour is added to the bottom of the skirts, which creates the effect of a frill. Women began wearing shoes in the summer a relatively long time ago, while continuing to wear boots in the winter. White stockings are worn with both shoes and boots.

The costume of *Kazár-Maconka* has a beauty all of its own, and here our attention is drawn first of all to the headdresses of married women (cf. Plate XIII). These are put together from many pieces: the ribbon frills, beads and golden lace arranged artistically, with colourful ribbons hanging down to the bottom of the skirt. On holidays women wear two blouses. One is starched, and on top of it they put a second blouse, made of tulle or cambric and cover it with a shoulder shawl tied across the chest. This is also a many-skirted costume, the top skirt often made of cashmere and joined to the bodice. An apron, sewn out of the same material as the top skirt, covered with embroidery, goes on in front. In the winter women wore a sheepskin *ködmön* embroidered with silk. The bridegroom presented the bride with a broadcloth short coat called *mente*, trimmed with braid and fox fur, and worn with a pair of red boots. This custom, however, survives today only in the memories of the older women. The men's top is of corduroy, specially ornamented with rows of white buttons.

It is also worth noting the costume of *Karancsság*. The headdress of the new bride, lavishly ornamented with white embroidery, roses, and

191. Girls and a young woman
Tard, Borsod-Abaúj-Zemplén County

192. Girls from the village Boldog
Boldog, Pest County

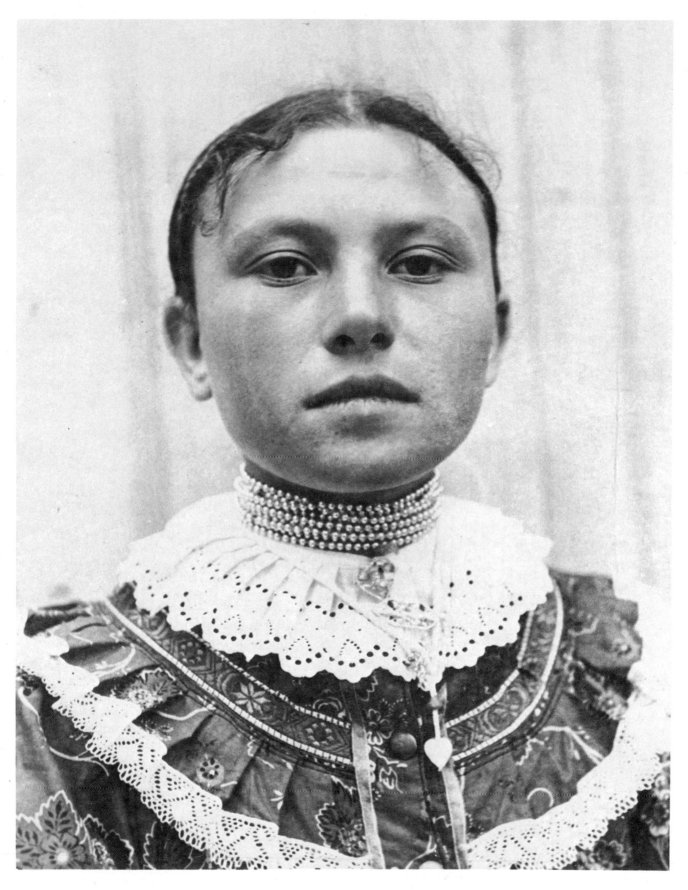

193. Young agrarian labourer in her best
clothes
Tard, Borsod–Abaúj–Zemplén County

ribbons, is quite special. The apron is made out of the same material as the skirts, so that it is no longer conspicuous and it is often left off. A colourful shoulder shawl is generally worn.

The rich folk costume of several villages along the *Galga* (Boldog, Galgamácsa, Tura) has begun to flower in this century. The headdress of the women of Tura, which is held out at the sides by the kerchief tied above it, deserves special mention. The girls of Galgamácsa tie a ribbon in their hair, which is braided into three strands; the headdress of the married women is decorated with gold lace, and the young women put a veil over it. The fine detailed embroidery with small-flower patterns ornamenting both the shirt sleeves and shoulder shawls of Tura are also very interesting. Dark-coloured cotton skirts are pleated into small folds and an apron of blue-dyed material is tied in the front. The girls of Galgamácsa wear a red skirt trimmed with black over 5 or 6 underskirts. This, with a blue apron and colourful shoulder shawl, gives an extremely lively colour effect. The older women edge their dark blue

348

195. Bride and bridegroom
Mezőkövesd

skirt with red. Shoes have been worn in the summer for a long time, but boots also survived until today as winter footwear. Many of the men from the village used to work for the railway, which meant an esteemed social rank, and the men's wear of Tura is based on this uniform. The suit was made of dark blue broadcloth with a red collar-patch, and trousers fitted to low boots or shoes. This suit was also worn by men who had no connection whatsoever with the railway. This example also shows that many divergent sources influence and affect folk costume.

The *Matyó* folk costume flourished in Mezőkövesd and Szentistván (cf. Ill. 37), but many of its attributes had an impact over a larger area, especially towards the north (cf. Ill. 18). The Matyó women's attire is unique, being seemingly Gothic in line. As opposed to the wearers of the other costumes, the silhouette of the women and girls is tall and slender. This effect is achieved by the headdress ending in a peak and by a skirt which is narrow at the waist and widening out only at the ankle, where it stands out in a circle and makes for a rhythmic movement. The bodice and shoulder shawl are worn over a shirt with wide silk sleeves. Various blouses came into use fairly early and turned the shirt into underwear. The material of the skirts was cashmere, silk or satin, or later artificial silk; under the top skirt is a shorter petticoat often made out of one hundred metres of material. The lower part of the long, narrow apron is richly embroidered, which further emphasizes the vertical line of the costume. The *Matyó* women's costumes were so expensive that girls of poor social standing had to work very hard for many years as day labourers and as seasonal workers to earn the price. They did this because the poor people did not want to be outdone by the rich, shown by the proverb: "Let it grumble, so long as it'll sparkle," meaning, they often had to starve in order to buy the extravagant outfit.

The sleeves of the *Matyó* young men's shirts are so loose and long that they cover the entire hand. The collar, shoulder, and front of the shirt are embellished with colourful embroidery. Pantaloons were worn with the shirts. They reached to mid-calf, were extremely loose, and fringed at the bottom. Wearing of broadcloth breeches commenced at the beginning of this century. On Sundays boots were worn with either the pantaloons or with trousers. Young men put a high hat on their head, with a big bouquet and a wide ribbon, the so-called *Barczi kalap*. According to tradition, there was a short lad, the son of a village judge, who made this kind of hat fashionable during the last century in order to make himself taller.

The *Matyó* child was dressed in a way similar to the adults. The first garment, cut very large, was given to the child by its godparents. Little boys' festive shirts were sewn just as loosely and were ornamented in the same way as those of the young men. Little boys also wore a hat with a bouquet on it. Little girls' skirts, like that of the adults, reached to the ankle, widening at the bottom; on holidays they also wore a short-sleeved silk blouse. Their embroidered aprons were fringed with silk, and their skirts were ornamented with lace.

The Great Plain is not as rich as Transdanubia or the Highlands in embroidered, colourful costumes made of various manufactured materials. These costumes are to be found mostly along border areas, among others, along the Danube.

The folk costume of *Kalocsa* and *Szakmár,* relatively new in origin and abundant in colour, is one of the most celebrated. The girls ornament their pinned-up hair with ribbons, pink or light blue in front, and tie it into a bow on the top. Married women cover their heads with embroidered, white linen bonnets. In the last century clothes were still mostly

Great Plain

196. Girls from Kalocsa
Kalocsa

197. Young wife from Kalocsa
Kalocsa

made of simple blue-dyed material. After the turn of the century, women began to embroider the sleeves of their blouses with dark blue and black yarn, they decorated the bodice with white flowers, and later on the embroidered flowers were worked in other colours. During the 1930s they tried even more colourful embroidery and began to use red, green, yellow, blue, and lilac yarn, so that today some articles are covered with large areas of multi-coloured needlework. Several petticoats are worn beneath the many-pleated skirt, which may be blue or

352

green, the front of which is covered by an apron, edged with white lace. Colourful slippers are worn with gay stockings. It is noteworthy that some time ago in Szakmár, just as at some other places in the Hungarian speaking region, brides dressed in dark, or even black clothes.

The folk costumes of the market towns between the Danube and Tisza had a singular position as these towns advanced in their economic development during the last century. This area was part of capitalist development early, and the more prosperous social groups could acquire factory-made products relatively easily. Women led the way in fashion, rejecting folk costume, as opposed to the kind of development which usually occurred in other parts of the Hungarian speaking territory. A note about *Kecskemét,* dating from 1845, may be quoted, as it is most characteristic: "The commoners' ladies appear in church and on the promenade in fashionably tailored frocks, made out of silk or some similar expensive material, holding parasols in their gloved hands, alongside the men wearing pantaloons or blue broadcloth pants and *suba*s."

The attire of the herdsmen of *Bugac* and the Kiskunság region in general preserves many old elements. The hat is high-topped and resembles the peaked fur cap, with only the rim differentiating the one from the other. A black waistcoat is worn with loose white pantaloons and over the loose white shirt. The waistcoat is decorated lavishly with silver buttons. Cattleherds wore a *suba* over that, the most beautiful examples of which can be found in the territory of the Kiskunság. The poorer herdsmen of Kiskunhalas used to wear frieze mantles *(szűr)* instead of sheepskin cloaks *(suba)*. A frieze jacket was called *szűrdolmány* or *kankó,* and although it provided less warmth, it was easier to work in. The *ködmön* (sheepskin jacket) or *dakuködmön* reached to below the waist; it has a 3 or 4-cm-wide red suede overlay sewn on its edges all around, and was embroidered with flowers in colourful yarn. The shepherds' trousers *(rajthuzli)* widened below the knee and with a row of yellow copper buttons on the side the lower part could be unbuttoned. Pointed-toe, high heeled boots were worn with this ensemble.

The costume of the herdsmen of the *Hortobágy* differs from the latter in many features although the clothes of the *Nagykunság* herdsmen were very similar to those of the Kiskunság. A wide-rimmed herdsmen's hat is worn on the Hortobágy to this day, and rubbing it with lard often makes it not only waterproof, but also so heavy that if a disobedient horse or donkey is hit on the nose with it, the animal immediately becomes docile. Bird feathers are pinned to the hat, always on the left side, all the more easy since the region is extremely plentiful in birds. Bustard, heron and egret feathers indicate the herdsman's rank, since a high price had to be paid for the feathers, especially those of the egret. The shirt and *gatya*s of the horseherds are blue. These elements of costume had spread in use in the middle of the last century, because some units among the cavalry in the Hungarian War of Independence in 1848–49 wore dark blue shirts and *gatya*s. Herdsmen usually liked to imitate the clothing of soldiers, especially those who fought for freedom. Horseherds and cattleherds wore boots; swineherds, on the contrary, usually wore laced-up sandals. Among the top wear they

198. Herdsmen from the puszta of Bugac
Bugac

generally wore the frieze mantle or *szűr,* and especially in winter, the sheepskin *suba* and *ködmön* were worn until recently. The shepherds' shirt and *gatya*s were of linen, and later on of cambric. Two white and two greased *gatya*s belonged to each shepherd's stock of clothes. The latter was soaked with ashes and tallow until it became impregnated to guard against rain. These clothes were worn for sheep shearing or any other dirty work. The *rajthuzli* made of leather or broadcloth became popular here in the winter, worn with cambric *gatya*s underneath. The

354

simplest among the garments were those made of skins, the *melles* and the *bőrlajbi* (sheepskin waistcoat), which here was buttoned in front. The sheepskin cloak was called *bunda* and was simple and generally made of six skins; or a *szűr* was used, the type without a stand-up collar.

The costume of the Hortobágy herdsmen influenced almost the entire central and northern section of the region beyond the Tisza. Similarly, *Debrecen* set the example in fashion for many of the towns and villages. Girls pleated their hair into a single braid and tied a wide ribbon on it; they decorated their heads with a beaded *párta,* and wore garnet necklaces. The head of a married woman was covered by a kerchief. The skirt and waistcoat were usually made of dark blue or black material. A short sheepskin cloak called *kis bunda* was worn in the winter, its leather tanned brown and flowers sewn with black silk. A broadcloth mantle with sleeves, similar to the hussar's pelisse or *mente,* was worn in the summer with decorated broadcloth appliqués. Shoes soon came into use as did cordovan holiday boots. The men's high-peaked hat came into fashion during the last century. Men wore a vest, embellished with silver or pewter buttons, over a shirt and *gatya*s made of cotton. In the winter they wore dark blue broadcloth and coat cut in Hungarian fashion, and wore a *suba* or a *szűr* over it. The feet were covered by boots, made of cordovan or other leather, and spurs with a point or a knob were fastened on its heels. This costume in its characteristic form lasted only until the First World War.

The many-skirted folk costume evolved only in a few places of the region beyond the Tisza (Tiszántúl). Among these, *Ajak* of Szabolcs County is one of the most interesting. In the last century women's costume was not as wide skirted, because fewer petticoats were worn and the top skirt was longer than mid-calf. Increasing the number of skirts simultaneously caused their further shortening. A flower-print apron covers the front of the top skirt. Different types of blouses have been made here for a long time, on which collars with a frill are worn for little girls, and collars with two frills for older ones. At the end of the 19th century the girls used to wear boots all winter from All Saints' Day until Palm Sunday. In summertime they wore shoes. Until recently a bride still wore a black shoulder shawl. Men's wear consisted of a shirt and *gatya*s, made of linen; they began to wear trousers only toward the end of the last century. Earlier gray, later black *guba*s were worn. In the summer men wore laced sandals as well as boots treated with oil.

No fanciful, attractive costume developed in the *Bodrogköz,* an area isolated by rivers and marshes from its surroundings. The girls braided their hair with colourful ribbons into three braids, and from the end of the last century, into two. They put on a little blouse *(litya),* made from colourful material, worn with a cambric blouse. Cashmere or silk skirts were put on over five to six starched petticoats which were called *kabát* and a *zsalikendő* (shoulder shawl of cashmere) was tied over their shoulders. Women also wore black boots, the heels studded with yellow copper nails and the fronts decorated with pale, yellowish-coloured braid. Women's short sheepskin jackets *(ködmön)* were richly embroidered. Young men wore loose-sleeved cambric shirts and wide *gatya*. They tied on a buttoned belt, from which colourful fringe and ribbons hung all the way down to their heels. The waistcoat, made of black material, was edged with wide trimming and braid. More prosperous people wore the black *guba*s of Ungvár and Debrecen.

<table>
<tr><td>*Transylvania*</td><td>

The folk costumes of Transylvania kept many antique elements, as western influences arrived there much later if at all. The readily-demonstrable mutual influences of the Rumanians and the Saxons in folk costume also lent special characteristics to Hungarian clothing. Several of the groups in Transylvania have kept their folk costumes even to this day. In what follows, we shall enumerate a few of the best known.

Many features of the folk costume of Hungarians living in the *valley of the Fekete Körös* river point toward the region beyond the Tisza, since at one time they went down the river to the plains to do their harvesting and other work. The two basic articles of the women's clothing, the blouse *(ing)* and the petticoat *(pendely),* were made of linen. The former is ornamented with two or three frills sewn on the end of its short sleeves. The petticoat is very full and the waist section is gathered into folds of palm-sized width. It is tied at the front with a linen ribbon. Girls wear white aprons trimmed with lace; married women wear a black, generously pleated apron. Skirts were worn only since the end of the last century, red for girls, blue for young wives, black for old women, and they are always worn with a bodice or blouse of similar colour. Bodices were embellished with braid trim, and flowers were also embroidered on them. Girls wore red boots, as they did in Kalotaszeg, using laced-up sandals *(bocskor)* only for field work. The shirt of the men was short-waisted and accompanied by a wide *tüsző* or *gyűszű* belt. Young men tied a white neckerchief, and the old men black cravats *(galand)* about their necks. The most widely used outer wear was the sleeveless, fur-collared, embroidered sheepskin vest *(kuzsók),* which they wore for work. The *suba* (sheepskin cloak), *guba* (frieze coat) and *cifra szűr* (embroidered frieze mantle) were all worn, but as these existed alongside each other, they indicated social differences. One characteristic coat-like garment was the *daróc,* sewn of homespun woollen cloth and devoid of ornamentation except for colourful stripes of broadcloth. Old men generally wore a black *daróc,* while the young men wore red. Laced sandals were worn to work, and in the winter they wrapped a woollen foot rag on the feet. In the second half of the 19th century, boots became primarily festive wear.

The folk costumes of *Kolozsvár,* specifically, the suburbs called Hostát and Hidelve, conformed largely with the clothing of the other towns of Transylvania and exercised great influence on its immediate and distant surroundings. As we have seen in the cases of Kecskemét and Debrecen, the women's wear of Kolozsvár began to be urbanized sooner that the men's wear. During the last century, several underskirts were worn beneath the relatively short skirt. The material of the top skirt was cotton in the summer, and, according to the dictates of fashion, some heavier material in the winter. The girls covered their shoulders with a white shawl *(hárászkendő).* Men wore pleated, full *gatya* and collarless, loose, flare-sleeved shirts. Breeches seem to have been an old article of

</td></tr>
</table>

199. Young wife from the district of
Kalotaszeg
Kalotaszeg, former Kolozs County

357

clothing here and were made of gray broadcloth for weekdays, and of blue for holidays. The breeches were trimmed with braid and equipped with a flap. On holidays a blue waistcoat ornamented with copper buttons was worn. Married men wore white *szűr*s and black soft-topped boots with pointed, turned-up toes.

The folk costume of *Kalotaszeg* is one of the most beautiful, both in form and in colour. The girls usually braided their hair, which they had earlier parted in the middle but more recently combed it straight back, and then braided it into one or, less frequently, two braids *(tyika)*. On weekdays they tied a narrow ribbon on the end, on holidays the ribbon was long enough to reach the bottom of the skirt. A beaded *párta* was worn on the head, with a ribbon attached to it (cf. Ill. 41). Married women put kerchiefs on their heads, as their hair was knotted into round buns. The kerchief was tied on the back of the head on weekdays and under the chin on holidays. There were many kinds of blouses for women. The collar, cuffs, and the tops of the sleeves were richly

200. Székely man coming home after field work
Máréfalva, former Udvarhely County

embroidered, sometimes with cross-stitch. The petticoat, made of linen or cambric, was pleated in a similar manner as the skirt, and on holidays, several of these were worn together. The characteristic skirt of Kalotaszeg, the *muszuj* or *bagazia,* was worn on top of these. It was made of black satin, lavishly pleated. They tucked the two corners of the skirt into the waistband, thus showing off the white petticoat underneath (cf. Ill. 199). Since the *muszuj* is only a loose, pleated back apron, the front opening was covered with an apron. In the winter fancy vests made of sheepskin were worn. The tops of the red boots of young women and girls recently were decorated with tulip motifs, embroidered with silk. More recently, black boots and different types of shoes are worn (cf. Szék, Ill. 42). The men used to let their hair grow long until the First World War. Their heads were covered by a hat with an oval-shaped top, or by a black cap. In the summer both men and women wear straw hats. The young men pin a bouquet of pearls *(gyöngyös bokréta)* on their hats, which is so large that it pulls the hat to the side. The loose-sleeved shirt was replaced by the narrow-sleeved, so-called *katonaing* (soldier's shirt) since the beginning of this century. Neckties are rarely worn. Wearing of white, loose *gatya*s and an accompanying small, flower-print apron ceased after World War I. Hose *(harisnya)* made of white cloth or frieze were a usual winter garment in the last century, resembling the Székelys' similar garment in appearance. The frieze mantle or *szűr,* ornamented by appliqué decoration, spread from the middle of the last century, from the direction of the Great Plain. Before its arrival, men used to wear white or brown frieze jackets *(daróc)* decorated with colourful stripes and fringes. They wore laced sandals *(bocskor)* to work, while in the majority of the villages of Kalotaszeg, boots became festive wear.

Much of the basic material of the rich, refined costume of Torockó was provided during the last century by factory production. This costume is essentially a peasant version of the 17th and 18th century costumes of the nobility and city dwellers. Women's blouses are richly smocked, their cuffs have fine ornamentation; the lace edging of the underclothes indicates the splendour and opulence of this costume. The bodice *(mellrevaló),* the cloak *(palást)* and the pelisse *(mente)* are richly ornamented. Red and blue are the favourite colours. Men's costumes are very similar to that of the Székelys in many ways, with sheepskin vests and jackets, tight breeches called *harisnya,* a black broadcloth vest, and a jacket made of frieze *(condra).* During the last century holiday boots were decorated with blue silk tassels.

Székely folk costumes, although similar in their basic elements, still differ in many details. Their common feature is that they themselves produced a significant part of the basic materials for their clothing until recently. The girls braid their two braids from three to four strands of hair, while married women tie a bonnet with frills *(csepesz)* on their hair, more recently a kerchief. Hair is pinned up in a knot. The blouses of women, made of linen, have a frilled collar and narrow cuffs; linen and cambric petticoats are generally worn. In the summer they wear a tight vest over the shirt, decorated with beading or braid and edged with colourful velvet. Their skirts were made of homespun material, with stripes of black, brown, red, and blue. This was later replaced by a cotton skirt *(rokolya).* A woollen or cotton apron of a different colour is always tied in front of it. In the winter they wore a sheepskin vest *(bundamellény)* or a *szokmány* or *kurti* (short coat), made of thick brown or gray homespun frieze. Feet were covered with soft-topped boots, later on with shoes. Beginning with the end of the last century, young men who had served in the army began to wear short hair instead of the usual long hair *(körhaj).* A wide-rimmed felt hat, or in the winter a fur cap, was worn on the head. Formerly men's shirts were without collar and cuffs, but these were replaced by linen shirts with collars and cuffs. Here the *gatya,* made of linen, became underwear at an early stage. The most characteristic garment of the Székely costume is the broadcloth hose *(harisnya)* (cf. Ill. 16), made primarily of white wool, flapped (with the opening on the two sides) and very tight, on which the decoration indicates social standing. The ornamentation of the sleeveless, braided vest, worn over the shirt in the summer, conforms to that of the hose. A sleeveless leather vest was worn during most parts of the year. The body is protected from winter cold by a brown homespun coat *(zeke, szokmány, cedele, bámbán)* or by a long leather coat. During the last century the laced sandal was worn on weekdays, the boots for holiday footwear.

202. Women and girls embroidering Lészped, Moldavia, Rumania

The Csángós, especially from Moldavia, have preserved several noteworthy ancient customs, including some in the area of folk costume (cf. Plates XV, XVI). Older girls rolled their hair on a split wicker ring, 20 to 30 cm in diameter, which brings to mind the 17th century custom of the nobility. The women place a bonnet *(csepesz),* or kerchief *(tulpa)* on their hair, which is fastened in a knot. Their necks are ornamented with several strings of beads. The blouse sleeves are richly embellished. A rectangular skirt goes over the long blouse. This skirt opens in front and its left edge is pinned up, so that the bottom of the long chemise can be seen under it. No apron is used in front of such skirts. Among the Hungarians of Moldavia, many men had their head shaved during Turkish rule, yet during the middle of the last century they usually wore their hair shoulder length. The high-topped felt hat represented an earlier style from Transylvania. Among their noteworthy articles of clothing are breeches made of homespun, the two legs of which were not sewn together, a survival of a 15th century western European custom.

Like the entirety of Hungarian folk culture, Hungarian folk costume amalgamates Eastern and Western influences, yet at the same time the results of its own internal development make it characteristically Hungarian. Because we lack the necessary preparatory work, it is extremely difficult to separate these factors, and it is rendered even more difficult by the development of well-defined areas of folk costumes with respect to colour and form during the last two centuries.

The Eastern origin of certain articles of clothing can be indicated not only by their names but much more by their straight-lined cut. This makes the task of sewing and piecing together easier, but almost completely eliminates waste and helps considerably to save on the basic material, which was difficult to obtain. This ancient method of cutting must have been reinforced by the coming and settling of the Cumanians and Jazygians, and later on by a century and a half of Turkish rule. Garments with this type of cut have survived almost until this day *(suba, guba, szűr,* certain kinds of shirts and *gatya*s, etc.). At the same time the curvilinear cut must have come from the west and became increasingly popular along with the diffusion of manufactured and factory-made materials.

Besides their cut, Hungarian folk costumes are also characterized by their colourful appearance. This is a relatively recent development, since a few centuries ago the natural colours of the materials dominated (white, yellowish, brown). The folk costumes that flourished in the last century were predominantly red, although blue was also much worn while the older people used the darker colours. With the spread of various types of broadcloth, darker colours became predominant in men's wear.

All of the above, together with the typical head and foot wear (boots), comprise the characteristic elements of the Hungarian folk costumes of the past one hundred years, which, though they differ by region, yet have much in common.

Ornamental Folk Art

Hungarian folk art embraces on the one hand traditionally ornamented objects and items of material culture, and on the other, the art of folk poetry, folk music and folk dance. However, this comprehensive use of the word has come to be established only in recent Hungarian ethnographical research. Formerly, Hungarian ethnographers and people at large used the concept of folk art to designate primarily and principally *ornamental folk art,* such as carving, weaving, embroidery, ceramics, etc. However, here and in what follows, we are using folk art as a comprehensive term, one of the important and generally known branches of which is ornamental folk art.

Ornamental folk art in its traditional form does not, in most cases, appear on objects without practical use; rather this type of decoration appears on functionally useful objects. Thus a richly patterned homespun may be made into an apron, embroidery may make articles of clothing more beautiful, a whip handle is embellished by colourful insets and is at the same time a constantly used tool of a herdsman, and more or less decorated pottery is used for drinking, or keeping milk in, or for cooking. From the point of view of its character, ornamental art stands closest to applied art, and during the last decades of development of ornamental folk art has approached the latter, which is the reason why we call the ornamental folk art of the most recent times *népi iparművészet* (popular applied arts).

Ornamental folk art is a historical formation always reflecting economic and social conditions. Its more detailed history is known only from the last two centuries, since few objects have survived from previous ages, and records referring to the existence of such are rare. From the end of the 18th century, and even more so since the beginning of the 19th, the peasantry has tried to make its environment more beautiful with objects increasingly decorated and colourful. After the liberation of the serfs in 1848 it was made possible, at least for one segment of the peasantry, to create a flourishing folk art with the aid of more expensive basic materials. From then until the First World War is the period of unfolding and fulfilling. Museums in Hungary primarily preserve works of art from this period. Between the two wars, ornamental folk art declined, and in certain areas ceased altogether.

The examination of ornamental folk art is a manifold and extremely complicated task. First of all, a certain work of art or group of such must be evaluated from the aesthetic point of view. However, this is by no means sufficient, because the characteristic tastes of its makers and users have to be taken into consideration, and these in many cases differ from the general norm. This norm, too, changed and is changing by periods, and accordingly, the investigation must be done from the historical point of view, each work being examined within the framework of its own period and, furthermore, always within a larger social, geographic,

363

and ethnic unit. We must also take into account internal development and historical influences, because only then can we survey the entire progress of development. Nor can we neglect social considerations, because certain branches of ornamental folk art are connected with social classes and strata, and naturally this connection is expressed in its forms. However, the points of view of ethnology are decisive, because these not only summarize the directions of the above investigation, but also elucidate the methods of creating art and functions to explain the symbolic system of ornamentations.

Ornamental folk art is a collective art, since generally a smaller or larger community uses and inspects its works; however, outstanding individuals have their role in developing and reshaping it. On the basis of patterns and traditions, many people could perform a certain decorating activity in a village. Thus, in the villages of certain regions almost every woman knew how to weave ornamental homespun, while in other places the men were masters of woodcarving. Even among the makers of the most widely spread kind of ornamental folk art outstanding artists were widely known. Thus, for example, in Mezőkövesd a few women excelled in the drawing of embroidery patterns, and they practically established a school around themselves. In every village there were one or two woodcarvers, from whose hands came the most beautiful grave posts and the most ornamented gates. They lived and worked just like everybody else in the village, but allowed the community to use their particular talents as a favour or for payments in kind.

In other cases, a certain decorating skill is attached to an entire social stratum. Thus in various parts of the Hungarian linguistic region the best woodcarvers came from among the herdsmen, who excelled first of all in the decorating of smaller utensils. In other places, entire villages were widely known for certain branches of ornamental folk art. A proverb says about Csíkmadaras of Székelyland:

> This village is Madaras
> Even the priest is fazekas [potter].

Among the pieces included in the concept of ornamental folk art, an outstanding place is due to those made by artisans who primarily worked for the peasantry. Some produced various basic material for clothing (weavers, tanners), while furriers and *szűr* makers not only made garments but also lavishly embroidered fur coats, vests, and *szűrs* mostly with flower designs. Certain centres for these skills played an important role in forming a taste of visual art over a large area. Such a centre was Jászberény, where in certain periods more than 300 furriers worked. The centres of pottery were known far and wide, thus for example, the products of Hódmezővásárhely's potters, whose members periodically exceeded 400, and which sold throughout the entire Southern Great Plain. Millers were regarded as the masters of large-scale woodcarving, since they built and maintained their mills themselves. And a string of such handicrafts existed in Hungarian villages and market towns (*szűr* tailors, comb makers, boot makers, honey-cake makers, etc.) who supplied ornate consumer commodities entirely or largely to peasants.

Such an artist often works for himself only, or else he still maintains a direct contact and acquaintance with his buyer or with the person commissioning his product, who can express his desires and criticize the exhibited objects at the fair, which are in most cases sold by the makers themselves.

The masters of ornamental art have remained anonymous in many cases. Stated so definitely, this observation is valid only when looking at folk art from the point of view of late posterity, and even then it is valid only with certain reservations. The memory of certain women excelling in weaving and embroidering as well as their relation to their products has survived not only in the tradition of their families but in the knowledge of the entire village. Other works of art—because they were made at a place distant from where they were sold—have been designated by the name of a village or town, e.g. water pitcher of Túr *(túri korsó)*, *suba* of Berény, *szűr* of Debrecen, jug of Csát. However, behind these always stand the makers, the masters, whose immediate and more distant surroundings not only know and keep track of them by name, but whose names, in the case of the most outstanding among them, have survived, their descendants talking about them as their masters.

So far we have only spoken of the ornamental objects, yet many objects exist which are artistic in form without any ornamentation at all. Let us refer to different plates and wooden mortars, seed holders, bread baskets, bee hives woven from bulrushes, carts made of wicker, and other wicker objects. Not only are their forms pleasing to the eye, but they are also ancient in origin. However, the majority of folk art includes ornamented objects on which the decoration usually expresses some inner content.

Therefore the outstanding works of ornamental folk art were attached to the great turning points and events of life. At the time of the child's birth the godparents carry an especially fine dinner to the mother tied in a homespun kerchief woven for this occasion. The kerchief given as an engagement pledge is also attached to certain forms and at some places to certain ornamental motifs. The kerchiefs given away to the officiating members of the wedding party have a different kind of embroidery than the ones presented to the priest or to the driver. Specific wine vessels were used for guild meetings of artisans, on which the symbols of the trade were depicted. Certain symbolically ornamented objects belong to burials, such as the tablecloths or the carvings and engravings of grave posts, from which it is possible to tell if it is a man or woman resting in the grave and, not infrequently, the name of his or her occupation as well. These are symbols, equally and similarly understood and appreciated by the smaller and larger community.

The entirety of peasant life was characterized by symbols, whose detailed analysis and introduction could fill a separate book. Therefore here we only want to indicate those territories from where significant results have already been brought to the surface by recent research.

Some objects express in their entirety a meaning seemingly far removed from their specific functions. The plough, for example, is not only the key implement of agriculture but has also been the symbol of agriculture for centuries. This is why from the 16th century on, we find the plough share and the coulter in the crests of a number of Hungarian villages. And where the cultivation of grapes is the basis of economic existence, we find the vine pruning knife occupying a similar position. The bed and the chest that contained the bride's trousseau was the symbol of the entire marriage; they were carried around the village, so that everyone could see their beauty and richness, then placed in a prominent part of the clean room.

An entire symbolic system of colours developed among the Hungarian peasantry. In general, the lighter, livelier colours designated youth, and the darker colours, old age. This can be measured especially in folk costumes, where the brightly coloured clothes of the young girls, then the more subdued coloured garments of the young wives, were replaced with age by brown and finally black. However, the meaning of the colours is not always the same. Thus, while red is generally connected with youth, it may also represent the death of a young person. In certain regions, the graves of those who died a violent death are also marked red. The colour of mourning is generally black, but in some areas even the old women mourn in white. The roots of all these symbolic significances must therefore be examined individually.

Certain motifs of folk art in ornamental art and in folk poetry are often similar in meaning. Let us consider the bird, which occurs so often in both areas. The single bird, "the dove who has lost its mate", is the symbol of the unlucky, unhappy lover. If the bird is holding a letter in its beak, it is a good friend bringing a message. We find pairs of birds on homespun prepared for weddings, since the two young people, just like the two birds, have found each other.

Symbols are important elements of folk culture, and they form and change along with it. That is why they are characteristic of certain periods, regions, social strata and groups, and they need to be evaluated accordingly.

The creative method of ornamental folk art is primarily determined by spontaneity rooted in tradition. Thus the women who do wood-painting, when starting to make a design on a surface, do not make divisions, but connect elements as they go along in such a way that finally the entire surface is covered meanwhile; also intuitively, they follow certain aesthetic rules. Such, among others, is the attempt at symmetry, which is omitted only as a rare exception. It is characteristic of Hungarian ornamental art that it favours bright, clear colours and strong contrasts, shades of red, black and blue. However, at the same time, although only rarely and just recently, yellow, green and purple occur. The colouring emphasizes the organization of the composition. Vigour, strength, vivid imagination, and, even on small objects, massivity characterize Hungarian ornamentation.

Hungarian ornamental folk art has begun to flourish anew during the last decades, and certain branches, extinct for a long time, have been successfully revived. However, this ornamental art still differs from its predecessor in many respects. This difference shows up not so much in the wealth of form, but primarily in content. The artist of today works more and more self-consciously. This consciousness was earlier manifested in the imitation of old forms of ornamentation; however, today this stage has been passed because the wealth of forms known from ethnographical collections has been further developed and completed with symbols of modern life. In addition, technique and basic material have changed to a significant degree, to which must be added the routine that comes from making things in larger quantities. The control or desire of the purchaser is not always asserted only through strong transpositions; various marketing organizations have come into existence intermediating between the buyer and the artist. Experts in ethnology and art do exercise control, but it does not in every case substitute for the direct influence coming from the public.

The function of the objects has also changed drastically. Previously the majority consisted of ornamented consumer commodities which had a function for carrying out work or storing products. Today the primary importance of objects lies in their ornamental character. The objects are made to decorate city apartments while most are almost completely missing from the life of their former makers. There are some experiments in embellishing various modern consumer commodities with traditional or new motifs of ornamental folk art. On this basis we can conclude that the expression, *popular applied art,* which points to the changing role of the arts and crafts in our time, is a correct one.

Works of art uniting the elements of fine art and ornamental art are on the borderline of folk art. Such for example is *glass painting,* which rustically imitates the excellent frescoes and panel paintings of churches, fills them with rustic content, sometimes switching over into profane depiction. A certain peasant artist may try to paint or draw the world around him. This is already *naive art,* even if it bears the marks of certain inner perspectives of ornamental folk art. Thus the painter does not make any sketch, nor makes designs ahead, but begins to work on one corner of the picture and finishes in the opposite corner. This happens because he visualizes what he wants to paint, has no model nor does he look at scenery. He paints, draws, or carves from memory. However, no matter how much these features resemble the creative method of ornamental folk art, the works of naive artists are not a topic of the more restricted circle of ethnological investigation.

Although we know most about the last two centuries of Hungarian ornamental folk art, we can attempt to point out certain historical roots. We can do so on the basis of the strongly conservative nature of ornamental folk art, which preserved specific elements and forms throughout the centuries. Then again, examination of this type is also helped by the phenomenon that certain great historical and artistic periods reached the peasantry in many instances through transposition and only after centuries of delay. This delay and conservatism assures a slight, yet still present chance, for historical examination.

Thus we can mention as a survival from the pre-Conquest period various vessels and boxes made mostly of birch bark. Not so much their ornamentation as their form and the method of joining them together indicate great antiquity. We can classify into the same group one form of the powder horns made of stag horn, the exact equivalents of which

Historical Strata of Ornamental Folk Art

served earlier for salt storage. The same can be said of those salt and grease containers, the etchings of which conjure up certain memories and rites of shamanism, even if they were made at the end of the last century or the beginning of the present by some herdsman of the Great Plain. Archeological finds prove that the ancestors of the Hungarians must have had some articles made of metal and leather, in which they kept the small implements that were used for making fire and for other purposes, utensils with which they carved a drinking vessel similar to today's water-dipper *(csanak)*, and the ornamented bone plates placed on their saddles. In both form and ornamentation, these utensils bear a remarkable resemblance to their 19th century equivalents.

The well developed metal and silver art of the Magyars was increasingly pushed into the background after the Conquest, yet part of the wealth of its motifs often returns in stone carving of Romanesque churches. Since the common people constantly saw these examples, they must certainly have made an effect on their art, especially that of carving. Furthermore, certain motifs from this period can still be found today. The history of the hewn chest *(szökröny)* can be traced all the way back to ancient times, but in Hungary it very likely gained ground during the Gothic period. The most characteristic elements of the notched ornamentation of wood can also be demonstrated from this time. Ornamental homespun may be seen on frescoes and on triptychs from the 13th century on. The starred and saw-toothed homespun patterns occur in this period and are a frequent motif in weaving to this day. The rich ornamentation of medieval fireplace tiles often echoes back to the past century.

Ornamental folk art preserved much from the elements, motifs, and creative methods of the Renaissance. Not only early 15th century influences are especially prominent, but also those of the 16th and 17th centuries, the so-called high Renaissance, which in some places of historical Hungary extended even to the beginning of the 18th century. While the influence can be well measured throughout the Hungarian linguistic territory, it was preserved longest in Transylvania, influencing almost to this day various branches of ornamental folk art. In this art, the rich ornamentation with winding stems *(indás)* and the many coloured varieties of different flowers and fruits played an especially important role. The Renaissance arrived primarily from the direction of Italy, bringing with it the carnation, the pomegranate, the vase and foliage, and the meander or wave-fret pattern called "big-snake" *(nagy kígyó)*. These can be found on folk homespun and embroidery as well as on the pottery and fireplace tiles of the potters or woodcarvings of the herdsmen. Characteristically, these spread and gained ground primarily at the time when the Hungarians and their country, torn into three parts, were languishing under Turkish and Habsburg rule, experiencing some semblance of freedom only in Transylvania. The diffusion of Renaissance influence clearly shows with what relative uniformity peasant culture developed and was formed throughout the entire Hungarian linguistic region, even during these difficult times.

It is worth mentioning several such Renaissance motifs that exist harmoniously on certain creations of folk art almost to this day. Thus at

XXII. Church ceiling. Magyarókereke, former Kolozs County

XXIII. Mirror–case
Transdanubia

XXIV. Mirror–case with floral decoration. Transdanubia

XXV. Mangling
board
Pusztasomorja,
Győr–Sopron
County

XXVI. Mirror-case.
Felsőzsid, Zala County

XXVII. Mirror-case with
sealing-wax inlay
Somogy County

XXIX. Two salt-cellars,
the one on the right, from 1893
Southern Transdanubia

XXX. Water-dipper
Somogy County

XXVIII. Mirror-case. Somogy County

XXXI. Cupboard for mugs,
1831. Homoródalmás, former
Udvarhely County

XXXII. Chest. Fadd, Tolna County

XXXIII. Chest painted with tulips
Hódmezővásárhely

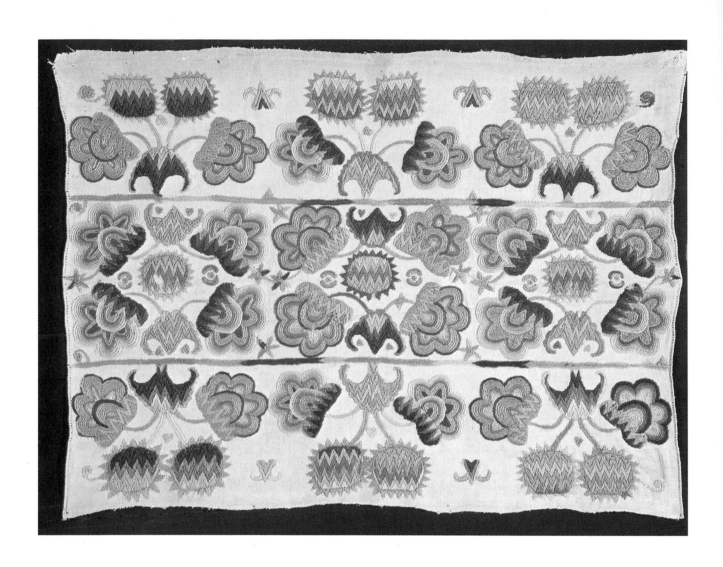

XXXIV. Crewelwork on a pillow–slip. Hódmezővásárhely

some period, the rigidity of the Italian tendril motifs was loosened with charming ease by the creative ability of the Hungarian folk, while at other times, on certain woodcarvings and chairs of the Dunántúl, these motifs were condensed. The vase and foliage motif appears on the most varied materials, but perhaps fit best into the ornamentation of the embroidery of Kalotaszeg, although in such an altered form that we can hardly notice its origin. The people of Transylvania favour patterns made of quadrangles standing on their peaks, but their rigidity loosened in various ways. Renaissance star motifs occur plentifully both on embroideries and homespuns, and these stars are connected in such a way that to the viewer they seem to be practically a mantle of stars. Székely embroideries and homespuns form even the frame structure out of floral elements, of leaves, following the Renaissance method of construction. We could make a lengthy list of the Renaissance elements, forms, and structural techniques that can be recognized without doubt in certain works of folk art, yet in spite of their descent, these designs are still different. The people have transformed them, altered them and made them into their own, according to their own taste and their own working method.

Turkish influence affected folk art about the same time as did the Renaissance. Often it is impossible to separate the two influences from each other, since the Italian Renaissance liked to borrow from Byzantine sources, out of which the Turks also drew, willingly or unwillingly, not to mention the fact that certain contacts existed between Italy and Turkey that made the exchange of cultural goods possible. Thus we can find tendrils, carnations, and pomegranates on Turkish ornamentation also. Turkish merchants travelled not only through the conquered territories, but also got as far as Transylvania and Upper Hungary. Since Turkish goods were much in fashion in the 16th and 17th centuries, their colourful, rich merchandise was always bought and was welcomed. In the occupied areas, Turkish potters, tanners, and furriers bustled about and spread their ornamentations along with their goods. Large numbers of Turkish embroidering women worked in the courts of great Hungarian lords, embroidering rich floral patterns on their especially fine Turkish basic materials. The Hungarian serf women who worked alongside them could easily learn these motifs.

Beginning in the first half of the 17th century, the so-called *Habán*s, Anabaptists some of whom may have originally come from Italy, arrived in Hungary through Moravia, and settled in those parts of Hungary where they could enjoy relative religious freedom, or at least could hope to enjoy it. They were active in different areas of craft and were primarily considered to be excellent potters and iron workers. Although their settlements disappeared in the 18th century, their artistic influence can be seen in certain areas of Hungary to this day.

The next great stylistic periods of ornamental folk art affecting Hungary, the Baroque, the Rococo, and the Neo-Classic, did not in any way leave the same deep and unmistakable mark as did the Renaissance. Although peasant chairs with Baroque-style carved backs occur already in the second half of the 18th century in Transdanubia (cf. Ill. 217), and although this same influence can also be discovered in the painted furniture, in general traces of this influence can rarely be found in embroidery, woven textiles or the woodcarvings of herdsmen. This is all the more interesting since Baroque architecture spread to Hungarian towns and villages during the 18th century, when churches, castles, manor houses were built in the Baroque style. The inside furnishing of churches, the statues in the streets primarily of Wendelin, Florian, St. John of Nepomuk, which have survived to this day, wear upon themselves the unmistakable signs of the Baroque. Scattered elements of Baroque can be found mostly in the folk art of Transdanubia. The elements of the Rococo and Neo-Classicism are also extremely rare, although the latter can be discovered in the folk architecture of the Great Plain.

Hungarian folk art has also been affected by certain characteristics of the ornamental art of the surrounding peoples. From the south, especially along the Danube, strong South Slav influence prevailed in the 18th–19th centuries. This manifested itself in ceramics, embroidery, in the use of certain types of basic materials, and especially in folk jewellery. The Slovaks and the Germans of Upper Hungary excelled at lace making and homespun weavings and carried their goods to the Great Plain and to Transylvania, where people not only bought their ware, but also imitated them. In the 18th and 19th centuries, Moravian shepherds who came with the Merino sheep and settled primarily in Transdanubia, brought with them the technique of ornamenting with sealing wax, which the Hungarian herdsmen quickly learned and they embellished their own carvings with motifs and structural patterns of local origin. The products of certain potters show that through the guilds, some potters may have had contacts with Austria. In Transylvania, the Rumanians, who live together with the Hungarians, are especially adept at woodcarving, which is why the Hungarian and Rumanian carvings often resemble each other. Certain centres of pottery patterned and coloured their vessels differently for the Hungarians and for the Rumanians, and the Saxons of Transylvania. Yet these vessels were so similar that it is often not easy to tell which nationality made or used certain pieces.

However, despite all these influences and regional divisions, Hungarian ornamental folk art still has a certain unity, which can be recognized not only by the expert, but by the maker and user as well. A good example is the common colour-scheme, the use of plain and clear colours: blue, red and black. In most cases, the colours are not even mixed, but used individually. The great colourfulness of Hungarian folk art is relatively recent; it appeared only in the second half of the 19th century, and even then only in certain regions. Earlier, the composition was such that the ornaments were never crowded but were rather emphasized by the open spaces around them. The crowding of ornaments began a century ago (embroidery, woodcarving, painting, etc.) and today has reached to the point where some completely cover the entire surface with ornaments and flowers. Such, together with many others, are the characteristic features differentiating Hungarian folk ornamental art from the art of other peoples.

It is very difficult to review the entirety of Hungarian ornamental folk art. Still, if we venture to do this, we first of all must separate the various branches from each other on the basis of material and technique. And even so we must accept the possibility that repetition will occur because several kinds of materials and techniques may be used in creating particular objects. Some less important areas shall not be discussed, or shall be mentioned only in passing. Thus we will talk about woodcarving, furniture making, about homespun textiles and embroidery, the products of potters, and a few rarer and less known branches of ornamental folk art, such as the working and ornamenting of metal.

Woodcarving

From the point of view of its basic material, carving can be of many different kinds. Wood is the most suitable, but horn and bone are also carved. So far we have become acquainted with two large-scale woodcarvings: the Székely gate and the grave posts and crosses of cemeteries (cf. p. 134). Similar monumental woodcarvings can also be found on houses. Primarily geometric patterns, developed mostly by applying compasses, were carved on the main girder beam, with sarmentose ornamentation and the depiction of living creatures only appearing sporadically. Geometric ornamentation, which can be looked upon as the oldest in time, survived primarily in Transylvania and between the Danube and the Tisza. For example, in Kalotaszeg they decorate the stand of the spinning distaff with such patterns. The most beautiful examples of these were carved by the young man for his intended wife

203. Carving tools. (Owned by Mihály Tóth, a herdsman specialist at carving) Felsősegesd-Lászlómajor, Somogy County

or by the husband for his new wife. If he did not possess the necessary skills the lad would turn to a master whose work he held in great esteem. In Kalotaszeg chiselled or carved geometric ornaments were carved even on hoe cleaners. This oldest style must have at one time been general through the entire Hungarian linguistic region, as is demonstrated by several mangle rollers carved to perfection in this manner which came to the Hungarian museums from western Transdanubia. Geometric ornamental form was popular throughout Europe, and is generally held to be the oldest type of decoration. Characteristically, it survived best in Transylvania, rich in wood, where the Hungarians and Rumanians know and use this ornamentation to this day. Most peasant men make these carved objects themselves, although there were popular masters who could carve especially well. Some *carpenters* and *millers* were famous far and wide for their woodwork.

Especially beautiful are relics left by windmillers of the area between the Danube and the Tisza, who not only erected complicated wooden

204. Mangling board, 1829
Győr-Sopron County

structures of windmills, but ornamented its inside with superb carvings. Worked in relief, these are sarmentous, flowery ornamentations, with decorative inscriptions in which the names of both maker and owner can be found. Another master of wood carving is the honey-cake maker (bábos) who used to make the wooden moulds for honey cake himself. Working with a chisel or a knife, he cut the pattern with a great deal of experience and artistic sense to a depth of 6 to 8 mm. Honey-cake making itself, like the trade of bluedyeing, came to Hungary from the West and so retained in its wealth of forms many Austrian and German

Fig. 173. Three salt-cellars made out of birch-bark, and the design on the surface of the middle piece. Székelyland, former Csík County. Middle of 19th century

206. Incised drinking horn of a herdsman Former Ung County

characteristics. The most beautiful examples are those which portray certain religious scenes, very likely on the basis of old woodcuts. Much livelier are those wooden forms that already show secular objects: a figure of a certain herdsman or outlaw, a heart, a bouquet, a hussar, a dancing pair. The numbers 3 and 8 occur often, especially on the heart shape wooden forms, the symbolic significance of which is the belonging together of a girl and young man.

Tree bark (elm, linden, pine, birch, poplar, etc.) is suitable for making various vessels. Noteworthy among these are the small, cylinder-like salt holders, the most beautiful examples of which have turned up in Transylvania, although we also know of similar ones from Upper Hungary and Transdanubia. The bark was peeled off in ribbons and the ends cut in such a way that by rolling them and sliding one on top of the other the box would be firmly fastened. The bottom and the top are closed with wooden plugs. The sides are ornamented with carved lines and circles, the equivalents of which, along with the technique of fastening, can be found among the various Finno-Ugric peoples. Thus these containers supposedly belong to the oldest layer of ornamental folk art.

From early times, herdsmen were regarded as the best carvers, as they

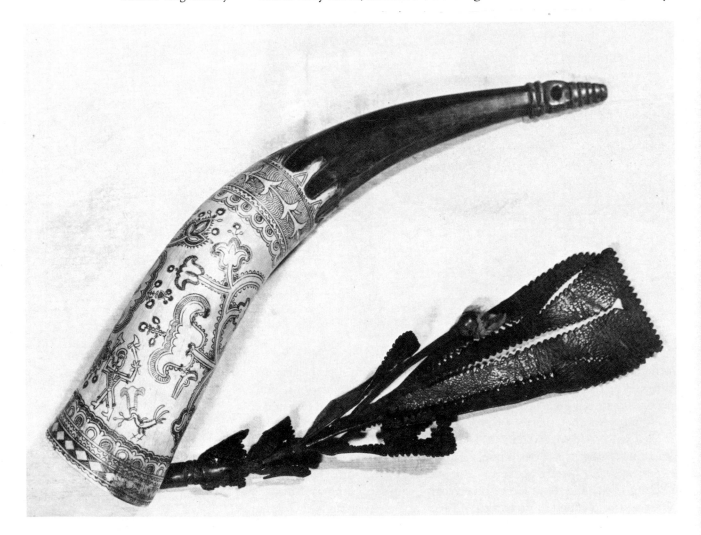

always had more time than the farmhands working on the large estates or the peasants who worked on their own land. When they followed the stock, or when the stock grazed peacefully, the herdsman took a jack-knife and a piece of wood from the bottom of his knapsack, and in a short time turned out some superb work of art. It is true that he had to do this mostly in secret, because the landlord, the bailiff, or the leaders of the village did not look favourably upon artistic herdsmen; these authorities regarded them as unreliable and were apt to send them packing. Fortunately, even the overseer got to the faraway pastures and endless meadows only rarely, so the herdsmen could keep on carving in peace. This is why herdsmen's art still existed in the first decades of our century, even when the peasants of the villages and the farmhands had already ceased to ornament their objects for quite a while.

The most characteristic basic materials of the carving herdsmen are wood and bone (horn). Most of the objects used by the herdsmen are made of wood: the richly decorated cudgel, the whip handle, the shepherd's crook, the axe handle, the wooden spoon to stir mush with, the jack-knife handle, the mirror holder, the drinking vessel, the razor case, the match box, the flute, and the pipe stem. The herdsman also carved smaller utensils for housekeeping out of wood, such as the beetle,

207. Detail of a mangling board
Hungary

mangle, wall salt holder, and children's toys. The horn, drinking gourd and holder for the scythe sharpener whetstone is made from horn left in its natural shape without changing it. It was necessary to saw the horn apart in order to shape smaller objects such as salt holder, mange-grease holder, and match holder.

When we consider the method of ornamentation, we find that geometric designs prevailed in Transylvania, while in Transdanubia, Upper Hungary and the Tiszántúl three clearly distinguishable styles of carving developed.

The earliest herdsmen's carvings of *Transdanubia* are known from the end of the 18th century. Pieces surviving from this period have been ornamented by chiselling and are geometric in character. Such objects, on which the engraved part was smeared with soot, gunpowder, and tallow mixed with oil to emphasize the incised lines of ornamentations appeared only at the beginning of the 19th century. The sealing wax process first occurred in the first quarter of the last century. The chiselled-out pattern was widened into inward-slanting grooves with the tip of a red-hot knife, and filled with black, green, blue, and red sealing wax; then the rough surface was smoothed out with a scouring rush or a piece of glass and brushed with beeswax (cf. Plates XXIII–XXVIII). Relief carving, which tried to fill as much as possible of the given surface, replaced the sealing wax and other techniques since the end of the last century, after which time it became the most widely spread carving technique in the western half of the linguistic territory.

The herdsmen's carvings of Transdanubia reflect their environment faithfully, and the entire world of their makers: colourful flowers, trees, bushes, and representatives of the animal world—sheep, pigs, foxes, rabbits, owls, and doves. We can see the shepherd walking behind his flock, the horseherd curbing his horse, the swineherd flashing his axe, the cattleherd parading in his embroidered fancy *szűr* coat, the tavern keeper and his wife, and the gypsies playing a song.

The favourite figure on Transdanubia wood carvings is the outlaw, the *betyár*. The outlaws of the 19th century came from among the

208. Water–dipper
Monostorapáti, Zala County

376

peasants whose land was taken from them, deserting soldiers, serfs, and peasants who could no longer bear the high-handedness of their land-lords. They did not harm the poor populace; instead they often helped them:

> *I blocked the roads,*
> *And plundered the lords.*
> *When I could take no more*
> *I gave all to the poor.*

—says the ballad about Andris Juhász of Somogy County. Many outlaws fought in the 1848–49 War of Independence against the oppressors, it is therefore natural that their popular figures frequently appear not only in folk poetry, but also among the scenes of herdsmen's carvings.

Originally the ornamentations on horns in Transdanubia were engraved and then coloured with nitric acid (cf. Plate XXIX). The ornamentation of the gourd reached a high artistic level and is related to similar work in the neighbouring Croat areas. A calabash suitable for use as a watering gourd must be carefully tended, run up on a trestle, shaped in a lath frame or glass jar, and decorated only after it is ripe. Its engraved ornamentations resemble those of wooden mirror-cases and of the horn salt holders. The herdsman tied the gourd filled with water on his belt and carried it with him into the fields (cf. Plate XXX).

Among the herdsmen of *Upper Hungary* the shepherds were especially great masters of wood carving. The most characteristic of their work is the drinking cup *(csanak),* which is tied on the knapsack of the herdsman, the hunter who walks the forest, and the peasant who tills his fields, in order to have it always on hand. The handles of Palots drinking cups are the most ornate, and often carved in the shape of a snake, dog, or sheep. The decoration shows a close relationship to work of the herdsmen-artists of the nearby Slovakian areas. The drinking cups are decorated on their sides with trees, flowers, and preferably with scenes taken from hunting, husbandry, or agriculture. Cudgels and axe handles are inlaid with lead, tin and pewter. Melted metal is poured into the carved-out, lace-like grooves of the wood, and when the metal cools, the geometric ornamentations are chiselled on the surface.

At one time it was impossible to find decent wood on the barren steppes of the *Great Plain* even after a day's walking, and yet excellent remains of wood carving have survived from this area also. The herdsman generally pilfered the plum trees of the vineyards and orchards which lay outside the villages in orde to get good material for the whip handle he was making. The most widespread method of wood decoration in the Great Plain is inlay with horn, brass, and recently with plastics. They sink the carefully cut-out figures into the wood and fasten them with tiny brass nails. By this method the herdsman of the Tiszántúl, the region east of the Tisza, decorates the handle of his whip, hatchet, and axe, his cudgel, and, more rarely, certain razor cases as well. Among the ornaments we often find entire compositions depicting scenes of the herdsman's life. At other times the objects of the herdsman's life are scattered seemingly without any particular connection:

Fig. 174. Intarsia design on a herdsman's staff. Hortobágy, former Hajdú County. 1920s

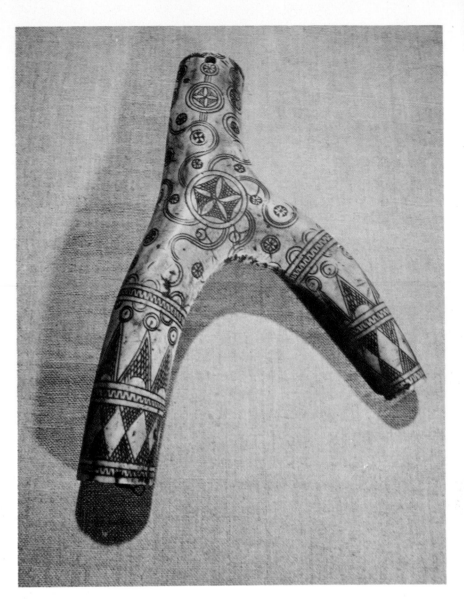

Fig. 175. Incised design on a drinking horn. Former Zemplén County. Second half of 19th century

axe, knife, fork, kettle, moon, sun, stars, gun, and pistol (referring to one-time outlaws), etc. On almost every piece the name or initials of its maker and owner are inscribed along with the year it was made.

Horn and bone carving has a great history in the Tiszántúl. The herdsman carves the ornamentation with the tip of his jack-knife and often tints the more important and outstanding sections yellow with nitric acid. Part of the ornamentation of the Tiszántúl herdsman's work is geometric, and often, though less frequently, sarmentous plants, herdsman's objects or scenes and depictions of outlaws occur on them. In the northern part of the Tiszántúl the huge horns of the grey Hungarian cattle are lavishly decorated with floral and geometric designs. A distinct feature of these outstanding works of art is a central circular design with tendrils and flowers branching out of it. Equivalents may be found among the Slovaks and Ruthenians.

The use and decoration of bone must be discussed separately, because these derive to our days from great antiquity. Geometrically patterned

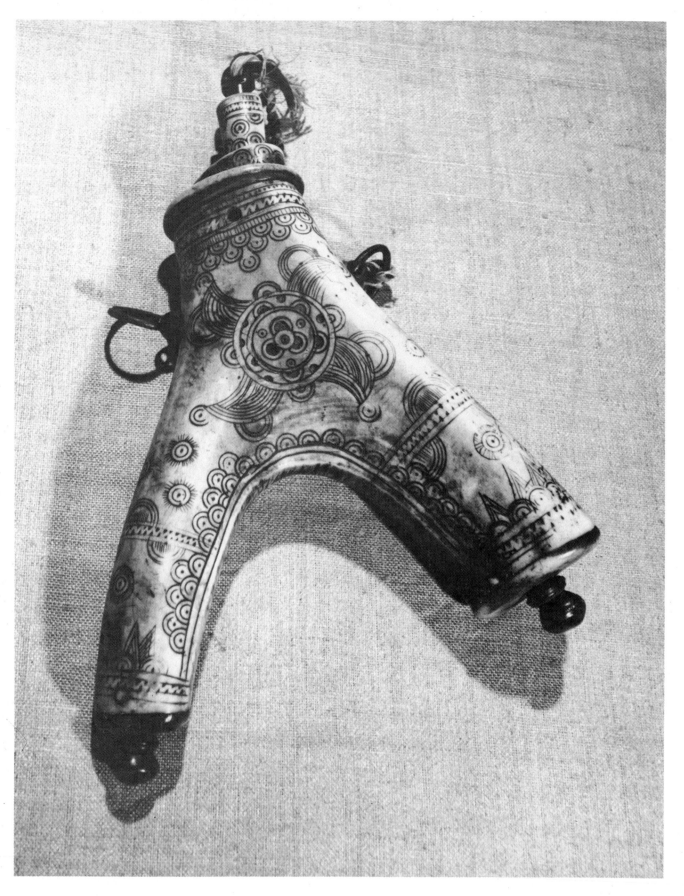

210. Powder-flask
Veszprém County

Fig. 176. Antropomorphic patterns on gunpowder flasks made from staghorn. Transylvania, 17th–18th century

bone dice, and different sized beads, made of sheep or dog bone, are strung on thongs by herdsmen. The geometric engraving is blackened with soot and tallow, and even if this was not done, time sooner or later would make the pattern show up. Such bead-like ornaments have been found in graves dating from the time of the Conquest, so that we can justifiably consider this type of ornamental folk art as being of the greatest antiquity.

Most of the powder horns *(porszaru)* that have been found in the eastern half of the linguistic region imply even greater antiquity. Hunters from the 16th and 17th centuries on kept their gunpowder, which was very sensitive to moisture, in these. They were made of the two-branched horn of the stag and outfitted on the top or bottom with a removable plug, carved out of bone. Two hangers on the side indicate that the hunter wore his powder horn hanging on his waist, as does the worn condition of usually the unadorned side. We do not exactly know what may have been kept in these horns before the discovery of gunpowder, but very likely it was salt, which is also sensitive to moisture.

Similar implements, decorated with small central circles, have also turned up, mostly from Avar graves of the Migration Period. The circular pattern can be found on 17th and 18th century samples also. Furthermore, whole lines of designs, indicating even greater antiquity, can be discovered on these horns. Thus the *swastika* (rotating rose), the various forms of which are traceable to antiquity, is often placed in the centre. Especially interesting are triangular human portrayals running along at the bottom of the two branches of the horn, which, as far as the composition is concerned, is the exact equivalent of the Halstatt type of human portrayal (early Iron Age, 10th to 5th centuries B.C.). It is interesting to note that the herdsmen of southern Transdanubia carved similar figures on their wood-framed mirrors at the end of the nineteenth century. Such motifs occur on hewn chests even in our century. All this is clear evidence that the survival of certain methods of portrayal is possible not only through a few centuries, but through thousands of years. The sarmentous pattern of certain examples resembles the metal purse-plates which date from the time of the Conquest. We often find simple animal portrayals, mostly stags, alongside of which they also engraved a flag. This indicates the magic with which they tried to assure the success of the hunt.

The comb maker *(fésűs)* is the professional master of horn processing. However, combs of great antiquity are not known, since the comb-making masters, who were organized into guilds, primarily travelled as journeymen in western countries and brought a significant part of their patterns from there. However, though they learned about their craft mostly in the West, they also got acquainted with the wealth of forms of the herdsman's art and *szűr* making, introducing such patterns to western countries. The fanciest combs were worn in the hair of married women, and though men did wear a curved comb, no ornamented piece has appeared so far. The comb-making master drew the pattern on paper and copied it from there onto horn, then cut out the filigreed, diaphanous ornaments with various tools, primarily with a saw. Certain

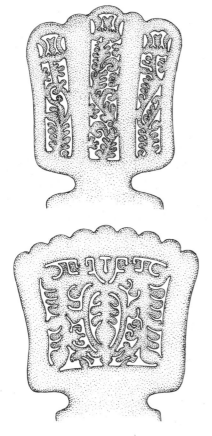

Fig. 177. Open-work top part of bone combs to hold a bun of hair. Eastern region of the Tisza. Second half of 19th century

masters possessed a collection of patterns in excess of one hundred, and they continually tried to complete and increase their designs in accord to changing fashion.

Furniture Making

In connection with the furnishing of the house we have already spoken above of the most characteristic types of furniture (cf. pp. 157-63), but we have not touched upon their forms and ornamentation.

The peasant who was able to carve could make the most simple furniture himself, but we know of cabinet makers' guilds from the Middle Ages, although these did not primarily work for peasants. The cabinet makers who lived in the market towns of the 17th and 18th centuries worked mostly for the nearby peasantry. However, they always maintained a lively contact with the masters who worked for the lords, and were often even apprenticed under them. In the course of their wanderings they not only became acquainted with new furniture forms, but also increased their store of ornamentation.

The oldest type of Hungarian peasant furniture was carved and made with a hewn technique. These are distinguishable from painted furniture, the earliest, undoubtedly peasant-used pieces of which are known from the 18th century.

We know of two large centres for making hewn chests *(ácsolt láda)*. One form developed in the south-eastern corner of Transdanubia. On each corner of its square top a kind of horn emerges (cf. Ill. 214). Its

211. Hewn chest *(szökröny)* Baranya County

212. Hewn chest (side view)
Baranya County

213. Hewn chest, 1889
Nógrád County

ornaments were mostly made with compasses or were linear. These were coloured black; other colours occur sporadically, although mostly on the rather new pieces. The other centre is the north-eastern part of Palócföld, the former Gömör County. Here the lid built on wooden corners is steeply pitched and the four horns are absent. Its ornamentation is always geometrical. Sometimes those triangular human portrayals may be seen that we observed above appearing on staghorns or on herdsmen's carvings. The works made by the people of Gömör can also be found in various parts of the Great Plain, carried by wandering merchants in a dismantled state. These chests were also hewn in the Székelyland. This is the piece of Hungarian furniture that has the longest history; we can follow its relations all the way to the times before Christ.

The carved pieces of furniture of the Palotses do not in any way appear to be so old, and their first makers were very likely herdsmen of the second half of the 19th century. The frame of the chair and bench was made of softwood and the carved, open-work panels, portraying various scenes, were fitted into it. Some show stags grazing in the forest, others show entire hunting scenes. There is the shepherd, herding his sheep and playing his bagpipe, the hussar and the *honvéd* (the soldiers of the 1848–49 War of Independence). In some cases subsequent panels tell an entire story in a surging, peasant-epic manner. Sometimes, although less frequently, cribs, the sides of tables, and plate holders were also decorated in this manner.

In Transdanubia, especially in the Bakony, furniture was carved out

Fig. 178. Hewn chest, called *szuszék*. Székelyvarság, former Udvarhely County. 1930s

214. Hewn chest
Hungary

215. Detail of the back of a bench
Nógrád County

216. Back of a bench
Nógrád County

384

217. Carved back of a chair
Veszprém County

218. Stool, 1838
Tiszafüred, Szolnok County

219. Armchair
Zádor, Baranya County

220. Church ceiling with painted panels
Magyarvalkó, former Kolozs County

221. Carved and painted chest
Komárom

of hardwood and decorated with simple intarsia. This was more frequent in the villages inhabited by the lesser nobility, in order to emphasize their belonging to the upper class.

The furniture of Kalotaszeg, which differs from that of the surrounding territories, has chiselled ornamentation, geometric in character, but a looser design which lends it a particular style.

The ornamental patterns of painted furniture are often rooted in the art of the Renaissance. Thus the choir, pulpit and ceiling paintings of the Calvinist churches (mostly of the 18th century, though a few earlier) had an unquestionable effect on the art of the peasant cabinet makers (cf. Plate XXII, Ill. 41). These occur throughout the entire Hungarian linguistic region, although the most beautiful works of art of the high Renaissance can be found in Transylvania. Tendrils and flowers fill certain panels, and although the motifs are repeated, every one of them is an independent work of art. Their connection with peasant furniture is made even more obvious by the fact that the wandering church painters happily took upon themselves the decorating of chests also, which then could provide immediate examples for the local cabinet makers.

A number of painted furniture centres developed in the Hungarian linguistic region. Several of the more important ones among these are worth mentioning (cf. Plate XXXII). We emphasize *Komárom* among the ones in Transdanubia, where the front of the chests were carved and smaller flowers and bouquets appeared along the central motif, painted with pale and subdued colours. Through the mediation of sailing the Danube, the chests travelled far south, in many cases even to the Balkans. The masters of Komárom themselves, as famous painters, embellished the ceilings and benches of churches not only in Transdanubia but in the Great Plain as well.

Hódmezővásárhely is the most important and most influential among

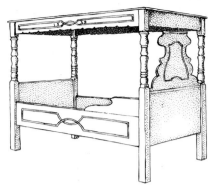

Fig. 179. Four-poster bed. Gyirmót, former Győr County. Second half of 19th century

222. Table. Mid-19th century Nógrád County

387

the furniture making centres of the Great Plain. The wealth of its motifs derives in most cases from the rich ornamentations in late Renaissance style of the local Calvinist church. The basic colour of the furniture is dark, in most cases dark blue, on which primarily red flowers dominate, at some places with paler yellow borders, while the green leaves blend into the dark background almost completely (cf. Plate XXXIII). The colouring of the neighbouring furniture from *Békés County* is livelier, and the open-work ornamentation of the chairs and benches differs from that of Hódmezővásárhely. The rich carvings and the open-work are always floral in character, and in many cases show Baroque influence.

In Upper Hungary the furniture painting of *Miskolc* and *Eger* was relatively similar. The most colourful pieces were made during the second half of the last century. On the brown, or more frequently red, ground colour were painted red and green and yellow or white and blue bouquets of flowers or wreaths. We often find ears of wheat among the flowers, which are the primary peculiarity of this centre. The basic colour of the furniture of *Sátoraljaújhely,* which lies in the north-eastern part of Upper Hungary, is black, on which is placed the central motif of a green, yellow, and red-blue bouquet in a vase or box. A garland is substituted for this on other pieces. Painted furniture was still produced here between the two world wars.

The rich ornamental wealth of *Torockó* stands out even among the numerous cabinet making centres of Transylvania. The basic colour of its products is mostly dark, primarily green, and less frequently blue or

223. Painted chest
Borsod-Abaúj-Zemplén County

brown. The flower patterns reflect Baroque and Rococo influence and always adjust to the background with blue-white-brown-red-orange colours. The composition is fairly severe, and the endeavour is to fill up the entire surface evenly.

One of the oldest among the numerous centres of painted furniture is *Vargyas*. The history of one of the cabinet-making families can be traced back to the late 16th century. In the 19th century they painted rich red-blue-yellow bouquets in pitchers, resembling Renaissance style, but wreaths, garlands and birds are also frequently portrayed. Here too, just as at other places, the date of production was written in the centre of the decoration (cf. Plate XXXI). The cabinet makers of Vargyas are still painting chests and other pieces of furniture today.

Homespuns

As we have already become acquainted with the production of plain homespun textiles (cf. pp. 302-9), we shall speak here only of the ornamented ones, which are also made of hemp, flax and cotton. The finest material is used for these, since ornamented homespun is the woman's "badge", and a number of its pieces are made for specific occasions.

Thus in the Bodrogköz, not long ago, a differently shaped and patterned homespun was attached to every significant event of human life, and in this way, accompanied man from the cradle to the grave. The marriageable girl and her mother prepared, well ahead of time, the various richly flowered homespun kerchiefs for the bridesmen, the best men, the priest, the drivers, and even for the gypsy band, in such a way as to show the maker's skill on each piece, say by using a different pattern. They handed out over a hundred kerchiefs at certain large weddings. The young wife had already started to prepare godparent kerchiefs before the wedding to take food in when she should invite one of her neighbours to stand as godparent. Textiles woven with red were put into the crib of a child, to ward off the evil eye. A flag-like homespun, hung out on the church tower, gave notice of a child's death. A table cover woven with black was put on the table the priest preaches from at burials. A richly decorated homespun shroud was spread on those who died young.

The basic colours of Hungarian homespuns are red and blue. Only rarely and more recently has some other colour been added to these. The technique of weaving makes right-angled ornamentations possible, but it makes continuous patterns very difficult to construct. Therefore, patterns are set up in slanting angles also, and with these expression becomes easier. In spite of this, weavers have recently generally aspired to portraying naturalistic roses, dolls, beets, etc., in such a way that they can be recognized by anyone. The closer they come to this goal, the higher the accomplishment is valued.

Simple, plain peasant weaving is, relatively speaking, not very difficult, but decorative weaving is all the more so, since the material has to be picked up. Even medieval sources mention the *szedett vászon* ("picked-up" linen), because of its greater value. The loom is warped as for plain linen, but before they begin weaving they pick up the warp on planks according to the pattern. This has to be done again each time for as many parts as there are to the stripe or pattern. The weaver's child also helps in this. Her task is only to make the rod behind the heddles stand up and lie down, according to the way her mother wants it.

The art of *rojtkötés* (macramé, fringe tying), which approaches lace in effect, is also connected to homespun textiles and to embroideries in certain areas, such as Bodrogköz, Sárköz, and among the Palotses and Matyós. The edges of tableclothes, aprons, towels, and godparent kerchiefs are decorated with hand-knotted fringes that are geometric in design and often four inches wide. Macramé frequently takes as much time as it does to weave the ornamented homespun itself.

The weaving masters *(takács),* organized in guilds, already worked in Hungary in the 14th and 15th centuries and jealously guarded the secrets and standards of their trade. The journeymen and apprentices could become masters only if they learned every technique of weaving and proved it by a superb piece of work, the masterpiece. But first they had to go for a long journey to foreign countries, to become acquainted with

224. Detail of a handwoven pillow-cover
Sárköz

all the tricks of weaving. Thus they brought back many new patterns with them, which they recorded in pattern-books and passed on within the family. These patterns made their way to the peasant women also, especially when they had the weavers weave their yarn into linen for them (cf. also p. 309).

In certain areas women were excellent masters of ornamental patterned weaving. The women of *Sárköz* were especially adept, and people from other villages turned to them eagerly for patterns or even for finished homespuns. Before the turn of the century they used mostly flax and hemp yarn that they had made themselves. From then on cotton, which had already been used earlier for the weaving of patterns, gained ground increasingly. At first only red was used, to which later came a few supplementary colours. Wider and narrower stripes follow each other on the design, the plain weaving in between emphasizing the pattern well. The stripes themselves do not end rigidly but playfully merge into the white background, their edges loosened up by some patterned detail. Stars, flowers, little birds, surrounded by geometric designs, often figure among the patterns. The ornamental homespuns were used mostly on the bed, made up into pillows, and on towels and kerchiefs. The tablecloths are the most ornamental, being entirely covered by designs. The weaving of Sárköz began to decline between the two world wars, but in 1952 a weavers' co-operative was formed in Decs, and its members, have created a new style.

In the southern part of Transdanubia, *Somogy* and *Baranya* were equally rich in homespuns. Several nationalities live together in the latter area. The patterns used by the South Slavs on woollen homespun differ from the homespuns of the Hungarians which are made of flax and hemp and decorated with red and black. They make tablecloths, aprons, and towels out of these. From the beginning of this century the older geometric designs—flowers, leaves, stars—were transformed into naturalistic ones. Patterns were arranged in stripes, the free area left plain, almost white in colour, which emphasized the richness of the homespun even more.

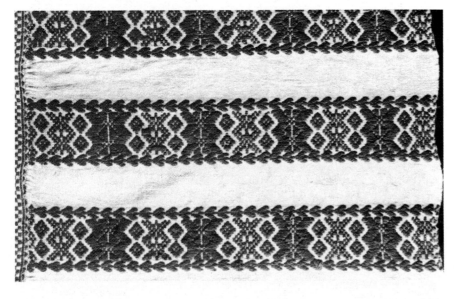

225. Detail of a handwoven tablecloth Somogy County

391

Weaving is very much alive to this day among the *Palots,* the largest and most widely spread ethnic group. Their work is the same in regard to material as the previous ones and differ perhaps only in that in some places woollen yarn was also used. Blue, green and pink colours have also spread alongside red. Such stripes, as they alternate, have a very special colour effect. They are placed at a relatively greater distance from each other, so that these forms make up a homespun different in character from the previous ones. Pillows and different kinds of kerchiefs are made from the woven material, primarily aprons from the ones with a geometric design. The co-operative that works in Szécsény and Heves further developed the old patterns and makes this Hungarian homespun, which is one of the most beautiful, famous far and wide.

The homespun of *Bodrogköz* is looser in construction than the ones mentioned above. In order to demonstrate the richness of the patterns, it is worth mentioning the following among the many designs: birch tree, cherry, pine tree, shamrock, rose, flower, beet, frog, June bug, rake,

226. Detail of a handwoven tablecloth
Baranya County

candle, small pipe, chain, clock, fritter, doll, star, buckle, etc., all well carried out by the weaving women. The way these are juxtaposed is so typical of certain weaving women that for decades afterwards the maker can be recognized from it.

The designs of the *Szabolcs* and *Szatmár* homespuns are also red, the white background appearing among them only rarely. They weave the pattern so close that certain ornamental elements are harder to differentiate. Thus the composition becomes more unified. They usually piece together two widths in the centre to make a square tablecloth out of it.

Weaving is alive to this day among the Hungarians of Transylvania, but here the importance of wool, along with flax and hemp, is especially great. The *Székelys of Kászon* still weave linen out of pure hemp, cotton, or a mixture of the two, into which they put striped patterns with motifs of a plate, star, rose, flower, bird, oakleaf, cockscomb. In the last century, the design was still made exclusively in red. Blue also appeared at the end of the last century, the two colours were not mixed until the 20th century. The motifs varied on pieces made for daily use: pillowcases, featherbeds, handcloths, and children's sheets. Occasional and

227. Homespun basket–cover for the godmother's present of food
Baranya County

393

special pieces were woven in a particularly ornate fashion. Such are the best man's kerchief, the baptismal sheet, the cloths to hang on a rod in a room, the ornamental pillow cover, the wedding tablecloths, etc. Their designs in many cases resemble that of medieval cloths called *bakacsin*.

According to our present knowledge, the majority of the Magyars of historical times did not weave rugs; we find these only in Transylvania. The warp of the *Székely rug,* or a kind of rug called *festékes* (dyed), is hemp, while its weft is home-dyed wool. This stands very close to those Eastern European rugs which, among others, are used practically to this day by the Russians, Ukrainians, and Rumanians, although the connection can be traced even further. These all are similar in that the majority of their designs are geometric, as a result of their weaving technique. Székely rugs spread throughout Transylvania in the 17th and 18th centuries, and we often find them mentioned in the inventories and last wills of this era. The dyed rug, however, differs from its neighbours in colour and arrangement. It is made with relatively few colours, and with pleasing geometric designs. Reserved modesty generally charac-

228. Knapsack worn on a pilgrimage
Nógrád County

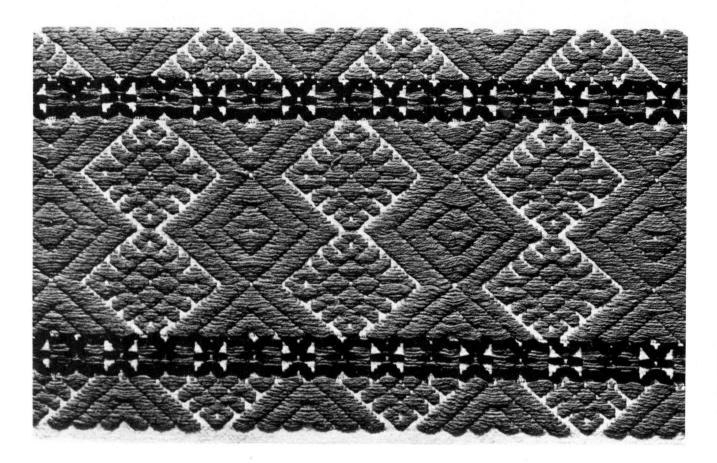

terizes it, perhaps precisely because it belongs to the earliest layers of folk art.

In *Kászon,* a region of Székelyland, they are still weaving the dyed rug, partly for their own use, partly to sell to their neighbours in Háromszék, where it is no longer made. The oldest known samples originate from the middle of the last century, and these are characterized by muted colours. They got the dye for the tobacco yellow (greenish ochre) and Indian red basic colours from plants and flowers grown on the mountainsides. They mixed this with raw-wool and blue-coloured yarn. More recently flaming red and green are often used as well as a combination of red and black, although naturally these are not coloured with plant dyes. Geometric patterns are composed into units of various sizes, such as the large rose that fills the entire centre of a rug, or four small roses, the centre motif of which is framed by ornate lines. Such rugs were originally used for covering the bed in such a way that they reached to the ground. More recently they are also used on tables, or to decorate the wall.

229. Handwoven pillow-cover
Székely of Bukovina, Transdanubia

Embroideries

Embroidery is one of the richest, most diverse branches of Hungarian ornamental folk art, and is extremely varied within a relatively small area. We can divide embroideries into two groups. One of these stands very close to woven textiles and is made by sewing the pattern into the plain homespun by counting threads. That is precisely why the elements

Fig. 180. Simple cross-stitch. General

of such cross and oblique cross-stitch embroidery *(keresztszemes, szálán-varrott hímzés)* are geometric, so that the insufficiently practised eye can easily confuse this form of embroidery with weavings. In contradiction to this, the freely drawn embroidery *(szabadrajzú hímzés)* is only slightly restricted by the basic material, so that it provides greater opportunity for variation of both the traditional and spontaneous elements.

Even little girls attempt to embroider, although the really good embroiderer is the one who is able to expertly vary and create new forms using the old wealth of motifs. Such women often become specialists who sometimes make the entire trousseau of marriageable girls in return for smaller or larger recompensation. The importance of the drawing women *(íróasszonyok),* who draw the most beautiful designs on the basic material that are brought to them, is especially great in the case of freely-drawn embroideries, so that women possessing less talent and practice can venture to embroider their designs.

Both ceremonial and plain pieces for everyday use were embroidered. That is why needlework has a great role, primarily on the visible parts of various folk costumes. The same can be said of pillow ends *(párnavég),* which are placed on the end of the pillow facing outwards on the bed,

230. Embroidery on communion-table
cover, 1755
Szirma, Borsod-Abaúj-Zemplén County

Fig. 181. Oblong cross-stitch, front and
back

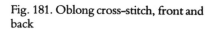

their ornament outwards, as well as of the various kerchiefs, covers,
tablecloths, and towels, so that the embroidered flowers may please not
only the family but visitors as well. However, no matter how ornate
these objects are, they all have some kind of a definite function.

Handwoven homespun or purchased linen of a later period provided
the basic material for embroidery, while the yarn for needlework was
either dyed at home with plant dyes or, in some areas, bought from
merchants. Among the various stitches the previously-mentioned cross
stitch, in which two or more stitches are placed cross-wise to create
a handwoven effect, is related to the geometric designs. One of its
versions is the oblique chain stitch embroidery, which makes the
embroidering of certain freer patterns possible. In this case two tiny
squares are sewn with three stitches instead of four. Several versions of
the satin stitch *(laposöltés)* are known over the Hungarian linguistic
region, depending on whether the threads line up partially or completely
next to each other. This is the most widely spread technique of
Hungarian embroidery. The common character of loop and chain stitch
(hurok- and *láncöltés)* is that a loop is formed on the face of the material.
The various methods of fastening this down assure the different characters of the embroideries.

Fig. 182. Simple satin stitch

Various principles prevail in Hungarian embroideries, not only in
technique, but in the composition of the stitches as well. However, the
most general and most classic is the three-part division. According to
this, the main motif, stretched in a longitudinal direction, is placed in the
centre of the surface to be ornamented. This motif is closed off at the top
and at the bottom by a border, the so-called *mesterke,* narrower than the
former, and mostly open towards the linen. This *mesterke* contains the
oldest design elements, which were slowly pushed out to the edges.

In some cases, embroidery was done by the men as well; these were
always artisans who, besides tailoring and sewing certain outer garments, also decorated them.

The material of the ornamental mantle *(cifraszűr)* is white or whitish
rough broadcloth, which was embroidered with black and red wool or
silk yarn, in some places with blue or even yellow. The designs, the
most frequent basic element of which are the rose, carnation, tulip, and
lily-of-the-valley, and the leaves that surround them, got onto the *szűr*
during the last two hundred years. The work of ornamentation is called
"flowering" *(virágozás)* by the mantle makers, and the flower bouquet
growing out of baskets and pots gave the inducement to its composition. Immoderate ornamentation became preponderant on mantl‹

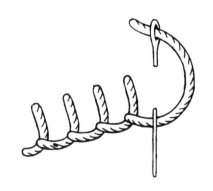

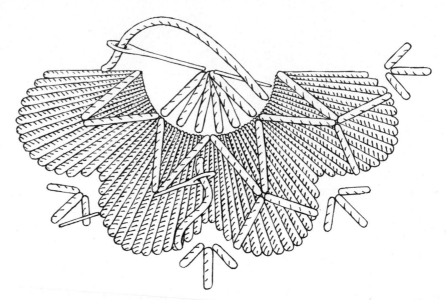

Fig. 184. Embroidered flower on a *szűr*
mantle from the Bakony hills. Veszprém
County. Early 19th century

from the middle of the last century. As far as possible, the embroiderer left no empty areas on the visible surfaces.

The most ornamental mantles were made in Eger with embroidered flowers covering the whole garment. In the Hajdúság they primarily embroider its two sides, the so-called *aszaj,* while the mantles of the Kunság can be recognized from their wreath motifs. Black appliqué designs are sewn on the mantles in the region east of the Tisza, chiefly in Bihar County, a practice which gained ground especially with the spread of sewing machines. This type of *szűr* even found its way to some places in Transylvania, such as Kalotaszeg (cf. p. 325). The mantles of Bakony and Somogy are not only distinguishable by their shortness, but also by their special world of design, in which, among other things, red appliqué also figures. This was even worn by the nobility in the middle of the last century as a sign of national resistance; furthermore they wore it when they went to the aid of the Italians in their war of liberation. That is why one version is called the Garibaldi *szűr.*

The embroidery of sheepskin garments along the seams (cf. also p. 332), is closely related to the embroidery on mantles. Such garments can still be found in many places, but really beautiful examples have survived primarily in Transylvania. They used furrier's silk, less frequently wool, to embroider the rich flower patterns with satin stitch. From the end of the 18th century various flower motifs, tied into bouquets, began to appear in increasingly·stylized forms as on the mantles. Certain differences in colour are apparent in the various parts of the linguistic territory. Thus in Kalotaszeg variations of the red colours dominate; they wore similar garments along the Homoród of Székelyland. Sheepskin garments were rarely ornamented in Csík; at most a bit of embroidery appears along the seam. The most ornamented are the jackets or *ködmön* of the Great Plain, the ones of Békés County standing out even among these, perhaps because here the influences of various nationalities met with those of the Hungarians (cf. Plate XXXVII). The short sheepskin mantles of the Hajdúság are embroidered mostly with black and the cloaks *(suba)* of Jászság with green. Between the Danube

Fig. 185. Decoration of a sheepskin jacket
(ködmön). Furrier's work. Region along
the river Ipoly, Nógrád County. Early
20th century

and the Tisza the Calvinists preferred a red colour scheme, while the Catholics preferred shades of blue and yellow. The *ködmön* of Transdanubia was embroidered with red, although other coloured yarns were also used in certain places.

Embroidery on linen was always done by women. Needlework is so varied over the different parts of the linguistic territory that we can undertake the introduction of only a few more characteristic and general versions.

One of the oldest known comes from the Great Plain, more specifically from Nagykunság, Hódmezővásárhely, and Orosháza, and is crewel-work called *szőrhímzés* (cf. Plates XXXIV, XXXVI). Such work was carried out with satin stitch, using woollen yarn in fine shades of blue, green, and red. Sometimes black was also used. The rose surrounded by flowers and leaves is the most popular motif, but tulips are also frequent. Similar designs have turned up recently from Transdanubia and Upper Hungary, evidence suggesting that their proliferation at one time may have been general.

On the *embroidery of Rábaköz,* we often find freely-drawn work alongside the cross stitch and laid stitch needlework (cf. Plate XXXV). Usually such cross stitch work was embroidered with red yarn and the pattern was fringed with small spiral lines. Flower motifs prevail primarily among the freely-drawn work, although sometimes birds also occur. In this type we often feel the influence of historical styles. Such embroidery has not been made for a long time, and can be studied only on museum pieces. A delicate kind of white embroidery

231. Border of a sheet, detail
Veszprém County

232. Border of a sheet, worked in white,
the owner's mark in the corner
Zala County

can be found around Kapuvár, principally in *Hövej*. Mainly head kerchiefs were ornamented with this type of work.

White embroideries form a separate group of their own, which are known in many places, or at least used to be known in the recent past. Some of these are related to button-hole embroidery. Such may be found in Somogy, Zala and Veszprém counties, where this needlework primarily adorned young men's shirts, especially those the bride gave the groom. The embroidery of Tura was also white originally, and cloths for food carrying, as well as shoulder-, head-, and handkerchiefs were decorated with it. The small flowers have become colourful and have grown in size during an observably short time, and along with the change in their composition, have also loosened up. This colourful type of satin-stitch embroidery then spread to the neighbouring villages.

The process of increased colouring is general among those embroideries that still exist today in the hands of the peasantry. *Kalocsa and its surroundings* give us the best examples. These originated from the factory-produced button-hole embroidery of the end of the last century, which the peasants began to imitate in red, blue, and black colours. During the last decades colouring has developed further, and today twenty-two shades of colour are used on the bodices, aprons, headdresses, and more recently on kerchiefs and coverings. The drawing women depart farther and farther away from the original patterns, and design richly ornamented, flowery, leafy, sarmentous patterns. This folk art did not stop at embroidery, but expanded to the painting of furniture,

400

XXXV. Border of a bed-spread. Region of Rábaköz

XXXVI. Border of a pillow-slip. Orosháza

XXXVII. Back of a woman's sheepskin jacket. Békés County

XXXVIII. Embroidery on the sleeves of a Matyó shirt. Mezőkövesd

XXXIX. The kiln of a potter. Csákvár, Fejér County

XLI. Wine-jug
Torda, former Torda-Aranyos County

XL. Plate, 1830. Debrecen

XLII. Plate, 1844. Debrecen

XLIII. Wine-jug
Torda, former Torda-Aranyos County

XLIV. Dish. Former Torda-Aranyos County

XLV. Dish. Sárköz region

XLVI. Jug, 1832. Debrecen

the walls of houses, and recently even to decorating Easter eggs and painting flowers on plates.

The people of *Sárköz* are outstanding masters not only of weaving but also of embroidery. The motifs of the red or black pillows to be put under the head of a corpse are connected with the Renaissance embroideries of the 16th and 17th centuries. Best known are headdresses embroidered in white on a black background. First the surface to be ornamented is outlined, then filled in richly, impromptu, without predrawing. Flowers, leaves, branches, even stylized birds, although less frequently, occurred in their patterns. Not everybody ventured to make the really ornate pieces, so women purchased or ordered the ones that suited their hearts' desire from outstanding sewing women *(var-róasszonyok)*. Young wives, called *menyecske* in Hungarian, wrapped a veil, the so-called *bíbor,* made out of voile, over their headdresses. Not only was the border of such a veil embroidered richly, but it was also embellished with metal sequins. It seems that this fashion came to the Sárköz district along the Danube from the Croatians and Serbians.

Matyó embroidery, in its present form, is fairly new in origin. The earlier designs were red and blue coloured cross stitched work, but the basic motif of even these was floral adapted to a geometric technique. A version of this form of embroidery exists to this day in Tard. Much more general, already in the last century, was the type of freely-drawn embroidery, the basic motif of which is a rose and leaves attached to it (cf. Plate XXXVIII). Earlier the colour was also red and blue, and such

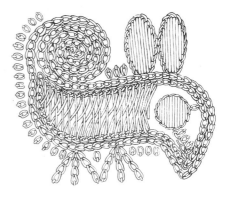

Fig. 186. Detail of the embroidery of a woman's coif, a motif called "little dog". Region of Sárköz, Tolna County. Early 20th century

233. A coif worn over the forehead, spread out
Sárköz

401

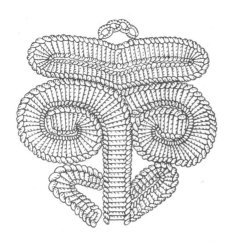

Fig. 187. Detail of embroidery worked in broad chain stitch, called *nagyírásos*. Region of Kalotaszeg. Early 20th century

234. *Matyó* embroidery, border of a sheet
Mezőkövesd

needlework was used to decorate the ends of sheets, pillows, and certain garments of men's wear. Since the turn of the century this embroidery became so densely worked with multi-coloured silk and wool yarn, that the basic material was completely covered with the roses and leaves. These compositions, drawn by the most outstanding "writing women" *(íróasszonyok)*, often resemble the ornamentation of furriers. Long after the furriers had stopped doing such work, drawing women still continued to sew old and new variations of their wealth of patterns.

The *kalotaszegi írásos* ("written" or pre-printed embroidery of Kalotaszeg) is one of the best known embroideries of Transylvania. Using a goose feather or the tip of the spindle dipped in a mixture of milk and soot, women draw the designs on the linen without any previous division of space, yet in such a way that it fits the given area exactly. The outlines were made by old women in whose heads and hands innumerable variations of the wealth of patterns existed. They ornamented sheets, pillowcases, coverings, and towels in this way. An increasing density in the pattern can be observed to have evolved here also; and not only was the closed square chain stitch used, but also the satin stitch to fill the left out areas. The most frequent colour of this work is red, but black

235. Embroidery to hang at the end of a bed
Kalotaszeg region, former Kolozs County

and dark blue also occur, usually just one or the other, because formerly such embroidery was always done in only one colour. The oldest *írásos* embroideries of Kalotaszeg still bore traces of the rigidity of their geometric ancestors, but at other times they evoke flower compositions, which through the mediation of the Renaissance can be traced to Italy.

Besides the freely pre-drawn type, the significant majority of embroideries in *Székelyland* are oblique chain stitch *(szálán varrott)* embroidery. Its ornamental elements have scarcely departed from those of the handwoven textiles. Often woven and embroidered pillowcases for marriageable girls are made with the same motifs. In the region of Kászon we can find almost all variations of the Székely oblique chain stitch embroidery. Their construction is well arranged and proportioned. The wide central motif that stretches in the middle gives the name to the different embroideries. They may call patterns various names, such as large plate, big or dense stars, dense rose, table leg, big apple, cockscomb, and wide stripe. These are borders on top and bottom of the central band, the so-called *mesterke*. In case of the oblique cross stitch embroideries of Székelyland, the two *mesterke*s together are not wider than one third or one half of the central band. Originally these

236. Embroidery to hang
at the end of a bed
Kalotaszeg region, former Kolozs County

237. Border of a pillowslip
Kalotaszeg region, former Kolozs County

patterns were worked with red yarn, but later blue, and at some places even black appeared. In many cases the designs show a relationship to the embroidery of the Saxons; in origin they can be traced back all the way to the Middle Ages.

We have already mentioned macramé fringe tying as one form of lace making *(csipkeverés).* The ornamental way of sewing together two widths of linen into either a sheet, a covering, or a tablecloth, can be compared to such work. However, we cannot really speak here of expressly Hungarian peasant lace making. This does not mean that lace

238. Border of a sheet, detail
Former Háromszék County

405

was not used; it was, but the lace was made by the Slovaks and the Saxons of Upper Hungary, and was sold on the greater part of the Hungarian linguistic region by wandering merchants. At the turn of the century, there were several attempts to adapt lace-making, but this succeeded only at Kiskunhalas and Karcag. The lace made here is enjoying great popularity to this day, both at home and abroad.

Pottery

Folk pottery, in form, colour and ornamentation, is one of the richest branches of Hungarian ornamental folk art. Its creators at all periods were professional masters who supplied a large area with their products, taking their ware on carts from market to market. Usually, they bargained not for money, but bartered, exchanging a selected vessel for grain with which it was filled once or twice, depending on the size and ornamentation of the vessel. This constant and direct contact with customers also made it possible for the request of the buyers to find expression in the size, function, and even ornamentation of the vessels. This is a factor, in every age, of the development of various centres of pottery (cf. Ill. 29).

At the time of the Conquest, the Magyars knew and used a number of unadorned clay vessels. Thus clay cauldrons, among others, appeared in the Carpathian Basin at the same time as did the Magyars, but shreds of a good many unadorned cups and pots have also been found by archaeologists. At the same time we know of vessels that may have come to the Hungarians from peoples living under Byzantine cultural influence. Excavations prove that in the 13th and 14th centuries Hungarian ceramics went through a great change in form and ornamentation, and began to adjust to Western forms. This became especially noticeable when, in the 15th century, lead glaze appeared. At first only green, brown and yellow spots and stripes, but gradually more and more definite ornaments and motifs emerged, which became general in peasant ceramics in the 17th and especially in the 18th centuries.

The simplest among the ornaments are the thumb-pressed strips of clay which have a long past. But on the edges of square candle-dipping vessels we find designs that imitate sewing, and which indicate that the predecessor of this type of vessel may have been made of leather (cf. Ill. 71). Some designs are partly incised into the clay and coloured pigments are trailed onto the vessels with a small earthenware utensil or pipette (íróka). Use of the paint brush became more general only in the second half of the 19th century, and even then only in a few places. Applied decorations occurred primarily on vessels made for the guilds, and on those used for ecclesiastical purposes. Such vessels were the kind the young potter created as his masterpiece. The pressing of clay into plaster moulds as a way of decoration spread sporadically only at the turn of the century, but this method has little to do with traditional ornamental folk art.

The technique of potters' work is divided into three clearly defined phases. The potter mined the clay himself, then cleaned it, mixed it according to need, stamped it with his bare feet, sliced it, and refined it. He prepared the well-worked clay with several days' work, and made it

239. János Horváth, Sr., potter
Mohács

into lumps of various sizes. The main element of the second phase of the work was the shaping that took place on the potter's wheel. The master treads on the larger, lower wheel of the potter's wheel with one bare foot, while he slaps clay sufficient for the size of a vessel on the smaller upper wheel. He shapes it and pulls the clay to the desired form and size. The potter always considered his wheel to be his most important tool; as a consequence, it appears on guild pitchers and badges as the symbol of the entire trade. The vessels are dried to a bone-dry state in a shady but warm place and this is followed by giving the basic colour and ornamentation. In the third phase comes the firing of the vessels. The first part of this is the so-called *zsengélés,* terracotta firing, when the designs get their colour. After this phase lead glaze is poured over the whole vessel, and the final firing follows. A great many different vessels are put into the kiln at one time. After firing the kiln is allowed to cool along with the pottery (cf. Plate XXXIX).

Some of the vessels are not glazed, such as those made for everyday use. These were either left unpainted, or were decorated with simple, undulating designs. Cabbage rolls were cooked in the oven in the so-called *vászonedény* ("linen" cooking pot), and water was carried to the fields in unglazed pitchers, because if dug a little into the ground, the water would evaporate and thus be kept cool. The *black vessels* are similar in shape to the former. After firing, they are brushed with a mixture of oil, petroleum, and industrial alcohol, and after drying they are buffed up with a piece of broadcloth. Afterwards their decoration is carried out with pebbles of various sizes, mostly plant and floral patterns, rarely a bird or dove motif. This kind of pottery is fired in the kiln by the usual method, except that for the last twenty minutes some wet straw and wood is placed into the kiln and gradually the kiln's openings are all shut. The trapped smoke penetrates the vessels and turns them black. This is how the potters of Nádudvar, Szentes, and Mohács fired their famous black pottery. The same firing was done with resinous pinewood in forest areas (Csíkmadaras, Madaras). The cooled pottery was wiped with a rag soaked in oil or lard, and in this way the designs emerged beautifully.

Often the masters who worked with clay did not make the same type of vessels even within the same settlement. The name *fazekas* or *gölöncsér* (potter) designates those who make the most simple commodities: pots, pans, fish and duck roasters, flower pots, chicken waterers, etc. The *tálas* (platter maker) and the *korsós* (pitcher maker) masters were held in higher esteem. The former also made other ornamental vessels besides platters and plates, such as milk and jam jugs, mugs, candle holders, and money boxes, while upright vessels, ornamental water pitchers, wine and brandy jugs and flasks were turned out by the pitcher maker. The platter and pitcher makers could also do the work of the potter, but he, on the other hand, could not do theirs.

Even during the last century most of the cooking and storing vessels of the Hungarians were earthenware, made out of clay. Their importance decreased gradually, but the census of 1890 still listed 5,300 independent master potters, among which 1,600 worked with one or more journeymen. However, their numbers continually decreased, and

240. The pitcher of the Peremarton
Bootmakers' Guild, 1770
Öskü, Veszprém County

between the two wars ornamental vessels were scarcely made. Today the best potters work in co-operatives and, with the help of ethnologists, are trying to develop new styles in the area of folk arts and crafts by starting out from the old patterns.

Some of the potters made glazed stove tiles *(kályhacsempe),* and starting from the Middle Ages, excellent artistic productions have survived. Although the ovens, built with cup or mug-like clay vessels, could be heated extremely well, they were not ornamental. However, plate-shaped tiles and especially square ones were suitable for decoration. The former were made on the potter's wheel, but the patterns of the latter were carved into wooden moulds and then the clay was pressed into it. The most beautiful rustic glazed tiles can be found in Transylvania, which, because of the beauty of their moulds belong among the loveliest works of art of ceramics and also of traditional carving. Most frequent among the patterns is the Renaissance bouquet in a two-handled vase, composed of tulips, carnations, georgina, and pomegranates. Geometric elements (rosette, star, peach stone, wolf tooth, etc.), which occur on wood carvings and even on weavings in Transylvania, may be found on the edge of the patterns.

The effect of a local majolica factory, established in the 18th century, can be seen on the pottery from *Tata,* one of the numerous pottery centres of Transdanubia. Since local potters also worked in the factory,

Fig. 188. Stove tiles. Korond, former Udvarhely County. 1. Unglazed tile. 1775. 2. A cornerpiece belonging to the former tile. 1776. 3. A tile glazed light green. 1875

241. Water jug. 1853 Tüskevár, Veszprém County

410

they probably learned the trade there. The basic colour of the Tata earthenware vessels is whitish. Their reticent designs are blue-green and bring to mind the majolica's wealth of patterns. The potters of the nearby *Csákvár,* operating to this day, made mostly fire-proof vessels, which were embellished with relatively few designs. The ceramics of *Sárköz* are richer. These are made at Szekszárd, Mórágy and Siklós in styles similar to each other (cf. Plate XLIV). The earlier vessels were light coloured, but later were replaced by dark brown. Green, reddish brown, and yellow dominate on its trailed designs, and flower and bird motifs are almost always present. Besides the many different kinds of dishes children's toys are also made, piggy banks and pear shaped boxes. The whistling cock, hen, and bird are favourite toys for children.

Hódmezővásárhely, in the Great Plain, has, during the last two centuries, always counted as the largest Hungarian pottery centre. The potters, platter and pitcher makers made here everything that could be formed of clay. Thus, alongside their multi-coloured, flowered plates, we find the so-called fritter platters with open-work, almost always coloured green. Their pitchers, with or without glaze, were famous far and wide. Here, and at nearby *Mezőtúr,* the most beautiful pocket-sized brandy flasks *(butella)* were made. These are always engraved and incised with floral and bird designs on a green background. We generally find a little verse on the side, which contains the name of the owner, and sometimes even of the maker:

> *Green* butella *my name be*
> *If there's brandy a-plenty be.*
> *If good brandy missing be*
> *My name's mere clay—no other be.*

> *Whose flask is this, you ask?*
> *István Marsi's, the carpenter's.*
> *He had it made for all his friends,*
> *Drinking alone meets not his ends.*

The most outstanding products of Hungarian folk pottery may be found along the Middle-Tisza region. The point of origin of these types, it seems, must have been *Debrecen,* whose traditions of pottery reach back to the Middle Ages. The guild has kept the list of masters from 1715 up to 1920. Debrecen was counted not just as an important centre, but as a market town as well. It enjoyed a certain independence during the Turkish occupation, and therefore all kinds of people came and went there, which made the assertion of many different influences possible on the art of pottery. The basic colour of its products is yellowish-white, ornamented with green, brown, yellow, red sarmentous and floral plant elements, and in some cases with birds. Debrecen was also one of the origins of anthropomorphic vessels (cf. Plates XL, XLII, XLVI).

From the beginning of the last century, the most beautiful examples of anthropomorphic pitchers were made at *Mezőcsát* (cf. Plates XLVII, XLVIII). The designs were incised, painted, and also carried out in relief on the yellowish-white basic colour. On the stomach of the wine pitcher in form of a man *(Miska* jug) a snake is often depicted, perhaps as

242. Decanters for Communion wine of
the Calvinist church of Báránd, 1797
Báránd, Hajdú-Bihar County

a warning to immoderate consumers of the danger contained in wine.
Nearby *Tiszafüred* worked primarily for the Matyó people, who liked
plenty of colour, and for the villages that lay at the foot of the mountains
(cf. Plates XLIX, L). Although they made wine pitchers similar to those
above, their main ware consisted of platters and plates. They flowered
the vessels in a most beautiful and diverse way, so that each composition
appears to be new and singular. Reddish-brown and bright green is the
most frequent on the light basic colour. We should mention among its
special dishes the *komaszilke,* which consists of several stackable pots and
lids, and in it the relatives and the *koma* (sponsor) women took dinner to
the newly-delivered mother. The pottery traditions of the Middle-Tisza
flourish today primarily in the shops of Karcag, on the level of folk arts
and crafts.

Among the pottery centres of Upper Hungary it is worth emphasizing the work of the masters in *Gyöngyös* and *Pásztó.* They worked with
blue, green, and, less frequently, red decorations on a whitish base. We

243. Dish decorated with the design of
a cock
Mórágy, Tolna County

244. Dish decorated with the design of
a bird, 1843
Mezőcsát, Borsod-Abaúj-Zemplén
County

413

often find gay little birds among the flower motifs. The so-called *csali kancsó* (puzzle-jug) has an open-work neck, while from the bottom several narrow tubes lead to the thickened edge; it is one of the characteristic products of the Gyöngyös and Pásztó regions. Only those who knew its trick were able to drink wine out of it, because they knew from which tube to suck the wine. In a cheerful company many jokes were played with such a vessel.

There were already potters in *Sárospatak* in the Middle Ages, although excavations have turned up ornamental and Turkish-style vessels only from the 16th century. Haban (Anabaptist) potters settled here in the middle of the 17th century, and the white basic colour they used here may perhaps be a survival, as opposed to the more general brown. Earlier they used trailed decoration, and from the second half of the 19th century brushwork for their geometric, floral designs in green, red, white and ochre colours. Sárospatak potters supplied earthenware dishes to a significant part of the north-eastern section of the Carpathian Basin.

414

There were few potters in Kalotaszeg in Transylvania, otherwise so rich in ornamental folk art; the people got most of their earthenware dishes from *Torda* and *Jára*. Among the richly ornamented vessels, the small pitcher, *bokály,* is typical of the entire Transylvania, which, if not used for drinking, decorated the walls. The white basic colour of the dishes of Torda often strongly recalls the wealth of motifs of Kalotaszeg embroidery. The potters of *Jára* used more colours. Red and black as basic colours also occurred as well as blue, and the colour of the motifs can be equally blue, yellow, and dark brown (cf. Plates XLI, XLIII, XLV).

In Székelyland, *Korond* is perhaps the largest, best-known potters' village. Here they made every kind of vessel, principally cooking pots, ornamental pitchers, plates, and stove tiles. The products of Korond were known through the entire area of Transylvania, and precisely because the potters worked for many areas, unity could not develop in their ornamental style. We find plant and animal motifs, the stag and the

246. Earthenware bowl
Sárospatak

415

bird being the most frequent among the latter. *Kézdivásárhely,* a market town, is also one of the important centres of pottery. The basic colour of the pitchers and plates is yellowish-white, on which are applied green and brown coloured geometric designs, and less frequently plant designs. Székely merchants of the last century transported the small pitchers often even over the Carpathians, so that we can also find some of them in the museums of Poland (Wrocław).

The artistic working of stone is of many kinds, but it is especially tied

416

to the place where the material is found. Therefore, the inhabitants of those villages around which suitable stone can be quarried usually excel in stone masonry and ornamentation. Its use is quite varied. Thus the door and the windows of a house may be made of stone, in which case mostly the upper sections are carved. Carved gate posts and roadside crosses may be met with, yet stone carving can be seen most frequently in cemeteries. The carvings of tombstones often show effects of relatively newer historical styles (Baroque, Rococo, Neo-Classical), as people try to imitate the tombstones of nobles, made in the city, or sometimes even abroad. Such a centre of stone masonry is Erdőbénye of the Hegyalja, which supplied the entire area. Several similar centres may be found in Transdanubia and in Transylvania. Most designs on stones were curved, sarmentous floral patterns, and even coloured in some places. Sometimes roughly-sketched human portrayals may be seen among them.

Other Branches of Ornamental Folk Art

Besides the main and most general branches, there are several kinds of Hungarian ornamental folk art that are worth mentioning briefly.

The extraordinarily rich metal art of the conquering Magyars barely left an impression on ornamental folk art in metal of the near past. We can even say that this branch of Hungarian ornamental folk art is relatively poor compared to the others, and it also did not participate in the great revival of the last century.

Peasant craftsmen are able to do certain types of metal ornamentation, and as we have seen, in some places the wood-carving herdsmen also apply metal. However, it is essentially still artisans, above all blacksmiths and locksmiths, who understand this branch of art best. A significant portion are Hungarian, but there are also a great many Gypsies among them, and excellent works of art are turned out of their hands. The Gypsies, who moved to Hungary during the Middle Ages, live scattered through the entire Carpathian Basin and pursue many different occupations. Thus there are among them musicians, wood carvers, trough carvers, reed makers for the loom, reed and tape weavers, but their main trade is still that of blacksmith and locksmith. They made various iron objects and work implements according to the taste of the persons who ordered them, and where there was an opportunity, they also ornamented it.

The young peasant man not only carved the distaff (guzsaly) of his beloved richly with flowers, but primarily in Upper Hungary decorated it with lead or tin casting, which he poured into a pre-hollowed hole. The designs were mostly geometric, and some can be traced back to the Gothic wealth of patterns. The relatively few elements were varied in such a way that they never became monotonous. In Kalotaszeg even spindle-weights were cast at home into moulds made of wood or alabaster. Initially geometric designs were also carved into these, then they put the mould away and used it when it was needed.

The blacksmiths and locksmiths ornamented even the simplest tools. Actually the brand mark is an elementary form of this practice and was used by its maker on the haycutter, vine pruning knife, and, less

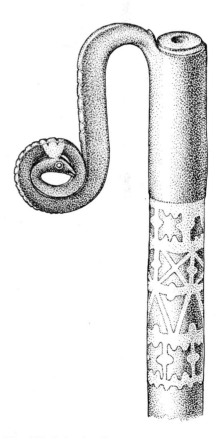

Fig. 189. A shepherd's crook with intarsia on its handle. Palotsland. Early 20th century

417

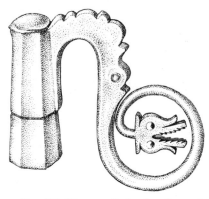

Fig. 190. The top of a shepherd's crook ending in a snake-head. Balmazújváros, former Hajdú County. 1908

Fig. 191. Metal buckles for the straps to hold cowbells. Kecskemét, Bács-Kiskun County. 19th century

frequently, even on the plough share. It might be a star, a roughly sketched heart, cross, half-moon, or a primitive flower consisting only of a few lines. But they also applied richer ornamentation by chiselling and punching. Sometimes we even find sarmentous floral motifs. The best blacksmiths decorated hatchets with copper or other metal inlay.

Blacksmiths also made objects which were first cast, then decorated, such as brass *buckles*. Some of these were used to fasten a bell to the leather strapped around the neck of oxen. An old, popular motif on such buckles is a pair of birds looking in opposite directions, though other animals were also frequently represented. After casting, the metal surface was refined and ivy, flower, linear or dotted ornamentation was applied. Of the moulds the most beautiful are the *shepherd's crooks,* made of brass, the outer loops of which were decorated with snake's heads, stars, and flowers. The smooth surfaces were decorated with metal buttons or incised with leaf and branch designes. Smaller and larger bells were made the same way, except that their decoration was only incised.

Blacksmiths also made objects which, though they had a function, still for the most part counted as ornaments. Such are the distaff nail (*guzsalyszeg*) and distaff pin (*guzsalytű),* with which they fasten the tow onto the distaff. The head of the nail gives an opportunity for embellishment, but the bottom was not altered because that was used to fulfil the original function. Hoops, leaves and squares were added on its upper section, and stretched spirals on its two sides, which lent a bouquet appearance to the whole thing.

The blacksmith made *coathangers* and lid holders usually out of barrel hoops. He worked the metal cold. He cut small pieces off the hoop, straightened them with a hammer, then shaped a coathanger out of it. He either decorated its upper part with simple notching, or perhaps shaped it in the form of a leaf or a flower. Animal figures were often added, especially the confronting cock and bird. The finished coathanger or lid holder was cleaned thoroughly, then painted with different colours, and in this way it became a favourite colourful spot of the house.

Ornaments made of wood or woven from straw were placed on the crest of the house in some places, but flowers made of wrought iron by the blacksmiths were considered the most beautiful. Although these can be found over the entire Hungarian linguistic region, the most superb pieces are known to us from the Great Plain. The star and half-moon motifs refer not only to the Calvinist religion of the inhabitants, but possibly to Turkish times. The ornamental cross is general among Catholics. Most crest-ornaments are flower shaped; thus tulips and carnations are the most frequent, but capitulum and pomegranates also occur. The majority of these iron ornaments carry a Renaissance heritage.

Besides beads, various pieces of *metal jewellery*—earrings, bracelets, necklaces, rings—also belonged to the Hungarian folk costume. Their makers are peasant silversmiths who congregated in certain larger cities such as Győr, Komárom, and Baja, and supplied huge areas from here. They worked mostly from silver, which they bought relatively cheaply; they also used silver coins, either melted down or with some transformation. Their designs are usually based on flowers and plants, and so clovers, six to eight petalled flowers and lentils appear among the patterns, while certain designs are named a shell, a star, or a butterfly. These *peasant silversmiths* worked until the most recent times, especially in the southern part of the linguistic territory.

Horsehair work is relatively rare; its masters are primarily men who work with horses (horseherds, drivers). Earlier they wove many consumer items out of the strong, ductile, and almost unbreakable horsehair (halter, rope, whip, shackle, etc.), but there were also some items which served primarily as ornaments. Such is, for instance, the pinholder, the centre of which is made of wood, birdbone, or feather, and was richly braided with horsehair all around. They also made rings, necklaces, and earrings out of horsehair. The technique and artistic character of these objects is of such high grade that it surpasses the professional button makers' lacings.

We have spoken of leather in several respects. The bootmakers ornamented women's footwear in different ways, and we also became acquainted with the colourful embroideries and appliqués of furriers, but beside these, ornamental leather had many more functions. The *harness maker* is also a professional master of leather processing. The main part of his work consists of making richly ornamented saddlery. One of its most important elements is the ornamental fringe *(sallang)*, made of leather and embellished in various ways. For example, they often saw red, yellow or green appliqué on black leather to emphasize the shape of the design. The edge of the harness formed into different shapes, and a whole composition created by cutting holes in it. There are also outstanding masters of weaving a flat braid out of thongs split very thin. These are fastened together with copper stars.

The distaff ribbons *(guzsalyszalag)* of the young Matyó wives and girls were ornamented mostly by the furriers. The women fastened the rolled-up tow with a string at the bottom, covering it with a leather strip embroidered in light brown, purple and light green. The strip widened towards the bottom and covered the top part of the tow entirely. It was decorated with circular, undulating rows of holes and its edges were laced. Such were given only by young men to young maidens.

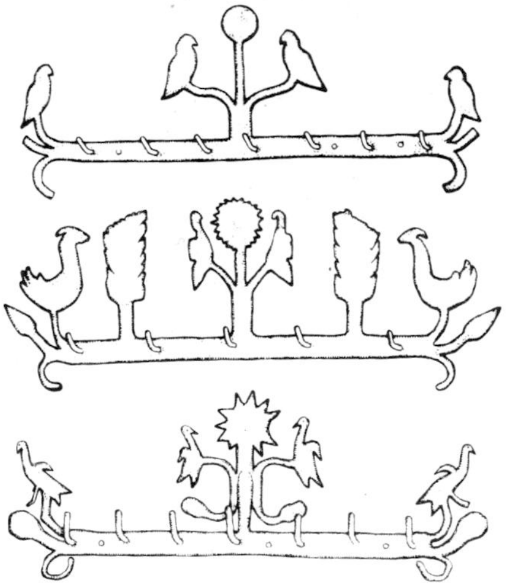

Fig. 192. Painted wrought-iron hangers. Hódmezővásárhely, Csongrád County. Early 20th century

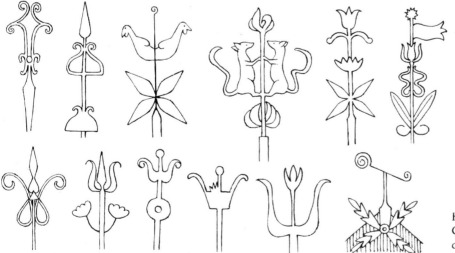

Fig. 193. Wrought-iron gable-tops. Great Cumania (Nagykunság). 19th–20th century

419

248. Woman painting eggs
Miske, Bács-Kiskun County

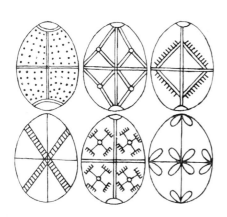

Fig. 194. Easter eggs painted with a resist
method. Ormánság region, Baranya
County. 1950s

The *painting of Easter eggs* is a branch of ornamental folk art especially tied to beliefs and customs (cf. pp. 645–6). The egg, as a symbol of fertility, plays an important role among beliefs, but the giving of ornamental egg itself is tied to the Easter holidays. This custom is actively alive to this day, both in villages and in cities. The long history of egg painting is demonstrated by the fact that such an egg has been found in an Avar grave from the period of the migration. The same is proved by such elements of design as one version of the swastika, as well as by a rake-like motif, and by many other geometric patterns that survived only on the Easter eggs. These are called both *ornamental* eggs in reference to their decoration, and *red* eggs, in reference to their colour. Among the many methods of making them, the resist technique is most frequent. With the help of a quill a pattern of melted wax is dripped on the cooled egg, then the whole egg is coloured. Afterward the wax is wiped off and the pattern underneath remains white. They rub the egg with an oiled rag to make it shiny. Sometimes the design is etched on the dyed surface with a sharp instrument. People know how to do egg painting, just as they know how to embroider, in every house, but this art too has outstanding specialists, usually old women who, for a kind word, or perhaps for a few eggs, will happily do the work of decorating.

III. Cultural Anthropology

So far we have tried to characterize the most important features of the social and material culture of the Hungarian people, the direction of their development, and the factors affecting them. In this chapter on the foundation of material and social culture, we shall introduce some important categories of folklore, folk poetry, the world of beliefs, and customs.

Folklore, cultural anthropology, or "intellectual culture", as it is called in Hungarian, is a superstructure of material culture; it is based on this foundation, although at times the transpositions are difficult to follow. As a consequence of altered economic and social circumstances, significant changes may also be observed in folklore. To mention only a few of the many examples, ornamental folk art flourished and became colourful, and a new type of Hungarian folksong became increasingly popular: the dance called csárdás.

Naturally, the superstructure did not change immediately in response to social and material transformations. Folklore changed in accordance with a rhythm all its own. Certain elements were introduced into the new type of culture while the traditions of centuries or even thousands of years were preserved. Sometimes, as in the case of beliefs and superstitions, certain details can greatly hinder even the process of economic production, while at other times production might be stimulated by intellectual factors. We shall try to point out certain characteristic elements and peculiarities of this intricate relationship.

In the Middle Ages, the intellectual culture of the lords and serfs stood quite close to one another. The Italian humanist Galeotto Marzio writes as follows about the court of King Matthias: "The Hungarians—whether nobles or peasants—use almost the same expressions and speak the same language... Poetry written in the Hungarian tongue is understood equally by peasants, town people, middle and upper nobility." During the following period, at the time of the unfolding and spread of Renaissance culture, a certain distance developed. This gap was increasingly widened by the spread of printing and schooling. Differences not only in the material culture of various social layers of the peasantry became increasingly apparent from the 18th century, but also in their intellectual culture as well. The reason is that upper social strata of the peasantry were trying to assimilate upward, but no such opportunity was available to the poorer strata of the peasantry. Since the poor and the indigent remained largely illiterate until the 20th century, they, if only for this reason, had to rely almost entirely on their traditional culture. That is exactly why the preservers, creators, further developers, and enrichers of, for example, folk poetry can be found among the poorest day-labourers, agrarian servants or small peasants.

Various professional groups also played a role in embellishing peasant culture and folklore as well. The small artisans of market towns differed even in their customs from the land-tilling peasantry, who, on the other hand, differed from the herdsmen, fishermen, pick and shovel men, and seasonal workers. We shall try to refer to these differences from time to time, but because of the unevenness of the available research, it is not possible to carry out a detailed analysis.

421

Instruments of Expression in Cultural Anthropology

Language, music, movement and dance have a relatively greater role in expressing and conveying folklore than they do in material and social culture. Therefore a few remarks shall be made in relation to them by way of introduction, sufficient to enable a more complete recognition of what follows. We must emphasize that language, music and dance are much more than just tools of expression, they are closely connected with the ethnic characteristics of the Hungarian people. Relics of centuries have been preserved through them, with new elements added by way of borrowing traits or by independent development. This is why the mentioned traits belong to the most prominent features of the Hungarians at large and of specific regions as well.

Hungarian Dialects

The best summary of certain characteristic features of the Hungarian language is given by Géza Bárczi in *A magyar nyelv életrajza* (The Biography of the Hungarian Language). The Hungarian vernacular and literary language developed on the basis of the spoken language and unity of dialects, so that folklore developed through the "folk language". It preserved the major inflectional and syntactical features of its Finno-Ugric origin, even through the thousands of years of its separation from the Ugric community. The significant majority of its stock of root-words developed and became enriched from the word stock of the Ugric period. Its vowel system is characterized by colourfulness aided by the variety of vowels, the sharp differentiation of long and short vowels, and the diphthongs. The richness of the consonant system is also worthy of attention. The Hungarian language avoids the excessive clustering of consonants and the monotony of vowel harmony. The system of accentuation emphasizing only the first syllable does not make cadence oscillate very much, but because of the flexibility of the language, Hungarian is one of the few living languages in which metrical poetry is possible with a cadence almost as perfect as in Greek or Latin. Through thousands of years the Hungarian language continually expanded and enriched the word stock of the Finno-Ugric original language without changing the inflectional and syntactical character; foreign words were incorporated into it, as into others, but this did not disturb the unity of the literary and vernacular language that developed after the 16th century. Furthermore, the word-building ability of the Hungarian language rests on its very rich system of suffixes and its tendency to create compound words. The entire character of the language (its system of verb conjugation and possessive conjugation, the system of verbal prefixes, etc.) is distinguished by an attempt at a great degree of conciseness and a synthetic creation of language. Thus, for example, certain conjugated verb forms can express time, mood, and aspect, and can also point out the person of the subject and the designated object. Along with its brevity and conciseness it remains clear and unambiguous. More recently, the analytical view of language, which favours subordinate clauses, has been showing up in Hungarian. So much for the language in a nutshell.

Besides the phonetic, inflectional, and syntactical peculiarities, the language and dialect of certain regions are differentiated by characteristic words, or by their characteristic meanings. Although certain elements of the dialects are usually clearly divided, a characteristic "transitional zone" generally exists among the individual dialects in which elements of two neighbouring dialects are mixed.

The Hungarian language belongs to the Finno-Ugric language family (cf. p. 26), but it could not have been uniform even at the time of its separation from it. Since at that period the way of life of the ancient Magyars involved dispersion over a large area, this separation would have led as a matter of course to the development of linguistic differences. Naturally, this is extremely hard to ascertain at a distance of many thousands of years, but numerous data testify to it.

Linguistic science has taken only the first steps in this area, but we can already refer to several basic observations. It is common knowledge that the Finno-Ugric consonant *k* generally becomes *h* in the Hungarian if followed by a velar vowel: an example is Ostyak *kul*, Cheremiss *kol*, Finnish *kala*, Hungarian *hal* (fish). However, this phonetic law, though widely proven, does not apply in every instance. For example, the Hungarian verb *huny* (close the eyes) also has a dialectical version, *kum*, with identical meaning. Its Vogul equivalent is *kőń*, Zyrian *kúnni*, Votyak *kiń*, Finnish *kyyny*. The earlier sound, therefore, was preserved in some of the Hungarian dialects, at least in a few words, most likely because even at that time there may have been certain dialectical differences in the ancient Magyar language.

Another phonetic phenomenon points to the groups of Finno-Ugric peoples the Magyars came into contact with even after separation. In the Hungarian as well as in the Permian languages, in the case of the Finno-Ugric *m, n, nj,* (Magyar *ny — ń*) + consonant, the *m, n, nj,* that is, the nasal consonants, largely disappear, for example, the Hungarian *ág* (branch), Votyak *vug,* Finnish *onke*. This indicates that some of the ancient Magyars who separated from the Finno-Ugric peoples must have been in some loose contact with certain Permian peoples.

The dual form of certain words suggests that among the ancient Magyars a dialect using *s* must have existed along with the prevailing dialect that used *sz,* and that generally the former succumbed in the struggle for survival between the two. Here are a few examples: *szőni* (to weave): *sövény* (hedge), *szem* (eye): *sömör* (ringworm), *szenved* (suffer): *senyved* (languish), *szőr* (hair): *sörény* (mane), *ország* (country): *uraság* (noble), etc.

We know considerably more of the Hungarian dialects from the time following the Conquest, especially from the 11th century. In fact, with the development of settlements, we can even relate them to specific places. Thus the use of *í* is a characteristic feature of some of the Hungarian dialects. It is possible to show the appearance of the sound *é* along with *í* in certain words and affixes very early: *néz* (look), *természet* (nature), versus *níz, termíszet*. The first Hungarian Bible translation in print, János Sylvester: *Újtestamentum magyar nyelven* (The New Testament in the Hungarian Language), Újsziget 1541, already reflects this dialectal peculiarity in a developed form.

By the end of the Middle Ages the characteristic phonetic phenomenon of the southern dialects, the use of the *ö,* had also begun to solidify. In certain areas the change e > ö took place in a great part of the words containing the sound *ö,* e.g. *kërëszt* (cross), *szëdër* (mulberry), *gërëndë* (beam) versus *köröszt, szödör, göröndö.* This change can be demonstrated primarily in the southern part of the dialectical region. However, its expansion toward the north must have been greater at one time, before it was limited by the depopulation caused by the Turkish occupation (16th and 17th centuries) and the resettlement that followed it. Perhaps the existence of distant linguistic islands using *ö* is also an outcome of this history.

We can find links between certain dialectical phenomena and localities as early as the Middle Ages. Such is the *-nott, -nól, -ni* triple suffix. This can be added to proper names and names of occupations. Its relations can be traced all the way to the Ugric period. Their meaning is as follows: *bírónott:* bírónál, bíróéknál (at the judge's, at the judge's family's); *bírónól:* bírótól, bíróéktól (from the judge, from the judge's family); *bíróni:* bíróhoz, bíróékhoz (to the judge, to the judge's family). In the past, as now, this pertained primarily to the north-eastern dialectical region.

Historical dialectal research is demonstrating and outlining more and more completely the characteristics of the predecessors of today's Hungarian dialects. It has also concluded that among the dialects of the more recent and remoter past, as well as in the present, the peoples of the two most distant parts of the Hungarian linguistic region, e.g. the Csángós of Moldavia and the Hungarians around Felsőőr, can understand each other, so that conversation does not pose any particular difficulty—apart from the use of a few unusual words, although the context can often facilitate comprehension. This uniformity of the Hungarian language permitting intelligibility through the entire linguistic region had already attracted the notice of Italian travellers of the 16th century. It contrasts with German, French, Spanish and Italian dialects, in which deviations are so great that they can practically be counted as separate languages, a state of affairs that in many cases made comprehension wellnigh impossible.

This fact also played an important role in the development of the literary language. No single dialect became the Hungarian literary language, as for example did Castilian in Spanish, or Tuscan in Italian, or the language around Paris in French. At the most we can say today that one or another of the Hungarian dialects stands closer to or farther from the literary language. Undoubtedly, the regional language of the Abaúj-Zemplén area is most in accord with the literary language, but perhaps this is because it occupies something of a central position among Hungarian dialects. Its dispersion was also aided by the fact that the first complete Protestant translation of the Bible (Gáspár Károlyi, 1590), and the life work of the great literary figure of the early 19th century, Ferenc Kazinczy (1759–1831), both reflected this dialect.

The beginnings of the formation of the Hungarian literary language can be traced back to the 16th century, when the writers, poets, and even the scribes of official documents and private letters began to use Hungarian instead of Latin. Naturally, at the beginning, the linguistic norm, an important part of which, spelling, was more or less a matter of habit, but especially from the 17th century, spelling gradually began to take on a definite form by separating more and more from the dialects and even by attempting to avoid certain of their characteristics (the latter's frequent use of *í, ö*, etc.). The wider proliferation of printing played a very great part in the development of the literary language, which also affected the dialects primarily through religious literature.

Literature gained a new momentum in the second half of the 18th century, the period of European Enlightenment. At this time it became apparent that no matter how melodious and flexible the Hungarian language might be, it had no words for the expression of numerous, especially new, concepts, objects, activities, so that as a consequence it had to borrow these from foreign languages. This was the time when the language reform movement, initiated by writers and poets, which enriched the Hungarian language with a great many new words, began. It is true that among these novel words many were rejected by common usage, while errors crept into the formation of others. By the end of the language reform movement in the first half of the 19th century, the literary language had reached maturity. This constantly growing and changing version of the tongue with its working vocabulary and grammatical structure is generally used today throughout the entire Hungarian linguistic region.

However, we must point out that the literary language in its growth and present form did not develop independently from the dialects. The greatest Hungarian writers and poets such as Ferenc Kazinczy, Mihály Csokonai Vitéz, Mihály Vörösmarty, János Arany, Sándor Petőfi, Mór Jókai, Kálmán Mikszáth and many others incorporated their own dialectal peculiarities in their works, and many of these found their way into the literary language. One of the sources of renewal of the literary language even today is the language spoken by the people. Thus from the 1930s the so-called populist writers have contributed many dialectal elements to the literary language.

Today the literary language, fixed in dictionaries and in its fundamental rules of grammar, is the standard against which we can measure the dialects. We shall use it in trying to define several characteristic large area groups on the basis of grammar and vocabulary.

Among the phonetic characteristics of the western Transdanubian dialects, instead of the vernacular *ú, ű, í*, short *u, ü, i* are generally used; and *l* is prominent—that is, it is pronounced instead of *ly*. The *l* that closes the syllable is often dropped. As regards vocabulary, Transdanubia is one of the most colourful large dialectal areas, where, in addition to the internal development, words of south Slav and German origin also appear.

The northern (Palots) dialectal region encompasses the greater part of the Hungarian linguistic region in the north. Its most characteristic phonic feature, unique in the area, is the *å* sound, made without the rounding of the lip, and the closely associated labial *ā*. Here, however, the use of the *l* is rather rare. From the standpoint of vocabulary, they generally keep contact with the northern part of the Great Plain. This has historical reasons. Mainly words of Slovak origin appear here, especially more recently, among their regional words.

The most characteristic peculiarity of the central part of the eastern dialectal region is the use of *í*. The lengthening of the syllable-closing *l, r, j* prevails, as it does over a much larger area. The pronunciation of *ly* as *j* is general, and other pronunciations are extremely rare. Closed and open *e* are not differentiated. This dialectal region, especially on the north-eastern areas, is closely connected to the Hungarian dialects of Transylvania, as can be easily seen in its vocabulary.

The most important phonic characteristic of the southern dialectal region is the profuse use of *ö,* which runs through the larger part of the southern linguistic region. The use of the *l* has become rare in this area. It also shows the least independence in its vocabulary. We can find here the characteristic regional words of south Transdanubia, or of the north, or of some parts of the eastern dialectal regions. The settlement history of the area explains this phenomenon. This area suffered most during the Turkish occupation, and afterwards a large part of it was resettled by people from different parts of the Hungarian linguistic territory.

The dialects of Transylvania can be divided into two large groups. One belongs to the Mezőség, to which can be related the dialect of Kalotaszeg. The Székely dialects are located in a homogeneous block at the lower slopes and valleys of the eastern Carpathians. It is difficult to summarize the extremely complicated and varied dialects of Transylvania according to homogeneous phonetic characteristic, because on this large territory the Hungarians live in numerous linguistic islands, restricted to small areas. This is why they have preserved many archaic features, while more recently Rumanian influence has appeared, especially in new cultural words.

There are transitional dialectal types among the large comprehensive dialectal groups, which have taken on many features from the regional dialect. Such are south Somogy, the area around Eger, around Hernád, along the northern part of the Danube, etc.

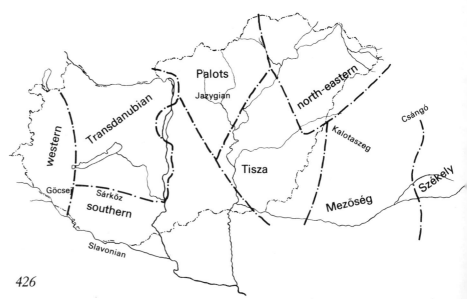

Fig. 195. Map of Hungarian dialects. 20th century

426

Linguistic islands are smaller units which have broken away from their mother language block and survive in a foreign language environment. Such is, for example, the linguistic island of Felsőőr, surrounded by Austrians, or the Csángós of Moldavia, who live among Rumanians. We can find many such linguistic islands in Transylvania, we can trace some in Slavonia, and in areas of Slovakia.

Dialectal islands came about through internal migration, primarily after the Turkish wars, when the resettled Hungarian population moved into an environment that spoke a different Hungarian dialect. Thus, among others, the Palots and Yazygians settled between the Danube and Tisza. Many people also came here from the southern part of Transdanubia. These people preserved part of their linguistic peculiarities even in the new environment, while at the same time they borrowed many characteristics from their neighbours. Such migration could also be witnessed during the Second World War, when smaller or larger groups settled into the south-eastern part of Transdanubia, from the southern part of Slovakia and from Bukovina of Rumania.

The question arises of just how closely the borders of ethnic groups (cf. pp. 34–47) coincide with those of dialect groups. We cannot answer this question unequivocally, since the separation of dialects takes place primarily from the phonetic point of view, and such separations do not necessarily coincide with the border lines of ethnic phenomena. In spite of this, we can find a good many smaller dialectal types which have also been identifed as ethnic groups. Such dialectical groups are in Hetés, Őrség, Kiskunság, Csallóköz, and Szigetköz. But we can to a certain degree look upon the Palotses as an example. Even ethnology draws the borderlines of this group in many cases on the basis of dialectal phonetic data. Although future research will have significant tasks in this area, it is already certain that among the characterizations of ethnic groups, dialects must also be taken into account.

Hungarian dialects, because they are bequeathed not in writing but by word of mouth, have preserved more archaisms than the standard language. This observation is especially true for folk poetry, which, because of the more or less fixed form, better preserved linguistic archaisms, the different idioms, and not infrequently extinct regional words. Furthermore, the language of folk poetry tends to carry some archaisms at the time of its inception. Especially verses of folk customs, idioms, proverbs and children's verses and rhymes have preserved a great many early features.

Hungarian dialects are still alive today, with more or less intensity. If, for example, one walks along the streets of Szeged in south Hungary, one immediately hears the most characteristic phonetic phenomenon, the use of *ö,* which is proudly assumed even by the intellectuals who come from this region. In Debrecen, however, where we can hear the use of *í* and the diphthongs, intellectual circles try to keep free from this. Among the Palotses even town folk differentiate in their language the *å* sound we have spoken about above. On the basis of the language of people interviewed in the course of a television or radio report, it is possible to tell the region from which they come. Nevertheless, dialectal characteristics are fading out of the language. The main reason for this is the growing literacy, which naturally supports literary usage. The school, the film, and the theatre also have a similar effect, but primarily the role of radio and television is extraordinary in this respect. However, in spite of the levelling influence of the last decades, dialect will remain for a very long time to come as a characteristic trait of certain regions.

The vernacular provides for the wealth, beauty, and strength of Hungarian folk poetry. In the past and present, students of Hungarian folk poetry have esteemed the power and tenderness of the vernacular very highly. Oral tradition has preserved folk poetry through the centuries; the power of the word is inseparable from the poetry of the people. Folk poetry is indebted to the language not only for the words, and for the words of the dialects that provide new colours in an unending stock of words, but also for the fine tones of phonetics almost beyond analysis as well as for the flexibility of the language which makes it adaptable to any genre, any subject, as an evocative, enlivening force. The lamentations of the wife of Mason Kelemen of the ballad can be heard in the language just as much as the soothing quality of a love song, the dirge of a soldier, the defiant song meant for the death of the outlaw, and the fiery verve of a dancing song. Similarly, we can hear at times the leisurely measures of a joke. The serenity, the unruffled superiority characteristic of the peasant radiates from the sentences, and the enchanting wonders of the fairy tales are made homely, turned into acceptable reality by the Hungarian language. It is the language of the people, the basis of a national literary language, a secure and inexhaustible treasure house. It is also the mainstay of folk poetry.

Hungarian Folk Music and Folk Instruments

As the result of the monumental work carried out by Béla Vikár, Béla Bartók, Zoltán Kodály, László Lajtha and others in the collection, publishing and adaptation of music, Hungarian folk music is famous far and wide.

Béla Bartók defined the most important traits of folk music as follows: "Folk music is the sum of all those melodies which were used in some kind of a human community over a smaller or larger area for a certain length of time, as spontaneous expressions of musical instinct. To put it simply, folk music is composed of melodies which were sung by *many* people and for a *long time*. But if melodies are sung by many from generation to generation, then on the one hand, these will undergo more or less of a transformation in one way or another, depending on the place, that is to say, variations in melody will occur. On the other hand, melodies originally dissimilar from one another in structure may undergo transformation and become similar; that is, melodies come into being with common characteristics and a homogeneous musical style." *(Népzenénk és a szomszéd népek zenéje* [Our Folk Music and the Folk Music of the Neighbouring Peoples], p. 3, Budapest, 1952.)

The basic melodies of the Hungarian treasury of folksongs exceed three thousand in number and naturally multitudes of innumerable and boundless variations are attached to these. Regardless of the homogeneity of such an enormous stock, certain historical strata can be differentiated of which only the most important shall be dealt with below.

Fig. 196. Melodies with the construction of alternating fifths. 1. Surd, Somogy County. 2. Rafajnaújfalu, former Bereg County. 1912

The oldest stratum of Hungarian folk music is characterized by the pentatonic scale and structure which repeats the melody a perfect fifth lower. If we take as our starting point the note "g", the outline of the scale is as follows: $g^1 - b^1 - c^2 - d^2 - f^2$. The missing notes often occur as unaccented passing notes. Today this structure is rarely found in a pure and untouched form, but if the influences of later centuries are stripped away, numerous melodies may be uncovered which were thought to be new. The texts in this kind of folk music comprise four lines: the third and fourth being sung a perfect fifth lower than the first two.

Although the pentatonic scale can be found in the music of practically every people, this melodic repetition at the interval of the perfect fifth is found mainly in areas of Hungary. Already a half century ago the idea emerged that this type of melody has its closest link with the melodies of the Mari (Cheremiss) people living in the Soviet Union. Often the similarity is so great that it is almost impossible to differentiate Hungarian and Cheremiss songs. This melodic form has also been found among the Chuvashes, where similarly it represents the oldest layer. Related forms occur even in Mongolia, so that this style can rightly be called Central Asian. We know what a great influence the Bulgaro-Turkish people, who spoke the language of the Chuvashes, exerted over the Hungarian language in the 7th to 8th centuries, and we have to suppose that musical connections also originate from this period.

The possibility also arose that the songs of mourning for the dead preserved Ob-Ugrian, or more precisely, Ostyak, connections. However the relationship is not that simple, because most likely this is a case of both having derived from the same source, the source from which the ancient Hungarian pentatonic world of melody, arising from North-Central Asia, could also have originated through appropriate transposition.

What we find in certain children's songs and minstrel songs (cf. pp. 654–8) appears to be another ancient layer of Hungarian folksongs. When we search for traces of the "hexachord-melodies", we know of parallels primarily among the Slav and German peoples. But in all likelihood this connection can be much wider because the twin bars, the prolonged repetition of short motifs, can be found in the basic layer of every people's music, and it has even survived in all the most ancient traditions.

The recording of music with notes started late, in the 8th and 9th centuries. In Hungary, musical notes appear much later. Thus free variations, especially in folk music, but in church music also, must have been extraordinarily extensive. Recorded folk music material also testi-

Fig. 197. Melody type A A⁵ A⁵ A. A ballad about highwaymen. Heves County

Fig. 198. Melody type A B B A. Heves County

430

♩ = 93

Fig. 199. Melody type A A⁵ B A. Bácsandrásszállás, Bács-Kiskun County. 1942

Fig. 200. Melody type A A B A. Fejér County. 1906

fies that Hungarian folk music assimilated many different elements. Influences came from Gregorian chants, just as sacred folk music has preserved a close connection with religious folksongs almost to this day. We know of several melodies that were sung with both religious and secular texts.

However, the repertoire of folk music has increased from the Middle Ages on, not only through religious written music but also through the influences of secular noted music. Some influences came from abroad, others evolved within the country. Foreign bards travelling to royal courts and to the upper nobility presented their songs. New vogues of dancing must also have introduced many new melodies. A detailed discovery of all these historical factors offers many tasks to the students of music history and music folklore.

Following the Western preliminaries that had already occurred in the Middle Ages, a new type of Hungarian folksong form arose in the 18th and 19th centuries, apparently under Western influence. Its characteristic traits are that the first and last lines of the four line melody are repeated, that is, we hear the opening line again as the conclusion. By disregarding variations few in number, these musical forms can be divided into four main groups: AA⁵ A⁵ A, ABBA, AA⁵BA, AABA. While about 200 melodies belong to the oldest layer of folk music, this newer group, not counting the minor variations, includes more than 800 basic variations. The new Hungarian folksong was dissimilated widely and thus restrained the inflow of foreign melodies.

At first glance there is a great deal of similarity among the melodies, but a more thorough examination also readily reveals the differences. Although this group is essentially a limited type, new melodies did come into existence, though in most cases these are only variants. Yet this melodic form maintains a close relation with the old structure. Thus the old form of A⁵ A⁵ AA can very easily, without any foreign influence, be

431

transformed into the form AA^5 A^5 A, and in that case connection with the old fifth-construction is already obvious. Similarly, we can find traces of the old stock of notes, even if the bulk of these are already pentatonic, because if we leave off the minor, weak beat notes, the heptatonic basic structure comes to light. Actually the new and the old songs are both symmetrical forms, and if we peel off the superimposed notes, we often discover the oldest layer of Hungarian folk music. This proves how very much the pentatonic structure and the fifth-construction are peculiarities of Hungarian folk music.

Songs composed in a popular form (*műdal,* e.g. artificial song) practically flooded the entire country from the end of the last century until the First World War and got even as far as the villages. Unfortunately, the composers of the verse and music are mostly not known, and today there is not much hope for discovering their identity. The majority of the songs, in both their lyrics and melody, are foreign to the spirit of the Hungarian folk; their composers were educated men, more familiar with foreign than with Hungarian folk music. The lyric text and the melodies both reflect resignation from life, hopelessness, not infrequently a desire to die. Thus these songs primarily expressed sentiments of the middle and lesser nobility, whose numbers were declining from the middle of the 19th century. However, the influence of these songs left their mark, especially in two respects. Lines that used to consist of 6 to 12 syllables were extended and often reached as many as 25 syllables. Through this type of songs the major and minor modes entered into Hungarian folk music to a significant degree for the first time. And yet, Hungarian folk music defended itself against their effect by trying to reshape such songs to its own image. Numerous folksongs are known which transform the mentioned type into pentatonic songs, although this did not in every case happen successfully and often resulted in some kind of a mixture. But even in such instances the value of the songs had been improved.

The question of the relationship between Hungarian folk music and gypsy music is closely related to this problem, all the more so since in the middle of the 19th century Ferenc Liszt in one of his works erroneously called Hungarian music "gypsy music". This notion became so deeply entrenched, especially abroad, that even today in many cases Hungarian folk music is equated with gypsy music. The truth is that gypsy orchestras of the cities played a shallow, folksy, composed music, suitable for satisfying wider audiences. Gypsies adjusted their musical repertoire to a great degree to their environment. As an earlier example, in Máramaros, Bihar, and also in some other places, in the first half of the last century the gypsy bands played, without any change, the repertoire inherited from bagpipers. But in and near cities their activity was limited almost exclusively to pseudo-folk music. As a result of more recently changing tastes, however, today they again frequently play old and new types of folksongs, true Hungarian folk music, even in cities.

Following the authority of Béla Bartók, we shall outline the reciprocal effect between the folk music of the Hungarians and that of the neighbouring peoples. Several instances are known: (1) only the structure and certain details are of foreign origin; (2) transforming the received melodies in a manner appropriate of the recipient people's music; (3) receiving the melody in a broader or more narrow form; (4) finally, complete reception of a melody without any change at all. We must note that there are also certain melodies which exist both among Hungarians and the neighbouring peoples (e.g. *Szeretnék szántani, Debrecenbe kéne menni,* etc.), yet are not characteristic of the music of either group.

Practically no direct reciprocal effect may be proved with respect to the style of German music. Melodies originating from the direction of Germany came to the Hungarians mostly through Czech-Moravian-Slovak transmission and transformation. It seems that, with the exception of the Central-European type German music of the late Middle Ages and the 16th to 18th centuries, there was such a fundamental difference between Hungarian and German music that it almost completely precluded borrowings.

The situation is entirely different with the Slovaks, not only within the region of the linguistic territory, but in more distant areas as well. The connection is most diverse, since Slovakian labourers travelled for centuries to the Great Plain, to do the harvesting, or earned their bread as travelling glaziers, tinkers, cambric merchants, etc. Interestingly, we either cannot find or find very rarely the traces of the old type of Hungarian folk music in Slovak music, yet the new type of folksong occurs all the more frequently. This was a genuine revolution of Hungarian folk music, which reached not only into Slovakia, but into Moravia and even into Galicia. The reason for this is possibly the strengthened relationship between these countries at the time. In the second half of the 19th century the rhythms of new folksongs were spread also by the soldiers. This is also a reason why we find so many corresponding melodies among Hungarian and Slovak songs.

The situation is again different in connection with the Transcarpathian Ruthenians. One part of Hungarian swineherds' songs, a group of about thirty variations, reflects an influence of the so-called *kolomejka.* We assume a sequence something like the following: Ruthenian *kolomejka* → Magyar swineherd songs → recruiting music → new type of Hungarian folk melodies. At the same time, the effects of the new Hungarian melodies and in many cases their complete reception shows up very strongly in this area. In some collections of folk music, the proportion of these songs reaches 20 to 40 per cent.

A different relationship developed with Rumanian folk music, which is worth examining primarily in Transylvania, where coexistence was extremely close both in the past and in the present. Rumanian folk music may be divided into several musical territories, each differing from the other to significant degrees. The pentatonic melodies of Hungarian origin are known in the majority of these areas; at the same time the new Hungarian music is almost completely unknown and occurs only perhaps in Máramaros, but here most likely as the result of Ruthenian transmission. The lack of the latter melodies can be explained among others by the different character of the fundamental Rumanian musical treasure by the attachment of Rumanians to that style, and also by a difference in musical taste.

433

It is futile to search for traces of Hungarian folk music in Serbia, Croatia and Slavonia. The influence is negligible on both sides. At the same time, in the Muraköz an extremely large number of songs were received from the old Hungarian material. We know of published collections where the influence of pentatonic music reached one-third of the melodies, proportionately greater than in Hungarian collections. However, the Muraköz district is a negligible part of the south Slav area, although it is extremely important for Hungarian folk music, precisely because of its conserving character.

We have surveyed certain layers of Hungarian folk music which, after the analysis of 2,600 melodies, was classified by Béla Bartók in the following way: (1) Old pentatonic melodies in approximately 200 groups of variations: approx. 1,000 songs (9%); (2) new type of melodies in approximately 800 groups of variations: approx. 3,200 (30%); (3) melodies composed in an artifical "Magyar" style in approx. 600 groups of variations: approx. 2,500 (23%); (4) foreign influence, approx. 100 groups of variations: approx. 4,000 (38%). The results of subsequent research have not changed the proportions of this survey, which shows clearly that prior to its fulfilment and general proliferation, the new Magyar folk music was threatened by strong foreign influence, which would have caused its Magyar character to be restricted to an extremely small area.

The fact that the grandparents stayed at home with the children while the parents and grown children worked in the fields and meadows determined over a very long period the method of transmitting folk music within the family. Thus the grandparents spent a great deal of time with the children and passed on their knowledge of folk music. This method of bequeathing broke up only in recent times with changes in the rhythm of village life.

There were a great many opportunities for singing in the past. Thus a whole series of communal activities could not have taken place without singing. Formerly the setting was given by the communal performance of feudal services, and later through day and seasonal labour on the large estates, though less frequently while working but rather during breaks. Corn husking, spinning, and grape harvesting provided opportunities for singing. Naturally, with the cessation of these types of work the opportunity for singing also decreased.

Singing was an indispensable part of children's games, of the gatherings of girls, and of Sunday afternoon strolls. Songs associated with occasions were tied to customs, and an entire system of these developed. Well-defined songs were sung at certain parts of the wedding. The songs of Christmas, Easter, and Palm Sunday were just as different as the songs of Shrovetide or the near-forgotten songs of the fire jumping on Midsummer Night. We shall speak of all these again in regard to customs (cf. pp. 637–659).

★

Peasants with a good ear and liking for music generally played instruments, and often made them themselves. But we also find instruments in the hands of bands who have joined together for certain occasions, and even more so in the hands of people who were regularly employed to play music.

Music and singing were already part of Hungarian village life in the Middle Ages. Sigismund, a Polish prince, spent a long time in Hungary around 1500, and on some occasion listened to the singing of men and women, and at another time to gipsies playing on the zither at their lodging. In the Vienna Codex from the middle of the 15th century we can read the following reference to musical instruments: "... at the time when I listened to the sounds of trumpets, pipes, fiddles and to the sound of the instrument made from elder-wood by minstrels, also to the voice of psalms and that of drums." Medieval sources bear witness that fiddlers, lute players, gleemen, bards, minstrels and flute players travelled throughout the country and played, sometimes sad, sometimes happy songs on the instruments with which they accompanied their singing. Since the way of life of the medieval nobility and of the peasantry did not differ greatly from one another, it is likely that many of the instruments were also the same.

The word *síp* (pipe or whistle) originates in the eastern dialectal areas from the word *sültü*, which was being mentioned in the middle of the 17th century in the form *süvöltyü*, and which originates from the very old onomatopoeic root word *sí, sív (sír*—howl, cry). Its wide diffusion is demonstrated not only by linguistic records but by children's poems, which look back to a much more distant past and preserves shamanistic elements:

> *Storkie, storkie, dickey bird,*
> *What has got your leg with blood?*
> *A Turkish lad has injured it,*
> *Magyar laddie cures it, with*
> *Piping, drum-beat, playing on the reed-strings.*
>
> Sárrét (Bihar County)

★

The traditional metre or prosody of any popular poetry is difficult to transpose into any other system of versification. If, as in our case, the traditions and conventions are so widely divergent for linguistic and cultural reasons as they are in Hungarian and English folk poetry, the task is nearly impossible. Nevertheless, I felt the task was worth the attempt. I have therefore accepted the challenge and tried to preserve as much as I could of the peculiar rhythms of my originals. I believe that doing (or at least seeking to do) justice to the prosodical features of foreign poetry, however outlandish and unusual they may be, is one of the translator's liabilities. If only because the original rhythm is no less part and parcel of the total effect than other ingredients of poetry, such as syntax, diction, rhyme, etc. And if we consider that the lyrics and ballads in this volume exist primarily as songs that are sung to this day, any adaptation of their prosodic structure to the English reader's accustomed native rhythms would have inevitably interfered with their appreciation as pieces of folk poetry and as folksongs. (Translation into prose, so often preferred in works of this kind, would have been, in my view, an even less acceptable solution.) The attempt to be faithful to the rhythmic form, I am aware, has no merit in itself; still, in order to be able to judge its success or otherwise, or even to be able to read or scan the lines as they are intended to be, the reader needs to be familiar with at least the basic principles of rhythm in Hungarian traditional verse. These principles are summed up and exemplified below.

Hungarian national versification is based on linguistic word stress, which invariably falls in speech on the first syllable. The periodically recurring *heavy* stresses in the poetic

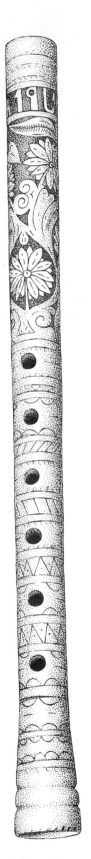

Fig. 201. Flute. Somogy County

line constitute the main principle of prosodic organization. The lines of varying syllabic length divide into units called *bars,* each beginning with a heavy stress—normally coming on a word initial syllable but the established and anticipated rhythmic pattern occasionally requiring it to be shifted—followed by 0, 1, 2, 3, 4 or 5 (relatively) unstressed syllables. A line usually consists of 2, 3, and 4 such *bars,* and each bar in turn may consist of the same or a varying number of syllables; if the *bars* are unequal in syllabic length, they are said (by one theory at least) to be equalized in time. This yields an extremely varied repertoire of rhythmic line patterns, some of which are more common or favoured than others. E. g.

1) Gólya, gólya || gilice,
 ‿ x x́ x || ‿ x x, where ‿ means heavy rhythmic stress, x́ light
   4   +   3   word stress, x unstressed syllable
Storkie, storkie, || dicky bird, (see p. 435)
:
:
Síppal, || dobbal || nádihege- || dűvel.
 ‿ x || ‿ x||‿ x x x || ‿ x
 2 + 2 + 4 + 2
Piping, || drumming, || playing on the || reed-strings.

2) Felszántom a || császár || udvarát,
 ‿ x x x ||‿ x || ‿ x x
   4   +   2   +   3
I shall go and || plough his ||Highness' land (cf. p. 470)

3) Tizönkét kőmijes || esszetanakodék,
 ‿ xxx́xx || ‿ x x x x x
   6   +   6
Once twelve master masons || put their heads together (cf. p. 524)

To help the reader establish the rhythm of the poems to follow, each different line structure will be provided with stress marks to show the beginning of each bar. In this simplified notation for convenience we shall dispense with double bars and the marking of light or subsidiary stresses. *(Translator's note.)*

*

The most primitive forms of such pipes or whistles were made of reed, and several varieties of them are known in the Hungarian linguistic region. One is made of a single reed, approximately 25 cm long. At one end it is stopped, and the reed-stops are placed at the other. Several holes, generally six, are bored along the side and the melody is played on these. Double reed pipes are also made, and people who intended to play the bagpipes later learned to play with the help of these. The reed pipe or whistle is mentioned in nursery rhymes. The counting-out rhyme below demonstrates the widespread existence of such musical instruments:

Once when I went down the cellar for to filch some butter,
Mother came soon after me and she did give me what for.
Hid in the reeds, I made myself a reed pipe;
This is what my reed piped: hee-how-hoy,
You are it, you big-mouthed boy.

This children's poem also records that when playing the pipe, the player would mutter into it ("hee, ho, hum"), in this way providing a background to the melody. Pipes were made from various kinds of

249. Old man playing the flute
Váralja, Tolna County

Fig. 202. Swineherd's horn. Former
Gömör County. 1906

wood or tree bark. Herdsmen were especially good at making these. Different sounds were produced by moving the lips and by blowing the right amount of air. It follows from all this that the sound and the register of every pipe is different.

However, as time went by, pipes descended the ladder of musical instruments and by and large became a children's toy. Pipes were replaced by flutes, the name of which, *furulya,* is a loan-word very likely from the language of Wallachian herdsmen. In general, two forms are known. One is long, with five holes, approaching one metre in length. The holes are placed near the end so that while blowing into it the player's head had to be raised high. The other is the short version, its length varying between 30 and 60 cm, and having six holes bored in its side. Generally, the players themselves make their own instruments out of maple or elder wood. Before the First World War, the Rumanians of Transylvania and the Slovaks of Upper Hungary made flutes for sale and travelled with them from village to village or to fairs.

The flute is an instrument played by men or boys. It was used during the last century primarily by herdsmen, who played it when alone, for their own enjoyment. With the exception of the Csángós, it is not used any more anywhere to play dance music. Because flutes are all tuned differently, their joint use in a band is impossible. Herdsmen, incidentally, especially in Transdanubia, often ornament their flutes with etched or embossed ornaments.

Herdsmen's horns *(pásztortülök)* were made out of the horns of cattle and were used not so much as musical instruments, but rather to signal. These signals, however, are musical in character. The horns of the gray Hungarian cattle were especially suitable for this purpose because of their length. Smaller horns were lengthened with copper plates. Horns gave an extremely high range, so that it is also possible to sound the keynote on them. (It follows that the four notes of the natural scale can also be sounded on them.) The signals for the most part imitate sounds such as the calls of pigs, horses, and cattle.

One of the most widely spread wind instruments among the Hungarians was the bagpipe *(duda),* which consisted of a large leather bellows and the pipes that were mounted on it. The word *duda* is of Slavic origin, but it cannot be determined where the Hungarians took it from, because both the name and the instrument can be found among all the surrounding Slavic peoples. Earlier they also called it *gajda,* especially in the eastern part of the linguistic region. This is a loan word, presumably of Slavic origin, that could have been spread by Wallachian herdsmen. The proliferation of the word is demonstrated by recordings of the family name Gajdos as early as the first years of the 15th century. We also have an 18th-century reference to another Hungarian name for the bagpipe: "A musical instrument, used habitually by the herdsmen, commonly called *tömlősíp* (bagpipe)."

One component of the bagpipe is the bellows, the function of which is to supply the two pipes evenly with air. They made it mostly from lambskin, less frequently from goat- or dogskin. Only the front part of the flayed skin is made use of and the stumps of the front legs. Thus, together with the neck, three openings are created on the skin. After-

438

wards the skin is prepared and used with the woolly side in the inside. They then make the bagpipe parts. First comes the blower through which the air is let into the bellows, then the deep toned bourdon pipe is fastened on, which has only one hole. The double melody pipe has $6+1$ holes. The single-tongued blowers of each, which are cut from reed, are hidden by a ram's or goat's head. In the Great Plain, we even find bagpipes shaped like heads of men or young women.

We know nothing of the tuning and pitch of bagpipes in the past, though we have adequate information from the 20th century. Their keynote lies between F and B. The scale of the melody pipe is mostly in the Mixolydian mode. If its first hole is opened up, then even deeper sounds than the keynote can be raised half a note. However, this is done only rarely, or rather just as an embellishment. Generally all together about eight notes can be sounded on a bagpipe.

From the 16th century the bagpipes became widespread. The players of bagpipes were greatly appreciated. For example, in 1666, of the eleven musicians of Prince Ferenc Rákóczi I, only the trumpet and violin players received higher salaries than the bagpipers. Among the princes of Transylvania, Mihály Apafi in particular loved the sound of the bagpipe, and when he went on a long trip he always took along his favourite bagpipers. This instrument had faded from the courts of the nobility by the 18th century and had found its place only in peasant bands. In the first half of the 19th century it was mostly used alone. The saying that "two bagpipers cannot fit into one tavern" was born at this time. People danced to a bagpipe at occasional and improvised dance gatherings, but the zither and especially the gipsy bands replaced it. Herdsmen played the bagpipe the longest, and were also the best bagpipers.

A good bagpiper was known far and wide, and even dance songs sung by herdsmen were written about him.

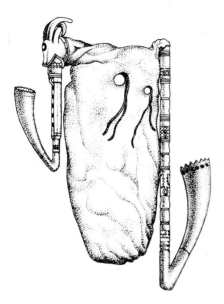

Fig. 203. Bagpipe. Palotsland. 1920s

> *He who wants to play the bagpipe,*
> *Needs to know Hell in and outside;*
> *Quite some time he must be stayin',*
> *Mastering his bagpipe playin'.*

Some learned to play with such virtuosity that legends were written about them. According to one, a bagpiper played so well in a tavern on the Nagykunság *puszta,* that as long as he played, the people couldn't stop dancing. There were also stories about others who hung their bagpipes on the main beam, and the instrument continued to play beautiful melodies by itself, and when four young men got tired of dancing they tried to take it outside into the yard, but could not move it. However, even famous bagpipers eventually got tired, and broke into the following song:

> *Weary am I, sick of livin',*
> *Good old bagpipe, I'am leavin'.*
> *Such a long time did I blow thee,*
> *Life is but a burden to me.*

Among the string instruments, several were used only in distant areas, such as the lute *(koboz)* in Moldavia, where it was preserved by contact with Rumanian gypsies. The word itself originates from one of the Turkic peoples, most likely from the Cumanians or Pechenegs, although it is also possible that these peoples revived a musical instrument that had existed earlier. Nothing shows better its general use than an observation about Hungary from the early 17th century, namely, that "in my country even the children are plucking it". It was still used in the second half of the last century: "The *koboz* is a guitar-like instrument having five ribs, a short neck, and eight strings, plucked by a quill. In the band it substitutes for the zymbalon, which is difficult to carry around." In the western areas it is an oval-shaped, narrow-necked musical instrument, fitted out with four or five guts or stranded cords. The player holds it in his right hand, half way in his lap, and plucks it with the fingers of his left hand. Its use was presumably limited by the lyre *(lant)* and harp *(hárfa),* of German origin, which at first did not much differ from the *koboz,* as is indicated by the fact that the words for these instruments sometimes occur as synonyms. Thus Comenius, among others, mentions them together in one of his books as "either *koboz* or harp".

The *tambura* is a stringed, plucked instrument, which came to the Hungarians presumably from the south. Different instruments were designated by this name through the centuries. Comenius writes about them in this way in the 17th century: "The *tombora* consists of strings, which are tightened by small string-tightening pegs"; a quotation from the 18th century says: "A horn out of which they make a *tombora*." It may be equated with the zither in the region between the Danube and the Tisza, or rather its larger version may be called by that name. However, the most general form is in which the pear-shaped body is covered with a plate in front, out of which the narrow and relatively short neck emerges. Usually four steel cords are fastened onto it, on two of which the melody is played, on the other two the accompaniment. It is generally played sitting down, by holding the instrument in the lap. In our century the instrument was replaced by the zither.

The hurdy-gurdy (*tekerőlant* or *tekerő,* or by its newer name the *nyenyere*) came to Hungary probably from the West. We can assume that the hand or street organ *(kintorna),* often mentioned in the 16th century,

251. Beggar with hurdy-gurdy
Great Plain

was its ancestor. This word took on the meaning "hurdy-gurdy" *(verkli)* only in the course of the language reform, during the 19th century. It appears in our sources as a ten-stringed musical instrument. And that the hurdy-gurdy and hand organ may have been some kind of closely related instrument is again suggested by Comenius: "Hurdy-gurdy, hand organ: lyre."

After its popularity in the 18th and 19th centuries, the hurdy-gurdy remained in the south Great Plain, primarily around Szentes, where its most eminent makers lived. Special tools and calculations are necessary to make the complicated mechanism, and these often passed on in a family from generation to generation as carefully guarded secrets. The majority of the instruments known today are four-stringed, a few of them five-stringed. The strings are sounded by a resined wheel, which rubs all four strings simultaneously and brings them into transversal vibration. The pitch of the sound is controlled with the help of a key. Although it was tuned in *a,* it cannot be controlled satisfactorily, so that it wavers between *g* and *c.* In general, people like to tune it higher than *a.*

The hurdy-gurdy players of Szentes know three different methods of playing. They turn the wheel smoothly for the quiet *(halk)* playing and play the melody with frequent flourishes, accompanied by the strongly buzzing-humming sound of the other three strings. The *friss* or *recsegős* (fresh, crisp) method of playing provides music for dancing. A small piece of wood is fastened under the rasping string and the wheel is turned with a rhythmic motion and brief interruptions. This makes the melody, played with a strict tempo without flourishes, characteristically rhythmical. Finally the instrument may imitate the bagpipe when the rasping string is disconnected with the help of a small hook. At the melody notes the key is let out periodically. This method provided an accompaniment similar to that of the second pipe of the bagpipe.

The makers and users of the hurdy-gurdy were poor day-labourers who supplemented their income with their music. They paired it off, earlier with the bagpipe and later on with the clarinet, which reinforced the melody considerably. Most recently the hurdy-gurdy player played alone in taverns and at pig-killing feasts, and was rewarded with money, drink, and food. Only men played on the hurdy-gurdy, but the instrument itself was often given a woman's name, usually the nickname *Bözsi* (Liz) or *Kati* (Kate).

The zither *(citera)* is a widely distributed string instrument still in use today. The origin of the word can be traced back to Latin, and the word was introduced into numerous European languages, but it is impossible to ascertain its exact transmission into Hungarian. At any rate it appeared fairly late, only in the 16th century. The Latin version of the word was already mentioned by the chronicle of Anonymus, although one cannot tell which kind of instrument could be hidden behind the name.

Several kinds of zithers are known in the Hungarian linguistic region. Among these the simplest is the so-called trough-shaped one, which is usually made of a single piece of soft or hard wood with its inside carved out. In a more widespread version, one side is gradually widened, creating the so-called kid- or lateral-headed zither. In the past the head

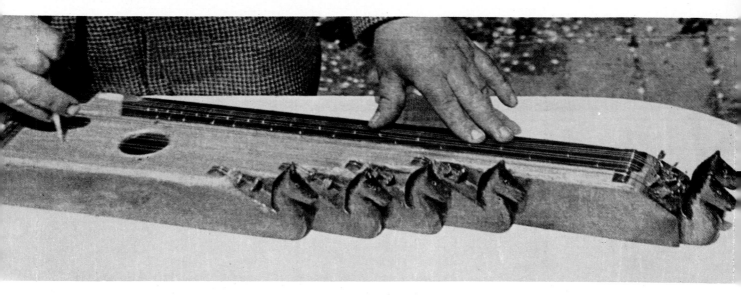

was adorned with fancy carvings, similar to a horse's head or to a snail, but more recently it has been simply rounded off, because fewer people are good at carving. The third type is the big-bellied zither, which can be differentiated from the former ones by the bulge on one of its sides. This came to the Hungarians from the Austrian–Styrian area, where they played it with the fingers as a plucking instrument. However, Hungarians use it in the same way as the above.

The great majority of the Hungarian zithers are tuned to the Mixolydian scale. The keynote of the larger-sized zithers, 70 to 80 cm in length, is around *g,* while the keynote of the smaller examples, 40 cm in length, is higher by an octave. The scale of the former includes as many as three octaves in itself, while the smaller includes at most two and a half octaves. According to the scales that can be sounded on the melody cords, diatonic zithers are used in Upper Hungary and Transdanubia, and their notes or scores are placed in one row. Chromatic zithers are general in the Great Plain, and their scores are grouped in two rows.

In the past, zither players used to play standing up, holding the instrument at a slant. More recently they sometimes sit on a low chair and place the instrument on a bigger chair. In his right hand the zither player clasps the pick, made of a goose feather, a piece of horn, or most recently of a small celluloid plate, while he holds down the cords made of steel with the help of the index finger or thumb of his left hand. As zither playing is learned easily and quickly, it was quite a widespread instrument. Generally men played it, although at some places the existence of outstanding female zither players has been recorded.

A zither, which any handy wood-working man could make himself,

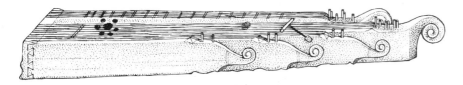

Fig. 204. Zither. Nagyszalonta, former Bihar County. Early 20th century

443

could be found in almost every house. That is precisely why the zither was always present at smaller gatherings. People also danced to the music of a zither at the conclusion of corn husking and spinning, for example. It was the most important instrument for dancing to at a Sunday afternoon gathering, and on winter evenings people liked to listen to its music even without dancing. Only in recent times has experimentation with zither bands begun, in which eight to ten participants play basically the same tune, while perhaps one or two more able rhythm players play a harmonic accompaniment.

During the last two centuries the *violin* has been the most important instrument of peasant bands and of gypsy bands. Undoubtedly this name designated some kind of string instrument during the Middle Ages, perhaps plucked, but from the 16th century it has become an instrument played with a bow. A traveller at the end of the 17th century noted with surprise that "the Hungarian violin players handle their instrument in a most peculiar manner; the stroke of the bow is very long, extended, with the kind of jerkings people from other nations cannot do". From the end of the 18th century the violin in Hungary more and more resembled its present form, following the general European development.

Cimbalom (or zymbalon) in Hungarian is a loan word of Latin origin, which spread over a great part of Europe. This originally meant the chiming of bells, but in the Hungarian language in the 15th century the name meant a percussion stringed instrument. "They sang to God with *cimbalom*", as it is written in one Hungarian codex, which shows that at this period it accompanied church music. In 1596 it was written: "... they do not pluck the cords with their fingers, but they beat them with wooden beaters and shout out the songs with full lungs". This reference is to a larger, trapezoid instrument with metal cords, which they beat with metal or wooden sticks. It was widespread in the 17th century and became an indispensable part of Hungarian orchestras from the end of the 18th century.

In the Middle Ages the majority of musical instruments mentioned above were not used solo but in bands. We can only deduce the structure of such bands from very sporadic records. One codex from the early 16th century records that after the death of King Stephen I (1038), "the playing of violins, pipes, and drums and dancing was forbidden in Hungary". These instruments presumably belonged together. Another codex originating from the same period records a search for "violin, lyre, drum, and zymbalon players" to play for a dance. A noted Calvinist preacher admonished his flock in 1563 in these words: "There are violins, lyres, flutes, and drums at your weddings, and there is no end to lyre, violin, and drum playing." Some still complain at the end of the following century: "God cries alas to those at whose weddings there is violin, lyre, pipe, drum, and wine."

At the end of the 17th century a foreign traveller described a peasant band, playing mostly stringed instruments. He observed that no matter how many there are in the band, the song is played on the same tune by the first descant and in the eighth note, which is called *contra*. The bagpipe accompanies violin players; its steady humming provides a good background to the melody. The first gypsy band—in the present meaning of the word—was, to our knowledge, formed in the middle of the 18th century by Panna Czinka (d. 1772). She herself played the first violin, accompanied by a second violin, a bass, and a *zymbalon* player. It seems that bands were expanding by the end of the century, as is testified to by the following lines of a contemporary poet:

> *One man his violin to his ear did press hard,*
> *His zither another to his knee placed up-right,*
> *To his bass violin a third hunched down crooked.*

And we can read the following from 1823: "An outstanding feature of Hungarian music is that it is ordinarily played by four instruments, such as two violins, one bass, and one *zymbalon;* however, in more recent times, they also use many kinds of wind instruments along with these." The *bass viol, cello,* and *bass* or "large violin" appeared in Hungary only in the second half of the 18th century, and from then on gradually pushed out the bagpipe by taking over its function. At the same time the clarinet also appeared, as indicated by our source quoted above.

Peasant orchestras, especially in Transylvania, where their archaic features are well preserved, retained almost till the present their extremely simple structure. The violin and cello formed a unit among the Székelys of Csík; a violin, and later on a clarinet were added to the bagpipe among the Palotses; the clarinet accompanied the hurdy-gurdy in the South Great Plain. The band of Szék in the Mezőség region (former Kolozs County) is already more complex, consisting of three

253. Musicians in a wedding procession Szék, former Szolnok-Doboka County

445

254. Drumming on the bass
Gyimesközéplok, former Csík County

255. Musicians at a wedding, with fiddle
and drum-bass
Gyimesközéplok–Görbepataka, former
Csík County

members: the violin player plays the leading melody, the viola player the harmony, the cellist usually the bass tune of the harmonies, although sometimes he plays the melody in unison with the violin. The violist brings out tunes created by treble stoppings, which are almost always major treble.

The so-called gypsy orchestras are largely a completed and enlarged version of this. The first violinist, the leader, plays the melody, and one or two viola players accompany him. They are completed by the large bass, less frequently by the small bass. In most cases the clarinet is as much of an indispensable part of this orchestra as is the zymbalon, which today stands on legs instead of being held on the player's knees. During the last decades, many of the gypsy musicians have attended music schools, which means that they became even more acquainted with the old and new style of Hungarian folk music.

Movement and Dance

Certain definite forms of movement are also very much part of ethnic and regional characteristics. Thus walking itself differs by regions, as may be observed in the difference between the gait of the people of the Great Plain and that of people from the mountain regions.

Those forms of crouching which include resting with or without a stick are most characteristic of herdsmen, especially those of the Great Plain, since mountain regions offer numerous possibilities for sitting down.

The ways of sleeping also vary, because the posture of the body is different in a feather bed and on a plank couch spread with straw, which serves as a place for an afternoon nap. During work, when someone did not want to fall into a very deep sleep, he would put a cut-down log under his head or perhaps rested on the satchel containing his scythe. Women also slept in a different posture during the break in work, lying in the straw, in contrast to their bed at night.

Certain rules existed regarding the way to wear and move in folk costumes. Thus, a woman of a Palots village, when sending off her little daughter in a longer dress, would instruct her how to step out quickly, so that her dress would not ripple like the skirts of the women from the next village, who take longer steps. The women and girls of Mezőkövesd moved in their costume with a taut body posture, chest thrown out, their skirts would swing at every step. When they left off wearing folk costumes, their way of walking changed and the body posture became less constrained.

The characteristic traits of simple and more complex movements are known today only fragmentarily, and in mentioning these we wish to provide a glimpse at opportunities given to research during the great transitions of the present.

Dancing is a form of movement regulated by tradition and bound to music, known equally in its historical depth and in its geographic distribution. The Hungarian word *tánc* (dance) is itself a European loan word which probably came into the language during the course of the Middle Ages from Middle High German, perhaps originally with reference to dancing in pairs, which was much condemned by the

256. Mangling board with sealing wax inlay showing dancers, 1868 Hövej, Győr-Sopron County

Protestant preachers of the 16th and 17th centuries. More and more dances are mentioned from the 16th century, but *Táncos* in the form of a family name may have been widespread even earlier. However, it is interesting that the peasants do not use the word, or do so only infrequently, to designate their dances. Instead they made the adjective of the dance independent: *karikázó* (rounder), *lépő* (stepping), *botoló* (cudgeller), *verbunk* (recruiter), *csárdás*. This shows that the word *tánc* remained strange to them even after several centuries.

We know that Hungarian dances have been occasionally mentioned and referred to from the Middle Ages. On the Runkelstein fresco in Austria (1320), the Hungarian queen of Polish origin, Elizabeth, leads the dance, which is similar to the round dance for girls of later times.

It seems that herdsmen were in every age not only masters but propagators and developers of Hungarian dances. The first great lyric poet, Bálint Balassi, introduced a dance during the course of the 1572 national assembly: "After the tables were removed the military youth and the grown children of the noblemen danced in the portico of the house; among them Bálint Balassa had no peer, this twenty-two-year-old son of János... in a dance form which is a speciality of shepherds, but which is held by foreign folks to be a common Magyar dance... the emperor and the king and the other princes regarded him with pleasure from a high platform, as he crouched down to the ground, snatched his legs together, then kicked them apart, then leapt up jumping high."

More than two and a half centuries later, in 1843, one outstanding Hungarian poet and lexicographer spoke of the herdsmen dances with the authority of an eye witness: "The herdsmen amuse themselves with peculiar music, singing, and dance. Their musical instrument is the bagpipe, or flute, less frequently a clarinet-like shawn (tárogató). Their songs, like the sound of a bagpipe, are muttering, and their dance, at least around the Bakony region, is a stamping dance, danced today only by swineherds, so that it is called swineherd dance. A brief outline of this dance is as follows: "The music consists of the sound of bagpipe or long flute, its rhythm entirely different from the various kinds of recruiting music or fresh [quick-tempoed] Hungarian music, and one's feet are almost compelled to stamp the rhythm when listening to it because of its very characteristic time measure. And while in the fresh dance man faces woman, here man faces man both stamping the ground, and both twirling a cudgel or stick or a shining hatchet with their fingers, and at times they throw the weapons to each other with frightening speed, and so it happens that, when the hands of one dancer are empty, the other one, armed in both hands, shows off his whirling dexterity; then they both put down their cudgels and jump over them from left to right and right to left, according to the rhythm; then one puts his cudgel between his legs and crouches down on it, while the other one circles it, sometime even jumping over it."

Historical sources often mention the *hajdú* or Heyduck dance among military dances. The Heyducks or foot-soldiers appear in the middle of the 16th century in Hungarian history (cf. p. 45). Half a century after the execution of György Dózsa (1514), a historical record already mentions that while the peasant leader was being tortured, his warriors were forced to dance a recruiting dance, also called *hajdú,* Heyduck dance. The recruiting dance here is still a "stamping dance", and the term *verbunk* (recruiting) is not used as that word appeared only after the language reform of the 19th century. In 1565, one of the Hungarian Calvinists wrote: "The bourdon pipe prompted the Heyducks to do the Heyduck dance." One Hungarian noble in 1615 sent some men with hatchets and weapons to perform a Heyduck dance to honour his son, a student in Wittenberg. They performed the dance to the sound of violins, trumpets, pipes and bagpipes. In the mid-18th century, Miklós Zrínyi wrote in regard to a celebration of the fight against the Turks:

> Some Croatian davorits★ holler'd fierce and loud;
> Some Heyducks hopped dancing with all their weapons proud.
>
> (The Zrínyiad, Canto IV.)

Brown, an English traveller passing through Hungary, also noted of this dance: "Before travelling in Hungary I had never seen the Pyrrhic dance as practised in the past by the ancients, and now by the Heyducks. They dance with naked swords, hit each other's swords, by which great

★minstrels

Fig. 205. The ways girls hold each other when dancing a round. a) Holding hands. b) Arm in arm. c) Loosely through hands crossed at the back. d) Holding on to the shoulder. e) Holding on to the neighbour's waist

clamour is created, they spin about, jump in the air, throw themselves onto the ground with surprising agility, and finally they sing in their own fashion." Three characteristic features of the Heyduck dance unfold from this description: the spinning, the jumping in the air, and throwing oneself on the ground. It is noteworthy that meanwhile the dancers also sang.

On the basis of historical notes, descriptions, and research which investigates dancing and music together and recorded them with the help of film, dances can now be divided into two large groups: the old type and the more recent. However, within these groups the possibility for further division is open.

If we look at the character of the dances, we can differentiate three large groups in the course of history. The rondes or chain-, circle-, or garland-dances belong to the first group, in which every member of the group does basically similar movements. These in part still-existing dance forms are characteristic of the Middle Ages, and their features are rooted in the collective spirit of the period. In the Balkans, where the long Turkish rule arrested and blocked development from general European trends, these dances continued to exist and in certain places 30 to 40 versions came into being. In Hungary, on the other hand, these types of dances have gradually been supplanted.

At the beginning of modern times, as an effect of Renaissance culture, the individual personality came more and more to the fore, even in dance. This is the time when a number of individual and couple-dances evolved. The ability of the dancer is clearly evident not only in solo but also in pair dancing, in which case both dancers moved independently of each other to the rhythm of the music. It is precisely in this area that Hungarian dance reached the highest degree of artistic achievement, the fulfilment of individual abilities. As is the case with folksongs, the possibilities for variation are so great that it is difficult to ascertain even the general rules of dancing. In this sense Dániel Berzsenyi, an early 19th century poet, writes the following about the Magyar dance:

> *Art cannot its hidden laws discover,*
> *Itself it obeys and its fiery soul.*

About two centuries ago and originating from the West, where the middle class rose earlier, a newer style of dancing gained ground, one regulating and binding the structure of couples dancing. Individual improvisation could not prevail in this latter form, or it prevailed to a much lesser degree. This layer of dancing spread in Hungary during the last century, but did not replace improvised dancing.

Let us consider some of the older forms of Hungarian dance, especially those that can be traced back to the Middle Ages. Such are the roundels or circle dances *(körtánc),* also known as ring *(karikás)* dances, of which some music and lyrics have come down to us, such as:

> *Ding-ho, way in, ring-ho way in,*
> *Hop in and do the round dance!*
> *Ding-ho, way in, ring-ho way in,*
> *Hop in and do the round dance!*

Up in front is justice Johnny,
Dressed in buckled jerkin,
At the back is goodwife Mary,
Oakum skirt a-swirlin'.

Most roundels are dances of girls, usually danced in the intermission of other types of dances, or as an introduction to the dancing gatherings of a Sunday afternoon, when finally the young men broke up the ring and selected their partners:

Let us stay yet for a while, for a while,
Then shall we go bye and bye, bye and bye.
We came here to dance the karikás
And wait for Mary with the bright blue eyes.

Törökkoppány (Somogy County)

The circle is always tight. Dancers hold each other's hand in various ways and, unlike the Balkan forms, they do not open the circle. Meanwhile, three kinds of movement are made. They all step inward or outward, so that the entire circle seems to be undulating. At other times they turn the circle in two ways. In the first they make two steps forward, one backward, but still moving forward with this asymmetrical form. Sometimes they all move around rapidly, taking small steps, at the same time regularly changing the direction of the ring. The roundels of girls are danced to their own singing.

In the eastern half of the linguistic region, mixed men and women roundels can be found, which fit organically into the sequence of dancing gatherings. Such are danced accompanied by musical instruments, but only two or three couples form a small circle. These are similar in form to those *csárdás* roundels that have been developing only since the middle of the last century, at the same time that certain circle-dances developed from the couples dances.

We find that the *herdsmen's dances* are a direct continuation of the Heyduck dances, and in general of weaponed dances. These are known not only in Hungary but also among the Slovaks, Gorals, Ruthenians, and the Rumanians of Transylvania. Today traces have remained in the north-eastern linguistic region and in the central part of Transdanubia.

The most beautiful forms of the cudgel *(botos)* dances are known from the north-eastern fringes of the Great Plain. The most important accessory of the dance is the herdsman's cudgel or stick. Dancers may dance alone, while trying to demonstrate their virtuosity at twirling and jumping over the cudgel. Or they may dance the paired men's dance with the cudgel, where they fence duel-like with each other to the rhythm of the music. Naturally, the striking and defending always creates new situations, so that there is much improvisation in the dance. More rarely, these dances are danced by a couple. The man playfully attacks the woman with the cudgel, who dodges away while trying to hinder the twirling of the weapon.

Although swineherd dances are known over the entire Hungarian linguistic regions, still, as we have said, the most beautiful versions have survived in Transdanubia. They use either a spontoon, hatchet or

Fig. 206. Tune of a swineherd's dance.
Dunafalva, Baranya County

cudgel, and usually jump over it after laying it on the ground. The form shows a certain relationship with Austrian and Slovenian dances, and with dances even farther afield. This also proves that predecessors of the weaponed dances existed all over Europe during the Middle Ages and flourished once more during the Turkish wars. Among the dance tunes the one below is the best known:

> *What's a-cooking, swineherd chap?—Lights with cabbage bacon!*
> *What's thou made it thick with?—Lots of belly-bacon!*
> *Tut, tut, no, no, no! what the heck thou saying.*
> *Easy it's to tell a herd by his shining hatchet,*
> *Easy it's to tell a herd by his shining hatchet,*
> *Raggle-taggle haversack and leather sandal latchet.*
> *Tut, tut, no, no, no, what the heck thou saying.*
> *Easy it's to tell a herd by his shining hatchet.*

Dunafalva (Baranya County)

The leaping dance *(ugrós)* relates in many regards to herdsmen's dances, except that it is always danced without accessories. In antiquity, *ugrós* often also meant dance in general. Therefore, we do not always know what exactly lies behind this designation. Certain of its forms were already mentioned in the 17th century: "The highest lords leap the dance with woman folk." The leaping wedding dance of Transdanubia *(lakodalmi ugrós)* is one of the most widely spread forms, although it is really a procession dance, performed when they follow the bride to church. The jumping dance of the Great Plain is danced to the same rhythms as the swineherd song, and a similar type of dance is known by the Bukovina Székelys.

The more primitive versions of the young men's dance *(legényes)* are known among the Székelys; however, this type of solo dance developed in its complexity in the Hungarian villages of Kalotaszeg and Mezőség. It is part of a whole dance programme: the young men dance it in front of the band, while the girls waiting to dance surround the lads in a rotating circle.

> Come on laddies, do a round!
> Let your boot-heels beat the ground!
> Here I help ye go around!
> Válaszút (former Kolozs County)

The *legényes* is one of the most developed, extremely varied forms of dancing. Its music and wealth of motifs are equally connected to the Heyduck and to the herdsmen's dances, and, after assimilating several European influences, it became the forerunner of the recruiting dance and its music.

Certain paired dances must also be briefly discussed, versions of which can be found in different parts of the linguistic region as the last remnant of the old style. Various western dances also affected these, and most of them can be viewed as a transformation, a Hungarianization of some of them. Among its motifs there are several resembling the *csárdás*, but differences in rhythm still preserve old traditions. Most of these dances have survived in Transylvania, where the rapid spread of the *csárdás* did not push out the older forms with such boisterous speed as it did in other parts of the linguistic territory. In Transylvania, the melodies of former paired dances are often sung to the more novel forms, such as the slow dance of Mezőség or the gypsy dance, and while singing the couples walk about for a while to the rhythm of the music.

As we end our review of old Hungarian dances, we ought to say that in the sequence of the dance programme mentioned above, a slow dance comes first, then a faster one, which is finally followed by a completely fast dance. The expression "three makes the dance" is a survival of this sequence. The expression already occurs in the 17th century: "They did not jump about goat-like, as they do now, but danced nicely and quietly, shouting every so often: 'Three makes the dance!'" The expression also appears among rhymes shouted out during dancing:

> Three the dances we are dancing
> Till the light of day be glancing!
> Mezőkövesd (former Borsod County)

The tradition of such a threefold sequence existed in the Hungarian villages right up to the most recent times.

The new Hungarian dance style reached maturity in the 19th century, but like the new folk music, it was closely linked to the traditions of previous centuries. Western paired dances became well known and served as a foundation for the development of new dances. The rhythm of dance music changed, the $\frac{2}{4}$ rhythm being replaced by $\frac{4}{4}$ rhythms, while for the faster dances the accelerating eighth note was added.

The most well known and most representative dance of the era is undoubtedly the *verbunk* or recruiting dance. The word itself, originating from the German *werben* (to recruit), was in some places replaced by the old dance name *toborzó*, revived by the language reform. At first the

257. The *legényes* dance at a wedding, in front of the church Méra, former Kolozs County

dance was closely related to the recruiting of soldiers. That is, the Austrian army supplemented its permanent soldiery from 1715 until 1868—when they introduced general compulsory military service—by means of recruiting. They determined the number of soldiers a certain market town or village had to muster and then the recruiting soldiers appeared, under the leadership of a corporal or sergeant. They praised the beauties of the soldier's life with songs and dances:

> *Kunhegyes's a fine old city,*
> *Every lad there looks so pretty.*
> *At his side a sword in scabbard,*
> *Copper chako on his forehead,*
> *Shining highboots very genteel,*
> *Tinkling spurs bedeck his boot heel,*
> *For his arse a saddle yellow,*
> *What a fine hussar's this fellow!*
> Kunmadaras (Szolnok County)

Any young man who drank from the wine and on whose head they placed a soldier's cap could no longer escape joining, and in many cases had to serve 10 to 12 years, far outside the country's borders, from where he was unable to come home on leave.

454

An excellent observer during the 1840s describes graphically the course of the recruiting dance: "... the young men stand in a circle, the corporal occupying the centre of it; the gipsy band—generally in uniform—starts up a new song, and the recruiting begins. While they are playing the first verse no kind of dance movement begins, rather the men either stand in their places making their spurs jingle, or walk around the circle, studying the ins and outs and the rhythm of the song, and sort of setting to the dance. Now come slow dance movements, in the course of which it is mostly determined who the dancer will hold eye contact with, or if it had not yet been decided then the corporal announces it, so that each takes care of the partner he has eye contact with. It is characteristic of this part of the dance that it is structured from systematized and less embellished steps, and if the song has eight beats, it goes two beats to the right, one to the left, again two to the right, one to the left, finished by a two-beat stamping back in place. After five or six such slow verses have been danced, the time comes for the embellishment, which is fresher, livelier than the former, so that now leaping here and there and up in the air follows. With the addition of the clattering of the tossed-about swords and the hesitant floating of the sporrans, the men project a real picture of a heroic dance."

One important accessory of the dance is a pair of spurs, differing from those of the horseman, which could easily have caused harm to the dancers with their point and blade. Therefore the young men wore clattering spurs, fastened to the counter of the boot, where a small piece of leather prevented them from sliding off. This type of spurs consisted of one or two rowels. On others a single or double rowel gave the sound. The young men wore those not only to dances but also on holidays, and because of them the girls recognized their coming from a long distance away:

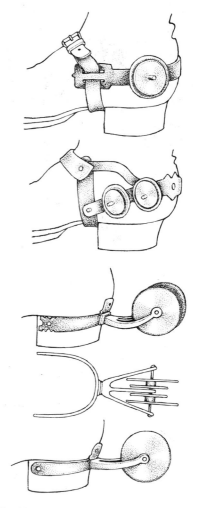

> *Late at night come not to see me,*
> *For they guard me vigilantly;*
> *See that noise of spurs you smother*
> *Just in case you wake my mother.*
>
> Hortobágy

The role of the spurs is especially great at recruiting dances, partly because they are an inevitable accessory of the equestrian soldier, partly because the rhythm of the dance is beaten with them.

The recruiting dance included the elements of several former men's dances (young men's dance, leaping dance, etc.); its unified style developed in the last century. It was generally the opening dance in the dance programme, and somewhat prepared the way for the paired dances. Two kinds can be differentiated. One is free in structure, assuring plenty of opportunity for improvisation and for displaying individual dancing skills. Mihály Csokonai Vitéz, the Hungarian poet of the turn of the 18th to 19th centuries, wrote the following, most certainly about the recruiting dance: "When during the time of the French war many English noblemen lived in Vienna, one Englishman counted 300 movements in the dance of the Hungarians who were there." We find the music and steps of the free-form recruiting dance

Fig. 207. Various forms of spurs for dancing and the ways they are fastened to the boot. Early 20th century

258. The dance called *forgatós*. Sandstone
relief
Region of Nyárád river, Rumania

among the Rumanians, the Slovaks, and even the Moravians. The
recruiting dance of the more regulated form consists of fewer and
mostly slow and brisk parts. They dance it in a half circle under the
direction of the dance leader. Certain versions are also known among the
Eastern Slovaks.

The best known dance of the Hungarians, the *csárdás,* expresses in its
name (*csárda,* tavern) the opposite of the *palotás* (*palota,* palace), the dance
of the nobility. It came into general fashion in the second quarter of the
19th century, when the recognition and discovery of the Hungarian
people's values, and the use of these values against Habsburg oppression, broke forth as a phenomenon involving national feelings. János
Garay, an eminent poet of this era, wrote: "Who would deny that the
dance is just as much of a permanent part of the nation as any other kind
of custom, its language and its songs, as well as its theatre, its music, its
costume, and its law? All these together mark a nation's identity,
making it different from any other; a nation that does not possess these is
no nation but a mass of people, not independent, the soulless imitator or
even the slave of others."

We first meet with the name *csárdás* in 1835, when the composer
Rózsavölgyi named one of his works *lassú csárdás* (slow csárdás). Very

456

soon it was danced over the entire country, and it gradually replaced various German and western dances. This dance, conceived in the spirit of national romanticism, occupied its rightful place alongside the new Hungarian folksong and the Hungarian language, and soon became all pervasive, so much so that in the second half of the century it pushed every dance into the background even among the peasantry.

The *csárdás* assimilated in itself the numerous traditions of the various paired dances which were increasingly gaining ground from the

Renaissance period on. The music itself grew out of the music of recruiting dances, to the tunes of which a great many different kinds of *csárdás* were danced among Hungarian ethnographical groups. Only men have an active role in paired dances, and in the Hungarian *csárdás* of ¼ beat, they do a movement at every quarter-value. The basic double step is partly repeated, partly the couples spin around in different fashions. As a relic of the old round dances, 2 to 4 pairs sometimes join together and dance in a circle.

261. Children's round dance
Szada, Pest County

We have already referred above (cf. p. 447) to the numerous occasions for dancing. The dancing games of children form a separate world of their own, and children learned to dance when they organized children's balls, or when at weddings the dancers attempted the first steps in a solo. The young celebrated the conclusion of certain bigger work projects (harvest, threshing, processing of flax, etc.) with dancing. Dance was an inevitable, important element of communal work (corn husking, hoeing, spinning, etc.), and such work was undertaken in the first place with the prospect of the celebration that followed it. Smaller gatherings (spinning, pig-killing feasts, stripping of feathers, etc.) have rarely taken place without dancing, when one instrument or another (zither, bagpipe, violin, flute, etc.) provided the music. At other times dance was the sole purpose for getting together among the young people (in a dance house, and at Sunday afternoon gatherings, etc.), and in the winter they even held balls. At baptisms, only a smaller dancing celebration was organized, but the entire wedding procession was built of the most varied dances. Records also show that at one time people even danced in the cemetery, and the funeral feast also had its characteristic dances.

In short, as we have said before, dance played a significant role in every aspect of the life of the Hungarians.

459

Folk Poetry and Prose

The Theory of Hungarian Folk Poetry and Prose

By folk poetry and prose we mean those works which were born among the wide masses of the working people, or those which spread and became popular among them. As we know, it has been customary to designate the entirety of all these works by the international term *folklore*. The word itself originally was intended to mean "folk learning", the knowledge and science of the people, "what the people know". It later began to be understood as the branch of knowledge engaged with various manifestations of the intellectual life of the people (folk poetry, folk music, ornamental folk art, customs, beliefs, etc.). In this sense, research on folk poetry and narrative can be looked·upon as one of the branches of folklore.

We must emphasize that when we speak of folk poetry and prose we use the word "folk" in the sense of "working people", so that we do not exclusively mean by it the peasantry, as did most of the authors of earlier works dealing with folk poetry and prose. Industrial labourers, the workers, also have their own folk poetry.

For that matter, the folklore of the industrial workers and working peasants is in contact in many ways, which is primarily explained, besides their fight against common exploiters, by the fact that a significant part of the industrial workers in Hungary have come and to this day are from among the peasantry, and bring along to their new employment the songs and stories of their village environment. The traditional contentual and formal world of these songs and stories continues to leave an impression on their literary creations.

A significant part of the commonly known works of Hungarian folk poetry and prose was born among the working peasantry. In Hungary old folkloristic traditions were preserved especially by rural workers, the small peasants who possessed a few acres, and the middle peasants. Béla Vikár had already ascertained by the end of the last century that only poor peasantry preserve the creations of folk poetry and prose. Similarly, Kodály and Bartók established that they could find valuable and ancient melodies only among poor peasants. Zsigmond Móricz also writes in his autobiography that it was unbecoming for a prosperous farmer to sing or tell stories: the well-to-do farmer listens to the tales in the spinning room, or at the scouring of the hemp; he goes to see the comic customs. He stands there and regards the poor folks enjoying themselves. But it was socially impossible for him to participate in the story telling or group singing. Therefore it was the working peasantry who basically created and preserved the oral traditions and customs of the peasantry. The contact of rich peasants with folk poetry and prose pertains to the narrow layer of jokes and anecdotes, to worthless "folksy", composed songs, and to certain forms of customs, which in the latter case are used precisely to show off the rich peasant's prosperity.

However, not infrequently certain poetic literature could become folk poetry and folklore. Among the poetry of the Hungarian poets, many songs of Petőfi especially became popular countrywide. The popularity of such poetic works is explained by their content, which expresses the sentiments and struggles of the people. "Hit" songs can become temporarily fashionable and may spread to folk poetry, but these, just like the sentimental composed folksongs of the second half of the last century, do not belong to folk poetry proper.

A significant part of folk poetry and prose reflect the life of the workers, as demonstrated not only by Hungarian folk poetry and prose, and by the folk poetry of the last 200 years, but by the tale set in Egypt, known by the title *Complaints of a Peasant,* which bewails the sufferings of the peasantry in 2000 B.C.

In relation to historical songs and myths, we shall speak in detail of what heroes the Hungarian folk remember from their wars of liberation, and, in the course of discussing certain literary forms, we shall also discuss the question of revolutionary traditions. However, in this connection a few, in themselves expressive, examples present themselves, and unmistakably manifest the revolutionary passion of the people, that explosive hatred with which they have wanted to strike back at those who have beaten them through centuries. Let us mention the popular group of tales called "Is the farmer angry?" *(Haragszik a gazda?),* which belongs to the humorous tales. When hiring his young farm hand, the farmer stipulates that he will not pay him if the farm hand gets angry during his service. The tale ends with the victory of the farm hand, who destroys the farmer's fields and house, sets a bear upon him, and always asks, "Are you angry, farmer?..." Or let us mention those story types known by the name *Nagy Kolos* (Big Kolos), *Kis Kolos* (Little Kolos) (cf. Ill. 270), as well as the story type of *Igazság és Hamisság* (Justice and Duplicity). In these, the rich peasant of the village is confronted by the poor man of the village. The rich walks over and tries to destroy the poor, but the poor peasant triumphs in the end. It is not surprising that one collector was told: "The only justice lies in stories; why can't people be like that?"

As a conclusion to these examples we shall quote a folk anecdote (recorded by Kálmány). It becomes obvious from it how clearly, also instinctively, the Hungarian folk saw in 1914 the connection between capitalism, imperialism, and the war. "When the war broke out, the king (Francis Joseph) sent a message to Rudolph, who was popular with the masses: 'I will pave your road with roses.' 'Pave it rather with the heads of the rich Rothschilds', was the message Rudolph sent back with the runner. 'That one thing I cannot do my dear son, because they print the money for my war.' That is the reason why prince Rudolph never came home."

However, the content of the previously quoted folk tale not only shows the close-knit unity of folk narrative and folk history, but also focuses on the great agitative power of the former.

Therefore, both folk and composed poetry, which in general we call literature, belong to the superstructure. Views which try to deny the superstructure character of folk poetry and prose and seek instead to emphasize that in folklore "permanent", "above-class", "continuous" elements can be found just as much as in language, are misleading. The misunderstanding in this case comes about in the following way: folk poetry and prose actually have formulas, motifs, formal elements which appear to be permanent and continuous and seem as if they have lived through centuries, up to the present day. However, these formulae and motifs reflect a given social and economic foundation, and detailed analysis also shows that after the foundation of certain such formulae and motifs has weakened, the motifs, by continuing to serve a new foundation themselves, become carriers of new content. One main characteristic of the elements of folk poetry and prose is continuous transformation and change. However, it is certain that the formulae and motifs of folk literature that developed in the past, and even its contextual elements in the feudal as well as in the capitalist period, often betray surprising relationships, although they are never completely identical.

It is indisputable that the development of folk poetry and prose depends on the laws of the superstructure, and thus is determined by the rules of social life, just like in composed poetry.

However, literature as superstructure and, within it, as ideological form, has its own particular character. It reflects reality through artistic method, it introduces reality, and by this means urges us to change it. This applies both to folk and regular literature.

The formal characteristics of literature and folk poetry and prose are also similar. Language provides the means of artistic expression in both, and their main genres (song, ballad, etc.) are related, or are frequently the same. Furthermore, many written works can become folk literature and thus part of folklore, or else help turn folk literature into "high" literature. Furthermore, the difference between the two forms is in the final stage of disappearance in socialist society, as the old folkloristic works are spread not just by word of mouth among the peasantry, but also through books, theatre and radio, and are becoming the treasure of the entire nation, its "literature".

While emphasizing the unity of folk and written literature, however, we must not forget that folk literature, right up to the present time, was transmitted through *oral tradition,* except for a slight layer expressed through written forms. Written poetry on the other hand has relied from the start on literacy and writing. That all this is not merely a formal difference we can ascertain, among other things, by the Latin name for literature, the word *literatura,* which originates from the word "letter", so that it includes in itself the concept of literacy. The Hungarian word *irodalom* (literature) also includes the concept of literacy (*írni,* to write). Literature, therefore, tried from the start to fix the work of art in writing, as opposed to folk literature, which has relied on the vitality of the living word of oral transmission. Of course, until the 18th century, the living word was strongly influential even in the sphere of composed literature. But while folk literature was not written down until the beginning of conscious collecting, composed literature has always been characterized by the intent to record, even in its earliest forms. For example, alongside the performers of Homeric poetry, the aidoses and rhapsodes, the preservers and explainers also appeared, who were the first developers of Homeric philology and pointed towards literature based on literacy.

One of the main characteristics of folk poetry and prose, on the other hand, is that it can be treated only *within* the framework of a *community*. Every episode of its birth and survival is passed from mouth to mouth; this, on the other hand, also means that it is under the judgement of a constantly changing, constantly correcting, creative community. Not counting a certain amount of isolated humming and singing, folk poetry and narrative is created in all its forms—the small stories of belief and superstition to the dramatic genres—in front of a communal presence, and with its creative participation. This is the cardinal rule characteristic of all folk poetry and prose. There are even some outstanding folklorists who see in this single feature the differentiating character of folk and written literature. Thus Bartók himself says in his definition of folksong that what can be considered as folksong is something the community has accepted, holds to be its own, and constantly lives with.

Literature also reflects the community, the class, the nation. However, there is still a difference between the two. In the world of literature, the reflection of community influence and social reality always takes place through individual creativity. This is demonstrated, for instance, by the different ways Goethe and Schiller, or their Hungarian contemporaries express the same social problems at the same time. Individual intention and talent in folk poetry and prose can only express themselves and their class within the traditional framework provided by the community.

We have, therefore, arrived at the point where, by examining the relations and quantitative differences of folk poetry and prose, we can establish that while in literature the community is reflected through the individual, and while all that is alive in the community is always expressed individually, the situation in folk poetry and prose is the opposite: individual quality and individual creative desire are expressed through the traditional forms and material of the community. All the succeeding conclusions follow from this law of ours.

One other basic difference comes from the fact that folk poetry and prose is tied to certain occasions. Folk poetry, especially until its old world of forms arrived at a state of decomposition, was strictly tied to occasions. Today in Hungarian folk poetry we rarely find this restriction to occasions and this rigidly consigned place of poetic manifestation in the life of society. The most characteristic feature of the restriction to occasions is that it was proper to sing or recite certain types of lyrics only on certain occasions and only by certain persons. For example, old women singing love songs were frowned upon. Béla Bartók and Zoltán Kodály often mention that it was precisely those old women who remembered the old material well, who were unwilling to sing the love songs. Or there are story types which could be told only by men, others that could be told only by women. Similar restrictions can also be found in plays and dramatic folk performances.

Because folk poetry and prose exists through oral tradition, and because it always occurs in some community, and within that, is generally tied to some occasion, it is constantly subject to *change*. For example, it is impossible to imagine that a novel would have as many versions as there are people who read it. On the other hand, a folksong or story often changes according to the character and composition of the community in which it is performed. Thus the story teller revises the story, weaves allusions into it, according to his audience. In folk plays the audience becomes a participant of equal rank in the play, a factor which also shapes and changes tradition. At the same time, in written poetry, from the beginning of the reign of literacy, every author, every poet strives for uniqueness, for unchangeability, insists on the finality of his rendering. The authors of antiquity were outraged if anybody changed their works. We know, for instance, that Horace attacked in his satires those who wanted to alter his work. Of course, variations of themes do appear within literature, yet if we regard the codexes either of antiquity or the Middle Ages, the number of versions is insignificant compared to the multitude of variations existing in folk poetry and prose. In short, a typical trait of folk poetry and prose is its existence in variations through transformations, and that its creations are never so final that time can no longer make an impression upon them.

In the course of the more recent research into folk poetry, the former mechanical view of evolution cannot be applied. It cannot be stated that individual works of ancient folk poetry and prose had an original "prototype", a so-called "archetype", the first and best formulation of individual texts and that afterwards every variation was a worse version, a mere corruption of the original form. It is evident, for example, that the recent recordings of numerous tales and ballads include motifs which appear much more lively in their recent form than in recordings made many decades ago. This is exactly why we must investigate individual texts, not from the point of view of the archetype, of "timelessness", but always in their own age and in the context of social relationships. Furthermore, comparison among the elements of form and content of some folk poetry and prose is possible in only such a way. Similarly, this view makes it possible to realize that a new creation can be even more beautiful and more valuable than the old.

Earlier folk poetry researchers also felt that it is difficult to grasp the phenomena of change and change itself. Among the Hungarian researchers, a music folklorist, János Seprődi, first noticed these phenomena at the beginning of the 20th century and pointed out that a whole lifetime would not be enough to gather all the variations of songs in even one village, because every melody is constantly changing: the same one singer changes the same song in the course of its repeated performance. Among the Hungarian researchers Zoltán Kodály pointed out in connection with the ballad *The Wife of Mason Kelemen* that within certain large epic songs the same melody and stanza structure alter from stanza to stanza in the course of the performance.

Since then, more and more researchers have become interested in the interrelation of change and traditional form. In this particular characteristic of folk poetry, important features of content, form, rhythm and stanza structure are repeated in the course of the performance, but at the same time they still go through some kind of a change. The changeability of folk poetry is a very significant factor, because it provides an opportunity for the old traditional form to become enriched with new content.

464

As we have already mentioned, certain rules can be set down about the question of change. Prose, narrative, and, in general, epic traditions are the most strongly subject to change; transformation by the individual is possible in these genres. We know of tales told for several days and reshaped by the teller. Ballads and historical songs belong to this category. Here we can observe a loose oscillation between the more rigid restrictions and free changeability, because the stanza structure and melody restrain the performer, and do not allow as much freedom as do prose presentations; yet opportunities for free interpretation are possible. There are also some transitional forms between ballads and prose epics: ballads that are sung may be transformed into prose epics. The most rigid restrictions is in the realm of small lyric units.

We must emphasize in this connection that folk poetry, the traditional oral lyric—with the exception of a very thin stratum—always exists together with melody. It is impossible either to understand or to explain correctly a folksong without its melody. Furthermore, the coexistence of poetry, melody and dance also characterizes a significant part of lyric oral tradition. János Erdélyi, the first great summarizer of Hungarian folk poetry, called the folk ballad the "opera of the people", with singing and dancing united in an organic whole. This refers again to one of the basic differences between folk poetry and prose and written literature, since in written literature, as the result of literacy, the interrelationship between lyric text and melody had ceased fairly early.

A further difference between the two is that while in written literature increasingly complex literary genres can be observed, folk poetry is characterized by relatively few literary forms, by repetition of content and motif, and by simplicity of structure. This difference is also expressed in the fact that folk poetry is generally shorter and smaller in scope than written poetry, although in some cases oral tradition has been capable of preserving works really large in scope.

However, in spite of its fewer literary forms, a limited number of themes and inner simplicity, folk poetry is still a monumental art form. It would be a mistake to believe that only intricacy and complex beauty represent the greatness of poetry. On the contrary, numerous examples of folksongs exist with emotional richness expressed in a simple pentatonic melody, and a short lyric folksong can approach in its own simplicity the greatest works of written poetry. The main aesthetic reason for this is that folk poetry gives a total reflection of its own society, fulfilling the theory of aesthetic completeness both from the point of view of form and of ideological content.

After all this, let us turn to one of the most important and most debated questions in the theory of folk poetry, namely the relationship between the individual and the community in creative activity. When interest in folk poetry was just making itself felt, the question had already appeared: who is it who creates works of folk poetry and prose? Is it individuals, or some kind of "mystical", anonymous community? Two points of view locked horns from the start. One—and Herder must be mentioned as first among its representatives—designated the "national community" as the originator of works of folk poetry. According to this view it was the community, and not an unknown individual creator, a poet, that produced folksongs. Hegel added to this that works of folk poetry came to life by involuntary, spontaneous creativity, so that it is their natural quality, directness, and character that speak to the entire nation. The theory of Herder and Hegel that folk poetry is "created" by a community can be traced to the most modern conceptions. Bartók on his part also pointed out that a nation would be unable to compose independent melodies by individual creation; he too claimed that the community itself, and the traditions of the community are responsible for creating, preserving and changing works of folk poetry and prose.

The theory of the communal origin of folk poetry clashes in many respects with the point of view of those who explicitly deny the folk origin and character of folk poetry and claim that because it is nearly impossible to find folk writers in person as authors of folk poetry, folk poetry is nothing else but the string of individual creations of "upper" social classes, descending down to the people through a corrupting process and thus turned into folk literature, evoking the feeling that it speaks of a separate poetic world, the world of folk poetry, only because it is primitive in nature.

The entire history of folk poetry and prose and the example of known folk authors prove the opposite of this theory. Naturally, we must not forget that the individual signs of creative activity are not as apparent in folk literature as they are in the sphere of written literature. Even the most talented story teller or singer hears from early childhood and then year after year, through innumerable versions, stories that the story tellers of previous generations have been telling. Tradition works in him when he starts telling stories and he tries to assert his own personality, to incorporate the experiences of his life and fate into the story through the bequeathed poetic material. The author's personality is expressed through given tradition, and it is also demonstrable that new types, new forms come into being under its influence which then, on the basis of the bequest of an important singer or story teller, can become new examples of community creation.

We know several characteristic types of story tellers. One is the faithful type of performer. He clings to the restrictions provided by tradition, and does not want to deviate from it at all. Many story tellers say that they heard the story in a certain way from their fathers, grandfathers—this was the custom in story telling, and they do not wish to deviate from the practice; should they make any changes, the tale would lose its meaning.

Another type of story teller asserts that someone who knows ten tales, if he has some imagination, can make even a hundred tales out of them. Such a story teller feels that he is able to recreate tradition, and therefore can be looked upon even as a kind of "poet". Within this type we can differentiate further types. One outstanding Soviet folklorist, Asodovsky, mentions a Siberian woman story teller, who always simplified the tales. She shaped the long and verbose tales into brief, epigrammatic ones and wove into them her own personal experiences, sorrows, wisdom, creating meanwhile veritable little masterpieces. Her opposite is one who elaborates, such as the famous Hungarian story teller Mihály Fedics, who often interweaves other tales into the main stream; remembering a new tale, he pays no attention to the trichotomy of the tale, but turns it upside down, connecting the old with the new tale, adding jokes to it, improvising according to the requirements of the audience.

A newer group among story tellers is represented by the type who explains, interprets the story, and tries to dress it up in more sober form and to bring it closer to reality. This type often simplifies and narrows down the world view of the tale. There are fine story tellers who try to connect the theme to historical events. They feel that the entire presentation, the entire spirit of the tales is irreconcilable with and unacceptable to the real world, and yet the inner truth of the tales' tradition is such a constraining factor for them that they must find an explanation for it.

Finally we must point out one more feature of folk poetry and prose that likewise points to a difference between folk and written literature. Among the listeners to oral folk poetry and prose, *credence,* the *desire to identify,* is much greater than among the readers of regular literature. We know that it is not possible to really experience and absorb a work of art if we do not accept that particular reality presented to us by the author in his work. However, in the case of literature, the identification is a paler factor than among the audience of folk poetry, ballads, and tales. Trust is much greater towards both folk theatre and the creations of the story tellers, than in the sphere of written poetry and prose.

The same applies to the self-consciousness that appears in a work. A writer is consciously the author of his work. The theory of conscious composition has a lesser role among the creators of folk poetry and prose, while instinctive creative force has the greatest role. However, we cannot accept in itself the romantic theory that only instinctive, communal folk creation exists, because within the restrictions already mentioned, folk poetry and prose also exhibit implicit creative consciousness. But behind every form of written composition, there stands the proud self-awareness of poetic immortality, the *exegi monumentum* of Horace, which looks beyond the poet's own existence. On the other hand—to quote Goethe—"collective modesty" characterizes folk poetry, that is to say, no feeling of authorship, no self-awareness of the immortality of the author's individuality is connected with its marvellous creations.

Folk Poetry Folksong

Patriots interested in literature read the following in the January 1782 issue of the *Magyar Hírmondó* (Magyar Courier) of Pozsony edited by Mátyás Ráth: "It is known with what great diligence the English and the French are gathering the old poems and songs not only of their ancestors but also of peoples living far away. Similar undertakings by the Italians are not less known. It is really necessary to bring up the Germans, since everybody noticed in what great respect old histories, epics and many similar kinds of songs are held among them. Who does not know how they are attracted by old poems heard from the lips of the common folk, called *Volkslieder?* They began to gather and value these since the time they started to cultivate their own language and with it the *belles lettres.*"

This is the way the first country-wide summons begins, which combined praise of the national language and of old literary works, urging the collection of Hungarian folk poetry. After a few preliminaries, after almost unconscious collecting, and after the copying of hand-written manuscripts, this summons looked upon research into the national language, the national literature and the poetry of the people as an inseparable unit. The credit for this belongs to the philologist Miklós Révai, who lived in Vienna and observed from there the Western European steps taken in the discovering of folk poetry. Révai's plan was a great Hungarian lyric collection, which would contain old lyric works, the material of collected manuscripts of songs, and folk poetry which preserved the characteristics of different types of dialects—a collection that would also be a good tool for studying the Hungarian language. Ráth supports this appeal; he refers to the European discovery of folk poetry, and urges its collecting at home. And so, though it came late, the collection of folk poetry was launched.

The reason for our limited knowledge of the history of Hungarian folksong is not least of all the persistent persecution of the people's songs by the Churches through the centuries. It is indeed true that for a long time only the voices of sharp criticism, disapproval and accusation could be heard in regard to folksongs and flower songs. In 1583 Miklós Telegdi raised the following among the questions of Confession: "Did you sing or listen to *flower songs* with remembrance to physical love and sensual feeling?" What was destroyed of folksongs can be well understood from this one question alone. For the Protestant and Catholic Churches, even listening to such songs constituted a grave sin. Péter Bornemisza, Calvinist preacher and writer, complained in 1578: "All ears are now wishing only for frivolous entertainment... to listen to flower and love songs..." The leading figure of the Hungarian Counter Reformation, Péter Pázmány, speaks of "repulsive flower songs". In 1679 the Cantus Catholici, in writing the following, represented the dangers even of sacred folk music when sung in the Hungarian vernacular: "The larger part of the congregation was drawn from the Roman Holy See by the sweetness of the sound of songs." At the same time puritan Calvinist village communities could be found even in the recent past, whose closed, rigid rule reflected the old preacher's antipathy towards singing.

And yet when we speak of Hungarian folksong, the Hungarian past is revealed to us in all its complexity; indeed, we may say that folksongs accompanied the nation's history. We know, for example, that lamentations and certain children's songs carry the memory of thousands of years; they speak to ethnomusicologists about the way the Magyars sang of the period of the Conquest. From later centuries, the legend of Bishop Gerhard recalls to us the serf girl singing while at work. We know that the armies of Dózsa sang their own fighting songs, which, however, have disappeared without a trace. *Kuruc* poetry flourished during the War of Independence led by Prince Rákóczi; the 1848–49 War of Independence was accompanied not only by Petőfi's fighting songs but also by longing, hopeful folksongs. That is why Béla Bartók and Zoltán Kodály maintained along with the poet Ady at the early part of the 20th century, that folksong and folk music are a sharp weapon of political opposition and struggle; that is why, between the two world wars, the outstanding poet Attila József made use of the metaphoric and structural forms of folksongs in his own poems.

Apart from a few sporadic notations, the discovery of the Hungarian folksong began at the end of the 18th century. Csokonai, poet of the Enlightenment in Hungary, wrote as follows: "Let us descend to the ignorant, simple peasant village, then there shall be less curious pronunciations before us." Next the words of Kölcsey during the age of literary romanticism, calling attention to the values of folk poetry: "We must seek the real spark of national poetry in the songs of the common people." Furthermore, János Erdélyi declared that the life and poetry of the people is like an ocean into which the poet must wade to rejuvenate himself. Kriza goes even further: he knows that folksongs, the material of folk poetry, have to be sought among people of the "true class", namely among the working peasantry. Along the path of such precedents Petőfi carried the Hungarian folksong to triumph.

However, it is unfortunate that we are only still at the very beginning of folksong research. Although Bartók and Kodály completed the major part of their work on the determination of musical structures, and Bence Szabolcsi has completed his into the research of melodic history, similarly complete examination of another important area, the lyric texts, has not yet been done, and the so-called hidden folksong material has not yet been recovered. Consequently, a great future task of research is to develop the progressive traditions which are expressed in folksongs, to develop the total wealth of the idealism and formality hidden in folksongs and to recover every episode of their historical eras. Our survey, therefore, can only be an outline, merely the designation of a few important aspects of the folksong. We owe the first significant examinations in this area to Imre Katona, who helped us with his essays in analysing prosodical, stylistic and formulaic matters, and his works defining categories of genre.

Here, by way of introduction, are a few words about the difficulties. The determination of classical aesthetic genres does not apply to folk poetry, where it is possible to encounter a series of contentual and formal genre transitions. We find strings of such genre transitions, or even the most varied genres, within the genre of the folksong. Lyric love songs, laments, merry lyric songs, work songs, soldier and outlaw songs, herdsmen's songs, the traditional forms of mocking rhymes and songs, dancing songs, songs of girls and young men may be mentioned, just to list the main types of the folksong. Through so many varieties of genre it would be difficult to find even in the work of a single poet that basic tone, that unified final message which his poetry is trying to express. What should we say about the folksong then? Among its "poets" are the Hungarian centuries, the bitterness, hope, sorrow, and happiness of an oppressed people, of the serfs at first, later on of the peasants, the lyric inspiration, rhythmic playfulness of anonymous poets, and the centuries-old reshaping, recreating, power of the anonymous community. But the influences which the people received and made use of are also present, shaped to their own language. All of this is therefore an extensive process, and it is in actuality a very difficult task to grasp its unified characteristics, to display the final meaning of the message, to research without controversy the theories organizing its forms, while seeming to fit these into a few generalizing formulae and beautiful expressions. The folksong is a reservoir of messages, genres, and poetic forms.

It is worth pointing out that besides transitions in genre, in general the entirety of folk poetry is interwoven with identical or similar formulae like very fine veins, and often with related content episodes. A widely-known example is an anti-clerical story. One of its suffering heroes is most often a priest, sometimes a cantor or a teacher, who hides in a chest or the fireplace in his fear of the husband, and whose seductive, adulterous intention is unmasked by a clever young servant lad. A song with this theme has also come down to us.

Ruddy tankard, red wine hot,
Up the flue the rector's got;
Come on down, your reverence,
Gone my man, and good riddance!

This song is known in several versions.

On leafing through the collections of folk poetry, the entire peasant life, work, and the customs of the most varied occasions are revealed to us. In truth, on the basis of folksongs a kind of summary could be written of peasant life, of its order, of the rules governing work, of exploitation, of the pains of the peasantry, and of the helpless abandonment, the consequence of which is that the working people—despite all their revolutionary temper and explosive, bloody rebellion—could not for a long time take its own fate into its own hands. The history, the limitations, the prison that was daily peasant life are all present in these folksongs. How clearly, for example, the following folksong speaks of the one-time fate of the Hungarian people!

I shall go and plough His Highness' land,
Sow my country's sorrows in that land.
Let it be known to His Majesty
All we reap is bitter agony.

Sorrow springs from bosoms, fields of woe,
Nothing but affliction Magyars know;
Bless him, God, His Royal Majesty,
He should on his subjects have mercy.

Though the song itself may have originated in the early 19th century, it could be the motto of the long centuries of Habsburg oppression. It presents a sombre picture of shackled humility, the bitterness of serfs, the abandonment of the Hungarians, and the hopelessness of failed rebellions. Often, though the fate of the working people appears in songs almost unnoticed:

Summer shower's coming down hard
On the kerchief of my sweetheart.
Gentlefolk it never falls on
Nor on them who rot in prison.

It would be interesting to analyse the hidden references of the song: the well-known opening formula of the "Kossuth Song", the nobility secure in their palaces and the suffering prisoners in the bottom of dungeons, as well as the figure of the peasant working on his field, woven into the lyric of the formula for a love song. An entire feudal society appears in the four lines of a gentle little tune. It is instructive to observe how the election songs *(kortesdal)* were passed on to the folk or were formulated and changed by the voice of the people. One version of a popularized election song addressed to Mihály Táncsics goes like this:

On my roof with holes and patches,
Not a stork alights or hatches;
And the taxes are so heavy
That the beam near falls upon me.

Sheriff he comes full of power,
Cares he not we cry or cover,
But he takes the clothes we have on,
With our wheat he loads his waggon.

Old King Joe said, just you listen,
He will teach us one good lesson.
Three can only buy one sheepskin,
Yet we bear the taxes' burden.

This is what the poor man's lot is,
No one comes to help the cotters;
From the cradle cares attend them.
And the grave alone will help them.

There are also innumerable versions of this song and of songs like it, various formulae which bear a relationship to historical songs. Songs of exile, songs of anger expressed against the Austrian tax assessors, election songs of 1848, dance songs mix and intertwine through the formulae, and what is even more decisive than the formulae, through the continuous reflection of class relations of the working peasantry.

There is no room to do so here, but the analysis of how the slogans of the Hungarian people's historical struggles and class warfare are expressed in folksongs, open parables and hidden formulae would deserve a special treatise. It would be worth examining how explicitly the folksong presents to us the layers of peasant class division, how precisely it differentiates between the prosperous farmer, the poor peasant eking out a living on his tiny strip of land, and the landless cottier; how it differentiates between the peasant, the pick and shovel man, and the herdsman; and how the separation from the village of the young men and girls, going off to industrial work, finds its way into the folksong. The folksongs tell what the peasantry thinks of a sly judge, of the servants of the nobility, of rascals who wander off after young wives, of the entire oppressing apparatus of the feudal state. All the oppression, the social conflicts and the alliance of the exploiters appear in the lively melodies of—let us say—an outlaw song or soldier song:

> *Russet trousers sheath and cover both my thighs,*
> *Under them the coarse cloth drawers none espies;*
> *Torn my shirt is, but it's hidden by my blouse,*
> *Still I have my beetle-bright-eyed lover's vows.*

However, to introduce the peasant songs that reflect the historical and social battles and the everyday work of the peasantry is an inexhaustibly great task, since to do so we would have to quote the entirety of the folksong wealth.

And just as the folksong reflects the historical and social battles of the people (to avoid misunderstanding, we might mention here that the everyday life of the peasantry, from the gentle forms of love to revelry, to social life, to work, etc., all find a place here), in like manner these songs reflect Hungarian history even in their style and not just in their message. However, this historical-stylistic aspect of the folksong has not yet been suitably defined. But we can confidently say that the stylistic directions of the feudal age can all be found in folksongs, right down to the more uniform, homogeneous peasant tones of the songs that suddenly flourished in the 19th century and created a new era of folksong. Because consciously initiated collecting is related to this period, most of our material is processed and published. It is remarkable that in the period of early capitalism, which fought for national markets and a national language, we can speak of a special blossoming of Hungarian folksongs and of their melodies. The new style of Hungarian folk melodies developed at this period, as has been observed by Bartók and Kodály. The uniform formula system and expressions of folksong lyrics also point at this time towards the development of a new, more permanent style. We can actually speak of the Renaissance of folksong. Folk costume and ornamental folk art also gained a new, enriched, and colourful direction at this time. It was as if during the ascending phase of capitalism the peasantry believed for a moment that the time of liberation had arrived. Briefly now let us take one by one the questions of form related to folksong. The first point is that the lyric text of the folksong is inseparable from the melody. Very often it is also inseparable from the dance of some rhythmic movement. This rule, the organic relatedness of melody, lyric, and dance, refers not only to folksongs but can also be found among certain groups of ballads. It is a normal phenomenon from the 19th century on that in the life of a folksong, melody and lyric can change hands easily, but the laws governing this have not been sufficiently researched.

The question of the verse forms of the Hungarian folksong is so complicated that we more or less have to be satisfied with simply referring to the problems. Some researchers hold that dance rhythm is the most ancient element of Hungarian verse, and that dance rhythm gives rise to verse through its effect on melody and lyric. Others believe that the structure of the language itself, its manner of presentation, the accentuation, the structure of the fluctuation of long and short syllables, determines the rhythm of Hungarian poetry. It was Kodály who first pointed out that prosody cannot be examined independently from melody.

It is generally held that the ancient structure of Hungarian verse has a strongly accented two-stress line, and has as its oldest structural formula the "ancient eight" and the subsequent folksongs of 3 to 4 beats, which give the basic elements from which Hungarian verse structure has developed. The Finnish *Kalevala* was built in the eight structure, and 70 per cent of the Hungarian folksongs were written in this form. Beside this, we also meet, although less frequently, with twelve-syllable, four-beat folksongs, which have descending rhythms. The lines become longer in the newer folksongs, and these in many cases form a transition in the direction of the written song.

One of the most characteristic features of Hungarian folksong is the end-of-the-line rhyme. A less frequently occurring form of this is the cluster rhyme, when all four lines rhyme. We find this mostly in historical songs. In a decisive majority of Hungarian folksongs, double rhymes harmonize at the end of the lines, when two lines following each other end in similar rhyme. The latter can also be looked upon as an old characteristic, because it prevails similarly in the poetry of the related nations.

According to Kodály, the Hungarian verse stanza is constructed on the base of the four-line stanza, and all subsequent narrowing or enlarging comes from this basic formula. Similarly, Kodály pointed out that Hungarian folksongs are characterized by a single-stanza structure in general, and that when several stanzas are also connected to each other in content, it is a later formation (we will not consider at this time the stanza structure of epic poetry).

Besides the inner content and formal elements, we must also speak of those modes of expression, the structural characteristics of the inner form, which are inseparable from the inner message and practically exhibit marks of definition by content. Among these features of Hungarian folk poetry which can be considered general, we shall emphasize the realistic nature of depiction, which insists on verity, and the dramatic method of depiction, the dramatic construction manifested in Hungarian folk poetry and prose.

Aesthetics justifiably distinguishes folk realism, or more precisely, the realism of folk poetry and prose. This realism is not an explicitly Hungarian feature of folk literature, but precisely because it is, in our case, the sensitive expression of Hungarian peasant reality, it is still a particular determinative.

Recently, more than one outstanding poet has mentioned the "surrealism" of Hungarian folk poetry. We think this is only a specious assertion. Even in the earliest poetic forms, playful and grotesque elements already occurred in use: the playful, meaningless mixing of merely tonal elements, the use of exaggerated images, and of comic adjectives and verbs. This method is also alive in Hungarian folk literature, from tall tales to comic folksongs, folk poetry employs the obviously unbelievable, grotesque elements of exaggeration and caricature. This method of characterization, by the way, exists in the often untranslatable idioms and playfulness of any language. It should suffice to refer to such adjectives as can be found in the expressions *tűzről pattant menyecske* (a young woman "popped off the hearth", i.e. lively as popcorn), or *hamvába holt* (a young man "died in his own ashes", i.e. very dull), for although we could analyse their folkloristic background, still they show the descriptive power of the language.

Among the stylistic methods of the Hungarian folksong, one of the most important is *contrast* or contradiction, by which the message is emphasized and underlined. Words, ideas, and expressions of contrary meaning appear within a single work, mostly within a four-line stanza.

> *I did give some* pure wheat
> *To the* gentle *pigeon,*
> *But not even* tailings
> *To the* churlish *pigeon.*

The contrasts that occur in Hungarian folksong are for the most part individual variants, although in the final analysis they can be simplified to positive-negative couplets. These behave completely independently and take their places in the centre of the songs. Sometimes the contrast runs through the entire work, at other times it is limited to certain words, in the majority of cases to the noun, less frequently to the adjective. We can assume that this is an old characteristic of the Hungarian folksong, and its occurrence is extremely frequent.

Among the stylistic features of Hungarian folksong, we direct attention to *exaggeration,* which lends it a graphic quality, expresses the content better, and thus increases its effect to a considerable degree. Two forms are frequent, overstatement and understatement.

> *Oh, my angel's* lips *and* eyes *are*
> *Worth much more than* Castle Buda,
> *'Cause up there the lords are owners*
> *But she mine is, I alone hers.*

> *Such is the world, such it now is,*
> *It is like the hazel's flowers;*
> Much *they promise,* scantily *yield,*
> *What they yield is* bitterest *yield.*

Exaggeration is a relatively frequent phenomenon of folk poetry, but overstatement, often of a cumulative nature, occurs much more frequently than understatement. However, the various phenomena of exaggeration can be observed not only in Hungarian folksong, but in other genres as well, primarily in the folk story.

At one time it was fashionable to discover mystical symbolism among the lyric symbols of Hungarian folksongs, and these symbolic systems were often explained on the basis of unhistorical, and sometimes idealistic theories, and at other times according to various false psychological explanations. Thus, some saw in the colour yellow, which occurs in folksongs, the hypothetical colour of ancient mourning. They tried to explain this among other things, by the yellow colour of barracks, county seats, and prisons in Hungarian songs. However, the county seat is yellow in folksongs for the simple reason that the hated county seats and barracks were yellow in reality, being plastered in the so-called "imperial yellow" or "Maria Theresa yellow", fashionable in the 18th century. The reason why the Austrian national colours of black and yellow showed up in Hungarian *soldiers' songs* to express a melancholic state of mind is just as obvious. This system of symbols, manifested in colours, is not some kind of an ancient system, a psychological mystery, but the combination of the colour of the oppressive authority with the black colour of mourning, strengthened by connecting black and yellow. We could quote folksongs in which yellow reflects a feeling of happiness and love, instead of separation, sadness, and death. Folksongs take their images, their natural depictions from everyday life.

Colour symbolism changes not only by region and area, but can acquire different meaning in the course of time even in the same place. To take yellow as an example, in a given case it can also mean passing, mourning, and sorrow. There is always a realistic ground for it in this case, since the sick and dead seem pale and yellow:

> *If you proved a faithless lover*
> *May the graveyard's clod you cover.*
> Yellow death *should bid you farewell,*
> *Take you in his wings to black hell.*

At the same time it can also mean love, and often such a meaning can be demonstrated in folk custom:

> *Sometimes we choose red apples to cut in two:*
> *Nutbrown lad you'd better not come me to woo.*
> *Don't sit on the edges of my* yellow *bed,*
> *If you love me, in the middle lie instead.*

In this case even the apple has a special significance. In some places the young man sent it to the girl if he wanted to ask for her hand. If the girl sent it back cut in half, she accepted his proposal.

All of this shows that in the historical research of symbols we must deal very carefully and circumspectly and can come to conclusions only on the basis of cautious and detailed examination of a large body of material.

The same also applies to the flower motifs, which from the earliest known times have been the inevitable elements of Hungarian folksongs, which is why these are called flower songs *(virágdal)*. In the historical songs, the flower generally meant the darling, the lover. Roses, carnations, gillyflowers, rosemary often appear in more recent times. All these are flowers that were generally grown in the gardens of medieval fortresses. Perhaps they found their way into the small gardens of the peasantry, which, placed in front of the house, were tended by the daughter, so the identification of the lover with the flowers growing there is easy to imagine:

Languish, rose mine, languish,
For you gave me anguish;
While to me belonged you,
What a red rose were you!

There's a woman with marrying daughters,
One is a pink, marjoram the other.
Pink says this to marjoram so calmly:
My sweet rose been pressed into the army.

These few examples demonstrate the development of a highly advanced symbolic system of folk poetry and, within it, of folksong. However, this system has changed and been reshaped constantly in its content and outer form, because it has always reflected the world around it and always adjusted to new circumstances.

We could build up all the details of peasant life, peasant work, and society from the various groups of Hungarian folksongs and ballads, and could get the entire world, living and inanimate, that surrounds the peasantry. The many images and turns of Hungarian song cannot be understood without a knowledge of the customs or activity of everyday life to which the songs refer. Not only was folk poetry embedded in the everyday life of the peasantry, not only did it reflect their most significant ideas, behaviour, and emotions, but it also took its adjectives, images and its figures of speech from the realm of peasant existence. We can take at random any one work of folk poetry and find that even the finest emotional vibration is expressed by symbols taken from everyday life.

For example, how realistic are these few lines of the following song, and what a great feeling of infinity they arouse:

Nutbrown lassie's sitting on a laddie's knee
By the Tisza under a great poplar tree;
Now the lad is gazing at the river's waves,
While the lass is gazing at her star a-blaze.

This is how the horizon of folk poetry expands to the cool stars, but all the feelings, thoughts, and total life it includes within this spacious infinity is expressed by the poetic methods of perceived, known, immediate reality. In this poetry, even symbols are expressed by the language of reality; they cling to reality and reality is the secret of their monumental simplicity, inner truth and pure power.

We believe, among other things, that exactly this feeling for reality, this folk realism of expression, makes Hungarian folk poetry so economical in its use of formal poetic means. Hungarian folksong applies adjectives sparingly, and positively avoids their accumulation. It does not customarily describe or characterize with adjectives, but rather with visual elements and with the rich uses of verb mood and verbal prefix. We hardly need to prove that this method of description is more compact, more realistic and related to reality. Hungarian folk poetry only uses a few permanent adjectives which really describe the subject and phenomenon, and if we read the Hungarian lyric folksongs with

476

attention, we are surprised at the almost puritan simplicity of their means of expression. Even in the songs that appear to be the most ethereal, folk poetry portrays, with clearly delienated pictures, a series of actions and scenes which follow one another. On the other hand, it always avails itself of adjectives precisely when the adjective gives a grotesque, peculiar effect, the power of a mood; at these outstanding turning points, certain adjectives glow with an almost conscious care, but to all the greater effect.

This expressive, descriptive method of realism in folk poetry is most certainly closely connected with another of its significant features, the methods of dramatic construction, dramatic condensation, and characterization. We cannot claim that dramatic character is an important feature of Hungarian folk poetry only, but neither can we say that it is a general and prevailing descriptive method of the entirety of European folk poetry. Among the surrounding peoples we find examples of the dramatic method of construction primarily in the Slavic lyric genres.

Can we really speak—no matter how figuratively—of the dramatic character of Hungarian folksongs? Do we have such structural elements as would testify without strain that the theory of dramatic construction can somehow also be achieved here? We must differentiate between the purely lyric folksongs and other folksongs, meaning by those, songs transitional to various epic songs, narrative songs, or to dance songs, to the groups of outlaw, soldier, and herdsmen's songs, and to those historical folksongs which cannot be classified unequivocally into some artistic category. In these groups of Hungarian folksong we can also find elements of dramatic construction, the active form of presentation, the construction by scenes, living images, dramatic dialogues, or forms of presentation resembling dramatic monologue. We cannot state that this dramatic method of construction is exclusively confined to these groups, since among them we can also find many songs possessing a narrative, epic character and unfolding more clearly. Often the drier, descriptive stanzas or more clumsy structures do not at all resemble a dramatically condensed performance. In other songs, the lyric elements prevail. Still, looking at the entirety of these groups of Hungarian folk poetry, we find that the decisive majority—and precisely the more valuable, the more poetically formed songs—are dramatic in character.

However, what can we say about the simple lyric songs composed of one or two stanzas, or the lyric stanzas independent of each other, and strung on a line of a single melody? What kind of elements of dramatic construction can be discovered in these lyric songs, commonly called folksongs? The goal of these small lyric masterpieces is often just the development of a single image, a single sentiment, a passing thought: it is not likely that they can be forced into the theory of dramatic construction. The overstraining of a thought, its application to everything, is always dangerous. Therefore we mention merely as a supposition that perhaps we could still discover one formal episode of dramatic construction in these small lyric songs, a sort of formal germ of the dramatic method of portrayal, of the dramatic construction which breaks into contrasts. We are thinking of a well-known, permanent characteristic of Hungarian folksong, the natural opening image, and of the theory of its structure and stanza construction and aesthetic effects. One characteristic of Hungarian folksong is the so-called *opening natural image*. This is the primary verse-opening element of Hungarian lyric folksong, and even more than that, it very often is not only an image initiating a verse, an opening image, but it appears in every stanza of the poem as well; that is to say, it is a structurally decisive element. The natural image divides the lyric song into two parts, an introductory part, which is the natural image itself, and the second part, which carries the emotional, intellectual content of the poem. The natural image may be an invocatory introductory image, but it can consistently move through the entire song and sometimes divides the stanza with a practically regular construction:

> *River Tisza rolls on downwards,*
> *Never will it flow up backwards.*
> *Still I have my sweetheart's kisses,*
> *Let her take back those she misses!*

Beside this division of the construction of the verse according to form and content, let us mention the division (of ancient origin) of the melody of the folksong: the so-called fifth construction also divides the melody. Therefore we can say—perhaps with a bit of exaggeration—that this peculiarity of the construction of Hungarian folksong pervades almost every one of its important elements. Insignificantly few are those lyric folksongs in which the natural opening image, or the natural image dividing the verse in two, would not appear in some form as one of the most important structural elements of the construction of the verse.

It is interesting to collect the most important groups of opening images, not as if we would expect from this to illuminate their origin, but rather to make it easier to look them over.

In many cases the opening image and the section following are parallel to each other; the emotional, speculative section that follows the opening image answers it almost as a reflection in the mirror:

> *Winds of spring the roads are drying,*
> *Chains of frost and ice untying;*
> *Seeking mates the birds are flying.*
> *"Say my sweet rose, who're you choosing?"*
> *"Lad as straight as reed I'm choosing:"*
> *When the winds begin a-playing,*
> *This way and that he'll be swaying.*
>
> Kibéd (former Maros-Torda County)

We can name another analogous group, but we can attach to these songs the so-called local and occasional associations, since they too are only drawn from among the analogous images of folk poetry:

> *Oh how tall you greenwood have grown!*
> *Oh how far you sweet dove have flown!*
> *If I could that greenwood hack down,*
> *I could take my sweetheart back home.*
>
> Tata (Komárom County)

478

The linking of contrasts is also frequent when the song expresses emotions and thoughts contrary to the mood the opening image:

> *In my garden skylarks sing so blissfully,*
> *Lover mine a sad letter has sent to me.*
> *Reading it my tears of sorrow fall like rain:*
> *Death alone will, death alone will part us twain.*
>
> Magyarpécska (former Arad County)

It happens that the natural opening image breaks away from its original setting and is used only as a formula:

> *Violets put forth blooms that are blue,*
> *Fall in love more, I shall not do.*
> *Rather I shall rein my heart in*
> *Than to let it do its harmin'.*
>
> Ipolybalog (former Hont Country)

Certain ones are used only for the sake of the rhyme, and these opening images have lost their logical-social connections:

> *Peeping from behind the trees, the moon has come.*
> *Lily of the valley mine, my peerless one.*
> *How I love that sweetly speaking tongue of yours,*
> *With which you so often have enticed me false.*
>
> Magyarpécska (former Arad County)

Finally, we also find some which have lost their meaning completely, have become obscure, at least for the purposes of today's examiner.

> *Aye the nut tree it has branches high and low,*
> *Only one girl gives me pleasure who I know.*
> *While in her weak mother's arms she carried her,*
> *Even then she gave me for to marry her.*
>
> Püspökbogád (Baranya County)

Grouping is not yet an explanation of origin, and it does not shed light on why such construction of the lyric song should be so popular. In the former question we can follow the idea of Béla Vikár, that the natural image developed from pairing and parallelism; at the beginning, the second part repeated the first verbatim, then the parallel image stepped into the place of one of the paired members, which essentially corresponds with the former, and from this beginning, supposedly, the many-branched Hungarian lyric song evolved. Most certainly this notion is attractive, since the repetitive structure indeed stands at the beginning of every versification. Hungarian versification became especially fond of this structure, which divides into two and makes lively even the most simple, small lyric unit.

Hungarian folksong created a marvellous variety of the application of the opening natural image. Often the opening image practically changes the lyric monologue to dialogue, gives room, as it were, to the inner tension of the lyric situation, builds a scene, makes the performance rich, enrapt, intimate. Lyric folksongs show at every step examples of this structure, just as do the examples above. To complete them, let one more stand here, collected by Béla Bartók:

Flowery hemp of mine,
It's in the retting-pit,
If you be cross with me,
Do not come spinning it.

I have dropped spindle mine,
No one does pick it up,
If my heart's sorrowing,
No one does cheer me up.

Gyergyóújfalu
(former Csík County)

We are thinking primarily of such songs when we look for the germ of dramatic character in the formal structural theory of the opening natural image, when we look, as it were, for its expressive character in the formal element. As we do not want to exaggerate and distort, we should add that this example (and we could point to lyric folksongs that display more or less dramatic liveliness) means only that even in the shortest lyric folksong the method of dramatic construction and portrayal can be found, along with the exposition of the opportunity provided by the natural image. We are thinking of the happy meeting between the melody building and the verse-building structural theory of the natural picture, of the opening picture, that is, and the tendency of Hungarian folk poetry to dramatic formation, its dramatic gift. This is why among the Hungarians the poetic tension, the tense balance of the natural opening image and of the second part that replies to it, emerged with special richness, creating numerous structural forms by starting out from the simple poetic device of the repetitive structure.

Application of the natural opening image has the further merit of helping to assure the purity, the simple beauty of rhyme in the folksong. That is, it deepens, it enriches the connection of the rhymed lines, because it is not only a mere tonal, outward, formal part of the pair of rhymes, but it reinforces emotionally, often even in content, the harmony of the rhymes. And it is unnecessary to emphasize that the perfect effect of rhyme is built on the best possible harmony of the already mentioned three factors—namely, when tonality, emotional mood, and the meaning of the message resound at the same time and together. The Hungarian folksong achieves this pure, inner sound precisely with the help of the natural image.

Comparative research into the opening natural image has taken only the initial steps. We already know that it is not exclusive to Hungarian folk poetry. Research to date has shown that it also occurs in the poetry of the peoples related to the Hungarians; it also shows surprising parallels with the folk poetry of the Bashkirs, Western European parallels have also been found in Italian and Swiss Ladin folk poetry. The further west we go, the less frequently this verse construction occurs. The Rumanian permanent opening natural image is known: it is the green leaf, the *frunza verde*. This structure is very frequent in the lyric folksongs of the Slavic peoples. The Ukrainian, Russian, and Slovak folksongs in particular favour introductory natural images of lyric tone.

Although this summary is very compact, with all the potential errors of enforced condensation, perhaps it still demonstrates the wealth, beauty, and power of Hungarian folk poetry. We thought that by way of introduction we should speak of the kinds of ideas which have directed the historical development of Hungarian folk poetry, and of the kind of inner, shaping force which has worked in every period of folk poetry in the most varied genres, and finally of how and through what creative theories the national form manifested itself in folk poetry.

We shall introduce in the following few groups the most characteristic types of the Hungarian folksong, but naturally we cannot attempt even an approximation of completeness.

From every perspective, love songs occupy a central position within lyric poetry, their numbers and proportion surpassing that of any other lyric group of songs. They are the ensemble of both the oldest and the newest types of works, that is, the most stratified lyric group of songs.

Love Songs

262. A peacock with a flowering bough, detail of a mirror-case. Somogy County

481

Through the stages of occasional songs, lyric development flows, the effect of love songs at the same time radiating to every neighbouring and related group of songs. If anywhere, it is here where barriers of genre cannot be lowered, so that it is also very difficult to group love songs according to uniform standards.

Predecessors of the love songs are the flower songs *(virágének)* of the medieval period. We are able to trace their influence and survival in phrase and images, and even in construction. In the notes written by János Sylvester Erdősy to accompany the first complete translation of the New Testament, published in 1541 at Sárvár, he observes that one must get used to the parables of Jesus, and that "it is easy for our people to get used to them, because the nature of such talk is not foreign to them. They live with such talk in their daily speech. It lives in songs, especially in the flower songs, through which every nation can admire the sharp nature of the Hungarian folk's inventiveness, which is nothing other than Hungarian poetry". This praise of János Sylvester Erdősy also gives the first brief formulation of the poetics of the Hungarian folksong. The comparison with the parables, the reference to speech in images, which may refer to the opening image of the folksongs and to their great variability, and the laudatory expression in regard to the adroïtness expressed in this "discovery", show that contrary to the opinion of his contemporaries, the famous translator felt the beauty and richness of the folk poetry of his era. Of course, at this time folk poetry and written poetry were not in any way sharply separated, so that the recognition could have been applied to both.

The sound of the flower songs often echoes in the love lyrics in the motif of the nest building bird, which is known in numerous variations:

Once a wee sweet birdie
Used to come to see me;
In my flower-garden
Made her nest and stayed she.

But the evil people,
They began to note it,
And the nest the bird built,
Off the tree they smote it.

Off the bird went flying,
Now her cage is empty;
These are words she sent back:
In the spring I'll see thee.

But she never came back,
Little bird came not she,
P'haps she found some new love,
And she did forsake me.

If she fails to come back,
I shall know she found one,
And her aching heart there
Someone else must have won.

If she fails to fly back
When the wheat grows ripe-red,
Then I'll know we won't be
Nevermore united.

Kászonimpér
(former Csík County)

Among the lyric songs the love songs are the least tied to occasion; most could be sung by anyone, regardless of difference in occupation or anything else. The great majority are typical and general; everybody can consider them his own. Although in lyric songs the individual does not express himself through the community but directly, he does so as one of the types of his society and not as a person different from others; the old types of songs spoke not of the emotions themselves, but rather of the effects of the emotions, and did not name the beloved, but rather mentioned her as a flower or bird.

In recent times we can observe the presence of many kinds of basic lyric situations, more shaded sentiments, various character types, etc. However, every basic situation, character type, and emotional state is almost immediately typified; instead of shading, praise or even judgement is expressed in effective images. Furthermore, sorrow appears to be a greater inspiration than happy love.

The result of the above-mentioned generalizing and typifying is to render fixtures, as it were, adjectives, personifications, etc., permanent, which sometimes creates a highly stylized atmosphere. It could easily appear as though in these love songs everything is symbolic, although in reality it is a matter of often repeated poetic devices, the legacy of the initial and, at the same time, elementary stages of the lyrical mode of expression, the meaning of which could already have faded away.

The extraordinarily rich love songs can be divided into a great many groups according to the basic lyrical situation and expression of sentiments. One or the other of these criteria can be distinguished from the other even historically. Thus the little bird who carries the love message is one of the most favoured elements:

Sweet birdie, sweet birdie,
Chattering sweet birdie,
Take what I've written her,
Take what I've written her,
Fly to fair Hungary.

If she asks who sent it,
Tell her, bird, he sent it,
Whose despair and sorrow
E'er his heart do harrow
Till the woes have rent it.

Szuha (Heves County)

The Hungarian folksong, which speaks of the garden of love, of its blossoming, its fragrant flowers, can be traced far back even historically. Songs recall the gardens of medieval fortresses, later the peasant gardens in front of the house, tended by the marriageable daughter:

Fig. 208. Carved decoration on grave-posts. Nagyszalonta, former Bihar County. Early 20th century

483

Hi, ho, marjoram,
Larkspur, pink and sweet William,
Lily of the valley!
If your garden I could see,
There I'd pick red roses free,
Right my heart would rally.

Hi, ho, marjoram,
Larkspur, pink and sweet William,
Redolent lavender.
If your garden I could see,
And I could your gard'ner be,
That would do such good to me.

However, most of the songs praise the beauty of the beloved with rich images or intone the sorrow of the abandoned lover:

Loveliest fair angel,
Our world adorning,
Brighter is your laughter
Than the rosy morning.
Whiter still your face is
Than a driven snow-field,
Blacker are your two eyes
Than the beetle's black wings.
Thank you sweetest angel,
That you so adored me,
But I thank you also
That from you you've shoved me.
On my life the sun shall
No more set nor rise up.
'Cause I have completely
Drained my bitter life's cup.
Now my mind goes wand'ring,
Of my love bereaven,
Like a lonely swallow
Wheels below the heavens.

Szaján (former Torontál County)

Others tell us that love means heartbreak, it is fleeting, that nobody should love deeply because it is not worth it, that it is also unpleasant, because the world with its gossip brings ruin on lovers whose mothers forbid them to meet:

Grass there grows not such aplenty
As they are that bear me envy.
Thorny briar that I live in,
Kapos town I must be leavin'.

Much as I have loved you ever,
Now it is, dear, through and over;
Our true love's done and ended
Just as your foes have intended.

They would banter as we chatted,
When I eyed you, they were at it.
Let their tongues wag, I don't worry,
If I loved you, I am sorry.

Mother, you can stop your prating,
And the whole world its berating.
Much too often did you scold me,
May your ill works harm you, oldie!

Lovers are separated from one another primarily not by envy and motherly prohibition, but by social circumstances, which at one time were not only kept account of in the Hungarian villages but often remained an insurmountable barrier between young lovers:

Born a poor man ever I stayed that way,
Though my rose I loved her truly alway;
Envy it has took her away from me,
Now it has all made a beggar of me.

I would go and dwell in a far country
Where I am all strange to all and sundry.
Gladly would I go unto the world's end,
So I don't get no one with me burdened.

Zsigárd (former Pozsony County)

Don't you come, don't you come at our door anockin',
If you should have less than three good pair of oxen.
To an ox-proud lad they gladly would me marry,
Down-and-outs are thrown out if too long they tarry.

Déva (former Hunyad County)

We find in these the pain of estrangement, abandonment, and permanent farewell, as well as refusal, rejection, and even a curse:

O I feel so poorly,
Death's upon me surely,
It is my betrothed lover's mother's curses
Must have done it to me.

Dare not no one curse me,
Not even his mother,
Just because her nutbrown, sloe-eyed darling son I
Never did love ever.

Had I loved him truly,
Now his wife I should be,
All under that church roof tall we should have sworn a
Marriage vow till doomsday.

Őcsény (Tolna County)

485

These groups of love songs are much more balanced than groups of other types of songs; the basic lyrics are strongly blended or "contaminated"; at the same time, it is precisely the love songs which were transformed most frequently into other kinds of songs (soldiers', harvesters', seasonal workers', etc.). It is no wonder, therefore, that we meet with certain stanzas in four or five groups of love songs or other kinds of songs. Naturally, being lyric, love songs bear the closest, most intensive and reciprocal relationship to the songs of wandering and soldiers' songs, though they are also related to love letters, cursing songs, and certain types of ballads as well as mocking songs and, in modern times, songs of migration to America and of seasonal workers.

The territorial division of various kinds of songs is fairly equally distributed. However, on the Great Plain the group of love songs is somewhat more accented than other groups. It is also true that the oldest love songs come in the largest numbers from the eastern edge of the Hungarian linguistic region (Székelys, Csángós of Moldavia).

Historical Songs and Songs of Valour	In this group of historical songs and songs of valour *(vitézi énekek),* we find a good number of songs, some that are partly folk in origin, some that have become folklore, and some connected with other events than their genre would indicate. At the same time they illuminate the historical awareness and knowledge of the people, which barely extends further than three or four generations, so that it is in vain to expect in these songs names of persons or exact time sequences. Folk poetry is not some kind of history of events but rather an emotional judgement of certain situations and groups of events, which can be manifested in identical or similar ways in difficult eras. Yet in spite of all this, in Hungarian folk poetry the turning points of history have been well selected, those moments when the cause of the people, the cause of freedom, came to a decisive turn. This is why we find a good number of folksongs referring to the devastation caused by the Mongolians and Turks, songs recording the feelings during the time of the 17th and 18th century insurrections under Thököly and Rákóczi, and during the 1848 War of Independence. Folk poetry selects heroes who truly represent the people: King Matthias, Rákóczi, Kossuth and others.

King Matthias (Mátyás), the Renaissance ruler who lived in the 15th century, is a frequent figure in folk poetry, but we meet him first of all in legends. The song below was supposedly sung at the time of his election as king, but it has also found its way into collections of folk poetry:

> *All his lands, not one excepted,*
> *Mátyás as their king elected;*
> *He it was that God has sent us*
> *For to keep Hungary protected.*
>
> *That is why we've chosen him, too,*
> *As a gift from God in heaven.*
> *Thanks be given for it to Him*
> *Ever and aye say we: Amen!*

The devastation caused by Turkish-Mongol troops has been preserved more by legend than by song; politically motivated and military men liked to repeat these even later on, which is why collectors found few such songs, and these are likely to have been born in later times:

> Do you see, my true-love,
> Yonder dry old asp-tree?
> When its leaves are greening,
> Then shall I, dear, see thee.
>
> God, I know my own tree
> Will again all green be,
> With the blooming spring-time
> Back again thou will be.
>
> Let us fell it, true-love,
> Yonder dry old asp-tree,
> Let us make it into
> A gallows high and sturdy!
>
> Let's the Turkish sultan
> Hang upon them gallows,
> Let him cause no mothers
> No more griefs nor sorrows.
>
> Hódmezővásárhely
> (Csongrád County)

A few scanty memories have remained from the time of Turkish rule, not infrequently in the songs of outlaws *(betyárdal):*

> Word I'll send the pasha up in Gyula town:
> He had better leave us outlaws well alone;
> If he does not, lordamighty! he'll repent it sore!
> I shall go and bring his head back beard, mustache and whiskers, all!
>
> Nagyszalonta (former Bihar County)

At the time of the Rákóczi War of Liberation (1703–1711) the hope glimmered that the Hungarians and the Carpatho-Ruthenian and Slovak peoples, who lived together with them, would be freed from Habsburg oppression. This is why the serfs poured out to serve under the flags of Prince Rákóczi and why songs about this can be found in the folk poetry of all three nations. The following is a successful version of a written work which became folklore:

> Swift the Garam's waters
> to the Danube hurry.
> Following its course down
> Storms a Magyar army.
>
> Gallant Magyar fighters,
> Briskly, at a gallop,
> Off they ride to battle,
> Legs both firm in stirrup.

487

Fain I would be riding,
With the horses flying,
For my dear old country
Gladly would be dying.

Koroncó
(former Győr County)

The following is the folksong most commonly known and most widely spread in the country, considered to be of Kuruc origin (the Kuruc were Rákóczi's soldiers).

Such fine man as you, Tyukodi comrade!
Not a Blaise Kucuk, who has us betrayed.
Let there be then in our land feast,
Wine to celebrate!
Many fillérs, many thalers
Costs this war, comrade!

Tyukod (Szatmár County)

After the defeat of the insurrection, Ferenc Rákóczi died in Turkish exile, but hope for his return echoed in folksongs for a long time to come:

O Rákóczi! O Bercsényi!
Victors proud of brave campaigns, ye!
Our wounds are still a-gaping,
Our pains are not abating.

O Rákóczi! O Bercsényi!
Victors brave of proud campaigns, ye!
Were you still among the living,
You would be this land defending.

Mezőberény (Békés County)

Soldiers' songs *(katonadal)* after the Kuruc era, just like songs later on, talk about the miseries of soldiering for foreign interests:

Up at the country's end
Stands there an apple-tree,
Singing are under it
Two men of cavalry.

Ever they keep singing:
Life is but bitterness,
Life is such bitterness,
If you go dinnerless.

All ye poor boys, listen,
Take good care and mark this:
Anyway keep out of
Military service.

For to join the army,
It is lifelong slav'ry;
For to join the army,
It is lifelong slav'ry.

Hadikfalva
(Bukovina)

The youngest shoots of the historical and heroic songs that live to this day are connected to the 1848–49 Hungarian War of Independence. At this time the Hungarian serfs were liberated from under feudal authority, and memories of this act are preserved in folksongs:

Eighteen hundred eight and forty
Was the year that freedom won we;
Serve we shall no lordships ever,
All the world is free forever!

I have land to plough at leisure,
Bide my lunch-time at my pleasure.
Love is all I have for dinner:
Hug my sweet rose for to win her.

Kalotaszentkirály
(former Kolozs County)

Lajos Kossuth, the leader of the nation that was fighting for its liberty, stands in the centre of the songs; more than five hundred songs about him have been recorded by the collectors. Over the entire country the well-known "Kossuth Song" in particular became virtually the symbol of the War of Independence. The following is one among the many versions:

Lajos Kossuth sent a summons:
He is short of troops, battalions.
If it's two or three that's missin',
Gladly we shall thirteen send him.
Long live the Magyar!

Lajos Kossuth sent a summons:
He has too few troops, battalions.
If he once more sends his callin',
All of us must go and fall in.
Long live the Magyar!

The Great Plain

The mention of the second message refers to an old tradition, namely, that, when in the Middle Ages the king called the nobility to arms, they gathered only at the second call. We also find the "Kossuth Song" among the neighbouring Carpatho-Ukrainians (Ruthenians) and Slovaks. The young men voluntarily joined up under the flag of Kossuth, because they knew that their blood would be spilled in the cause of liberty:

Now the rose is putting forth its tender buds,
Lajos Kossuth's flag is unfurled, hoisted up.
Many fine lads swear allegiance under it;
Each would die if Magyars' country wanted it.

I shall also join a fighting company,
Petals strewn by girls will me accompany.
In the ranks shall I be known for bravery,
And before long captain they shall make of me.

I shall have a sword of steel made unto me,
Stamp on it the coat-of-arms of Hungary;
I shall cut of walnut tree a haft for it,
Have the name of Lajos Kossuth carved on it.

Borsodszentgyörgy (former Borsod County)

This successful, half-folk creation already appeared in newspapers during the War of Independence, and it spread widely among the people. And when, faced with the superior number of the enemy, the Hungarians surrendered on the field of Világos, near Arad, songs like the following took wing:

Silken flags in battle field are fluttering,
Round them mourning Magyar lads are gathering.
Don't be crying cavalrymen's faithful band,
With your blood must you redeem your motherland!

Arad heard the band still play a merry tune;
Then Világos came to be the country's tomb.
God Himself bemoaned us and he seemed to doubt
If one Magyar e'er could ride that tempest out.

Sorrow gripped the heart of every soldier
When he fled to Hungary's fair frontier.
Up to knees his horse had waded in the blood,
Yet they nipped the country's freedom in the bud.

Galgahévíz (Pest County)

Afterwards the Hungarians in their songs continued to expect Kossuth's return, along with the return of his generals and that of the leader of the Italian wars of unification, Garibaldi:

Dirty is my tunic,
Soiled my underpants too.
Kossuth brings us clean ones,
Stevie Türr the brass guns.

Kossuth, Klapka, and Türr,
All will come again in,
Marching with an army,
Twenty thousand—thirty.
Long live Garibaldi!

490

> *Ravens wait for corpses;*
> *Few the swords and horses!*
> *We shall get 'em, shan't we?*
> *To the last must fight we.*
> *Long live Garibaldi!*

The songs of the War of Independence were collected primarily from the centre of the country, from the Great Plain, and only much less frequently has a version or two come to light from the peripheries of the linguistic territory.

The songs of wandering *(bujdosóének)* stand in close relationship with the corresponding songs of the Kuruc period; at other times they harmonize with the outlaw and soldier songs. There are many songs of pseudo-folk origin among these as well, songs which more or less became folklore and spread over larger or smaller areas. These half lyric, half epic works tell about the sorrowful feelings of various people excluded from society (deserting soldiers, orphans, disappointed lovers), usually in the first person. When the text speaks of a strange environment we do not need to think directly of a foreign country, since most of them sing only about the bitter parting from the place of their birth.

Songs of Wandering and Captivity

As to the content, many songs sing the sorrow of parting, of the separation from country, lover, and family, and of the feeling of uncertainty in a strange land:

> *I did leave behind my country,*
> *Famous dear old little Hung'ry;*
> *As I looked back, half the way gone,*
> *From my eyes the tears did roll down.*
>
> *Woe my dinner, woe my supper,*
> *Woeful is my every hour.*
> *As I watch the starry heaven,*
> *Of my crying there's no ending.*
>
> *God I beg you give me lodging,*
> *Tired I have grown of wand'ring,*
> *Living aye a lonely outcast,*
> *Day and night my tears roll down fast.*
>
> Gyula (Békés County)

This song is known, at least in its components, from the beginning of the 18th century; it exists in many versions, primarily in the eastern half of the linguistic region.

Criminal offence often figures among the reasons for wandering, something that has no remedy:

> *Murky, foggy weather, bracing winds a-blowing,*
> *Time when but an hour thousand years is showing.*
> *Up among the clouds, the moon is brightly riding,*
> *Over hills and dales, a boy goes there a-hiding.*

Father, mother oft would warn and bid me do good,
Yet I turned a deaf ear like a naughty boy would:
Leaving home I went out, outlaws' life to lead there,
Of a robbers' gang I soon became the leader.

Palotsland

This was recorded in the 1840s, and the influence of one of Petőfi's folksong-like poems is strongly felt in it. We often encounter in these songs a sense of longing for the lost lover, mentioned as a bird:

Bonny bird it goes a-hiding,
Calls at every wood, alighting.
Such a poor and lonely critter,
Just as mine, its lot is bitter.

Bonny bird it goes a-hiding,
Calls at every wood, alighting.
Now you see, they cast me out too,
Sweet, I wander all without you.

Vojlovica
(former Torontál County)

Variants of this song known throughout the country barely differ from one another. Sending mail by birds is very frequent in wandering songs, which we can often trace to the 16th and 18th centuries:

Yond a cloud is coming, dark, so black and stormy,
There she preens one corbie, black as black she can be.
Bide you raven, come down, take my letter, fly ye
To my folks and also ringed betrothed bridie.

If they ask about me, say that I am ailing,
In a strange land hiding, no more than a strayling.
Those that I have loved so, if but once could see them,
That would give my sorrowing heart quick and soothing balsam.

Diósad (former Szilágy County)

Sometimes the hope of returning glimmers through; at other times the wanderer returns to visit the parental home in a sort of vision:

Dear old home, my land beloved,
Wish I saw the borders of it!

Skyward, dimly, in the distance,
Smoke I see arise in wisp thence.

Light the candle, light it, mother,
I shall see you, wait me supper.

Boil some sweet milk, now your son comes,
Put into it fresh-baked bread-crumbs.

> *Let me have a cheerful supper,*
> *Such as none makes but you, mother.*
> Székelyland

The songs of captivity *(rabének)* and prison songs *(börtöndal)* are related
to the songs of wandering, and we can trace certain of them back to the
18th century. These also speak in the first person, grieving about the
sorrow of prison life and about the separation from homeland, family,
and beloved. The songs are often related to outlaw or soldiers' songs,
although they may be considered an independent group because their
permanent framework is the prison and loss of freedom. There are also
epic features in them, especially as they tell about the judicial trial and
everyday life of the prison. Prisons of the past century were important
places to learn songs, and among these songs, prison songs were
naturally the first acquired. Some songs give an account of the beginning
and end of prison life with epic authenticity in three stanzas, but with the
idioms of folksong:

> *'Twas when I to Komárom town*
> *Came in fetters, hands and feet bound.*
> *All the girls they wept like raining,*
> *When they spied me iron chains in.*
>
> *Don't be crying, little shy 'uns*
> *That you see me put in irons.*
> *Day will come when they release me,*
> *Not for aye shall I in jail be.*
>
> *When the clock strikes and has struck one*
> *To the door the gaoler will come.*
> *"Get your things, rogue, go you, get hence,*
> *You have done your lawful sentence."*
> Alsóegerszeg (Baranya County)

In general, the reason why the prisoner suffers appears only infrequently
in prison songs.
  However, once in a while it does come up:

> *In my life one mishap right another follows,*
> *Day to day my heart is filled with woes and sorrows.*
> *Day to day my heart is filled with woes and sorrows,*
> *'Cause my life free till now, knows no free tomorrows.*
>
> *Cast am I in dungeon all for six wild cattle,*
> *Clink my iron fetters for some steeds with saddle.*
> *All the lamp I have is eyes of snakes and paddocks.*
> *For to cover me in, prison walls with padlocks.*
>
> *Do not marvel, darling, at my face so sallow,*
> *Nine twelve-months I have been rotting in this cellar!*
> *Nine full years I've spent here, down this gloomy dungeon,*
> *Now eleven years more I have got to serve on.*
> Sárköz (Tolna County)

The following song is a virtual summary of prisoner songs. Its first stanza is a lyric cliché from the Middle Ages, while the second derives from one of the oldest Hungarian prisoner songs, and the third stanza has lines from a song about an outlaw languishing in the prison of the county hall, of which there is a wealth of similar songs:

Tisza fleed, Danube fleed, if all ink they could be,
Leaves in the green forest, if all paper could be,
Blades of grass in meadow, if all quills they could be,
And the stars in heaven, if all scribes they could be,
Still my griefs could no one never set down fully.

'Twas in County Bihar that they took and catched me,
Then to dungeon dark they right away dispatched me.
Prison roof will do me as a winding-sheet well,
Jangling of the gyves as ringing of my death-bell,
Glare of serpent's eyes as lighting in my death-cell.

Down flew then the peacock, lighted on the gaol's well,
For to free the poor lads, free them from the gaol cell.
"Captive ay, captive, I long to get my freedom,
God knows when they free me, when it chance to please them."
"Sick at heart I shall be while you are in fetter,
When they free you, sweetheart, I shall be much better."

Nagyszalonta (former Bihar County)

Prisoner songs were generally collected in the same places as herdsmen's and outlaw songs. The greatest numbers come from the south Great Plain, where between 1868–1871 the outlaw-exterminating court of law of Count Gedeon Ráday operated. This area coincided with that of the most intensive early folksong collecting. It is true that prisoner songs have also turned up from Transylvania and Moldavia, from places where outlaw songs occur as an exception, but their atmosphere and form is of much older style.

Herdsman and Outlaw Songs

While not large in numbers, there is a well defined goup of folksongs related to herdsman songs *(pásztordal),* and these are mostly related to outlaw songs. Herdsmen lived among somewhat better conditions in the past century, and it appeared that they even received a greater share of freedom than peasants or the agricultural labourers of the large estates. Therefore, in many cases they were as heroes to the people of the villages and feudal manors, who liked to take up and sing the songs about them. The reverse of this practice was not frequent, because newer songs, especially composed songs, did not filter through to the isolated world of the herdsmen, or did so only rarely. Thus, the wealth of songs about herdsmen and outlaws are much more archaic than that of the village peasantry from the point of view of lyrics and melody.

Naturally, many songs speak of the livestock that was entrusted to the herdsmen, of their care and troubles, of the pasture, watering, guarding—i. e. of everything that fills up the major part of the herdsman's day:

494

Down around those triple hillocks
Cattle graze with calves and bullocks.
Let 'em graze, if graze they want to:
It's the herd my rose attends to.

Last year we'd a drought that parched us,
All my cattle starved for pastures.
Rough time of it we were having,
Lots of nights we spent in waking.

Plenty rain will fall next summer,
All my cattle will have pasture.
No more nights we spend in waking,
Thirst in pubs we will be slaking.

Broke the well-pole—what I oughter
Do my herd at noon to water?
Fasten on the pole a ribbon,
Come what may I'll water give 'em.

Ormánság (Baranya County)

263. *Betyárs,* or outlaws. Detail of a salt-cellar
Transdanubia

Water or watering is the greatest problem of the herdsman, especially in the Great Plain, and so it is in the Hortobágy. Therefore the appreciation of water reverberates through many songs:

495

> *Debrecen town has a river,*
> *Hortobágy's the name we give her.*
> *There's a stone bridge spans athwart it,*
> *Piers and arches nine support it.*
>
> *Debrecen town has a river,*
> *Hortobágy's the name we give her.*
> *At the edge a water-mill stands,*
> *Cattle graze near in the lowlands.*

Hortobágy

The love songs of the herdsmen mostly begin with an image taken directly from their environment, but the majority are less shaded than the love songs of peasants:

> *Evening's fallen, dark the fields grown everywhere;*
> *Do you love me still so true, my sweetheart fair?*
> *I have plucked this red rose for your lovely hair,*
> *Yours shall it be Carnival time for to wear.*

Kiskunhalas (Pest County)

A certain system of rank developed among the herdsmen over the entire linguistic region. Shepherds were the wealthiest, swineherds the poorest. The latter were looked down on and mocked even in songs:

> *If a man lives merrily,*
> *It's the shepherd verily:*
> *In the greenwoods, on the lowlands,*
> *Walks he, pipes he, plays the flute;*
> *Ambles, stops and shuffles foot.*
>
> *If a man's lot's misery,*
> *It's the swineherd's verily:*
> *All the winter, all the summer*
> *Tends his pigs out on a limb;*
> *Shepherd lads poke fun at him.*

Balatonboglár (Somogy County)

The horseherds thought themselves at all time to be the best among the herdsmen:

> *Look at me a horseherd,*
> *Pride of Hortobágy land.*
> *Cowherd, though he looks good,*
> *After me he must rank.*
>
> *Rarely will I hobnob*
> *With some hook-staff shepherds,*
> *Even less palaver*
> *With some dirty swineherds.*

Hortobágy

However, the life of the herdsmen was completely vulnerable, since it always depended upon the owner of the stock. They were at a disadvantage at the time of hiring and firing, and even when wages were paid. It is no wonder that herdsmen often complain about their low esteem in songs:

> Cheap is here the herdsman,
> Unesteemed by masters,
> Commonly they call him
> Just a worthless bastard.
> If he should have something,
> People say he plunders.
> If he has got nothing,
> That he drinks and squanders.
> When he goes to buy bread,
> Well, the weight is shorter,
> When he goes for bacon,
> Loses by a quarter.
> All the wheat he gets is
> Bottom of the mortar.
> For the wretched herdsman
> Has a hard time ever
> Do he whatsoever
> Never can he prosper.
>
> Békés (Békés County)

The territorial division of herdsmen's songs is different from that of others. We find them in greatest numbers in places where at one time great extensive husbandry went on, that is to say, primarily in the Great Plain. Within this area, most herdsmen's songs derive from east of the Tisza, while there is rarely a trace of any in the more eastern linguistic territory.

Although the main genre of *outlaw poetry* is the ballad and not the song (cf. p. 539), it is very difficult to draw a boundary between the two, since ballads contain lyric parts in a fair number, as do the songs epic characteristics. The *betyár* songs stand close to herdsman songs in both form and content, and frequently herdsman and outlaw appear together, just as in life.

In much of the 18th century the word *betyár* (outlaw) itself meant a manual labourer who wandered about looking for work and was employed for a longer or, more often, a shorter period. Young men more and more mixed with these men driven away from their birth place by the tyranny of the landlord or by the ever-increasing burden of feudal obligations, and men escaping army service. These were pursued by the authorities and were thus willy-nilly confronted with the state authorities. As a consequence, they tried to acquire a means of survival by violence.

However, the *betyár* and the bandit were differentiated by general folk wisdom. The latter were ordinary robbers and murderers, while the former only took away what they absolutely needed, and took even that from the lords, the rich—primarily, that is, from the exploiters of the poor. Therefore it comes as no surprise that many supporters could be found for them among the social strata from which they derived. It was

264. Mirror-case with sealing-wax inlay, 1885
Nagydobsza-Istvánmajor, Somogy County

mainly herdsmen, labourers, and poor peasants who saved and hid these people. Stories circulated about their deeds and lives, and these soon found composers who put them into poetic or song forms, thus further disseminating this poetry.

The increasingly vigorous growth of peasant farms in the Great Plain during the first part of the 19th century favoured them, while the forests of Transdanubia and the north provided good hiding places. Most herdsman's dwellings and the taverns admitted the outlaws. They lived in groups, often under military discipline. Besides bands consisting of 2 or 3 men, the most numerous were of 10 to 15 men, although contemporary records also mention bands with 50 to 60 or even more members. Their activities were revitalized in the late 19th century, and showed a definite anti-Habsburg tendency, which increased the sympathy towards them and lent further romantic colouring to their figures.

The poor peasantry idealized the outlaws at every period, feeling that they behaved towards the rich and the landlords in a way they themselves would have liked to. Poor people often looked upon some of the outlaws as heroes, although in reality they could hardly be considered as anything but ordinary robbers. In 1848 the most famous outlaw, Sándor Rózsa, joined the War of Independence together with his band and caused considerable losses to the Imperial troops. That is why the outlaws appear in songs and ballads as defenders of social justice and liberty:

Thus the Lord said when he made the Universe:
Let's the World with betyár outlaws intersperse.
If the World were lacking all its betyár boys,
Godly masters would not know their prayer's joys.

Nagysárrét (former Bihar County)

People also liked to recall that outlaws easily and quickly became soldiers of liberty:

Betyár I am, betyár called by everyone,
Yet ashamed I won't be before anyone.
Time may come too, and it might be soon enough,
That the country needs hussars and soldiers tough.

Kiskunhalas (Pest County)

For most outlaws, life had taken a bad turn somewhere, and there was good reason why each of them had got into trouble; others blamed their parents for not raising them strictly enough:

I have had my horse lost
In a cedar forest.
I have torn in searching for it
Both my buskin boots best.

"Do not go and search it,
For the horse is pound' in.
In a stable new with floorboards
Are its bells resoundin'."

"Well I ken my own horse
When I hear its bells ring,
Street and stye I ken my true love
By her prideful stepping."

"Oh you were my mother,
Why did you not learn me?
I was but a tender tree shoot,
Why did you not bend me?"

"I did try to bend thee,
But thou proved'st the harder;
With the betyárs and the cowherds
Drank you in the csárda.

Kiskunhalas (Pest County)

The outlaws were not only pursued by the pandours and the gendarmes, but they also had to fight the elements, rain, storm, and snow:

Drink up, betyár, summer's over!
Can't be long a lawless rover:
Poplar leaves are starting to fall;
Where then betyárs go and hide them?
Soon the burdock sheds its leaves all,
Outlaws wrap their leaves around them.

Tiszaladány (former Zemplén County)

265. Shepherd lad. Detail of a razor-case, 1842
Bakonybél, Veszprém County

Outlaws could be best encircled and captured in the winter and they were often hanged on the first tree without the verdict of a judge or a court of law:

> *There's a poplar stands beyond the common,*
> *With a betyár one of its boughs hung on.*
> *When he drops the beasts will come and eat him,*
> *And the birds of heaven will be weepin'.*
>
> *Oh my God when I do look around, too,*
> *What's my life worth, what has it all come to?*
> *I shall end up drying on the gallows,*
> *Wither like the green grass of the fallows.*
>
> Nagyszalonta (former Bihar County)

Soldiers' Songs

In both significance and in number, soldiers' songs *(katonadal)* follow love songs and mocking songs. They are near relatives of the historical, heroic, and wandering songs, but more than anything they tell about the hard fate, the life and death of the Hungarian soldier serving in foreign lands. Such songs really began to appear from the 18th century, but the bulk are from the second half of the 19th century, and their revival was largely over by the end of the First World War. Their tone is gloomy and embittered, since with the exception of the War of Independence, Hungarian soldiers always have had to spill their blood for foreign interests.

The soldiers' song is very varied and by its content has the most varied relationships, that is to say, it is open towards every group of songs. One significant part of them actually continues to speak of civilian life, of recruiting, of the preparation for joining. Bitterness also finds expression, since social discrimination prevails even in the songs:

> *"Tell me, mother, tell me please the reason,*
> *Why do press gangs only poor men seize on?"*
> *"I shall tell you, sonny, be it treason:*
> *Poor men have no patrons in no season."*
>
> Magyarszentmárton
> (former Torontál County)

It is mostly self-consolation to sing about what a fine soldier the poor and the orphan will become:

> *In the town hall at Vásárhely,*
> *There I had my measure taken;*
> *There I had my measure taken,*
> *There the army me did break in.*
>
> *Butter pear is not a field pear;*
> *Orphans make the model soldier;*
> *Orphans make the model soldier,*
> *'Cause they have no high protector.*
>
> Hódmezővásárhely (Csongrád County)

Because recruiting still counted as a celebration, the ones who proved unfit were ashamed of themselves; however, by the time of joining up, the lads turned uncertain, and the mothers lamented their sons just as they did their dead loved ones:

> I've become a soldier,
> Native land's defender,
> Mother is a-crying,
> Now I'm taken from her.
>
> Mother is a-crying,
> And my rose in sorrow:
> Blossom black of mourning
> Sorrows in her window.
>
> Farewell my rose dear,
> I am off and leaving,
> Don't forget me ever,
> I shall not you either.
>
> Egyházaskér
> (former Torontál County)

In the first half of the 19th century soldiers were still recruited (cf. p. 454); they were induced to join military service with singing and music, but mostly by force, often for six, but sometimes for twelve years:

> Now the drum is rolling
> In the city market,
> Now the flag is hoisted
> High atop the turret.
>
> Now must they be marching,
> Poor and helpless fellows,
> They must leave behind them
> Many wives and widows.
>
> When the rose's root's cut,
> Then the bloom is fading,
> When a bird has no mate,
> Then her heart is aching.
>
> Okorág (Baranya County)

The songs about training in the barracks recall the prisoner song; some, on the other hand, maintain close relationships with the songs of wandering, since wandering or soldiering far away from home, often in foreign countries, are related to each other in many ways:

> Sick I am and sore with hiding,
> Up hill, down dale, walking, riding.
> Holy Script befits the clerics,
> Down-and-outs must keep to barracks:

Western winds blow over hill's edge,
Padua town sent her message:
Everyone must to the army,
'Cause there will another war be.

They who live at home in leisure
Lead a life that's not all pleasure;
For they too must kick the bucket,
Linger abed till they cop it.

Soldier's life's for lords, not goners,
All the world must pay him honours;
Needs like salt, wine, he's just scoffin'
Has no care for pomp nor coffin.

Never's seen he by his mother,
Neither mourned by cherished lover;
But his comrades will bemoan him.
They at home will hear their mournin'.

Kisdobsza (Somogy County)

The semi-folk rhymed letters also belonged to the soldier's life. These spread and improved with the help of printed and handwritten letter-books. The songs of battle, war, marching, and of prisoners of war are equally sad in tone. Those which depict the difference between branches of military service are lighter in mood; and naturally—just as among the herdsmen—those on horseback, the *huszár*s, think of themselves as the best:

Horseman I am, not one of them paddlefoots,
'Cause my feet would noway suffer ankle boots;
Why hussar's pelisse with braids looks nice on me,
Few the lassies who can take their eyes off me.

'Twas the Germans put me in the cavalry,
And they gave a hoss so I may travel free;
Mounted on a thoroughbred with stockings white,
I shall, sweetkins, come and see you every night.

Köröstarcsa (Békés County)

There are also many epic characteristics in soldier songs, some of which are entirely ballad-like: they speak of forcible enlistments, the hardship of marching, heavy punishments, battles. Everybody was just counting days and waited for the day of discharge, when the officers and drill sergeants could no longer order them about:

Don't be sorry, little horse, and don't shed tears,
I have taken care of you for three full years.
"Thank you, Captain, thank you for your kindness, too,
But I give my bleeding badges back to you!
I have done my three years time and seven days,
I shall not my hand to you saluting raise!"

Captain he would give us orders, boss around
That we have to groom and rub his hosses down.
Let his damn old mother take his ordering,
Not a hussar who did three years' soldiering.

Szeged (Csongrád County)

266. Back of a mirror-case with sealing-
wax inlay, 1885
Nagydobsza-Istvánmajor, Somogy
County

And if they had to go to war, they could hardly wait for it to end. Such peace songs were by and large left out of folklore collections, since their content was contrary to the interests of the ruling class. They were therefore sung mostly in secret:

Far off in Odessa's port a man-of-war lies anchored,
On her top is flying high the red, white and green standard
Blown by the wind, blown high, homeward it is waving...
Come ye girls of Hungary, for peace let us be praying!

In the sandy steppes of Russia lies a trench of ours,
Gay it is and all adorned with laurel sprigs and flowers.
Blown by the wind, blown high, homeward they are waving...
Back at home now wreaths for peace lovely girls are weaving.

Áj (former Abaúj County)

Rural Workers' Songs The poorest social layers in the Hungarian village contracted in groups for share harvesting in the summer (cf. pp. 82–4). They often worked far away from their own village, under very hard conditions. This is reflected in their characteristic songs, sung during breaks in the work:

All the summer I was reaping,
Rarely lay in bed a-sleeping:
Now I slept in field or greenwood,
Now on stubble, best as I could.

Oh, my Lord, say, why you keep me?
Why was I born poor and needy?
Had I not been such a poor lad,
I would reap and eat my own bread.

Bodrogköz
(former Zemplén County)

The major part of these songs is known country-wide. It is noteworthy that among them relatively many are composed, artificial songs. Since the foremen came mostly from among those who could read and write, they themselves made up and wrote lyrics to existing melodies, and these show relationship primarily with the news-verse. The songs object not so much to the poor provisions, as to the mean treatment. Special songs developed about concluding the work and are generally the most light-hearted in tone:

Now that harvest is completed,
Harvest-home is celebrated.
Supper, goodwife! Call your guests in!
Give us, God, a good night's restin'.

Gerencsér (former Nyitra County)

At the same time, harvesting was regarded as providing an important chance for finding a mate. Many marriages came about from harvesting together:

When I go a-reaping to the farmstead land,
She will be the lass to set the sheaves on end.
After we have gathered in the corn so ripe,
I shall take that lassie for my wedded wife.

When I go a-reaping to the farmstead land,
He will be the lad to come and lend a hand.
After we have gathered in the corn so ripe,
I shall be that laddie's lawful wedded wife.
And I'll fry him tarhonya★ so nice and crisp
If he eats it, I shall kiss him on the lip.

Apátfalva (former Csanád County)

★*Granulated dried pastry made of flour and eggs.*

504

We know relatively few of these songs of farm hands *(cseléddal)* and rural servants *(szolgadal)*, because collecting them began only after they had nearly sunk into oblivion. However, the songs we do know expose the hard life on the large estates, where the indigent labourers were not counted as human beings (cf. pp. 87-90). The peasantry did not take over these songs, since they expressed sentiments, questions, sufferings unknown to them. As a rule, they consequently did not become known in wider circles, being at most perhaps carried over certain areas by the agricultural labourers who were compelled to change their place of work frequently.

There are relatively few songs telling about the grief of the servants hired at the house of the big peasant farmers:

> *As a tender boy came I to orphanhood,*
> *When I grew up I fell into servitude;*
> *Then it was I learnt endurance, hardihood:*
> *How to bear this world's insults and turpitude.*
>
> *I have tended four oxen all properly,*
> *All four were my master's beasts and property.*
> *I shall teach these oxen how to bear the yoke:*
> *I, too, plough the furrows of some other folk.*
>
> Székelyland

What embittered the young servant men most was that no matter how much they worked from dawn to dusk, they were given poor provisions and little payment in kind:

> *Grapes they are growing,*
> *Vines are a-groaning*
> *Under their heavy weight.*
> *Two needy farmhands*
> *Want to go ploughing*
> *But have no bread to take.*
>
> *'Tis but some onion*
> *They have to munch on;*
> *It has a bitter smack.*
> *Shallow the ladle,*
> *Long is the table,*
> *What a poor, meagre snack!*
>
> *Roguish the master*
> *Chases girls after;*
> *Keeps of the 'days' no track.*
> *But the day lab'rer,*
> *Every poor neighbour*
> *Gets but a meagre snack.*
>
> Generally known

Continual moving on was hardest to take for the agricultural labourer, farm hand, and servant. He never knew, once the year was over, when

505

the farmer might send him away, not because of his work, but perhaps because he had talked back to him. Most servant songs deal, in one way or another, with this theme:

> *Servant I am, servant,*
> *Soon I must engage me.*
> *With the new year coming,*
> *Comes the cart to fetch me.*
>
> *Sure I'll miss my oxen,*
> *And my iron yoke-pin,*
> *Ornamented goad stick,*
> *And my nutbrown darlin'.*
>
> *Oxen stray in meadow,*
> *Barrow's left in furrow;*
> *Cowherd mine still farther;*
> *Myself in the csárda.*
>
> Rábaszovát (former Sopron County)

The tobacco growers formed a separate group on the large estates. Although they were tenants and entrepreneurs, they still depended entirely on the landlord. Their hard work was never really repaid. Only a few among their characteristic songs have survived:

> *Uncle Pista goes out to the drying-shed,*
> *Takes an armful baccy leaves right off the peg.*
> *"Why, tonight you not sleep, my lazy souls,*
> *Till you tied this heap of baccy up in rolls."*
>
> *"Uncle Pista, come out to us, come out please,*
> *Bring with you our papers and dismissories.*
> *Write me one discharge ticket too, signed and sealed,*
> *Well enough we toiled on your tobacco field."*
>
> Verpelét (Heves County)

Songs of Seasonal Workers

The seasonal workers *(summás)* (cf. pp. 82–84) spent half of the year far from their place of residence. On Sundays, in their free time, there was plenty of time for singing. Thus a relatively rich and typical group of folksongs have survived. These are mostly the new type of folksongs, which, along with the soldiers' songs of the world wars, are the most lively offshoots of Hungarian folksong.

The seasonal workers sang about every episode of their life, from recruiting to returning home, so accordingly almost their entire life and work can be put together from their songs. However, the central question of these songs is mean treatment and bad food:

> *In the courtyard of the bailiff stands a tree,*
> *Under it are labourers in groups of three.*
> *Mister Bailiff shouts at season labourers:*
> *"Get a move on, God's sakes and our Saviour's!"*

> *"May God bless you, Mister Bailiff, evermore!*
> *Of your bacon don't allot us any more.*
> *Tuck it in or give it to your rabid curs,*
> *But not to the six month contract labourers!"*
>
> Bélapátfalva (former Borsod County)

There was often trouble not only with the food but with lodgings as well, because the seasonal workers had to take shelter in the cattle barn, sheep-pen, or some kind of barracks:

> *Through the barn door's chinks the breezes*
> *Keep a-blowin' when it freezes.*
> *Chilly breezes blow and murmur:*
> *Who shall free the season worker?*
>
> Mezőkövesd (former Borsod County)

In general, seasonal workers' songs *(summásdal)* were not just means of amusement and entertainment, but were also weapons in the fight against the employer because the poetic form, the song, assured a certain opportunity to recount grievances. The tone of the songs becomes especially harsh when the contract is nearing its end:

> *Standing 'fore the bailiff man's house is a tree,*
> *Hanged upon it Mister Bailiff oughta be!*
> *For to see him swingin' it's my only hope:*
> *And to put around his neck the halter-rope.*
>
> Sarkad (Bihar County)

In general, songs of seasonal workers appear in those areas from which at one time seasonal workers came in large numbers, so that the songs are local in character. Most come from Heves and Borsod Counties, fewer from the southern Great Plain and Transdanubia.

Songs of Pick and Shovel Men

Among those working in the Hungarian village, the pick and shovel men (cf. pp. 84–7) came closest to organized workers. That is to say, the building of railroads and the raising of dikes and other earthworks demanded strong organization, which also developed among them into a defence against the employer. Some of their songs are related to the soldiers' and herdsmen's songs, from which they came. Others tell about the hardships of work:

> *'Neath the sky we have our dwellin',*
> *For a quilt the stars of heaven.*
> *All day we have slaved as navvies,*
> *Where the thicket, there our bed is.*

> *Creakily the barrow's wheels are gratin',*
> *Full of murky mud it is all laden.*
> *When my arms and feet are to buckle,*
> *Then would I change with the dead nettle.*
>
> Zsadány (former Bihar County)

The constant coming and going habituated the pick and shovel man to the tavern and to the pub:

> *Why a navvy has no house nor shanty*
> *Is because his wages go for brandy.*
> *And the barman spends the navvy's money*
> *Playing cards and on a sloe-eyed honey.*
>
> Szentes (Csongrád County)

Among their songs, mixed in origin and new in style, the most frequent is the cocky, taunting, or perhaps bitter-toned drinking and revelling song. Songs that speak of wandering, of working places, and of taking leave are more individualistic and more suited to occasions:

> *No one's life's as bloody hard and heavy*
> *As the girl's whose lover is a navvy.*
> *For a digger has to keep a-going,*
> *And must leave his lass at home sorrowing.*
>
> Hódmezővásárhely (Csongrád County)

Songs of the pick and shovel men are primarily known in the southern part of the Great Plain. In other places, such songs were only occasionally sung, primarily at places where the pick and shovel men had worked for a longer time.

Songs of Revellry Drinking Songs

The group of revellry *(mulatónóta)* and drinking or wine songs *(bordal)* consists of a wide range of songs. Noticeably, the influence in this group of written songs, of literature, and of Latin verse predominates. Just as in love songs, here, too, we find many characteristics related to herdsmen's and outlaws' songs. In fact, because the connection between them has been continuous, it is not possible to draw fixed and final boundaries.

Wine songs and songs of revellry are all connected to some occasion, and these may be quite varied. Songs are sung at the most different folk gatherings: name days, pig-killing feasts, merrymaking in the tavern, weddings, grape harvesting, drinking in the wine cellar, or just simply drinking wine. They are often tied to one or another occasion in their content. Thus the tavern or pub are often mentioned:

> *Every time I turn up at the Kustány Inn,*
> *I do eat and drink on tick, there revellin',*
> *'Cause I have all plenty enough credit there;*
> *Take my word that all my debts I'll square up fair.*
>
> *Barman's wife, go fetch me of your scarlet wine,*
> *No matter how much it costs, never you mind;*
> *Though I sell my crescent horned, mottled cow,*
> *I shall pay the price of that wine anyhow!*
>
> Felsőkustány (Zala County)

Drinking songs often like to contrast work with drinking wine.

While I have a horse in harness,
I'll be drinking in the csárda.
Little grey I'll loose from swinking,
Let 'im earn some dough for drinking.

Folks dare call me rakehell drunkard,
And a slacker, workshy sluggard.
Nay, I do work as become me,
When I'm running short of money.

Ormánság (Baranya County)

No drinking can take place without praising the wine and drink, especially as high spirits mount:

Wine, wine, wine,
Did you drink such good red wine!
If the women start a-sipping,
Soon their topknots go a-slipping.

Nagyszalonta (former Bihar County)

In company, the song in praise of wine *(bordicsérő)* is followed by the drink-giving *(itató)* and glass-touching *(koccintó)* songs, into which they often weave the names of those present. At other times they urge with well-known phrases those who for some reason are reluctant to drink:

God created cockerels,
Cockerels and pickerels,
And he made some water wells
For to water animals.

But as even quacks do claim
Drinking from a well is shame:
Toads and frogs infest the same,
And a man's life mar and maim.

Mohács (Baranya County)

Afterwards, songs dealing with drunkenness and its consequences are also sung.

To the vineyard I was going,
Hoe in hand to do some hoeing;
But I did not feel like swinkin'
Damn it all, I started drinkin'.

I have drunk, and like a drunkard,
Noway can I leave the vineyard;
Anyone who knows should come, say
Where to find the homeward highway.

'Tis a shame what friends and foes said
That the wine has made my nose red;
What makes red the gander's pecker
When in wine he dips it never?

509

> *Women say amongst each other*
> *Wine does make me reel and totter.*
> *Why, a reed-stalk sways a-rocking,*
> *Though in water lays a-soaking!*
>
> Tálya (former Zemplén County)

We could continue to list the glass-touching and drink-giving songs, those about fights in the tavern, and those in which the real drinkers take the bottle with them even into the grave. The following is a link in the direction of outlaw songs, since outlaws favoured wine, women, and gypsy musicians very much:

> *When all outlawed betyárs*
> *From this world have vanished,*
> *Rich innkeepers have to*
> *Beg alms from the parish.*

> *Then all pretty damsels will*
> *Go in dresses tattered;*
> *And the gypsy fiddlers*
> *Will have by then scattered.*
>
> Szaján (former Torontál County)

Most wine songs are known in important grape-growing areas. Thus every important wine region has its characteristic wealth of wine songs, without which no worthwhile merrymaking could take place.

Mocking Songs, Humorous and Satirical Songs

This complex group of songs is one of the largest in the Hungarian linguistic region. It is placed according to numerical proportion between the love and soldiers' songs. The tradition of mocking songs goes back many centuries; it is permeated by the candour, the turbulent gaiety of goliardic poetry, and by the Latin humour of the 16th to 18th centuries, the connection with which it can be demonstrated in many cases.

The triple title of mocking songs *(csúfoló),* humorous *(tréfás)* and satirical songs *(gúnydal)* designates groups close to each other, yet still separate, so that it would be very difficult to characterize them uniformly. A concept applicable to very many occasions and to a whole string of lyric songs is more or less open in the direction of every other folksong.

Their presentation, one following the other, was occasioned by cheerful social gatherings. They mocked, with poignant and sharp humour, certain groups of people, girls, women, young men, priests, and masters. This versified judgement is cutting, stinging to the quick, and often very ruthless, especially when they substitute in a suitable fashion places and names and in this way actualize the song. As is also apparent, numerous examples of this group of songs are partly or entirely improvised.

To arrange them according to content is nearly impossible, especially if we list the parodies as well. The most frequent form is when the girls sing about the young men, or vice versa, and list their assumed or real qualities:

Puszta lads are hard-up fellers, hard-up fellers,
All the money that they earn is merely fillérs.
Though they search their trouser pockets, trouser pockets,
All they find there is but pumpkin seeds or peanuts.

Hódmezővásárhely (Csongrád County)

This is how the town folks mocked the generally poorer people of peasant farmsteads. At other times they sang about other qualities than material attributes:

Hardly is a young lad worth a wrinkled punkin
Who besides his lass sits like a pipsqueak mankin,
Casting sheepish looks and gaping like a bunkin,
Bugger such a booby, fuddy, duddy dumbling!

Generally known

Naturally, the young men were not to be outdone, and they caricature the girls freely, especially those girls who dote too much on them:

In the town of Szentgyörgy girls were laying hen,
Under each they lay some twenty eggs and ten.
Of the thirty hatched a single cockerel then,
Alas, fair Szentgyörgy girls, where'll you find your men?

Sepsiszentgyörgy (former Háromszék County)

The mocking of men and women often contains erotic features, which made the songs even more popular:

Corn-cake, milky, sugar-coated,
Soon I will become betrothed:
Bride today and wife tomorrow,
Goodwife then, a year tomorrow.

Corn-cake, stodgy, made with flour,
Old man am I, past my flower,
Got one thing to pin my hope on:
I have such a sprightly woman.

Generally known

Lizzy's busy lentils shuckin'
Waitin' till her great goodluck's in.
When she is not all alone in,
O the bench goes creakin', groanin'!

Pusztafalu (former Abaúj County)

In Europe, spinsters and women were always targets of mockery, so that it is natural that they are not left out of Hungarian folksongs either. On the contrary, most of these are about them:

Fillet, fillet, damn my maiden-fillet,
May a fire burn it up or grill it!
I have worn all thirteen fillets threadbare,
But saw not a pair of drawers lads wear.

Nagymegyer (Komárom County)

511

Out the house went, through the windows,
Still the old hag stays she indoors.
Teeth she lacks all three and thirty,
Still she calls her lover birdie.

Nagyszalonta (former Bihar County)

Stunted carrot, parsley, chervil,
Old women are danger, peril.
I can hardly bide the Devil
For to take 'em critters evil.

For a crone it would be better
If she was in hell in fetters;
Withered is the skin upon her,
Makes a man recoil in horror.

Nemespátró (Somogy County)

Naturally, the clerical and secular leaders of the village could not avoid being caricatured. The priest and the cantor in particular are the recurring actors of songs:

I for one detest a person
If he speaks ill of a parson;
For a cleric wears no sheepskin,
In his cassock he is freezin'.
Whippy, whoopee, hop!

I for one detest such persons
Who on tradesmen cast aspersions;
For the tradesmen have no pot-hats,
On the street, too, wear their cloth-caps.
Whippy, whoopee, hop!

Whippy, whoopee, hopsy-skipsy,
Strike up, play my tune you gypsy!
Come on, lovey, let's be dancin'
Foot it gayly, lively prancin'!
Whippy, whoopee, hop!

Generally known

They also excoriated the village mayor. The social content of the song is also clear, since the mayor came from among the more prosperous peasants, whom he therefore supported:

Down the gardens is a mare,
Confiscated by the mayor.
So she kicked his Excellence,
Three day's time he'll exit hence.

O the poor man, magistrate,
He was such good give-and-take:
What he plundered from the poor,
Gave the rich to have some more.

512

Come rejoice ye farmer folk,
'Cause your mayor died, he croaked,
What you never hoped could be,
That your grey mare accomplished beautifully.

Szend (former Szabolcs County)

This genre is known throughout the entire country. Most of the songs were collected in Transylvania and the Great Plain. Not that humour was stronger in these regions, but most likely the unevenness of collecting has caused it to seem so.

★

Naturally, we have been able to introduce above only a few groups of Hungarian folksongs, and can only refer to the rest of them. We have left out the cradle-songs, children's ditties and games, lyrical maxims, riddles, match-making songs, love letters in verse, verses of the witnesses at weddings, wedding songs, dance songs, toasts and festive songs, night watchmen's songs, beggar songs, songs at fairs and vendor songs, mourning songs, wandering songs, and a few more. We shall deal with part of these when discussing customs. We think it important to list them only because they indicate the impressive richness of Hungarian folksong.

If, by way of summary, we try finally to characterize Hungarian folksong in general, we must emphasize the characteristic breadth, the clarity, the artistic simplicity in their message, and, through this, the manifold, intricate artistic expression of life and society that make up Hungarian folksong. Many folksongs could conjure up through a four-line stanza contemporary Hungarian society. They seem, however, to always tell the problems of the individual personally, to express in this way the sentimental attitudes, emotions, passions, thoughts, value judgement of the entire community. In folksong the entire community speaks through the voice of the individual, so that the expressions "individual" and "communal" with regard to Hungarian folk poetry are, in the final analysis, inseparable.

Folk Ballad

The Hungarian folk ballad is one of the most attractive areas both of folk poetry research and literary history. From the first moment of its discovery, the consensus of literary opinion has held it to be the most beautiful "flower" of Hungarian poetry; and indeed, it was received with the enthusiasm due to a new discovery. This high esteem was undoubtedly encouraged by the expectation of recovering the lost ancient Magyar epic through the folk ballad. The disappointment of this expectation explains why János Arany, the 19th century poet who borrowed abundantly from folk tradition, mentions, at first bitterly, in his great study of the Hungarian folksong, that the Hungarians did not preserve the history of the nation in their songs save for "some bandit songs". However, not much later he writes: "The German ancient epos, the Czech manuscript from the king's court, the Serbian smaller narratives, the northern ballads and Spanish romances, and in our country the adventures of *Szilágyi and Hajmási* and the often mentioned few ballad-type poems show such internal completeness in the respective genres of narrative, that written poetry can compete with them but has never surpassed them anywhere."

The Hungarian folk ballad did not develop in isolation from the European, especially not from Eastern European balladry. On the contrary, every one of the factors bringing about its historical and artistic development and alteration is related to the Eastern European and European ballad. Therefore, it is impossible to answer, even in general outlines, questions about the folk ballad without taking at least a brief look at the history of European folk balladry. This is why it is worth our while to consider attempts at defining the folk ballad in general, and to deal with theories on the origin of European balladry and with the history of its artistic development, themes, and forms.

In defining the concept of the ballad, one runs into many difficulties, as is also shown by the uncertainty of creative poets, that is, the versed authors, who compose in this genre. Thus, Goethe discovers the ancient form of poetry precisely in the ballad, which contains, like a primitive ovum, all the genres of poetry in a condensed unit. Herder, trying to differentiate the ballad from the romance, could not find a better method than the geographical one, and expounds the difference between the grim northern ballads and the southern romances. These definitions strongly affected the theoretical literature of later times.

History of the Ballad

It is understandable that those theoretical attempts which did not apply to historical-social perspectives were faced with almost insurmountable difficulties: mythicizing attempts, aesthetic formulae, geographical or nationalistic theories were not suited to condensing into a single formula the creations of many eras and social forms, which had been related to each other and had been drawn under a single collective noun. These are works of art that, although containing many differences, still contain something common in spite of national, historical and artistic differences. Furthermore, it was also hard to find the root of this "something common". It is the centre from which the variations have unfolded some kind of an ancient mode of performing, some epic that was combined with dance, the effect of the Christian Middle Ages, or is it the effect of geographic regions? The Italian *ballata* (dance song), the Celtic *gwaelawd* (epic song), the Russian *bilina*, the Ukrainian *dumi*, the South Slav *narodne pesme, junačke pesme,* the Spanish *románce,* the Danish, Norwegian *folkeviser,* the Hungarian *ballada* are the same genre; they fulfil the same function, that of the short epic song, often dramatic in character. Still there are great differences among them, or, more precisely, they incorporated other genres, until in the end the amalgamation of genres, the separate national development of the ballad, produced different forms everywhere. All this explains the uncertainties of theoretical definitions and of generalizing formulae.

Soviet researchers, although duly separating literary and folk ballads and exploring the connections between the two types, do not attempt an unequivocal definition in regard either to the ballad or to the *bilinas,* but they consider it their task to draw the definite social and historical background of folk epic poetry, and to analyse the historical layers deposited one over the other in epic song recital.

There is an element in defining the ballad which leads closer to the question of the origin of the ballad, and at the same time is an aid to apprehending the two decisive elements of the ballad. These two elements are the dance song and the epic song, and both are ballads. One is derived from the verb *ballare* (to dance), and primarily can be discovered in the refrained stanzas, the feature of dance songs; the other is from the Celtic expression *gwaelawd* (hero). However, according to some people, the epic song that was sung and the dance separated in the course of their development, so that their growth diverged. It is certain, however, that at the birth of the European folksong, the dance song and epic song were equally functioning, and we can even look upon it as symbolic that in the attempt to explain the word, the two genres have met.

To the researcher, the ballad is a characteristically European genre, in spite of its many artistic colourations and divergences. And even if there is considerable debate about the factors and history of its development, it is obvious that the development itself took place within Europe. Where epic songs similar to the ballad genre can be discovered outside Europe, this is always an effect of traditions brought by European settlers. Thus the Russian epic song-writing spread to Siberia; French and English settlers carried their own ballads to Canada and North America; the Spanish *romancero* became the new type of ballad, called *corrido,* which developed in Mexico. When Jorge Amado speaks of the blind singers who sang about the fight of the exploited workers of the cocoa fields, he tells us about a type of poetry which was further shaped from Portuguese balladry and was thus also able to express new ideas. This is a way the European-born ballad became enriched with novel elements and expanded its geographic boundaries.

There is much less agreement about the origin of the ballad. Since the discovery of the Greek ballads in Akritas, we can push the earliest time limit of the data referring to the ballad to the 9th to 10th centuries A.D. Until now, 12th century France and early 12th century Scandinavia were considered as the points of origin, and supposedly the epic-dramatic dancing song moved from there to England after the Norman Conquest. It spread in the German linguistic region in the 13th century.

The balladry of the Slavic peoples, or rather, the development of their ballad–like epic songs, was also estimated to have been somewhere in the 11th to 13th centuries. The 11th to 16th centuries saw the maturation of the ballad. Indeed, this is when it unfolded in the complete wealth of the variety of its artistic form, this is when the concise, dramatic structural form of its themes developed which assures the ballad such a special place in epic song writing.

The question, therefore, is not whether the epic can originate from the ballad, or whether every epic originates from a ballad song. For us it follows that the ballad did not appear in the poetry of European peoples earlier than the feudal period. It is another question whether the epic poems reflecting clan organization or various phases of feudalism were or were not preceded by smaller epic forms (this can be verified in certain cases), and this question of genre history cannot be confused with the question of the development of the ballad as such. The folk ballad (and this also applies to the beginnings of the written ballad) was born in Europe; its form began to take shape during the early phase of the stabilization of feudalism, and it reached the height of its flowering during the zenith of feudal society. It then declined, only to leap into a new flowering in written poetry, during the period of Romanticism.

Naturally, it would hardly be possible to characterize European balladry in a uniform way. Still, in broad outline, three major layers are differentiated in the themes of the European ballad, and the entire balladry of Europe is divided into these three thematic cycles, no matter which ballad is in question, that of the Slavic peoples, the Northern, English-Scotch, or the Romance (French, Walloon, Spanish, Portuguese, Rumanian, Italian) ballad, the German, or the Hungarian ballad. The earliest ballads are characterized by mythological themes, and such songs actually turn up among the *bilinas* as much as among the South Slav or Norwegian and Scottish ballads. The next group consists of historical epic themes, a sub-group of which comprises the epic songs of Eastern European peoples about their struggles with the Turks. This group can equally be found among the Bulgarian, Rumanian, South Slav and Hungarian ballads, and also in the Ukrainian and Russian material. The third group containing the most general, most varied material is made up of the epic songs that tell about individual and family tragedies and comedies in song and dance. These provide us with the most effective picture of actual social conflicts.

Although the development of the Hungarian folk ballad is related in many ways to the general European development, still it has a character all its own.

Naturally, an examination of the Hungarian folk ballad will not solve the mysteries of the lost Hungarian epic poetry and heroic poetry, just as on the other hand, neither the Vogul heroic song nor the Finnish *Kalevala* direct us in questions of the Hungarian folk ballad. This is especially so as the balladry of the Finno-Ugric peoples related to the Hungarians shows more common characteristics with Northern Slav and Germanic folk poetry than with ours. With respect to the ancient Magyar epic poetry, of the few motif and melody fragments left to us, as well as the interpretation of the historical data relevant to old epic minstrelsy, are extremely hard tasks, and even after much critical scientific examination, we are only beginning to explore this field.

This does not mean that the folk ballad does not give valuable information of the past of the Hungarian epic and the long road it has traversed, especially as the existence and beauty of the folk ballad, and the spread of almost every type of ballad over a large part of the Hungarian linguistic region, testify in themselves to the epos-making talent of the Hungarian people. Certain researchers have doubted this talent. Unscientific "theories" relying on insinuated or open racial prejudices have announced that the Hungarian folk has talent only for lyric songs, and that epic poetry received both the topics and the manner of performing from the German fiddlers and Slavic minstrels. Or, as one researcher explained the matter, the pride of the Magyar folk did not

permit them to "demean" themselves by becoming entertainers. Others proclaimed that only a highly cultivated aristocratic class is able to create epic poetry, and listed the epos-creating and preserving talent of the Hungarian people as the fantasy of folklorists.

We hardly need to waste many words on refuting such theories, since even the negative arguments testify that the practice of epic minstrelsy was constant and powerfully alive among the Hungarian people. Let us consider the chronicle of Anonymus (12th century), in which he tells how unseemly it would be to hear the origins and heroic history of the Magyars only from the false stories of the peasants and the prattling songs of the minstrels. This sentence, evidencing the contemptuous attitude of this master of letters, actually acknowledges that through three hundred years folk poetry and story telling had lived among the Hungarians in oral tradition, and this preserved historical traditions better than written records, which only salvaged fragments of it. How this type of heroic minstrelsy was transformed into relating and singing

517

other types of epics, we do not know. However, we do know that even in its transformation it tenaciously preserved its earlier heroes and created new ones.

Mátyás Bél, a scientist interested in literature and folklore, mentions in the 18th century stories about Toldi, a folk hero known for his superhuman strength, to live on the lips of the people—also through the distance of several centuries. We need to think only of the writings of Zoltán Kodály, the musicological studies of Bence Szabolcsi, to know what ancient inheritance is preserved by Hungarian folk music, by its pentatonic system, and what ancient memories of melody forming, verse structure and rhythm live precisely in the older groups of ballads. There are also themes which, on the lips of peasant performers, call to life whole centuries. We can therefore rightly suppose that even if folksongs do not give definite support to the understanding of old Hungarian heroic epic poetry, they still have preserved many principles of the ancient epic method of performance, singing, hero forming, and the epic and dramatic method of construction. Therefore we can look upon the older strata of the Hungarian folk ballad—and the peculiarities of these older strata are in the process of reshaping, transforming almost in front of our eyes, while still retaining old characteristics—as the continuation of ancient epic minstrelsy, as receiver of the role of ancient epic minstrelsy.

This much is certain, that contrary to the theories of oblivion and conscious destruction, we have continuous information up to the 16th century of the lively practice by the jesters, lyrists and violinists of the royal court of singing merry, comic songs. We also know that bards, minstrels and lyrists lived not only at the courts, but also among the people. The supposition is by no means arbitrary that these minstrels played themes related to each other in their material. The nature of the tunes appears just as certain as the invocation, the poetic introduction addressed to the audience—which shows relationship not only between the songs of Sebestyén Tinódi Lantos, best known singer-chronicler of the 16th century, and folk ballads, but also between ballads and 19th century broadsheet or chapbook ballads—a relationship reaching back even further, and to be found not infrequently also in melody and rhythm. Furthermore, just as the survival of archaic pre-Conquest heroic songs recited in first person may be found in Latin chronicles, similarly the captive of the Turks or of the lords would speak in the first person as would the 19th century hero of outlaw ballads. Just as many theorists see the song of lament at the cradle of the epic, a song which both laments the hero and tells of his deeds, so too we may discover among the ballads the dirge which, though disguised in the form of new epic song, bears an obvious relationship in its intonation to the ballad. In the way Tinódi asks his listeners if they had heard about the siege of the town Lippa, or in the way he begins the history of Ali *pasha* of Buda with a similar formula, so for centuries before his time singers used to speak the same way, as for instance in the 18th century the ballad of "Izsák Kerekes" addresses its audience with such a question, and printed texts of murder ballads, which became broadsheet or chapbook ballads in the 19th and 20th centuries, also phrase their question thus. And we could

268. Woman singing a ballad
Moldavia, Rumania

519

continue making this list, without even dealing with the distant past of historical songs or the ancient method of versification.

The minstrel's role must be certainly evaluated as the most important in preserving epic traditions and in the development of its forms, and it is also certain that the Hungarian people, fond of songs, have preserved the bulk of their individual creative talent through the centuries even though it has been wrapped in anonymity. However, this does not in any way mean that only the compositions of court minstrels got down to the people and changed there in a certain way. Our data about the role of court and folk minstrels, about their historical fate, prove precisely that the art of minstrels was connected inseparably to the traditions of the Hungarian people. Minstrels' songs received inspiration from folk poetry, melodic language and traditional image appear moulded with novel contributions, a new voice and erudition. In the course of this process, anonymous oral tradition reshaped and polished the repeated meetings of old and new through the constant practice of centuries. Minstrels sang both among urban and rural people and at the tables of the lords. Gianmichele Bruto, Italian historiographer of István Báthori (1533–1586), the Polish king of Hungarian descent, writes the following about the importance of minstrels: "They sing the praise of ancestors in verse accompanied by the sounds of a violin, to fire up the youth so that they aspire to military glory by competing in valour. In these songs their heroic deeds are collected chronologically, as in a yearbook, and because these songs remain so solidly preserved in the memory of the Hungarians from childhood on now, when the largest part of the country, along with its royal seat, is destroyed, there is no better recollection of the past than that which can be found recorded in these songs."

This beautiful observation also illustrates how important epic minstrelsy was for the entire nation and how comprehensive the role of minstrels was.

The analysis of the ballads of romance also indicates that the written form was preceded by oral tradition, which to this day carried vestiges of the original ancient form. We also know that songs of wandering composed by people whose names have come down to us accommodated and adapted themselves to oral tradition. Thus, oral tradition plays a significant role in both creating and preserving balladry. Among the transmitters of this tradition were the many singers, from court singers and minstrels, beggar-singers at fairs, warriors, and Kuruc heroes forced into wandering, through wandering students and their teachers. They sang of the fate of the people, their hard lives and wars, in the voice of the people, just as later on, in the 19th century, chapbook merchants took to the fairs those books whose language and themes were familiar to the rural populace. They sang about the fights with Turks and Serbs, the sufferings and adventures of prisoners in Turkish captivity, family, love tragedies, the voices and dramas of passion, hatred and love.

The Hungarian folk always had a great respect for those who had the talent for epic singing, and loved the minstrels who could do it well. In this manner, the minstrel, at one with the people and speaking in their language, preserved through changes in form and content, and through songs with new content preserved his role through the centuries.

520

Therefore, not only certain subjects and motifs were left to us of pre-Conquest times, but the traditional, oral traditional way of performance and the role of the singer as well. In this way, we can come upon the relationship between the ancient epic and Hungarian folk ballad.

Alongside epic minstrelsy, dance songs also played an important role in the European development of the folk ballad. There were places where their significance was greater than elsewhere, at other places their role was considerably less, but yet could be found everywhere. The texts and melodies of this layer of the Hungarian folk ballad prove that one group of the merry and tragic ballads were originally dance ballads. In the past, methods of collecting strove simply to record only the texts yet even so ballads refer to dance songs, and dance-games possess refrains or structures with repeated lines. There are also recordings of ballad-like songs sung to children's roundels, as for example the tragic ballad of the three orphans written down by Kodály in 1922.

In the development of the Hungarian folk ballad the same two artistic factors operate that created the European folk ballad, namely the historical and narrative song. This does not mean that we should doubt the national character of the Hungarian ballad, nor its individual development; it only means that great historical, social, and literary factors exercised their legitimate effects in the development of the poetry of the Hungarian people. The researcher has to be careful to show precisely those peculiarities which determine its history, in addition to the common development and general characteristics of balladry, to show that surplus it brought to the common treasure house of peoples, nations, and of mankind.

How did the Hungarian folk ballad develop historically and what strata does it have? Recording of Hungarian folk ballads began only in the 19th century, but that does not mean that further tracing of the history of Hungarian folk ballads is an impossibility. We have tried to show above that Hungarian folk ballads were part of a lively process, the older links of which can only be inferred, but the certainty of their existence is demonstrated by their artistic forms.

We can trace the oldest, historically determinable layer of Hungarian folk ballads to the 15th and 17th centuries. References, historical atmosphere, and subject matter place them into that period. However, there are ballads whose age can hardly be determined because their plot, structure, connection to more ancient beliefs (e.g. building sacrifice, motifs signalling trouble) offer a possibility of dating this type of ballad much earlier. At the same time, presumably only some of the elements of these ballads are truly more ancient, but their generic development cannot be put earlier than the 15th to 16th centuries. It is certain that some of the mythical story motifs of the European ballad, not infrequently beliefs going back to the age of a tribal community, also indicate earlier centuries, yet the genre of the ballad itself still was not born earlier than the turn of the 9th to 10th centuries. In short, we can say this much with certainty, that some elements of the Hungarian folk ballad are survivals of more ancient memories, but the artistic form of the ballad did not evolve in Hungary earlier than the 13th to 14th centuries, and the first verifiable references in our recorded ballads refer to the 16th century. The collections of folklorists have placed in front of us the evaluation, the flourishing, and the power of the ballad to create new layers and new groups, and we can see that this creative force in folk ballad poetry has remained a force, although the tradition-destroying effect of developing capitalism can also be traced.

Today, historical periodization of Hungarian folk ballads and their division according to subjects and eras is carried out with a great deal of difficulty. How hard such an experiment is can be shown by the introduction of different classifying experiments, in which the most varied and most arbitrary viewpoints are mixed with correct historical interpretation. Perhaps those researchers proceeded most consistently who simply divided Hungarian folk ballads by centuries. However, this division, although suitable for determining starting points, in no way marks off the larger units. That historical aspects have to be connected with aspects of genre also makes the division more difficult. Therefore, here we are first providing only an experiment in historical periodization according to subject, keeping in mind that the characteristic but understandable conservatism of the cultural elements of peasant class society does not permit closed time limits in any direction. At the same time this division by period is also suitable for briefly characterizing how the folk ballads have reflected the picture of society and how the development of the peasantry's fate can be read from it.

Narrative Ballads

There is a group among Hungarian folk ballads which bears the marks of great antiquity, and both the construction and conclusion of these is fable-like in character. In the technical literature this ballad is designated with the name "Miraculous Dead" or *Ilona Görög* (Helen Greek in English translation) and was found primarily in Transylvania and the north-western linguistic region:

"O indeed I die for,
Mother dear, my mother,
Helen Greek, my fair one,
Waist of hers so lithesome,
Waist of hers so lithesome,
Ruddy cheeks so wholesome,
Ruddy cheeks so wholesome,
Lips of hers so playsome,
Lips of hers so playsome,
Buttocks round and buxom,
Eyes of hers like flax bloom,
Helen Greek, my fair one."
And between them will be,
Magic mill a-seeing,
Helen Greek your true love."

"Dearest, sweetest mother,
Give me leave to go for
Magic mill a-seeing."

"Do not go, my daughter,
Helen Greek, my fair one,
'Tis a net they're casting
For the fish to catch in."

"O indeed I die for,
Mother dear, my mother,
Helen Greek, my fair one,
Waist of hers so lithesome,
Waist of hers so lithesome,
Ruddy cheeks so wholesome,
Ruddy cheeks so wholesome,
Lips of hers so playsome,
Lips of hers so playsome,
Buttocks round and buxom,
Eyes of hers like flax bloom,
Helen Greek, my fair one."

"Do not die, my dear son,
László Zetelaki!
I shall have all made you
Wondrous magic tower,
Breadthwise river Danube
With its walls will touch it,
Heightwise will it reach up
Heaven's highest summit.
Maidens, comely virgins
Sure they must come there for
Magic tower seeing,
And between them will be
Magic tower seeing,
Helen Greek your true love."

"Sweetest, dearest mother,
Give me leave to go for
Magic tower seeing."

"Do not go, my daughter,
Helen Greek, my fair one,
'Tis a net they're casting
Barbel for to catch in."

"O indeed I die for,
Mother dear, my mother,
Helen Greek, my fair one,
Waist of hers so lithesome,
Waist of hers so lithesome,
Ruddy cheeks so wholesome,
Ruddy cheeks so wholesome,
Lips of hers so playsome,
Lips of hers so playsome,
Buttocks round and buxom,
Eyes of hers like flax bloom
Helen Greek, my loved one."

"Do not die, my dear son,
László Zetelaki!
I shall have all made you
Such a magic hand-mill
As the first mill-stone will
Cast forth pearls the purest,
Second of the mill-stones
Cast forth silver farthings,
And the third will cast forth
Swishing fine silk fabric.

"Go and die, my son dear,
László Zetelaki!
Sure they must come there for,

Famous, fairest maidens,
Magic dead a-seeing,
'Mong the women will be,
Magic dead a-seeing,
Helen Greek, your true love."

"O my dearest mother,
Give me leave to go for
Magic dead a-seeing,
Magic dead to see who
Gave for me his ghost up."
"Do not go, my daughter,
Magic dead a-seeing,
'Tis a net they're casting
Barbel for to catch in,
Helen Greek, the fair one,
From her mother snatching."

★

But she would not heed her,
Hies she to her chamber,
There she goes to dress up,
Slips her blue silk gown on,
Puts a pair of red and
Iron-studded boots on;
On her head she ties a
Scarlet silken head-cloth,
Down the front she ties a
Clean and snow-white apron.

"Rise, my son, rise now,
László Zetelaki!
For the one you died for
There she comes the road up;
Rise my son, arise now,
László Zetelaki!
For the one you died for
There she comes the door in."

★

I have seen some dead men,
Never once like this one!
One whose feet should rise up
Ready for a-jumping,
One whose arms should stretch out
Ready for a-hugging,
One whose lips should open
Ready for a-kissing,
And who should right wake up
Soon as I have kissed him!

523

It is a theme widespread in European ballad literature that the young man entices his beloved by pretending he is dead. The variations, however, are very different. The Hungarian versions indicate northern connections (e.g. miraculous mill). From the point of view of their form, on the other hand, they can be classified into the newer ballads, which reflect the message and attitude of the folk tale, from ballads of romance character. The condensed method of performance, the administering of justice, the good humoured strength and finesse of the folk tale are asserted in these ballads.

Fig. 209. One of the melodies of the ballad "The Wife of Mason Kelemen". Korond, former Udvarhely County. 1955

The ballad of *Kőműves Kelemenné* (The Wife of Mason Kelemen) belongs to the same group, but it no longer sounds the happy, victorious voice of the tales, but rather that of inevitable tragedy (although in the Hungarian material of this group we know of tale-like prosaic endings, built on the elements of tales). In it the tragic conflict is built simultaneously on the motif of inhuman exploitation and greed and on an ancient belief, the belief of the building sacrifice (cf. pp. 158–9), data supporting this belief have been recovered at excavations of the city of Ur, from the fifth millennium B.C.

> *Once twelve master masons put their heads together,*
> *Déva's lofty castle that they would erect there.*
> *They would erect it for two full pecks of silver,*
> *Two full pecks of silver, two full pecks of guilder.*
> *Thereupon they set out, Déva town they went to,*
> *Déva's lofty castle building they did set to.*
> *What they built by midday, down it fell by evening,*
> *What they built by evening, down it fell by morning.*
>
> *Once more they took counsel, all twelve master masons,*
> *How to stop walls crumbling, how the building hasten;*
> *Till at last agreed they, came to this solution,*
> *All between themselves they made a resolution:*
> *"Any of our wives who be the first arriver,*
> *Gently we should take her, throw her in the fire,*
> *Mix with lime her ashes, tender ashes softly*
> *For to strengthen with it Déva's castle lofty."*

"Coachman mine, coachman mine, eldest of my servants,
Hark my hest which is to go and see my husband,"
Spoke and said the wife of Kelemen the mason,
"Hitch the horses quickly, harness them, come, hasten,
Hitch the horses quickly, bring them up the drive-way,
Let's set out for Déva, take we to the highway."

When that they were gone but half the journey forward,
Came there such foul weather, fast it rained and showered.
"Mistress mine, my starlet, let us stop, go backward:
Yesternight I had a bad sign in my sleeping,
In my sleep at night I such a dream was dreaming,
Kelemen the mason's courtyard I was treading,
Why his yard was all round covered in black mourning,
Right there in the middle stood a deep well yawning,
And his little son was dead in it all drownded;
Now this dream today might prove itself well-founded.
Mistress mine, my starlet, let us stop and turn back!"
"Coachman mine, coachman mine, never shall we turn back,
Nor the horses yours are, nor the carriage yours is,
On you drive the coach and crack whip on the horses."

Towards Déva's castle as they went advancing,
Kelemen the mason saw them at a glancing;
Sore afraid became he, uttered loud this prayer:
"O my God and Lord, please, take them away from here!
May the legs be broken of my chestnut steeds four,
May the spokes be shattered of my coach's wheels all,
May the Lord Almighty's thunderbolt come strike down,
May my horses snort and turn the carriage right home!"
Towards Déva's castle on the coach advances,
Neither horse nor coach did meet with no mischances.

"Good morrow, good morrow, all twelve master masons,
Good morrow to you, Kelemen the mason,"
So the woman hailed them and her husband answered:
"Good morrow, my wife, to you too," he at once said,
"Why did you come here to meet your death so dire,
Gently we should take you, throw you in the fire.
We the twelve stonemasons came to this agreement:
If a wife should come here, this should be her treatment:
We should take her gently, throw her in the fire,
Mix with lime her ashes taken from the pyre,
Déva's lofty castle make thereby well strengthened,
Only that way can we gain the hard-won payment."

Mistress Kelemen no sooner saw the meaning
Than a woeful heart with thus began a-moaning:
"Pray wait you, pray wait you, twelve who mean to murder
Till I take my farewell, wait you till no further,

Till I take my farewell women-friends of mine from,
From my women-friends and bonny little son from;
For the dead they're ringing, three times rings the church-bell,
But my lonely soul for none will toll the dead-knell."
With that Kelemen's wife home she went departing
For to say her farewells and take her final parting,
Take her final farewell women-friends of hers from,
From her women-friends and bonny little son from.

Mistress Kelemen then back she went a-hieing,
Towards Déva's castle all the way a-crying;
There they took her gently, throwed her in the fire,
Mixed with lime her ashes taken from the pyre,
Only thus could build they Déva's castle higher,
And the full tall price win which they did require.

Kelemen the mason when he went his gate in,
Saw his little son come running for to greet him:
"Welcome home, my father, dear beloved father!
Where is she, where is she, mother, dear my mother?"
Then his father answered, thus began a-speaking:
"Never you mind, dear son, she'll be home by evening."

"Lackaday, welladay, evening's come and sun set,
Still my mother dear she failed to come back home yet!
O my father, father, tell me, tell me truly
Where's my mother gone to, where my mother could be."
"Go you, son, you go to Déva's castle lofty,
There your mother's walled in, midst the stones lies coldly."

Up and went his son then, set out tears a-falling,
Set out for to find her Déva's castle tall in;
Three times did he shout on Déva's castle lofty:
"Mother, mother, speak up, speak to me once softly!"
"Son, I cannot speak up, for the stone wall presses,
Heavy stones lie o'er me, body, limbs and tresses."

There her heart did break and under her the ground, too,
And her little son he fell the chasm into.

This ballad is one of the most frightening symbols of the feudal, land-tied, completely exploited fate of the peasants. It tells of the dreadful inhumanity of class society, where not only the sweat and blood of the worker must be built into the fortress under erection, but if needs be, he must wall into it his own wife alive, or mix her gentle ashes into the lime in order for the wall to remain standing. And what is so tragic in this ballad, and in the belief itself, is that the peasantry looked upon the sacrifice as a matter of course; although presentiment, the anxious prayer of her husband and the force of nature all attempted to stop her, the order satisfying the pleasures of the lords must be carried out—the woman must sacrifice her life. What is so shocking is that for the peasantry, this story had great "epical authenticity".

The foundation of these ballads of belief is that at the raising of buildings there is a need to make a sacrifice. In ancient times this may have been human sacrifices, but later they tried to assist the structure to bind together by sacrificing only the blood or hair of men. Animal sacrifices (e.g. a rooster) were customary until the most recent times: this they placed mostly under the threshold or built into the wall. Remnants of these sacrifices often turn up even today from pulled down buildings. The belief in building sacrifice and the ballads expressing it are best known in Eastern Europe, especially in the Balkans.

Ballads attached to folk beliefs, or emphasizing the epic role of such beliefs, can be found in many groups, which makes their classification difficult. Thus the ballad of *Kata Kádár* contains more than one belief (bloody kerchief signalling trouble, the flower that grows out of the grave and begins to speak; both motifs are frequent in other ballads and tales), although the style of this ballad puts it more naturally among the songs of romance. Belief-like and story-like motifs both help the escape of "Gorgeous Kata Bán" *(Gyönyörű Bán Kata)* and explain the "Complaints of the Three Orphans", and such motifs appear even in the outlaw ballads, reflecting many centuries of observation of nature and beliefs. All of this proves that a rigid division is difficult, and that folk poetry can bring to life ancient motifs and fill them with new content.

Ballads containing religious motifs also belong to the rank of ballads built on motifs based on superstition. We can find ballads of arresting beauty among these also, such as the ballad "Julia, Fair Maiden" *(Júlia szép lány)*, certain of whose motifs remind some Hungarian researchers of the religious images of the pagan period, others of the religious images of the Christian era.

Ballads of Belief

> *Julia, fair maiden, walked abroad one morning,*
> *Cornflowers to gather out the fields of corn in,*
> *Cornflowers to gather, garlands for to bind there,*
> *Garlands for to bind there, for a while amuse her.*
> *High above in heaven as she looked up sunward,*
> *There a pleasant pathway came a-winding downward,*
> *Curly milk-white lamb came down upon it frisking,*
> *Lo, the sun and moon he mid his horns was bringing;*
> *On its brow it carried, ay, a shining starlet,*
> *Hanging from its horns each, ay, a red-gold bracelet,*
> *Both its sides bedight with two fair lighted candles,*
> *Hairs as many had it, all were sparkling spangles.*
>
> *Curly milk-white lamb did speak to her and say then:*
> *"Dont't be frightened of me, Julia, fair maiden,*
> *Holy host of virgins fell by one short lately,*
> *If thou wilt not say nay, I anon should take thee*
> *Up to Heaven's choir of saintly virgins thankful,*

527

Lead thee there amongst them, with thee make their ranks full,
Heaven's key I'd give thee, there to enter freely;
At the cock's first crowing I should come and see thee,
At the second crowing ask thee me to marry,
At the cock's third crowing off I should thee carry."

Julia, fair maiden, turned she to her mother:
"Mother dear, my mother," these words she did utter,
"As I walked out one day, cornflowers to gather,
Cornflowers to gather, for to bind some garlands,
Garlands for to bind and play amidst the corn lands,
High above in heaven as I looked up sunward,
There a pleasant pathway came a-winding downward,
Curly milk-white lamb came down upon it frisking,
Lo, the sun and moon he mid his horns was bringing;
On its brow it carried, ay, a shining starlet,
Hanging from its horns each, ay, a red-gold bracelet,
Both its sides bedight with two fair lighted candles,
Hairs as many had it, all were sparkling spangles.

Curly milk-white lamb did speak to me and said then:
'Don't be frightened of me, Julia, fair maiden,
Holy host of virgins fell by one short lately.'
If I wilt not say nay, he anon should take me
Up to Heaven's choir of saintly virgins thankful,
Lead me there amongst them, with me make their ranks full,
Heaven's key he'd give me, there to enter freely;
At the cock's first crowing he should come and see me,
At the second crowing ask me him to marry,
At the cock's third crowing off he should me carry.
Mourn for me, my mother, let me hear it living,
Living let me hear it how you mourn my leaving."

"O my daughter, dear one! Honeycomb so tender
Made by bees not swarmed yet★ from my flowers' nectar,
Yellow beeswax of my honeycomb so mellow,
Shroud of smoke a-spreading of the beeswax yellow,
Shroud of smoke a-spreading, flame that leaps to Heaven!

All the bells of Heaven, unrung, they were ringing,
Heaven's gates wide open, unflung, they were flinging,
There, alas, they just now led my little girl in."

We know this ballad, singular in its religious rapture, in relatively few versions. Its roots reach back to medieval poetry. This type of ballad is frequent and manifold in Western Europe, but those versions resemble the Hungarian version only in the taking of a girl to heaven for a bride.

★*'Virgin-honey', gathered by young bees before they have swarmed, is finer than honey from old hives.*

However, alongside certain elements of the Christian system of symbols (the lamb of God, candle of the Mass), the elements of the earlier world of belief can also be found in it (mythical stag, a guiding light). It may have been born in the Middle Ages, so that the possibility existed for uniting the two symbolic systems in one marvellous ballad.

The songs reminiscent of medieval Latin kinds *(disputatio)* also belong to this group, such as the Disputation of the Flowers *(Virágok vetélkedése).* However, this latter, with is conclusion, is not exactly sacred but rather like a secular love song. Less valuable, epic religious songs, which were sold in broadsheets or chapbooks, also belong here, and more remotely, the similar songs sung by beggars.

The next and very significant group of Hungarian folk ballads consists of historical ballads *(széphistóriás ballada),* associated with the 15th to 17th centuries and with themes of romance and the Turkish period. Even earlier researchers thought of these ballads as the most eloquent examples of the old ballad style; indeed, on the basis of their rhythm, structure, language, and melodies they can be listed among the ballads which preserve the oldest elements. The ballads of *Anna Molnár* and *Kata Kádár,* the ballads of *Szilágyi and Hajmási, Julia Szép* and *Julia Kis,* as well as *István Fogarasi* and its companions belong here. Naturally, references to the Turkish period, to the prison of the Sultan, etc., belong only to the paraphernalia of romance such as the following ballad of *Szilágyi and Hajmási,* and not to the basic story:

Ballads of Romance and of the Turkish Period

> *"Buddy, my good buddy, on the same bread living!*
> *Seven years have gone by since they took us captive*
> *To the Sultan's prison, for a bunch of grapes each;*
> *Never since then have we seen the sun a-burning,*
> *Nor the moon and stars in all their ceaseless turning..."*

> *This the Sultan's daughter, standing by the door, heard,*
> *Sultan's fairest daughter spoke to them with these words:*
> *"Hark you two Hungarians, hark to me and listen,*
> *You're to be set free soon from my father's prison:*
> *If I now release you, will you pledge yourselves too,*
> *For to take me in to Hungary's land with you?"*
> *Great Miklós Szilágyi made her right this answer:*
> *"Sure we pledge ourselves, ay, Sultan's fairest daughter!..."*
> *Straightaway she went back, Sultan's fairest daughter,*
> > *To her father's chamber.*
> *There she took the gaol key, with that to unlock it,*
> *And a few gold pieces put she in her pocket.*
> *Back again she went then, and the gaol door opened.*
> *Hardly had they left there, going in a hurry,*
> *When the girl began to glance back in a flurry,*
> > *Sultan's fairest daughter.*
> *"Hark, you two Hungarians, hark to me and listen,*
> *Young men just released from my father's prison:*

Look, there comes, look, there comes, all my father's army!
If they overtake us, o alas, they'll slay you,
                    And they'll take me back home."
"Do not fear, do not fear, Sultan's fairest daughter!
Neither will they slay us if our swords do serve us,
Nor will take you back home if the Lord preserve us."

Soon the camp came rolling, merciless great army—
"Buddy, my good buddy, look ye to the damsel,
                    Let us never say die!"
As the army caught up, he engaged in battle.

Through their ranks he made a footpath rushing forward,
Then he cut a cartway on the sally backward,
Leaving of the huge host but a single coward;
For to tell the news he run for hide all homeward.

When this had been over, they resumed their journey,
Spoke László Hajmási, this is what his words be:
"Buddy, my good buddy, let us try each other,
Which of us can win her, Sultan's fairest daughter!"
"Hark you two Hungarians, hark to me and listen,
Young men just released from my father's prison:
Do not cross you swords or fight you for me ever
Here I kneel, come, my head from neck you sever...!"

Brave Miklós Szilágyi speaks at once and says this:
"Buddy, my good buddy, on the same bread living!
Willingly I give you Sultan's fairest daughter,
For I have at home a ring betrothed woman,
Lawful wedded wife and helpmate of my bosom."

When the Sultan's daughter heard Szilágyi say so,
Readily she joined the other knight called László.
Brave Miklós Szilágyi went his way then homeward,
And László Hajmási took the damsel with him.

These ballads are often differentiated by passing nuances only from another group which portrayed the conflict, tragedies, and comedies of feudal social structure. This latter group is characterized by poetic formulations which carry the traces of both older and newer poetic styles. The story of the girl sold to the Turks and preferring to die is also revived in a more modern version dealing with the tragedy of the girl sold to the village miller *(István Fogarasi).* This group of the ballads of romance is linked together not only by the manner of presenting the themes and the narrative structure, but above all, by the folk-tale and narrative elements in its mirroring of society. It is not by chance that the 14th to 16th century literature of short stories and romance made use of this method of description throughout Europe. The phenomenon of the double influence could be verified by hosts of examples in this area also.

The images of the structured society and its confined laws still vividly remind one of folk tales, but in the plot, the conflict already begins to fill up with elements of reality, of real conflicts. This characteristic duality, the innate contrast of description is one of the reasons for the captivating charm of this cycle of ballads, e.g. *Barcsai*.

> *"Go, my husband, go to Kolozsvár up northward,*
> *Kolozsvár up northward, to my father's courtyard,*
> *Fetch from there, fetch from there great big rolls of linen,*
> *Great big rolls of linen, cambric freely given."*
> *"Do not go, my father, leave not home, I pray thee,*
> *Mother loves Barcsai, sure does as I say thee!"*
> *"Do you hear, my woman, what this child is saying?"*
> *"Heed him not, my sweet lord, sure he is but raving."*
> *With that he departed for to do as bidden,*
> *For to do as bidden, off to town was ridden.*
> *When he was but half-way, half-way of the journey,*
> *Came into his mind the words said by his bairn wee;*
> *Thereupon he turned back, went his way all homeward,*
> *Went his way all homeward, stepped into his courtyard.*
> *"Open the door, open up, quick, my wedded woman!"*
> *"Right I will, right I will, sweet my wedded husband!*
> *Only wait till I can put my workday skirt on,*
> *Only wait till I can tie around my apron."*
> *"Open the door, open up, quick, my wedded woman!"*
> *"Right I will, right I will, sweet my wedded husband!*
> *Only wait till I can pull my new-soled boots on,*
> *Only wait till I can tie my workday scarf on."*
> *"Open the door, open up, quick, my wedded woman!"*
> *What was she to do but went the door to open.*
> *"Go and get the key, the key to my big coffer!"*
> *"Nay, I cannot give you the key to the big coffer:*
> *Going through the garden for to visit next door,*
> *I must have dropped it, the key of the big chest there,*
> *But I'm sure we'll find it when the day is dawning,*
> *When the day is dawning, in the crimson morning."*
> *Thereupon he kicked his ornamented chest in,*
> *Ripping one side right off, wrenching it and wresting:*
> *Out of it came Barcsai, out he fell and rolled there,*
> *Ay, he snatched his sword and severed head from shoulder.*
> *"Do you hear, you woman, do you hear, you woman,*
> *From among these three deaths ay you must to choose one:*
> *Either choose that I should cut your head off right here*
> *Or that I sweep with your silken hair the house clear,*
> *Else you keep a vigil till the light breaks palely,*
> *Seven boards of guests to hold a candle gaily."*
> *"From among the three deaths sure I choose the last one,*
> *Seven boards of guests to holding candle gaily."*
> *"My servant, my servant, littlest of my servants,*
> *Bring you forth, bring you forth that big bowl of pitch bring,*

Bring you forth, bring you forth those big rolls of linen,
Those big rolls of linen, cambric freely given.
Start it at her head and wind her in them wholly,
Take those piles of cambric, round her head all roll ye,
Start it at her head and top to toe you tar her,
Start it at her toes and set it all on fire.
At her head I'll set a Wallachian piper,
At her feet I'll set a gypsy fiddle-player;
Come and blow, Wallachian, blow your olah★ *wood pipe,*
Come and play you, gypsy, play your gypsy fiddle;
Blow it to the four winds, come and play, don't tarry,
Let my wife be gay now, let her heart make merry."

The figure of the wife punished for her infidelity is frequent in European folk poetry; variations of it can also be shown in the *Gesta Romanorum*. Equivalents of this ballad can be traced all the way to the Spanish ballads. It can be compared to certain creations of Eastern European, primarily Russian ballad poetry, but the form of punishment by burning occurs rarely. The roots of this cruel but beautiful Hungarian ballad reach far back into the Middle Ages.

Here we will simply mention that one of the informative, word of mouth phenomena in the development of ballads which belongs precisely to this cycle is the shaping of the ballad towards prose structure. We can observe in this group the different degrees of development towards a completely prose version, through the lines of which still throbs the rhythm of the verse. This is the secret of its strange, spontaneous beauty, and it is also an example of the creation of figures, not necessarily corrupted but sometimes of new beauty, by oral transformation, or as certain theoretical schools have called it with sharp disparagement, "by singing asunder". It appears as if the development of the epic method of presentation created the conditions for prose transformation; however, so far few of us have examined the rules of this transformation.

Ballads of Wandering and Captivity

The ballads of wandering *(bujdosó ballada)* and captivity *(rabballada)*, which can be dated to the 17th and 18th centuries, represent a separate group. This delimitation of time cannot be taken rigidly; rather it indicates a period of development, the rise of characteristic features, since frequently a phrase, a strophe, or an entire connected section of such ballads of wandering and captivity went into the songs of the period that followed the defeat of the wars of liberation. Other parts have been integrated into the 19th century ballads of outlaws *(betyár ballada)*. The fate of the Hungarians fighting for their national freedom during the devastating Turkish occupation appears in these balladic laments with the validity of true poetry. This is no longer the world of the ballads of romance conjuring up royal, lordly courts. Neither is the cocky good spirit present, the resolute firmness of the Kossuth songs and soldiers' songs of 1848. The themes are of ravaged, smoking peasant

★ *Wallachian*

villages, deserted manors, the desperation of lost battles, the entreaty of captives to the miserly families, the lover waiting in vain, the soldier wandering in the pathless winter forest. Songs of particular authors might be supposed among these songs, laments of students and wandering soldiers, epic songs striking the chord of older ballads. However, their unity has absolute validity and clearly shows what differentiates poetic inspiration from recreations by the people, from continual polishing, and the monumental power of oral tradition. These songs and fragments give us a lyric, poignant portrait of the period through the eyes of the serfs. Let us mention here also that these were the centuries in which a characteristic stratum of the so-called "Turkish" soldier songs developed, the Hajdú and wandering songs of Rumanian, Bulgarian, Albanian and South Slav folk poetry. Comparative examination of these songs (one part of the Ukrainian folk poetry can also be included here) is one of the many tasks Eastern European folklore studies have still ahead. While the epic character defines the method of performance of the ballads in the first group—even of those constructed through dramatic dialogues—this group of ballads is characterized by lyric presentation.

The next group of ballads is defined by their dramatic construction and mode of depiction. These are characteristically composed so as to condense the story into one or more powerful dramatic scenes, and if there are more scenes, each is an almost independent dramatic whole, filled, in spite of the small scope, with terrific tension, with the clashing of emotions and passions. The historical dimensions of these ballads may be placed at about the periphery of the 17th and 18th centuries, although there are some, stylistically not part of the old ballad style, such as the ballad of *László Fehér,* which uses motifs that go back at least to the 16th century, and at the same time several elements foreshadowing the outlaw ballads:

Fig. 210. One of the melodies of the ballad László Fehér

533

László Fehér
(The Convict's Sister)

László Fehér roped some mounts in
Down below the black wood mountain.
Some he whipped off, some he snaffled;
Görc town was dismayed and baffled.

"Come on, come on, men of Görc town;
László Fehér we have run down.
Put the irons on the brigand,
Chain the left leg with the right hand."

"Give yourself up, doggone betyár,
Say your name, you outlawed beggar!
Give yourself up, doggone betyár,
Else your name speak, outlawed beggar!"

"Stockings white my horse's legs wear,
Sister mine's called Anna Fehér."
"What's your horse like asked you not we,
Nor about your sister haughty."

"Give yourself up, doggone betyár,
Say your name, you outlawed beggar!
Give yourself up, doggone betyár,
Else your name speak, outlawed beggar!"

"Stockings white my horse's legs wear,
And my name is László Fehér."
"Put the irons on the brigand,
Chain the left leg with the right hand."

Off to take him they were risen,
For to take him to the prison.
Off to take him they were risen,
Rode him off to darkest prison.

Anna Fehér when they told her
That they caught and jailed her brother,
Gave her coachman orders, said she,
"Get the coach-and-six all ready.

Get the coach-and-six all ready,
Put some gold on, gold with pecks three,
Put some gold on, gold with pecks three,
I shall get my brother set free."

Anna Fehér could not wait more,
Hied she to the iron-shod door:

"Brother, brother, László Fehér,
Are you sleeping, resting in there?"

"Neither resting nor a-sleeping,
On you, sister, I am thinking.
Neither resting nor a-sleeping,
On you, sister, I am thinking."

Anna Fehér could not wait more,
Hied she to the iron-shod door:
"Brother, brother, László Fehér,
What's he called, the magistrate here?"

"Justice Horvát is the villain,
He's the rascal fit for swinging.
Justice Horvát is the villain,
He's the rascal fit for swinging."

Anna Fehér none could hinder,
She will to the judge's winder:
"Justice Horvát, Lordship listen,
Get my brother out of prison.

Get my brother out of prison,
I shall give you gold in ransom."
"Keep your gold, I don't want any,
All I want is, lie down with me."

Anna Fehér could not wait more,
Hied she to the iron-shod door:
"Brother, brother, László Fehér,
Justice told me, this he did say:

"He'll today be freed of fetter
If we were to sleep together;
He'll today be freed of fetter
If we were to sleep together."

"Sister, sister, Anna Fehér,
Do not go to spend the night there;
For he shall your maidenhead take
And he shall your brother's head take."

Anna Fehér could not wait there
She will to the judge's chamber;
She did aye spend one night with him,
Gilded poster bed they lay in.

When it struck one midnight after,
From the courtyard came a clatter;

"Oh, Your Worship, Justice Horvát,
What's that clatter down the courtyard?"

"That's my coachman makes his horse drink,
It's the curb-bit makes that clinking.
That's my coachman makes his horse drink,
It's the curb-bit makes that clinking."

Anna Fehér could not wait more,
Hied she to the iron-shod door:
"Brother, brother, László Fehér,
Are you sleeping, resting in there?"

"Sister, sister, Anna Fehér,
Do not seek your brother in here;
O'er greenwood, o'er meadows,
There he hangs high from the gallows!"

Anna Fehér none could hinder,
She will to the judge's winder:
"Judge, Your Lordship, Justice Horvát,
May the horse you're riding stumble,

May the horse you're riding stumble,
May you from the saddle tumble,
May the horse you're riding stumble,
May you from the saddle tumble.

Thirteen cartloads' straw for palliasse
Go a-rotting in your mattress;
Thirteen years you lie on straw-sacks
Till their bottom with your weight sags.

Thirteen doctors be all busy,
With your sores should grow a-weary.
Thirteen stores of chemists, druggists
Empty for you all their physics.

Hark you, judge, what I am saying:
Be it blood you wash your face in,
Fire set your towel blazing,
May you never God's good grace win!"

This ballad is known throughout the entire Hungarian linguistic region, and new variations of it are still being discovered. Its archaic characteristics point to medieval origin; its main theme is widespread over Western Europe, so that it was even written up in literature, for example in Shakespeare's "Measure for Measure" or Sardou–Puccini's "Tosca". The subject is probably Italian in origin, and passed on into French and English collections of tales through Latin transmission. This ballad probably came to Hungary from the Italians, perhaps through Dalmatian transmission, after the middle of the 16th century.

This group contains whole strings of beautiful ballads, among them the ballads about the great mountain robbers, Ilona Budai, Beautiful Anna Bíró, Boldizsár Bátori, Anna Bethlen, and also the ballad of the girl who was danced to death (cf. Plate XXVIII).

Sheriff's wife of Sár Town
(The Girl who was Danced to Death)

"Good morrow, good morrow,
Sheriff's wife of Sár town,
Sheriff's wife of Sár town,
Kate, your daughter nutbrown!"

"Come in, daughter Kati,
Young men came to see you:
There's to be in Sár a
Wedding and a ball too."

"Nay, I go not, mother,
For it can't but bad bring:
'Tis János Árvadi
Has today his wedding."

"Come, my daughter Kati,
Put your skirt of silk on;
Put your feet and legs in
Boots of leather crimson.

Pull a pair of gold rings
On your every finger;
May they give your lover
Each of them a stinger."

"Good evening to János,
Árvadi, good evening!
I have come along too
For to grace your wedding."

"Come and hop it with me,
Merrily and briskly."
"Nay, I won't go with you
For your sleeves are filthy."

"Come and hop it with me
Merrily and briskly."
"Ay, I shall go with you:
Your sleeves are not filthy."

"Gypsy, play till midday,
Then on till the evening,
All the night till morning,
Till the day is dawning."

"Let me go, let me go,
Life is me a-leaving,
Silken skirt of mine is
To my body cleaving."

"I don't care a farthing
From this world your parting:
If you will not have me,
No one else should have ye."

"Let me go, let me go,
I am near a-dying,
In my clotted blood are
Both my legs a-lying."

"I don't care a farthing
From this world your parting,
If you will not have me,
No one else should have ye."

"Gypsy, play till midday,
Then on until evening,
All the night till sun-up
Till the girl is laid up."

"Coachman, bring the horses,
Let us with her home ride!..."
"Open, mother, open,
Open quick the gates wide!

Make your bed, make your bed,
Hurry with its making,
Let me rest awhile my
Limbs and body aching."

"Good morrow, good morrow,
Sheriff's wife of Sár town,
Sheriff's wife of Sár town,
Kate your daughter nutbrown!

Will you tell me, mother,
How's your daughter Kati?
Will you tell me, mother,
How's your daughter Kati?"

"Kati she is better,
As fit as a fiddle,
And she is all laid up
In her chamber's middle."

"Say if you will make a
Walnut coffin for her?"
"Sure I'll make a coffin
Made of marble for her."

"Say if you will have the
Triple bells a-ringing?"
"Mother, I shall have them
Singing all the sixteen."

"Say if you will have her
Taken to some clay-pit?"
"Mother, I shall have her
To the graveyard carried."

"Say if you will have her
By a beggar buried?"
"Mother, I shall have her
By the gendarmes carried."

Cursed be the father,
Seven times the mother,
Who will let their daughter
Go a wedding ball to;

Let her go at even,
Miss her not next morning;
On the third day after,
She is brought home dying.

In these epic songs of dramatic force, the merciless, closed system of feudalism is manifested much more than before; and, contrary to the conclusions of earlier researchers, it can be ascertained that the cause of these dramatic clashes is precisely the social and family order that suppressed individual feeling and proved how much the individual was at the mercy of the blind and wild forces of society. All conflicts arise from this. Passions, too, all run in the same closed electric circuit; hatred, jealousy, greed, violation and murder fill the stories. Not a word is mentioned about the tragedies of Christian freedom of choice; rather it keeps coming to light that it is impossible to break out of this predetermined closed system. The power of these ballads to describe human beings, their method of shaping human fates through certain passions, is unmatched in its kind. The story begins immediately with an explosive, tense scene, and one of the great marvels of these ballads is precisely that the very few scenes and characters provide the tragic tension of great drama. The apparent great difference between epic and ballad can be found, among other things, in this method of construction, in such a dramatic and concise method of composing the story of the ballad. It is also characteristic that, while in the dramatic ballads of the 16th and 18th centuries the peasants already appear with their own social clashes among the characters, and while in the folk tale and historic ballads they almost never appear, or infrequently as secondary characters, the situation is reversed in dance ballads, where, with the exception of the ballad about the prince, the characters come exclusively from peasant class society.

Dance ballads *(táncballada)* make up a separate group within the ballads with dramatic construction. It is perhaps even harder to place them within a time period than is the case with other Hungarian ballads, since we have reason to suppose that this ballad group follows its genre almost from the inception of the genre and is a characteristic part of it. The period of its flourishing in Hungary probably falls within the 16th century, when it acquired its characteristic features. There are some among these dance ballads that follow a tragic course. Not infrequently, the merry counterpart of a tragic ballad can be found among the dance ballads, such as the story of the punishment of the unfaithful wife or the tragedy of overbearing pride, or the story of the bride who became pregnant before the wedding. At the same time we can find in this ballad cycle a whole row of realistic, ironic depictions and sharply observed comic scenes. It is instructive to consider how great a part is played in their tone by "Latin education", to which significant style-forming power is attributed—not without reason—in folk music. However, this alone cannot be considered to be determinative of period and style.

Dance Ballads

We also know the clumsy, literary originals of some merry ballads *(víg ballada)*, such as "The Cuckolded Husband". However, the merry folk versions of these, which spread throughout the country, are not only more valuable, but also have amalgamated into the popular ballad stylistic characteristics that existed in the literary form. Or let us refer to the difference that shows up, despite the connection, between the repetitious (often comically meaningless) lines and refrain-like sections of dance ballads and similar stylistic traits of 17th century poets. In these dance ballads a new kind of voice arises trying to express the disintegration of the closed feudal structure. A more liberated way of handling the story and a certain irony reflect an encounter with society as a whole, and in it of the serfs, with the newly established economic and social forces. Naturally, all of this is reflected through an indirect mode of expression, but in the development of the ballad genre it is precisely dance ballads that show this supposition to be correct.

Merry Ballads

Therefore, to all intents and purposes the genre of the dance ballad leads us from the ballad poetry of previous centuries to the group of ballads that developed in the 19th century. Needless to say, these 19th-century folk ballads are also connected by numerous links to the tradition that developed in previous periods, even though at the same time their evolving new genre and stylistic characteristics separate them from their predecessors as well. It is usual to term this group the new-style ballad, on the example of melodic categorization.

The first and most important group of new-style or 19th-century ballads still echoes the tone of 18th-century ballads in a number of ways. This is the cycle of the ballads of outlaws *(betyárballada)* (cf. also pp. 495-500). One of the main reasons for their widespread distribution and popularity was discovered early: the poor and oppressed people saw in the heroes of the outlaw ballads its own heroes, the defenders of the poor and the

Ballads of Outlaws

punishers of the lords. The people took pleasure in the outlaws' show of courage, and all their sympathy belonged to the chained or hanged outlaw. These ballads already use a new poetic language and a new method of description.

> *Rózsa Sándor's saddling up his Velvet horse,*
> *Thirty-three gendarmes pursue his trail and course;*
> *Rózsa Sándor didn't take it for a joke,*
> *Jumping on his horse named Velvet off he rode.*
>
> *"Publican's wife, good day give the Lord to you,*
> *Have the mounted gendarmes been here, tell me true!"*
> *"No, the mounted gendarmes were not here today,*
> *Szeged betyárs only just have gone away."*
>
> *"Publican's wife, pour out some wine in this cup,*
> *Send your maid and as a look-out set her up!"*
> *All at once the frightened maid comes scurrying:*
> *"Nine gendarmes are coming this way hurrying!"*
>
> *Rózsa Sándor didn't take this for a joke,*
> *Riding to the crown-land puszta out he broke.*
> *Stumbling in a hole the horse did throw him down:*
> *Rózsa Sándor was arrested lying down.*
>
> *"All I ask you, corporal of gendarmerie,*
> *Here my right arm, will you please my arm set free?"*
> *But the corporal listened not to what he said:*
> *All the nine let fly in his arm shots of lead.*
>
> *Rózsa Sándor's led by the constab'lary*
> *Up the prison steps of the gendarmerie.*
> *Town of Szeged, yellow★ city, dark yellow!*
> *Rózsa Sándor's locked up there, all brought down low.*

Sándor Rózsa (1813–1878) was the best known Hungarian outlaw and there are ballads and songs about him throughout the entire linguistic territory. At the age of 23 he was already prisoner in the notorious prison of Szeged, from which he escaped; that escape and a whole string of other adventures are associated with his name. During the War of Independence of 1848–49, he formed a "free troop" that fought against the oppressors, thus further increasing his earlier popularity. After the war was lost, Rózsa and his mates continued their outlaw existence, taxing primarily the rich. He was captured twice and condemned to death both times, although there was very little evidence against him. His punishment in both cases was commuted to life imprisonment, and he lived out his life in prison.

In the outlaw ballad the epic-lyric tone once again returns. It sings about its hero not by means of dramatic condensation, but rather

---

★ *Yellow, a colour of the Habsburgs, was symbolic of Austrian oppression.*

through realistic portrayal. At times this calm, realistic tone, telling the cruellest story, is truly astounding. We can say that it is indeed a novel voice, looser, more informal, not containing the sultry tension and suffocating density of the ballads of earlier periods. It is, by the way, precisely this liberated tone, this simple method of description of the Hungarian outlaw ballad that differentiates it from its Russian, Ukrainian relatives, from the cruel-toned Spanish robber ballads, or from the English Robin Hood ballads. Although outlaw ballads display connections with the murder ballads from this period that were sold as broadsheets, and other broadsheet ballads, the outlaw ballad is much more mature, more artistic than those and was better filtered through the sieve of oral tradition:

> *Where's Péter supping, poor man so forsaken?*
> *By a little greenwood he is toasting bacon.*
>
> *Poor man Péter Barna stole and sold some horses,*
> *Both the Roman daughters clothed them from these sources.*
>
> *Poor man Péter Barna 'twixt gendarmes is walking*
> *With the Roman daughters through the window gawking.*
>
> *Poor man Péter Barna two gendarmes cross-question,*
> *Mrs Roman's daughters in the doorway listen.*
>
> *"O you ill-famed lady, don't you make them listen,*
> *'Cause it is for you three I must go to prison.*
>
> *Gentlemen of Kálló they are four and twenty,*
> *Who is hauled afore them suffers more than plenty.*
>
> *All the four and twenty torture me and question,*
> *Any man they keep in learns a painful lesson.*
>
> *'Bring him to the gallows,' one of them is saying,*
> *But another thinks that 'He is not past saving.'*
>
> *And the twenty-fourth is entering my name in,*
> *But the dame beside him is the one dictatin'.*
>
> *O you ill-famed lady, don't my name you utter,*
> *'Tis alone for your sake all this I must suffer."*

This ballad probably originated in the first half of the 19th century. It describes without any romanticism the life of the lonely outlaw, who in most cases finally faces death.

Ballads of Lament   The epic manner of performance of the outlaw ballads is somewhat related to those ballads of lament *(sirató ballada)* which tell their tragic story in the first person singular, about the high point of death, as it were. The construction and handling of the story of the outlaw ballads is in many ways similar, and the first person singular method of story telling—perhaps after an introductory section—is not infrequently characteristic of it. Here also the hero of the ballad reviews and laments his life in its concluding moment, at the moment of his capture and before the sentence is carried out. Structural analyses of these two ballad groups proves undeniably what a formative role was played by the laments in the birth of epic genres, also by the first-person singular method of narration. The ballads of lament demonstrate the way literary works "coming from above", cantorian songs and the like, take on the popular manner of performance and become artistically transformed.

Broadsheet Ballads   The group of sheet or broadsheet ballads *(ponyva ballada)* which tell about so-called true events—love, infidelity, murder originating from jealous love, family revenge, murder by family members pursuing wealth, infanticide, and similar themes (see Ill. 269-272)—is probably not earlier than the 19th century. We can feel in these ballads that they have just come off the huckster's spread-out canvas (hence the Hungarian name *ponyva,* meaning canvas), and that oral tradition has as yet barely started its work of altering and transforming them. The verse is frequently jolting, the construction of the theme reminds one of primitive wood engravings or the depictions of scenes by picture exhibitors at fairs, its moral lessons connected unnaturally to the conclusion of its story as if the story itself was felt to be lacking in strength to publicize its inner truth.

Náni Bereg
(The Murderous Unwed Mother)

Debrecen town has a greenwood, greenwood,
Yellow bird is keeper of that greenwood;
I was once the keeper of that forest,
Náni Bereg's faithful lover honest.

Náni's flowing ribbon, as I guesses,
Never will she weave it in her tresses.
"Put it, Náni, put it in your drawer there,
It may come in handy for your daughter."

"Oh good Lord, it gives me woe and sadness
When I see my life become so hapless.
Bitterly I weep and burst out crying
Though my lips took as if they're smiling."

Náni Bereg to the greenwood rode she,
Made herself a bed under an oak tree.

I did shout and call to her and cry too:
"Get up, Náni, lest a body spy you!"

Náni rose, and putting feet in stirrup,
To a csárda went she at a gallop.
As she was the Arad Inn to enter,
Nine gendarmes did get her to surrender.

Náni bids the goodwife of the tapster:
"Four-score quarts o'wine and four score candles,
Let the gendarmes, all nine lads be drinkin'!"

As she is escorted by these fellows,
Náni's mother watches through the windows.
"Don't look on my shame and scandal, mother,
'Cause it is for you I have to suffer."

"Come tell, Náni, is your heart not achin',
For to have your new-born child forsaken?"
"Yea, it is, oh sure my heart is breakin',
Till I die the chains I shall be shakin'."

Brass straps do my door of jail cell fasten,
And my berth is whitewashed in the 'mansion'.
I must thank the gracious noble county
For their kindness granting me such bounty.

Tisza river, Tisza flows so murky,
Swimming 'cross it naught avails a birdie.
Have you heard such a word under heaven
That to love my sweetheart is forbidden?

In my mind with Kálmán I am drinkin',
On my parents rarely am I thinkin'.
I forget all, scarce do I remember,
Captive to him I must be forever.

The ballad develops its themes in rather rigidly juxtaposed images, jolting along like the performance of historical songs, in which the conflicts of peasant class society, its tensions, and problems are already expressed, often describing through the story of one single family an entire society.

There appears before us in these stories a new method of reflecting society, the peasant picture of feudalism in its state of capitalization, and also an emerging new form. Although in Hungary the broadsheet ballad cannot look back to such a distant past as it does in the rest of Europe, we do know that János Arany, who was very much interested in folk poetry, saw in the middle of the last century picture-exhibiting singers whose primitive manner of performance inspired him to write his most artistically constructed ballads, and we do know that one of the well-known figures of Hungarian rural fairs was the huckster with his calendars and his poetic or prose stories (cf. Ills. 269–272).

However, the broadsheet ballad is instructive not only because through oral tradition it can take on an ever finer, ever more clear form (as in the case of the well-known ballad of *Kláris Szücs*), but also because in this area the increasingly class-conscious, creative, peasant talent can be observed, peasant poets striving to be individual artists and do so, although a long and difficult struggle still awaits them.

Kláris Szücs

Soon the clock will strike eight, evening is beginning,
Every maid gets ready for to go a-spinning.
Poor maid Kláris Szücs too she would like to go there,
But the sky above her gathered clouds all over.

Heaven's overcast and dark with dismal warning,
Poor maid Kláris Szücs put herself in mourning;
Come to the spinning-room, scarcely was she seated,
When a lad came up and called her out a minute.

Says the eldest woman: "Who is she, I wonder?"
"She's my sweetheart," said he, giving her the answer.
Then he called her out and took her down the valley.
There she will be murdered in th' "Italian gully".

When he struck the first blow: up and gleamed the fokos,★
When he struck the second: oh, it made her blood gush.
"Come ye girls, come ye girls, come my friends and help me,
Never shall I come more to the Sunday spinn'ry."

Out they went, lifted her, put her on the ground dead,
All the blood was in her made the earth around red.
"Dear my friends, dear my friends, learn of me this lesson:
Shun all jealous young men, don't get friendly with them.

Do not carry distaffs when you go a-spinning,
Taking 'em along there might be your undoing;
You shall be all wordless by the Monday morning,
In th' 'Italian gully' you will meet your ruin..."

Write this on the headboard, on my mournful grave-post...
Every virgin maid her chastity should guard most.

This is the area in which we can trace most easily the century-long process of peasant creativity. Although the figure of a shepherd who knew Latin and wrote poetry had already appeared in the correspondence of the *literati* during the first quarter of the 19th century (Ferenc Kazinczy and Ádám Pálóczi Horváth), notice has been taken of creative,

★ *A Hungarian folk weapon resembling a long-handled ax*

peasant poetic talent only very late. Since that discovery, and by means of the broadsheet and oral tradition, we now know the identity of an increasing number of peasant poets who, by using the turn of oral tradition and by serving the demands of their audience, endeavoured to recount events in verse. From these versifiers who wrote not only in the manner of the historical song writers but who also frequently made use of Tinódi-like phrases, a long road leads to the time when from among these cumbrous versifiers poets were born, those true poets who sang about the deepest sorrows of the Hungarian people.

The last group of ballads from the 19th century and the turn of the century already speak about the theme of capitalization. The village encounters the machine, and it appears in ballads as something unknown and frightening, the cause of tragedies. Ballads are known about the peasant girl's fate in the factory, her misfortune, and these similarly reflect a fear of the machine:

New Ballads

Julcsa Farkas
(The girl who fell into the threshing machine)

Harvesters began to work at Beremend,
On the feed-plate Julcsa Farkas had to stand;
Julcsa Farkas to the feed-plate up she went;
She did tumble in the drum by accident.

Shouts the feeder high up on the thresher's top,
"Hey, machinist, bring the engine to a stop!
Hey, machinist, bring the engine to a stop!
'Cos the drum my lil' sister swallowed up."

Julcsa Farkas they did bundle on a cart,
Took her to dear Doctor King, in his backyard.
Doctor he just looked at her, and this he said:
"But for God's grace she is now as good as dead."

Floating wicks are lighted at the Farkas's,
'Tis her folks are keeping watch, or so I guess.
Julcsa Farkas has around her flower wreaths,
By the bed her mother wakes and sore she grieves.

Every time Ol' Farkas goes to see her there,
Droops he o'er his walnut table in despair.
"Lord, you have deprived me of my only child,
God, your frightful punishment near drives me wild!"

That machinist goes out to the cemet'ry,
And before the cross he falls down on his knee:
"Good my Lord, do take my soul to you above
Once you have deprived me of my only love!"

The steam-driven threshing machine was the first machine to appear in the Hungarian village and also to spread rapidly during the second half of the last century. Naturally, people not used to machinery often fell victim to the turning wheels, primarily those girls who fed the sheaves into the threshing machine. Ballads about them spread over the entire linguistic territory during the last decades of the 19th century, and in these the balladic manner of description can still be found.

The stories in the ballads of emerging capitalism show the bleakness, hopelessness of peasant fate; the songs of migration recall the tone of the ballads of wandering; in others, the evicted kills the auctioneer, and the religious stanzas that are linked to the ballad do not alleviate the barren, cruel mood. In these ballads, even if not always in artistically ripened forms, the image of the plundered, aimlessly lost, tortured peasantry is frequently conjured up.

Forms of the Folk Ballad

So far we have been discussing the development of the ballad, those factors which influenced its development, about its performers, and the nameless peasant community which polished and perfected the ballad. We have considered the link between the ballad and the elements of fairy stories, short stories, of belief and superstition and the historical, epic manner of performance, the principle of dramatic construction both in the epic and dance song versions of ballads. In the course of outlining this genre, we have also had the opportunity to consider the "message" of the Hungarian folk ballads through their symbols and themes, as well as through their manner of depiction.

During this historical review, it has, hopefully, become evident that the Hungarian folk ballad incessantly gave voice, from its earliest periods, to the feelings and world of ideas of the entire nation, singing about the life of the hopeless, ill-fated people from the willingness to fight for their cause, to the bitter fate of the fugitive. Now, let us look at the question of the artistic form of the Hungarian folk ballad. It is evident that the folk ballad represents a literarily complex poetic world which actually fuses the essential features of every genre, and might demand the formal analysis of the complete storehouse of Hungarian folk poetry. Its complex literary nature created an immense wealth of forms: all the formative achievements and mature results of folk poetry flowed into the channel of folk ballad; we can find here the uncertain tone of early development just as much as infinitely chiselled poems of flawless cadence and full sounding melody.

First, let us make a few comments about the language and richness of poetic expression of the Hungarian folk ballads. In the middle of the 19th century, János Erdélyi had already called attention to the significance of the language in folk poetry: "In what, therefore, does the strength of folk poetry lie? It lies primarily in the language, in transparent, clear, noble performance... Therefore literary poetry is to take up the clarity of folk poetry, its brave linking of words, its idioms independent of all rules..."

At another place he pointed to the straightforward, concise forms of balladic expression, its economic use of adjectives, while the elucidation of repetition as a linguistic form carried him to the questions of versification. In the folk ballad the adjective does not have only orna-mental value, but rather always appears at crucial moments of descrip-tion and expression. Therefore the people use it infrequently, only at the important turns of the poem. Economy of adjectives and adverbs is not a sign of poverty but rather represents the inner strength and richness of forms that are well condensed and welded. In the poetry of the people this especially applies to ballads, where each adjective has an outstanding syntactical and poetic value. Historically, we could say that the later Hungarian ballad increasingly uses a structure of adjectives and similes, and as we approach our times, it seems as if folk poetry would permit more and more concessions. In certain older ballads, however, the accumulation of adjectives might be a sign of interference by a writer or recorder.

Verbs are used richly and in a diversified way in folk ballads. The descriptiveness and power of expression in the use of verb tense and moods, as well as the diversified and not infrequently incremental use of verbs in the Hungarian ballads would deserve a separate essay. This is in large part connected with their dramatic construction and with the folk ballad's method of dramatic condensation. In an epic genre of such a small calibre as the ballad, dramatic conflicts, the antagonism of characters, and the expression of actions can only be achieved by the courageous and incisive use of verb forms, of which the folk ballad is a master.

All that is called to our attention by the syntax of folk poetry could be considered a special chapter on Hungarian verse syntax. The folk ballad, and indeed folk poetry in general, sets a good example to the poet by the perfect coincidence of the expressive sentence with the structure of the poem and thus with the emphatic part of the poetic message. Unification of the intellectual and expressive with the poetic and descriptive aspects of the sentence is perfectly attained here. It would be worth while analysing the dramatic dialogues and clashes from the point of view of the peculiar syntax of the verse, or the development of the ballad-type sentence according to the lyric, dramatic, or epic progress of the poem. The flexible shaping of the ballad type sentence, its tightening in dramatic ballads, its harsh explosiveness or lyric softness at other places, all this praises the wealth of folk language. Thus the ballad shows poets how they can apply the vast potential of the language for the expression of the most complicated message.

As we said above, to speak of ballad versification almost amounts to speaking about the most important questions of versification for the entirety of folk poetry. At the outset our researchers found in ballad versification the example of ancient Hungarian versifying, although attention must be called to the difference among certain ballad groups, and to the difference in the historical period of their verse forms. Some people emphasize even the geographic element of the difference: those from the Great Plain are more melodic and lyric than the ones from Transylvania, the epic character of which is more conspicuous. Those from the Great Plain have stanzas and rhymes, while those from Transylvania are often without stanza and rhyme and use only the caesura, stress, alliteration, and parallelism.

One characteristic of Hungarian folk ballad versification is alliteration, or rather the fact that the structure of word repetition often also determines the form and character of the stanza, replaces the refrain or rather develops it. We can look upon this conspicuous method of repetition in the ballad as a genuinely Hungarian rhythmic tradition. It would be a gratifying task to systematize these types of repetitions, and to examine their regularity. The character of repetition which creates a poetic atmosphere and emphasizes the importance of the message clearly manifests itself in the Hungarian folk ballad. Repetition in folk ballads is not merely an old technique, the survival of which would be understandable anyway as an aspect of oral tradition, but it is rather a poetic means of expression and exists for the sake of the message. In the innumerable shades of repetition we can see one of the most significant elements of the formation of Hungarian folk ballads.

Furthermore, in their rhythms, verse and stanza structure, these folk ballads reflect every aspect of the development and flowering of written Hungarian poetry. We can perhaps look upon rhyme technique as the least rich and polished, and we are indeed more likely to find the newer ballads among those in rhymed forms, although even this is not exclusively so. At a number of points, precisely in playful, merry ballads, rhyme technique meshes with the forms of European versifying, with forms also affecting Hungarian poets. Therefore we can state that the entire progress of Hungarian historical prosody can be found in ballads.

The problem of the dramatic structure and construction of the Hungarian ballad belongs to the questions of artistic form, in the narrow sense, of "national form". Even if we accept the earlier observation —which, however, applies to the totality of the Hungarian ballad genre and not to individual ballads—that through historical development epic, dramatic, and lyric elements equally have become amalgamated into the ballad, the fact remains that the dramatic element had the greatest formative role in the ballad's development. Within the body of the European ballads, the Hungarian folk ballads are dramatically constructed epic or lyric songs, with the dramatic principle taking precedence. The architectural structure of folk ballads, the confrontation and intensification of situations, the dramatic composition of the dialogues, the introduction of the characters through these dialogues almost as heroes as well as individual personalities, all testify to a high degree of poetic awareness. Indeed, the concept of creative awareness may safely be applied to those anonymous authors and subsequent re-tellers who gave these ballads their shape. Dramatic character permeates every group of folk ballads—with the exception of a number of more recent broadsheet ballads, in which the historical narrative voice still greatly dominates.

Obscure and spasmodic style is by no means necessarily dramatic in effect. Drama always develops from and seeks solutions to great conflicts, tragedies or comedies of the clash of ideologies, morals and characters. Hungarian folk ballads show a special propensity for the creation of such characters and situations through dialogue—and not infrequently, by telling the story in the first or third person. One characteristic of the thrice-repeating structure, which, by the way, is related to folk tales even in its form, is also suitable for dramatic intensification. While the thrice-repeating structure of the folk tale (three adventures, three deals with the dragon, etc.) more likely uses the methods of *quantitative* intensification, this intensification in the ballad is *qualitative:* repetition (cf. *Ilona Görög, Wife of Mason Kelemen, Anna Fehér,* etc.) makes the situation increasingly dramatic, it more and more exposes the worthless, bad wife, the daughter deserted by her parents and saved only by her lover, the dead man who begins to respond only to the words of his lover, etc. Increasing intensification also makes the fate of the wife of the Mason Kelemen even more ominous. Yet not only intensification, but the use of scenes antithetical to each other, the dramatic buildup of unexpected situations, also emphasize this characteristic quality of the Hungarian ballad. Most definitely, one of the greatest poetic values of the Hungarian folk ballads lies in their dramatic nature. The ballad in this sense is really a *dramatic* song.

The examination of melody also falls within the scope of the question of ballad form. We know that ballads always appear in the union of lyrics and melody, and today we see increasingly clearly that this union is not the only thing characterizing ballads, since a play-like dancing performance was also characteristic, and is characteristic in many places even today, including both tragic and merry themes. This intertwining of lyrics and melody does not mean that the same melody was always connected to a certain lyric. Bartók warned us that even melodies of the old-style Székely ballads are not inseparable from their lyrics, that other ballads of similar rhythm or lyric songs are sung to the same beautiful melodies. However, Bartók also notes that this separating, this teaming up with a novel text is not old in origin. Naturally, this separating and switching do not moderate but rather increase our problems in this area.

Bartók analyzed the melodic peculiarities of Hungarian folk ballads, the four-line isometric stanza construction and the largely pentatonic scale; we also know that ballads, in the course of their historical development, behaved similarly in the matter of prosody, and we could quote a series of significant parallels in the history of Hungarian folk melodies. Most distant historical perspectives and relationships to historic melodies have been increasingly discovered. We know of ballads which have been stamped by the sign of Latinate, collegiate music, by the ecclesiastic scale, and by 16th–17th century Hungarian folk music; and we identify as well one stratum of ballads with widespread, new-style melodies, which, however, have centuries-old antecedents.

Folk Tales and Legends

The genres of narrative folklore are extraordinarily varied, and although they can be clearly separated from one another by their principal traits, we can still find numerous points of transition and interconnection. The Hungarian material, that is, the folk tale, different groups of sagas, legends, anecdotes, true stories, the increasingly popular short stories, memoirs, idioms, proverbs and riddles, can be mentioned here only in broad outline. Even among these, we must restrict ourselves to those genres that are most general and teach us the most about the subject.

Certain groups of place names infer that fairy tales and tales of belief have an extensive past. We can find these place names in documents and historical notations from the 11th century among the most diverse Hungarian ethnic groups and in different parts of the country. So far, research has paid little attention to such data. Let us quote a few examples: 1075/1217: *Usque ad caput laci qui* (ÖRDÖG SARA) (devil's soil) *uocatur* (the numbers indicate the date of the document, or perhaps the date of its recopying); 1270: *Quod quidem fossatum vulgariter* ÖRDÖGBARÁZ-DÁJA (devil's furrow) *noncupatur*." We will not quote further sentences from documents but will introduce instead a few examples of place names that fit here and demonstrate that epic tales, local epic histories, and short stories of belief were very much alive. 1342: *ördögkútja* (devil's well); 1344: *ördög szántása* (devil's plough land); 1416: *ördög-kő* (devil's stone); 1446: *bába völgye* (witch's valley); *ördögmaró völgye* (devil's grass valley, here the reference is to a magic grass); 1500–1580: *ördög eresz-kedője* (devil's slope); 1295/1403: *ördöngős fő* (devilish head). We find the following among proper names: Anthonio *Ördögűző* (Anthonio the Exorcist), 1454, Johanne *Ördöngős* (Devilish John), 1429, etc. Another group of place names includes: 1256/1270: *Sárkány-hegy* (dragon hill); 1262: *Sárkány-fő* (dragon head); 1391: *Sárkány szigete* (dragon's island); 1418: *Sárkánykő* (dragon stone); 1462: *Sárkány ároka* (dragon's ditch), etc.; also 1476: *Bűbájos tó* (enchanted lake). Similarly, we could list data from 1279 about, e.g. *kígyókő* (snake stone), *kígyólyuk* (snake hole). For example, a local document dated 1390 allows us to infer the existence of both a local legend and of a myth of origin: *Iungit vnum magnum lapidem* MEDVEKŐ (bear stone) *nuncupatum*.

These data on selected place names and proper names demonstrate that in oral tradition and in the circle of epic prose various stories of magic and belief must have existed; there were also local legends and myths of origin. We find references in documents which may refer to a fabulous content, but it is not possible to solve them; such is, e.g. the mention from 1578 of the "two fools' plate", which might be based on a true story associated with King Matthias. We could continue mention-ing such problematical names, e.g. 1520: Demetriusz *Babszem,* meaning Bean, but being the equivalent of Tom Thumb, a name which would verify the suspicion that the family name of the hero of the folk tale "Babszem Jankó" (Johnny Bean) was not a new invention. However, the occurrence of *Babszem* is rare, and this tale probably came to the Hungarians later in the wake of the Grimm Tales; therefore we need not concern ourselves with listing data of this type. We think that for the time being, we can be satisfied with the evidence provided by documented material from as early as the first centuries after the Conquest, of the existence through oral tradition of epic prose and fabulous narratives.

Besides the testimony of documents, the history writers of the royal courts of the House of Árpád can also bear witness to the existence of oral tradition and of fabulous epics. These chroniclers tried to serve the consolidating central power of the kings, and the difference between the authenticity of their manuscripts and scorned oral tradition was further sharpened by the existence in oral tradition of an attitude opposed to the consolidating feudal state and regime. And yet, in spite of this, and despite the scorn of courtly chroniclers, the legends that existed in oral tradition and the mythical or fabulous stories that were connected with (or that interfered with) them seeped into the official historical narration. And it is interesting that despite Anonymus' reproving and slighting comments, such fabulous histories of oral tradition not only were preserved but in the narrations of Hungarian chroniclers written between the 12th to 14th centuries, but tale-type details increasingly proliferated. The *Chronicle of Kézai* (1280), among others, reports many legendary elements surviving in the wake of the lost 11th century ancient gestes, the sources of which can be found in Persian tales.

We can trace the fabulous and legendary elements to a great past. Thus for example, the legend of the chieftain Lél (Lehel) belongs to the Salamon-legend cycle, widely known during the Middle Ages. The duel of Botond, the small-statured Hungarian common soldier, with six huge Byzantine soldiers recalls the fight of David and Goliath.

The chronicles and historical works of the 16th century both offered a great deal to oral tradition and also preserved much of it. Thus in 1559, in the work of István Benczédi Székely published in Cracow and entitled *Chronicle of the Outstanding Things of the World,* or in the work of Gáspár Heltai that appeared in 1575, entitled *Chronicle of the Affairs of the Magyars,* several more significant stories about King Matthias are included, which refer, furthermore, to the existence of these stories in oral folk tradition, a reference which is especially interesting because in another of his works Heltai simply abstracts his work in Latin from the Italian Bonfini.

All this means that after the passage of a century, oral folk tradition surrounding the figure of this great king had already begun to develop. For our purposes, this proves the power of oral tradition.

We will not trace all the way through the literature of chronicles. Among the examples that can be given perhaps these will serve to demonstrate that Hungarian historical writing between the 12th and 16th centuries preserved a number of elements of local legends and anecdotal stories taken over from the oral tradition of peasants and serfs, and through various transfers, from the legends of chronicle literature. More elements filtered in from oral tradition.

The various genres of religious literature, the effects of cloister literature between the 13th and 16th centuries (sermons, parables, meditations, biographies of saints, etc.) also have significant source value for us. Just as European folklore has taken notice of material from the *Legenda Aurea,* the *Scala coeli,* the various *Speculums,* the *Catalogus de Sanctorum,* so Hungarian prose folk poetry also drew from similar sources. But folk poetry in its turn also effected religious literature: the works of Pelbárt Temesvári (1435–1504) and Osvát Laskai (1450–1511), which appeared in many reprintings, contain legendary episodes, motifs, and anecdotal stories. In these the short story-like narrative method, the tone of adventurous, romantic story telling also appears from time to time. The mutual effect of written records and of oral tradition on each other, and their simultaneous development, can be demonstrated in this area also. We are not willing to suppose only a one-directional influence originating from literature, because effects of oral folk poetry in prose can also be found in religious literature.

Not only Catholic religious literature, but the religious literature of the Reformation also had a direct contact with narrative folklore. Its most outstanding example is one of the famous works of Péter Bornemisza (1535–1585), *Ördögi kísértetek* (Devilish Spectres), published in 1578. This collection of sermons dips generously into the European, especially Italian and German sources of short story and true story literature. Markalf and his colleagues were not the only ones appearing in its parables, nor were the most diversified stories of belief, devilish temptations, magical incantations; there were also such fabulous topics as understanding the talk of animals. Local legends and myths of creation, short story-type and magic tales, true stories, various groups of trials of wisdom, all can be found in this large artistic reservoir.

These religious works of different genre and character prove clearly—precisely because of the peculiar character of their transmission—that they generously handed over the epic treasure of this period to the people, and at the same time they also made use of the existing oral tradition, thus testifying to its existence.

The Folk Tales

Fig. 211. Hungarian hero fights a twelve-headed dragon. A design from a swineherd's horn. Tolna County. 19th century

The Hungarian word *mese* is an ancient inheritance from the Ugric period; it can be found both among the Voguls and Ostyaks, with the basic meaning "tale, legend". The "e" sound at the end of the word is either a possessive suffix or diminutive suffix, which developed separately in the Hungarian language. The word *mese* appeared at the end of the 14th century, when riddles were marked by this word, which also proves its antiquity. The word occurs more generally from the 15th

552

century, meaning "narrated, imagined story, a parable, an enigma". In the 1533 dictionary of Murmelius, the translation of fable is still *beszéd* (i.e., "talk"), and with this definition he differentiates it from *história* (history), which he translates as "true event", making a distinction between the "lying" fable and real history. The present meaning of *mese* developed only in the 18th century, thus following the same path as other European languages, i.e., by being restricted to signifying a particular genre.

Before turning to the discussion of Hungarian folk tales, let us take a quick look at its most important general characteristics.

Especially if as collectors we sit down next to the story teller in some village where the practice of story telling still exists, and listen for long hours to adventures and tales, our first surprise will be that nothing unbelievable takes place in the stories: everything is in its place and seems absolutely necessary, reflecting things as they should be. This sounds strange at first hearing, but it is true. Only an uninitiated person, the one who is left out of the magic circle of the tales, views the adventures happening to the heroes—to young swineherds or to princesses—as an impossible miracle. Naturally, to the unbelieving listener who thinks only in terms of this world of reality, the transformation of the fugitive pair of lovers into a lake and a duck swimming on it, the misleading of the wicked pursuer, the little prince who turns into a fawn, the princesses in the castle rotating on a duck's foot, carried away by dragons, all these occurrences are totally improbable and miraculous. But those who listen to the tales, or read them with true identification, do not observe a special emphasis, a stressing of the miracle, when these miraculous parts are told. In tales on the lips of the people, the miracle is a natural element of the story; only on the literary level does it become a strange, or romantically emphasized detail.

Fairy Tales　The wondrous miracle provides the meaning, ultimate principle, and at the same time the atmosphere of the fairy tales *(tündérmese),* the most important group of Hungarian folk tales. These stories are inevitable and habitual, the best known genre of the corpus of Hungarian peasant tales, and makes up approximately fifty per cent of the entire Hungarian treasury of tales. In order to provide a base for further explorations of the tale, we shall now tell a short fairy tale. It is from the county of Háromszék and is known in Hungarian ethnological literature by the title *Rózsa vitéz* (Rózsa the Brave) (AaTh 401). It has been recorded in several parts of the Hungarian linguistic region, but this type of tale also occurs in Sicily, Germany, and in other parts of Europe as well. This tale also provides an illustration of how an internationally known tale can become Hungarian, that not only the motif and type is of importance, but also the specific national versions.

A king had three sons. An enemy attacked the country and occupied it. The king fell. The princes were good hunters, and the three, with three hunting hounds, made off from the danger. They walked for a long time, not even knowing where; finally, on the highest snowy mountain top, where the road branched off, they decided to part from each other and try their fortunes separately.

They agreed to put up a long pole with a white kerchief on it on top of the mountain on the summit of a tall tree; each one of them was to be on the lookout for that, and if he saw blood on it, he was to get going after his brothers, because then one of them would be in danger.

The youngest, who was called Rózsa, started off to the left, the other two to the right. Rózsa, when he had passed well into the seventh snowy mountain, saw a beautiful castle and turned in as a tired traveller to sleep there. He settled in a house.

In the evening the gate of the castle opened with much clatter, and seven huge giants walked into the yard and from there to the house! They were as big, every one of them, as a big tower.

Rózsa in his fright scurried under the bed; but one of the giants, just as soon as they entered, said: Yech! What Adam stink! They looked for Rózsa, caught him, chopped him up like a stalk, and cast him out of the window.

In the morning the giants left again to make their living. A snake with the head of a beautiful girl crawled out of the bush and gathered every little piece of Rózsa's body and put it nicely together, saying: this goes here, this goes there. She rubbed mending herb on it and brought living-dead water from a nearby spring and sprinkled it with that. All of a sudden Rózsa jumped to his feet and became seven times more handsome and stronger than before. Then the snake with the girl's head came out of that snake skin to the armpits.

Rózsa, since he had become so strong, became confident and in the evening did not hide under the bed but waited for the giants at the gate. Those arrived and sent their servants ahead to grind up that wretched Adam left-over, but they could not handle him, and the giants themselves had to chop him up.

Next morning the snake with the girl's head brought him to life again, and she herself climbed out of the snake skin to the waist. Rózsa became twice as strong now as each giant was separately.

That night the seven giants killed him again; he, however, killed all the servants and wounded many of the giants.

In the morning, the giants left by themselves. The snake again resurrected Rózsa. Rózsa became stronger than the seven giants together and so handsome that it was possible to gaze at the sun, but not at him. The girl came completely out of the snake skin. What a dear and beautiful creature she was!

Then they told each other their affairs and lives. The girl said that she too was of royal blood; that her father had been killed by the giants, who occupied her country; that the castle used to be her father's; that the giants go out every day to extort from the people; that she, however, became a snake with the help of a good magician-nurse, and swore that she would stay in the snake skin until she could take revenge on the giants; but that as he can now well see, though the snake skin has split off her, she can now achieve her goal because Rózsa is strong enough to take care of all seven giants. "Now Rózsa, destroy them! I won't be ungrateful."

Rózsa answered the following: "Dear and beautiful girl! You gave me back my life three times, wouldn't I owe it to you to pay you back for that? My life is yours and so am I!"

They swore everlasting love to each other, and the day passed very pleasantly until evening.

When the giants arrived in the evening, Rózsa spoke to them as follows: "Didn't you, all you scoundrels, kill me three times? Now I say that today none of you will step across this gate, do you believe it? Let us fight!" They fell upon him with great anger, but it did not happen as it had twice before; he killed them all in order, then he took in his hand the keys from their pocket, rummaged every nook and cranny of the castle, and saw that they need not fear because the castle was theirs. They spent the night quietly. In the morning Rózsa looked over the snowy mountain top toward the white kerchief and saw that it is soaked in blood. He saddened and told his sweetheart: "I must go to seek out my brothers, because they are in trouble; wait for me, because if I find them, I am sure to return!" With that he got ready, took along his sword, arrow, mending herb, and living-dead water, and went exactly to the place where they had parted. He shot a rabbit on *his way. When he arrived there, he started off on the road his brothers had taken. He found a little house, and a tree in front of it; he settled there, and there were the two hunting dogs of his brothers tied up with chains! He untied them, built a fire, and began to roast the rabbit, and just as he was about to roast it, he heard somebody shouting on the tree, shivering: "Oh, how cold I am!" He called out and said: "If you are cold, come down, warm yourself." The voice said: "Yes, but I am afraid of the dogs!"—"Don't be afraid, they don't attack honest people!"—"I believe it," says the one on the tree, "but still, throw this hair among them, let them smell it first, so that they can recognize me from it!" Rózsa took the hair and threw it in the fire. An old witch descended from the tree and went inside to warm up, she also put a warty toad on a spit and began to roast it. As she roasted it, she started to tell Rózsa: "that is mine, this is yours!" With that she threw some toward him. Rózsa couldn't stand it, pulled out his sword, and struck toward the witch, but the sword became a log of wood!*

The witch fell on Rózsa, to kill him. She said: "Now this is the end of you! I already killed your brothers to revenge your killing my seven giant sons!" Rózsa set the dogs on her and they held her down long enough to make her blood run; the blood dripped on the log of wood, which turned it back into a sword; Rózsa grabbed it and cut off the witch's left arm with it; then the witch showed him where she buried his brothers; Rózsa smote once more with the sword, and with that he dispatched the witch to Pluto.

Rózsa dug up his brothers, put together their chopped-up bodies, mended them with mending herb, and resurrected them with living-dead water. When they opened their eyes and saw Rózsa, both said: "Oh, how long I have slept!" "Yes, a long time," said Rózsa, "and if I hadn't come here you would have slept even longer!" They told him that soon after they parted they heard that the enemy had left the country, and as they returned they decided that one of them, the older one, should go home and govern the country, the other go to find Rózsa. They turned into the little house, and there the old witch handled them in the same way as she wanted to handle Rózsa.

Rózsa also told them what he had gone through and said: "You, my older brother, go home, take our father's place! And you, my other brother, come with me and let the two of us govern that big country where the giants ruled!"

Here they parted and all of them went to their places. Rózsa found his beautiful sweetheart, who was grieving after him so much that she had nearly pined away, but when Rózsa arrived she became very happy. They took over the country they had saved from the giants, and Rózsa and his sweetheart married, put on a great wedding, and had many guests who danced much with the bride. And if they're not dead yet, they are still alive to this day. Round them up in an eggshell, and may they be your guests tomorrow!

Though this tale is the shortest among its group, still it contains fully every characteristic of the genre: the wondrous miracle, mysterious assistance, magical transformation, the kerchief that signals danger, giants, witches, the motifs of the resurrection of the dead. At the same time, its style has about it epic authenticity, the confident faith of the narrator. In the peasant community, fairy tales had a complete epic credibility; it is a later phenomenon which identifies the tale with the made-up story. We can often see how much, during the story telling, the listeners and narrator identify with the heroes of the story, and even people who already have heard it a great many times continue to worry and rejoice with the other listeners. In no other community can we find identification to such a degree as among the story-telling peasantry.

While the previous tale appears in a number of places in Europe, the following, which is known in Hungarian folk tale literature as *The Tree That Reached Up To the Sky*, contains elements of shamanism.

Once upon a time, beyond the beyond, there was a king and he had a beautiful wife. But she was so beautiful that... that in the whole wide world nobody had such a beautiful wife as he. And they had a very beautiful little daughter, and the little daughter was just as beautiful as her mother. They rejoiced much in her and loved her.

When the little girl came of school age her mother sickened and died. The king grieved so much that he didn't eat or sleep night or day and just cried for his wife. But the little girl always consoled him:

"You know very well, we are not born at once and neither do we die at once. One must be resigned to God's will."

The king thought, "My God, how young this little girl is! I should not cry so much, I can't resurrect her that way." At once he said:

"My sweet daughter, I declare that I will never remarry, because I can never find the like of your mother, there is none like her. I would rather stay as I am."

The girl says:

"My father, don't stay this way. I will not be here forever, and then what will you do alone?"

The king says:

"I don't care, my daughter, but I will not marry again. I would rather stay like this, a widower."

The girl says:

"Then, my father, I will not marry either. I will not leave you in this great sorrow."

This king had a flowering garden, and it may be that in the whole world there wasn't another garden as beautiful as that. All the flowers that grow in the world were present in that garden, fragrant flowers, one more beautiful than the other. And in the middle of the garden there was a tree so tall that its top reached up to the sky. Well, one day the king's daughter went for a walk in the garden. During her walk she was thinking:

"My God, why indeed should I get married, when I could never again find a garden the equal of the one I have."

Just as she said this, a wind began to blow so hard, she thought the tree would pull away from its core. This wind picked up the girl and took her to the top of that big tree. But nobody had seen the girl disappearing. Well, her father waited, time passed, still he was waiting for her to return. She didn't come. Right away he sends his cook, but she doesn't return. She searched every nook and cranny of the flower garden, but couldn't find her anywhere. He ordered the soldiers to the city to search for her from street to street. They couldn't find her anywhere. The king didn't know what to do. He put out an announcement that his daughter had got lost, and if anybody knows about her, to report where she is. But all this was in vain, so now he cried for his daughter until his heart almost broke. He gathered his advisors: what is he to do? How to find out where his daughter is? Nobody had a guess where that girl could be.

When one night the king lay down and fell into slumber, he saw in his dream how on that Saturday, when that big wind blew, the whirlwind had picked up the girl and carried her to the top of the big tree. She is in the castle of a twenty-four headed dragon. Well, he saw this dream, and when he woke up he said, "My God, this is a very telling dream!"

The king announced that if there can be found a brave man who will bring his daughter down from the tree top, he will give him his daughter, half his kingdom, and after his death, his entire realm. To be sure, when this was announced there came princes, barons, and handsome, finely built, brave lads, straight as beautiful, lit candles. They passed through the door one after the other, volunteering that they will bring her down. But there wasn't one among them who could get up on that tree. They went up a way, then fell back down, some breaking their arms, others their necks. Oh, the king was always sad, crying all the time, because nobody could go up, he will never see his daughter again.

The king had a young swineherd, a herdsman caring for the pigs. He was a little boy fifteen or sixteen years old. His name was Johnny. He went daily to the forest with the pigs. Well, as he is going out one day with the pigs—Johnny too was very sad, he too was sorry for the princess—suddenly he stops by a tree and leans on his stick. There as he was thinking he says:

"Oh, the dear and good hearted princess is lost, we shall never see her again."

Suddenly a little pig goes up to him and says:

"Don't grieve Johnny, because you will bring down the princess."

Johnny looks at the little pig because he had not heard him talk before.

"What are you saying, you little pig, talking such folly?"

He says:

"I am not talking folly, Johnny. You just listen to me. Go to the king, present yourself, tell him you will bring her down and that then he must give his daughter to you for a wife. Only before starting out after the maiden you tell the king: 'Your Majesty, I will bring her down, but first you must have a cow-buffalo slaughtered and have seven pairs of sandals and seven suits of clothes made out of her skin for me. By the time they wear out, I will be back.'"

The little pig says:

"Johnny, I will also tell you that when you get up to the middle of the tree you will reach a slender limb, but that limb is so long that it is the length of a world and a half, but slender. You must slide along it, go out to the end of it, and if you are able to get through it, then you can surely get up to the tree top. Only be careful not to fall down, because if you fall from there even your bones will be smashed to smithereens. There you will arrive at the leaves of the tree, for until then the tree has no leaves. It has leaves so big that a country can fit onto each one separately. Once you see yourself up there, you can trust that you will get the princess. You will be able to find her."

Now then, he thanked the little pig for the good advice and the same evening presented himself to the king. He knelt before the king and greeted him nicely.

"Well," asks the king, "what is the matter, my son?"

"Your Majesty, I hope I am not offending you, but I would have a request to make of you."

"What? Tell me Johnny, go ahead, tell me!"

"Your Majesty, if you will permit me, I will go up after the princess to the top of the tree and bring her down."

The king had never laughed since his wife had died. But now he burst out laughing.

"Oh, you Johnny, Johnny, what ideas you do bring before me!"

"The idea that I will go up and bring her down, if only you tell me that you permit it."

"My God," he says, "such fine, well built, brave men could not go up, and such a child as you want to bring her down?"

"That is my problem. You just promise that you will permit it."

"Well, my son, if you want to go so badly I permit it, but you'd better die on the spot should you fall back, because if you don't, I will kill you on the spot for pressing me like this."

"Well, Your Majesty, if you permit it, have a cow- buffalo butchered, have seven sandals and seven suits of clothes made for me from her skin, and I will return in that yet, bring down the princess, for God will help me."

Well, the king had the cow-buffalo slaughtered, had seven suits of clothes and seven sandals made for him.

Well, the clothes were ready, Johnny dressed in one suit and packed up the rest and took them with him. The king packed food for him for the road, so he would have something to eat and drink.

The king says to him:

"Well, Johnny, God help you, and I hope you return with my daughter, because then you will be fortunate."

So many gathered together for the marvel of his going up that there were terribly many, to see how he could go up. Johnny always carried a hatchet with him, so he took that along, and when he arrived at the bottom of the tree, he cut the hatchet into the tree and climbed like a cat, but took farewell of the world on the ground. Then he pulled out the hatchet and cut into the tree again, further up. The trunk of the tree was very long, so it was late by the time he reached the branches. That was why it was so hard to go up. Up there he kept taking out the hatchet and cutting in with it higher and higher until he reached the branch of the tree. Then one minute here, two minutes there and Johnny was lost among the branches and they could not see him from the ground. Johnny went on up and up and up until he reached the long branch mentioned by the little pig.

"Aha," he says, "the little pig was not speaking in vain, it is difficult to slip through here."

The branch was very slender. He couldn't go on foot, but laid belly down and crawled like a caterpillar. When he reached the leaves, he stood up, closed his eyes and said:

"Goodbye world," and jumped onto a leaf like a frog.

Well, then he rested a little, because he was very tired, and when he had rested himself, he looked around carefully and said:

"By God, the world here is just like home. They are ploughing and sowing."

There were cities where some houses were even twenty stories high. He walked on and on but didn't meet anybody, didn't see either man or beast, although the city was very beautiful. Well, as he was walking in front of the big, many-storied houses, he kept a lookout this way and that, to the right and the left. He heard a voice:

"Where are you going hereabouts?"

This was spoken from the upper storey, but the princess spoke to him.

"Where are you going?"

"I am looking for you, princess."

The princess motions like this:

"Psst, quietly," she says, "so my husband won't hear, or he will promptly kill you. Come on up to the top floor."

She came out for him and took him inside.

"Come on in, because my husband is not at home. I would like to talk to you before he returns."

"Oh, Johnny, do you know that my husband is the twenty-four headed dragon? If he should learn that you have come to take me back, it would be the certain end of you. What is my father doing?"

"God knows what he is doing," he says. "He is crying all the time. His eyes are never dry from his tears."

He told her quickly how many princes had tried to go up after her, but that nobody could get up there. The king said that he will give her as a wife to the one who can bring her down. So he says:

"I tried it too and God helped me get here, but I will not go down without you for anything, until I can carry you down."

"Please, Johnny, be quiet so the dragon won't hear this."

She promptly gave him food and drink so he could eat and drink.

"I tell you now, Johnny, that I will hide you so my husband won't find you when he comes home," she says. So she hid him under a tub. "First I will tell him who came here, because he is mighty nervous. Then I'll hide you."

At once, the dragon came. But when he was still seven miles away, he came with such force that he cast his mace ahead and opens the gate asunder.

"See, Johnny, he is coming. He already has cast his mace ahead."

At once he comes in and bellows:

"What kind of a stranger do I smell in here? Who was here?" says he. "I could feel it on the way already that a stranger was here."

"Oh," she says, "don't be angry, dear husband. Our swineherd has come up from the fields in order to find me. He is very sorry about no longer seeing me and has come to continue to serve me here."

"Well, where is he? Bring him forth."

"I would bring him forth, only please don't hurt the poor thing, since he came to serve me here further."

She lifted the tub and let Johnny out. The dragon stood in front of him, looked him over, then put him in his mouth, swallowed him, and spit him out. He did this to him three times.

"Well," he says, "if you have come to serve your queen, I shall see if what you eat is a total loss or just half. Well, sit down and eat with me!"

So Johnny ate and drank. When the dragon had also eaten, they went out to the stable. He showed him his horses, his cattle, and what work he had to do.

But among the other horses, lying in the innermost corner, there was a colt. The colt was so skinny that he could not get up and could not part his legs in his great skinniness. The other horses, on the other hand, were so fat they were rotting in their great fatness. The dragon said to Johnny:

"You know, Johnny, you water, feed, and clean these. But you needn't clean that colt lying there, nor should you give it the same things as the others. Instead, when he asks for hay, give him oats, and when he asks for oats, give him water, but never give him what he asks for."

So he showed him everything. Johnny stayed in the stable, and he went inside.

560

So this happened today, that tomorrow. The young man sat there for a month and behaved himself very well. He did what the dragon told him to do, and he was by now so well trusted that he need not tell him anything. He did everything as if he had been born there. That pleased the dragon a lot. He did everything.

One day the dragon went hunting, and as Johnny was feeding in the stable, he stopped once by the back of the skinny colt.

"You poor colt, why are you so skinny? Can't you get up from here, you poor thing?"

Suddenly the colt begins to speak:

"Johnny, I see you have a kind heart, but there is no time to talk now. I'll tell you more some other time."

There was no time because the dragon was coming home.

Well, the dragon looked over everything and found all in order. He liked Johnny, who ate at his table. Next day the dragon went away again, and Johnny also went out to the stable and took care of the cattle. Then the colt started to speak again.

"Johnny, I see that you are a kind-hearted young man, and I know why you came here, but to carry the princess back from here is very hard. But if you listen to me," he says, "you will be lucky. Look here, Johnny, tomorrow is Sunday. Now you go in and tell the princess that by using guile, by questioning him with sweet words, she must find out where he keeps his power. Look here, she should question him. He won't want to tell, she will have to caress him, but she is to get it out of him somehow and then you tell it to me!"

And so that is what happened. Johnny went in and told the queen.

"Princess, Your Majesty, I am telling you, find out from your husband where he keeps his power. Queen, Your Majesty, I tell you, if you ever want to see your father again, question him about where he keeps his power."

"Oh, Johnny, that will be hard to question him about, because he won't tell," she says. But with some sweet, guiling talk she will get it out of him.

So suddenly the dragon is coming and throws his mace so that the gate falls in two halves. Seven-foot flames come out of his throat as he comes. She gives him supper and they eat and drink. Next day he is about to leave again. His wife says to the dragon:

"My sweetheart, don't go hunting again today, rest instead at home. I am always by myself. I am very tired of this. I wish you would just spend a day sitting at home with me."

She leaned against him and began to caress and fondle him. Well, the dragon was mighty happy. He thought she loved him, although she loved him like manure. But she had no other choice.

"Well," she says, "my dear husband, if you are just to me, don't deny me if I ask you something."

"What, my dear wife? What do you want from me?"

"I don't want anything else," she says, "only tell me where you keep your power?"

"Oh, my dear wife, why do you want to know this from me? We have never talked about this. And nobody but I know where my power is."

"Can't you tell me? Am I not your wife?"

"Well, I won't tell you. I will tell you everything, but I will not tell you this."

The woman says:

"Then you don't really love me, that is why you won't tell. Because if you loved me better, then you would not deny me." And so the woman began to cry.

And then her husband felt sorry for her:

"Oh, don't cry my sweetheart," he says.

"How could I help crying, my sweetheart, when you just admitted that you don't really love me."

"Of course, I love you."

"If you loved me, then you would tell me."

"Look here, my sweet wife, this is a great secret. And nobody must know it."

"I always heard that once a woman is married to a man, then there must be one heart and one soul, so why do you deny me?"

"Well, listen here, my dear wife, but nobody else is to learn this!"

"Of course not! What kind of talk is this?"

"Well, I'll tell you. My power is there in the forest, where there is a silver bear, and here and thereabouts is a stream, and every noon to this stream he comes for a drink of water. If somebody should shoot that bear and split his head in two, he would find there a wild boar. The boar would then jump out of it, and if someone should shoot that wild boar and split his head in two, a rabbit would jump out of it. If somebody should shoot that rabbit and split his head in two, a box would jump out of it. If somebody should break that box with two stones, he would find nine wasps in that, and that is my power. If they destroy these wasps, I will not have as much power as a sick fly. This is why it is a great secret, and why nobody should know where I keep my power."

"Well," said his wife to him, and kissed him, "oh, my sweetheart, you didn't want to tell, although there is no man born on this earth to whom I would betray you. Now, my dear husband, let us drink together."

So she brought up a jug of wine of the strongest kind and then they sat down.

"Well, let us drink to your health!"

They filled their cups and made a toast. The man drank it, the woman acted as if she had drunk it but poured it on the ground instead.

"Well," said the man, "now let us drink a cupful to your health as well."

So they filled the cups again. The husband drank that too, but the woman only pretended to be drinking and poured the wine down her chest. Then the woman said:

"Now let us also drink to Johnny's health!"

So they drank to that too, and then talked for a little while. But the woman saw that her husband was a little drunk from the terribly strong wine.

The woman said:

"My dear husband, let us drink one more to a long life together."

They drank that too, and then the man toppled over and fell down like a log of wood. He slept and snored as if he had no trouble in the world.

After that the woman went out and called in Johnny.

"Well, my Johnny, I questioned him and learned where his power is."

She told him right away what she learned, and then Johnny went out to the stable to the colt and told him:

"Look, here's where he keeps his power, there is a silver bear in the forest, and at noontime he goes to the golden stream for a drink. If he could be shot there and his head split in two, a wild boar would jump out of it, if someone would shoot that boar and split his head in two, a rabbit would jump out of it, if he would also shoot the rabbit, a box would come out of his head, and in it there are nine wasps.

That is his power. If someone could break this box so that the wasps be destroyed, then he would not have as much power as a fly."

"Well," says the colt, "go on Johnny, light a log of wood, and when it has burned, bring in to me three buckets full of embers."

Johnny ran and made a good fire. When a log of wood had burned down and became pure embers, he took three buckets-full to the colt. The colt licked it up. When he had licked it up, he got on his knees.

"Now then, let me out of the stable!"

He let the colt out, and the colt licked up all the embers of the log of wood. When he had licked it all up, he became a steed with pure golden hair, and he had five legs.

"Well now, Johnny, now run down to the cellar. You know where the key is!"

"Yes," he says.

"Run down to the cellar. There hangs a golden saddle and a suit of golden clothes for you. Get dressed quickly, bring up the saddle, and put it on my back. There is also a sword hanging on a nail. Take it down, too!"

Well, Johnny did just as he was told. He brought the saddle and the hung-up sword, and he dressed up in the suit of clothes.

"Now get on my back, and let's go!"

So they left. When they arrived in the forest, the colt knew exactly where he wanted to go, for he was familiar with the place.

When they arrived, the bear was just drinking from the stream, and when he saw them, he began to howl and came at them. The colt said: "Don't be afraid John, be brave!"

When the bear tried to close in on him, the colt kicked him so hard with his fifth leg that he toppled over, and then Johnny jumped down and cut his head in two with the sword. And he split the head so much that the boar jumped out of it. He too fell upon Johnny to kill him, but the colt kicked him so hard with his fifth leg that he too tumbled over, and Johnny ran with the sword and cut his head in half. Then the rabbit jumped out of it and began to run, but the colt could run even faster and kicked him so hard that he too tumbled over. Then Johnny split his head also, and that box jumped out. It hopped and jumped about but John took out two big stones and broke it up so hard that nothing was left of it.

"Well," said the colt, "we can go home now, we need no longer fear them."

So they went home, and the dragon was lying there where he had fallen, and said:

"Did you take away my power, Johnny? Well, it doesn't matter even though you took it, but at least leave me my life."

"I'll leave it right now!"

He grabbed his sword and cut off the dragon's twenty-four heads right there. So the dragon finally was finished, he perished right there and then.

"Well," says the colt, "now you tell me, John, what you want to do! Do you want to be king in this country? You can be, it is now yours, but if you want to take the princess home you can do that, too."

John says:

"Well, thank you for offering me this country, but I have no desire to stay here. I would like to go home. I feel very sorry for the old king, and I want to take his daughter home."

"Well," he says, "if you want to take her home, you certainly may go. Take *as much of the treasure and gold as you can carry, for there is plenty here. And sit on my back, both of you, and I'll take you."*

When they were seated upon his back, he said:

"Now close your eyes."

They closed their eyes and by the time they could have said "hip-hop, where I think, there I'll be," they were in the king's courtyard.

They went in. The old king by then was on his deathbed. He was nearly gone from sorrow.

Johnny went to him and reported that he had returned: "Your Majesty, I brought your dearest daughter, for whom you have grieved so much."

He says:

"Where is she?"

The king opens his eyes, and the maiden begins to speak:

"My father, I am here."

At once she embraces her father, and first both cried together with joy, then all three of them.

"Well," he says, "my son John, you have brought me my daughter. From now on you are the king of this country, and I give you my daughter, my country, I hand over everything to you."

And as the king said this and gave them his blessing, he died forthwith. John married the king's daughter and if they are not dead, they are still alive today.

The tree that reached up to the sky is one of the oldest motifs of Hungarian folk tales. A significant number of researchers connect it with the shamanistic ceremony of the Uralic-Altaic peoples (cf. pp. 671-2). Thus Vilmos Diószegi writes the following: "This tree reaching to the sky is nothing other than the *világfa* (world tree) of the shamanistic religion, and the great deed of the swineherd is the memory of the old *shaman initiating ceremony*, that is to say, of the ceremony when the candidate for shaman had to climb up on the notched tree that had been prepared for this purpose and that represented the world tree." This element occurs in the Hungarian treasury of the various types of tales, and sometimes can also be found as an opening phrase.

Humorous Tales Another outstanding group of folk tales is the so-called humorous tales *(tréfás mese),* which form about twelve per cent of the Hungarian folk tale corpus. Although they frequently slip into the world of fairy tales, with which they are interwoven by the presence of the miraculous, they are more robust and more realistic, and at times lash out with rather unsparing humour at the stumblings of the weak. Furthermore, if the villain comes to grief in humorous tales, he receives his punishment soundly. This is a harsh, almost cruel way of amusement. We can immediately see that these jokes were born or became rooted in the tradition of people having a hard, often barely tolerable fate. Thus, in these humorous tales the reigning element is not the miraculous, but the grotesque.

The world often turns topsy-turvy in humorous little stories, but that is not always in order to find solace in the symbols of higher justice, as in the moral lesson of the fairy tales, but rather it is merely to create

564

A kis Kolozs

és

a nagy Kolozs.

Felette tréfás és víg történet.

Öt szép képpel.

Pest, 1873.

Nyomatott és kapható Bucsánszky Alajosnál. Ösz-utcza 20. szám.

discomfiture and to raise a laugh. Certain tales from this genre often rival the most artful, modern, grotesque short stories. As an example, we shall introduce a tale of lying *(hazudós mese)* that was recorded a hundred years ago in Hódmezővásárhely (AaTh 852). This tale, by the way, offers not only the simple ridiculing of human vanity, and self-conceit but also a social judgement, the victorious, sardonic laughter of the poor peasantry.

Once upon a time, beyond the seven seas and beyond their farthest shores, there was a poor man, and he had three sons.

Once the king declared throughout the entire country that he will give his daughter to anyone who can tell him something that he will not believe. The oldest son of the poor man, a boy called Peter, heard of this, prepared himself, and went to the king, where he told the servant that he wanted to talk to the king. The king saw straight away what the young man wanted but said nothing to anybody, only ordered them to let him in forthwith. Although by then as many princes as there are stars in the sky, as there are blades of grass in the meadow, and God knows how many of what kind of great lords, had come before the king—every one among them wanting to marry the princess—still none of them could say anything the king would not have believed. So Peter went in to the king and greeted him:

"God give you a good day, My Lord King!"

"To you too, my son! What brings you here?"

"I would like to get married, my Lord King!"

"Very good, son, but tell me, how would you keep a wife?"

"God knows! I would keep her somehow... my father has a house and also a small field."

"I believe it, son," says the king.

"And we also have three cows."

"I believe that, too."

"Now, not long ago, so much peat collected in our yard that we hardly had any room left."

"I believe it."

"Once, my father said: My sons, carry these weeds out to that little field. Perhaps it will do it some good."

"I believe it."

"However, by mistake we carried it, to the last blade, to the neighbour's field."

"I believe it."

"When it was all done, I went home and told my father."

"I believe it."

"Then I, my father, and my two younger brothers, the four of us together went out to our field."

"I believe it."

"Then we got hold of the four corners of the neighbour's four fields, lifted it, as you lift up a table cloth, and turned the weeds from it onto our field."

"I believe it."

"Then we sowed our field with grass seeds."

"I believe it."

"And a thick forest grew on it such that no one has ever seen the like."

"I believe it."

"Then my father was sorry to have those beautiful trees cut down, so he bought a herd of pigs."

"I believe it."

"Then he hired Your Majesty's grandfather for the swineherd."

"You lie! You rascal!"

But the king suddenly remembered his wager, called the priest and the hangman, and married his daughter to the poor man's son. They had a wedding big enough to be heard of beyond seven counties, gave sweetcakes as big as my arm

"Now, Peter, pick up the bones to the last piece!"

Peter did as he was told and picked them up. Jesus then put them away in the sleeve of his szűr. In the evening, after the shepherd had fallen asleep, the Lord went to the fold and threw the bones among the sheep, and each of the pieces turned into a sheep, with the brand of the shepherd on the rear of every one of them.

When this was done Jesus and St. Peter left the fold and went on without a word.

When the shepherd got up next morning, he looked at the sheep in the fold and saw that there were lots of strange sheep among them, perhaps three times as many as the master's, and what was miraculous about it all was that his brand was stamped on the rear of each one of them. He couldn't figure out how this could be when he had no sheep, not even half of one, since he had slaughtered the last one just the night before for his guests. Then he started looking for his guests but could find them nowhere. It was then he realized that nobody but God himself could have given those sheep to him, and he pledged that from then on he would always help the needy as much as he can, even if he has only a penny.

Animal fables *(állatmese)* occur in the Hungarian treasury of tales in relatively small numbers (3.5 per cent). These can be divided into two large groups: moralizing tales, which are Hindu in origin and came to us partly through Eastern European oral tradition, partly by written Greek–Latin interposition. Many of these found their way into the Hungarian folk tale corpus through sermons. The other group originates in ancient European animal myths. Literature and folk tradition closely intertwine in this genre. We meet them on the one hand in the fables of Aesop, and on the other, the Aesopean collections of tales also have often preserved texts taken over from oral tradition. An animal fable characteristic of this group is *The Fox and the Wolf* (AaTh 1+AaTh 34 B AaTh 3★ "AaTh 23★):

Animal Fables

There was once in the world a wolf and a fox. The fox lay down on the cartroad. A driver who was going by put him up on the forage ladder, where there were three cheeses. The fox hung them on his neck, jumped down, and ran off. Then the wolf said to the fox:

"Where did you get this cheese?"

The fox said:

"Come right on, I will show you some cheese!"

They went to a lake. It was night, and the moon shone on the water, so he said:

"If you drink up all this water, that cheese will be there underneath it."

Then the wolf got to work but could not drink it all up. He got sick from it.

So they went to a house where a wedding was being held, and music played on and on. Suddenly he said:

"We will play even more beautifully if you let us up onto the attic where the hens and strudels are kept."

They let them up. When they had their fill, they jumped down and ran away.

They kept running, and found a big pointed stake. The fox said:

"You can't jump across it!"

So the wolf jumped across it.
"Well, jump across it this way, with your back to it!"
The wolf tried to jump across it that way, but the stake went into his belly.
The fox told him:
"Shake yourself, then you will get loose!"
The stake went in even further. Then the fox said:
"In the name of the Father and the Son,
I used to torture you for what you'd done
Because you devoured a horse
That never was."

Besides those we have discussed, there are other different kinds of fables, and groups of various genres can be found in greater and lesser numbers in Hungary. Among these are noteworthy the short-story tales *(novellamesék)* (8.5 per cent), the foolish-devil tales *(ostoba ördögmesék)* (1.5 per cent), and the fool's tales *(bolondmesék)* (6.5 per cent). Only a small fraction of tales (1 per cent) cannot be classified into any group.

The Form and Content of Folk Tales

Let us now continue our discussion by a closer investigation of the historical, contextual, formal, social, and functional questions of the Hungarian folk tale.

Research on the historical problems of the Hungarian folk tale must go in several directions. Thus scholars have examined the question: in researching Hungarian folk tales may typical strata of Hungarian folk tales be found, which refer back to pre-Conquest times, to Oriental connections? Is there such a stratum, and can one distinguish it from the types, motifs, and perhaps certain forms of the more generally known West European tales? Naturally, the earlier romantic view regarded most of Hungarian tales as an inalienable national possession. Even after a great deal of comparative examination and debate, no ultimate conclusion can be drawn. The tales that have been examined above call attention to the fact that some shamanistic images of the pre-Conquest Magyars do appear among the motifs of folk tales, and as we cannot find their western equivalents in the western material, we must regard the so-called oriental shamanistic stratum as the most ancient portion of Hungarian folk tales (cf. pp. 670-2). One motif thought to have originated from such shamanistic religious belief is the frequent motif of the castle that rotates on a duck's (or other bird's) foot. This, however, is not by any means characteristic of the Hungarian tales alone, for it is encountered frequently in other tales, especially those from Russia and East Europe. The motif of the rotating castle occurs at a very early stage in Celtic epic, and other West European analogues of it also indicate a wide distribution of the motif. More recent researchers have taken the standpoint that generally it is not the case of an isolated motif but that more likely several elements and motifs from images and narratives of shamanistic ceremonies and rites can be found, presumably in a genetic connection, in Hungarian folk tales. Recently, a Soviet researcher has observed the transmission of elements and stories of belief of shamanistic rites into tales of entertainment. While these rites had a claim to authenticity, and while they possessed a socially obligatory validity, the stories attached to them were not able to be included among the tale-type narratives. However, when their social authenticity and validity began to break down, and eventually ceased, elements and motifs fell one after the other into the simple entertaining tale-type stories. More and more of the Hungarian stories of folk belief got into the world of the Hungarian folk epic tales (cf. pp. 588-9). This process can be looked upon as normal, and the religious and semi-religious element must have become, during various historical periods, part of the material of fanciful, fairy tale stories.

Naturally, in the following we shall refer only in very broad outline to some traits of the very complex historical process. The oldest elements of the Hungarian tales that were also connected to each other genetically could have issued from pre-Conquest, shamanistic rites. We can thus look upon the following as such motifs: the topless tree, the castle rotating on a duck's foot, the learning and trial of the shaman's apprentice (the sorcerer's apprentice in fairy tales), the cutting to pieces of the hero, and also the formula of the sigh of the hero when he is resurrected after being dismembered ("Oh, what a strange dream I have had"). Furthermore, we may list here the motif of the mirror that can see the whole world (namely the magic mirror of the shaman), although we know that this motif occurs elsewhere as well, e.g. in the motif corpus of the *Gesta Romanorum*. Although many among these motifs are related to folk-tale elements from other circles, still their appearance in tales of a similar type and their consistent, living existence in the Hungarian tale corpus permit the supposition that they are the surviving remnants of an older, uniform, shamanistic type of religious imagery.

Otherwise, as we have said, if it is difficult to isolate one by one these motifs from the material that is known in other places as well, it is even more difficult to isolate certain types of formulae. Since the previously mentioned formula "Oh, what a strange dream I have had," can also be found outside the circle of shamanistic rite, our supposition here can be justified only by the non-accidental, non-sporadic occurrence of these elements.

It is a harder task to attach the opening formula "Once upon a time" *(hol volt, hol nem volt)* to the oldest layer of Hungarian narrative. Some people list it among the polarizing tale-openings of Slavic origin, while others feel that this type of formula is frequent in the Caucasian corpus of tales (Mingrel, Georgian, Armenian, etc.) and from there it got by chance to other places. As its occurrence in the Seldjuk–Turkish, Caucasian, and Hungarian material is normal, while in other places it is accidental, this formula too seems to belong to the pre-Conquest layer of the Hungarian corpus of tales.

We can add many more tale-type idioms, such as the question "What are you doing here where even the birds don't fly?", and the answer the helpful old witch gives to the hero of the tale: "You are lucky that you called me grandma!" Some researchers consider this formula also as a survival of the matriarchal state of society. This is all we can say so far about the oldest layer of the Hungarian folk tale, of the stratum that is most divergent from West European tales. Although even this difference is subject to debate, still we can consider these motifs and formulae as a uniformly related group, belonging to the shamanistic culture of the Hungarians.

Stith Thompson, in his great work on folk tales, devotes a few words to the place of the Hungarian folk tale in the European corpus. It seems that he considers significant only the unmistakably German features in the Hungarian folk tale (and in the Czech and South Slav tales as well), although in his reference he also speaks of the situation between the East European and West European domains of tales. Just as it is hard to introduce a nation's corpus of tales in a brief survey, it is equally difficult to emphasize a few of its characteristic features, those that would primarily apply to this particular treasury of tales. There are separable, larger domains of tales in the European treasury of tales, and it is without a doubt that the place of the Hungarian folk tale is among the East European tales. And still, in not just one episode, the Hungarian folk also assimilated among its tales a more ancient heritage. The Magyars, Finno-Ugric in origin, inseparably amalgamated with Turkic tribes thousands of years before the Conquest, and this duality determined the basic tone of their culture even before the Conquest. It is also certain that the Inner Asian, Caucasian, Iranian cultures also influenced the Magyars before they arrived in our present homeland, when they then came into contact with Ancient Slavic and Byzantine culture. Furthermore, after 896 A.D., Hungary became one of the sensitive focal points connnecting different cultures between East and West (cf. pp. 694–700). Undoubtedly all this added to the complexity of the history of Hungarian culture, and within it the culture of the peasantry; at the same time, it made Hungarian culture into a unifier, a synthesizer of many contradictory elements.

Indeed, Hungarian folk tales stand at the border of the West European world of tales, their colourful, rich character originating from this position. There are tales which give opportunity for discovering numerous historical and cultural layers: in a single tale many centuries and cultural currents may meet. If, therefore, we want to speak of characteristic features of Hungarian folk tales, we must first and foremost mention their being situated between East and West as a characteristic feature, side by side with what has been said of their narrative style and stylistic features. The geographical location assuring many different contacts is one of the major causes of the multi-layered nature of Hungarian folk tales and of their wealth, which suggests many complicated historical and ethnic contacts. And finally, we cannot overlook the recognition of the already often mentioned shamanistic elements in these tales, which can no longer be explained by the situation that the Hungarians are wedged between the great Slavic and Germanic blocks, but which rather suggest their historical past and also their more ancient ethnic connections.

After these questions of the contents of the tale, let us take a brief, closer look at the relationship between the customs of story telling and of social classes. Certain documents tell us that during the 18th century, story telling was frequent even among young men and women of the nobility. We know that the spoken tale, the comic story, was fashion-

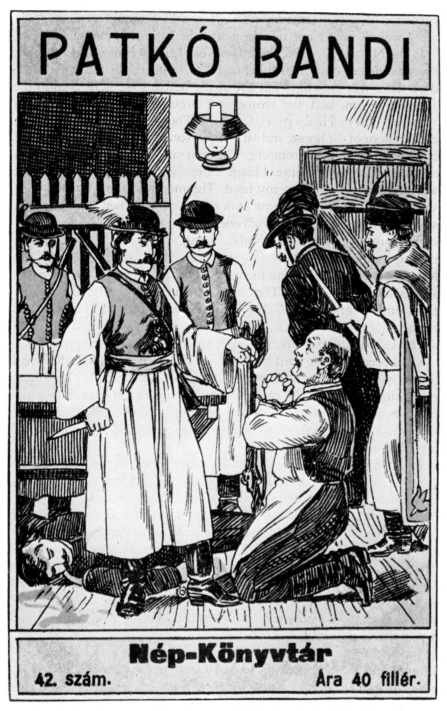

able among burghers. In the 13th to 16th centuries people also listened to the "godless entertainers" and tellers of merry tales in front of the church. Data exist from the 18th century indicating that during the hard and long years of military service the telling of tales was one of the comforts to that small community of men which happened to be formed in a regiment. They took turns in telling tales, and if a man could not tell a tale, he was humiliated through certain ceremonial forms. There was also a way for the story teller to find out if his tale still interested his audience, or if it was better to finish it. If to the question "Bone?" they answered "Meat", or in other places "Crock!", he could continue. If the reply was silence or one or two words, he had to end his tale.

In the Nyírség, in 1938, the 86-year-old Mihály Fedics told about the story telling customs of his childhood. What did he say? "Back in the old days there was no lamp. The fire in the hearth gave light even in the spinning room, and the women sat around that... The men also gathered. They all had a *guba* (cf. p. 326). They folded it, put it down on the dirt floor of the house, and sat on it, or some liked to spread it out and lie down on it on their stomachs. The men sang and told stories there on the floor. There was silence. I listened mostly in the corner of the hearth and gathered all of it into my head. The men told the tales, and there were some who just said 'now I am taking over!' When he finished the story, another volunteered to tell one, or even if no one volunteered, the others passed it on to somebody, saying, 'You tell it!' When I was cutting cordwood, I told stories at the clearing of the forest, and I too learned. There was a big hut there, and seventy of us slept in it. We told stories in this hut all night. The one who told the story yelled out sharply from time to time: 'Bone.' Then if they answered 'Crock!' he continued telling it, but if only two or three answered, then he didn't go on anymore, because one after the other had fallen asleep during the tale as we had been working hard all day long. But I, even if story telling had gone on for weeks, could not have shut my eyes..." This is the confession of a passionate story learner and story teller, and at the same time an authentic narrative of story telling custom—or at least of its more major characteristics—of the rest and work periods, going back at least one or two centuries.

It is common knowledge that the solitary humming of a folksong is possible, but the folk tale can live only in a small, live community. There is no such thing as solitary story telling. Therefore, the relationship between the audience and the story teller is a more important factor than anything else. This relationship determines the very existence of the tale, the methods of transmitting it, and the artistic-narrative processes of retelling, and recreating. Good story tellers do not like to tell stories for just one or two listeners, and our experience is that it harms the performance and stylistic effect of the tale if the folklore collector shuts himself up with the story teller and does not record the narration amidst a participating, laughing, excited audience.

Researchers throughout Europe have observed how much the community and the repeated, diversified narration of certain tales help to develop stabilized forms. In the course of the narration these two forces continually battle with each other: on the one hand there is the story teller's demand for recreation (this is often demanded by the listeners, who expect something new as well), and on the other hand, there is loyalty to tradition.

Examination of the Hungarian peasant story telling communities gives evidence that bigger or smaller story telling communities practically cover the entire peasant existence with a network. We know the small communities, restricted only to the family, where the parents, or even more the grandparents tell stories to the young ones; but we should also know that it is customary in certain places that the young husband tells stories to his wife. In telling stories to the children, the role of the mother is usually the most significant, alongside that of the grandparents, but this is not a rule.

We differentiate the communities and occasions of story telling according to whether they are within or outside the village. The communities of village story telling can develop during the various work opportunities. Even when resting at night during the hard work of harvesting, and during the bundling of tobacco, the harvesting of corn, the various occasions of field and vineyard work, during the evening rest of woodcutters, or during the long rest periods of village life (the late afternoons and evenings of winter months, in the spinneries that were still fashionable at the end of the last century and the first part of this one)—on all such occasions, besides games and songs of the young people, listening to the stories of the old folk was the main entertainment. Outside the village, we find communities of story telling primarily among the herdsmen and fishermen, who did not consider themselves peasants, and among the groups of soldiers and woodcutters, and men who did work in cities (e.g. in the building trade). But we also know of story-listening communities in men's dormitories, among the industrial workers, as well as in workshops among the village artisans.

In our opinion the communities may be more permanent, or even if the community breaks up from time to time, similar periodically reform. Such are the communities outside the village. The two types also leave a mark on the transmission of stories. The permanent type of audience in the village assures a stability, the repetition of types and structures, and relative continuity, while the ones outside the village make possible the infiltration of new elements and content into the village corpus of tales.

It is among the characteristics of Hungarian communities that there are actual specialists in certain genres of tales. There are some who like to tell merry, erotic tales, others who like telling religious or magic stories, and their listeners keep demanding the same kind from them. There are some story tellers who are masters of weaving up-to-date material and references into the tale, which gives opportunity for interruption and comic comments. In fact, audience demands and expectations prompt the good story teller to chisel out the forms and structures of his most popular, most successfully narrated tales, to colour up the more interesting episodes, and with these changes make his tales even more memorable. These listening audiences are sharp critics of a bad performance, and put beginners at story telling and over-hasty performers into their place. We also know that certain story telling communities (and the occasional story listening communities—woodcutters, soldiers, fishermen, herdsmen—lead the way in this especially) like to listen to very long tales that last for days, with interruptions that understandably follow from their situation. During such occasions the story tellers actually strive to lengthen, to colour their tales more and more. All of this has a direct effect on the text of the tale itself and on the development of the tale and the method of its transmission.

But we also know of special occasions for telling tales. In the course of big fairs, migrations, servant work on estates or at the far end of the country, and even abroad, the Hungarian peasant story teller moved into newer and newer, strange communities of audiences as late as the turn of the last century and the beginning of our century, where he became acquainted with always newer story tellers and themes. These contacts and the common ethnic and linguistic boundaries made possible the often seemingly abrupt "migration" of the tales.

If the occasions for story telling and an attentive audience can be proved to have a direct or indirect effect on the text and the transmission of tales, a story teller's personality may affect the development of the text at least as strongly. Today we see with increasing clarity that both communities of listeners and the custom of story telling truly exist and flourish only at places where a talented story teller is active. In the course of collecting folklore, we repeatedly meet cases when the genre of the folk tale, the prose epic flourishes in villages, in communities where story telling is still in practice and where several story tellers function, each with a different degree of talent. From similar observations it is certain that this was always the case in other countries also. Even in literary life, there are many mediocre imitators or retellers who swarm around outstanding authors.

We must attempt to collect the total repertoire of the greatest possible number of story tellers, and with this method open the way for an understanding of the nature of transmission better, to discover the laws of creative and destructive processes during the course of retelling. That is to say, oral tradition is in no way destructive, as many people used to claim.

Our experience is that a certain ballad or tale begins to "fall apart", to get "spoiled" when the community no longer uses its traditions, when it is preserved only in the uncertain memory of individuals. Since records note only certain stages in such processes, the idea of splitting asunder, of falling apart, developed with erroneous one-sidedness.

Our own personal folklore collecting experience has proven that in numerous cases stories told in fragments or outlines, and generally told poorly, are inseparable from their narrators, and that when we have listened to the really good story teller, it turned out that the text that had been "told to shreds" could come to a new life and become enriched with new colours. Many of the tales recorded during the past decades are like this. Of course, these tales are full of carelessly spoken language; there are no finishing touches by an author. We have also noticed that the same story teller might relate the same story—even within a short span of time—either in a more rich form or more poorly.

The personality of story tellers is known only since recent research. Although János Kriza, collector of ballads and folk tales mentioned some Székely story tellers with great affection and noted their names already in 1863, that is all that is known about the persons who told the stories.

In the same year Ágost Greguss, an outstanding researcher of the Hungarian folk ballad, wrote the following in one of his articles: "Much depends on the man who told the tale, whether he was an accomplished or a clumsy story teller. That is the reason why collectors seek for those who are excellent at telling stories." The correct basic theory was present; it just was not put into practice.

Good story tellers generally come from among the poor peasantry, even from the poorest, the rural labourers, as much foreign data also testifies. According to peasant etiquette, telling stories or even listening to them was not proper; if a well-to-do farmer told a story he usually just told an anecdote or two. Story telling flourished, and still exists sporadically even today, among the poor peasantry, and the best story tellers are found among them. Such was Mihály Fedics, one of the best known of the Hungarian story tellers, who was a day-labourer throughout his life and lived in the greatest poverty, and who in the last years of his life became a beggar, earning his way from village to village; Mihály Lacza, who lived in similar circumstances until 1945; the widow Mrs. Palkó, who came from a landless, small-peasant family and struggled with serious cares. Almost without exception, all those herdsmen, fishermen and peasant story tellers known from the Hungarian linguistic territory belonged to the poorest layer of the Hungarian peasantry.

Coming from a certain social class determines a person's outlook, which is one basic reason why in folk tales an awareness of the social position and the oppression of the peasantry developed with such a definite sharpness both in symbolic stories as well as in clearly pointed remarks. In the narratives of poor peasant story tellers, who lived in poverty themselves, the bitter anger and often wild passion of the oppressed intensifies unrelentingly, and shines through the medieval parable or fires up the story of a poor young servant man. Furthermore, the desire for the poorest and weakest to be victorious in the tales, and for the haughty and evil lords to be humiliated, the power of the dragon to be broken by the son who was ridiculed and considered stupid, these features gain especially strong authenticity when narrated by a poor rural peasant worker. All these seemingly worn-out themes come to vigorous life on the lips of story tellers in the community of their similarly hard-up listeners, and carry the promise of oncoming justice.

Among Hungarian story tellers we can find all the examples of those types who, according to foreign descriptions, can be found among tellers in other nations. We know of story tellers who try to relate with the greatest possible authenticity what they learned from their predecessors and not only do they not alter the structure of the story, but cling even to the sentences. Naturally this authenticity in reproduction is relative. Others actually relish making changes. We know of numerous statements by Fedics in which he asserts that he freely varied the motif stock of his tales, and that the value of his narration lay in his ability to make the story ever more varied. This is the method of many good story tellers in Hungary, as the text analysis of old collections also testifies, and this is the reason why the Hungarian tale does not exhibit the rigid construction characteristic of many West European tales.

The life, the personal experience of the Hungarian story teller is also woven into the tale, and the vocabulary of the tale itself shows what sort of peasant work, what craft the narrator is at home with. And we can also follow with attention those characteristics of the narrator's style which testify to the faithful preservation of dialectical peculiarities, or to the mixing of certain of their elements with foreign influences; we can observe the linguistic influences of the city, which increasingly have been stolen into the style of story tellers, the imitation of the so-called gentlemanly, city-like speech, etc. Naturally, the differences between male and female story tellers also unfold, showing up in textual construction and in the development and elaboration of peculiar episodes.

In short, the development of the text of the tale, its future fate, and the sequence of its variations and transitions depend in a great many ways on the story teller. Therefore recently we have been trying to observe who is likely to become "an apprentice" from among the listeners of an outstanding story teller, who shall only retell the story, how the content of the story is retained in the memory of ten- to twelve-year-old children, and what development is shown in content. Long years are necessary for such study, and although the results may be less than the energy spent, we think it is worth the while.

Earlier folklore records and observations of village life show that story telling was alive everywhere in Hungary: the audience liked to listen to lengthy fairy tales, quick rolling, fresh anecdotes, and high-spirited, mocking village tales. According to the recollection of the old story tellers, the village always respected the story tellers of "beautiful words and a great memory". To learn tales never heard before and the words of home stories was an organic part of village life and of military life, of the bleak evenings itinerant workers spent away from home. Telling stories does not function in peasant existence the way it used to do. Story-telling occasions are coming to an end, or rather the character and content of communal gatherings is changing, and the old story themes are no longer part of the audience's interest. Instead, they increasingly discuss the questions and events of everyday life.

The anecdotes and local mocking stories cling most adamantly to life. Listening to fairy tales, and the re-creation of that peculiar, magical atmosphere that lifts the unbelievable adventures of the tale into the world of reality, where the listeners identify with the hero, is an increasingly rare experience. Naturally, we no longer have many good story tellers. We do know of ethnic groups where tradition is still alive, even though the custom of story telling itself is becoming increasingly rare. Still we must see two processes: the gradual relegation to the background of magic tales and fairy tales, and the listener's slow desertion of the story tellers, which also means that the active role played by the audience in the preservation and verification of the tale is about to end. More and more story tellers are becoming isolated in Hungary.

If we consider the formal, stylistic characteristics of story telling and tale narration, we first of all must say a few words about the strong dramatic character of performance and style. We cannot state that this dramatic manner of performance and structure is an exclusive charac-teristic of the Hungarian folk tale. Several researchers claim the same characteristic for Russian story telling, and we ourselves also have listened to Czech and Slovak story tellers whose performance testified to their great ability to dramatize, to create freshness and brilliant dia-logues, even in the telling of brief, joking stories. Comparative examin-ation has discovered numerous examples of this both in and outside of Europe.

Naturally, when we deal with the structure of the tales, we have in mind primarily the fairy tale as an example of dramatic structure: the three adventures which follow the introduction and in which the hero must struggle with increasing difficulties, and in which the third, the hardest of the adventures, already carries in itself the concluding events which relieve the tension. Although it seems to work through primitive devices, this structure resembles drama in its composition.

The Hungarian folk tale is dramatic in other ways as well. Drama is expressed by the way almost every good story teller, in the course of telling a story, builds it up through dramatically powerful scenes, a procedure that also testifies that this is not a matter of individual invention but a common tradition of Hungarian story telling, not because of chance, but in accordance with certain rules. The scenes which follow each other are always played through the dialogues of the participating characters; the more description of action, related by a third person, is rare. There are Hungarian tales in which the interpolated descriptive and explanatory parts almost disappear and are barely more than a signal, so that the entire story, which is now a series of scenes, appears through many witty, lively disputes and dialogues. And he who has been able to follow the events of a tale right to the end in the company with a devotedly listening peasant community, can testify to the dramatic method of a good story teller's performance. The story tellers build up the climaxes of the dialogues, practically change tone as the different characters speak, and use every tool to arouse interest and create tension before their enthusiastic audience.

In the course of analyzing the formal concerns of the Hungarian tale, we must mention again a trait that we have already spoken of in regard to the story teller. At first, on the basis of older, formerly collected folk tales which have been somewhat "corrected", we could scarcely believe how very lengthily, and with what great attention to detail, story tellers spin their tale, especially a wondrous fairy tale. It is true that some such authentic tales are known even from older collections. This generous expanding of details is characteristic of Hungarian tales, and is achieved without sacrificing the dramatic strength of the performance. Good story tellers are proficient at amassing even small incidents; they like to enlarge the story's structure and fit in newer motifs.

When in 1872 László Arany said in conjunction with his volumes of Hungarian folk poetry collection (*Magyar Népköltési Gyűjtemény*) that he wanted to answer the question "what characterizes the Hungarian tale", he wrote the following: "In our Hungarian tales it is primarily the complexity that differs from the tales of neighbouring peoples. None of them connect the various parts in such a random way as the Hungarian folk, especially those from the Great Plain; among the Germans it is more likely that the narrator forgets and leaves something out, and the Grimm brothers mention in regard to numerous tales that they have created the tale from two; our Hungarian collector runs into problems precisely because of the length of the tales, and the complications that get them into trouble in the narration. I believe the style of life of our people to be responsible for this situation..., their days spent with animals, their free evenings on the farmstead, their naturally silent character makes them very patient in listening to narratives."

That slow pastoral and country life to which László Arany attributes this method of construction has long ceased to exist, but our good story tellers still narrate tales this way. They like prolonging the narrative so much that even the tale's introductory formula is made into a separate, comic little story to mock the audience, and in tall tales the number of climaxes are expanded and increased. Among the best performers we can observe a tendency to enlarge the numerous small episodes, which results in performances that freely expand the motifs, to the brink of loquacity.

580

This is why as regards the types of the Hungarian folk tale we can always observe that transitional characters abound and that many types are amalgamated into an untroubled construction. Recently we have begun to investigate the laws with which certain types and motifs are more frequently attached to each other, and the regularity of affinity that can be demonstrated in these attractions and linkages. That is to say, we think that the law of affinity is one of the many theories to explain the development of new types, groups of types, and of historical changes within oral tradition. In our opinion this is how actual groups of types developed from types that stand near each other, yet each type possesses an individual character, such as, e.g. the tales of the type of *Amor and Psyche* (AaTh 425), the *Grateful Dead* (AaTh 505–508), etc.

But the related affinity of motifs and types makes it possible while relating the tale to unify the identical, the variable, and the many transitional forms. Therefore, a frequent practice in Hungarian folk tale is to mingle together several types, or at least to enrich them with motifs, freely borrowing from other story types. As Mihály Fedics, one of the best known Hungarian story tellers, mentioned on one occasion: "Somebody who knows only a few tales, even only ten, can make as many as a hundred out of them if he has a talent for it." At another place he explained that the good story teller can shorten or enlarge according to his taste: "The end of the tale can be here on the porch, or far over there at the edge of the forest." The story tellers boldly exercised this sovereign talent for forming and varying and are exercising it even today. We know a beautiful confession by one of the most outstandingly talented story tellers with the inclination to reshape, a forty-three-year-old fisherman, Ferenc Czapár: "It might go on even for a week before I finish a tale. It could be started about anything. About a table, a plate, whatever came to mind. The story is exactly like a small sapling. It grows. Man cuts it back, grafts it, cleans it, it will have leaves, fruit. A life is developing, just like man's. Who would think what is going to become of it? The tale is just like that. Once I started a tale about how a young lady found a wooden box. She picked it up, and looked to see what was in it. She opened it, and it was a dragon. He then picked her up and carried her off. I was telling for a week what happened to her. The tale goes the way we want it, only the foundation is needed, and everything else can rest on that."

A third formal feature of Hungarian folk tales, their colourfulness and perceptive strength, is connected with these features. We do not think that we are biased when we call attention to the sparkling brilliance, the formal wealth, the joke-spinning witticism of Hungarian tales, since such wonders of the folk tale also ornament all people's treasury of tales.

There is a wondrous duplicity in the method of narrating a Hungarian tale—although it is not alone in this in Europe. This characteristic duplicity consists in a realistic method of depicting a ceaselessly flying wonder, the expression of magic. But it is precisely the realistic depiction of small details that continually are brought into the tales, motifs told in Hungarian and known all over Eurasia, details from the Hungarian countryside, from Hungarian peasant life, and also about heroes that accord with Hungarian temperament. And it cannot be otherwise.

Among other characteristics, this poetic method of realistic depiction is what is a distinctive feature of Hungarian tales. No matter where the hero of the tale travels, the scene of the adventures in the Hungarian folk tale takes place is the world of the Hungarian peasant, in the village, in a farmstead's yard; and even the royal city is more like a little village than one of the small towns. The royal court very often recalls the prestigious household of a prosperous farmer, and one of the fascinating contradictions of the folk tale are the mysterious adventures, the enchantments and miracles that transcend this world, all woven together with the small realities of everyday life. Even the magic tools in tales—a spittle, a drop of blood, a comb, a starving nag and other such things—form an inseparable bond of the most unbelievable adventures with the everyday sights of peasant observation. Let us not even analyse what peculiar charm is provided by features of folk tales which permit to tell about the most impossible adventures, the most grotesque ideas, with a matter-of-fact naturalness. Most certainly this mode of performance is the reason that folk tales were listened to with such identification within rural cottages in wintertime, and in the herdsmen's quarters out on the faraway *puszta*s.

However, this is not the only reason to believe in the folk tale, and for the anxiety and joy that comes from identification with its adventures. The Hungarian folk tale, in almost all its genres, is first of all the expression of the social desires of the people, of its self esteem, its longing for justice and revenge.

Many people already have spoken of this matter in many different ways and have looked upon the reverent miracles of the tales, and the victory of the youngest and weakest son as expressing a desire for some kind of normative world of the desires. Perhaps we need to speak some more of the social tendencies expressed in folk tales. People preserved, listened to, and continued to create folk tales not least of all because this poetic genre expressed more completely than others, either in clear world-parables or in very understandably pictured parables, the people's concerns, their feeling of exposure among cruel oppressors, and their triumphant hope for the victory of the weakest. We know from the statement of many peasants how much they identify their peasant fate with the fate of the hero who fights it out with dragons, wicked warriors, mendacious friars. The statements explain the symbols very clearly.

It is also very instructive that the tale of the young servant man who took cruel revenge on his evil master and priest (AaTh 1000–1029) belongs among the most popular, most often repeated tales, and we know many versions of this type. Our experience is that the telling of such tales has a liberating effect on the audience, who do not deny why they are fond of these very tales. There is playfulness, the pleasure taken in wonders, fondness for adventure, everything in the narrative that for many centuries has been able to please peasant listeners who wish to learn about unknown worlds. And the greater the oppression, the more peasants have to stoop under their cruel fate, the more their tales are expressions of social tension, one of the most important factors in retaining folk tales. Barren, disconsolate poverty, newer and newer sufferings were the lot of the Hungarian peasantry for many centuries. This peasant past still comes through the meandering, light, colourful sentences of their tales.

The Legend

The Hungarian word *monda* (legend) dates from the end of the 18th century and comes from the twin words *mende-monda* (hearsay). The Hungarian folk does not know the designation *monda*, for what the literary language calls myth they call "history" *(história)*, "story" *(történet)*, and with that designation they differentiate it from the tale *(mese)* genre. Two of its large groups, historical legends and legends of superstition and belief, can be clearly distinguished from each other.

Historical Legends

The kern of the historical legend *(történeti monda)* is actually always realistic and has some foundation in truth. However, this kern of reality is coloured generally, often by tale-like elements. The kern of the legend is usually as old as the central historical fact, but in the course of time more and more recent elements, such as folk-story motifs, and even new historical facts, become attached to certain legends. It also happens that during the passing of time a legend becomes attached to new heroes of new times, without any significant change in its action. Some of the legends attached to Ladislas I (11th century) seem to have developed from the legends of an earlier folk hero, and we also know a Kossuth legend (19th century), the seed of which corresponds in all its important features to a well-known tale about King Matthias (15th century).

The first written survival of Hungarian legends is preserved for us by medieval Hungarian chronicles, but a good part of them supposedly originated from before the Conquest. One is the dream of Emese *(Emese álma)*, a totemic myth of the Árpád clan. The founding mother Emese sees an eagle and a glorious river flows from her womb, the family of rulers from the House of Árpád; first among them is Álmos, the one dreamed of and whose coming has been foretold. The totemic ancestor of the clan and the woman Emese herself appear to preserve traditions dating back to the time of matriarchal society. The Magyar myth of origin, the Legend of the White Stag *(Csodaszarvas monda)*, is related to the history of the Árpád clan, which was preserved by a 13th-century chronicle, although most likely its source was an 11th-century ancient geste.

The giant Ménrót moved to the land of Eviláth following the (Babylonian) confusion of tongues... and here he had two sons, namely Hunor and Mogor, born to him from his wife Ene, and from these descend the Huns and Magyars. However, the giant Ménrót also had other wives, and from these many sons and daughters descended. And because Hunor and Mogor were his first born sons, they lived in a tent separate from their father's. And it happened on one occasion that they went hunting. A deer [roe] rose in front of them, and as she fled from them they chased her into the bogs of Maeotis. There they lost her completely and could not find her even after much searching. Finally, after they had wandered back and forth through the bog, they decided that it was suitable for the grazing of

583

animals. They then returned to their father, and as soon as they gained his consent, they went on together with all their stock, to the bogs of Maeotis, in order to settle there. The region of Maeotis borders on the province of Persia; except for a narrow crossing, it is surrounded on all sides by the sea. It has no flowing waters, but it is abundant in grass, trees, birds, fish, and wild beasts. Getting in and out was difficult. When they settled down in the bogs of Maeotis, they did not budge from there for five years. But when they ventured out once in the sixth year, they met, purely by chance, with the children and wives of the sons of Belár, as they were camping in the puszta without their husbands; and, riding fast, they carried them off with all their belongings to the bogs of Maeotis. It so happened that they had caught the two daughters of Dula, the chieftain of the Alans, among these children; Hunor married one of them, Mogor the other. From these women descend the Huns and Magyars, everyone of them.

The mythical stag that showed the new homeland seems to be connected with an ancient totemic animal. The pursuit of an enticing animal belongs among the known mythic, legend-type stories, and, for example, is an important tale in the Persian collection titled *A Thousand and One Nights*. The motif of abducting women, on the other hand, reflects the connection of the Árpáds' ancestors, the clan of the "Gyulák", with the famous Bulgarian dynasty (Belár–Bolgár), and in general the historical contacts of Magyars and Bulgaro-Turks.

The final source of the Botond legend can be found in the wars waged by the Hungarians against Byzantium, and from a closer view, it preserves memories of the ancient Magyar ceremonies of declaring war, which began with nicking a spear of pickaxe into the enemy's gate. The hero of the Lél (Lehel) legend had fallen captive to the German emperor. Knowing that the emperor would condemn him to death, he hit the emperor on the head with his bugle and said: "You go ahead of me and be my servant in the other world." This is connected with one of the historical episodes in the Magyars' roaming after the Conquest, and its action preserves the belief that existed among the ancient Magyars, namely, that the hero is served after his death by those he had killed in battle during his lifetime. Here let us mention the legendary text of the battles fought for the new homeland. The "Myth of the White Horse" *(Fehér ló mondája)* preserves the peace-making ceremonies of the Magyars, which consisted of an animal sacrifice, pouring water on the ground, touching the earth, turning a saddle around, and lifting a handful of soil toward the sky.

The oldest legends, therefore, give interesting and, from the point of view of their final kern, historically authentic pictures of ancient Magyar history; we learn from them the heroic fight waged in conquering the new homeland.

These legends were probably spread and kept alive for long centuries by professional singers. The texts of these minstrels must have seemed to the writers of the chronicles to be evidence, and with the help of the chronicles' text it is even possible to ascertain that the heroic legends were sung as if the hero himself were giving an account of his deeds in the first person. The tale-type legend form developed early. The already mentioned opinion of Anonymus about "the idle talk" of minstrels and jokers, and the "false tales of the peasants", therefore, refers to the story-like genres as well.

Otherwise, in absence of records, we know little of the folk legends from the centuries following the Conquest, since at this time only distinguished clerical men were literate. Songs and tales that gave form to complaints and desires of the oppressed were persecuted. But no matter how much the church persecuted folk poetry with iron and fire, the songs passed from mouth to mouth. Telling such tales made heavy peasant work more tolerable and related the deeds of conquering heroes. Besides the old songs, legends and tales, new ones also arose about heroes, personifying the virtues and desires of the people, especially those who excelled in beating back enemy intervention that endangered the entire country. One of the most popular figures of heroic songs is King Ladislas (11th century), hero of battles against foreign invaders, whose person and deeds are mingled in the imagination of the people with what seem to be the deeds and the characters of a heroic epic originating in the earlier homeland.

It seems that conflicts within the feudal ruling class played a large role also in legends of the Hungarian folk. Feudal rebels who rose against the king appear, in the imagination of the people, as heroes of a rebellion against the entire feudal society. The murderous attempt of Felicián Zách against the royal family in the time of the Hungarian king Charles Robert (14th century), and the consequent punishment of the Zách family, their total extermination, were suitable events for the emergence of a legend.

The legend of "Lőrinc Tar's Descent to Hell' (Tar Lőrinc pokoljárása) belongs to the class that came into existence around the 14th–15th centuries and was later worked up by the famous minstrel of the 16th century, Sebestyén Tinódi Lantos. Tinódi himself reveals that he heard the story in a song. Although some motifs of the song are not of folk origin, it seems that the story of Lőrinc Tar, who met the king in hell, as well as the archbishop who had collected false tithes, the bishop and the noble lords who ravaged the property of the peasants, must have been popular for a long time throughout the country. The international parallels of the story can be traced quite far.

Today this old material barely survives in the Hungarian wealth of legends, or only fragments are being related at some places. A part of the historical legends still living on the lips of the people is not connected with popularly known historical persons, and perhaps these myths reflect most authentically the national catastrophes that primarily troubled the suffering, working peasants. The oldest of the legends belonging to this group are the *myths of the Mongol invasion*. These are often identical with the myths of the Turkish occupation, a fact that permits the assumption that one or two myths belonging to this category are connected not with the Mongol invasion of the 13th century but rather with the intrusions of the Mongols frequent during the wars with the Turks. At any rate, the legends of the Mongol invasion and the Turkish occupation resemble each other in many respects. The following similar type of legend, recorded in Karcsa (Zemplén county), also proves this contention:

"... Then once the Turks came, but they did not call them Turks, they called them the dogheaded Mongols. What shall we do? They will eat us! People took food with them, everything that will last so that they shouldn't starve to death. And there was kotorca *[the floury stem of the rush], and there were roots, and later they opened up the rush and ate it. So they had food.*

They had little horses no bigger than a cat or a dog. They lay low on their backs and the horses carried them to the top of the sandy hill of grapes. They started to shout:

"Sári, Zsuzsi, Borcsa, Mari, come on out! The dogheaded Mongols are no longer here. They have gone, come on home. The dogheaded Mongols are not here!"

But they did not stir, so one of them says:

"You just wait, I know where you are. You are in the rushes. I am going in there, going to ride in with my horse. Here is the way, here they are. Come on boys, it is not deep, not deep."

The others stopped at the edge of the water, along the sedge. He then rode in, until even the foam disappeared after him. He was not seen anywhere.

Then a long time passed, and when the waters had subsided and left, the lake dried out. Well, a great, enormous walnut tree grew out of the Turk's pocket. Beautiful. That tree may have been even two hundred years old. Nobody harmed it. But the Jews and the barons moved here and they got tired of it, did not like it on their land. It was on the boundary or some such place, so they cut down the walnut tree. And the folks of Karcsa wept for it bitterly, because it has been preserved from father to son that this tree and these nuts had come from the pocket of the Turk and had grown out of there.

The story in most of these legends is about the successful flight of the populace from a superior force. However, it is their cunning and resourcefulness that is responsible for their great success. Other legends that belong to this group tell about brave heroes who triumph over superior forces; the legends also tell about cowards and traitors with contempt.

Local Legends The legends of the Mongol invasion and Turkish occupation consist usually of one element and for this reason alone exhibit a close relationship with one of the large groups of historical legends, the local legends *(helyi monda)*. Numerous versions of these are known. The most frequent are legends explaining the foundation of a place, legends of treasure, legends about the mountains, hills, waters, legends about someone turning into a stone, etc. Most of them coincide in many respects with the historical legends, and furthermore the types mentioned are frequently attached to a person or historical figure. According to one such a legend, a man was obliged either to pay a piece of gold to the landlord or to hoe for him for three days in his vineyard. King Matthias, as he passed through that place, also tackled the hoeing in company with a peasant mate. Unseen by him, the king threw a gold piece in front of his mate, but the latter would not leave until the king also threw a piece in front of himself. The king then sent the bailiffs for the landlord, who tried to flee but fell into the Danube with his carriage and they caught him only at the ferry, which was called by the name "Vörösmarti-ferry" even after.

The Hungarians have rich traditions regarding King Matthias, the Renaissance ruler of the 15th century. According to the legends he himself came from a peasant background, and he brings to heel great lords, oppressing nobles, in some cases the village magistrates (the representatives of the wealthier peasantry), in order to improve the lot of the poor peasants. Some of the legends about King Matthias were later transferred to Lajos Kossuth or even to other heroes whom the people felt to be their own.

The figure of King Matthias plays a role not only in traditions of Hungarian folk poetry but also in those of the Ukrainians, Croats, Slovenes, Czechs, and Slovaks. We can say that among the peoples of East Europe the figure of Matthias is a symbolic hero much like Nasreddin Hodja in the Near East, or the similar hero of Russian folk poetry, Ilya Muromets, or even Robin Hood.

Few well formulated legends in Hungarian folk poetry recall Prince Ferenc Rákóczi, leader of the anti-Habsburg War of Liberation. Only fragments mentioning Rákóczi as a liberating hero have survived, yet his figure lives even today in Ukrainian and Slovak traditions. Formerly, on the basis of existing knowledge, our opinion was that the memory of Rákóczi as a liberating hero was not as alive in the mind of the Hungarian people as the figure of King Matthias or Kossuth. However, after the meagre results of earlier collecting, Imre Ferenczi amassed a whole volume of material testifying that the Rákóczi War of Liberation, and especially the figure of Ferenc Rákóczi, is very much alive in oral tradition, as historical legends not infrequently are mixed with legends on belief.

One of the most popular heroes of Hungarian legend is the leader of the 1848–49 War of Independence Lajos Kossuth. He often appears in folksongs also (cf. p. 489). Forms of costume, hats, even beards were designated with his name, which also appeared frequently in idioms and proverbs. In the myths the people endowed Kossuth with all those characteristics and deeds possessed by his predecessors, including Matthias. Thus Matthias myths often appear with Kossuth's name, as in the following myth, recorded in Debrecen (MNK 921 X^x):

Once upon a time Kossuth gathered the lords around him and right there on the spot he asked them:

"Who deserves the juice of the grape?"

The lords, all of them, answered that it is the one who owns the land.

"Well then, lords, let us get hoeing!"

So they started on it. Lajos Kossuth hoed up in front, not just the ordinary way, but uphill. A little time passed, and he then allowed them a little rest and asked:

"Who deserves the juice of the grape?"

To this the lords again replied that it is the one who owns the land.

"Well, lords, let us go and hoe some more!"

So they started up again, and the lords were really sweating at it.

Kossuth asked again:

"Who deserves the juice of the grape?"
"Both the one to whom the land belongs, and the one who sweats on it."
But even this was not enough for Kossuth, so he again said:
"Well, lords, let's get hoeing!"
They hoed for a good while, then Kossuth asked again:
"Who deserves the juice of the grape?"
And to this all the lords answered, he who hoes it, and it is a good thing that a little is left for those who just dangle their legs.

The Kossuth legends are in many cases just narratives; their form is not mature, but still they show that the process of becoming a legendary figure has already started around the figure of Kossuth.

The cycle of outlaw legends *(betyár monda)* forms a separate world of its own. (Cf.: outlaw songs, outlaw ballads, pp. 494, 539). The story told about Sándor Rózsa by a Great Plain peasant well represents the way of thinking of these stories:

Don't you, for any sake, think that Sándor Rózsa was a robber or a brigand! He was a great man who loved justice! But in those days he handed out justice the only way possible. He took money from the rich and gave it to the paupers. Once a poor cotter's house burned down, and so Sándor Rózsa gave him money to build it up. And he didn't kill the rich either; yes indeed, he never got mixed up in murder. Other outlaws killed and robbed, and the Austrian lords blamed it all on Sándor Rózsa, because they hated Sándor very much. It is true that he joined Kossuth's army together with other outcast highwaymen, and where the band of Sándor Rózsa fought, they were sure to win. Bullets didn't harm Sándor, he was always in front of the troops. Gun in his hand, carbine on his shoulder, in linen shirt and white trousers, oh, what a handsome young man he was.

So goes the remembrance. People looked upon outlaws as fighters for liberty who seized the excess money from the hands of the rich and handed it over to the penniless.

A significant part of the Hungarian historical legends not only records events but also selects among them. It primarily rewards those who really defended the poor, who fought for the freedom of the entire nation. Thus these legends not only testify to a historical sense of value but also that this type of folk poetry came from the poor peasants.

Legends of Belief

The attention of Hungarian research has been directed to legends of belief *(hiedelemmonda)* most vigorously only during the last decades. Although several versions were known earlier, this group was not discussed separately from other genres. In consequence, collecting these could not have become systematic. The definition of the group, despite serious Hungarian and European research, cannot in every respect be looked upon as final. It is indisputable that we are dealing with an epic genre that surrounds one kern of belief, but not every belief becomes a legend, that is to say, the totality of the legends does not simultaneously provide all the material. Only those beliefs become legends that are connected to some action. Then again, not every kern of a legend of belief is part of the whole world of beliefs, so that for example, legends of belief about giants also occur within the Hungarian linguistic region, while at the same time they do not belong to the body of beliefs of the Hungarian folk. According to the most recent knowledge, the kern of belief and the action attached to it, the local story, characterize the genre of the legends of belief.

Legends of belief are partly national in character, partly international, so that they can be found both among the Hungarians and the European peoples.

A survey of these legends can be carried out only on the basis of the belief elements, according to which they are divided into two large groups: legends about men, beasts, plants, and objects possessing supernatural strength; and myths about supernatural beings. It is characteristic of the entirety of the Hungarian legends that the first group dominates, and legends of the second group occur in much smaller numbers than do those of the first group. In the treasury of similar European legends, the situation is exactly the opposite, and this lends a special significance to the Hungarian legends of belief.

First, let us discuss some human figures possessing supernatural power, since from a calculation supported by 3,000 legends, it is evident that these make up almost 60 per cent of the corpus of Hungarian beliefs. Significant among these is the group of shaman *(táltos)* legends, which undoubtedly contain shamanistic features. In spite of their long history, their numbers barely reach 3 per cent, and in many cases the story is mixed with the legend about the *garabonciás,* an occidental wandering student. Similarly, this group also makes up 3 per cent of the Hungarian legends of belief.

The essence of the *táltos* legends (cf. pp. 672-3) is a struggle for "knowledge", the knowledge of magic power, the struggle fought by those who were born with teeth, or with six fingers, in the disguise of a bull or a fiery wheel. The following legend, recorded at Karcsa (former Zemplén county), tells about this:

Afterwards we went to the lower end of the village. We used to go there to talk with one of our neighbours. And during the talk such matters came up. Old Ferenc Nagy said that he too had heard from an old cattleherd that there was a boy, he came to a pasture. There was a big herd of cattle, and alongside of them a man between forty-five or fifty, a herdsman. He greeted him:

"God give you good day!"

He asks him, doesn't he need a young herdsman.

"Indeed I do," he says, "I used to have a young herdsman but he was no satisfactory, so now I need one who is. So son," he says, "if you think that you can take care of the responsibilities, I'll take you on."

So he took him on as his young herdsman, but he was really more like a cattleherd. The days passed one after the other, but he didn't admit to his gazda that he is a garabonciás.

Then time went on, and once it began thunder and lightning, and a great black cloud was coming. Well, this young herdsman knew what was going to happen, but the old herdsman didn't know. It is enough to say that the herdsman spoke thus:

"Well son," he says, "let us drive the cattle toward the fold, because we might have such a storm that we can't handle the cattle."

Then they drove the cattle into the corral, and afterwards the boy says to the gazda:

"Well," he says, "my gazda, let's go to the hut, but take the best cudgel in hand. Furthermore," he says, "you urge the two dogs when the time comes."

"Well," he says, "then I'll go into the hut, and you on the other hand stay outside at the mouth of the hut. Then," he says, "I am going to turn into a bull, and I have to fight it out with that bull. But if I don't have any help he will be stronger than I am. So, my gazda, take the cudgel and beat the small toenail of the bull as hard as you possibly can. And urge the dog, both dogs, to rip the balls of that bull who comes down from the cloud. This way somehow I might be able to fight him."

And so this is what happened. When the bull came down from the cloud, the boy also turned into a bull, jumped out of the hut, and they fell upon each other, that is how they fought. Then when the gazda saw that he was weakening, he began to beat the back small toenail on the other bull's leg. And he urged the dogs to rip at his balls as much as they can.

Well, then the gazda saw that that one was weakening. And when the cloud descended as low to the ground as when he had come out of it, the bull climbed into the cloud and left. The other one then changed back into a man.

Then he told his gazda what this was all about.

"He came for me just now. If I don't fight him now, if I don't break him down, then they would take me away. But because I fought him, they will leave me now in peace, so now I am free."

One interesting group of Hungarian legends of belief is connected with the person of the *Clever Coachman (tudós kocsis)* (cf. p. 676). His most frequently occurring characteristic trait is his power to bind, to stop man or beast so it cannot move. Parallels to this motif can be found equally in east and west. Less frequently it happens that he brings to life a horse skin stuffed with straw and travels great distances by rising into the air with this horse. These features point more in the direction of the Orient, and we can find their equivalents in the world of beliefs of those peoples who were related to the Magyars or were in contact with them at some time. This form of the legend of belief is known primarily in the eastern half of the linguistic region. The following was recorded in Tyukod (former Szatmár County):

"My father was an apprentice in Porcsalma, at the lord's. There, he met this wise man. Terge had a coachman. It is he I want to tell a story about now. This Terge brought the horses from Transylvania, to sell them here. He had a coachman who knew about horses and also other things. Terge didn't know about this. Once Terge got a letter from along the Tisza that there will be a wedding. He wanted to go there. He was supposed to be there by morning. Because he was going off, Terge told the coachman to be quick about his work. The coachman said nothing but just went to the tavern and paid no attention to the horses. He went home in the evening, and it was getting very late when he brought the cart out."

"Well, we are going to be late because of you," Terge said to him.

590

"Don't you worry, we'll be there by the time we have to. It isn't far from here, only one stroke, two strokes, and we are already there," answered the coachman.

When they got going, the coachman asked:

"How should we go: like the wind or like a thought?"

He only just answered, "Go like the wind. Then he suddenly saw that he was being lifted up because the wheels didn't touch the ground. So they went over the tree tops, over the water on the Szamos [river]. It wasn't yet dawn when they arrived. Only then did Terge realize who his coachman was. He could hardly wait to get there and discharged him immediately. But the horses were unable to budge. He got frightened again, but he finally found a coachman who was able to drive them. The other one also knew how to do it, that's why."

The figure of the Cunning Shepherd *(tudós pásztor)* (cf. p. 675) is related to the magic coachman. It makes up more than 4 per cent of the Hungarian legends of belief, and is mostly restricted to the eastern part of the country where the extensive keeping of animals, and along with that, the less tied-down life of the herdsmen, survived the longest. The herdsmen possessing supernatural knowledge and power excelled in healing, in the scattering of animals and herds, and in keeping them together under any circumstance. They send the stock, generally the bull, against their enemies, and at the same time they not only avert similar attempts against themselves but they even turn them around in the other direction. There are many legends of experiences among such stories, and legends heard firsthand, but there are also some among them the forms of which have solidified and are identical over a large area.

Most widely spread over the entire Hungarian linguistic region are the legends about witches *(boszorkánymonda)*, which comprise over one-fourth of the known material (cf. pp. 673-4). These tell about the acquisition of magic, the spoiling of milk, the witch's turning into some animal. The most general are still those recounting different versions of the one about being pressed by a witch. The following from Kishartyán (Nógrád County) is a version of such a myth:

This is what happened in Cserhátsurány to two brothers. They lay in the same bed every night, and the younger one was pressed every night. This went on for a whole year. Of course the boy didn't dare tell anybody. One time his older brother told him:

"Younger brother, what is with you? You are getting skinnier each day."

But he was secretive then and didn't want to tell. His parents also questioned him the same way. They said "do tell us," and his brother was questioning him,—he must be helped somehow. Finally the boy tells his older brother,

"I am being pressed every night, so much so that I almost die, since I cannot get any air at all."

"Well, brother, it is a good thing that you finally told us about is. Now we are going to change places. I will wait for it."

The older brother had a sleep already in the daytime, so that he would be alert at night. And the witch came around midnight. I heard when the door opened, I was not sleepy, but when she approached the bed sleep overcame me. I did notice the witch when she put her weight on me. But because he was awake, he didn't lose consciousness and started to wrestle with the witch. They wrestled for a half an hour, but he could not overcome the witch. But while we were struggling there, her small finger was caught in my mouth. I held that with all my might and bit down on it. I made only one mistake, and that is when I spat out the piece of the finger onto the floor of the house. So the witch became obedient right away, left me in the bed, and took the piece of finger along. Then my mother said, now we must watch carefully whose hand is going to be bound up.

So the next day several of us met that certain woman who was otherwise a midwife. So he questioned her like this:

"Aunt Mari, what happened to your hand?"

"Oh, my dear son, I was chopping wood and cut my hand. I am going to the doctor—she said.

Meanwhile my mother also met her:

"Aunt Mari, what is the matter with your hand?"

"Oh," she says, "I was chopping wood!

But she didn't tell her that she had cut her finger, only that she cut her hand. Then the mother of the boy told her:

"Oh the plague should fall on you, Aunt Mari! Aren't you ashamed of yourself for wrecking that poor boy for an entire year? Now, if it wasn't for his brother changing place with him, you could have finished him off. You should be ashamed of yourself, you dirty old witch. Isn't it enough that you sucked on every cow in the neighbourhood in the shape of a cat? It had already come to light at the neighbours' that when they poured the milk into the pigs' trough and beat the milk in the trough with a willow twig, even then you went there saying "don't you hurt that milk!" It came to light, didn't it, that as they beat the milk, you felt the pain, but they just kept beating the milk all the more. Isn't it true that since then there has been no milk missing from a single cow? You dirty old witch, and on top of all this you think we need you as midwife? You should be kicked out of the village!" she says.

From then on the boy got livelier and better every day, and he was not pressed any more.

The legends about witches vary greatly in form and content. The majority are stories of experiences which coincide in content with the world of beliefs and can be looked upon as manifestations of it. Their construction is often loose, and only in the versions of certain story-tellers do these tales become more permanent as the result of frequent repetition. Although the second group maintains contact with the world of beliefs, still some tales become more entertaining in content and form, and their legendary traits wear off. At the same time the form of these legends crystallizes, and it becomes more and more apparent that they deal with wanderers of far-away lands.

Supernatural beings are not present in this category of Hungarian legends. So far it has not been possible to ascertain satisfactorily the reason for this. However, this is compensated for by the wealth of material relating to the figure of death, haunting spirits, ghosts, that is to say, everything that is connected to the still existing world of belief or to beliefs which had existed in the near past. Legends about the returning dead, whose desire was not fulfilled, are very frequent. The following comes from the Palots region and dates from the late 19th century:

All of a sudden some rumbling was heard from outdoors, like when the wind is bending the trees; I look over at the window and I see someone looking in and then disappears. At first I thought that somebody was just curious, but it came to the window for the second time and third time, so I went out of the house to see who it was, but there wasn't a soul anywhere. Well, I thought to myself, I am not going back now. The hour was getting late, so I went on.

But I had hardly gone ten steps when somebody is coming exactly towards me in a white dress, boots on its feet, lace made of gold on its head, like the one young wives wear here, and it held a rosary in its hand. I saw it clearly in the moonlight. So the woman comes straight to me and tells me:

"Do not be afraid, my dear son. I am your godmother. Tell my daughter that I never rest in the other world. If my dotted skirt and two clean gangas (a pure white apron made from hemp linen) are in the chest she should sell them and pay for two masses for me."

With that she became like a piece of smoke or fog and disappeared from in front of my eyes. And it is true, as God is guarding us in heaven; if I didn't see it, I would not tell about it.

So I go next day to the daughter of my godmother and tell her about it. But the young woman just didn't want to believe it, except when I mentioned the dotted skirt and two gangas. Then she said:

"Now, brother-in-law, I believe that you spoke to my mother, because in truth she left me nothing else but those. But if that is her wish I will sell those also, so that she won't be lacking in the other world, as she always lacked in this one."

Hungarian legends are connected to the still existent or formerly existing world of belief. Belief in the existence of people possessing supernatural knowledge and ability (*táltos, garabonciás,* coachman, miller, ferryman, herdsman, etc.) has ceased almost entirely, yet the form of the legends has become solidified and polished in style. The other group of legends is attached to the still valid or dormant world of belief. Legends about witches, supernatural beings, and the haunting dead speak about certain experiences that justify the local world of belief and direct the listeners in their behaviour with supernatural beings. Their moral is at least as important in these as the aim of entertaining. Generally, the form has not yet solidified and is interwoven with a great deal of individual colour. Naturally, innumerable transitions are possible between the two groups, according to the desuetude of the religious base and the crystallization of form.

The experts and best relaters of legends of belief are generally former labourers on the large estates, or the peasant strata close to them socially (day labourers, share croppers, poor peasants). Yet social references are rare because of the character of the genre. We can still find some legends, especially those about magic coachmen or herdsmen, where in the narration people hit back for the many injuries they had suffered from their lord or his steward. It seems as if supernatural power and its qualities serve precisely this same purpose.

There are no traditional phrases for beginning these legends as there are for fairy tales. The action usually starts off with the precise designation of the locality, the time, and perhaps the participants. The style of the majority of legends, consisting mostly of one or two elements, is extremely simple. However, their content and form do influence their style to a significant degree. If the legend is similar to a tale, then its language and mode of performance also becomes similar. Still, the style is mainly determined by the desire to disclose some peculiar event in such a way that the audience should be able to learn from it, and not primarily by wanting to entertain. This is why its mode of delivery is objective: it does not move about the topic but proceeds directly towards the goal. Simple language completes the clear, translucent form, which even more underlines the clarity of the legend.

Those who relate legends of belief are mostly not identical with the standing story tellers. Generally they also know tales as well, but they value their own genre much more than fairy stories, saying that those stand much closer to everyday life. The occasions for story telling also conform in broad outline with those for reciting legends. The herdsmen, day labourers, and labourers on the large estates were glad to relate such stories when work provided an opportunity, and similar tales were also certainly told at wakes.

Other Types of Folk Narrative

Besides tale and legend, there are several other genres that also belong to folklore. The anecdote *(anekdota)* is a humorous, snappy, short narrative, mostly connected in action with a definite person and place. It contains a great many itinerant elements, which assures the genre's mobility. It is still a live and expanding genre today. The *trufa* is also a humorous story, its humour usually coarse. This was also the name for the uproariously funny theatrical performances at fairs or other folk gatherings in the Middle Ages. While the *trufa* achieved a more or less permanent form, narrative accounts *(elbeszélés)* about personal adventures (soldiering, work, family, etc.) became polished during the course of frequent repetition.

We shall discuss in more detail the idioms, proverbs, and riddles, which are the smallest, yet important creations of folk prose.

Proverbs *(közmondás)* and idiomatic sayings *(szólás)* are condensed expressions of the people's wisdom, of their often ironic, mocking cleverness, of their sagacity hardened by painful and victorious battles over the centuries, and these idioms also had their effect in literature. Shakespeare, Pushkin, Tolstoy, the Hungarians János Arany, Sándor Petőfi, Mór Jókai, Kálmán Mikszáth, all use such condensing, prosaic and yet epigrammatic elements of folk poetry. Idomatic sayings and proverbs have a power of expression which is the innermost property of the language and at the same time is more than a matter of mere linguistics, of simple sentence structure; the condensing power of folk experience and adventures, parables is alive in it.

Proverbs and idiomatic sayings demonstrate best the social and collective nature of folklore. Individual creation is wrapped in deeper anonymity in them than in any other genre. Even in literature there are characters who constantly use proverbs, who answer the most varied phenomena of life with sayings, etc. Furthermore, ethnographers often have the good fortune to meet inexhaustible knowers and inventors of proverbs. However, when we consider the characteristic features of

594

idiomatic sayings and proverbs, first the communal nature and lack of individual character must be mentioned.

Secondly, a trait which may be called "general usage" characterizes idiomatic sayings, which means that in a given time—because idioms also have a historical age—the community, mostly the entire community of the nation, consistently uses such idioms and proverbs. They are used almost spontaneously and with identical meaning, part of the vocabulary, but more meaningful than a mere linguistic expression, and they appear to be something like a communal poetic quotation of common origin.

The third characteristic of idiomatic sayings and proverbs is their stabilizing formal structure, which follows from this and is related to all that we have said so far. In proverbs, stable formal structure is primarily expressed by the aspiration to condensation and brevity. We must emphasize also that idioms and proverbs differ significantly from simple linguistic expressions.

Let us now look more closely at what is strictly considered to be an idiom. There are two kinds, idiomatic expression *(szólásmód)* and idiomatic simile *(szóláshasonlat)*. These are more elementary forms, and almost approach the mere stylistic formation of words, although they are emphatically differentiated by their consolidated form and their contentual excess. The simplest formula is the idiomatic expression, an idiomatic formula consisting of one part. It is characterized by the many kinds of varied ideas used in place of simple linguistic expressions. Here, for example, are a few of the common sayings applied to a miser: "he beats the penny to his teeth"; "he keeps count even of his gulps"; "he would make two of one coin if he could"; "he would skin even the stone if it only had skin"; "he would charge rent even for air"; etc. It can be felt that these common sayings express a complex judgement of the community and that they are not simply elementary linguistic forms.

Another kind of idiomatic saying is the idiomatic simile. Its name implies that it seemingly is one of the species of simile and could also appear as some simple, linguistic, stylistic device. However, the idiomatic simile does not belong within the circle of simple, arbitrary similes, something which exists in language and poetry in innumerable varieties, but lives in the consciousness of the community and revives at given times in its fixed form. This constancy, this fixity and communal character lift it out of the world of similes. Sometimes it appears that there is hardly any difference between the ordinary simile and the idiomatic simile, but still the two types, the linguistic (pure simile) and the folk poetic (idiomatic simile), can be distinctively separated. "Blinks like one who has dust in his eyes", for example, is only a simple simile, but if we say "blinks like the Miskolc *kocsonya*" (cold pork in aspic), we have already used an idiomatic simile, which has a consolidated foundation, and an emotional, humorous background that comes alive in the entire community alike. Of course both kinds of similes in their consolidated form always come alive and gain shape by being related to certain persons and events, so that in themselves they are incomplete:

Idiomatic Sayings

595

"X.Y. sleeps like a marmot", etc., "X.Y. would skin even the stone". Therefore, the structure of the simile is in open contrast to that of the proverb, which is a closed formal and contextual unit in itself.

Proverbs The proverb *(közmondás)* covers three groups, which can be differentiated primarily according to whether their content is statement, judgement, or advice. The first form, the statement, expresses public opinion without any elaboration, judgement, or moral comment: "The dog barks, the caravan moves on"; "You can't make a silk purse out of a sow's ear"; "Good wine needs no sign-board"; "Who comes earlier will be happy earlier"; "The runaway servant is paid by the stick" (a historical survival of social conditions), etc. Proverbs may express a valuation in their judgement, often of a political or class nature, as expressed in the statements: "It is not good to eat cherries out of the same bowl with high lords"; "Better a lean compromise than a fat lawsuit"; "It is not all true what the lords lie about"; "Better a sparrow today than a partridge tomorrow".

The third group most resembles the so-called worldly wisdom of maxims, which—especially at one time—were almost a literary fashion. These are advice-giving proverbs. For example, "Bend the twig while it is young"; "Stretch only as far as your cover reaches", etc.

The picture of social life, along with the mental attitude of how the people view the surrounding world, is reflected in the proverb, this most simple branch of folk poetry which virtually appears to be a linguistic form of folk poetry. In the expression "a poor man stuck to the ground", there lives the historical and class memory of the serfs' being bound to the land, of permanent bondage! "A priest does not levy a tithe on a priest", brings to mind the tithe of the time of church taxes. And the following need no further explanation: "The peasant lives by his ten fingers"; "A rich widow is always 30 years old"; "The rich have two nostrils like those of the poor man's pig"; and so on.

Other proverbs carry memories of cultural history: thus, for example, "Many notches are against him" is a reference to the old way of counting by notches. Many proverbs by now appear to be only humorous common sayings. The saying, "There is neither money nor broad-cloth", has a time-defining—i.e. historical—value; it refers to the life of the soldiers who defended the border fortresses in the 16th to 17th centuries and received their payment either in money or in kind, or did not get it at all. "I tie back your heel"; "I will teach you to play the pipe in your glove"; "Keep denying until the fingernail breaks", come from the circle of medieval torture procedures and are not at all a reminder of humorous practices. In the same way "Play his song for him on the violin", or "Learned to dance the *Kállai kettős*" recall through common sayings the harsh methods of interrogating captives. There are still a great many proverbs about the justice of King Matthias. Kossuth also is remembered through proverbs.

We have mentioned conciseness as a basic characteristic of all proverbs, the attempt to formulate as finally and simply as possible, using either an open linguistic structure or a closed linguistic structure.

Conciseness is so characteristic of this group that it is not necessary to justify it with separate examples; still, it can be said that this conciseness stands even the greatest tests of poetic condensation and often surpasses the best expressions of authors. It can also be stated as a rule that the more concise and simple a proverb, the more certain is its long past, the broader its communal character, and the more frequent its usage.

Another structural characteristic is the proportioned structure. The much liked double measure can be found, but there are also proverbs in great numbers that are measured out into three and four parts. The following are virtually rhythmical structures: "Today a bride, tomorrow a wife, the day after tomorrow a *koma* [godmother] woman"; "The table is wide, the tablecloth is narrow, the dinner is sparse." In four parts: "If you come, you'll be there; if you bring, you'll have food." Because of this condensation and attempt at giving proportion, a significant part of Hungarian proverbs and idiomatic sayings show a certain rhythmic regularity, fit into a rhythmic structure, and often take on a rhymed, lyric form.

It is also possible to construct the metrics of Hungarian idiomatic sayings and proverbs: the ancient six syllable (*lassú víz partot mos*—slow water washes the shore); seven syllable (*eső után köpönyeg*—raincoat after the rain); eight syllable (*késő bánat eb gondolat*—late sorrow, dog idea), (*olcsó húsnak híg a leve*—cheap meat makes thin soup), etc. We can find regular lines of three measures (with a ten, eleven, twelve formula), compound lines with various rhythmic formulae, and besides these rhythmic structures, a regular alliterative form (*vak vezet világtalant*—blind leads the blind) and final rhyme forms as well. Often the rhythmic formula tries to become verse-like through echo words and phonetic effects. All this shows that the proverb not only tries to attain its intellectual function—that is, to close debate with judgement, advice, and parables—but also that it tries to give a transformed, shaped form, that is to say, a poetic expression, to its message.

Finally it is hardly necessary to point out that connections with the European treasury of idiomatic sayings and proverbs can also be found in the Hungarian material. Apart from the earlier Hungarian antecedents, there is György Gaál, who published folk tales in Vienna in 1829 and had earlier edited a volume of comparative proverbs. This is understandable, since one of the sources of European proverbs and idiomatic sayings was the Bible, the other the tradition of ancient maxims. It is also understandable that the way of looking at nature and agriculture, and at the related situation of peasant labour and society could also have created a string of related and identical or similar proverbs. However, those proverbs and idioms that preserve local stories and anecdotes—by now "worn" into the form of proverbs and one or another idioms—are tied to certain ethnic groups or nations. There are also plenty of these in the Magyar material of the genre.

Riddles   The riddle *(találós kérdés)* is a roundabout description of unidentifiable objects, with the help of the features of another object that are either identical with or refer to the unidentified ones. Riddles therefore stand close to metaphors, which is to say that on the basis of similarity they transfer the identifying features of the identifiable object onto another object, or phenomenon, generally identified in the question.

We can suppose that the Hungarians liked riddles from the earliest of times. They called them tales *(mese)* or riddle tales *(találós mese)* even in the 17th century: "I'll marry my daughter to the one who can solve my tale." We differentiate two kinds in Hungarian folklore. One is the "riddle tale", that, is a question shaped into some tale form and related to a story; however, the most frequent are the shorter, actual riddles, generally consisting of only one sentence. The Hungarian people prefer the latter type. However, only since the middle of the last century has attention been paid to collecting and recording them.

Among all nations, hence among the Hungarians as well, one of the prime opportunities for asking riddles is the time of communal work, e.g. at corn husking in the autumn and in the spinnery during long winter evenings. In many places asking riddles is customary when asking for the daughter's hand in marriage. There are many roguish questions among these, worded with a double meaning that suits the occasion.

The time when riddles originated can be ascertained in only a few cases and even then only approximately. This much seems indisputable, that certain riddles could not have been born before the existence of the objects mentioned or to be identified by them. Thus, for example, the riddle "knaggy-knotty blackness, burns like a house on fire", could have originated only after coal came into common use for heating in the Great Plain, that is in the middle of the 19th century.

The most ancient riddles are very likely those referring to the phenomena of nature: e.g. "The big hive swarms often"; "When the sun shines on it, it all melts" (snow); "It goes without stopping, lies down but never stands up, has branches and knots yet never grows leaves" (river); "A golden button is thrown over the mountain" (sun). Similarly, riddles related to parts of the body also represent old types.

With a knowledge of the life of the Hungarian peasantry, it is understandable that a significant part of their riddles reflect the world of agriculture and animal husbandry: "Ten pulls four" (milking the cow); "Butter on ladder climbs, sits on my leather chair, cuts iron with bone" (stirrup iron, saddle, bridle-bit and horse tooth); "Round like an apple, pleated like a skirt. If you can tell what it is, I'll put a penny in your palm" (onion).

Riddles that carry direct social messages deserve special attention, but the folklore collections of the past published few of these. In the questions belonging here one hears expressed the condemnation of class society and the self-assertion of the working people: e.g., "I am dear to the lords, I commit much chicanery, but I am not responsible for any of it" (writing pen); "I pour out my poppy seeds and ask my crawfish to pick them up and not to wish me ill" (administration of justice).

The artistic form of riddles betrays unheard-of richness and testifies to the quick wit and inventiveness of the people. A significant part of Hungarian riddles have an etymological base. Belonging here are questions based on word analysis ("Which hog was never a piglet? The hedgehog"), and especially on change of meaning ("What does the wine do/make in the bottle? Moisture").

Another large group of Hungarian riddles hinges on emphasizing a single word and precisely evaluating its real meaning ("How many stitches are needed for a well-sewn shirt? None, since it is well-sewn"). Related to these are the so-called "why" questions, where the question does not refer to the entire content of the sentence but only to one word ("Why do you look for the thing you have lost? Because you don't know where it is").

While speaking about the form taken by riddles, we must also mention that a large part of riddles, as in the case of idiomatic sayings and proverbs, are also characterized by rhythmic, proportioned structure, and there are even riddles with alliterative, final-rhyme structure. All of this bears witness that even in the case of riddles the people tried to express their message poetically.

Folk Customs and Dramatic Traditions

Dramatic traditions appear in many areas of Hugarian peasant culture. The beginning and end of harvest have dramatic traditions, as does the story teller's performance of the hero's adventures, the gestures with which a ballad singer accompanies the events he relates, and the games of children, all are interwoven with various dramatic traditions. Naturally, it is the area of folk customs where dramatic elements occur most often, and in the widest sphere. Therefore, it is reasonable to discuss folk customs together with dramatic traditions, because it is not possible to separate the two in life.

Consequently, we should emphasize, by way of introduction, that peasant theatricals are not limited to Nativity plays and to certain customs similar to carol singing, such as the celebration of St. Gregory's day *(gergelyjárás),* Whitsuntide greeting *(pünkösdölő),* and the celebration of St. Blaise's day *(balázsolás),* or to the old custom of *regölés* at Christmas and New Year, a custom nearly extinct today. When speaking of the dramatic traditions of the Hungarian folk, people think, first and foremost of Nativity plays or the customs referred to above. Excluded in this way are a large and varied number of games with which young people entertained themselves at the conclusion of a substantial piece of work (e.g. harvesting) or in the spinnery. Among these are several humorous ones acted by members of a spinnery who go over to a neighbouring spinning house to perform their scenes. And if we want to pursue the simile further, at some places the welcome "actors" even got a "payment" in food for their "play". Although the message of these scenes has no dramatic or, traditional text, the audiences were highly amused. The basic forms of these scenes were preserved by tradition.

Even though the text is often a mixture of insignificant and meaningless jokes, it gives all the more chance for invention and ingenuity, so that the amused audience rewarded such jokes and unexpected broadsides, well suited to the occasion, by grateful approval. A large part of wedding customs must also be added here, while the rest belong to cultic customs. The jokes and competitions of the best men, or even earlier, the traditional ways of proposing to the bride are all the popular offspring of the people's desire for theatricals. The role and task of these plays are significant in the world of dramatic folk customs, although in basic form they differ from the Nativity and other plays, which are plays to be performed and which have faithfully preserved texts. However, these customs cannot be excluded from this group. Anybody who has witnessed a peasant or a Nativity play can see that the acting has two basic forms: the improvised performance, and the faithful repetition of the fixed text. We cannot neglect either to the advantage of the other.

To throw a little more light on the subject, let us consider a sample of Hungarian wedding customs. The following comes from Szabolcs

County, although we could bring up examples quite similar in structure from other places as well.

The *koma*s of the groom-to-be gather in the best room of the house. The expression *koma* means those friends and relations who shall be later invited as godparents: in this case the *koma* are young men, the brothers of the groom, his future brothers-in-law, but only those who are already married. The relatives of the young girl are already in the room. The suitors come in saying that they are men who have travelled a long distance and are very tired. Would they give them lodging? (We need not call special attention to the fact that with this entry we are already in the middle of a theatrical performance, into acting out a fictitious situation.) A star has led them here, which they took as a good omen. Thus it is revealed that the theatricals of the marriage suit are woven throughout with biblical allusions. Naturally, the hosts receive the guests readily. They tell them to rest, even though they do not yet know if they can give them lodging. What has brought them here? The suitors sit down comfortably and say that they have brought a flower, and they are seeking a mate for it. On their way, after much searching, they were directed here. At this point the hosts pretend that they do not understand the allusion, and quickly bring out a flower and offer it to the visitors. They shake their heads: no, that is not the kind they want, they want a larger flower; it would not be worth while to travel so far for this little one. The hosts cut down a largish bough and offer it. But the suitors do not want that either; they want a live flower. The hosts are puzzled; they wonder, what is it they want? "Perhaps they want a walking flower?" "Yes, that is it!" So they bring in a kitten and tie a flower on its neck. But this is no good either, because they want a flower that walks on two legs. They quickly bring in a frightened, clucking hen, and tie a flower on its neck. No matter, the suitors are still dissatisfied and now they say that they want a flower who can talk. They bring in a small child, dressed up in mummery: she is grinning in awe. "We need a bigger one," they say, rejecting the offer. All this time, they would in no way shorten the ceremony. They bring in an older girl. "We want one even bigger than this: bigger and fuller in body."

And we should not think that this detailed banter and delay tires out the ingenuity of the hosts or the demands of the suitors. The actors whole-heartedly enjoy the new and present alteration in the known and proper turn of events, and they watch their own behaviour excitedly. One would think that following this latest request, they would finally bring forth the long-awaited bride-to-be. But it is still not her turn; there is time left for a word game or two. A young wife comes in amidst much swishing of skirts; perhaps she will be full bodied enough? But they do not want her either; she already has a flower, so the travellers reject the offering. Now they bring in an oldish widow, since she has no mate. No, they don't want her. She used to be a flower, they say; but now she is wilting away.

By now they have run out of jokes and bring in the bride-to-be. She is reluctant and blushing, as is required by propriety and the situation itself. Many people are watching her, so she must properly abide by the rules. Of course the custom set by the rules as well as the emotions of her

soul—these great inner treasures of peasant culture—join anyway and further strengthen the girl in playing the role and in the new situation of her life. "This is the one, this is the one!"—exult the suitors all together, "this is the flower we were looking for!" The girl takes the hand of the young man and the two sit down. Only after this do they start to eat and drink with good appetite; up to now they had offered food and drink to the tired "travellers" to no avail. Then, singing loudly, they celebrate until morning.

If we were simply to list this custom among the so-called wedding customs and not see in it a propensity of the folk spirit for play-acting, and at the same time the inner, self-actualizing working out of dramatic folk plays, we would fail to understand folk plays themselves and their essence. These wedding customs are filled with inexpressibly deeper experiences than the Nativity plays or greetings, which have been rattled off even in the recent past by schoolchildren, and even today they intertwine the permanent framework of traditional customs with multi-personal inspiration. Naturally, descriptions of these details are very scanty, showing only the framework and course of the custom. It is something like trying to summarize the contents of a lyric poem in a few prose sentences.

In the following, therefore, we shall try to introduce the most important customs and dramatic traditions in the way they really lived at one time, and how the way they were interwoven with a great many beliefs.

Human customs and traditions already accompany the moment of birth. According to records and recollections, some women at the beginning of the last century gave birth in a standing position, leaning against the door post, perhaps clinging to a rope tied to the main girder beam. And sources also recall giving birth squatting down or in a chair.

Customs and Feasts

274. Carrying a present of clothes to the godchild
Méra, former Kolozs County

The bed entirely eliminated these ways by the second half of the 19th century. An older, experienced woman assisted the birth, but in the last two centuries mostly a midwife, assisted by woman relatives. No man could be present at the birth until after the child was born, and if it was a boy, they gave it to the father to hold. At such times the farmers who had horses took the infant to the stable and set him on the back of a horse, so that he should become a fine, horse-loving man.

Certain customs regulated the selection of names. Thus the first son inherited the name of the father, the first daughter the name of the mother, then the names of the grandparents, uncles, aunts, or respected relatives followed in order. The Matyós (cf. p. 43), however, because they tied their naming to King Matthias, liked to christen their children after him. At other places, especially in Protestant areas, biblical names were frequent (Samuel, Jeremiah, Rachel, etc.).

Baptism

The selection of godparents and others who stand in some ceremonial relationship to the parents, known as *koma,* had generally already taken place before the birth (cf. p. 70). Baptizing in the church followed two or three days after the birth, usually during the morning hours. The child, carried by the midwife, was taken to church by its godmother, where the godfather and the *koma*s had already gathered. When they arrived back home they entered saying the proverb known throughout Europe: "We took away a pagan, and brought home a Christian." The baby's father or grandmother lifted it across the threshold and with this, the infant became a full-fledged member of the family. Now they called it by its name for the first time, because before baptism they had called it only "Little One", "Little Don't Know", "No Name", or other similar names in order to protect it from evil spells.

A feast is held either just after the baptism or on the following Saturday; mostly only the members of the family and the godparents and other *koma*s participate in this, although, of course, the midwife cannot be left out of it. We do not know of traditional dishes common to the entire linguistic region, although in some places milk loaf and particularly large pretzels can be looked upon as traditional. Good wishes are expressed in prose, although at times, in verse:

> *Godmother I ask you, prithee,*
> *Take good care and raise this kiddie,*
> *So he will a handsome man be*
> *Such as takes the lassies' fancy,*
> *Hay-hey, hey-hey, hey!*
> Magyarvista (former Kolozs County)

Children's Games

The bulk of children's poetry forms part of children's communal games. From the point of view of their substance, children's games are related to dramatic customs, and this relationship finds expression in the dialogue form, as well as in the presence of dance and song and mimicry, although there are games in which the last has no role. The number of

275. A swaddled babe lying in a tub
Lészped, Moldavia

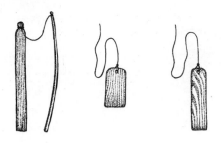

Fig. 212. Three types of bull-roarers called *zugattyu*. Great Plain. 1930s

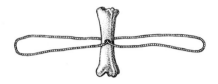

Fig. 213. A buzzer made out of a pork-bone. Debrecen. 1930s

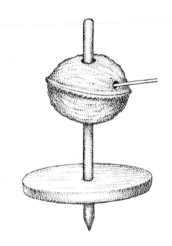

Fig. 214. A top turned with the aid of a walnut. Vásárosnamény, former Bereg County. 1930s

such games, considering their many variations, is so numerous that we can survey even the most important ones only with great difficulty. Games for groups can be summed up in the following way: "In one type of group game (with roles and/or changing roles, e.g. tag, 'white lily', blind man's bluff, ring games, etc.), the group itself remains basically unchanged, except that one child playing a certain role is then *replaced*, handing the brief role over to another, which mostly lasts until the song is sung. One child steps into the place of the other when the predecessor designates his successor. This *change* that hands over a role is the chief distinguishing sign of this type of game. The games in which couples are exchanged (ex: pillow dance) are the more adult versions of the former games, and they are closer to folk customs. And games containing competitive changing are the reversed versions of this type; these games allow the right of choice to the group.

Decreasing-increasing games constitute another large category of group games. These differ from all previous ones in having the group itself change: the circle becomes a disbanded (counted-out) group, the inward-turning circle becomes an outward turning circle, the standing circle becomes a chain that goes around ('bride-asking games', e.g. 'walking around the castle', line games), a bridge is built from a moving chain (bridge games and their relatives), a bunch of children are caught from a freely grazing 'herd' (goose games and their relatives). Certain selected players (if there are such) function only to effect orderly transitions: they call out the counting-out verse, designate the next child for turning out of the ring, or to lead the walk around the 'castle', etc. They take care that the movement from one to the other should connect them smoothly.

The game of *forfeits* is a substituting increasing-decreasing game. The child next in turn who makes a mistake pays a forfeit, which represents him.

The playing group arrives to the end of its career—to the border of its adult life—in the last group of games. Here the society of children, who used to change roles, now belongs into a community which dances and plays in a unified unchanging group (somewhat theatrical); neither change nor increasing-decreasing disrupts their community (Cf. György Kerényi).

This division organizes our children's games only from a formal viewpoint. However, it allows a good glimpse into the rich and colourful world of games. The investigator of folk poetry is primarily interested in the text of children's games. The most varied types of folk poetry can be found in these texts. Lajos Kálmány aptly says that

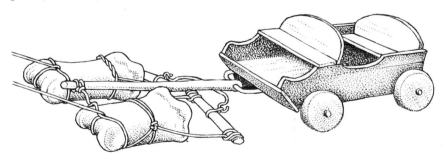

Fig. 215. A toy cart drawn by bone-horses. Poroszló, Heves County. 1930s

606

276. Bird-shaped earthenware whistle
Budapest, Ethnographical Museum

277. Child pushing a cart
Szentistván, Borsod-Abaúj-Zemplén
County

278. Goose-girl
Nógrád County

Fig. 216. Hanging decoration to
symbolize the company of unmarried
young men. Szigetköz, on the Danube.
Early 20th century

607

children's poetry is a "virtual repository, a virtual asylum of folk poetry... There are in them every branch of folk poetry and every activity that happens in life... from the simple rhymed lines and lullabies to survivals of ballads. The tree of folk poetry is a very labyrinthian tree: its branches reach across each other, but nowhere else do so many branches come together as here among children's games, which is why I have called it a virtual repository; if the wind catches and breaks some branches of folk poetry, they lean left and right until they tumble onto this branch, the branch of children's games, then they join onto it, and that is why it is a virtual asylum."

Indeed, a significant part of textual children's games appear to preserve survivals of Hungarian folk poetry and constitute a priceless source for the historical researchers' of folklore. Nursery rhymes to scare away animals or to call them have preserved numerous historical memories. For example, one of the actors of a stork-scaring little poem is a Turkish child, and this undoubtedly preserves the memory of the centuries-long fight against the Turks, while one snail-calling verse speaks, in its various versions, of Turks and Mongols, and the threatening words of the text refer to their cruelty. We could continue to make a long list of such historical references. In the bridge games there is reference to "Our good King Lengyel László" and the fight of Hungarians and Germans. The memory of King Matthias survives in a game played with a ball. We can recognize in other children's games the custom of recruiting soldiers. And the figures of the cruel oppressors of the people, landlords, wily judges, and pandours, also live in games.

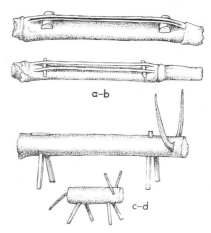

Fig. 217. Toys made out of maize. a–b) Fiddle. Gige, Somogy County. c–d) Ox. Galgamácsa, Pest County. Early 20th century

279. Children at play Galgamácsa, Pest County

280. The dance of the youngsters
Szék, former Kolozs County

However, not only the memory of historical characters and events can be discovered in children's poetry but also remnants of numerous old customs as well. The reason for this is that children naturally imitate adults. In certain animal-imitating games (goose game, goat game, etc.), research has discovered the late descendants of ancient animal descriptions, while other games have preserved in their songs and dances wedding customs that are in the process of disappearing.

Beside far-reaching historical roots of children's games, we must also remember that these games exist in the present life of children, and the long survival of their motifs, which themselves can be traced far back into the past, can be explained only by their continual expansion with newer and newer elements, the creation of newer versions by children. These games have followed the transformations of social history, which influenced even the world of children. At times only a formula has been changed; at other times entire games have been transformed or have gained a new role.

Historical survivals, however, represent only the most interesting elements of children's games, but scarcely the most important. What is significant is that children's games, precisely because of the afore-mentioned inclination of the child to imitate, observe the events of real life. Even little short poems are full of references to nature and to the animal kingdom, and the realistic images of everyday work are also to be found in them. "We crack salt, we crack pepper, we ring with a gourd" reads one sun-calling verse, and there are hardly any children's games that do not refer to the most varied manifestations of farm work (guarding the animals, taking them to pasture, hoeing, spinning and weaving, sowing, harvesting, cooking and baking, etc.), not only in the text but also in the gestures that accompany the game.

After the age of twelve, children were counted less and less as children, but the young lads and girls did not yet admit them into their company. This mostly came about at the age of 16 to 18, and for boys, initiation took place usually in the tavern. The young man to be initiated invited the older ones, and while drinking they accepted him into their community. At such times one older lad adopted the boy like a god-father with the following words: "I have held you to be my good friend until now, but now I hold you as my good godson. At every step, if someone insults you, I will take care of you" (Garam Valley). Then the young man, thus initiated, could go to the tavern, to the spinnery, to dances, to girls' houses; he could ask any girl to dance, and if someone attacked him the others hurried to his aid. Each year they elected anew the leader of the young men, the *legénybíró* (leader of the lads); the landlord and the leaders of the village also had a voice in this act, since they paid for his wine, while he was helped by the young men with his daily work. In some places the election was held at Whitsuntide, when he who defeated the others in horse-racing, or wrestling or bull wrestling, thus proved his suitability.

The organization of young girls was not as precisely regulated as that of the young men. In general, after her fourteenth birthday, a girl invited the older girls for dinner, who then accepted her among them. Although older records mention the election of the "queen of Whitsuntide", who

Fig. 218. The emblem of the leader of the lads. Barskapronca, former Bars County. Late 19th century

611

afterwards became the leader of the girl's group for a year. This custom later was transformed into a children's game.

The grown girls and young men did not use the familiar form of address towards each other. They met at work, on Sunday afternoon walks, in the spinnery and dance houses. Young men could go to the house of a girl only on definite days, generally on Saturday. If a young man and a girl had already come to an understanding, and if the parents did not see any obstacles to the marriage, then the boy visited the house more often. The girl could stay out longer when she saw him out, and among the Palotses they could even stay together in the sleeping room. At such times other young men would drop away.

Wedding

The *wedding,* and the great body of customs related to it, are most enthusiastically described by amateur folklore collectors and are generally well known. Although the details of courting which are governed by certain unwritten conventions shall not be described, wedding customs must be conceived as a virtually theatrical custom including the ritual of proposing. Suitors appear at the house of the marriageable girl, where they are already expected, although the hosts do not in any way show this. After much banter and jokes the marriageable girl finally turns up. If the suit was not well received, they let him know about that too. The saying "they put his *szűr* out", meaning the proposal was rejected, came about because at some places this was a way to indicate that the suitor's request was not well received. The young man, who found his frieze coat *(szűr),* which he had purposely left behind, put out under the eaves, could go somewhere else in search of a wife.

If the proposal is a kind of theatre, the wedding is even more so. It is a composition starting with the march to church, then putting the bride's belongings on a cart, the wedding feast, the bridal dance, and so on, to knotting the bride's hair in the fashion of young wives. The director and master of ceremonies for these theatricals is the first best man *(első vőfély)* who makes the audience laugh or cry with his serious or humorous verses, and who, in the tradition of dell'arte, memorably improvises jokes suited for the occasion, within the framework provided by the centuries. It is like a primitive yet eternal human comedy with constantly changing characters, which, though it makes fun of the institution of marriage, is yet very much for it. For example, a comic best man's saying claims that:

> *Marriage is a pillory,*
> *Out of it you'd better be!*

Still, according to the villagers, spinsterhood and bachelorhood are shameful and a condition not in accord with village laws.

The great majority of marriages in the Hungarian linguistic region are endogamous; that is to say, the young man generally chooses a mate for himself from his own village, and even from his part of the village. The ones who tried to break this order were often forced to observe it by bloody fights. Less frequently, in certain smaller groups of villages, intermarrying was considered permissible. The earlier order began to disintegrate at the end of the 19th century as young men moved on to other areas to work or as soldiers.

The main "characters" and directors of Hungarian weddings are by and large the same over the entire linguistic region. The bride and the groom both have a *násznagy* (witness, or more precisely, master of ceremonies), who, though they are most respected elderly married men, still have to put up with a whole series of jokes. They play an active role at the time of proposing for the girl, when she is handed over, and at meals. The organizer and director of the whole wedding is the *első vőfély* (the first best man), who must possess outstanding abilities. Thus, he is a first-rate organizer who staves off difficulties and quarrels, who knows the entire process of the wedding and all the verses and appropriate songs. He deals with the music and makes sure that everybody is supplied with food and drink. He leads the wedding procession and performs a personal dance through the street. Only a few such organizers can be found in each village, and they are constantly called upon to arrange big events. At both the house of the bride's family and that of the groom, there are several *kis vőfélys* (young best men), who conduct the invitations and serve up the food. The *szakácsasszony* (woman cook) is a person who directs, with the help of the hosting family, the large scale cooking and baking, which requires a great deal of circumspection.

The Hungarian words for wedding teach us an interesting lesson. The word *menyegző* (wedding, nuptials), today very much relegated to the background, appears to be the oldest. It has been known from the end of

281. Seeing off the bride
Buják, Nógrád County

the 14th century and originates from a word of the Uralic period, *meny* (daughter-in-law). The word *házasság* (marriage), the existence of which is known from the first half of the 15th century, connects the concept of wedding to the *ház* (house), just as in Bulgarian, Ottoman Turkish, and other languages. *Lakodalom* (wedding), the word most frequently used in the present, originates from the verb *lakik* (to dwell), and has been used since the beginning of the 16th century and earlier, meaning every kind of feasting, banquets. This latest name demonstrates without doubt what an important role eating and the drinking connected with it have played on festive occasions.

The folk poetry of the wedding is extraordinarily rich. Among this, we must first mention the *vőfélyvers* (best man's verses), the bulk of which is the product of rural choir-masters. These were distributed in both handwritten and printed form and thus produced similarities among certain areas. They were recited by the first best man or, less frequently, by one of the witnesses. A few taps of a stick accompanied by a flourish played by the gypsy called everybody's attention before the

282. Carrying the bride's bed
Balavásár, former Szolnok-Doboka
County

verses were begun. Today these verses are in all cases without melody, but we know about sung versions a few centuries ago. These verses follow the programme of the wedding, and the books which publish them also follow in this sequence.

The *wedding songs* include virtually every layer of Hugarian folksong. Thus during the meal almost every genre can be performed: wine songs, toasts as well as entertaining and humorous songs, or even biblical or moralizing songs. Most of them are closely tied to the ceremonies of the wedding. Many among them are sung only at weddings, and these must be brought forth no matter what.

The customs, dramatic traditions, lyrics and narrative folklore of Hungarian wedding customs is uncommonly rich and diverse, and we can also vouch for strong regional variations. Precisely for this reason we shall introduce here only a general framework, common to weddings everywhere, the varieties of which can be found in different parts of the linguistic region almost to this day.

Once the proposal is over, the betrothal *(eljegyzés, kézfogó)* takes place. Gardezi, a Persian historian, wrote about the Magyars in about the middle of the 11th century, that they "buy" girls for furs and stock. Perhaps as a memory of this, it is said even today about girls of 16 to 18 years of age that they have grown into "girls for sale" *(eladólány)*. During the betrothal the groom-elect gave a gold or silver coin, either stuck in an apple or wrapped in decorated paper, to the bride-elect. Beginning in the second half of the last century, this custom was more and more generally replaced by a golden wedding ring. In many places, the young man received a bouquet for his hat, which he wore up to his wedding day. At the end of the festivity the witness of the groom *(kikérő násznagy)* blessed the engaged couple, and then both he and the witness for the bride received a richly embroidered scarf from the bride-elect. Thanks was expressed for this in Cigánd (former Zemplén County) in the following way:

> She who's made these kerchiefs, weaving 'em and spinnin'
> 'Tween her gentle fingers, twistin' yarn on bobbin,
> Sewin' 'em keepin' 'em but for us, no others,
> May God give her blessin'!
>
> May the hemp of women grow as tall as ever,
> May the hailstorm spare it, and its stalks not sever!
> May God speed its needs in any thing whatever:
> Standin' up, unlaid, it other winters weather.

After all this, preparations were begun, an important stage in which was reached when the engaged couple, accompanied by the *násznagy* and an older woman relative, went to the clergyman to register. Their names were read out on the following three Sundays, and it was proper that the engaged couple should listen to this on at least one occasion. After the last reading, the time was right for the wedding. Although the day varied according to time and place, it generally was held on Wednesday, or more often on Saturday. Most weddings were held in the early winter period of the year or after Shrovetide, because in this way they did not interfere with work.

The preparation of food began a day or two before the wedding. The women made a pastry in the shape of spirals *(csiga)* which was served in the soup at the wedding, but only in the region of the Great Plain. The cabbage rolls were also made ahead, and the chickens and hens were plucked. The women who participated in this afterwards organized a smaller dancing gathering, also attended by the best men and the masters of ceremony, or witnesses.

The younger best men *(kis vőfély)* were responsible for inviting the guests, primarily from among the family, relatives up to third, fourth, and in some places, fifth cousins. (Cf. p. 67.) Naturally, neighbours and village leaders were never left out of the invitation. The two young men delivered the invitation in the name of the bride's or the groom's family, with regionally varying rhymes:

> *We have brought you goodwill as we are here treading,*
> *Asking all this household to a modest wedding.*
> *Just as our forebears about to be united*
> *Every brother, neighbour, duly they invited.*

> *'Tis an ancient custom, hardly needs explaining:*
> *Magyar folks are fond of guests and entertaining.*
> . . . .
> *We expect you kindly, come without one failing,*
> *None of you should stay home, not even the ailing!*
> *So to make your word good, give a sign you mean it:*
> *Put your hand, good brother, into my mine this minute!*
> *That you should come all and should not fail the wedding—*
> *May God give this household all his gracious blessing!*
>
> Great Plain

One way of accepting the invitation was for the guests to carry their presents, consisting of useful commodities and various kinds of food, to the wedding house a day before the wedding. In most places wedding cakes have become widely used as gifts since half a century ago. They are always offered by those who baked them at the conclusion of dinner.

On the afternoon preceding the wedding-day, the bride's hope chest, perhaps other pieces of furniture, and her bedding and clothes were taken by cart to the house of the groom, where the couple were going to live. They chose the longest possible route so that the entire village could see what the bride was taking with her. During the trip songs, varying by regions, were sung under the leadership of the best man:

> *With the bed of girl to marry*
> *Off the bridegroom's peace they carry.*
> *Off the bridegroom's peace they carry.*

> *Wish the Lord their bed would bless*
> *Year hence with a lovely lass!*
> *Year hence with a lovely lass!*
>
> Geszte (former Nyitra County)

616

283. Carrying the bride's dowry
Vista, former Kolozs County

284. Carrying the bride's bed
Vista, former Kolozs County

285. Going off to church
Szentistván, Borsod-Abaúj-Zemplén
County

The parade would not be easily allowed to depart from the bride's house with all her belongings, and had to endure even more banter until they got inside the groom's house. At this time they danced around the feather bed placed in the yard, then rolled a boy on the bedding so the first child should be a boy.

On the morning of the wedding, the two wedding parties, gathered at the house of the bride and at that of the groom. The groom put on the wedding shirt he had received from the bride, then his first best man would bid him goodbye in the name of his unmarried male friends and they would start off on foot or on carts for the house of the bride. However, they would not be able to get in there immediately because the gate would be blocked against them, and only after lengthy bargaining between the best man of the groom and the best man of the bride, would the gate be opened. Meanwhile the bridesmaids would be dressing the bride and combing her hair. Most brides in the last century still wore dark clothes in Hungary, and the generally prevailing white bride's robe of today came into fashion only at the turn of the century.

The *kikérő násznagy* who asks for the bride in the name of the groom would keep on demanding her from the family so that the parade could start off for church. First he would be shown an old hunch-backed woman, then one of the bridesmaids or a boy dressed up as a girl, and only after he had refused to accept these, would the real bride be presented. At this point the first best man would start saying the farewell of the bride to her family:

> *Hush the fiddles playing, hush the voices singing,*
> *And I ask the dancers cease the spurs from ringing,*
> *For my speech of godspeed right now is beginning,*
> *Listen to my speech, please, till the very ending.*
> *Now the bride says farewell to her father, mother*
> *And to her beloved sister and good brother.*
> *She would speak herself, but oh! her heart is sinking,*
> *Let me say then for her what her mind is thinking.*

286. Wedding cakes and pastries
Méra, former Kolozs County

Gathering of guests I ask for your forebearance,
Children at the back, please, be awhile in silence!

Great Plain

The first best man always said the farewell verse in first person, in the name of the bride who was herself sobbing. When the ceremony was over, the procession would parade out of the yard. Regionally divergent forms are known, but generally the wedding party of the groom walked in front, followed by the wedding party of the bride; the bride was either surrounded by the bridesmaids or led by one of her best men (cf. Plate LI). As they turned out of the gate they would begin a particular song:

Look out, mother, through your window,
See me last with bitter sorrow
As they lead me, lead the gate through;
Will you see me, shall I see you?

620

Of my mother's blooming rose-tree,
Last I blossomed in her posy.
Wish she had not ever bore me,
Had I stayed a-budding only!

Sweetest mother's blooming rose-tree,
For her finest shoot she growed me,
But a lad came for to take it,
In his arms I withered, faded!

Szögliget (former Abaúj County)

The *násznagy,* or witness, kept order at the end of the procession, and on the way they treated the onlookers with wine from bottles and flasks. The two wedding parties would stop once more and dance in front of the church. Then the religious wedding ceremony followed in the church, during which the bride would secretly try to step on the

288. Wedding feast
Püspökhatvan, Pest County

groom's foot to assure her domination in the future. The best man thanked the clergyman for celebrating the wedding and in thanks handed him a bottle of wine, a milk loaf, and a homespun kerchief. The two wedding parties—still unmixed—then marched out of the church.

At this time the two witnesses would argue about what was to happen to the bride, and they generally agreed that for the time being she was to go back to her parents' house. After this the two wedding parties parted and, if possible, each went back, by a different route, to their own hosts, where they were to be served lunch. After lunch one emissary after the other came to the bride's house demanding that she be handed over. Finally, in the afternoon the groom would set forth with his entire wedding party and go himself to redeem his bride. Naturally, this did not happen either without jokes and shamming games. The groom would have to pick out his bride from among three veiled figures. Finally, the two wedding parties set off to the house of the groom and arrived there with a song, like this example from Transylvania:

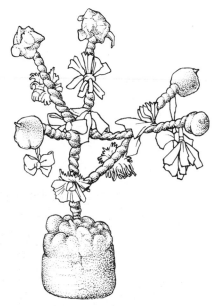

> Nice we are and nicely tread
> But the bride is nicer yet;
> Nice her fame and nice her name too,
> Nice the maiden's dress and hairdo.
>
> Come my rose to Enyed town,
> All the world revolves it round,
> There they sell the rose of spring,
> Lillyflower, blooming pink. O-ho!
>
> Bridegroom's mom you come out quick
> To the gate and open it!
> Such a good help we have brought you
> And a good wife for your son, too.
> Szépkenyerüszentmárton
(former Szolnok-Doboka County)

Here too, the gate would be opened only after lengthy goading, after much banter among the best men. The bride was either carried in, or a chair put to the cart and she stepped down on it. They led her around the porch and fireplace, and thus she would become a member of the family. After this, the first best man, acting as the master of ceremonies, would again ask for attention and recite the following verse:

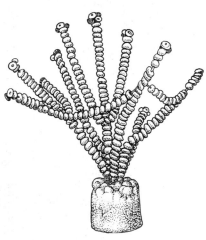

Fig. 219. Pastries baked for a wedding, called *prémes*. Former Udvarhely County. 1920s

> Ladies and gentlemen! All dear guests and neighbours,
> Not in vain have been my troubles, pains and labours:
> We have got the groom a comely bride so ruddy,
> They are one another's, one in soul and body.
> Let's rejoice then at their luck and life in clover,
> Also that the rites of marriage are now over.
> What's to follow is a fam'ly feast and banquet;
> Sit down at the table for a little junket!
> More, I say, strike up, get your fiddle playing,
> Look at all the folks how merry they are making!
> Sepsibesenyő (former Háromszék County)

The young people would spend the afternoon with games, the older people with conversation and singing. The gypsies would play the so-called sad songs *(hallgató)*. Meanwhile the women, under the direction of the cook, were preparing dinner. All the furniture would have been moved out of the house, so that only the tables, chairs, and benches would be left inside. If the weather was pleasant, a tent was pulled up in the backyard and the dinner was served out there.

In some areas the order of sitting at the dinner was fixed, but this practice varies according to regions. In some places the witnesses sat in the centre and the young couple next to them, while in other places it was just the opposite, where the young couple sat next to each other and the witnesses one on each side. The relatives followed them according to their position in the extended family. A place of honour was provided for the invited office holders of the village. In most places the young couple ate out of one plate and drank out of one cup, to show in this way that they belonged together. Serving was the job of the best men, while the first best man, after everyone had settled down, announced each course with the appropriate rhyme:

> *Good luck and good evening, everyone I'm greeting,*
> *All the wedding crowd, guests in this house a-meeting;*
> *I have brought some dainty from my goodman neighbour,*
> *Which he sends to thank you for your kindly labour;*
> *'Tis good chicken soup with pastry I deliver,*
> *Boiled in it are heart and lungs, and legs and liver.*
> *Each of you come forward, for himself to see it,*

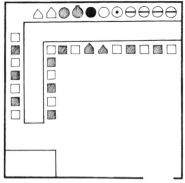

Fig. 220. Seating order at the wedding table. Nemespátró, Somogy County. 1930s. 1. Bridegroom. 2. Bride. 3. The witness who made the proposal *(kérő násznagy)*. 4. Best man *(vőfély)*. 5. The father of the bridegroom. 6. The mother of the bridegroom. 7. The father of the bride. 8. The mother of the bride. 9. Bride's maid *(nyoszolyó lány)*. 10. Married woman called *nyoszolyó asszony*. 11. Relative of the bridegroom. 12. Relative of the bride.

289. Wedding feast
Homokmégy, Bács-Kiskun County

Make good cheer my wish is, with keen relish eat it,
But I put it down now, here, receive it bestman,
Don't turn up your noses, that's how says my goodman.

Tetétlen (former Hajdú County)

The courses came one after the other: paprikash meat, cabbage rolls, roast meat—all, including the wine, offered with the appropriate rhyme. In the Great Plain, where they were called "Cumanian captains", merry young people sat across from the *násznagy*. They tried to make a joke out of everything, and for that reason the first best man *(nagyvőfély)* would especially offer them wine:

Hi, Cumanian captains, welcome and good even'!
Take this flask of wine and share between you even!
Come on, eat and drink you, everyone make merry,
Says the host you should now cares and woes all bury.

Tetétlen (former Hajdú County)

Then they served up the traditional mush, which later on was replaced by pastries and cakes. However, in spite of this, the cook still appeared after dinner and the first best man announced in the following way the great mishap that had befallen her:

Marred by a misfortune, our feast is saddened,
In the hustle-bustle something awful's happened:
As the cook with laddle portioned out the corn-mash,
She did have a blob o't on her hand and arm splashed,
And she got her arm all scalded in the mischief;
Now that ugly burn she's bandaged in a kerchief.
Poor soul, she is crying, watching it is torment,
Someone from the chemist's ought to bring some ointment.
But to purchase medicine, money, sure, is needed,
I appeal for help then, asking you to heed it:
Every man jack fork up, just as much as each can,
So we may thus speed the healing of the cook's hand.

Great Plain

So everybody would put money on the plate, at the same time lifting the cloth on the cook's hand and even her skirt, while she would whack good and hard at the pesterers with the wooden spoon she held in her other hand.

Meanwhile, the onlookers had gained admittance, dressed up in mummery. Others performed a parody of a burial, in which a young man dressed as a clergyman holds a farewell sermon—interwoven with coarse jokes—over the fake dead, covered with a white sheet. The mummers got food and drink for this and also could participate in the dance. The gypsies would be playing through dinner, the men would order songs for money, the women for nothing. When dinner was over the gypsies began to eat, while the best men carried the chairs and tables out so that the dance could start. The older folks withdrew into the smaller room to drink and to talk.

We shall in the following introduce three episodes of the wedding which, although they are known in a large part of the linguistic region, vary in regard to their order by regions or often by villages.

Time came for the *fektetés* (bedding down) after dancing, when the best man again would bid farewell to the family and girlfriends of the new wife in her name, and lead her out of the house. Here the woman attendants of the bride took her over and led her and her husband to the attic or pantry, when they prepared the wedding bed for them. Then the young wife took off her bridal garland, which the best man pinned on his staff and took back among the dancers and revellers.

The *felkontyolás* (putting up of the hair) is the actual acknowledgement that the girl had become a woman and that this state must also be given expression in her attire. They usually put up the hair in the sleeping quarters of the young people, and during this time only women and girls could be present, except for the husband. While they knotted the young wife's hair, she kept crying, as was required by propriety. In the meantime they sang appropriate songs:

> *I shall lead a life all happy*
> *Till my ribbon goes flip-flappy.*
> *Ribbons are but light apparel,*
> *In the wind they flipper-flapper.*
>
> *But the clothes are clumsy wearing,*
> *Ever fraught with woes, despairing.*
> *Oh, the clothes are clumsy wearing,*
> *Fraught till death with woes, despairing.*
>
> Hertelendyfalva (former Torontál County)

When they were done putting up her hair, they again handed the new wife over to the best man for some kind of a ransom, and he led her back among the wedding party with the following words:

> *I can see no maiden but a married woman,*
> *And a coil of hair, where used to be a ribbon.*
> *Wear in good health your tresses gathered in a topknot,*
> *Go through life happy, may you thrive and lack not!*
>
> *May the Lord God bless you with your loving helpmate,*
> *May you live contented, never part or sep'rate;*
> *Satisfied and happy, always merry, joyous,*
> *Live a life becoming, God-fearing and pious.*
>
> Kovácsvágás (former Abaúj County)

The *menyasszonytánc* (bride's dance) or, as it is also called, the *menyecs-ketánc* (young wife's dance), was one of the closing elements of the wedding. At this time the first best man introduced the new wife with the following words:

> *Lo! behold the sweet bride, here before us standin',*
> *First time since she's married, she is on the randan;*
> *To each guest that asks her, she a dance is grantin'*
> *For to buy her shoes with gifts that you must hand in.*

Come on folks and ask her for a round of dancin';
Look out for her shoe-caps as you are advancin'!
Not for nothing were those pretty little shoes made!
Then when you have finished, see to it your due's paid.

There's an empty plate lies in the table's middle;
I shall have the first dance, you can wait a little.
Meanwhile go get money, banknotes or else metal.
Long live the new couple!—gypsy, play your fiddle!

Bodroghalász (former Zemplén County)

They also place a bottle of wine and a glass next to the plate, and with this gesture the dance really begins. When the first best man has finished, he shouts "the bride is for sale", and then the best men and the relatives throw money on a plate or into a box and take a few turns with the young wife. As they hand her over to the next one, they drink a toast to her health. When everybody—even the older children—had danced with the bride, then the new husband throws a larger sum on the plate and the two finish the dance together. Meanwhile, the first best man counts up the money, which eases the young couple's start in life. This motif of the wedding not only has survived but is again in vogue even in the cities.

In the past, weddings lasted for two or three days among the more prosperous, and contained details that varied according to numerous ethnic and regional groups. At the end they served up "push-out mush" *(kitoló kása)* to those who were reluctant to leave, and the best man, the first best man, let them know that the wedding was over:

Had enough of merry making,
Time it is your leaves were taking.
Stir your legs, host, harness horses,
Put your guests on homeward courses.

Hertelendyfalva (former Torontál County)

Afterwards only those gather together who had helped carry out the wedding. At this time they eat the cooking of the new wife and praise it with the following good wish:

Tattered though the wedding cap be,
May the young wife live long, happy!

This extremely sketchy survey will serve to draw several conclusions. First, it shows what a close unit customs, beliefs, domestic traditions, and folkloristic creations are. It also shows what a complicated system developed out of all this. Historical research has demonstrated that marriage customs have shifted significantly in the direction of eating, drinking and revelling, so that in many cases it has become *lakodalom* in the original meaning of the word. This at the same time also means that to organize a very expensive wedding was possible only for the well-to-do peasants, even if a lot of the expenses were recovered from the presents and the bridal dance. The poorer people, if they held a big wedding, often groaned under the consequences of bearing heavy debts through half their lives.

The customs and world of belief attached to death and burial are not nearly so diverse and extensive as the customs of weddings, yet at the same time these have preserved greater antiquity and in many cases extraordinarily archaic traits. The reason is that descendants did not dare change the sequence of customs for fear that the spirit of the dead might return. Yet, only a few of these customs survived, which may be attributed to persecution by various churches as they tried to exterminate all traditions not agreeing with or opposed to articles of faith.

The expressions relating to death and to burial look back upon a long past. Thus the words *hal* (die), *halál* (death), *sír* (grave), *temet* (bury), *temető* (cemetery) are Finno-Ugric derivatives, and the word *koporsó* (coffin) and perhaps *tor* (burial feast) are of ancient Turkic origin. We know well from archaeological excavations the burial style of the Magyars of the Conquest. The more distinguished, prosperous warrior was buried with the head and four legs of his horse placed beside his body, as well as his saddle, stirrups, and bridle with the bit. Among his weapons usually the bow and the arrows were placed into the grave. The sword represented power, as did the rich, sarmentously ornamented purse plate, of which so far 23 have been found. It has been possible to estimate the position occupied in life by the dead from the number of arrow points. A horse's skull and legs were placed in a woman's grave only very rarely, probably only in cases when with the death of the male members of the family, the leadership fell to her. In the graves of common people the quantity of buried objects is much less. Poor and rich graves alike were situated facing east-west, thus the dead were laid facing the rising sun. Burial customs show many common characteristics related with those of the nomads from the steppes of Central Asia and South-Eastern Europe, some of which have been preserved almost to this day.

After conversion to Christianity, grave furnishings quickly disappeared from Magyar graves. Burials were conducted with a church ceremony, and in order to oversee this most thoroughly, it was decreed that the dead be buried around the church. The formerly sacrificed horse itself, or its price, was given to the church. Magyar burial ceremonies, changing because of Christianity, began to resemble those of neighbouring peoples, and only fragments survived of ancient traditions.

It is believed that certain occurrences foretell death. Thus if a picture or mirror falls off the wall, if a clock stops without reason, if the dog howls or the hooting of an owl can be heard about the house, then someone from the family will die. When members of the family thought that the condition of an ill person was beyond recovery, they called the priest. The sick person, if a Catholic, was given extreme unction, if a Calvinist, the Lord's Supper. Then, a bed out of straw was made on a rush mat under the main girder beam, in the belief that a man can die more easily if close to the ground. The window was opened but the doors shut, even the drawers of the chests, so that the departing soul could find its way out easily and could not hide away somewhere in the house.

When death came, the chin of the dead was tied up, the eyes closed, and coins or bits of clay put on them, which were made especially for this occasion. The clock was halted, the mirror covered, the fire extinguished, and not relit so long as the dead remained in the house. Those who were asleep were woken up and people shouted the news that the farmer or his wife had died into the barn and even into the apiary.

The preparation of the body followed. First it was washed, a service done in most places by women, regardless of the sex of the dead. The water was thrown in a place where nobody could step on it, and the soap was thrown away. The dead man was shaved, and in some places the face smeared with vinegar or wine to keep it from changing, that is, so that it remained rosy. Next, they dressed the corpse in his best Sunday suit, although footwear was generally not put on. Then they laid him on the bier, which was placed in the middle of the room. This is made of two or three planks laid on chairs or trestles and covered with homespun. Often the custom was to make it up into a bed. In some places people laid out the dead on the bed, taking care to place the bed parallel to the main girder beam. Sometimes a sickle was put on the stomach to prevent swelling. This is noteworthy because sickles were also found in some of the graves of the Conquest, although only in the graves of women.

It is proper for relatives, acquaintances, and neighbours to visit the body lying in state. In the Hajdúság they enter with the following words: "God console the sad-hearted ones who are left behind, and take the dead into the kingdom of heaven." The relations of the dead reply to this: "May God hear you." The visitors look at the face of the dead and praise his good character, his humanity, and deeds. Then they bid good-night and leave.

However, relatives and older women and men stay and sit around the dead, praying and singing, generally religious songs. The men usually gather separately, where they talk and play cards but may not fall asleep. Later they put together the data that will help the minister or cantor to bid farewell at the burial. Some records testify that at one time various games may have been played at the wake, as is hinted by a description from western Transdanubia, dated 1818: "The young men used to take rattling sticks along. These are sticks split in five or six ways at the end, and they hit each other on the back with them for entertainment. They pull somebody down, cover his eyes, and two, three, or more hit him. If he can tell who has hit him, they pull that one down; if he cannot tell, he is pulled down again until he guesses who hit him." At other times, as a consequence of the wine and even brandy that has been consumed, secular songs as well as religious songs turn up, especially those the deceased himself used to like singing.

The carpenter took the measurement of the coffin with a stick or reed. Then he painted the box, which narrowed towards the foot, according to the deceased's age: white for children, blue for the young, brown for the middle aged, black for the old. In some places tulips and roses were painted on the coffins of the young, just as they did on chests used in the rooms. The small pillow that was put under the head of the dead was filled with the shavings from making the coffin.

Certain objects are put into the coffin when the body is laid out. Men get their pipe and pipe pouch, perhaps their favourite walking stick,

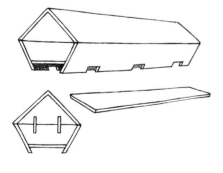

Fig. 221. The construction of a coffin. Désháza, former Szilágy County. 1950s

herdsmen their ringed whip, often a razor and soap. Mostly a needle, yarn, and kerchief are put into the coffins of women, while the children take along their toys, books, and copybooks. Often, fruit or other kinds of food are included. Sometimes a Bible, a prayer book, holy medals, small statues, a rosary or psalter are placed at the feet.

The tolling of the church bell has a great role in saying farewell to the dead. The smallest bell, called the soul-bell, is rung at the hour of death for Catholics. Among Protestants, the tolling of one or more bells identifies the sex of the dead. The bells give notice that the funeral gathering is beginning, and its sound follows the dead on its last journey. This is why it is written on bells all over Europe: "I am calling the living and lament the dead."

The dead is covered with a shroud before beginning the burial, but a small opening is cut into it at the face. After closing the coffin and nailing down the lid, it is carried out of the house usually feet first, and the carriers knock with it three times on the threshold, so that the dead will not find its way back. They place the coffin in the yard on a so-called St. Michael's horse, which is actually two trestles. A small table stands at the foot of it for the clergyman and the cantor. The family takes its place around the coffin. The men are on one side, the women on the other, in the sequence of their position within the extended family. Often two

290. Lamentation
Magyarszovát, former Kolozs County

kerchiefs are put on the table, which are given to the clergyman and the cantor after the ceremony.

Lamenting the dead *(siratás)* was an inevitable part of burial until the most recent past. Only the women lamented by wailing, and this survived in spite of strict prohibition by the churches. Laments consist of reminiscences about the time spent together, and leave-taking, which is always in the first person. There is much reality in them alongside the religious content. The form is not fixed, but improvised according to the situation of the moment. The text is partly sung, partly recited. Such lamentations were also recited when seeing off soldiers or immigrants, the content in that case, of course, suited to the occasion. The loved ones who died far away were also lamented. The following song of lament is an example:

Oh, my sweet son, my dear son!
Oh, what a sad letter I received in the mail!
Oh, where in that far-off place did you meet your death?
Only the birds are hovering above you now!
My sweet son, my dear son, my beloved child!
Oh, my child of great skill and learning, my bright and smart son, where shall I
*   look for you, where can I find you?*
Oh, how far you are, death has so utterly parted me from you!
Only the bullets went flying over your head, my sweet child, my dear son!
Oh, Gossip, a very bad morning we are having.
Oh, the sun has risen very sadly on us, we have a very sad goodmorning, my dear
*   Gossip.*
Oh, my sweet child, my dear son, where shall I look for you, which way shall I
*   start to find you?*
No longer will you come to knock at the fence.
Who shall I be waiting for every morning, every evening;
*   —Mother, come out please a moment!—*
Oh, who shall I go to, who shall I look for, who shall I watch for every morning
*   which way he is coming?*
I have nobody left!
Oh, my sweet and dear child, my smart and shrewd son!
Oh, death has so utterly parted me from you!
There is no one to walk the length of your coffin, only the birds are hovering above
*   you there, my dear, sweet son!*
Oh, when you were home but a year ago you said as we went a-hoeing
beet—Mother, look at those nice baking taters yonder, if we live next year,
*   we should get some seeds and sow them!*
Oh, but you didn't live, my sweet son, to get some of those nice baking taters!
Oh, how glad you were to see them though!
You were much amazed and said:—Oh, Mother, I have never seen the like of
*   them.*
Who shall I go to now, who shall I talk to, my dear son?
Oh dear, oh dear, motherless, fatherless meek little bird of mine, out there in a far-
*   off land, where you have nobody!*
Oh, my God, my God, where shall I look for you, where shall I find you?

Cigánd (former Zemplén County)

Fig. 222. Detail of a song of lament. Cigánd, former Zemplén County. 1957

291. Lamentation
Rimóc, Nógrád County

Fig. 223. Song of lament. Kapospula,
Somogy County. 1961

Fig. 224. Song of lament. Nagyszalonta,
former Bihar County. 1917

Although the majority of the lamentations are improvisations in prose, certain permanent expressions and combinations of words are repeated in them.

"What wrong have I done to the Almighty Lord that he has taken away my loving mate? Oh, Ferkó, Ferkó, Ferkó Buda! Oh, what shall I do, where shall I turn? Oh, who is to comfort me? Oh, I have heard say that a widow's life is happy: nay it is sad! Oh because I am like the mateless bird wandering from bough to bough. Oh, I must go to that garden of mourning and bewail my lot to the earth which does not tell anybody about it. Oh, my dear God, my dear God, where shall I go, where shall I turn? I have nobody to comfort me, I have nobody to speak for me. Oh, oh, oh, oh, oh, oh!"

Kapospula (Somogy County)

Some rhyming lines occur in the lamenting song above, but there are also a great many in which the pain of the ones left behind is told entirely in verse. Zoltán Kodály recorded the following song of lament of fixed structure in 1917:

I was left here lonely
Like a field of stubble
All the pride of which is
Cut down by the sickle.

Thank him so much, thank him,
Thousand times I thank him
For his every goodness
That he always showed us.

Let him rest, let him rest
Till the Day of Judgement.
Jesus Christ our Lord came
When his need was urgent.

Jesus Christ our Lord came
Bringing ample medicine,
And a balmy ointment
Bathed his sores and wounds in.

Nagyszalonta (former Bihar County)

The melodies of some Hungarian songs of lament can be traced back to pre-Conquest times; parts indicative of great antiquity can also be discovered in their formulae and expression. Lamenting songs were already recorded in the 16th–17th centuries. These already bore a close resemblance to those of the recent past.

After the lamenting and the church ceremony has been concluded, the funeral procession is formed. In a significant part of the linguistic region, the relatives and friends carry the coffin on foot by means of poles placed under it. In the Great Plain, they generally put it on a cart along with the grave post or wooden cross. It was the custom in many places not to go directly to the cemetery but to stop in front of the church instead and sing a church song. In the past century it has even happened that they carried the coffin into the church and the minister preached there over it, while at other places they left it in the churchyard during the church service. The minister and cantor walked at the head of the funeral procession, perhaps with the children, who sang all the way. The immediate relations followed the coffin, but there men and women were already mixed.

The burial of young men and girls who were brides- and grooms-to-be resembled a wedding in many aspects. Although there were no best men, the girls and young men walked on both sides of the coffin dressed as for a wedding. Thus among the Csángós of Hétfalu (former Brassó County) they sang the following while the coffin was carried out of the house by the maids and young men of honour:

> I am too a bridegroom [or a bride]
> Ready for to go soon.
> Folk come here a-treading
> To a woeful wedding.
> I was once a flower,
> But I won't bloom ever
> Laid at rest in coffin.
> In my parents' garden
> I was once a flower,
> Rose that won't bloom ever,
> For the Reaper cut me
> When a youth unwary

292. Funeral procession
Magyarszovát, former Kolozs County

293. Lamentation
Átány, Heves County

294. Funeral meal (the men)
Magyarszovát, former Kolozs County

634

The grave was dug on the day of the burial, or a day before. This, in the Hungarian villages, is community work to this day, and it is proper for the relatives, friends, and neighbours to attend. Afterwards they are treated in the most simple way with brandy, bread, and bacon. Many versions of digging a grave exist in the Hungarian linguistic region. The simplest is when they dig a single hole approximately 2 to 2.5 metres deep. In most family graves a so-called *padmaly* (floor) is cut into the two sides of the grave, level with the bottom of the grave and matching the height of the coffin. In other places they put planks on the coffin that lies at the bottom of the grave and place another coffin over that. Where the cemetery has not been laid out in rows, the direction of the graves is east–west. However, they also try to arrange rows in such a way as to make it

295. Funeral meal (the women)
Magyarszovát, former Kolozs County

635

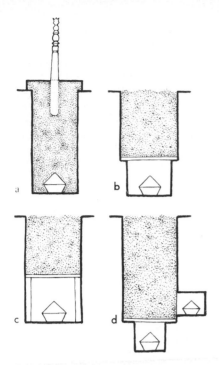

Fig. 225. Various types of graves.
a) Simple grave with a gravepost. b–c) The
type in which the coffin is closed off by
boards *(padmalyos)*. Diósháza, former
Szilágy County. d) Grave with both the
upper solution and a nook on the side.
Sámson, former Szilágy County. 1950s

296. All Saints' Day in the cemetery
Tiszaörs, Szolnok County

possible to retain this orientation. Leafy branches and twigs are placed over the dug-out grave, so that evil spirits cannot move into it in the dark.

The funeral procession stops at the gate of the cemetery (cf. p. 129), and from here they carry the coffin by hand to the open grave and lay it on poles placed over the opening. The leave-taking follows, then the religious ceremony, and finally they slowly lower the coffin into the grave with ropes. At this time the relatives, and often all participants throw a handful of soil on the coffin, sometimes also throwing in those kerchiefs they had cried their sorrow into, so as not to take their sadness home. At some places it is also customary to walk around the grave.

On the grave posts, wooden crosses, or grave stones not only the name of the dead were written, but, especially from the last century, their lives and virtues were also mentioned in shorter or longer verses. The half-folk verses in many cases preserved older traditions:

> *After all my sufferings ended,*
> *Here this grave enclosed my body.*
> *Here my broken bones found at last their resting place.*
> *We shall meet hereafter, God be with you all.*
>
> Kömörő (former Szatmár County)

Gravepost poems became increasingly parodistic, and reciting them at evening gatherings became a favourite pastime.

The concluding act of the funeral is the burial feast *(tor)*, that is to say, the treating of the participants. In the Middle Ages it was held in the cemetery itself and, as a memory of this, it has been arranged there sporadically even in this century. Already in 1279 the council of Buda prohibited entertainment and dancing in the graveyard; the churches

always looked upon the custom with disfavour. Thus at the beginning of the 17th century it was written: "The annual feast making for the dead is the invention of the devil." Comenius, in the middle of the same century, has more to say about it: "Heaping praises on the dead by the droning of the funeral feast." Dancing in the cemetery survived in a few places where the episodes of the young man's or young woman's burial imitated the progression of the wedding. The treating of beggars with food and drink at the gate of the cemetery also recalls the memory of the funeral feast.

In this century the burial feast was held in the house of the deceased. Bread and bacon were offered, and at some places, milk loaf, or a cooked meal, generally paprikash meat, was served. Brandy was given with the former, more likely wine with the latter. A place was set for the dead also.

Time passed with quiet talking and singing: then, as the effect of the brandy and wine took hold, they turned to more merry songs and usually sang the favourite song of the departed. When the funeral feast began to turn into entertainment, then, at the suggestion of one of the older relatives, the visitors all left together.

The colour of mourning used to be white, that is, light. The wearing of black for grieving spread among the peasants from the West and through the intermediation of the upper classes. Women still mourned in white half a century ago in the Ormánság. The time and limits to mourning are not uniform among the Hungarian peasantry. It is certain that for a few years the deceased is remembered on his name day and on the day he died, people abstaining from entertainment at such times. Later on the family remembers all its dead on Good Friday, when they put the graves in order, and on the eve of All Saints' Day (November 1), when they take flowers to the cemetery, and when not only Catholics but even Protestants burn candles. At such times members of the family, even those who live far away, come home if possible so that the living can meet the dead. Today All Saints' Day observation, while it has partly lost its religious character, is general not only in the villages but in the cities as well.

Customs of the Calendar Year

The calendar customs are grouped around the spring equinox and the winter and summer solstices, but in order to survey them more easily we will introduce them in chronological order. The number and variety of these customs, interwoven and coloured with dramatic elements, is extremely varied by regions and ethnic groups, which is precisely why we venture to introduce only the most general, the most beautiful, that is to say, the most archaic forms.

It is very difficult to distinguish those customs which belong to New Year's Day. The reason is to be found in the fact that up to the 16th century the New Year was counted from Christmas. Therefore, in many cases the customs cannot precisely be fixed in relation to a certain day. In the Middle Ages the serfs and servants visited their landlord and took him gifts. Perhaps as a direct continuation of this, herdsmen, servants, and also children used to visit the houses of more prosperous

637

farmers on New Year's morning and wish happiness for the following year with verse and song:

May God give us everything
In the year to follow:
May the white bread swell up in
Hutches made of willow;
Wine, wheat and sausage
None of us need borrow;
Let us all forget all medicine
In the year to follow.

Orosháza (Békés County)

Children and young men made a great noise with cowbells, bells, and bits of iron to scare away evil from the house, its inhabitants and the stock. In part of the Székelyland we know of "burying" the winter, in which young men buried a straw doll representing winter. Around Lake Balaton they chased a hunchback through the streets and beat him with switches; they called this the "expulsion of winter".

Many customs of mainly religious content are attached to Epiphany, January 6 *(Vízkereszt),* since this is the twelfth and concluding day of Christmas. The custom of the Three Magi *(Háromkirályok)* shows much similarity with Christmas carolling, although it makes less use of dialogue form. Its most important props is the star, which shows the way to Bethlehem for the Three Magi. In a letter from Somogy County this is mentioned as early as 1540: "Then send on the star songs, if you have them; try all the more to find other songs if you can because I have a good child here, whom I will send on to you if I cannot protect him [e.g. from the Turks]." The star is carried by one of the Three Magi, dressed in white, on a pole or on an expandable and contractable sectional implement, used for this purpose. They smear soot on the face of Balthazar, to indicate his being a Saracen. They go from house to house and enter with this song:

Eastern wise men three went on a journey,
The star is a-twinkling!
Now it is standing over the stable,
The star is a-twinkling!
Eastern wise men three went on a journey,
The star is a-twinkling!
Kings they are saying good day to the Virgin,
The star is a-twinkling!
Kings they are bowing heads to the Maiden,
The star is a-twinkling!

(Veszprém County)

After each of the three has said his verse, they get food and money from the master of the house.

In many regions even today the clergyman and the cantor, with a few altar boys, go through the village and consecrate the houses. They write the year on the door and under it the initials of the Three Wise Men: GMB. At such times the faithful give food and money, which the

297. Epiphany: the Three Magi
Szakmár, Bács-Kiskun County

children collect in baskets and bags. This custom was mentioned in 1783: "On the day of Epiphany the clergy go to every house with a cross and prayers and together they ask for alms *(kolendálnak),*" that is, they collected gifts. The term *kolendálni* is used even when just children go alone and collect gifts for themselves.

The custom of celebrating St. Blaise *(Balázs,* called *Balázsolás,* on February 3), is known primarily in the western half of the Hungarian linguistic region. St. Blaise is the patron saint of children, he is not only a teacher but also protected children from sickness. A *Balázsoló* group consisted of several members. In Zala, at the beginning of the century their names were recorded in this way: warrior *(vitéz),* general *(generális),* bishop *(püspök),* corporal *(káplár),* standard bearer *(zász-lótartó),* sergeant *(strázsamester),* keeper of the bacon *(szalonnás),* alphabetizer *(ábécés).* The many military ranks can be explained by the children's entering the houses under the pretext of recruiting for school:

> 'Tis today Saint Blaise's Day;
> Long it's been a folkway,
> Ancient custom,
> That this day the schoolkids
> All their fellows, pals with
> Go recruiting.
>
> Taught by our teachers
> How to be good creatures
> Came we hither:
> Every sluggard, wagger,
> Every truant, slacker
> For to gather.
>
> Is there in this house then
> Any of such children?
> If so, hurry,
> Join our little group, too,
> Come away to school, you
> Won't be sorry!

However, the purpose of the custom was collecting, as was often indicated also by the naming of some participants: Satchel Carrier *(Tarisznyás),* Skewer *(Nyársas),* Basket Carrier *(Kosaras),* Keeper of the Bacon *(Szalonnás).* In return for the alms, they asked that the sore throat (diphteria) should not take its victims from among the little ones.

> You we are now begging,
> Grant your holy blessing:
> From our throats please chase away and
> Save it from all evil.
> For a sore throat, Saint Blaise's ill,
> Go away and heal it will
> If you make a woman

Give us children sausage, bacon,
So we swallow often!
                    Szántó (Tolna County)

In its history, the custom of celebrating St. Gregory's Day *(Gergelyjárás,*
March 12), appears to be older than the *Balázsolás,* but similarly, it is
a custom of students. Greetings for St. Gregory's (Gergely) Day have
been passed down to us from as early as the 17th century, one of the
most beautiful versions of which is preserved by Csángó folk poetry.
The two stanzas below are from there and, like the entire poem, they
evoke medieval traditions:

Doctor St. Gregory,
Holy of memory,
On this thine day,
Heeding old tradition
And the Lord's provision
Go to school we.

Lo, the little birds too
Multiply in number
For to grow up later;
Now the spring is come in,
Day and night are singing
Very sweetly.

Students who collected alms for their school in the Middle Ages, and
later their Protestant successors, certainly played a significant role in
making the customs of *Balázsolás* and *Gergelyjárás* known. These late
successors are the mendicants, who even a few decades ago went around
the villages on large holidays and collected for Protestant schools.

Carnival *(farsang)* starts with Epiphany and lasts until Ash Wednesday, but is especially festive from the Sunday before Ash Wednesday
until Tuesday evening, which is generally called the "tail of Farsang".
This is one of the joyful holidays of spring, which had overcome winter,
cold, and darkness. Medieval sources already recall it. Most certainly the
custom came to the Hungarians from the West, as is shown by its
Austrian–Bavarian name, which appeared in the form of a family name
as early as the 14th century. The churches always persecuted carnival and
its most varied manifestations, as is demonstrated by a notation originating from 1757: "The Hungarians took over that famous *Farsang* from the
Germans, who formed it from the deeds of *cantu circulatorum,* pursuer of
playful jokes and dirt; who initiated many kinds of games and foolish-
ness on this day, and at this time entertain guests and rush around having
a good time."

At the end of Carnival the names of those girls who had not succeeded
in getting married were shouted out. The young men, amidst a great
deal of noise, recited different songs and rhymes in front of the houses
where such girls lived:

Shrovetide, Shrovetide, three days bother,
Off she went my daughter's mother.

You can come home, Uncle Pesta,
Married off are all the daughters:
Some for corn-cake, some for worser,
Kati Bagi for a milk-cow,
Missus swine-herd for a big sow,
Missus cantor for a frilly,
And the groom's wife for a filly.

Maconka (Heves County)

In the western part of the linguistic region, the custom of stump dragging *(tuskóhúzás)* falls at the end of Carnival, a mocking ceremony organized by the young men. An 1820 description says as follows: "In the past, on Ash Wednesday, in Hungary, those marriageable girls who had not got married during the days of *farsang* were made to drag tree stumps like some unbroken mares." In some parts of the Great Plain the young men raised a great clamour with pots and pieces of iron under the window of the girl and shouted the following:

Pancake Day! Shrove Tuesday!
Some girls would now maidens stay.
Those who have a girl to wed,
Lead her to the herd instead.

(former Szabolcs County)

642

Alongside the great many mummeries of Carnival there also occur the customs of driving out evil and working magic on the crop. At such times they threaten the fruit trees with an axe that if they do not yield enough, they will cut them down.

At the northern edge of the linguistic region the *kiszehajtás* comes about at the end of winter and beginning of spring, generally on Palm Sunday. The word *kisze* originally means a typical Lenten food: sour fruit- or bran-soup, which people became very tired of through the winter and want to get rid of. The girls dress up a straw doll in the clothes of a young wife who was married in the previous year (this symbolizes the *kisze)* and carry it singing to the nearest river, stream, or lake. They take the clothes off the straw doll and throw the doll into the water. At this time they foretell the marriages of those present from where and how the water carries the straw and doll. To this day some of the songs still recall the memory of getting free from Lent:

> *O kisze, oh!*
> *Bring the gammon in!*
> *Out with kisze, kisze dear,*
> *Come in gammon, all good cheer!*
>
> *Margit Szabó she be*
> *Such a famous woman,*

299. Masquerading on Shrove Tuesday
Moha, Fejér County

For a dress we asked her,
She the kisze gave one.

Felsőszemeréd (former Hont County)

They ridiculed the young wife who had refused to give her clothes. They also believed that by taking the *kisze* out they put a stop to illness and fog. There are also data showing that at some places they burned the straw doll instead of throwing it in the water:

Kisze burns, it burns anew,
Wisps of smoke a-twining;
Spring is near, the sky is blue,
Warm the sun is shining.
When its smoke does disappear,
Frosty fogs we need not fear:
Spring is come and stayeth here.

(former Hont County)

One important area within the spring circle of celebrations is *Easter*. Easter Monday sprinkling is general in the whole country, and in the past used to be done at a well with buckets (cf. Plate LIII). If the girls did not come by themselves, then the young men dragged them there by force. Basically, sprinkling with water is connected to fertility rites. Later sprinklers began to use perfumed water, but received coloured and decorated eggs (cf. p. 420) just as before. This custom is still flourishing today. Sprinkling poems spread and differ according to time and region.

301. Preparing the *kisze* doll
Szandaváralja, Nógrád County

300. Carnival masquerades
Moha, Fejér County

302. Easter sprinkling
Acsa, Pest County

On a Ducking Monday fun to see the people
Go out in the streets and one another sprinkle.
We shall duck the master, mistress with her daughter:
Painted eggs we ask for, two each for the water.
If you give us two each, we shall thank you gladly;
If you give but one each, we'll return them sadly.
Kézdimárkosfalva (former Háromszék County)

The Easter egg, one of the most general symbols of fertility, has significance even on the so-called White Sunday that follows Easter. This is the time when godparents send a so- called *"koma* platter" to their grandchildren, and the smaller girls present them to those to whom they want to show their respect, and want for a friend. This custom survived longest in Transdanubia and the Palots region. Thus in Somogy they put a bottle of wine, a few red eggs, and pretzels on a plate, cover it with a white or colourful cloth, and carry it ceremoniously to the selected *koma*. The girl who hands it over recites the following little poem:

Koma-plate I brought you,
I had it adorned, too.
Gossip sends it, relative,
Gossip should a present give.
(Somogy County)

In Gyöngyös and its surroundings the girls receive a *koma* platter from their lovers and the young men receive them from the girls. If they accept the *koma* platter, this means that sentiments are mutual.

646

May Day has for long centuries been the joyous celebration of spring. One of its most beautiful features in European practice is putting up a *Maypole*.

Young men went out to the forest and selected a long-trunked, fine, leafy, branchy tree. This they put up in front of the window of a girl one of their mates was courting, and in this way he showed his intentions towards her. In some places the young men set up the tree while the girl and her mother provided its colourful decoration. When the tree began to wither, it was "danced out", that is, young people organized a smaller dance at its felling. On this ancient day of celebration, since a very long time, city dwellers used to go out to the forests and amuse themselves until evening. After such antecedents, and beginning with 1890, May the First has become the holiday of workers in Hungary. The day is celebrated with a parade, with outings and picknicking.

The summer circle of calendar holidays begins with *Whitsuntide,* when the children go around greeting:

647

What's today? What's today?
Pinky Pinkster Sunday;
On the morn, on the morn
Will be Pinkster Monday.
Andy so dandy,
Has a wife and dances well;
Pull 'em in, pull 'em hard,
Bridles of the horses,
So they shall not, so they shall not
Trample on the roses.
All along the road it's
Full of Whitsun roses,
Come you bride and pick 'em up,
Tie them up in posies.

Szeged (Csongrád County)

Another version of the custom of choosing a king and queen at Whitsuntide occurs among the games of little girls. A little girl—the "Queen of Whitsuntide"—is covered with a kerchief and the group of girls enter every house, raise the kerchief for a moment, and show the "Queen" with the following words:

God has brought us Whitsun,
Pinky Pinkster Sunday.
All around we carry
Whitsun queen for one day.

Gencsapáti (Vas County)

304. Taking the Queen of Whitsuntide
around Vitnyéd,
Győr-Sopron County

Fertility rites are also connected to this custom in western Transdanubia; they lift a little girl up really high and shout, "May your hemp grow this high". At Apáca, in Transylvania, "cock shooting" or "cock hitting" (kakaslövés) took place at Whitsuntide. The boys used to shoot arrows at a live cock, and later on at a target. The shooting lasted until they hit the heart, or the centre. Meanwhile humorous mourning songs were recited, and in the evening a cock supper was held.

Most significant among the customs of the summer is lighting the fire of Midsummer Night (szentiváni tűzgyújtás) on the day of St. John (June 24), when the sun follows the highest course, when the nights are the shortest and the days the longest. The practice of venerating St. John the Baptist developed in the Catholic church during the 5th century, and at this time they put his name and day on June 24. Naturally, the summer solstice was celebrated among most peoples, so the Magyars may have known it even before the Conquest. Although the Arab historian Ibn Rusta speaks of the Magyars' fire worshipping, we so far have no data that could connect it to this day. At any rate, in the Middle Ages it was primarily an ecclesiastical festivity, but from the 16th century on the sources recall it as a folk custom. The most important episode of the custom is the lighting of the fire:

> Lay we fire, pile it,
> Lay it out to square shape:
> In one of its corners
> Sitting are fine old men,
> In the second corner
> Sitting fine old women,
> In the third again are
> Sitting lusty laddies,
> In the fourth are sitting
> Lovely maiden lassies.
> Kolony (former Nyitra County)

The custom survived longest and in the most complete form in the north-western part of the linguistic region, where as late as the 1930s they still lit a Midsummer Night fire. The way of arranging the participants by age and by sex has suggested the possibility that these groups sang by answering each other, but there are hardly any remnants that appear to support this possibility. People jumped over the fire after they lit it. This practice is mentioned as early as the 16th century, although at that time in connection with a wedding; still, it is called "Midsummer Night fire". The purpose of jumping over the fire is partly to purify, partly because they believed that those whose jump is very successful will get married during the following carnival:

> Make the fire, darling, make its flames leap higher;
> For my tender arms to warm me by the fire!
> Forth I went, back I came, everywhere I been to,
> Come, my sweetest darling love, hop it right across too!

305. Leaping over the Midsummer
Night fire
Kazár, Nógrád County

Come, my darling, pile it up, let the sparks be flying,
Spread your sheepskin coat down, on it we'll be lying!
Forth I went, back I came, everywhere I been to,
Come, my sweetest loving lad, come and warm yourself, too!

Tild (former Bars County)

Lighting and jumping over the Midsummer Night fire also had a definite match-making role, and can be compared with the customs and folk poetry of the winter solstice.

Customs relating to agriculture predominate among the customs of the autumn, and perhaps the extremely large amount of work to be done then is the reason for the much smaller number of other types of customs at this time.

One of the richest circles of celebrations are attached to Christmas *(karácsony)*. The pagan world of tradition, itself related with older anniversaries, as well as the more recently developed peasant customs, both fused into the holiday circle of the ecclesiastical year. Religious customs and celebrations of the ecclesiastical year in their reality could not be understood without considering such an interlacement. We need not think that in all cases we are dealing with survivals of traditions from the pagan period, but it is certain that anniversaries so important for the peasantry, the customs, traditions, and beliefs of spring, summer, autumn and winter equinoxes or solstices, are connnected with and have melted into the traditions of the ecclesiastical year. The church, faithful to its thousand-year-old and well-established methods, has outright consecrated some of these customs and installed them among the

650

religious holidays, while it has quietly overlooked others, due to their important function in the life of the people. Thus we can observe in the holiday customs of the people, in their beliefs tied to the ecclesiastical year, the peaceful co-existence of the most varied strata. Ancient beliefs of the pagan period, more newly developed peasant superstitions, Germanic and Slavic influence—and accompanying these, customs that spread because of the influence of Christianity as well as certain elements of the religious concepts of antiquity—all of these can be found in the folk customs and celebrations that are attached to the holidays of the ecclesiastical year. The best example of this is the holiday cycle of Christmas.

Christmas celebrations really begin with *Advent,* the first day of which is the Sunday that falls closest to St. Andrew's Day (November 30). In some places they signalled its beginning by ringing the bells at midnight, and from then on all loud musical entertainment was prohibited. The girls and women went to church in black, or at least in dark-coloured dresses.

The celebrating of *Saint Nicholas' Day* (December 6) is one of our newer folk customs. Thus the giving of gifts to children began to spread in the Hungarian villages only in the last century. The Hungarian peasantry also took over mummery *(alakoskodás)* from the West, but that seems to be older than gift giving. Thus in Csepreg in 1785 they were already prohibiting this custom: "And because it has been experienced from ancient times that some among the citizens, on the evening or during the night before the day of Bishop Saint Nicholas, go from house to house in various garbs and frighten the young children with scary, ugly figures, contrary to common sense, it is strictly ordered that nobody among the citizens shall dare to permit their children or their servants to go around in such colourful garbs on the night before Saint Nicholas' Day."

Before the Gregorian calendar reform, St. Lucy's Day, December 13 *(Luca-nap)* was the shortest day of the year, which is why in many places until quite recently the Hungarian peasants counted the lengthening of the days from here. The women did not work on this day. The men began to make the "Lucy chair" *(Luca szék),* carving a separate piece one day at a time from different kinds of wood, so that the chair would be finished exactly by the time of the Christmas Eve Mass. He who sat on it during Midnight Mass would see the big-horned witches in the church, but then he had to run homeward immediately because if they recognized him he would have been torn apart by them. (Géza Róheim wrote one of his first large-scale monographs about the beliefs of Lucy's Day, the historical precedents for the making of the *Lucy chair,* its international connections, and its ethno-psychological meaning.) In Transdanubia, children go from house to house on this day and charm the hens with ditties so that they will lay eggs all the year around. They wish everything good to the people of the house with a poem:

> *Lucy, Lucy, cackle cock,*
> *Sharp, sharp, croo, croo, cuckuricoo!*
> *May you have as many chickens*
> *As there are stars in the heavens!*

651

May you have much wheat and money,
Blades of grass be not so many!
May you have so big a sausage
As the country's longest passage!
May you have bacon, fat,
As big as the courtyard gate!
Doctors go in hunger crazy,
Let their beasts go push the daisy!
Never be the goodwife lazy!
Lucy, Lucy, cackle cock
Cuckuricoo!

A custom called "looking for lodgings" *(szálláskeresés)* is a recent religious custom. Nine families got together and from December 15 on carried the picture of the Holy Family to a different house every day, singing and praying in front of it. Then they gave gifts to a poorer family, as if they were giving them to the Holy Family.

The most popular Christmas custom is the Nativity play *(Betlehemezés)*, which was known in the near past throughout the entire Hungarian linguistic region and was played even in cities. Records speak of mystery plays in the church as early as the 11th century, but later these were ousted from the churches and in the 17th to 18th centuries were

306. "Bethlehem" Nativity players
Szakmár, Bács-Kiskun County

performed in schools and by religious societies. It seems that the custom became general only in the last century, at least in the form and by the name known currently (cf. Plates LIV, LV).

Generally 16 to 18-year-old boys played in the Nativity play, girls doing so only among the Matyós (cf. p. 43), where the Nativity in the shape of a church was carried by an older woman. A runner *(kengyelfutó)* from among the players went ahead of the rest, who in Torda of Transylvania asks for admission with verses like this:

> *Praised be the Lord Our Jesus Christ!*
> *Holy day, the brightest feast day*
> *Breaks for Christians with this morning,*
> *Though the Holy Church of Nature*
> *Clad she is in silent mourning.*
> *Long ago in Bethlehem town*
> *Shepherds sang about the Saviour,*
> *Who descended and redeemed us*
> *And has always helped poor people.*
> *Honoured Host and meekly masters!*
> *Outside are my friends awaiting;*
> *What, my good man, is thine answer:*
> *Wilt thou let my friends advance here?*

On an affirmative answer the participants come in. Two "angels" bring in the church-shaped Nativity, and they are followed by King Herod, Joseph the father, and two or three shepherds who lie down in front of the Nativity. Only when everybody has settled down do they start to pretend awakening and begin songs the content of which varies by regions:

> *Rise, shepherds, rise up, men,*
> *Go we quick to Bethlehem!*
> *Haste as we are able*
> *To a ragged stable!*
> *Start we now, e'en tonight,*
> *So we get there still before the morning light,*
> *And we pay our Lord respect as best we might.*
> *Oh he's cold, the poor thing,*
> *How his tears are pouring!*
> *Pillows soft prop not his head,*
> *Nor he lies on feather bed*
> *But in hay and straw instead,*
> *For a stove to keep him warm there all he hath*
> *Is from cows' and donkeys' mouth the steaming breath.*
>
> Pásztó (Heves County)

Usually after such an introduction comes the brief description of the birth of Christ, then Joseph tells how he tried without success to find lodging, and then the shepherds render homage in front of the infant Jesus. A comedy follows, the humorous rivalry and squabble of the shepherds, and after the performers have been treated to food and drink, the players sing their blessing together:

Fig. 226. A "Bethlehem" or miniature church used as a stage for showing puppets at Christmas. Lengyeltóti, Somogy County. Early 20th century

Fig. 227. Figures of the puppet-show (above). Lengyeltóti, Somogy County. Early 20th century

Fig. 228. A "bagpipe" imitation made out of a milk jug, used by minstrels called *regös*. Jákfa, Vas County. First half of 20th century

Hurry, goodman, if you would,
Give us speed for go we should.
May God give you every good,
You, your house and neighbourhood.

Tiszakarád (former Zemplén County)

Numerous other variations have also been recorded, especially if we take in consideration the puppet Nativity plays *(bábtáncoltató betlehem),* the most complete form of which were recorded in the north-eastern and western parts of the linguistic territory. The Szatmárcseke version has seven different puppets: two old shepherds, two shepherd boys, two angels, King Herod, the Devil, Death, Small Mike, and the one who collects the candle money *(gyertyapénzszedő).* The sequence of the play and the songs are similar to those in other Nativity plays, but here a single child moves the puppets on the church-like, towered stage, made especially for this purpose. As a conclusion, the candle-money collector puppet comes on stage and recites the following verse:

Here this box of copper,
Hungry pot of money,
Waits for you to drop a
Penny as is proper.
Make it all the richer,
For today was born little Jesus.

Szatmárcseke
(former Szatmár County)

Nativity players began to prepare their equipment at Advent, when they learned the poems and songs, and they went about in the village often for ten days, certain groups of them even going to neighbouring settlements.

One of the oldest Hungarian customs, the *regelés* or *regölés* (minstrelsy) (cf. p. 36), is connected with the second day of Christmas, Saint Stephen's Day. According to philological findings the word *reg* may have meant an occasion of royal and lordly entertainment in the Middle Ages, during which the *regös* men (minstrels) entertained their lords. The word itself is connected to the shamanistic word *révülés* (entrancement), so that it can be supposed that at least in part it is traceable to pre-Conquest times, while on the other side it has links with the different types of European mummers' plays. The main role of the songs, melodies, and jokes of medieval minstrels was entertainment, but they often included social wrongs that the country or the leaders of certain large regions would otherwise not have heard about.

However, the custom of minstrelsy associated with a certain time of year must also have been known among the people. In a note from 1552 referring to Transylvania, we can read: "After the birthday of our Lord Jesus Christ comes the big celebration of the Devil, the week of minstrelsy... There is no end to the plentiful drinking and abundant song."

In the last century the custom of minstrelsy was practised in almost two hundred villages of Transdanubia, especially in its western part, as well as in certain parts of the Székelyland. Children and young men

307. "Bethlehem" Nativity play
Kéty, Tolna County

Fig. 229. Minstrels called *regös*. Alsóhahót, Zala County. Early 20th century

went around the village mostly dressed in pelts. They rattled their scary-sounding chained cudgels and tried to make as much noise as possible with their jug pipe—which is nothing other than an earthenware jug covered with a membrane—and in many other ways. They went from house to house and entered with such greetings as the following: "We, the servants of Saint Stephen, have arrived from a cold and snowy country, our ears and feet are frozen, and we want to cure them with your gifts. Shall we tell it or press it?" If they got permission from the farmer to tell their story, they started on the song full of character and implying mythical, archaic connections. One of its parts, coming just after the introduction, are words wishing the magic of plenty, wishing every kind of good, heaped up to overflowing, to all the people in the house. (The ancient refrain in this and the following song have since become obscure in meaning):

> *Here there sprang up one*
> *Wonderful pond;*
> *And around this pond some*
> *Wonder-working stags stand:*
> *Horns a-locked in tangles*
> *Are a thousand candles:*
> *Unlit, they be lighted,*
> *With the night benighted*
> *In the coming new year!*
> *May the great God give this goodman*
> *Six times seven pecks of grain an acre!*
> Régi rejtem, régi rejtem,
> Sej, regü rejtem!
> *O the God Almighty*
> *This too did He grant thee.*
> *May the great God give this goodwife*
> *Eggs a hundred for her every layer!*
> Régi rejtem, régi rejtem,

656

Sej, regü rejtem!
O the God Almighty
This too did He grant thee.

Nyögér (Vas County)

In the second part comes the turn of those girls and young men who are going to be paired off or "minstreled" together. It is believed that those whose turn comes in this way will get married after the next Carnival:

Here we know a lassie
By the name of Julcsa;
There we know a laddie
By the name of Pista.
May God not defend him,
In his bosom tend him!
Chase him from the garden,
Let him have no pardon,
Choke him in a pillow
Make him cry and bellow
Like a sow her farrow,
But a little still more so!
Haj, regő, rejtő!
This too grant He might thee,
God our Lord Almighty!

Miháld (Somogy County)

Fig. 230. A staff with chains rattling on it, used by the minstrels. Region of Göcsej, Zala County. 1930s

A mummer disguised as a bull usually runs in after the song and keeps frightening the children and girls, after which the minstrels ask for a reward for their song. One of the earliest recorded versions from Transdanubia even tells about this:

Goodman is abed a-lying,
Tied around his waist his wallet;
In it are two hundred forints,
Half belongs to regös minstrels,
Half goes to its owner.

Gowns we have of buckwheat stalks,
Shoes we have of oak-tree bark.
If you let us out now,
Off we go a-skating!

Various versions often mention the oak- or birch-bark sandal *(bocskor)*, and the minstrels usually call themselves the servants of Saint Stephen. Undoubtedly all of this refers to great antiquity. Besides the young men, married men also indulge in minstrelsy in the Székelyland, but they formed a group of their own. They generally sang a verse at the house of young married couples rather than at those of girls, and to this verse is attached the *De hó reme róma* refrain, the content of which is not quite clear.

Grains of snow do fall and flurry,
De hó reme róma

Foxes, rabbits romp and scurry.
De hó, etc.
Off we trudged into the village,
De hó, etc.
To the yard of Mózes Illés.
De hó, etc.
There we found a chock-full household,
De hó, etc.
In it saw a bed all tumbled,
De hó, etc.
In the bed there lies the goodman,
De hó, etc.
By the wall there lies his woman,
De hó, etc.
Mid them lies their rose-cheeked sonny.
De hó, etc.
Thus he urged his father, mother:
Get up, father, rise up, mother
Reges men came, let them come in.

Kénos (former Udvarhely County)

The Transylvanian version also differs in talking about the "red ox" rather than the stag, so that this is some custom of mummery in which at one time the bull, the ox, stood at the centre. Hungarian ethnology has occupied itself considerably with the customs and poems of minstrelsy, but in this regard it has not yet been able to arrive at a confident, final solution.

Holy Innocents' Day whipping (December 28) belongs among the old customs of ecclesiastical origin, although in the final count we can follow its trail back to antiquity. They beat the children with switches in memory of King Herod's killing of the infants. The following was written in an 18th century notation from Transylvania: "On this day the fathers or others hit the little children with switches early in the morning, in memory of the suffering of the infants for Christ, and because they too shall have to suffer in this worldly life." But the switch was also used on those they wanted to urge to do more diligent work. People also tried to get rid of sickness and boils with their ditties, among others, this one:

Do as told and be good,
If they send you upward, down you go,
If they send you downward, up you go,
If to fetch some water, wine you bring,
If they send some wine for, water bring,
Be you hale and hearty, lively, never have no sores!

Zalaistvánd (Zala County)

We have mentioned only the most important among the calendar customs of the year, but the celebration of *Name's Day* also belong here and is practiced throughout the country. Among these the most important are precisely those attached to Christmas: St. Stephen's day and

St. John's day. At this time the children go from house to house, recite their verses, and expect gifts. Many of the verses are of half-folk origin, having been written by cantors, but there can also be found among them some really beautiful ones:

> *Up and get, good men meek, for the dawn's breaking there,*
> *Angel-like hovers on wings of gold, bright and fair.*
> *Every flower will deck itself as it blows*
> *And it will dry itself on a soft lily-rose.*
> *As many grass-blades do grow in the motley mead,*
> *As many water drops lie in the ocean bed,*
> *So many blessings shall fall on St. Johnny's head!*
> *All of us wish him well!*

Nagyszalonta (former Bihar County)

Customs not Tied to the Calendar Year

In this book we have already dealt at several places with the customs not tied to specific dates. At this point we call attention only to customs that were not mentioned at all or mentioned from another point of view.

The spring inspection of landmarks *(határjárás)* took place when the snow had already melted but the spring work had not yet begun. The leader of the village and the representatives of the landlord participated, but they also took with them a few old men blessed with good memory, and a few young men who would be witnesses in the future. One of the most important tasks of the land inspectors is to verify precisely boundaries, boundary mounds, and boundary stones. These often are altered by individuals or even entire villages in accord with their interest, in order to increase their own land holdings by doing so. At such times the boundaries have to be reestablished. The young people raised a mound at the meeting point of the boundaries and perhaps put a stone on top of it. At the conclusion of the work the youngest were lifted off their ten toes and beaten soundly with a switch so that they would be able to remember the spot even in their old age.

In some places people were not satisfied with mounds alone but also drew a ditch around the village boundary with a plough. This custom survived the longest in Kalotaszeg, where in Körösfő, eight pairs of buffalo pulled the huge boundary marking plough, which was three metres long. They took the plough out in early May, amidst much celebrating. All the people of the village, great and small, followed it in their Sunday best. The more prosperous farmers provided the buffalos and two selected young men held the plough handles. Then ploughing began, followed finally by a toast.

The toast *(áldomás,* "wetting the bargain") (cf. pp. 117-8), is the concluding act of bigger work and more significant sales and purchases. It usually consists of treating with food and drink. The one for whom the work was done, or the disposer, provides for this, and not only can the buyer count on it but generally even those who participated either officially or as helpers. Thus, for example, the "cup of the law" *(törvénypohár)* was due also to the members of the council in Tokaj-Hegyalja, when the selling of a vineyard was registered.

We also know of customs by which the community tries to maintain its own laws. Such are, among others, the *zángozás* or *kongózás,* known in certain villages of Bihar County. If a married couple divorce and then move back together again, or if a couple live together without marriage, or if they are unfaithful to each other, a large group of people go to their window. They make a public announcement, amidst much bell ringing and shouting, of all the sins the couple have committed or are believed to have committed. Another way of expressing public opinion is a mock wedding, and the "clergyman" shouts out, in an unprintable fashion, all the things attributed to the married couple. Such serious insults may result in physical violence, while the offended couple might prefer to move out of the village rather than to tolerate such ridicule from the community.

Numerous customs are attached to the *building of a house*. When the top of the wall is reached, a garland is pinned up, and then the farmer treats the builders. The practice of a building sacrifice has already been illustrated in one of the most beautiful ballads (cf. pp. 524-7). A more gentle version of such a sacrifice is the placing of a lock of hair into the building, as was done in one of the medieval buildings of Eger's fortress. Nowadays, when old houses are demolished, the walling in of smaller and larger animals often are brought to light. Sometimes these were buried under the threshold. Building sacrifices are often mentioned, especially in Transylvania, not only in regard to peasant houses but to castles as well. Thus, when the castle of the lord at Gerend (former Torda-Aranyos County) was built, the masons noticed with dismay that the walls were cracking and crumbling at some places. They thought that walling in a few sheep or a calf would stop the crumbling, but the miserly lord was unwilling to provide for this, saying it was not in the contract. What was to be done? The poor masons caught a dog and a cat nearby and walled those into the new building. Although in this way they assured the solidity of the walls, the family of the count consequently quarelled like cats and dogs, and there was no blessing on the inhabitants of the castle—so says a local legend.

Recruiting *(sorozás)* was a great event in every village after the introduction of general compulsory military service in 1868 (cf. pp. 500-4). People prepared for this well ahead of time. The young men decked their hats with ribbons and went to the nearby town or larger village together on a cart, where they had to appear in front of the recruiting committee. On the way they sang a recruiting song:

> *Szeged town has such a yellow County Hall,*
> *There I go for military overhaul.*
> *On the floor I throw my knickers, shirt and all,*
> *As I face the officers, my tears do fall.*
>
> *This inspecting doctor he is such a crook,*
> *For he found me fit and saw no fault to book;*
> *One fault you can certainly find, come and touch:*
> *Here this heart for lover mine aches very much.*
>
> Szeged (Csongrád County)

660

Those who proved fit for military service arrived back in the village amidst much singing, while those who were unfit slunk home one by one under cover of the gardens, because no matter how miserable the three years of military service were, still they were ashamed of being unfit for it. Time for joining up came in the autumn, when there was a big farewell ball. The women and girls accompanied their sons and lovers to the nearest railway station and lamented them as if they had died. The young men took leave with songs like this:

> *Three times does the cart in the yard turn about:*
> *Mother, mother, will you bring my kit-box out!*
> *Bring it also, bring it to me my call-up card,*
> *Nagykászon forgets me soon as I depart.*

> *Mother dear, please, grieve not for me, shed no tear,*
> *Go back home and rear my little brother dear!*
> *Let him be an able-bodied fighting jack,*
> *Bold hussar who never falls from horse's back.*
>
> Kászon (former Csík County)

We have already spoken of ecclesiastical customs (cf. pp. 104–9) above. Here we need only mention the blessing of the fields in the spring *(határszentelés)*, practised only by Catholics (cf. Ill. 38). The procession marched singing and carrying flags to the field, trying to assure a good harvest in this way, and the successful gathering of the crop.

The grown children's acceptance into the Church took place with a certain festivity and in folk style. The Catholics decorate the church with green boughs and flowers for First Communion *(első áldozás)* and Confirmation, and on both occasions the boys get a bouquet to pin on their chests, the girls a wreath of flowers, and then the godparents give them further gifts. After Confirmation *(konfirmálás)*, the Protestants in many places thank the clergyman for the preparation and the initiation of the children into the teachings of the Church and give him small gifts: flower baskets, a few red-coloured eggs.

Certain forms of selecting the Queen of Whitsuntide (cf. p. 647) survived longer among Church customs. The ornately dressed Matyó "Daughters of Mary" may be regarded as such. Their dresses, made for the occasion, increased the festive splendour of the holidays. Such were also the "rose-girls", among whom the clergyman designated a queen and whose head was adorned with a garland of roses or wheat. In the evening a dance was organized in her honour, and afterwards they all accompanied her home and at this time gave her money they had collected for her dowry.

The guilds (cf. p. 91) preserved numerous customs, primarily the dance gatherings, which were called *lakozás* in Baja and were generally held around Carnival time. People went to Mass early in the morning, and then the journeymen marched out with the flags and emblems of the guild and invited the masters and their families, amidst loud music-playing. In the afternoon they gathered where the emblems were kept, and the masters offered wine to the journeymen. Afterwards they went together to the scene of the entertainment and placed their emblems in the hall where it was to take place. Here by late afternoon they were already dancing, but the ceremonious customs really started with dinner at eight o'clock. The kitchen master tapped the door frame with a stick mounted with bells and in this way announced the next course to the accompaniment of a poem, just as though he were the first best man at a wedding. Such parties lasted until noon the next day, but at more prosperous guilds, such as, for example, the millers', it often lasted for two days.

Work Customs

We have already considered customs associated with certain tasks in their appropriate place (cf. pp. 215-19). Here, therefore, we wish to examine the relationship between work and custom, rite and belief. In general we can state that the majority of customs relate to the beginning and conclusion of work. The customs at the beginning of work are interwoven with beliefs meant to assure the success of the work, whilst the emphasis at the conclusion is simple but liberated celebration, joy over the results won. It is worth taking some examples into consideration from this point of view. Thus, at the time of sowing, people try to influence the coming crop in the most diverse manner. Water was sprinkled on the first carts going out to the fields in the spring, to assure a plentiful crop, also by ploughing an egg into the first furrow. On the first day of sowing, tradition prescribed a special diet and abstention from certain dishes. Besides these customs, people did not forget to ask the Church's blessing either; the sower took off his hat, and before he started work he asked God's blessing in a brief prayer. How different is the conclusion of harvesting and threshing (cf. Ill. 26)! At that time, there is no forbidden food, and celebration takes place with songs, dancing, and a rich dinner, during which various jokes, bantering, and mummery were also practised. The same can be observed in relation to work in the vineyards, at the end of which a happy celebration, the *szüret* (wine harvesting) (cf. pp. 226-31), concludes the work (cf. Plate LII).

Numerous customs and beliefs are also attached to driving out the animals in the spring. Since much trouble could come to the stock on the plains of the Great Plain and on the mountain pastures, this was prevented with various actions, actions which a herdsmen's song from Csík has virtually gathered into a bouquet:

> *Herdsman go and gather*
> Ching-a, ling-a, long-a
> *Cattle droves together;*
> Ching-a, ling-a, long-a
> *Little bullocks bawling, mooing*
> Ching-a, ling-a, long-a
> *Go the roads along-a.*
>
> *Fasten chains on threshold*
> Ching-a, ling-a, long-a
> *So the herds of cattle all told*
> Ching-a, ling-a, long-a

308. Harvest festival
Kazár, Nógrád County

May return home in the autumn —
Neither thieves nor wolves maraud 'em —
Ching-a, ling-a, long-a
Safe where they belong-a!

Grass it grow before them,
Ching-a, ling-a, long-a
Let diseases spare them!
Ching-a, ling-a, long-a
Let them fatten while a-grazing,
Folks their price should keep on raising
Ching-a, ling-a, long-a
In the market throng-a.

(former Csík County)

How different is the "crowding in the fold", that is to say, the stock's return in the autumn, when on St. Andrew's Day (November 30) or, in some places, at the first snow fall they drive the flocks home:

Would it rained and wind was blowing,
Setting cows and horses homing;
Herdsman he could make his tally,
Shepherd's boy was free to dally.

Györgytarló (former Zemplén County)

Afterwards follows the "wetting of the bargain" *(áldomás),* the celebration of their having successfully protected the stock from all dangers.

We can also make similar observations in connection with the building of the house. The lifting of the first soil from the foundation, the already mentioned building sacrifice (cf. p. 660), are all attempts to influence the success of building the house. The first occasion for celebration is when the wall and roof structures are already upright. Celebration reaches its peak when the house is completed and, after the family has moved in, they hold a house-warming, the expression of joy at the completion of work.

We shall also mention customs not directly connected to work but to occupations. Noteworthy among these are the days that refer to predicting the weather and crop yield. A few of the more important ones follow:

If the snow is melting on *St. Vincent's Day* (January 22), the time of thawing, then the vine growers think they can hope for a plentiful and good harvest, while if the sun shines on the Day of the Feast of the Purification of the Virgin Mary *(Gyertyaszentelő Boldogasszony,* February 2), then a much longer winter can be expected, as is told by a short ditty:

If bright on Candlemas Day,
Get you out your chaff and hay!

Báránd (Bihar County)

If the ice is still firm on *Icebreaking Matthias' Day* (February 24), the fishermen expect plentiful fishing, especially the fisherman who on this day succeeds in catching a pike. If the first warm day is St. Joseph's Day (March 19), then everybody must start ploughing that day.

St. George's Day (April 24) is an ancient holiday celebrating the beginning of spring. On this day the stock is driven out and the spring hiring-market for servants is held. According to tradition, cows had to be guarded from witches with special care on this day, because witches were said to collect dew on the fields to acquire the benefit of the milk. On *St. Mark's Day* (April 25), the day of the cattle men, the owners of the stock they guard would bake strudel for them.

The *Day of St. John of Nepomuk* (May 13) is the holiday for men connected with water: fishermen, sailors, millers, who on this day organize a big celebration on the Danube in Baja and parade with illuminated boats.

St. Urban (May 25) is the patron of bee keepers, and the bees begin to swarm on this day. But the vine dressers paid respect to him as well as to *Donát*. The statue of Saint Urban stood on the path to the vineyards, and on this day the vine dressers put flowers on the statue to protect the vines from hail and other damage. Péter Bod, an 18th century historian from Transylvania, related that: "They held this day as a *Dies criticus,* from which the ignorant tell fortunes: a plentiful yield of wine if there is bright sunshine; scarcity if there is rainy weather. In this regard there was in Alsace a custom that if there was bright sunshine they took the wooden image of Urban through the streets with much joy and singing of songs; if the weather was rainy, they tied a rope on his neck and dragged him through the mud."

Peter–Paul (June 29) played an extremely important role in agricultural life because the stalk of the wheat breaks off then, and it is time to start harvesting. The day is also celebrated by the fishermen, whose patron saint is St. Peter. They organized parades at this time and invited the leaders of the village to a dinner made of fish.

St. Michael's Day (September 29) begins the autumn quarter of the agricultural year, was also the day by which all payments in kind had to be taken care of. The mountain herdsmen at this time held the celebration that was to ward off losses to wolves. From this day on the bees did not go out to collect honey. The oak forest was freed, and the herd could be driven into it.

The statue of *St. Wendelin* (October 20), the patron saint of herdsmen, can still be seen frequently, especially in Transdanubia. On St. Wendelin's Day the herdsmen held a great celebration. The name Wendelin *(Vendel)* was specially frequent in herdsmen's families.

Days of celebration related to occupations are eclipsed by the general days of celebration throughout the year. On *St. Martin's Day* (November 11), city dwellers and in some places even the peasants, killed a goose and tasted the new wine. It was a day of much eating and drinking, to ensure abundance until spring. At this time the herdsmen went around to the farmers and got from them cakes or, in place of cakes, money.

St. Andrew's Day (November 30) is the last day before Advent that is still free for entertainment. This is the time people begin to slaughter pigs and hold pig- killing feasts *(disznótor)*. St. Ambrose (December 7) is the patron saint of bee keepers and honeycake makers. His day was celebrated even in Budapest between the two wars, and a procession with church flags was held.

★

One fundamental feature of Hungarian folk customs emerges from the above: the community, whether a village or a market town, or only a group of peasant homesteads, remained unconditionally loyal to the social conventions indispensable to its members. In descriptions of the customs of certain villages we never find it said that a certain custom was practised one way in one house, another way in the next. The proverb, "There are as many customs as houses", does not apply to the main events of village life, such as the customs of celebrating holidays. It happened of course that the various nationalities in a village followed different traditions; this is only natural, and goes to show that even a single village is comprised of distinct, well-defined communities. Social categories also created differences, but these differences are observable in the "pomp and circumstance" of life. A wedding, an Easter or a funeral feast was held by the poor, too, in accordance with

309. Saint Wendelin, the patron saint of
herdsmen
A wayside statue
Jászberény

village custom, though more often than not, at the price of great sacrifice.

Naturally, there were fastidiously observed unwritten agreements regarding what was proper for a poor man, whom he may ask to be a *koma,* with how much splendour he could celebrate his wedding, what his clothes, his food should be like, etc. In many places they reprimanded the poor if they wanted to imitate the big farmers. In other places, the poor held themselves aloof voluntarily and evolved separate forms for celebrating important moments of their life. All these ethnic and social differences verify that peasant life submitted itself to the discipline of the community even in the looser moments of celebration; for example, in many villages young men could visit the house of their chosen ones only on prescribed days, and the laws of the village even watched over love. And needless to say, anyone breaking these laws received his just punishment.

The World of Hungarian Folk Beliefs

In speaking of the world of Hungarian folk beliefs we must first of all think of the age-old sense of unity it assumes between the supernatural on the one hand, and nature and man on the other. Without this, much would remain obscure for us in the system of folk beliefs. The Hungarian peasantry carry from the past not only certain motifs and remnants of memory but also many fundamental ideas from their archaic religious beliefs and their world view in general, all of which lies hidden in their world of beliefs.

The majority of researchers, confronted with the existence of various primitive and peasant beliefs, superstitious customs, and naive religious behaviour, have posed the question this way: How is the world of beliefs possible? On the basis of what logic? How could otherwise capable hunters, fishermen, stockmen, and peasants, who can find their way in the midst of the dangers and cares of practical life, believe in these misconceptions so obviously false to us? Various theories about the origin and history of the development of beliefs were conceived to answer this question. All these theories usually examine only the superstition itself and want to derive its meaning in and of itself. Needless to say, what these mean is a decisive and necessary question, but it still does not answer the problem posed above: Why did people hold for such a long time, and why do some still hold, these different beliefs?

We could give a complete and detailed answer to this query only if we took under observation the entire peasant culture and social structure from this point of view, throughout the course of its own development. If we consider, out of context, only the fact that the Hungarian peasantry believed in the evil eye *(rontás),* in the taking of cow's milk, in the shaman *(táltos),* in incubi *(lidérc),* and in many other things, this can appear really nonsensical to us. However, it is even more nonsensical and unaccountable that to this day high European culture and, within that, city life is full of superstitious behaviour, gestures, and obedience to magic effects.

If we examine the history of Hungarian culture, we can see that peasant culture was not in organic but only in occasional contact with the developing intellectual awareness of the ruling classes. In general this differentiation was a European phenomenon, so that not only can we find it in Hungary, but the following remarks are applicable *mutatis mutandis* to the peasantry of other nations as well. The ethnic groups and social layers of the Hungarian peasantry could not develop together with either the nobility or the middle class of the cities. The situation of the peasant class, their being tied to the land, and the nature of peasant agricultural work prevented them equally from joining in the rhythm of European culture and intellectual awakening that has been rapidly developing since the Renaissance, and from taking over directly the results of European rationalism. Peasants were also influenced from the direction of the ruling classes, although these influences did not affect precisely the fundamental traits and characteristics of their thinking and culture but rather, for example, changed their customs, certain of their tales, and melodies. The peasantry's opinion about the final affairs of the world, about life and death and their own place in the world, has continued in the same tracks through centuries.

Essentially, peasant culture and what we have called their world view were strongly self-sufficient, having to answer questions without an intermediary, just as the peasant on his little property had to be simultaneously the house building architect and the expert who knows about animal husbandry, farming, weather, singing, and many other things. Peasant life was involuntarily universalist, involuntarily all encompassing. Therefore, as we have said, the peasant largely had to find for himself the hopefully correct answers to his own final questions. This is why a different world view evolves from his beliefs, a view that in many cases resembles that ancient shamanistic perception from which it originates historically. In this perception, too, the supernatural powers, nature, and man are in the closest relationship, the ties are not to be severed. Besides, it is evident from these beliefs that the supernatural world and our earthly world have not yet clearly been separated from each other, that they interpenetrate, so that miracles can happen at any time. A piece of iron, a hatchet, can be at once a useful agricultural tool and a magical aid that prevents damage by the storm, prevents hail. Naturally, this connection, this interpretation is more easily recognizable and perceptible in the cults of the archaic tribal cultures and in the world of ancient beliefs than in peasant cultures.

The peasantry had to invent theories of explanation, or, more correctly, they had to cling, for lack of better ones, to those ancient theories of explanation with which they could interpret the phenomena of the world and thus help them do a good job in their affairs. This is why we are not to think that superstition and belief were just some kind of a subsidiary factor in the peasant world of old; it was one of the main factors and directors in their life; complicated customs and prohibitions followed them through life, from birth to death, and they had to cling to them. Magic and beliefs were woven into the activities even of economic life. Fertility and guidance magic, as well as beliefs connected with domestic stock and their products, milk and eggs, all show that every area of the peasants' life was interwoven with these beliefs. According to the peasant view, superstitions in economic processes had just as important a role as the strictly economic working processes. Sowing beliefs are closely attached to sowing, and, by the terms of their faith, they could confidently attribute a good harvest to the carefully carried out ceremonies of fertility magic.

Nothing proves better how much peasant life was affected by this world of beliefs than the fact that for centuries it could live its own life among both Catholic and Protestant peasants. We know well that the peasantry throughout Europe was characterized by a peculiar mixture of peasant religiosity and intertwining of Christianity with the older world of beliefs. Christian customs and devotional exercises were mixed with pagan traditions, ancient memories, and later developed peasant super-stitions. In the course of the centuries, peasant religiousness has grown into a really intricate system consisting of parts that contradict each other, so that the researcher faces a real task in trying to distinguish elements so diverse in origin. And he is not always successful, as certain beliefs have taken on a newer shape, have changed roles, have been transformed through the centuries. Often we cannot even decide for sure about some belief whether it is a pagan tradition, or has developed in Christian Europe, or is a rural development of recent times.

At any rate, beyond these historical strata, the decisive finding is the verification that for various historical, social, and cultural reasons the intellectual make-up and world view of the Hungarian peasantry remained such that superstitious forms of behaviour could, as in a re-vival, reawaken in it, that the beliefs had their beaten, almost precon-ditioned tracks, in which superstition could always appear, in a new situation, as the tool and interpretive theory for a solution.

The world of beliefs influenced the religious picture of the world as well as the social life, economic activities, and everyday customs of the Hungarian peasantry. It also enmeshed one of the most significant areas of peasant creation, the folk tales (cf. pp. 554–64). One of the richest, most complex areas of peasant creative talent could not have developed if the peasantry had not thought in terms of its system of beliefs. The spirit of wonder and of magic penetrates the atmosphere of folk epics; their credibility and the interest in transmitting them can occur only in a society cherishing a picture of the world that is not determined solely by rationalism and everyday reality but also by this luxuriant growth of a network of beliefs. In such a society, in such a cultural form, the fairy-story was, through long centuries, a good and credible entertainer of the peasantry. The present fate and transformation of the folk tales can also verify this: with the destruction of the world of beliefs, tales that were full of miracles are the earliest to die, to wither away, whereas the anecdote and the local epic can maintain themselves longer, apparently because there is much in common in these forms of literature with the perceptible world.

The world of peasant beliefs—as we have said—encompassed every area of life. Therefore we cannot provide a full discussion but will instead just highlight a few characteristic and important questions. We have already referred to certain traits of belief in the course of discussing various areas of folk culture.

Figures of the World of Beliefs

First among the figures of the world of beliefs of the Hungarian peasantry, we will mention the *táltos,* as one in whom the features of the pre-Conquest shamanistic faith can be found most prominently. The word *táltos* itself is presumably Finno-Ugric in origin, and its Finnish equivalent means "learned", which is just what regional dialects of Hungarian call people endowed with supernatural powers. Today, the characteristics and equipment of the *táltos* can be analyzed mostly from the legends of belief (cf. p. 675) that still live in the memory of old people living primarily in the eastern half of the country.

The *táltos* is generally supposed to be well-meaning rather than punitive. He does not gain his knowledge by his own will, but receives it, as one of them bore witness during the course of an interrogation in 1725: "Nobody taught me to be a *táltos*, because a *táltos* is formed so by God in the womb of his mother." Therefore no matter how much his parents and relatives might oppose it, he who has been ordered to his fate must carry it through.

A child was carefully examined at birth to see if he had any teeth or perhaps a sixth finger on one of his hands. One extra bone already foretold that with time the child would become a *táltos*. However, to become one, it was also necessary that the ancestors steal him for three or more days. One accused said, when interrogated for charlatanry in 1720: "… lying dead for nine days, he had been carried off to the other world, to God, but he returned because God sent him to cure and to heal." They called this state *elrejtezés,* being in hiding, which is also a word of Finno-Ugric origin, and we can find its equivalent both in form and content among the related and various peoples of Siberia.

They maintain that while the *táltos*-designate is asleep, the others cut him to pieces to see if he has the extra bone. This motif also occurs in the Hungarian version of the generally known tale, "The Magician and his Apprentice" (AaTh 325): the kidnapped youth is cut up, usually put together on the third day, and by this gains for himself a previously unknown knowledge.

However, the *táltos*-designate's struggle and trial is not over then, because he has to take a test. One way of doing this is by climbing up a tree that reaches to the sky, and if he returns without trouble, he can practise his newly acquired knowledge.

Tradition also tells about the equipment of the táltos. Among these we shall mention various headdresses: the feather duster and the horns. In most cases it is possible to ascertain that the horns resemble the horns of cattle, but less frequently stag horns also occur. Memory of the shaman drum also lives vividly, often paired off with a sieve, which occurs even in children's verses (cf. p. 610) and Midsummer Night songs:

> *May God give us gentle rainfall,*
> *May He wash them both in one, all;*
> *Sift in sieve on Friday,*
> *Loving be on Thursday,*
> *Drum Wednesday.*

The magical mummers of the Hungarians of Moldavia go about on New Year's Day with a sieve, on the side of which they fasten rattles and bells. At one time the *táltos* used this for curing sicknesses, for divining, and for conjuring up abundance, just as did the shamans of Siberia. The Táltos Tree, already mentioned at the time of the pagan revolts (11th century), was known nearly up to the present. As late as the beginning of the past century, they wrote the following about a táltos of the Sárrét: "He goes down, he knows where, and by climbing up the big tree, he will find out what a bad man the village magistrate is. And he can cause what he wants to happen to the village magistrate and to the village." Thus the tree, usually depicted in folk art with a little bird sitting on top,

Fig. 231. The decoration on a horn salt-cellar with the Tree of Life and herdsmen's scenes. Sárrétudvari, former Bihar County. Second half of 19th century

Fig. 232. The intarsia decoration on the handle of a whip with the Tree of Life, the sun and the moon. Biharnagybajom, former Bihar County. Late 19th century

was at once one of the *táltos*'s instruments and the symbol of his power.

Among the activities of the *táltos* we must especially emphasize ecstasy, which the Hungarian language calls *rejtezés* (hiding) and *révülés* (ecstasy). Both words in their foundations can be traced back to the Finno–Ugric period, and it can be ascertained that they were related to shamanistic rites. However, we know that the religio-psychological meaning of ecstasy was not part of the shaman religious world view alone, for it was also known among the archaic beliefs in ancient religious traditions. The *táltos*, the learned one, can create contact with supernatural beings and with the spirits of the dead ancestors only in the state of ecstasy.

The other activity known from stories of belief (cf. p. 589) throughout the entire Hungarian linguistic region is the *táltos* combat (*táltosviaskodás*). The *táltos* from time to time had to fight the *táltos*es of the neighbouring areas in the shape of a bull, stallion, or perhaps a fiery wheel, just as described in a lawsuit of the Great Plain about a village boundary in 1620: "… The *táltos* of Békés fought the *táltos* of Doboz, but the *táltos* of Doboz was a match for the *táltos* of Békés." The strange bull usually came down from a cloud and brought along a storm, while the people were able to help the local bull.

We have reason to suspect that remnants of a one-time *táltos* song survive in the *"haj, regő rejtem"* line of the minstrel songs (cf. p. 657), which supposedly means "I conjure with magic", or in these words even closer to shamanism, *"révüléssel révülök"* ("I am ecstatic in a trance"). Indeed, the language of our nearest linguistic kindred, the Ob-Ugrians, the name of the shaman song developed from the *kai, kei* word, which is the exact etymological equivalent of our *haj, hej* interjection, and the name of the Hungarian shaman song may have been *hajgatás*.

The recently deceased Vilmos Diószegi, who made a great contribution to the field of *táltos* and shaman research, observed as the summary of his investigation: "The selection of the *táltos*-designate by illness, lengthy sleep, as well as by the cutting up of his body, that is, his gaining knowledge by way of finding the 'extra number' of bones in his body, his initiation by climbing the tree reaching to the sky—all this projected, even in its details and also in its entirety, the images formed by the Magyars of the Conquest of the *táltos*-designate. The single-bottomed drum with rattles on it in the hand of the *táltos,* which also serves as his saddled animal, as well as his owl-feathered or horned headgear, his notched or ladder-shaped 'tree' with the sun and moon on it disclose the equipment of the *táltos* of the Magyars of the Conquest, and his ecstasy, the combat that followed it, his conjuring of ghosts with interjections also reveal his activities." Therefore the *táltos* figure of the world of Hungarian folk beliefs even today is closely attached to the shamanism of Eastern Europe and Asia.

The figure of the *garabonciás* was strongly mixed during the centuries with that of the *táltos,* but this figure originates from the West. The name itself is perhaps connected with the Italian word *gramanzia,* "enchantment, devilry". He is equally supposed to be ready to do good or evil, to conjure up storms, and he reads enchantments from his book because, strictly speaking, he is a version of the medieval journeying student who had finished the seven or thirteen years of schooling at the university. In the course of this he had also acquired black magic, which he passed on to the peasants during his wanderings. The Wandering Scholar knocked on the doors of the peasant houses and asked for milk or eggs to eat. If they refused his request or gave sparingly, he conjured up a storm and sent hail to the fields of the entire village, while he rode away on the back of a dragon. His figure appears to be more revengeful and dangerous than that of the *táltos* and undoubtedly, in the world of beliefs of the Hungarian peasantry, he represents European black magic.

Boszorkány (witch) is a word of ancient Turkish origin, in the vernacular meaning a woman, although in the minds of the people either a man or woman can be a witch. In many areas witches are called *bába* or *vasorrú bába* (iron-nosed witch). The word *bába* is a Slavic derivative where the meaning "old woman, witch" can equally be found. As the names differ, so too the features which characterize Hungarian witches originate from several layers. Many different kinds of practice, procedure, and what the Hungarian language collectively calls *babona* (superstition) cling to this figure. The word *babona* is also Slavic in origin, perhaps taken over by the Magyars from some ancient Russian dialect, since numerous elements within this circle of belief can be found that indicate pre-Conquest Eastern Slavic contact.

According to Hungarian folk belief, the acquiring of a witch's knowledge is generally an active step (cf. p. 591). Most frequently it was learned at midnight at crossroads, where the person would draw a circle around herself with a stick, which he or she was forbidden to move out of or even if a four-horse carriage or a bull charged or if a millstone on a thread was rolled over him or her. If the seeker of witchcraft could overcome her fear, she then could become a witch. At other times, the meat of a black cat was consumed for the same reason, or skill was acquired in the cemetery at midnight, but it could also happen that a person climbed a tree or a dry stalk of a weed, just like a *táltos,* and came back from there with the acquired knowledge. Witchcraft was most often transmitted within the family. It was passed on to the younger generation on the deathbed with a handshake. But no matter how it happened, the designate had to do something to get the power, while at the same time a chance to refuse it also existed.

However, once the witch had acquired her knowledge, she then could not put it down, because her colleagues would not leave her in peace and she became unlucky all her life. They believed that a witch is punished for her sins after death; she goes to hell, where snakes and frogs rip apart her guilty soul.

A wave of witch-persecutions passed through all of Europe in the 16th to 18th centuries, and these, in a somewhat weakened form, also reached Hungary. We first hear of them in more detail from the second half of the 16th century: "I could also tell a lot about women getting around at night, jumping in the form of cats and going among themselves like many gallants, ravers, dancers, drunkards, lechers, who with a half foot push little children into the sea, who cause damage and much mischief, and among whom many were burned, not long ago, around Pozsony, in the year 1574, after having testified to their terrible deeds. They also have a queen, and on her word the devil does horrible things."

Witches were regarded with caution mixed with a certain fear, so that at times even the tithe collectors avoided their houses. Although witch trials were fairly frequent in Hungary, large scale witch burnings like those in the West were rare. Nevertheless, in Szeged in 1728 nine women believed to be witches and in Debrecen a decade later three others met their death by burning at the stake.

Witches were supposed to have formed certain organizations, which differed from region to region. The leaders were generally men, as in 1722 in Békés County: "András Harangöntő was a very famous master witch who not only practised healing, cast spells, and practised enchantment, but was also the head, the master of that army of witches that, according to him, formed and organized a collective within the area of our county." In such organizations captain, lieutenant, flag-bearer, corporal, and scribe are mentioned. The organization, as in the case of western, primarily German witches, imitated the army. It has also come to light from the data that, from the middle of the 17th century, a strong German influence showed up in Hungarian belief about witchcraft, elements of which survived almost to this day.

However, contrary to this, shamanistic features were undoubtedly preserved also, a few of which are worth mentioning. Thus witches had "horns", which could be seen by a knowledgeable man who sat on the Lucy Chair at Christmas during the Midnight Mass. Documents from witch trials also mention the drum among the equipment of a witch. According to an 18th century confession from Szeged: "... a stout beggar woman at Felsőváros has the copper drum, because she wants to teach her son, who is 18 years old. She wants to enlist him into the order of captains Dániel Rósa and Ferenc Borbola. The stout beggar is such a witch, because the plaintiff is old and cannot carry the drum, which is why they ordered it. Like a pint pot, it was that big." It is presumably not because of the weight of the drum but because of the exhausting nature for body and soul of the ecstasy that they wanted to initiate the young man into the knowledge. We know from Bodrogköz that witches were supposed to take the bones out of sleeping people, which brings to mind the search for the extra bone of the *táltos*. That is to say, the witches wanted to acquire knowledge through possession of these bones.

Witches gathered together regularly to carouse and dance on one of the hills or islands, or at the edge of the forest. Therefore there is hardly a settlement in Hungary where a certain geographic name does not preserve this practice. Even so, the Gellért Hill in the middle of Budapest, rising on the bank of the Danube, was the most famous and central place for such gatherings in the whole country. It should be noted that according to tradition the pagan Magyars, who did not want to be converted, rolled or, more correctly, threw Bishop Gellért, nailed up in a barrel, into the Danube from the top of Gellért Hill. Stories of the witches' visit to Gellért Hill and their flights of many hundreds of kilometres from there have also survived. Thus in Kassa, in a collection of sermons published in 1794, a preacher chastises the faithful in this way: "They say that witches and he-devils saddle people and ride to Saint Gellért Hill, or to where, they alone know, that with a mere look they stop empty carts so that that cannot move an inch, that they can bewitch cow, calf, and small children in thousands and thousands of different ways merely by the spell of eyes or look. But you know better than I what else is believed about witches and what is not." Research during the near past has also disclosed the belief that witches gather at the Gellért Hill from within a 200–300-kilometre radius, flying there even from as far as Székelyland.

A witch carried out her bewitching usually not in her own form but after she had changed into some kind of an animal. Most often she appeared in the form of a cat. Then, primarily on the night of St. George's Day (April 24), she would try to take the milk yield of the stock. As a precaution, the farmers would put some kind of spiky object, usually a harrow, in the door while they themselves kept watch with a pitchfork so that no cat could sneak into the barn. Witches are also believed to take on the shape of a goose, duck, hen, brooding hen, and chicken, as well as the shape of a dog and horse. Interestingly the cow does not appear among these domestic animals, only its horn, imagined as an attribution, the witch herself maintaining her human body. The fox and the rabbit are most frequently encountered as figures into which witches change from among wild animals. Equivalents may be looked for and similar beliefs demonstrated in the West.

The extremely wide strata of beliefs about witches extend to every area of life, but to speak very generally, the majority belong to the category of bewitching with the Evil Eye *(rontás)* (cf. p. 685). Thus witches harm small children by the Evil Eye, and break up or bring together young couples as they wish. They might bring sickness on man and beast equally, cause damage to the crop, and secure the yield of animals for themselves. However, a witch would be compelled to bow to and withdraw in front of one with greater knowledge and power.

Such a person could be, as was considered especially in the Great Plain, a Cunning Shepherd *(tudós pásztor),* who could defend not only his own stock and his interests with supernatural power, but also tried to help others and to fend off the bewitching of witches (cf. p. 675). A Cunning Shepherd, similarly to witches, also acquired his knowledge in an active way, at the crossroads or by the acceptance of some kind of a herdsman's tool—a cudgel, satchel, or ringed whip—or by a hand-shake with an older wise herdsman who was dying.

The Cunning Shepherd had power over the stock in every respect. If he wished, he was able to scatter the flock of others, so that the animals wandered off to several days' walking distance, but if he climbed his special tree and called the beasts back, then they returned even from several days' walking distance. A shepherd of lesser knowledge could not scatter the stock of the Cunning Shepherd, because on the Day of St. George he had encircled the pasture and fold of his own with smoke so that his cattle could not break out. The power of the herdsman was thought to lie in his cudgel and in his whip. The skin of a snake that had come out on St. George's Day was braided into the latter, because it gave them power over the stock.

Cunning Shepherds as rivals often set two bulls against each other. The shepherd of greater knowledge was either protected by a circle of smoke, or tamed his attacker with salt poured out on a hat. At such times he could turn the bull around to chase or even destroy the one with lesser knowledge. A runaway herd of horses could be brought back from great distances by beating on a *szűr* spread on the ground.

Herdsmen were forever in a state of feud with witches, especially for bewitching cows and taking away the milk yielded. Not only were they able to discover who had taken the milk away, but by beating the milk with a hatchet, by smoking one garment of the bewitcher, and by other methods, they forced the person to appear on the scene of the witchcraft and somehow repair the damage done. A Cunning Shepherd was able to cure his own stock and the stock of others by both practical and supernatural methods. He had knowledge of many crafts, among others, how to bind by supernatural power *(kötés)* or to release *(oldás)*.

The latter is the most characteristic attribute of the Clever Coachman *(tudós kocsis)* (cf. p. 590). A Clever Coachman gained his knowledge with the help of some kind of implement. Thus a horseshoe nail or a magic whip assured supernatural power, which could, however, only be purchased for a symbolic sum. The main power of a Clever Coachman was to halt and bind horse carriages, but he could also reverse this no matter who had done it, he or someone else. At such times the Clever Coachman hit a spoke of the wheel with his hatchet, or struck the end of the carriage beam with an axe or a wine bottle. At other times, with the button tied to the tip of his whip, he struck out the eye of the horseman who had bound his carriage, even though he was at a great distance, thus freeing his carriage to go on. If the situation required, he was able to rise up in the air with his horses and carriage, and if on the way the horse died of the great strain, he could still go home with it, and the horse dropped out of harness only when they reached their destination.

One interesting feature of the Clever Coachman's knowledge is his power to turn a straw mattress into a horse and start out on the road with that. We can suspect the elements of certain pre-Conquest shamanistic procedures in this as the skin of a sacrificed horse was stuffed with straw, so that it could come back to life and be at the disposition of the dead in the other world. The most polished, well-rounded myths developed in the region east of the Tisza, especially around the figure and activities of the Clever Coachman and Cunning Shepherd (cf. p. 591).

The *millers* were also thought to possess supernatural power. The knowledge of sending and chasing away rats was attached to them throughout the entire linguistic region.

Faith in the power of "seeing women" *(léleklátó asszony)* and healers *(javasember)* lives on almost to this day. Their activity is manifold. Thus there were some who could make contact with and transmit messages to the spirits of people who had died in the near or distant past. People came from far away to consult certain highly reputed seers *(látóasszony)*, especially during wartime, when they wanted to find out something about their dead or missing relatives.

There were among them some who achieved cures with prayers and incantations, while others practised the art of divination. Although the majority of such persons were strongly religious, in the 20th century they came into conflict with both the Church and secular authorities. Some of these persons were supposed to have acquired their supernatural knowledge during sleep, during "hiding", just as the *táltos* did, a fact which demonstrates how the oldest forms of belief continued to exist among newer circumstances.

The characters listed above are all persons who belonged to some community, or at least appeared there from time to time. What differentiated them from average, everyday people was only that in one or another area of life they commanded supernatural power and used it for good or evil purposes, for the benefit or the ruin of themselves or of others. However, there exist also some truly supernatural figures in the world of Hungarian beliefs, although their number is significantly smaller.

The origin of the Hungarian word *lidérc (Ignis Fatuus incubus)* has not yet been successfully resolved. Many characters, and accordingly many different kinds of Eurasian beliefs, are concealed in the figure. Thus it can mean a special kind of *lidérc* chicken, hatched by someone from an egg held under his armpit. This will acquire everything its master wishes to make him rich, but it may also endanger his health. Furthermore, as long as it is alive, its master cannot free himself from it, or can do so only with great difficulty. In some places *lidérc* means a lover who appears in human or animal form and destroys a man or woman, often by tormenting him or her to death. Finally we also meet with its meaning as will-o'-the-wisp, usually wandering, like a dead spirit who for some reason cannot come to rest, over the area where at one time he had lived.

The belief in the ghost of a Wandering Surveyor *(bolygó mérnök)* is connected with the *lidérc*. The surveyor falsely measured the land during his life, cheated the poor people, and this is why he cannot rest. He walks the fields with a lantern and a measuring chain, remeasuring the land that has already been divided. Because he has no help, he must run from one end of the land-measuring chain to the other. They believe him to be generally friendly, but if somebody meets him directly or hinders him in his work, then he hits the man in the chest with his lantern.

It is traditionally held that the soul of the dead man leaves his body but still wanders about the house and watches to see if the burial (cf. pp. 627-37) takes place in an orderly fashion. Afterwards the soul stands in the cemetery gate until it is relieved by another one, at which time the soul is finally freed. But according to folk belief, this does not happen in the case of every soul, because there are some who cannot rest, and return from time to time. The reason may be that the person had not bidden goodbye to his relatives or had some other affairs on earth to be disposed of. And he who was miserly in his life, who had cheated or stolen and in general caused losses for others, or he whose requested things had not been put in his coffin, was also believed to come back. A soul cannot rest if its small children are ill-treated or if the heirs cannot agree on the division of property. At such times it returns, turns everything upside down, and knocks pictures and plates off the wall. The relatives would try to find out the reason for its return, but if they failed, they dug the body up, turned it over, and nailed it with a long nail to the bottom of the coffin.

The ghost is a soul who for some reason is condemned to wander eternally or until it is in some way freed from its fate. Therefore, the Palots people, when they met such a ghost, greeted him the following way:

"All souls praise the Lord!"

Amidst great sighs the wandering soul answered:

"I would praise Him, too, if only it were possible!"

Then it wailed in a voice of pain, since it forever has to haul along that boundary stone he once moved further, in order to enlarge his plough land:

"Oh so heavy! Where am I to put it?"
"If it's heavy, put it back where you found it!"

If the ghost did so, then under fortunate circumstances, it was freed from the curse and found peace. A ghost could appear in many forms. Most frequently, it haunted people in the shape of a horse, calf, piglet, rabbit, dog, cat, or goose. In most cases these ghosts are of good will and do no harm; at the most, the ghost follows those who get in its way and appears in the shape of a familiar man or woman asking for a ride on a cart; but the cart can then go no further, because it cannot carry the great weight, while the horses, sensing the ghost, run wild. A ghost might appear in a familiar shape leading his victim into a swamp or river to meet his death. This meaning is hidden in the Hungarian word *kísértet* (ghost), which through the metastasis *kísért* (haunt) can be traced back to the Ugrians.

The Székelys' Wild Girl *(vadleány)* belongs to the group of ghosts having a female form. It is called Fair Maid *(kisasszony)* in the rest of Transylvania and in the Bodrogköz. In the latter region, they believe her to be generally good-natured. If one does not speak to her, she just walks about quietly and perhaps sits up on a cart. However, if they oppose or taunt her, or perhaps swear in front of her, then in her anger, she breaks everything she finds in her proximity. In the Transylvanian version, it is even possible to capture and marry her, and she also lures men.

Many more less frequent figures, or figures not occurring in a larger area, could be mentioned among the characters of the world of beliefs of the Hungarian peasantry. In general, we can observe that among these, dwarfs, giants, fairies, elves, water sprites, house spirits, and others, all of which are fairly frequent among the surrounding peoples and especially among peoples to the west of us, occur relatively rarely.

The Peasant World View

The Hungarian peasant had a command of certain ideas and knowledge of the surrounding world, our earth and the Universe. By "world view" we mean the entirety of these ideas and knowledge, which are interwoven into every phase of life. We also include in this terminology experience acquired at school and from reading, or just learned from the teachings of religion. Beside the rational elements, irrational elements played an extraordinarily great role in developing this world view.

There is a stratum that can be traced right back to the Finno-Ugric period, while other parts are survivals of ancient European cultures. Much was learned from the surrounding peoples; some of this knowledge originates from the literature of the Middle Ages, while other ideas were developed by the Hungarian peasantry itself on this multi-layered foundation. Naturally, all of these were more or less influenced by Christian perception. We cannot venture to do more than throw light on a few areas and illuminate certain characteristic parts of the picture.

According to folk belief, water surrounds the entire universe, and water holds up both earth and sky. Three worlds are nestled in this water, and mankind lives on the middle one. There is an upper world, with a lake of milk lying in it. Angels bathe in this and frequently visit heaven from there. The lower world can be reached through a hole. It is called Dragon Country *(Sárkányország),* or sometimes hell *(pokol).* The end of the world is located where these worlds come in contact. The concept of this layered universe is fairly widespread in the Hungarian world of beliefs, but in some places it is made up of even layers in people's imagination.

The most important element of the system is the *sun,* which rises in the east, and in the evening sinks into the sea in the west. In the course of the night it wanders back to the east under the sea, so that at dawn it can re-emerge at the usual spot. This is precisely why the appearance and warming of the sun is connected in many ways to peasant life. In the spring, the children call the heat-giving sun this way:

> *Sun shine, pray,*
> *Saint George Day!*
> *Frisky lambkins*
> *In yond meadow*
> *Freeze all day!*
> *Spread on ground your*
> *Coat of leather,*
> *May God give us*
> *Best of weather!*
> Szőreg
> (former Torontál County)

Incantations to ward off illness and bring it to an end are most successful when recited at sunrise:

> *Even as the sun goes up,*
> *Even as the sun goes down,*
> *You should go away.*
> *Neither sent for,*
> *Nor awaited,*
> *Whence you came, thither you should disappear.*
> Zagyvarékas (Szolnok County)

Even more beliefs are attached to the *moon* than to the sun, since it changes in size constantly. It is generally believed that St. David is sitting in the moon playing the violin or the harp:

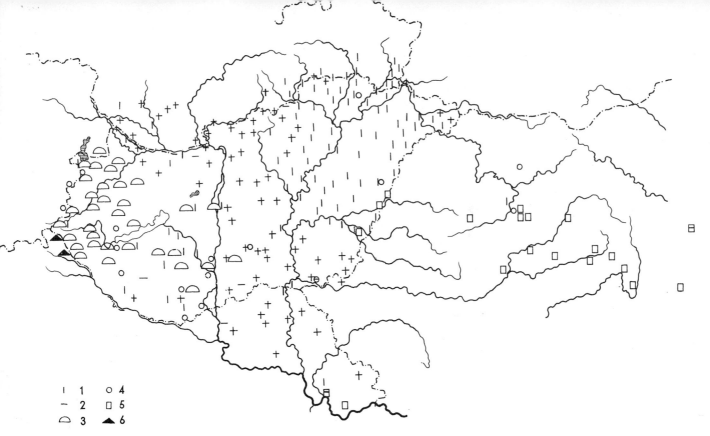

Fig. 233. Explanations of the spots on the moon. 1. David making music. 2. Cicelle is dancing (or both together). 3. A man (David) chopping wood. 4. A man (David) carrying straw, hay, vineshoots or firewood. 5. A herdsman (David) drying his footrag. 6. A man ploughing with an ox.

I	1	o	4
–	2	□	5
◠	3	▲	6

In the moon Saint David sits,
Fiddles when his fancy bids.
Báránd (former Bihar County)

So says a children's ditty from the Sárrét about the moon. In other places they believe that the easily visible spots on the full moon are the footrags of St. David. They also attribute a special importance in agriculture to the new moon and to the full moon. We know of far-reaching traditions of this. Thus the pedagogue Comenius writes the following in the middle of the 17th century: "Cut down the trees after the full moon, so they will not become worm-eaten." It is also generally believed that plants growing above ground need to be planted with the waxing moon, and plants growing underground with the waning moon, that is, at the time when the moon is "underground". And the moon also has a significant role in weather prediction. If its halo is large, rain is expected. Longer-range weather may also be predicted from its position. It is believed in the Jászság that if the tip of the new moon is upright, there will be much rainfall during the month; if it is downwards, little rain can be expected.

Investigation of peasant knowledge about the *starry sky* has already elicited good results. The Kolozsvár calendar at the end of the 16th century acknowledged that comets cause wars and disasters. This belief is still general today, and naturally, not just in the Hungarian linguistic region. The three stars located next to each other in the Orion constellation are called Reaper *(Kaszás)* or Three Reapers *(Három Kaszás)*. In the same connection Sirius is mentioned as the Lame Girl *(Sánta Leány)* or Lame Kate *(Sánta Kata)*. It is thought that she carries dinner to the three reapers working out in the field. In Transylvania the name of Orion is St. Peter's Rod *(Szent Péter pálcája)*. The Hungarian names for the constellation Orion are rooted in European traditions, which also preserved the classical Greek and Roman antecedents. The most widely known constellation is the Big Dipper, which is considered to be an ox cart *(göncölszekér)*, with four wheels and a pole. On beautiful summer nights even the young manservant can be seen by its central star, when the Milky Way also appears. Someone from Szőreg (former Torontál County) said about this: "The Big Dipper cart belonged to St. Peter. St. Peter went off to steal straw, and the field-guard caught him at it; he didn't want to let him take the straw. Then, as St. Peter drove the oxen fast, he scattered the straw, and since that time the Milky Way has been seen in the sky." This is again a belief connecting the Hungarians not only with Europe but also with the Near East.

According to folk belief, the *rainbow* is a sign that God will not destroy the world again by flood. They hold that where it reaches the ground is the end of the world, and if somebody points at it with a finger, they immediately make him bite it, so as not to cause calamity. People also predict the crop from it; if there is much yellow in the first rainbow of the spring, then there will be much corn, if the green stripe is wide, then the wheat harvest will be good, and much red promises a rich yield of wine.

Peasants predict *wind* a day in advance. If the sun goes down in a red cloud, there will be much wind the next day. They hold this to be true in case of sunrise also. The *whirlwind* was held to be the most dangerous among the winds, because a *táltos, garabonciás* or witch could travel in them from one place to another. Therefore a sickle, clods of earth, or other things were thrown into whirlwinds, but they had to be very careful that the one inside the whirlwind should not take revenge on them. Sometimes, they would grab a sieve, because by looking through it, the witch inside could be seen.

People tried to find satisfactory explanations for various natural phenomena which could not be explained rationally. Such explanations and beliefs not only took root but were also further developed. Similarly various metals were endowed with supernatural characteristics and power. Part of these beliefs derive from ancient times when various metals, because of their scarcity, represented a particular value. In the Hungarian language, the name of gold *(arany)*, silver *(ezüst)*, tin *(ón)*, lead *(ólom)*, and iron *(vas)* originate from the Finno-Ugric period, so it is likely that traditions of a long past adhere to them.

Beliefs connected with *gold* are often mixed with those referring to treasure in general. It is believed that gold gets purified every seven years, mostly on the night of St. George's Day (April 24), when it burns with a blue flame that can be seen above the ground. At this time people throw a piece of rag or a footrag on the flame so that the treasure should not sink back into the depths again. However, they usually chide gold and other treasure with a curse to insure that it will be dug up only at the cost of some sacrifice, generally a chicken or a cock. A man could not utter a sound or curse while digging for treasure, because then it would disappear into the depths and no trace of it could be found for the next seven years.

The largest number of beliefs are attached to *iron* and to objects made from it. Some of these may originate from the period when iron, a new metal, eclipsed everything else in the making of articles of consumption. Beliefs connected with *horseshoes* are known even to this day. Horseshoes can be found in many places nailed to the threshold even of city apartments. If they are turned inward, so that their shanks face towards the apartment and their curvature outward, they ward off trouble coming from the outside; if they face in the opposite direction, that means that the horseshoe is not allowing good fortune to leave the house. Horseshoes were also held to be capable of counteracting the bewitching of milk and sickness of animals, and their power could be increased by making them red hot. But any kind of iron material is suitable for warding off troubles, such as storm or hail. During a hailstorm, they throw an ax into the yard, blade up. If the ax cuts a piece of ice in half, then the clouds part immediately. In other places a fork and knife are crossed on the table or a sickle is thrown in the direction of the storm during thunder and lightning. All this is connected with the belief that the storm was let loose by the *garabonciás,* or by witches, or evil spirits who have to be wounded and chased away by various kinds of iron objects.

Iron objects were considered to be suitable for preventing and warding off many forms of witchcraft. Here, again, we can speak only of the defence against bewitching spirits who were supposed to be afraid of iron and tools made out of iron. Thus a knife was put into the boot of the bridegroom to preserve him from illness, or a dismantled ax was hidden under the bed of a woman in childbirth to ease her labour. They bathed the child in water that was poured into the tub on the blade of a scythe. On the other hand, they took away all iron from the clothes and boots of the dead and from the hair of dead women, so that these would not cause difficulties for them in the other world. There must have been some idea in this that ghosts are afraid of iron, perhaps because they had once been defeated by iron implements. For the same reasons, a significant role was also attributed to iron objects in preventing the bewitching of animals. The following, dated 1731, was written during a witch trial: "He bid him drive his cattle to him; then, on driving them home, he pulled a chain through the gate and drove the cattle through it, so that no harm should ever come to them." To counteract milk being bewitched, people stuck a knife or knocked an ax into the milk poured into the trough, or they milked onto a red-hot plough iron, sickle, or horseshoe, which made the witch who caused the trouble appear.

We have spoken about *fire* in regard to iron; purifying powers were generally attributed to fire. This is why people jump over a fire during certain customs (cf. p. 649), and that is why they heat iron with it. Fire is generally held to be good-natured because it warms, cooks, and bakes for people and carries out other useful activities. If wet food makes a "crying" sound there will be quarrelling in the house. To ward that off, people spit into the fire, but never pour water on it.

Naturally, many beliefs are attached to the person who works with iron and fire, to the *smith* in particular. He already enjoyed a great deal of respect among the conquering Magyars. Many distinguished families of the Conquest period claim their origin from smith ancestors. Besides working with iron, smiths were knowledgeable about curing illnesses. The best teeth pullers and removers of cataracts came from among them. They were also excellent animal doctors, mixing both rational and irrational elements in their curing work.

A great number of irrational beliefs are also attached to cultivated plants. Thus, for example, people believed that the wheat will be blighted if it is sown while the church bell rings, if they smoke a pipe or put a hat on the table during the time of sowing, or if bread is baked on the day of the sowing or on Friday. On the other hand, they thought that if peals of thunder can be heard in the sky before St. George's Day, or if it rained on the way home from Christmas Mass, there was prospect for a good harvest. If poppy seeds are sown on Shrove Tuesday the crop will not be wormy, but in order to avoid this pest, it was prohibited to talk to anybody during the time of sowing, and the peasants did not accept even greetings then.

Many of the notions connected with plants that grow wild are related to St. George's Day. The herdsmen went at this time to collect those grasses they used for smoking the pasture and the fold so that the stock could never break out from that circle. The women at this time collected nine kinds of herbs from nine fields, and the cow they fed it to was sure to give plenty of milk that year. They searched for a long time for vervain, because if someone held it in his hand he could open shackles and every lock with it, and some even believed that it could make its owner invisible.

A vast amount of knowledge of different origins adhered to domestic animals as well as to wild beasts. Thus it was held that birds speak to each other. Certain people were said to understand the speech of animals. The greatest number of beliefs was undoubtedly attached to the *snake*. Its name, *kígyó*, is one of the oldest words of Finno-Ugric origin and was known already in the Ural period. Still, in certain regions the word is not uttered even today, although everybody knows it; people prefer to call it *csúszó* (glider) after its characteristic movement. We find similar naming procedures, precisely in connection with animals, in fairly large numbers in the Hungarian language. It was believed that some snakes were related to dragons, and this kind was in most cases malicious and equally dangerous to man and beast. The house snake and the white snake mentioned in the various sources were considered to be good-natured. They wrote in 1805 about such a white snake: "All animals, wild creatures, birds, grass, and trees will be understood by the one who eats the flesh of the white snake or at least sucks on its bones; and the white snake lives at the root of such hazelnut trees on the top of which mistletoe grows." It was believed that snakes climb into the sick man and clean out his insides. In the spring, the snakes gather in a large group and, led by the king of the snakes, blow stones. The serpentine *(kígyókő)* is, so they say, the size of a diamond and is guarded by the snake king. A man can acquire it by rolling a cart among them; when they disperse, the stone left behind will assure invisibility to the man.

In connection with *bees,* they believed that the farmer should not give out anything from the house until Joseph's Day (March 19), because if he did, he would deliver the yield of the honey with it. If the queen bee is stolen, then the entire hive of bees dies of sorrow. But a hive which has been stolen collects and proliferates especially well, so that this kind of stealing was condemned less severely.

In regard to *parts of the human body*, right and left sides were differentiated. The former is the lucky side which is why people get off the bed on that side, just as the proverb says: "He got up with the left foot," which is to say, someone is angry, ill-tempered. Furthermore, witches work with their left hand to carry out all activities that have some kind of supernatural connection. Important trips are started on the right foot; going off to work, to hunt, or to get married, etc. These superstitions are still alive in many areas even today.

Special magic qualities were attributed to *hair*. That is why a little was cut from the hair of infants and hidden under the threshold. Women collected the hair they daily combed out, and after their death it was put in their coffin, because those who burned it were not able to find it any more at Resurrection. Similarly, *fingernails* were cherished very carefully. The nails of infants were not cut until one year of age, but were chewed off instead. The cut off nails always had to be collected and burned or, even better, buried somewhere, because otherwise there would be no rest after death for the spirit continually coming back to collect its nails.

What has been said so far gives only a glimpse of the world of beliefs that extended to every area of life and naturally was equally tied to buildings, transportation, cleansing one's body, washing, and every kind of housework, as it was also to certain occupations, to sicknesses, and to the great turning points of life.

This world of belief, living and lifeless things, were populated with good and bad spirits, whose characteristics had to be known exactly so that it would be possible to live with them, or rather to influence their power.

Actions Connected with the World of Beliefs

The Hungarian peasants' world of belief consisted not only of facts, prescriptions, prohibitions, and certain premonitory signs of predictions, but also of a series of differently motivated actions. Some of these are attempts to bring about certain goals, others are used for bewitching, and still others, for curing. There are also activities aimed at prevention and avoidance. Naturally, these actions were often related to one another, in which case we, too, shall introduce them together.

We know of numerous procedures to assure *health* and *beauty*. Thus before sunrise on Good Friday, girls brought water from the river or the well, because those who wash in this will be healthy all the year around. During the holy week before Easter, some people threw a red apple into the well and both man and beast drank of it in order to keep their health throughout the year. It was said that eating bread crust keeps you red-cheeked all year, while girls liked to eat lentils on Saturday so as to make themselves beautiful for Sunday. Lentil was also consumed in the food for New Year to help preserve health and good looks. Children rolled in the first snow to improve their health. Washing the face in March snow

promised beauty for girls. Little girls stood outside in pouring rain and
waited for their hair to grow with the following ditty:

> *Rain, raining rain,*
> *Till tomorrow rain.*
> *Thrive and thicken wheat,*
> *Speed the crop of oat.*
> *Let my head of hair be*
> *Like the filly's tail,*
> *Nay a little longer,*
> *Like the Danube's length,*
> *Nay a little longer,*
> *Like the ocean's breadth.*
> Csongrád (Csongrád County)

In the interest of increasing the yield of *milk* and *butter*, the Palotses fed
the cow bloodgrass *(sanguisorba),* dried, crushed and mixed with salt.
They tried, among the Hungarians of Nyitra County, to put a spell on
the new churn so that it would curdle the greatest possible amount of
cream to make butter. To do so they rinsed it with water dipped from
three rivers, in which they had boiled pebbles collected on the river
shore; others claimed that the juice of grass picked from nine boundaries
or from a grave was the best charm. There is a legend about a woman
who walked about the room or went to the crossroads with the churn on
her back, and by the time she had returned, there was already butter
inside. If milk was difficult to curdle, then it was urged with songs. One
such was recorded in Zagyvarékás (Szolnok County):

> *Maiden girl, Saint Margaret,*
> *Turn our milk and clot it;*
> *Girl with child lives down the way*
> *Wishes for some butt'ry whey.*
> *Milk, curd, clotted cream,*
> *Miska, wake up from your dream.*
> *Curdle, curdle, churn it,*
> *Into butter turn it!*
> *Down the village lives a maid*
> *Butter, milk is what she craves.*
> *Curdle, curdle, churn it,*
> *Into butter turn it!*
> *Holy Philip, Holy Paul,*
> *Come here straight,*
> *Come and put in it some five or six*
> *Like this little Tibi's pate.*

At such times they would weave into the song the name of a child who
happened to be pottering about waiting for the buttermilk.

Among the agriculture tasks, people naturally tried to influence *sowing*
(cf. pp. 203-5) not only with prohibitions but also by actions, in the
interest of a better harvest. Thus, in Kalotaszeg, if there was a nursing
mother in the house, she dribbled a few drops of her milk on the grain to
be sown, so that it would be good and "milky". Or a man mixed his

fingernail trimmings with the grain and during sowing said the following words: "Nobody is to hurt you when I am not here," that is to say, his nails were to act as a substitute for the presence of the farmer. On the night of the Day of the Blessed Virgin (September 8), in Göcsej, they spread out the grain to be sown, so that it would take the "blessing of the Lord" and yield a plentiful harvest. Along the Rába river they dribbled the millet through a hole on a wheel to assure the secrecy of the sowing and thus protect it from the birds.

Growing *maize* (cf. p. 217) became general in Hungary only from the 18th century on, and as we have seen above, numerous urgings are attached to its sowing. Around Pécs, they threw the first seeds under the hoe through a split in the skirt, so as to keep the gophers from finding them. They likewise held a corn seed under the tongue during sowing so that the mice should not find the sown seeds. In the Kiskunság they poured the left-over seeds back into the sack and tied the mouth of the sack so as to keep the crows from eating the sown seeds. The mouth of the sack was not opened until the corn had sprouted. In the Jászság, when the sack that hung on the neck of the sower was emptied, they threw it high up in the air so that the corn would grow high, then rolled on the ground so there would be an ear on every stalk.

People watered the *melon* seed with sweet milk before sowing to assure the growth of sweet fruit. They jump up and hurry from one hill to the other at the time of sowing *gourd,* so that its tendrils should also run fast. At the conclusion of sowing, they touch their bottom to the ground so that the gourd should be equally large.

Some of the people who are said to possess supernatural power, witches especially, are supposed to bewitch people, animals, and plants equally. Small children had to be the most cared for, because if a witch only looked at them, they might become sick immediately, or cry until they died of it. The other group of victims of witchcraft comes from among lovers. If a girl wanted to charm a lover, she would bake his hair or its ashes into biscuits, thus binding the boy to her.

The *curse* is one of the most general forms of bewitching, and its concealed forms can be found in the vernacular to this day: e.g. "the devil get into him", "confound him", "a pox on him". Curses called down on thieves were the most frequent, and we know the most about these. People tried to get hold of some article of clothing belonging to the suspected thief, and while burning it at a crossroads, they said: "I am not burning this clothing, I am burning your soul and bones, you should have no rest until you return it [the stolen article]." And he whose bees were stolen said this curse: "The one who stole my bees should not be able to die until he calls me to him." The other big group of curses was attached to lovers. Thus the abandoned girl shaped a human form out of mud picked up from the footsteps of the young man, and spoke this curse: "You are not to have peace and rest until you return and marry me." It was also common for the abandoned girl to utter curses in verse or song:

Love, it's not my custom, still I curse you,
Wish your washing water blood may turn to,
May your drying towel scorch and burn you,
Till you die convulsions shake and jerk you,
Parch, dry, swell and go down, wither,
Where you sit now, darling, let you stick there.
(former Szatmár County)

If they wanted to take away somebody's luck, they spoke this curse over his reversed footprint: "Let him lose his luck, let his arms and legs dry up." There are also some curses that wish good luck to their teller in the first part, while cursing in their second part. Such a one, among others, is the magic ditty of the *gazdasszony* who is poking at the hens on Lucy's Day (December 13):

Lay eggs, lay eggs, hatch 'em all,
Woman next door, ill you fall!

Witches could do evil *(rontás;* cf. p. 675) by pouring *(öntés)*. Thus in the Székelyland a witch would cook beans and, when the cock crew at dawn, poured them on the spot where the person to be bewitched usually goes. If he walked over it, whatever evil the witch wished on him came true. Pouring the water which had been used to wash a dead person into someone else's yard caused sickness. In other places witches were said to scatter money about and, if someone picked it up, blisters would appear on him. If the roots of belladonna were dug secretly under the threshold, the occupants of the house would be bewitched by it. In the Bodrogköz, it was said that if dolls had been dug into the road that led out of the village, these kept the stock from being driven out; the animals simply turned back.

Curing consists partly of rational procedures based on experience, partly on survivals of medieval medical procedures. A significant amount are irrational methods of curing human and animal illness. Such methods pervaded every type of curing and provided protection against curses and bewitching also by incantation *(ráolvasás)*.

Incantations, as do curses, look back to an extremely distant past. Perhaps they were already present in the procedures of the pagan Magyars of the 11th century, who said the Christian prayers backwards in order to break their power and to reverse them. In Tiszaigar (Szolnok County) they expelled worms from a cow with these words:

'Tis you I say St. Ivan,
In this cow of Imre Csató,
In the speckled cow, the Pink,
Dwell nine maggots all.
Not nine, but eight.
Not eight, but seven,
Not seven, but six,
Not six, but five,
Not five, but four,
Not four, but three,
Not three, but two,

Not two, but one,
Not one, but none,
Get out of it, get out!

There is hardly any illness not connected with some kind of incantation. If somebody grew a sty, called *árpa* (barley) in Hungarian, on the eye, they chased it away with this saying: "Run away barley, or I will harvest you, thresh you, grind you, bake you, and eat you." They said the following over a broken or sprained leg: "Mend bone to bone, blood to blood, flesh to flesh, and as it was, so be it now also." They kept repeating this little ditty to put an end to toothache:

New moon, new king
I greet him with wormy teeth,
Praised be the name of Jesus!

In the Great Plain they tried to cure erysipelas with this poem:

Dry day, headache,
Leave this man's head,
May its spell break,
Seek the greenwoods,
Live in tree roots,
Find you here no rest.
Jesus, my King,
Pray be listening:
Blessing is mine,
Healing is thine.

Generally differentiation was made between illness that came from bewitching and illness coming from fright. The latter was cured by *tin-pouring women* who poured out hot tin, and the shape of the tin showed what or who had caused the illness. If, for example, a dog appeared, then by the mere ascertainment of the cause the sickness would depart.

Rabies *(veszettség)* was one of the most dangerous sicknesses for both man and animals; *rabies' doctors,* famous far and wide dealt with curing it. Their knowledge was generally passed on within the family from father to son. They kept their procedure completely secret, because if it became known it lost its power and effectiveness. The most important component of their medicine was the powder of the cantharis, which was mostly administered with brandy. The cattle was driven through the smoke of such powder, and the animal which hesitated and would not go through had the sickness already hidden in it. They therefore separated that animal from the others and tried to cure it.

Various methods were known to prevent bewitching. Among these *smoking* played an especially important role. A fire was made from nine corn cobs, three beans, three cloves of garlic, the skin of three potatoes, a handful of sugar, and a pinch of incense, lit with the help of a bundle of straw, and the bewitched child was held over it. To fend off the evil eye the child had to be bathed in milk before sunrise. If the child was a girl, they gave the milk it was bathed in to a female dog; if it was a boy, they gave it to a male dog. They bathed a sick person in juices boiled from the

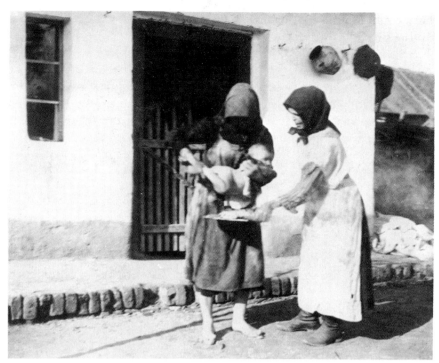

310. Smoking against the evil eye
Tunyog, Szabolcs-Szatmár County

311. Spinning the sieve
Beregújfalu, former Bereg County

leaves of nine kinds of fruit trees, then poured the juice out backhandedly in the direction of the west.

Activities serving the *warding off* of bewitching, sickness, and trouble make up a significant part of the world of folk beliefs. To prevent bewitching, the bride-to-be put money in her shoe and walked on it. Pregnant women lay under a cobweb for the same reason. They tied a red ribbon on the small child's arm to protect him from the Evil Eye. If someone was eating something for the first time that year, then he first said this little poem:

> *Take in novelty,*
> *Pox on lords and royalty!*

A few stalks of grain were left on the field after harvest to keep the birds from damaging the next year's crop. To protect the new-born colt from witchcraft, they tied about its neck a few hairs from a mare's tail.

Prevention is an action or procedure carried out against an external

312. Divination with beans on a sieve Hajcsána, Moldavia (Egyházaskozár, Baranya County)

force. Thus they put the baker's shovel and the poker in front of the house to keep the lightning from striking. Even today, and in many settlements, the belief exists that ringing bells against the storm keeps destruction from the fields and from the village.

The world of folk beliefs, by losing its social and economic foundation, gave way to rational knowledge and has in large part disappeared. However, the survival of it still lives in everyday speech. If we cannot explain someone's behaviour, we say that "the devil got into him", or if someone does his work well and quickly that he "became *táltos*-like." We could give a long list of such expressions, now detached from their original content. However, certain remnants of beliefs do exist to this day, not only among village dwellers but among city dwellers as well. Thus many people still show their money to the new moon with these words: "May your father and mother come here," hoping that their money will grow in direct proportion with the moon. It is not customary to say "thank you" for medicine given as a present, because it will lose its efficacy. Pricking or cutting tools should not be given as presents, because they cut off friendship, or, if such a gift is given, then the giver pricks the finger of the new owner and in this way insures that there will not be any more trouble. Nobody spends money on Monday if possible. The first customer, because he brings luck, is valued even by the market women of the capital. However, meeting a woman first in the morning does not bring luck. Hunters and fishermen also believe in this. If someone has already stepped over the threshold, he should not come back, because then he will not have luck that day; on the other hand, clothes put on inside-out mean good luck, just as do spiders, which should not be killed. It is best not to praise someone too loud, because he'll get spoiled easily; if someone sleeps in a new place where he never slept before, he ought to count the corners and then his dream will come true. If a black cat crosses the road in front of an automobile, many a driver still feels a sense of apprehension.

We have listed these few examples only in order to demonstrate how adamantly the world of beliefs of the past survives even among those who obviously know that these beliefs are mere superstition.

IV. The Past and Future of Hungarian Folk Culture

We have referred many times to the source, origin and integration of certain elements of Hungarian folk culture. We still feel, however, that at the end of our book we must summarize the situation of this cultural heritage within Europe. Furthermore, if we are to speak of its past, we should attempt to designate its present place and its place in Hungarian culture of the future, that is to say, we shall attempt to outline the ways folk culture continues to exist within socialist culture.

Between East and West

Recognizing Hungary's position "between East and West" as a matter of its geographic and historic fate, has long ago become a significant component in the concept of the national self. The concept of a "lonely" nation, formulated as "we are alone" by King Béla IV (13th century) and by the painful and proud expression, "the shield of Christianity", as the poet and warrior Miklós Zrínyi expressed it, determined almost for centuries the tragic-pessimistic tone of common thinking about the dilemma of the country lying between the East and West.

This recognition became more and more warped later on, especially between the two world wars, and by becoming part of the official reactionary-nationalistic ideology of the time, it became the source of self-deluding illusions instead of national self-knowledge, and distracted attention from the real social and historical problems that awaited solution. All of this did not help the objective and scientifically valid exploration of the special features of Hungarian culture.

We hardly need to prove that such a fundamental stand on the part of our poets, scientists, and politicians regarding the historical situation of the Hungarians as well as the judgement of foreign countries about us, made its impression on the newly developed Hungarian ethnology; its effects are undeniable. However, we want to summarize, not on an emotional basis but by examining facts, what its location between East and West has really meant for Hungarian folk culture.

A fundamental task for Hungarian research is to examine the complexity of folk culture and to analyze ever more carefully its proportions, infra-structural relations, and ways of functioning. Furthermore, it is our conviction that a really workable European ethnology is inseparable from the thorough examination of such complex national units as Hungarian folk culture.

Considering the social-economic foundation that has determined the life of the Hungarian people, and within it the order and forms of cultural creativity, the situation of the Hungarians between East and West must again be stressed. Recent historical research shows that in Hungarian history the development of feudalism was strongly determined by East European precedents, and that post-Conquest society was built on the social fabric of that society. Just as in its origin, so in the course of its historical development, Hungarian feudalism, and within it the ethnic groups, the serfs and landless cotters who evolved from various social strata, showed significant deviations from western development as well as related and parallel features. And it is instructive that on this basis the Hungarian peasantry developed similarly and also differently in more ways than one, from the kind of development traced by the general history of the peasants of Eastern Europe, which shows various degrees of retardedness. Ferenc Erdei examined in several of his works this retardedness in the process of social development of the Hungarian peasantry, and he also pointed out that the so-called classic peasant culture of the oral tradition could live its own life only within this backward social structure. The most recent historical analysis also shows that the historical development of the Hungarian peasantry and the system of its social-economic restrictions are related to the more backward Eastern types. This relationship determined the economic system of its services, the forms of taxes and labour surviving even 1848, backwardness in schooling, and the order of strict obligations that existed even in the semi-feudal, semi-capitalist recent past.

The East European peoples occupied the same scale of backwardness, although in different degrees; social oppression and economic exploitation characterized the histories of them all. At the same time we can list those social groups that transmitted to Hungary, already in the feudal period, influences deriving from various cultural levels and from various peoples. There were the scribes who wrote the complaining letters of serfs, a small number of schoolmasters, and groups of landless cotters who had learnt how to read and write. Through the migration of landless peasants, through soldiering at home and abroad, and from the 18th century on, through the travels of journeymen, among whom the working songs were born, the world of ideas and the sound of songs of the European working class reached Hungary. There were the bitter songs of peasants and workers migrating to and returning from America, songs about sailing on the sea and life abroad. The Hungarians learned these from Czech, Moravian, Slovak, Rumanian, and Russian migrants and amalgamated them with their own songs. This already shows to what a great extent Hungarian folk culture is capable of accepting influences, working with them, and making them into its own.

However, this did not take place equally in every area. Material culture, for example, preserved fewer archaic features than folklore, since it was much more strongly determined by changing economic, social, historical and geographic factors. Furthermore, transmitting and taking on cultural influences did not succeed in the same way in every direction, even geographically, neither in Hungary, nor among other peoples.

Still, looking at its historical past and relationships, we can say that the Hungarian people constitute a cultural and ethnic research unit indispensable for the effective research of European ethnology. We see more and more how true was the observation of János Csaplovics, who said in 1829 that "Hungary is Europe in a nutshell."

The type of peasant culture with oral traditions which is the subject of our examination, includes fishing implements of the Ugric period as well as forms of melody, shamanistic beliefs, and epic myths; it was a participant in that continuum that preserved many characteristic features of the ancient European cultural whole, and preserved signs of newer European cultural inheritances, as well as self-created autochthonous forms and contents. If we talk about investigations of folklore and material culture in Hungary, we can first point out that research up to now has uncovered primarily those structural components and their proportions which characterize Hungarian peasant culture and ethnic individuality in the situation between East and West.

Anthropological research has explored those physical anthropological components which are characteristic of Hungarian ethnic groups. Philology has illuminated even in its details the inner independence of the Hungarian language, preserved through its historical development, and the organic unity and rich variations of the Indo-European strata that it has incorporated. The study of the language has already shown that the Hungarian people have been inclined to preserve their traditions tenaciously, to maintain inner independence, and that simultaneously, they have been willing to adopt outside influences, though at the same time organically transforming them. *Mutatis mutandis,* this applies to other peoples as well, but still it is especially obvious in the history of the Hungarian language, wedged as it is among languages of different structure. And the dual nature of this tradition that preserved independence and is willing to assimilate shows up in every other area of the cultural creations of the Hungarian people.

Eastern and Western components have been examined by researchers in almost every area. Research has explored every historical stratum of folksong melodies, from the lamenting and historic melodies and the primitive order of sounds; from children's songs of the Ugric period to pentatonic melodies; to the Western influences that were built into this melody order; through the Gregorian and the effects of feudal court music and its world of melody to the most recent ethnic influences. We shall refer to just one example, to the problems of the melody and dance form of Hajdú dance, which cannot be regarded as anything other than the joint creation of several peoples: Hungarians, various Slavic peoples, and Rumanians. Accordingly, it makes much good sense to draw the historical and ethnological problems of the Hajdú question (cf. p. 449) within the circle of common Bulgarian, Rumanian, Ukrainian, Slovak, and Hungarian research. But the genres of the ballad, folk tale, and true story *(trufa)* also show the organic, historical intertwining of Eastern and Western cultural layers; and in fact, not only the genres alone, but often a certain ballad or story itself shows the organic relationship of motifs and thousands of years old elements. This is why we research the historical and motivational connection of a certain tale, ballad and other epic creation, and analyze the process of how verbal creations or pieces of ornamental folk art become aesthetic unified works in form and content. Thus, for example, the many-sided analysis of the "Kossuth Song" (cf. p. 489) shows how the tradition of numerous historical periods can melt in the lyrics of a single little folksong into one unit with formal beauty of expression.

We could go on listing examples. Animal husbandry, agriculture and beliefs about these, folk rhymes, customs, dramatic plays, all carry the historical layers of East and West and show their dovetailing. The witch trials, the formulas for interrogating the defendants, show instructively the copying of Western procedures and the linkage of these with the more archaic beliefs brought along by the Hungarian people. How the archaic beliefs attached to witch trials—which survive more tenaciously than in the formulae of Western interrogations—lived on, is especially instructive.

In the course of our work we not only explore the historical strata in certain areas of folk culture, or even in certain works of art. The task of historical analysis is certainly important and is inseparable from comparative analysis. We also adopt an analytical point of view that makes a historical comparative system more effective.

For example, we have been investigating with greater care than before, through certain genres and through the works of a genre, those propositions in the area of folklore that can be looked upon as characteristic of the ethnic make-up of just one people. Hungarian philology can already be credited with significant results in the exposition of the proportions of historical strata. Researchers of the Hungarian folk tale have also made attempts to achieve this. We ourselves referred to the instability of these experiments and comparisons, to the disproportionate nature of collecting, and not infrequently to the methodological dangers of given comparisons within this area. Such misgivings do not mean the postponement of research. As we think it necessary to prepare international and national type- and motif-catalogues, so in the same way we take into account the compound proportion of certain genres and areas of creativity, the proportions of historical and ethnic elements. It is clear that this proportion-assembling, this making of charts, the assembling of strata statistics, will be incomplete, and that from decade to decade the results will need to be corrected in the light of new collecting and new analysis, but this is also the way it is with the catalogues of tales or big dictionaries that contain the treasure house of languages.

But if we really want to complete the summary of European ethnology on the basis of facts and interrelationships, we must undertake to measure by nations, ethnic units, genres and subject groups the historical and ethnic proportions of organically or externally interwoven elements. Another regularity and system of affinity evolves in front of us. It may come to light how strongly certain peoples, ethnic units, preserve their traditional forms and contents, what formal solutions and expressions of content are more likely to be used, from which ethnic group, neighbouring or distant people they prefer to adopt creations and methods of solution, what group or people is the one they prefer to ignore or to maintain only superficial contact with. It may come to light what historical period can be called more extensive (cf. pp. 26-34), more permanent in its effect on certain people; where a break in continuity, oblivion shows up; what genres, groups of themes, and forms drop out of memory and out of the custom of cultural recreation—all this may come to light. The analysis and comparison of proportions gives firmer foundations to analyzing certain types and motifs, to recognizing formal signs in the making, and to their ethnic and national fixing.

The examination of such proportions also helps us understand how a certain ethnic unit, a people or a nation is able to preserve its independent inner style—that is, in its historical evolution and degree of social development, to what extent it builds its culture organically or superficially, and what the characteristic marks and creative methods of its culture are. Today even research in comparative literary history and the history of civilization emphasizes the mistake formerly made in old methods of comparison: they examined only the print of transmission in certain cultural creations, objects, institutions, or genres, as though they were some kind of invading foreign element, although in the process of transmission and adoption, the process itself and the evolving results are equally important.

According to an old and antiquated theory on the history of Hungarian civilization, every significant creation of Hungarian culture arrived through the "Vienna Gate", that is, from the West. In making their examinations, those holding to this conception placed weight only on the process of transmission. Today nobody can doubt that mutual influence in culture develops among peoples who live close to each other.

At this time, it is enough to specify a few such instances. The history of Hungarian civilization proves that the pre-Conquest civilization of the Magyars was composed of many different layers (cf. p. 26-28). And even later on, Europe came to Hungary through not just one gate. There were Byzantine traditions, the Avars lived here, many different kinds of Slavic traditions lived on locally, and there are the strata of Italian, French, and German influences, just to mention some of the main groups besides the Finno-Ugric foundation, and influences coming first from Turkic, later from Ottoman Turkish groups affecting the Magyars.

It is really not commonplace facts that we want to refer to here, nor how geographic factors aided renewed contacts in Hungary; how the Carpathian Mountain system created particular economic and cultural forms and the contacts of the peoples living here, how the water system of the Danube and also the Tisza was a geographic and economic prerequisite for the complicated network of contacts. Nor do we need to expound in detail how much European migratory processes and settlements passing through the entirety of Hungary's national history contributed to the colourfulness, historical changeability and unity of the Hungarian ethnic map.

All this belongs to the fundamental factors of cultural, creative processes. However, besides keeping in mind these foundations, and besides examining the effects of transmission and integration, the primary task of researchers is to examine within this process its stages as well as its manifested results and deviations. When we spoke of the proportion of foreign or assimilated elements in a cultural creation, we raised problems related to this theme.

While examining the music of the Hungarian and neighbouring peoples, Béla Bartók introduced a decisively important methodological theory into comparative research. We must extend this theory to every branch of ethnological research, for only then will their comparison be real and observant of creative processes as a whole. Béla Bartók examined, that is to say, not only what elements and what melody forms Hungarian folk music took over and assimilated into the system of Hungarian folk music, but he also observed the stages of assimilation, and from what neighbouring peoples the Hungarians borrowed, what had no effect on them, and what the ethnic character of a melody is, what kind of formal element is consistently left out of the Hungarian world of melody even though every historical and social reason make the materialization of its effect possible. We are trying to apply this fundamentally significant theory of research in different areas of ethnology.

When measured against other European folk units, Hungarian peasant culture is especially well suited to such examinations, precisely because its pre-Conquest historical and ethnic contacts and later on its post-settlement history show, that in spite of many different kinds of influence, it was able to preserve the traditional forms of its ethnic character and has built the new influence organically into the means and contents of expression of its cultural forms. Hungarian researchers are increasingly stepping out of the circle of one-directional examination of effect, pointing out in their analyses that between East and West the Hungarians were not only takers but were also transmitters and creators. Most instructive are those examinations of folk tales that show the Hungarian forms of appearance, or rather the complete or almost complete lack of the most generally known story-types from the western treasury of tales. We know Hungarian versions of the European redactions from the European treasury of tales that are practically mirror images of the European version, and at the same time there are tales that do not appear in Hungarian peasant tradition. For example although the Grimm tales got to the then still illiterate Hungarian peasantry in several waves, through numerous editions, through textbooks, and through chap-books, still they were never generally accepted.

Bartók mentions German melody types that reached the Hungarians only through Czech-Moravian transmission. Certain layers of the corpus of Hungarian beliefs can be traced back to the Ugric period, and some medieval borrowings were assimilated easily into it, while others were never borrowed.

The social structure of the Hungarian peasantry displays a disparate, belated development compared to the western structure, yet transmission layers always functioned between East and West, and on this Hungarian pivotal point the work of cultural transmission, recreation, and reshaping was continuous. What has surprised the Western researcher even in the past decades is the creative liveliness of this oral tradition. Thus, for example, western research in general no longer knew the richness of story-telling recreation still flourishing in Hungary. Researchers occasionally find excellent story tellers or recreators even today. Given its retardedness, this creative situation of oral tradition belongs among the ethnological peculiarities of the Magyar people, wedged between East and West.

While this situation between East and West was a source of Hungarian tragedy and loneliness for the poets of the nobility and middle class, and for philosophers of history as well as politicians, ethnological research today does not look at the past with this view. It does not forget tragic events either, but those do not influence investigations. Instead we have found within this historical-social situation one of the most prolific points in comparative research. We see that in the great Eurasian area, and within that, in Europe, the Hungarian people have represented an ethnically very sensitive focal point, a receiving and radiating centre, and at any rate, one interesting station for reshaping and forming common European traditions.

Folk Culture Today and Tomorrow

In class-based societies not only the entirety of the nation is divided into two classes, but culture as well. Accordingly, two readily definable cultures live next to each other in every capitalist nation: one is the culture of the ruling class, the other is that of the working classes. This was the case in feudal society as well, although in the Middle Ages the differences were not nearly of the size of later centuries, as a significant part of the nobles and landlords could neither read nor write, and so could gain their culture also by way of oral tradition. For this reason, their culture was very close to the culture of the peasantry. Although belonging to the upper house of magnates, Bálint Balassi, the outstanding poet of the 16th century, was still a virtuoso artist of the shepherd dance, and it is recorded that he danced before the royal court.

With time, the culture of the ruling classes increasingly departed from that of the people. That the schools assured literacy and cultural opportunities primarily to the privileged, which at the same time meant their joining universal European culture, played a significant role in this change. Something from all this could filter down to the illiterate peasantry only by passing through certain intermediaries. Therefore, the large masses of the peasantry had to rely primarily on their own resources in every area of life. Thus in production, culture, and art they created their particularly coloured peasant culture, which was defined by the historical past, by the present, and by socio-economic circumstances, so that consequently it was regionally diversified.

One of the most important characterizations of this culture is *bequeathing,* turning to tradition, that is, the phenomenon of passing on from generation to generation the totality of a culture or certain elements of it orally and by other means. These elements were not recorded in writing for centuries. Another characteristic also attached to bequeathing tradition is its extreme changeability, and at the same time its ability to preserve archaic traits. The contradiction is only on the surface, because while certain elements adamantly maintain themselves, others, for example songs, tales and legends, are shaped by their performers according to their ability; they connect certain elements and motifs according to their own knowledge and taste, and thus content and form change and become more nearly perfect in the performance of certain outstanding individuals. This was so in the area of material culture also, since during the centuries there were many peasant men, blessed with excellent technical ability, who shaped and made perfect implements such as the hoe, the plough, or the cart, thus raising the level of production.

Reciprocity between the two cultures occurred within every area of life, as we have mentioned in many parts of our book. We can show, from the 18th century on, increasingly more elements that moved, to a certain degree consciously, into the culture of the ruling classes.

Attention really turns to the peasantry and their culture in the first half of the 19th century, with the appearance of some poets who themselves came from among the peasantry. It is at this time that the discovery and increasingly systematic collecting begins, the recording and publishing of Hungarian folk poetry. In this period János Arany, Sándor Petőfi, and many others not only introduced folk themes into their poetry but also implanted the language, form, and expression of the folk. Thus certain of their poems became folksongs, while sometimes they themselves took over lines, and perhaps stanzas from folk poetry, so that in some cases it is difficult to ascertain if one or another folksong came from among the peasantry into the work of the poet or the other way around. This can be considered an intentional procedure practised regularly by poets. Once Sándor Petőfi told János Arany that he would give a good part of his poetry in exchange for being able to condense his sentiments into a few round lines as folksongs are capable of doing.

From the end of the past century there have been numerous experiments at incorporating folk traditions into the national culture in the area of folk music, folk dance, and ornamental art. István Györffy, the outstanding Hungarian ethnographer, interested himself most widely in this question. He wanted to confront Hitlerist expansion with folk culture. In the last work of his life, entitled *Folk Tradition and National Culture* (1939), he endeavoured to make folk tradition the foundation of Hungarian culture. Though today we do not agree with all of his basic statements, we still must say that numerous of his valuable and useful recommendations have been realized during the last decade.

The greatest achievement was that made by the composers Béla Bartók, Zoltán Kodály and László Lajtha, who raised folk music to the rank of written music. They were at the same time outstanding researchers and adapters of Hungarian folk music. Zoltán Kodály wrote in 1937: "Folk tradition did not fulfil its role by taking care of the musical life of the people. It is still close to life. It contains the kernel and the design of a great national music culture. The development and completion of this is the job of the educated class. But they will have the strength to do it only through spiritual unity with the people."

We could go on listing examples of how the most outstanding scientists of Hungarian intellectual life and Hungarian anthropological sciences have attempted from as early as the end of the last century to build folk culture into national culture. That this did not succeed always, or succeeded only in certain areas, followed from the structure of society, from economic conditions, that is to say, from the essence of class society.

Let us see what, after certain experiments and antecedents, the role of folk culture is in socialist society, in socialist culture. In order to find directions in this extremely complex question, we need by way of introduction to clear up a few questions. First of all, socialist culture does not arise ready made, nor is it the invention of experts, but "it has to come into existence by way of that normal development of accumulated knowledge, which mankind has worked out under the pressure of capitalist and bureaucratic society" (Lenin). As we have seen, culture was divided into two parts in a capitalist society, as was the entirety of the nation. This division is eliminated in a socialist society. Thus it is without doubt that the culture created by the working class from their own resources during the centuries of oppression must also play a serious role in the socialist culture that extends to the entire nation. Today, the method of this and the way about it is not entirely clarified yet, and we see only the outlines.

And here is where the question of instinct and consciousness emerges. In the development of societies preceding ours, instinct played a definitive role. People were not acquainted with those laws and rules of development by which economic life, society and culture came about; therefore they could not take advantage of the opportunities presented to them. This is especially true of folk culture, which was not recorded in writing and was passed on orally. The outstanding singer, story teller, wood carver, or potter created instinctively, without "expertly" knowing, or being familiar with the inner process of creating and its developmental laws. Consciousness is a characteristic feature of the building of a socialist society. We know what we want and we determine in what way we want to achieve it, and what laws, what rules we must apply and take into consideration. This is true in relation to building socialist culture as well.

Consciousness must be expressed first of all in selection. What do we want to incorporate into our new culture, and what shall we leave behind? In connection with this, let us get acquainted with the concept of *progressive tradition*. The adjective "progressive" means that those traditions are valuable for us which speak to the entire society and nation, which are in accord with our educational objectives, and help to realize these as soon as possible. Therefore, wide-ranging expert knowledge, a clear definition of goals, that is to say, consciousness, is necessary for such a selection.

Everything of value can be and must be made use of in socialist culture. Part of the agricultural techniques of the folk can equally be built into more highly developed forms of agriculture, horticulture, and animal husbandry; collective farming would commit the greatest sin against itself if it cast away usable, well-tried experience. And we do not believe that these well-suited local experiences would hinder, or make altogether unnecessary, the results of modern socialist agriculture. Today, of course, nobody wants to thresh with a flail and plough with a cow instead of a tractor, in the interest of the old techniques. This usable knowledge refers mostly to soil conditions, and to the local knowledge of climates. Since, for example, collective farms themselves determine where, when, and what to plant, crop yields have increased significantly.

Folk culture, as we have said, is the creation of illiterate people, using only oral tradition, and arose amidst a great deal of hardship. But oral tradition creates new works in traditional style only up to the time when it reaches a certain cultural level. After stepping out of illiteracy, the people of the villages still create culture, but this is no longer the world of folksongs and folk tales. We can rightly say that between the two world wars there was a great deal of refuse (sentimental chapbook novels, bad films, corny music, etc.) in urban culture given to the village by

702

313. Decorated gourd, 1969
Made by Mihály Tóth, Master of Folk Art
Segesd, Somogy County

capitalism; all this did not mean a cultural ascent for the village people; compared to these products of capitalism, classic peasant creations of well-defined form and passionate power were unattainable heights. But we need not worry about the village today, for peasant ascent in the area of culture is not a slogan any more, it is living reality. The culture created

703

314. Cigarette-case
Made by István Kálmán, Master
of Folk Art
Balatonfenyves, Somogy County

315. Water-dipper
Made by Dénes Sztelek, Master
of Folk Art
Palóc region

704

XLVII. Brandy flask
Mezőcsát, former Borsod County

XLVIII. *Miska*-jug
Mezőcsát, Borsod-Abaúj-Zemplén
County

XLIX. Brandy flask
Tiszafüred, Szolnok County

LI. Wedding. Vista, former Kolozs County

L. Brandy flask. Tiszafüred, Szolnok County

LII. Vintage festival. Sióagárd, Tolna County

LIII. Easter sprinkling. Galgamácsa, Pest County

LIV. The Bethlehem Nativity play of the Székelys from
Bukovina. Kakasd, Tolna County

LV. Bethlehem Nativity play. Kéty, Tolna County

LVI. Figure of a woman holding a dish for fruit
Made by Sándor Kántor, Master of Folk Art
Karcag

LVII. Dish decorated with a rosette
Made by Sándor Kántor, Master of Folk Art
Karcag

LVIII. Embroidery to hang on the wall
Made by Mrs. M. Sárosi, Master of Folk Art
Hódmezővásárhely

LIX. Coverlet in Sióagárd style ▷
Made by Anna Király. Baja

LX. Embroidery to hang on the wall in ▷
the style of Matyó shirts
Made by Mrs. M. Fazekas, Master of Folk Art
Mezőkövesd

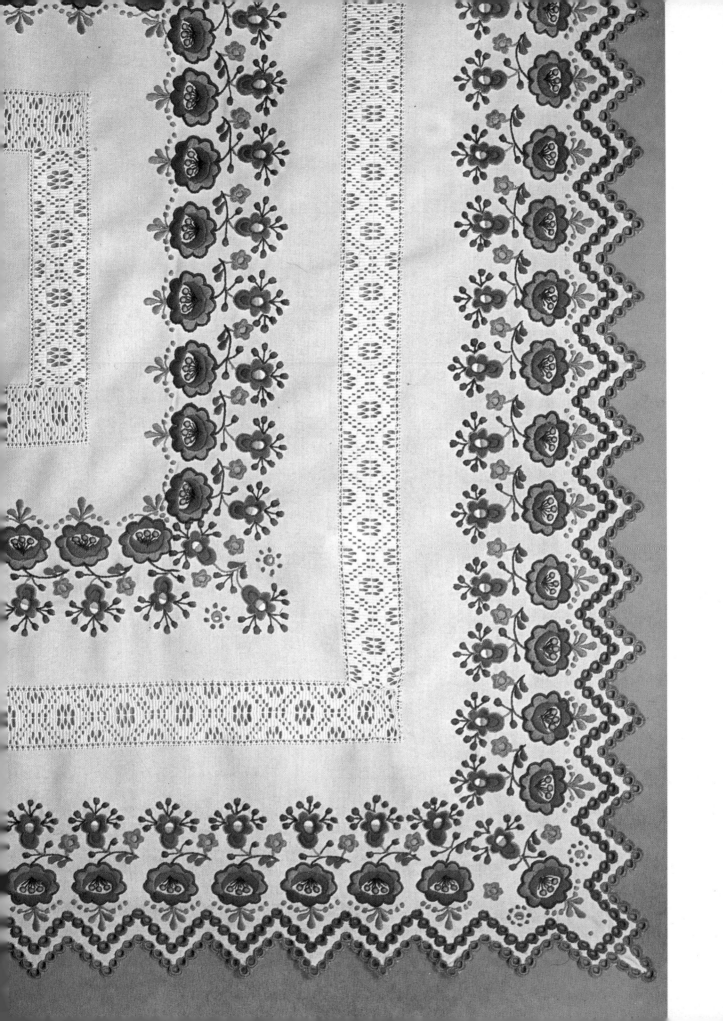

LXI. Woven textile in the style of the Palots
(from a pillow-slip). Balassagyarmat

LXII. Woven textile from Majos
Majosháza, Pest County

LXIII. Textile to hang on the wall from Bihar
Made by Mrs. M. Nyakas. Debrecen

LXIV. The house of Bori Kis Jankó. Mezőkövesd ▷

LXV. The interior of Bori Kis Jankó's house. Mezőkövesd ▷

by socialism in Hungarian society in the most varied areas of cultural life really leads our peasantry along the road of development.

In practice, the great work of incorporating folk tradition into socialist culture may be divided into two parts. The objective of ethnology, as a historical science, is to examine the traditional culture of the working classes in different periods and in different social formations. In the course of collecting and processing its material, ethnology attempts to grasp the whole culture, trying to place even the details into their place. It follows that every detail of the working people's life is of interest; research does not select, and it does not carry out observation as, for example, what trait will prove usable, what not, from the viewpoint of the future. That is, its task is to provide as much material as possible for the purpose of historical knowledge, and to provide a most plentiful choice for progressive traditions to pick from for future use. It happens only as a rare exception that an excellent collector is also an adopting artist, able to build into the new culture the traditional elements of the people, as we can see in the case of folk music researchers and in the case of folk dance.

Opinion varied for a long time regarding traditional folk culture, its elements, and how and in what way it can be built into the new culture. There were some researchers who claimed that no changes should be made, but that folk culture should be received with both content and form preserved. They consequently wanted to teach wood carvers and potters to copy the old classic pieces and, at best, to imitate them. Those who recommended this did not know at all, or grossly misjudged, folk art, since one of its major characteristics is constant change and reshaping. The creative folk artists themselves felt this and protested against stagnating with their talent on the level of mere copying. Folk culture, therefore, is not to be copied, but to be lived and further developed, because the opportunity to do so is there.

Great European composers, Bach, Mozart, Beethoven, learned from folksongs just as did Bartók and Kodály, but the historical strata of folk music are also bound by the effects of professional European music. And the peoples living in close proximity and suffering under the weight of the same fate have continually passed on to each other their cultural treasures. Bartók analysed in detail how much the Hungarians gave to the folk music of neighbouring peoples and how much they received in return. Furthermore traditional folk culture also changed continually through its history and is inseparable from the historical development of the Hungarian people. Why should we want to lead it back to ancient forms, in part living, in part already only reconstructed, and fix it there? On the contrary, the more courageously cultural mass movement approaches the topic, the more courageously it continues to build on the folk forms, the more it enhances the birth of new forms of folk culture. Just as the people continued to build the old tradition in their small, illiterate communities, and just as they kept reacting vigorously to new things, so the task today is similarly to aid the development of the nascent culture, and we cannot be satisfied with simply repeating the foregoing forms of folk art.

After all this, it is worth while to take a moment and look at what kind

316. Puzzle jug *(csalikancsó)*
Made by Imre Jakucs, Master of Folk Art
Mezőtúr

of results have been born recently in the area of incorporating the traditional elements of folk culture into today's culture. Our experiences so far have shown that fewer opportunities are offered for this activity in the areas of social and material culture than in the area of intellectual culture or folklore. Therefore, we shall mention a few examples only from the latter.

Ornamental folk art (cf. pp. 363–420) has again come to the fore, especially during the last two decades, in spite of the fact that between the two world wars many branches of handicrafts disappeared, especially the most artistic kinds. Ornamental folk art has begun to flourish again, and it has often been possible to revive even those branches which earlier had died out completely or partly (leather work, appliqué, *szűr* making, etc.). However, this new ornamental folk art differs, naturally, in many ways from its predecessors. This difference is partly expressed in the wealth of form, and more so in inner content and technique. Earlier, the peasant or handicraft master worked instinctively, that is, unintentionally followed the road prescribed by tradition; today, he is working increasingly more consciously. This consciousness was first expressed in the faithful or little altered way of decoration, in colours, and composition, but today the best artists not only apply new elements but also invent individual compositions. New basic materials and more highly developed techniques, supported by experience as well as by artistic talent, further underline this line of development.

The function of objects of ornamental folk art has also fundamentally changed. Earlier, these were consumer objects or vessels for everyday use, and their makers tried to make them more attractive with ornamentation. Today, however, it is not the function but the ornamentation of the objects that has become primarily important, while the meaning of the function has become completely rudimentary. This explains why these objects today are not made any more for peasant house-keeping —which itself has undergone a fundamental change—but serve to make city homes more attractive and homely. All of this clearly shows that ornamental folk art today is approaching the arts and crafts; therefore today we often call it popular applied art *(népi iparművészet)*.

Formerly, folk artists worked for their immediate surrounding (family, village, region). This meant that the lesser or greater community could directly express its approval or disapproval, and so could directly influence the craftsman's work. Today this happens in a different way, since the most outstanding creators of folk art and craft are known by the entire country. The best among them receive the honorary title of "Master of Folk Art" each year and their experiments are regularly supported. At the same time, the immediate control and guidance of the larger community is made felt on their work only by transmission. A smaller circle of artists and professional ethnographers express an opinion on their work, while the only way the artists can learn the judgement of the community is through how well they sell in the shops. From this example it is clear how many theoretical and practical problems arise even in areas where both professional know-how and material support are available (cf. Plates LVI–LXV).

Let us now turn to the children's games, music and dance, where we meet with another question. We had thought that internationally well-known games have completely erased former village children's games from memory. Such indeed eclipsed the larger part of so-called folk sporting games. An experiment, promising success, was initiated only recently in reviving various ball games of folk origin. The singing children's games of the youngest ones—the nursery-school age (3–6 years)—are drawn increasingly from folk traditions, especially during the last decade. This is particularly important since more than 70 per cent of the little ones attend some nursery or day-care centre where they are taught nursery rhymes, children's songs, and games largely of peasant origin. These children, when grown, will most certainly show greater susceptibility towards folksong and folk music than the preceding generations from the cities and often even from the villages.

Zoltán Kodály called folk music the "musical mother tongue", and because he was not only a great folk music researcher and composer but an outstanding musical educator as well, he did all he could in the interest of the most extensive incorporation of Hungarian folk music into the entirety of Hungarian musical life. Today we speak of the "Kodály method", and its pedagogical methodology is known and practised not only in Hungary but all through Europe and even beyond it.

While the acquaintance of children with folk music seems to be reassuring, we have failed to reach real results among the adult generations. However, even here we can speak of new initiatives during the past years. Such, for example, is the movement of the "Peacock Circle", which received its name from the peacock that plays an outstanding role not only in folksong but in the motif treasury of ornamental folk art as

317. Bowl
Made by Mrs. B. Szkircsák, Master
of Folk Art
Sárospatak

708

318. Water-jug
Made by János Horváth, Master
of Folk Art
Mohács

well. These circles have been formed mostly in villages or in smaller towns, and especially welcome those older members who are themselves still familiar with the folksong treasury and folk music of the village or region and can pass it on to interested young people. Today hundreds of such circles function all over the country; from time to time they participate at meetings regionally and nationally, and with the help of radio and television, the best of them become known to the whole country. The great value of the Peacock Circles is that, because of them the villages themselves become aware of their own values. Where earlier not much else besides operetta songs and hit-tunes could be heard, today folksongs are again increasingly popular. This movement helped the revival of certain customs to a great degree—among them the wedding —which is unthinkable without singing. Today collective farms organize some of the village weddings, and the old songs, rhymes, and customs, rewritten according to the situation and circumstances, are increasingly growing roots.

In some respect, the situation is again different with folk dances, since from the middle of the past century the simplified *csárdás* largely unified the previously rich dance tradition. This is why a large part of the strata of old dances with a long past was already lost by the turn of the century, when dance teachers appeared in the villages and domesticated there the modern European dances of the age. The excellent researchers into Hungarian folk dance of the last decades had to mine the old material from ever greater depths and with even greater difficulty than did the researchers into Hungarian folk music a few decades ahead of them.

Village folk dance groups were created as early as the 1930s; then in the 1950s there were hardly any Houses of Culture which did not have a dance group. These tried to stage not only local dances but also to display local folk costumes. However, most of them did not rise to sufficient artistic levels and stopped at the point of having learned a few dances still known to the older people. However, we can now witness not only the performance of old dances by excellent folk dance ensembles who give authentic performances of the dances, but choreographers of these ensembles also create new works by applying suitable elements. Thus new culture has arisen on the old foundation.

Film, radio, and television play a vital role in making folk dance and folk music familiar to the public. Films introducing one or another branch of folk culture are made in good numbers and can be seen by the public in cinemas or on television. Folk music constitutes a very significant part of the musical broadcasts on the radio, and the regularly returning programme series also introduces the folksong treasury of certain regions. Television has accomplished much in the way of introducing dances and those traditions where visual experience is indispensable.

Besides good examples—and we could continue to enumerate them, let us mention some that we look upon with reservations. Here we are thinking, among others, of that wave of fashion in the wake of which some people have tried to acquire objects of folk art in masses, and stuff their apartments with them. An institutional version of this is when in a restaurant or especially in the so-called *csárda* (tavern) the walls are

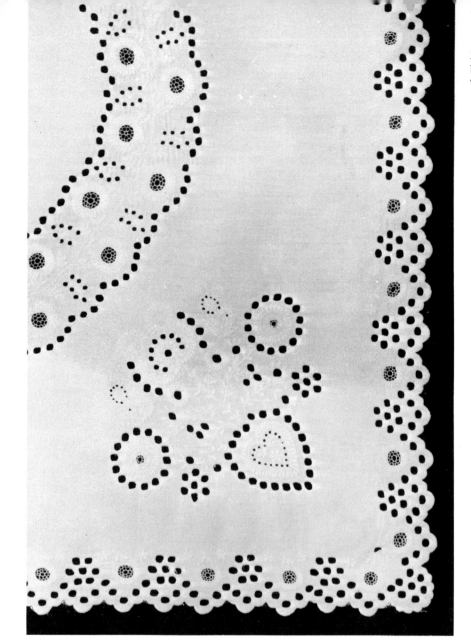

319. Embroidered coverlet, detail. Made by Mrs. M. G. Tóth
Tura, Pest County

hung with too many objects of folk arts and crafts of unequal quality. Furthermore, uncomfortable chairs and tables try to imitate certain rural predecessors. Added to all this is the professional and artistic dilettantism expressed in the entire interior that makes such furnishings worthy of the adjective "national trash". Here two things meet or, rather, clash with each other. There is a wide range of interest in and definite demand for ornamental folk art and for old forms of furniture on the one hand, and there is a lack of knowledge that is expressed in selection, over-crowding, and disproportion on the other. This poses a serious danger, since for the well-meaning but ignorant person this can give a false impression of what should be incorporated of the progressive traditions into the new culture.

Ethnology as science, a thorough acquaintance with folk art and old traditions, must also be placed at the service of education. Knowledge of folk culture brings the lesson of what excellent art our predecessors were

711

able to create under very difficult economic and social conditions, such work that can justifiably be listed among the nation's universal values. At the same time, it also appears that this culture is characteristic of the Hungarian people in its entirety, while certain elements of it unite enormous territories across linguistic, ethnic, and political boundaries. But it is clear that other peoples, too, possess folk culture, which, although different from that of the Hungarians, is similarly precious for the people who created it. So the knowledge of folk culture can be a source of national and international education.

The active period of folk art is still alive in certain areas. Its effect is important both from the social and artistic points of view, and it seems as if this effect has increasingly intensified during the last decades. We cannot look upon a significant part of the elements, the visual and creative method of folk culture, as dead material, since it flows into the culture of the future. Today we do not yet always see clearly the ways and means of this flow, but from the summation of numerous up-to-date results and initiatives, we are learning more and more about the natural laws of development.

V. Literature and Appendix

In what follows we have compiled a bibliography drawn primarily from among the more recent publications in Hungarian ethnological science. We have in no way attempted completeness but have aimed at giving the reader and researcher as much material concerning each chapter of the book as could satisfy their more particular interest. At the same time, the articles and books listed here are primarily the references used in writing our chapters. To make the bibliography easier to use, we have avoided abbreviations. We have not marked the page numbers of the articles in certain publications as these can be found from the table of contents.

After the literature we have also included the sources and other data for our pictures and figures, as well as the present-day names of places now falling outside the borders of Hungary.

ACTA ARCHAEOLOGICA Academiae Scientiarum Hungaricae (Journal). Budapest.
ACTA ETHNOGRAPHICA Academiae Scientiarum Hungaricae (Journal). Budapest.
ACTA HISTORICA Academiae Scientiarum Hungaricae (Journal). Budapest.
ACTA LINGUISTICA Academiae Scientiarum Hungaricae (Journal). Budapest.
AGRÁRTÖRTÉNETI SZEMLE Historia Rerum Rusticarum. (Journal). Budapest.
ALBA REGIA (Annales Musei Stephani Regis). Székesfehérvár.
ARCHEOLÓGIAI KÖZLEMÉNYEK (Archaeological Bulletin. Journal.) Budapest.
ARRABONA. Les annales du musée de Győr (Hongrie). Győr.
A BÉKÉS MEGYEI MÚZEUMOK KÖZLEMÉNYEI (Publications of Békés County Museums). Békéscsaba.
BÉKÉSI ÉLET (Scientific and educational journal). Békéscsaba.
CUMANIA (Acta Museorum ex comitatu Bács-Kiskun). Kecskemét.
A DEBRECENI DÉRI MÚZEUM ÉVKÖNYVE (Annales Musei Debreceniensis de Frederico Déri nominati). Debrecen.
DISSSERTATIONES ETHNOGRAPHICAE (Publication of the Institute of Ethnography of the Hungarian Academy of Sciences). Budapest.
DUNÁNTÚLI SZEMLE (Scientific and educational journal). Szombathely.
AZ EGRI MÚZEUM ÉVKÖNYVE (Annales Musei Agriensi). Eger.
EGYETEMES PHILOLÓGIAI KÖZLÖNY (Archivum Philologicum. Journal). Budapest.
ÉLETÜNK (Journal). Szombathely.
ERDÉLYI MÚZEUM (Transylvania Museum. Journal). Kolozsvár — Cluj-Napoca.
ETHNOGRAPHIA (Journal of the Hungarian Ethnographical Society). Budapest.
EUROPA ET HUNGARIA. Congressus ethnographicus in Hungaria. 16–20. X. 1963. Budapest. Ed. Gy. Ortutay — T. Bodrogi. Budapest, 1965.
FOLKLÓR ARCHIVUM (Publication of the Ethnographical Research Group of the Hungarian Academy of Science). Budapest.
FÖLD ÉS EMBER (Journal of the Anthropology Department of the Hungarian Ethnographical Society). Szeged.
FÖLDRAJZI KÖZLEMÉNYEK (Bulletin International de la Société Hongroise de Géographie). Budapest.
A HAJDÚSÁGI MÚZEUM ÉVKÖNYVE (Yearbook of the Hajdúság Museum [Hungary]. Hajdúböszörmény.
A HERMAN OTTÓ MÚZEUM ÉVKÖNYVE (Yearbook of the Herman Ottó Museum, Miskolc [Hungary]). Miskolc.
HÍD (Journal of literature, art and the social sciences). Újvidék — Novi Sad.
A JANUS PANNONIUS MÚZEUM ÉVKÖNYVE (Annales Musei de Iano Pannonio nominati). Pécs.
JÁSZKUNSÁG (Journal). Szolnok.
LÉTÜNK (Journal of literature, science and culture). Újvidék — Novi Sad.
LUD SŁOWIAŃSKY (Journal). Wrocław.
MAGYAR NÉPKÖLTÉSI GYŰJTEMÉNY (Collection of Hungarian Folklore). I–XIV. Pest–Budapest, 1872–1924.
A MAGYAR NÉPZENE TÁRA (Corpus musicae popularis hungaricae). I–V. Budapest, 1951–1966.
A MAGYARSÁG NÉPRAJZA (Ethnography of the Hungarians). I–IV. 2nd. ed., Budapest, 1941.
A MAGYAR TUDOMÁNYOS AKADÉMIA NYELV- ÉS IRODALOMTUDOMÁNYI OSZTÁLYÁNAK KÖZLEMÉNYEI (Bulletins of the Language and Literature Faculty of the Hungarian Academy of Sciences). Budapest.
A MAGYAR TUDOMÁNYOS AKADÉMIA TÁRSADALMI-TÖRTÉNETI TUDOMÁNYOS OSZTÁLYÁNAK KÖZLEMÉNYEI (Bulletins of the Faculty of Social Science and History of the Hungarian Academy of Sciences). Budapest.
A MISKOLCI HERMAN OTTÓ MÚZEUM KÖZLEMÉNYEI (Communications of the Herman Ottó Museum). Miskolc.
MÓRA FERENC MÚZEUM ÉVKÖNYVE (Annales du Musée Ferenc Móra). Szeged.
MŰVELTSÉG ÉS HAGYOMÁNY (Culture and Tradition. Annual of the Ethnological Institute of the University Lajos Kossuth

in Debrecen [(Hungary]). Debrecen.
NÉPI KULTÚRA — NÉPI TÁRSADALOM
(Folclorica et ethnographica. Yearbook of
the Ethnographical Research Group of the
Hungarian Academy of Sciences).
Budapest.
NÉPÜNK ÉS NYELVÜNK (Journal of the
Section of Ethnography, Social Sciences
and Linguistics of the Alföld [Great
Plain]). Research Committee of Szeged
(Hungary). Szeged.
NÉPRAJZ ÉS NYELVTUDOMÁNY (Acta
Universitatis Szegediensis de Attila József
nominatae. Sectio ethnographica et
linguistica). Szeged.
NÉPRAJZI ÉRTESÍTŐ. (Yearbook of the
Ethnographical Museum). Budapest.
NÉPRAJZI KÖZLEMÉNYEK (Ethnographical
Bulletin). Budapest.
NÓGRÁD MEGYEI MÚZEUMI KÖZLEMÉNYEK
(Bulletins of the Nógrád County
Museums). Balassagyarmat —
Salgótarján.
A NYÍREGYHÁZI JÓSA ANDRÁS MÚZEUM
ÉVKÖNYVE (Jahrbuch des Jósa András
Museums von Nyíregyháza).
Nyíregyháza.
ORVOSTÖRTÉNETI KÖZLEMÉNYEK
(Communicationes de historia artis
medicinae). Budapest.
SAVARIA (Bulletin der Museen des
Komitats Vas). Szombathely.
SOMOGYI MÚZEUMOK KÖZLEMÉNYEI
(Mitteilungen der Museen des Komitates
Somogy). Kaposvár.
SOPRONI SZEMLE (Ödenburger
Rundschau. Lokalhistorische
Quartalschrift). Sopron.

STUDIA COMITATENSIA (Studies published
by the Museums of Pest County).
Szentendre.
STUDIA SLAVICA ACADEMIAE SCIENTIARUM
HUNGARICAE (Journal). Budapest.
SZÁZADOK (Bulletin of the Hungarian
Historical Society). Budapest.
SZEGEDI FÜZETEK (Journal of language and
literature). Szeged.
A SZEKSZÁRDI BÉRI BALOGH ÁDÁM
MÚZEUM ÉVKÖNYVE (Annales Musei
Szekszárdiensis de Béri Balogh Ádám
nominati). Szekszárd.
SZÍNHÁZTÖRTÉNETI ÉRTESÍTŐ (Bulletin of
Theatrical History). Budapest.
SZOLNOK MEGYEI MÚZEUMI ÉVKÖNYV
(Jahrbuch der Museen des Komitats
Szolnok). Szolnok.
TELEPÜLÉSTUDOMÁNYI KÖZLEMÉNYEK
(Studies by the Department of Urban
Architecture of the College of
Construction and Technology).
Budapest.
ÚJ MAGYAR NÉPKÖLTÉSI GYŰJTEMÉNY
(New Collection of Hungarian Folklore).
I–XVIII. Budapest, 1940–1975.
UNGARISCHE JAHRBÜCHER (Yearbook).
Berlin.
URAL-ALTAISCHE JAHRBÜCHER
(Yearbook). Göttingen.
VASÁRNAPI ÚJSÁG (Weekly newspaper).
Budapest.
VASI SZEMLE (Scientific and educational
journal). Szombathely.
A VESZPRÉM MEGYEI MÚZEUMOK
KÖZLEMÉNYEI (Publicationes Museorum
Comitatus Vesprimiensis).
Veszprém.

Introduction—The History and Present Organization of Hungarian Ethnography

VISKI, K., Die ethnographische Tätigkeit in Ungarn. *Lud Słowiański*, 1931;
ORTUTAY, GY., *Magyar népismeret* (Hungarian Folk Knowledge). Budapest,
1937; MARÓT, K., Zur Entwicklungsgeschichte der Volkskunde in Ungarn.
Ungarische Jahrbücher, 1938; ORTUTAY, GY., A magyar népköltési gyűjtemények története (History of Collections of Hungarian Folklore). *Ethnographia*, 1939; TÁLASI, I., *Néprajzi életünk kibontakozása* (Development of Hungarian Folk Life). Budapest, 1948; BALASSA, I., Néprajzi múzeológiánk tíz éve
(Zehn Jahre unserer volkskundlichen Museologie). *Néprajzi Értesítő*, 1955;
ORTUTAY, GY., The Science of Folklore in Hungary between the Two World
Wars and during the Period Subsequent to the Liberation. *Acta Ethnographica*,
1955; TÁLASI, I., Az anyagi kultúra néprajzi vizsgálatának tíz éve (L'étude
ethnographique de la culture matérielle. Rassemblement de matériaux et
recherches. 1945–1955). *Ethnographia*, 1955; BALASSA, I.–SZOLNOKY, L., *Ethnographische Sammlungen der Museen in Ungarn*. Budapest, 1964; *A magyar néprajztudomány bibliográfiája*, 1945–1954 (Bibliographie der ungarischen ethnographischen Literatur in den Jahren 1945–1954). Ed.: SÁNDOR, I., Budapest, 1965; the
same for 1955–1960. Budapest, 1971 and 1850–1870. Budapest, 1977; HOFF-
MANN, T., 100 Jahre Ethnographisches Museum. *Néprajzi Értesítő*, 1972; SZA-

BÓ, L.–CSALOGH, ZS., *Szolnok megye néprajzi atlasza* (Volkskundlicher Atlas des Komitates Szolnok). Szolnok, 1974–1975/1976); *Magyar Néprajzi Lexikon* I. A–E; II. F–Ka; III. K–Né; IV. N–Szé; V. Sz–Zs. ed. ORTUTAY, GY., Budapest, 1977, 1979, 1980, 1981, 1982; VOIGT, V., *Bevezetés a szemiotikába*. (Introduction to Semiotics). Budapest, 1977.

So far two volumes of the bibliography of Hungarian ethnography have been published (see above). Further volumes will continue to be published. Those interested will find the most important Hungarian ethnographic books and studies in certain volumes of the Internationale Volkskundliche Bibliographie (International Folklore Bibliography. Red.: Wildehaber, R. and Brednich, R. W.). Since 1973 Néprajzi Hírek has published annually the complete ethnographic bibliography of the previous year.

The Ethnogenesis of the Hungarian People and Their Place in European Culture

MOÓR, E., Studien zur Früh- und Urgeschichte des ungarischen Volkes. *Acta Ethnographica,* 1951; SEBESTYÉN, I., Zur Frage des alten Wohngebietes der uralischen Völker. *Acta Linguistica,* 1951–52; HAJDÚ, P., *A magyarság kialakulásának előzményei* (The Prehistory of the Magyars). Budapest, 1953; VÉRTES, E., Randbemerkungen zu den neuesten Forschungen auf dem Gebiete der ungarischen Vorgeschichte. *Acta Linguistica,* 1954; MOLNÁR, E., *A magyar nép őstörténete* (Ancient History of the Magyars). Budapest, 1954; BOGYÁN, T., Forschungen zur Urgeschichte der Ungarn nach dem zweiten Weltkrieg. *Ural-Altaische Jahrbücher* (Göttingen), 1957; LÁSZLÓ, GY., Contribution à l'archéologie de l'époque des migrations. *Acta Archaeologica,* 1957; LIPTÁK, P., Awaren und Magyaren im Donau-Theiss Zwischenstromgebiet. Zur Anthropologie des VIII–XIII. Jahrhunderts. *Acta Archaeologica,* 1957; FEHÉR, G., Zur Geschichte der Steppenvölker von Südrussland im 9–10. Jahrhundert. *Studia Slavica* (Budapest), 1959; GYÖRFFY, GY., *Tanulmányok a magyar állam eredetéről* (Studies on the Origin of the Hungarian State). Budapest, 1959; SZŐKE, B., Über die Beziehungen Morawiens zu dem Donaugebiet in der Spätawarenzeit. *Studia Slavica,* 1960; BARTHA, A., Hungarian Society in the Tenth Century and the Social Division of Labour. *Acta Historica,* 1963; SZABÓ, I., *A falurendszer kialakulása Magyarországon. X–XV. század* (Development of the Village System in Hungary between the 10th and 15th Centuries). Budapest, 1966; SZABÓ, I., Ungarns Landwirtschaft von der Mitte des 14. Jahrhunderts bis zu den 1530er Jahren. *Agrártörténeti Szemle,* 1966. Supplementum; VAJAY, SZ., *Der Eintritt des ungarischen Stammbundes in die europäische Geschichte.* München, 1968; HOFFMANN, T., Vor- und Frühgeschichte der ungarischen Landwirtschaft. *Agrártörténeti Szemle,* 1969. Supplementum; SZABÓ, I., *A középkori magyar falu* (The Hungarian Village in the Middle Ages). Budapest, 1969; LÁSZLÓ, GY., *Őstörténetünk legkorábbi szakaszai. A finnugor őstörténet régészeti emlékei a Szovjetföldön* (The Earliest Phases of Our Ancient History. The Archaeological Remnants of Finno-Ugric Ancient History in the Soviet Area). 2nd ed. Budapest, 1971; LÁSZLÓ, GY., *Steppenvölker und Germanen. Kunst der Völkerwanderungszeit.* Berlin–Budapest, 1971; DIENES, I., *A honfoglaló magyarok* (The Conquering Magyars). Budapest, 1972; BARTHA, A., *A IX–X. századi magyar társadalom* (Hungarian Society of the 9th–10th Centuries). 2nd ed. Budapest, 1973; BALASSA, I., Mivel járulhat hozzá a néprajztudomány a honfoglaló magyarság életmódjának kutatásához (How Can Ethnography Contribute to the Research on the Life of the Conquering Magyars). *Ethnographia,* 1974; ZSIGMOND, G., *A magyar társadalomnéprajz kezdetei. Beöthy Leó (1839–1886)* (The Beginnings of Hungarian Social Anthropology). Budapest, 1974; GYÖRFFY, GY., *A magyarok elődeiről és a honfoglalásról* (On the Predecessors and the Conquering of the Homeland of the Magyars). Budapest, 1975; HAJDÚ, P., *Uráli népek. Nyelvrokonaink kultúrája és hagyományai* (Uralian

Peoples. The Culture and Traditions of our Linguistic Kindred). Budapest, 1975; VERES, P., A gazdálkodási specializáció és a termelőerők fejlődése a magyar őstörténet folyamán (Economic Specialization and the Development of the Forces of Production in the Course of Hungarian Prehistory). *Néprajzi Értesítő*, 1975; ZSIGMOND, G., *Az ősi társadalom magyar kutatói* (Hungarian Scholars of Ancient Society). Budapest, 1977.

Hungarian Ethnic Groups, Ethnographic Regions and Pockets of Survival

VISKI, K., *Etnikai csoportok és vidékek* (Ethnic Groups and Regions). Budapest, 1938; BARABÁS, J., Az etnikai csoport fogalmának kérdéséhez (Zum Begriff der ethnischen Gruppe). *Néprajzi Értesítő*, 1958; GUNDA, B., A kultúra integrációja és az etnikai csoportok alakulása (Die Integration der Kultur und die Ausgestaltung der ethnischen Gruppen). *Műveltség és Hagyomány*, 1963; KÓSA, L.–FILEP, A., *A magyar nép táji-történeti tagolódása* (The Regional, Historical Division of the Hungarians). Budapest, 1975.

Transdanubia

KISS, G., *Ormánság*. Budapest, 1937; KODOLÁNYI, J., Problémák az ormánsági etnikai csoport körülhatárolásában (Probleme der Grenzziehung der ethnischen Gruppe des Ormánság). *Néprajzi Értesítő*, 1958; VAJKAI, A., *A Bakony néprajza* (The Ethnography of the Bakony). Budapest, 1959; VAJKAI, A., *Szentgál. Egy bakonyi falu néprajza* (The Ethnography of a Bakony Village). Budapest, 1959; VÉGH, J., *Őrségi és hetési nyelvatlasz* (Linguistic Atlas of Őrség and Hetés). Budapest, 1959; DÖMÖTÖR, S., *Őrség*. Budapest, 1960; KODOLÁNYI, J., *Ormánság*. Budapest, 1960; KATONA, I., *Sárköz*. Budapest, 1962; VAJKAI, A., *A Balatonmellék* (The Balaton Region). Budapest, 1962; SZENTMIHÁLYI, I., XVII. századi adatok Göcsej nevéről, területéről (Data from the 17th Century on the Name and Territory of Göcsej). *Ethnographia*, 1969; CSISZÁR, K., *Az Őrség földje és népének élete* (Das Leben und die Geschichte des Volkes von dem Őrség). Budapest, 1973; IMRE, S., Az ausztriai (burgenlandi) magyar népcsoport szórványok (Ungarische Streusiedlungen in Österreich (Burgenland). *Népi kultúra – Népi társadalom*, 1973; TIMAFFY, L., *Szigetközi krónika* (Chronicle of Szigetköz). Mosonmagyaróvár, 1975; SZENTMIHÁLYI, I., A történeti Hetés (Die Gegend von Hetés in der Geschichte). *Ethnographia*, 1977.

Upper Hungary

HERKELY, K., *A mezőkövesdi matyó nép élete* (The Life of the Matyós of Mezőkövesd). Budapest, 1939; DIÓSZEGI, V., A palóc etnokulturális csoport határa és kirajzása (Die Grenzen und das Ausschwärmen der palozischen ethnokulturellen Gruppe). *Népi kultúra – Népi társadalom*, 1968; PALÁDI–KOVÁCS, A., A barkó etnikai csoport (Die ethnische Gruppe "Barkó"). *Műveltség és Hagyomány*, 1968; SELMECZI–KOVÁCS, A., *Reguly Antal palóc jegyzetei 1857* (Ethnographische und anthropologische Aufzeichnungen von Antal Reguly in Ungarn bei den Paloczen in 1857). Eger, 1975; BALASSA, I., *Lápok, falvak, emberek. Bodrogköz* (Marshes, Villages, People. Bodrogköz). Budapest, 1975.

Great Plain

SZŰCS, S., *A régi sárrét világa* (The World of Old Sárrét). Budapest, n. d. (1943); SZŰCS, S., *Pusztai krónika* (Chronicle of the *Puszta*). Budapest, 1946; GYÖRFFY, I., *Nagykunsági krónika* (Chronicle of Nagykunság). Budapest, 1955. 2nd ed.; KISS, L., *Régi Rétköz* (Old Rétköz). Budapest, 1961; BÁLINT, S., *A szegedi nép* (The People of Szeged). Budapest, 1968; BALOGH, I., *Hajdúság*. Budapest, 1969; BALOGH, I., *A civisek világa* (The World of the *Civis*). Budapest, 1973; PALÁDI–KOVÁCS, A., Az anyagi kultúra alakulása néhány délalföldi (bánsági) magyar faluban (Die Entwicklung der materiellen Kultur in einigen ungarischen Dörfern des südlichen Tieflands [Banats]), *Népi kultúra – Népi társadalom,* 1973; ERDÉSZ, S., *Nyírség.* Budapest, 1974; BÁLINT, S., A szögedi nemzet. A szegedi nagytáj népélete (Das "Geschlecht von Szöged". Das Volksleben der Gegend um Szeged) I–II. *A Móra Ferenc Múzeum Évkönyve,* 1974–1975 [1976], 2; 1976–1977 [1977]. 2; PAPP, Z. S., *A beregdaróci emberek élete a századfordulón* (Life of the People of Beregdaróc at the Turn of the Century). Budapest, 1975; SZŰCS, S., *Régi magyar vízivilág* (Old Hungarian Aquatic Life). Budapest, 1977; TÁLASI, I., *Kiskunság* (The Kiskunság Region). Budapest, 1977; *Szőreg népe* (The People of Szőreg). ed. HEGYI, A. SZEGED, 1977.

Transylvania

KÓS, K., *Népélet és néphagyomány* (Folk Life and Folk Tradition). Bucharest, 1972; KÓS, K.–SZENTIMREI, J.–NAGY, J., *Kászoni székely népművészet* (Székely Folk Art of Kászon). Bucharest, 1972; SEBESTYÉN, Á., *A bukovinai andrásfalvi székelyek élete és története Madéfalvától napjainkig* (The Life and History of the Székelys of Andrásfalva in Bukovina from Madéfalva to the Present). Szekszárd, 1972; ANDRÁSFALVY, B., A bukovinai székelyek kultúrájáról (Über die Kultur der Buchenlandszekler). *Népi kultúra – Népi társadalom,* 1973; KÓS, K. –NAGY, J.–SZENTIMREI, J., *Szilágysági magyar népművészet* (Hungarian Folk Art of the Szilágyság). Bucharest, 1974; KÓS, K., *Tájak, falvak, hagyományok* (Regions, Villages, Traditions). Bucharest, 1976.

I. Social Anthropology—General Works

FÉL, E., *A magyar népi társadalom életének kutatása* (Research into the Life of Hungarian Folk Society). Budapest, 1948; BODROGI, T., A néprajzi terminológia kérdéséhez (A Contribution to the Question of Ethnographical Terminology). *Ethnographia,* 1957; ORTUTAY, GY., Az iskolai nevelés szerepe parasztságunk kultúrájában (The Role of Public Education in the Culture of our Peasantry). *Ethnographia,* 1962; SZABÓ, L., *A társadalom-néprajz alapvető kérdéseiről* (On Questions of Social Ethnography). Szolnok, 1970; BALOGH, I., *A parasztság művelődése a két világháború között* (The Culture of the Peasants between the Two World Wars). Budapest, 1973; *Paraszti társadalom és műveltség a XVIII–XIX. században ([Faluk – Mezővárosok – Tanyák]).* (Peasant Society and Culture in the 18th and 19th Centuries [Villages — Country Towns — Farmsteads]). Budapest–Szolnok, 1974.

On the History of Family Organization

ACSÁDY, I., *A magyar jobbágyság története* (History of the Hungarian Serfs). Budapest, 1944; LÁSZLÓ, GY., *A honfoglaló magyar nép élete* (Life of the Conquering Magyars). Budapest, 1944; MOLNÁR, E., *A magyar társadalom története az őskortól az Árpád-korig* (History of Magyar Society from Ancient Times to the House of Árpád). Budapest, 1949; VERESS, É., *Jobbágytelek és parasztság az örökös jobbágyság kialakulásának korszakában* (Land Held in Villeinage and Peasantry during the Era of the Development of Perpetual Serfdom). Budapest, 1966; SZABÓ, I., *A középkori magyar falu* (The Medieval Hungarian Village). Budapest, 1969; DIENES, I., *A honfoglaló magyarok* (The Conquering Magyars). Budapest, 1972; SZABÓ, I., *Jobbágyok–parasztok. Értekezések a magyar parasztság történetéből* (Serfs — Peasants. Studies in the History of the Hungarian Peasantry). Budapest, 1976.

Family Organization

SZENDREY, ZS., A magyar nemzetségi szervezet emlékei (Denkmäler der Sippen-Organisation). *Ethnographia,* 1936; PAPP, L., *Kiskunhalas népi jogélete* (Folk Laws of Kiskunhalas). Budapest, 1941; FÉL, E., *Egy kisalföldi nagycsalád*

718

társadalom-gazdasági vázlata (Wirtschaftlich-gesellschaftliche Skizze einer Grossfamilie im Kisalföld). Érsekújvár, 1944; FÉL, E., *A nagycsalád és jogszokásai a Komárom megyei Martoson* (Die Grossfamilie und deren Rechtsbräuche in Martos, Komitat Komárom). Budapest, 1944; TÁRKÁNY SZŰCS, E., *Martély népi jogélete* (Das völkische Rechtsleben in Martély). Kolozsvár, 1944; SZ. MORVAY, J., *Asszonyok a nagycsaládban* (Women in the Large Family). Budapest, 1956; MORVAY, J., A had és nemzetség fogalmának körülhatárolása (Bestimmung der Begriffe "Had" [Kriegsvolk] und "Nemzetség" [Sippe]), *Ethnographia*, 1966; ANDORKA, R., Paraszti családszervezet a XVIII–XIX. században (Peasant Family Structure in the 18th and 19th Centuries). *Ethnographia*, 1975; CSEH, I., A nagycsalád-rendszer emléke a szlavóniai magyaroknál (The Memories of the Large Family-System in a few Villages in Slavonia, where Hungarian People live). *Néprajz és Nyelvtudomány*, 1975–1976.

Classes and Social Strata in the Hungarian Village

SZENDREY, Á., A népi társadalom tagozódása (Die Zergliederung der volkischen Gesellschaft). *Ethnographia*, 1937; ORTUTAY, GY., *Parasztságunk élete* (Life of Our Peasantry). Budapest, 1937; ERDEI, F., *A magyar falu* (The Hungarian Village). Budapest, 1941; ERDEI, F., *Magyar paraszttársadalom* (Hungarian Peasant Society). Budapest, 1941; TÁRKÁNY SZŰCS, E., *Martély népi jogélete* (Das völkische Rechtsleben in Martély). Kolozsvár, 1944; VERES, P., *Falusi krónika* (Village Chronicle). Budapest, 1956; ERDEI, F., *Parasztok* (Peasants). Budapest, 1973; SZABÓ, I., *Jobbágyok, parasztok* (Serfs, Peasants). Budapest, 1976; EGYED, Á., *A parasztság Erdélyben a századfordulón* (The Peasantry in Transylvania at the Turn of the Century). Bucharest, 1975; SZABÓ, K., A kecskeméti pásztorok nemzetisége a XVI–XIX. században (Nationalität der Kecskeméter Hirten im XVI–XIX. Jh.). *Cumania* II. 1974; SZILÁGYI, M., Mezővárosi társadalom és műveltség (Society and Culture in Country Towns). In: *Gyomai tanulmányok*. Gyoma, 1977; BENCSIK, J., Adatok a hajdúsági pásztorok származás szerinti összetételéhez (Data about Places of Origin of Herdsmen in the Hajdú District). *Ethnographia*, 1977.

Share Labourers

BALASSA, I., Adatok a Békés és Csongrád megyei részesmunka és ledolgozás kérdéséhez (1850–1944) (Landwirtschaftliche Arbeitsorganisation in den Komitaten Békés und Csongrád [1850–1944]). *Ethnographia*, 1955; GYÖRFFY, L., A női munka a régi arató- és cséplőbandákban (Frauenarbeit in den alten Schnitter- und Drescher-Banden). *Néprajzi Közlemények*, 1959; SZABÓ, F., Dél-tiszántúli munkásszerződések 1889–1944 (Erdarbeiterkontrakte aus dem südlichen Teil des Gebietes jenseits der Theiss [1889–1944]). *Néprajzi Közlemények*, 1966; BALASSA, I., *A magyar kukorica*. Néprajzi tanulmány (Der ungarische Mais. Ethnographische Studie). Budapest, 1960; NAGY, G., A képések munkaszervezete és életmódja a Bodrogközben (Lebensweise und Arbeitsorganisation der Erntearbeiter im Bodrogköz). *A Miskolci Herman Ottó Múzeum Évkönyve*, 1975.

Seasonal Workers

KOÓS, I., *Summásélet* (Life of the Seasonal Workers). Miskolc, 1956; SÁNDOR, I., Otthon és summásság a mezőkövesdi matyók életében (Heimat und Saisonarbeit bei den Matyó in Mezőkövesd). *Néprajzi Értesítő*, 1956; SÁRKÖZY, Z., A summások (Seasonal Workers). In: *A parasztság Magyarországon a kapitalizmus korában 1848–1914*. Ed., SZABÓ, I. Budapest, 1965; BORSAI, I., *A parasztdaltól a munkásdalig* (From the Peasant Song to the Workers' Song). Budapest, 1968.

Kɪss, L., *A szegény emberek élete* (The Life of the Poor). Budapest, 1955; Katona, I., A "csikó". A kubikosok talicskahúzó segédmunkása (The "Colt"). *Ethnographia,* 1957; Katona, I., *A magyar kubikosok élete* (Life of the Hungarian Pick and Shovel Men). Budapest, 1957; Katona, I., Az emberhámok főbb típusai és a kubikosnyakló (Die Haupttypen der Menschengeschirre und der Schulterriemen der Erdarbeiter in Ungarn). *Ethnographia,* 1960; Katona, I., Rigmusmondó és versíró kubikosok (Reimevorsagende und Verse schreibende Erdarbeiter). *Ethnographia,* 1960; Katona, I., A kubikoskordé és a kordésmunka (Der Pferdekarren und die Kärrnerarbeit). *Ethnographia,* 1961; Katona, I., A kubikosok ideiglenes hajlékai (Provisorische Behausungen der Erdarbeiter). *Néprajzi Közlemények,* 1962; Katona, I., A kubikostalicska és talicskamunka (Der Schubkarren der ung. Erdarbeiter und die Arbeit mit dem Schubkarren). *Ethnographia,* 1962, 1963.

Agricultural Hands on Large Estates

Illyés, Gy., *Puszták népe* (People of the *Puszta*). Budapest, 1953; Petőcz P., *Cselédsors az ellenforradalmi Magyarországon* (Labourers on Large Estates in Counter-revolutionary Hungary). Budapest, 1954; Kardos, L., Jegyzetek a volt uradalmi cselédek kultúrájának és életmódjának alakulásáról (Szentgyörgy-puszta) (Notes on the Formation of the Culture and Manner of Life among the Former Agricultural 'Servants'). *Ethnographia,* 1955; Veres, P., *Falusi krónika* (Village Chronicle). Budapest, 1956.

Artisans

Szádeczky, L., *Iparfejlődés és a céhek Magyarországon* (Industrial Development and Guilds in Hungary). Budapest, 1913; Szűcs, J., *Városok és kézművesség a XV. századi Magyarországon* (Cities and Craftsmanship in 15th Century Hungary). Budapest, 1955; Tolnai, Gy., A parasztipar kialakulása és tőkésiparrá fejlődése Magyarországon 1842–1849 (The Emergence of Cottage Industry and its Development into Capitalist Production in Hungary between 1842–1849). *Századok,* 1956; Eperjessy, G., *Mezővárosi és falusi céhek az Alföldön és a Dunántúlon* (1686–1848) (Market-town and Village Guilds in the Great Plain and Transdanubia: 1686–1848). Budapest, 1967; Domonkos, O., Magyarországi festőcéhek (Ungarische Färberzünfte). I–II. *Arrabona* 1974, 1976; *A magyarországi céhek kézművesipar forrásanyagának katasztere* (Register of Sources Relating to Crafts and Guilds in Hungary). Ed. Éry, I.–Nagybákay, P. I–II. Budapest, 1975; Domonkos, O., Céhkoszorú, céhkorona (Guildchaplet, Guild Crown). *Népi kultúra – Népi társadalom* 1976 [1977].

Collective Work and Social Gatherings

Szendrey, Á., A népi társas munkák és összejöveteleik (Die gesellschaftlichen Arbeiten und Zusammenkünfte des Volkes). *Ethnographia,* 1938; Fél, E., Társaságban végzett munkák Martoson (Die gemeinschaftlich ausgeführten Arbeiten in Martos). *Néprajzi Értesítő,* 1940; Szabó, L., A paraszti munkaszervezet és termelékenység a zempléni hegyvidéken (Die bäuerliche Arbeitsorganisation und die Gemeinschaftsarbeiten im Zempléner Bergland). *Néprajzi Értesítő,* 1965; Janó, Á., A társas munkák és a kendermunkák társas jellege Szatmárban (Die Kollektivarbeiten und das kollektive Gepräge der Hanfarbeiten in Szatmár). *Ethnographia,* 1966; Szabó, L., *Munkaszervezet és termelékenység a magyar parasztságnál a XIX–XX. században* (Work Organization and Productivity among the Hungarian Peasantry in the 19th and 20th Centuries). Szolnok, 1968; Heckenast, J., *Szövetkezések a századforduló paraszti gazdálkodásában* (Associations in Peasant Agriculture at the Turn of the Century). Budapest, 1969; Kós, K., Kalákák és egyéb munkaformák a régi Bodonkúton *(Kaláka* and Other Forms of Work in Old Bodonkút). In: *Népélet és Néphagyomány.* Bucharest, 1972.

Self-governing Bodies of the Village

Szendrey, Á., A közigazgatás népi szervei (Popular Organizations of Local Government). *Népünk és Nyelvünk,* 1929; Szendrey, Á., Néprajz és jogtörténet (Volkskunde und Rechtsgeschichte). *Ethnographia,* 1936; Papp, L., *A magyar népi jogélet kutatása* (Research into the Legal Life of the Hungarian Folk). Budapest, 1948; Szűcs, S., *Pusztai krónika (Puszta* Chronicle). Budapest, 1946; Szomjas-Schiffert, Gy., *Énekes éjjeliőrök a falu társadalmában* (Singing Night Watchmen in Village Society). Budapest, 1969; Imreh, I., *A rendtartó székely falu* (Order in the Székely Village). Bucharest, 1973; Tárkány Szűcs, E., Makói parasztok végrendeletei (Testamente von Makóer Bauern). *Ethnographia,* 1974.

The Churches and Religious Life

Bálint, S., *Sacra Hungaria.* Budapest, 1943; Manga, J., *Magyar katolikus népélet képekben* (Hungarian Catholic Folk Life in Pictures). Budapest, 1948; Manga, J., A hasznosi tömegpszihózis (Relationships between the Places of Pilgrimages and the "Miracle at Hasznos"). *Ethnographia,* 1962; Kardos, L., *Egyház és vallásos élet egy mai faluban (Bakonycsernye)* (The Church and Religious Life in a Contemporary Village [Bakonycsernye]). Budapest, 1969; Bálint, S., *Ünnepi kalendárium a Mária-ünnepek és jelesebb napok hazai és közép-európai hagyományvilágából. I–II* (A Festive Calendar of Hungarian and Central European Traditions Connected with Festivities of the Holy Virgin and Important Holidays. I–II). Budapest, 1977; Fügedi, E., Kapisztrán János csodái. Találkozás a középkori népi vallásossággal (Die Wunder des Johannes Capistranus. Ein Einblick in die volkstümliche Religiosität des Mittelalters). *Ethnographia,* 1977.

Parish Feasts, Markets, Fairs

Bálint, S., Adatok a magyar búcsújárás néprajzához (Data on the Ethnography of Hungarian Pilgrimages). *Ethnographia,* 1939; Szendrey, Á., A népi élet társas összejövetelei (Die gesellschaftlichen Zusammenkünfte des volklichen Lebens). *Ethnographia,* 1938; Banner, B., Házalók népünk szolgálatában a XIX. század második felében (Marchands et artisans ambulants au service du peuple hongrois dans la seconde moitié du XIXe siècle). *Ethnographia,* 1948; Kiss, L., *Vásárhelyi híres vásárok* (Famous Fairs of Vásárhely). Szeged, 1956; Dankó, I., *A gyulai vásárok* (The Fairs of Gyula). Gyula, 1963; Kirner, A. B., *A békési vásár* (The Fair of Békés). Gyula, 1964, Dankó, I., The Functions of Hungarian Fairs. In: *Studia ethnographica et folkloristica in honorem Béla Gunda.* Debrecen, 1971; Dankó, I., A lacikonyha (Cook's Stall at Fairs). In: *Emlékkönyv a Túrkevei Múzeum fennállásának 20. évfordulójára.* Túrkeve, 1971; Dankó, I., A magyar vásárok funkciói (Die Funktion der ungarischen Messen). In: *A Hajdúsági Múzeum Évkönyve,* 1973; Kós, K., Az árucsere néprajza (The Ethnography of the Interchange of Goods). In: *Népélet és Néphagyomány.* Bucharest, 1972; Dankó, I., A gyöngyösi vásárok–piacok néprajza (Die Ethnographie der Messen und Märkte von Gyöngyös). *Az Egri Múzeum Évkönyve,* 1973/1974; Dankó, I., A hortobágyi hídi vásár (Hortobágyer Jahrmarkt). *Műveltség és Hagyomány,* 1972/1974; Schram, F., A máriabesnyői búcsújáróhely (Der Wallfahrtsort Máriabesnyő). *Studia Comitatensia,* 1975; Szőllősi, Gy., *Vásártörténet, hídivásár* (Market History, Bridge Market). Debrecen, 1976; Dankó, I., A mintából való árusítás (Selling from Sample). *Ethnographia,* 1977.

PAPP, L., Ásatások az elpusztult Kecskemét vidéki falvak helyén (Ausgrabungen an der Stelle der im XVI. Jh. zugrundegegangenen Dörfer in der Umgebung von Kecskemét). *Néprajzi Értesítő,* 1931; BÁTKY, Zs., Házvidékek és kultúrmozgalmak Kelet-Közép-Európában (Hauslandschaften und Kulturbewegungen im östl. Mitteleuropa). *Néprajzi Értesítő,* 1934; BALOGH, I., *Magyar fatornyok* (Hungarian Wooden Belfries). Budapest, 1935; BÁTKY, Zs., Das ungarische Bauernhaus. *Ungarische Jahrbücher,* 1938; BÁTKY, Zs., Építkezés (Building Construction). In: *Magyarság Néprajza II.* Budapest, 1941; GYÖRFFY, I., *Magyar nép, magyar föld* (Hungarian People, Hungarian Land). Budapest, 1942; GYÖRFFY, I., *Magyar falu, magyar ház* (Hungarian Village, Hungarian House). Budapest, 1943; VAJKAI, A., *A magyar népi építkezés és lakás kutatása* (Research on Hungarian Building Construction and Dwellings). Budapest, 1948; GUNDA, B., A népi építkezés kutatásának módszere (Methods of Research in Folk Architecture). *Magyar Tudományos Akadémia Nyelv- és Irodalomtudományi Osztályának Közleményei,* 1954; GUNDA, B., A magyar népi építkezés kutatása a két világháború között és annak kritikája (Research on Hungarian Building Construction between the Two World Wars and its Critique). *Magyar Tudományos Akadémia Társadalmi Történeti Tudományos Osztályának Közleményei,* 1954; KÁROLYI, A.–PERÉNYI, I.,–TÓTH, K.–VARGHA, L., *A magyar falu építészete* (Architecture of the Hungarian Village). Budapest, 1955; VARGHA, L., Die Baudenkmäler des ungarischen Volkes. *Ethnographica* (Brno), 1960; PRAŽAK, V., Közép-Európa népi építkezésének néhány fejlődéstörténeti kérdése (Einige Fragen der Entwicklungsgeschichte der Wohnkultur in Mitteleuropa). *Műveltség és Hagyomány,* 1960; TÓTH, J., *Népi építészetünk hagyományai* (Traditions of Our Folk Architecture). Budapest, 1961; VARGHA, L., A magyar népi építészeti vizsgálatok napjainkban (Die Untersuchungen der ungarischen Volksarchitektur in unseren Tagen). *Ethnographia,* 1962; MÉRI, I., *Árpád-kori népi építkezésünk emlékei Orosháza határában* (Remnants of Folk Architecture of the age of the Árpáds near Orosháza). Budapest, 1964; IKVAI, N., Földalatti gabonatárolás Magyarországon (Unterirdische Getreidelagerung in Ungarn). *Ethnographia,* 1966; SZABÓ, I., *A középkori magyar falu* (The Medieval Hungarian Village). Budapest, 1969; ERDEI, F., *Város és vidéke* (The City and its Environs). Budapest, 1971; BAKÓ, F., *Visonta. Fejezetek a falu történetéből* (Visonta. Chapters from the History of the Village). Eger, 1975; UJVÁRY, Z., Hajdúszoboszló népélete (The Life of the People in Hajdúszoboszló). In: *Hajdúszoboszló monográfiája.* Hajdúszoboszló, 1975.

Settlement

GYÖRFFY, I., Az alföldi kertes városok (Die Garten-Städte in der ungarischen Tiefebene). *Néprajzi Értesítő,* 1926; GYÖRFFY, I., Telekformáink (Hungarian Plots). *Földrajzi Közlemények,* 1935; ERDEI, F., *Magyar tanyák* (Hungarian Farms). Budapest, 1942; MÁRKUS, I., *Kertek és tanyák Nagykőrösön a XVII–XVIII. században* (Gardens and Farms in Nagykőrös in the 17th–18th Centuries). Kecskemét, 1943; BELÉNYESY, M., *Adatok a tanyakialakulás kérdéséhez* (Data on the Problems of the Development of Farms). Budapest, 1948; HOFER, T., Dél-Dunántúl településformáinak történetéhez (Zur Geschichte der Siedlungsformen im südlichen Transdanubien). *Ethnographia,* 1955; HOFER, T., Csűrök és istállók a falun kívül (Scheunen und Ställe ausserhalb des Dorfes). *Ethnographia,* 1957; HOFER, T., A magyar kertes települések elterjedésének és típusainak kérdéséhez (Zur Frage der Verbreitung eines charakteristischen ungarischen Siedlungstypes). *Műveltség és Hagyomány,* 1960; MAJOR, J., Telektípusok kialakulásának kezdetei Magyarországon (Early Development of Plot

Types in Hungary). *Településtudományi Közlemények,* 1960; Barabás, J., A szórványtelepülések kialakulása Közép-Európában (Die Entstehung der Einzelsiedlungen in Mitteleuropa). *Műveltség és Hagyomány,* 1960; Balogh, I., *Tanyák és majorok Békés megyében a XVIII–XIX. században* (Farms and Manors in Békés County in the 18th–19th Centuries). Gyula, 1961; Porpáczy, M., A gazdálkodás módjának és a település rendszerének kapcsolata az Őrségben (The Relation between the Method of Farming and the Order of the Settlements in the Őrség). *Vasi Szemle,* 1963; Holub, J., *Zala megye középkori vízrajza* (Medieval Hydrography of Zala County). Zalaegerszeg, 1963. Szabó, I., *A falurendszer kialakulása Magyarországon. X–XV. század* (The Development of the Village System in Hungary in the 10th–15th Centuries). Budapest, 1966. 2nd ed. 1971; Hoffmann, T., A magyar tanya és a hagyományos mezőgazdaság üzemszervezetének felbomlása Európában (The Disintegration of the Hungarian Peasant Farmstead and the Traditional Organization of Agriculture in Europe). *Ethnographia,* 1967; Éri, I., Veszprém megye középkori településtörténeti vázlata (Abriss der mittelalterlichen Siedlungsgeschichte des Komitats Veszprém). *Veszprém megyei múzeumok közleményei,* 1969; Györffy, Gy., A magyar falurendszer kialakulásának kérdéséhez (Zur Frage der Ausbildung des ungarischen Dorfsystems). *Ethnographia,* 1970; Müller, R., *Régészeti terepbejárások a göcseji "szegek" vidékén és településtörténeti tanulságaik* (Archäologische Bodenforschungen im Göcsejer "szegek"-Gegend und ihre Siedlungsgeschichte Lehren). Zalaegerszeg, 1971; Maksay, F., *A magyar falu középkori településrendje* (Medieval Settlement Structure of the Hungarian Village). Budapest, 1971; Hofer, T., A magyar kettősudvarok kérdéséhez (Zur Frage der ungarischen Doppelhöfe). *Ethnographia,* 1972; Tálasi, I., Adatok és szempontok a szálláskertes települések kutatásához (Data and Aspects in the Research of Settlements with Double Plots). *Ethnographia,* 1972; Bárth, J., A kalocsai Sárköz népének települése és gazdálkodása a XVIII–XIX. században. A kalocsai szállások településnéprajzi sajátosságai (Geteilte Siedlungsgebiete der Stadt Kalocsa im XVIII. und XIX. Jahrhundert. Siedlungsprobleme der Weiler von Kalocsa). In: *Dissertationes ethnographicae* I., 1973; Bárth, J., Kalocsa környéki ártéri kertek a XVIII–XIX. században (On the 18th–19th Century History of the Gardens in the Flood Area near Kalocsa). *Agrártörténeti Szemle,* 1974; Bárth, J., Migráció és kontinuitás egy Duna melléki táj népesedéstörténetében (Migration und Kontinuität in der Bevölkerungsgeschichte eines Gebietes an der Donau). *Cumania* II, 1974; Erdei, F., *Magyar falu* (Hungarian Village). Budapest, 1974; Juhász, A., Telekrendezés a szegedi tanyákon (Hofanlage in den Gehöften um Szeged). *Ethnographia,* 1974; Mezősi, K., Kiskunfélegyháza településtörténete és XVIII. századi társadalma (Die Siedlungsgeschichte der Stadt Kiskunfélegyháza und ihre Gesellschaft im XVIII. Jahrhundert). *Cumania* II., 1974; Fehér, Z., A bátyai szállások (Die Standplätze von Bátya). *Cumania* II., 1974; Bárth, J., *A kalocsai szállások településrajza* (The Settlement Pattern of Satellite Settlements ["szállás"]). Kalocsa, 1975; Bárth, J., A szállás fogalma és típusai Kalocsa környékén (Types of Satellite Settlements ["szállás"] around Kalocsa). *Ethnographia,* 1975; Juhász, A., Adatok a szegedi tanyák kialakulásához (Beiträge zur Entstehung des Gehöftsystems um Szeged). *Ethnographia,* 1975; Kresz, M., Nyíljegyek Nyárszón (Eigentumszeichen in Nyárszó). *Néprajzi Értesítő,* 1975; Novák, L., Gyoma településrajzi viszonyai és hagyományos paraszti gazdálkodása (The Settlement Pattern and Traditional Agricultural Activity in Gyoma). In: *Gyomai tanulmányok.* Gyoma, 1977.

Cemeteries, Gates, Wells

Solymossy, S., Ősi fejfaformák népünknél (Eine uralte Grabmalform bei unserem Volke). *Ethnographia,* 1930; Morvay, P., Emberalakú fejfák a börvelyi temetőben (Anthropomorphe hölzerne Grabmäler auf dem Friedhof von

Börvely). *Ethnographia*, 1958; Timaffy, L., Emberalakú fejfák, sírkeresztek kisalföldi temetőkben (Anthropomorphe Grabhölzer und Grabkreuze auf den Friedhöfen der Kleinen Tiefebene). *Arrabona*, 1963; Zentai, J., Ormánsági fejfák (Wooden Grave-posts of Ormánság). *A Janus Pannonius Múzeum Évkönyve*, 1964; Kós, K., A székely sírfák kérdéséhez (On Wooden Grave-posts of Transylvania). In: *Népélet és Néphagyomány*. Bucharest, 1972; Balassa, I., A magyar temetők néprajzi kutatása (Ethnographische Erforschung der ungarischen Friedhöfe) *Ethnographia*, 1973; Olasz, F.–Kós, K., *Fejfák* (Grave-posts). Budapest, 1975; Novák, L., Halottkultusz és fejfatípusok Albertirsán (Totenkult und Grabholztypen in Albertirsa). *Studia Comitatensia*, 1973; Nagy, D., A magyar fejfák és díszítményeik (Ungarische Grabhölzer und ihre Ornamentik). *Folklór Archivum*, 1974. Szinte, G., A kapu a Székelyföldön (The Gate in Székelyland). *Néprajzi Értesítő*, 1909, 1910; Viski, K., Adatok a székely kapu történetéhez (Beiträge zur Geschichte des Széklertores). *Néprajzi Értesítő*, 1929; Cs. Sebestyén, K., A székely kapuk pálmafája (Die Palmen der Széklertore). *Ethnographia*, 1939; Cs. Sebestyén, K., A magyar gémeskút (The Hungarian Sweep-well). *Szegedi Füzetek*, 1934; Gönczi, F., Göcseji kutak és hácskuk (Wells and *hácsku* of Göcsej). *Néprajzi Értesítő*, 1905; N. Bartha, K., A kötött kapu faragása és állítása Bágyban (Zur Geschichte der Tore in Bágy). *Néprajzi Értesítő*, 1933.

The Houses and the Farm Buildings

Jankó, J., *Az ezredéves országos kiállítás néprajzi faluja* (The Ethnographic Village at the National Millennial Exhibition). Budapest, 1898; Hermann, A., Az építő áldozatról (Building Sacrifices). *Ethnographia*, 1903; Bátky, Zs., Parasztházak építőanyag szerint való elterjedése hazánkban (The Diffusion of Peasant Houses in our Country According to Building Material). *Föld és Ember*, 1921; Cs. Sebestyén, K., A székely sütőkemence keletkezése (The Origin of the Székely Oven). In: *Emlékkönyv a Székely Nemzeti Múzeum ötvenéves jubileumára*. Sepsiszentgyörgy, 1929; Bátky, Zs., Magyar tűzhelyek és háztípusok (Magyarische Feuerstätten und Haustypen). *Néprajzi Értesítő*, 1930; Bátky, Zs., A magyar istálló (ól) eredetéhez (On the Origin of the Hungarian Stable [sty]). *Népünk és Nyelvünk*, 1932; Cs. Sebestyén, K., Der Ursprung des ungarischen Bauernhauses. *Ungarische Jahrbücher*, 1936; Bátky, Zs., A magyar "konyha" története (Die Geschichte der ungarischen Küche). *Néprajzi Értesítő*, 1937; Márkus, M., A magyar népi világítás (Die ungarische Volksbeleuchtung). *Néprajzi Értesítő*, 1940; Cs. Sebestyén, K., A magyar ház ősi magyar műszavai (Die ältesten Hausbestandteil-Benennungen des ungarischen Hauses). *Ethnographia*, 1941; Barabás, J., Scheunentypen in Göcsej. *Acta Ethnographica*, 1956; Szolnoky, L., Az udvar és építménye Vajdácskán (Der Hof und dessen Bauwerke in der Dorfgemeinde Vajdácska). *Ethnographia*, 1956; Füzes, E., A magyarországi szántalpas hombár (Kornspeicher mit Schlittenkufe in Ungarn). *Ethnographia*, 1964; Füzes, E., A gerendavázas gabonás (Kornbehälter mit Balkengerüst). *Ethnographia*, 1970; Barabás, J., A lakóház füsttelenítéséről (Über das Abrauchen des Wohnhauses im ungarischen Sprachgebiet). *Ethnographia*, 1970; Selmeczi-Kovács, A., Az építőközpontok kérdéséhez (Building Centres). *Ethnographia*, 1971; Füzes, E., A gabonásvermek problematikájához (Zur Problematik der Getreidegruben). *Ethnographia*, 1973; Szász, J.–Sziget-vári, J., *Népi építészetünk nyomában* (In Search of our Folk Architecture). Budapest, 1976; Balassa, M. I., Az ágasfás-szelemenes tetőszerkezet a magyar népi építkezésben (Das Pfettendach in der ungarischen volkstümlichen Baukunst). *Ethnographia*, 1977.

NAGY, J., A Hegyhát-vidék építkezése (The Architecture of the Hegyhát). *Néprajzi Értesítő,* 1900; GÖNCZI, F., A göcseji és hetési falvak, házak elhelyezkedése (The Arrangement of the Houses in Göcsej and Hetés). *Néprajzi Értesítő,* 1914; SEEMAYER, V., Pajtáskertek Nemespátrón (Scheuergarten in Nemespátró [Kom. Somogy]). *Néprajzi Értesítő,* 1934, 1935; GUNDA, B., A lakóház kialakulása az Ormánságban (Die Entstehung des Wohnhauses in der Ormánság). *Ethnographia,* 1936; BÁT KY, ZS., Az ormánsági lakóház kialakulásának kérdéséhez (Zur Frage der Entwicklung des Wohnhauses in der Ormánság [Süd-Baranya]). *Ethnographia,* 1936; CSALOG, J., Talpas sövényházak a tolnamegyei Dunaszakaszon (Flechthäuser mit Holzaufsatz an der Donau im Kom. Tolna). *Néprajzi Értesítő,* 1939; TÓTH, J., *Göcsej népi építészete* (Folk Architecture of Göcsej). Budapest, 1965; BARABÁS, J., Füstös ház Zalában (Rauchstube im Kom. Zala). *Ethnographia,* 1969; BÍRÓ, F., Jobbágyparaszti ház- és lakáskultúra az őrségi Szalafőn (Haus- und Wohnkultur der Leibeigenzeit in Szalafő [Südwest-Ungarn, Őrség]). *Néprajzi Értesítő,* 1969; BÍRÓ, F., A falusi ház és lakás, mint a hagyományos paraszti-népi életforma tárgyi kerete (The Village House and Dwelling as the Objective Framework of Traditional Peasant Life-style). Fejezetek a Vas megyei Őrség ház- és lakásműveltségének köréből. *Életünk,* 1971; MÜLLER, R., Adatok a Nyugat-Dunántúl középkori népi építészetéhez (Angaben zur mittelalterlichen Volksarchitektur West-Transdanubiens). *Veszprém megyei múzeumok közleményei,* 1972; KNÉZY, J., A favázas lakóházépítkezés emlékei a belső-somogyi Csököly, Gige, Rinyakovácsi és Kisbajom községekben (Denkmäler von Balkengerüsthäusern [Fachwerk] in den Dörfern Csököly, Gige, Rinyakovácsi und Kisbajom im inneren Somogy). *Somogyi Múzeumok Közleményei,* 1973; BÍRÓ, F., *Az Őrség ház- és lakáskultúrája a XVIII. század végétől napjainkig* [1972] (Houses and Dwellings in the Őrség from the end of the 18th Century to our Times [1972]). Szombathely, 1975; TÓTH, J., *Az Őrségek népi építészete* (Folk Architecture in the Őrség). 2nd ed. Budapest, 1975.

West and Central Transdanubia

VISKI, K., *A bakony-balatonvidéki kőépítkezés.* Budapest, 1926; ÉBNER, S., Adatok a Bakony északi községeinek építkezéséhez (Beiträge zum Bauwesen des nördlichen Bakony-Gebirges). *Néprajzi Értesítő,* 1933; PADÁNYI GULYÁS, J.–MISKOLCZY, L.–TÓTH, K., *A Fertő-vidék népének építészete* (Folk Architecture of the Fertő Region). Budapest, 1937; TÓTH, J., *Így épít a vasi nép* (Vasi Folk Architecture). Szombathely, 1938; VAJKAI, A., Veszprém megye népi építészete (Volkstümliche Bauweise im Komitat Veszprém). *Néprajzi Értesítő,* 1940; VAJKAI, A., Élet a cserszegtomaji házban (Fonction des maisons d'une commune de montagne en Transdanubie). *Ethnographia,* 1948; VAJKAI, A., Présházak és pincék a XVIII. századból a Balaton északi partján (Kelterhäuser und Weinkeller aus dem 18. Jahrhundert am Nordufer des Balatons). *Ethnographia,* 1956; VAJKAI, A., Balatonfelvidéki és Bakony vidéki falusi épületek a XVIII. századból (Dörfliche Gebäude aus dem XVIII. Jahrhundert im Plattensee-Oberland und im Bakonyer Wald). *Ethnographia,* 1957; VARGHA, L., Családi és közösségi hagyomány az építkezésben (Gemeinschaftliche und Familientradition in der Bauweise). *Ethnographia,* 1972; VAJKAI, A., Füstös konyhás házak a Balaton környékén (Rauchstubenhäuser in der Balatongegend). *Ethnographia,* 1973.

Palots Dwelling Sites of Upper Hungary

PÁPAI, K., A palóc faház (The Palots Wooden House). *Ethnographia,* 1893; BÁTKY, ZS., Barlanglakások Borsod vármegyében (Cave Dwellings in Borsod County). *Néprajzi Értesítő,* 1906; ISTVÁNFFY, GY., A palócok lakóháza és berendezése (Palots Dwellings and Furnishings). *Néprajzi Értesítő*, 1911; VISKI, K., Bódvakörnyéki tűzhelyek (Feuerungsanlagen im Kom. Borsod). *Néprajzi Értesítő*, 1933; VAJKAI, A., Adatok az Alsó–Hernádvölgye és az abaúji Cserehát népi építkezéséhez (Beiträge zum Hausbau des Volkes im Komitat Abaúj-Torna). *Néprajzi Értesítő*, 1937; NAGY, B., A társadalmi szervezet befolyása egy palóc falu építkezésére (Der Einfluss der Gesellschaftsorganisation auf das Hauswesen eines Palócz-Dorfes). *Műveltség és Hagyomány*, 1960; BAKÓ, F., A faépítkezés emlékei Heves megyében (Alte Hausbauten im Komitat Heves). *Az Egri Múzeum Évkönyve*, 1967; SELMECZI-KOVÁCS, A., A zsupfedél készítése a keleti palócoknál (Strohdächer bei den Palozen). *Ethnographia*, 1968; BAKÓ, F., Népi építkezés Eger környékén a XVIII. század derekán (Bautätigkeit des Volkes in der Gegend von Eger im J. 1765). *Az Egri Múzeum Évkönyve*, 1969; SELMECZI-KOVÁCS, A., Hof- und Scheunengemeinschaft bei den Paloczen. *Műveltség és Hagyomány*, 1971; BAKÓ, F., Kőházak és barlanglakások Észak-Hevesben (Maisons de pierre et habitations troglodytiques dans la partie septentrionale du Comitat Heves). *Az Egri Múzeum Évkönyve*, 1972; BAKÓ, F., A föld- és téglafalazat az észak-magyarországi népi építkezésben (Das Lehm- und Ziegelmauerwerk in der Volksbaukunst Nordungarns). *Az Egri Múzeum Évkönyve*, 1972; BAKÓ, F., Észak-magyarországi parasztházak tüzelőberendezésének történeti előzményei (Das historische Hervorgehende der Heizeinrichtung von der Bauernhäusern Nordungarns). *Az Egri Múzeum Évkönyve*, 1973–1974; BAKÓ, P., A parasztház alaprajzi fejlődése Észak-Magyarországon (Die Entwicklung der Grundrisszeichnung des Nordungarischen Bauernhauses). *Az Egri Múzeum Évkönyve*, 1975; SELMECZI KOVÁCS, A., Csürös építkezés és gazdálkodás Észak-Magyarországon (Scheunenbau und Scheunenwirtschaft in Nordungarn). *Műveltség és Hagyomány*, 1976; BAKÓ, P., Tetőformák, homlokzatok a Bükk és a Mátra vidékének parasztházain (Dachformen, Fassaden der Bauernhäuser der Bükk- und Mátragegend). *Az Egri Múzeum Évkönyve*, 1976; BAKÓ, F., *Bükki barlanglakások* (Höhlenwohnungen im Bükk-Gebirge). Miskolc, 1977; BAKÓ, F., *Parasztházak és udvarok a Mátra vidékén* (Peasant Houses and Courtyards in the Mátra Region). Budapest, 1978.

Dwelling Sites of the Great Plain

GYÖRFFY, I., A Nagykunság és környékének népies építkezése (Folk Architecture of Great Cumania and its Environs). *Néprajzi Értesítő*, 1908, 1909; GYÖRFFY, I., A nagykun tanya (The Farms of Great Cumania). *Néprajzi Értesítő*, 1910; DEÁK, G., Az ung vármegyei "Tiszahát" népi építkezése és művészete (Folk Architecture and Art of the Tiszahát of Ung County). *Néprajzi Értesítő*, 1910; BANNER, J., A békési magyarság népi építkezése (Folk Architecture of the Hungarians of Békés). *Néprajzi Értesítő*, 1911; ECSEDI, I., A debreceni népi építkezés (Folk Architecture of Debrecen). *Néprajzi Értesítő*, 1912; GYÖRFFY, I., Dél-Bihar falvai és építkezése (Villages and Architecture of South-Bihar). *Néprajzi Értesítő*, 1915; Cs. SEBESTYÉN, K., A Szeged vidéki parasztház és az alföldi magyar háztípus (Peasant Houses of the Szeged Region and the Hungarian Houses of the Great Plain). *Népünk és Nyelvünk*, 1933; NYÁRÁDY, M., A Nyírség nemesházai (Häuser des Adels in der Nyírség). *Néprajzi Értesítő*, 1935; VARGHA, L., *A tilalmasi tanyák építkezése* (The Construction of the Farms of Tilalmas). Budapest, 1940; SZŰCS, S., Sárréti nádház és élete (Das Schilfrohrhaus im Sárrét and sein Leben). *Néprajzi Értesítő*, 1943; BALOGH, I., Adatok az alföldi magyar ház tüzelőhelyéhez (Angaben zur Kenntnis der Feuerungsstelle des ungarischen Hauses im Alföld). *Ethnographia*, 1947; KISS, L., A boglyakemence és élete Hódmezővásárhelyen (Der Bauernofen und das Leben um den Ofen in Hódmezővásárhely). *Ethnographia*, 1953; KURUCZ, A., A népi építkezés emlékei a konyári szőlőkben (Die Überreste des bäuerlichen Bauwesens in den Weingärten von Konyár). *Műveltség és Hagyomány*, 1961;

DANKÓ, I., Házformák Hajdúnánáson (Morphologie des Hajdúnánáser Hauses in kurzen Umrissen). *Ethnographia*, 1964; GYÖRFFY, L., Nagykunsági házorom-díszek (Façade Decorations in Great Cumania). *Ethnographia*, 1967; SZABÓ, L., Mereglyés építkezés Szabolcs megye keleti részén (Der Bau eines Hauses mit "Mereglye"-Wand in Oros. Ungarn, Kom. Szabolcs). *Ethnographia*, 1968; FILEP, A., A kisalföldi lakóház helye népi építkezésünk rendszerében (Die Bauerhäuser in der kleinen Ungarischen Tiefebene und ihre Einordnung im System der ungarischen Volksbaukunst). *Ethnographia*, 1970; BARNA, G., Kerekólak a Hármas-Körös mentén (Rundställe den Fluss Körös entlang). *Ethnographia*, 1971; DÁM, L., A hajdúböszörményi szőlők népi építkezése (Folk Architecture of the Vineyards of Hajdúböszörmény). Debrecen, 1972; GILYÉN, N.–MENDELE, F.–TÓTH, J., A Felső-Tisza-vidék népi építészete (Folk Architecture of the Upper Tisza Region). Budapest, 1975; DÁM, L., A Nagy-Sárrét népi építészete (Volksarchitektur des Gross-Sárrét). *Műveltség és Hagyomány*, 1975; PALÁSTI, P., Csongrádi házak oromdíszei (Crest Ornamentation on Houses in Csongrád). Szeged, 1977.

Székely Dwelling Sites of Transylvania

HUSZKA, J., A székely ház (The Székely House). Budapest, 1895; JANKÓ, J., A székely ház (The Székely House). *Ethnographia*, 1895; SZINTE, G., A székely csűr (The Székely Shed). *Néprajzi Értesítő*, 1903; Cs. SEBESTYÉN, K., A három-széki Szentföld székely háza (The Székely House of the Holy Land of Három-szék). *Néprajzi Értesítő*, 1905; BÁTKY, Zs., Néhány adat Bánffyhunyadnak és környékének népies építkezéséhez (Data on the Folk Architecture of Bánffy-hunyad and its Surroundings). *Néprajzi Értesítő*, 1907; KÓS, K., A székely ház (The Székely House). In: *Emlékkönyv a Székely Nemzeti Múzeum ötvenéves jubileumára.* Sepsiszentgyörgy, 1929; VISKI, K., Székely tűzhelyek (Feuerstätte im Széklerland). *Néprajzi Értesítő*, 1931; Cs. SEBESTYÉN, K., A székely-ház eredete (Die Herkunft des Székler-Hauses). *Néprajzi Értesítő*, 1941; Cs. SEBES-TYÉN, K., *Krassó-Szörény vármegye parasztháza* (The Peasant House of Krassó-Szörény County). Kolozsvár, 1944; MÁRKOS, A., Homoródalmási szállások (Hüttenbauten in Homoródalmás). *Ethnographia*, 1958; KÓS, K., A Kisküküllő menti népi építkezés (Ungarische volkstümliche Baukunst am Fluss Klein-Kükel). *Ethnographia*, 1964; KÓS, K., Építkezés (Architecture). In: *Kászoni székely népművészet.* Bucharest, 1972; BARABÁS, J., A székely ház alaprajzi fejlődéséről (Die Entwicklung des Grundrisses des Szeklerhauses). *Népi kultú-ra – Népi társadalom*, 1973; KÓS, K., Lakóház, lakásbelső (Houses, Interiors). In: *Szilágysági magyar népművészet.* Bucharest, 1974.

Acquiring Raw Materials from Flora and Fauna
Food Gathering

RAPAICS, R., *A kenyér és a táplálékot szolgáltató növényeink története* (The History of Bread and Our Food-providing Plants). Budapest, 1934; GYÖRFFY, I., Viricselés a Székelyföldön (Das Sammeln des Birkensaftes im Széklerland). *Ethnographia*, 1937; VAJKAI, A., Adatok a Bakony gyűjtögető és vadfogó életmódjához (Data on the Foraging and Trapping Life of the Bakony). *Vasi Szemle*, 1938; GUNDA, B., Sammelwirtschaft bei den Ungarn. *Ungarische Jahrbücher*, 1938; VAJKAI, A., A gyűjtögető gazdálkodás Cserszegtomajon (Sammelwirtschaft in einer Berggemeinde des Plattenseegebietes). *Néprajzi Értesítő*, 1941; GYÖRFFY, I., Gyűjtögetés (Food Gathering). In: *Magyarság Népraj-za.* II. Budapest, 1941; SZŰCS, S., A régi Sárrét világa (Old Sárrét). Budapest (1941); TÁLASI, I., Adatok a Bakony erdei életéhez (Beiträge zum Leben im Bakonyer Wald). *Néprajzi Értesítő*, 1942; HAÁZ, F., *Udvarhelyszéki famesterségek* (Woodcrafts of Udvarhelyszék). Kolozsvár, 1942; TAGÁN, G., Fakitermelés és szénégetés Székelyvarságon (Holzausbeute und Kohlenbrennerei in Székelyvarság). *Néprajzi Értesítő*, 1943; BÖDEI, J., Adatok Zalabaksa gyűjtögető gazdálkodásához (Beiträge zur Sammelwirtschaft des Dorfes Zalabaksa). *Néprajzi Értesítő*, 1943; VAJKAI, A., Adatok Szentgál gyűjtögető életmódjához (Angaben zur Sammelwirtschaft aus Szentgál). *Ethnographia*, 1945; GUNDA, B., *A magyar gyűjtögető és zsákmányoló gazdálkodás kutatása* (Research on Hungarian Gleaning and Predatory Culture). Budapest, 1948; BARABÁS, J., Nádvágás a Velencei-tavon (Schilfschneiden am See von Velence). *Ethnographia*, 1950; BOROSS, M., Az Országos Néprajzi Múzeum nádvágó gyűjteménye (Die Sammlung von Schilfschneidegeräten im Ethnographischen Museum von Budapest). *Néprajzi Értesítő*, 1954; BABUS, J., Nádvágás és tetőfedés a Bereg megyei Lónyán (Schilfschneiden und Dachdecken in der Ortschaft Lónya [Komitat Bereg]). *Ethnographia*, 1954; E. FEHÉR, J., Adatok Bernecebaráti gyűjtögető és zsákmányoló gazdálkodásához (Angaben zur Sammel- und Ausbeutungswirtschaft des Dorfes Bernecebaráti [Komitat Nógrád]). *Néprajzi Közlemények*, 1957; HEGYI, I., Erdei fakitermelés Bakonycsernyén (Die Waldholzgewinnung in Bakonycsernye). *Néprajzi Közlemények*, 1957; UJVÁRY, Z., A vadontermő növények szerepe a táplálkozásban az abaúj-zempléni hegyvidéken (Die Rolle der im Bergland Abaúj-Zemplén wild wachsenden Pflanzen in der Ernährung der Bevölkerung). *Néprajzi Értesítő*, 1957; ERDÉLYI, Z., Faközelítés a Bernecebaráti környéki erdőkben (Das Rücken des Holzes in den Forsten um Bernecebaráti). *Ethnographia*, 1958; UZSOKI, A., Egy szigetközi aranyász és felszerelése (Ein Goldwascher und seine Geräte von Szigetköz [Westungarn]). *Néprajzi Közlemények*, 1959; GUNDA, B., A gyűjtögető életmód emlékei a gyalui havasokban (Sammelwirtschaft im Gyaluer Gebirge). *Műveltség és Hagyomány*, 1960; HEGYI, I., Gyűjtögető gazdálkodás az északkeleti Bakonyban (Sammelwirtschaft im nordöstlichen Bakonygebirge). *Ethnographia*, 1970; MIKLÓS, Zs., A debreceni vákáncsosok (Die Debrecener Vakanzleute). *A Debreceni Déri Múzeum Évkönyve*, 1972/1974; Sz. FUTÓ, R., A sulyom gyűjtése és felhasználása a Takta mellékén (The Collection and Utilization of Waterchestnuts along the Takta). *A Miskolci Herman Ottó Múzeum Közleményei*, 1974; GUNDA, B., Ősi gyűjtögető tevékenység a mocsárvilágban (Primitive gathering activity in the moors of the Great Hungarian Plain). *A Hajdúsági Múzeum Évkönyve*, 1975; HEGYI, I., A népi erdőkiélés jogszokásai (1848–1945) (The legal customs of popular forest usage [1848–1945]). *Néprajzi Értesítő*, 1975; SZABÓ, T. E. A.–PÉNTEK, J., *Ezerjófű* (Centaury). Etnobotanikai útmutató, Bucharest, 1976.

Farming

BÁTKY, Zs., Aratósarlók a Néprajzi Múzeumban (Sicheln des Ethnographischen Museums). *Néprajzi Értesítő*, 1926; GYÖRFFY, I., A takarás és nyomtatás az Alföldön (Das Einsammeln und Treten in der ungarischen Tiefebene). *Néprajzi Értesítő*, 1928; KISS, L., *Földmívelés a Rétközön* (Farming in Rétköz). Debrecen, 1929; NYÁRÁDY, M., Az őszi rozs termelése Ramocsaházán (Bau des Herbstroggens in Ramocsaháza). *Néprajzi Értesítő*, 1930; GUNDA, B., Népi mezőgazdálkodás a Boldva völgyében (Volkswirtschaft im Boldvatal). *Néprajzi Értesítő*, 1937; K. KOVÁCS, L., A Néprajzi Múzeum magyar ekéi (Die ungarischen Pflüge des Ethnographischen Museums zu Budapest). *Néprajzi Értesítő*, 1937; K. KOVÁCS, L., Acker Geräte in Ungarn. *Ungarische Jahrbücher*, 1938; BALASSA, I., *A debreceni civis földművelésének munkamenete és műszókincse* (The Process and Nomenclature of the *civis* Farms in Debrecen). Debrecen, 1940; GYÖRFFY, I., Földművelés (Farming). In: *Magyarság Néprajza*. II. Budapest, 1941; IMRE, S., *A felsőőrsi földművelés* (Farming at Felsőőrs). Debrecen, 1941; SÁNDOR, G., *A hóstátiak szénavontatása* (The Hauling of Hay at Hóstát). Kolozsvár, 1944; KÓS, K., Az Erdélyi Nemzeti Múzeum Néprajzi Tárának faekéi (The Wooden Ploughs of the Ethnographic Collection of the Transylvanian National

Museum). *Erdélyi Múzeum*, 1947; K. Kovács, L., *A magyar földművelő gazdálkodás kutatása* (Research on Hungarian Agriculture). Budapest, 1948; Balassa, I., A Néprajzi Múzeum favillagyűjteménye (The Wooden Pitchfork Collection of the Ethnographical Museum). *Ethnographia*, 1949; K. Kovács, L., Die Ungarischen Dreschflegel und Dreschmethoden. *Acta Ethnographica*, 1950; László, Gy., Székely faeke a XV. századból (La représentation d'une charrue de bois sicule du XVe siècle). *Ethnographia*, 1951; Balogh, I., Határhasználat Hajdúböszörményben (Flurbenutzung in Hajdúböszörmény im XVIII. Jahrhundert). *Ethnographia*, 1954; Belényesy, M., A földművelés fejlődésének alapvető kérdései a XIV. században (Die grundlegenden Fragen der Entwicklung der Landwirtschaft im XIV. Jahrhundert). *Ethnographia*, 1954; Nyárády, M., A tengeri népi termelése Ramocsaházán (Bäuerlicher Maisbau in Ramocsaháza). *Néprajzi Értesítő*, 1955; Balassa, I., Adatok a Békés és Csongrád megyei részesmunka és ledolgozás kérdéséhez (1850–1944) (Landwirtschaftliche Arbeitsorganisation in den Komitaten Békés und Csongrád [1850–1944]). *Ethnographia*, 1955; Balassa, I., A kévébe kötött szálasgabona összerakása és számolása (Das Zusammenlegen und die Berechnung des in Garben gebundenen Halmgetreides in Ungarn). *Ethnographia*, 1956; Boross, M., A nagybudapesti és Pest környéki paradicsomkultúra gazdasági és néprajzi vizsgálata (Wirtschaftliche und ethnographische Untersuchung der Tomatenkultur von Gross-Budapest und seiner Umgebung). *Néprajzi Értesítő*, 1956; Penyigey, D., *A dohány elterjedése, hazai termesztésének kialakulása* (The Spread of Tobacco and the Domestic Development of its Growing). Budapest, 1957; Boross, M., A csányi dinnyetermesztés eszközei (Die Geräte des Melonenbaus in Csány). *Néprajzi Értesítő*, 1957; Nagy, Gy., Adatok Doboz gabonatermesztéséhez (Grain Production in Doboz). Gyula, 1959; Balassa, I., *A magyar kukorica* (Der ungarische Mais). Néprajzi tanulmány. Budapest, 1960; Takács, L., *A dohánytermesztés Magyarországon* (Tobacco Growing in Hungary). Budapest, 1962; Bálint, S., *A szegedi paprika* (The Paprika of Szeged). Budapest, 1962; Hoffmann, T., *A gabonaneműek nyomtatása a magyar parasztok gazdálkodásában* (Processing Grain in Hungarian Husbandry). Budapest, 1963; Boross, M., A kecskeméti homoki zöldségtermelés (Gemüseanbau auf dem Sandboden von Kecskemét). *Ethnographia*, 1963; Andrásfalvy, B., *Duna menti gyümölcsöskertek* (Orchards Along the Danube). Pécs, 1963; Nagy, Gy., *Hagyományos földművelés a Vásárhelyi-pusztán* (Traditional Farming on the Vásárhely *puszta*). Budapest, 1963; Balassa, I., *Földművelés a Hegyközben* (Ackerbau im Hegyköz). Budapest, 1964; Pais, S., A becsvölgyi gazdálkodás (Farming in Becsvölgy). *Néprajzi Közlemények*, 1964; Ikvai, M., Földművelés a Zempléni-hegység középső részén (Landwirtschaft im Zempléner Gebirge). *Műveltség és Hagyomány*, 1967; Takács, L., Kaszasarlók Magyarországon (Sensensicheln in Ungarn). *Ethnographia*, 1967; Kósa, L., A dél-somogyi burgonyatermelés (Die Kartoffelproduktion im südlichen Somogy). *Ethnographia*, 1968; Kósa, L., A magyar burgonyakultúra történetének és néprajzának kutatása (Die Untersuchung der Geschichte und Ethnographie der ungarischen Kartoffelkultur). *Népi kultúra – Népi társadalom*, 1968; Takács, L., Kaszaszerű vágóeszközök történetéhez I–II (Zur Geschichte unserer sensenartigen Schneidegeräte). *Néprajzi Értesítő*, 1968, 1969; Boross, M., A makói hagymatermesztés eszközanyaga (Geräte des Zwiebelbaus in Makó). *Néprajzi Értesítő*, 1968; Selmeczi-Kovács, A., Adatok a nyomtatómunka termelékenységéhez Észak-Magyarország középső területéről (Angaben zur Produktivität der Drescharbeiten im mittleren Teil Nordungarns). *Agrártörténeti Szemle*, 1971; Balassa, I., Fejezetek az eke és szántás Balaton környéki történetéből (Abschnitte aus der Geschichte des Pfluges und Pflügens in der Balaton-Gegend). *Veszprém Megyei Múzeumok Közleményei*, 1972; Boross, M., Bolgár és bolgár rendszerű kertészek Magyarországon. 1870–1945 (Bulgarische Gärtnereien und Gärtnereien von bulgarischem System in Ungarn. 1870–1945). *Ethnographia,* 1973; Balassa, I., Möglichkeiten der Erforschung der frühesten Pflugsbenutzung in Mitteleuropa. *A Magyar Mezőgazdasági Múzeum Közleményei,* 1971–1972; Balassa, I., *Az eke és a szántás története Magyarországon* (Die Geschichte des Pfluges und Pflügens in Ungarn). Budapest, 1973; Bellon, T., *Karcag város gazdálkodása (Földművelés)* (Die Landwirtschaft der Stadt Karcag. Ackerbau). Szolnok, 1973; Kósa, L., A magyar burgonyakultúra néprajza. A magyarországi burgonyatermelés kiterjedése (Ethnographie der ungarischen Kartoffelkultur. Entwicklung des Kartoffelbaus in Ungarn). In: *Dissertationes Ethnographicae I,* 1973; Fél, E.,–Hofer, T., *Geräte der Átányer Bauern.* Budapest, 1974; Andrásfalvy, B., *Dunamente népének ártéri gazdálkodása Tolna és Baranya megyében az ármentesítés befejezéséig* (The Farming of Catchment Basins by People along the River Danube in Tolna and Baranya Counties up to the Completion of Protection against Flooding). Szekszárd, 1975; Nagy. Gy., *Parasztélet a Vásárhelyi-pusztán* (Peasant Life on the Vásárhely puszta). Békéscsaba, 1975; Selmeczi-Kovács, A., Akklimatisation und Verbreitung der Sonnenblume in Europa. *Acta Ethnographica,* 1975; Bencsik, J., Gazdálkodás a Kecskéspusztán Kisújszállás külső legelőjén (Wirtschaft auf Kecskéspuszta, auf der äusseren Weide der Stadt Kisújszállás). *A Hajdúsági Múzeum Évkönyve,* 1975; Varga, Gy., Hajdúszoboszló agrártörténete (The History of Agriculture in Hajdúszoboszló). In: *Hajdúszoboszló monográfiája.* Hajdúszoboszló, 1975; Takács, L., *Egy irtásfalu földművelése* (Die Landwirtschaft eines Rodungsdorfes). Budapest, 1976; Gunst, P.–Hoffmann, T., *A magyar mezőgazdaság a XIX–XX. században* [1848–1949] (Hungarian Agriculture in the 19th and 20th Centuries [1848–1949]). Budapest, 1976; Takács, L., Foglaló jelek és foglalkozási módok a hazai irtásföldeken (Property Marks and Ways of Marking Acquisitions on Cleared Land in Hungary). *Ethnographia,* 1976; Knézy, J., *Csököly népének gazdálkodása és táplálkozása [XVIII–XX. sz.]* (The Farming Methods and the Eating Customs of the People of Csököly [18th–20th c.]). Kaposvár, 1977; Kós, K., A faluekéről (Über den Gemeindepflug). *Ethnographia,* 1977; Paládi–Kovács, A., Munkaerő és munkaszervezet a magyar parasztok rétgazdálkodásában (Manpower and Organization of Labour in the Meadow Farming of the Hungarian Peasantry). *Népi kultúra – Népi társadalom,* 1977; Selmeczi-Kovács, A., Mezőgazdasági eszközkapcsolatok [Marokszedő kampókévekötőfa] (Landwirtschaftliche Arbeitsgeräte und ihre Zusammenhänge [Abraffhaken und Garbenbindestock]). *Ethnographia,* 1977; Szilágyi, M., A Békés megyei mezővárosok termelési szervezete a XVIII–XIX. század fordulóján (Production Structure of Agrotowns in Békés County at the Turn of the 18th-19th Centuries). *Ethnographia,* 1977; Takács, L., Részes aratás a Várong körüli pusztákon (Share-harvesting on the Farms around Várong). *Népi kultúra – Népi társadalom,* 1977; Takács, L., A "vész" mint irtási szakkifejezés (Das ung. Wort "Vész" als Fachausdruck der Rodung). *Ethnographia,* 1977.

Processing Cereals

Madarassy, L., A kiskunsági szélmalom (The Windmills of Kiskunság). *Néprajzi Értesítő,* 1903; Cs. Sebestyén, K., A krassovánok kanalas malma (The Scoopwheel Mill of the Krassovans). *Néprajzi Értesítő,* 1908; Lambrecht, K., A magyar szélmalom (The Hungarian Windmill). *Ethnographia,* 1911; Lambrecht, K., *A magyar malmok könyve* (The Book of Hungarian Mills). Budapest, 1915; Nagy, Gy., Az utolsó működő szárazmalom (Die letzte funktionierende Rossmühle). *Néprajzi Értesítő,* 1956; Szabó, K., Zsákhúzó a tornyos szélmalmokban (Aufziehapparat für Getreidesäcke in türmigen Windmühlen). *Néprajzi Közlemények,* 1956; Pongrácz, P., *A mezőgazdasági jellegű ipari építészet műemlékei. A malmok* (The Relics of Industrial Construction of Agricultural Character. The Mills). Budapest, 1957; Gunda, B., Prehisztorikus őrlőkövek a Kárpátokban (Milling Stones of Prehistoric Type in the Area of the Carpathians). *Ethnographia,* 1958; JUHÁSZ, A., Vízimalmok a szegedi Tiszán (Schiffmühlen auf der Theiss in Szeged). *Móra Ferenc Múzeum Évkönyve,* 1958; NAGY, GY., A vámosoroszi szárazmalom (Moulin à manège de Vámosoroszi). *A nyíregyházi Jósa András Múzeum Évkönyve,* 1959; CZIGÁNY, B., Adatok a Győr megyei hajómolnárok életéhez (Beiträge zur Geschichte des Schiffsmüller im Komitat Győr). *Arrabona* (Győr), 1962, 1963, 1965, 1967, 1968, 1970; VARGHA, GY., Az uszodi hajómalom (Die Schiffsmühle von Uszod). *Néprajzi Értesítő,* 1965; NAGY, GY., A népi olajütő technológia Baranya megyében (Bauerliche Ölkeltertechnologie im Kom. Baranya). *Ethnographia,* 1966; SELMECZI-KOVÁCS, A., A Mátra vidéki molnárok élete (Das Leben der Müller der Mátragegend am Ende des 19. Jh.). *Ethnographia,* 1967; PALOV, J., *A szarvasi szárazmalom* (The Horse-driven Mill in Szarvas). 2nd rev. ed. Szarvas, 1976.

Grapes and Wine

ZOLTAI, L., A debreceniek szőlőműveléséről és szőlőskertjeiről (On the Vineyards and Viniculture of the People of Debrecen). *Néprajzi Értesítő,* 1914; SZABÓ, K., *Kecskemét szőlő- és gyümölcstermelésének múltja* (The History of Kecskemét's Wine and Fruit Production). Kecskemét, 1934; VAJKAI, A., A paraszt szőlőművelés és bortermelés Veszprém megye déli részében (Das bäuerliche Weinbau im südlichen Teil des Komitats Veszprém). *Néprajzi Értesítő,* 1938; GYÖRFFY, I., Szőlőmívelés (Viniculture). In: *A magyarság Néprajza.* II. Budapest, 1941; BELÉNYESY, M., Szőlő- és gyümölcstermesztésünk a XIV. században (Unser Weinbau und Gartenbau im 14. Jahrhundert). *Néprajzi Értesítő,* 1955; VINCZE, I., Magyar szőlőmetsző kések és metszésmódok (Die ungarischen Rebmesser und Schnittarten). *Néprajzi Értesítő,* 1957; ANDRÁSFALVY, B., A vörös bor Magyarországon. Szőlőművelésünk balkáni kapcsolatai (Der Rotwein in Ungarn. Balkanische Beziehungen des ungarischen Weinbaus). *Néprajzi Értesítő,* 1957; VINCZE, I., Magyar borpincék (Ungarische Weinkeller). *Néprajzi Értesítő,* 1958; VINCZE, I., Magyar borsajtók (Ungarische Weinpressen). *Ethnographia,* 1958; VINCZE, I., A borkészítés módjai és eszközei, különös tekintettel a borsodi Hegyközre (Arten und Mitteln des Kelterns mit besonderer Rücksicht auf die Borsoder Hegyköz-Gegend). *Ethnographia,* 1960. BAKÓ, F., *Egri borpincék* (Wine Cellars of Eger). Budapest, 1961; KURUCZ, A., *Az észak-bihari szőlőművelés és borgazdálkodás* (Viniculture and Wine Production of North Bihar). Debrecen, 1964; KECSKÉS, P., A szőlő talajművelése Észak-Magyarországon (Bodenarbeiten in den nordungarischen Weinbergen). *Néprajzi Értesítő,* 1967; KÓS, K., Népi szőlőművelés Szászmuzsnán (Folk Viniculture in Szászmuzsna). In: *Népélet és Néphagyomány.* Bucharest, 1972; BALASSA, I., A szőlőművelés és borkezelés változása a XVI–XVII. században Tokaj-Hegyalján (Der Wandel des Weinbaus in Tokaj-Hegyalja im 16.–17. Jahrhundert). *Agrártörténeti Szemle,* 1973; ÉGETŐ, M., A szőlőművelés átalakulása a századfordulón a Solt-vidéken (Veränderungen in der Bearbeitung der Weingärten in der Solt-Gegend um die Jahrhundertwende.—Transformation de la viticulture au tournant du siècle dans la région de Solt). *Cumania* II, 1974; HUSZKA, L., *Szatymazi szőlőhegyek* (The Vine Hills of Szatymaz). Szeged, 1975; NOVÁK, L., A szőlő Albertirsa és Pilis hagyományos telekrendszerében és üzemszervezetében (Der Weinbau im traditionellen Bodensystem und in der Betriebsorganisation der Gemeinden Albertirsa und Pilis). *Studia Comitatensia,* 1975; VINCZE, I., Taposók és prések. Adatok a kelet-európai borkultúra történetéhez (Tretgeräte und Pressen. Beiträge zur Geschichte der osteuropäischen Weinkultur). *Ethnographia,* 1975; VARGA, GY., *Az érmelléki szőlőkultúra* (The viniculture of Érmellék). Berettyóújfalu, 1976; SUGÁR, I., Adatok az egri vörös bor történetéhez. A bikavér kialakulása (Indications concernant l'histoire du vin rouge d'Eger. Le développement du "sang de taureau"). *Az Egri Múzeum*

Évkönyve, 1976; VAJKAI., A., Szőlőprések és díszítésük a Balaton északi mellékén (Weinpressen und ihre Verzierung in der Nordgegend des Balaton).
Ethnographia, 1977.

Animal husbandry—Bee-keeping

LÜKŐ, G., Régimódi méhészkedés Moldovában (Altertümliche Bienenzucht in
der Moldau). *Néprajzi Értesítő,* 1934; GÖNYEY, S., Ősfoglalkozások a Börzsöny
hegységben (Urbeschäftigungen im Börzsönyer Gebirge). *Néprajzi Értesítő,*
1935; GYÖRFFY, I., Vadméhkeresés Biharban (Looking for Wild Bees in Bihar).
Népünk és Nyelvünk, 1935; TAGÁN, G., Erdei méhkeresés Székelyvarságon
(Bienen-Suche in Székelyvarság). *Néprajzi Értesítő,* 1941; SZŰCS, S., A régi
Sárrét világa (The World of Old Sárrét). Budapest, 1941; GYÖRFFY, I., Méhészet
(Apiculture). In: *A magyarság néprajza.* II. Budapest, 1941; GUNDA, B., *A magyar
gyűjtögető és zsákmányoló gazdálkodás kutatása* (Research on Hungarian Gleaning
and Predatory Culture). Budapest, 1948; SZABÓ, M., Primitív sonkolypréselő
eljárás Algyőn (Primitives Presseverfahren für Wachskuchen in Algyő). *Nép-
rajzi Értesítő,* 1956; SZABADFALVI, J., Méhészkedés a szatmári Erdőháton
(Imkerei im Erdőhát-Gebiet des Komitats Szatmár). *Ethnographia,* 1956; MOL-
NÁR, B., Méhkeresés és mézzsákmányolás Domaházán (Waldbienensuchen und
Honigraub in Domaháza). *Ethnographia,*1957; GUNDA, B., A méhvadászat
(Hunting for Bees). In: *Ethnographia Carpatica.* Budapest, 1966; H. KERECSÉNYI,
E., A népi méhészkedés története, formái és gyakorlata Nagykanizsa kör-
nyékén (The History, Forms and Practice of Folk Apiculture around Nagy-
kanizsa). *Néprajzi Közlemények,* 1969; BALASSA, M. I., Élőfás méhtartás a Kár-
pát-medencében (Waldbienenzucht im Karpatenbecken). *Ethnographia,* 1970;
FÜVESSY, A., A méhészettel kapcsolatos vándorkereskedelem Észak-Borsodban
(Wanderhandel verbunden mit Bienenzucht im nördlichen Teil vom Komitat
Borsod). *Ethnographia,* 1971; BALASSA, M. I., Méhesek a Hegyközben és
a Bodrogközben (Bienengürten im Hegyköz und Bodrogköz). *Néprajzi
Értesítő,* 1971; CSABA, J., Adatok a vend vidék népi méhészkedéséhez (Data
Concerning the Apiculture of the Wendish Region). *Ethnographia,* 1971;
FÜVESSY, A., A méhlakások Észak-Borsodban (Bienenhäuschen in Nord-
Borsod). *A Miskolci Herman Ottó Múzeum Évkönyve,* 1972; SAÁD, A., Adatok
a kaptárkövek eredetének, korának és rendeltetésének meghatározásához
(Angaben zum Ursprung, zum Alter und zur Bestimmung der Bienenstock-
steine). *A Miskolci Herman Ottó Múzeum Évkönyve,* 1972; BALASSA, M. I.,
A hegyközi és bodrogközi méhészet. A méhtartás egész évi menete (Bienen-
zucht der Gebiete Hegyköz und Bodrogköz. Jahreslauf der Bienenzucht). In:
Dissertationes Ethnographicae I., 1973; BALASSA, M. I., Waldbienenzucht im
Karpatenbecken. *Acta Ethnographica,* 1975; SZABÓ, K., Méhészkedés ősi módon
Debrecenben (Bee-keeping in Debrecen). *Agrártörténeti Szemle,* 1977.

Hunting

KOVÁCS, A., A csikle (The Snare). *Néprajzi Értesítő,* 1904; KOVÁCS, A.,
A csikkentő és tőr (The Noose and the Trap). *Néprajzi Értesítő,* 1905; ECSEDI, I.,
Népies vadfogás és vadászat a debreceni határban és a Tiszántúlon (Volkstümlicher
Wildfang und Jagd im Debrecener Gebiet und jenseits der Theiss [Tiszántúl]).
Debrecen, 1933; GÖNYEY, S., Ősfoglalkozások a Börzsöny hegységben (Urbe-
schäftigungen im Börzsönyer Gebiet). *Néprajzi Értesítő,* 1935; MÁRKUS, M.,
Népi vadfogás módjai Nyíregyháza vidékén (Volklicher Wildfang in der
Umgebung von Nyíregyháza. Kom. Szabolcs). *Néprajzi Értesítő,* 1937; BÖDEI,
J., Madárfogók Göcsejből (Bird Snares from Göcsej). *Vasi Szemle,* 1939;
KOROMPAY, B., Finnugor eredetű csapdáink kérdéséhez (Zur Frage der ungari-
schen Fallen finnisch-ugrischer Herkunft). *Néprajzi Értesítő,* 1939; GUNDA, B.,
Adatok a bukovinai és moldvai magyarok vadfogó eszközeihez (Beiträge zu den

Jagdfallen und -schlingen der Magyaren von Bukowina und der Moldau). *Néprajzi Értesítő,* 1940; GYÖRFFY, I., Vadászat (Hunting). In: *A magyarság néprajza.* II. Budapest, 1941; SZŰCS, S., *A régi Sárrét világa* (Old Sárrét). Budapest n. d. (1941); PÁVEL, Á., Rigászás a vend vidéken és az Őrségben (Kramtsvogelstellen im Wendischen Gebiet und im Őrség). *Néprajzi Értesítő,* 1942; GUNDA, B., *A magyar gyűjtögető és zsákmányoló gazdálkodás kutatása* (Research into Hungarian Gleaning and Predatory Culture). Budapest, 1948; MÉSZÖLY, G., Az ugorkori vadászélet magyar szókincsbeli emlékei (Das Jägerleben der ugrischen Zeit im ungarischen Wortschatz). *Ethnographia,* 1951; KOROMPAY, B., A csiklétől a csikkentőig (Von den Csikle-Fallen zu den Csikkentő-Fallen); *Néprajzi Értesítő,* 1956; HOFER, T., Vadfogó vermek a töröknek hódolt Baranyában (Fallgruben im Komitat Baranya im XVII. Jahrhundert). *Ethnographia,* 1957; GUNDA, B., Vadfogó hurkok a Keleti-Kárpátokban (Wild Game Snares in the Eastern Carpathians). In: *Ethnographia Carpatica,* 1966; CSABA, J., Népi vadfogó eszközök és eljárások Csákánydoroszlón (Geräte und Verfahren des Wildfangs beim Volk von Csákánydoroszló). *Savaria,* 1971–1972 [1975].

Fishing

HERMAN, O., *A magyar halászat könyve,* I–II (The Book of Hungarian Fishing, I–II). Budapest, 1887; MUNKÁCSI, B., A magyar népies halászat műnyelve (The Nomenclature of Hungarian Folk Fishing). *Ethnographia,* 1893; JANKÓ, J., *A magyar halászat eredete* (Herkunft der magyarischen Fischerei). Budapest –Leipzig, 1900; SZTRIPSZKY, H., Adatok Erdély őshalászatához (Data on the Ancient Fishing of Transylvania). *Néprajzi Értesítő,* 1903; SZTRIPSZKY, H., A Feketeügy halászatához (About Feketeügy Fishing). *Néprajzi Értesítő,* 1903; KOVÁCS, A., Sárköz régi halászatához (On Old Fishing in Sárköz). *Néprajzi Értesítő,* 1904; SZABÓ, K., Ősi halászat nyomai Kecskemét környékén (Ancient Survivals of Fishing around Kecskemét). *Ethnographia,* 1918; BANNER, J., *A szegedi halászbárka* (The Fishing Boat of Szeged). Szeged, 1926; GÖNYEY, S., Adatok a Bodrog halászatához (Beiträge zur Fischerei des Bodrog). *Néprajzi Értesítő,* 1926; M. KISS, L., A Sajó népi halászata (Die volkstümliche Fischerei an der Sajó [Komitat Borsod]). *Néprajzi Értesítő,* 1931; VISKI, K., Tihany őshalászata (Urfischerei in Tihany). *Néprajzi Értesítő,* 1932; ALAPI, GY., *A csallóközi halászat története* (The History of Fishing at Csallóköz). Komárom, 1933; GYÖRFFY, I., Az Ipoly menti halászat (Fischerei an der Ipoly). *Néprajzi Értesítő,* 1933; ECSEDI, I., *Népies halászat a Közép-Tiszán és a tiszántúli kisvízeken* (Volkstümliche Fischerei im Gebiet der mittleren Theiss und jenseits der Theiss). Debrecen, 1934; MORVAY, P., Adatok az Alsó-Szamos halászatához (Beiträge zur Kenntnis der Fischerei auf der Unteren Szamos). *Néprajzi Értesítő,* 1937; SZABÓ, K., Kecskeméti Múzeum halászati gyűjteménye (Die Fischerei-Sammlung der Kecskeméter Museums. Kom. Pest). *Néprajzi Értesítő,* 1937; GÖNYEY, S., A néprajzi Múzeum szigonygyűjteménye (Die Fischgabelsammlung des Ethnographischen Museums in Budapest). *Néprajzi Értesítő,* 1937; GUNDA, B., A magyarországi halászó hurkok eredete (Herkunft der ungarländischen Fischschlingen). *Néprajzi Értesítő,* 1938; NYÁRÁDY, M., A Rétköz régi halászata (Die alte Fischerei des Rétköz). *Ethnographia,* 1938; DEGRÉ, A., *Magyar halászati jog a középkorban* (Hungarian Fishing Rights in the Middle Ages). Budapest, 1939; ROSKA, M., Az erdélyi halastavak őskori vonatkozásai (Die vorgeschichtlichen Beziehungen der siebenbürgischen Seen). *Néprajzi Értesítő,* 1939; CSALOG, J., A Tolna megyei Sárköz népi halászata (Volkliche Fischerei im Sárköz). *Néprajzi Értesítő,* 1940; GUNDA, B., *A magyar gyűjtögető és zsákmányoló gazdálkodás kutatása* (Research on Hungarian Gleaning and Predatory Culture). Budapest, 1948; DIÓSZEGI, V., A zsákos tapogató kialakulása a Velencei-tavon (Die Entstehung eines mit Sack versehenen Deckkorbes am Velenceer See).

Ethnographia, 1950; L∪κάϲs, K,. Tiszai hatás a balatoni halászatban (L'influence des pêcheurs de la Tisza sur la pêche au lac Balaton). *Ethnographia*, 1951; Belényesy, M., A halászat a XIV. században (Der Fischfang im XIV. Jahrhundert). *Ethnographia*, 1953; L∪κάϲs, K., Adatok a Fertő és Rábaköz halászatának történetéhez (Beiträge zur Fischerei im Fertő-See und im Rábaköz). *Ethnographia*, 1953; Solymos, E., A borító halászszerszámok fejlődése Magyarországon (Entwicklung der Deckfischereigeräte in Ungarn). *Ethnographia*, 1957; Solymos, E., *Rekesztő halászat a Velencei-tavon* (Fish Mooring on Lake Velencei). Székesfehérvár, 1958; Solymos, E., Halászélet a Duna magyarországi szakaszain (Das Leben der Fischer am ungarischen Abschnitt der Donau). *Ethnographia*, 1959; Bárdosi, J., A magyar Fertő tapogató halászata (Die Stülpfischerei des ungarischen Fertő-Teiches). *Arrabona*, 1959; Babus, J., A lónyai vizek néprajza (Zur Volkskunde der Gewässer von Lónya [Komitat Bereg]). *Néprajzi Közlemények*, 1959; Khin, A., *A Velencei-tó halászata* (Fishing on Lake Velence). Budapest, 1960; Solymos, E., *Adatok a Fehér-Körös halászatához* (Data on Fishing in the Fehér-Körös). Gyula, 1960; Solymos, E., *Dunai halászat a magyar Dunán* (Fishing on the Hungarian Danube). Budapest, 1965; Solymos, E., A termelési mód változásainak hatása a magyar népi halászatra (Einfluss der Veränderungen der Produktionsweise auf die Fischerei des ungarischen Volkes). *Ethnographia*, 1970; Andrásfalvy, B., A paraszti halászati jog a Duna mentén Tolna és Baranyában (Fischerei der Bauern entlang der Donau in den Komitaten Tolna und Baranya). *Ethnographia*, 1970; Szilágyi, M., Tiszaverés ("Tiszaverés" [eine Art der Koppelfischerei an der Theiss]). *Szolnok Megyei Múzeumi Évkönyv*, 1973; Fábián, M., Halászat a bukovinai Andrásfalván (Fischfang in der Gemeinde Andrásfalva in Bukowina). *Ethnographia*, 1973; Andrásfalvy, B., *A Sárköz és a környező Duna menti területek ősi ártéri gazdálkodása és vízhasználata a szabályozás előtt* (Die Wassernutzung im Sárköz und in den umgebenden Überschwemmungsgebieten der Donau — vor den Gewässerregulierungen). Budapest, 1973; Solymos, E., Typenkatalog der Fischereisammlung des Türr István Museums zu Baja. *Cumania* II, 1974; Szilágyi, M., Halászati üzemformák a Tisza vidékén a XVIII–XIX. században (Fischereibetriebesformen in der Theissgegend im 18. und 19. Jahrhundert). *Ethnographia*, 1975; *Studien zur europäischen traditionellen Fischerei*. Ed. Solymos, E., Baja, 1976; Szilágyi, M., A szárított hal [Halkonzerválási módok a magyar halászok gyakorlatában] (Das Trocknen des Fisches. Fischkonservierungsmethoden in der Praxis der ungarischen Fischer). *A szekszárdi Béri Balogh Ádám Múzeum Évkönyve*, 1975–1976; Szilágyi, M., A rekesz [Az áradások jelentősége a tiszai halászatban] (The Importance of Flood with Regard to Fishing in the River Tisza). *Népi kultúra – Népi társadalom*, 1977; Takács, L., Rákászat a Kis-Balaton mentén (Krebsfang um den Kleinen Balaton). *Ethnographia*, 1977.

Animal Husbandry—General works

Herman, O., *A magyar ősfoglalkozások köréből* (From the Circle of Ancient Magyar Occupations). Budapest, 1899; Herman, O., *A magyarok nagy ősfoglalkozása* (The Great Ancient Occupation of the Magyars). Budapest, 1909; Madarassy, L., *Nomád pásztorkodás a kecskeméti pusztaságon* (Nomad Husbandry on the Kecskemét *puszta*). Budapest, 1912; Herman, O., *A magyar pásztorok nyelvkincse* (The Vocabulary of the Hungarian Herdsmen). Budapest, 1914; Ecsedi, I., *A Hortobágy-puszta élete* (Life on the Hortobágy *puszta*). Debrecen, 1914; Györffy, I., *Nagykunsági krónika* (Chronicle of Nagykunság). Karcag, 1922; Györffy, I., *Das Bauwesen der Hirten im ungarischen Tiefland*. Budapest, 1928; Györffy, I., *A szilaj pásztorok* (Extensive Herdsmen). Karcag, 1928; Tálasi, I., *A Kiskunság népi állattartása* (Folk Animal Husbandry of the Kiskunság). Budapest, 1936; Györffy, I., Állattartás (Animal Husbandry). In: *A magyarság néprajza*. II. Budapest, 1941; Luby, M., *Fogyó legelőkön* (On Decreasing

734

Pastures). Budapest, n. d.; Szűcs, S., *A régi Sárrét világa* (Old Sárrét). Budapest, n. d. (1941); László, Gy., *A honfoglaló magyar nép élete* (The Life of the Conquering Magyars). Budapest, 1944; Szűcs, S., *Pusztai krónika* (Chronicle of the *Puszta)*. Budapest, 1946; K. Kovács, L., *A magyar állattartás kutatása* (Research on Hungarian Animal Husbandry). Budapest, 1948; Belényesy, M., Az állattartás a XIV. században Magyarországon (Viehhaltung in Ungarn im 14. Jahrhundert). *Néprajzi Értesítő*, 1956; Szűcs, S., *Pusztai szabadok* (The Free Ones of the *Puszta)*. Budapest, 1957; Nagy, Cz. L., *Pásztorélet a Kiskunságon* (Herdsmen's Life in the Kiskunság). Budapest, 1959; Földes, L., *Az állattartás és pásztorélet néprajzi szakirodalma* (Ethnographical Literature on Animal Husbandry and the Life of the Herdsmen). Budapest, 1963; Bartha, A., *A IX–X. századi magyar társadalom* (Magyar Society in the 9th and 10th Centuries). Budapest, 1968; Bökönyi, S., A háziasítás kérdése a legújabb kutatások fényében (The Question of Domestication in Light of the Most Recent Research). *Ethnographia*, 1969; Szabadfalvi, J., *Az extenzív állattenyésztés Magyarországon* (Extensive Viehzucht in Ungarn). Debrecen, 1970; *Tanulmányok a Hortobágy néprajzához* (Studies on the Ethnography of the Hortobágy). Debrecen, 1972–74; Matolcsi, J., *A háziállatok eredete* (The Origin of Domesticated Animals). Budapest, 1975.

Detailed Studies

Málnási, Ö., A szoboszlai juhászat (Die Schäferei in Szoboszló). *Néprajzi Értesítő*, 1928; Szabó, K., A jószág jegye és billege Kecskeméten (Viehbrandzeichen bei den Hirten in Kecskemét). *Néprajzi Értesítő*, 1932; Szabó, K., Csengetyű és kolomp a kecskeméti pásztorság kezén (Vieglocken der Hirten von Kecskemét). *Néprajzi Értesítő*, 1932; Gönyey, S., A zselicségi kanászélet (Das Leben der Schweinehirten in Zselic). *Ethnographia*, 1933; Györffy, I., Juhtartás és tejgazdaság Kalotaszegen (Schafzucht und Milchwirtschaft im Kalotaszeg). *Néprajzi Értesítő*, 1934; Borzsák, E., A régi istállók élete és a jószág takarmányozása Pest vármegye északi felében (Das Leben der alten Ställe und die Futterung des Viehes). *Néprajzi Értesítő*, 1936; Szabó, K., Az állatok betegsége és gyógyítása a kecskeméti pusztán (Krankheit und Heilung der Tiere auf den Puszten von Kecskemét). *Ethnographia*, 1937; Györffy, I., Nomád település és szilaj pásztorkodás a székelyeknél (Nomadische Siedelung bei den Széklern). *Ethnographia*, 1937; Balogh, I., *A jószág teleltetése Debrecen környékén* (Wintering the Stock around Debrecen). Debrecen, 1938; Szabó, K., Kecskemét pásztorélete I. Juhászat (Das Kecskeméter Hirtenleben). *Néprajzi Értesítő*, 1942; Kós, K., A kalotaszegi kosarazó juhászat (Sheepkeeping in Kalotaszeg) *Miscellanea Ethnographica* Tom. I. Kolozsvár, 1947; K. Kovács, L., Adatok a bálványosváraljai fejősjuhászathoz (Angaben zur Melkschäferei in Bálványos-váralja). *Ethnographia*, 1947; Csermák, G., Az istensegítsiek állatorvoslása (La pratique vétérinaire des habitants d'Istensegíts). *Ethnographia*, 1949; Nagy, Cz. L., Pásztortörvények és szabályok, ún. regulák a Kiskunságban (Gesetze und Regel der Hirten in der Klein-Kumanei [Kom. Pest]). *Néprajzi Értesítő*, 1954, 1955; Balogh, I., A pusztai legeltetés rendje Debrecenben a XVIII–XIX. században (Die Weidegerechtigkeit auf den Puszten bei Debrecen im XVIII.—XIX. Jahrhundert). *Ethnographia*, 1958; Zólyomi, J., Cserhátsurány népi állattartásának másfél százada (Anderthalb Jahrhunderte Viehhaltung in Cserhátsurány [Im Komitat Nógrád]). *Ethnographia*, 1960; Földes, L., Egy alföldi juhtartó gazdaság (Eine traditionelle Bauerngenossenschaft für Schafhaltung in der Grossen Ungarischen Tiefebene). *Néprajzi Értesítő*, 1962; Szebeni, G., A csíki juhászat (Die Schafhaltung im Komitat Csík). *Ethnographia*, 1962; Paládi–Kovács, A., A keleti palócok pásztorkodása (La bergerie des Paloczes Orientaux). *Műveltség és Hagyomány*, 1965; Bencsik, J., *Pásztorkodás a Hortobágy északi területén a XVIII. század végétől* (Herding on the Northern

Hortobágy from the End of the 18th Century). Debrecen, 1969; Csiszár, Á., A beregi sertéstenyésztés (Schweinezucht in Bereg). *Ethnographia,* 1971; Papp, Z. S., A bivalytartás Beregdarócon (Buffalo Raising at Beregdaróc). *Ethnographia,* 1971; Bencsik, J., *Paraszti állattartás Hajdúböszörményben* (Bäuerliche Viehhaltung in Hajdúböszörmény). Debrecen, 1971; Szabadfalvi, J., Az extenzív sertéstenyésztés emlékei Magyarországon (Überlieferungen der extensiven Schweinezucht in Ungarn). *A debreceni Déri Múzeum Évkönyve,* 1970; Balassa, I., Makkoltatás a Kárpát-medence északkeleti részében a XVI–XIX. században (Eichelmast im nordöstlichen Teil des Karpatenbeckens im XVI–XIX. Jahrhundert). *Ethnographia,* 1973; Petercsák, T., Szarvasmarhatartás egy hegyközi faluban (Rinderzucht in einem Dorf von Hegyköz). *A Miskolci Herman Ottó Múzeum Évkönyve,* 1973; Béres, A., Erdélyi purzsások teleltetése a Hortobágyon (Überwinterung von siebenbürgischen rumänischen Schäfern in der Hortobágy). *Műveltség és Hagyomány,* 1972–1974; Bencsik, J., *A szarvasmarha paraszti tartása Hajdúnánáson a XVIII. század végétől* (Die Rinderzucht der Bauern in Hajdúnánás von Ende des 18. Jahrhunderts). Hajdúböszörmény, 1974; Tábori, Gy., Tótkomlós állattartása (Viehhaltung in Tótkomlós). *A Békés Megyei Múzeumok Közleményei,* 1974; Szabadfalvi, J., Die natürlichen Wetterschutzanlagen und Bauwerke der extensiven Viehzucht in Ungarn. *Acta Ethnographica,* 1975; Pusztainé, Madar, I., Adatok a sárrétudvariak gazdálkodásának történetéhez, különös tekintettel a lótartásra (Contributions to the History of Farming at Sárrétudvari with Special Regard to Horse Maintenance). *Agrártörténeti Szemle,* 1976; Gémes, B., A juhászok ládái és a juhászcéh kérdése Mezőföldön a XVIII—XIX. században (Die Schäferladen und die Schäferzunft in Mezőföld im 18.–19. Jh.). *A Szekszárdi Béri Balogh Ádám Múzeum Évkönyve,* 1975–1976 [1977]; Paládi-Kovács, A., A gömöri magyar pásztorkodás (Hungarian Herdsmen's Life in the Region Gömör [Gemer, Slovakia]). *Ethnographia,* 1977; Markuš, M., A kelet-szlovákiai sertéskupecek életéből (East-Slovakian Peasant Pig-dealers), *Ethnographia,* 1977.

Breaking in Stock and the Means of Transportation

Réthei, P. M., A kocsi eredete (The Origin of the Cart). *Egyetemes Philológiai Közlöny,* 1897; Herman, O., *Debreceni lófogatok* (Horse Carriages of Debrecen). Budapest, 1910; Ecsedi, I., A debreceni fogatok (Carriages of Debrecen). *Néprajzi Értesítő,* 1911; Pettkó-Szandtner, T., A magyar kocsizás (Hungarian Carriage Driving). Budapest, 1931; Gunda, B., A magyar kétrúdú szekér eredete és a régi magyar ajonca szekér (Ursprung d. ung. Wagen mit zwei Femerstangen und der alte ung. Ajonca-Wagen). *Néprajzi Értesítő,* 1934; Tálasi, I., A járó- és vonójószág betanítása a Kiskunságban (Die Einschulung der Pferde und Ochsen in der Klein-Kumanei). *Néprajzi Értesítő,* 1935; Márkus, M., A nyíregyházi taliga (Nyíregyházaer Karren). *Néprajzi Értesítő,* 1938; Sándor, G., *A kolozsvári Hóstát emberi erővel végzett teherhordási módjai és eszközei* (Methods and Means of Hauling Loads by Manpower in Hóstát of Kolozsvár). Kolozsvár, 1942; K. Kovács, L., *A magyar népi közlekedés kutatása* (Research on Hungarian Folk Transportation). Budapest, 1948; Betkowski, J., Adatok a szolnoki hajósok életéből (Contributions à l'étude de la vie des bateliers de Szolnok). *Ethnographia,* 1954; Nagy, B., Adatok a magyar teherhordó eszközök használatához és elterjedéséhez (Angaben zum Gebrauch und zur Verbreitung eines ungarischen Traggerätes). *Ethnographia,* 1954; Csalog, Zs., A kocsi és szekér Szentes vidékén (Der Wagen und das Fuhrwerk in der Umgebung von Szentes [Kom. Csongrád]). *Néprajzi Közlemények,* 1965; Tarr, L., *A kocsi története* (History of the Carriage). Budapest, 1968; Cseglédy, J., Tutajozás a Maroson a múlt században (Flossfahrt auf der Maros im vorigen Jahrhundert). *Ethnographia,* 1969; Gráfik, I., Szállítás és közlekedés Szentendrei-szigeten (Beförderung und Verkehr auf der Szentendre-Insel).

Néprajzi Közlemények, 1971; BODÓ, S., Az igavonó szarvasmarha a Hortobágy vidékén (Das Rind als Zugtier in der Umgebung der Puszta Hortobágy). *Műveltség és Hagyomány,* 1972–1974; PALÁDI-KOVÁCS, A., A magyar parasztság kerekes járműveinek történeti és táji rendszerezéséhez (Zur historischen und regionalen Systematisierung der Wagen der ungarischen Bauernschaft). *Néprajzi Közlemények,* 1973; P. MADAR, I., Szekérkészítés és használat a székelyföldi Atyhán és az alföldi Sárrétudvariban (Cart Making and Use at Atyha of the Székelyland and at Sárrétudvari of the Great Plain). *Néprajzi Közlemények,* 1973; PALÁDI-KOVÁCS, A., Néhány megjegyzés a magyar parasztság teherhordó eszközeiről (Einige Bemerkungen über die Traggeräte der ungarischen Bauern). *Ethnographia,* 1973; GRÁFIK, I., Az állati erővel végzett folyami vontatás (Rendszerelemzési kísérlet) (Schiffschleppen mit tierischer Zugkraft auf ungarischen Flüssen). *Ethnographia,* 1973; GRÁFIK, I., Hajóvontatók (Die Treidler). *Néprajzi Értesítő,* 1975; KUCZY, K., *Vízi élet, népi hajózás Foktőn* (Aquatic Life, Folk Shipping at Foktő). Kalocsa, 1976; PALÁDI-KOVÁCS, A., Egy népi teherhordó eszköz magyarországi elterjedtségének tanulságai [Hátitarisznya a palócoknál a XIX–XX. században] (Belehrungen über die Verbreitung eines Volkstraggerätes in Ungarn. Der Ranzen bei den Palozen im 19.–20. Jahrhundert). *Az Egri Múzeum Évkönyve,* 1976.

Alimentation—Comprehensive and General Works

GÖNCZI, F., A göcseji s hetési nép étele, itala és étkezése (The Food, Drink and Eating Habits of the People of Hetés and Göcsej). *Néprajzi Értesítő,* 1907; ECSEDI, I., *A debreceni és tiszántúli magyar ember táplálkozása* (The Alimentation of the Hungarians of Debrecen and Tiszántúl). Debrecen, 1935; GUNDA, B., Magyarországi primitív sütő-főző eljárások (Die ungarischen primitiven Koch- und Bratverfahren und ihre völkerkundlichen Zusammenhänge). *Néprajzi Értesítő,* 1935; BÁTKY, Zs., A magyar konyha története (Die Geschichte der ungarischen Küche). *Néprajzi Értesítő,* 1937; BOLLA, J., *A népi konyhamesterség műszókincse Felsőgörzsönyben (Bakonyalja)* (The Nomenclature of Hungarian Folk Gastronomy in Felsőgörzsöny [Bakonyalja]). Debrecen, 1939; BÁTKY, Zs., Táplálkozás (Alimentation). In: *A magyarság néprajza.* I. Budapest, 1941; KARDOS, L., *Az Őrség népi táplálkozása* (Folk Alimentation of the People of Őrség). Budapest, 1943; VAJKAI, A., *A magyar népi táplálkozás kutatása* (Research of Hungarian Folk Alimentation). Budapest, 1947; MORVAY, J., Az ünnepi táplálkozás a Boldva völgyében (Les repas des fêtes dans la vallée de la Boldva). *Ethnographia,* 1950; BELÉNYESY, M., Egy XVI. századi főúri étrend kultúrtörténeti tanulságai (Die kulturhistorische und ethnographische Bedeutung einer Speisefolge auf dem Tisch des Gutsherren Nádasdi aus dem XVI. Jahrhundert.) *Néprajzi Értesítő,* 1958; SCHRAM, F., Összefüggések az úri és a népi konyha között (Beiträge zur Beziehung der herrschaftlichen und bauerlichen Speisen). *Ethnographia,* 1961; BÓNA, J., *Haraszti táplálkozási hagyományai* (The Traditions of Alimentation of Haraszti). Szeged, 1963; KISBÁN, E., A népi táplálkozás alakulásának problémái (Die Probleme der Umwandlungen in der Ernährung des Volkes). *Műveltség és Hagyomány,* 1963; KISBÁN, E., Újítások Észak-Dunántúl újkori népi táplálkozásában (Neuerungen in der neuzeitlichen Volksnahrung im nördlichen Transdanubien). *Ethnographia,* 1970; ERDEI, F., *Népi ínyesmesterség* (Folk Gastronomy). Budapest, 1971; SCHRAM, F., Némelly étkek készítési módgya (XVIII. századi kéziratokból...) (The Method of Preparing Certain Dishes [from 18th c. manuscripts]). Budapest, 1972; SZIGETI, GY., Az apátfalvi nép táplálkozása (Die Ernährung des Volkes von Apátfalva). *A Móra Ferenc Múzeum Évkönyve,* 1972–1973 [1974]; MORVAY, J.,–KRESZ, M., Táplálkozás, konyha, cserépedények (Eating, Cuisine, Earthenware Dishes). *Néprajzi Közlemények,* 1977.

MADARASSY, L., Szárított juhhús (Dried Mutton). *Ethnographia*, 1903; GYÖRFFY, I., A Szatmár megyei szilvaaszaló (The Plum-drier of Szatmár County). *Néprajzi Értesítő*, 1911; NYILASSY, J., Gyümölcsaszalás Zengővárkonyban (Das Obstdörren in Zengővárkony [Kom. Baranya]). *Néprajzi Közlemények*, 1957; BARABÁS, J., Adatok a népi húskonzerváláshoz (Beiträge zur volkstümlichen Fleischkonservierung). *Ethnographia*, 1959; DOBROSSY, I., Az aszalás, mint konzerválási mód a Zempléni-hegység falvaiban (Das Dörren als Konservierungsmethode in den Dörfern des Zempléner Gebirges). *Ethnographia*, 1969; PALÁDI-KOVÁCS, A., Szárított hús a pásztoroknál (Dörrfleisch bei den Hirten). *Műveltség és Hagyomány*, 1972–1974.

Vegetable Dishes

KISS, L., A hódmezővásárhelyi ember eledelei (Die Speisen der Leute von Hódmezővásárhely). *Ethnographia*, 1923/24; PALOTAY, G., Lakodalmi torták Boldogon (Hochzeitkuchen in Boldog [Kom. Pest]). *Néprajzi Értesítő*, 1929; NÉMETHY, E., Két régi kemenesaljai nagyböjti tészta: a málé és a szalados (Two Traditional Dishes Connected with Lent, at Kemenesalja). *Ethnographia*, 1949; BAKÓ, F., Az erdőhorváti perecsütő asszonyok (Die brezelbackenden Frauen aus Erdőhorváti). *Ethnographia*, 1952; H. FEKETE, P., Tésztás kása-e az öhöm? (Eine Breispeise der ungarischen Hirten). *Ethnographia*, 1957; KISBÁN, E., Nyersanyag és technika. Pépes ételeink típusai (Ungarische breiige Speisen). *Néprajzi Értesítő*, 1960; BALASSA, I., *A magyar kukorica* (Der ungarische Mais). Budapest, 1960; DÖMÖTÖR, S., Dunántúli és alföldi édeslepények (Süsse Fladen jenseits der Donau [Dunántúl-Transdanubien] und auf der ungarischen Tiefebene). *Ethnographia*, 1960; ENYEDI, J., A káposzta jelentősége a nép életében Hajdúhadházon (Die Bedeutung des Weisskohls im Leben des Volkes von Hajdúhadház [Komitat Hajdú-Bihar]). *Ethnographia*, 1962; HEGYI, I., A lisztminőség és a tésztaételek összefüggése (Zusammenhänge der Mehlqualität und der Mehlspeisesorten). *Ethnographia*, 1964.

Bread and Milk Loaf

KISS, L., A kenyérsütés Hódmezővásárhelyen (Bread Baking in Hódmezővásárhely). *Néprajzi Értesítő*, 1908; GUNDA, B., A kenyérsütés Orosháza környékén (Brotbacken in der Umgebung von Orosháza). *Néprajzi Értesítő*, 1932; VÉGH, J., Rozskenyérsütés Kiskunhalason (Das Roggenbrotbacken in Kiskunhalas [Kom. Pest]). *Ethnographia*, 1940; PERESZLÉNYI, M., Adatok a kenyérsütéshez Balaton környékéről (Beiträge zum Brotbacken der Plattenseegegend). *Néprajzi Értesítő*, 1941; KISBÁN, E., A gyümölcskenyér elterjedésének tanulságai (Bemerkungen zur Verbreitung des Früchtebrotes). *Ethnographia*, 1961; BÁLINT, S., A kenyér és kalács a szegedi néphagyományban (Bread and Milk Loaf in the Folk Tradition of Szeged). *Néprajz és Nyelvtudomány*, 1962; DÖMÖTÖR, S., Lakodalmi kalácsok Vas megyében (Wedding Milk Loaves in Vas County). *Savaria*, 1965; GUNDA, B., A sütőkövek és ősi kenyérfélék (Baking Stones and Ancient Bread Types). In: *Ethnographica Carpatica*. Budapest, 1966; KISBÁN, E., A kenyér a táplálkozási struktúrában (Das Brot in der Ernährungsstruktur). *Népi kultúra – Népi társadalom*, 1970; SCHWALM, E., Kenyérsütés Hevesaranyoson és Egerbocson (Das Brotbacken in Hevesaranyos und Egerbocs). *Az Egri Múzeum Évkönyve*, 1975.

Meat Dishes

GYÖRFFY, I., Ló- és szamárhúsevés a magyar népnél. *Ethnographia*, 1936; BORZSÁK, E., Juhhús a népi táplálkozásban (Hammelfleisch in der Volksernahrung). *Ethnographia*, 1937; BÓNA, J., *Haraszti népi táplálkozási hagyományai* (The

Traditions of Alimentation of Haraszti). Szeged, 1963; MÁRTON, B., A nyári és téli ételek Bihardiószegen 1944-ben (Summer and winter life in Bihardiószeg in 1944). *Ethnographia*, 1968; BALÁZS, L., A szalonna és háj szerepe Nádudvaron a XIX. században. *Ethnographia*, 1968; KISBÁN, E., Vom Speck zum Schmalz in der ländlichen ungarischen Speisekultur. In: *In Memoriam António Jorge Dias* II. Lisbon, 1974.

Milk and Milk Processing

ECSEDI, I., Hogy készül az ótó, a gomolya és a zsendice a szilaj pásztorok kezén? (Wie wird der Gärstoff [aus Kalbmagen], der Topfen und die Molke von den Schafhirten im Alföld erzeugt?). *Néprajzi Értesítő*, 1929; MADARASSY, L., Gulyások tarhója ("Tarhó" ein Milcherzeugnis der ungarischen Hirten). *Ethnographia*, 1932; GYÖRFFY, I., Juhtartás és tejgazdaság Kalotaszegen (Schafzucht und Milchwirtschaft im Kalotaszeg). *Néprajzi Értesítő*, 1934; MÁRKUS, M., Gomolyakészítés Nyíregyházán (Zubereitung des Topfens in Nyíregyháza). *Néprajzi Értesítő*, 1938; NAGY, J., Juhsajtkészítés (bácsolás) a kalotaszegi Magyarvalkón (Die Zubereitung der Schafkäse in Magyarvalkó [Kom. Kolozs]). *Ethnographia*, 1943; K. KOVÁCS, L., Adatok a bálványosváraljai fejősjuhászathoz (Angaben zur Melkschäferei in Bálványosváralja). *Ethnographia*, 1947; ZÓLYOMI, J., Tejnyerés és tejfeldolgozás Cserhátsurányon (Gewinnen und Bearbeiten der Milch in Cserhátsurány). *Néprajzi Közlemények*, 1957; B. BENE, Zs., A tejjel kapcsolatos hiedelmek és szokások a Csereháton (Die mit Milch verbundenen Glauben und Bräuche in Cserehát [Nordost-Ungarn]). *Néprajzi Közlemények*, 1957; ANDRÁSFALVY, B., A lótej erjesztése és fogyasztása Bogyiszlón (Die Gärung und Verzehrung der Pferdemilch in Bogyiszló [Kom. Tolna]). *Néprajzi Közlemények*, 1958; KISBÁN, E., A joghurt helye és szerepe a délkelet-európai tejfeldolgozási rendszerekben (Place and Role of the Dairy-Product "Yogurt" within the Milk-Processing Systems of South-East Europe). *Ethnographia*, 1967; K. KOVÁCS, L., Adatok tejkonzerválásunk egyik régi módjához (Daten zu einem alten System der Milchkonservierung bei den Ungarn). *Ethnographia*, 1970; GY. KOVÁCS, I., A tehéntej feldolgozása és hiedelmei Karcagon (Die Kuhmilchwirtschaft, ihre Bräuche und Glauben in Karcag [Grosse Ungarische Tiefebene]). *Szolnok Megyei Múzeumi Évkönyv*, 1973.

Drinks

GYÖRFFY, I., Viricselés a Székelyföldön (Das Sammeln des Birkensaftes im Széklerland). *Ethnographia*, 1937; BALASSA, I., Adatok a székely népi italok ismeretéhez (Volkliche Getränke der Székler). *Ethnographia*, 1944; NÉMETHY, E., Adatok egy primitív pálinkafőző eljárás előfordulásához (Angaben zu einer anfänglichen Vorrichtung zum Branntweinbrennen). *Ethnographia*, 1945; CSATKAI, E., A márc. Egy letűnt népi csemege ("Márc", friandise disparue du peuple). *Ethnographia*, 1948; SZABÓ, L., Az almabor és almaecet készítése a Tiszaháton (Die Bereitung von Apfelwein und Apfelessig in der Theissgegend). *Ethnographia*, 1961; SZABADFALVI, J., A magyar mézsörkészítés (Die Zubereitung des ungarischen Honigbiers). *Műveltség és Hagyomány*, 1961; PALÁDI-KOVÁCS, A., A boza kultúrtörténeti hátteréhez (Zum kulturhistorischen Hintergrund des Bauerngetränks "boza"). *Műveltség és Hagyomány*, 1966; BÖRCSÖK, V., A szőlő és must a szegedi tanyák népének téli táplálkozásában (Grape and Grape Juice in the Winter Alimentation of the People on the Farms of Szeged). *Néprajzi dolgozatok* 14. Szeged, 1963.

Folk Costumes—General, Historical Works

KŐVÁRY, L., *A magyar családi s közéleti viseletek és szokások a nemzeti fejedelmek korában* (The Magyar Family and Public Costumes and Customs During the Time of the National Princes). Pest, 1860; NEMES, M.–NAGY, G., *A magyar viseletek története* (The History of Hungarian Costumes). Budapest, 1905; SZENDREY, J., *A magyar viseletek történeti fejlődése* (The Historical Development of Hungarian Costumes. Budapest, 1905; GYÖRFFY, I., A nagykun viselet a XVIII. században (Die grosskumanische Tracht im XVIII. Jh.). *Ethnographia,* 1837; PAPP, L., A kecskeméti viselet múltja (Vergangenheit der Kecskeméter Tracht). *Néprajzi Értesítő,* 1930; ZOLTAI, L., A debreceni viselet a XVI–XVIII. században (Die Tracht in Debrecen im XVI–XVIII. Jahrhundert). *Ethnographia,* 1938; BALOGH, J., Mátyás kori, illetve későközépkori hagyományok tovább-élése műveltségünkben (La survivance de quelques traditions de l'époque du roi Mathias c'est-à-dire de la fin du Moyen Age dans la civilisation hongroise). *Ethnographia,* 1948; KRESZ, M., *Magyar parasztviselet 1820–1867* (Hungarian Peasant Costumes 1820–1867). Budapest, 1956. (Also in German: Ungarische Bauerntrachten 1820–1867. Budapest–Berlin, 1957.)

General Works on the Recent Past

MALONYAI, D., *A magyar nép művészete* (The Art of the Hungarian People). I–V. Budapest, 1907–1922; BÁTKY, Zs.–GYÖRFFY, I.–VISKI, K., *Magyar népművészet* (Hungarian Folk Art). Budapest, 1928; PALOTAY, G.–KONECSNI, GY., *Magyar népviseletek* (Hungarian Folk Costumes). Budapest, 1938; GYÖRFFY, I., Viselet (Costume). In: *A magyarság néprajza.* I. Budapest, 1941; PALOTAY, G., *A magyar népviselet kutatása* (Research into Hungarian Folk Costume). Budapest, 1948; PALOTAY, G., A viselésmód ruhaformáló szerepe (Einfluss der Tragweise auf die Kleiderform). *Ethnographia,* 1948; FÉL, E., Újabb szempontok a viselet kutatásához. A test technikája (Neue Gesichtpunkte der Trachtforschung). *Ethnographia,* 1952; *Magyar népi díszítőművészet* (Ungarische Volkskunst [German ed.], L'art populaire hongrois [French ed.], Hungarian Decorative Folk Art [English ed.]. Budapest, 1954; FÉL, E., *Népviselet* (Folk Costume). Budapest, 1962; FÉL, E.–HOFER, T.–K. CSILLÉRY, K., *A magyar népművészet* (Hungarian Folk Art). Budapest, 1969; (English ed., Hungarian Folk Art, Budapest, 1979). GÁBORJÁN, A., *Magyar népviseletek* (Hungarian Folk Costumes). Budapest, 1969. (German ed., Ungarische Volkstrachten. Budapest, 1974.); GÁBOR-JÁN, A., Magyar népviseletek. Kísérlet egy összefoglalásra (Hungarian Peasant Costumes. A Tentative Approach to a Summary). *Néprajzi Értesítő,* 1976/1977.

Processing Hemp and Flax

BÁTKY, Zs., A kenderrel való munka Kalotaszegen (Working with Hemp at Kalotaszeg). *Néprajzi Értesítő,* 1905; KÓRIS, K., Matyó kendermegmunkáló szerszámok (*Matyó* Implements for Processing Hemp). *Néprajzi Értesítő,* 1907; ÉBNER, S., A Budapest környéki községek népi kendermunkája és eszközei (Der Hanfbau und seine Werkzeuge beim Volke in der Gegend Budapest). *Néprajzi Értesítő,* 1927; DOMOKOS, P. P., A kender feldolgozása és eszközei Menaságon (Die Bearbeitung des Hanfes im Menaság [Komitat Csík]). *Néprajzi Értesítő,* 1930; GÖNYEY, S., A kendermunka népi szerszámai Magyarországon (Volkliche Bearbeitung des Hanfes in Ungarn). *Néprajzi Értesítő,* 1936; NAGY, J., *A népi kendermunka műszókincse Magyarvalkón (Kalotaszeg)* (The Nomenclature of Hemp Processing in Magyarvalkó [Kalotaszeg]). Debrecen, 1938; NÉMETHY, E., A kender termesztése és feldolgozása Kemenesalján (Der Hanfbau und die Bearbeitung des Hanfes in Kemenesalja). *Néprajzi Értesítő,* 1938; SZOLNOKY, L., A kender és feldolgozója Kemencén (Le travail du chanvre à Kemence). *Ethnographia,* 1949; SZOLNOKY, L., Minőségi csoportok, mennyiségi egységek és a fonalrendezés számolási rendje a kenderfeldolgozásban (Groupes qualitatifs, unités quantitatives et dénombrement de fils dans le travail du chanvre). *Ethnographia,* 1950; SZOLNOKY, L., *Az Országos Néprajzi Múzeum guzsalygyűjte-ménye* (The Distaff Collection of the National Ethnographical Museum). Budapest, 1951; GÁBORJÁN, A., A kenderfeldolgozás és a nyert termékek felhasználása Tardon (Die Bearbeitung des Hanfes und die Verwendung der gewonnenen Produkte in Tard). *Néprajzi Értesítő,* 1955; Szolno-ky, L., Das Rösten des Hanfes bei den Ungarn. *Acta Ethnographica,* 1959; La-jos, Á., *Borsodi fonó* (Spinnery in Borsod). Miskolc, 1965; Szolnoky, L., *Alakuló munkaeszközök. A magyar népi kenderrost megmunkálása* (Arbeitsgeräte im Wandel. Volkstümliche Hanfbearbeitung bei den Ungarn). Budapest, 1972; Szolnoky, L., Zwei weniger bekannte Hanfbrechgeräte. *Acta Ethnographica,* 1974; Szabó J., A kendermunka és szókincse Nagykónyiban (Working with Hemp and its Vocabulary in Nagykónyi). *Néprajz és Nyelvtudomány,* 1975–1976.

Processing Wool

Bátky, Zs., A nemez- és posztógyártás (The Making of Felt and Broadcloth). In: *A magyarság néprajza.* I. Budapest, 1941; Luby, M., A gubakészítés módja és a gubásmesterség (Der "Guba" und dessen Herstellung). *Néprajzi Értesítő,* 1927; N. Bartha, K., A debreceni gubacsapó céh (The *Guba*-making Guild of Debrecen). Debrecen, 1929; N. Bartha, K., A cserge készítése az Udvarhely megyei Bágy községben (Verfertigung des "csörge" [zottiger Webstoff] in Bágy [Kom. Udvarhely]). *Néprajzi Értesítő,* 1932; Haáz, F. R., A székely ványoló (Die Székler Walkmühle). *Néprajzi Értesítő,* 1931; Béres, A., Adatok a debreceni gubás mesterséghez (Materialien zur Geschichte der Wollmantelverfertigung in Debrecen). *A Debreceni Déri Múzeum Évkönyve,* 1958–1959; Kós, K.–Szent-imre, J.–Nagy, J., *Kászoni székely népművészet* (Székely Folk Art of Kászon). Bucharest, 1972.

Processing Leather

Lázár, I., Bőrcserzés Nagyenyeden (Tanning Skin at Nagyenyed). *Néprajzi Értesítő,* 1900; Ferenczi, I., A tímármesterség Nyíregyházán (Das Gerberhandwerk in Nyíregyháza). *Néprajzi Értesítő,* 1927; Pető, J., *A debreceni tímárok céh- és mesterségszavai* (The Guild and Trade Vocabulary of the Tanners of Debrecen). Debrecen, 1938; Bátky, Zs., A bőrmunka (Leather Work). In: *A magyarság néprajza.* I. Budapest, 1941; Dorogi, M., A juhbőr népi kikészítése a Hajdúságban és a Nagykunságban (Die Bearbeitung und Benutzung der Schaffelle bei den Heidukken and Kumanen [in Hajdúság und Nagykunság]). *Ethnographia,* 1956; Takáts, Gy., A szömörce aratásról és a tobakról (Die Ernte des Gerbersumachs [Rhus Cotinus] und die "Tobak" Handwerker). *Ethnographia,* 1956; Gáborján, A., A magyar módra való bőrkikészítés problematikája (Fragen der Ledererzeugung auf ungarischer Art). *Néprajzi Értesítő,* 1962; Nagy, L., A veszprémi tobakok. Egy bőrkészítő kismesterség és művelői a XVIII–XIX. században (Die Tobaken aus der Stadt Veszprém). *Veszprém Megyei Múzeumok Közleményei,* 1971.

Elements of Folk Costume—Hair and Headdresses

Garay, Á., Régi magyar hajviseletek (Old Hungarian Hair Styles). *Néprajzi Értesítő,* 1911; Lükő, G., A moldvai magyarok hajviselete és fejrevalói (Haartracht und Kopfbedeckung der moldauischen Ungarn). *Néprajzi Értesítő,* 1935; Újváriné Kerékgyártó, A., *A magyar női haj- és fejviseletek* (Hair and Headdresses of Hungarian Women). Budapest, 1937; Luby, M., A kézi gyapjúkalap készítése (Der handgearbeitete Filzhut). *Ethnographia,* 1951, 1952; Kerecsé-nyi, E., Az asszonyok fejviseletének kialakulása Kiskomáromban és környékén az elmúlt 90 év alatt (Die Entwicklung der weiblichen Kopfbedeckung in Kiskomárom und Umgebung während der letzten 90 Jahre). *Néprajzi Értesítő,* 1957; Domokos, O., A süvegviselés történetéhez (Zur Geschichte der Filzmützentracht). *Néprajzi Értesítő,* 1962; Dömötör, S., Fehér fejrevalók Vas megyében (Weisse Kopftücher im Komitat Vas). *Savaria,* 1964; Zentai, J., Baranya magyar főkötői (Ungarische Hauben aus Komitat Baranya). *A Janus Pannonius Múzeum Évkönyve*, 1969–1970.

Underwear

PALOTAY, G., A magyarországi női ingek egy szabástípusa (Ein Schnittypus der ungarländischen Frauenhemden). *Néprajzi Értesítő*, 1931; GYÖRFFY, I., Az alsóruha (Underwear). In: *A magyarság néprajza*. I. Budapest, 1941; KRESZ, M., Adatok a palóc pendely szabásához (Angaben zum Schnitt des "pendely"). *Ethnographia*, 1947; MORVAY, J., Korc nélküli pendely Nagybalogról (Ein Schlupfloser Unterrock aus Nagybalog). *Néprajzi Értesítő*, 1957; K. CSILLÉRY, K., Rövid derekú női ing és a hozzávaló pendely Faddról (Das kurze Frauenhemd und der dazugehörige Unterrock von Fadd). *Néprajzi Értesítő*, 1958.

Outer Wear

FÉL, E., Magyarországi ujjatlan felső ruhák (Die ungarländischen ärmellosen Oberkleider). *Néprajzi Értesítő*, 1936; PALOTAY, G., A "harisnya" szabása Csík megyében (Schnitt der Hosen bei den Széklern und Csángó im Kom. Csík). *Néprajzi Értesítő*, 1937; GYÖRFFY, I., A felsőruha (Outer Wear). In: *A magyarság néprajza*. I. Budapest, 1941; GÁBORJÁN, A., Adatok a tardi "felszúrt" szoknyaviselethez (Contribution à la question des jupes épinglées). *Ethnographia*, 1948; NAGY, J., *Adatok a székely posztóharisnya fejlődéstörténetéhez* (Contribution to the History of the Development of the Székely Broadcloth hoses). Kolozsvár, 1957; KÓS, K., A kalotaszegi muszuj (Ein althergebrachtes Kleidungsstück in Kalotaszeg). *Műveltség és Hagyomány*, 1964.

Coat-like Outer Garments

SZABÓ, K., A "suba" és mestersége Kecskeméten (Der ungarische Bauernpelz und seine Verfertigung in Kecskemét). *Ethnographia*, 1923–1924; KISS, L., A szűcsmesterség Hódmezővásárhelyen (Das Kürschnerhandwerk in Hódmezővásárhely). *Néprajzi Értesítő*, 1926; KISS, L., *A nyíregyházi szűcsmesterség és ornamentika* (The Furrier Trade and Ornamentation of Nyíregyháza). Debrecen, 1929; GYÖRFFY, I., *Magyar népi hímzések I. A cifraszűr* (Hungarian Folk Embroidery I. The Ornamented *Szűr*). Budapest, 1939; DAJASZÁSZYNÉ DIETZ, V., A mezőkövesdi kozsu (Der kurze Pelzrock "kuzsu" aus Mezőkövesd). *Néprajzi Értesítő*, 1956; DOROGI, M., *A kunsági kisbunda* (The Short Furcoat of Kiskunság). Szolnok, 1962; GÁBORJÁN, A., Adatok a szűr kialakulásához (Daten zur Ausgestaltung einer Art des Bauernmantels [ung. Szűr]). *Ethnographia*, 1970; GÁBORJÁN, A., Három magyar népi posztóruha (Trois manteaux de bure des paysans hongrois). *Néprajzi Értesítő*, 1972; DOROGI, M., Sárréti és nagykunsági adatok a kacagány viseletéről (Angaben aus dem Sárrét [Grosse Ungarische Tiefebene] und Grosskumanien zum Überwurfsfell). *Szolnok Megyei Múzeumi Évkönyv*, 1973; GERVERS-MOLNÁR, V., *The Hungarian Szűr, an Archaic Mantle of Eurasian Origin*. Toronto, 1973; GÁBORJÁN, A., A magyar szűr eredetének kérdéséhez (Zur Frage der Entstehung des ungarischen Szűrs). *Néprajzi Értesítő*, 1975.

Footwear

GÖNYEY, S., Bocskorformák Csonka-Szatmár és Bereg megyében (Riemenschuhformen in den Kom. Szatmár und Bereg). *Néprajzi Értesítő*, 1932; GYÖRFFY, I., A lábbeli és a kesztyű (Footwear and Gloves). In: *A magyarság néprajza*. I. Budapest, 1941; BÁLINT, S., *A szegedi papucs* (The Slippers of Szeged). Szeged, 1955; GÁBORJÁN, A., A szolnoki hódoltságkori ásatási lábbelianyag magyar viselettörténeti vonatkozásai (Die Beziehungen des bei den Ausgrabungen in Szolnok gefundenen Fussbekleidungsmaterials zur ungarischen Trachtentwicklung). *Ethnographia*, 1957; GÁBORJÁN, A., Két magyar hosszú szárú lábbelitípus viselettörténeti elemzése (Trachtenhistorische Analyse zweier ungarischer langschäftiger Fussbekleidungen). *Néprajzi Értesítő*, 1958; GÁBORJÁN, A., A Néprajzi Múzeum lábbeli gyűjteménye. I. Csizmák (Die Stiefelsammlung des Ethnographischen Museums zu Budapest). *Néprajzi Értesítő*, 1959; FÜR, I., *Bocskortípusok a Dél-Alföldön* (The Types of Laced Sandals of the South Alföld). Néprajzi Dolgozatok 27. Szeged, 1972.

Regional Forms of Hungarian Folk Costume—Transdanubia

JANKÓ, J., *A balatonmelléki lakosság néprajza*. Budapest, 1902. Also in German: Ethnographie der Bevölkerung der Umgebung des Balatonsees. Wien, 1906; BELLOSICH, B., A hetési magyarság viselete (The Costumes of the Hungarians of Hetés). *Néprajzi Értesítő*, 1903; GÖNCZI, F., A göcseji és hetési népviselet (The Folk Costumes of Göcsej and Hetés). *Néprajzi Értesítő*, 1910; KISS, G., Az ormánsági népviselet (Die Volkstracht in Ormánság). *Ethnographia*, 1931; FÉL, E., A női ruházkodás Martoson (Die Frauentracht in Martos). *Néprajzi Értesítő*, 1942; PETÁNOVITS, K., A sármelléki női viselet a századfordulótól napjainkig (Wandel der Frauentracht in der transdanubischen Ortschaft Sármellék zwischen der Jahrhundertwende und heute). *Veszprém Megyei Múzeumok Közleményei*, 1971; HORVÁTH, T., Kapuvár népviselete (Die Volkstracht von Kapuvár). *Néprajzi Közlemények*, 1972.

Upper Hungary

PALOTAY, G., Egy palóc falu ruházata (Die Tracht eines Palowzendorfes in dem Komitate Nógrád). *Néprajzi Értesítő*, 1930; FÉL, E., A turai viselet (Die Tracht in Tura. Komitat Pest). *Néprajzi Értesítő*, 1937; GÖNYEY, S., A Zagyva felső völgyének palóc népviselete (Die Volkstracht der Palozen in der oberen Flussgegend der Zagyva). *Néprajzi Értesítő*, 1938; HERKELY, K., A szokolyai viselet (Die Tracht von Szokolya). *Néprajzi Értesítő*, 1938; GYÖRFFY, I., *Matyó viselet (Matyó Costumes)*. Edited and prepared for publication by FÉL, E., Budapest, 1956; FLÓRIÁN, M., *Rimóc népviselete* (Folk Costumes of Rimóc). Balassagyarmat, 1966.

Great Plain

CSERZY, M., Népviselet és népszokások Szeged vidékén (Folk Costume and Customs around Szeged). *Néprajzi Értesítő*, 1906; ECSEDI, I., A hortobágyi pásztorviselet (Herdsmen's Costumes of the Hortobágy). *Néprajzi Értesítő*, 1914; NYÁRÁDY, M., Az ajaki népviselet (Die Volkstracht von Ajak). *A nyíregyházi Jósa András Múzeum Évkönyve*, 1961; PÉCSINÉ ÁCS, S., *Kalocsa népművészete* (The Folk Art of Kalocsa). Kalocsa, 1970.

Transylvania

GYÖRFFY, I., A Fekete-Körös völgyi magyarság viselete (The Costume of the Hungarians of Fekete-Körös Valley). *Néprajzi Értesítő*, 1912; SZABÓ, I., A dévai csángó viselet (The Costumes of the *Csángó* of Déva). *Néprajzi Értesítő*, 1904; HAÁZ, F. R., Egy székely falu (Lövéte) öltözete (The Costume of a Székely Village [Lövéte]). In: *Emlékkönyv a Székely Nemzeti Múzeum ötvenéves jubileumára*. Sepsiszentgyörgy, 1929; NAGY, J., A kalotaszegi népi öltözet (The Folk Costumes of Kalotaszeg). Bucharest, 1957; NAGY, J., *A torockói magyar népi öltözet* (Hungarian Folk Costume of Torockó). Bucharest, 1957; KRESZ, M., A gyermekek és fiatalok viselete a kalotaszegi Nyárszón (Die Tracht der Kinder und Jugendlichen im Dorfe Nyárszó des Gebietes Kalotaszeg). *Néprajzi Értesítő*, 1957; NAGY J., Adalékok a székely népi öltözet fejlődéséhez (Zur Untersuchung der Entwicklung der Volkstrachten der Székler). *Ethnographia*, 1958; NAGY, J., A szilágysági Tövishát magyar népi öltözetének vizsgálatához (Contribution to the Research on the Hungarian Folk Costumes of Tövishát in the Szilágyság). *Ethnographia*, 1959; FÉL, E.–HOFER, T., A kalotaszentkirályi kelengye (Die Aussteuer in Kalotaszentkirály). *Néprajzi Értesítő*, 1969; PAP JÁNOSSY, M., Györgyfalva viselete (Volkstracht in Györgyfalva). *Ethnographia*, 1971; KÓS, K., Ismeretlen magyar népviseletekről (On Unknown Hungarian Folk Costumes). In: *Népélet és Néphagyomány*. Bucharest, 1972; NAGY, J., Öltözet (Costume). In: KÓS, K.–SZENTIMREI, J.–NAGY, J., *Kászoni székely népművészet* (Folk Art of Kászon). Bucharest, 1972; NAGY, J., Öltözet (Dress). In: *Szilágysági magyar népművészet*. Bucharest, 1974; FARAGÓ, J.–NAGY, J.–VÁMSZER, G., *Kalotaszegi magyar népviselet [1949–1950]* (Hungarian National Costume in Kalotaszeg [1949–1950]). Bucharest, 1977.

Ornamental Folk Art—Comprehensive and General Works

HOLME, CH., *Peasant Art in Austria and Hungary*. London–Paris–New York, 1911; MALONYAY, D., *A magyar népművészet* (Hungarian Folk Art). I–V. Budapest, 1907–1922; BÁTKY, ZS.–GYÖRFFY, I.–VISKI, K., *A magyar népművészet* (Hungarian Folk Art). Budapest, 1928; VISKI, K., A székely népművészet (Székely Folk Art). In: *Emlékkönyv a Székely Nemzeti Múzeum ötvenéves jubileumára*. Sepsiszentgyörgy, 1929; ORTUTAY, GY., *A magyar népművészet* (Hungarian Folk Art). I–II. Budapest, 1941; PALOTAY, G., *A magyar népművészet kutatása* (Research on Hungarian Folk Art). Budapest, 1948; KRESZ, M., Népi díszítőművészetünk fejlődésének útjai (Les tendences dominantes de l'évolution de l'art populaire hongrois). *Ethnographia*, 1952; *Magyar népi díszítőművészet* (Ungarische Volkskunst [German edition], L'art populaire hongrois [French edition], Hungarian Decorative Folk Art [English edition]). Budapest, 1954; FÉL, E.–HOFER, T., *Parasztok, pásztorok, betyárok. Emberábrázolások a magyar népművészetben* (Husaren, Hirten, Heilige. Menschendarstellungen in der ungarischen Volkskunst). Budapest, 1966; BALOGH, J., Népművészet és a történeti stílusok (Volkskunst und geschichtliche Stile). *Néprajzi Értesítő*, 1967; KRESZ, M., A magyar népművészet felfedezése (Die Entdeckung der ungarischen Volkskunst). *Ethnographia*, 1968; DOMANOVSZKY, GY., Személytelen-e a népművészet? (Is Folk Art Impersonal?) *Ethnographia*, 1969; FÉL, E.–HOFER, T.–K. CSILLÉRY, K., *A magyar népművészet* (Hungarian Folk Art). Budapest, 1969; MANGA, J., A népi díszítőművészet stíluselemzésének történeti tanulságai (Die historischen Lehren der Stilanalyse in der Volksornamentik). *Népi kultúra – Népi társadalom*, 1971; HOFER, T.–FÉL, E., *Magyar népművészet* Budapest, 1975. (English ed., *Hungarian Folk Art,* Budapest, London, 1979). DOMONKOS, O., A kisiparok néprajzi kutatása (Die ethnographische Untersuchung des Handwerks). *Ethnographia,* 1974; HOFER, T.–FÉL, E., *Magyar népművészet* (Hungarian Folk Art). Budapest, 1974; ANDRÁSFALVY, B.–SIPOS, ZS., *A népművészet tegnap és ma* (Folk Art Yesterday and Today). Budapest, 1976; CSILLÉRY, K., A magyar népművészet változása a XIX. században és a XX. század elején (Changes of Hungarian Folk Art in the 19th and Early 20th Centuries). *Ethnographia,* 1977; HOFER, T., XIX. századi stílusváltozások: az értelmezés néhány lehetősége (Stiländerungen der ungarischen Volkskunst im 19. Jahrhundert: einige Möglichkeiten der Interpretation). *Ethnographia,* 1977; HOFER, T.–FÉL, E., *Magyar népművészet* (Hungarian Folk Art). 2nd. ed. Budapest, 1977.

Wood Carving

JANKÓ, J., Régi hazai lőportartók szarvasagancsból (Old Domestic Powder Horns Made from Stag Horn). *Archaeologiai Közlemények,* 1890; HERMAN, O., Magyar pásztoremberek remekelése (Masterpieces of Hungarian Herdsmen). *Ethnographia,* 1892; BÁTKY, ZS., Mángorló lapickák (Mangle Dollies). *Néprajzi Értesítő,* 1905; MADARASSY, L., *Vésett pásztortülkök* (Engraved Herdsmen's

744

Horns). Budapest, 1925; BÁTKY, Zs., *Pásztor ivópoharak* (Hirten Schöpfkellen). Budapest, 1928; MADARASSY, L., *Dunántúli tükrösök* (Transdanubian Mirror-cases [English edition]). Budapest, 1932; MADARASSY, L., *A palóc fakanál* (Holzlöffel [Kelle] bei den Palowzen). *Néprajzi Értesítő*, 1932; MADARASSY, L., *Művészkedő magyar pásztorok* (Artistic Hungarian Herdsmen). Budapest, 1934; VÉGH, S., Mézesbábsütő-minták faragása a Tiszántúlon (Das Gravieren der Lebzeltenformen der ungarischen Tiefebene). *Néprajzi Értesítő*, 1938; LÜKŐ, G., *A hortobágyi pásztorművészet* (The Herdsmen's Art of the Hortobágy). Debrecen, 1940; VISKI, K., Díszítőművészet (Ornamental Art). In: *A magyarság néprajza*. II. Budapest, 1941; HAÁZ, F. R., *Udvarhelyszéki famesterségek* (Wood Trades of Udvarhelyszék). Kolozsvár, 1942; DOMANOVSZKY, GY., *Magyar pásztorművészet* (The Art of the Hungarian Herdsmen). Budapest, 1944; SZŰCS, S., Ősi mintájú ábrázolások pásztori eszközökön (Ancient Decorative Patterns on Herdsmen's Implements). *Ethnographia*, 1952; KOVÁCS, D., *Írott botok és guzsalyok mintái* (Patterns on Inscribed Cudgels and Distaffs). Csíkszereda, 1954; DOMANOVSZKY, GY., *A két faragó Kapoli* (The Two Carving Kapolis). Budapest, 1955; BÉRES, A., A Déri Múzeum Debrecen környéki díszes pásztorbotjai (Geschmückte Hirtenstöcke des Déri Museums aus der Umgebung von Debrecen). *A debreceni Déri Múzeum Évkönyve*, 1957; LENGYEL, GY., *Faragás* (Carving). Budapest, 1961; DOMONKOS, O., Sopron megye pásztorművészete (Herdsmen's Art of Sopron County). *Soproni Szemle*, 1962, 1963; MANGA, J., Hirtenkunst in Transdanubien. *Acta Ethnographica*, 1961; MÁNDOKI, L., Pásztor faragóiskola ("Schnitzschule" der Hirten). *A Janus Pannonius Múzeum Évkönyve*, 1963; MANGA, J., *Pásztorművészet* (Herdsmen's Art). Budapest, 1963; WEINER, P., *Geschnitzte Lebkuchenformen in Ungarn*. Budapest, 1964; KÓS, K., *Népélet és Néphagyomány* (Folk Life and Folk Tradition). Bucharest, 1972; KÓS, K., Fafaragás (Wood Carving). In: *Szilágysági magyar népművészet*. Bucharest, 1974; KÓS, K.–OLASZ, F., *Fejfák* (Wooden Crosses). Budapest, 1975.

Furniture Making

SZABÓ, I., A dévai csángó–székely telepesek lakása és lakásberendezése (The Dwellings and Furnishings of the Csángó–Székely Settlers of Déva). *Néprajzi Értesítő*, 1903; VISKI, K., *Dunántúli bútorok I. Székek* (Furniture of the Dunántúl I. Chairs). Budapest, 1925; Cs. SEBESTYÉN, K., A magyar parasztbútor (Hungarian Peasant Furniture). *Népünk és Nyelvünk*, 1929; Cs. SEBESTYÉN, K., Falitéka (Wall Rack). *Népünk és Nyelvünk*, 1930; Cs. SEBESTYÉN, K., Magyar parasztszékek (Hungarian Peasant Chairs). *Népünk és Nyelvünk*, 1937; Cs. SEBESTYÉN, K., Ungarische Bauernmöbel. *Ungarische Jahrbücher*, 1938; K. CSILLÉRY, K., Le coffre de charpenterie. *Acta Ethnographica*, 1950; MÁNDOKI, L., A kisgyermek állni és járni tanulását szolgáló eszközök a Néprajzi Múzeumban (Stehstühle, Gehschulen und Laufgeräte für Kleinkinder im Ethnographischen Museum, Budapest). *Néprajzi Értesítő*, 1960; MÁNDOKI, L., Baranyai székek (Stühle im Komitat Baranya). *A Janus Pannonius Múzeum Évkönyve*, 1962; DOMANOVSZKY, GY., Népi bútorok (Folk Furniture). Budapest, 1964; TOMBOR, I., *Régi festett asztalosmunkák a XV–XIX. században* (Alte ungarische Schreinermalereien. 15.–19. Jahrhundert). Budapest, 1967; K. CSILLÉRY, K., *A magyar nép bútorai* (Ungarische Bauernmöbel). Budapest, 1972; KÓS, K., *Népélet és néphagyomány* (Folk Life and Folk Tradition). Bucharest, 1972; KÓS, K., *A vargyasi festett bútor* (The Painted Furniture of Vargyas). Kolozsvár, 1972; K. CSILLÉRY, K., Egy németalföldi eredetű magyar népi bútor: a csuklós támlájú pad (Die Bank mit umlegbarer Lehne, ein ungarisches Bauernmöbelstück niederländischen Ursprungs). *Néprajzi Értesítő*, 1975. Foreign language edition: *Un meuble régional hongrois originaire des anciens Pays-Bas; le banc à dossier mobile*. In: *Miscellanea K. C. Peeters*. Antwerp, 1975.

Homespuns

Fábián, Gy., *A népies szövés művészete* (The Folk Art of Weaving). Budapest, 1911; Ébner, S., *Bodrogközi szőttesek* (Homespuns of Bodrogköz). Budapest, 1924; Viski, K., *Székely szőnyegek* (Székely homespuns). Budapest, 1928; Szabó, T. A., A festékes és társai (Der "festékes" [farbige Wirktteppich] und ähnliche Teppichgewebe). *Ethnographia*, 1956; Kodolányi, J., *Baranyai szőttesek* (Homespuns of Baranya). Pécs, 1957; Szentimrei, J., *Székely festékesek* (The "festékes" Homespuns of the Székelys). Bucharest, 1957; Kántor, M., *Len és kender feldolgozása a Bodrogközben* (Processing of Hemp and Flax in Bodrogköz). Sárospatak, 1961; Perczel E., *Szőttes* (Homespuns). Budapest, 1962; Szolnoky, L., Falusi takácscéhek Magyarországon (Weberinnungen in den Dörfern Ungarns). *Ethnographia*, 1972; Manherz, K., Beiträge zur volkskundlichen Beschreibung des Weberhandwerks aus Pula (Plattenseeoberland). *Acta Ethnographica*, 1972; Lőrincz, A., *Tolna megyei székely szőttesek és hímzések* (Webereien und Stickereien der Székler im Komitat Tolna). Budapest, 1973.

Embroideries

Gyarmathy, Zs., *A kalotaszegi varrottas (Peasant Embroidery of Kalotaszeg)*. Budapest, 1899; Bátky, Zs., *Rábaközi hímzések* (Embroideries of Rábaköz). I. Budapest, 1924; Bátky, Zs., *Kalotaszegi varrottasok (Peasant Embroidery of Kalotaszeg)*. Budapest, 1924; Györffy, I., *Szilágysági hímzések* (Embroideries of the Szilágyság). I. Budapest, 1924; Györffy, I., *Jászsági szűcshímzések* (Furrier's Embroideries of the Jászság). Budapest, 1924; Viski, K., *Székely hímzések. I. Csík megyeiek* (Székely Embroideries I. Csík County). Budapest, 1924; Györffy, I., *Nagykun szűrhímzések (Szűr* Embroideries of Nagykunság). Budapest, 1925; Viski, K., A pávaszem (Das Pfauenauge). *Néprajzi Értesítő*, 1926; Palotay, G., Sárközi "rostkötés"-ek (Fransenknüpfmuster aus dem Sárköz [Macramé-Arbeit]). *Néprajzi Értesítő*, 1936; Ferencz, K., *A tűzött csipke* (Stitched Lace). Budapest, 1937; Palotay, G., Die historische Schichtung der ungarischen Volksstickerei. *Ungarische Jahrbücher*, 1938; Herkely, K., A mezőkövesdi matyók rojtkötése (Das Fransenknöpfen der Matyó's von Mezőkövesd). *Néprajzi Értesítő*, 1939; Palotay, G., *Oszmán-török elemek a magyar hímzésben* (Les éléments turcs-ottomans des broderies hongroises [bilingual ed.]). Budapest, 1940; Ferencz, K., Subrikálásszerű csipkeverő-technika (Technik einer durchbruchartiger Klöppelspitze). *Néprajzi Értesítő*, 1940; Haáz, F. R.–Palotay, G.–Szabó, T. A., A Néprajzi Múzeum erdélyi vászonhímzésanyaga (Die Siebenbürger Leinenstickereien des Ethnographischen Museums). *Néprajzi Értesítő*, 1940; Palotay, G.–Szabó, T. A., Ismeretlenebb magyar hímzéstípusok (Einige ungarische Stickereitypen aus Siebenbürgen). *Néprajzi Értesítő*, 1941; Gönyey, S., *Drávaszögi hímzések* (Stickereien aus dem Drauwinkel). Budapest, 1944; Palotay, G., *A szolnok-dobokai Szék magyar hímzései* (Hungarian Embroidery of Szolnok-Doboka). Kolozsvár, 1944; Fél, E.–Dajaszászyné, D. V., *Borsod megyei régi keresztszemes hímzések* (Alte Kreuzstich-Stickereien aus dem Komitat Borsod in Ungarn). Budapest, 1951; Dajaszászyné, D. V., *Keresztöltéses párnavéghímzések. A Dél-Dunántúlra telepített bukovinai székelyek varrásai* (Cross-stitch Pillow Case Embroideries of the Székelys of Bukovina Who Settled in South Transdanubia). Budapest, 1951; Dajaszászyné, D. V., Adatok a matyó íróasszonyok életéhez (Lebenslauf und Stilarten der Mezőkövesder Musterzeichnerinnen). *Ethnographia*, 1952; Dajaszászyné, D. V., *Mezőkövesdi hímzések* (Mezőkövesd Embroidery). Budapest, 1953; Dajaszászyné, D. V.–Manga, J., *Nógrád megyei szabadrajzú hímzések* (Free-drawn Embroideries of Nógrád County). Budapest, 1954; Szirmai, F. M., *Tisza-vidéki keresztszemes hímzésminták* (Cross-stitched Embroidery Patterns of the Tisza Region). Budapest, 1960; Vajkai, A., *Bakony-vidéki kereszt-*

szemes hímzésminták (Cross-stitched Embroidery Patterns of the Bakony Region). Budapest, 1960; Fél, E., *Ungarische Volksstickerei*. Budapest, 1961; Varga, M., *Turai hímzések* (Embroideries of Tura). Budapest, 1965; Fél, E., *Bevezetés a magyar népi hímzések ismeretébe* (Introduction to Hungarian Folk Embroidery). Budapest, 1964; Fél, E., *Hímzésminták Baranyából* (Embroidery Patterns from Baranya). Budapest, 1966; Hegedűs, M., *Népi öltéstechnikák* (Folk Stitching Techniques). Budapest, 1967; Csulak M., *Árapataki varrottasok* (Ungarische Volksmuster in Kreutzstichen). Sepsiszentgyörgy, 1972; Seres, A., *Népi hímzéseink. Barcasági csángó férfiingek, menyecskeingek, öregasszonyingek és díszkendők hímzésmintái* (Our Folk Embroideries. Embroidery Patterns of Csángó Men's Shirts, Young Women's Shirts and Ornamental Kerchiefs from the Barcaság). Sepsiszentgyörgy, 1973; Csiszér, I.–Kovács, D., *Csíkszentkirályi keresztszemesek* (Cross Stitchery of Csíkszentkirály). Csíkszereda, 1974; Kocsis, A.–Kunszabó, J., *Székely varrottasminták*. Budapest, 1974; Fél, E., *Magyar népi vászonhímzések* (Also in English: Peasant Embroidery on Linen and Hemp in Hungary). Budapest, 1976.

Ceramics

Herman, O., Magyar bokály, magyar tál (Hungarian Jugs and Plates). *Vasárnapi Újság*, 1887; Tömörkény, I., Feliratos agyagedények (Inscribed Clay Vessels). *Néprajzi Értesítő*, 1912; Kiss, L., A hódmezővásárhelyi tálasság (The Pottery of Hódmezővásárhely). *Néprajzi Értesítő*, 1915, 1916; Viski, K., *Tiszafüredi cserépedények* (Also in English: Tiszafüred Pottery). Budapest, 1932; Fábián, Gy., *A jáki gerencsérek* (The Potters of Ják). Szombathely, 1934; Beczkóyné, R. Á., Adatok a gyöngyösi régi cserépedények kérdéséhez (Angaben zu den Fragen der Töpferei vom Ende des XIX. Jahrhunderts in Gyöngyös. Kom. Heves). *Néprajzi Értesítő*, 1937; Beczkóyné, R. Á., A mórágyi és gyüdi fazekasság (Die Volkskeramik Mórágy und Gyüd). *Néprajzi Értesítő*, 1938; Viski, K., Cserépmunka (Pottery Work). In: *A magyarság néprajza*. II. Budapest, 1941; Kós, K., A züricvölgyi gerencsérség (Pottery of Züricvölgy). *Dunántúli Szemle*, 1944; Domanovszky, Gy., *Mezőcsáti kerámia* (Mezőcsát Pottery). Budapest, 1953; Kresz, M., Évszámos hódmezővásárhelyi cserépedények a Néprajzi Múzeumban (Dated Pottery from Hódmezővásárhely in the Ethnographical Museum). *Néprajzi Értesítő*, 1954; Román, J., *Sárospataki kerámia* (German edition: Die Töpferei von Sárospatak). Budapest, 1955; Soproni, O., Bizánci hatások a felső-tiszai kerámiában (Byzantinische Einflüsse in der Keramik des Gebietes der oberen Theiss). *Néprajzi Értesítő*, 1959; Szabadfalvi, J., Die Ornamentik der ungarischen Schwarzkeramik. *Acta Ethnographica*, 1960; Szabadfalvi, J., A magyar fekete kerámia és kelet-európai kapcsolatai (Die ungarische schwarze Keramik und ihre osteuropäischen Zusammenhänge). *Műveltség és Hagyomány*, 1960; Kresz, M., Fazekas, korsós, tálas (Potter, Jugmaker, Dishmaker). *Ethnographia*, 1960; Kresz, M., Magyar népi cserépedények kiállítása a Néprajzi Múzeumban (Ausstellung ungarischer Bauerntöpferei im Ethnographischen Museum, Budapest). *Néprajzi Értesítő*, 1961; Dankó, I., A gyulai fazekasság (The Pottery of Gyula). Gyula, 1963; Molnár, L., *Fazekasság* (The Potter's Craft). Budapest, 1963; Herepei, J., *Az aradi és szegedi bokály* (The Jugs of Arad and Szeged). Szeged, 1963; J. István, E., Sárközi népi cserépedények (Bauernkeramik aus Sárköz). *Néprajzi Értesítő*, 1964; Kresz, M., Maksa Mihály tálas (Mihály Maksa, der "Schüsselmacher"). *A Móra Ferenc Múzeum Évkönyve*, 1964, 1965; Körmendi, G., *A tatai fazekasság története* (History of the Potter's Craft of Tata). Tatabánya, 1965; Béres, A., *A nádudvari fekete kerámia* (Die Schwarzkeramiksammlung der Bauerntöpferei von Nádudvar im Museum Déri [Debrecen]). Debrecen, 1965; Nagybákay, P., Veszprémi és Veszprém megyei céhkorsók (Zunftkrüge aus Stadt und Komitat Veszprém). *A Veszprém megyei Múzeumok Közleményei*, 1965; Kné-

ZY, J., *A hedrehelyi gölöncsérek* (The Potters of Hedrehely). Kaposvár, 1966; KRESZ, M., A Nagykunság fazekassága (The Pottery of Nagykunság). *Jászkunság,* 1971; KRESZ, M., Emberkorsók. Adatok az antropomorf korsók funkcióihoz (Menschenförmige Krüge. Angaben zu der Funktion antropomorpher Krüge). *Néprajzi Értesítő,* 1971; KRESZ, M., A borsodi fazekasság (Die Töpferei im Komitat Borsod). *A Miskolci Herman Ottó Múzeum Közleményei,* 1972; SAROSÁCZ, GY., *A mohácsi kerámia és története* (Zur Geschichte der Mohácser Keramik). Pécs, 1972; KRESZ, M., Illusztrációk az erdélyi fazekasság történetéhez különös tekintettel a késő-habán kerámiára (Beiträge zur Geschichte der Keramik in Siebenbürgen). *Ethnographia,* 1972; BALOGH, Ö., A marosvásárhelyi fazekasmesterség (The Potter's Craft of Tîrgu-Mureş [History, Technics, Vocabulary]). *Ethnographia,* 1972; KÓS, K., Népi kandallók és kályhacsempék az erdélyi magyarság körében (Folk Fireplaces and Stove Tiles among the Magyars of Transylvania). In: *Népélet és Néphagyomány.* Bucharest, 1972; GYÖRFFY, I., Feliratos butellák a túrkevei Finta Múzeumban (Trinkflaschen mit Inschrift aus dem Finta Museum in Túrkeve). *Szolnok Megyei Múzeumi Évkönyv,* 1973; BUNTA, M., *Az erdélyi habán kerámia* (Die Habaner Keramik in Siebenbürgen). Bucharest, 1973; DOMANOVSZKY, GY., *Magyar népi kerámia* (Ungarische Keramik). Budapest, 1973; KATONA, I., *A habán kerámia Magyarországon* (*Haban* Ceramics in Hungary). Budapest, 1974; KÓS, K., Agyagmunka (Claywork). In: *Szilágysági magyar népművészet.* Bucharest, 1974; BÁRDOSI, J.– DORNER, M., Adatok a sárvári (és kőszegi) fazekas céh történetéhez (Beiträge zur Geschichte der Hafnerzünfte von Sárvár und Kőszeg). *Savaria,* 1971–1972, 1975; GECSEI, L.–TÁBORI, H., *Cseréptárgyak* (Earthenware Objects). Békéscsaba, 1975; G. VÁMOS, M., A szakcsi fazekasság az anyakönyvek tükrében (Die Töpferei von Szakcs im Spiegel der Personenstandsbücher). *A Szekszárdi Béri Balogh Ádám Múzeum Évkönyve,* 1975–1976/1977; DOMANOVSZKY, GY., *Kántor Sándor* (Sándor Kántor). Budapest, 1977; VÉGH, O., *A kalotaszegi fazekasság* (Pottery in Kalotaszeg). Bucharest, 1977.

Other Branches of Ornamental Folk Art

GYÖRFFY, I., *Magyar hímes tojások* (Hungarian painted eggs). Budapest, 1925; ECSEDI, I., Csengőöntés ősi módon Hajdúböszörményben (Bell Casting in the Ancient Manner in Hajdúböszörmény). *Jelentés Debrecen Déri Múzeumának 1930. évi működéséről.* Debrecen, 1931; SZABÓ, K., Csöngettyű és kolomp a kecskeméti pásztorság kezén (Vichglocken der Hirten von Kecskemét). *Néprajzi Értesítő,* 1932; VISKI, K., Díszítőművészet (Ornamental Art). In: *A magyarság néprajza.* II. Budapest, 1941; BÉRES, A., Adatok a juhászkampó készítéséhez és használatához Hajdú-Bihar megyéből (Angaben zur Verfertigung und des Gebrauchs des Hakenstockes der Hirten aus dem Komitate Hajdú-Bihar). *Ethnographia,* 1953; BOGDÁL, F., A rézöntés technikájához (Az edelényi juhászkampó) (Zur Technik des Kupfergusses [Der Haken des Schäferstabes in Edelény]). *Ethnographia,* 1959; BOGDÁL, F., Az ároktövi kovácsok (Schmiede von Ároktő). *Ethnographia,* 1967; BOGDÁL, F., Kovácsremekek, kovácscégérek (Iron-smith Masterpieces and Guild Signs). *A Miskolci Herman Ottó Múzeum Közleményei,* 1971; HORVÁTH, T., Fülbevaló viselet Baja környékén (Das Tragen des Ohrschmucks in der Gegend von Baja). *Néprajzi Értesítő,* 1972; GYÖRGYI, E., A tojáshímzés díszítménykincse (Der Ornamentschatz der verzierten Eier). *Néprajzi Értesítő,* 1974; JANÓ, Á.–VORÁK, J., *Halasi csipke* (Halas Lace). Kiskunhalas 1975; CSONTOS, G., *A nánási szalmaipar* (The Straw Industry in Nánás). Hajdúnánás, 1975.

III. Cultural Anthropology—Instruments of Expression in Cultural Anthropology—Hungarian Dialects

BALASSA, J., *A magyar nyelvjárások osztályozása és jellemzése* (Classification and Description of Hungarian Dialects). Budapest, 1891; HORGER, A., *A magyar nyelvjárások* (Hungarian Dialects). Budapest, 1934; CSŰRY, B., *A népnyelvi búvárlat módszere* (The Method of Investigating Folk Languages). Budapest, 1936; LAZICZIUS, GY., *A magyar nyelvjárások* (Hungarian Dialects). Budapest, 1936; BÁRCZY, G., *A régi magyar nyelvjárások* (Old Hungarian Dialects). Budapest, 1947; DEME, L., *A magyar nyelvjárások néhány kérdése* (Some Problems Concerning Hungarian Dialects). Budapest, 1953; BENKŐ, L., *Magyar nyelvjárástörténet* (History of Hungarian Dialects). Budapest, 1957; VÉGH, J., *Őrségi és hetési nyelvatlasz* (Linguistic Atlas of the Őrség and Hetés). Budapest, 1959; BÁRCZI, G., *A magyar nyelv életrajza* (A Biography of the Hungarian Language). Budapest, 1963; PAPP, L., *Nyelvjárástörténet és nyelvi statisztika* (History of Dialect and Linguistic Statistics). Budapest, 1963; KÁLMÁN, B., *Nyelvjárásaink* (Our Dialects). Budapest, 1966; *A magyar nyelvjárások atlasza* (Atlas of Hungarian Dialects). Budapest, from 1968; IMRE, S., *A mai magyar nyelvjárások rendszere* (The System of the Present Hungarian Dialects). Budapest, 1971; *A Magyar Nyelvjárások Atlaszának elméleti-módszertani kérdései* (Theoretical and Methodological Problems of the Atlas of Hungarian Dialects). Budapest, 1975; SZABÓ, T. A., *Erdélyi magyar szótörténeti tár* (Wortgeschichtlicher Thesaurus der Siebenbürgisch-Ungarischen Sprache). I–II. A–Elsz. Bucharest, 1975, 1978; VÉGH, J.–PAPP, L., *Heves megye földrajzi nevei 2. A füzesabonyi járás* (The Geographical Names of Heves County 2. The Füzesabony District). Budapest, 1976.

Hungarian Folk Music and Folk Instruments

SZTRIPSZKY, H., Igriczek, énekes koldusok (Minstrels, Singing Beggars). *Ethnographia,* 1908; KODÁLY, Z., *Ötfokú hangsor a magyar népzenében* (The Pentatonic Scale in Hungarian Folk Music). Temesvár, 1917; BARTÓK, B., *A magyar népdal* (Hungarian Folksong). Budapest, 1924; BARTÓK, B., *Das ungarische Volkslied.* Budapest, 1925; BARTÓK, B., *Hungarian Folk Music.* Oxford, 1931; SZABOLCSI, B., Egyetemes művelődéstörténet és ötfokú hangsorok (Die Verbreitung der Pentatonie und ihre Bedeutung für die Kulturgeschichte). *Ethnographia,* 1936; SZABOLCSI, B., Két zenetörténeti előadás I. Írott hagyomány – élő hagyomány. II. Makám-elv a népi és művészi zenében (Two Lectures on the Relation of Folk Music and Art Music. I. Oral Tradition and Ancient Musical Records. II. The Principle of the maqam in Folk Melodies and Art Music). *Ethnographia,* 1949; KERÉNYI, GY., *Gyermekjátékok* (Children's Games). Budapest, 1951. *A Magyar Népzene Tára I;* BARTÓK, B., *Népzenénk és a szomszéd népek zenéje* (Our Folk Music and the Music of the Neighbouring Peoples). Budapest, 1952; KODÁLY, Z., *A magyar népdal* (Hungarian Folksong). Budapest, 1952; KERÉNYI, GY., *Jeles napok* (Special Days). Budapest, 1953. *A Magyar Népzene Tára II;* FARAGÓ, J.–JAGAMAS, J., *Moldvai csángó népdalok és népballadák* (Moldavian *Csángó* Folksongs and Folk Ballads). Bucharest, 1954; LAJTHA, L., *Széki gyűjtés* (A Collection from Szék). Budapest, 1954; LAJTHA, L., *Szépkenyerűszentmártoni gyűjtés* (A Collection from Szépkenyerűszentmárton). Budapest, 1954; SZABOLCSI, B., *Népzene és történelem* (Folksong and History). Budapest, 1954; VARGYAS, L.–NAGY CZIROK, L., *Régi népdalok Kiskunhalasról* (Old Folksongs from Kiskunhalas). Budapest, 1954; KISS, L., *Lakodalom* (Wedding). Budapest, 1955. *A Magyar Népzene Tára III;* AVASI, B., *Ötfokúságból hétfokúság* (The Development of Pentatonic Scales into Diatonic Scales). *Ethnographia,* 1956; BARTÓK, B., *Válogatott írásai* (Selected Writings). Budapest, 1956; DOMOKOS, P. P.–RAJECZKY, B., *Csángó népzene* (La musique populaire csángó (Die Volksmusik der Tschangos). I–II. Budapest, 1956–1961; KODÁLY, Z., *Die ungarische Volksmusik.* Budapest, 1956; LAJTHA, L., *Sopron megyei virrasztó énekek* (Dirges from Sopron County). Budapest, 1956; HALMOS, I., *A zene Kérsemjénben* (Music in Kérsemjén). Budapest, 1959; KERÉNYI, GY., *Párosítók* (Pairing Songs). Budapest, 1959. *A Magyar Népzene Tára IV;* KODÁLY, Z., *Folk Music of Hungary.* Budapest, 1960; VARGYAS, L., *Áj falu zenei anyaga* (Das Musikmaterial des Dorfes Áj). Budapest, 1960; JÁRDÁNYI, P., *Magyar népdaltípusok* (Hungarian Folksong Types). I–II. Budapest, 1961; KERÉNYI, GY., *Népies dalok* (Folk-like Songs). Budapest, 1961; LAJTHA, L., *Dunántúli táncok és dallamok* (Dances and Melodies from Transdanubia). Budapest, 1962; KISS, L.–RAJECZKY, B., *Siratók* (Laments). Budapest, 1966. *A Magyar Népzene Tára V;* KODÁLY, Z., *Ötfokú zene. 100 magyar népdal* (Pentatonic Music, 100 Hungarian Folksongs). 8th edition. Budapest, 1966; MANGA, J., *Magyar népdalok, népi hangszerek* (Hungarian Folksongs, Folk Instruments). Budapest, 1960; BARTÓK, B.–KODÁLY, Z., *Népdaltípusok* (Volksliedertypen). 1. Ed. JÁRDÁNYI, P.–OLSVAI, I. Budapest, 1973. *A Magyar Népzene Tára VI;* SÁROSI, B., *Zenei anyanyelvünk* (Our Musical Mother Tongue). Budapest, 1973; VARGYAS, L., *Népzene és zenetörténet* (Folk Music and Music History). Budapest, 1974; MADARASSY, L., Palóc duda (Palowzischer Dudelsack). *Néprajzi Értesítő,* 1934; DINCSÉR, O.–LAJTHA, L., A tekerő (Der Drehleier). *Néprajzi Értesítő,* 1939; DINCSÉR, O., *Két csíki hangszer. Muzsika és gordon* (Two Musical Instruments from Csík. Music and Cello). Budapest, 1943; MANGA, J., *Nógrádi dudások* (Bagpipers of Nógrád). Budapest, 1950; AVASI, B., A széki banda harmonizálása (L'harmonisation de l'orchestre tzigane de Szék). *Néprajzi Értesítő,* 1954; LAJTHA, L., *Kőrispataki gyűjtés. Erdélyi táncok kis zenekarra* (Collection from Kőrispatak. Dances of Erdély for Small Bands). Budapest, 1955; TAKÁCS, L., Síp cseresznyefa héjából (Die Pfeife aus Kirschbaumrinde). *Néprajzi Közlemények,* 1956; VARGYAS, L., A duda hatása a magyar népi tánczenére (The Effect of the Bagpipe on Hungarian Folk-dance Music). *MTA Nyelv- és Irodalomtudományi Osztályának Közleményei,* 1956; FÜZES, E., A duda (gajda) készítése Mohácson (Die Verfertigung des Dudelsackes [Gajda] in Mohács). *A Janus Pannonius Múzeum Évkönyve,* 1958; AVASI, B., A magyarországi tekerő hangkészlete (Die Töne der ungarischen Drehleier). *Néprajzi Értesítő,* 1959; SCHRAM, F., Egy bernecebaráti furulyakészítő (Ein Flöteerzeuger aus Bernecebaráti). *Ethnographia,* 1960; SÁROSI, B., Citera és citerajáték Szeged környékén (Zither und Zitherspiel in der Umgebung von Szeged). *Ethnographia,* 1961; MANGA, J., Die Harfner der Plattenseegegend. *Acta Ethnographica,* 1962; SÁROSI, B., A magyar népi furulya (Die ungarische Flöte). *Ethnographia,* 1962; SZŰCS, S., *Szól a duda, verbuválnak* (The Bagpipe's Playing, They're Recruiting). Budapest, 1962; DOMOKOS, P. P., Szültü (Egy moldvai csángó hangszer) ("Szültü" [ein Musikinstrument bei den Csángós]). *Ethnographia,* 1963; MANGA, J., Hungarian Bagpipers. *Acta Ethnographica,* 1965; SÁROSI, B., Die ungarische Flöte. *Acta Ethnographica,* 1965; MANGA, J., *Magyar népdalok, népi hangszerek* (Ungarische Volkslieder und Volksmusikinstrumente). Budapest, 1969; SÁROSI, B., *Magyar népi hangszerek* (Hungarian Folk Music Instruments). Budapest, 1973.

Movement and Dance

FARAGÓ, J.–NAGY, O., *Előbb a tánc, aztán a lakoma* (First the Dance, then the Wedding Feast). Bucharest, n.d.; RÉTHEI PRIKKEL, M., *A magyarság táncai* (Hungarian Dances). Budapest, 1924; LAJTHA, L.–GÖNYEY, S., Tánc (Dance). In: *A magyarság néprajza.* IV. Budapest, 1941; VISKI, K., *Hungarian Dances.* Budapest, 1937; LUGOSSY, E.–GÖNEY, S., *Magyar népi táncok* (Hungarian Folk Dances). Budapest, 1947; MOLNÁR, I., *Magyar tánchagyományok* (Hungarian Dance Traditions). Budapest, 1947; FARAGÓ, J.–ELEKES, D., *Táncoljunk, daloljunk! Székely néptáncok* (Let's Dance, let's Sing! Székely Folk Dances). Bucharest, 1949; MORVAY, P., A templomkertben, temetőben és halotti toron táncolás, s a halottas-játék népszokásához (Zur Volkssitte des Tanzes im Kirchengarten, im Friedhof und bei dem Totenmahle, und des Leichenspieles). *Ethnographia,* 1951; LUGOSSY, E., *77 leánytánc* (77 Girls' Dances). Budapest, 1952; MOLNÁR, I., *Pusztafalutól Karcsáig* (From Pusztafalu to Karcsa). Budapest, 1953; SZENTPÁL, O., *Sióagárdi táncok* (Dances of Sióagárd). Budapest, 1953; LUGOSSY, E., *39 verbunktánc* (39 Recruiting Dances). Budapest, 1954; MORVAY, P.–PESOVÁR, E., *Somogyi táncok* (Dances of Somogy). Budapest, 1954; RÁBAI, M., *Szatmári táncok* (Dances of Szatmár). Budapest, 1954; Sz. SZENTPÁL, M., *Felsőtárkányi táncok* (Dances of Felsőtárkány). Budapest, 1954; SZENTPÁL, O., *A csárdás* (The *csárdás*). Budapest, 1954; MARTIN, GY., *Bag táncai és táncélete* (The Dances and Dancing-life of Bag). Budapest, 1955; VARGA, GY., *Ajaki leánytánc* (The Girls' Dance of Ajak). Budapest, 1955; MORVAY, P., Az egykori verbuválás és régi népi táncaink ismeretéhez (Beiträge zum ehemaligen Werbetanz und zu anderen Volkstänzen in Ungarn). *Néprajzi Közlemények,* 1956; BELÉNYESY, M., *Kultúra és tánc a bukovinai székelyeknél* (Kultur und Tanz der umgesiedelten Bukowiner Szekler). Budapest, 1958; KAPOSI, E.–MAÁCZ, L., *Magyar népi táncok és táncos népszokások* (Hungarian Folk Dances and Folk Customs Related to Dance). Budapest, 1958; MAÁCZ, L., Adalékok csürdöngölő táncunk ismeretéhez (Contributions à la dance hongroise "csürdöngölő"). *Ethnographia,* 1958; KAPOSI, E.–PETHES, I., *Magyar tánctörténeti áttekintés* (Historical Survey of Hungarian Dance). Budapest, 1959; PESOVÁR, E., Alapi táncok (Dances d'Alap). *Alba Regia,* 1960; RÁBAI, M., *Kun verbunkos* (Cumanian Recruiting Dance). Budapest, 1960; MARTIN, GY.–PESOVÁR, E., Determination of Motive Types in Dance Folklore. *Acta Ethnographica,* 1963; MARTIN, GY., *A sárközi Duna menti táncok motívumkincse* (Motifs of the Dances of Sárköz along the Danube). Budapest, 1964; MARTIN, GY., East-European Relations of Hungarian Dance Types. *Europa et Hungaria.* Budapest, 1965; PESOVÁR, E., Der Tändel Tschardasch. *Acta Ethnographica,* 1969; MARTIN, GY., *Magyar tánctípusok és táncdialektusok* (Types and Dialects of Hungarian Dance). I–III. Budapest, 1970; BERKES, E., A szlavóniai magyar népsziget tánchagyományai (Dance Traditions of the Hungarian Ethnic Enclave in Slavonia). *Létünk,* 1973; MARTIN, GY., *Ungarische Volkstänze.* Budapest, n.d. 1973; MARTIN, GY., A táncos és a zene. Tánczenei terminológia Kalotaszegen (The Dancer and the Music. Dance Musical Terminologies at Kalotaszeg). *Népi kultúra – Népi társadalom,* 1977; MARTIN, GY., Az új magyar táncstílus jegyei és kialakulása (Development and Distinguishing Marks of the "New Style" in Hungarian Folk Dancing). *Ethnographia,* 1977; ESZE, T., Rákóczi tánca (Der Tanz Ferenc Rákóczis). *Ethnographia,* 1977.

Hungarian Folk Poetry and Prose—The Theory of Hungarian Folk Poetry and Prose Collections

KRIZA, J., *Vadrózsák* (Wild Roses). Kolozsvár, 1863. ARANY, L.–GYULAI, P., *Elegyes gyűjtések* (Mixed Collections). Pest, 1872. *Magyar Népköltési Gyűjtemény* I; TÖRÖK, K., *Csongrád megyei gyűjtés* (Collections from Csongrád County). Pest, 1872; *Magyar Népköltési Gyűjtemény* II; KÁLMÁNY, L., *Koszorúk az Alföld vadvirágaiból* (Wreaths from the Wild Flowers of the Great Plain). I–II. Arad, 1877–78; KÁLMÁNY, L., *Szeged népe* (The People of Szeged). I–III. Arad–Szeged, 1881–1891; KRIZA, J.–ORBÁN, B.–BENEDEK, E.–SEBESI, J., *Székelyföldi gyűjtés* (Collection from the Székely Region). Budapest, 1882. *Magyar Népköltési Gyűjtemény* III; Pest, 1882. LÁZÁR, I., *Alsófehér vármegye magyar népe* (The Hungarians of Alsófehér County). Nagyenyed, 1896; MAJLAND, O., *Székelyföldi gyűjtés* (Collection from the Székely Region). Budapest, 1905. *Magyar Népköltési Gyűjtemény* VII.; VIKÁR, B., *Somogy megye népköltése* (Folk Poetry and Prose of Somogy County). Budapest, 1905. *Magyar Népköltési*

Gyűjtemény VI.; SEBESTYÉN, GY., *Dunántúli gyűjtés* (Collection from Transdanubia). Budapest, 1906. *Magyar Népköltési Gyűjtemény* VIII.; KÁLMÁNY, L.; *Hagyományok és rokonneműek* (Traditions and the Like), I–II. Vácz, 1914—Szeged, 1914; SZENDREY, ZS.; *Nagyszalontai gyűjtés* (Collection from Nagyszalonta). Budapest, 1924. *Magyar Népköltési Gyűjtemény* XIV; ORTUTAY, GY., A magyar népköltési gyűjtemények története (History of Collections of Hungarian Folklore). *Ethnographia, 1939*; BERZE NAGY, J., *Baranyai magyar néphagyományok* (Hungarian Folk Traditions from Baranya). I–III. Pécs, 1940; DOMOKOS, P. P., *Moldvai magyarság* (The Hungarians of Moldavia). Kolozsvár, 1941; GÖNCZI, F., *Göcsej népköltészete* (The Folk Poetry of Göcsej). Zalaegerszeg, 1948; MARÓT, K., *A népköltészet elmélete és magyar problémái* (The Theory and Problems of Hungarian Folk Poetry and Prose). Budapest, 1949; ORTUTAY, GY., *A magyar népköltészet* (Hungarian Folk Poetry and Prose). Budapest, 1952; ORTUTAY, GY., *Magyar népköltészet* (Hungarian Folk Poetry). I–III. Budapest, 1955; KRIZA, J., *Székely népköltési gyűjtemény* (Collection of Székely Folk Poetry and Prose). I–II. Budapest, 1956; KONSZA, S.–FARAGÓ, J., *Háromszéki magyar népköltészet* (Hungarian Folk Poetry and Prose of Háromszék). Marosvásárhely, 1957; KOVÁCS, F.–FARAGÓ, J., *Iratosi kertek alatt (Kisiratosi népköltészet)* (In the Gardens of Iratos [Folk Poetry of Kisiratos]). Bucharest, 1958; ORTUTAY, GY., Variáns, invariáns, affinitás, a szájhagyományozó műveltség törvényszerűségei (Variant, Invariant, Affinity. The Laws of Orally Transmitted Culture). *MTA Társadalmi-Történeti Osztályának Közleményei,* 1959; ORTUTAY, GY., A szájhagyományozódás törvényszerűségei (Regularities in the Oral Transmission of Popular Tradition). *Ethnographia, 1965*; VOIGT, V., A néprajztudomány elméleti terminológiai kérdései (Theoretical and Terminological Problems in Recent East European Ethnology, Ethnography and Folklore). *Ethnographia, 1965*; DÖMÖTÖR, T.–ORTUTAY, GY.–KATONA, I., *A magyar népköltészet.* (Egyetemi jegyzet.) (Hungarian Folk Poetry [Lecture Notes]). Budapest, 1966; ORTUTAY, GY., *Halhatatlan népköltészet* (Immortal Folk Poetry and Prose). Budapest, 1966; HONT, F., Folklore und Theaterwissenschaft. *Acta Ethnographica,* 1970; ISTVÁNOVITS, M., Beiträge zur belletristischen Verwendung folkloristischer Texte. *Acta Ethnographica,* 1970; VOIGT, V., Vom Neofolklorismus in der Kunst. *Acta Ethnographica,* 1970; VOIGT, V., *A folklór esztétikájához* (On the Aesthetics of Folklore). Budapest, 1972; ORTUTAY, GY., *Hungarian Folklore.* Essays. Budapest, 1972; DÖMÖTÖR, T.–KATONA, I.–ORTUTAY, GY.–VOIGT, V., *A magyar népköltészet* (Hungarian Folk Poetry and Prose). Budapest, 1974; EGYÜD, Á., *Somogyi népköltészet* (Folk Poetry and Prose of Somogy). Kaposvár, 1975; VOIGT, V., *A szájhagyományozás törvényszerűségei* (Regularities of oral tradition). Budapest, 1974; VOIGT, V., A népköltészet változása a XIX. században (Die Veränderung der ungarischen Volksdichtung im 19. Jahrhundert). *Ethnographia, 1977.*

The Folksong

DÁVID, GY.–TORDAI, Z., *A kuruckor költészete* (History of the *Kuruc* Era). Bucharest, n.d.; FARAGÓ, J.–JAGAMAS, J.–SZEGŐ, J., *Moldvai csángó népdalok és népballadák* (Folksongs and Ballads of the *Csángó* of Moldva). Budapest–Bucharest, n.d.; ERDÉLYI, J., *Népdalok és mondák* (Folksongs and Legends). Pest, 1846–1848; BARTALUS, I., *Magyar népdalok* (Hungarian Folksongs). I–VII. Budapest, 1873–1896; KÁLMÁNY, L., *Koszorúk az Alföld vadvirágaiból* (Wreaths from the Wild Flowers of the Great Plain). I–II. Arad, 1877–1878; KÁLMÁNY, L., *Szeged népe* (The People of Szeged). I: *Ős-Szeged népköltése* (Folklore of Ancient Szeged); II: *Temesköz népköltése* (Folklore of Temesköz); III: *Szeged vidéke népköltése* (Folklore around Szeged). Arad, 1881–1882, Szeged, 1891; IMRE, S., *A népköltészetről és a népdalokról* (On Folk Poetry and Folksong). Budapest, 1906; BARTÓK, B.–KODÁLY, Z., *Erdélyi magyarság. Népdalok* (The Hungarians of

Transylvania. Folksongs). Budapest, 1923; BARTÓK, B., *Das ungarische Volkslied*. Budapest, 1925; HORVÁTH, J., *A magyar irodalmi népiesség Faluditól Petőfiig* (Hungarian Literary Populism. From Faludi to Petőfi). Budapest, 1927; ECSEDI, I.–BODNÁR, L., *Hortobágyi pásztor- és betyárnóták* (Herdsmen's and Outlaws' Songs of the Hortobágy). Debrecen, 1927; KISS, L., *Régi népdalok Hódmezővásárhelyről* (Old Folksongs from Hódmezővásárhely). Karcag, 1927; ORTUTAY, GY., *Mondotta Vince András béreslegény, Máté János gazdalegény. Nyíri, rétközi balladák, betyár- és juhásznóták* (Thus Said András Vince Young Hired Hand, János Máté Young *gazda,* Ballads from Nyír and Rétköz, Outlaws' and Herdsmen's Songs). Szeged, 1933; BERZE NAGY, J., *Baranyai magyar néphagyományok* (Hungarian Folk Traditions of Baranya). I. Pécs, 1940; VARGYAS, L., *Áj falu zenei anyaga* (Musical Material of the Village Áj). Budapest, 1941; JÁRDÁNYI, P., *A kidei magyarság világi zenéje* (The Secular Music of the Hungarians of Kide). Kolozsvár, 1943; KÁLMÁNY, L., *Történeti énekek és katonadalok* (Historical Songs and Soldiers' Songs). (Prepared for publication by DÉGH, L.–KATONA, I.). Budapest, 1952; ORTUTAY, GY., Kossuth Lajos a magyar nép hagyományaiban (Lajos Kossuth in Hungarian Popular Tradition). *Ethnographia,* 1952; DÉGH, L., *A szabadságharc népköltészete* (Folk Poetry of the War of Independence). Budapest, 1953; ESZE, T.–KISS, J.–KLANICZAY, T., *Magyar költészet Bocskaytól Rákócziig* (Hungarian Folk Poetry from Bocskay to Rákóczi). Budapest, 1953; FARAGÓ, J.–JAGAMAS, J., *Moldvai csángó népdalok és népballadák* (Moldavian *Csángó* Folksongs and Ballads). Budapest–Bucharest, 1954; VARGYAS, L.–NAGY CZIROK, L., *Régi népdalok Kiskunhalasról* (Old Folksongs from Kiskunhalas). Budapest, 1954; LAJOS, Á., *Borsodi népdalok* (Folksongs from Borsod). Miskolc, 1955; ORTUTAY, GY., *Magyar népköltészet. I: Népdalok* (Hungarian Folklore. I: Folksongs). Budapest, 1955; STOLL, B., *Virágénekek és mulatónóták. 17–18. század* (Flower Songs and Songs of Merrymaking). Budapest, 1956; KONSZA, S.–FARAGÓ, J., Háromszéki magyar népköltészet (Hungarian Folk Poetry of Háromszék). Marosvásárhely, 1957; KERÉNYI, GY., Párosítók (Pairing Songs). Budapest, 1959. *A Magyar Népzene Tára IV;* LAJOS, Á., Egy archaikus dallamsajátság Észak-Borsodban (Eine archaische Eigenschaft der Volksweisen in Nord-Borsod). *Ethnographia,* 1960; MARÓTHY, J., Az európai népdal születése (The Birth of European Folksong). Budapest, 1960; KERÉNYI, GY., Népies dalok (Folk-like Songs). Budapest, 1961; SÁROSI, B., Magyar népi líra (The Hungarian Folk Lyric). Budapest, 1961; KATONA, I., Historische Schichten der ungarischen Volksdichtung. Helsinki, 1964; FFC 194; ORTUTAY, GY., A magyar népdal (Hungarian Folksong). In: Kis magyar néprajz (Short Hungarian Ethnography). Budapest, 1966; KATONA, I.–MARÓTHY, J.–SZATMÁRI, A., A parasztdaltól a munkásdalig (From the Peasant Song to the Workers' Song). Budapest, 1968; KODÁLY, Z., A magyar népdal (Hungarian Folksong. 4th ed. Collection edited by VARGYAS, L.). Budapest, 1969; DÖMÖTÖR, T., Mythical Elements in Hungarian Midwinter Fête Songs. *Acta Ethnographica,* 1970; KATONA, I., Die Gliederung der ungarischen Volkslyrik nach Kunstgattungen und Thematik. *Acta Ethnographica,* 1970; ORTUTAY, GY.–KATONA, I., Magyar népdalok (Hungarian Folksongs). I–II. Budapest, 1970; ÁG, T., Édesanyám rózsafája. Palóc népdalok (My Mother's Rose Bush. Palots Folksongs). Bratislava–Budapest, 1974; JAGAMAS, J.–FARAGÓ, J., Romániai magyar népdalok (Hungarian Folksongs from Rumania). Bucharest, 1974; EGYÜD, Á., Somogyi népköltészet (Folk Poetry from Somogy). Kaposvár, 1975; ORTUTAY, GY.–KATONA, I., *Magyar népdalok I–II.* (Hungarian Folksongs I–II.). 2nd ed. Budapest, 1976; SEBESTYÉN, Á., *Bukovinai, andrásfalvi népdalok* (Folksongs of Bukovina and Andrásfalva). Szekszárd, 1976; BORSAI, I., Régi stílusú elemek megjelenése az új magyar népdalstílusban (Elemente des "alten Stils" im "neuen ungarischen Volksliedstil"). *Ethnographia,* 1977; NAGY, Z., *Nógrádi summásdalok* (The Songs of Seasonal Labourers in Nógrád). Salgótarján, 1977.

ORTUTAY, GY., *Székely népballadák* (Székely Folk Ballads). Budapest, 1935; TAKÁCS, L., Népi verselők és hírversírók (Bauerndichter ungarischer Nachrichtenreime). *Ethnographia*, 1951; TAKÁCS, L., A képmutogatás kérdéséhez (Zur Frage der Bänkelsänger). *Ethnographia*, 1953; CSANÁDI, I.–VARGYAS, L., *Röpülj páva, röpülj. Magyar népballadák és balladás dalok* (Fly Peacock, Fly. Hungarian Folk Ballads and Ballad Songs). Budapest, 1954; KÁLMÁNY, L., *Alföldi népballadák* (Folk Ballads of the Great Hungarian Plain). Edited by ORTUTAY, GY. Budapest, 1954; TAKÁCS, L., A históriások alkotásmódja (The Way of Composing Verse-Chronicles). *Ethnographia*, 1956; UJVÁRY, Z., Árgirus nótája egy népi énekes könyvében (Das Argirus-Lied eines Volksliederbuches). *Ethnographia*, 1956; TAKÁCS, L., *Históriások, históriák* (Chroniclers, Chronicles). Budapest, 1958; DOMOKOS, P. P., Júlia szép leány. Ballada monográfia (Beautiful Maiden Julia. Monograph of a Ballad). *Ethnographia*, 1959; DOMOKOS, P. P., A pávát őrző leány balladája (Die Ballade vom Mädchen, das einen Pfauen hütet). *Ethnographia*, 1959; SZŰCS, S., *Békési históriák* (Chronicles from Békés). Gyula, 1959. *A gyulai Erkel Ferenc Múzeum Közleményei*, 6; VARGYAS, L., Kutatások a népballada középkori történetében (Forschungen zur Geschichte der Volksballade im Mittelalter). I–III. *Néprajzi Értesítő*, 1959, *Ethnographia*, 1960; ÁG, T., "Kőműves Kelemen" a Zoborvidéken (Die Ballade von der eingemauerten Frau in der Umgebung des Berges Zobor [im ehemaligen Komitat Nyitra]). *Néprajzi Közlemények*, 1961; ERDÉSZ, S., A "sárga kígyó" ballada Nyírbátorból (The Ballad of the "yellow snake" from Nyírbátor) *A nyíregyházi Jósa András Múzeum Évkönyve*, 1963–64; KRIZA, I., Affinitás a népballadában (Affinität in der Volksballade). *Ethnographia*, 1965; JEVSEYEV, V., A Kőműves Kelemen ballada történetéhez (Zum Ursprung der Ballade von der eingemauerten Frau). *Ethnographia*, 1967; KRIZA, I., *A halálra táncoltatott lány* (The Girl who was Danced to Death). Budapest, 1967; VARGYAS, L., *Researches into the Mediaeval History of Folk-ballad.* Budapest, 1967; ORTUTAY, GY.–KRIZA, I., *Magyar népballadák* (Hungarian Folk-ballads). Budapest, 1968; FARAGÓ, J.–RÁDULY, J., A népballadák egy romániai falu mai köztudatában (Volksballaden im heutigen Bewusstsein eines ungarischen Dorfes in Rumänien). *Ethnographia*, 1969; KALLÓS, Z., *Balladák könyve. Élő hazai magyar népballadák* (The Book of Ballads. Living Hungarian Folk-ballads in Hungary); Bucharest, 1970; ALBERT, E.–FARAGÓ, J., *Háromszéki balladák* (The Ballads of Háromszék). Bucharest, 1973; KRUPA, A., *Újkígyósi népballadák* (Folk-ballads of Újkígyós). *Békési Élet*, 1974; KOVÁCS, I., *Gombosi népballadák* (The Folk-ballads of Gombos). Újvidék, 1975; RÁDULY, J., *Kibédi népballadák* (The Folk-ballads of Kibéd). Bucharest, 1975; VARGYAS, L., *A magyar népballada és Európa* (The Hungarian Folk-ballad and Europe). I–II. Budapest, 1976.

Folk Poetry in Prose—The Folk Tale

ERDÉLYI, J., *Magyar népmesék* (Hungarian Folk-Tales). Pest, 1855; GAAL György magyar népmesegyűjteménye (György Gaal's Collection of Hungarian Folk-Tales). I–II. Pest, 1861; ARANY, L., *Eredeti népmesék* (Original Folk-Tales). Pest, 1862; MERÉNYI, L., *Sajóvölgyi eredeti népmesék* (The Original Folk-Tales of the Sajóvölgy). I–II. Pest, 1862; MERÉNYI, L., *Dunamelléki eredeti népmesék* (The Original Folk-Tales of the Dunamellék); I–II. Pest, 1863–64; MAILÁTH, J., *Magyar regék, mondák és népmesék* (Hungarian Fables, Sagas and Folk-Tales). Pest, 1864; ISTVÁNFFY, GY., *Palócz mesék a fonóból* (Palóts Tales from the Spinning Room); Lipótszentmiklós, 1890; BENEDEK, E., *Magyar mese- és mondavilág* (The World of Hungarian Stories and Sagas). I–IV. Budapest, 1894–1896; BERZE NAGY, J., *Népmesék Heves és Jász-Nagykun-Szolnok megyéből* (Folk-tales from Heves and Jász-Nagykun-Szolnok Counties). Budapest, 1907. *Magyar*

Népköltési Gyűjtemény IX; Horger, A., *Hétfalusi csángó népmesék* (The Csángó Folk-Tales of Hétfalu). Budapest, 1908. *Magyar Népköltési Gyűjtemény* X; Ipolyi Arnold *népmesegyűjteménye* (Arnold Ipolyi's Collection of Folk-tales). Budapest, 1918. *Magyar Népköltési Gyűjtemény* XIII; Buday, Gy.–Ortutay, Gy., *Nyíri és rétközi parasztmesék* (Peasant Tales from Nyír and Rétköz). Gyoma, 1935; Dégh, L., *Pandur Péter hét bagi meséje* (Péter Pandur's Seven Tales from Bag). Budapest, 1940; Ortutay, Gy., *Fedics Mihály mesél* (Mihály Fedics Tells Stories). Budapest, 1940. *Új Magyar Népköltési Gyűjtemény* I; Banó, I., *Baranyai népmesék* (Folk-tales from Baranya). Budapest, 1941; *Új magyar Népköltési Gyűjtemény* II; Dégh, L., *Pandur Péter meséi* (The Tales of Péter Pandur). I–II. Budapest, 1942. *Új Magyar Népköltési Gyűjtemény* III–IV; Kovács, Á., *Kalotaszegi népmesék* (The Folk-tales of Kalotaszeg). Budapest, 1944. *Új Magyar Népköltési Gyűjtemény* V–VII; Végh, J., *Sárréti népmesék és népi elbeszélések* (Folk-tales and Folk Narratives from Sárrét). Debrecen, 1944; Dégh, L., *Bodrogközi mesék* (Tales from Bodrogköz). Budapest, 1945; Beke, Ö.–Katona, I., *Csalóka Péter* (Tricky Peter). Budapest, 1947; Ortutay, Gy., *Adalék a mese és ballada összefüggésének kérdéséhez* (Beiträge zur Frage des Zusammenhangs zwischen dem Märchen und der Ballade). *Ethnographia*, 1938; Ortutay, Gy.–Katona, I., *Magyar parasztmesék* (Hungarian Peasant Tales). I–II. Budapest, 1951–1956; Béres, A., Mai mesélő alkalmak (Opportunities for Story-telling To-day). *Ethnographia*, 1955; Dégh, L., *Kakasdi népmesék* (The Folk-tales of Kakasd). I–II. Budapest, 1955–56. *Új Magyar Népköltési Gyűjtemény* VIII–IX; Faragó, J., *A szegény ember vására* (The Poor Man's Fair). Bucharest, 1955; Berze Nagy, J., *Magyar népmesetípusok* (Hungarian Folk-tale Types). I–II. Pécs, 1957; Dégh, L., Adalékok a "hálás halott" epizód mesei és mondai formálódásához (Zur Gestaltung der Episode des "dankbaren Toten" in Märchen und Sage). *Ethnographia*, 1957; Földy-Virány, J., *A bodrogközi Láca népmeséiből* (From the Folk-tales of Láca, Bodrogköz). Sárospatak, 1957; Ortutay, Gy., *Ungarische Volksmärchen*. Berlin, 1957; Berze Nagy, J., *Égig érő fa* (The Tree that Reached up to the Sky). Pécs, 1958; Kovács, Á., *Magyar állatmesék típuskatalógusa* (The Type-catalogue of Hungarian Animal Tales). Budapest, 1958; Nagy, O., *A három táltos varjú. Mezőségi népmesék* (The Three Magic Crows. Folk-tales from the Mezőség). Bucharest, 1958; Dégh, L., *Az egyéniségvizsgálat perspektívái* (The Individual Factor in the Development of Folk-tales). *Ethnographia*, 1960; Erdész, S., Egy szamosháti termelőszövetkezet mesemondója (The Story-teller of an Agricultural Co-operative in Szamoshát). *A nyíregyházi Jósa András Múzeum Évkönyve*, 1960; Ortutay, Gy., *Magyar népmesék* (Hungarian Folk-tales). I–III. Budapest, 1960; Banó, I.–Dömötör, S., *Régi magyar népmesék Berze Nagy János hagyatékából* (Old Hungarian Folk-tales from the Legacy of János Berze Nagy). Pécs, 1961; Dobos, I., *Egy somogyi parasztcsalád meséi* (The Tales of a Peasant Family from Somogy). Budapest, 1962; Honti, J., *Válogatott tanulmányok* (Selected Studies). Budapest, 1962; Voigt, V., Elemente des Vorstellungeskreises vom "Herrn der Tiere" im ungarischen Volksmärchen). *Acta Ethnographica*, 1962; Ortutay, Gy., Das ungarische Volksmärchen. In: *Kleine ungarische Volkskunde*. Weimar, 1963; Kovács, Á., Register der ungarischen Schildbürgerschwank-Typen (Rátótiaden). (ATH 1200–1349 MT). *Acta Ethnographica*, 1964; Kovács, Á., *A rátótiádák típusmutatója* (Directory of the Types of Counting Games). Budapest, 1966; Kovács, Á., *Ungarische Volksmärchen*. Düsseldorf-Cologne, 1966. *Die Märchen der Weltliteratur*; Domokos, S., A kétnyelvű mesemondás problémái (Probleme zweisprachiger Märchenerzähler). *Ethnographia*, 1967; Faragó, J., Kurcsi Minya a havasi mesemondó (Minya Kurcsi der Märchenerzähler aus dem Hochgebirge). *Ethnographia*, 1967; Sándor, I., Dramaturgy of Tale-telling. *Acta Ethnographica*, 1967; Erdész, S., *Ámi Lajos meséi* (The Tales of Lajos Ámi). Budapest, 1968. *Új Magyar Népköltési Gyűjtemény* XIII–XV; Faragó, J., Az emberevő nővér meséjéhez (Zum Märchen von der menschenfressenden Schwester). *Ethnographia*, 1968; Kiss, G., Hungarian Redactions of the Tale type 301. *Acta Ethnographica*, 1968; Faragó, J., A Contribution to the Table Motif of the Bird Concealed in the Vessel. *Acta Ethnographica*, 1970; Nagy, G., *Mesék, mondák Karcsáról és Karosból* (Popular Tales and Legends from Karcsa and Karos). Karcsa, 1973; Vekerdi, J., *A cigány népmese*. Tanulmány és antológia (The Gypsy Folk-tale. A study and anthology). Budapest, 1975; Bálint, S., *Tombácz János meséi* (The Tales of János Tombácz). Budapest, 1975. *Új Magyar Népköltési Gyűjtemény* XVII; Nagy, O., *A szegény ember táltostehene. Mérai népmesék* (The Poor Man's Magic Cow. Folktales from Méra). Cluj-Napoca, 1976; Nagy, O., *Széki népmesék* (The Folktales of Szék). Bucharest, 1976.

The Legend

Ortutay, Gy., *Rákóczi két népe* (Rákóczi's Two Peoples). Budapest, 1939; Ortutay, Gy., Kossuth Lajos a magyar nép hagyományaiban (Lajos Kossuth in Hungarian Popular Tradition). *Ethnographia*, 1952; Maácz, L., Adatok a hiedelmek és az epikus műfajok összefüggéséhez (Contributions to the Relation between Beliefs and the Epic Genres). *Ethnographia*, 1956; Szentmihályi, I., *A göcseji nép eredethagyománya* (Tales of Origins of the People of Göcsej). Budapest, 1958; Penavin, O., Mátyás-mondák a Vajdaságból (Mathias-Sagen aus der Vojvodina [Jugoslavien]). *Néprajzi Közlemények*, 1959; Ferenczi, I., Rákóczi alakja az abaúj-zempléni néphagyományban (Die Gestalt von Franz Rákóczi in der Volksüberlieferung des nordungarischen Gebiets von Borsod-Abaúj-Zemplén). *Ethnographia*, 1960; Ferenczi, I., Bocskai István és szabadságharcának emléke a néphagyományban (The Memory of István Bocskai and his War of Independence in Popular Tradition). *A debreceni Déri Múzeum Évkönyve*, 1960–61; Ferenczi, I., A népmondakutatás néhány elvi kérdése (Einige prinzipielle Fragen der Volkssagenforschung). *Műveltség és Hagyomány*, 1961; Ferenczi, I., A török küzdelmek emléke Hajdú-Bihar mondahagyományában (The Memory of the Struggle Against the Turks in the Legend Tradition of Hajdú-Bihar). *A debreceni Déri Múzeum Évkönyve*, 1962; Balassa, I., *Karcsai mondák* (Legends from Karcsa). Budapest 1963. *Új Magyar Népköltési Gyűjtemény* XI; Ferenczi, I., Huszita emlékek és a néphagyomány (Die Hussiten und die Volksüberlieferung). *Műveltség és Hagyomány*, 1963; Vargyas, L., Keleti párhuzamok Tar Lőrinc pokoljárásához (Östliche Parallelen zu der Höllenfahrt von Lőrinc Tar). *Műveltség és Hagyomány*, 1963; S. Dobos, I., Az "igaz" történetek műfajának kérdéséről (Über die Dichtungsart der "Wahren" Geschichten). *Ethnographia*, 1964; Voigt, V., A mondák műfaji osztályozásának kérdéséhez (Some Questions of Cataloguing Folk Legends). *Ethnographia*, 1965; Balassa, I., Die Sagen eines Dorfes. *Acta Ethnographica*, 1966; Ferenczi, I., Mondaterminológiák és műfajkritériumok (Legend Terminologies and Genre Criteria). *Néprajz és Nyelvtudomány*, 1966; Ferenczi, I., Történelem, szájhagyomány, mondahagyomány (Geschichte, mündliche Überlieferung, Sagenüberliefrung). *Ethnographia*, 1966; Körner, T., A magyar hiedelemmondák rendszerezéséhez (Zur Systematisierung der ungarischen mythischen Sagen). *Ethnographia*, 1967; Dám, L., A kővé vált kenyér hiedelme a Nagysárréten (The Fable of the Bread Turned to Stone at Nagysárrét). *Ethnographia*, 1968; Körner, T., Mutatvány a készülő magyar hiedelemmonda-katalógusból. (A halál és a halottak (Ein Kapitel aus dem in der Vorbereitung befindlichen Glaubensagen-Katalog). *Ethnographia*, 1970; Dobos, I., *Tarcal története a szóhagyományban* (The History of Tarcal in Oral Tradition). Budapest, 1971; Szabó, L., *Taktaszadai mondák* (The Legends of Taktaszada). Budapest, 1975. *Új Magyar Népköltési Gyűjtemény* XVIII.

KERTÉSZ, M., *Szólásmondások* (Proverbs). Budapest, 1922; CSEFKÓ, GY., *Szállóigék, szólásmondások* (Adages, Proverbs). Budapest, 1930; BERZE NAGY, J., *Magyar szólásaink és a folklór* (Our Hungarian Proverbs and Folklore). Budapest, 1932; KERTÉSZ, M., *Szállok az Úrnak* (Collection of Hungarian Sayings and Proverbs). Budapest, 1933; O. NAGY, G., *Mi a szólás?* (What is a Proverb?). Budapest, 1954; O. NAGY, G., *Mi fán terem?* (What is It?). Budapest, 1957; O. NAGY, G., *Magyar szólások és közmondások* (Hungarian Adages and Proverbs). 2nd ed. Budapest, 1976; VANKÓ, DUDÁS, J., Falum Galgamácsa (My Village, Galgamácsa). *Studia Comitatensia* 4.

Folk Customs—Dramatic Traditions

RÉSŐ-ENSEL, S., *Magyarországi népszokások* (Hungarian Folk Customs). Pest, 1860; KODÁLY, Z., Zoborvidéki népszokások (Folk Customs of the Zoborvidék). *Ethnographia*, 1909; SZENDREY, ZS., A magyar népszokások osztályozása (Klassifizierung der ungarischen Volksbräuche). *Ethnographia*, 1933; LUBY, M., *A parasztélet rendje* (The Order of Peasant Life). Budapest, 1935; DÖMÖTÖR, T., Állatalakoskodások a magyar népszokásokban (Animal Masks in Hungarian Folk Customs). *Ethnographia*, 1940; SZENDREY, ZS., Magyar népszokások ősi elemei (Urtümliche Elements der ungarischen Volksbräuche). *Ethnographia*, 1940; VISKI, K., Drámai hagyományok (Dramatic Traditions). In: *A Magyarság Néprajza*. III. 2nd ed. Budapest, 1941; SZENDREY, Á.–SZENDREY, ZS., Szokások (Customs). In: *A Magyarság Néprajza* IV. 2nd. ed. Budapest 1941; MANGA, J., *Ünnepi szokások a nyitramegyei Menyhén* (Folk Customs in Menyhe, Nyitra County). Budapest, 1947; DÖMÖTÖR, T., Történeti rétegek a magyar népi színjátszásban (Couches historiques dans les jeux dramatiques populaires hongrois). *Ethnographia*, 1957; UJVÁRY, Z., Az átadás, átvétel és funkció kérdései egy népszokásban (Die Fragen der Übergabe, Übernahme und Funktion bei einem ungarischen Volksbrauch). *Műveltség és Hagyomány*, 1961; DÖMÖTÖR, T., *Naptári ünnepek — népi színjátszás* (Calendar Holidays — Popular Drama). Budapest, 1964; UJVÁRY, Z., Az egyén szerepe a népszokásokban (Die Rolle des Individuums in den Volksbräuchen). *Ethnographia*, 1965; DÖMÖTÖR, T., Masken in Ungarn. *Schweizerisches Archiv für Volkskunde,* 1967; DÖMÖTÖR, T., Népi színjátéktípusok (Types de drames populaires). *Műveltség és Hagyomány,* 1968; MANGA, J., *Ünnepi szokások az Ipoly mentén* (Festive Customs along the River Ipoly). Budapest, 1968; DÖMÖTÖR, T., *A népszokások költészete* (The Poetry of Folk Customs). Budapest, 1974; MANGA, J., Szokások Tótkomlóson (Brauchtum in Tótkomlós). *A Békés Megyei Múzeumok Közleményei,* 1974; BECK, Z., *Népszokások Békés megyében* (Folk Customs in Békés County). Békéscsaba, 1974; KAPROS, M., A keresztelés szokásai az Ipoly menti falvakban (Baptizing Customs of the Villages along the River Ipoly). *Nógrád Megyei Múzeumok Közleményei,* 1975;

Children's Toys

KRESZ, M., *A magyar gyermekjáték-kutatás* (Hungarian Research into Children's Toys). Budapest, 1948; GÖNCZI, F., *Somogyi gyermekjátékok* (Children's Toys in Somogy). Kaposvár, 1949; KERÉNYI, GY., *Gyermekjátékok* (Children's Toys). Budapest 1951. *A Magyar Népzene Tára* I; SZENDREY, Á., Legényavatás (Jünglingsweihe). *Ethnographia,* 1952; BAKOS, J., *Mátyusföldi gyermekjátékok* (Children's Toys in Mátyusföld). Budapest, 1953; ENDREI, W., Két gyermekjáték eredetéről (Zum Ursprung von zwei Kinderspielzeugen). *Ethnographia,* 1957; KISS, L., Hódmezővásárhelyi sárjátékok (Mud Games in Hódmezővásárhely). In: *Vásárhelyi hétköznapok.* Budapest, 1958; KRESZ, M., Játék a kalotaszegi Nyárszón (Kinderspiel in Nyárszó [Kalotaszeg, Siebenbürgen]). *Néprajzi Köz-*

lemények, 1959; Fresz, M., A kisbaba és anyja Nyárszón (Die gemeinschaftlichen Gebräuche der Jugend in Nyárszó [Kalotaszeg, Siebenbürgen]). *Néprajzi Közlemények,* 1960; Ortutay, Gy., Le rôle de l'éducation scolaire dans la culture de notre paysannat. *Acta Ethnographica,* 1962; Pácsi-Ács, S., Kalocsa vidéki népi gyermekjátékok (Bäuerliche Kinderspiele der Kalocsaer Landschaft). *Cumania* II, 1974.

The Wedding

Ortutay, Gy., A szerelem Ajakon a házaséletig (Love before Married Life in Ajak). *Népünk és Nyelvünk,* 1934; Bakó, F., Felsőtárkány község lakodalmi szokásai (Wedding Customs in the Village of Felsőtárkány). *Ethnographia,* 1955; Kiss, L., *Lakodalom* (Wedding Feast). Budapest, 1955–1956. *A Magyar Népzene Tára* III/A–B; Lugossy, E., A lakodalom táncai (The Dances of the Wedding Feast).Budapest, 1956. In: *A Magyar Népzene Tára* III/B; Szendrey Á., Die Vorbereitung der Hochzeit und der Abschluss des Ehevertrages bei den Ungarn. *Acta Ethnographica,* 1957–1958; Manga, J., Die Hochzeitsbräuche der Paloczen und ihre slowakischen Analogien. *Acta Ethnographica* 1957–1958; Dömötör, S., Lakodalmi kalácsaink néprajzához (Zur Volkskunde der ungarischen Hochzeitskuchen). *Néprajzi Értesítő,* 1959; Manga, J., Varianten der Hochzeitslieder eines Dorfes. *Acta Ethnographica* 1970; Szathmári, I., Lakodalmi szokások Hajdúszováton (Hochzeitsbräuche in Hajdúszovát). *A debreceni Déri Múzeum Évkönyve,* 1974/1975; Csilléry, K., A szerelmi ajándék a magyar parasztságnál (Das Liebesgeschenk bei den ungarischen Bauern). *Ethnographia* 1976.

The Burial

Szendrey, Á., Az ősmagyar temetkezés (Altungarische Grablegungssitten). *Ethnographia,* 1928; Kovács, L., A kolozsvári hóstátiak temetkezése (Burial Customs of the "Hostatis" in Kolozsvár). *Ethnographia,* 1928; Ferenczi, I., Egy temetési rítus magyar párhuzamai és történeti összefüggései (The Hungarian Parallels and Historical Interconnections of a Burying Ritual). *Néprajz és Nyelvtudomány,* 1965; Kiss, L.–Rajeczky, B., *Siratók* (Laments). Budapest, 1966. *A Magyar Népzene Tára* V; Ujváry, Z., Das Begräbnis parodierende Spiele in der ungarischen Volksüberlieferung. *Österreichische Zeitschrift für Volkskunde,* 1966; Nagy, D., A magyar fejfák és díszítmények (Ungarische Grabhölzer und ihre Ornamentik). *Folklór Archívum,* 1974.

The Customs of the Calendar Year

Sebestyén, Gy., *Regös-énekek* ("Regös Songs"). Budapest, 1902. *Magyar Népköltési Gyűjtemény* IV; Sebestyén, Gy., A regösök (Minstrels). Budapest, 1902. *Magyar Népköltési Gyűjtemény* V; Sebestyén, Gy., A pünkösdi király és királyné (The King and Queen of Whitsuntide). *Ethnographia,* 1960; Szendrey, Zs., A tavasz, nyár és ősz ünnepkörének szokásai és hiedelmei (Bräuche und Aberglauben in den Festkreisen von Frühling, Sommer und Herbst). *Ethnographia,* 1941; Szendrey, Zs., A tavaszelő ünnepkörének szokásai és hiedelmei (Bräuche und Aberglauben des Frühlingseintritts). *Ethnographia,* 1941; Benedek, A.–Vargyas, L., *Az istenesi székelyek betlehemes játéka* (The Nativity Play of the Székelys in Istenes). Kolozsvár, 1943; Bálint, S., Adatok Luca-napi néphagyományainkhoz (Beiträge zu den ungarischen Volkstraditionen am Luzientag). *Ethnographia,* 1948; Faragó, J., Betlehemezés Csíkcsobotfalván 1946-ban (The Bethlehem-play in Ciobotani). *Ethnographia,* 1949; Dömötör, T., Adatok a magyar farsangi játékok történetéhez (Contributions to the History of Carnival Festivities in Hungary). *Színháztörténeti Értesítő,* 1953; Kerényi, Gy., *Jeles napok* (Special Days). Budapest, 1953. *A Magyar Népzene Tára* II; Dömötör, T., Regélő hétfő (Der erste Montag, nach Epiphania).

Ethnographia, 1958; R<small>AJECZKY</small>, B., Regélni (Zur Verbreitung des Wortes "regö-lés" in Ungarn). *Néprajzi Közlemények*, 1959; F<small>ERENCZI</small>, I.–U<small>JVÁRY</small>, Z., Far-sangi dramatikus játékok Szatmárban (Fastnachtspiele aus den Dörfern im Gebiet von Szatmár). *Műveltség és Hagyomány*, 1962; Z<small>ENTAI</small>, J., Tojáshímzés az Ormánságban (Eierverzierung im Ormánság). *Ethnographia*, 1962; D<small>IÓSZEGI</small>, V., Luca napi kotyoló szövegek (Zauberliedertexte beim "kotyolás" am Luzien-Tag). *Néprajzi Közlemények*, 1963; K<small>ERÉNYI</small>, G<small>Y</small>., A regös ének magva (The Core of the "Regös Song"). In: *Emlékkönyv Kodály Zoltán 70. születésnap-jára* (Commemorative book for the 70th birthday of Zoltán Kodály). Budapest, 1963; L<small>ÉVAY-GÁBOR</small>, J., Komatál. A barátságkötés és ennek változatai az énekes népszokások között (The Sponsor's Dish [komatál]). *Ethnographia*, 1963; S<small>ZABÓ</small>, L., Húsvéti tojások a beregi Tiszaháton (Die Ostereier in Tiszahát, ehem. Kom. Bereg, Nordostungarn). *Ethnographia*, 1963; U<small>JVÁRY</small>, Z., Hahnenschlagen und Hahnenschiessen in Ungarn. Die Frage der Übergabe und Übernahme. *Acta Ethnographica*, 1965; U<small>JVÁRY</small>, Z., Kecskemaszkos szokás Hajdúdorogon (Zie-genmaskenbrauch in Hajdúdorog). *A debreceni Déri Múzeum Évkönyve*, 1965; B<small>AKÓ</small>, F., A májusfa és a májusi kosár Heves megyében (Der Maibaum und der Maikorb im Komitat Heves). *Az Egri Múzeum Évkönyve*, 1966; D<small>ÖMÖTÖR</small>, T., Das Blochziehen in Rábatótfalu 1968. In: *Kontakte und Grenzen. Festschrift für G. Heilfurth zum 60. Geburtstag*. Göttingen, 1969; V<small>ÁMSZER</small>, G., Adatok a csíki farsangi szokásokhoz (Angaben zu den Fastnachtsbräuchen in Csík). *Ethnogra-phia*, 1959; E<small>GYÜD</small>, Á., Csodatévő szarvasnak ezer ága-boga. Adatok a somogyi regöléshez (Beitrag zur Problematik der "Regös"-Gesänge im Komitat Somogy). *Somogyi Múzeumok Közleményei*, 1975; B<small>URÁNY</small>, B., Adalékok a jeles napok népszokásainak megismeréséhez. A betlehemezés Zentán és vidékén (Contributions to the Presentation of the Folk Customs of Important Occa-sions. Christmas Carol Singing in Zenta and its Environs). *Hid*, 1975; B<small>ÁLINT</small>, S., *Ünnepi Kalendárium* (Festive Calendar). I–II. Budapest, 1977.

Work Customs

S<small>ZENDREY</small>, Z<small>S</small>., *Magyar népszokások a fonóban* (Die ungarischen Volksgebräuche in der Spinnstube). *Ethnographia*, 1928; S<small>ZENDREY</small>, Á., A népi élet társas összejövetelei (Die gesellschaftlichen Zusammenkünfte des volklichen Lebens). *Ethnographia*, 1938; L<small>AJOS</small>, Á., *Borsodi fonó* (Spinnery in Borsod). Miskolc, 1966; L<small>AJOS</small>, Á., *Este a fonóban. Borsodi népszokások* (An Evening in the Spinnery. Folk Customs in Borsod). Budapest, 1974; M<small>ANGA</small>, J., Aratószokások, aratóénekek (Harvesting Customs–Harvest Songs). *Népi kultúra – Népi társadalom, 1975 (1977)*.

Popular Beliefs in Hungary

R<small>ÓHEIM</small>, G., A Lucaszék (St. Luca's Chair). Budapest, 1920. In: *Adalékok a magyar néphithez* II; R<small>ÓHEIM</small>, G., *Magyar néphit és népszokások* (Hungarian Popular Beliefs and Folk Customs). Budapest, 1925; I<small>POLYI</small>, A., *Magyar mythologia* (Hungarian Mythology). 3rd ed. Budapest, 1929; L<small>UBY</small>, M., *Bába-lelte babona* (The Midwife-found Superstition). Budapest (1930s); S<small>ZENDREY</small>, Z<small>S</small>., Népszokásaink és hiedelmeink eredetének kérdéséhez (Unsere Sitten und Bräuche und unser Volksglauben). *Ethnographia*, 1935; D<small>ÖMÖTÖR</small>, S., *Szent Gellért hegye és a boszorkányok* (Saint Gerhardt's Hill and the Witches). Budapest, 1940. S<small>ZENDREY</small>, Z<small>S</small>., Évnegyedi szokásaink és babonáink (Ungarische Viertel-jahrsbräuche und aberglauben). *Ethnographia*, 1941; V<small>AJKAI</small>, A., *Népi orvoslás a Borsavölgyében* (Ethnomedicine in Borsavölgye). Kolozsvár, 1943; S<small>ZENDREY</small>, Á., A magyar lélekhit (Popular Beliefs Concerning the Soul). *Ethnographia*, 1964; S<small>ZENDREY</small>, Á., *A magyar néphit kutatása* (Research into Hungarian Popular Beliefs). Budapest, 1948; S<small>ZŰCS</small>, S., A nagyétű boszorkányról (The Voracious Witch). *Ethnographia*, 1954; D<small>IÓSZEGI</small>, V., A novaji tudósasszony (Die "Weisc

Frau" von Novaj). *Néprajzi Közlemények,* 1956; H. FEKETE, P., Állatgyógyítás a Hajdúságon (Tierheilkunde in der Hajdúság [Gegend um Debrecen]). *Ethnographia,* 1956; OLÁH, A., Népi orvoslás, orvoslástörténet, orvostudomány (Ethnomedicine, the History of Medicine, Medical Science). *Communicationes ex Bibliotheca Historiae Medicae Hungarica,* 1956; DIÓSZEGI, V., Dobbal való kötés, oldás (Ein Andenken des Schamanen-Zauberns in Kinderreimen). *Néprajzi Közlemények,* 1957; GUNDA, B., A totemizmus maradványa a magyar táltoshagyományokban. *A debreceni Déri Múzeum Évkönyve,* 1957; BERZE NAGY, J., *Égigérő fa* (The Tree that Reached up to the Sky). Pécs, 1958. *Magyar mitológiai tanulmányok;* DIÓSZEGI, V., *A sámánhit emlékei a magyar népi műveltségben* (Traces of Shamanism in Popular Hungarian Culture). Budapest, 1958; DIÓSZEGI, V., Die Überreste des Schamanismus in der ungarischen Volkskultur. *Acta Ethnographica,* 1958; DIÓSZEGI, V., Embergyógyítás a moldvai székelyeknél (Volksheilkunde bei den Moldauer Szeklern). *Néprajzi Közlemények,* 1960; DIÓSZEGI, V., A magyar néphagyomány és a sámánhit kapcsolatai (Die Andenken des Schamanismus in der ungarischen Volkskultur). *Műveltség és Hagyomány,* 1960; FERENCZI, I., Az animizmus világa és a magyar erdőkultusz (Die Welt des Animismus und der ungarische Waldkult). *Műveltség és Hagyomány,* 1960; Cs. PÓCS, É., Étel és étkezés a magyar néphitben és népszokásban (Speisen und Mahlzeiten im ungarischen Volksglauben und Brauchtum). *Néprajzi Értesítő,* 1961; BALÁZS, J., Über die Ekstase des ungarischen Schamanen. In: *Glaubenswelt und Folklore der sibirischen Völker.* Budapest, 1963; ERDÉSZ, S., The Cosmogonical Conception of Lajos Ámi, Storyteller. *Acta Ethnographica,* 1963; DÖMÖTÖR, T., A magyar néphit és népszokások Kelet és Nyugat között (Hungarian Popular Belief and Customs between the East and West). *Ethnographia,* 1964; CSISZÁR, Á., Gyógyítás emberkoponyával (Das Heilen durch Menschenschädel im Kom. Bereg). *Ethnographia,* 1965; Cs. PÓCS, É., A karácsonyi vacsora és a karácsonyi asztal hiedelemköre (Der Aberglaubenkreis um das Weihnachtsmahl und den Weihnachtstisch). *Néprajzi Közlemények,* 1965; Cs. PÓCS, É., Zagyvarékás néphite (Der Volksglaube von Zagyvarékás). *Néprajzi Közlemények,* 1964; DIÓSZEGI, V., *A pogány magyarok hitvilága* (The Beliefs of the Pagan Hungarians). Budapest, 1967; PÓCS, É., Binde- und Lösungszauber im ungarischen Volksglauben. *Acta Ethnographica,* 1967; UJVÁRY, Z., Theriomorphe Korndämonen in der ungarischen Volksüberlieferung. *Acta Ethnographica,* 1967; Cs. PÓCS, É., A magyar ráolvasások műfaji és rendszerezési problémái (Gattungs- und Systematisierungsprobleme der ungarischen Beschwörungsformeln). *Népi kultúra – Népi társadalom,* 1968; UJVÁRY, Z., Anthropomorphe mythische Wesen in der agrarischen Volksüberlieferung Ungarns und Europas. *Acta Ethnographica,* 1968; DIÓSZEGI, V., A honfoglaló magyarok hitvilágának történeti rétegei. I. A világfa (Die historischen Schichten der Glaubenswelt der Ungarn der Landnahmezeit. I. Der Weltbaum). *Népi kultúra – Népi társadalom,* 1969; HOPPÁL, M., A magyar lidérc-hiedelemkör szemantikai modellje (Das semantische Modell des ungarischen Lidérc-Glaubenkomplexes). *Ethnographia,* 1969; KÖRNER, T., Boszorkányszervezetek Magyarországon (Die ungarischen Hexenorganisationen). *Ethnographia,* 1969; UJVÁRY, Z., Az agrárkultusz kutatása a magyar és az európai folklórban (Forschung des Agrarkults in der ungarischen und europäischen Folklore). *Műveltség és Hagyomány,* 1969; SCHRAM, F., *Magyarországi boszorkányperek* (Witch Trials in Hungary). I–II. Budapest, 1970; DIÓSZEGI, V., A táltos alakjának földrajzi elterjedéséhez (Der ungarische Schamane [táltos] in Transdanubien). *Szolnok Megyei Múzeum Évkönyve,* 1973; DIÓSZEGI, V., A tótkomlósiak hitvilága (Die Glaubenswelt der Tótkomlóser). *A Békés Megyei Múzeumok Közleményei,* 1974; KÁLMÁN, E., *Népi gyógyítás a Tiszaháton* (Ethnomedicine in Tiszahát). Nyíregyháza, 1974; KRUPA, A., *Hiedelmek, varázslatok, boszorkányok* (Beliefs, Magic, Witches). Békéscsaba, 1974; PAIS, D., *A magyar ősvallás nyelvi emlékeiből* (The Relics of Hungarian Prehistorical Religion). Budapest, 1975; UJVÁRY, Z., *Varia folkloristica. Írások a néphagyomány köréből* (Varia folkloristica. Studies in popular tradition). Debrecen, 1975; HOPPÁL, M.–TÖRŐ, L., Ethnomedicine in Hungary. *Orvostörténeti Közlemények,* 1975; GULYÁS, É., Jászdózsai hiedelmek (Folk Beliefs from Jászdózsa). *Folklór Archívum,* 1976; SÁNDOR, M., Mrs, Egy bihari parasztasszony hiedelmei (Beliefs of a Hungarian Peasant Woman). *Folklór Archívum,* 1976.

List of Sources and Other Data Relating to Figures

Abbreviations: Bp.=Budapest; *Ethn.*=*Ethnographia* (periodical); *Hung. Ethn.²*=*Hungarian Ethnography*, 2nd ed.; *EB.*=*Ethnographical Bulletin* (periodical, yearbook).

Figure   1. Zsigray, M., *Finnugor rokonságunk* (Finno-Ugric Kinship). Bp., 1939. 13. Vogul-Mansi, Ostyak-Khanty, Komi-Zyrian, Votyak-Udmurt, Cheremiss-Mari, etc.

Figure   2. Pamlényi, E. (ed.), *Die Geschichte Ungarns*. Bp., 1971. Based on No. 13.

Figure   3. Sources used for designing the map: *Hung. Ethn.²* 1:23–27; Ortutay, Gy., *Kis Magyar Néprajz* (Short Hungarian Ethnography). Bp., n.d.; Balassa, I., *Magyar néprajz* (Hungarian Ethnography). Bp., 1947. 17; Kósa, L.–Szemerkényi, Á., *Apáról fiúra* (From Father to Son). Bp., 1973 and other sources.

Figure   4. Based on Bátky, Zs., *Útmutató néprajzi múzeumok szervezésére*. Bp., 1906. 83. Plate No. 201.

Figure   5. *Hung. Ethn.²* 2:103.

Figure   6. Based on Kós, K., *Népélet és néphagyomány* (Folk Life and Folk Tradition). Bucharest, 1972. Diagram No. 242.

Figure   7. Based on Kós, K., *Népélet és néphagyomány* (Folk Life and Folk Tradition). Bucharest, 1972. Diagram No. 243.

Figure   8. Based on Morvay, J. *EB* 49(1967), 29. Page 151/1 of *Magyar Néprajzi Atlasz* (An Ethnographical Atlas of Hungary).

Figure   9. Based on Katona, I., *Ethn.* 74(1963), 17. Diagram No. 6.

Figure 10. Authors' own survey.

Figure 11. 1–2. Based on Balassa, I., *Az eke és a szántás története Magyarországon* (The History of the Plough and Ploughing in Hungary). Bp., 1973. 535–7; *Tápé története és néprajza* (The History and Ethnography of Tápé). Cover. Tápé, 1971.

Figure 12. Based on *Hung. Ethn.²* Photograph of Plate No. 4:XLI.

Figure 13. Based on Dankó, I., *A gyulai vásárok* (Fairs in Gyula). Gyula, 1963.

Figure 14. Based on Dankó, I., *A gyulai vásárok* (Fairs in Gyula). Gyula, 1963.

Figure 15. Based on Molnár, Gy., *Ethn.* 78(1967), 595. Diagram No. 2.

Figure 16. Based on Gilyén, N.–Mendele, F.–Tóth, J., *A Felső-Tisza-vidék népi építészete* (Folk Architecture of the Upper Tisza Region) Bp., 1975. 24. Diagram No. 15.

Figure 17. Based on Bárth, J., *Ethn.* 86(1975), 249. Diagram No. 5.

Figure 18. Survey ordered by Emperor Joseph II. Courtesy of T. Hofer.

Figure 19. Based on Szinte, G., *EB* 10(1911), 176–7. Plate No. 23.

Figure 20. Based on Gilyén, N.–Mendele, F.–Tóth, J., *op.cit.* 185. Diagram No. 275.

Figure 21. Based on Bátky, Zs., *EB* 26(1934), 46. Diagram No. 1.

Figure 22. Based on Bátky, Zs., *Hung. Ethn.²* Diagram No. 1:114.

Figure 23. Courtesy of T. Hofer.

Figure 24. Based on Györffy, I., *EB* 9(1908), 15. Diagram No. 7. The length of the plot is approx. 40 m, its width 16 m.

Figure 25. Based on Gönyey, S., *EB* 34(1942), 221. Diagram No. 1.

Figure 26. Based on Cs. Sebestyén, K., *EB* 33(1941), 39. Diagram No. 4.

Figure   27. Based on Cs. Sebestyén, K., *EB* 33(1941), 41. Diagram No. 5.

Figure   28. Based on Gilyén, N.–Mendele, F.–Tóth, J., *op.cit.* 164. Diagram No. 254.

Figure   29. Based on sketches by Balassa, M.I.

Figure   30. Based on Barabás, J., *EB* 49(1967), 16, page 54/a of *Magyar Néprajzi Atlasz* (An Ethnographical Atlas of Hungary).

Figure   31. Gönyey, S., *EB* 23(1931), 108. Plate II/1.

Figure   32. Based on Bátky, Zs., *EB* 30(1938), 7. Diagrams 26, 28, 29.

Figure   33. Based on Bátky, Zs., *Hung. Ethn.*[2] Diagram No. 1:37.

Figure   34. Based on Gönyey, S., *EB* 23(1931), 9. Diagram 1.

Figure   35. Based on Bátky, Zs., *Hung. Ethn.*[2] Diagram No. 1:198.

Figure   36. Based on Végh, J., *Ethn.* 51(1940), 424. Diagram No. 7.

Figure   37. Based on Bátky, Zs., *Hung. Ethn.*[2] Diagram No. 1:174.

Figure   38. Based on Bátky, Zs., *Hung. Ethn.*[2] Diagram No. 1:175.

Figure   39. Based on Viski, K., *EB* 24(1932), 22. Diagram No. 1.

Figure   40. Based on Bátky, Zs., *Hung. Ethn.*[2] Diagram No. 1:200.

Figure   41. 1–2. Based on Márkus, M., *EB* 32(1940), 98. Diagram No. 10.5,11; Diagram No. 3. Iváncsics, N., *Ethn.* 69(1958), 416. Diagram No. 3.

Figure   42. Based on Márkus, M., *EB* 32(1940), 115. Diagram No. 21/4, 8, 9.

Figure   43. Based on Bátky, Zs., *Hung. Ethn.*[2] Diagram No. 1:204.

Figure   44. Based on Balassa, I., *Földművelés a Hegyközben* (Land Cultivation in Hegyköz). Bp., 1964. 104. Diagram No. 81.

Figure   45. Based on Gönyey, S., *Ethn.* 68(1957), 505. Diagram No. 1.

Figure   46. Based on Kós, K.,–Szentimrei, J.–Nagy, J., *Kászoni székely népművészet* (Székely Folk Art in Kászon). Bucharest, 1972. 78. Diagram No. 38.

Figure   47. Based on Novák, I. L., *EB* 14(1913), 53.

Figure   48. Based on Györffy, I., *Hung. Ethn.*[2] 124.

Figure   49. Based on Iváncsics, N., *Ethn.* 77(1966), 363. Plate No. II.

Figure   50. Based on Kardos, L., *Az Őrség táplálkozása* (Eating Habits of the People of the Őrség). Budapest, 1943. 220. Diagram No. 172.

Figure   51. Based on sketch by M.I. Balassa. Total length of building: 13.21 m; width: 5.24–1.10 m terrace.

Figure   52. Based on Bátky, Zs., *Hung. Ethn.*[2] 1:117.

Figure   53. Based on sketch by M.I. Balassa. Greatest length of building: 23.27 m, one wing: 13.85 m; other wing: 15.33 m.

Figure   54. Based on sketch by M.I. Balassa. Length of building: 23.34 m; width: 7.13 m.

Figure   55. Based on sketch by M.I. Balassa. Length of building: 11.60 m; width: 4.70 m.

Figure   56. Based on Balassa, I., *Magyar Néprajz* (Hungarian Ethnography). Bp., 1947. 124. Drawing by T. A. Csikós.

Figure   57. Based on Györffy, L., *EB* 10(1909). 73. Diagram No. 8.

Figure   58. Based on Vargha, L., *Ethn.* 73(1962), 182.

Figure   59. Based on Gilyén, N.–Mendele, F.–Tóth, J., *op.cit.* Diagram No. 43.

Figure   60. Based on Cs. Sebestyén, K., *EB* 33(1941), 46. Diagram No. 10.

Figure   61. Based on Kós, K., *op.cit.* 1972. 46. Length of house: 10.00 m; width: 7.90 m.

Figure   62. Based on Ecsedi, I., *Népies halászat a Közép-Tiszán és a tiszántúli kisvizeken* (Popular Fishing on the Middle Tisza and in the Shallow Waters Beyond the Tisza). Debrecen 1934. 290. Diagram No. 74.

Figure   63. Based on Ecsedi, I., *op.cit.* 1934. 219. Diagram No. 75.

Figure 64. Based on Barabás, J., *Ethn.* 61(1950), 83. Diagram 1.
Length: 3.00 m.

Figure 65. Based on Bátky, Zs., *op.cit.* 1906. Plate No. 2., Diagrams No. 1–3.

Figure 66. Based on Balassa, I., *A magyar kukorica* (Hungarian Maize). Bp. 1960. 163. Diagram 59. *Ibid.,* cf. sources of map.

Figure 67. Based on Kovács, L, *EB* 29(1937), 21. Diagram No. 31.

Figure 68. Based on Kovács, L., *EB* 29(1937), 32. Diagram No. 47.

Figure 69. Based on Kovács, L., *EB* 29(1937), 17. Diagram No. 26.

Figure 70. Based on Kovács, L., *EB* 29(1937), 37. Diagram No. 58.

Figure 71. Based on Balassa, I., *op.cit.* 1964. 54. Drawing by D. Nagy.

Figure 72. 1–4. Based on Kántor, M., *EB* 18(1926), 84. Diagrams No. 1; 5–7. Györffy, I., *Hung. Ethn.*[2] Diagram No. 2:172.

Figure 73. Based on Balassa, I., *op.cit.* 1964. 76. Drawing by D. Nagy.

Figure 74. Based on Györffy, I., *Hung. Ethn.*[2] Diagram No. 2:178

Figure 75. Based on Györffy, I., *Hung. Ethn.*[2] Diagram No. 2:177.

Figure 76. Based on Szolnoky, L., *EB* 49(1967), 7. Page 15/1 of *Magyar Néprajzi Atlasz* (An Ethnographical Atlas of Hungary).

Figure 77. Based on Nagy, Gy., *Ethn.* 65(1954), 508. Plate No. 508.

Figure 78. Based on Balassa, I. *Ethn.* 60(1949), 113. Diagram No. 1.

Figure 79. Based on Nagy, Gy., *Ethn.* 69(1954), 493. Drawings of Plate No. VII.

Figure 80. Based on Györffy, I. *Hung. Ethn.*[2] Diagram No 2:186.

Figure 81. Based on Balassa, I., *Acta Ethnographica* 10(1961), 348–357. Diagrams No. 1, 6, 11. Drawings by T. A. Csikós.

Figure 82. Based on Bálint, S.; *EB* 28(1936), 120.

Figure 83. Based on Balassa, I., *op.cit.* 1960. 209. Diagram No. 88. Drawings by T. A. Csikós.

Figure 84. Based on Balassa, I., *op.cit.* 1960. Diagram No. 236. Drawings by T. A. Csikós.

Figure 84. Based on *Hung. Ethn.*[2] Diagram No. 1:42.

Figure 86. Based on Gunda, B., *EB* 29(1937), 65. Diagram No. 40.

Figure 87. Based on Nagy, Gy., *EB* 38(1956), 90. Diagram No. 3.

Figure 88. Based on Domanovszky, Gy., *EB* 32(1940), 173. Diagram No. 7.

Figure 89. Based on Nagy, Gy., *Ethn.* 77(1966), 287. Plate No. 287.

Figure 90. Based on Kecskés, P., *Ethn.* 77(1966), 507. Diagram No. 14 Different names for each wine region.

Figure 91. Based on Györffy, I., *Hung. Ethn.*[2] Diagram No. 2:198.

Figure 92. Based on Vincze, I., *Ethn.* 71(1960), 12. Diagram No. 12.

Figure 93. Based on Vincze, I., *Ethn.* 69(1958), 2. Diagram No. 1.

Figure 94. Based on Bátky, Zs., *Hung. Ethn.*[2] Diagram No. 1:50.

Figure 95. Based on Molnár, B., *Ethn.* 8(1957), 486. Diagram No. 5.

Figure 96. Based on Kós, K., *Ethn.* 60(1949), 162. Diagram No. 5.

Figure 97. Based on Szabadfalvi, J., *Ethn.* 67(1956), 465. Diagram No. 12.

Figure 98. Based on Györffy, I., *Hung. Ethn.*[2] Diagram No. 2:12.

Figure 99. Based on Györffy, I., *Hung. Ethn.*[2] Diagram No. 2:18.

Figure 100. Based on Ecsedi, I., *Népies vadfogás és vadászat a debreceni határban és a Tiszántúlon* (Game Killing and Hunting in the Outskirts of Debrecen and in the Region beyond the Tisza). Debrecen, 1933. 211. Diagram No. 54.

Figure 101. Based on Kovács, A., *EB* 5(1904), 51. Diagram No. 1.

Figure 102. Based on Györffy, I., *Hung. Ethn.*[2] Diagram No. 2:37.

Figure 103. Based on Ecsedi, I., *op.cit.* 1933. 159. Diagram No. 16. Drawing by T. A. Csikós.

Figure 104. Based on Kiss, L., *Ethn.* 54(1943), 35.

Figure 105. Based on Végh, J., *EB* 31(1939), 47. Diagram No. 10/F.

Figure 106. Based on Györffy, I., *Hung. Ethn.*[2] Diagram No. 2:51.

Figure 107. Based on Györffy, I., *Hung. Ethn.*[2] Diagram No. 2:55.

Figure 108. Based on Ecsedi, I., *op.cit.* 1934. 158. Diagram No. 11; and Györffy, I., *Hung. Ethn.*[2] Diagram No. 2:57.

Figure 109. Based on Györffy, I., *Hung. Ethn.*[2] Diagram No. 2:58.

Figure 110. Based on Kiss, L., *EB* 29(1937), 164. Diagram No. 2.

Figure 111. Based on Györffy, I., *Hung. Ethn.*[2] Diagram No. 2:78.

Figure 112. Based on Györffy, I., *Hung. Ethn.*[2] Diagram No. 2:106.

Figure 113. Based on Béres, A., *A Déri Múzeum Évkönyve* (Yearbook of the Déri Museum) 1960–61. 188. Diagram No. 6.

Figure 114. Béres, A., *Ibid.*

Figure 115. Béres, A., *Ibid.*

Figure 116. Based on Györffy, I., *Ethn.* 48(1937), 119.

Figure 117. Based on Györffy, I., *Hung. Ethn.*[2] Diagram No. 2:95.

Figure 118. Based on Bátky, Zs., *op.cit.* 1906. 86. Plate No. 21. Drawings No. 1–4.

Figure 119. Based on K. Kovács, P., *Ethn.* 62(1951), 376. Diagram No. 1. Drawing by T. A. Csikós.

Figure 120. Based on Garay, Á., *EB* 27(1935). Drawing No. 115.

Figure 121. Based on Györffy, I., *Hung. Ethn.*[2] Diagram No. 2:111.

Figure 122. Based on Györffy, I., *Hung. Ethn.*[2] Diagram No. 2:115.

Figure 123. Based on Tálasi, I., *Ethn.* 47(1936),170. Diagram No. 11.

Figure 124. Based on Balassa, I., *op.cit.* 1947. 85. Drawing by T. A. Csikós.

Figure 125. Based on Györffy, I., *Hung. Ethn.*[2] Diagram No. 2:117.

Figure 126. Based on Kiss, L., *EB* 29(1937), 319. Diagram No. 25.

Figure 127. Based on Balogh, I., *Ethn.* 76(1965), 182. Diagram No. 20.

Figure 128. Based on Bátky, Zs., *op.cit.* 1906. 82. Plate No. 20. Diagram No. 7.

Figure 129. Based on Garay, Á., *EB* 28(1936), 111.

Figure 130. Based on Balogh, I. *Ethn.* 76(1965), 178. Diagram No. 14.

Figure 132. Based on Bogdál, F., *Ethn.* 71(1960), 525. Diagram No. 1.

Figure 133. Based on Balassa, I., *op.cit.* 1964. 154. Diagram No. 139. Drawing by D. Nagy.

Figure 134. Based on Balogh, I., *Ethn.* 77(1966), Diagram No. 77.

Figure 135. Based on Bátky, Zs., *op.cit.* 1906. Plate No. 62. Diagrams No. 2.

Figure 136. Based on Borzsák, E., *EB* 33(1941), 214. Diagrams No. 5/10–11.

Figure 137. Based on Borzsák, E., *EB* 33(1941), 228. Diagram No. 8.

Figure 138. Based on Kardos, L., *op.cit.* 162. Diagrams No. 80–81.

Figure 139. Based on Bátky, Zs., *Hung. Ethn.*[2] Diagram No. 1:52.

Figure 140. Based on Balassa, I., *op.cit.* 1947. 54. Drawing by T. A. Csikós.

Figure 141. Based on Kardos, L., *op.cit.* 106. Diagram No. 29.

Figure 142. Based on Bátky, Zs., *op.cit.* 1906. 183. Plate No 57. Diagram No. 10.

Figure 143. Based on Kardos, L., *op.cit.* 107. Diagram No. 31–33.

Figure 144. Based on Bátky, Zs., *op.cit.* 1906. 183. Plate No. 57. Diagram No. 12.

Figure 145. Based on Bátky, Zs., *op.cit.* 1906. 183. Plate No. 57. Diagram No. 15.

Figure 146. Based on Bátky, Zs., *op.cit.* 1906. 177. Plate 55. Diagrams No. 1–213.

Figure 147. Based on Kardos, L., *op.cit.* 136. Diagrams No. 47–49.

Figure 148. Based on Kardos, L., *op.cit.* 142. Diagram No. 56.

Figure 149. Based on Kardos, L., *op.cit.* 141. Diagram No. 55.

Figure 150. Based on Kovács, L., *EB* 33(1941), 121. Diagram No. 2.

Figure 151. Based on Kovács, L., *EB* 33(1941), 122. Diagram No. 4.

Figure 152. Based on Nagy, J., *A népi kendermunka műszókincse Magyarvalkón*

(Kalotaszeg) (The Terminology of Hemp Cultivation in Magyar-
valkó [Kalotaszeg]). Debrecen, 1938. 23. Diagrams No. 23–24.
Figure 153. Based on Nagy, J., *op.cit.* 28. Diagram No. 27.
Figure 154. Based on Kós, K., *op.cit.* 1974. 218. Diagram No. 8.
Figure 155. Based on Kovács, L., *EB* 33(1941), 129. Diagram No. 14.
Figure 156. Based on Kovács, L., *EB* 33(1941), 132. Diagram No. 18.
Figure 157. Based on Dorogi, M., *Ethn.* 67(1956), 303. Plate No. 1. Diagrams
No. 1–7.
Figure 158. Based on Domokos, P.P., *EB* 27(1935), 109. Plate No. 1. Diagram
No. 4.
Figure 159. Based on Bátky, Zs., *op.cit.* 1906. 83. Plate No. 20. Diagram No.
10.
Figure 160. Based on Garay, Á., *Hung. Ethn.*[2] Drawing No. 1:328.
Figure 161. Based on Györffy, I., *Hung. Ethn.*[2] Drawing No. 1:338.
Figure 162. Based on Györffy, I., *Hung. Ethn.*[2] Drawing No. 1:341.
Figure 163. Based on Györffy, I., *Hung. Ethn.*[2] Drawing No. 1:341.
Figure 164. Based on Fél, E., *EB* 34(1962), 97. Diagram No. 4.
Figure 165. Based on Palotay, G., *EB* 29(1937), 338. Diagram No. 2.
Figure 166. Based on Kós, K., *op.cit.* 1974. 196. Drawing No. 19.
Figure 167. Based on Györffy, I., *Cifraszűr* (Embroidered *Szűr* Coat). Bp.
1930. Diagram No. 91.
Figure 168. Based on Györffy, I., *Hung. Ethn.*[2] Diagram No. 1:348.
Figure 169. Based on Györffy, I., *Hung. Ethn.*[2] Diagram No. 1:356.
Figure 170. Based on Balogh, I., *Ethn.* 70(1959), 306. Diagram No. 4.
Figure 171. Based on Gönyey, S., *EB* 24(1932), 127. Size of leather: 17 by 28
cm.
Figure 172. Based on Györffy, I., *Hung. Ethn.*[2] Diagram No. 1:363.
Figure 173. Based on Szebeni, G., *Ethn.* 73(1962), 80. Diagram No. 36. The
piece was assembled with the so-called *farkasfog* technique.
Figure 174. Based on Béres, A., *Debreceni Déri Múzeum Évkönyve* (Yearbook of
the Debrecen Déri Múzeum). 111. Diagram No. 19.
Figure 175. Based on Viski, K., *Hung. Ethn.*[2] Diagram No. 2:246.
Figure 176. Based on Viski, K., *Hung. Ethn.*[2] Drawings No. 2:243.
Figure 177. Based on Viski, K., *Hung. Ethn.*[2] Drawings No. 2:251.
Figure 178. Based on Haáz, F., *EB* 33(1941), 96. Diagram No. 1.
Figure 179. Cs. Sebestyén, K., *Ethn.* 65(1954), 379. Drawing by B. Csete.
Figure 180. Based on Ferencz, K.,–Palotay, G., *Hímzőmesterség.*[2] (The Art of
Embroidery). Bp. 1940. 17. Diagram No. 20.
Figure 181. Based on Ferencz, K.,–Palotay, G., *op.cit.* 17. Diagram No. 21.
Figure 182. Based on Ferencz, K.,–Palotay, G., *op.cit.* 12. Diagram No. 1.
Figure 183. Based on Ferencz, K.,–Palotay, G., *op.cit.* 20. Diagram No. 36. 18.
Figure 184. Based on Ferencz, K.,–Palotay, G., *op.cit.* 28. Diagram No. 59.
Figure 185. Based on Viski, K., *Hung. Ethn.*[2] Diagram No. 2:284.
Figure 186. Based on Ferencz, K.,–Palotay, G., *op.cit.* 36. Diagram No. 76.
Figure 187. Based on Ferencz, K.,–Palotay, G., *op.cit.* 58. Diagram No. 145.
Figure 188. Based on Kós, K., *op.cit.* 1972. 158. Diagrams No. 60–62.
Figure 189. Based on Béres, a., *Ethn.* 64(1954), 274. Diagram No. 29.
Figure 190. Based on Béres, A., *Ethn.* 64(1953), 270. Diagram No. 19.
Figure 191. Based on Szabó, K., *EB* 24(1932). 74. Diagrams No. 1–4.
Figure 192. Based on Kiss, L., *EB* 20(1928), 49.
Figure 193. Based on Györffy, I., *Ethn.* 78(1967). 266. Diagrams No. 34–37.
Figure 194. Based on Zentai, J., *Ethn.* 73(1962), 456. Diagram No. 2.
Figure 195. Based on Kálmán, B., *Nyelvjárásaink* (Hungarian Dialects). Bp.
1971. 119.
Figure 196. Collected by Béla Bartók. Manga, J., *Magyar népdalok, népi hang-*

szerek (Hungarian Folksongs, Hungarian Folk Instruments). Bp. 1969. 15.

Figure 197. Collected by Béla Bartók. Manga, J., *op.cit.* 20.

Figure 198. Collected by J. Manga. Manga, J., *op.cit.* 20.

Figure 199. Manga, J., *op.cit.* 21.

Figure 200. Collected by Béla Bartók, Manga, J., *op.cit.* 21.

Figure 201. Manga, J., *Ethn.* 50(1939). Diagram No. 1.

Figure 202. Kodály, Z., *Hung. Ethn.*[2] Plate No. 4:VIII.

Figure 203. Based on Kodály, Z., *Hung. Ethn.*[2] Diagram No. 4:381.

Figure 204. Based on Lajtha, L.–Gönyey, S., *Hung. Ethn.*[2] Diagrams No. 4:82.

Figure 205. Martin, Gy., *A magyar nép táncai* (Dances of the Hungarian People). Bp., 1974. 28.

Figure 206. Based on Lajtha, L.–Gönyey, S., *Hung. Ethn.*[2] Diagrams No. 4:78.

Figure 207. Based on Viski, K., *Hung. Ethn.*[2] Diagram No. 2:302.

Figure 208. Jagamas, J.–Faragó, J., *Romániai magyar népdalok* (Hungarian Folksongs in Rumania). Bucharest, 1974. 220. Tune No. 220.

Figure 209. Albert, E.–Faragó, J., *Háromszéki népballadák* (Folk Ballads of Háromszék). Bucharest, 1973. 137. Tune No. 59.

Figure 210. Based on *Hung. Ethn.*[2] Plate No. 3:XII.

Figure 211. Based on N. Bartha, K., *Hung. Ethn.*[2] Diagram No. 4:385.

Figure 212. Based on N. Bartha, K., *Hung. Ethn.*[2] Diagram No. 4:409.

Figure 213. Based on N. Bartha, K., *Hung. Ethn.*[2] Diagram No. 4:405.

Figure 214. Based on N. Bartha, K., *Hung. Ethn.*[2] Diagram No. 4:410.

Figure 215. Based on Balassa, I., *op.cit.* 1960. 440. Diagram No. 214.

Figure 216. Based on Viski, K., *Hung. Ethn.*[2] Diagram No. 2:347.

Figure 217. Based on Viski, K., *Hung. Ethn.*[2] Diagram No. 2:348.

Figure 218. Based on Haáz, F.—Siklódi, P., *EB* 23(1932), 118-9.

Figure 219. Based on Seemayer, V., *Ethn.* 47(1936), 75.

Figure 220. Based on Kós, K., *op.cit.* 1972. 229. Diagram No. 20/2.

Figure 221. Kiss, L.–Rajeczky, B., *Siratók* (Mourners). Bp., 1966. 473-4. Tune No. 120.

Figure 222. Kiss, L.–Rajeczky, B., *op.cit.* 315-6. Tune No. 62.

Figure 223. Kiss, L.–Rajeczky, B., *op.cit.* 741. Tune No. 202.

Figure 224. Based on Kós, K., *op.cit.* 1972. 229. Diagram No. 20.

Figure 225. Based on Viski, K., *Hung. Ethn.*[2] Diagram No. 2:355.

Figure 226. Based on Viski, K., *Hung. Ethn.*[2] Diagram No. 2:356.

Figure 227. Based on Viski, K., *Hung. Ethn.*[2] Diagram No. 2:376.

Figure 228. Based on Viski, K., *Hung. Ethn.*[2] Diagram No. 2:352.

Figure 229. Based on Balassa, I., *op.cit.* 1947. 169. Drawing by T. A. Csikós.

Figure 230. Based on Szűcs, S., *Ethn.* 63(1952), 161. Diagram No. 2.

Figure 231. Szűcs, S., *Ethn.* 63(1952). 165. Diagram No. 7.

Figure 232. Based on Diószegi, V., *EB* 49(1967). 31. Page 185/1 of *Magyar Néprajzi Atlasz* (An Ethnographical Atlas of Hungary).

List of Sources for Black-and-White Photographs

1. The Village Museum of Göcsej
   Zalaegerszeg
   Tamás Kovács

2. The Village Museum of Göcsej
   Zalaegerszeg
   Tamás Kovács

3. The Village Museum of Vas
   County
   Szombathely
   Miklós Lantos

4. The Hungarian Ethnographical
   Village Museum
   Regional unit from former
   Szatmár County
   Szentendre
   Jenő Szabó

5. The Hungarian Ethnographical
   Village Museum
   Farmsteads from Kispalád and
   Botpalád
   Szentendre
   Jenő Szabó

6. The Hungarian Ethnographical
   Village Museum
   House from Kispalád
   Szentendre
   Jenő Szabó

7. The *Palots* house
   Balassagyarmat, Palóc Museum
   Jenő Szabó

8. The Outdoor Ethnographical
   Museum
   Tihany
   Jenő Szabó

9. Rural buildings
   Szigliget, Veszprém County
   Miklós Lantos

10. A wine-cellar built of logs
    Csurgó–Nagymarton, Somogy
    County
    Miklós Lantos

11. A dwelling in the vineyard
    Nagykutas, Zala County
    Jenő Szabó

12. Catholic church
    Hollókő, Nógrád County
    Jenő Szabó

13. Cumanian men
    Kunszentmiklós, Bács-Kiskun
    County
    Jenő Szabó

14. Village scene
    Jászjákóhalma, Szolnok County
    Iván Hevesy, Union
    of Photographers

15. Calvinist church
    Magyarvalkó, former Kolozs
    County
    Péter Korniss

16. Men going off on a Sunday
    Jobbágytelke, former Maros-
    Torda County
    Péter Korniss

17. Rural scene
    Antalok-pataka, former Csík
    County
    Zoltán Móser

18. *Matyó* family
    Mezőkövesd
    Herman Ottó Museum, Miskolc

19. Old peasant
    Szany, Győr-Sopron County
    Kata Kálmán

20. Cumanian peasant *(gazda)*
    Great Plain
    Kata Kálmán

21. Wife of a landless peasant
    Boldog, Pest County
    Kata Kálmán

22. Middle peasant man
    Jászalsószentgyörgy, Szolnok
    County
    Kata Kálmán

23. A cotter woman
    Öszöd, Somogy County
    Kata Kálmán

24. Harvesting
    Great Plain
    Ernő Vadas, Union
    of Photographers

25. Harvest festival
    Boldog, Pest County
    Rudolf Balog, Union
    of Photographers

26. Harvesters eating their midday
    meal
    Great Plain
    Károly Escher, Union of
    Photographers

27. Pick and shovel men awaiting
    employment
    Budapest, Teleki Square
    Kata Sugár, Union
    of Photographers

28. Pick and shovel men at work
    Great Plain
    Károly Escher, Union
    of Photographers

29. The sign-board of a potter
    Nagyatád, Somogy County
    Kaposvár, Rippl-Rónai Museum
    Miklós Lantos

30. Front of a guild chest, 1800
Miskolc
Miskolc, Herman Ottó Museum
Tamás Broczkó

31. Summoning tablet of the tailors'
guild
Fertőszentmiklós, Győr-Sopron
County
Veszprém, Bakony Museum
László Nagy

32. Reverse side of the above tablet
Fertőszentmiklós, Győr-Sopron
County
Veszprém, Bakony Museum
László Nagy

33. Reaping hay
Szék, former Szolnok-Doboka
County
Péter Korniss

34. Breakfast during maize
harvesting
Átány, Heves County
Budapest, Ethnographical
Museum
Tamás Hofer

35. Men playing cards
Méra, former Kolozs County
Budapest, Ethnographical
Museum
Tamás Hofer

36. Men having a talk in the stable
Átány, Heves County
Budapest, Ethnographical
Museum
Tamás Hofer

37. Drumming out the news
Szentistván, Borsod-Abaúj-
Zemplén County
Budapest, Ethnographical
Museum
Sándor Gönyey

38. Maidens of Mary, ready
for procession
Mezőkövesd
Budapest, Ethnographical
Museum

39. Procession for blessing the wheat
Nádújfalu, Heves County
Budapest, Ethnographical
Museum
Márton Kankovszky

40. Interior of a Calvinist Church
Szenna, Somogy County
Jenő Szabó

41. In church
Vista, former Kolozs County
Péter Korniss

42. Sunday, after church
Szék, former Szolnok-Doboka
County
Péter Korniss

43. Market
Jászberény
Kata Kálmán

44. Selling cow-bells
Hortobágy, near Debrecen
Budapest, Ethnographical
Museum
István Györffy

45. The fair at the Hortobágy bridge
near Debrecen
Rudolf Balogh, Union
of Photographers

46. Farmstead
Kecskemét
Photograph taken from the air
by the MTI

47. Farmstead
Székkutas, Csongrád County
Photograph taken from the air
by the MTI

48. Farmsteads
Kecskemét
Photograph taken from the air by
the MTI

49. Farmstead
Jászárokszállás, Szolnok County
Budapest, Ethnographical
Museum
Sándor Gönyey

50. A well with a steep
on a farmstead
Karcag
Jenő Szabó

51. A grave-post in the cemetery
Magyarvalkó, former Kolozs
County
Péter Korniss

52. Cemetery
Szentegyházasfalu, former
Udvarhely County
Péter Korniss

53. Cemetery
Szatmárcseke, Szabolcs-Szatmár
County
Zoltán Móser

54. Grave-post
Szenna, Somogy County
Jenő Szabó

55. Heart-shaped grave-post
Karancsság, Nógrád County
Péter Korniss

56. Tombstone, 1791
Tök, Pest County
Zoltán Móser

57. Székely double-gate
Máréfalva, former Udvarhely
County
Péter Korniss

58. A single gate
Szombathely, Village Museum
of Vas County
Jenő Szabó

59. Settlement around a medieval
fortress
Nagyvázsony, Veszprém
County
Photograph taken from the air
by the MTI

60 Village with streets
Tab, Somogy County
Photograph taken from air by the
MTI

61. Village with streets
Erdőbénye, Borsod-Abaúj-
Zemplén County
Photograph taken from the air by
the MTI

62. Wooden belfry
Nemesborzova, Szabolcs-
Szatmár County
Miklós Lantos

63. Chimneyless kitchen
of a cottage built on a log
foundation
Szenna, Somogy County
Miklós Lantos

64. Kitchen interior
Bogyoszló, Győr-Sopron
County
Jenő Szabó

65. Székely open fire-place
Székelyland, Rumania
Rudolf Balogh, Union
of Photographers

66. Open fire-place with chimney
Gyimesközéplok, former Csík
County
Budapest, Ethnographical
Museum

67. Oven in a Palots house
Balassagyarmat, Palóc Museum
Jenő Szabó

68. Open fire-place with cooking
stove
Ziliz, Borsod-Abaúj-Zemplén
County
Miskolc, Herman Ottó
Museum
Géza Megay

69. Round oven
Tápé, Csongrád County
Miklós Lantos

70. Tile-stove with "eyes"
Szenna, Somogy County
Miklós Lantos

71. Vessel for dipping candles
Kecskemét, Katona József
Museum
Tamás Kovács

72. Corner of a room
Sióagárd, Tolna County
Miklós Lantos

73. Room interior
Hollókő, Nógrád County
Péter Korniss

74. Highly stacked bed in the
"Sárköz House"
Decs, Tolna County
Miklós Lantos

75. Interior of a peasant house
Mezőkövesd
Jenő Szabó

76. Sleeping chamber in a Palots
house
Parád, Heves County
Jenő Szabó

77. Interior of the best room
Mátisfalva, former Udvarhely
County
Budapest, Ethnographical
Museum
István Kovács

78. Cellar built of logs
Vineyard in Csurgó-
Nagymárton, Somogy County
Miklós Lantos

79. Barn built on a structure of logs
Szenna, Somogy County
Miklós Lantos

80. Grain bin
Magyarbóly, Baranya County
Miklós Lantos

81. Barn with triple sections
Inaktelke, former Kolozs
County
Budapest, Ethnographical
Museum
Sándor Gönyey

82. Barn built of logs with a thatched
roof
Székelyvarság, former
Udvarhely County
Budapest, Ethnographical
Museum
Galimdsán Tagán

83. A storehouse (kástu)
Szalafő, Pityerszer, Vas County
Miklós Lantos

84. Wicker-work maize bin
Berzence, Somogy County
Miklós Lantos

85. Farmhouse
Szalafő, Pityerszer, Vas County
Jenő Szabó

86. House
Szalafő, Pityerszer, Vas County
János Reismann

87. Façade decoration on a house
Szentbékkálla, Veszprém
County
Jenő Szabó

88. House
Kővágóőrs, Veszprém County
Kata Kálmán

89. House
Balatonzamárdi, Somogy
County
Kata Kálmán

90. Log cottage
Ájfalucska, former Abaúj-Torna
County
Iván Hevesy, Union
of Photographers

91. A cave dwelling
Alsóborsod, former Borsod
County
Miskolc, Herman Ottó Museum
Kálmán Kóris

92. House
Borsod County
Miskolc, Herman Ottó Museum

93. House
Komádi, Hajdú–Bihar County
Budapest, Ethnographical
Museum
Dezső Antal

94. House
Torockó, former Torda-
Aranyos County
Jenő Szabó

95. House
Mikóújfalu, former Háromszék
County
Budapest, Ethnographical
Museum
Dezső Antal

96. Sewing a bulrush mat
Great Plain
Rudolf Balogh, Union
of Photographers

97. Splitting wicker
Kiskunfélegyháza
Kálmán Kónya

98. Ploughing
Kökényespuszta, Nógrád
County
Budapest, Ethnographical
Museum
Sándor Gönyey

99. Sowing
Kazár, Nógrád County
Budapest, Ethnographical
Museum
Sándor Gönyey

100. Reaping with a sickle
Szentgál, Veszprém County
Veszprém, Bakony Museum
Aurél Vajkai

101. Reaping with scythes
Diósjenő, Nógrád County
Kata Sugár, Union
of Photographers

102. a. Wooden holder for whetstone
Budapest, Ethnographical
Museum
b. Corn dolley
Gégény, Szabolcs-Szatmár
County
c. Corn dolley
Sárospatak, Calvinist Collection
Tamás Kovács

103. Treading out the corn
Átány, Heves County
Budapest, Ethnographical
Museum
Tamás Hofer

104. Winnowing the corn
Mezőkövesd
Miskolc, Herman Ottó Museum
Kálmán Kóris

105. Threshing with a flail
Óbánya, Baranya County
Miklós Lantos

106. Threshing with a flail
Szentgál, Veszprém County
Veszprém, Bakony Museum
Aurél Vajkai

107. Potato picking
Bercel, Nógrád County
Péter Korniss

108. Utensil for chopping tobacco
Botpalád, Szabolcs-Szatmár
County
Szentendre, Hungarian
Ethnographical Village Museum
Tamás Kovács

109. Corn husking
Mezőkövesd
Miskolc, Herman Ottó Museum
István Györffy

110. A "dry" mill drawn by a horse
Szarvas
Jenő Szabó

111. Working in a mill
Gyimesközéplok, former Csík
County
Péter Korniss

112. Windmill
Kiskundorozsma, Csongrád
County
Tamás Kovács

113. Preparations for vintage
Sióagárd, Tolna County
Péter Korniss

114. Wine-press from 1750
Hills north of Balaton
Veszprém, Bakony Museum
Levente Szepsi Szűcs

115. Bottom of barrel with the relief
of St. Urban
Hungary
Budapest, Ethnographical
Museum
Tamás Kovács

116. Beehive
Vajdácska, Borsod-Abaúj-
Zemplén County
Sárospatak, Calvinist Collection
Tamás Kovács

117. Drumming the bees into a new
hive
Komádi, Hajdú-Bihar County
Budapest, Ethnographical
Museum
Tamás Hofer

118. Placing fish-traps in front of
a large fish-net
Kopács, former Baranya
County
Budapest, Ethnographical
Museum
Sándor Gönyey

119. Fisherman with his net
Komádi, Hajdú-Bihar County
Budapest, Ethnographical
Museum
Balázs Molnár

120. Gourd for keeping mudfish
Haraszti, former Verőce County
Budapest, Ethnographical
Museum
Tamás Kovács

121. Fishing under the ice
Sára, Borsod-Abaúj-Zemplén
County
Budapest, Ethnographical
Museum
Sándor Gönyey

122. Cattleherd
Borsod-Abaúj-Zemplén County
Kata Kálmán

123. The chief cattleherd
Dévaványa, Békés County
Kata Kálmán

124. Cattleherds having their noon
meal
Hortobágy
Budapest, Ethnographical
Museum

125. Driving the cattle out in the
morning
Szék, former Szolnok-Doboka
County
Péter Korniss

126. Shepherd leaning on his crook
Hortobágy
Budapest, Ethnographical
Museum

127. Driving out the swine
Hollókő, Nógrád County
Kata Sugár, Union
of Photographers

128. Milking sheep
Szék, former Szolnok-Doboka
County
Péter Korniss

129. Sheep shearing
Great Plain
Rudolf Balogh, Union
of Photographers

130. Sheep shearing
Szék, former Szolnok-Doboka
County
Péter Korniss

131. Watering the flock
Hortobágy
István Moser

132. Mowing with scythes
Szék, former Szolnok-Doboka
County
Péter Korniss

133. Gathering hay
Maconka, Heves County
Budapest, Ethnographical
Museum
Sándor Gönyey

134. Collecting hay
Vista, former Kolozs County
Péter Korniss

135. Sheep fold
Gyimes, former Csík County
Tamás Hofer

136. A flock of sheep
Szék, former Szolnok-Doboka
County
Péter Korniss

137. The cabin of the shepherd who
guards the flock at night
Csíkszentdomokos, former
Csík County
Budapest, Ethnographical
Museum
Tamás Hofer

138. Women carryings sacks
Vista, former Kolozs County
Péter Korniss

139. Women carrying bundles
Hollókő, Nógrád County
Péter Korniss

140. On the way home from reaping
Galgagyörk, Pest County
Péter Korniss

141. Sleighing
Drágszél, Bács-Kiskun County
Péter Korniss

142. Horses drinking
Jászjákóhalma, Szolnok County
Kata Kálmán

143. Kitchen with stove
Bábonymegyer, Somogy
County
Miklós Lantos

144. Cauldron in the sheep fold
Gyimes, former Kolozs County
Budapest, Ethnographical
Museum
Tamás Hofer

145. Spoon-rack
Semjén, Borsod-Abaúj-
Zemplén County
Sárospatak, Calvinist Collection
Tamás Kovács

146. Wooden bowl with two handles
Szuhahuta, Heves County
Budapest, Ethnographical
Museum
Tamás Kovács

147. Two pottery dishes
Budapest, Ethnographical
Museum
Tamás Kovács

148. Baking bread: mixing leaven
Komádi, Hajdú-Bihar County
Budapest, Ethnographical
Museum
Balázs Molnár

149. Baking bread: forming the
dough into loaves
Komádi, Hajdú-Bihar County
Budapest, Ethnographical
Museum
Balázs Molnár

150. Basket for the dough of a loaf
Cigánd, Borsod-Abaúj-
Zemplén County
Sárospatak, Calvinist Collection
Tamás Kovács

151. Bread basket
Cigánd, Borsod-Abaúj-
Zemplén County
Sárospatak, Calvinist Collection
Tamás Kovács

152. Bread inside an oven
Átány, Heves County
Budapest, Ethnographical
Museum
Tamás Hofer

153. Baking pastry horn wound
around a stick
Jobbágytelke, former Maros-
Torda County
Péter Korniss

154. Making strudel
Buzsák, Somogy County
Péter Korniss

155. Churning butter
Kazár, Nógrád County
Rudolf Balogh, Union
of Photographers

156. Wine-flasks covered with leather
Hungary
Budapest, Ethnographical
Museum
Tamás Kovács

157. Salt-cellar
Balassagyarmat, Palóc Museum
Tamás Kovács

158. Breaking hemp: a swingle
Gyimes-Bükkhavas, former
Csík County
Albert Kresz

159. Combing out hemp
Karcsa, Borsod-Abaúj-Zemplén
County
Kata Kálmán

160. Working on a spinning wheel
Sukoró, Fejér County
Jenő Szabó

161. The loom of a professional
weaver
Nagyvázsony, Veszprém
County
Tamás Kovács

162. Beating out the wash at the river
Miske, Bács-Kiskun County
Tamás Kovács

163. Beating out the wash
Kalotaszentkirály, former
Kolozs County
Péter Korniss

164. Woman spinning from a distaff
Lészped, Moldavia
Péter Korniss

165. Shoemakers at work: detail
of a painted guild-chest, 1800
Borsod-Abaúj-Zemplén County
Miskolc, Herman Ottó Museum
Tamás Broczkó

166. A hide-dresser at work: detail
from a painted guild chest, 1800
Borsod-Abaúj-Zemplén
County
Miskolc, Herman Ottó
Museum
Tamás Broczkó

167. Guild's tablet for announcements
Bács-Kiskun County
Kecskemét, Katona József
Museum
Tamás Kovács

168. Woman braiding her hair
Boldog, Pest County
Kata Kálmán

169. Two young wives (menyecske) in
festive headdress
Kazár, Nógrád County
Károly Koffán

170. Arranging the headdress of
a young wife (menyecske)
Kazár, Nógrád County
Károly Koffán

171. Headdress of a middle-aged
woman
Kazár, Nógrád County
Károly Koffán

172. Headdress of an aged woman
Kazár, Nógrád County
Károly Koffán

173. Married young woman's
headdress
Kalocsa
Kata Kálmán

174. Bride in her bridal wreath
Boldog, Pest County
Kata Kálmán

175. The back of an embroidered szűr
mantle
Veszprém County
Veszprém, Bakony Museum
Levente Szepsi Szűcs

176. Horseherd wearing a szűr mantle
Hortobágy
Kata Kálmán

177. Men and woman wearing the
guba mantle
Tunyog, Szabolcs-Szatmár
County
Budapest, Ethnographical
Museum
Margit Luby

178. The embroidery of a suba
sheepskin cloak
Kisújszállás, Szolnok County
Budapest, Ethnographical
Museum

179. Women wearing ködmön jackets
Nagycigánd, Borsod-Abaúj-
Zemplén County
Budapest, Ethnographical
Museum

180. Short sheepskin bunda of the
Hajdú district
Debrecen
Károly Koffán

181. Young married woman
Kapuvár, Győr-Sopron County
Kata Kálmán

182. Bride and groom
Kapuvár, Győr-Sopron County
Budapest, Ethnographical
Museum
Sándor Gönyey

183. Young man dressed as
a bridesman
Martos, former Komárom
County
Budapest, Ethnographical
Museum
Sándor Gönyey

184. Middle-aged couple and their
young son wearing
second-best clothes in
summertime
Martos, former Komárom
County
Budapest, Ethnographical
Museum
Edit Fél

185. Young girl dressed in Sunday
clothes in summertime
Martos, former Komárom
County
Edit Fél

186. Young women in their best
clothes
Érsekcsanád, Bács-Kiskun
County
Kata Kálmán

187. Young wives in their costumes
Decs, Tolna County
Budapest, Ethnographical
Museum
Sándor Gönyey

188. Girl
Sióagárd, Tolna County
Miklós Lantos

189. Dressing the newly wed wife
Kazár, Nógrád County
Klára Langer, Union
of Photographers

190. Young Palots wives
Lúdány, Nógrád County
Kata Kálmán

191. Girls and a young woman
Tard, Borsod-Abaúj-Zemplén
County
Kata Kálmán

192. Girls from the village Boldog
Boldog, Pest County
Kata Kálmán

193. Young agrarian labourer in her
best clothes
Tard, Borsod-Abaúj-Zemplén
County
Kata Kálmán

194. Old woman wearing a sheepskin
kuzsu
Mezőkövesd
Budapest, Ethnographical
Museum
Edit Fél

195. Bride and bridegroom
Mezőkövesd
Budapest, Ethnographical
Museum
György Kemény collection

196. Girls from Kalocsa
Kalocsa
Kata Kálmán

197. Young wife from Kalocsa
Kalocsa
Kata Kálmán

198. Herdsmen from the puszta
of Bugac
Bugac
Kata Kálmán

199. Young wife from the district
of Kalotaszeg
Kalotaszeg, former Kolozs
County
Kata Kálmán

200. Székely man coming home after
field work
Máréfalva, former Udvarhely
County
Péter Korniss

201. Men in their Sunday suits
Nagykapus, former Kolozs
County
Kata Kálmán

202. Women and girls embroidering
Lészped, Moldavia
Péter Korniss

203. Carving tools. (Owned by
Mihály Tóth, a herdsman
specialist at carving)
Felsősegesd-Lászlómajor,
Somogy County
Miklós Lantos

204. Mangling board, 1829
Győr-Sopron County
Sopron, Liszt Ferenc Museum
Tamás Kovács

205. A shaving horse
Borsod-Abaúj-Zemplén County
Miskolc, Herman Ottó Museum
Tamás Kovács

206. Incised drinking horn
of a herdsman
Former Ung County
Sárospatak, Calvinist Collection
Tamás Kovács

207. Detail of a mangling board
Hungary
Budapest, Ethnographical
Museum
Jenő Szabó

208. Water-dipper
Monostorapáti, Zala County
Veszprém, Bakony Museum
Levente Szepsi Szűcs

209. Powder-flask
Veszprém, Bakony Museum
Levente Szepsi Szűcs

210. Powder-flask
Veszprém County
Veszprém, Bakony Museum
Levente Szepsi Szűcs

211. Hewn chest *(szökröny)*
Baranya County
Pécs, Janus Pannonius Museum
Miklós Lantos

212. Hewn chest (side view)
Baranya County
Pécs, Janus Pannonius Museum
Miklós Lantos

213. Hewn chest, 1889
Nógrád County
Budapest, Ethnographical
Museum
Tamás Kovács

214. Hewn chest
Hungary
Budapest, Ethnographical
Museum
Jenő Szabó

215. Detail of the back of a bench
Nógrád County
Budapest, Ethnographical
Museum
Jenő Szabó

216. Back of a bench
Nógrád County
Budapest, Ethnographical
Museum
Kálmán Kónya

217. Carved back of a chair
Veszprém County
Veszprém, Bakony Museum
Levente Szepsi Szűcs

218. Stool, 1838
Tiszafüred, Szolnok County
Budapest, Ethnographical
Museum
Kálmán Kónya

219. Armchair
Zádor, Baranya County
Budapest, Ethnographical
Museum
Kálmán Kónya

220. Church ceiling with painted
panels
Magyarvalkó, former Kolozs
County
Péter Korniss

221. Carved and painted chest
Komárom
Budapest, Ethnographical
Museum
Kálmán Kónya

222. Table. Mid-19th century
Nógrád County
Budapest, Ethnographical
Museum
Kálmán Kónya

223. Painted chest
Borsod-Abaúj-Zemplén County
Miskolc, Herman Ottó Museum
Tamás Broczkó

224. Detail of a handwoven pillow-
cover
Sárköz
Budapest, Ethnographical
Museum
Tibor Gyerkó

225. Detail of a handwoven tablecloth
Somogy County
Budapest, Ethnographical
Museum
Tibor Gyerkó

226. Detail of a handwoven tablecloth
Baranya County
Budapest, Ethnographical
Museum
Tibor Gyerkó

227. Homespun basket-cover for the
godmother's present of food
Baranya County
Budapest, Ethnographical
Museum
Tibor Gyerkó

228. Knapsack worn on a pilgrimage
Nógrád County
Budapest, Ethnographical
Museum
Tibor Gyerkó

229. Handwoven pillow-cover
Székely of Bukovina,
Transdanubia
Budapest, Ethnographical
Museum
Tibor Gyerkó

230. Embroidery on communion-
table cover, 1755
Szirma, Borsod-Abaúj-
Zemplén County
Sárospatak, Calvinist
Collection
Tamás Kovács

231. Border of a sheet, detail
Veszprém County
Budapest, Ethnographical
Museum
Tibor Gyerkó

232. Border of a sheet, worked in
white, the owner's mark in the
corner
Zala County
Budapest, Ethnographical
Museum
Tibor Gyerkó

233. A coif worn over the forehead,
spread out
Sárköz
Budapest, Ethnographical
Museum
Tibor Gyerkó

234. *Matyó* embroidery, border
of a sheet
Mezőkövesd
Miskolc, Herman Ottó Museum
Tamás Broczkó

235. Embroidery to hang at the end
of a bed
Kalotaszeg region, former
Kolozs County
Budapest, Ethnographical
Museum
Tibor Gyerkó

236. Embroidery to hang at the end of
a bed
Kalotaszeg region, former
Kolozs County
Budapest, Ethnographical
Museum
Tibor Gyerkó

237. Border of a pillowslip
Kalotaszeg region, former
Kolozs County
Budapest, Ethnographical
Museum
Tibor Gyerkó

238. Border of a sheet, detail
Former Háromszék County
Budapest, Ethnographical
Museum
Tibor Gyerkó

239. János Horváth, Sr., potter
Mohács
Miklós Lantos

240. The pitcher of the Peremarton
Bootmakers' Guild, 1770
Öskü, Veszprém County
Veszprém, Bakony Museum
Levente Szepsi Szűcs

241. Water jug, 1853
Tüskevár, Veszprém County
Veszprém, Bakony Museum
Levente Szepsi Szűcs

242. Decanters for Communion wine
of the Calvinist church
of Báránd, 1797
Báránd, Hajdú-Bihar County
Debrecen, Déri Museum
Tamás Kovács

243. Dish decorated with the design
of a cock
Mórágy, Tolna County
Budapest, Ethnographical
Museum
Tamás Kovács

244. Dish decorated with the design of
a bird, 1843
Mezőcsát, Borsod-Abaúj-
Zemplén County
Miskolc, Herman Ottó Museum
Tamás Broczkó

245. The *Miska*-jug of the
Locksmiths' Guild
Mezőcsát, Borsod-Abaúj-
Zemplén County
Miskolc, Herman Ottó
Museum
Tamás Broczkó

246. Earthenware bowl
Sárospatak
Sárospatak, Calvinist Collection
Tamás Kovács

247. Crosses
Csíksomlyó, Salvator Chapel,
former Csík County
Zoltán Móser

248. Woman painting eggs
Miske, Bács-Kiskun County
Klára Langer, Union
of Photographers

249. Old man playing the flute
Váralja, Tolna County
Kata Kálmán

250. Head of a bagpipe
Kaposvár
Károly Koffán

251. Beggar with hurdy-gurdy
Great Plain

252. Playing the zither
Sándorfalva, Csongrád County
Budapest, Ethnographical
Museum
Bálint Sárosi–Margit Tóth

253. Musicians in a wedding
procession
Szék, former Szolnok-
Doboka County
Péter Korniss

254. Drumming on the bass
Gyimesközéplok, former Csík
County
Budapest, Ethnographical
Museum
Zoltán Kallós–Tamás Hofer

255. Musicians at a wedding, with
fiddle and drum-bass
Gyimesközéplok-Görbepataka,
former Csík County
Péter Korniss

256. Mangling board with sealing
wax inlay showing dancers,
1868
Hövej, Győr-Sopron County
Budapest, Ethnographical
Museum
Jenő Szabó

257. The *legényes* dance at a wedding,
in front of the church
Méra, former Kolozs County
Péter Korniss

258. The dance called
forgatós. Sandstone relief
Region of Nyárád river
Zoltán Móser

259. Dancing the *forgatós* at a wedding
Méra, former Kolozs County
Péter Korniss

260. Dancing the *forgatós* at a wedding
Méra, former Kolozs County
Péter Korniss

261. Children's round dance
Szada, Pest County
Budapest, Ethnographical
Museum
Sándor Gönyey

262. A peacock with a flowering
bough, detail of a mirror-case
Somogy County
Budapest, Ethnographical
Museum
Jenő Szabó

263. *Betyárs,* or outlaws. Detail of
a salt-cellar
Transdanubia
Budapest, Ethnographical
Museum
Jenő Szabó

264. Mirror-case with sealing-wax
inlay, 1885
Nagydobsza-Istvánmajor,
Somogy County
Kaposvár, Rippl-Rónai
Museum
Tamás Kovács

265. Shepherd lad. Detail of a razor-
case, 1842
Bakonybél, Veszprém County
Veszprém, Bakony Museum
Tamás Kovács

266. Back of a mirror-case with
sealing-wax inlay, 1885
Nagydobsza-Istvánmajor,
Somogy County
Kaposvár, Rippl-Rónai
Museum
Tamás Kovács

267. Woman singing a ballad
Moldavia
Budapest, Ethnographical
Museum
Tamás Hofer

268. Woman singing a ballad
Moldavia
Budapest, Ethnographical
Museum
Tamás Hofer

269. Cover of a chapbook novel

270. Cover of a chapbook novel

271. Cover of a chapbook novel

272. Cover of a chapbook novel

273. Christening
Lészped, Moldavia
Péter Korniss

274. Carrying a present of clothes to
the godchild
Méra, former Kolozs County
Budapest, Ethnographical
Museum
Tamás Hofer

275. A swaddled babe lying in a tub
Lészped, Moldavia
Péter Korniss

276. Bird-shaped earthenware whistle
Budapest, Ethnographical
Museum
Tamás Kovács

277. Child pushing a cart
Szentistván, Borsod-Abaúj-
Zemplén County
Miskolc, Herman Ottó Museum
Olga Leszik

278. Goose-girl
Nógrád County
Kata Sugár, Union
of Photographers

279. Children at play
Galgamácsa, Pest County
Péter Korniss

280. The dance of the youngsters
Szék, former Kolozs County
Péter Korniss

281. Seeing off the bride
Buják, Nógrád County
Budapest, Ethnographical
Museum
János Manga

282. Carrying the bride's bed
Balavásár, former Szolnok-
Doboka County
Rudolf Balogh

283. Carrying the bride's dowry
Vista, former Kolozs County
Péter Korniss

284. Carrying the bride's bed
Vista, former Kolozs County
Péter Korniss

285. Going off to church
Szentistván, Borsod-Abaúj-
Zemplén County
Klára Langer

286. Wedding cakes and pastries
Méra, former Kolozs County
Péter Korniss

287. Wedding
Szentistván, Borsod-Abaúj-
Zemplén County
Klára Langer

288. Wedding feast
Püspökhatvan, Pest County
Zsuzsa Sándor

289. Wedding feast
Homokmégy, Bács-Kiskun
County
Klára Langer

290. Lamentation
Magyarszovát, former Kolozs
County
Budapest, Ethnographical
Museum
Tamás Hofer

291. Lamentation
Rimóc, Nógrád County
Péter Korniss

292. Funeral procession
Magyarszovát, former Kolozs
County
Budapest, Ethnographical
Museum
Tamás Hofer

293. Lamentation
Átány, Heves County
Budapest, Ethnographical
Museum
Tamás Hofer

294. Funeral meal (the men)
Magyarszovát, former Kolozs
County
Budapest, Ethnographical
Museum
Tamás Hofer

295. Funeral meal (the women)
Magyarszovát, former Kolozs
County
Budapest, Ethnographical
Museum
Tamás Hofer

296. All Saints' Day in the cemetery
Tiszaörs, Szolnok County
Péter Korniss

297. Epiphany: the Three Magi
Szakmár, Bács-Kiskun County
Péter Korniss

298. Smutting the face at Carnival
Moha, Fejér County
Péter Korniss

299. Masquerading on Shrove
Tuesday
Moha, Fejér County
Péter Korniss

300. Carnival masquerades
Moha, Fejér County
Jenő Szabó

301. Preparing the *kisze* doll
Szandaváralja, Nógrád County
Albert Kresz

302. Easter sprinkling
Acsa, Pest County
Péter Korniss

303. Raising the May Tree
Mezőkövesd
Budapest, Ethnographical
Museum
Sándor Gönyey

304. Taking the Queen of
Whitsuntide around
Vitnyéd, Győr-Sopron
County
Péter Korniss

305. Leaping over the Midsummer
Night fire
Kazár, Nógrád County
Budapest, Ethnographical
Museum
Gertrúd Palotay

306. "Bethlehem" Nativity players
Szakmár, Bács-Kiskun County
Péter Korniss

307. "Bethlehem" Nativity play
Kéty, Tolna County
Péter Korniss

308. Harvest festival
Kazár, Nógrád County
Rudolf Balogh

309. Saint Wendelin, the patron saint
of herdsmen
A wayside statue
Jászberény
Miklós Lantos

310. Smoking against the evil eye
Tunyog, Szabolcs-Szatmár
County
Budapest, Ethnographical
Museum
Margit Luby

311. Spinning the sieve
Beregújfalu, former Bereg
County, Soviet Union
Budapest, Ethnographical
Museum
Béla Gunda

312. Divination with beans on a sieve
Gajcsána, Moldavia
(Egyházaskozár, Baranya
County)
Budapest, Ethnographical
Museum
Vilmos Diószegi

313. Decorated gourd, 1969
Made by Mihály Tóth, Master of
Folk Art
Segesd, Somogy County
Gábor Minarik

314. Cigarette-case
Made by István Kálmán, Master
of Folk Art
Balatonfenyves, Somogy
County
Gábor Minarik

315. Water-dipper
Made by Dénes Sztelek, Master
of Folk Art
Palots region
Gábor Minarik

316. Puzzle jug *(csalikancsó)*
Made by Imre Jakucs, Master of
Folk Art
Mezőtúr
Gábor Minarik

317. Bowl
Made by Mrs. B. Szkircsák,
Master of Folk Art
Sárospatak
Gábor Minarik

318. Water-jug
Made by János Horváth, Master
of Folk Art
Mohács
Gábor Minarik

319. Embroidered coverlet, detail.
Made by Mrs. M. G. Tóth
Tura, Pest County
Gábor Minarik

List of Sources for Colour Plates

I. Székely gate
Máréfalva,
former Udvarhely
County
Péter Korniss

II. Blue-dyers at work.
A signboard for the hostel
of journeymen, 1862
Sopron

III. A stall for indigo-dyed
cottonware at a fair
Véménd,
Baranya County
János Szerencsés,
from the book by
Ottó Domokos

IV. Wine cellar
Upper Balaton region
Károly Szelényi

V. Vintage
Upper Balaton region
Károly Szelényi

VI. Hay-making women
Vista, Former
Kolozs County
Péter Korniss

VII. Treading out grain on an
estate, 1855
Great Plain
(Gábor Prónay: *Vázlatok
Magyarhon népéletéből.*
Pest, 1855)
Attila Károly

VIII. Shepherds, 1855
Great Plain
(Gábor Prónay: *Vázlatok
Magyarhon népéletéből.*
Pest, 1855)
Attila Károly

IX. Catching a horse
with a lasso, 1855
Great Plain
(Gábor Prónay: *Vázlatok
Magyarhon népéletéből.*
Pest, 1855)
Attila Károly

X. Buffalo herdsman, 1855
Upper Balaton region
(Gábor Prónay: *Vázlatok
Magyarhon népéletéből.*
Pest, 1855)
Attila Károly

XI. A young wife *(menyecske)*
Kapuvár,
Győr-Sopron County
Károly Koffán

XII. Women and girls
in festive costume
Sióagárd, Tolna County
Jenő Szabó

XIII. Girls wearing
their costumes
Kazár, Nógrád County
Károly Koffán

XIV. A girl dressed in her
Sunday best
Vista,
former Kolozs County
Péter Korniss

XV. A couple wearing
everyday clothes
Gyimes-Bükkhavas,
former Csík County
Albert Kresz

XVI. Men wearing
their costumes
Gyimes-Bükkhavas,
former Csík County
Albert Kresz

XVII. A woman's
sheepskin jacket
Tordaszentlászló, former
Torda-Aranyos County
Budapest,
Ethnographical Museum
Károly Szelényi

XVIII. Back of woman's
sheepskin jacket
Transdanubia
Budapest,
Ethnographical Museum
Károly Szelényi

XIX. Woman's sheepskin
jacket
Maconka, Heves County
Budapest,
Ethnographical Museum

XX. Sleeves of women's
sheepskin jackets
Transdanubia
Budapest,
Ethnographical Museum
Károly Szelényi

XXI. Detatil of a *suba*
(sheepskin cloak)
Kisújszállás,
Szolnok County
Budapest,
Ethnographical Museum
Károly Szelényi

XXII. Church ceiling
Magyarókereke, former
Kolozs County
Budapest,
Ethnographical Museum
Károly Szelényi

XXIII. Mirror-case
Transdanubia
Budapest,
Ethnographical Museum
Károly Szelényi

XXIV. Mirror-case with
floral decoration
Transdanubia
Budapest,
Ethnographical Museum
Károly Szelényi

XXV. Mangling board
Pusztasomorja,
Győr-Sopron County
Budapest,
Ethnographical Museum
Károly Szelényi

XXVI. Mirror-case
Felsőzsid, Zala County
Budapest,
Ethnographical Museum
Károly Szelényi

XXVII. Mirror-case with
sealing-wax inlay
Somogy County
Budapest,
Ethnographical Museum

XXVIII. Mirror-case
Somogy County
Budapest,
Ethnographical Museum
Károly Szelényi

XXIX. Two salt-cellars, the one
on the right from 1893
Southern Transdanubia
Budapest,
Ethnographical Museum

XXX. Water-dipper
Somogy County
Budapest,
Ethnographical Museum

XXXI. Cupboard for mugs, 1831
Homoródalmás, former
Udvarhely County
Budapest,
Ethnographical Museum
Károly Szelényi

XXXII. Chest
Fadd, Tolna County
Budapest,
Ethnographical Museum
Károly Szelényi

XXXIII. Chest painted with tulips
Hódmezővásárhely
Budapest,
Ethnographical Museum
Károly Szelényi

XXXIV. Crewelwork
on a pillow-slip
Hódmezővásárhely
Budapest,
Ethnographical Museum
Károly Szelényi

XXXV. Border of a bed-spread
Region of Rábaköz
Sopron,
Liszt Ferenc Museum
János Szerencsés

XXXVI. Border of a pillow-slip
Orosháza
Budapest,
Ethnographical Museum
Károly Szelényi

XXXVII. Back of a woman's
sheepskin jacket
Békés County
Budapest,
Ethnographical Museum
Károly Szelényi

XXXVIII. Embroidery on the
sleeves
of a Matyó shirt
Mezőkövesd
Budapest,
Ethnographical Museum

XXXIX. The kiln of a potter
Csákvár, Fejér County
Albert Kresz

XL. Plate, 1830
Debrecen
Debrecen, Déri Museum
Károly Koffán

XLI. Wine jug
Torda, former
Torda-Aranyos
County
Budapest,
Ethnographical Museum
Károly Szelényi

XLII. Plate, 1844
Debrecen
Debrecen, Déri Museum
Károly Koffán

XLIII. Wine jug
Torda, former
Torda-Aranyos
County
Budapest,
Ethnographical Museum
Károly Szelényi

XLIV. Dish
Former Torda-Aranyos
County
Budapest,
Ethnographical Museum
Károly Szelényi

XLV. Dish
Sárköz region
Budapest,
Ethnographical Museum
Károly Szelényi

XLVI. Jug, 1832
Debrecen
Debrecen, Déri Museum
Károly Koffán

XLVII. Brandy flask
Mezőcsát,
Borsod-Abaúj-Zemplén
County
Budapest,
Ethnographical Museum
Károly Szelényi

XLVIII. *Miska*-jug
Mezőcsát,
Borsod-Abaúj-
Zemplén County
Budapest,
Ethnographical Museum
Albert Kresz

XLIX. Brandy flask
Tiszafüred,
Szolnok County
Budapest,
Ethnographical Museum
Albert Kresz

L. Brandy flask
Tiszafüred,
Szolnok County
Budapest,
Ethnographical Museum
Károly Szelényi

LI. Wedding
Vista, former
Kolozs County
Albert Kresz

LII. Vintage festival
Sióagárd, Tolna County
Károly Koffán

LIII. Easter sprinkling
Galgamácsa, Pest County
Péter Korniss

LIV. The Bethlehem Nativity
play of the Székelys
from Bukovina
Kakasd, Tolna County
Péter Korniss

LV. Bethlehem
Nativity players
Kéty, Tolna County
Péter Korniss

LVI. Figure of a woman
holding a dish for fruit
Made by Sándor Kántor,
Master of Folk Art
Karcag
Károly Szelényi

LVII. Dish decorated
with a rosette
Made by Sándor Kántor,
Master of Folk Art
Karcag
Károly Szelényi

LVIII. Embroidery to hang on
the wall in the
style of Matyó
shirts
Made by Mrs. M. Sárosi,
Master of Folk Art
Hódmezővásárhely
Károly Szelényi

LIX. Coverlet in Sióagárd style
Made by Anna Király
Baja
Károly Szelényi

LX. Embroidery to hang on
the wall in the style
of Matyó shirts
Made by Mrs. M.
Fazekas, Master
of Folk Art
Mezőkövesd
Károly Szelényi

LXI. Woven textile in the style
of the Palots
(from a pillow-slip)
Balassagyarmat
Károly Szelényi

LXII. Woven textile
from Majos
Majosháza, Pest County
Károly Szelényi

LXIII. Textile to hang on the
wall from Bihar
Made by
Mrs. M. Nyakas
Debrecen, Déri Museum
Károly Szelényi

LXIV. The house
of Bori Kis Jankó
Mezőkövesd
Gábor Minarik

LXV. The interior of Bori Kis
Jankó's house
Mezőkövesd
Gábor Minarik

LXVI. Figure of a woman
holding a dish for fruit
Made by Sándor Kántor,
Master of Folk Art
Karcag
Károly Szelényi

LXVII. Dish decorated
with a rosette.
Made by Sándor Kántor,
Master of Folk Art
Karcag
Károly Szelényi

LXVIII. Embroidery to hang on
the wall
Made by Mrs. M. Sárosi,
Master of Folk Art
Hódmezővásárhely
Károly Szelényi

782

List of Place Names Now Outside Hungary

Alsóőr	Unterwart	Austria
Apáca	Apața	Rumania
Asszonyvására	Targușor	Rumania
Áj	Háj	Czechoslovakia
Barskapronca	Koprivnice	Czechoslovakia
Bánffyhunyad	Huedin	Rumania
Belényes	Beiuș	Rumania
Bécsújhely	Wiener Neustadt	Austria
Bény	Biňa	Czechoslovakia
Bogdánfalva	Valea Seaca	Moldavia, Rumania
Bozók	Bzovík	Czechoslovakia
Brassó	Brașov	Rumania
Csíkmadaras	Mădăraș	Rumania
Csíkmenaság	Armășeni	Rumania
Csíksomlyó	Șomleu	Rumania
Csíkszenttamás	Tomești	Rumania
Csíkszereda	Miercurea Ciuc	Rumania
Csütörtökhely	Spišsky Štvrtok	Czechoslovakia
Darufalva	Drassburg	Austria
Désháza	Deja	Rumania
Déva	Deva	Rumania
Diósad	Dioșod	Rumania
Egyházaskér	Vrbica	Yugoslavia
Erked	Archita	Rumania
Eszék	Osijek	Yugoslavia
Esztelnek	Estelnic	Rumania
Felsőőr	Oberwart	Austria
Gerencsér	Nitrianske Hrnčiarovce	Czechoslovakia
Gerend	Grind	Rumania
Geszte	Host'ová	Czechoslovakia
Gyergyóújfalu	Suseni	Rumania
Gyimes	Lunca	Rumania
Györgyfalva	Gheorgheni	Rumania
Hadikfalva	Dornești	Bukovina, Rumania
Haraszti	Hrastin	Yugoslavia
Hertelendyfalva	Vojlovica	Yugoslavia
Inaktelke	Inucu	Rumania
Ipolybalog	Balog nad Ipl'om	Czechoslovakia

Jákótelke	Horlacea	Rumania
Jára	Iara	Rumania
Jobbágyi	Rohrbach an der Teich	Austria
Kalotaszeg	Zona Calata	Rumania
Kalotaszentkirály	Sîncraiu Silvanici	Rumania
Kassa	Košice	Czechoslovakia
Kászonimpér	Imper	Rumania
Kémer	Camăr	Rumania
Kénos	Chinuşu	Rumania
Kézdimárkosfalva	Mărcuşa	Rumania
Kézdivásárhely	Tîrgu-Secuiesc	Rumania
Kibéd	Chibed	Rumania
Kisborosnyó	Boroşneu Mic	Rumania
Kolony	Kolinany	Czechoslovakia
Kolozsmonostor	(belongs to Kolozsvár)	
Kolozsvár	Cluj	Rumania
Komárom	Komárno	Czechoslovakia
Kórógy	Korog	Yugoslavia
Korond	Corund	Rumania
Körösfő	Izvorul Crişului	Rumania
Lippa	Lipova	Rumania
Magyarpécska	Rovine	Rumania
Magyarszentmárton	Sînmărtinu Maghiar	Rumania
Magyarvalkó	Văleni	Rumania
Magyarvista	Viştea	Rumania
Marosvásárhely	Tîrgu-Mureş	Rumania
Martos	Martovce	Czechoslovakia
Mezőség	Cimpia Ardealului	Rumania
Munkács	Mukachevo	U.S.S.R.
Nagymegyer	Calovo	Czechoslovakia
Nagyszalonta	Salonta	Rumania
Nagyvárad	Oradea	Rumania
Olasztelek	Talişoara	Rumania
Oltszem	Olteni	Rumania
Őrisziget	Siget in der Wart	Austria
Pozsony	Bratislava	Czechoslovakia
Radna	Radna	Rumania
Rafajnaújfalu	Rafainovo	U.S.S.R.
Rákosd	Răcăştia	Rumania
Rétfalu	Retfala	Yugoslavia
Sámson	Şamşud	Rumania
Sepsibesenyő	Beşeneu	Rumania
Sepsiszentgyörgy	Sfîntu Gheorghe	Rumania
Siklód	Şiclod	Rumania

Szaján	Sajan	Yugoslavia
Szakadát	Sacadate	Rumania
Szamosfalva	Somoşeni	Rumania
Szentlászló	Laslovo	Yugoslavia
Szék	Sic	Rumania
Székelyudvarhely	Odorheiu	Rumania
Székelyvarság	Vârşag	Rumania
Szépkenyerű-szentmárton	Sînmărtin	Rumania
Szér	Ser	Rumania
Szimő	Zemné	Czechoslovakia
Szotyor	Coşeni	Rumania
Tardoskedd	Tvrdošovce	Czechoslovakia
Tild	Teldince	Czechoslovakia
Torda	Turda	Rumania
Torockó	Rimetea	Rumania
Torockószentgyörgy	Colţeşti	Rumania
Tövishát	Teiuş	Rumania
Udvarhelyszék	Judetul Odorheiu	Rumania
Ungvár	Uzhgorod	U.S.S.R.
Uzon	Ozun	Rumania
Vargyas	Vîrghiş	Rumania
Válaszút	Răscruci	Rumania
Zsére	Žirany	Czechoslovakia
Zsigárd	Žihárec	Czechoslovakia

785

Subject index

acacia
  —beam 173
  —flower 288
accordion 84
acorn 266
adobe 144, 170, 174, 225
  —brick 144
  —making pits 144
adoption 70
adventurous story 115
agricultural
  —equipment 65, 75
  —hands 88, 89
  —annual payment 88
  —common kitchen 88
  —dwelling 87, 89
  —order for the work 88
  —Sunday 89
  —implement 66
  —tool 58
  —work 62, 88
agriculture 26, 36, 39–41, 45, 47, 127, 196
  extensive— 46, 215
  plough— 28
Alan 45
Albanian 533
alfalfa 258
All Saints' Day 355, 636
alliteration 547, 548
alliterative
  —final-rhyme structure 597
  —regular form 597
almanac 115, 118
Alpine husbandry 50
St. Ambrose Day 665
American Indians 219
Anabaptists 369
Ananyno culture 27
ancient eight (rhythm) 473
andiron 151
St. Andrew's Day 651, 664, 665
anecdote 549, 579, 694
animal
  —doctor 264
  domestic— 246
  draught— 270
  driving out animal in the spring 662
  extensive keeping— 33, 45, 591
  —fable 569, 570
  —fair 117, 118
  forest animal husbandry 48
  —healing 264
  —husbandry 36, 37, 244–246

  —mark 65
  —myth 569
  —portrayal 380
  —power 222
  —sacrifice 27, 574
  speech of the— 683
  —trade 117
  unbroken— 270
anis 300
anthropomorphic
  —pitcher 411
  —vessel 412
apiary 233
  fenced— 233
  partly roofed— 233
apiarist 232
apiculture 232, 235
  tools of— 233
  Hungarian peasant— 235
  live tree— 233
apple 282
apprentice 93, 94, 390
  first— 243
apricot 282
apron 324, 335, 337, 343, 345, 348, 350, 353, 355, 356, 360, 392, 400
  back— 323
  —of blue-dyed material 348
  bridal— 324
  cotton— 361
  embroidered— 345, 350
  flower-print— 355
  homespun— 324, 344
  long— 350
  loose— 324
  loose, pleated back— 360 (muszuj)
  narrow— 324, 350
  satin— 345
  —with trimmed lace 356
archeology 26
architecture 334
  cave— 140
  European form of— 30
armchair 385
art
  applied— 363
  collective— 364
  creating— 364
  decorative— 47, 51
  naive— 367
  ornamental— 363, 367
  ornamental folk— 367, 406, 701
  popular applied— 363

artificial song 432
artisan 30, 31, 89–94, 112, 113
ash 286
attic 151, 152, 153, 169, 283, 625
  smoky— 283
Austrian 171, 323, 373, 454
  —Bavarian 93, 641
  —German 32
  —kitchen 291
Avar 206, 698
  —grave 380, 420
axe 121, 219, 682
  —handle 375, 377
  pick— 121
axle 274
  —grease 195

baby
  newborn— 68
bachelorhood 612
bacon 86, 278, 280, 284, 295
badger
  holes of— 237
bag
  sheepskin— 298
bagpipe 219, 435, 438, 439, 440, 442, 445, 449, 459
  keynote of the— 439
bagpiper 432, 440, 445
bailiff (ispán) 87
baker's shovel 291
baking 153, 189, 286, 288
  —bell 151, 177
  —bread 60, 291
  —house 153
  —oven 153, 155
  —pan 277
ball 190
  —roarer 606
ballad (also folk ballad) 31, 38, 115, 472, 515, 516, 521, 549, 696
  —of belief 527–529
  broadsheet— 519, 542–545
  —of captivity 532–538
  chapbook— 519
  dance— 521, 539
  historical— 529
  —of lament 542
  merry— 521, 539
  narrative ballad— 522–529
  new— 545–546
  outlaw— 519, 527, 532, 542, 539–541
  —of romance 520, 529–532

Scottish— 516
Székely— 549
thematic cycle of the—
  historical epic themes 516
  mythological themes 516
  individual family tragedies 516
tragic— 521
—of Turkish period 529
—of Wandering 532–538
ballata 514
band 84, 85
bandagazda 83, 85
bandit 497
bank 151
—of clay 157, 185
—of the hearth (padika) 175
wooden— 157
baptism 105, 107, 126, 459
baptismal
—feast 190
—sheet 394
bard 31, 435, 519
pagan— 31
bargaining 117
"wet the—" 117, 664
barley 203, 204, 220, 286, 287
—straw 258
barn 64, 72, 79, 84, 89, 118, 136, 163–167, 179, 181, 186, 197, 210, 213, 214, 258
—built of logs 167
—built on structure of logs 164
closed— 163
division of the— 165
"branch" (csűrág) 165
"drawer" (fiók) 165
"threshing ground" (szérű) 165
"throat" (szénűtorok) 165
plastered— 166
threshing— 208
—with wattle walls 166
—made of wood 166
yoke-like— 166
Baroque 131, 189, 369, 370, 388, 389, 417
barrack 84
—for sheltering hay 169
barrel 66, 170, 282
barrow 282
hand— 85
—man 273
wheel— 85
bass 445
drum— 446
—viol 445
basket 220, 289, 291
bread— 290
bulrush— 289, 290
straw— 289, 290
wicker— 240
willow— 230

Baskhir 480
Bavarian-Austrian 30
bead 362
bean 284, 285
divination with— 690
bear 237
—dancer 115
beard 318
—made from maize silk 219
beating 236
beauty
procedures to assure— 684
bed 64, 65, 115, 160, 366
—chamber 175, 177
four-poster— 387
—of grain 212
—resting on poles hammered into the ground (dikó) 169
bedding down 625
bee 683
—dwelling 234
—garden 233
—hive 233, 235, 240, 365
——made out of planks 234
——woven out of bulrush 234, 235
——woven out of straw 234
wooden—— 235
—keeper 233, 235
—keeping 90, 232
——wax 156
beef 295
beer 95, 299
home-made— 298
beet 282
thinning of— 84
beetle 375
belfry 139, 140, 141, 188
belief 42, 209, 217, 281, 420, 521, 524, 546
folk— 235, 321, 668, 679, 684, 781,
irrational— 683
—about the soul 26
traditional— 317
world of— 30, 31, 44, 45, 47, 324, 592, 593, 627, 668, 691
bell 261, 418
baking— 151, 177
church— 261
cow— 114, 261
—ringer 107
bellow 438, 439
—of dogskin 438
—of goatskin 438
—of lambskin 438
belt 315, 325
buttoned— 355
bench 115, 152, 158, 160, 161, 183, 291, 383, 384
clay— 169
wooden— 157
best man 616, 622, 625, 626

——of the bride 618, 620
first—— 612, 613, 618, 620, 622, 623, 626
——of the groom 618
——'s verses 614
young—— 613, 616
betrothal 615
bewitching
—of animals 686
—with the Evil Eye 675
—by incantation 687, 688
methods to prevent— 688
—people 686
—plants 686
preventing the bewitching of animals 682
—spirits 682
warding off— 690
Bible 160, 597
bier 628
"bilina" 514
bill-hook 122
bin 172
corn— 170
maize— 172, 173, 177
plastered wicker— 170
wickerwork maize— 173
wooden framed— 172
binder 79
bird 194, 236, 366
—catching 237
frighten— 99
—lime 237
singing— 237
single— 366
water— 236
birch bark 367
birth
child's— 365
biscuit
—baked in ashes 286
bison 202, 247, 262
black magic 673
blacksmith 89, 192, 200, 262, 417, 418
village— 200
St. Blaise Day
celebration of—— 600
Blessed Virgin's Day 686
Blighted Peter's Day 204
blind man's buff 600
blood
—contract 70
—feud 68
bloody kerchief signalling trouble 527
blouse 322, 341, 345, 355, 356, 360, 362
cambric— 355
linen— 356
blower 439
single-tongued— 439
blue-dyed material 324, 345, 348, 352

bluedyer 323
bluedying 373
boat 240, 241, 244
—mill 221
bodice 323, 324, 335, 338, 343, 344, 352,
  356, 360, 400
  embroidered leather— 345
bone 371, 375
  —bead 380
  —dice 380
bonnet 360, 362
  white linen— 351
book of Psalms 160
  —seller 115
boot 58, 63, 315, 333, 337, 345, 350, 353,
  355, 360, 361
  ankle— 334
  black— 338
  coloured— 333
  cordovan holiday— 355
  high heeled— 353
  leather soled boots with felt top part
  333–334
  —maker 91, 114, 364, 419
  red— 333, 338, 343, 345, 356
  yellow— 333
border
  —of a pillowslip 405
  —of a sheet 399, 400, 402, 405
border-guards
  Székely— 324
bottle of wine 622
boundary mark 120
bouquet 337, 345, 350
  —of pearls 360
bowl 708
  earthenware— 415
  wooden— 279
bowling alley 95
box 367
bracelet 418, 419
braid 318, 325, 326
  —maker 46, 325
braiding 324, 325
  —trim 324, 328
bran 284, 288
brand 65
  —mark 66, 417
  —the rump of the animal 259
branding 259
  —iron 259
brandy 58, 84, 95, 281
  apricot— 298
  —flask 408
  pocket sized—— 411
  fruit— 298
  —jug 408
  plum— 298
brass
  buckle— 418

bread 78, 86, 107, 175, 194, 280, 281, 284,
  287, 290
  baking— 60
  —basket 365
  flat— 291
  loaf of— 153
  —rack 291
  —tub 291
breakfast 280, 281
breaking hemp 305
breaking in the stock 270
breeches 324, 335, 356, 359
  broadcloth— 350
  —made of home spun 362
  tight— 360
breed 246
  western— 247
brick 144
  baked— 225
bridal
  —dance 612
  —garland 625
  —wreath 158
bride 61, 293, 366, 345, 349, 353, 355,
  622
  —bed 616, 617
  —bedding 616
  —'s belongings 612
  —dance 625
  —'s dowry 617
  —'s hope-chest 616
  —house 322
  seeing off the— 613
  bridegroom— 322, 345, 349
bridesmaid 618, 620
bridle 271
  —bit 271
brine 283
broadcloth 302, 311, 324, 326, 328, 333,
  334, 335
  blue— for holidays 359
  —breeches 324, 350
  gray— for weekdays 359
  —jacket 328
  —mantle 355
  —short coat (mente) 329, 355, 360
  suit of— 344, 350
broadsheet 541, 545
broadside pamphlet ("canvas" literature)
  115
Bronze Age 142
browning 283
brush 289
bucket 174, 228, 255, 256, 278
  wooden— 278
buckwheat 36, 203, 220, 284, 286
  —mush 285
building
  brick— 187
  —construction 28

pine log— 187
rural— 38
—sacrifice 521, 660, 664
—for stock and herdsmen (temporary)
264–270
stone— 187
—style 36
timber— 188
Bukovina Székely 452
Bulgarian 29, 533, 614, 696
—Khaganate 198
Bulgaro-Turk 196, 198, 244, 315, 584
bullock 270, 271
bulrush
  —basket 289, 291
  —mat 193
  processing of— 37, 47
bun 291, 318
bunch 197
bunda 331
bundle 271
bungler 91
buoy made of hollowed out gourd 241
burial 28, 68, 69, 105, 126, 624,
  627–637
  day of the— 635
  —feast 190, 636, 637 (see also funeral
  feast)
"bury the winter" 638
bushel 211
bustard
  —feathers 353
butcher 95, 295
butt 228, 229
butter 283, 292, 296, 685
  —milk 296
button 325
  —maker 301, 325
  copper— 353
  pewter— 355
  silver— 353, 355
buzzer 606
Byzantine 29, 369, 406, 572, 698
  —source 28

cabbage 47, 282
  —roll 282, 408, 616, 624
  stuffed— 277
  —soup 284
cabin
  —of the shepherd 269
cabinet maker 381, 389
  peasant—— 387
  —'s guild 381
cabinet making 381
  ——center 388
  ——family 389
caesura 547
cake 293
  —pan 286

wedding— 293
calabash 377
calendar 160
calf 65, 270, 296
Calvinist 44–46, 131, 381, 418
Calvinist church
    ceiling painting of the—— 387
    choir painting of the—— 387
    pulpit painting of the—— 387
cambric 322
camomile 194
cantor 75
candle 156, 157, 637
    —from beeswax 156
    —dipping 157
    —dipping vessel 406
    —maker 157
    —making 235
    ——from tallow 156
    ——from stearin 156
cap
    Cumanian— 261, 318
    fur— 318, 337
    high fur— 341
    —maker 114
    ——of high caps 311
    peaked— 315, 316
    peaked fur— 353
carnation 368
Carnival 94, 641, 642
Carpatho-Ruthenian 487–489
carpenter 91, 115, 220, 372
carpentry work 225
carol 26
carriage 676
carrier 91
cart 80, 82, 92, 165, 188, 192, 210, 212,
    229, 271–273, 365, 632
    —driver 86
    —ladder 210, 264
    —rope 263
    two-wheeled, square— 85–86
carter 251, 275, 333
carting 82
cartwright 89, 199
carver 374
carving 363, 370, 371, 381, 388
    herdsmen's— 376
    relief— 376
    —of the Székely gate 189
    —of tombstone 417
    —tools 371
casting
    lead— 417
    tin— 417
castle
    —rotating on duck's foot 571
Catalogus de Sanctorum 551
catching
    —birds with an eagle 238

————a falcon 238
fish— 238
—game in a pit 237
Catholic 104, 105, 131, 158, 281, 291, 418,
    661
    —church 43
    Greek— 109
    Roman— 42, 45
cattle 50, 65, 100, 202, 219, 220, 253, 261,
    262, 265, 269, 270, 281
    —driving road 117
    grey Hungarian horned— 246, 263
    —herd 89, 248, 249, 262
    virgin flock or— 252
    western breeds of— 245
cauldron 148, 151, 157, 278
    —clay— 406
    copper— 175
cave dwelling 182
celebration 208, 209, 228, 229
cellar 173, 231, 232
    —built of logs 39, 163
    cave-like— 231
cello 445
celtic epic 570
Celts 29, 227, 570
cemetery 68, 126, 127, 129–131, 190, 417,
    459, 636, 673
    dancing in the— 459, 636, 637
    —ditch 129
    gate of the— 637
    last trip to the cemetery 107
ceramics
    Hungarian— 406
    peasant— 406
cereal crops 206
chaff 142, 164, 165, 204, 211–214
    —shed 186
chaffy grain 214
chair 157, 383, 385
    shelling— 220
charcoal 192, 195
cheese 285
    cottage— 296, 298
    round— 298
chemise 322, 362
Cheremissian 26, 429
chest 64, 65, 115, 157, 269, 366,
    387
    carved— 386
    dower— 65
    of drawers 160
    guild— 92–94, 312
    hewn— 368, 380–383
    painted— 386, 388
    —seat 162
chest warmer 330
chicken 59, 62, 247, 294
    —coop 167, 169, 172, 179
    —waterer 408

children's
    —dance 707
    —ditties 513
    —games 26, 38, 434, 604–612, 707, 708
    bride asking— 606
    decreasing-increasing— 606
    —of forfeits 606
    group— 606
    line— 606
    ring— 606
    testual— 609
    —music 707
    —poetry 609, 611
    —song 708
    —toy 438
chimney 147, 179
    open— 151
    perpendicular— 186
    skirted— 185
    —stack 152
chisel 373
Christening 602
Christian era 527
Christianity 30, 31, 71
Christmas 254, 295
    —carolling 638
    —Eve 281
    —Mass 683
chronicle 551
chronicler 115, 550, 551
church 75, 104–108, 109
    Calvinist— 48, 106
    Catholic— 104, 105
    —ceiling with painted panels 386
    —council 105
    —holiday 31
    —as landlord 105
    Lutheran— 104
    —music 108
    Protestant— 104, 106
    —Reformed Presbyterian 104
    sleeping in— 109
    —tower 139
    —yard 129, 633
churn 296, 297, 685
Chubashes 429
civis (civilian) 46
clan 67–69
    head of the— 68
clarinet 445
    —like shawn 449
clay 155, 162, 174, 175, 408
    —bank 157
    —corner bank 151
    —floor 190
    —house 187
    —soil 140
clearing 122
    —field 121
    —swampy areas 122

Clever Coachman 676
cloak 360, 398
  —like garment 329
  sheepskin— 353, 354, 356
clog 262
cloth 291
  —garment 60
clothes 61
clothing 60
clover 258
clown 115
coach 275
  mail— 275
  —man 89
coarse meal 284
coat 58
  broadcloth short— 345
  frieze— 356
  —hanger 418
  homespun— 361 *(zeke)*
  —like garment *(daróc)* 356
  —like outer wear *(szűr)* 325
  sheepskin—
    short sheepskin coat of homespun
    frieze 361 *(szokmány, kurti)*
"cock hitting" 649
"cock shooting" 649
coffin 628, 629, 632, 635, 636
coif 321, 344, 401
  conical— 321
collar 322, 326, 329, 359
  —with a frill 355
  stand-up— 326, 329
collecting of
  —herbs 193
  —mushrooms 193
  —raspberry 193
  —wild strawberry 193
collective work 96–100
collectivization 127
collegiate music 549
colour symbolism 475
colt 263, 272
comb 338
  —maker 364, 380
  —making masters'guild 380
comet 680
common land 103
communal
  —activity 434
  —gathering 579
  —job 307
  —work 68, 459, 598, 635
Confirmation 661
congregation 106
Conquest (pre Conquest) 30, 35, 56, 67,
  70, 130, 131, 139, 168, 196, 197, 198,
  206, 226, 236, 243, 244, 247, 256, 272,
  296, 302, 314–316, 318, 367, 368, 380,

406, 550, 572, 583, 584, 627, 628, 649,
  654, 672, 673, 676, 698, 699
contract with share harvesters 81
cooking 153, 189
  —pot 408
cooks'stall 116–118
copper 192
  —heel iron 333
  —inlay 418
  —nails for heels 355
  —smith 115
  —star 419
co-operative work *(kaláka)* 50
corn 284
  —barn 131
  —dolly 208, 209
  —field 215
  hoeing of— 84, 459
  —husking 191, 218, 434, 444, 459
  —stalk 90
cornice beam 165, 172
corrido 515
costume 33, 42, 50
  archaic— 41
  folk— 360
  —of the nobility 360
  Székely folk— 360
cot 64
cottage 76, 78
  —cheese 283, 292
  —industry 37, 91, 93
cottier 103
cotton 393
coulter 200, 202, 260, 366
Counter-Reformation 104
cover 397
  communion table— 396
covered structures on the pastures 266
covering 400, 402, 405
  reed— 185
  rush— 185
  sedge— 185
cow 61, 65, 88, 296
  —bell 114, 241, 261, 418
  —'s milk taking 668
  —put to the yoke 202
crackling 292
craft 261, 380, 410
crampoon 243
cranberry 194
cravat 356
cream 296
  sour— 291, 296
crest-ornament 418
crewel-work 399
crib 194, 383
Croat, Croatian 36, 172, 316, 334, 377,
  401, 587
crook 117, 250, 262

crop 81, 89, 117
  —gate 133
  working magic on the— 643
cross 158, 161, 416
  roadside— 417
  stone— 131
  wood— 131
Crusades 223
Csángó 51, 157, 187, 318, 332, 362, 641
  —of Gyimes 52, 123, 156
  —of Hétfalu 52, 633
  —of Moldavia 52
Csárdás (a dance) 453, 456, 457, 458
cucumber 282
cudgel 449, 451, 452
cuff 322, 359
culture
  field— 28
  garden— 28
  grape— 28
  intellectual— 78
  traditional— 78, 89
Cumanian, Cuman 31, 41, 44, 45, 47,
  50, 69, 245, 247, 263, 316, 317, 362,
  440
  Great— 44
  Little— 44
"Cunning Shepherd" 591, 675, 676
cup
  unadorned— 406
  "—of law" 659
cupboard 280
  corner— 160, 161
  flat— 161
curing 687
currier 301
curse 686, 687
cushion
  rear— 339
custom 38, 603
  —of celebrating St. Blaise 640
  —of choosing a king and a queen at
  Whitsuntide 648
  —at the beginning of work 662
  —at the conclusion of work 662
  cultic— 600
  dramatic— 604
  —of driving out evil 643
  ————of animals 662
  —called "looking for lodgings" *(szálláskeresés)* 652
  wedding— 600
  work— 662
Czech 572, 579, 587, 695
Czech-Moravian 323

Dalmatian 537
damage 219
dance 49, 99, 167, 447–459, 472

chain— 450
—in the cemetery 459
circle— 450
couple— 450
csárdás— 453, 456–458
children's— 459
cudgel— 451
"forgatós"— 457, 458
—at funeral feasts 459
garland— 450
gypsy— 453
—house 459
Heyduck (Hajdú)— 449, 451, 453, 696
herdsman's— 449, 451–453
individual— 450
jumping— 452
leaping— 452
"legényes"— 453, 454
men's— 455
—music 438, 453
paired— 453, 457
recruiting— 453, 455, 458
ring— 450
round— 458
roundel— 451
slow— 453
stamping— 449
swineherd's— 449, 451, 452
weaponed— 451, 452
wedding— 452
young men's— 452–455
—wife's— 625
dancer 448, 450, 459
dancing 89, 228, 306, 333, 444, 447, 459
—games of children 459
—in the graveyard 636, 637
improvised— 450
Daughters of Mary 661
St. David 679, 680
day-labourer 76, 112, 294, 442
day of Demetrius (Dömötör) 117, 251
decanter for the Communion wine 412
deer 237, 238
devastation caused by the
—Mongolians 486, 487
—Turks 486, 487
dialect 41
dill 300
dinner 79
dish 413
ceremonial— 294
distaff 305, 306, 311, 371, 417, 418
—nail 418
—pin 418
—ribbon 419
ditch 133
divination 690
divorce 62
doctor 76

dog 191, 238, 247, 261, 262, 264
naming dogs after rivers 264
dolman coat (szűrdolmány) 341
—like mente 329
domestic fowl 247
domestication
—of cattle 28
——horses 28
——sheep 28
donkey 247, 273
double-inner holding
——plot 133
——system 131
dough 194, 286, 288, 289, 291
bread— 287
leavened— 287
raised— 291, 292
rising of the— 287
dovecote 169
Dömötör Day 117
dragon 683
Dragon Country 679
drainage 47
dramatic
—character 477
—condensation 477
—constructions 477
—folk custom 600
—play of religious content 108
—song 549
—tradition 600
drawers (gatya) 355
drawing women 396
dream of Emese 583
drinking
—cup 377
—gourd 376
—horn 374
—vessel 375
driver 272, 365, 419
drover 117
drum 435, 444
—beat 435
single bottomed— 672
drumming 102
—out new 102
dry mill 222
drying 283
duck 247, 294
wild— 236
dummy 42
dumpling 292
round— 292
dwelling 88, 89, 127
—house 132, 133, 136, 157
permanent— 126, 127
semipermanent— 28
—in the vineyard 40
dyed rug 494

eagle 238
earthenware 408
—dish 283, 414, 415
—tile 155
—utensil 406
—vessel 46, 58, 155
earthwork 27
Easter 293
—egg 401, 646
—holiday 420
holy week before— 684
—Monday sprinkling 645, 646
—Sunday 281
ecclesiastic scale 549
economic unit (of the extended family) 183
egg 59, 62, 281, 291, 292
coloured— 645
decorated— 645
Easter— 401, 646
painting of—— 420
ornamental— 426
red— 420
—yolk 217
egret feathers 353
eight stcture (folksong) 473
einkorn 220
Elek Day 117
ember
—fire 177
—hearth 175
—peel 289
embers 278, 286, 289, 294
embroidery 33, 43, 47, 50, 75, 323, 324, 330, 332, 337, 341, 343, 348, 350, 352, 353, 363, 368, 369, 371, 395–406, 419
colourful— 41
—on communion table cover 396
Matyó— 401, 402
multicoloured— 46
—patterns 364
white— 37, 41, 399
enclosure
—for cattle 266
—for horses 266
—for sheep 266
endogamy 612
English 449, 455, 467, 515, 516, 536
enterpreneur 95
entertainment 216, 219, 305, 306
epic myth 695
Epiphany 638, 640
equites (Székely) 50
estate 81–84, 89, 121
large— 79, 81, 87, 89, 91, 215, 216, 218, 247
Estonian 26
ethnic groups
Great Plain 44–47
emigrants 52

Transdanubia 36–41
Transylvania 47–52
Upper Hungary 41–47
eve of All Saints' Day 637
evil
  do evil by pouring 687
  driving out— 643
  scare away— 638
  —spirit 682
Evil Eye 668, 675, 688–690
exogamy 67
expulsion of the winter 638
extasy 672
extended family 183

fabulous epic 550
fair 58, 95, 109, 111, 113, 117, 118, 286
  animal— 116, 117
  —for crop 113
  goods— 113
  livestock— 114
  presents from the— 161
  —for stocks 113
fairy
  —story 546
  —tale 89, 554–564
falcon 238
falling 311
fallow 122, 197
  —field 214
  —land 266
  —system 197
family 60
  —burial 55, 56, 61
  extended— 54, 55, 62, 64, 67, 69, 76,
  183
  daughters in the—— 59, 60, 61
  daughters-in-law—— 59, 60, 62
  education in the—— 59
  farmhand in the—— 63
  head of the—— see: gazda
  inheritance in the—— 65
  youngest son in the—— 65
  oldest son in the—— 61, 65
  sons in the—— 59, 62
  sons-in-law in the—— 59, 61
  history of the— 54
  joint— 43, 59
  —mark 66
  medieval— 54
  nuclear— 54, 67
  one-child— 40
  organization of the— 54–60
  patriarchal— 54, 55, 64
famine food 194, 196
farm
  —building 76
  —hand 64, 76, 169, 219, 252, 375
  ——'s salary 63
  —house 175

—implement 165, 166
scattered— 46
—stead 89, 121–129, 132, 168, 218, 270
——center 127
—tool 89, 95
—yard 132, 163, 168
farmer 260
farming
  collective 34
  Great Plain style of— 197
  peasant— 270
  rotation— 197, 203, 253
  —system of Hungarian— 196
fashion 355
fasting
  —dish 284
  —food 286
  —regulations 281
feasts 283, 285, 603
feather 194, 353
  bustard— 318, 353
  crane— 318
  eagle— 318
  egret— 353
  heron— 353
feeding
  —trough 169
felloe 275
felt 302, 311, 325, 333, 334
fence 72, 117, 131, 133, 179, 307
  —from corn stalks 134
  —from lath 134
  —from planks 134
  —from reeds 134
  —from rod iron 134
  —from sunflower 134
ferry 244
fertility
  —rites 645, 649
  symbol— 646
fetter 262
fiddle 435, 446
fiddler 435
field 216
  cleared— 122
  common— 257
  cultivated— 122
  fallow— 122
  reclaimed— 121
  —gard 90
  ——'s hut 90
  —keeper 218, 219
  ploughed— 214, 217
  —worker 284
fifth-construction 432
  perfect— 429
fight for independence (1703–1711) 32
fingernails 684
Finnish 670
Finns 26

Finn-Permian 26
Finno-Ugric 26, 27, 54, 133, 144, 198, 232,
  237, 238, 244, 269, 272, 296, 302, 315,
  332, 374, 627, 670, 671, 679, 681, 683,
  698
fire 682
  open— 149, 150, 151, 183, 185, 268,
  269, 294
  —watcher 103
fireplace 129, 149, 158, 168, 175, 189, 286
  built-in— 278
  closed— 151, 277
  open— 149, 151, 153, 155, 175, 178,
  183, 277
  ——with cooking stove 153
  permanent— 149
  —tile 368
First Communion 661
fish 90, 194, 281
  preparing— 294
  —soup 294
  —spear 239
  —trap 239, 240
  —weir 240
fisher-hunter 34
fisherman 46, 90, 91, 238, 240, 241, 243,
  244, 578
fishing 37, 40, 47, 90, 238–244
  —ark 244
  —with bare hands 238
  —pond 242
  —cast 240
  —cluster 242
  —group 242
  —implements 695
  —sect 242
  —under ice 243
flag 94
flail 165, 213
  —threshing 165, 210
flax 58, 301, 302, 305, 309, 393
  —linen 302, 322
  processing of— 60, 99, 302, 309, 359, 459
  —yarn 309
flock 248, 252, 254, 261
  —of the community 91
  extensive— 245, 246
  semi-extensive— 245, 246, 254
  —of sheep 267
  short— 252
  virgin— 252
  wild— 252
flour 282, 286, 287, 291, 292
  —of corn 284
  —of wheat 284
flower 216
  —cult 130
  —motif in folksongs 475
  —that grows out of the grave 527
flute 375, 436–438, 459

fodder 59, 61, 118, 131, 164, 165, 203, 214, 219, 220, 245, 246, 253, 256, 258, 278
—crop 258
fold 265, 267
—sheep— 265
folk
—architecture 75, 188, 189
—art 363, 366, 368, 369
Master of—— 704, 706, 709
ornamental—— 363–420
—artist 705
—ballad 51, 513–549
forms of the—— 546–549
history of the—— 514–522
—belief 264, 527, 668
—costume 47, 49, 301, 315, 334
—culture 334, 366
—custom 600
—dance 51, 710
——groups 710
—gathering 508
—industry 94
—music 47, 51, 428–434, 698, 705, 710
——instruments 434–447
pseudo—— 432
sacred—— 431, 468
—play 602
—poetry 41, 42, 44, 47, 78, 366, 614
——and prose 460–599
theory of—————— 460–467
—realism 476
—song 28, 51, 87, 431, 460–469, 477, 482, 513, 705
contradictions in—— 474
four-beat in—— 473
historical—— 477
lyric—— 477, 479, 480
religious—— 431
—tale 51, 549, 570, 696, see also: tale
"folkeviser" 514
folklore 28, 31, 47, 51, 551
food 81
famine— 194, 196
—gathering 192, 193, 196
—gathering figure of the Great Plain swamp (pákász) 194
—staple 214
foot-cloth (kapca) 333
——maker 311
foraging 256, 258
forecarriage 199, 201, 271
forest 122
communalty 103
—right 103
forester 89
—'s house 122
forestry work 42
fork
wooden— 211, 212
fortune-teller 115

foundation
—sacrifice 158
stone— 164
wooden— 164
foundry 198
four-line stanza 473, 549
fowl 277, 281
fox holes 237
frame
wagon equipped with a— (vendégoldal) 275
lower framework of the wagon 274
freeman 31
French 30, 455, 515, 536, 698
—settlers 333
frieze 311
—coat (szűr) 612
—jacket (szűrdolmány) 353, 360
—maker (gubacsapó) 301
—mantle (szűr) 58, 311, 353
—jacket (daróc, condra) 360
fringe
ornamental— 419
—tying 390
frog closing (sujtás) 325
front (ingmell) 322
fruit
—growing 42
—production 46
—tree 130
"frunza verde" 480
fuel for heating 88
fulling 311
—mill 311
funeral 322
—feast 459
—meal 634, 635
—procession 633, 636
funnel 240
fur 325
furniture 65, 157, 381, 383, 387, 388, 389
factory-made— 78
painted— 33, 89, 381, 387, 388, 389
painting— 400
—making 371, 381–389
—centres:
Bakony 383
Békés 388
Eger 388
Hódmezővásárhely 387–388
Komárom 387
Miskolc 388
Sátoraljaújhely 388
Torockó 388
Vargyas 389
furrier 91, 114, 301, 364, 369, 402
German— 332
Hungarian 330, 332
peasant— 114
fustic 315

gable 169, 179
—top 419
gaff
curved— 239
gall 312
gait 447
game (see: children's game)
game 194, 236, 237
preparing— 294
catching— 237
garabonciás (see wandering scholar) 672, 682
garden 60, 127, 133, 135, 214, 215
—of the nobility 216
vegetable— 88, 166
gardener
Bulgarian— 216
garland 388, 660
—celebration 97
—out of grapes 229
garlic 300
garment
cloth— 60
leather— 330
outer— 60, 65, 322, 323
under— 60, 65, 322, 323
garnishing 294
gate 133, 179
—with bindings 134
carved— 134
—of the cemetery 636
—with dove-cots 134
ornamental— 130, 364
painted— 134
plank— 134
—post 417
—roofed small— 134
single— 136
Székely— 188, 371
Székely double— 134
wicker— 134, 164
gathering (work)
—of beets 84
—of corn 84
gathering
—in the barn 73
dance— 84
—of girls 434
—of men 72, 78, 96
social— 78, 96
Sunday afternoon— 95, 434, 444, 451, 459
winter evening— 283, 444
"gatya" (pantaloons, trousers) 335, 353, 356
cambric— 354
greased— 354
linen— 354
loose— 323, 360
"gazda" 56–63, 70, 79, 80, 82–84, 91, 97, 98, 100, 101, 103, 112, 169

unrestricted authority of the— 57
"gazdaasszony" (wife of the gazda) 59–62, 64, 84
Gellért Hill 674, 675
gendarmes 80
geometric
—design 376
—element 410
—ornamentation 371, 372
St. George's Day 205, 217, 255, 297, 665, 675, 681, 683
Sunday before— 252
German 29, 30, 32, 33, 36, 37, 42, 46, 93, 144, 226, 276, 316, 323, 373, 440, 447, 457, 552, 572, 641, 674, 698, 699
Germans of Upper Hungary 370
Gesta Romanorum 532, 571
ghost 678, 682
Fair Maid 678
—having a female form 678
Wild Girl 678
girl market 110
—"for sale" 615
glass painting 367
gleeman 435
goad 199
—pattle 201
godmother 281
main— 71
godparent (koma) 70–72, 190, 350, 604
—main koma pair 71
gold 681
Good Friday 281, 637, 684
goods
cultural— 275
goose 59, 247, 294
—wing 291
Goral 451
gopher
catching— 237
—hole 237
Gothic 139, 188, 189, 350, 368, 417
goulash
—meat 295
—soup 295
gourd 241, 242, 377, 686
decorated— 703
hollowed out— 241
—for keeping mudfish 242
grain
autumn— 203
—bin 165, 171
clearing of— 167
—market 115
—merchant 95
seed— 203
spring— 203
storing of— 165, 167
threshing of— 99, 167
treading out of— 99, 164

winnowing the— 167
gramanzia 672
granary 58, 89, 133, 164, 166, 171, 172, 179, 186, 190, 216
grape 226, 229
aszu- 231
cultivation of the —s 226, 232
desiccation of the —s 230
foam of fementing— 288
—growing region 123
—harvest 229, 434, 508
skins of pressed —s 288
gratc 278
grave 130, 194, 635
—cross 371
directions of the— 636
—furnishing 627
—post 50, 130, 371, 483, 632, 636
colour of the—— 131
anthropomorphic— 131
——poem 636
—stone 636
types of— 636
—yard 129
grazing 253, 256, 269
—land 122
grease
container 368
Great Cumanian 44
Greek 42, 681
Greek-Latin interposition 569
Gregorian chants 431, 696
St. Gregory's Day
celebrating St. Gregory a custom of students 600, 641
grey Hungarian cattle 378
Grimm tales 550, 699
grinder
home— 282
—for oily seeds 225
grinding of cereal seeds between two stones 221
grits 285
groom 293, 336, 613, 619, 622
—'s house 618
groper 239
wicker— 239
grower
—of paprika 216
—of tobacco 216
guard 133
—'s tree 269
guarding 261
—the grapes 99
guba (overcoat made of woollen sloth) 46, 328, 355, 356, 362
—maker 114
guiding light 529
guild 30, 93, 94

—charter 93
—chest 92–94, 312
guild of
—cabinet makers 381
—millers 662
—tailors 301
—weaving masters 390
—'s customs 94
head master of the— 94
—member 93
—meeting 365
—pitcher 409
—'s regulations 94
—'s rules 95
guinea-fowl 247
gunpowder 376
St. Guy's Day 205
gwaelawd 514, 515
Gypsy 118, 228, 229, 417, 435, 623, 624
—band 432, 445
—clan 261
—colony 138
—herdsman 249
—horse dealer 117
—music 209, 432
—musician 219
—occupation 144
—orchestra 432, 447
Rumanian— 440

Habán (Anabaptist) 369
—potters 414
Habsburg oppression 368, 487
hadas
—settlement 43, 69
hair 684
married woman's— 321
pinning up of the— 318
Hajdú, Heyduck 45, 47, 69
—towns 45, 132
—villages 45
—privileges 45
to halt and bind horse carriages 676
halter 419
ham 281
handcloth 394
handicraft 364
handkerchief 400
hands
agricultural— 87
hired— 87
hardware merchant 115
harness 272, 419
breast— 272
collar— 272
driving— 272
—maker 46, 115, 419
harp 440

harpoon 239
harrow 202
  spike— 203
  toothed— 203
harvest 78, 98, 281, 459
  conclusion of the— 209
  —day 205
  —festival 82, 663
  —garland 209
harvester 79, 99, 294
  share— 209, 281
  —strike 81
harvesting 59, 79, 80, 81, 205–209, 433
  —contract 79
  —couples 79
  —customs 205–209
  —gazda 79
  —labourer 80
  —with sickle 206
  share— 78
  songs about— 82
  —strike 80
hat 318
  felt— 361, 362
  high— 350
  high-peaked— 355
  high-topped— 353, 362
  "peasant outlaw—" 318
  ornamental— 301
  smaller-rimmed— 318
  straw— 318, 360
  wide-rimmed— 318, 341
  wide-rimmed herdsmen's— 353
  wide-rimmed felt— 318, 361
hatmaker 114, 333
hatchet 243, 262, 449
  —handle 377
hatter 301
haulier 91, 100, 273, 275
hauling 59, 89, 91, 275
  —or the manure 98
hay 164, 258
  —carrying 98
  —collecting 259
  —cutter 417
  —field 121, 257
  —gathering 98, 258
  —holding structure 169
  —loft 258
  —market 111
  —shed 136
  —stacking 98
head
  —of the family 291
headcovering 321
head-dress 315, 319–321, 338, 339, 340, 343, 345, 348, 400, 401
  —ending in a peak 350
  maiden's— 321
  —of white linen 334

headgear 322, 338
headkerchief 322, 400
head master (guild) 94
hearth 151, 152, 157, 183, 277, 286, 291
  drying— 282
  open— 153, 188
healer 676
healing
  animal— 264
health
  procedures to assure— 684
heating
  —equipment 129
  —fuel 220
heddle 309
hedge 72, 133
  —of box-thorn 133
help
  mutual— 97
hemp 189, 301, 305
  —linen 302, 322
  —processing of— 28, 60, 99, 302, 309, 311
  —yarn 309
hen house 88
herb
  medicinal— 194
herd
  breeding of—
  fancy— 252
  —of horses 252
  lazy— 252
  —of swine 47, 252, 254
  wild— 252
herding 44
herdsboy 280
herdsman 45, 89–91, 103, 116, 117, 219, 248, 249, 251, 254, 255, 259–261, 266–271, 329, 330, 353–355, 374, 375, 377, 378, 380, 438, 440, 447–449, 578
  —'s hay 269
  food of— 284
  gypsy— 249
  —'s horn 438
  Hortobágy— 355
  —'s household 282
  —hut 268, 269
  —'s rank 353
  Wallachian— 268, 438
  woodcarving of— 370
herdsmen
  —'s market 252
  organization of the— 248–252
  —'s staff 377
  —'s superstition 262, 263
heron
  —feathers 353
hewn
  —chest 381, 382, 383
  —technique 381

Heyduck see: Hajdú
hide-dress 312
hiding see: rejtezés
highland pastures 311
hill villages 123
Hindu 569
hip cushion 323
hired hands 61, 91
hobble 262
hoe 198, 214, 219
  flat— 122
  two-pronged— 121
hoeing 218, 227, 459
holder
  —for scythe sharpener whetstone 376
holding 232
  —with double courtyard 136
  ribbon— 174, 187
  street— 187
holiday 293
  —s of the village 110
Holy Communion 107
  —image 158
  ——Innocents' Day whipping 658
homespun 33, 41, 42, 47, 50, 323, 389–395
  —of cotton 389
  —of hemp 389
  —of flax 389
  —kerchief 365, 389
  ——for best men 389
  ——for bridesmen 389
  ——for drivers 365, 389
  ——for godparents 389
  ——for the gypsyband 389
  ——for the priest 365, 389
  ornamental— 364, 368, 391
  saw-toothed homespun pattern 368
  shroud— 389
  starred homespun pattern 368
  —textile 371, 389
  —weaving 370
  —woollen cloth 356
honey 232, 287
  —cakes 235
  —cake maker 299, 364, 373
  ——making 373
hook 208, 241, 262
  bill— 122
  fishing with a— 241
  slashing— 122
hop 288
horn 103, 271, 371, 375
  —carving 378
  —for catching bees 232
  —of the grey Hungarian cattle 438
  powder— 367
  processing of— 380
  stag— 367, 380
  swineherd's— 438, 552

two-branched— 380
horse 50, 61, 65, 100, 117, 118, 202, 208, 212, 246, 248, 261, 262, 265, 270–273
—dealer 117
—hair 262
——work 419
—herd 248, 261, 262, 263, 327, 353, 419
—hoe 218
—man 29
—radish 281, 300
—scrub 246
—shoes 682
—'s skull and legs 246, 627
—traction 274
hose ("harisnya") 360
broadcloth— 361
Székely— 324
hothouse 216
house
bake— 188
baking— 153
—on beams 40
fenced— 179
—frontispiece 188
one-unit smoke— 179
Palots— 183
reed thatched— 178
single-room— 149
smoke— 178, 179
three-unit— 32, 185
two-roomed smoke-kitchen— 179
two-unit— 179
wattle— 179
—warming 97
wooden— 139
—work 61
household
—altar 158
herdsman's— 282
peasant— 282, 294, 296
housewife 287, 288, 291
humanism 32
Hun 206
Hungarian
——dialects 422–428
ethnogenesis of the Hungarian people 26–34
hunter 89, 380
—implement 236
—peasant 238
—tool 237
hurdle
reed— 267
wicker— 266
hurdy-gurdy 441, 442
four-stringed— 442
ten-stringed— 442
—player 442
husband 625, 626
husbandman 43, 196, 318

—'s building 273
husbandry 26, 38, 41
animal— 28, 36, 37, 39, 40, 42, 49, 232, 252
extensive— 245, 246
forest-animal— 48
half-extensive— 251
meadow— 47
nomadic— 28, 245
semi-nomadic— 245
husking 219
—cobs 219
—corn 218
hussar
Hungarian— 272
—'s pelisse (mente) 355
hut 86, 129, 218, 266
dug-out— 86
herdsman's— 122, 265
rick-shaped— 269
round— 269
—on sledge runners 172
—on wheels 268
hydromel 299

Icebreaking Matthias' Day 664
idiom 549, 594, 597
idiomatic
—saying 594, 595
metric of—— 597
—simile 595
Ignis Fatuus incubus 677
illiterate 89
illness 78
—from bewitching 688
—from fright 688
implement
commonly owned— 78
—for cutting veins 264
hand— 84
one-wheeled— 85
work— 118
improvised performance 600
incubi 668
Indo-European 45, 696
industrial crops 81
industry
clothing— 94
cottage— 37, 91, 93
folk— 94
home— 49
rural— 91
inheritance 64
initials of the owner 259
initiations of the young man 611
inlay
—with brass 377
—with horn 377
inn 111, 118
inner holding 133

instrument
musical— 444
stringed— 444
insurrection of Ferenc Rákóczi 488
intarsia 387
intellectual
—culture 115
—need 118
Iron Age 380
iron 682
—anvil 207
—crampon 243
—grass 262
—implement 682
—mining 50
—objects preventing witchcraft 682
—ax 682
—blade of scythe 682
—horseshoe 682
plough iron 682
—sickle 682
—pellet 261
—pestle 220
—shoe 197, 682
—"slippers" of wooden spades 198
—tool 29, 682
Illés Day 117
Italian 30, 168, 276, 536, 537, 552, 698

jack-knife 375, 378
—handle 375
jacket (dolmány; ködmön) 329, 330, 332, 398
frieze— 353, 360
sheepskin (ködmön)— 343, 355, 356, 398
jam 196, 282
—jug 408
—pocket 292
jar 282
Jazygian 31, 44, 316, 362
St. John the Baptist's Day 649
St. John's day 649, 659
St. John of Nepomuk's day 665
joke 87
—master 229
St. Joseph' Day 665, 683
journeyman 93, 94, 380, 390, 408
itinerant— 94
judge 77, 101
field— 102
law— 102
jug 278, 279, 414
brandy— 408
—of Csát 365
jam— 408
milk— 408
Miska— (anthropomorphic) 411
puzzle— 706
water— 709
"junačke pesme" 514

junk dealer 115
juryman 102, 103

Kabar 28
kaláka (mutual help) 50, 97, 98
    housebuilding— 97
Kalevala 473, 516
keeper 227
    field— 218, 219, 236
kerchief 322, 348, 355, 359, 360, 362, 365,
    389, 397, 636, 648
    best man's— 394
    embroidered white— 337
    head— 400
    homespun— 365
kettle 278, 280, 282
    copper— 151, 177
keynote 439, 443
Khanti 26
Khazar Khaganate 28, 196, 198, 226
kiln 140, 408
kindred 67, 69
    artificial— 70
King Stephen I. 29, 30
kings of the House of Árpád 31
kisze (is a straw dummy, symbolic object)
    42, 643
    —hajtás (throwing the straw dummy
    into the brook) 42, 643, 645
    preparing the "kisze" 645
kitchen 149, 151, 175, 185, 188, 277, 280
    Austrian— 285
    chimneyless— 148
    Hungarian— 216
    peasant— 235
    smoky— 148, 151
    summer— 174
    —utensils 162
knapsack 269, 280
    —worn on a pilgrimage 394
kneading 287, 288
knife 373, 376, 692
    —maker 46
    vinepruning— 366, 417
knot 318
knotting the bride's hair 612
"kolomejka" 433
Komi 26
komondor (sheepdog) 247
Kossuth beard 318
ködmön (coat) 332
    sheepskin— 345
Kuruc (Prince Rákóczi's soldiers) 488
    —era 488
labourer 90, 350
    day— 78, 112
    farm— 75, 79
    rural— 83, 577
    agrarian— 78
    agricultural— 75, 78, 79

seasonal— 33, 43
    share— 77, 79
    wage— 78
lace 406
    —making 370, 405, 406
lad
    unmarried— 61
lamb
    spring— 281
lament 469
lamentation 26, 190, 468, 629, 631, 632, 634
    —song 632
lamp
    kerosene— 157
land
    cultivated— 214
    —holding 77
    leaving—uncultivated 196
    —lord 31, 33, 37, 121
landmark 120
    inspection of the— 120
landowner 80
land-use 196
lantern 157
Lapp 26
lard 284, 285, 287, 291, 292, 295
lariat 263
lash 262
lasso 263
Latin 442, 444, 536, 539, 544
Latinate 549
lead glaze 406, 408
leader
    —of the lads 611
    election of—— 611
    —of the village 101
leather 302, 325, 419
    —bellow 438
    cordovan— 315
    processing of— 419
leaven 287, 288
    maturing of the— 287
    —stick 288
    —wood 287
leavening 287
    —agent 288
lees 196
lebbencs (pastry cut into big squares) 86
legend 31, 549, 551, 583
    —of belief 588–594
    —of the Clever Coachman 590
    Christ— 568
    —about the haunting dead 593
    heroic— 584
    historical— 583–586, 588
    —about King Matthias 586, 587
    —about King Ladislas I. 583, 585
    —about Lajos Kossuth 587, 588
    local— 551, 552, 586–588
    —of the Mongol Invasion 586

—about an accidental wandering stu-
    dent (garabonciás) 589
    outlaw— 588
    —about Prince Rákóczi 587
    religious— 568, 569
    —about the returning dead 592
    shaman— 589
    superstitious— 219
    —of the Turkish occupation 586
    —about the White Stag 583
    —about witches 591, 592
Legenda Aurea 551
legendary tale 568
legging 333
Lent 643
lentil 284
    —in the world of beliefs 281
lid holder 418
lighting of the evening light 157
lime 140, 192
    —burner 140
    —burning 140
    —washing 140
limestone 140
liming 237
linear village 136
linden tree 194
linen 301, 322
Little Cumanian 44
livelihood 83
livestock 61, 247, 249, 252, 266, 270
    —dealer 25
    —fair 114
living quarter 131
loaf 287, 289
    breaking of the— 64
    milk— 59, 281, 287, 291
    tart— 286
lock of hair
    placing a ——— into the building
    660
locksmith 89, 417
locust-tree 130
lodging 123
loft 163
long pantaloon (gatya) 323
loom 306, 308, 309, 311, 389
    vertical 308
    warping of the— 307
lord 74
lot 135
    "ribbon lot" system 135
    settlements with street lots 135
    square— 135
    rectangular-shaped— 135
luck 281
"Lucy chair" 651, 674
Lucy's Day 651, 687
lute 440
    —player 435

lyre 440, 444
lyric text 472
lyrical maxims 513
lyrist 519

macramé 390
—fringe 405
magic
—to assure success of the hunt 380
—coachman 593
—ditty 687
—herdsman 593
—horseshoe nail 676
—of plenty 656
—whip 676
working magic on the crops 643
Maidens of Mary 104, 661
maidservant 62, 63
maize 33, 88, 89, 216–219, 220, 284, 286, 287
biscuit 287
—closely sown for fodder 258
—flour 282
gathering in of— 99
—meal 285
—porridge 285
—shelling 220
—stalk 258
major mode 432
mange-grease holder 376
manger 169
mangle 376
—roller 372
mangling board 372, 375, 448
manor 12, 87, 89, 90
manpower 79
Mansi 26
mantle (szűr) 114, 325, 327
belted— 315
broadcloth— 355
embroidered frieze— 356
frieze— 353, 354, 360
—maker 397, 364
ornamental— 397–399
—tailor 364
Mari (Cheremiss) 26, 429
marjoram 300
St. Mark's Day 665
mark 259, 260
branding— 260
family— 66
identifying— 260
—of stamps used by village communities 101
market 37, 38, 60, 62, 89, 95, 109–111, 115, 270, 275, 406
—day 111
livestock— 116
men— 112
right to —s 111

—town 32, 37, 44, 46, 69, 90, 112, 118, 353, 364, 381
marketing 126
wheat— 116
marriage 107
marrying 105
St. Martin's Day 665
mask
—from a pumpkin 219
masquerading 219
master (gazda) 243
—of ceremony 613, 616
—craftsman 94
mat 193, 282
match
—box 375
—holder 376
material culture 26, 31
Matthias (King) 43
Matyó 42, 83, 168, 321, 325, 350, 390, 412, 604, 653
—embroidery 401–402
mayor 101
May Day 647
Maypole 647
May Tree 647
meal 79, 280, 281
funeral— 634
midday— 83
meat 84, 285
—dish 294
dried— 280
paprikash— 624
smoked— 284
medicine 216
melodic history 469
melody 472
—with the construction of alternating fifths 429
—a fifth lower 28
forms of— 695
pentatonic— 28
melon
—grower 79
—picker 33
—seed 686
memorabilia 160
menu
standard— 281
merchandise
article of merchandise 227
merchant 112, 113
clothes— 114
Merino sheep 247, 264, 266, 294, 370
merry-go-round 115
———men 110
metal
—art 368
—buckle 418
—inlay 418

—jewellery 418
—ornamentation 417
—purse-plate 380
supernatural characteristic of— 681
St. Michael's Day 117, 227, 254, 665
"——horse" (two trestle) 629
Middle Ages 31, 50, 51, 74, 101, 102, 108, 109, 111, 112, 120, 121, 129, 133, 157, 192, 197, 202, 203, 208, 226, 237, 238, 244, 246, 275, 294, 299, 301, 309, 314, 316, 381, 405, 417
Midsummer Night fire 649, 650
midwife 604
migrant 219
migration 29, 32, 78, 420
—period 380
milk 59, 60, 62, 284, 287, 291, 292, 296
—"brotherhood" 70
increasing the yield of— 685
—jug 227, 408
—loaf 59, 281, 287, 291, 604, 622
—pot 296
—product 283
—processing 60, 296
—profit 91
—to take away the— 676
mill 95, 221, 282
boat— 221
—driven by animals 221
dry— 222, 270
horse-walk of a—— 222
turning tent of a—— 222
fulling— 311
hand— 221, 298
miraculous— 524
tower— 225
tread— 222, 225
water— 220
overshot—— 221
undershot—— 221
wind— 220, 222, 223, 225
—house 222
—stone 222
miller 91, 95, 220–222, 225, 364, 372
—'s family 221
millet 203, 220, 281, 284
—mush 285
minister 75, 106
minor mode 432
minstrel (regős) 430, 519, 520, 584, 656, 657
miraculous— 524
—'s song 332, 520
minstrelsy 36, 517, 654, 657, 658
mirror 160, 162, 190, 380, 627
—case 377, 481, 498, 503
—holder 375
Miska jug 411
monastic orders 105
money box 408

monoxylon 244
moon 679, 680
Moravian 29, 370, 456, 695
Mordvinian 26, 287
mortar 140
   wooden 216, 220, 365
motif
   Renaissance star— 369
   tendril— 369
   vase and foliage— 369
mould 292, 298
mouldboard 201
mourning
   colour of— 366, 637
   white colour of— 40, 637
moustache 317
   —made from maize silk 219
mowing 206, 257
mud
   —ball 143
   plastering with— 40
mug 408
mummer 624, 657
   magical— 671
mummery 624, 651, 658
   —of Carnival 643
mush 284, 286, 287, 295
   "farewell"— 285
   goose— 285
   meaty— 285
   millet— 285
   —with mutton 284, 294
mushroom 195, 282
music 44
   church— 430
   dance— 438
   German 433
   gypsy— 432
   Hungarian— 445
   recruiting— 433, 449
   Slovak— 433
   Rumanian— 433
   zither— 306
musical
   —instruments 434, 435, 438, 444
   —structures 469
musicians 417
   —at weddings 445, 446
mutton 294
mutual help (kaláka) 97, 98
myth 31, 82, 108
   European animal— 569
   totemic— of the Árpád clan 583
   —of the Mongol invasion 585
   —of the Turkish occupation 585
   —of the White Horse 584
mythical stag 629, 584
Myxolydian
   —mode 439
   —scale 443

name day of a church's saint 110
Name's Day 658
narodne pesme 514
násznagy (see also witness) 613, 615, 624
narration 87
national fair 112
Nativity Play 600, 603, 652, 653
   —player 652, 654
   puppet—— 654
navvy 273
neckerchief 356
necklace 341, 345, 418
   garnet— 338, 355
needlework 399
   colourful— 323, 401, 402
   white— 322
neighbour 72, 73
neighbourhood 72, 73
   —relationship 73
Neo-Classical 369, 417
Neo-Classicism 370
net 237, 240, 241, 244
   bicentral— 242
   dipping— 240
   drag— 242, 243
   fouling— 237
   large— 242
   old— 242
New Stone Age 142, 145, 189, 203
New Year 281, 684
newspaper 160
St. Nicholas's Day 651
nicking 260
night manure 266
   —watchman 102
ninth of produce 31, 57, 216
nobility 301, 302, 440
   western— 302
nobles 74, 75
   common— 74
noggin 211
nomadic 28
   —husbandman 34
   —husbandry 28
   —half-nomadic way of life 29
noodle 86, 292, 293
notary 76
notched tree 564
notching
   carry on— 260
   —the car of pigs 66
   —the ear of sheep 66
   half— 260
   paired— 260
   stock— 260
nursery rhyme 609

oak forest 246, 254
   —apple 312
oat 203

oil 215, 376
   —lamp 156
   ——with candlestick 156
Ob-Ugrian 27, 429
onion 86, 280, 284, 285, 295, 300
   —grower 79
Onugrian 28
open fire 278, 291
   openwork 388
   ——panel 383
opening 226
opening natural image 477–480
oral tradition 517, 520, 541, 545, 548
orchard 37, 129, 166
orchestra
   gypsy— 447
   peasant— 445
organ
   hand— 441
   street— 441
ornamental folk art 363–420
ornamentation with winding stem 368
ornamented bone plate 368
Ostyak 26, 27, 429, 552
Ottoman Turkish 32, 698
outlaw 117, 130, 374, 497
   —poetry 497
outskirt of the settlement 120–133
oven 149, 151, 152, 153, 154, 175, 178,
   179, 184, 185, 287, 289, 290, 410
   baking— 155
   cooking— 153
   low— 282
   open-air baking— 154
   plum drying— 174
   round— 152, 154
   —with a chimncy 153
ox 61, 202, 208, 261, 271
   —traction 274

pagan 31, 527
paganism 104
pail 228, 297
paint brush 406
Palm Sunday 42, 355, 434
Palots (palóc) 41, 43, 45, 64, 69, 132, 152,
   156, 157, 161, 165, 170, 183, 200, 206,
   297, 317, 325, 344, 383, 445, 685
   —house 183
pan
   baking— 277
   cast-iron— 278
   —cake 286
   earthenware— 277
   frying— 294
panel 387
   painted— 386
   openwork— 383
pantaloon (gatya) 323, 350
   loose, white— 353

pantry 136, 149, 169, 170, 173, 179, 183, 282, 291, 625
  one-level—building (kástu) 170, 171, 181
  separate— (kástu) 179
  two-level—building 181
paprika 216, 284, 300
  —grower 79
  —growing 46
  —mill 216
parade 229
parallelism 547
parish clerk 76
parson 105
pasta 283
  cooked— 292
  kneaded— 283
pasture 59, 90, 91, 121, 125, 129, 197, 246, 253–255, 258, 264, 266, 268–270
  —association 103
  caring for— 96
  common— 253
  —ground 133
  upkeep of the— 103
pasturing 28
pastry 281
  baked— 293
  —cut into big squares 86
  —in the shape of spirals (csiga) 616
  —horn 291, 292
  fritter-like— 292
  leavened— 281
  raised— 291
  —without lard 281
payment
  daily— 81
  —in kind 102, 103, 105
pea 284
"Peacock Circles" 708, 710
pear 282
peasant 43, 76, 78, 90, 275, 375, 434
  —architecture 180
  —band 440, 444
  —doctor 264
  —house 280
  —household 282, 283
  —housekeeping 95
  —life 365
  middle— 77–79
  —orchestra 445
  poor— 33, 78, 83, 91, 100, 218, 593
  —rebellion 31
  —uprising 31
  rich— 33, 76, 77, 79
  —wedding 76
  —world of beliefs 684
peasantry 74–76, 284, 302, 364, 577, 578
  poor— 578
peat cutting 37
Pecheneg 29, 50, 316, 440

peel 289
pelisse (mente) 355, 360
pen 168, 186, 262, 266
  chaff— 167
  covered— 245
  duck— 172
  —with a fireplace 168
  goose— 167, 172
  pig— 131, 167, 169, 172, 179, 183
  —for the small livestock 169
penny novel 160
pentatonic 432
  —melody 28, 433, 696
  —music 434
  —scale 429, 549
  —world 430
pepper 285, 300
  green— 33
peripatetic vendor (bosnyák-Bosnian) 114
Permian 287, 423
pestle
  iron— 220
  wooden— 221
Peter-Paul (day of) 205, 665
Peter's pence 105
petticoat 322, 323, 338, 341, 352, 355, 360
  starched— 355
phylloxera 226
pick and shovel man (kubikos) 33, 84, 507
pickling 282
picture 162
  —of the master of the house 160
  —"pointers" (képmutogató) 115
pig 66, 78, 88, 247, 261, 265
  —herd 38, 266
  —killing 283, 665
  —feast 295, 298, 442, 459, 508, 665
  —lard 215
  —pen 131, 167, 169, 172, 179, 183
  —built on logs, bridge-like (hidas) 169
  —sty 88, 169
pilgrimage 109, 110, 111, 118
pillory 103, 108
pillow
  —case 394, 402, 404
  —cover 394, 395
pinewood 139
pipe (musical instrument) 435, 436, 438, 444, 449
  bourdon— 439, 449
  double melody— 439
  double reed— 436
  reed— 436
pipe 628
  —pouch 628
  —stem 375
pipette 406
pit 170, 173, 186, 215, 266
  —cutter 170
  grain— 170

grave— 170
house— 148
pear-shaped— 170
prism-shaped— 215
"stack-" 173
temporary— 173
underground— 170, 197
  —for wild boar 237
wolf— 237
pitcher 192, 298, 409, 411, 416
  anthropomorphic— 411
  —maker 408, 411
  ornamental— 415
  small— 415
  unglazed— 408
  water— 408
  wine— 411, 412
pitchfork 238, 257, 258
pixidarii (székely) 50
plank 148
  —door 164
  —gate 165
plate 162, 192, 408, 415, 416
  —holder 383
platter 280, 408, 411
  —maker 408, 411
play-like dancing performance 549
plough 75, 214, 215, 365
  all iron— 201
  asymmetrical—share 199, 200
  —beam 199, 202
  —cultivation of fields 28
  —culture 198, 199
  detour— 202
  —farming 198
  —field 197, 215
  forecarriage of the— 199, 201, 202
  asymmetrical——— 201
  symmetrical—— 201
  frame of the— 199
  furrow-turning— 200
  —handle 202
  half iron— 200, 201
  iron— 199, 200, 201, 682
  —iron 260
  —land 197, 215
  ——cultivation 214
  —maker 199
  mould board— 200, 201, 202
  reversible— 200–202
  rooting— 201
  —share 199, 200, 366
  slip— 201
  stilt-sole type of— 200
  symmetrical— 200
  wheeled— 28
  wooden— 200, 201
plough agriculture 37
ploughing 202, 203, 205
  —apart 202

first spring— 202
joint— 202
ridge and furrow— 202
plum 282, 292
poker 291
Pole 145
pole 210, 271, 272
hay— 210
Polish 42, 316
Poljan 28
pomegranate 368
pommel 272
popcorn 281
poppy-seed 281, 292
porch 64, 151, 153, 162, 183, 188, 190,
  216, 307
pork 281, 295
—stew 97
porridge
  maize— 285
  mashed— 285
—plant 220
portico
  colonnaded— 181, 185
  pillars of the— 189
portion
  —of the crop 79
  —of the yield 79
portrayal
  animal— 380
  human— 383
post 275
pot 408
  castiron— 278
  clay— 283
  cooking— 277
  earthenware— 277
  flower— 408
  unadorned— 406
potter 92, 112, 114, 275, 369, 408, 411,
  415
  —wheel 408, 410
  —'s co-operation 410
pottery 277, 364, 368, 371, 406
  black— 408
  centre 192, 410–412
  —centres:
    Csákvár 411
    Debrecen 411
    Gyöngyös 412
    Hódmezővásárhely 411
    Mezőcsát 411
    Mezőtúr 411
    Pásztó 412
    Sárköz 411
    Tata 410
  —dish 280
potash 40, 195
potato 33, 47, 88, 214, 215, 285, 295
  gathering in—s 99

—picking 215
poultry 60, 88, 169, 294
pounded wall 143
powder
  —horn 367, 380
  —flask 378–380
prayer book 115
predicting
  —cropyield 664
  —the weather 664
preparing
  —chicken 294
  —fish 294
  —game 236, 294
presbitery 106
present (vásárfia) son of the fair 113
press 229–232
  —with a large beam 229
  middle spindle— 230
pretzel 286, 291, 604
prevention 690
priest 75, 105, 291, 365
"primor" (Székely) 50
privilege 45, 46, 74
privy 173
processing
  —bulrush 47
  —reed 47
production
  large-scale— 215
producing
  —for the market 214
professional master 406
progeny profit 91
proposal 612, 613
Protestant 104, 110, 160
  —sect 105
proverb 549, 594–597
  European— 597
  metrics of— 597
prune 282
pruner 227
pruning 226, 227
  —knife 227
  —scissors 227
pseudo folk music 432
pub 118
puli (kind of sheepdog) 247
Purification of the Virgin Mary 664
"push-out mush" (kitolókása) 626
putting up the hair (felkontyolás) 625
puzzle-jug 414

quail 237
quiver 315

rabies' doctor 688
rabbit 236, 238
rack 274
  bread— 291

three-legged— 258
racka sheep 247
raft 195, 244
rafter 165
railed—off counter 95
railway worker 283
rainbow 681
rake 166, 197, 207, 211, 257, 258
rattle 261, 338
raw meat 282
razor-case 375, 377, 499
reaping hay 96, 207
recruiting 501
"red ox" 658
reed (plant) 142
  —cutter 219
  —fence 194
  —house 142, 417
  —pipe 436
  processing of— 37, 47
  —for roofing the house 194
  —string 435
  —weaver 417
  wind screen made of— 264
reed (tool) 86, 90, 309
  —maker for the loom 417
  wool-weaving— 311
reel
  four-forked turnable— 306
  one-forked hand— 306
Reformation 32, 131
Reformed Presbyterian 104
"rejtezés" (hiding) 671, 672
relief carving 376
religious
  —legend 568–569
  —life 104
  —literature 551, 552
  Catholic—— 552
  —literature of the Reformation 552
  —text 431
Renaissance 32, 139, 152, 188, 189, 322,
  368, 387–389, 401, 404, 410, 450, 458,
  486
repetitive structure 479
repetition
  —in the ballads 548
  —of the fixed text 600
resist technique 420
rhyme 547, 548
  nursery— 708
rhymed saying 87
rhythmic
  —formula 597
  —tradition 548
rice 295
rick 258
riddle 513, 549, 594, 598, 599
  —tales 598
ring 262, 418, 419

ritual
—role 293
roaster
—duck 408
—fish 408
Robin Hood 541, 587
Rococo 369, 370, 389, 417
Roman 29, 177, 221, 681
—tradition 226
romance 514
"romancero" 515
Romanesque 368
roof 164, 253
gable of the— 164
hipped— 163
liftable— 169
reed— 168, 174, 185
rush— 185
sedge— 185
shingle covered— 166, 167, 171
straw— 185
—standing on poles 168
—structure 144–148, 163, 167
chair-leg type of—— 145, 146
half-a post structure— 145
—purlin type 145, 178, 185
—rafter type 145, 167, 183, 188
—ridge beam supported by forked post 145
—ridge beam supported by scissor beams 145
thatched— 165, 166, 168, 171, 188
tile covered— 166
room
"clean"— 161, 190
"best"— 161, 162
—of the young couple 179
rooster 158
rope 241, 271
—made of hemp 241
—made of horsehair 241
—maker 115
round-about of a dry mill 222
round cloak (suba) 329
roundel 451
rotation system 214
rug 394
Rumanian 32, 33, 35, 46, 51, 186, 220, 266, 316, 333, 356, 370, 372, 394, 438, 451, 456, 533, 695, 696
runic script 28
rural
—agricultural labourer 78–90
—hands on large estates 87–91
—melon picker 33
—pick and shovel man 33, 84–87
—seasonal worker 82–84
—share labourer 79–82
—tobacco picker 33

—industry 91
—worker 83
rush 86
—matting 86
Russian 42, 394, 532, 541, 568, 579, 695
Ruthenian 378, 433, 451
rye 203, 286

sack 172, 204, 270
sacred corner 158, 162
sacrifice 527
animal— 527, 584
building— 524, 527
foundation— 158
human— 527
sacrificing the blood of man 527
—the hair of man 527
sacristan 105
saddle 271, 272, 315, 368
wooden— 271
saddle-back 227 (bakhát)
saffron 300
saga 549
salt 88, 285–295, 299, 380
—cellar 300, 374, 495
—container 368
—holder 376, 377
sample (kóstoló) 296
—of bread 73
—of fresh baking 73
—when the pig was killed 68, 73
sandal (bocskor) 332, 335
birch-bark— 332, 657
covered— 33
laced-up— 332, 353, 355, 360, 361
oak-bark— 657
sarmentous floral motif 417, 418
——pattern 380
saru (a kind of sandal) 333
sauerkraut 282
sausage 295
blood— 278, 295
liver— 295
—making 295
Saxons 32, 186, 187, 356, 405
—of Transylvania 32, 370
—of Upper Hungary 406
saw 380
Scala coeli 551
scale
ecclesiastic— 549
pentatonic— 549
scare away evil from the house 638
scarecrow 205
scissor beam 178
scoop 240
scorching 295
Scottish ballad 516
scutcher 305

scythe 59, 62, 197, 206–208, 257
—blade 219, 682
long-handled— 194
twinhandled— 206
—with a slasher 206
sealing wax 370
seating order
——at the dinner 623
——at the wedding 623
seasonal worker 33, 82, 84, 294, 350
——'s lodging 84
——'s working hours 84
Second Day of Our Lady 70
secular text 431
seed holder 365
seedling 216
"seeing woman" 676
selection of names 604
Serbian, Serb 42, 226, 316, 333, 334, 401, 520
Catholic— 216
serf 74, 79, 121, 139, 489
free— 31
freeing of the —s 33, 79
liberation of the —s 103
permanent 31
serpentine 683
servant 62, 89
servants of Saint Stephen 656, 657
settlement 37, 38, 69, 72, 120, 123, 135, 232
clan— 187
closed— 126, 129
divided— 183
double inner-lot type of— 131, 132, 174, 177, 187
kinship (szer)— 123
order of the— 69
outskirt of the— 120–138
parent— 126, 127
"ribbon lot" system of— 135
scattered— 123
"spindle" type of— 183
—with street lots 135
street type of— 178
Severjan 28
sexton 105, 106
shackle 419
shaman (see also táltos) 28, 564, 668, 670–672
—drum 671
—initiating ceremony 564
shamanism 26, 28, 368, 557, 672
shamanistic
—belief 570, 695
—ceremony 564
—faith 670
—features 670
—image 570
oriental shamanistic stratum 570

—procedures 676
share 80, 82
  —harvester 79, 81, 82
  —labourer 79, 81
  —maize 80
  ratio of the— 79
sharing of the milk 297
shaving horse 372
shawl 332, 338, 345
  shoulder— 343–345, 348, 350, 355
  white— 356
shearing 311
sheave 59, 194, 197, 206–208, 210, 213
  stocking of the— 80
shed 84, 129, 131, 173, 177, 188
  —for beehives 174
  cart— 173, 186
  chaff— 186
  cutting— 173
  half-roofed— 72
  woodcarving— 173
sheep 50, 66, 91, 252, 261, 266, 298, 311
  —fold 266, 278, 311
  mangy— 264
  Merino— 370
  —shearing 255
  scrub— 247
  —stock 296
sheeppen 131
sheepskin 302, 312, 318
  —bag 283
  —cloak (suba) 329, 353
  —cloak (bunda) 316, 355
  —coat (ködmön) 114, 267, 355
  —garment 316, 329
  —jacket (ködmön) 301, 345, 353, 398, 399
  —vest 356
  —waistcoat 355
sheet 402, 405
  ends of the— 402
shelling
  —chair 220
  —machine 220
  —maize 220
shepherd 91, 247, 248, 250, 260, 264, 266, 268, 329, 354, 377, 496
  common— 296
  —'s crook 375, 417, 418
  wages of the— 103
shepherding 42
  alpine— 50
shift 322
shingle 148, 187
shipping 37
shirt 315, 322, 350, 355
  of the bridegroom 322
  brokade— 337
  dark blue— 323
  embroidered linen— 345, 348

festive— 322
  —with folded collar 322
  —loose-sleeved 355, 356, 360
  loose white— 353
  men's— 361
  narrow-sleeved— 360
  narrow-waisted— 343
  "soldier's—" 322
  tulle— 340
shock (kepe) 80
  —of corn (kalangya) 208
  double—— 208
shoe 333, 350, 355, 361
  —maker 312
shop
  —keeper 95
  local— 95
shoulder (ingváll) 322
  —kerchief 400
shovel 85
  woodden— 214
showman 110, 115
shroud 629
Shrove Tuesday 643, 683
shuttle 309
sickle 62, 197, 205–207, 219, 628, 681, 682
  harvesting with— 206
  smooth bladed— 206
  toothed— 206
sideboard 162, 163
sieve
  divination with beans on a— 690
  grab a— 681
  leather— 283
  spinning the— 689
Simon-Jude's Day 228
singer 78, 520
  beggar—at fairs 520
singing 89, 209, 434, 435, 468
  opportunities for— 434
single stanza structure 473
silk
  —skirt 355
  —yarn 402
silver 418
  —art 368
  —chain 338
  —coin 418
  peasant silversmith 418, 419
skin 301
  ox— 314
  processing of— 192, 312, 315
skirt 323, 337–339, 343–345, 348, 355, 356, 360, 362
  cashmere— 350, 355
  cotton— (rokolya) 361
  linen— (bikla) 339
  silk— 355
  holiday— 339

linen— 334
  many-pleated— 352
  outer— 323
  satin— 350
  silk— 350
slashing hook 122
slate 148
slaughterer 295
Slav, Slavic 28–30, 33, 41, 71, 72, 142, 168, 197, 198, 208, 221, 238, 245, 256, 276, 284, 291, 302, 315, 316, 333, 430, 438, 447, 515
  Eastern— 28, 196, 221, 243, 278, 296, 673
  South— 32, 35, 40, 145, 220, 226, 316, 333, 334, 370, 533, 572
slay 273
sleeping places
  barn 64
  chamber 64
  stable 169
  room 64
sleeve 315, 322
  top of the— 359
sleighing 273
sling shot 236
slipper 334, 353
  cloth— 343
  —maker 46, 114, 334
Slovak, Slovakian 29, 30, 32, 35, 36, 42, 46, 145, 170, 181, 183, 316, 318, 370, 377, 378, 406, 433, 438, 451, 487, 489, 579, 587, 695, 696
Sloven, Slovenian 29, 171, 334, 587
smallholder 165
smith 682
smocking 323
smoke
  trapped— 408
smoking 216, 283
  —against the evil eye 689
  —to prevent bewitching 688
smoky
  —house 151
  —kitchen 148
snail shaped noddles 283
snake 190, 683
snare 237
  horsehair— 237
  —pulling 237
social gatherings 295
  —tendencies in folk tales 582
sod 86, 175
  virgin— 121
soil 140, 215
  clay— 226
  —cultivation 197
  sandy— 226
Sokác (Catholic Serbian) 172
song 49, 59, 219

—of anger 471
artificial— 504
—of battle 502
—beggars 513, 529
biblical— 615
—of captivity 491–494
children's— 430, 468, 606, 708
—of Christmas 434
cradle— 513
cursing— 486
dance— 469, 471, 477, 515
dramatic— 549
drinking— 508–510
drink-giving— 509, 510
—of Easter 434
election— 471
epic— 477, 515, 542
—of exile 471
—at fairs 513
—of farmhands 505, 506
festive— 513
fighting— 468
—of firejumping on Midsummer Night 434
"flower"— 468, 475, 482
—of girls 469
glass-touching— 509, 510
harvesters'— 486
herdsmen's— 452, 477, 494–500
heroic— 489, 500, 585
historical— 486–491, 500, 545
humorous— 510, 615
Kossuth— 489, 532
—of the kuruc period 491
lamenting— 632
love— 469, 480, 483, 510
lyric— 469, 483
—of marching 502
—of migration to America 486
minstrel— 430
mocking— 486, 500, 510,
moralizing— 615
mourning— 429, 513
narrative— 477
night watchman's— 513
outlaw— 469, 477, 491, 493, 494–500, 510
—of Palm Sunday 434
peasant— 472
—of pick and shovel men 507, 508
prisoner— 493, 494, 501, 502
religious— 628
—of revelry 508–510
—rural servants 505, 506
—rural workers 504
satirical— 510–513
—of seasonal workers 486, 506, 507
secular— 628
—of Shrovetide 434

soldiers'— 469, 477, 486, 488, 491, 493, 500, 502–510, 532
—of valour 486–491
vendor— 513
—of war 502
wandering— 486, 491–494, 500, 501, 513
wedding— 513, 615
wine— 508–510, 615
work— 469
—of young men 469
soot 376, 380
soul of the dead man 677
soup 86, 277
bean— 281
cabbage— 281, 284
chicken— 281
fasting— 282
fish— 294
hen-meat— 294
—made with pasta 283
meat— 283
sour— 281, 284
sparerib— 296
sow
undomesticated— 266
sower 204, 205
sowing 203–205, 217, 685
date of— 203, 204, 217
device of— 217
Spanish 247, 532, 541
spade 85, 198
—handle 86
two-forked— 214
—with two-sided blade 197
—with one-sided blade 198
wooden— 197, 198
spear 243
—fisher 239
Speculum 551
speech of animals 683
spelt 203, 284
spice 216
spindle 305, 306
—weight 417
spinery 611
spinning 305, 306, 434, 444, 459
conclusion of— 190
—distaff 305
—house 305, 306
—wheel 305
spinsterhood 612
"spitting place" 112
spoke 275
spoon-rack 279
spreading news 222, 275
spring 109
respect for—s 109
spring inspection of landmarks 659
spur 455

clattering— 455
stable 88, 131, 133, 136, 167, 169, 177, 179, 245, 246
heatable— 131
—keeping 246
stack 206, 208, 258
stag 380
stag horn 367, 380
staff (tool) 377
staggers 264
stalk
—of the corn 219
———as fodder 219
—cutter 219
stampede of the herd 262, 263
stamping dance 449
stanza 547, 548
starry sky 680
steerman 243
St. Stephen's Day 658
steward 87
stitch
chain— 397
closed square chain— 49
cross— 397, 399, 401
laid— 399
loop— 397
oblique chain— 397, 404
oblique cross— 396, 404
oblong cross— 397
satin— 398, 399
simple cross— 396
stick 236, 261, 449
flinging— 236
hitting— 236
planting— 214
stock 58, 76, 89, 117, 197, 245–247, 249, 251–256, 261, 278
animal— 252
breaking in the— 270
common— 260
live— 116
—market 116
—'s return in autumn 664
small— 60
village— 252
wild— 264
stocking 343, 353
white— 345
stoke hole of the room 185
stone 140
—foundation 164, 166
storage room 183
store
—boat 221
—house (kástu) 171
story 59, 84
—telling 72
stove 154, 155, 277
—cooking 286

—tile 410, 415
glazed—— 410
tile— 155, 177, 179
stool 385
storing 282
story
    anti-clerical— 470
    —of belief 550
    fabulous— 551
    —of magic 550
    —listening community 575, 576
    local mocking— 579
    —teller 78, 306, 574–580
    —telling 87, 216, 219, 572, 576, 579, 580
story telling communities 574, 575
    outside the village:
        among fishermen 575
        among herdsmen 575
        among industrial workers in men's
            dormitory 575
        among soldiers 575
        among village artisans in workshops
            575
        among wood cutters 575
    within the village:
        after bundling tobacco 575
        after fieldwork 575
        after harvesting 575
        in spineries 575
        after vineyard work 575
    special occassions for telling tales
        575–576
        abroad 575
        in the course of big fairs 575
        at the far end of the country 575
        in the course of migration 575
        in the course of servant work on esta-
            tes 575
    ——custom 574, 579
    ——occasion 575, 594
    "true"—— 82, 89, 549, 552, 696
straw 79, 142, 146, 164, 211, 213, 215
    buckwheat— 147
    —doll, representing winter 638, 643
    pea— 147
    —roof 147
    rye— 147
    —thatched house 147, 174
stretcher 274
string instrument 440
stripping of feathers 459
sturgeon 241
suba (round sheepskin coat) 329, 330, 344,
    353, 355, 362
    embroidered— 341
    —of Berény 365
süveg (a cap) 329
sugar 287
    —beet 81
suicide 130

suitors 612
sun 679
    —flower 215
Sunday 281
    —afternoon stroll 434
    —service 107
superstition 131, 209, 217, 262, 263, 306,
    317, 546
supper 79
"swallow walling" 143
swamp 121
swastika 380, 420
swath 59, 62, 257, 258
swineherd 39, 258, 262, 269, 353, 496
    —'s dance 449
    —'s horn 438
    —'song 433
swingle 302, 303
Swiss 247
Swiss-Ladin 480
sword 315
Székely 50, 51, 123, 167, 186–188, 273,
    287, 311, 318, 332, 393, 416, 445, 452,
    678
    —ballad 549
    —of Bukovina 51, 67, 70, 395
    —equites 50
    —gate 50
    —primor 50
    —rug 394
szűr (overcoat of thick woollen cloth or
    frieze) 46, 326, 355, 362, 398
    collared— 326
    —of Debrecen 365
    —dolmány 341
    embroidered— 341
    Garibaldi— 398
    —and guba maker 91, 301
    large— 335
    —making 380
    —mantle 301, 311, 326, 327
    short— 335
symbol 365, 366, 476, 529
    —of agriculture 365
    —of fertility 420
symbolic system
—of colours 366
    ——of folk poetry 476
symbolically ornamented objects 365
system of sixty 208

table 157, 158, 387
    —cloth 204, 391, 392, 394, 397, 405
    —drawer 291
    drawered— 158
    —with a "pantry" below 158
tailor 114
tale 47, 59, 82, 108, 286, 306
    —of belief 550
    fairy— 550, 554, 579

folk— 549
foolish devil— 570
fool's— 570
humorous— 564–567
legendary— 568
—of lying 565
magic— 552
scary— 306
telling of tales 573
village mocking— 567, 568, 579
tale's introductory formula 580
tallow 156, 157, 314, 376, 380
    cow— 156
    sheep— 156
táltos (shaman) 28, 670–672
    equipment of the— 671, 674, 681
    extra bone of the— 672
    —tree 671
tanner 91, 312, 314, 364, 369
tanning 314
taper-wood 156
    crane to hold— 155
tarhonya 86
tarragon 300
tart 286
    —bread 286
    flat— 286
tart-loaf
    hard— 286
    soft— 286
Tartar 44, 245
tavern 84, 95, 103, 110, 111, 118, 122, 611
    —keeper 95
tawer 301
tax 105
taxation 126
teacher 75
teasing of the wool 311
tendril motif 369, 387
tent 190
terracotta firing 408
tether 263, 271
thatch 147, 163, 164
    reed— 174
    straw— 174, 183
    —work 183
thatched roof 165, 166, 168, 171, 188
thatching 147
thief 113, 117, 118
    —' fine 219
Thousand and One Nights 584
Three Magi 638
Three Wise Men 638
thresher 213
threshing 61, 80, 82, 84, 131, 165–167,
    197, 210–214, 281, 459
    —barn 133, 208
    —flail 163, 165, 197, 210, 213
    —floor 211, 212
    —grain 99, 185

—ground 165, 166, 213
machine— 163,
—machine 164
mechanical— 214
—yard 164, 166, 197, 200
thrice-repeating structure 549
thumb-pressed strips of clay 406
tile
  cup or mug like— 410
  earthenware— (kályhaszem) 155
  plate-shaped— 410
  rustic glazed— 410
  —stove 155
  stove— 410
timber framework 140
tin
  —dish 283
  —pouring woman 688
tithe 57, 105, 214, 216
toast 97, 513, 659
  —asking for blessing 97
tobacco 33, 216
  —grower 79, 216
  —picker 33
tolling of the church bell 629
tombstone 130
  carving of— 417
tool 188
  agricultural— 38, 192
  hand— 197
  —for home use 38
  repairing of—s 189
totemic animal 584
towel 402
tower 188, 225
toy car 606
trade 30
  rural— 91
tradition 301
  intellectual— 222
  oral— 517, 550, 551
traditional folk culture 705
transportation
  means of— 270
trap
  bow— 237
  crushing— 237
  fishing— 240
  mouse— 237
  rat— 237
trapping 238
travelling glazier 433
  —tinkers 433
treading 185, 210–214
treading out corn 61, 210, 212
  ——grain 99, 131
  ——with horses 197, 212
  ——with oxen 212
tree bark 374
Tree of Life 671, 672

—that Reached up to the Sky 557, 564
  topless— 571
  world—of shamanistic religion 564
triangular human portrayal 380, 383
trimming the ear of sheep and pigs 66
tripod 277
  iron— 277
had (= troop) smaller unit than the clan 67, 69
troubled spirit 121
trough 174, 256
  —carver 417
trousseau
  bride's— 366
  —of clothes 61
trousers 315
trumpet 435
tub 287–289
  perforated— 231
  wooden— 287
tulip motif 360
tumbril 273
Turk 28, 32, 93, 143, 177, 184, 196, 216, 316
  fight with the—s 520, 609
Turkic peoples 27, 28, 54, 276, 296, 333, 440, 698
Turkish 244
  —devastation 487
  —Empire 32
  —influence 369
  —industrial product 32
  —occupation 532
  —origin 44, 109, 673
  Ottoman— 315, 333, 614
  —people 429
  —period 529
  —rule 120, 183, 188, 210, 226, 317, 362, 368, 450, 487
  —soldier songs 533
  —style 414
  —times 418
  —wars 452
turnip 282
turnover 281
turret 139, 188
tussock 255

Udmurt 26
Ugric period 26, 54, 144, 315, 552, 695, 696
Ukrainian 145, 394, 541, 587, 696
unbaptized infant 130
underskirt 348
underwear 322
undulating design 408
union of lyrics and melody 549
Unitarian 110
unmarried lad 61
unpaid work 82

Ural period 683
Uralic-Altaic peoples 564
St. Urban's Day 311, 665

vegetable 84
  —production 46
vehicle
  light— 273
  two-wheeled— 273
velvet 337, 339
Vendel's day 117
vendor 112, 114
  occasional— 112
  peripatetic— 114
  permanent— 112
vessel 278, 280, 367, 374, 408, 415
  anthropomorphic— 411
  black— 408
  candle-dipping— 406
  churning— 296
  cooking— 277, 408
  drinking— 368
  earthenware— 58, 155, 411
  fireproof— 411
  iron— 278
  —made out of horn 232
  ———————wood 232
  storing— 408
  unadorned clay— 406
  unpainted— 408
vest 355
  black— 345
  embroidered sheepskin— 356
  sheepskin— 355, 356, 361
  sleeveless leather— 361
village 89, 90, 95, 96, 100–102
  agglomerated— 135, 183, 187
  —artisan 192
  —chest 101
  —community 90, 95, 97
  —drummer 102
  —farmyard 131
  —grocery 95
  —hall 102
  —intellectuals 75, 76
  —law 101
  leader of the— 101
  linear— 136
  —mayor 102–103
  —mayoral election 101
  —mocking tale 567, 568, 579
  —staff 101
  street— 136
  —with stable-yard (szálláskert) 132
villeinage 56
St. Vincent's Day 664
vine 36
  —culture 47
  —growing 28, 42, 46, 196
vinegar 299

apple— 299
wine— 299
vineyard 129, 227, 231
viniculture 30, 226
vintage 227, 228, 229
   beginning of the— 227
   completion of the— 229
viola 447
violin 440, 444, 445, 447, 459
Virgin Mary's birthday 216
Vogul 26, 27
voluntary co-operative work see: kaláka
Votyak 26, 287

wage 81, 83, 84
wagon 273, 274
   four-wheeled low— 208
waistcoat 325, 355
   black— (lajbi) 352
   —with braidings 325
   —with cut-out neck 325
   —with high collar 325
   —with ornated buttons 325
   —sleeveless 324
wake 628
wall
   adobe— 185
   mud— 184
   —painting 46
   plank— 166
   plastered wicker— 173
   pounded— 142
   reed— 142
   sod— 143
   wattle— 142, 164–166, 233
   wicker— 40, 184, 233
walling 142
   —material 142
Wallachian 266, 268, 438
Walloon 30, 31, 226, 227
wandering
   —merchant 383
   —scholar 673
   —student (garabonciás) 589, 681
Wandering Surveyor 677
War of Independence (1848–1849) 318,
   468, 489–491, 587
War of Liberation (1703–1711) 487, 532,
   587
warding off 690
   ——bewitching 690
   ——sickness 690
   ——trouble 690
wardrobe 162
warp 309
warping 308, 311
   —of the loom 307
   —wheel 308
water
   —bird 236

—chestnut 193, 194
—dipper 368, 376, 704
—fowl 194
—jug 410
—mill 122
—pitcher of Tur 365
watering 255
wattle 174
   —fence 268, 270
   —fold 268
   —matting 143
   —of willow 142
   —wall 142, 164, 166, 233
wax
   bees— 376
   sealing— 376
ways of sleeping 447
weapon 262
weather prediction 680
weaver 91, 275, 301, 364
   artisan— 309
   —'s co-operative 391
weaving 91, 307, 311, 363, 410
   —of homespun 60
   —master 390
wedding 28, 68, 69, 126, 190, 277, 284,
   285, 291, 293, 318, 322, 434, 444, 459,
   508, 612–626
   —bed 625
   —cake 616, 619
   —dinner 283
   —feast 281, 612, 621, 623
   —mush 281
   —pastry 619, 622
   —party 291, 365, 621, 622
   peasant— 76
   religious wedding ceremony 621
   —tablecloth 394
weeding 205
weft 309
well
   cleaning of— 103
   draw— 174
   sweep-pole— 174
St. Wendelin 255, 665, 666
wheat 89, 203, 286, 287
   blessing of the— 105
wheel 274, 275
   warping— 308
   —wright 112, 192, 199, 275
whetstone 207, 208
whey 285, 298
whip 117, 236, 248, 262, 272, 419
   —handle 375, 377
   magic— 676
whirlwind 681
whisk 291
whisker 317
whistle 435, 436
   bird-shaped earthenware whistle 607

whitewash 190
Whitsuntide 611, 647
   —greeting 600
   King of— 648
   Queen of— 611, 648, 661
wicker 40, 142, 143
   —gate 164
   —groper 240
   —wall 40, 173, 184, 233
   willow— 142
   —work 142
wild
   —boar 237, 238
   —duck 236
   —stock 264
wind
   —break 267
   —grinder 223
   —mill 75, 225, 273
   —miller 225
   —screen 253, 264
wine 42, 58, 95, 107, 118, 196, 226, 227,
   298, 444
   —flask 299
   —house 231
   —pitcher in a form of man (Miska jug)
   411
   —press 229
   pressed— 230
   pure— 230
   vessel— 365
winehouse
   —in vineyard 231
   —within the settlement in a cluster 232
winnowing 203, 213
   —the corn 211
   shade for the— 211
   —spade 214
   mechanical— 214
witch 28, 121, 673, 681, 682, 686
   —changed into an animal 675
   gathering of witches 674
   iron-nosed— 673
   organization of—es 674
   —persecution 673
   —trial 674
   —craft 673, 682
witness (násznagy) 613, 615, 619, 620, 622,
   623
   —of the groom 615, 619
woman in confinement 281
wondrous duplicity 581
wood
   —building 148
   —carver 364, 417
   —carving 38, 49, 50, 130, 364, 369–371,
   373, 376, 377, 410
   —cut 374
   dog— 262
   —lock 167

oak— 262
pear— 262
plum— 262
processing of— 39
—work 372
—working 38
wooden
   —architecture 139
   —bank 157
   —bench 157
   —board 262, 285
   —box-body 273
   —building 139, 140
   —cross 632, 636
   —fork 165
   —foundation 164
   —holder for whetstone 208
   —hook 208
   —house 139
   —ladder 171
   —mirror case 377
   —mortar 221
   —mould for honey-cake 373
   ——for plate shaped tiles 410
   —opener 219
   —peg for husking cobs 219
   —pestle 220

—screw 230
—spoon 375
—structure 139
wool 58, 301, 309, 311, 325, 393
   —comb 311
   oily— 311
   —processing 192
   unwashed— 311
woollen
   —foot rag 356
   —yarn 392, 402
world
   —of belief 684–691 (see belief)
   —view 678
   peasant—— 678–684
work
   agricultural— 62, 82
   —band 84
   —bench 165
   collective, common, communal, community— 78, 96, 216
   farm— 61
   house— 61
   —room 171
   —tools 166
working magic on the crops 643
workshop of the farmer 165, 181

yard (garden) 59, 64, 118, 133, 135, 163–165, 167, 174, 179, 186, 188, 190, 213, 216, 220, 262
   threshing— 166
yarn 306, 309, 399
   —washing 307
   woollen— 392, 399, 402
yeast 288, 289
yield
   portion of the— 79
yoghurt 296
yoke 270, 271
   —pin 271
young wife (menyecske) 60, 62

zymbalon 444, 445
   —player 444, 445
zither 84, 219, 435, 440, 441, 442, 444, 459
   —band 445
   big-bellied— 443
   chromatic— 443
   diatonic— 443
   music— 306
Zyrian 26, 287

Geographical index

Abaúj (County) 129, 155, 164, 166, 202, 205, 214, 275, 503, 511, 621, 625
Abaúj-Torna (County) 181
Abaúj-Zemplén area 424
Acsa 646
Ajak 355
Áj 503
Ájfalucska 181
Almáspatak 49
Alps 36, 37
Alsóborsod 182
Alsóegerszeg 493
Alsóhahót 656
Alsónyék 41
Alsóőr 37
Alsóőrség 123
Alszeg 49
America 52, 78, 214, 695
Andocs 109
Antalokpataka 51
Apáca 649
Apátfalva 504
Apáti-puszta 317
Arad (County) 479
Arad 490
Aranyosszék 50
Asia 672
Asia Minor 315
Asszonyvására 111
Átány 97, 99, 210, 290, 634
Augsburg 29
Austria 34, 370, 448, 452
Austrian-Styrian area 123, 443
Austro–Hungarian Monarchy 33

Bábonymegyer 277
Bácsandrásszállás 431
Bács (County) 132, 227, 272, 329
Bács-Kiskun (County) 44, 152, 267, 273, 307, 313, 340, 418, 420, 431, 623, 638, 652
Bácska (Southern Great Plain) 45, 46, 51
Baja 418, 661, 665
Bakony (Hills, Mountain, Region) 38, 109, 140, 164, 177, 221, 247, 383, 398, 449
Bakonybél 499
Bakonypeterd 225
Balassagyarmat 24, 152, 300, 344
Balaton (Lake) 21, 36, 39, 174, 177, 181, 240, 241, 244, 315, 638
Balaton (Hills north of —) 140, 229
Balatonboglár 496

Balatonfelvidék 38, 226
Balatonfenyves 704
Balatonhenye 179
Balatonzamárdi 180
Balavásár 614
Balkans 151, 177, 198, 247, 268, 387, 450, 451, 527
Balkan Peninsula 221
Balmazújváros 329, 418
Bán 41
Bánát (Southern Great Plain) 45, 46
Bánffyhunyad 49
Báránd 412, 664, 680
Baranya (County) 39, 40, 41, 51, 165, 174, 212, 239, 381, 382, 385, 391, 392, 393, 420, 452, 479, 493, 495, 501, 509, 690
Barcaság (region of —) 52
Bars (County) 611, 650
Barskapronca 611
Báta 41
Békés 46, 143, 497, 672
Békés (County) 47, 113, 114, 211, 212, 219, 222, 225, 240, 248, 388, 398, 488, 491, 497, 502, 638, 674
Bélapátfalva 507
Belényes 48
Bény 169
Bercel 215
Bereg (County) 221, 429, 606, 689
Beregújfalu 689
Berek 185
Berettyó (river) 47
Berzence 173, 199
Bihar (County) 47, 103, 125, 173, 184, 185, 314, 398, 432, 435, 443, 483, 487, 494, 499, 500, 507, 509, 512, 632, 659, 660, 664, 671, 672, 680
Biharnagybajom 672
Bihartorda 184, 185
Black Sea 37, 241
Bodrog (river) 181
Bodroghalász 626
Bodrogköz (island of Bodrog–Tisza–Latorca) 47, 69, 147, 240, 286, 287, 305, 307, 324, 355, 389, 390, 392, 504, 674, 678, 687
Bódva 42
Bogyoszló 149
Boldog 63, 82, 293, 317, 321, 346, 348
Borsa (Valley) 49
Borsod-Abaúj-Zemplén (County) 102, 138, 153, 233, 243, 248, 279, 289, 290,

303, 312, 330, 346, 347, 372, 388, 396, 413, 414, 607, 618, 620
Borsod (County) 41, 153, 182, 213, 221, 232, 235, 453, 459, 490, 507
Borsodszentgyörgy 490
Botpalád 22, 217
Bozok 156
Brassó 52, 116
Brassó (County) 633
Buda 74, 140, 229, 275
Budapest 85, 111, 607, 666, 674
Bugac-puszta 272, 353, 354
Buják 323, 345, 395, 613
Bükk (Mountains) 140
Bukovina 51, 67, 70, 395, 427, 452, 489
Burgenland 37
Buzsák 293
Byzantium 31, 584

Canada 515
Carpathian Basin 11, 28, 29, 30, 31, 34, 35, 36, 42, 71, 139, 140, 142, 170, 172, 184, 196, 197, 199, 200, 201, 202, 203, 206, 210, 220, 221, 229, 232, 233, 236, 245, 246, 247, 256, 264, 273, 286, 287, 302, 305, 308, 323, 406, 414, 417
Carpathians 51, 52, 254, 416, 698
Caucasus 28, 278, 572
Cegléd 46
Central Asia 314, 429, 627
Central Europe 11, 34, 136, 139, 210
Central Transdanubia 177, 287
Cigánd 206, 289, 290, 615, 631
Croatia 434
Csákvár 411
Csallóköz 37, 133, 338, 427
Csanád (County) 504
Csepreg 651
Cserehát 42
Cserfő 230
Csík (basin of —) 50
Csík (County) 51, 150, 167, 186, 187, 223, 265, 269, 303, 324, 326, 374, 398, 416, 445, 446, 480, 483, 661, 662, 664
Csíkmadaras 364, 408
Csíkménaság 187
Csíksomlyó 109, 416
Csíkszék 50, 105, 326
Csíkszentandrás 324
Csíkszentdomonkos 269
Csíkszereda 111
Csongrád 154, 685
Csongrád (County) 85, 101, 121, 211, 214,

810

219, 225, 262, 264, 419, 443, 487, 500,
503, 508, 511, 648, 660, 685
Csurgó-Nagymarton 39, 163
Csütörtökhely 111
Czechoslovakia 23, 30, 34, 185

Dacia 29
Dunafalva 452
Danube (river) 36, 37, 38, 41, 51, 131, 185,
241, 254, 287, 328, 334, 340, 351, 353,
370, 371, 387, 401, 426, 586, 607, 665,
674, 698
Danube (between the — and the Tisza) 44,
46, 125, 129, 131, 132, 155, 183, 200,
216, 226, 268, 270, 280, 287, 353, 371,
372, 398, 427, 441
Danube-Drava (region) 171
Darufalva 151
Debrecen 46, 110, 111, 112, 114, 116, 151,
194, 236, 252, 254, 260, 261, 271, 272,
273, 274, 286, 316, 321, 329, 331, 355,
356, 365, 411, 427, 496, 587, 606, 674
Decs 41, 154, 159, 341, 391
Derecske 173
Désháza 47, 305, 628
Déva 158, 485
Dévaványa 248
Diósad 47, 492
Diósháza 636
Diósjenő 207
Doboz 211, 672
Domaháza 232
Drágszél 274
Dráva (river) 36, 39, 40, 174, 221
Drávaszög 40
Dunafalva 452

East Asia 323
Eastern Carpathians 36, 50, 299, 426
Eastern Europe 136, 332, 394, 527, 532,
533, 570, 572, 587, 672, 694
Eastern Transdanubia 140, 163, 210, 341
Eger 226, 388, 398, 426, 660
Egyházaskér 501
Egyházaskozár 690
England 515
Erdőbénye 138, 417
Erdőház 41
Erdővidék 50
Erked 328
Érmellék (part of the plains of Bihar) 47
Érsekcsanád 41, 340
Eszék 40
Esztelnek 109
Esztergom (County) 169
Europe 29, 109, 125, 174, 272, 314, 315,
323, 333, 372, 452, 511, 515, 530, 543,
554, 557, 574, 670, 673, 681, 693, 698,
699

Fadd 341
Fejér (County) 101, 194, 431, 642, 643, 645
Fekete-Körös (Valley of the —) 48, 356
Felsőkustány 508
Felsőőr 37, 424, 427
Felsőőrség 37
Felsősegesd-Lászlómajor 371
Felsőszemeréd 645
Felszeg 48
Fertőszentmiklós 93
France 29, 515
Füzér 214

Galga 348
Galgagyörk 272
Galgahévíz 490
Galgamácsa 348, 609
Galgamente 41
Galicia 433
Garam (river) 29, 41, 181, 611
Gárdony 194
Gégény 208
Gellért Hill 674, 675
Gencsapáti 648
Gerencsér 504
Gerend 660
Germany 29, 433, 554
Geszte 616
Gige 609
Göcsej (region of —) 36, 123, 139, 163,
179, 181, 218, 221, 296, 334, 657, 686
Gömör (County) 200, 206, 383, 438
Great Cumania see Nagykunság
Great Plain 32, 33, 36, 41, 42, 43, 44, 45,
46, 47, 48, 49, 51, 58, 59, 61, 64, 72, 75,
76, 81, 82, 83, 84, 86, 87, 90, 112, 120,
123, 129, 132, 133, 136, 139, 140, 143,
144, 145, 147, 153, 157, 163, 168, 169,
170, 172, 173, 174, 181, 183, 184, 186,
187, 189, 192, 193, 194, 195, 196,
197–199, 201, 203, 206, 207, 208, 210,
214, 223, 227, 237, 245, 246, 247, 248,
251, 253, 254, 255, 256, 257, 260, 262,
263, 266, 269, 270, 271, 275, 277, 278,
279, 281, 282, 283, 284, 285, 286, 288,
291, 294, 296, 298, 299, 306, 314, 316,
317, 318, 322, 329, 330, 332, 333, 334,
351, 360, 368, 370, 377, 383, 387, 388,
398, 399, 411, 418, 426, 433, 439, 441,
442, 443, 447, 451, 452, 486, 489, 491,
495, 497, 498, 507, 508, 513, 547, 580,
598, 606, 616, 620, 624, 632, 642, 662,
672, 675, 688
Gyenesdiás 129
Gyergyó (basin of —) 50
Gyergyóújfalu 480
Gyimes 52, 56, 186, 187, 265, 278
Gyimes-Bükkhavas 303
Gyimesközéplok 150, 223, 446
Gyirmót 387

Gyöngyös 226, 229, 412, 414, 646
Győr 418
Győr (County) 387, 488
Győr-Sopron (County) 57, 93, 149, 335,
336, 373, 448, 648
Györgyfalva 233
Györgytarló 664
Gyula 112, 113, 114, 491

Hadikfalva 489
Hajcsána 690
Hajdú (County) 261, 262, 263, 268, 318,
377, 418, 624
Hajdú-Bihar (County) 45, 184, 234, 241,
288, 289, 412
Hajdú (district) 45, 69, 331, 398, 628
Hajdúböszörmény 280
Hajdúszoboszló 297
Hangony 41
Hanság 37
Haraszti 40, 242
Háromszék (County) 50, 135, 186, 187,
214, 313, 326, 395, 405, 511, 622, 646
Hasznos 109
Hegyalja 417
Hegyhát 41
Hegyköz 42, 166
Hejce 155
Hernád (river) 42, 181, 426
Hertelendyfalva 625, 626
Hetés 36, 334, 427
Heves 392
Heves (County) 97, 99, 105, 161, 210, 258,
279, 290, 430, 483, 506, 507, 606, 634,
642, 653
Hidelve 49, 356
Highlands 351
Hódmezővásárhely 46, 111, 223, 291, 364,
387, 388, 399, 411, 419, 487, 500, 508,
511, 565
Holland 75, 225
Hollókő 43, 159, 251, 271, 345
Homok 41
Homokmégy 623
Homoród 398
Hont (County) 41, 156, 479, 645
Hortobágy 114, 116, 249, 250, 256, 260,
261, 262, 263, 268, 269, 318, 323, 327,
353, 355, 377, 455, 495, 496
Hóstát 49, 356
Hövej 400, 448
Hunyad (County) 68, 485

Inaktelke 166
Inner Asia 28
India 568
Indonesia 568
Ipolybalog 479
Iran 572
Istanbul 37
Italy 29, 368, 369, 404

Jákfa 654
Jákótelke 156
Jára 415
Jászalsószentgyörgy 77
Jászapáti 290
Jászárokszállás 123
Jászberény 110, 206, 364, 666
Jászjákóhalma 45, 274
Jászság 69, 294, 398, 660, 686
Jobbágyi 37
Jobbágytelke 40, 292

Kadarkút 148
Kalocsa 46, 216, 318, 321, 351, 352, 400
Kalota (river) 48
Kalotaszeg (region of—) 48, 49, 98, 130,
    134, 135, 139, 166, 291, 321, 322, 323,
    325, 333, 356, 357, 359, 360, 369, 371,
    372, 387, 398, 402, 403, 404, 405, 415,
    417, 426, 453, 659, 685
Kalotaszentkirály 308, 489
Kapospula 632
Kaposvár 39, 439
Kapuvár 37, 335, 336, 337, 400
Karancsság 130, 345
Karcag 44, 124, 135, 261, 266, 406, 412
Karcag-Berek 185
Karcsa 150, 303, 585, 589
Kardoskút 211, 212
Kassa 674
Kászon 167, 326, 393, 395, 404, 661
Kászonimpér 167, 483
Kazár 204, 297, 298, 319, 320, 343, 663
Kazár-Maconka 345
Kecskemét 46, 66, 111, 120, 122, 156, 260,
    353, 356, 418
Kemenesalja 37, 214
Kemeneshát 37
Kémér 211
Kénos 658
Kerka 36
Kéty 654
Kézdimárkosfalva 696
Kézdivásárhely 111, 187, 313, 416
Kibéd 478
Kiev 31
Kisborosnyó 135
Kisdobsza 502
Kishartyán 591
Kiskundorozsma 225
Kiskunfélegyháza 44, 195
Kiskunhalas 152, 353, 406, 496, 499
Kiskunság see Little Cumania
Kislőd 101
Kispalád 22, 23
Kissárrét 47
Kisújszállás 325, 329
Kocs 275
Kolony 649
Kolozs (County) 48, 98, 107, 125, 135,

156, 166, 198, 233, 259, 270, 278, 303,
    305, 308, 357, 359, 386, 403, 404, 405,
    445, 453, 454, 457, 458, 489, 603, 604,
    610, 617, 619, 629, 633, 634, 635
Kolozsmonostor 49
Kolozsvár 49, 111, 356
Komádi 142, 184, 234, 241, 288, 289
Komárom 37, 386, 387, 418
Komárom (County) 198, 275, 322, 337,
    338, 339, 478, 511
Kondorfa 155
Konyár 125
Kopács 239
Kórógy 40
Koroncó 488
Korond 410, 415, 524
Kökényespuszta 199
Kömörő 636
Körös (river) 47
Körösfő 659
Köröstarcsa 502
Kovácsvágás 625
Kővágóőrs 180
Kraszna (river) 240
Krasznokvajda 202
Kunhegyes 454
Kunmadaras 199, 454
Kunság 45, 69, 299, 398
Kunszentmiklós 44

Lengyeltóti 654
Lészped 311, 361, 602, 604
Little Cumania (Kiskunság) 45, 142, 236,
    251, 252, 254, 267, 353, 427, 686
Lippa 519
Little Plain 134, 163, 183, 185, 201
Lóc 322, 345
Losonc 344
Ludány 344

Maconka 258, 642
Madaras 408
Magyaralmás 101
Magyarbóly 165
Magyarpécska 479
Magyarszentmárton 500
Magyarszerdahely 213
Magyarszovát 629, 633, 634, 635
Magyarvalkó 49, 125, 198, 303, 305, 386
Magyarvista 604
Máramaros (County) 432, 433
Máréfalva 134, 359
Márianosztra 183
Máriapócs 109
Marosszék 50, 299
Maros–Torda (County) 49, 292, 478
Marosvásárhely 111
Martonvásár 111
Martonyi 153
Martos 322, 337, 338, 339

Mátisfalva 162
Matolcs 328
Mátra (Mountains) 227
Mátraverebély 109
Mátyusföld 37
Matyóföld 323
Mediterranean 223, 241, 314
Medvesalja 41
Mekényes 225
Méra 98, 454, 457, 458, 603, 619
Meszlen 151
Mexico 515
Mezőberény 143, 365, 488
Mezőcsát 365, 411, 413, 414
Mezőföld 41
Mezőkövesd 42, 55, 83, 84, 104, 160, 211,
    218, 302, 333, 348, 349, 350, 364, 402,
    447, 453, 507, 647
Mezőség (central area of Transylvania) 49,
    144, 187, 426, 445, 453
Mezőtúr 411, 706
Miháld 657
Mikóújfalu 187
Milota 185
Miske 307, 420
Miskolc 92, 116, 129, 273, 388, 595
Moha 642, 643, 645
Mohács 32, 406, 408, 509, 709
Moldavia 51, 52, 200, 247, 298, 311, 361,
    362, 424, 427, 440, 486, 494, 517, 519,
    602, 604, 671, 690
Mongolia 429
Monor 277, 278
Monostorapáti 376
Mór 226
Mórágy 411, 413
Moravia 369, 433
Munkács 316
Muraköz 434

Nádaspatak 48, 49
Nádudvar 408
Nádújfalu 105
Nagyabony 132
Nagyatád 92
Nagyborzova 205
Nagycigánd 330
Nagydobsza-Istvánmajor 498, 503
Nagyecsed 332
Nagykálló 239
Nagykapus 359
Nagykőrös 46
Nagykunság 129, 254, 353, 399, 419, 440
Nagykutas 40
Nagymegyer 510
Nagysárrét 47, 499
Nagyszalonta 103, 443, 483, 487, 494, 500,
    509, 512, 632, 659
Nagyszekeres 129
Nagyvárad 112, 143

Nagyvarsány 239
Nagyvázsony 137, 306
Near East 314, 681
Nemesborzova 141
Nemespátró 512, 623
Nógrád (County) 41, 43, 130, 159, 183, 199, 204, 207, 215, 251, 271, 297, 319, 320, 322, 323, 329, 333, 343, 344, 382, 384, 387, 394, 398, 591, 607, 613, 631, 645, 650, 663
North America 515
Northern Europe 568
Nyárád (river) 456
Nyír 47
Nyíregyháza 116, 273
Nyíri 164, 202, 275
Nyírség 69, 183, 214, 216, 217, 287, 574
Nyitra (County) 504, 616, 649, 685
Nyögér 657

Óbánya 212
Okor (river) 39
Okorág 501
Olasztelek 109
Oltszem 214
Orgovány 265
Ormánság 39, 136, 170, 177, 339, 420, 495, 509, 637,
Orosháza 399, 638
Öcsény 41, 485
Őrhalom 323
Őrhalom-Hugyag 344
Őriszentpéter 278
Őrség 36, 181, 285, 289, 296, 427
Őrisziget 37
Öskü 409
Öszöd 80

Palotsland (Palócföld, Palóc Region) 109, 140, 145, 146, 148, 152, 153, 163, 166, 170, 186, 200, 322, 333, 383, 392, 417, 440, 447, 492, 592, 646, 704
Pannonia 29, 36
Parád 161
Pásztó 412, 414, 653
Pécs 686
Péntekfalu 111
Penyige 134
Peremarton 409
Pereszteg 170
Pest 46
Pest (County) 63, 82, 130, 132, 136, 265, 272, 277, 278, 293, 317, 321, 346, 459, 490, 496, 499, 609, 621, 646, 711
Petneháza 239
Pinka (river) 37
Poland 275, 416
Poroszló 606
Pozsony 74, 467, 673
Pozsony (County) 485

Pusztafalu 511
Püspökbogád 479
Püspökhatvan 621

Rába (river) 37, 686
Rábaköz 37, 337, 399
Rábaszovát 506
Rábca (river) 37, 179
Radna 109
Rafajnaújfalu 429
Rákosd 68
Rátót 567
Rétköz 47
Rima (river) 41
Rimóc 333, 345, 631
Rumania 34, 46, 47, 52, 150, 361, 427, 456, 517, 519
Russia 200, 275, 570

Saint Gellért Hill 674, 675
Sajó (river) 41, 264
Sámson 636
Sándorfalva 443
Sára 143, 243
Sarkad 507
Sárköz 41, 99, 236, 321, 322, 340, 343, 390, 391, 401, 411, 493
Sárospatak 208, 414, 415, 708
Sárpilis 41
Sárrét 47, 142, 435, 671, 680
Sárrétudvari 314, 671
Sárvár 482
Sárvíz 41
Sátoraljaújhely 388
Scandinavia 515
Sebes-Körös (river) 48
Segesd 703
Semjén 279
Sepsibesenyő 622
Sepsiszentgyörgy 129, 511
Serbia 434
Siberia 200, 515, 671
Sicily 554
Siklód 150
Siklós 411
Sió (river) 41
Sióagárd 158, 228, 318, 343
Slavonia 40, 41, 156, 263, 427, 434
Slovakia 36, 37, 42, 200, 427, 433
Slovenia 452
Sokoró 37
Sokoróalja 37
Somogy 322, 398
Somogy (County) 39, 80, 92, 106, 128, 136, 137, 148, 155, 163, 164, 173, 174, 177, 180, 199, 214, 277, 284, 293, 322, 338, 371, 391, 400, 426, 429, 436, 451, 481, 496, 498, 502, 503, 512, 609, 623, 632, 638, 646, 654, 657, 703, 704
Sopron 226

Sopron (County) 151, 170, 506
Sóstó 21
South-Eastern Europe 210, 326, 627
Southern Great Plain 273, 334, 364, 445, 494, 507, 508
South Russian Plain 138, 145
Southern Transdanubia 109, 170, 171, 172, 174, 175, 217, 218, 247, 287, 318, 332, 338, 380, 426
Soviet Union 34, 429
Spain 29
St. Anna (Lake) 109
Surd 429
Switzerland 29
Szabolcs (County) 140, 239, 244, 271, 284, 355, 393, 513, 600, 642
Szabolcs-Szatmár (County) 127, 141, 208, 217, 328, 689
Szabolcsbáka 140
Szada 136, 459
Szaján 484, 510
Szakadát 50
Szakmár 351, 353, 638, 652
Szalafő 155, 170, 171, 175, 177, 287, 296
Szalonna 213, 221
Szamos (river) 47
Szamosfalva 49
Szamoshát (plain south of the —) 47
Szandaváralja 645
Szántó 641
Szany 57
Szarvas 75, 222
Szatmár 112, 393
Szatmár (County) 21, 129, 133, 134, 185, 217, 235, 282, 328, 332, 488, 590, 636, 654, 687
Szatmárcseke 127, 654
Szécsény 345, 392
Szeged 46, 126, 216, 334, 427, 503, 540, 648, 660, 674
Szegvár 211, 214
Szék 49, 96, 108, 109, 250, 253, 255, 257, 267, 445, 610
Székelyland 50, 67, 96, 97, 98, 109, 129, 130, 133, 134, 139, 140, 150, 152, 153, 173, 174, 187, 198, 203, 240, 245, 283, 287, 291, 296, 298, 299, 323, 326, 333, 364, 374, 383, 395, 398, 404, 415, 493, 505, 638, 654, 657, 675, 687
Székelyudvarhely 109
Székelyvarság 168, 383
Székesfehérvár 227
Székkutas 121
Szekszárd 226, 411
Szend 513
Szenna 106, 128, 148, 155, 164
Szentbékkálla 178
Szentegyházasfalu 126
Szentendre 21, 22, 23
Szentes 85, 262, 264, 408, 442, 508

Szentgál 205, 213
Szentistván 42, 102, 350, 607, 618, 620
Szentlászló 40
Szepes (region of —) 30
Szépkenyerűszentmárton 622
Szer 47
Szeremle 41, 132
Szigetköz 37, 427, 607
Szigliget 38
Szilágy (County) 211, 305, 328, 492, 628, 636
Szilágyság (hilly area in the western half of Transylvania) 47, 49
Szimó 198
Szrima 396
Szolnok (County) 45, 77, 123, 135, 185, 199, 206, 241, 261, 266, 274, 290, 325, 329, 385, 454, 636, 679, 685, 687
Szolnok-Doboka (County) 96, 108, 250, 253, 255, 257, 267, 445, 614, 622
Szombathely 20, 21, 111, 136
Szomoróc 297
Szögliget 621
Szőreg 679, 681
Szuha 483
Szuhahuta 279

Tab 137
Takta 302, 303, 308, 309
Taktaköz 47
Tállya 510
Tápé 101, 154
Tard 346, 347, 401
Tardoskedd 111
Tarna (river) 41
Tata 410, 411, 478
Telkibánya 129
Tetétlen 624
Tihany 21, 25, 227
Tild 650
Tisza (river) 193, 254, 299, 371, 698
    region east of the — (Tiszántúl) 44–47, 104, 125, 131, 132, 143, 147, 184, 200–203, 245, 262, 268, 280, 287, 297, 325, 333, 355, 356, 376, 377, 378, 380, 398, 497, 676
    middle region of the — 411, 412
    plain north of the — (Tiszahát) 47, 134, 139, 188
    upper region of the — 134, 169, 206
    valley of the — 185
Tiszabercel 271
Tiszacsege 263
Tiszadob 47
Tiszafüred 385, 412
Tiszaigar 687
Tiszakarád 654
Tiszakóród 133
Tiszaladány 499

Tiszaörs 636
Tiszaörvény 241
Tokaj 47, 227, 229
Tokaj-Hegyalja 42, 140, 226, 227, 228, 230, 232, 275, 659
Tolna (County) 41, 51, 154, 158, 159, 228, 317, 323, 341, 343, 401, 413, 436, 485, 493, 552, 641, 654
Torda 415, 653
Torda (County) 50
Torda-Aranyos (County) 186, 660
Torockó 50, 186, 187, 321, 325, 360, 388
Torockószentgyörgy 50
Torontál (County) 227, 484, 492, 500, 501, 510, 625, 626, 679, 681
Tök 130
Törökkoppány 338, 451
Tövishát 47
Transdanubia (Dunántúl) 29, 33, 36, 40, 41, 51, 67, 82, 99, 104, 109, 123, 132, 140, 143, 144, 147, 151, 155, 156, 163, 169, 170, 171, 174, 183, 189, 200, 202, 207, 208, 210, 216, 220, 223, 226, 227, 230, 231, 237, 245, 247, 257, 262, 278, 285, 286, 291, 315, 321, 323, 325, 330, 333, 334, 338, 340, 351, 369, 370, 372, 374, 376, 377, 381, 383, 387, 391, 395, 399, 410, 417, 427, 438, 443, 451, 452, 495, 498, 507, 628, 646, 649, 651, 654, 657, 665
Transylvania (Erdély) 29, 30, 32, 36, 42, 46, 47, 48, 49, 50, 51, 52, 68, 105, 111, 112, 115, 131, 136, 139, 140, 144, 146, 151, 152, 163, 170, 172, 173, 186, 187, 188, 189, 200, 201, 202, 220, 221, 227, 235, 245, 246, 247, 254, 268, 273, 278, 284, 285, 287, 291, 294, 297, 298, 300, 311, 316, 325, 330, 332, 356, 362, 368, 369, 370, 371, 372, 374, 376, 380, 387, 388, 393, 394, 398, 402, 410, 415, 417, 426, 427, 433, 438, 440, 445, 451, 453, 494, 513, 522, 547, 622, 649, 653, 654, 658, 660, 665, 678, 681
Tunyog 328, 689
Túr 365
Tura 348, 350, 400, 711
Turkey 369
Tüskevár 410
Tyukod 488, 590

Udvarhely (County) 126, 134, 150, 162, 168, 318, 359, 383, 410, 524, 622, 658
Udvarhelyszék 50, 187
Ukraine 145, 199, 200
Ung (County) 374
Ungvár 316, 356
Uplands 323
Upper Hungary (Felföld) 33, 36, 41, 42, 46, 131, 132, 140, 146, 169, 170, 181, 207, 254, 273, 298, 316, 343, 369, 370, 374, 376, 377, 388, 399, 406, 412, 417, 438, 443
Upper Tisza (region) 169, 172
USA 34, 79
Uzon 186

Vajdácska 233
Válaszút 453
Váralja 436
Vargyas 389
Várvölgy 47
Vas (County) 136, 151, 155, 170, 171, 174, 175, 177, 214, 278, 287, 291, 296, 297, 648, 654, 657
Vásárosnamény 606
Velem 291
Velence (Lake) 41
Vencsellő 244
Verőce (County) 242
Verpelét 506
Veszprém (County) 38, 101, 137, 156, 178, 179, 180, 205, 213, 225, 306, 326, 378, 379, 385, 398, 399, 400, 409, 410, 499, 567, 638
Vienna 37, 74, 275, 435, 455, 468, 597, 698
Világos 490
Villány 226
Vista 107, 259, 270, 617
Vitnyéd 648
Vojlovica 492
Vukmaroca 263

Western Europe 52, 94, 136, 275, 314, 362, 480, 528, 536, 568, 570, 572
Western Transdanubia 115, 139, 140, 145, 156, 163, 169, 177, 201, 286, 287

Yugoslavia 23, 34, 36, 40, 46

Zádor 174, 385
Zagyva 44
Zagyvarékas 679, 685
Zala 36
Zala (County) 40, 129, 163, 213, 221, 229, 230, 264, 376, 400, 508, 656, 657, 658
Zalaegerszeg 18, 19
Zalaistvánd 658
Zemplén (County) 143, 150, 206, 302, 303, 308, 309, 378, 499, 504, 510, 585, 589, 615, 626, 631, 654, 664
Zemplén Mountains 42
Ziliz 153
Zobor (region) 38, 185
Zsadány 507
Zselickislak 136
Zselicség (region) 39
Zsigárd 485

Table of Contents

Preface   *5*
Foreword   *11*
Introduction   *15*
The history and present-day organization of Hungarian ethnography   *15*
*The ethnogenesis of the Hungarian people and their place
   in European culture*   *26*
Hungarian ethnic groups, ethnographic regions and pockets of survival   *34*
      Transdanubia   *36*
      Upper Hungary   *41*
      Great Plain   *44*
      Transylvania   *47*

I. SOCIAL ANTHROPOLOGY   *53*

The nuclear and the extended family   *54*
On the history of family organization   *54*
Family organization   *56*
The troop, clan, kindred   *67*
Artificial kindred, neighbourhood   *70*
Classes and social strata in the Hungarian village   *74*
Nobles and lords   *74*
The village intelligentsia   *75*
The rich peasants   *76*
The middle peasants   *77*
The poor peasants   *78*
The rural agricultural labourers   *78*
      Share labourers   *79*
      Seasonal workers   *82*
      Pick and shovel men   *84*
      Agricultural hands on large estates   *87*
      Smaller groups and occupations   *90*
      Artisans   *91*
      Entrepreneurs   *95*
Collective work and social gatherings   *96*
Self-governing bodies of the village   *101*
The Churches and religious life   *104*
Parish feasts, markets and fairs   *109*

II. MATERIAL ANTHROPOLOGY   *119*

Settlement building, house furnishing   *120*
The outskirts of the settlement   *120*

Patterns of village settlement and the organization of lots   133
The houses and the farm buildings   138
   The walling of the houses   138
   Roof structure and roofing   144
   Layout, fireplace and lighting   148
   Furniture arrangement in the dwelling houses   157
   Outbuildings of the farmyard   163
Regional differences in Hungarian architecture   174
   Southern Transdanubia   174
   Western and Central Transdanubia   177
   Dwelling sites of Upper Hungary and the Palots region   181
   Dwelling sites of the Great Plain   183
   Dwelling sites of Transylvania and the Székely region   186
   The influence of historical styles on folk architecture   188
   Life in the house and the farmyard   189
Acquiring raw material from flora and fauna   192
Food gathering   192
Farming   196
   The system of Hungarian farming   196
   Soil cultivation   197
   Sowing   203
   Harvesting and harvesting customs   205
   Treading and threshing   210
   Hoed plants   214
   Processing cereals   220
   Grapes and wine   226
Animal husbandry   232
   Apiculture   232
   Hunting   236
   Fishing   238
   Animal husbandry   244
   Regional varieties of breeds   246
   The organization of the herdsmen   248
   Flocks   252
   Grazing and watering   253
   Foraging   256
   Branding and guarding   259
   Animal healing   264
   Buildings for the stock and herdsmen   264
   Breaking in stock and the means of transportation   270
Alimentation   276
Furnishing the kitchen   277
The order of meals   280
Storing and preserving raw materials   282
Soups   284
Preparation of plant foods   284
   Porridges, mushes   284
   Tarts   286
   Bread and milk loaf   287
   Noodles   292

    Baked pastries   293
Meat dishes   294
Milk and milk processing   296
Drinks and spices   298
Folk costumes   *298*
Raw materials   301
    Processing hemp and flax   302
    Processing wool   309
    Processing skin   312
Elements of folk costume   315
    Historical strata   315
    Hair and headdress   317
    Underwear   322
    Outer wear   323
    Mantles and coat-like outer wear   325
    Footwear   332
Regional forms of Hungarian folk costumes   334
    Transdanubia   334
    Upper Hungary   343
    Great Plain   351
    Transylvania   356
Ornamental folk art   *363*
Historical strata of ornamental folk art   367
Woodcarving   371
Furniture making   381
Homespuns   389
Embroideries   395
Pottery   406
Other branches of ornamental folk art   417

III. CULTURAL ANTHROPOLOGY   *421*

Instruments of expression in cultural anthropology   *422*
Hungarian dialects   422
Hungarian folk music and folk instruments   428
Movement and dance   447
Folk poetry and prose   *460*
The theory of Hungarian folk poetry and prose   460
Folk poetry   467
Folksong   467
    Love songs   481
    Historical songs and songs of valour   486
    Songs of wandering and captivity   491
    Herdsman and outlaw songs   494
    Soldiers' songs   500
    Rural workers' songs   504
    Songs of farm hands and rural servants   505
    Songs of seasonal workers   506
    Songs of pick and shovel men   507

     Songs of revellry, drinking songs 508
     Mocking songs, humorous and satirical songs 510
  Folk ballad 513
     History of the ballad 514
     Narrative ballads 522
     Ballads of belief 527
     Ballads of romance and of the Turkish period 529
     Ballads of wandering and captivity 532
     Dance ballads 539
     Merry ballads 539
     Ballads of outlaws 539
     Ballads of lament 542
     Broadsheet ballads 542
     New ballads 545
     Forms of the folk ballad 546
  Folk tales and legends 549
  The folk tales 552
     Fairy tales 554
     Humorous tales 564
     Village mocking tales 567
     Religious legends 568
     Animal fables 569
     The form and content of folk tales 570
  The legend 583
     Historical legends 583
     Local legends 586
     Legends of belief 588
  Other types of folk narrative 594
  Idiomatic sayings 595
  Proverbs 596
  Riddles 598
  Folk customs and dramatic traditions 600
  Customs and feasts 603
     Baptism 604
     Children's games 604
     Wedding 612
     Burial 627
  Customs of the calendar year 637
  Customs not tied to the calendar year 659
  Work customs 662
  The world of Hungarian folk beliefs 668
  Figures of the world of beliefs 670
  The peasant world view 678
  Actions connected with the world of beliefs 684

  IV. THE PAST AND FUTURE
  OF HUNGARIAN FOLK CULTURE 693

  Between East and West 694
  Folk culture today and tomorrow 700

V. LITERATURE AND APPENDIX *713*

List of sources and other data relating to figures *763*
List of sources for black-and-white photographs *769*
List of sources for colour plates *780*
List of place names now outside Hungary *783*

Index 787